Craftsman 2005 NATIONAL RENOVATION & INSURANCE REPAIR ESTIMATOR

with data from the Rutlidge Institute

Ri RUTLIDGE institute

edited by Jonathan Russell

Includes inside the back cover:

- An estimating CD with all the costs in this book, plus,
- An estimating program that makes it easy to use these costs,
- An interactive video guide to the National Estimator program,
- A program that converts your estimates into invoices,
- A program that exports your estimates to QuickBooks Pro.

Monthly price updates on the Web are free and automatic all during 2005. You'll be prompted when it's time to collect the next update. A connection to the Web is required.

Craftsman

Craftsman Book Company
6058 Corte del Cedro / P.O. Box 6500 / Carlsbad, CA 92018

© 2004 Craftsman Book Company   ISBN 1-57218-146-X   Published October 2004 for the year 2005.

contents

▶ **USING THIS BOOK** **4–14**
  about this book 4-6
  abbreviations and acknowledgements 7
  area modification factors 8-11
  using the unit price pages and the time & material charts 12-13
  crews 14

① **ACOUSTIC CEILINGS** **15–16**
  time & material charts 17-18

② **APPLIANCES** **19–34**
  gas cook tops, ranges, ovens 19-21
  electric cook tops, ranges, ovens 21-25
  range hoods 26
  dishwashers, garbage disposals 26-28
  microwaves 28-29
  refrigerators 29-31
  trash compactors 31
  washing machines, dryers 31-32
  time & material charts 33-34

③ **AWNINGS** **35–40**
  time & material charts 38-40

④ **BATHROOM HARDWARE** **41–46**
  time & material charts 46

⑤ **CABINETS** **47–54**
  time & material charts 53-54

⑥ **CLEANING** **55–70**
  time & material charts 68-70

⑦ **COLUMNS** **71–82**
  time & material charts 81-82

⑧ **CONCRETE** **83–98**
  repair 83
  footings, foundations 83-85
  piers, grade beams 86-88
  flatwork, steps 89-90
  sawing, core drilling 90-91
  pump truck costs, rebar, foundation coating 91
  foundation buttressing, compaction grouting 91-92
  time & material charts 92-98

⑨ **DEMOLITION & HAULING** **99–100**
  time & material charts 100

⑩ **DOORS** **101–126**
  folding doors, bypassing doors 101-103
  jamb and casing for closet doors 102-103
  interior doors 103
  French doors 103-104
  full- and half-louvered doors 104
  jamb and casing for interior doors 104-105
  pocket doors 105-106
  panel doors 106-109
  batten doors, storm doors 109-110
  exterior French doors, exterior veneer doors 110

  additional costs for lites in doors 110
  Dutch doors 110-111
  entry doors and side lites 111-116
  jamb and casing for entry and exterior doors 116-117
  entry door fanlites, transoms 117-118
  cafe doors 118-119
  sliding patio doors 119-120
  pet doors 120-121
  garage doors, garage door openers 121-123
  time & material charts 124-126

⑪ **DOOR HARDWARE** **127–132**
  time & material charts 131-132

⑫ **DRYWALL** **133–138**
  time & material charts 137-138

⑬ **ELECTRICAL** **139–176**
  complete house 139
  outlets, switches, covers 139-141
  wiring runs, conduit, wire 141-146
  breaker panels, electrical service, breakers 146-148
  door bells 148-149
  bath fans, kitchen fans, whole-house fans 149-150
  intercoms 150-151
  sound systems 151
  check circuits 151
  smoke, carbon monoxide, and radon detectors 151-152
  thermostats and TV antennas 152
  wall heaters, resistance heating, baseboard heaters 152-153
  light fixtures 153-173
  time & material charts 173-176

⑭ **EXCAVATION** **177–184**
  time & material charts 181-184

⑮ **FEES** **185–186**

⑯ **FENCES** **187–198**
  board 187-189
  chain link 189-192
  vinyl 192-195
  ornamental iron, electric gate openers 195-196
  time & material charts 197-198

⑰ **FINISH CARPENTRY** **199–240**
  base, casing 199-204
  curved casing, wood keys, base blocks, head blocks 204-205
  overdoor molding, architraves, door and window surrounds .205-209
  stool, apron, chair rail, drip cap, astragal, cove 209-214
  half-round, quarter-round, corner bead 214-216
  bed mold, crown, hand rails 216-217
  specialty molding, custom-milled molding, inside radius ...217-222
  closet work, bookcases, mantel beams, mantels 222-225
  coffered ceilings, niches 225-226
  gingerbread trim and woodwork 226-231
  porch posts 231-232
  onlays, finish boards, finish plywood 232-234
  time & material charts 235-240

18 FIREPLACES **241–256**
  standard, prefabricated, forms 241-244
  fire brick, chimneys, chimney repair, caps, pots, screens 244-246
  grates, screens, doors, clean-out doors, dampers 246-248
  chimney pipes, gas fireplace equipment 248-249
  fireplace faces and hearths 249-252
  time & material charts 253-256

19 FLOORING **257–272**
  carpet, stone, marble, slate, tile, terrazzo 257-261
  vinyl, linoleum, wood 261-268
  time & material charts 269-272

20 HAZARDOUS MATERIALS **273–274**
  time & material charts 274

21 HVAC **275–280**
  time & material charts 279-280

22 INSULATION **281–284**
  time & material charts 283-284

23 MASKING & MOVING **285–286**
  time & material charts 286

24 MASONRY **287–330**
  brick walls, brick and block walls, cavity walls 287-295
  brick veneer, other brick wall and veneer costs 296-298
  concrete block, tile, gypsum tile, glass block, pavers 298-305
  stone walls, stone veneer walls, keystones, quoins 305-309
  stone veneer panels 309-310
  stone door and window architraves, cut stone trim 310-317
  wall caps, wall coping 317-318
  repoint brick and stone, brick and stone wall repair 318-321
  clean masonry, cut hole in masonry and shore, lintels 321-322
  time & material charts 323-330

25 OUTBUILDINGS **331–332**

26 PAINTING **333–346**
  time & material charts 343-346

27 PANELING **347–352**
  time & material charts 351-352

28 PLASTER & STUCCO **353–360**
  time & material charts 359-360

29 PLUMBING **361–390**
  supply pipe, DWV pipe 361-364
  exterior lines, pressure valves, underground repairs 364
  rough plumbing by complete house, room, and fixture 365-368
  faucets, fixtures, tub surrounds, showers, shower doors 368-381
  water heaters, water softeners 381-382
  septic tanks with leach fields, pumps 382-383
  antique style faucets and fixtures 384-387
  time & material charts 387-390

30 RETAINING WALLS **391–392**
  time & material charts 392

31 ROOFING **393–408**
  steep and complex roof costs, metal shingles 393
  asphalt shingles, roll roofing, slate, wood shingles, shakes ..393-396
  fiber & cement shingles, granular coated metal tile, clay tile ..396-399
  furring strips, concrete tile, sheet fiberglass, sheet metal ..399-403
  built-up roofs, single ply membranes 403-405
  time & material charts 406-408

32 ROUGH CARPENTRY **409–452**
  interior and exterior walls per lf, per sf, and per bf 409-415
  top plates, sill plates, headers, posts, precast piers 415-417
  jackposts, lally columns, glu-lam and micro-lam beams 417-420
  pine and oak beams 420-423
  pine and oak post and beam bents with trusses, joints 423-429
  deck joist systems, decking, railings, stairs and landings ..429-430
  furring strips, joist systems per sf 430-432
  I joists, floor trusses, hand-framed roofs and dormers 432-439
  roof trusses, sheathing 439-443
  interior soffits, factory built wall panels, chimney crickets ..443-444
  time & material charts 445-452

33 SECURITY SYSTEMS **453–454**
  time & material charts 454

34 SIDING **455–464**
  siding, fascia, soffits, gutters, downspouts, conductors, shutters .455-463
  time & material charts 463-464

35 STAIRS **465–482**
  stair framing, prefabricated spiral stairs, attic stairs 465-471
  balustrades, brackets, tread trim, newels 471-480
  time & material charts 480-482

36 SUSPENDED CEILINGS **483–488**
  time & material charts 487-488

37 SWIMMING POOLS **489–490**

38 TEMPORARY **491–492**
  time & material charts 492

39 TILE **493–494**
  time & material charts 494

40 WALL COVERINGS **495–498**
  time & material charts 497-498

41 WATER EXTRACTION **499–500**
  time & material charts 500

42 WINDOWS **501–512**
  aluminum, vinyl, wood, skylights, storm, reglazing, repair .501-511
  time & material charts 512

MANUFACTURED HOUSING mini price list **513–528**

MOLD REMEDIATION special price list **529–536**

QuickCALCULATORS **537–558**

INDEX **559–572**

about this book

WHAT'S NEW IN 2005

A strengthing economy and the overall strength of the construction industry point to another good year in 2005.

Spot shortages of some materials such as copper and plywood will most likely lead to unpredictable prices in some trades. Be sure to check for the most up-to-date prices at costbook.com. Craftsman's new feature allows you to get pricing updates to this costbook each month.

A TOOL

This book is a tool and like all tools it can be misused. It is an excellent tool for the renovation and repair professional. It is not a substitute for experience, skill, and knowledge.

Prices in this book are based on research of actual jobs and successful estimates. They represent an average of the typical conditions.

Estimators should compare the conditions described in this book with actual conditions on site and adjust the price accordingly.

UNIQUE TO RENOVATION AND REPAIR WORK

This book is compiled specifically for the unique problems and conditions found in renovation and repair work. *It is not a new construction cost book.*

Renovation and repair work involve different circumstances than those found in new construction.

For example, the renovation or repair professional must work around existing conditions including home contents, access problems, out-of-plumb or out-of-square buildings, outdated materials, and existing conditions that violate current building codes.

New-construction professionals have the luxury of placing items in a logical order, but the renovation, remodel, or repair professional must deal with conditions as they find them.

This means that joists have to be replaced in an existing floor system, paint has to be applied in a room where stain-grade base and carpeting are already installed, structures may have to be braced, contents have to be moved or worked around, and materials and installation techniques must be matched.

DETERMINING COSTS

All costs in this book are based on typical conditions and typical problems found when remodeling or repairing a structure.

This means a door takes 10 to 15 minutes longer to install than it would in the ideal circumstances found in new construction.

Stairs are more difficult to install around pre-existing walls, wall framing takes longer when walls are typically splicing into existing work, and so on.

Some prices in this book will closely match prices used in new construction. Other prices will reflect the complex conditions found in renovation and repair and will be dramatically different.

For example, using this book's stair building prices to estimate stair work in a series of 150 tract homes will result in an estimate that is far too high.

THE ART OF ESTIMATING

Estimating is part art, part science. Estimators must consider many factors, including access, crew productivity, special techniques, special abilities, temperament of the owner, and how busy the company is.

A contractor who is desperate for work will estimate much lower than a contractor who is swamped with work.

All of these factors—and many other similar ones—cannot be included in this or any other price book. They are part of the art of estimating.

The science of estimating, which includes prices, typical techniques, and materials, *is* included in this book.

This book is designed to make the *science* of estimating easier, which allows you to spend much more time focusing on the *art* of estimating, where your skill is crucial to the success of your company.

GENERAL vs. SPECIFIC

It is important to note that the more specific the estimator is, the more accurate the final estimate will be.

For example, when an estimator calculates all electrical costs for a typical home using a square foot cost, it may not be as accurate as if the estimator priced each fixture, outlet, and appliance hook-up.

Since the square foot price is based on a typical installation, it will not be exact for a home that is atypical in any way–for example, one with special outdoor lighting or with an expensive crystal fixture in the entry.

The more specific the item, the more exact the prices. The more general an item, the more assumptions must be made.

rounding

This book rounds hourly wage rates and the material, labor, and equipment components of a unit price.

These prices are rounded to "three significant digits." This means that prices under three digits (including two to the right of the decimal) are not rounded. Prices four digits and larger are rounded to the third digit from the left.

For example:
.23 is not rounded
2.33 is not rounded
23.33 is rounded to **23.30**
233.33 is rounded to **233.00**
2,333.33 is rounded to **2,330.00**
23,333.33 is rounded to **23,300.00**

To help ensure the accuracy of your estimates we describe any assumptions made when determining general items.

For example, the *Rough Carpentry* chapter contains a square foot price for estimating 2" by 4" wall framing. To help you make sure that this price will work for you, we describe our assumptions: the stud centers, the number of openings, headers, corners, plates, and so forth, that would typically be found in a wall.

In most cases the square foot price will apply, but you will always want to carefully consider items that are more general, and if needed, adjust them to fit the conditions.

In the case above, the estimator may want to use the square-foot price for average fixtures, then add an allowance for the crystal fixture and the outdoor lighting.

TIME AND MATERIAL CHARTS

Almost all chapters include time and material charts at the end. These time and material charts are designed to show you the materials used, waste, labor rates, labor burden costs, and labor productivity.

When materials with a range of sizes appear, only the small and large size are usually listed.

When materials with a range of qualities appear, often only the low and high prices are listed.

These charts are designed to give you accurate detail on the exact prices used. When prices change, this book does not become obsolete. Compare current prices with those used and factor accordingly.

MATERIAL COSTS

National average material costs are compiled from surveys of suppliers throughout the country.

Costs for some materials, such as clay tile, building stone and hardwood, will vary a great deal from region to region.

For example, clay tile plants are located near naturally occurring clay sources. Because clay tiles are heavy, the further the tiles have to be shipped, the more expensive the tiles will be. The user of this book must be aware of local price variations.

Materials commonly found in every city are priced based on local delivery. In most cases this will be delivery no greater than 20 miles away from a local source. However, many rural areas have lumber yards that will deliver to a wider area at no additional charge.

Materials that are not commonly available locally, like hand-carved moldings or historical wallpaper, include shipping costs anywhere in North America. Estimators in Hawaii, Alaska and remote areas of Canada should add for additional shipping costs when applicable.

Material waste is often indicated with the items, but it's always a good idea to check the time and material charts for the exact waste calculated for all the components of an item.

Waste indicates material that is discarded during installation. It does not include waste that occurs when materials are taken to storage and ruined, run over at the job site, spilled, improperly cut, or damaged due to mishandling.

These types of occurrences are kept to a minimum by every good contractor, but will still occur on any job site.

Another common waste issue in renovation and repair is when a contractor must buy a minimum quantity for a small repair. For example, to replace a six-inch section of base, it is necessary to buy a piece of base that is eight-feet long or longer. In these cases, use the minimum price.

Material prices may not be listed with the time and material charts in some chapters. In these chapters little new information would be provided by the materials chart so the space is saved for other information.

For example, a materials chart in the *Appliance* chapter will not provide an estimator with any new information.

The materials component of the unit price for an oven as listed in the main body of the chapter will tell the estimator how much the oven and connections cost.

Relisting these appliances in a materials chart wastes valuable space.

LABOR COSTS

Labor costs are national average rates that usually are consistent with union labor wages.

See the time and material charts for specific costs and labor rates.

Crew labor rates are an average hourly rate for each member of the crew. For example, a masonry crew might consist of a mason, a mason's helper, and a hod carrier.

The hourly rate for this crew is the average cost of all three. In other words, the hourly rate is for 20 minutes work by the mason, 20 minutes work by the mason's helper, and 20 minutes work by the hod carrier.

Separation of labor in renovation and insurance repair work is much more difficult than is separation of labor on large commercial construction projects.

On a typical repair or renovation job a carpenter may participate in demolition, frame walls, set doors, set toilets, install electrical outlets and fixtures, and do a little painting.

In the jobs analyzed for this cost book, well over 40 percent of the demolition work was done by skilled workers. This is because demolition is often selective, requiring a skilled worker to ensure that additional damage does not occur.

Many renovation and repair companies are also relatively small, so skilled workers participate in all phases of construction.

These realities are reflected in the labor costs used in this book. This means that a demolition laborer's hourly rate may seem higher than is normal for an unskilled worker.

The time and material charts show all items that are built into each labor rate.

Some contractors may not provide health insurance or retirement plans to some or all of their workers. Estimators can "back-out" these expenses from the labor costs.

It is critical that estimators examine the Worker's Compensation costs calculated in the wage rates. Some states have Worker's Compensation rates that are double, triple, or even quadruple the national average rates used in this book.

Worker's Compensation rates should be adjusted to match local conditions.

Labor productivity is based on observation of work performed in renovation and repair conditions.

These conditions differ from new construction in many ways, but a few of the most common are:
❶ difficulty matching existing work, ❷ access problems, ❸ materials that must be more carefully shaped and attached than is typical in new construction, ❹ out-of-plumb or out-of-square structures, ❺ reinforcing, ❻ more trips and effort are required to find materials, ❼ much more travel time is required because most jobs will have a relatively small amount of work in some trades, ❽ more vehicles are required by the renovation or repair contractor because many tradespeople are often traveling between jobs, compared to new construction where crews may spend weeks or months on one job, and because crews tend to be smaller and each crew may need a vehicle, ❾ more unexpected problems, and ❿ more restrictions in established neighborhoods.

Labor productivity is based on a clean job site where tools are put away and secured at the end of each day.

Depending on the trade, 20 to 30 minutes per eight hours is allowed for cleanup and putting away tools. Normally skilled workers spend half as much time cleaning up as do unskilled workers.

As is typical in new construction, labor includes unpacking and in some cases unloading materials from

a truck on site, some travel to pick up minor materials (e.g. a forgotten tube of caulk, or a forgotten tool), typical breaks, lay-out, planning, discussion, coordination, mobilization (many companies meet at a central location each morning to receive instructions), recording hours (including specific information needed for job costing), occasional correction of mistakes in installation, and so forth.

Supervision is not included in these costs but should not generally be required. This is because each crew includes a skilled tradesperson who normally would not require supervision beyond the normal dispatch and mobilization discussed previously.

EQUIPMENT COSTS

Equipment costs are included only when equipment will be used that is not typically a part of the tools used by the majority of renovation or repair contractors.

For example, each carpenter should have a worm-drive saw, miter box, compressor, nail guns, and so forth. These types of tools are not included in the equipment costs.

However, equipment like cranes, backhoes, concrete saws, and jack hammers are not assumed to be part of the equipment and tools owned by a typical renovation or repair contractor. When these are needed, equipment rates are included in the unit price.

Equipment costs include the typical cost to rent the equipment from a local equipment rental shop. When applicable, they also include fuel or blade costs.

Check each item to determine if it includes delivery to the job site or operator labor. Also be careful to note minimum costs for work where rented equipment is needed.

MARKUP

Prices in this book do not include markup. Insurance repair markup is almost always 20 percent: 10 percent for overhead and 10 percent for profit.

In renovation work on historical structures, markup may be as high as 30 percent, although markup over 20 percent may be "hidden" inside the unit cost. Typical remodeling work markup varies from 15 percent to 25 percent. The most common markup for all types of work is 20 percent.

REGIONAL DIFFERENCES

Construction techniques vary from region to region. Different climates and local customs provide a variety of unique regional methods.

For example, in southern Florida it is common to build the first floor of a home from concrete block capped with a spandrel beam. This method won't be found in Colorado.

Similarly, coral stone walls aren't common in Denver, although they are often seen in Miami.

Slate roofs are common on historical homes and newer custom homes in Philadelphia but are virtually nonexistent in Rapid City.

Homes in the south often include screened porches which aren't nearly so common in the west.

A Georgia home is much more likely to include a series of architecturally-correct columns with Corinthian capitals than is a home in Minnesota.

A Hawaii home may be built entirely from treated wood, when an Arizona home only uses treated lumber when it contacts dirt or concrete.

Many regional materials and techniques are priced in this book. Keep in mind that you should not use these prices if the item is not common to your area.

WE WANT TO HEAR FROM YOU

If you have questions or concerns about this cost book, let us hear from you. Send letters to:

**Craftsman Book Company
NRI Editor
P.O. Box 6500
Carlsbad, CA 92018-9974**

abbreviations

ABS....Acrylonitrile butadiene styrene	**lf** ....lineal foot	**SBS**.....................styrene butyl styrene
ac ....alternating current	**li** ....lineal inch	**sf** ....square foot
bf ....board foot	**m** ....one thousand	**sh** ....sheet
btu.....................British thermal units	**mbf** ....1,000 board feet	**si** ....square inch
CEC........California Earthquake Code	**mBtu**.........1,000 British thermal units	**sq** ....100 square feet
(also see page 83)	**mh** ....man hour	**st** ....step
cf ....cubic foot	**mi** ....mile	**sy** ....square yard
cfm ....cubic foot per minute	**mlf**...........................1,000 lineal feet	**t&g** ....tongue-&-groove edge
ci ....cubic inch	**mm** ....millimeter(s)	**TV** ....television
cy ....cubic yard	**mo** ....month	**UBC**.............Uniform Building Code
ea ....each	**mph** ....miles per hour	**UL** ....Underwriters' Laboratory
FUTA.............Federal Unemployment	**msf**..........................1,000 square feet	**vlf** ....vertical lineal foot
Compensation Act tax	**no.**....................................number	**wk**..week
gal ....gallon	**oc** ....on center	**w/** ....with
GFCI ..ground fault circuit interrupter	**oz**.......................................ounce	**x** ....by or times
gph ....gallon(s) per hour	**pr** ....pair	
gpm ....gallon(s) per minute	**psi** ....pounds per square inch	**SYMBOLS**
hp ....horsepower	**PVC**....................polyvinyl chloride	**/** ....per
hr(s) ....hour(s)	**qt** ....quart	**-** ....through or to
IMC ....intermediate metal conduit	**R/L** ....random length(s)	**@** ....at
kd ....kiln dried	**R/W/L** ......random widths and lengths	**%** ....percent
kv ....kilovolt(s)	**RSC** ....rigid steel conduit	**$** ...........................U.S. dollars
kva ....1,000 volt amps	**S1S2E**...........surfaced 1 side, 2 edges	**'** ....feet
kw....................................kilowatt(s)	**S2S** ....surfaced 2 sides	**"** ....inches
lb(s) ....pound(s)	**S4S** ....surfaced 4 sides	**#**..............................pound or number

acknowledgements

The editor wishes to gratefully acknowledge the contribution of the following: 18th Century Hardware Co., Inc. ~ A-Ball Plumbing Supply ~ A&Y Lumber ~ American Building Restoration Chemicals, Inc. ~ American Custom Millwork, Inc. ~ American Society for Testing and Materials (ASTM) ~ Anderson Windows ~ Anthony Lombardo Architectural Paneling Inc. ~ Anthony Wood Products Incorporated ~ The Antique Hardware Store ~ Architectural Components, Inc. ~ Architectural Woodwork Institute ~ The Balmer Architectural Art Studios ~ Bathroom Hardware, Inc. ~ Bathroom Machineries ~ Bendix Mouldings, Inc. ~ Brass Reproductions ~ Brick Institute of America ~ C & H Roofing, Inc. ~ C. G. Girolami & Sons ~ Caradco ~ Cataumet Sawmills ~ CertainTeed ~ Chadsworth Incorporated ~ Chelsea Decorative Metal Company ~ Classic Accents, Inc. ~ Classic Ceilings ~ CMW, Inc. ~ Conant Custom Brass ~ Conklin Metal Industries ~ Craftsman Lumber Company ~ Crown City Hardware Co. ~ Cumberland General Stores ~ Cumberland Woodcraft Co. Inc. ~ Designs in Tile ~ Dimension Hardwood ~ Donnell's Clapboard Mill ~ Driwood Moulding ~ Eisenhart Wallcoverings ~ Empire Wood Works ~ Raymond Enkeboll Designs ~ James Facenelli, *CGR #28* ~ Focal Point Architectural Products ~ Four Seasons Sun Rooms ~ Futurbilt ~ Garland ~ Gates Moore ~ General Electric Company ~ George Taylor Specialties Co. ~ Goodwin Heart Pine Company ~ Gougeon Brothers, Inc. ~ Grand Era, Inc. ~ Granville Manufacturing Company ~ Groff & Hearne Lumber ~ Hampton Decor ~ Harris-Tarkett, Inc. ~ Heatway ~ Heritage Vinyl Products ~ Michael Higuera ~ Italian Tile Center ~ J. G. Braun Company ~ Jeffries Wood Works, Inc. ~ Jennifer's Glass Works ~ JGR Enterprises ~ Johnson Paint Company, Inc. ~ Joseph Biunno Ltd ~ Kenmore Industries ~ King's Chandelier Company ~ Kraftmaid Cabinetry, Inc. ~ David Lawrence, illustrator ~ Lasting Impression Doors ~ Lehman's ~ Linoleum City, Inc. ~ Ludowici-Celadon, Inc. ~ MCA, Inc. ~ Millwork Specialties ~ The Millworks, Inc. ~ Mountain Lumber Co. ~ National Oak Flooring Manufacturers Association (NOFMA) ~ National Wood Flooring Association ~ Northwest Energy, Inc. ~ Oak Flooring Institute ~ The Old Fashioned Milk Paint Company, Inc. ~ Ole Fashion Things ~ Omega Too ~ Pagliacco Turning & Milling ~ Pella Corporation ~ Permaglaze ~ Piedmont Home Products, Inc. ~ Piedmont Mantel & Millwork Ltd ~ Pinecrest ~ Radiantec ~ The Readybuilt Products Company ~ Rejuvenation Lamp & Fixture, Co. ~ Runtal Radiators ~ The Saltbox ~ Salvage One Architectural Artifacts ~ Silverton Victorian Millworks ~ Stairways Inc. ~ Steptoe and Wife Antiques Ltd ~ Stromberg's Architectural Stone ~ The Structural Slate Co. ~ Sunbilt ~ Supradur Manufacturing Corporation ~ Taylor Door ~ Touchstone Woodworks ~ Turncraft ~ USG Company ~ Vande Hey's Roofing Tile Co., Inc. ~ Velux-America Inc. ~ Vixen Hill Manufacturing Co. ~ W. F. Norman Corporation ~ Watercolors, Inc. ~ WELco ~ Western Wood Products Association ~ Williamsburg Blacksmiths ~ Windy Hill Forge ~ Wolverine Technologies ~ The Wood Factory ~ Worthington Group Ltd ~

area modification factors

Construction costs are higher in some cities than in other cities. Use the factors on this and the following page to adapt the costs listed in this book to your job site. Increase or decrease your estimated total project cost by the percentage listed for the appropriate city in this table to find your estimated building cost.

These factors were compiled by comparing the actual construction cost of residential, institutional and commercial buildings in 740 communities throughout the United States. Because these factors are based on completed project costs, they consider all construction cost variables, including labor, equipment and material costs, labor productivity, climate, job conditions and markup.

Use the factor for the nearest or most comparable city. If the city you need is not listed in the table, use the factor for the appropriate state. Note that these location factors are composites of many costs and will not necessarily be accurate when estimating the cost of any particular part of a building. But when used to modify all estimated costs on a job, they should improve the accuracy of your estimates.

ALABAMA	–1%
Anniston	–1%
Birmingham	0%
Coosa	0%
Dothan	–4%
Huntsville	0%
Jasper	0%
Mobile	2%
Montgomery	0%
Sheffield	–4%
Troy	–2%

ALASKA	74%
Aleutian Islands	90%
Anchorage	70%
Barrow	77%
Clear	76%
Delta Junction	73%
Fairbanks	75%
Galena	73%
Gambel	73%
Goodnews Bay	75%
Haines	74%
Huslia	74%
King Salmon	86%
Nome	73%
Whittier	73%

ARIZONA	2%
Douglas	0%
Flagstaff	5%
Gila Bend	6%
Holbrook	0%
Mesa	0%
Phoenix	0%
Sierra Vista	2%
Tuba City	5%
Tucson	0%
Yuma	1%

ARKANSAS	–2%
Arkadelphia	–2%
Blytheville	–2%
Camden	–2%
Conway	–2%
El Dorado	–2%
Fayetteville	0%
Fort Smith	–1%
Harrison	–2%
Hot Springs	–2%
Jonesboro	–2%
Little Rock	–2%
Pine Bluff	–1%

CALIFORNIA	17%
Alameda	19%
Bakersfield	18%
Barstow	12%
Centerville	15%
Concord	24%
Coronado	13%
Desert Area	13%
El Centro	12%
El Monte	18%
El Toro	13%
Forestville	25%
Fresno	18%
Hanford	18%
Herlong	19%
Jolon	15%
Lathrop	13%
Lawndale	17%
Lompoc	15%
Long Beach	22%
Los Alamitos	22%
Los Angeles	26%
Marysville	12%
Modesto	13%
Mojave	13%

CALIFORNIA	continued
Monterey	16%
Novato	25%
Oakland	27%
Oceanside	14%
Oxnard	14%
Paso Robles	18%
Rancho Cordova	13%
Ridgecrest	13%
Rio Vista	20%
Riverbank	13%
Riverside	16%
Sacramento	11%
Salinas	17%
San Bernardino	15%
San Bruno	27%
San Diego	17%
San Francisco	88%
San Jose	24%
San Leandro	25%
San Mateo	25%
San Pablo	25%
Santa Rosa	25%
Seal Beach	18%
Stockton	13%
Sunnyvale	19%
Tracy	20%
Tustin	18%
Twentynine Palms	13%
Ukiah	20%
Upland	18%
Vallejo	19%
Victorville	18%

COLORADO	3%
Colorado Springs	7%
Denver	5%
Fort Carson	4%
Grand Junction	2%

COLORADO	continued
La Junta	2%
Lakewood	2%
Pueblo	–5%
Ski resorts	32%

CONNECTICUT	12%
Bridgeport	13%
Cromwell	12%
Fairfield	12%
Hartford	12%
Milford	11%
New London	11%
Stratford	11%
West Hartford	12%

DELAWARE	5%
Dover	4%
Kirkwood	6%
Lewes	6%
Milford	4%
Wilmington	7%

DISTRICT OF COLUMBIA	4%
Washington	4%

FLORIDA	4%
Baldwin	9%
Jacksonville	9%
Key West	22%
Lakeland	2%
Lynn Haven	0%
Melbourne	10%
Miami	6%
Milton	0%
Ocala	2%
Ocean City	–4%
Orlando	10%
Palatka	2%

FLORIDA	continued
Panama City	2%
Pensacola	0%
St Petersburg	1%
Tampa	1%

GEORGIA	3%
Albany	–1%
Athens	2%
Atlanta	12%
Augusta	–5%
Chamblee	2%
Columbus	–3%
Dublin	2%
East Point	2%
Forest Park	13%
Fort Valley	2%
Hinesville	0%
Kings Bay	2%
Macon	2%
Marietta	2%
Rome	2%
Savannah	0%
Tifton	12%
Valdosta	2%

HAWAII	82%
Alimanu	82%
Ewa	82%
Halawa Heights	82%
Hilo	82%
Honolulu	82%
Kailua	90%
Lualualei	82%
Mililani Town	82%
Pearl City	82%
Wahiawa	82%
Waianae	82%
Wailuku (Maui)	82%

IDAHO	0%
Boise	4%
Coeur d'Alene	2%
Idaho Falls	-1%
Mountain Home	-1%
Twin Falls	-2%

ILLINOIS	5%
Addison	5%
Arlington Heights	5%
Aurora	5%
Belleville	3%
Bloomington	5%
Champaign	5%
Chicago	16%
Decatur	5%
Forest Park	9%
Galesburg	5%
Gibson City	5%
Granite City	5%
Green River	5%
Hanover	1%
Harvey	5%
Highland Park	5%
Homewood	5%
Joliet	5%
Kankakee	5%
Mascoutah	3%
North Chicago	9%
North Park	5%
Northfield	5%
Orland Park	5%
Peoria	5%
Peru	5%
Rantoul	5%
Rock Island	4%
Rockford	5%
Springfield	5%
Urbana	5%

INDIANA	0%
Bloomington	1%
Crane	-2%
Fort Wayne	1%
Gary	1%
Indianapolis	-1%
Jeffersonville	1%
Kokomo	1%
Lafayette	1%

INDIANA	continued
Lawrence	-1%
Logansport	1%
New Albany	1%
North Judson	1%
Peru	1%
Porter	1%
Richmond	1%
Rushville	1%
South Bend	1%

IOWA	-1%
Ames	3%
Burlington	-2%
Cedar Rapids	-2%
Cherokee	-2%
Council Bluffs	-2%
Davenport	0%
Decorah	-2%
Des Moines	-3%
Keokuk	-2%
Mason City	-2%
Pocahontas	-2%
Sac City	-2%
Sioux City	-2%
Washington	-2%
Waterloo	-2%

KANSAS	-1%
Atchison	-1%
Emporia	-1%
Hays	-1%
Independence	-1%
Junction City	-1%
Kansas City	-1%
Lawrence	-1%
Leavenworth	7%
Manhattan	-4%
Olathe	-1%
Osage City	-1%
Parsons	-1%
Pittsburg	-1%
Topeka	-1%
Wichita	3%

KENTUCKY	-3%
Ashland	-3%
Bardstown	-3%
Bowling Green	-3%

KENTUCKY	continued
Fort Thomas	-3%
Hopkinsville	-1%
Lexington	-5%
Louisville	-1%
Madisonville	-3%
Paducah	-3%
Radcliff	-1%
Richmond	-3%
Russell	-3%

LOUISIANA	-4%
Alexandria	-4%
Baton Rouge	-4%
Bogalusa	-4%
Bossier Base	-8%
Hammond	-4%
Leesville	-7%
Monroe	-4%
New Orleans	11%
Shreveport	-4%

MAINE	2%
Auburn	1%
Bangor	-1%
Brunswick	4%
Caribou	1%
Cutler	1%
Dexter	1%
Northern Area	1%
Portland	3%
Winter Harbor	1%

MARYLAND	2%
Aberdeen	0%
Annapolis	2%
Baltimore	1%
Bel Air, Hartford	1%
Bethesda	3%
Cascade	0%
College Park	1%
Cumberland	1%
Curtis Bay	1%
Edgewood	1%
Frederick	1%
Hagerstown	1%
Hyattsville	3%
Indian Head	3%
Lexington Park	3%

MARYLAND	continued
Olney	1%
Patuxent River Area	3%
Prince Georges	3%
Westminster	1%
White Oak	1%

MASSACHUSETTS	15%
Ayer	15%
Bedford	15%
Boston	15%
Brockton	15%
Chicopee	15%
Fitchburg	15%
Hingham	15%
Lawrence	15%
Natick	15%
Pittsfield	15%
Quincy	15%
Roslindale	15%
South Weymouth	15%
Springfield	15%
Taunton	15%
Watertown	15%

MICHIGAN	4%
Ann Arbor	5%
Bad Axe	5%
Battle Creek	5%
Bay City	5%
Carleton	5%
Detroit	16%
Flint	5%
Grand Rapids	5%
Grayling	5%
Inkster	5%
Ishpeming	-1%
Lansing	5%
Livonia	5%
Marquette	-1%
Muskegon	5%
Newport	15%
Northern Area	5%
Oscoda	-1%
Pontiac	5%
Republic	-1%
Saginaw	5%
Southfield	5%
Traverse City	-6%

MICHIGAN	continued
Warren	5%

MINNESOTA	5%
Brainerd	5%
Buffalo	5%
Duluth	2%
Fairbault	5%
Fergus Falls	5%
Fort Ripley	5%
International Falls	5%
Mankato	5%
Minneapolis	8%
New Brighton	8%
Rochester	5%
St Cloud	5%
St Paul	8%
Walker	5%
Willmar	5%

MISSISSIPPI	-4%
Bay St Louis	-5%
Biloxi	-5%
Clarksdale	-5%
Columbus	-7%
Greenville	4%
Greenwood	-5%
Gulfport Area	-3%
Jackson	-5%
Laurel	-5%
Meridian	-5%
Pascagoula	-3%
Tupelo	-5%
Vicksburg	-5%

MISSOURI	1%
Belton	0%
Bolivar	0%
Caruthersville	0%
Farmington	0%
Independence	0%
Kansas City	2%
Kirksville	0%
Knob Noster	-1%
Lebanon	2%
Portageville	0%
St Louis	4%
Washington	4%
Weldon Springs	4%

MONTANA .... **−1%**	**NEW JERSEY** ...*continued*	**NEW YORK** .....*continued*	**NORTH CAROLINA** ...*continued*	**OKLAHOMA** ....*continued*
Billings ....−1%	Browns Mills...............11%	Corning 12%	Jacksonville...............−4%	Altus ....−4%
Butte ....−1%	Burlington..................11%	Lockport 12%	Kinston ....−4%	Ardmore...................−2%
Cut Bank.................−1%	Camden....................11%	Long Island................76%	New Bern ....−4%	Bartlesville ....−2%
Fairview..................−1%	Earle 11%	Malone 12%	Raleigh.....................−4%	Chickasha.................−2%
Glasgow..................−1%	Edison.......................11%	Manhattan Beach.......32%	Salisbury...................−4%	Clinton.....................−2%
Great Falls...............−1%	Freehold....................11%	Massena....................12%	Southport..................−4%	Durant......................−2%
Havre ....−1%	Highlands..................11%	Mattydale.................12%	Wilmington...............−4%	El Reno.....................−2%
Helena.....................−1%	Lakehurst 11%	Montauk 12%	Wilson......................−4%	Enid.........................−2%
Kalispell...................−1%	Lodi..........................11%	New York City............84%	Winston-Salem...........−4%	Lawton ....−2%
Lewistown ....−1%	Long Branch..............11%	New York City (Manhattan) .84%		McAlester ....−6%
Miles City.................−1%	Middletown 11%	Newark-Arcadia 11%	**NORTH DAKOTA**. **−3%**	Miami ....−2%
Missoula ....−1%	Mount Hope...............12%	Newburgh...................11%	Bismarck ....−3%	Midwest City..............−2%
	Newark 12%	Niagara Falls..............10%	Grand Forks...............−4%	Muskogee 0%
NEBRASKA .... **−1%**	Pedricktown...............11%	Niskayuna..................11%	Minot ....−1%	Norman ....−2%
Ashland....................0%	Red Bank 11%	Penn Yan...................11%	Nekoma ....−2%	Oklahoma City............0%
Bellevue....................0%	Trenton 11%	Plattsburgh.................4%	Williston ....−2%	Okmulgee ....−2%
Fremont....................0%	Wallington 11%	Rochester...................10%		Ponca City.................−2%
Grand Island ....−4%	Wrightstown 11%	Rockaway...................12%	**OHIO** **3%**	Shawnee...................−2%
Lincoln....................−4%		Rome 12%	Akron 3%	Stillwater ....−1%
Omaha.....................1%	**NEW MEXICO** **2%**	Schenectady...............11%	Chillicothe.................3%	Tulsa........................−1%
	Alamogordo................2%	Seneca Falls................5%	Cincinnati..................3%	
NEVADA................**4%**	Albuquerque...............4%	Staten Island..............77%	Cleveland...................4%	**OREGON** **6%**
Carson City...............5%	Clovis 1%	Stewart 11%	Columbus...................3%	Coos Bay...................6%
Fallon.......................7%	Fort Sumner...............3%	Syracuse....................12%	Dayton 2%	Pendleton 6%
Hawthorne................6%	Gallup 3%	Utica.........................12%	Fairborn 2%	Portland 5%
Las Vegas.................14%	Las Cruces 2%	Watertown 4%	Fremont 4%	Salem.......................6%
North Las Vegas........14%	Sandia Base...............3%	Wayland....................10%	Lima.........................4%	Umatilla....................7%
Reno.......................12%	Santa Fe 3%	West Point 12%	Marietta 3%	
Yerington...................5%			Newark 3%	**PENNSYLVANIA** **3%**
	NEW YORK **17%**	**NORTH CAROLINA** .. **−3%**	Sandusky...................4%	Allentown 4%
NEW HAMPSHIRE..**1%**	Albany 7%	Albemarle..................−4%	Springfield.................3%	Altoona 4%
Claremont..................1%	Amherst 12%	Asheville ....−4%	Steubenville...............2%	Annville.....................4%
Concord.....................1%	Amityville...................12%	Burlington ....−4%	Toledo.......................4%	Bristol 4%
Dover 1%	Auburn 12%	Camp Mackall............−4%	Warren 3%	Brookville..................4%
Manchester 1%	Batavia 12%	Charlotte...................−4%	Wooster.....................3%	Butler 4%
New Boston................1%	Bellmore....................12%	Cherry Point...............−3%	Youngstown...............3%	Carlisle.....................−2%
Portsmouth 1%	Brooklyn....................12%	Durham ....−4%	Zanesville..................3%	Chambersburg............−3%
	Buffalo 12%	Fayetteville...............−4%		Clearfield 4%
NEW JERSEY **11%**	Canandaigua 11%	Goldsboro..................−4%	**OKLAHOMA**........ **−2%**	Erie..........................4%
Bayonne....................11%	Canton 12%	Greensboro ....−4%	Ada ....−2%	Frankfort...................4%

PENNSYLVANIA ...continued

City	%
Gettysburg	4%
Johnstown	4%
Kittanning	4%
Lancaster	4%
Meadville	4%
Mechanicsburg Area	4%
New Castle	4%
New Cumberland	-2%
Oakdale	1%
Philadelphia	7%
Pittsburgh	1%
Punxsutawney	4%
Scranton	4%
Tobyhanna	3%
Valley Forge	4%
Warminster Area	7%
Wilkes Barre	4%
Willow Grove	4%

RHODE ISLAND 9%

City	%
Bristol	9%
Coventry	9%
Cranston	9%
Davisville	9%
Narragansett	9%
Newport	9%
Providence	9%
Warwick	9%

SOUTH CAROLINA ... -1%

City	%
Anderson	-12%
Beaufort Area	5%
Charleston	1%
Clemson	-2%
Columbia	-2%
Greenville	-2%
Myrtle Beach	1%
Rock Hill	-2%
Spartanburg	-2%
Sumter	-2%

SOUTH DAKOTA -2%

City	%
Aberdeen	-3%
Box Elder	1%
Hot Springs	-3%
Mitchell	-3%
Rapid City	1%
Sioux Falls	-4%

TENNESSEE 2%

City	%
Chattanooga	2%
Greeneville	2%
Kingsport	2%
Manchester	0%
Memphis	4%
Milan	2%
Oak Ridge	2%

TEXAS 2%

City	%
Abilene	1%
Alice	1%
Amarillo	1%
Austin	1%
Bay City	1%
Beaumont	1%
Beeville	1%
Brownsville	1%
Bryan	1%
Corpus Chrsti	1%
Dallas	8%
Del Rio	12%
Del Valle	1%
El Paso	1%
Ft Worth	8%
Harlingen	1%
Houston	1%
Huntsville	1%
Killeen	1%
Kingsville	1%
Laredo	1%
Longview	1%
Lubbock	4%

TEXAS ....continued

City	%
Marshall	1%
McAllen	1%
Mineral Wells	1%
Paris	1%
Pasadena	1%
Port Arthur	1%
Rio Grande City	1%
San Angelo	-1%
San Antonio	4%
San Marcos	1%
Sinton	1%
Texarkana	6%
Victoria	1%
Wichita Falls	1%
Yoakum	2%

UTAH 4%

City	%
Brigham City	5%
Clearfield	-6%
Green River	-6%
Logan (Cache Valley)	5%
Ogden	5%
Price	-4%
Provo	5%
Salt Lake City	5%
St. George	5%
Tooele	4%

VERMONT .... -1%

City	%
Burlington	0%
Chester	-1%
Montpelier	-1%
Rutland	-1%

VIRGINIA 2%

City	%
Abingdon	1%
Alexandria	15%
Arlington	15%
Berryville (Winchester)	1%
Blackstone	3%

VIRGINA ....continued

City	%
Bowling Green	4%
Charlottesville	1%
Chesapeake	1%
Chincoteague	1%
Churchland	1%
Dahlgren	-3%
Dam Neck	1%
Dublin (Radford)	1%
Galax	1%
Hampton	3%
Herndon	1%
Marion	1%
Newport News	3%
Norfolk	3%
Petersburg	2%
Quantico	-1%
Richmond	1%
Vint Hill Farms	-1%
Virginia Beach	3%
Warrenton	1%
Williamsburg	3%
Woodbridge	1%
Yorktown	1%

WASHINGTON 7%

City	%
Bangor	7%
Bremerton	10%
Keyport	6%
Lakewood	6%
Olympia	6%
Pacific Beach	6%
Pasco	6%
Puget Sound Area	6%
Seattle	6%
Spokane	9%
Tacoma	6%
Trentwood	7%
Vancouver	6%
Whidbey Island	6%
Yakima	1%

WEST VIRGINIA.. -3%

City	%
Bluefield	-5%
Charleston	-1%
Dawson	-3%
Fairmont	-3%
Grafton	-3%
Huntington	-3%
Martinsburg	-3%
New Martinsville	-3%
Parkersburg	-3%
Ripley	-3%
Romney	-3%
Sugar Grove	-5%
Weirton	-3%
Wheeling	-3%

WISCONSIN 1%

City	%
Clam Lake	1%
Cornell	1%
Dodgeville	1%
Fond du Lac	1%
Junction City	1%
Kewaunee	1%
La Crosse	1%
Ladysmith	1%
Madison	-5%
Milwaukee	6%
Oshkosh	1%
Wausau	1%

WYOMING .... -8%

City	%
Casper	-4%
Cheyenne	-4%
Cody	0%
Evanston	-6%
Gillette	-8%
Jackson	6%
Laramie	-8%
Powell	-9%
Sheridan	0%
Star Valley	4%

unit price pages

The unit price pages have six columns. ❶ The column in the outside margin is the QuickFinder column. It contains headings and information designed to help you quickly find the item you need. ❷ The second column contains the item description along with applicable material, labor, and equipment prices and any necessary item information. ❸ The third column contains a two-letter abbreviation that indicates the unit of measure. ❹ The fourth column contains the price to tear out the item and place the debris in a dumpster on site. ❺ The fifth column contains the price to install the new item. ❻ The sixth column gives the total remove and replace cost.

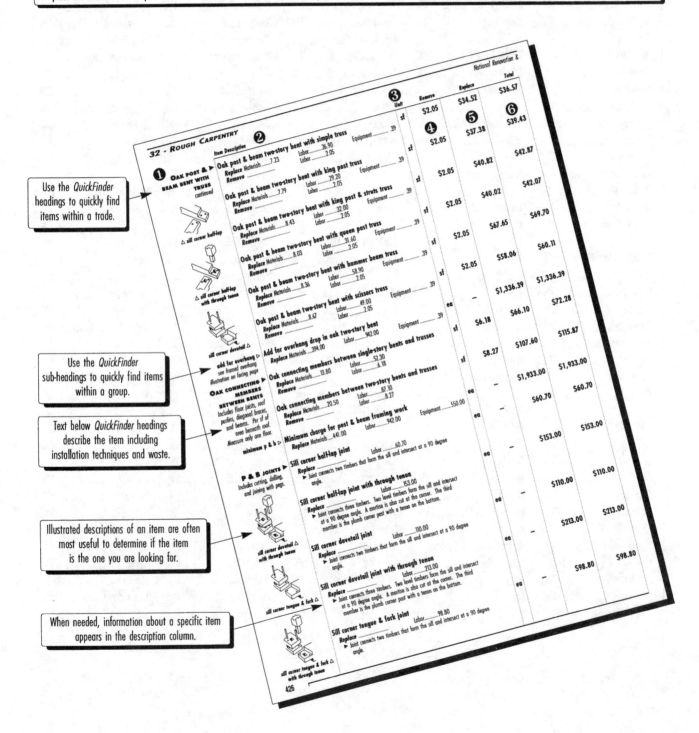

Use the *QuickFinder* headings to quickly find items within a trade.

Use the *QuickFinder* sub-headings to quickly find items within a group.

Text below *QuickFinder* headings describe the item including installation techniques and waste.

Illustrated descriptions of an item are often most useful to determine if the item is the one you are looking for.

When needed, information about a specific item appears in the description column.

time & material charts

Material charts show the material description, the material cost priced per typical unit purchased, the gross coverage, the typical waste, the net coverage after waste has been subtracted, and the resulting materials price including waste and often converted to a different unit of measure.

TIME & MATERIAL CHARTS (selected items)

Concrete Materials

DESCRIPTION	MATERIAL PRICE	GROSS COVERAGE	WASTE	NET COVERAGE	UNIT PRICE
Ready mix concrete delivered					
5 bag mix 2,500 psi, per cy	$96.40 cy	1	6%	.94	$103.00 cy
5.5 bag mix 3,000 psi, per cy	$96.90 cy	1	6%	.94	$103.00 cy
6 bag mix, 3,500 psi, per cy	$101.00 cy	1	6%	.94	$107.00 cy
6.5 bag mix, 4,000 psi, per cy	$101.00 cy	1	6%	.94	$107.00 cy
7 bag mix, 4,500 psi, per cy	$104.00 cy	1	6%	.94	$111.00 cy
7.5 bag mix, 5,000 psi, per cy	$106.00 cy	1	6%	.94	$113.00 cy
add for synthetic fiber reinforcing	$11.90 cy	1	6%	.94	$11.90 cy
add for high early strength	$12.70 cy	1	6%	.94	$12.70 cy
minimum ready mix charge	$124.00 each	1	0%	1	$124.00 ea
Concrete form materials					
form ties	$48.50 box	1	0%	1	

Concrete Rental Equipment

DESCRIPTION	PRICE	COVERAGE		UNIT PRICE
Forms				
plywood wall forms (per sf of form)		400	5%	380
steel curb & gutter forms				$.13 sf
Tractor-mounted auger				
hourly charge	$.19 per day			
delivery and take-home charge	$.93 per day	.25 per sf		$.76 sf
Concrete pump truck		1 lf		$.93 lf
foundation wall	$220.00 per hour			
footings	$465.00 each	90 lf		$2.44 lf
flatwork		1 each		$465.00 ea
piers	$135.00 hour			
grade beam	$135.00 hour	450 sf of wall		$.30 sf
pressure grout	$135.00 hour	112 lf of footing		$1.21 lf
	$135.00 hour	475 lf of flat		$.28 sf
	$135.00 hour	78 lf or pier		$1.73 lf
	$135.00 hour	146 lf of beam		$.92 lf
		4 lf 2" pipe		$33.80 sf

Concrete Labor

LABORER	BASE WAGE	PAID LEAVE	TRUE WAGE	FICA	FUTA	WORKER'S COMP.	UNEMPLOY. INSUR.	HEALTH INSUR.	RETIRE (401k)	LIABILITY INSUR.	COST PER HOUR
Concrete form installer	$23.80	1.86	$25.66	1.96	.21	6.21	2.23	2.92	.77	3.85	$43.80
Concrete finisher	$23.60	1.84	$25.44	1.95	.20	6.16	2.21	2.92	.76	3.82	$43.50
Concrete finisher's helper	$19.20	1.50	$20.70	1.58	.17	5.01	1.80	2.92	.62	3.11	$35.90
Equipment operator	$30.80	2.40	$33.20	2.54	.27	7.38	2.89	2.92	.71	3.82	$53.80
Plasterer	$23.60	1.84	$25.44	1.95	.20	6.04	2.21	2.92	1.00	4.98	$44.70
Concrete saw operator	$22.00	1.72	$23.72	1.81	.19	4.33	2.06	2.92	.76	3.56	$39.30
Compaction grouter	$34.30	2.68	$36.98	2.83	.30	8.96	3.22	2.92	1.11	5.55	$61.90
Laborer	$16.60	1.29	$17.89	1.37	.14	4.33	1.56	2.92	.54	2.68	$31.40
Demolition laborer	$14.40	1.12	$15.52	1.19	.12	5.01	1.35	2.92	.47	2.33	$28.90

Concrete Labor Productivity

WORK DESCRIPTION	LABORER	COST PER HOUR	PRODUCTIVITY	UNIT PRICE
Demolition				
remove footings including rebar	demolition laborer	$28.90		
remove footings including CEC rebar	demolition laborer	$28.90	1.64	$47.40 cy
remove footings with rebar	demolition laborer	$28.90	1.96	$56.60 cy
remove footings with CEC rebar	demolition laborer	$28.90	.121	$3.50 lf
remove foundation including rebar	demolition laborer	$28.90	.147	$4.25 lf
remove foundation including CEC rebar	demolition laborer	$28.90	2.44	$70.50 cy
remove 5" or 6" foundation with rebar	demolition laborer	$28.90	2.94	$85.00 cy
remove 5" or 6" foundation with CEC rebar	demolition laborer	$28.90	.073	$2.11 sf
remove 8" or 10" foundation with rebar	demolition laborer	$28.90	.088	$2.54 sf
remove 8" or 10" foundation with CEC rebar	demolition laborer	$28.90	.076	$2.20 sf
remove footing & foundation with rebar	demolition laborer	$28.90	.092	$2.66 sf
			1.96	$56.60 cy

Equipment charts show the cost to rent equipment, the amount of work that can be done with the equipment per period of time, and the resulting unit price.

Labor charts show the base wage, then add all additional costs that are based on wage. More information is always listed below this chart. It's important to note the "True" wage before adding labor related expenses. The true wage is the wage rate plus an allowance for vacation time. Since all the other costs must be paid even when an employee is on vacation, it is important that they become a component in the cost calculations when estimating work.

Labor productivity charts show the description of the work, the laborer or crew who will do the work, the average cost per man hour, the productivity and the resulting cost per unit.

crews

Craft Code	Avg. Cost per Hour	Crew Composition
1A	$34.20	acoustic ceiling installer
2A	$38.60	appliance installer
3A	$47.80	appliance refinisher
4A	$42.80	awning installer
5A	$32.10	awning installer's helper
6A	$37.50	awning installer awning installer's helper
1B	$25.70	cleaning laborer
2B	$55.20	post & beam carpenter
3B	$39.00	post & beam carpenter's helper
4B	$47.10	post & beam carpenter post & beam carpenter's helper
1C	$43.50	carpenter
5C	$32.10	carpenter's helper
6C	$37.80	carpenter carpenter's helper
1D	$28.90	demolition laborer
2D	$37.90	drywall hanger drywall hanger's helper
3D	$43.40	drywall hanger
4D	$32.30	drywall hanger's helper
5D	$43.70	drywall taper
6D	$39.80	drywall hanger drywall hanger's helper drywall taper
5E	$31.10	excavation laborer
6E	$42.50	excavation laborer equipment operator
7E	$45.30	electrician
8E	$33.50	electrician's helper
9E	$39.40	electrician electrician's helper
1F	$43.80	concrete form installer
2F	$31.40	concrete laborer
3F	$37.60	concrete form installer concrete laborer
4F	$37.80	carpenter (fence installer) carpenter's helper
5F	$44.60	painter
6F	$43.50	concrete finisher
7F	$35.90	concrete finisher's helper
8F	$39.70	concrete finisher concrete finisher's helper
9F	$38.70	concrete form installer concrete laborer concrete finisher concrete finisher's helper
1G	$61.90	compaction grouting specialist
2G	$46.70	compaction grouting specialist concrete laborer
1H	$44.80	hazardous materials laborer
2H	$48.40	HVAC installer
3H	$36.70	wallpaper hanger

Craft Code	Avg. Cost per Hour	Crew Composition
1I	$31.80	insulation installer
2I	$36.00	cabinet installer laborer
3I	$43.30	flooring installer
4I	$32.00	flooring installer's helper
5I	$37.70	flooring installer flooring installer's helper
6I	$43.50	paneling installer
7I	$32.10	paneling installer's helper
2L	$28.40	cabinet installer's helper
3L	$27.50	masking & moving laborer
1M	$48.00	mason
2M	$44.00	mason's helper
3M	$33.60	hod carrier
4M	$41.90	mason mason's helper hod carrier / laborer
5M	$46.00	mason mason's helper
6M	$112.00	stone carver
7M	$33.50	mobile home repair specialist
1O	$53.80	equipment operator
2O	$39.30	concrete saw operator
4P	$44.70	plasterer
5P	$38.30	plasterer's helper
6P	$41.50	plasterer plasterer's helper
7P	$46.70	plumber
8P	$37.80	paneling installer paneling installer's helper
9P	$39.80	plumber's helper
3R	$42.20	retaining wall installer
4R	$52.30	roofer
5R	$44.00	roofer's helper
6R	$48.20	roofer roofer's helper
1S	$35.30	susp. ceiling installer susp. ceiling installer's helper
2S	$40.50	susp. ceiling installer
3S	$30.10	susp. ceiling installer's helper
4S	$43.10	siding installer
5S	$31.90	siding installer's helper
6S	$37.50	siding installer siding installer's helper
7S	$39.90	security system installer
8S	$53.10	swimming pool installer
9S	$37.10	water extractor
1T	$40.70	tile layer
7Z	$72.40	mildew remediation specialist
8Z	$44.20	mildew remediation assistant
9Z	$58.30	mildew remediation specialist mildew remediation assistant

1 .... *Acoustic Ceilings*

Item Description	Unit	Remove	Replace	Total	
Minimum charge for acoustic ceiling tile work	ea	–	$60.30	$60.30	◀ **MINIMUM**
Replace Materials.......17.50 Labor..........42.80					
1/2" ceiling tiles on furring strips, smooth face	sf	$.35	$1.94	$2.29	◀ **1/2" ON STRIPS**
Replace Materials ...... 1.08 Labor............ .86					*12" x 12" tiles stapled in place. Does not include furring strips. Includes 3% waste.*
Remove .... Labor............ .35					
1/2" ceiling tiles on furring strips, fissured face	sf	$.35	$2.25	$2.60	
Replace Materials........1.39 Labor............ .86					
Remove .... Labor............ .35					
1/2" ceiling tiles on furring strips, textured face	sf	$.35	$2.45	$2.80	
Replace Materials........1.59 Labor............ .86					
Remove .... Labor............ .35					
1/2" ceiling tiles on furring strips, patterned face	sf	$.35	$2.56	$2.91	
Replace Materials........1.70 Labor............ .86					
Remove .... Labor............ .35					
1/2" ceiling tiles on flat ceiling, smooth face	sf	$.46	$2.07	$2.53	◀ **1/2" ON FLAT**
Replace Materials ...... 1.08 Labor............ .99					*12" x 12" tiles glued in place. Includes 3% waste.*
Remove .... Labor............ .46					
1/2" ceiling tiles on flat ceiling, fissured face	sf	$.46	$2.38	$2.84	
Replace Materials........1.39 Labor............ .99					
Remove .... Labor............ .46					
1/2" ceiling tiles on flat ceiling, textured face	sf	$.46	$2.58	$3.04	
Replace Materials........1.59 Labor............ .99					
Remove .... Labor............ .46					
1/2" ceiling tiles on flat ceiling, patterned face	sf	$.46	$2.69	$3.15	
Replace Materials........1.70 Labor............ .99					
Remove .... Labor............ .46					
5/8" ceiling tiles on furring strips, smooth face	sf	$.35	$2.25	$2.60	◀ **5/8" ON STRIPS**
Replace Materials........1.39 Labor............ .86					*12" x 12" tiles stapled in place. Does not include furring strips. Includes 3% waste.*
Remove .... Labor............ .35					
5/8" ceiling tiles on furring strips, fissured face	sf	$.35	$2.45	$2.80	
Replace Materials........1.59 Labor............ .86					
Remove .... Labor............ .35					
5/8" ceiling tiles on furring strips, textured face	sf	$.35	$2.66	$3.01	
Replace Materials........1.80 Labor............ .86					
Remove .... Labor............ .35					
5/8" ceiling tiles on furring strips, patterned face	sf	$.35	$2.76	$3.11	
Replace Materials........1.90 Labor............ .86					
Remove .... Labor............ .35					
5/8" ceiling tiles on flat ceiling, smooth face	sf	$.46	$2.38	$2.84	◀ **5/8" ON FLAT**
Replace Materials........1.39 Labor............ .99					*12" x 12" tiles glued in place. Includes 3% waste.*
Remove .... Labor............ .46					

RELATED ITEMS
Cleaning 55
Painting 333
Suspended Ceilings......483

	Item Description	Unit	Remove	Replace	Total
5/8" ON FLAT ► *continued*	**5/8" ceiling tiles on flat ceiling, fissured face**	sf	$.46	$2.58	$3.04
	Replace Materials........1.59 Labor............99				
	Remove .... Labor............46				
	5/8" ceiling tiles on flat ceiling, textured face	sf	$.46	$2.79	$3.25
	Replace Materials........1.80 Labor............99				
	Remove .... Labor............46				
	5/8" ceiling tiles on flat ceiling, patterned face	sf	$.46	$2.89	$3.35
	Replace Materials........1.90 Labor............99				
	Remove .... Labor............46				
3/4" ON STRIPS ► *12" x 12" tiles stapled in place. Does not include furring strips. Includes 3% waste.*	**3/4" ceiling tiles on furring strips, smooth face**	sf	$.35	$2.35	$2.70
	Replace Materials........1.49 Labor............86				
	Remove .... Labor............35				
	3/4" ceiling tiles on furring strips, fissured face	sf	$.35	$2.56	$2.91
	Replace Materials........1.70 Labor............86				
	Remove .... Labor............35				
	3/4" ceiling tiles on furring strips, textured face	sf	$.35	$2.70	$3.05
	Replace Materials........1.84 Labor............86				
	Remove .... Labor............35				
	3/4" ceiling tiles on furring strips, patterned face	sf	$.35	$2.86	$3.21
	Replace Materials........2.00 Labor............86				
	Remove .... Labor............35				
3/4" ON FLAT ► *12" x 12" tiles glued in place. Includes 3% waste.*	**3/4" ceiling tiles on flat ceiling, smooth face**	sf	$.46	$2.48	$2.94
	Replace Materials........1.49 Labor............99				
	Remove .... Labor............46				
	3/4" ceiling tiles on flat ceiling, fissured face	sf	$.46	$2.69	$3.15
	Replace Materials........1.70 Labor............99				
	Remove .... Labor............46				
	3/4" ceiling tiles on flat ceiling, textured face	sf	$.46	$2.83	$3.29
	Replace Materials........1.84 Labor............99				
	Remove .... Labor............46				
	3/4" ceiling tiles on flat ceiling, patterned face	sf	$.46	$2.99	$3.45
	Replace Materials........2.00 Labor............99				
	Remove .... Labor............46				
ADDITIONAL ► **COSTS**	**Add for 3/4" tiles with fire rating**	sf	—	$.29	$.29
	Replace Materials 29				
	Add for aluminum-coated tiles	sf	—	$.43	$.43
	Replace Materials 43				
FURRING STRIPS ► *Nailed and glued to joists or flat ceiling. Includes 4% waste.*	**1" x 2" furring strips 12" on center**	sf	$.26	$.48	$.74
	Replace Materials ....24 Labor............24				
	Remove .... Labor............26				
REPAIR ► **LOOSE TILE**	**Repair loose acoustic tile**	ea	—	$8.79	$8.79
	Replace Materials ....14 Labor 8.65				
ANGLED INSTALL ►	**Add 24% for diagonal install**				
	Add 31% for chevron install				
	Add 40% for herringbone install				

TIME & MATERIAL CHARTS (selected items)

Acoustic Ceiling Materials

DESCRIPTION	MATERIAL PRICE	GROSS COVERAGE	WASTE	NET COVERAGE	UNIT PRICE
1/2" thick acoustic tile (per 12" x 12" tile)					
smooth face	$.90 each	1	3%	.97	$.93 sf
fissured face	$1.20 each	1	3%	.97	$1.24 sf
textured face	$1.40 each	1	3%	.97	$1.44 sf
patterned face	$1.50 each	1	3%	.97	$1.55 sf
5/8" thick acoustic tile (per 12" x 12" tile)					
smooth face	$1.20 each	1	3%	.97	$1.24 sf
fissured face	$1.40 each	1	3%	.97	$1.44 sf
textured face	$1.60 each	1	3%	.97	$1.65 sf
patterned face	$1.70 each	1	3%	.97	$1.75 sf
3/4" thick acoustic tile (per 12" x 12" tile)					
smooth face	$1.30 each	1	3%	.97	$1.34 sf
fissured face	$1.50 each	1	3%	.97	$1.55 sf
textured face	$1.64 each	1	3%	.97	$1.69 sf
patterned face	$1.79 each	1	3%	.97	$1.85 sf
Additional material costs					
add for fire rating	$.28 per sf	1	3%	.97	$.30 sf
add for aluminum-coated face	$.42 per sf	1	3%	.97	$.46 sf
add **5%** for diagonal installation					
add **10%** for chevron installation					
add **15%** for herringbone installation					
Tile adhesion					
adhesive	$13.90 per gallon	102	2%	99.96	$.14 sf
staples	$8.60 per box	1,200	4%	1,152	$.01 sf
1" x 2" furring strips 12" on center	$.80 per 8' strip	6.77	4%	6.5	$.12 sf
construction adhesive (for furring strips)	$5.40 per cartridge	87	4%	83.52	$.06 sf
nails (for furring strips)	$54.00 per box	3,212	4%	3,083.52	$.02 sf

Acoustic Ceiling Labor

LABORER	BASE WAGE	PAID LEAVE	TRUE WAGE	FICA	FUTA	WORKER'S COMP.	UNEMPLOY. INSUR.	HEALTH INSUR.	RETIRE (401k)	LIABILITY INSUR.	COST PER HOUR
Acoustic ceiling installer	$19.80	1.54	$21.34	1.63	.17	2.47	1.86	2.92	.64	3.20	$34.20
Demolition laborer	$14.40	1.12	$15.52	1.19	.12	5.01	1.35	2.92	.47	2.33	$28.90

Paid Leave is calculated based on two weeks paid vacation, one week sick leave, and seven paid holidays. Employer's matching portion of **FICA** is 7.65 percent. **FUTA** (Federal Unemployment) is .8 percent. **Worker's compensation** for the acoustic ceiling trade was calculated using a national average of 11.57 percent. **Unemployment insurance** was calculated using a national average of 8.7 percent. **Health insurance** was calculated based on a projected national average for 2005 of $580 per employee (and family when applicable) per month. Employer pays 80 percent for a per month cost of $464 per employee. **Retirement** is based on a 401(k) retirement program with employer matching of 50 percent. Employee contributions to the 401(k) plan are an average of 6 percent of the true wage. **Liability insurance** is based on a national average of 14.0 percent.

Acoustic Ceiling Labor Productivity

WORK DESCRIPTION	LABORER	COST PER HOUR	PRODUCTIVITY	UNIT PRICE
Demolition				
tiles attached with adhesive	demolition laborer	$28.90	.016	**$.46** sf
tiles attached with fasteners	demolition laborer	$28.90	.012	**$.35** sf
ceiling furring strips	demolition laborer	$28.90	.009	**$.26** sf
Repair				
repair loose tile	installer	$34.20	.253	**$8.65** ea
Installation				
tiles on furring strips	installer	$34.20	.025	**$.86** sf
tiles on flat ceiling	installer	$34.20	.029	**$.99** sf
furring strips	installer	$34.20	.007	**$.24** sf
Additional labor costs				
minimum labor charge	installer	$34.20	1.25	**$42.80** ea
add **55%** for diagonal installation				
add **65%** for chevron installation				
add **85%** for herringbone installation				

NOTES: _____

_____

_____

_____

_____

_____

_____

_____

_____

_____

_____

_____

_____

_____

_____

_____

_____

_____

_____

_____

_____

_____

_____

_____

_____

_____ end

2 .... *Appliances*

Item Description	Unit	Remove	Replace	Total	
Minimum charge for appliance work	ea	–	$110.30	$110.30	◄ **MINIMUM**
Replace Materials ......35.00 Labor 75.30					
Gas cook top, standard grade	ea	$28.20	$522.90	$551.10	◄ **GAS COOK TOP**
Replace Materials ....430.00 Labor 92.90					
Remove .... Labor 28.20					
► Baked enamel finish, standard burners, pilotless ignition.					
Gas cook top, high grade	ea	$28.20	$652.90	$681.10	
Replace Materials ....560.00 Labor 92.90					
Remove .... Labor 28.20					
► Tempered glass or brushed chrome finish, sealed burners, pilotless ignition, automatic reignition. May have retractable downdraft unit.					
Gas cook top with grill / griddle	ea	$28.20	$852.90	$881.10	
Replace Materials ....760.00 Labor 92.90					
Remove .... Labor 28.20					
► Tempered glass or brushed chrome finish, two sealed burners, downdraft exhaust unit, gas grill with griddle attachment, pilotless ignition, automatic reignition.					
Remove gas cook top for work, then reinstall	ea	–	$175.00	$175.00	
Replace Materials ....3.00 Labor 172.00					
Gas range, economy grade	ea	$29.80	$605.70	$635.50	◄ **GAS RANGE**
Replace Materials .....510.00 Labor 95.70					
Remove .... Labor 29.80					
► Free-standing with standard-clean oven, chrome drip pans, analog clock and timer.					
Gas range, standard grade	ea	$29.80	$775.70	$805.50	
Replace Materials ....680.00 Labor 95.70					
Remove .... Labor 29.80					
► Free-standing with continuous-clean oven, chrome drip pans, digital clock and timer.					
Gas range, high grade	ea	$29.80	$1,015.70	$1,045.50	
Replace Materials ....920.00 Labor 95.70					
Remove .... Labor 29.80					
► Free-standing with self-clean oven, sealed burners, digital clock and timer.					
Gas range with grill / griddle	ea	$29.80	$1,328.10	$1,357.90	
Replace Materials ...1230.00 Labor 98.10					
Remove .... Labor 29.80					
► Free-standing with self-clean oven, two sealed burners, grill, digital clock and timer.					
Space-saver gas range, standard grade	ea	$29.80	$752.90	$782.70	◄ **SPACE SAVER GAS RANGE**
Replace Materials ....660.00 Labor 92.90					
Remove .... Labor 29.80					
► 20" free-standing with continuous-clean oven, chrome drip pans, digital clock and timer.					
Space-saver gas range, high grade	ea	$29.80	$942.90	$972.70	
Replace Materials ....850.00 Labor 92.90					
Remove .... Labor 29.80					
► 20" free-standing with self-clean oven, sealed burners, digital clock and timer.					

RELATED ITEMS

Electrical *(wiring)*
  gas oven or range 143

Item Description	Unit	Remove	Replace	Total
HIGH-LOW ▶ GAS RANGE				
High-low gas range with microwave high, standard grade	ea	$34.10	$2,109.00	$2,143.10
Replace Materials...2010.00 Labor 99.00				
Remove .... Labor 34.10				
▶ 1.4 cf microwave with touch-pad controls. Range with continuous-clean oven, chrome drip pans, digital clock and timer.				
High-low gas range with microwave high, high grade	ea	$34.10	$2,309.00	$2,343.10
Replace Materials...2210.00 Labor 99.00				
Remove .... Labor 34.10				
▶ 1.4 cf microwave with touch-pad controls. Range with self-clean oven, chrome drip pans, digital clock and timer.				
High-low gas range with microwave high, deluxe grade	ea	$34.10	$2,599.00	$2,633.10
Replace Materials..2500.00 Labor 99.00				
Remove .... Labor 34.10				
▶ 1.4 cf microwave with touch-pad controls. Range with self-clean oven, chrome drip pans, digital clock and timer, integrated hood and venting system.				
Remove gas range for work, then reinstall	ea	–	$193.00	$193.00
Replace Materials........3.00 Labor 190.00				

RESTAURANT ▶ GAS RANGE

Some common manufacturers are Viking, Thermador and Garland. Many of these manufacturers also deliver economy models starting at around **$1,390**. Also beware of "mimicked" restaurant styles from prominent manufacturers of standard ranges that sell from **$890** to **$2,250**.

Item Description	Unit	Remove	Replace	Total
Restaurant-style gas range, standard grade	ea	$86.70	$2,967.00	$3,053.70
Replace Materials...2760.00 Labor.........207.00				
Remove .... Labor 86.70				
▶ Stainless-steel or black epoxy finish, zero clearance, insulated handles, stainless-steel upper shelf, electronic ignition, push-to-turn controls, six burners, single oven with in-oven infrared gas broiler.				
Restaurant-style gas range, high grade	ea	$86.70	$6,247.00	$6,333.70
Replace Materials..6040.00 Labor.........207.00				
Remove .... Labor 86.70				
▶ Stainless-steel or colored epoxy finish, zero clearance, insulated handles, stainless-steel upper shelf, electronic ignition, push-to-turn controls, four burners with griddle, and single oven.				
Restaurant-style gas range, deluxe grade	ea	$86.70	$9,707.00	$9,793.70
Replace Materials..9500.00 Labor.........207.00				
Remove .... Labor 86.70				
▶ Stainless-steel or colored epoxy finish, zero clearance, insulated handles, stainless-steel upper shelf, electronic ignition, push-to-turn controls, six burners with griddle, and convection oven.				
Remove restaurant-style gas range for work, then reinstall	ea	–	$274.00	$274.00
Replace Materials........6.00 Labor.........268.00				
GAS WALL OVEN ▶				
Gas wall oven, economy grade	ea	$38.70	$645.80	$684.50
Replace Materials ....562.00 Labor 83.80				
Remove .... Labor 38.70				
▶ Standard-clean oven, pilotless ignition.				
Gas wall oven, standard grade	ea	$38.70	$731.80	$770.50
Replace Materials ....648.00 Labor 83.80				
Remove .... Labor 38.70				
▶ Standard-clean oven, pilotless ignition, electronic pad controls.				
Gas wall oven, high grade	ea	$38.70	$909.80	$948.50
Replace Materials ....826.00 Labor 83.80				
Remove .... Labor 38.70				
▶ Continuous-clean oven, pilotless ignition, electronic pad controls with clock.				

Item Description	Unit	Remove	Replace	Total
Gas wall oven, deluxe grade	ea	$38.70	$1,103.80	$1,142.50
Replace Materials ..1020.00 Labor 83.80				
Remove .... Labor 38.70				
▶ One self-clean oven, pilotless ignition, electronic pad controls with clock.				
Remove gas wall oven for work, then reinstall	ea	–	$159.00	$159.00
Replace Materials ....5.00 Labor 154.00				
Gas double wall oven, economy grade	ea	$56.40	$1,254.00	$1,310.40
Replace Materials ....1100.00 Labor 154.00				
Remove .... Labor 56.40				
▶ Two standard-clean ovens with pilotless ignition.				
Gas double wall oven, standard grade	ea	$56.40	$1,414.00	$1,470.40
Replace Materials ....1260.00 Labor 154.00				
Remove .... Labor 56.40				
▶ One standard-clean oven, one continuous-clean oven, pilotless ignition, electronic pad controls with clock.				
Gas double wall oven, high grade	ea	$56.40	$1,764.00	$1,820.40
Replace Materials ...1610.00 Labor 154.00				
Remove .... Labor 56.40				
▶ One continuous-clean oven, one self-clean oven, pilotless ignition, electronic pad controls with clock.				
Gas double wall oven, deluxe grade	ea	$56.40	$2,144.00	$2,200.40
Replace Materials ....1990.00 Labor 154.00				
Remove .... Labor 56.40				
▶ Two self-clean ovens, pilotless ignition, electronic pad controls with clock.				
Remove gas double wall oven for work, then reinstall	ea	–	$285.00	$285.00
Replace Materials ....6.00 Labor 279.00				
Electric cook top, standard grade	ea	$29.80	$460.20	$490.00
Replace Materials ....380.00 Labor 80.20				
Remove .... Labor 29.80				
▶ Baked enamel finish with Calrod coil burners.				
Electric cook top, high grade	ea	$29.80	$560.20	$590.00
Replace Materials ....480.00 Labor 80.20				
Remove .... Labor 29.80				
▶ Brushed chrome finish with Calrod coil burners.				
Electric cook top with grill / griddle	ea	$29.80	$650.20	$680.00
Replace Materials ....570.00 Labor 80.20				
Remove .... Labor 29.80				
▶ Tempered glass or brushed chrome finish, downdraft exhaust unit, two Calrod burners, grill with griddle attachment.				
Solid-disk electric cook top, standard grade	ea	$29.80	$680.20	$710.00
Replace Materials ....600.00 Labor 80.20				
Remove .... Labor 29.80				
▶ Solid cast-iron burners, rotary heat controls.				
Solid-disk electric cook top, high grade	ea	$29.80	$750.20	$780.00
Replace Materials .....670.00 Labor 80.20				
Remove .... Labor 29.80				
▶ Solid cast-iron burners, rotary heat controls, low profile, brushed chrome finish.				

RELATED ITEMS

Electrical *(wiring)*
gas oven or range 143
electric appliance 142
cook top 144
Cleaning 55

◀ **GAS DOUBLE WALL OVEN**

◀ **ELECTRIC COOK TOP**

◀ **SOLID-DISK ELECTRIC COOK TOP**

	Item Description	Unit	Remove	Replace	Total
SOLID-DISK ► ELECTRIC COOK TOP *continued*	**Solid-disk electric cook top with grill / griddle** *Replace* Materials ....740.00 Labor ....80.20 *Remove* .... Labor ....29.80 ► Downdraft exhaust unit, two solid cast-iron burners, grill with griddle attachment.	ea	$29.80	$820.20	$850.00
FLAT-SURFACE ► ELECTRIC COOK TOP *For halogen instant-heat burners instead of radiant heat burners add $130 per burner.*	**Flat-surface radiant electric cook top, standard grade** *Replace* Materials ....720.00 Labor ....80.20 *Remove* .... Labor ....29.80 ► White on white or almond on almond, 30" smooth surface, fingerprint and scratch resistant.	ea	$29.80	$800.20	$830.00
	Flat-surface radiant electric cook top, high grade *Replace* Materials ....830.00 Labor ....80.20 *Remove* .... Labor ....29.80 ► Black on black radiant cook top, 30" smooth surface, fingerprint and scratch resistant.	ea	$29.80	$910.20	$940.00
	Flat-surface radiant cook top with grill / griddle *Replace* Materials ....880.00 Labor ....80.20 *Remove* .... Labor ....29.80 ► Two flat radiant burners, center down draft unit, grill with griddle attachment.	ea	$29.80	$960.20	$990.00
MODULAR ► ELECTRIC COOK TOP UNIT	**Modular electric cook top, two coil (Calrod) burners** *Replace* Materials ....300.00 Labor ....28.50 *Remove* .... Labor ....14.70 ► Two Calrod coil burners module.	ea	$14.70	$328.50	$343.20
	Modular electric cook top, two solid-disk burners *Replace* Materials ....350.00 Labor ....28.50 *Remove* .... Labor ....14.70 ► Two solid-disk cast-iron burners module.	ea	$14.70	$378.50	$393.20
	Modular electric cook top, two flat-surface radiant burners *Replace* Materials ....400.00 Labor ....28.50 *Remove* .... Labor ....14.70 ► Two smooth-surface radiant heat burners module. For halogen instant-heat burners instead of radiant heat burners add $130 per burner.	ea	$14.70	$428.50	$443.20
	Modular electric cook top, griddle *Replace* Materials ....420.00 Labor ....28.50 *Remove* .... Labor ....14.70 ► Griddle module. (See grill for units with a griddle attachment that fits on top of the grill module.)	ea	$14.70	$448.50	$463.20
	Modular electric cook top, grill *Replace* Materials ....450.00 Labor ....28.50 *Remove* .... Labor ....14.70 ► Grill module with one-piece grill and removable porcelain enamel reflector pan. Includes griddle accessory.	ea	$14.70	$478.50	$493.20
	Modular electric cook top, downdraft unit *Replace* Materials ....220.00 Labor ....22.10 *Remove* .... Labor ....14.70 ► Two- to three-speed fan, 350 to 500 cfm. Add $150 for telescopic downdraft unit.	ea	$14.70	$242.10	$256.80
REMOVE & ► REINSTALL COOK TOP	**Remove modular cooking unit for work, then reinstall** *Replace* .... Labor 53.50	ea	–	$53.50	$53.50
	Remove modular downdraft unit for work, then reinstall *Replace* Materials ....2.00 Labor 40.00	ea	–	$42.00	$42.00

Item Description	Unit	Remove	Replace	Total	
Remove electric cook top for work, then reinstall	ea	–	$149.00	$149.00	
Replace Materials........2.00 Labor 147.00					
Electric range, standard grade	ea	$28.20	$648.40	$676.60	◄ **ELECTRIC RANGE**
Replace Materials ....570.00 Labor...........78.40					
Remove .... Labor 28.20					
► Free-standing range with standard-clean oven, four Calrod coil burners, chrome drip pans, analog clock and timer.					
Electric range, high grade	ea	$28.20	$848.40	$876.60	
Replace Materials ....770.00 Labor...........78.40					
Remove .... Labor 28.20					
► Free-standing range with continuous-clean oven, four Calrod coil burners, chrome drip pans, digital clock and timer.					
Electric range, deluxe grade	ea	$28.20	$1,068.40	$1,096.60	
Replace Materials ....990.00 Labor...........78.40					
Remove .... Labor 28.20					
► Free-standing range with self-clean oven, four Calrod coil burners, chrome drip pans, digital clock and timer.					
Electric range with grill / griddle	ea	$28.20	$1,298.40	$1,326.60	
Replace Materials...1220.00 Labor...........78.40					
Remove .... Labor 28.20					
► Free-standing range with self-clean oven, two Calrod coil burners, grill with griddle accessory and cover, digital clock and timer.					
Solid-disk electric range, standard grade	ea	$28.20	$868.40	$896.60	◄ **SOLID-DISK ELECTRIC RANGE**
Replace Materials ....790.00 Labor...........78.40					
Remove .... Labor 28.20					
► Free-standing range with standard-clean oven, four cast-iron solid-disk burners, chrome drip pans, analog clock and timer.					
Solid-disk electric range, high grade	ea	$28.20	$918.40	$946.60	
Replace Materials ....840.00 Labor...........78.40					
Remove .... Labor 28.20					
► Free-standing range with continuous-clean oven, four cast-iron solid-disk burners, chrome drip pans, digital clock and timer.					
Solid-disk electric range, deluxe grade	ea	$28.20	$1,118.40	$1,146.60	
Replace Materials ..1040.00 Labor...........78.40					
Remove .... Labor 28.20					
► Free-standing range with self-clean oven, four cast-iron solid-disk burners, digital clock and timer.					
Solid-disk electric range with grill / griddle	ea	$28.20	$1,358.40	$1,386.60	
Replace Materials ..1280.00 Labor...........78.40					
Remove .... Labor 28.20					
► Free-standing range with self-clean oven, two cast-iron solid-disk burners, grill with griddle accessory and cover, digital clock and timer.					
Flat-surface radiant electric range, standard grade	ea	$28.20	$1,038.40	$1,066.60	◄ **FLAT-SURFACE ELECTRIC RANGE**
Replace Materials ....960.00 Labor...........78.40					*For halogen instant-heat burners instead of radiant heat burners add $130 per burner.*
Remove .... Labor 28.20					
► Free-standing range with standard-clean oven, four smooth-surface burners, chrome drip pans, analog clock and timer.					
Flat-surface radiant electric range, high grade	ea	$28.20	$1,178.40	$1,206.60	
Replace Materials ...1100.00 Labor...........78.40					
Remove .... Labor 28.20					
► Free-standing range with continuous-clean oven, four smooth-surface burners, chrome drip pans, digital clock and timer.					

RELATED ITEMS

Electrical *(wiring)*
electric appliance............142
cook top 144
electric oven or range......144

Item Description	Unit	Remove	Replace	Total
FLAT-SURFACE ► **Flat-surface radiant electric range, deluxe grade**	ea	$28.20	$1,428.40	$1,456.60
ELECTRIC RANGE *Replace* Materials...1350.00 Labor.........78.40				
continued *Remove* .... Labor 28.20				
► Free-standing range with self-clean oven, four smooth-surface burners, digital clock and timer.				
Flat-surface radiant electric range with grill / griddle	ea	$28.20	$2,068.40	$2,096.60
Replace Materials...1990.00 Labor..........78.40				
Remove .... Labor 28.20				
► Free-standing range with self-cleaning oven, two smooth-surface burners, grill with griddle accessory and cover, digital clock and timer.				
Remove electric range for work, then reinstall	ea	–	$168.00	$168.00
Replace Materials........4.00 Labor 164.00				
DROP-IN OR ► **Drop-in or slide-in electric range, standard grade**	ea	$35.30	$814.20	$849.50
SLIDE-IN *Replace* Materials....720.00 Labor.........94.20				
ELECTRIC RANGE *Remove* .... Labor..........35.30				
► Drop-in or slide-in range with standard-clean oven, four Calrod coil burners, chrome drip pans, analog clock and timer.				
Drop-in or slide-in electric range, high grade	ea	$35.30	$1,054.20	$1,089.50
Replace Materials ....960.00 Labor..........94.20				
Remove .... Labor..........35.30				
► Drop-in or slide-in range with continuous-clean oven, four solid-disk cast-iron burners, chrome drip pans, digital clock and timer.				
Drop-in or slide-in electric range, deluxe grade	ea	$35.30	$1,224.20	$1,259.50
Replace Materials ...1130.00 Labor..........94.20				
Remove .... Labor..........35.30				
► Drop-in or slide-in range with self-clean oven, four smooth-surface burners, digital clock and timer.				
Drop-in or slide-in electric range with grill / griddle	ea	$35.30	$1,474.20	$1,509.50
Replace Materials ..1380.00 Labor..........94.20				
Remove .... Labor..........35.30				
► Drop-in or slide-in range with self-clean oven, two smooth-surface burners, grill with griddle accessory and cover, digital clock and timer.				
Remove drop-in or slide-in electric range, for work, then reinstall	ea	–	$184.00	$184.00
Replace Materials........5.00 Labor 179.00				
SPACE-SAVER ► **Space-saver electric range, standard grade**	ea	$28.20	$1,036.00	$1,064.20
ELECTRIC RANGE *Replace* Materials ....960.00 Labor..........76.00				
Remove .... Labor 28.20				
► 20" free-standing range with standard-clean oven, four Calrod coil burners, and chrome drip pans.				
Space-saver electric range, high grade	ea	$28.20	$1,106.00	$1,134.20
Replace Materials ..1030.00 Labor..........76.00				
Remove .... Labor 28.20				
► 20" free-standing range with continuous-clean oven, four Calrod coil burners, and chrome drip pans.				
HIGH-LOW ► **High-low electric range with microwave high, standard grade**	ea	$29.80	$1,941.10	$1,970.90
ELECTRIC RANGE *Replace* Materials ..1860.00 Labor..........81.10				
Remove .... Labor 29.80				
► 1.4 cf microwave with touch-pad controls. Range with continuous-clean oven, four Calrod burners, chrome drip pans, digital clock and timer.				

Item Description	Unit	Remove	Replace	Total
High-low electric range with microwave high, high grade	ea	$29.80	$2,141.10	$2,170.90
Replace Materials ..2060.00 Labor...........81.10				
Remove .... Labor 29.80				
► 1.4 cf microwave with touch-pad controls. Range with self-clean oven, four Calrod burners, chrome drip pans, digital clock and timer.				
High-low electric range with microwave high, deluxe grade	ea	$29.80	$2,371.10	$2,400.90
Replace Materials ..2290.00 Labor...........81.10				
Remove .... Labor 29.80				
► 1.4 cf microwave with touch-pad controls. Range with self-clean oven, four Calrod burners, chrome drip pans, digital clock and timer, integrated hood and venting system.				
Electric wall oven, economy grade	ea	$34.10	$609.30	$643.40
Replace Materials ....534.00 Labor...........75.30				
Remove .... Labor 34.10				
► Standard-clean oven.				
Electric wall oven, standard grade	ea	$34.10	$693.30	$727.40
Replace Materials .....618.00 Labor...........75.30				
Remove .... Labor 34.10				
► Continuous-clean oven, electronic pad controls with clock.				
Electric wall oven, high grade	ea	$34.10	$859.30	$893.40
Replace Materials ....784.00 Labor...........75.30				
Remove .... Labor 34.10				
► Self-clean oven, electronic pad controls with clock.				
Electric wall oven, deluxe grade	ea	$34.10	$1,047.30	$1,081.40
Replace Materials ....972.00 Labor...........75.30				
Remove .... Labor 34.10				
► Convection oven, electronic pad controls with clock.				
Remove electric wall oven for work, then reinstall	ea	–	$141.00	$141.00
Replace Materials ....2.00 Labor 139.00				
Electric double wall oven, economy grade	ea	$47.10	$1,179.00	$1,226.10
Replace Materials ..1040.00 Labor 139.00				
Remove .... Labor 47.10				
► Two standard-clean ovens.				
Electric double wall oven, standard grade	ea	$47.10	$1,349.00	$1,396.10
Replace Materials ...1210.00 Labor 139.00				
Remove .... Labor...........47.10				
► One continuous-clean oven, one self-clean oven, electronic pad controls with clock.				
Electric double wall oven, high grade	ea	$47.10	$1,669.00	$1,716.10
Replace Materials ...1530.00 Labor 139.00				
Remove .... Labor..........47.10				
► Two self-clean ovens, electronic pad controls with clock.				
Electric double wall oven, deluxe grade	ea	$47.10	$2,029.00	$2,076.10
Replace Materials ..1890.00 Labor 139.00				
Remove .... Labor...........47.10				
► One self-clean oven, one convection oven, electronic pad controls with clock.				
Remove electric double wall oven for work, then reinstall	ea	–	$238.00	$238.00
Replace Materials ....3.00 Labor 235.00				

◄ **ELECTRIC WALL OVEN**

◄ **ELECTRIC DOUBLE WALL OVEN**

RELATED ITEMS

Cleaning....................55
Electrical *(wiring)*
    electric oven or range......144

Item Description	Unit	Remove	Replace	Total
RANGE HOOD ▶ **Range hood, economy grade**	ea	$21.30	$125.70	$147.00
Replace Materials ......62.00 Labor 63.70				
Remove .... Labor..........21.30				
▶ 30" wide, two-speed fan, light, non-vented with disposable charcoal filter, baked enamel finish.				
Range hood, standard grade	ea	$21.30	$167.70	$189.00
Replace Materials ....104.00 Labor 63.70				
Remove .... Labor..........21.30				
▶ 30" or 36" wide, two-speed fan, light with night setting, vented with up to 16 lf duct, baked enamel finish.				
Range hood, high grade	ea	$21.30	$188.70	$210.00
Replace Materials .....125.00 Labor 63.70				
Remove .... Labor..........21.30				
▶ 30" or 36" wide, variable-speed fan, two lights, vented with up to 16 lf duct, baked enamel finish.				
Range hood, deluxe grade	ea	$21.30	$216.70	$238.00
Replace Materials .....153.00 Labor 63.70				
Remove .... Labor..........21.30				
▶ 30" or 36" wide, variable-speed fan, two lights, vented with up to 16 lf duct, brushed chrome finish.				
Range hood, custom grade	ea	$21.30	$264.70	$286.00
Replace Materials ....201.00 Labor 63.70				
Remove .... Labor..........21.30				
▶ 30" or 36" wide, variable-speed fan, two lights, vented with up to 16 lf duct, specialty deep design, copper finish.				
OVERSIZED ▶ **Oversized range hood, standard grade**	ea	$25.60	$398.10	$423.70
RANGE HOOD *Replace* Materials .....319.00 Labor...........79.10				
Remove .... Labor 25.60				
▶ 42" wide, two-speed fan, light with night setting, vented with up to 16 lf duct, baked enamel finish.				
Oversized range hood, high grade	ea	$25.60	$462.10	$487.70
Replace Materials ....383.00 Labor...........79.10				
Remove .... Labor 25.60				
▶ 42" wide, variable-speed fan, two lights, vented with up to 16 lf duct, baked enamel finish.				
Oversized range hood, deluxe grade	ea	$25.60	$548.10	$573.70
Replace Materials ....469.00 Labor...........79.10				
Remove .... Labor 25.60				
▶ 42" wide, variable-speed fan, two lights, vented with up to 16 lf duct, brushed chrome finish.				
Oversized range hood, custom grade	ea	$25.60	$696.10	$721.70
Replace Materials .....617.00 Labor...........79.10				
Remove .... Labor 25.60				
▶ 42" wide, variable-speed fan, two lights, vented with up to 16 lf duct, specialty deep design, copper finish.				
Remove range hood for work, then reinstall	ea	–	$136.00	$136.00
Replace Materials ....2.00 Labor 134.00				
PUSH-BUTTON ▶ **Push-button dishwasher, economy grade**	ea	$40.20	$485.30	$525.50
DISHWASHER *Replace* Materials .....410.00 Labor...........75.30				
Remove .... Labor 40.20				
▶ Three cycles, five options, standard insulation package.				

Item Description	Unit	Remove	Replace	Total
Push-button dishwasher, standard grade	ea	$40.20	$615.30	$655.50

Replace Materials....540.00   Labor...........75.30
Remove ....   Labor 40.20

▶ Five cycles, eight options, standard insulation package.

Push-button dishwasher, high grade	ea	$40.20	$745.30	$785.50

Replace Materials.....670.00   Labor...........75.30
Remove ....   Labor 40.20

▶ Five cycles, fourteen options, deluxe insulation package.

Push-button dishwasher, deluxe grade	ea	$40.20	$855.30	$895.50

Replace Materials....780.00   Labor...........75.30
Remove ....   Labor 40.20

▶ Six cycles, eighteen options, deluxe insulation package.

Electronic dishwasher, economy grade	ea	$40.20	$905.30	$945.50

Replace Materials....830.00   Labor...........75.30
Remove ....   Labor 40.20

▶ Electronic touch-pad control, six cycles, twelve options, deluxe insulation package, specialty racks.

◀ **ELECTRONIC DISHWASHER**

Electronic dishwasher, standard grade	ea	$40.20	$985.30	$1,025.50

Replace Materials.....910.00   Labor...........75.30
Remove ....   Labor 40.20

▶ Electronic touch-pad control, seven cycles, twenty-three options, deluxe "quiet" insulation package, water saver cycle, delayed start option, specialty racks.

Electronic dishwasher, high grade	ea	$40.20	$1,165.30	$1,205.50

Replace Materials ..1090.00   Labor...........75.30
Remove ....   Labor 40.20

▶ Electronic touch-pad control, seven cycles, twenty-three options, deluxe "quiet" insulation package, water saver cycle, delayed start option, specialty racks, self-cleaning filter system.

Electronic dishwasher, deluxe grade	ea	$40.20	$1,235.30	$1,275.50

Replace Materials ...1160.00   Labor...........75.30
Remove ....   Labor 40.20

▶ Electronic touch-pad control, seven cycles, twenty-three options, deluxe "quiet" insulation package, water saver cycle, delayed start option, specialty racks, self-cleaning filter system, smooth-surface exterior panels that can integrate with cabinet design.

Convertible (portable) dishwasher, standard grade	ea	$40.20	$475.50	$515.70

Replace Materials....430.00   Labor...........45.50
Remove ....   Labor 40.20

▶ Push-button control, four cycles, seven options, standard insulation package, plastic laminate top.

◀ **CONVERTIBLE DISHWASHER**

Convertible (portable) dishwasher, high grade	ea	$40.20	$595.50	$635.70

Replace Materials ...550.00   Labor...........45.50
Remove ....   Labor 40.20

▶ Push-button control, four cycles, thirteen options, deluxe insulation package, specialty racks, wood veneer top.

Convertible (portable) dishwasher, deluxe grade	ea	$40.20	$695.50	$735.70

Replace Materials....650.00   Labor...........45.50
Remove ....   Labor 40.20

▶ Push-button control, four cycles, fourteen options, deluxe insulation package, specialty racks, solid wood top (often butcher block), delay start option.

RELATED ITEMS

Cleaning...................55
Electrical *(wiring)*
  range hood..................143
  dishwasher..................142
Plumbing
  dishwasher..................368

Item Description	Unit	Remove	Replace	Total
SPACE-SAVER ► UNDER-SINK DISHWASHER  **Space-saver under-sink dishwasher, standard grade** *Replace* Materials....600.00 Labor..........116.00 *Remove* .... Labor..........40.20 ► Push-button control, four cycles, seven options, standard insulation package.	ea	$40.20	$716.00	$756.20
 **Space-saver under-sink dishwasher, high grade** *Replace* Materials....710.00 Labor..........116.00 *Remove* .... Labor..........40.20 ► Push-button control, five cycles, eight options, deluxe insulation package.	ea	$40.20	$826.00	$866.20
Remove dishwasher for work, then reinstall *Replace* Materials........5.00 Labor..........142.00	ea	–	$147.00	$147.00
GARBAGE ► DISPOSAL **1/3 hp garbage disposal** *Replace* Materials....122.00 Labor..........74.70 *Remove* .... Labor..........37.60 ► Continuous feed.	ea	$37.60	$196.70	$234.30
1/2 hp garbage disposal *Replace* Materials....146.00 Labor..........74.70 *Remove* .... Labor..........37.60 ► Continuous feed, sound shield.	ea	$37.60	$220.70	$258.30
1/2 hp stainless steel garbage disposal with auto-reverse *Replace* Materials....340.00 Labor..........74.70 *Remove* .... Labor..........37.60 ► Continuous feed, sound shield, auto-reverse.	ea	$37.60	$414.70	$452.30
3/4 hp garbage disposal *Replace* Materials....409.00 Labor..........74.70 *Remove* .... Labor..........37.60 ► Batch feed, deluxe "quiet" sound shield, non-corroding, glass-filled polyester drain housing and hopper.	ea	$37.60	$483.70	$521.30
3/4 hp stainless steel garbage disposal with auto-reverse *Replace* Materials....486.00 Labor..........74.70 *Remove* .... Labor..........37.60 ► Batch feed, deluxe "quiet" sound shield, non-corroding, glass-filled polyester drain housing and hopper, with auto-reverse.	ea	$37.60	$560.70	$598.30
1 hp garbage disposal *Replace* Materials....708.00 Labor..........74.70 *Remove* .... Labor..........37.60 ► Batch feed, deluxe "quiet" sound shield, non-corroding, glass-filled polyester drain housing and hopper.	ea	$37.60	$782.70	$820.30
1 hp stainless steel garbage disposal with auto-reverse *Replace* Materials....770.00 Labor..........74.70 *Remove* .... Labor..........37.60 ► Batch feed, deluxe "quiet" sound shield, non-corroding, glass-filled polyester drain housing and hopper, with auto-reverse.	ea	$37.60	$844.70	$882.30
Remove garbage disposal for work, then reinstall *Replace* Materials........5.00 Labor........140.00	ea	–	$145.00	$145.00
MICROWAVE ► Microwave oven, standard grade *Replace* Materials....294.00 Labor..........15.10 *Remove* .... Labor..........14.50 ► To 800 watts, defrost, multiple power levels, time cook.	ea	$14.50	$309.10	$323.60

Item Description	Unit	Remove	Replace	Total
Microwave oven, high grade	ea	$14.50	$424.10	$438.60

   Replace Materials....409.00   Labor...........15.10
   Remove ....   Labor...........14.50

  ▶ To 800 watts, defrost, popcorn pad, 10 power levels, time cook, reheat pad.

Microwave oven, deluxe grade	ea	$14.50	$577.10	$591.60

   Replace Materials....562.00   Labor...........15.10
   Remove ....   Labor...........14.50

  ▶ To 800 watts, defrost, popcorn pad, 10 power levels, time cook, reheat pad, roasting and defrost automatic sensing controls.

Microwave oven, custom grade	ea	$14.50	$709.10	$723.60

   Replace Materials.....694.00   Labor...........15.10
   Remove ....   Labor...........14.50

  ▶ To 800 watts with convection heating, defrost, popcorn pad, 10 power levels, time cook, reheat pad, baking, defrost sensing controls.

Microwave oven, under cabinet, standard grade	ea	$14.50	$720.30	$734.80

   Replace Materials....645.00   Labor...........75.30
   Remove ....   Labor...........14.50

◀ **UNDER CABINET MICROWAVE**

  ▶ To 750 watts (many models around 550 to 600 watts), defrost, popcorn pad, 10 power levels, time cook, reheat pad, baking, defrost sensing controls, with high-capacity exhaust vent fan (includes up to 16 lf of duct).

Microwave oven, under cabinet, high grade	ea	$14.50	$1,044.30	$1,058.80

   Replace Materials.....969.00   Labor...........75.30
   Remove ....   Labor...........14.50

  ▶ To 750 watts (many models around 550 to 600 watts) with convection, defrost, popcorn pad, 10 power levels, time cook, reheat pad, baking, defrost sensing controls, with high-capacity exhaust vent fan (includes up to 16 lf of duct).

Side-by-side refrigerator / freezer, 24 to 27 cf capacity, standard grade	ea	$28.20	$1,851.40	$1,879.60

   Replace Materials ..1820.00   Labor...........31.40
   Remove ....   Labor 28.20

◀ **SIDE-BY-SIDE REFRIGERATOR / FREEZER**

  ▶ Standard-style shelves, energy efficient.

Side-by-side refrigerator / freezer, 24 to 27 cf capacity, high grade	ea	$28.20	$2,321.40	$2,349.60

   Replace Materials ..2290.00   Labor...........31.40
   Remove ....   Labor 28.20

  ▶ Specialty-style shelves, deep doors, energy efficient.

Side-by-side refrigerator / freezer, 24 to 27 cf capacity, deluxe grade	ea	$28.20	$2,781.40	$2,809.60

   Replace Materials ..2750.00   Labor...........31.40
   Remove ....   Labor 28.20

  ▶ Specialty-style shelves and doors, deep doors, highly energy efficient.

Side-by-side refrigerator / freezer, 20 to 23 cf capacity, standard grade	ea	$28.20	$1,211.40	$1,239.60

   Replace Materials ...1180.00   Labor...........31.40
   Remove ....   Labor 28.20

  ▶ Standard-style shelves, energy efficient.

Side-by-side refrigerator / freezer, 20 to 23 cf capacity, high grade	ea	$28.20	$1,731.40	$1,759.60

   Replace Materials...1700.00   Labor...........31.40
   Remove ....   Labor 28.20

  ▶ Specialty-style shelves, deep doors, energy efficient.

Side-by-side refrigerator / freezer, 20 to 23 cf capacity, deluxe grade	ea	$28.20	$2,011.40	$2,039.60

   Replace Materials...1980.00   Labor...........31.40
   Remove ....   Labor 28.20

  ▶ Specialty-style shelves and doors, deep doors, highly energy efficient.

RELATED ITEMS

Cleaning...............55
Electrical *(wiring)*
  dishwasher....................142
  garbage disposal...........143
  electric appliance...........142
Plumbing
  dishwasher................368

Item Description	Unit	Remove	Replace	Total
SIDE-BY-SIDE CABINET MATCH ▶ **Add for side-by-side refrigerator / freezer with cabinet-matching doors**	ea	–	$361.00	$361.00
Replace Materials.....361.00				

Item Description	Unit	Remove	Replace	Total
OVER-UNDER REFRIGERATOR / FREEZER ▶ **Over-under refrigerator / freezer, 21 to 25 cf capacity, standard grade**	ea	$24.50	$1,277.90	$1,302.40
Replace Materials ..1250.00 Labor..........27.90				
Remove .... Labor..........24.50				
▶ Standard-style shelves, energy efficient.				
Over-under refrigerator / freezer, 21 to 25 cf capacity, high grade	ea	$24.50	$1,447.90	$1,472.40
Replace Materials...1420.00 Labor..........27.90				
Remove .... Labor..........24.50				
▶ Specialty-style shelves, deep doors, energy efficient.				
Over-under refrigerator / freezer, 21 to 25 cf capacity, deluxe grade	ea	$24.50	$1,797.90	$1,822.40
Replace Materials...1770.00 Labor..........27.90				
Remove .... Labor..........24.50				
▶ Specialty-style shelves and doors, deep doors, highly energy efficient.				
Over-under refrigerator / freezer, 17 to 20 cf capacity, standard grade	ea	$24.50	$1,127.90	$1,152.40
Replace Materials...1100.00 Labor..........27.90				
Remove .... Labor..........24.50				
▶ Standard-style shelves, energy efficient.				
Over-under refrigerator / freezer, 17 to 20 cf capacity, high grade	ea	$24.50	$1,277.90	$1,302.40
Replace Materials ..1250.00 Labor..........27.90				
Remove .... Labor..........24.50				
▶ Specialty-style shelves, deep doors, energy efficient.				
Over-under refrigerator / freezer, 17 to 20 cf capacity, deluxe grade	ea	$24.50	$1,537.90	$1,562.40
Replace Materials ...1510.00 Labor..........27.90				
Remove .... Labor..........24.50				
▶ Specialty-style shelves and doors, deep doors, highly energy efficient.				
Over-under refrigerator / freezer, 13 to 16 cf capacity, standard grade	ea	$24.50	$964.90	$989.40
Replace Materials ....937.00 Labor..........27.90				
Remove .... Labor..........24.50				
▶ Standard-style shelves, energy efficient.				
Over-under refrigerator / freezer, 13 to 16 cf capacity, high grade	ea	$24.50	$1,127.90	$1,152.40
Replace Materials...1100.00 Labor..........27.90				
Remove .... Labor..........24.50				
▶ Specialty-style shelves, deep doors, energy efficient.				
Over-under refrigerator / freezer, 13 to 16 cf capacity, deluxe grade	ea	$24.50	$1,307.90	$1,332.40
Replace Materials ..1280.00 Labor..........27.90				
Remove .... Labor..........24.50				
▶ Specialty-style shelves and doors, deep doors, highly energy efficient.				
Over-under refrigerator / freezer, 10 to 12 cf capacity, standard grade	ea	$24.50	$804.90	$829.40
Replace Materials ....777.00 Labor..........27.90				
Remove .... Labor..........24.50				
▶ Standard-style shelves, energy efficient.				
Over-under refrigerator / freezer, 10 to 12 cf capacity, high grade	ea	$24.50	$978.90	$1,003.40
Replace Materials ....951.00 Labor..........27.90				
Remove .... Labor..........24.50				
▶ Specialty-style shelves, deep doors, energy efficient.				

Item Description	Unit	Remove	Replace	Total
Over-under refrigerator / freezer, 10 to 12 cf capacity, deluxe grade	ea	$24.50	$1,117.90	$1,142.40
Replace Materials ..1090.00 Labor...........27.90				
Remove .... Labor...........24.50				
▶ Specialty-style shelves and doors, deep doors, highly energy efficient.				
Remove refrigerator for work, then reinstall	ea	–	$58.30	$58.30
Replace .... Labor 58.30				
Add for refreshment center in refrigerator / freezer	ea	–	$512.00	$512.00
Replace Materials ....396.00 Labor..........116.00				
Disconnect refrigerator water line for work, then re-connect	ea	–	$13.90	$13.90
Replace Materials .... .70 Labor...........13.20				
Refreshment center plumbing hook-up in existing building	ea	–	$331.00	$331.00
Replace Materials ......27.00 Labor.........304.00				
Refreshment center plumbing hook-up, new construction	ea	–	$177.00	$177.00
Replace Materials ......25.00 Labor 152.00				
Refinish refrigerator	ea	–	$409.00	$409.00
Replace Materials ......42.00 Labor.........367.00				
Refinish and recondition refrigerator	ea	–	$483.00	$483.00
Replace Materials ......62.00 Labor.........421.00				
Trash compactor, economy grade	ea	$24.50	$560.70	$585.20
Replace Materials ....507.00 Labor 53.70				
Remove .... Labor...........24.50				
▶ Convertible or built-in, 12".				
Trash compactor, standard grade	ea	$24.50	$698.70	$723.20
Replace Materials ....645.00 Labor 53.70				
Remove .... Labor...........24.50				
▶ Convertible or built-in, 12" to 15", key lock, automatic anti-jam, reversible panel.				
Trash compactor, high grade	ea	$24.50	$782.70	$807.20
Replace Materials ....729.00 Labor 53.70				
Remove .... Labor...........24.50				
▶ Convertible or built-in, 12" to 15", key lock, automatic anti-jam, heavy gauge construction, reversible panel.				
Remove trash compactor for work, then reinstall	ea	–	$112.70	$112.70
Replace Materials .... .70 Labor..........112.00				
Clothes washing machine, economy grade	ea	$15.70	$446.70	$462.40
Replace Materials ....430.00 Labor...........16.70				
Remove .... Labor...........15.70				
▶ Large capacity, five cycles, three water levels, bleach dispenser.				
Clothes washing machine, standard grade	ea	$15.70	$550.70	$566.40
Replace Materials ....534.00 Labor...........16.70				
Remove .... Labor...........15.70				
▶ Large capacity, six cycles, two speeds, two wash / spin combinations, three water levels, bleach dispenser.				
Clothes washing machine, high grade	ea	$15.70	$634.70	$650.40
Replace Materials .....618.00 Labor...........16.70				
Remove .... Labor...........15.70				
▶ Extra large capacity, nine cycles with pre-wash, three speeds, four wash / spin combinations, three water levels, bleach dispenser.				

RELATED ITEMS

Cleaning......................55
Electrical *(wiring)*
  trash compactor 143
  clothes washer 142
Plumbing
  clothes washer 368
  ice maker 368

◀ **REFRESHMENT CENTER**

◀ **REFRESHMENT CENTER PLUMBING**
With supply lines and hookup to appliances. For installation of supply lines only see Plumbing on page 368.

◀ **REFINISH REFRIGERATOR**

◀ **TRASH COMPACTOR**

◀ **WASHING MACHINE**

Item Description	Unit	Remove	Replace	Total
WASHING ▶ MACHINE *continued*				
Clothes washing machine, deluxe grade	ea	$15.70	$835.70	$851.40
Replace Materials.....819.00 Labor..........16.70				
Remove .... Labor..........15.70				
▶ Extra large capacity, programmable, ten cycles with pre-wash, four programmable speeds, four programmable wash / spin combinations, variable water levels, bleach / fabric softener dispenser.				
Remove washing machine for work, then reinstall	ea	–	$31.40	$31.40
Replace .... Labor..........31.40				
CLOTHES DRYER ▶ *Electric dryers with up to 20' of vent pipe. Add $133 for gas dryer (includes additional cost of dryer and additional cost to install).* **Clothes dryer, electric, economy grade**	ea	$14.50	$362.10	$376.60
Replace Materials ....347.00 Labor..........15.10				
Remove .... Labor..........14.50				
▶ Large capacity, two cycles, three heat selections.				
Clothes dryer, electric, standard grade	ea	$14.50	$445.10	$459.60
Replace Materials ....430.00 Labor..........15.10				
Remove .... Labor..........14.50				
▶ Large capacity with automatic drying control, six cycles, four heat selections.				
Clothes dryer, high grade	ea	$14.50	$570.10	$584.60
Replace Materials ...555.00 Labor 15.10				
Remove .... Labor..........14.50				
▶ Extra large capacity with electronic drying control, five cycles with delicate fabrics option, four heat selections, drum lamp.				
Clothes dryer, deluxe grade	ea	$14.50	$716.10	$730.60
Replace Materials.....701.00 Labor..........15.10				
Remove .... Labor..........14.50				
▶ Extra large capacity with electronic drying control, six cycles with delicate fabrics option, four heat selections, drum lamp.				
Remove clothes dryer for work, then reinstall	ea	–	$27.90	$27.90
Replace .... Labor..........27.90				

✍ NOTES: _____

_____

_____

_____

_____

_____

_____

_____

_____

_____

_____

_____

_____

_____

_____ end

TIME & MATERIAL CHARTS *(selected items)*

Appliance Materials

See **Appliance** material prices with the line items and other information in the **QuickFinder** column.

Appliance Labor

LABORER	BASE WAGE	PAID LEAVE	TRUE WAGE	FICA	FUTA	WORKER'S COMP.	UNEMPLOY. INSUR.	HEALTH INSUR.	RETIRE (401K)	LIABILITY INSUR.	COST PER HOUR
Appliance installer	$22.40	1.75	$24.15	1.85	.19	3.08	2.10	2.92	.72	3.62	**$38.60**
Appliance refinisher	$25.50	1.99	$27.49	2.10	.22	7.71	2.39	2.92	.82	4.12	**$47.80**
Electrician	$26.90	2.10	$29.00	2.22	.23	3.16	2.52	2.92	.87	4.35	**$45.30**
Plumber	$26.70	2.08	$28.78	2.20	.23	4.85	2.50	2.92	.86	4.32	**$46.70**
Demolition laborer	$14.40	1.12	$15.52	1.19	.12	5.01	1.35	2.92	.47	2.33	**$28.90**

Paid Leave is calculated based on two weeks paid vacation, one week sick leave, and seven paid holidays. Employer's matching portion of **FICA** is 7.65 percent. **FUTA** (Federal Unemployment) is .8 percent. **Worker's compensation** was calculated using a national average of 12.71 percent for the appliance installer; 27.98 percent for the appliance refinisher; 10.86 percent for the electrician; 16.80 percent for the plumber; and 32.20 percent for the demolition laborer. **Unemployment insurance** was calculated using a national average of 8.7 percent. **Health insurance** was calculated based on a projected national average for 2005 of $580 per employee (and family when applicable) per month. Employer pays 80 percent for a per month cost of $464 per employee. **Retirement** is based on a 401(k) retirement program with employer matching of 50 percent. Employee contributions to the 401(k) plan are an average of 6 percent of the true wage. **Liability insurance** is based on a national average of 14.0 percent.

Appliances Labor Productivity

WORK DESCRIPTION	LABORER	COST PER HOUR	PRODUCTIVITY	UNIT PRICE
Demolition				
remove gas cook top	demolition laborer	$28.90	.975	**$28.20** ea
remove gas range	demolition laborer	$28.90	1.03	**$29.80** ea
remove high-low gas range	demolition laborer	$28.90	1.18	**$34.10** ea
remove restaurant-style gas range	demolition laborer	$28.90	3.00	**$86.70** ea
remove gas wall oven	demolition laborer	$28.90	1.34	**$38.70** ea
remove gas double wall oven	demolition laborer	$28.90	1.95	**$56.40** ea
remove electric cook top	demolition laborer	$28.90	1.03	**$29.80** ea
remove modular electric cook-top unit	demolition laborer	$28.90	.510	**$14.70** ea
remove electric range	demolition laborer	$28.90	.975	**$28.20** ea
remove drop-in or slide-in electric range	demolition laborer	$28.90	1.22	**$35.30** ea
remove high-low electric range	demolition laborer	$28.90	1.03	**$29.80** ea
remove electric wall oven	demolition laborer	$28.90	1.18	**$34.10** ea
remove electric double wall oven	demolition laborer	$28.90	1.63	**$47.10** ea
remove range hood	demolition laborer	$28.90	.736	**$21.30** ea
remove over-sized range hood	demolition laborer	$28.90	.886	**$25.60** ea
remove dishwasher	demolition laborer	$28.90	1.39	**$40.20** ea
remove garbage disposal	demolition laborer	$28.90	1.30	**$37.60** ea
remove microwave oven	demolition laborer	$28.90	.500	**$14.50** ea
remove side-by-side refrigerator / freezer	demolition laborer	$28.90	.975	**$28.20** ea
remove over-under refrigerator / freezer	demolition laborer	$28.90	.848	**$24.50** ea
remove trash compactor	demolition laborer	$28.90	.848	**$24.50** ea
remove clothes washing machine	demolition laborer	$28.90	.542	**$15.70** ea
remove clothes dryer	demolition laborer	$28.90	.500	**$14.50** ea

. . . More ➢

Appliances Labor Productivity *continued*

WORK DESCRIPTION	LABORER	COST PER HOUR	PRODUCTIVITY	UNIT PRICE
Install appliances				
gas cook top	plumber	$46.70	1.99	$92.90 ea
gas range	plumber	$46.70	2.05	$95.70 ea
gas range with grill / griddle	plumber	$46.70	2.10	$98.10 ea
space-saver gas range	plumber	$46.70	1.99	$92.90 ea
high-low gas range with microwave high	plumber	$46.70	2.12	$99.00 ea
restaurant-style gas range	plumber	$46.70	4.43	$207.00 ea
gas wall oven	installer	$38.60	2.17	$83.80 ea
gas double wall oven	installer	$38.60	3.98	$154.00 ea
electric cook top	electrician	$45.30	1.77	$80.20 ea
modular cooking unit	electrician	$45.30	.629	$28.50 ea
modular electric cook top downdraft unit	electrician	$45.30	.488	$22.10 ea
electric range	installer	$38.60	2.03	$78.40 ea
drop-in or slide-in electric range	installer	$38.60	2.44	$94.20 ea
space-saver electric range	installer	$38.60	1.97	$76.00 ea
high-low electric range with microwave high	installer	$38.60	2.10	$81.10 ea
electric wall oven	installer	$38.60	1.95	$75.30 ea
electric double wall oven	installer	$38.60	3.61	$139.00 ea
range hood	installer	$38.60	1.65	$63.70 ea
oversized range hood	installer	$38.60	2.05	$79.10 ea
dishwasher	installer	$38.60	1.95	$75.30 ea
convertible (portable) dishwasher	installer	$38.60	1.18	$45.50 ea
space-saver under-sink dishwasher	installer	$38.60	3.00	$116.00 ea
garbage disposal	plumber	$46.70	1.60	$74.70 ea
microwave oven	installer	$38.60	.390	$15.10 ea
microwave oven under cabinet	installer	$38.60	1.95	$75.30 ea
side-by-side refrigerator / freezer	installer	$38.60	.813	$31.40 ea
refreshment center in side-by-side refrigerator / freezer	installer	$38.60	3.00	$116.00 ea
over-under refrigerator / freezer	installer	$38.60	.722	$27.90 ea
refreshment center in over-under refrigerator / freezer	installer	$38.60	3.00	$116.00 ea
refreshment center plumbing hook-up in existing building	plumber	$46.70	6.50	$304.00 ea
refreshment center plumbing hook-up, new construction	plumber	$46.70	3.25	$152.00 ea
trash compactor	installer	$38.60	1.39	$53.70 ea
clothes washing machine	installer	$38.60	.433	$16.70 ea
clothes dryer	installer	$38.60	.390	$15.10 ea

✎ NOTES: _____

_____

_____

_____

_____

_____

_____

_____

_____

_____

_____

_____

_____

_____

_____

_____

_____ end

3

Awnings

Item Description	Unit	Remove	Replace	Total	
Free-standing aluminum carport, 150 sf or less *Replace* Materials ......16.50 Labor ....2.89 *Remove*....................... Labor 1.45	sf	$1.45	$19.39	$20.84	◄ **FREE-STANDING CARPORT** *40 psf. Aluminum with baked enamel finish. With 4 posts under 200 sf. With 6 posts over 200 sf.*
Free-standing aluminum carport, 151 to 250 sf *Replace* Materials ......14.30 Labor ....2.89 *Remove*....................... Labor 1.45	sf	$1.45	$17.19	$18.64	
Free-standing aluminum carport, 251 to 480 sf *Replace* Materials.......13.70 Labor ....2.89 *Remove*....................... Labor 1.45	sf	$1.45	$16.59	$18.04	
Remove free-standing aluminum carport for work, then reinstall *Replace* Materials .... .40 Labor 6.04	sf	–	$6.44	$6.44	
Attached aluminum carport or patio cover, 150 sf or less *Replace* Materials.......15.00 Labor ....2.66 *Remove*....................... Labor 1.56	sf	$1.56	$17.66	$19.22	◄ **ATTACHED CARPORT** *40 psf. Aluminum with baked enamel finish. With 3 posts under 200 sf. With 4 to 5 posts over 200 sf.*
Attached aluminum carport or patio cover, 151 to 250 sf *Replace* Materials.......13.10 Labor ....2.66 *Remove*....................... Labor 1.56	sf	$1.56	$15.76	$17.32	
Attached aluminum carport or patio cover, 251 to 480 sf *Replace* Materials ......12.50 Labor ....2.66 *Remove*....................... Labor 1.56	sf	$1.56	$15.16	$16.72	
Remove attached aluminum carport or patio cover for work, then reinstall *Replace* Materials .... .40 Labor 5.63	sf	–	$6.03	$6.03	
Minimum charge for carport or patio cover work *Replace* Materials ......49.00 Labor...........69.40	ea	–	$118.40	$118.40	◁ minimum
Add for heavy gauge aluminum carport or patio cover *Replace* Materials........3.70	sf	–	$3.70	$3.70	◁ add for heavy gauge
Carport or patio cover post *Replace* Materials ......55.40 Labor...........41.50 *Remove*....................... Labor 8.10	ea	$8.10	$96.90	$105.00	◁ post
Remove carport or patio cover post for work, then reinstall *Replace* Materials ....2.20 Labor...........67.40	ea	–	$69.60	$69.60	
Carport or patio cover post scroll *Replace* Materials ......66.00 Labor...........15.60 *Remove*....................... Labor 2.78	ea	$2.78	$81.60	$84.38	◁ scroll
Remove carport or patio cover post scroll for work, then reinstall *Replace* Materials ....1.00 Labor...........25.30	ea	–	$26.30	$26.30	
Carport or patio cover aluminum fascia *Replace* Materials ......14.00 Labor ....4.70 *Remove*....................... Labor .... .80	lf	$.80	$18.70	$19.50	◁ fascia

Item Description	Unit	Remove	Replace	Total
Remove carport or patio cover aluminum fascia for work, then reinstall	lf	–	$7.90	$7.90
Replace Materials......... Labor 7.90				
Carport or patio cover roof panel	ea	$14.10	$112.00	$126.10
Replace Materials......83.00 Labor 29.00				
Remove.................... Labor 14.10				
Remove carport or patio cover roof panel for work, then reinstall	ea	–	$50.40	$50.40
Replace Materials.......4.00 Labor 46.40				
Carport or patio cover downspout	ea	$2.81	$59.10	$61.91
Replace Materials ......55.00 Labor 4.10				
Remove...................... Labor 2.81				
Remove carport or patio cover downspout for work, then reinstall	ea	–	$6.20	$6.20
Replace Materials......... Labor 6.20				
Aluminum door awning with 42" projection, 2 to 4 lf	lf	$13.90	$188.40	$202.30
Replace Materials.....171.00 Labor 17.40				
Remove...................... Labor 13.90				
Aluminum door awning with 42" projection, 5 to 8 lf	lf	$13.90	$162.40	$176.30
Replace Materials.....145.00 Labor 17.40				
Remove...................... Labor 13.90				
Aluminum door awning with 42" projection, 9 to 12 lf	lf	$13.90	$148.40	$162.30
Replace Materials.....131.00 Labor 17.40				
Remove...................... Labor 13.90				
Aluminum door awning with 54" projection, 2 to 4 lf	lf	$14.50	$247.20	$261.70
Replace Materials....229.00 Labor 18.20				
Remove...................... Labor 14.50				
Aluminum door awning with 54" projection, 5 to 8 lf	lf	$14.50	$210.20	$224.70
Replace Materials.....192.00 Labor 18.20				
Remove...................... Labor 14.50				
Aluminum door awning with 54" projection, 9 to 12 lf	lf	$14.50	$189.20	$203.70
Replace Materials.....171.00 Labor 18.20				
Remove...................... Labor 14.50				
Remove aluminum door awning for work, then reinstall	lf	–	$42.20	$42.20
Replace Materials........6.20 Labor 36.00				
3' high aluminum window awning, 2 to 4 lf	lf	$11.60	$68.30	$79.90
Replace Materials .....55.30 Labor 13.00				
Remove...................... Labor 11.60				
3' high aluminum window awning, 5 to 8 lf	lf	$11.60	$56.30	$67.90
Replace Materials......43.30 Labor 13.00				
Remove...................... Labor 11.60				
3' high aluminum window awning, 9 to 12 lf	lf	$11.60	$53.60	$65.20
Replace Materials......40.60 Labor 13.00				
Remove...................... Labor 11.60				
Remove 3' high aluminum window awning for work, then reinstall	lf	–	$37.30	$37.30
Replace Materials........6.20 Labor 31.10				

Side notes (left margin):

roof panel ▷

downspout ▷

42" ALUMINUM ▶ DOOR AWNING
25 to 40 psf.
Aluminum with baked enamel finish. Includes all hardware and adjustable supports.

54" ALUMINUM ▶ DOOR AWNING
25 to 40 psf.
Aluminum with baked enamel finish. Includes all hardware and adjustable supports.

3' HIGH WINDOW ▶ AWNING
25 to 40 psf.
Aluminum with baked enamel finish. Includes all hardware and adjustable supports.

Item Description	Unit	Remove	Replace	Total	
4' high aluminum window awning, 2 to 4 lf	lf	$12.00	$78.00	$90.00	◄ **4' HIGH WINDOW**
Replace Materials......64.70 Labor..........13.30					**AWNING**
Remove................. Labor..........12.00					*25 to 40 psf. Aluminum*
4' high aluminum window awning, 5 to 8 lf	lf	$12.00	$66.80	$78.80	*with baked enamel finish.*
Replace Materials......53.50 Labor..........13.30					*Includes all hardware and*
Remove................. Labor..........12.00					*adjustable*
4' high aluminum window awning, 9 to 12 lf	lf	$12.00	$63.20	$75.20	*supports.*
Replace Materials......49.90 Labor..........13.30					
Remove................. Labor..........12.00					
Remove 4' high aluminum window awning for work, then reinstall	lf	–	$37.90	$37.90	
Replace Materials........6.20 Labor..........31.70					
5' high aluminum window awning, 2 to 4 lf	lf	$12.20	$99.60	$111.80	◄ **5' HIGH WINDOW**
Replace Materials......86.10 Labor..........13.50					**AWNING**
Remove................. Labor..........12.20					*25 to 40 psf. Aluminum*
5' high aluminum window awning, 5 to 8 lf	lf	$12.20	$91.50	$103.70	*with baked enamel finish.*
Replace Materials......78.00 Labor..........13.50					*Includes all hardware and*
Remove................. Labor..........12.20					*adjustable*
5' high aluminum window awning, 9 to 12 lf	lf	$12.20	$75.30	$87.50	*supports.*
Replace Materials......61.80 Labor..........13.50					
Remove................. Labor..........12.20					
Remove 5' high aluminum window awning for work, then reinstall	lf	–	$38.50	$38.50	
Replace Materials........6.20 Labor..........32.30					
6' high aluminum window awning, 2 to 4 lf	lf	$12.40	$113.40	$125.80	◄ **6' HIGH WINDOW**
Replace Materials......99.60 Labor..........13.80					**AWNING**
Remove................. Labor..........12.40					*25 to 40 psf. Aluminum*
6' high aluminum window awning, 5 to 8 lf	lf	$12.40	$108.50	$120.90	*with baked enamel finish.*
Replace Materials......94.70 Labor..........13.80					*Includes all hardware and*
Remove................. Labor..........12.40					*adjustable*
6' high aluminum window awning, 9 to 12 lf	lf	$12.40	$86.50	$98.90	*supports.*
Replace Materials......72.70 Labor..........13.80					
Remove................. Labor..........12.40					
Remove 6' high aluminum window awning for work, then reinstall	lf	–	$39.10	$39.10	
Replace Materials........6.20 Labor..........32.90					
Minimum charge for door or window awning work	ea	–	$118.40	$118.40	◁ **minimum**
Replace Materials......49.00 Labor..........69.40					
Door or window awning slat	ea	$6.71	$35.30	$42.01	
Replace Materials......21.00 Labor..........14.30					
Remove................. Labor..........6.71					
Roll-up aluminum awning, 2 to 5 lf	lf	$12.10	$72.40	$84.50	◄ **ROLL-UP**
Replace Materials......62.10 Labor..........10.30					**AWNING**
Remove................. Labor..........12.10					*Security awning that*
Roll-up aluminum awning, 6 to 12 lf	lf	$12.10	$57.80	$69.90	*covers window.*
Replace Materials......47.50 Labor..........10.30					*Aluminum with baked*
Remove................. Labor..........12.10					*enamel finish. Includes*
					all hardware and
					adjustable
					supports.

Item Description	Unit	Remove	Replace	Total
Remove roll-up aluminum window awning for work, then reinstall	lf	—	$27.60	$27.60
Replace Materials........4.80 Labor 22.80				
Canvas awning with 24" drop, 2 to 3 lf	lf	$9.36	$105.90	$115.26
Replace Materials ......87.40 Labor............18.50				
Remove........................ Labor 9.36				
Canvas awning with 24" drop, 4 to 5 lf	lf	$9.36	$100.00	$109.36
Replace Materials ......81.50 Labor............18.50				
Remove........................ Labor 9.36				
Canvas awning with 30" drop, 2 to 3 lf	lf	$9.36	$121.70	$131.06
Replace Materials ....102.00 Labor............19.70				
Remove........................ Labor 9.36				
Canvas awning with 30" drop, 4 to 5 lf	lf	$9.36	$109.60	$118.96
Replace Materials ......89.90 Labor............19.70				
Remove........................ Labor 9.36				
Canvas awning with 30" drop, 5 to 6 lf	lf	$9.36	$100.70	$110.06
Replace Materials ......81.00 Labor............19.70				
Remove........................ Labor 9.36				
Canvas awning with 30" drop, 7 to 8 lf	lf	$9.36	$91.80	$101.16
Replace Materials ......72.10 Labor............19.70				
Remove........................ Labor 9.36				
Canvas awning with 30" drop, 9 to 10 lf	lf	$9.36	$78.90	$88.26
Replace Materials ......59.20 Labor............19.70				
Remove........................ Labor 9.36				
Canvas awning with 30" drop, 11 to 12 lf	lf	$9.36	$74.50	$83.86
Replace Materials ......54.80 Labor............19.70				
Remove........................ Labor 9.36				
Remove canvas awning for work, then reinstall	lf	–	$48.10	$48.10
Replace Materials........5.00 Labor 43.10				
Minimum charge for canvas awning work	ea	–	$103.90	$103.90
Replace Materials ......42.00 Labor............61.90				
Vinyl awning with 24" drop, 2 to 3 lf	lf	$9.36	$70.30	$79.66
Replace Materials ......51.90 Labor............18.40				
Remove........................ Labor 9.36				
Vinyl awning with 24" drop, 4 to 5 lf	lf	$9.36	$66.10	$75.46
Replace Materials ......47.70 Labor............18.40				
Remove........................ Labor 9.36				
Vinyl awning with 30" drop, 2 to 3 lf	lf	$9.36	$80.20	$89.56
Replace Materials ......60.70 Labor............19.50				
Remove........................ Labor 9.36				
Vinyl awning with 30" drop, 4 to 5 lf	lf	$9.36	$72.80	$82.16
Replace Materials ......53.30 Labor............19.50				
Remove........................ Labor 9.36				
Vinyl awning with 30" drop, 5 to 6 lf	lf	$9.36	$68.00	$77.36
Replace Materials ......48.50 Labor............19.50				
Remove........................ Labor 9.36				

CANVAS ▶ AWNING
Waterproof acrylic duck colorfast fabric with retractable metal frame and hardware.

minimum ▷

VINYL AWNING ▶
Vinyl awning with acrylic coating. Includes metal frame and all hardware.

Item Description	Unit	Remove	Replace	Total
Vinyl awning with 30" drop, 7 to 8 lf *Replace* Materials......38.80 Labor..........19.50 *Remove*........................ Labor 9.36	lf	$9.36	$58.30	$67.66
Vinyl awning with 30" drop, 9 to 10 lf *Replace* Materials......35.50 Labor..........19.50 *Remove*........................ Labor 9.36	lf	$9.36	$55.00	$64.36
Vinyl awning with 30" drop, 11 to 12 lf *Replace* Materials......34.50 Labor..........19.50 *Remove*........................ Labor 9.36	lf	$9.36	$54.00	$63.36
Remove vinyl awning for work, then reinstall *Replace* Materials........5.10 Labor..........42.40	lf	–	$47.50	$47.50
Minimum charge for vinyl awning work *Replace* Materials......29.00 Labor..........55.10	ea	–	$84.10	$84.10 ◁ minimum

✍ NOTES: _____

_____

_____ end

TIME & MATERIAL CHARTS *(selected items)*

Awning Materials

DESCRIPTION	UNIT PRICE
Aluminum carport	
free-standing, 151 to 250 sf	$14.30 sf
attached, 151 to 250 sf	$13.10 sf
Aluminum door awning	
with 42" projection, 5 to 8 lf	$145.00 lf
with 54" projection, 5 to 8 lf	$192.00 lf
Aluminum window awning	
3' high, 5 to 8 lf	$43.30 lf
4' high, 5 to 8 lf	$53.50 lf
5' high, 5 to 8 lf	$78.00 lf
6' high, 5 to 8 lf	$94.70 lf
Roll-up aluminum awning	
2 to 5 lf	$62.10 lf
6 to 12 lf	$47.50 lf
Canvas awning	
24" drop, 2 to 3 lf	$87.40 lf
24" drop, 4 to 5 lf	$81.50 lf
30" drop, 2 to 3 lf	$102.00 lf
30" drop, 7 to 8 lf	$72.10 lf
30" drop, 11 to 12 lf	$54.80 lf
Vinyl awning	
24" drop, 2 to 3 lf	$51.90 lf
24" drop, 4 to 5 lf	$47.70 lf
30" drop, 2 to 3 lf	$60.70 lf
30" drop, 7 to 8 lf	$38.80 lf
30" drop, 11 to 12 lf	$34.50 lf

Awning Labor

LABORER	BASE WAGE	PAID LEAVE	TRUE WAGE	FICA	FUTA	WORKER'S COMP.	UNEMPLOY. INSUR.	HEALTH INSUR.	RETIRE (401K)	LIABILITY INSUR.	COST PER HOUR
Awning installer	$23.80	1.86	$25.66	1.96	.21	5.20	2.23	2.92	.77	3.85	$42.80
Awning installer's helper	$17.40	1.36	$18.76	1.44	.15	3.80	1.63	2.92	.56	2.81	$32.10
Demolition laborer	$14.40	1.12	$15.52	1.19	.12	5.01	1.35	2.92	.47	2.33	$28.90

Paid Leave is calculated based on two weeks paid vacation, one week sick leave, and seven paid holidays. Employer's matching portion of **FICA** is 7.65 percent. **FUTA** (Federal Unemployment) is .8 percent. **Worker's Compensation** for the awning trade was calculated using a national average of 20.22 percent. **Unemployment insurance** was calculated using a national average of 8.7 percent. **Health insurance** was calculated based on a projected national average for 2005 of $580 per employee (and family when applicable) per month. Employer pays 80 percent for a per month cost of $464 per employee. **Retirement** is based on a 401(k) retirement program with employer matching of 50 percent. Employee contributions to the 401(k) plan are an average of 6 percent of the true wage. **Liability insurance** is based on a national average of 14.0 percent.

Awning Labor Productivity

WORK DESCRIPTION	LABORER	COST PER HOUR	PRODUCTIVITY	UNIT PRICE
Demolition				
remove free-standing aluminum carport	demolition laborer	$28.90	.050	$1.45 sf
remove attached aluminum carport or patio cover	demolition laborer	$28.90	.054	$1.56 sf
remove 42" projection aluminum door awning	demolition laborer	$28.90	.481	$13.90 sf
remove 54" projection aluminum door awning	demolition laborer	$28.90	.500	$14.50 sf
remove 3' high aluminum window awning	demolition laborer	$28.90	.403	$11.60 lf
remove 4' high aluminum window awning	demolition laborer	$28.90	.415	$12.00 lf
remove 5' high aluminum window awning	demolition laborer	$28.90	.423	$12.20 lf
remove 6' high aluminum window awning	demolition laborer	$28.90	.429	$12.40 lf
remove roll-up aluminum window awning	demolition laborer	$28.90	.417	$12.10 lf
remove canvas or vinyl window awning	demolition laborer	$28.90	.324	$9.36 lf
Awning Installation Crew				
install, awnings and patio covers	awning installer	$42.80		
install, awnings and patio covers	awning installer's helper	$32.10		
awning installation crew	awning installation crew	$37.50		
Install aluminum carport or patio cover				
free-standing carport	awning installation crew	$37.50	.077	$2.89 sf
attached carport or patio cover	awning installation crew	$37.50	.071	$2.66 sf
Install aluminum door awning				
42" projection	awning installation crew	$37.50	.463	$17.40 lf
54" projection	awning installation crew	$37.50	.484	$18.20 lf
Install aluminum window awning				
3' high	awning installation crew	$37.50	.346	$13.00 lf
4' high	awning installation crew	$37.50	.354	$13.30 lf
5' high	awning installation crew	$37.50	.361	$13.50 lf
6' high	awning installation crew	$37.50	.368	$13.80 lf
Install roll-up aluminum awning				
per lf	awning installation crew	$37.50	.274	$10.30 lf
Install canvas awning				
24" drop	awning installation crew	$37.50	.493	$18.50 lf
30" drop	awning installation crew	$37.50	.526	$19.70 lf
Install vinyl awning				
24" drop	awning installation crew	$37.50	.491	$18.40 lf
30" drop	awning installation crew	$37.50	.520	$19.50 lf

NOTES: _____

_____ end

4 .... *Bathroom Hardware*

Item Description	Unit	Remove	Replace	Total	
Minimum charge for bathroom hardware work	ea	–	$46.50	$46.50	◀ **MINIMUM**
Replace Materials......22.00 Labor..........24.50					
Bath hardware for complete bathroom, economy grade	ea	$64.20	$288.00	$352.20	◀ **COMPLETE BATH**
Replace Materials.....113.00 Labor..........175.00					*Bathroom with toilet,
Remove .... Labor..........64.20					sink, and bathtub / shower. Includes towel bar,
Bath hardware for complete bathroom, standard grade	ea	$64.20	$387.00	$451.20	wash cloth bar, door-
Replace Materials.....212.00 Labor..........175.00					mount robe hook, toilet
Remove .... Labor..........64.20					paper dispenser, and cup / toothbrush holder.
Bath hardware for complete bathroom, high grade	ea	$64.20	$483.00	$547.20	
Replace Materials....308.00 Labor..........175.00					
Remove .... Labor..........64.20					**HARDWARE QUALITY**
Bath hardware for complete bathroom, deluxe grade	ea	$64.20	$592.00	$656.20	Some "rules of thumb" for determining bathroom
Replace Materials.....417.00 Labor..........175.00					hardware quality:
Remove .... Labor..........64.20					**Economy:** Light-gauge
Bath hardware for complete bathroom, custom grade	ea	$64.20	$650.00	$714.20	metal, chrome plated. May
Replace Materials....475.00 Labor..........175.00					have some plastic compo-
Remove .... Labor..........64.20					nents. Little or no pattern.
Bath hardware for complete bathroom, antique reproduction	ea	$64.20	$953.00	$1,017.20	**Standard:** Heavier gauge metal, chrome or brass
Replace Materials....778.00 Labor..........175.00					plated with little or no
Remove .... Labor..........64.20					pattern or wood hardware made of ash or oak.
1/2 bath hardware for complete bathroom, economy grade	ea	$46.20	$131.40	$177.60	◀ **1/2 BATH**
Replace Materials......37.00 Labor..........94.40					*Bathroom with toilet, and
Remove .... Labor..........46.20					sink. Includes wash cloth bar, towel ring, and toilet
1/2 bath hardware for complete bathroom, standard grade	ea	$46.20	$166.40	$212.60	paper dispenser.
Replace Materials......72.00 Labor..........94.40					
Remove .... Labor..........46.20					**QUALITY** *continued*
1/2 bath hardware for complete bathroom, high grade	ea	$46.20	$198.40	$244.60	**High:** Brass, chrome over brass, or nickel over brass
Replace Materials....104.00 Labor..........94.40					with minimal detail, or plated
Remove .... Labor..........46.20					hardware with ornate detail, or European style curved plas-
1/2 bath hardware for complete bathroom, deluxe grade	ea	$46.20	$235.40	$281.60	tic, or hardware with porcelain
Replace Materials.....141.00 Labor..........94.40					components, or wood hard-
Remove .... Labor..........46.20					ware made of walnut, cherry, or similar wood.
1/2 bath hardware for complete bathroom, custom grade	ea	$46.20	$255.40	$301.60	**Deluxe:** Brass, chrome over
Replace Materials.....161.00 Labor..........94.40					brass, or nickel over brass
Remove .... Labor..........46.20					with ornate detail.
1/2 bath hardware for complete bathroom, antique reproduction	ea	$46.20	$369.40	$415.60	**Antique Reproduction / Custom:** Brass, chrome over
Replace Materials....275.00 Labor..........94.40					brass, or nickel over brass
Remove .... Labor..........46.20					with ornate and/or antique style detail.
Glass bathroom shelf	ea	$9.39	$91.30	$100.69	◀ **GLASS SHELF**
Replace Materials......79.00 Labor..........12.30					*21" x 5-1/2" glass shelf.*
Remove .... Labor..........9.39					
▶ With plated chrome hardware.					

	Item Description	Unit	Remove	Replace	Total
GLASS SHELF ▶ *continued*	**Glass & brass bathroom shelf** *Replace* Materials .....115.00 Labor ....12.30 *Remove* .... Labor ....9.39 ▶ With solid brass or chrome-plated brass hardware.	ea	$9.39	$127.30	$136.69
	Remove glass bathroom shelf for work, then reinstall *Replace* .... Labor 14.40	ea	–	$14.40	$14.40
CUP & TOOTH- ▶ **BRUSH HOLDER** *For quality indicators* *see page 41.*	**Cup & toothbrush holder, standard grade** *Replace* Materials.......11.00 Labor ....7.35 *Remove* .... Labor 4.71	ea	$4.71	$18.35	$23.06
	Cup & toothbrush holder, high grade *Replace* Materials.......17.70 Labor ....7.35 *Remove* .... Labor 4.71	ea	$4.71	$25.05	$29.76
	Remove cup & toothbrush holder for work, then reinstall *Replace* .... Labor 9.44	ea	–	$9.44	$9.44
DOOR CLOTHES ▶ **HANGER** *For quality indicators* *see page 41.*	**Door-mounted clothes hanger, standard grade** *Replace* Materials ......10.00 Labor ....6.13 *Remove* .... Labor 4.02	ea	$4.02	$16.13	$20.15
	Door-mounted clothes hanger, high grade *Replace* Materials ......16.10 Labor ....6.13 *Remove* .... Labor 4.02	ea	$4.02	$22.23	$26.25
	Remove door-mounted clothes hanger for work, then reinstall *Replace* .... Labor 7.61	ea	–	$7.61	$7.61
ROBE HOOK ▶ *For quality indicators* *see page 41.*	**Robe hook, standard grade** *Replace* Materials.......11.00 Labor ....6.13 *Remove* .... Labor 4.02	ea	$4.02	$17.13	$21.15
	Robe hook, high grade *Replace* Materials ......18.00 Labor ....6.13 *Remove* .... Labor 4.02	ea	$4.02	$24.13	$28.15
	Remove robe hook for work, then reinstall *Replace* .... Labor 7.61	ea	–	$7.61	$7.61
SOAP HOLDER ▶ *For quality indicators* *see page 41.*	**Soap holder, standard grade** *Replace* Materials ......39.00 Labor ....7.35 *Remove* .... Labor 4.71	ea	$4.71	$46.35	$51.06
	Soap holder, high grade *Replace* Materials ......64.00 Labor ....7.35 *Remove* .... Labor 4.71	ea	$4.71	$71.35	$76.06
	Remove soap holder for work, then reinstall *Replace* .... Labor 9.44	ea	–	$9.44	$9.44
RECESSED ▶ **SOAP HOLDER** *For quality indicators* *see page 41.*	**Recessed soap holder, standard grade** *Replace* Materials ......21.00 Labor ....8.74 *Remove* .... Labor 4.71	ea	$4.71	$29.74	$34.45
	Recessed soap holder, high grade *Replace* Materials ......53.00 Labor ....8.74 *Remove* .... Labor 4.71	ea	$4.71	$61.74	$66.45

Item Description	Unit	Remove	Replace	Total
Remove recessed soap holder for work, then reinstall	ea	–	$11.60	$11.60
Replace .... Labor 11.60				
Soap dispenser, standard grade	ea	$4.71	$25.92	$30.63
Replace Materials ......18.00 Labor 7.92				
Remove .... Labor 4.71				
Soap dispenser, high grade	ea	$4.71	$48.92	$53.63
Replace Materials ......41.00 Labor 7.92				
Remove .... Labor 4.71				
Remove soap dispenser for work, then reinstall	ea	–	$9.74	$9.74
Replace .... Labor 9.74				
Recessed tissue holder, standard grade	ea	$4.02	$47.44	$51.46
Replace Materials ......40.00 Labor 7.44				
Remove .... Labor 4.02				
Recessed tissue holder, high grade	ea	$4.02	$70.44	$74.46
Replace Materials ......63.00 Labor 7.44				
Remove .... Labor 4.02				
Remove recessed tissue holder for work, then reinstall	ea	–	$10.80	$10.80
Replace .... Labor 10.80				
Shower curtain rod	ea	$2.57	$44.92	$47.49
Replace Materials ......40.00 Labor 4.92				
Remove .... Labor 2.57				
Remove shower curtain rod for work, then reinstall	ea	–	$5.66	$5.66
Replace .... Labor 5.66				
Towel bar, economy grade	ea	$9.39	$34.10	$43.49
Replace Materials ......17.00 Labor 17.10				
Remove .... Labor 9.39				
Towel bar, standard grade	ea	$9.39	$41.10	$50.49
Replace Materials ......24.00 Labor 17.10				
Remove .... Labor 9.39				
Towel bar, high grade	ea	$9.39	$56.10	$65.49
Replace Materials ......39.00 Labor 17.10				
Remove .... Labor 9.39				
Towel bar, deluxe grade	ea	$9.39	$75.10	$84.49
Replace Materials ......58.00 Labor 17.10				
Remove .... Labor 9.39				
Remove towel bar for work, then reinstall	ea	–	$24.50	$24.50
Replace .... Labor 24.50				
Toilet paper dispenser, economy grade	ea	$9.39	$39.18	$48.57
Replace Materials ......31.00 Labor 8.18				
Remove .... Labor 9.39				
Toilet paper dispenser, standard grade	ea	$9.39	$47.18	$56.57
Replace Materials ......39.00 Labor 8.18				
Remove .... Labor 9.39				

◄ **SOAP DISPENSER**
For quality indicators see page 41.

◄ **RECESSED TISSUE HOLDER**
For quality indicators see page 41.

◄ **SHOWER ROD**
For quality indicators see page 41.

◄ **TOWEL BAR**
For quality indicators see page 41.

◄ **TOILET PAPER DISPENSER**
For quality indicators see page 41.

RELATED ITEMS
Cleaning 56

	Item Description	Unit	Remove	Replace	Total
TOILET PAPER ▶ **DISPENSER** *continued*	**Toilet paper dispenser, high grade** *Replace* Materials......54.00 Labor ....8.18 *Remove* .... Labor 9.39	ea	$9.39	$62.18	$71.57
	Toilet paper dispenser, deluxe grade *Replace* Materials......63.00 Labor ....8.18 *Remove* .... Labor 9.39	ea	$9.39	$71.18	$80.57
	Remove toilet paper dispenser for work, then reinstall *Replace* .... Labor..........10.70	ea	–	$10.70	$10.70
TOWEL RING ▶ *For quality indicators* *see page 41.*	**Towel ring, economy grade** *Replace* Materials.......17.00 Labor..........10.40 *Remove* .... Labor 9.39	ea	$9.39	$27.40	$36.79
	Towel ring, standard grade *Replace* Materials ......21.00 Labor..........10.40 *Remove* .... Labor 9.39	ea	$9.39	$31.40	$40.79
	Towel ring, high grade *Replace* Materials ......24.00 Labor..........10.40 *Remove* .... Labor 9.39	ea	$9.39	$34.40	$43.79
	Towel ring, deluxe grade *Replace* Materials......28.00 Labor..........10.40 *Remove* .... Labor 9.39	ea	$9.39	$38.40	$47.79
	Remove towel ring for work, then reinstall *Replace* .... Labor..........13.00	ea	–	$13.00	$13.00
WASH CLOTH BAR ▶ *For quality indicators* *see page 41.*	**Wash cloth bar, economy grade** *Replace* Materials ......14.00 Labor ....17.10 *Remove* .... Labor 9.39	ea	$9.39	$31.10	$40.49
	Wash cloth bar, standard grade *Replace* Materials ......18.00 Labor ....17.10 *Remove* .... Labor	ea	$9.39	$35.10	$44.49
	Wash cloth bar, high grade *Replace* Materials ......25.00 Labor ....17.10 *Remove* .... Labor 9.39	ea	$9.39	$42.10	$51.49
	Wash cloth bar, deluxe grade *Replace* Materials ......33.00 Labor ....17.10 *Remove* .... Labor 9.39	ea	$9.39	$50.10	$59.49
	Remove wash cloth bar for work, then reinstall *Replace* .... Labor..........24.50	ea	–	$24.50	$24.50
RECESSED ▶ **MEDICINE CABINET**	**Recessed medicine cabinet, economy grade** *Replace* Materials......53.00 Labor..........57.00 *Remove* .... Labor..........17.60 ▶ Plastic or polystyrene box with two to three shelves. Up to 16" wide and up to 25" tall. Mirror doors with chrome-plated trim.	ea	$17.60	$110.00	$127.60
	Recessed medicine cabinet, standard grade *Replace* Materials ......65.00 Labor..........57.00 *Remove* .... Labor..........17.60 ▶ Plastic or polystyrene box with two to three shelves. Up to 16" wide and up to 25" tall. Mirror door with brass-plated or wood trim or vinyl shutter door.	ea	$17.60	$122.00	$139.60

Item Description	Unit	Remove	Replace	Total
Recessed medicine cabinet, high grade	ea	$17.60	$151.00	$168.60
Replace Materials ......94.00　　Labor...........57.00				
Remove ....　　Labor...........17.60				
▶ Steel box with adjustable shelves. Up to 16" wide and up to 25" tall. Mirror door with chrome-plated or wood trim; or real wood door (includes stain & varnish). May have beveled mirror with no trim.				
Recessed medicine cabinet, deluxe grade	ea	$17.60	$168.00	$185.60
Replace Materials .....111.00　　Labor...........57.00				
Remove ....　　Labor...........17.60				
▶ Steel box with adjustable shelves. Up to 20" wide and up to 32" tall. Arched mirror door with brass or wood trim; or real wood door (includes stain & varnish). May have beveled mirror with no trim.				
Recessed medicine cabinet, custom grade	ea	$17.60	$194.00	$211.60
Replace Materials.....137.00　　Labor...........57.00				
Remove ....　　Labor...........17.60				
▶ Steel box with adjustable shelves. Up to 20" wide and up to 32" tall. Arched or oval mirror door brass or wood trim; or real wood door (includes stain & varnish). May have beveled mirror with no trim.				
Remove recessed medicine cabinet for work, then reinstall	ea	–	$81.80	$81.80
Replace ....　　Labor...........81.80				
Surface-mounted medicine cabinet, economy grade	ea	$18.80	$131.70	$150.50
Replace Materials......66.00　　Labor...........65.70				
Remove ....　　Labor...........18.80				
▶ Plastic or polystyrene box with two to three shelves. Up to 16" wide and up to 25" tall. Hinged mirror doors with chrome-plated trim; or vinyl shutter door. Also larger mirror styles with small sliding door cabinet below mirror.				
Surface-mounted medicine cabinet, standard grade	ea	$18.80	$160.70	$179.50
Replace Materials ......95.00　　Labor...........65.70				
Remove ....　　Labor...........18.80				
▶ Metal box with adjustable shelves. Up to 16" wide and up to 25" tall. Hinged mirror doors with chrome-plated trim or wood trim; or wood shutter door (includes stain & varnish).				
Surface-mounted medicine cabinet, high grade	ea	$18.80	$226.70	$245.50
Replace Materials .....161.00　　Labor...........65.70				
Remove ....　　Labor...........18.80				
▶ Metal box with two to three shelves. Up to 16" wide and up to 25" tall. Hinged mirror doors with chrome-plated trim or wood trim; or wood shutter door (includes stain & varnish). Also up to 30" by 30" cabinets with bypassing mirror doors.				
Surface-mounted medicine cabinet, deluxe grade	ea	$18.80	$337.70	$356.50
Replace Materials ....272.00　　Labor...........65.70				
Remove ....　　Labor...........18.80				
▶ Wood plastic laminate coated box with two to three shelves. Up to 30" wide and up to 30" tall. 3 door hinged doors usually with oak trim.				
Surface-mounted medicine cabinet, custom grade	ea	$18.80	$453.70	$472.50
Replace Materials ....388.00　　Labor...........65.70				
Remove ....　　Labor...........18.80				
▶ Metal box (may be chrome) with two to three shelves. Up to 38" wide and up to 32" tall. 3 hinged doors usually with oak trim.				
Remove surface-mounted medicine cabinet for work, then reinstall	ea	–	$85.70	$85.70
Replace ....　　Labor...........85.70				
Bathroom mirror with stainless-steel trim	sf	$1.18	$22.61	$23.79
Replace Materials ......18.00　　Labor 4.61				
Remove ....　　Labor 1.18				

◀ **SURFACE-MOUNT MEDICINE CABINET**

RELATED ITEMS
Cleaning 56

◀ **BATHROOM MIRROR**

Item Description	Unit	Remove	Replace	Total
BATHROOM ▶ **MIRROR** *continued*				
Bathroom mirror with brass-finished trim	sf	$1.18	$23.61	$24.79
Replace Materials........19.00 Labor ....4.61 *Remove* .... Labor 1.18				
Bathroom mirror with wood frame	sf	$1.18	$24.61	$25.79
Replace Materials......20.00 Labor ....4.61 *Remove* .... Labor 1.18				
Bathroom mirror beveled glass	sf	$1.18	$24.61	$25.79
Replace Materials......20.00 Labor ....4.61 *Remove* .... Labor 1.18				
Remove bathroom mirror for work, then reinstall	sf	–	$7.35	$7.35
Replace .... Labor 7.35				

TIME & MATERIAL CHARTS *(selected items)*

Bathroom Hardware Materials

See **Bathroom Hardware** material prices with the line items and other information in the **QuickFinder** column.

Bathroom Hardware Labor

LABORER	BASE WAGE	PAID LEAVE	TRUE WAGE	FICA	FUTA	WORKER'S COMP.	UNEMPLOY. INSUR.	HEALTH INSUR.	RETIRE (401k)	LIABILITY INSUR.	COST PER HOUR
Carpenter (installer)	$24.30	1.90	$26.20	2.00	.21	5.15	2.28	2.92	.79	3.93	$43.50
Demolition laborer	$14.40	1.12	$15.52	1.19	.12	5.01	1.35	2.92	.47	2.33	$28.90

Paid Leave is calculated based on two weeks paid vacation, one week sick leave, and seven paid holidays. Employer's matching portion of **FICA** is 7.65 percent. **FUTA** (Federal Unemployment) is .8 percent. **Worker's compensation** for the bathroom hardware trade was calculated using a national average of 19.63 percent. **Unemployment insurance** was calculated using a national average of 8.7 percent. **Health insurance** was calculated based on a projected national average for 2005 of $580 per employee (and family when applicable) per month. Employer pays 80 percent for a per month cost of $464 per employee. **Retirement** is based on a 401(k) retirement program with employer matching of 50 percent. Employee contributions to the 401(k) plan are an average of 6 percent of the true wage. **Liability insurance** is based on a national average of 14.0 percent.

Bathroom Hardware Labor Productivity

WORK DESCRIPTION	LABORER	COST PER HOUR	PRODUCTIVITY	UNIT PRICE
Demolition				
hardware for complete bathroom	demolition laborer	$28.90	2.22	$64.20 ea
hardware for complete 1/2 bathroom	demolition laborer	$28.90	1.60	$46.20 ea
recessed medicine cabinet	demolition laborer	$28.90	.609	$17.60 ea
surface-mounted medicine cabinet	demolition laborer	$28.90	.650	$18.80 ea
bathroom mirror attached with glue	demolition laborer	$28.90	.041	$1.18 sf
Install complete bathroom hardware				
full bathroom	carpenter	$43.50	4.02	$175.00 ea
1/2 bathroom	carpenter	$43.50	2.17	$94.40 ea
Install hardware				
soap holder	carpenter	$43.50	.169	$7.35 ea
recessed tissue holder	carpenter	$43.50	.171	$7.44 ea
towel bar	carpenter	$43.50	.393	$17.10 ea
toilet paper dispenser	carpenter	$43.50	.188	$8.18 ea
towel ring	carpenter	$43.50	.238	$10.40 ea
wash cloth bar	carpenter	$43.50	.393	$17.10 ea
recessed medicine cabinet	carpenter	$43.50	1.31	$57.00 ea
surface-mounted medicine cabinet	carpenter	$43.50	1.51	$65.70 ea
bathroom mirror	carpenter	$43.50	.106	$4.61 sf

5 .... *Cabinets*

Item Description	Unit	Remove	Replace	Total	
Minimum charge for cabinet work *Replace* Materials......46.00 Labor..........96.10	ea	–	$142.10	$142.10	◄ **MINIMUM**
Lower kitchen cabinets, standard grade *Replace* Materials......90.00 Labor..........13.00 *Remove* .... Labor..........7.57	lf	$7.57	$103.00	$110.57	◄ **LOWER CABINETS**
Lower kitchen cabinets, high grade *Replace* Materials.....116.00 Labor..........13.00 *Remove* .... Labor..........7.57	lf	$7.57	$129.00	$136.57	
Lower kitchen cabinets, deluxe grade *Replace* Materials....164.00 Labor..........13.00 *Remove* .... Labor..........7.57	lf	$7.57	$177.00	$184.57	
Lower kitchen cabinets, custom grade *Replace* Materials....234.00 Labor..........13.00 *Remove* .... Labor..........7.57	lf	$7.57	$247.00	$254.57	
Lower kitchen cabinets, custom deluxe grade *Replace* Materials....303.00 Labor..........13.00 *Remove* .... Labor..........7.57	lf	$7.57	$316.00	$323.57	
Remove lower kitchen cabinets for work, then reinstall *Replace* .... Labor..........22.90	lf	–	$22.90	$22.90	
Upper kitchen cabinets, economy grade *Replace* Materials......63.00 Labor..........12.60 *Remove* .... Labor..........6.82	lf	$6.82	$75.60	$82.42	◄ **UPPER CABINETS**
Upper kitchen cabinets, standard grade *Replace* Materials......84.00 Labor..........12.60 *Remove* .... Labor..........6.82	lf	$6.82	$96.60	$103.42	
Upper kitchen cabinets, high grade *Replace* Materials....104.00 Labor..........12.60 *Remove* .... Labor..........6.82	lf	$6.82	$116.60	$123.42	
Upper kitchen cabinets, deluxe grade *Replace* Materials.....151.00 Labor..........12.60 *Remove* .... Labor..........6.82	lf	$6.82	$163.60	$170.42	
Upper kitchen cabinets, custom grade *Replace* Materials.....218.00 Labor..........12.60 *Remove* .... Labor..........6.82	lf	$6.82	$230.60	$237.42	
Upper kitchen cabinets, custom deluxe grade *Replace* Materials....277.00 Labor..........12.60 *Remove* .... Labor..........6.82	lf	$6.82	$289.60	$296.42	
Remove upper kitchen cabinets for work, then reinstall *Replace* .... Labor..........22.00	lf	–	$22.00	$22.00	

CABINET CONSTRUCTION

STOCK CABINETS Stock-grade cabinets are manufactured in standard sizes and warehoused until sold.

SEMI-CUSTOM CABINETS Semi-custom grade cabinets are available in a wide variety of styles and shapes. Within limits, the manufacturer builds the cabinets to match the kitchen.

CUSTOM CABINETS Custom-grade cabinets are built specifically for the kitchen and include specialty doors, woods and construction.

CABINET GRADES

ECONOMY GRADE Stock-grade cabinets with flush-face doors. Doors made from veneered particle board.

STANDARD GRADE Stock-grade cabinets with raised panel or cathedral doors. Interior panel may be plywood. Lower grade plastic-laminate face cabinets.

HIGH GRADE Semi-custom cabinets with raised panel or cathedral doors. Higher grade plastic-laminate face and foil-face cabinets.

continued on next page

RELATED ITEMS
Cleaning 56

Item Description	Unit	Remove	Replace	Total
LOWER ISLAND ▶ CABINETS — **Lower kitchen island cabinets, economy grade** *Replace* Materials ......74.00 Labor ....13.40 *Remove* .... Labor 7.31	lf	$7.31	$87.40	$94.71
Lower kitchen island cabinets, standard grade *Replace* Materials ......94.00 Labor ....13.40 *Remove* .... Labor 7.31	lf	$7.31	$107.40	$114.71
Lower kitchen island cabinets, high grade *Replace* Materials .....121.00 Labor ....13.40 *Remove* .... Labor 7.31	lf	$7.31	$134.40	$141.71
Lower kitchen island cabinets, deluxe grade *Replace* Materials .....171.00 Labor ....13.40 *Remove* .... Labor 7.31	lf	$7.31	$184.40	$191.71
Lower kitchen island cabinets, custom grade *Replace* Materials ....243.00 Labor ....13.40 *Remove* .... Labor 7.31	lf	$7.31	$256.40	$263.71
Lower kitchen island cabinets, custom deluxe grade *Replace* Materials .....315.00 Labor ....13.40 *Remove* .... Labor 7.31	lf	$7.31	$328.40	$335.71
Remove lower kitchen island cabinets for work, then reinstall *Replace* .... Labor 23.50	lf	–	$23.50	$23.50
UPPER ISLAND ▶ CABINETS — **Upper kitchen island cabinets, economy grade** *Replace* Materials ......66.00 Labor ....12.90 *Remove* .... Labor 6.88	lf	$6.88	$78.90	$85.78
Upper kitchen island cabinets, standard grade *Replace* Materials ......87.00 Labor ....12.90 *Remove* .... Labor 6.88	lf	$6.88	$99.90	$106.78
Upper kitchen island cabinets, high grade *Replace* Materials ....108.00 Labor ....12.90 *Remove* .... Labor 6.88	lf	$6.88	$120.90	$127.78
Upper kitchen island cabinets, deluxe grade *Replace* Materials .....157.00 Labor ....12.90 *Remove* .... Labor 6.88	lf	$6.88	$169.90	$176.78
Upper kitchen island cabinets, custom grade *Replace* Materials ....227.00 Labor ....12.90 *Remove* .... Labor 6.88	lf	$6.88	$239.90	$246.78
Upper kitchen island cabinets, custom deluxe grade *Replace* Materials ....288.00 Labor ....12.90 *Remove* .... Labor 6.88	lf	$6.88	$300.90	$307.78
Remove upper kitchen island cabinets for work, then reinstall *Replace* .... Labor 22.80	lf	–	$22.80	$22.80
FULL-HEIGHT ▶ UTILITY CABINET — **Full-height utility cabinet, economy grade** *Replace* Materials .....172.00 Labor ....21.30 *Remove* .... Labor 9.57	lf	$9.57	$193.30	$202.87
Full-height utility cabinet, standard grade *Replace* Materials .....217.00 Labor ....21.30 *Remove* .... Labor 9.57	lf	$9.57	$238.30	$247.87

CABINET GRADES

continued from prior page

DELUXE GRADE Semi-custom cabinets with raised panel or cathedral doors. May include special slide-out drawers, pull-out baskets, glass doors, foil-face, cherry, pecan, or Shaker style maple or pine.

CUSTOM GRADE Custom cabinets with raised panel or cathedral doors. May include specialty slide-out drawers, pull-out baskets, glass mullion or leaded glass doors, cherry, pecan, or Shaker style maple or pine.

CUSTOM DELUXE GRADE Same as Custom Grade may have some curved wood cabinets and more custom features.

Item Description	Unit	Remove	Replace	Total
Full-height utility cabinet, high grade	lf	$9.57	$286.30	$295.87
Replace Materials ....265.00 Labor..........21.30				
Remove .... Labor 9.57				
Full-height utility cabinet, deluxe grade	lf	$9.57	$359.30	$368.87
Replace Materials ....338.00 Labor..........21.30				
Remove .... Labor 9.57				
Full-height utility cabinet, custom grade	lf	$9.57	$390.30	$399.87
Replace Materials ....369.00 Labor..........21.30				
Remove .... Labor 9.57				
Full-height utility cabinet custom, deluxe grade	lf	$9.57	$435.30	$444.87
Replace Materials .....414.00 Labor..........21.30				
Remove .... Labor 9.57				
Remove full-height kitchen cabinets for work, then reinstall	lf	–	$25.40	$25.40
Replace .... Labor 25.40				
Full-height built-in oven cabinet, economy grade	lf	$9.57	$184.30	$193.87
Replace Materials .....163.00 Labor..........21.30				
Remove .... Labor 9.57				
Full-height built-in oven cabinet, standard grade	lf	$9.57	$227.30	$236.87
Replace Materials ....206.00 Labor..........21.30				
Remove .... Labor 9.57				
Full-height built-in oven cabinet, high grade	lf	$9.57	$273.30	$282.87
Replace Materials ....252.00 Labor..........21.30				
Remove .... Labor 9.57				
Full-height built-in oven cabinet, deluxe grade	lf	$9.57	$342.30	$351.87
Replace Materials ....321.00 Labor..........21.30				
Remove .... Labor 9.57				
Full-height built-in oven cabinet, custom grade	lf	$9.57	$372.30	$381.87
Replace Materials ....351.00 Labor..........21.30				
Remove .... Labor 9.57				
Full-height built-in oven cabinet, custom deluxe grade	lf	$9.57	$414.30	$423.87
Replace Materials ....393.00 Labor..........21.30				
Remove .... Labor 9.57				
Remove full-height built-in oven cabinets for work, then reinstall	lf	–	$25.40	$25.40
Replace .... Labor 25.40				
Full-height built-in double oven cabinet, economy grade	lf	$9.57	$179.30	$188.87
Replace Materials .....158.00 Labor..........21.30				
Remove .... Labor 9.57				
Full-height built-in double oven cabinet, standard grade	lf	$9.57	$221.30	$230.87
Replace Materials ....200.00 Labor..........21.30				
Remove .... Labor 9.57				
Full-height built-in double oven cabinet, high grade	lf	$9.57	$265.30	$274.87
Replace Materials ....244.00 Labor..........21.30				
Remove .... Labor 9.57				
Full-height built-in double oven cabinet, deluxe grade	lf	$9.57	$332.30	$341.87
Replace Materials ....311.00 Labor..........21.30				
Remove .... Labor 9.57				

◄ **FULL-HEIGHT OVEN CABINET**

FOIL-FACE CABINETS

Foil-faced cabinets (also called thermo foil) are coated with rigid polyvinyl chloride (PVC) that has been heated and pressed. The interior core is usually medium density particleboard.

Currently, there is no good way to repair scratched or dented foil-face cabinets. Although colors do not fade from foil-faces, it is almost impossible to replace doors or other parts with colors that will match.

Foil-face cabinets are high to custom deluxe quality depending on the interior features and the complexity of the design.

◄ **FULL-HEIGHT DOUBLE OVEN CABINET**

RELATED ITEMS

Cleaning 56

Item Description	Unit	Remove	Replace	Total
FULL-HEIGHT ▶ **Full-height built-in double oven cabinet, custom grade**	lf	$9.57	$360.30	$369.87
DOUBLE OVEN *Replace* Materials ....339.00　　Labor...........21.30				
CABINET *Remove* ....　　Labor 9.57				
continued				
Full-height built-in double oven cabinet, custom deluxe grade	lf	$9.57	$402.30	$411.87
Replace Materials ....381.00　　Labor...........21.30				
Remove ....　　Labor 9.57				
Remove full-height built-in double oven cabinets for work, then reinstall	lf	–	$25.40	$25.40
Replace ....　　Labor 25.40				
CABINET ▶ **Cabinet drawer front**	ea	$4.16	$18.25	$22.41
DRAWER FRONT *Replace* Materials ......14.00　　Labor 4.25				
Remove ....　　Labor 4.16				
CABINET DOOR ▶ **Flush-face cabinet door**	ea	$7.72	$27.07	$34.79
Replace Materials ......18.00　　Labor 9.07				
flat panel *Remove* ....　　Labor 7.72				
Flat panel cabinet door	ea	$7.72	$34.07	$41.79
Replace Materials ......25.00　　Labor 9.07				
Remove ....　　Labor 7.72				
raised panel **Raised panel cabinet door**	ea	$7.72	$46.07	$53.79
Replace Materials ......37.00　　Labor 9.07				
Remove ....　　Labor 7.72				
Raised panel cathedral cabinet door	ea	$7.72	$55.07	$62.79
Replace Materials ......46.00　　Labor 9.07				
raised panel *Remove* ....　　Labor 7.72				
cathedral **Cabinet door with glass**	ea	$7.72	$65.07	$72.79
Replace Materials ......56.00　　Labor 9.07				
Remove ....　　Labor 7.72				
with leaded				
glass **Cabinet door with leaded glass per door**	ea	$7.72	$121.07	$128.79
Replace Materials ......112.00　　Labor 9.07				
Remove ....　　Labor 7.72				
REFINISH CABINET ▶ **Refinish cabinet drawer front**	ea	–	$11.37	$11.37
Cabinets are stripped and *Replace* Materials ....1.60　　Labor 9.77				
restained. Edge surfaces				
that are **Refinish cabinet door**	ea	–	$26.50	$26.50
finished with 1/4" hard- *Replace* Materials ....3.60　　Labor 22.90				
wood plywood are				
replaced. **Refinish cabinet door with glass**	ea	–	$24.70	$24.70
Replace Materials ....1.70　　Labor 23.00				
Refinish cabinets & doors, re-face plywood ends	lf	–	$64.40	$64.40
Replace Materials ......14.00　　Labor 50.40				
Refinish island cabinets & doors, re-face plywood ends & faces	lf	–	$80.60	$80.60
Replace Materials ......15.00　　Labor...........65.60				
repair gouge or hole ▷ **Repair gouge or hole in cabinet, grain patch to match finish**	ea	–	$60.10	$60.10
Replace Materials ....7.00　　Labor 53.10				
▶ Gouge or hole is filled, then "grained" by the painter to look like natural wood grain, matched to the finish of the cabinets.				

Item Description	Unit	Remove	Replace	Total	
Post-formed plastic laminate countertop	sf	$3.81	$14.30	$18.11	◄ **PLASTIC LAMINATE COUNTERTOP**
Replace Materials......4.00 Labor..........10.30					*Most commonly known by the trade name "Formica." Add 6% for installation on bathroom vanity.*
Remove .... Labor 3.81					
► Backsplash is integrated into countertop with a rounded cove transition.					
Flat-laid plastic laminate countertop	sf	$3.81	$14.90	$18.71	
Replace Materials........3.80 Labor..........11.10					
Remove .... Labor 3.81					
► Countertop butts into wall with flat edge.					
Cultured marble countertop	sf	$3.81	$29.30	$33.11	◄ **CULTURED MARBLE COUNTERTOP**
Replace Materials ......18.00 Labor..........11.30					*Add 6% for installation on bathroom vanity.*
Remove .... Labor 3.81					
Add for integrated sink in cultured marble countertop	ea	–	$156.00	$156.00	
Replace Materials.....156.00					
Cultured granite countertop	sf	$3.81	$35.30	$39.11	◄ **CULTURED GRANITE COUNTERTOP**
Replace Materials ......24.00 Labor..........11.30					*Add 6% for installation on bathroom vanity.*
Remove .... Labor 3.81					
Add for integrated sink in cultured granite countertop	ea	–	$196.00	$196.00	
Replace Materials.....196.00					
Onyx countertop	sf	$3.81	$35.30	$39.11	◄ **CULTURED ONYX COUNTERTOP**
Replace Materials ......24.00 Labor..........11.30					*Add 6% for installation on bathroom vanity.*
Remove .... Labor 3.81					
Add for integrated sink in onyx countertop	ea	–	$190.00	$190.00	
Replace Materials.....190.00					
Solid-surface countertop, economy grade	sf	$3.81	$120.90	$124.71	◄ **SOLID-SURFACE COUNTERTOP**
Replace Materials ....109.00 Labor..........11.90					*Commonly known by the trade name Corian. Other trade names include Avonite, Surell, Gibraltar, and Fountainhead. Add 9% for installation on bathroom vanity.*
Remove .... Labor 3.81					
► Off-white colors, bull-nose edge.					
Solid-surface countertop, standard grade	sf	$3.81	$167.90	$171.71	
Replace Materials.....156.00 Labor..........11.90					
Remove .... Labor 3.81					
► All standard colors, patterned edge detail, with thin strip inlay.					
Solid-surface countertop, high grade	sf	$3.81	$228.90	$232.71	
Replace Materials.....217.00 Labor..........11.90					
Remove .... Labor 3.81					
► All standard colors, patterned edge detail, with wood or strip inlay.					
Solid-surface countertop, deluxe grade	sf	$3.81	$273.90	$277.71	
Replace Materials ....262.00 Labor..........11.90					
Remove .... Labor 3.81					
► Layered with alternating colored layers, wood strip inlays, custom edge detailing.					
Solid-surface countertop, custom grade	sf	$3.81	$304.90	$308.71	
Replace Materials ....293.00 Labor..........11.90					
Remove .... Labor 3.81					
► Layered with alternating colored layers, wood strip inlays, custom edge detailing, inlaid patterns in countertop.					
Granite countertop	sf	$3.81	$181.90	$185.71	◄ **GRANITE COUNTERTOP**
Replace Materials.....167.00 Labor..........14.90					*Add 6% for installation on bathroom vanity.*
Remove .... Labor 3.81					

	Item Description	Unit	Remove	Replace	Total
STAINLESS STEEL ▶ COUNTERTOP	**Stainless steel countertop** *Replace* Materials ......26.00 Labor ....13.60 *Remove* .... Labor 3.81	sf	$3.81	$39.60	$43.41
BUTCHER-BLOCK ▶ COUNTERTOP Add **6%** for installation on bathroom vanity.	**Butcher-block countertop** *Replace* Materials ......23.00 Labor ....11.30 *Remove* .... Labor 3.81	sf	$3.81	$34.30	$38.11
SOLID WOOD ▶ COUNTERTOP Add **6%** for installation on bathroom vanity.	**Solid wood countertop** *Replace* Materials ....8.10 Labor ....10.50 *Remove* .... Labor ....3.81 ▶ Maple or oak.	sf	$3.81	$18.60	$22.41
	Remove countertop for work, then reinstall *Replace* .... Labor 16.10	sf	–	$16.10	$16.10
TILE ▶ COUNTERTOP Add **6%** for installation on bathroom vanity.	**Tile countertop, economy grade tile** *Replace* Materials ....13.00 Labor ....9.04 *Remove* .... Labor ....6.62 ▶ Average priced tile set in thinset mortar bed over cement backer board.	sf	$6.62	$22.04	$28.66
	Tile countertop, standard grade tile *Replace* Materials ....19.00 Labor ....9.04 *Remove* .... Labor ....6.62 ▶ Average priced tile set in mortar bed or higher priced tile set in thinset mortar over cement backer board.	sf	$6.62	$28.04	$34.66
	Tile countertop, high grade tile *Replace* Materials ......24.00 Labor ....9.04 *Remove* .... Labor ....6.62 ▶ Higher priced tile set in mortar bed or deluxe priced tile set in thinset mortar over cement backer board.	sf	$6.62	$33.04	$39.66
	Tile countertop, deluxe grade tile *Replace* Materials ......38.00 Labor ....9.04 *Remove* .... Labor ....6.62 ▶ Deluxe priced tile set in mortar bed.	sf	$6.62	$47.04	$53.66
REPAIR TILE ▶ COUNTERTOP	**Replace tile in tile countertop to match** *Replace* Materials ......31.00 Labor 33.10	ea	–	$64.10	$64.10
	Re-affix loose tile in tile countertop *Replace* Materials ......20.00 Labor 22.50	ea	–	$42.50	$42.50
	Minimum charge for tile countertop work *Replace* Materials ......21.00 Labor 79.90	ea	–	$100.90	$100.90
BATHROOM ▶ VANITY CABINET	**Bathroom vanity cabinet, economy grade** *Replace* Materials ......73.00 Labor ....13.40 *Remove* .... Labor 7.80	lf	$7.80	$86.40	$94.20
	Bathroom vanity cabinets, standard grade *Replace* Materials ......93.00 Labor ....13.40 *Remove* .... Labor 7.80	lf	$7.80	$106.40	$114.20
	Bathroom vanity cabinets, high grade *Replace* Materials .....119.00 Labor ....13.40 *Remove* .... Labor 7.80	lf	$7.80	$132.40	$140.20
	Bathroom vanity cabinets, deluxe grade *Replace* Materials .....169.00 Labor ....13.40 *Remove* .... Labor 7.80	lf	$7.80	$182.40	$190.20

Item Description	Unit	Remove	Replace	Total
Bathroom vanity cabinets, custom grade	lf	$7.80	$254.40	$262.20
Replace Materials.....241.00 Labor..........13.40				
Remove .... Labor...........7.80				
Bathroom vanity cabinets, custom deluxe grade	lf	$7.80	$325.40	$333.20
Replace Materials.....312.00 Labor..........13.40				
Remove .... Labor...........7.80				
Remove bathroom vanity cabinet for work, then reinstall	lf	–	$23.50	$23.50
Replace .... Labor..........23.50				

RELATED ITEMS

Cleaning 56

✍ NOTES: _____

_____

_____ end

TIME & MATERIAL CHARTS (selected items)

Cabinets Materials

See **Cabinets** material prices with the line items and other information in the **QuickFinder** column.

Cabinets Labor

LABORER	BASE WAGE	PAID LEAVE	TRUE WAGE	FICA	FUTA	WORKER'S COMP.	UNEMPLOY. INSUR.	HEALTH INSUR.	RETIRE (401K)	LIABILITY INSUR.	COST PER HOUR
Cabinet installer	$24.30	1.90	$26.20	2.00	.21	5.15	2.28	2.92	.79	3.93	$43.50
Painter	$23.90	1.86	$25.76	1.97	.21	6.91	2.24	2.92	.77	3.86	$44.60
Tile layer	$22.80	1.78	$24.58	1.88	.20	4.50	2.14	2.92	.74	3.69	$40.70
Laborer	$15.30	1.19	$16.49	1.26	.13	3.24	1.43	2.92	.49	2.47	$28.40
Demolition laborer	$14.40	1.12	$15.52	1.19	.12	5.01	1.35	2.92	.47	2.33	$28.90

Paid Leave is calculated based on two weeks paid vacation, one week sick leave, and seven paid holidays. Employer's matching portion of **FICA** is 7.65 percent. **FUTA** (Federal Unemployment) is .8 percent. **Worker's Compensation** was calculated using a national average of 19.63 percent for the cabinet installer and helper; 26.77 percent for the painter; and 18.26 percent for the tile layer. **Unemployment insurance** was calculated using a national average of 8.7 percent. **Health insurance** was calculated based on a projected national average for 2005 of $580 per employee (and family when applicable) per month. Employer pays 80 percent for a per month cost of $464 per employee. **Retirement** is based on a 401(k) retirement program with employer matching of 50 percent. Employee contributions to the 401(k) plan are an average of 6 percent of the true wage. **Liability insurance** is based on a national average of 14.0 percent.

Cabinets Labor Productivity

WORK DESCRIPTION	LABORER	COST PER HOUR	PRODUCTIVITY	UNIT PRICE
Demolition				
remove lower kitchen cabinets	demolition laborer	$28.90	.262	$7.57 lf
remove lower island kitchen cabinets	demolition laborer	$28.90	.253	$7.31 lf
remove upper kitchen cabinets	demolition laborer	$28.90	.236	$6.82 lf
remove upper island kitchen cabinets	demolition laborer	$28.90	.238	$6.88 lf
remove full-height kitchen cabinets	demolition laborer	$28.90	.331	$9.57 lf
remove bathroom vanity cabinet	demolition laborer	$28.90	.270	$7.80 lf

... More ➤

Cabinets Labor Productivity *continued*

WORK DESCRIPTION	LABORER	COST PER HOUR	PRODUCTIVITY	UNIT PRICE
remove countertop	demolition laborer	$28.90	.132	$3.81 sf
remove tile countertop	demolition laborer	$28.90	.229	$6.62 sf
remove cabinet door	demolition laborer	$28.90	.267	$7.72 ea
remove cabinet drawer front	demolition laborer	$28.90	.144	$4.16 ea
Cabinet crew				
install cabinets & countertop	cabinet installer	$43.50		
install cabinets & countertop	laborer	$28.40		
cabinet installation	*installation crew*	$36.00		
Install kitchen cabinets				
lower kitchen cabinets	installation crew	$36.00	.360	$13.00 lf
upper kitchen cabinets	installation crew	$36.00	.349	$12.60 lf
lower kitchen island cabinets	installation crew	$36.00	.371	$13.40 lf
upper kitchen island cabinets	installation crew	$36.00	.359	$12.90 lf
full-height cabinet	installation crew	$36.00	.593	$21.30 lf
Install cabinet drawer fronts & doors				
drawer front	installation crew	$36.00	.118	$4.25 ea
door	installation crew	$36.00	.252	$9.07 ea
Refinish cabinets				
cabinet drawer front	painter	$44.60	.219	$9.77 ea
cabinet door	painter	$44.60	.513	$22.90 ea
cabinet door with glass	painter	$44.60	.515	$23.00 ea
cabinets & doors, re-face plywood ends	painter	$44.60	1.13	$50.40 lf
island cabinets & doors, re-face plywood ends & faces	painter	$44.60	1.47	$65.60 lf
Cabinet repair				
repair gouge or hole in cabinet, grain to match	painter	$44.60	1.19	$53.10 ea
Install countertop				
post-formed plastic laminate	installation crew	$36.00	.286	$10.30 sf
flat-laid plastic laminate	installation crew	$36.00	.309	$11.10 sf
cultured material	installation crew	$36.00	.314	$11.30 sf
solid-surface	installation crew	$36.00	.330	$11.90 sf
granite	installation crew	$36.00	.415	$14.90 sf
stainless steel	installation crew	$36.00	.377	$13.60 sf
butcher block	installation crew	$36.00	.314	$11.30 sf
solid wood	installation crew	$36.00	.292	$10.50 sf
tile	installation crew	$36.00	.251	$9.04 sf
Install bathroom vanity cabinet				
bathroom vanity cabinet	installation crew	$36.00	.371	$13.40 lf

NOTES: _____

_____

_____

_____

_____

_____

_____

_____

_____

_____

_____ end

6 .... *Cleaning*

Item Description	Unit			Total	
Minimum charge for cleaning work *Clean* Materials............2.00 Labor 46.30	ea	–	–	$48.30	◀ **MINIMUM**
Clean acoustic ceiling tiles *Clean* Materials .... .02 Labor .... .36	sf	–	–	$.38	◀ **ACOUSTIC TILE**
Clean cook top *Clean* Materials .... .90 Labor 22.50	ea	–	–	$23.40	◀ **APPLIANCES**
Clean range *Clean* Materials............1.60 Labor 39.60	ea	–	–	$41.20	
Clean space-saver range *Clean* Materials............1.50 Labor 37.30	ea	–	–	$38.80	
Clean high-low range *Clean* Materials............2.10 Labor...........51.90	ea	–	–	$54.00	
Clean restaurant-style gas range *Clean* Materials............2.20 Labor 54.20	ea	–	–	$56.40	
Clean wall oven *Clean* Materials............1.30 Labor 32.60	ea	–	–	$33.90	
Clean double wall oven *Clean* Materials............2.20 Labor 54.20	ea	–	–	$56.40	
Clean modular electric cook top unit *Clean* Materials .... .50 Labor 11.30	ea	–	–	$11.80	
Clean drop-in or slide-in range *Clean* Materials............1.40 Labor 36.00	ea	–	–	$37.40	
Clean range hood *Clean* Materials .... .40 Labor 11.00	ea	–	–	$11.40	
Clean oversize range hood *Clean* Materials .... .50 Labor 11.70	ea	–	–	$12.20	
Clean dishwasher *Clean* Materials .... 1.00 Labor 25.70	ea	–	–	$26.70	
Clean microwave *Clean* Materials .... .50 Labor..........12.50	ea	–	–	$13.00	
Clean side-by-side refrigerator *Clean* Materials............1.90 Labor 46.30	ea	–	–	$48.20	
Clean over-under refrigerator *Clean* Materials............1.70 Labor...........41.60	ea	–	–	$43.30	
Clean trash compactor *Clean* Materials .... .60 Labor...........14.40	ea	–	–	$15.00	

CLEANING

Unless otherwise noted, all cleaning prices are for items typically smoke stained. For lightly stained items deduct **10%**.

For heavily stained items add **15%**.

RELATED ITEMS

Acoustic Ceilings............15
Appliances....................19

Item Description	Unit			Total
APPLIANCES ▶ **Clean clothes washing machine** *Clean* Materials .... .70 Labor 16.50	ea	–	–	$17.20
continued				
Clean clothes dryer *Clean* Materials .... .50 Labor 12.20	ea	–	–	$12.70
AWNINGS ▶ **Clean aluminum or steel carport or patio** *Clean* Materials .... .02 Labor .... .49	sf	–	–	$.51
Clean aluminum or steel door or window awning *Clean* Materials .... .20 Labor 4.96	lf	–	–	$5.16
BATHROOM ▶ **Clean complete bathroom fixtures and hardware** *Clean* Materials .... 4.10 Labor 103.00	ea	–	–	$107.10
HARDWARE				
Clean complete 1/2 bathroom fixtures and hardware *Clean* Materials .... 2.60 Labor 66.00	ea	–	–	$68.60
Clean bathroom hardware (per piece) *Clean* Materials .... .25 Labor 6.32	ea	–	–	$6.57
Clean medicine cabinet *Clean* Materials .... .58 Labor 14.60	ea	–	–	$15.18
Clean bathroom mirror *Clean* Materials .... .03 Labor .... .67	sf	–	–	$.70
CABINETS ▶ **Clean lower cabinets** *Clean* Materials .... .46 Labor 11.50	lf	–	–	$11.96
Clean upper cabinets *Clean* Materials .... .43 Labor 10.70	lf	–	–	$11.13
Clean lower island cabinets *Clean* Materials .... .47 Labor 11.70	lf	–	–	$12.17
Clean upper island cabinets *Clean* Materials .... .53 Labor 13.20	lf	–	–	$13.73
Clean full-height cabinets *Clean* Materials .... .77 Labor 19.20	lf	–	–	$19.97
countertop ▷ **Clean plastic laminate countertop** *Clean* Materials .... .04 Labor .... .90	sf	–	–	$.94
Clean cultured stone countertop *Clean* Materials .... .04 Labor .... .98	sf	–	–	$1.02
Clean solid-surface countertop *Clean* Materials .... .04 Labor 1.00	sf	–	–	$1.04
Clean granite countertop *Clean* Materials .... .04 Labor 1.11	sf	–	–	$1.15
Clean stainless steel countertop *Clean* Materials .... .04 Labor 1.03	sf	–	–	$1.07
Clean wood countertop (butcher block or solid wood) *Clean* Materials .... .05 Labor 1.16	sf	–	–	$1.21

Item Description	Unit			Total
Clean tile countertop *Clean* Materials .... .06 Labor 1.59	sf	–	–	$1.65
Clean bathroom vanity cabinet *Clean* Materials .... .36 Labor 8.89	lf	–	–	$9.25
Clean column *Clean* Materials .... .16 Labor 4.06	lf	–	–	$4.22 ◄ **COLUMNS**
Clean pilaster *Clean* Materials .... .09 Labor 2.24	lf	–	–	$2.33
Clean capital *Clean* Materials ....1.42 Labor 35.50	ea	–	–	$36.92
Clean ornate capital (Corinthian) *Clean* Materials ....2.53 Labor 63.20	ea	–	–	$65.73
Clean column base *Clean* Materials .... .88 Labor 22.00	ea	–	–	$22.88
Clean pilaster base *Clean* Materials .... .47 Labor 11.80	ea	–	–	$12.27
Clean concrete wall *Clean* Materials .... .02 Labor .... .36	sf	–	–	$.38 ◄ **CONCRETE**
Clean concrete floor *Clean* Materials .... .02 Labor .... .31	sf	–	–	$.33
Clean concrete step (per step) *Clean* Materials .... .23 Labor 5.71	lf	–	–	$5.94
Clean door jamb and casing (per lf) *Clean* Materials .... .02 Labor .... .51	lf	–	–	$.53 ◄ **DOORS**
Clean door jamb and casing (per door) *Clean* Materials .... .36 Labor 8.97	ea	–	–	$9.33
Clean folding door *Clean* Materials .... .27 Labor 6.68	ea	–	–	$6.95
Clean louvered folding door *Clean* Materials .... .45 Labor 11.30	ea	–	–	$11.75
Clean bypassing door *Clean* Materials .... .48 Labor 11.90	ea	–	–	$12.38
Clean louvered bypassing door *Clean* Materials .... .64 Labor 16.00	ea	–	–	$16.64
Clean French door *Clean* Materials .... .84 Labor 21.00	ea	–	–	$21.84
Clean standard flush door *Clean* Materials .... .45 Labor 11.30	ea	–	–	$11.75
Clean pocket door *Clean* Materials .... .46 Labor 11.50	ea	–	–	$11.96

RELATED ITEMS

Bathroom Hardware 41
Cabinets 47
Columns 71
Concrete 83
Doors 101

Item Description			Unit			Total
DOORS ▶ continued	**Clean panel door**		ea	–	–	$12.27
	Clean Materials .... .47	Labor 11.80				
	Clean transom		ea	–	–	$6.15
	Clean Materials .... .24	Labor 5.91				
	Clean batten door		ea	–	–	$12.79
	Clean Materials .... .49	Labor 12.30				
	Clean storm door		ea	–	–	$12.17
	Clean Materials .... .47	Labor 11.70				
	Clean exterior door side lite		ea	–	–	$9.89
	Clean Materials .... .38	Labor 9.51				
	Clean Dutch door		ea	–	–	$12.38
	Clean Materials .... .48	Labor 11.90				
	Clean fan lite		ea	–	–	$9.06
	Clean Materials .... .35	Labor 8.71				
	Clean cafe doors		ea	–	–	$9.41
	Clean Materials .... .36	Labor 9.05				
sliding patio door ▷	**Clean 6' wide sliding patio door**		ea	–	–	$28.30
	Clean Materials 1.10	Labor 27.20				
	Clean 8' wide sliding patio door		ea	–	–	$32.00
	Clean Materials 1.20	Labor 30.80				
	Clean 12' wide sliding patio door		ea	–	–	$36.90
	Clean Materials 1.40	Labor 35.50				
garage door ▷	**Clean 8' wide garage door**		ea	–	–	$41.70
	Clean Materials 1.60	Labor 40.10				
	Clean 9' wide garage door		ea	–	–	$44.10
	Clean Materials 1.70	Labor 42.40				
	Clean 10' wide garage door		ea	–	–	$46.50
	Clean Materials 1.80	Labor 44.70				
	Clean 12' wide garage door		ea	–	–	$48.90
	Clean Materials 1.90	Labor 47.00				
	Clean 14' wide garage door		ea	–	–	$51.60
	Clean Materials 2.00	Labor 49.60				
	Clean 16' wide garage door		ea	–	–	$54.50
	Clean Materials 2.10	Labor 52.40				
	Clean 18' wide garage door		ea	–	–	$57.70
	Clean Materials 2.20	Labor 55.50				
	Clean garage door opener		ea	–	–	$25.80
	Clean Materials 1.00	Labor 24.80				
DRYWALL OR ▶ PLASTER	**Clean wall**		sf	–	–	$.35
	Clean Materials .... .02	Labor .... .33				

Item Description	Unit			Total	
Clean ceiling *Clean* Materials .... .01 Labor .... .36	sf	—	—	$.37	
Clean ceiling acoustic texture *Clean* Materials .... .02 Labor .... .44	sf	—	—	$.46	
Clean outlet or switch *Clean* Materials .... .09 Labor 2.16	ea	—	—	$2.25	◄ **ELECTRICAL**
Clean breaker panel *Clean* Materials .... .71 Labor 17.80	ea	—	—	$18.51	
Clean circuit breaker *Clean* Materials .... .23 Labor 5.83	ea	—	—	$6.06	
Clean door bell or chime button *Clean* Materials .... .03 Labor .... .87	ea	—	—	$.90	
Clean bathroom exhaust fan *Clean* Materials .... .30 Labor 7.45	ea	—	—	$7.75	
Clean bathroom exhaust fan with heat lamp *Clean* Materials .... .33 Labor 8.25	ea	—	—	$8.58	
Clean kitchen exhaust fan *Clean* Materials .... .31 Labor 7.68	ea	—	—	$7.99	
Clean whole-house exhaust fan *Clean* Materials .... .36 Labor 9.05	ea	—	—	$9.41	
Clean intercom system station *Clean* Materials .... .20 Labor 4.96	ea	—	—	$5.16	
Clean detector *Clean* Materials .... .19 Labor 4.75	ea	—	—	$4.94	
Clean thermostat *Clean* Materials .... .22 Labor 5.42	ea	—	—	$5.64	
Clean light fixture *Clean* Materials .... .46 Labor 11.50	ea	—	—	$11.96	◁ light fixtures
Clean bathroom light bar (per light) *Clean* Materials .... .16 Labor 4.11	ea	—	—	$4.27	
Clean chandelier, typical detail *Clean* Materials .... 1.30 Labor 32.90	ea	—	—	$34.20	
Clean chandelier, ornate detail *Clean* Materials .... 2.05 Labor 51.40	ea	—	—	$53.45	
Clean chandelier, very ornate detail *Clean* Materials .... 3.05 Labor 76.80	ea	—	—	$79.85	
Clean crystal chandelier, typical detail *Clean* Materials .... 4.60 Labor 115.00	ea	—	—	$119.60	
Clean crystal chandelier, ornate detail *Clean* Materials .... 5.95 Labor 149.00	ea	—	—	$154.95	

RELATED ITEMS

Drywall 133
Plaster & Stucco 353
Electrical 139
light fixtures 153

Item Description	Unit			Total
ELECTRICAL ▶ (light fixtures) *continued* **Clean crystal chandelier, very ornate detail** *Clean* Materials..........8.05 Labor........201.00	ea	–	–	$209.05
Clean fluorescent light fixture *Clean* Materials............55 Labor..........13.30	ea	–	–	$13.85
Clean ceiling fan *Clean* Materials............60 Labor..........14.90	ea	–	–	$15.50
Clean ceiling fan with light *Clean* Materials............70 Labor..........17.60	ea	–	–	$18.30
Clean recessed spot light fixture *Clean* Materials............40 Labor..........10.07	ea	–	–	$10.47
Clean strip light (per spot) *Clean* Materials............20 Labor............5.01	ea	–	–	$5.21
Clean exterior flood light fixture (per spot) *Clean* Materials............21 Labor............5.32	ea	–	–	$5.53
Clean exterior light fixture *Clean* Materials............50 Labor..........12.50	ea	–	–	$13.00
Clean exterior post light fixture *Clean* Materials............60 Labor..........14.90	ea	–	–	$15.50
FENCES ▶ **Clean 4' high wood fence** *Clean* Materials............07 Labor............1.64	lf	–	–	$1.71
Clean 6' high wood fence *Clean* Materials............08 Labor............2.00	lf	–	–	$2.08
Clean 8' high wood fence *Clean* Materials............10 Labor............2.57	lf	–	–	$2.67
Clean 4' high chain-link fence *Clean* Materials............05 Labor............1.13	lf	–	–	$1.18
Clean 6' high chain-link fence *Clean* Materials............05 Labor............1.29	lf	–	–	$1.34
Clean 8' high chain-link fence *Clean* Materials............06 Labor............1.49	lf	–	–	$1.55
Clean 4' high vinyl fence *Clean* Materials............06 Labor............1.44	lf	–	–	$1.50
Clean 6' high vinyl fence *Clean* Materials............07 Labor............1.72	lf	–	–	$1.79
Clean 8' high vinyl fence *Clean* Materials............08 Labor............2.11	lf	–	–	$2.19
Clean 60" high ornamental iron fence *Clean* Materials............08 Labor............2.00	lf	–	–	$2.08
Clean 72" high ornamental iron fence *Clean* Materials............07 Labor............1.77	lf	–	–	$1.84

Item Description	Unit			Total	
Clean molding *Clean* Materials .... .02 Labor .... .39	lf	–	–	$.41	◄ **FINISH CARPENTRY**
Clean interior wood architrave *Clean* Materials .... .04 Labor .... .95	lf	–	–	$.99	
Clean exterior wood architrave *Clean* Materials .... .04 Labor 1.08	lf	–	–	$1.12	
Clean exterior door surround *Clean* Materials .... .08 Labor 2.11	lf	–	–	$2.19	
Clean exterior window surround *Clean* Materials .... .07 Labor 1.85	lf	–	–	$1.92	
Clean closet shelf and brackets *Clean* Materials .... .04 Labor .... .98	lf	–	–	$1.02	
Clean closet organizer *Clean* Materials .... .03 Labor .... .77	sf	–	–	$.80	
Clean linen closet shelves *Clean* Materials .... .04 Labor .... .93	sf	–	–	$.97	
Clean closet rod *Clean* Materials .... .02 Labor .... .51	lf	–	–	$.53	
Clean bookcase *Clean* Materials .... .03 Labor .... .75	sf	–	–	$.78	
Clean fireplace mantel *Clean* Materials .... 1.00 Labor 25.10	ea	–	–	$26.10	
Clean ceiling with exposed beams *Clean* Materials .... .03 Labor .... .72	sf	–	–	$.75	
Clean coffered ceiling *Clean* Materials .... .04 Labor .... .95	sf	–	–	$.99	
Clean wall niche *Clean* Materials .... .23 Labor 5.83	ea	–	–	$6.06	
Clean gingerbread trim *Clean* Materials .... .03 Labor .... .64	lf	–	–	$.67	
Clean gingerbread bracket *Clean* Materials .... .20 Labor 4.96	ea	–	–	$5.16	
Clean gingerbread corbel *Clean* Materials .... .22 Labor 5.50	ea	–	–	$5.72	
Clean gingerbread spandrel *Clean* Materials .... .20 Labor 4.96	lf	–	–	$5.16	
Clean gingerbread cornice *Clean* Materials .... .18 Labor 4.39	lf	–	–	$4.57	
Clean gingerbread gable ornament *Clean* Materials .... .45 Labor 11.30	ea	–	–	$11.75	

RELATED ITEMS

Fences........................187
Finish Carpentry...........199

Item Description		Unit			Total
FINISH CARPENTRY ▶ *continued*	**Clean gingerbread finial** *Clean* Materials .... .37 Labor 9.23	ea	–	–	$9.60
	Clean porch post *Clean* Materials .... .04 Labor 1.08	lf	–	–	$1.12
FIREPLACES ▶	**Clean fireplace screen** *Clean* Materials ....1.15 Labor 28.80	ea	–	–	$29.95
	Clean fireplace door *Clean* Materials .... 1.09 Labor 27.20	ea	–	–	$28.29
	Clean marble fireplace face *Clean* Materials .... .05 Labor 1.21	sf	–	–	$1.26
	Clean brick fireplace face *Clean* Materials .... .06 Labor 1.39	sf	–	–	$1.45
	Clean stone fireplace face *Clean* Materials .... .06 Labor 1.49	sf	–	–	$1.55
	Clean tile fireplace face *Clean* Materials .... .06 Labor 1.44	sf	–	–	$1.50
	Clean marble fireplace hearth *Clean* Materials .... .10 Labor 2.44	lf	–	–	$2.54
	Clean brick fireplace hearth *Clean* Materials .... .11 Labor 2.72	lf	–	–	$2.83
	Clean stone fireplace hearth *Clean* Materials .... .12 Labor 2.88	lf	–	–	$3.00
	Clean tile fireplace hearth *Clean* Materials .... .11 Labor 2.72	lf	–	–	$2.83
FLOORING ▶	**Clean carpet** *Clean* Materials .... .02 Labor .... .59	sf	–	–	$.61
	Clean wool carpet *Clean* Materials .... .03 Labor .... .85	sf	–	–	$.88
	Clean carpet cove *Clean* Materials .... .02 Labor .... .54	lf	–	–	$.56
	Add per step for carpet cleaning *Clean* Materials .... .16 Labor 3.98	ea	–	–	$4.14
	Clean stone floor *Clean* Materials .... .03 Labor .... .64	sf	–	–	$.67
	Clean tile floor *Clean* Materials .... .03 Labor .... .87	sf	–	–	$.90
	Clean tile base *Clean* Materials .... .02 Labor .... .41	lf	–	–	$.43
	Clean and wax vinyl floor *Clean* Materials .... .03 Labor .... .72	sf	–	–	$.75

Item Description	Unit			Total
Clean vinyl cove	lf	–	–	$.43
Clean Materials .... .02 Labor............. .41				
Clean and wax wood floor	sf	–	–	$.94
Clean Materials .... .04 Labor............. .90				
Clean and deodorize ducts (per lf of duct)	lf	–	–	$4.17 ◀ HVAC
Clean Materials .... .16 Labor 4.01				
Clean furnace	ea	–	–	$78.85
Clean Materials...........3.05 Labor............75.80				
Clean heat pump	ea	–	–	$34.20
Clean Materials...........1.30 Labor 32.90				
Clean humidifier	ea	–	–	$25.25
Clean Materials .... .95 Labor............24.30				
Clean through-wall AC unit	ea	–	–	$29.95
Clean Materials...........1.15 Labor 28.80				
Clean evaporative cooler	ea	–	–	$36.90
Clean Materials...........1.40 Labor...........35.50				
Clean evaporative cooler grille	ea	–	–	$6.69
Clean Materials .... .26 Labor 6.43				
Clean heat register	ea	–	–	$6.42
Clean Materials .... .25 Labor 6.17				
Clean cold-air return cover	ea	–	–	$6.50
Clean Materials .... .25 Labor 6.25				
Clean brick wall	sf	–	–	$.67 ◀ MASONRY
Clean Materials .... .03 Labor............. .64				
Clean block wall	sf	–	–	$.61
Clean Materials .... .02 Labor............. .59				
Clean slump block wall	sf	–	–	$.67
Clean Materials .... .03 Labor............. .64				
Clean fluted block wall	sf	–	–	$.78
Clean Materials .... .03 Labor............. .75				
Clean glazed block wall	sf	–	–	$.75
Clean Materials .... .03 Labor............. .72				
Clean split-face block wall	sf	–	–	$.85
Clean Materials .... .03 Labor............. .82				
Clean split-rib block wall	sf	–	–	$.80
Clean Materials .... .03 Labor............. .77				
Clean stone wall	sf	–	–	$.88
Clean Materials .... .03 Labor............. .85				
Clean glazed structural tile wall	sf	–	–	$.64
Clean Materials .... .02 Labor............. .62				

RELATED ITEMS
Fireplaces....................241
Flooring....................257
HVAC 275
Masonry...................287
clean masonry...........321

Item Description	Unit			Total
MASONRY ▶ *continued* **Clean glass block wall** *Clean* Materials .... .02 Labor .... .62	sf	–	–	$.64
Clean pavers *Clean* Materials .... .03 Labor .... .64	sf	–	–	$.67
Clean stone veneer panels *Clean* Materials .... .03 Labor .... .64	sf	–	–	$.67
Clean cultured stone veneer panels *Clean* Materials .... .03 Labor .... .64	sf	–	–	$.67
Clean stone architrave *Clean* Materials .... .05 Labor 1.16	lf	–	–	$1.21
Clean stone trim stones *Clean* Materials .... .04 Labor 1.03	lf	–	–	$1.07
PANELING ▶ **Clean wood paneling** *Clean* Materials .... .02 Labor .... .44	sf	–	–	$.46
Clean wood paneling with moldings or onlays *Clean* Materials .... .02 Labor .... .54	sf	–	–	$.56
Clean panel wall *Clean* Materials .... .04 Labor .... .90	sf	–	–	$.94
Clean pegboard *Clean* Materials .... .02 Labor .... .46	sf	–	–	$.48
Clean rough-sawn wood paneling *Clean* Materials .... .02 Labor .... .59	sf	–	–	$.61
Clean tongue-and-groove paneling *Clean* Materials .... .02 Labor .... .51	sf	–	–	$.53
STUCCO ▶ **Clean stucco** *Clean* Materials .... .02 Labor .... .62	sf	–	–	$.64
Clean stucco architrave *Clean* Materials .... .05 Labor 1.18	lf	–	–	$1.23
PLASTER ▶ See **Drywall** heading in this chapter for prices to clean interior plaster walls. **Clean plaster molding** *Clean* Materials .... .04 Labor .... .90	lf	–	–	$.94
Clean plaster architrave *Clean* Materials .... .04 Labor 1.08	lf	–	–	$1.12
Clean ceiling medallion *Clean* Materials .... .57 Labor 14.30	ea	–	–	$14.87
Clean ceiling rose *Clean* Materials .... .97 Labor 24.30	ea	–	–	$25.27
PLUMBING ▶ **Clean sink faucet** *Clean* Materials .... .49 Labor 12.20	ea	–	–	$12.69
Clean shower faucet and head *Clean* Materials .... .60 Labor 14.90	ea	–	–	$15.50

Item Description	Unit			Total
Clean tub faucet	ea	–	–	**$13.31**
Clean Materials .... .51 Labor 12.80				
Clean tub faucet and shower head	ea	–	–	**$16.54**
Clean Materials .... .64 Labor 15.90				
Clean wet bar sink	ea	–	–	**$10.45**
Clean Materials .... .40 Labor 10.05				
Clean bathroom sink	ea	–	–	**$11.13**
Clean Materials .... .43 Labor 10.70				
Clean kitchen sink, per bowl	ea	–	–	**$11.44**
Clean Materials .... .44 Labor 11.00				
Clean laundry sink, per bowl	ea	–	–	**$11.96**
Clean Materials .... .46 Labor 11.50				
Clean visible sink supply lines	ea	–	–	**$6.86**
Clean Materials .... .26 Labor 6.60				
Clean toilet	ea	–	–	**$17.78**
Clean Materials .... .68 Labor 17.10				
Clean bidet	ea	–	–	**$18.51**
Clean Materials .... .71 Labor 17.80				
Clean toilet seat	ea	–	–	**$4.82**
Clean Materials .... .19 Labor 4.63				
Clean porcelain enamel finish tub	ea	–	–	**$26.73**
Clean Materials .... 1.03 Labor 25.70				
Clean porcelain enamel finish tub with whirlpool jets	ea	–	–	**$34.20**
Clean Materials...........1.30 Labor 32.90				
Clean fiberglass finish tub	ea	–	–	**$32.05**
Clean Materials...........1.25 Labor 30.80				
Clean fiberglass finish tub with whirlpool jets	ea	–	–	**$43.60**
Clean Materials...........1.70 Labor...........41.90				
Clean tub and shower combination	ea	–	–	**$43.60**
Clean Materials...........1.70 Labor...........41.90				
Clean fiberglass or metal shower stall	ea	–	–	**$31.30**
Clean Materials...........1.20 Labor 30.10				
Clean glass shower stall	ea	–	–	**$39.30**
Clean Materials...........1.50 Labor...........37.80				
Clean tub surround	ea	–	–	**$14.55**
Clean Materials .... .55 Labor...........14.00				
Clean shower door	ea	–	–	**$23.50**
Clean Materials .... .90 Labor 22.60				
Clean sliding glass tub door	ea	–	–	**$31.50**
Clean Materials...........1.20 Labor 30.30				

RELATED ITEMS

Masonry 287
 clean masonry 321
Paneling 347
Plaster & Stucco 353
Plumbing 361

Item Description	Unit			Total
PLUMBING ▶ *continued* **Clean folding plastic tub door**	ea	–	–	$32.05
Clean Materials............1.25 Labor..........30.80				
Clean water heater	ea	–	–	$25.25
Clean Materials .... .95 Labor..........24.30				
Clean claw-foot tub faucet	ea	–	–	$13.30
Clean Materials .... .50 Labor..........12.80				
Clean claw-foot tub faucet and shower conversion	ea	–	–	$18.20
Clean Materials .... .70 Labor..........17.50				
Clean freestanding water feeds	ea	–	–	$7.60
Clean Materials .... .30 Labor 7.30				
Clean pedestal sink	ea	–	–	$13.75
Clean Materials .... .55 Labor..........13.20				
Clean pill-box toilet	ea	–	–	$21.85
Clean Materials .... .85 Labor..........21.00				
Clean low-tank toilet	ea	–	–	$28.30
Clean Materials .... 1.10 Labor..........27.20				
Clean high-tank toilet	ea	–	–	$36.90
Clean Materials............1.40 Labor..........35.50				
Clean antique tub	ea	–	–	$31.30
Clean Materials............1.20 Labor 30.10				
SIDING ▶ Clean fiberglass corrugated siding	sf	–	–	$.38
Clean Materials .... .02 Labor............ .36				
Clean metal or vinyl siding	sf	–	–	$.41
Clean Materials .... .02 Labor............ .39				
Clean wood lap siding	sf	–	–	$.41
Clean Materials .... .02 Labor............ .39				
Clean vertical wood siding (board on board, etc.)	sf	–	–	$.41
Clean Materials .... .02 Labor............ .39				
Clean cement fiber shingle siding	sf	–	–	$.46
Clean Materials .... .02 Labor............ .44				
Clean shake or wood shingle siding	sf	–	–	$.51
Clean Materials .... .02 Labor............ .49				
Clean hardboard or plywood siding	sf	–	–	$.41
Clean Materials .... .02 Labor............ .39				
Clean tongue-and-groove siding	sf	–	–	$.43
Clean Materials .... .02 Labor............ .41				
Clean metal or vinyl fascia	sf	–	–	$.43
Clean Materials .... .02 Labor............ .41				
Clean wood fascia	sf	–	–	$.43
Clean Materials .... .02 Labor............ .41				

Item Description	Unit			Total	
Clean metal or vinyl soffit	sf	–	–	$.37	
Clean Materials .... .01 Labor .... .36					
Clean wood soffit	sf	–	–	$.41	
Clean Materials .... .02 Labor .... .39					
Clean rough-sawn wood soffit	sf	–	–	$.48	
Clean Materials .... .02 Labor .... .46					
Clean shutter	ea	–	–	$9.60	
Clean Materials .... .37 Labor 9.23					
Clean wood stair tread	ea	–	–	$4.36	◄ STAIRS
Clean Materials .... .17 Labor 4.19					
Clean spiral stair balustrade	lf	–	–	$3.02	
Clean Materials .... .12 Labor 2.90					
Clean stair balustrade	lf	–	–	$3.05	
Clean Materials .... .12 Labor 2.93					
Clean disappearing attic stair	ea	–	–	$64.15	
Clean Materials............2.45 Labor 61.70					
Clean stair bracket	ea	–	–	$8.29	
Clean Materials .... .32 Labor 7.97					
Clean suspended ceiling grid	sf	–	–	$.28	◄ SUSPENDED CEILING
Clean Materials .... .02 Labor .... .26					
Clean tile shower	ea	–	–	$36.90	◄ TILE
Clean Materials............1.40 Labor............35.50					
Clean tile tub surround	ea	–	–	$48.15	
Clean Materials............1.85 Labor 46.30					
Clean vinyl wallpaper	sf	–	–	$.41	◄ WALLPAPER
Clean Materials .... .02 Labor .... .39					
Clean paper wallpaper	sf	–	–	$.46	
Clean Materials .... .02 Labor .... .44					
Clean grass or rice cloth wallpaper	sf	–	–	$.67	
Clean Materials .... .03 Labor .... .64					
Clean window up to 8 sf	ea	–	–	$10.92	◄ WINDOWS
Clean Materials .... .42 Labor 10.50					
Clean window 9 to 14 sf	ea	–	–	$12.69	
Clean Materials .... .49 Labor 12.20					
Clean window 15 to 20 sf	ea	–	–	$15.50	
Clean Materials .... .60 Labor 14.90					
Clean window 21 to 30 sf	ea	–	–	$22.88	
Clean Materials .... .88 Labor 22.00					
Clean window, per sf	sf	–	–	$.80	
Clean Materials .... .03 Labor .... .77					

◄ TILE

See **Cabinet** heading in this chapter for prices to clean tile countertops and **Flooring** for prices to clean tile floors and base.

RELATED ITEMS

Bathroom Hardware 41
mirrors 45
Siding 455
Stairs 465
Wall Coverings 495
Windows 501

	Item Description	Unit			Total
WINDOWS *continued*	**Clean skylight up to 8 sf** *Clean* Materials .... .44 Labor 11.00	ea	–	–	$11.44
	Clean skylight 9 to 14 sf *Clean* Materials .... .51 Labor 12.80	ea	–	–	$13.31
	Clean skylight 15 to 20 sf *Clean* Materials .... .64 Labor 15.90	ea	–	–	$16.54
	Clean skylight 21 to 30 sf *Clean* Materials .... .92 Labor 23.10	ea	–	–	$24.02
	Clean skylight per sf *Clean* Materials .... .03 Labor .... .82	sf	–	–	$.85
	Add 15% to clean windows with multiple, small panes				
MIRROR ▶ *Also see* **Bathroom** **Hardware** *heading.*	**Clean wall mirror** *Clean* Materials .... .03 Labor .... .69	sf	–	–	$.72
FINAL CLEAN ▶	**Final construction clean-up to broom clean** *Clean* Materials .... .02 Labor .... .31	sf	–	–	$.33

✐ NOTES: _____

_____ end

TIME & MATERIAL CHARTS *(selected items)*

Cleaning Materials

See **Cleaning** material prices with the line items and other information in the **QuickFinder** column.

Cleaning Labor

LABORER	BASE WAGE	PAID LEAVE	TRUE WAGE	FICA	FUTA	WORKER'S COMP.	UNEMPLOY. INSUR.	HEALTH INSUR.	RETIRE (401K)	LIABILITY INSUR.	COST PER HOUR
Cleaning laborer	**$14.20**	1.11	**$15.31**	1.17	.121	2.09	1.33	2.92	.46	2.30	**$25.70**

Paid Leave is calculated based on two weeks paid vacation, one week sick leave, and seven paid holidays. Employer's matching portion of **FICA** is 7.65 percent. **FUTA** (Federal Unemployment) is .8 percent. **Worker's compensation** for the cleaning trade was calculated using a national average of 13.62 percent. **Unemployment insurance** was calculated using a national average of 8.7 percent. **Health insurance** was calculated based on a projected national average for 2005 of $580 per employee (and family when applicable) per month. Employer pays 80 percent for a per month cost of $464 per employee. **Retirement** is based on a 401(k) retirement program with employer matching of 50 percent. Employee contributions to the 401(k) plan are an average of 6 percent of the true wage. **Liability insurance** is based on a national average of 14.0 percent.

Cleaning Labor Productivity

WORK DESCRIPTION	LABORER	COST PER HOUR	PRODUCTIVITY	UNIT PRICE
Clean appliances				
cook top	cleaning laborer	$25.70	.876	$22.50 *ea*
range	cleaning laborer	$25.70	1.54	$39.60 *ea*
wall oven	cleaning laborer	$25.70	1.27	$32.60 *ea*
				. . . More ➤

Cleaning Labor Productivity *continued*

WORK DESCRIPTION	LABORER	COST PER HOUR	PRODUCTIVITY	UNIT PRICE
Clean appliances *continued*				
range hood	cleaning laborer	$25.70	.428	$11.00 ea
dishwasher	cleaning laborer	$25.70	1.00	$25.70 ea
microwave	cleaning laborer	$25.70	.486	$12.50 ea
side-by-side refrigerator	cleaning laborer	$25.70	1.80	$46.30 ea
over-under refrigerator	cleaning laborer	$25.70	1.62	$41.60 ea
trash compactor	cleaning laborer	$25.70	.561	$14.40 ea
Clean awnings				
aluminum or steel carport or patio	cleaning laborer	$25.70	.019	$.49 sf
aluminum or steel door or window awning	cleaning laborer	$25.70	.193	$4.96 lf
Clean bathroom hardware				
bathroom hardware (per piece)	cleaning laborer	$25.70	.246	$6.32 ea
medicine cabinet	cleaning laborer	$25.70	.570	$14.60 ea
Clean cabinets				
lower cabinets	cleaning laborer	$25.70	.446	$11.50 lf
upper cabinets	cleaning laborer	$25.70	.418	$10.70 lf
full-height cabinets	cleaning laborer	$25.70	.749	$19.20 lf
plastic laminate countertop	cleaning laborer	$25.70	.035	$.90 sf
tile countertop	cleaning laborer	$25.70	.062	$1.59 sf
Clean concrete				
wall	cleaning laborer	$25.70	.014	$.36 sf
floor	cleaning laborer	$25.70	.012	$.31 sf
Clean door				
folding door (per section)	cleaning laborer	$25.70	.260	$6.68 ea
bypassing door	cleaning laborer	$25.70	.462	$11.90 ea
door	cleaning laborer	$25.70	.438	$11.30 ea
storm door	cleaning laborer	$25.70	.454	$11.70 ea
Clean drywall or plaster				
wall	cleaning laborer	$25.70	.013	$.33 sf
ceiling	cleaning laborer	$25.70	.014	$.36 sf
ceiling acoustic texture	cleaning laborer	$25.70	.017	$.44 sf
Clean electrical				
light fixture	cleaning laborer	$25.70	.449	$11.50 ea
bathroom light bar (per light)	cleaning laborer	$25.70	.160	$4.11 ea
chandelier, typical detail	cleaning laborer	$25.70	1.28	$32.90 ea
fluorescent light fixture	cleaning laborer	$25.70	.519	$13.30 ea
ceiling fan	cleaning laborer	$25.70	.580	$14.90 ea
ceiling fan with light	cleaning laborer	$25.70	.686	$17.60 ea
Clean fence				
4' high wood	cleaning laborer	$25.70	.064	$1.64 lf
4' high chain-link	cleaning laborer	$25.70	.044	$1.13 lf
4' high vinyl	cleaning laborer	$25.70	.056	$1.44 lf
60" high ornamental iron	cleaning laborer	$25.70	.078	$2.00 lf
Clean finish carpentry				
molding	cleaning laborer	$25.70	.015	$.39 lf
Clean fireplace				
screen	cleaning laborer	$25.70	1.12	$28.80 ea
door	cleaning laborer	$25.70	1.06	$27.20 ea
Clean flooring				
carpet	cleaning laborer	$25.70	.023	$.59 sf
stone floor	cleaning laborer	$25.70	.025	$.64 sf
tile floor	cleaning laborer	$25.70	.034	$.87 sf
vinyl floor and wax	cleaning laborer	$25.70	.028	$.72 sf
wood floor and wax	cleaning laborer	$25.70	.035	$.90 sf
Clean HVAC				
furnace	cleaning laborer	$25.70	2.95	$75.80 ea
through-wall AC unit	cleaning laborer	$25.70	1.12	$28.80 ea
evaporative cooler	cleaning laborer	$25.70	1.38	$35.50 ea

. . . More ➤

Cleaning Labor Productivity *continued*

WORK DESCRIPTION	LABORER	COST PER HOUR	PRODUCTIVITY	UNIT PRICE
Clean masonry				
brick wall	cleaning laborer	$25.70	.025	$.64 sf
block wall	cleaning laborer	$25.70	.023	$.59 sf
stone wall	cleaning laborer	$25.70	.033	$.85 sf
glass block wall	cleaning laborer	$25.70	.024	$.62 sf
stone veneer panels	cleaning laborer	$25.70	.025	$.64 sf
Clean paneling				
wood paneling	cleaning laborer	$25.70	.017	$.44 sf
wood paneling with moldings or onlays	cleaning laborer	$25.70	.021	$.54 sf
panel wall	cleaning laborer	$25.70	.035	$.90 sf
rough-sawn wood paneling	cleaning laborer	$25.70	.023	$.59 sf
tongue-and-groove paneling	cleaning laborer	$25.70	.020	$.51 sf
Clean plaster *(also see clean drywall)*				
stucco	cleaning laborer	$25.70	.024	$.62 sf
Clean plumbing				
sink faucet	cleaning laborer	$25.70	.473	$12.20 ea
tub faucet	cleaning laborer	$25.70	.499	$12.80 ea
tub faucet and shower head	cleaning laborer	$25.70	.620	$15.90 ea
bathroom sink	cleaning laborer	$25.70	.418	$10.70 ea
kitchen sink, per bowl	cleaning laborer	$25.70	.428	$11.00 ea
laundry sink, per bowl	cleaning laborer	$25.70	.449	$11.50 ea
toilet	cleaning laborer	$25.70	.665	$17.10 ea
bidet	cleaning laborer	$25.70	.691	$17.80 ea
porcelain enamel finish tub	cleaning laborer	$25.70	1.00	$25.70 ea
fiberglass finish tub	cleaning laborer	$25.70	1.20	$30.80 ea
tub and shower combination	cleaning laborer	$25.70	1.63	$41.90 ea
fiberglass or metal shower stall	cleaning laborer	$25.70	1.17	$30.10 ea
glass shower stall	cleaning laborer	$25.70	1.47	$37.80 ea
tub surround	cleaning laborer	$25.70	.544	$14.00 ea
shower door	cleaning laborer	$25.70	.881	$22.60 ea
sliding glass tub door	cleaning laborer	$25.70	1.18	$30.30 ea
pedestal sink	cleaning laborer	$25.70	.513	$13.20 ea
pill-box toilet	cleaning laborer	$25.70	.817	$21.00 ea
Clean siding				
fiberglass corrugated	cleaning laborer	$25.70	.014	$.36 sf
metal or vinyl siding	cleaning laborer	$25.70	.015	$.39 sf
wood lap siding	cleaning laborer	$25.70	.015	$.39 sf
vertical wood siding (board on board, etc.)	cleaning laborer	$25.70	.015	$.39 sf
cement fiber shingle siding	cleaning laborer	$25.70	.017	$.44 sf
shake or wood shingle siding	cleaning laborer	$25.70	.019	$.49 sf
plywood siding	cleaning laborer	$25.70	.015	$.39 sf
tongue-and-groove siding	cleaning laborer	$25.70	.016	$.41 sf
Clean stairs				
wood stair tread	cleaning laborer	$25.70	.163	$4.19 ea
stair balustrade	cleaning laborer	$25.70	.114	$2.93 lf
disappearing attic stair	cleaning laborer	$25.70	2.40	$61.70 ea
Clean tile				
tile shower	cleaning laborer	$25.70	1.38	$35.50 ea
tile tub surround	cleaning laborer	$25.70	1.80	$46.30 ea
Clean wallpaper				
vinyl wallpaper	cleaning laborer	$25.70	.015	$.39 sf
paper wallpaper	cleaning laborer	$25.70	.017	$.44 sf
grass or rice cloth wallpaper	cleaning laborer	$25.70	.025	$.64 sf
Clean window				
window up to 8 sf	cleaning laborer	$25.70	.408	$10.50 ea
window 21 to 30 sf	cleaning laborer	$25.70	.856	$22.00 ea
window, per sf	cleaning laborer	$25.70	.030	$.77 ea
skylight up to 8 sf	cleaning laborer	$25.70	.428	$11.00 ea
skylight 21 to 30 sf	cleaning laborer	$25.70	.898	$23.10 ea
skylight per sf	cleaning laborer	$25.70	.032	$.82 ea

7 .... *Columns*

Item Description	Unit	Remove	Replace	Total	
Minimum charge for column or pilaster work *Replace* Materials......30.00 Labor...........87.00	If	—	$117.00	$117.00	◄ **MINIMUM**
12" round column made from composite materials *Replace* Materials ......42.00 Labor...........14.50 *Remove*....................... Labor 6.13	If	$6.13	$56.50	$62.63	◄ **12" COLUMN** *Round columns with no taper. See page 72 to add for taper, fluting, and architecturally correct taper.*
12" round pine column *Replace* Materials......44.10 Labor...........14.50 *Remove*....................... Labor 6.13	If	$6.13	$58.60	$64.73	
12" round redwood column *Replace* Materials ......52.40 Labor...........14.50 *Remove*....................... Labor 6.13	If	$6.13	$66.90	$73.03	
12" round oak column *Replace* Materials......58.10 Labor...........14.50 *Remove*....................... Labor 6.13	If	$6.13	$72.60	$78.73	
12" round stone column *Replace* Materials ......78.00 Labor...........14.50 *Remove*....................... Labor 6.13	If	$6.13	$92.50	$98.63	
12" round synthetic stone column *Replace* Materials ......72.90 Labor...........14.50 *Remove*....................... Labor 6.13	If	$6.13	$87.40	$93.53	
12" round aluminum column *Replace* Materials......44.50 Labor...........14.50 *Remove*....................... Labor 6.13	If	$6.13	$59.00	$65.13	
12" round interior plaster column *Replace* Materials ......42.40 Labor...........14.50 *Remove*....................... Labor 6.13	If	$6.13	$56.90	$63.03	
12" round exterior stucco column *Replace* Materials ......41.10 Labor...........14.50 *Remove*....................... Labor 6.13	If	$6.13	$55.60	$61.73	
12" round pilaster made from composite materials *Replace* Materials ......26.80 Labor...........12.70 *Remove*....................... Labor 3.87	If	$3.87	$39.50	$43.37	◄ **12" PILASTER** *Half-round pilaster with no taper. See page 72 to add for taper, fluting, and architecturally correct taper.*
12" round pine pilaster *Replace* Materials ......28.30 Labor...........12.70 *Remove*....................... Labor 3.87	If	$3.87	$41.00	$44.87	
12" round redwood pilaster *Replace* Materials ......33.50 Labor...........12.70 *Remove*....................... Labor 3.87	If	$3.87	$46.20	$50.07	
12" round oak pilaster *Replace* Materials ......37.10 Labor...........12.70 *Remove*....................... Labor 3.87	If	$3.87	$49.80	$53.67	

COLUMN MATERIALS

Composite materials: A combination of marble (or similar material) polymers, and fiberglass or columns made from high-density polyurethane.

Pine: Made from laminated staves of Douglas fir or Ponderosa pine.

Redwood: Made from laminated staves of redwood.

Oak: Made from laminated staves of red oak.

Stone: Crushed and reconstructed limestone reinforced with glass fibers.

Synthetic stone: Lightweight simulated stone which are either cement or gypsum-based fiberglass.

Aluminum: Cast aluminum.

continued on next page

RELATED ITEMS

Cleaning.....................57
Finish Carpentry...........199
Painting......................333

Item Description	Unit	Remove	Replace	Total

12" PILASTER ▶
continued

12" round stone pilaster — If — $3.87 — $62.60 — $66.47
Replace Materials ......49.90   Labor 12.70
Remove.........................   Labor 3.87

COLUMN MATERIALS

continued from prior page

Plaster: Made from fibrous plaster and gypsum products reinforced with fiberglass or jute, or steel or sisal for use on interior of structure.

Stucco: Made from fibrous plaster products reinforced with fiberglass or jute or steel or sisal for use on exterior of structure.

12" round synthetic stone pilaster — If — $3.87 — $59.30 — $63.17
Replace Materials ......46.60   Labor 12.70
Remove.........................   Labor 3.87

12" round aluminum pilaster — If — $3.87 — $41.20 — $45.07
Replace Materials ......28.50   Labor 12.70
Remove.........................   Labor 3.87

12" round interior plaster pilaster — If — $3.87 — $39.70 — $43.57
Replace Materials ......27.00   Labor 12.70
Remove.........................   Labor 3.87

12" round exterior stucco pilaster — If — $3.87 — $39.00 — $42.87
Replace Materials ......26.30   Labor 12.70
Remove.........................   Labor 3.87

ADDITIONAL ▶ COLUMN COSTS

Add 18% for round fluted column or pilaster

Add 13% for tapered column or pilaster
▶ Consistent taper from bottom to top.

Add 65% for architecturally correct tapered column or pilaster
▶ Columns that taper according to the classic Greek or Roman styles.

12" SQUARE ▶ COLUMN

12" square column made from composite materials — If — $6.13 — $68.80 — $74.93
Replace Materials ......55.40   Labor 13.40
Remove.........................   Labor 6.13

12" square pine column — If — $6.13 — $71.70 — $77.83
Replace Materials ......58.30   Labor 13.40
Remove.........................   Labor 6.13

12" square redwood column — If — $6.13 — $82.50 — $88.63
Replace Materials ......69.10   Labor 13.40
Remove.........................   Labor 6.13

12" square oak column — If — $6.13 — $90.20 — $96.33
Replace Materials ......76.80   Labor 13.40
Remove.........................   Labor 6.13

12" square stone column — If — $6.13 — $116.40 — $122.53
Replace Materials ....103.00   Labor 13.40
Remove.........................   Labor 6.13

12" square synthetic stone column — If — $6.13 — $109.70 — $115.83
Replace Materials ......96.30   Labor 13.40
Remove.........................   Labor 6.13

12" square aluminum column — If — $6.13 — $72.20 — $78.33
Replace Materials ......58.80   Labor 13.40
Remove.........................   Labor 6.13

12" square interior plaster column — If — $6.13 — $69.40 — $75.53
Replace Materials ......56.00   Labor 13.40
Remove.........................   Labor 6.13

Item Description	Unit	Remove	Replace	Total
12" square exterior stucco column	lf	$6.13	$67.80	$73.93
Replace Materials......54.40 Labor..........13.40				
Remove..................... Labor..........6.13				
12" square pilaster made from composite materials	lf	$3.87	$47.00	$50.87
Replace Materials......35.30 Labor..........11.70				
Remove..................... Labor..........3.87				
12" square pine pilaster	lf	$3.87	$49.00	$52.87
Replace Materials......37.30 Labor..........11.70				
Remove..................... Labor..........3.87				
12" square redwood pilaster	lf	$3.87	$56.00	$59.87
Replace Materials......44.30 Labor..........11.70				
Remove..................... Labor..........3.87				
12" square oak pilaster	lf	$3.87	$60.80	$64.67
Replace Materials......49.10 Labor..........11.70				
Remove..................... Labor..........3.87				
12" square stone pilaster	lf	$3.87	$77.50	$81.37
Replace Materials......65.80 Labor..........11.70				
Remove..................... Labor..........3.87				
12" square synthetic stone pilaster	lf	$3.87	$73.30	$77.17
Replace Materials......61.60 Labor..........11.70				
Remove..................... Labor..........3.87				
12" square aluminum pilaster	lf	$3.87	$49.30	$53.17
Replace Materials......37.60 Labor..........11.70				
Remove..................... Labor..........3.87				
12" square interior plaster pilaster	lf	$3.87	$47.30	$51.17
Replace Materials......35.60 Labor..........11.70				
Remove..................... Labor..........3.87				
12" square exterior stucco pilaster	lf	$3.87	$46.30	$50.17
Replace Materials......34.60 Labor..........11.70				
Remove..................... Labor..........3.87				
Repair wood column or pilaster with wood patch	ea	—	$31.70	$31.70
Replace Materials......3.60 Labor..........28.10				
Repair fluted wood column or pilaster with wood patch	ea	—	$38.50	$38.50
Replace Materials......3.60 Labor..........34.90				
Repair wood column or pilaster by replacing section	ea	—	$84.30	$84.30
Replace Materials......6.40 Labor..........77.90				
Repair fluted wood column or pilaster by replacing section	ea	—	$109.00	$109.00
Replace Materials......8.00 Labor..........101.00				
Repair dry rot in column or pilaster with epoxy	ea	—	$119.40	$119.40
Replace Materials......6.40 Labor..........113.00				
Repair dry rot in fluted column or pilaster with epoxy	ea	—	$133.40	$133.40
Replace Materials......6.40 Labor..........127.00				
Add for column repair if column is removed from structure	ea	—	$469.00	$469.00
Replace Materials......64.00 Labor..........405.00				
► Additional cost to build temporary brace wall and remove column from structure.				

◄ **12" SQUARE PILASTER**

◄ **COLUMN REPAIR**

RELATED ITEMS

Cleaning.....................57
Finish Carpentry..........199
Painting.....................333

Item Description	Unit	Remove	Replace	Total
COLUMN REPAIR ▶ *continued* **Minimum charge for column or pilaster repair** *Replace* Materials ......18.00 Labor 101.00	ea	—	$119.00	$119.00
CONTEMPORARY ▶ CAPITAL *Capital up to 4" high. Includes load-bearing plug.* **Contemporary capital made from composite materials** *Replace* Materials.....160.00 Labor...........24.60 *Remove*....................... Labor...........24.60	ea	$24.60	$184.60	$209.20
Contemporary capital made from pine *Replace* Materials ....184.00 Labor...........24.60 *Remove*....................... Labor...........24.60	ea	$24.60	$208.60	$233.20
Contemporary capital made from redwood *Replace* Materials.....212.00 Labor...........24.60 *Remove*....................... Labor...........24.60	ea	$24.60	$236.60	$261.20
Contemporary capital made from oak *Replace* Materials ....243.00 Labor...........24.60 *Remove*....................... Labor...........24.60	ea	$24.60	$267.60	$292.20
Contemporary capital made from stone *Replace* Materials....324.00 Labor...........24.60 *Remove*....................... Labor...........24.60	ea	$24.60	$348.60	$373.20
Contemporary capital made from synthetic stone *Replace* Materials ....301.00 Labor...........24.60 *Remove*....................... Labor...........24.60	ea	$24.60	$325.60	$350.20
Contemporary capital made from aluminum *Replace* Materials ....183.00 Labor...........24.60 *Remove*....................... Labor...........24.60	ea	$24.60	$207.60	$232.20
Contemporary capital made from interior plaster *Replace* Materials.....174.00 Labor...........24.60 *Remove*....................... Labor...........24.60	ea	$24.60	$198.60	$223.20
Contemporary capital made from exterior stucco *Replace* Materials.....170.00 Labor...........24.60 *Remove*....................... Labor...........24.60	ea	$24.60	$194.60	$219.20
CORINTHIAN ▶ CAPITAL *Capital up to 14" high. Includes load-bearing plug.* **Corinthian capital made from composite materials** *Replace* Materials ....490.00 Labor...........24.60 *Remove*....................... Labor...........24.60	ea	$24.60	$514.60	$539.20
Corinthian capital made from pine *Replace* Materials ....870.00 Labor...........24.60 *Remove*....................... Labor...........24.60	ea	$24.60	$894.60	$919.20
Corinthian capital made from redwood *Replace* Materials ....998.00 Labor...........24.60 *Remove*....................... Labor...........24.60	ea	$24.60	$1,022.60	$1,047.20
Corinthian capital made from oak *Replace* Materials .1,150.00 Labor...........24.60 *Remove*....................... Labor...........24.60	ea	$24.60	$1,174.60	$1,199.20
Corinthian capital made from stone *Replace* Materials....653.00 Labor...........24.60 *Remove*....................... Labor...........24.60	ea	$24.60	$677.60	$702.20
Corinthian capital made from synthetic stone *Replace* Materials ....607.00 Labor...........24.60 *Remove*....................... Labor...........24.60	ea	$24.60	$631.60	$656.20

Item Description	Unit	Remove	Replace	Total
Corinthian capital made from aluminum *Replace* Materials....368.00 Labor..........24.60 *Remove*....................... Labor..........24.60	ea	$24.60	$392.60	$417.20
Corinthian capital made from interior plaster *Replace* Materials ....352.00 Labor..........24.60 *Remove*....................... Labor..........24.60	ea	$24.60	$376.60	$401.20
Corinthian capital made from exterior stucco *Replace* Materials....342.00 Labor..........24.60 *Remove*....................... Labor..........24.60	ea	$24.60	$366.60	$391.20
Doric or Tuscan capital made from composite materials *Replace* Materials.....167.00 Labor..........24.60 *Remove*....................... Labor..........24.60	ea	$24.60	$191.60	$216.20
Doric or Tuscan capital made from pine *Replace* Materials......191.00 Labor..........24.60 *Remove*....................... Labor..........24.60	ea	$24.60	$215.60	$240.20
Doric or Tuscan capital made from redwood *Replace* Materials.....219.00 Labor..........24.60 *Remove*....................... Labor..........24.60	ea	$24.60	$243.60	$268.20
Doric or Tuscan capital made from oak *Replace* Materials ....252.00 Labor..........24.60 *Remove*....................... Labor..........24.60	ea	$24.60	$276.60	$301.20
Doric or Tuscan capital made from stone *Replace* Materials ....337.00 Labor..........24.60 *Remove*....................... Labor..........24.60	ea	$24.60	$361.60	$386.20
Doric or Tuscan capital made from synthetic stone *Replace* Materials.....312.00 Labor..........24.60 *Remove*....................... Labor..........24.60	ea	$24.60	$336.60	$361.20
Doric or Tuscan capital made from aluminum *Replace* Materials ....189.00 Labor..........24.60 *Remove*....................... Labor..........24.60	ea	$24.60	$213.60	$238.20
Doric or Tuscan capital made from interior plaster *Replace* Materials ....180.00 Labor..........24.60 *Remove*....................... Labor..........24.60	ea	$24.60	$204.60	$229.20
Doric or Tuscan capital made from exterior stucco *Replace* Materials.....175.00 Labor..........24.60 *Remove*....................... Labor..........24.60	ea	$24.60	$199.60	$224.20
Empire capital made from composite materials *Replace* Materials.....312.00 Labor..........24.60 *Remove*....................... Labor..........24.60	ea	$24.60	$336.60	$361.20
Empire capital made from pine *Replace* Materials....554.00 Labor..........24.60 *Remove*....................... Labor..........24.60	ea	$24.60	$578.60	$603.20
Empire capital made from redwood *Replace* Materials ....637.00 Labor..........24.60 *Remove*....................... Labor..........24.60	ea	$24.60	$661.60	$686.20

◄ **DORIC OR TUSCAN CAPITAL**
Capital up to 4" high.
Includes load-bearing plug.

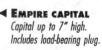

◄ **EMPIRE CAPITAL**
Capital up to 7" high.
Includes load-bearing plug.

RELATED ITEMS

Cleaning...............57
Finish Carpentry...........199
Painting...................333

	Item Description	Unit	Remove	Replace	Total
EMPIRE CAPITAL ▶ *continued.*	**Empire capital made from oak** *Replace* Materials ....732.00 Labor..........24.60 *Remove*..................... Labor..........24.60	ea	$24.60	$756.60	$781.20
	Empire capital made from stone *Replace* Materials .....417.00 Labor..........24.60 *Remove*..................... Labor..........24.60	ea	$24.60	$441.60	$466.20
	Empire capital made from synthetic stone *Replace* Materials ....386.00 Labor..........24.60 *Remove*..................... Labor..........24.60	ea	$24.60	$410.60	$435.20
	Empire capital made from aluminum *Replace* Materials....234.00 Labor..........24.60 *Remove*..................... Labor..........24.60	ea	$24.60	$258.60	$283.20
	Empire capital made from interior plaster *Replace* Materials....223.00 Labor..........24.60 *Remove*..................... Labor..........24.60	ea	$24.60	$247.60	$272.20
	Empire capital made from exterior stucco *Replace* Materials.....217.00 Labor..........24.60 *Remove*..................... Labor..........24.60	ea	$24.60	$241.60	$266.20
ERECHTHEUM ▶ **CAPITAL** *Capital up to 7" high.* *Add **50%** for necking.* *Includes load-bearing plug.* 	**Erechtheum capital made from composite materials** *Replace* Materials....303.00 Labor..........24.60 *Remove*..................... Labor..........24.60	ea	$24.60	$327.60	$352.20
	Erechtheum capital made from pine *Replace* Materials....538.00 Labor..........24.60 *Remove*..................... Labor..........24.60	ea	$24.60	$562.60	$587.20
	Erechtheum capital made from redwood *Replace* Materials .....617.00 Labor..........24.60 *Remove*..................... Labor..........24.60	ea	$24.60	$641.60	$666.20
	Erechtheum capital made from oak *Replace* Materials ....709.00 Labor..........24.60 *Remove*..................... Labor..........24.60	ea	$24.60	$733.60	$758.20
	Erechtheum capital made from stone *Replace* Materials....403.00 Labor..........24.60 *Remove*..................... Labor..........24.60	ea	$24.60	$427.60	$452.20
	Erechtheum capital made from synthetic stone *Replace* Materials ....375.00 Labor..........24.60 *Remove*..................... Labor..........24.60	ea	$24.60	$399.60	$424.20
	Erechtheum capital made from aluminum *Replace* Materials....228.00 Labor..........24.60 *Remove*..................... Labor..........24.60	ea	$24.60	$252.60	$277.20
	Erechtheum capital made from interior plaster *Replace* Materials....217.00 Labor..........24.60 *Remove*..................... Labor..........24.60	ea	$24.60	$241.60	$266.20
	Erechtheum capital made from exterior stucco *Replace* Materials.....212.00 Labor..........24.60 *Remove*..................... Labor..........24.60	ea	$24.60	$236.60	$261.20

Item Description	Unit	Remove	Replace	Total
Roman Ionic capital made from composite materials	ea	$24.60	$340.60	$365.20
Replace Materials.....316.00 Labor...........24.60				
Remove....................... Labor...........24.60				
Roman Ionic capital made from pine	ea	$24.60	$584.60	$609.20
Replace Materials....560.00 Labor...........24.60				
Remove....................... Labor...........24.60				
Roman Ionic capital made from redwood	ea	$24.60	$667.60	$692.20
Replace Materials....643.00 Labor...........24.60				
Remove....................... Labor...........24.60				
Roman Ionic capital made from oak	ea	$24.60	$763.60	$788.20
Replace Materials ....739.00 Labor...........24.60				
Remove....................... Labor...........24.60				
Roman Ionic capital made from stone	ea	$24.60	$445.60	$470.20
Replace Materials ....421.00 Labor...........24.60				
Remove....................... Labor...........24.60				
Roman Ionic capital made from synthetic stone	ea	$24.60	$414.60	$439.20
Replace Materials ....390.00 Labor...........24.60				
Remove....................... Labor...........24.60				
Roman Ionic capital made from aluminum	ea	$24.60	$261.60	$286.20
Replace Materials ....237.00 Labor...........24.60				
Remove....................... Labor...........24.60				
Roman Ionic capital made from interior plaster	ea	$24.60	$250.60	$275.20
Replace Materials ....226.00 Labor...........24.60				
Remove....................... Labor...........24.60				
Roman Ionic capital made from exterior stucco	ea	$24.60	$244.60	$269.20
Replace Materials ....220.00 Labor...........24.60				
Remove....................... Labor...........24.60				
Scamozzi capital made from composite materials	ea	$24.60	$356.60	$381.20
Replace Materials ....332.00 Labor...........24.60				
Remove....................... Labor...........24.60				
Scamozzi capital made from pine	ea	$24.60	$612.60	$637.20
Replace Materials....588.00 Labor...........24.60				
Remove....................... Labor...........24.60				
Scamozzi capital made from redwood	ea	$24.60	$699.60	$724.20
Replace Materials.....675.00 Labor...........24.60				
Remove....................... Labor...........24.60				
Scamozzi capital made from oak	ea	$24.60	$799.60	$824.20
Replace Materials....775.00 Labor...........24.60				
Remove....................... Labor...........24.60				
Scamozzi capital made from stone	ea	$24.60	$466.60	$491.20
Replace Materials ....442.00 Labor...........24.60				
Remove....................... Labor...........24.60				
Scamozzi capital made from synthetic stone	ea	$24.60	$434.60	$459.20
Replace Materials.....410.00 Labor...........24.60				
Remove....................... Labor...........24.60				

◀ **ROMAN IONIC CAPITAL**
Capital up to 5" high. Includes load-bearing plug.

◀ **SCAMOZZI CAPITAL**
Capital up to 5" high. Includes load-bearing plug.

RELATED ITEMS
Cleaning.................57
Finish Carpentry..........199
Painting...................333

Item Description	Unit	Remove	Replace	Total
SCAMOZZI CAPITAL *continued.* **Scamozzi capital made from aluminum** *Replace* Materials ....248.00 Labor...........24.60 *Remove*..................... Labor...........24.60	ea	$24.60	$272.60	$297.20
Scamozzi capital made from interior plaster *Replace* Materials ....237.00 Labor...........24.60 *Remove*..................... Labor...........24.60	ea	$24.60	$261.60	$286.20
Scamozzi capital made from exterior stucco *Replace* Materials ....231.00 Labor...........24.60 *Remove*..................... Labor...........24.60	ea	$24.60	$255.60	$280.20
TEMPLE-OF-THE-WINDS CAPITAL *Capital up to 12" high. Includes load-bearing plug.* **Temple-of-the-Winds capital made from composite materials** *Replace* Materials ....379.00 Labor...........24.60 *Remove*..................... Labor...........24.60	ea	$24.60	$403.60	$428.20
Temple-of-the-Winds capital made from pine *Replace* Materials ....673.00 Labor...........24.60 *Remove*..................... Labor...........24.60	ea	$24.60	$697.60	$722.20
Temple-of-the-Winds capital made from redwood *Replace* Materials ....772.00 Labor...........24.60 *Remove*..................... Labor...........24.60	ea	$24.60	$796.60	$821.20
Temple-of-the-Winds capital made from oak *Replace* Materials ....887.00 Labor...........24.60 *Remove*..................... Labor...........24.60	ea	$24.60	$911.60	$936.20
Temple-of-the-Winds capital made from stone *Replace* Materials ....504.00 Labor...........24.60 *Remove*..................... Labor...........24.60	ea	$24.60	$528.60	$553.20
Temple-of-the-Winds capital made from synthetic stone *Replace* Materials ....469.00 Labor...........24.60 *Remove*..................... Labor...........24.60	ea	$24.60	$493.60	$518.20
Temple-of-the-Winds capital made from aluminum *Replace* Materials ....284.00 Labor...........24.60 *Remove*..................... Labor...........24.60	ea	$24.60	$308.60	$333.20
Temple-of-the-Winds capital made from interior plaster *Replace* Materials ....272.00 Labor...........24.60 *Remove*..................... Labor...........24.60	ea	$24.60	$296.60	$321.20
Temple-of-the-Winds capital made from exterior stucco *Replace* Materials ....264.00 Labor...........24.60 *Remove*..................... Labor...........24.60	ea	$24.60	$288.60	$313.20
CAPITAL REPAIR **Repair wood capital with wood patch (each patch)** *Replace* Materials........2.80 Labor 46.10	ea	—	$48.90	$48.90
Repair wood capital by replacing section *Replace* Materials ......26.00 Labor 169.00	ea	—	$195.00	$195.00
Repair dry rot in capital with epoxy *Replace* Materials........2.80 Labor 90.50	ea	—	$93.30	$93.30
Minimum charge for capital repair *Replace* Materials ......31.00 Labor 127.00	ea	—	$158.00	$158.00

Item Description	Unit	Remove	Replace	Total	
Add 78% for spiral column or pilaster					◄ **ADDITIONAL COLUMN SIZES** Add or deduct from the costs for 12" columns, pilasters, capitals and bases. (Bases are built to hold columns of the size indicated.)
Deduct 45% for 6" column, pilaster, capital, or base					
Deduct 35% for 8" column, pilaster, capital, or base					
Deduct 17% for 10" column, pilaster, capital, or base					
Add 59% for 14" column, pilaster, capital, or base					
Add 81% for 16" column, pilaster, capital, or base					
Add 115% for 18" column, pilaster, capital, or base					
Add 185% for 20" column, pilaster, capital, or base					
Column base made from composite materials	ea	$22.70	$73.60	$96.30	◄ **COLUMN BASE**
Replace Materials......49.00 Labor..........24.60					
Remove..................... Labor..........22.70					
Column base made from pine	ea	$22.70	$76.60	$99.30	
Replace Materials......52.00 Labor..........24.60					
Remove..................... Labor..........22.70					
Column base made from redwood	ea	$22.70	$85.60	$108.30	
Replace Materials.......61.00 Labor..........24.60					
Remove..................... Labor..........22.70					
Column base made from oak	ea	$22.70	$92.60	$115.30	
Replace Materials......68.00 Labor..........24.60					
Remove..................... Labor..........22.70					
Column base made from stone	ea	$22.70	$115.60	$138.30	
Replace Materials......91.00 Labor..........24.60					
Remove..................... Labor..........22.70					
Column base made from synthetic stone	ea	$22.70	$109.60	$132.30	
Replace Materials......85.00 Labor..........24.60					
Remove..................... Labor..........22.70					
Column base made from aluminum	ea	$22.70	$76.60	$99.30	
Replace Materials......52.00 Labor..........24.60					
Remove..................... Labor..........22.70					
Column base made from interior plaster	ea	$22.70	$73.60	$96.30	
Replace Materials......49.00 Labor..........24.60					
Remove..................... Labor..........22.70					
Column base made from exterior stucco	ea	$22.70	$72.60	$95.30	
Replace Materials......48.00 Labor..........24.60					
Remove..................... Labor..........22.70					
Column pedestal, standard grade	ea	$11.80	$553.00	$564.80	◄ **COLUMN PEDESTAL**
Replace Materials....184.00 Labor.........369.00					
Remove..................... Labor.........11.80					
► Pedestal framed with 2" x 4" up to 3' high. Outside trimmed with paint-grade pine or poplar. Moldings around top of pedestal and bottom.					

RELATED ITEMS

Cleaning....................57
Finish Carpentry..........199
Painting....................333

Item Description	Unit	Remove	Replace	Total
COLUMN ▶ PEDESTAL *continued*				
Column pedestal, high grade	ea	$11.80	$652.00	$663.80
Replace Materials ....243.00 Labor 409.00				
Remove....................... Labor 11.80				
▶ Pedestal framed with 2" x 4" up to 3' high. Outside trimmed with paint-grade pine or poplar. Moldings around top of pedestal and bottom. Each of the four sides also includes panel molding. Or standard grade from stain-grade fir.				
Column pedestal, deluxe grade	ea	$11.80	$821.00	$832.80
Replace Materials ....360.00 Labor 461.00				
Remove....................... Labor 11.80				
▶ Pedestal framed with 2" x 4" up to 3' high. Outside trimmed with paint-grade pine or poplar. Moldings around top of pedestal and bottom. Each of the four sides includes a recessed raised panel. Or standard grade from red oak or mahogany.				
Column pedestal, custom grade	ea	$11.80	$933.00	$944.80
Replace Materials.....424.00 Labor 509.00				
Remove....................... Labor 11.80				
▶ Pedestal framed with 2" x 4" up to 3' high. Outside trimmed with paint-grade pine or poplar. Moldings around top of pedestal and bottom. Each of the four sides includes a recessed raised cathedral panel. Or deluxe grade from red oak or mahogany.				
PILASTER ▶ PEDESTAL				
Pilaster pedestal, standard grade	ea	$9.65	$374.00	$383.65
Replace Materials .....113.00 Labor 261.00				
Remove...................... Labor 9.65				
▶ Pedestal framed with 2" x 4" up to 3' high. Outside trimmed with paint-grade pine or poplar. Moldings around top of pedestal and bottom.				
Pilaster pedestal, high grade	ea	$9.65	$437.00	$446.65
Replace Materials .....147.00 Labor 290.00				
Remove...................... Labor 9.65				
▶ Pedestal framed with 2" x 4" up to 3' high. Outside trimmed with paint-grade pine or poplar. Moldings around top of pedestal and bottom. Each of the three sides also includes panel molding. Or standard grade from stain-grade fir.				
Pilaster pedestal, deluxe grade	ea	$9.65	$542.00	$551.65
Replace Materials .....217.00 Labor........325.00				
Remove...................... Labor 9.65				
▶ Pedestal framed with 2" x 4" up to 3' high. Outside trimmed with paint-grade pine or poplar. Moldings around top of pedestal and bottom. Each of the three sides includes a recessed raised panel. Or standard grade from red oak or mahogany.				
Pilaster pedestal, custom grade	ea	$9.65	$618.00	$627.65
Replace Materials ....256.00 Labor........362.00				
Remove...................... Labor 9.65				
▶ Pedestal framed with 2" x 4" up to 3' high. Outside trimmed with paint-grade pine or poplar. Moldings around top of pedestal and bottom. Each of the three sides includes a recessed raised cathedral panel. Or deluxe grade from red oak or mahogany.				
ADD FOR OTHER ▶ WOOD SPECIES **Add 12% for stain-grade redwood materials**				
▶ Add to the cost of any redwood item listed above.				
Add 16% for mahogany materials				
▶ Add to the cost of any redwood item listed above.				

standard △   △ high

deluxe △   △ custom

✍ NOTES: _____

_____end

TIME & MATERIAL CHARTS *(selected items)*

Columns Materials

DESCRIPTION	MATERIAL PRICE	GROSS COVERAGE	WASTE	NET COVERAGE	UNIT PRICE
Minimum materials charge for column or pilaster work					
minimum	$30.00 ea				$30.00 ea
12″ round column					
composite materials	$336.00 8′	8	0%	8	$42.00 lf
pine	$353.00 8′	8	0%	8	$44.10 lf
12″ round pilaster					
composite materials	$214.00 8′	8	0%	8	$26.80 lf
pine	$226.00 8′	8	0%	8	$28.30 lf
12″ square column					
composite materials	$443.00 8′	8	0%	8	$55.40 lf
pine	$466.00 8′	8	0%	8	$58.30 lf
12″ square pilaster					
composite materials	$282.00 8′	8	0%	8	$35.30 lf
pine pilaster	$298.00 8′	8	0%	8	$37.30 lf
Contemporary capital					
composite materials	$160.00 ea				$160.00 ea
pine	$184.00 ea				$184.00 ea
Corinthian capital					
composite materials	$490.00 ea				$490.00 ea
pine	$870.00 ea				$870.00 ea
Doric or Tuscan capital					
composite materials	$167.00 ea				$167.00 ea
pine	$191.00 ea				$191.00 ea
Empire capital					
composite materials	$312.00 ea				$312.00 ea
pine	$554.00 ea				$554.00 ea
Erechtheum capital					
composite materials	$303.00 ea				$303.00 ea
pine	$538.00 ea				$538.00 ea
Roman Ionic capital					
composite materials	$316.00 ea				$316.00 ea
pine	$560.00 ea				$560.00 ea
Scamozzi capital					
composite materials	$332.00 ea				$332.00 ea
pine	$588.00 ea				$588.00 ea
Temple-of-the-Winds capital					
composite materials	$379.00 ea				$379.00 ea
pine	$673.00 ea				$673.00 ea
Column base					
composite materials	$49.00 ea				$49.00 ea
pine	$52.00 ea				$52.00 ea
Column pedestal					
standard grade	$184.00 ea				$184.00 ea
custom grade	$424.00 ea				$424.00 ea
Pilaster pedestal					
standard grade	$113.00 ea				$113.00 ea
custom grade	$256.00 ea				$256.00 ea

Columns Labor

LABORER	BASE WAGE	PAID LEAVE	TRUE WAGE	FICA	FUTA	WORKER'S COMP.	UNEMPLOY. INSUR.	HEALTH INSUR.	RETIRE (401k)	LIABILITY INSUR.	COST PER HOUR
Carpenter	$24.30	1.90	$26.20	2.00	.21	5.15	2.28	2.92	.79	3.93	$43.50
Demolition laborer	$14.40	1.12	$15.52	1.19	.12	5.01	1.35	2.92	.47	2.33	$28.90

Paid Leave is calculated based on two weeks paid vacation, one week sick leave, and seven paid holidays. Employer's matching portion of **FICA** is 7.65 percent. **FUTA** (Federal Unemployment) is .8 percent. **Worker's compensation** for columns was calculated using a national average of 19.63 percent. **Unemployment insurance** was calculated using a national average of 8.7 percent. **Health insurance** was calculated based on a projected national average for 2005 of $580 per employee (and family when applicable) per month. Employer pays 80 percent for a per month cost of $464 per employee. **Retirement** is based on a 401(k) retirement program with employer matching of 50 percent. Employee contributions to the 401(k) plan are an average of 6 percent of the true wage. **Liability insurance** is based on a national average of 14.0 percent.

Columns Labor Productivity

WORK DESCRIPTION	LABORER	COST PER HOUR	PRODUCTIVITY	UNIT PRICE
Demolition				
remove column	demolition laborer	$28.90	.212	$6.13 lf
remove pilaster	demolition laborer	$28.90	.134	$3.87 lf
remove column or pilaster capital	demolition laborer	$28.90	.850	$24.60 ea
remove column or pilaster base	demolition laborer	$28.90	.785	$22.70 ea
remove column pedestal	demolition laborer	$28.90	.410	$11.80 ea
remove pilaster pedestal	demolition laborer	$28.90	.334	$9.65 ea
Install column				
round	finish carpenter	$43.50	.333	$14.50 lf
square	finish carpenter	$43.50	.308	$13.40 lf
Install pilaster				
round	finish carpenter	$43.50	.292	$12.70 lf
square	finish carpenter	$43.50	.270	$11.70 lf
Install capital				
column or pilaster capital	finish carpenter	$43.50	.566	$24.60 ea
Install column or pilaster base				
column or pilaster base	finish carpenter	$43.50	.566	$24.60 ea
Repair column or pilaster				
round with wood patch	finish carpenter	$43.50	.706	$30.70 ea
fluted with wood patch	finish carpenter	$43.50	.863	$37.50 ea
round by replacing section	finish carpenter	$43.50	1.94	$84.40 ea
fluted by replacing section	finish carpenter	$43.50	2.59	$113.00 ea
round dry rot with epoxy	finish carpenter	$43.50	2.74	$119.00 ea
fluted dry rot with epoxy	finish carpenter	$43.50	3.24	$141.00 ea
minimum charge	finish carpenter	$43.50	2.33	$101.00 ea
Repair wood capital				
with wood patch	finish carpenter	$43.50	1.06	$46.10 ea
by replacing section	finish carpenter	$43.50	3.88	$169.00 ea
dry rot with epoxy	finish carpenter	$43.50	2.08	$90.50 ea
minimum charge	finish carpenter	$43.50	2.91	$127.00 ea
Build and install column pedestal				
standard grade	finish carpenter	$43.50	8.49	$369.00 ea
custom grade	finish carpenter	$43.50	11.7	$509.00 ea
Build and install pilaster pedestal				
standard grade	finish carpenter	$43.50	6.01	$261.00 ea
custom grade	finish carpenter	$43.50	8.33	$362.00 ea

8 .... *Concrete*

Item Description	Unit	Remove	Replace	Total	
Minimum charge for concrete repair *Replace* Materials ......65.00 Labor 348.00	ea	–	**$413.00**	**$413.00**	◄ MINIMUM
Concrete crack repair with pressurized epoxy injection *Replace* Materials .... .74 Labor ....4.83 Equipment............1.56 ► A pressure pot is used to inject pressurized epoxy into a concrete crack. Care is taken to fill and plug areas where the epoxy could escape.	lf	–	**$7.13**	**$7.13**	◄ EPOXY REPAIR
Minimum charge for pressurized epoxy injection concrete crack repair *Replace* Materials ......70.00 Labor ....128.00 Equipment 97.00	ea	–	**$295.00**	**$295.00**	
Concrete hole repair with epoxy system per cubic inch of hole *Replace* Materials .... .03 Labor ....2.31 ► Epoxy is poured or injected into a hole. Priced per cubic inch of the hole.	ci	–	**$2.34**	**$2.34**	
Minimum charge for concrete hole repair with epoxy system *Replace* Materials ......63.00 Labor 21.80	ea	–	**$84.80**	**$84.80**	
Concrete crack repair with caulking gun epoxy injection *Replace* Materials .... .43 Labor 1.09	lf	–	**$1.52**	**$1.52**	
Minimum charge for concrete crack repair with epoxy injection *Replace* Materials ......70.00 Labor 21.80	ea	–	**$91.80**	**$91.80**	
Repair spalled concrete with concrete resurfacer *Replace* Materials .... .86 Labor .... .39	sf	–	**$1.25**	**$1.25**	
Minimum charge to repair spalled concrete *Replace* Materials ......41.80 Labor 43.50	ea	–	**$85.30**	**$85.30**	
Concrete footings including rebar package & forming *Replace* Materials .....124.00 Labor..........94.40 *Remove*..................... Labor..........47.40 Equipment..........58.90	cy	$106.30	$218.40	$324.70	◄ FOOTING
Concrete footings including CEC rebar package & forming *Replace* Materials .....151.00 Labor..........114.00 *Remove*..................... Labor ....56.60 Equipment..........98.30	cy	$154.90	$265.00	$419.90	
16″ wide by 10″ deep concrete footings with rebar *Replace* Materials........5.40 Labor ....5.81 *Remove*..................... Labor ....3.50 Equipment............3.03	lf	$6.53	$11.21	$17.74	
16″ wide by 10″ deep concrete footings with CEC rebar *Replace* Materials........6.93 Labor ....6.98 *Remove*..................... Labor ....4.25 Equipment............3.67	lf	$7.92	$13.91	$21.83	
20″ wide by 10″ deep concrete footings with rebar *Replace* Materials........6.48 Labor ....6.17 *Remove*..................... Labor ....3.50 Equipment............3.03	lf	$6.53	$12.65	$19.18	
20″ wide by 10″ deep concrete footings with CEC rebar *Replace* Materials........8.15 Labor ....7.34 *Remove*..................... Labor ....4.25 Equipment............3.67	lf	$7.92	$15.49	$23.41	

CALIFORNIA EARTHQUAKE CODE

Items that include "CEC" in the description are priced according to California earthquake code requirements.

Although these *Universal Building Code* or similar standards are also required in other areas of the country, they are most commonly associated with efforts initiated in the State of California to improve the construction and engineering of structures in quake zones.

◄ FOOTING
Standard 16″, 20″, and 24″ footings include 3 horizontal lengths of #4 rebar. Standard 32″ footing includes 4 horizontal lengths of #4 rebar. CEC 16″ and 20″ footings include 3 horizontal lengths of #5 rebar. CEC 24″ and 32″ footings include 4 horizontal lengths of #5 rebar. Tie-in rebar from foundation wall bent continuously into the footing is included in the foundation wall prices.

CEC = California Earthquake Code.

	Item Description	Unit	Remove	Replace	Total
FOOTINGS ▶ continued	**24" wide by 12" deep concrete footings with rebar**	lf	$6.53	$15.63	$22.16
	Replace Materials........9.18 Labor...........6.45				
	Remove................... Labor...........3.50 Equipment...........3.03				
	24" wide by 12" deep concrete footings with CEC rebar	lf	$7.92	$18.65	$26.57
	Replace Materials.......11.03 Labor...........7.62				
	Remove................... Labor...........4.25 Equipment...........3.67				
	32" wide by 14" deep concrete footings with rebar	lf	$6.53	$20.44	$26.97
	Replace Materials.......13.60 Labor...........6.84				
	Remove................... Labor...........3.50 Equipment...........3.03				
	32" wide by 14" deep concrete footings with CEC rebar	lf	$7.92	$23.51	$31.43
	Replace Materials.......15.50 Labor...........8.01				
	Remove................... Labor...........4.25 Equipment...........3.67				
minimum ▷	**Minimum charge for concrete footing work**	ea	–	$88.30	$88.30
	Replace Materials.......48.60 Labor...........39.70				
FOUNDATION ▶	**Concrete foundation wall including rebar package & forming**	cy	$144.20	$252.80	$397.00
Standard foundation walls include horizontal and vertical lengths of #4 rebar 24" on center. Vertical rebar is bent continuously into footing. CEC foundations include horizontal and vertical lengths of #5 rebar 12" on center. Vertical rebar is bent continuously into footing.	*Replace* Materials......118.00 Labor.........104.00 Equipment...........30.80				
	Remove................... Labor.........70.50 Equipment...........73.70				
	Concrete foundation wall including CEC rebar package & forming	cy	$183.30	$290.80	$474.10
	Replace Materials......139.00 Labor.........121.00 Equipment...........30.80				
	Remove................... Labor.........85.00 Equipment...........98.30				
	5" wide concrete foundation wall	sf	$3.93	$4.68	$8.61
	Replace Materials........1.65 Labor.........2.27 Equipment 76				
	Remove................... Labor.........2.11 Equipment...........1.82				
	Rebar package for 5" wide concrete foundation wall	sf	–	$1.63	$1.63
	Replace Materials .... .24 Labor...........1.39				
	CEC rebar package for 5" wide concrete foundation wall	sf	–	$3.27	$3.27
	Replace Materials .... .75 Labor...........2.52				
	6" wide concrete foundation wall	sf	$3.93	$5.22	$9.15
	Replace Materials........1.99 Labor.........2.47 Equipment .... .76				
	Remove................... Labor.........2.11 Equipment...........1.82				
	Rebar package for 6" wide concrete foundation wall	sf	–	$1.63	$1.63
	Replace Materials .... .24 Labor...........1.39				
	CEC rebar package for 6" wide concrete foundation wall	sf	–	$3.27	$3.27
	Replace Materials .... .75 Labor...........2.52				
	8" wide concrete foundation wall	sf	$4.29	$6.28	$10.57
	Replace Materials........2.65 Labor.........2.87 Equipment .... .76				
	Remove................... Labor.........2.20 Equipment...........2.09				
	Rebar package for 8" wide concrete foundation wall	sf	–	$1.63	$1.63
	Replace Materials .... .24 Labor...........1.39				
	CEC rebar package for 8" wide concrete foundation wall	sf	–	$3.27	$3.27
	Replace Materials .... .75 Labor...........2.52				
	10" wide concrete foundation wall	sf	$4.29	$7.35	$11.64
	Replace Materials........3.32 Labor.........3.27 Equipment .... .76				
	Remove................... Labor.........2.20 Equipment...........2.09				

CEC = California Earthquake Code.

Item Description	Unit	Remove	Replace	Total
Rebar package for 10" wide concrete foundation wall	sf	–	$1.63	$1.63
Replace Materials .... .24 Labor 1.39				
CEC rebar package for 10" wide concrete foundation wall	sf	–	$3.27	$3.27
Replace Materials .... .75 Labor 2.52				
Add for insulating foam stay-in-place foundation wall forms	sf	–	$3.16	$3.16
Replace Materials ...... 1.47 Labor 1.69				
Minimum charge for concrete foundation wall work	ea	–	$317.00	$317.00
Replace Materials ......62.00 Labor ....155.00 Equipment 100.00				
Single-pour footing and foundation wall with rebar package	cy	$122.80	$169.90	$292.70
Replace Materials .....109.00 Labor ....22.80 Equipment 38.10				
Remove .... Labor ....56.60 Equipment 66.20				
Single-pour footing and foundation wall with CEC rebar package	cy	$138.60	$176.70	$315.30
Replace Materials .....111.00 Labor ....27.60 Equipment 38.10				
Remove .... Labor ....67.30 Equipment 71.30				
Single-pour footing with 6" wide by 3' stem wall	lf	$19.30	$29.46	$48.76
Replace Materials.......11.50 Labor ....13.40 Equipment 4.56				
Remove .... Labor ....10.00 Equipment 9.30				
Single-pour footing with 8" wide by 3' stem wall	lf	$19.30	$31.46	$50.76
Replace Materials.......13.50 Labor ....13.40 Equipment 4.56				
Remove .... Labor ....10.00 Equipment 9.30				
Single-pour footing with 10" wide by 3' stem wall	lf	$19.30	$31.76	$51.06
Replace Materials.......13.80 Labor ....13.40 Equipment 4.56				
Remove .... Labor ....10.00 Equipment 9.30				
Rebar package for single-pour footing & 3' stem wall	lf	–	$6.97	$6.97
Replace Materials.......1.74 Labor 5.23				
CEC rebar package for single-pour footing & 3' stem wall	lf	–	$13.31	$13.31
Replace Materials.......4.17 Labor 9.14				
Single-pour footing with 6" wide by 4' stem wall	lf	$21.50	$36.48	$57.98
Replace Materials.......13.50 Labor ....16.90 Equipment 6.08				
Remove .... Labor ....12.20 Equipment 9.30				
Single-pour footing with 8" wide by 4' stem wall	lf	$21.50	$39.08	$60.58
Replace Materials.......16.10 Labor ....16.90 Equipment 6.08				
Remove .... Labor ....12.20 Equipment 9.30				
Single-pour footing with 10" wide by 4' stem wall	lf	$21.50	$41.78	$63.28
Replace Materials.......18.80 Labor ....16.90 Equipment 6.08				
Remove .... Labor ....12.20 Equipment 9.30				
Rebar package for 6" wide by 4' single-pour footing & stem wall	lf	–	$7.72	$7.72
Replace Materials.......2.00 Labor 5.72				
CEC rebar package for 6" wide by 4' single-pour footing & stem wall	lf	–	$14.24	$14.24
Replace Materials.......4.65 Labor 9.59				
Minimum charge for single-pour footing & stem wall work	ea	–	$280.00	$280.00
Replace Materials.......25.00 Labor ....155.00 Equipment 100.00				

◁ minimum (Minimum charge for concrete foundation wall work)

◀ **SINGLE-POUR FOOTING & FOUNDATION** Single-pour footing and foundation wall. See footings on page 83 and foundations on 84 for explanations about the rebar included in each system.

◁ minimum (Minimum charge for single-pour footing & stem wall work)

CEC = California Earthquake Code.

RELATED ITEMS
Cleaning....................57
Painting 333

Item Description	Unit	Remove	Replace	Total

DRILL PIER HOLE ▶
Pier hole from 12" to 24" in diameter. (Most common sizes are 16" and 18".)

Item Description	Unit	Remove	Replace	Total
Delivery & take home charge for tractor-mounted auger (mobilization)	ea	–	$801.00	$801.00
Replace .... Labor ....336.00 Equipment 465.00				
Drill concrete pier hole for hillside home construction	lf	–	$6.91	$6.91
Replace .... Labor ....4.47 Equipment 2.44				
Minimum charge to drill concrete pier	ea	–	$828.00	$828.00
Replace .... Labor ....268.00 Equipment 560.00				

PIER ▶
Pier from 12" to 24" in diameter. (Most common sizes are 16" and 18".) In most cases piers are not removed. When removed they are pulled from the ground with a crane or trackhoe. An engineer should be consulted when piers are removed and a new structure will be built on the same site.

Item Description	Unit	Remove	Replace	Total
Concrete pier including rebar cage	cy	$76.20	$1,026.00	$1,102.20
Replace Materials ....449.00 Labor 577.00				
Remove .... Labor ....20.20 Equipment 56.00				
Concrete pier with up to 36" fiber tube wrapped cap	lf	$8.89	$84.80	$93.69
Replace Materials ......16.90 Labor 67.90				
Remove .... Labor ....2.37 Equipment 6.52				
Above-grade concrete pier with fiber tube wrap	lf	$8.89	$112.20	$121.09
Replace Materials ......42.10 Labor 70.10				
Remove .... Labor ....2.37 Equipment 6.52				
Rebar cage for concrete pier (meets CEC requirements)	lf	–	$43.42	$43.42
Replace Materials ......40.00 Labor 3.42				
Minimum charge for concrete pier work	ea	–	$841.00	$841.00
Replace Materials ....332.00 Labor 509.00				

JACKET PIER ▶

Item Description	Unit	Remove	Replace	Total
Jacket concrete pier with new concrete and rebar ties	ea	–	$265.80	$265.80
Replace Materials ......39.10 Labor ....191.00 Equipment 35.70				
▶ Existing pier is jackhammered. Holes are drilled for rebar. Rebar is secured with epoxy. Pier is formed and concrete jacket poured.				

minimum ▷

Item Description	Unit	Remove	Replace	Total
Minimum charge to jacket a concrete pier with concrete and rebar	ea	–	$527.00	$527.00
Replace Materials ......98.00 Labor ....309.00 Equipment 120.00				

SHALLOW PIER ▶
Usually poured in hand-dug holes for light structures or decks.

Item Description	Unit	Remove	Replace	Total
Shallow concrete pier (less than 3' deep) for deck or light structure	ea	$32.90	$133.90	$166.80
Replace Materials ......20.10 Labor 113.80				
Remove .... Labor 32.90				
Pre-cast concrete pier for deck or light structure	ea	$6.73	$33.10	$39.83
Replace Materials ......23.00 Labor 10.10				
Remove .... Labor 6.73				

GRADE BEAM ▶
Grade beams include pre-fabricated rebar cage. All rebar cages are to CEC standards. When removed, grade beams are detached from piers with a jackhammer or concrete saw. The beams are broken into manageable chunks and loaded by crane or backhoe into a truck. (Does not include hauling or dump fees.)

Item Description	Unit	Remove	Replace	Total
Grade beam with rebar cage per cy	cy	$108.00	$796.00	$904.00
Replace Materials ....641.00 Labor 155.00				
Remove .... Labor ....67.30 Equipment 40.70				
12" wide by 18" deep grade beam with rebar cage	lf	$9.38	$59.24	$68.62
Replace Materials ......46.00 Labor ....10.20 Equipment 3.04				
Remove .... Labor ....5.03 Equipment 4.35				
12" wide by 20" deep grade beam with rebar cage	lf	$9.38	$60.83	$70.21
Replace Materials ......46.60 Labor ....11.19 Equipment 3.04				
Remove .... Labor ....5.03 Equipment 4.35				
12" wide by 22" deep grade beam with rebar cage	lf	$10.93	$63.44	$74.37
Replace Materials ......47.30 Labor ....13.10 Equipment 3.04				
Remove .... Labor ....5.64 Equipment 5.29				

CEC = California Earthquake Code.

Item Description	Unit	Remove	Replace	Total
12" wide by 24" deep grade beam with rebar cage	lf	$10.93	$61.84	$72.77
Replace Materials......48.00 Labor...........10.80 Equipment............3.04				
Remove........................ Labor ....5.64 Equipment............5.29				
14" wide by 18" deep grade beam with rebar cage	lf	$9.38	$62.04	$71.42
Replace Materials......47.00 Labor...........12.00 Equipment............3.04				
Remove........................ Labor ....5.03 Equipment............4.35				
14" wide by 20" deep grade beam with rebar cage	lf	$9.38	$65.04	$74.42
Replace Materials......47.70 Labor...........14.30 Equipment............3.04				
Remove........................ Labor ....5.03 Equipment............4.35				
14" wide by 22" deep grade beam with rebar cage	lf	$11.14	$65.84	$76.98
Replace Materials......48.50 Labor...........14.30 Equipment............3.04				
Remove........................ Labor ....5.75 Equipment............5.39				
14" wide by 24" deep grade beam with rebar cage	lf	$11.14	$68.94	$80.08
Replace Materials......49.30 Labor...........16.60 Equipment............3.04				
Remove........................ Labor ....5.75 Equipment............5.39				
16" wide by 18" deep grade beam with rebar cage	lf	$12.10	$72.34	$84.44
Replace Materials......48.00 Labor...........21.30 Equipment............3.04				
Remove........................ Labor ....6.24 Equipment............5.86				
16" wide by 20" deep grade beam with rebar cage	lf	$12.10	$77.84	$89.94
Replace Materials......48.80 Labor...........26.00 Equipment............3.04				
Remove........................ Labor ....6.24 Equipment............5.86				
16" wide by 22" deep grade beam with rebar cage	lf	$12.49	$74.04	$86.53
Replace Materials ......49.70 Labor...........21.30 Equipment............3.04				
Remove........................ Labor ....6.44 Equipment............6.05				
16" wide by 24" deep grade beam with rebar cage	lf	$12.49	$79.64	$92.13
Replace Materials......50.60 Labor...........26.00 Equipment............3.04				
Remove........................ Labor ....6.44 Equipment............6.05				
18" wide by 18" deep grade beam with rebar cage	lf	$12.10	$64.04	$76.14
Replace Materials ......49.00 Labor...........12.00 Equipment............3.04				
Remove........................ Labor ....6.24 Equipment............5.86				
18" wide by 20" deep grade beam with rebar cage	lf	$12.10	$67.34	$79.44
Replace Materials......50.00 Labor...........14.30 Equipment............3.04				
Remove........................ Labor ....6.24 Equipment............5.86				
18" wide by 22" deep grade beam with rebar cage	lf	$12.49	$68.24	$80.73
Replace Materials......50.90 Labor...........14.30 Equipment............3.04				
Remove........................ Labor ....6.44 Equipment............6.05				
18" wide by 24" deep grade beam with rebar cage	lf	$12.49	$71.54	$84.03
Replace Materials ......51.90 Labor...........16.60 Equipment............3.04				
Remove........................ Labor ....6.44 Equipment............6.05				
Minimum charge for concrete grade beam work	ea	–	$480.70	$480.70
Replace Materials ....341.00 Labor ....39.70 Equipment.........100.00				
Jacket concrete grade beam with new concrete and rebar ties	lf	–	$37.56	$37.56
Replace Materials ......12.00 Labor ....20.80 Equipment............4.76				

▶ Existing grade beam is jackhammered. Holes are drilled for rebar. Rebar is secured with epoxy. Grade beam is formed and concrete jacket poured.

RELATED ITEMS

Cleaning.........................57
Masonry
  grade beam wall cap 303
Painting 333

◁ minimum

◀ JACKET GRADE BEAM

	Item Description	Unit	Remove	Replace	Total
JACKET ▶ **GRADE BEAM** *continued*	**Minimum charge to jacket grade beam with concrete and rebar** *Replace* Materials ......57.00 Labor ....309.00 Equipment 120.00	ea	—	$486.00	$486.00
LIGHTWEIGHT ▶ **FLATWORK**	**Lightweight concrete flatwork per cy (no rebar)** *Replace* Materials ....134.00 Labor ....78.90 *Remove* .... Labor ....67.90 Equipment 53.20	cy	$121.10	$212.90	$334.00
	2" lightweight concrete slab *Replace* Materials .... .83 Labor .... .89 *Remove* .... Labor .... .75 Equipment .... .68	sf	$1.43	$1.72	$3.15
	4" lightweight concrete slab *Replace* Materials ....1.65 Labor .... .93 *Remove* .... Labor .... .75 Equipment .... .68	sf	$1.43	$2.58	$4.01
	6" lightweight concrete slab *Replace* Materials ....2.48 Labor .... 1.01 *Remove* .... Labor .... .75 Equipment .... .68	sf	$1.43	$3.49	$4.92
minimum ▷	**Minimum charge for lightweight concrete slab work** *Replace* Materials ......64.00 Labor 155.00	ea	—	$219.00	$219.00
FLATWORK ▶	**Concrete flatwork by cy (no rebar)** *Replace* Materials .....107.40 Labor ....78.90 *Remove* .... Labor ....69.10 Equipment 53.60	cy	$122.70	$186.30	$309.00
	4" concrete slab *Replace* Materials ....1.33 Labor ....1.36 *Remove* .... Labor .... .78 Equipment .... .68	sf	$1.46	$2.69	$4.15
	6" concrete slab *Replace* Materials ....1.99 Labor ....1.84 *Remove* .... Labor .... .78 Equipment .... .68	sf	$1.46	$3.83	$5.29
	8" concrete slab *Replace* Materials ....2.65 Labor ....1.84 *Remove* .... Labor .... .78 Equipment .... .68	sf	$1.46	$4.49	$5.95
minimum ▷	**Minimum charge for concrete slab work** *Replace* Materials ......51.00 Labor 155.00	ea	—	$206.00	$206.00
UTILITY ▶ **FLATWORK**	**Concrete footing for chimney** *Replace* Materials ....2.89 Labor ....1.71 *Remove* .... Labor .... .87 Equipment .... .76	sf	$1.63	$4.60	$6.23
	Concrete slab for exterior heat pump, condenser, etc. *Replace* Materials ....1.57 Labor ....1.71 *Remove* .... Labor .... .78 Equipment .... .68	sf	$1.46	$3.28	$4.74
REBAR FOR ▶ **FLATWORK**	**Rebar for concrete slab, #4 24" on center** *Replace* Materials .... .54 Labor 1.35	sf	—	$1.89	$1.89
	Rebar for concrete slab, #4 12" on center *Replace* Materials ...... 1.11 Labor 3.01	sf	—	$4.12	$4.12
	Wire mesh for concrete slab, 6" x 6" #10 *Replace* Materials .... .17 Labor .... .56	sf	—	$.73	$.73
FLATWORK ▶ **BASE**	**2" aggregate slab base** *Replace* Materials .... .05 Labor .... .52 Equipment .... .12	sf	—	$.69	$.69

Item Description	Unit	Remove	Replace	Total
4" aggregate slab base	sf	–	$.79	$.79
Replace Materials .... .09 Labor............ .58 Equipment .... .12				
2" sand slab base	sf	–	$.60	$.60
Replace Materials .... .05 Labor............ .43 Equipment .... .12				
4" sand slab base	sf	–	$.70	$.70
Replace Materials .... .09 Labor............ .49 Equipment .... .12				
6 mil slab membrane	sf	–	$.10	$.10
Replace Materials .... .04 Labor............ .06				
5 mil slab membrane	sf	–	$.10	$.10
Replace Materials .... .04 Labor............ .06				
Concrete sidewalk per cy	cy	$122.70	$280.00	$402.70
Replace Materials .....119.00 Labor 161.00				
Remove........................ Labor............69.10 Equipment..........53.60				
▶ Sidewalks 4" to 6" thick.				
3" concrete sidewalk	sf	$1.66	$2.60	$4.26
Replace Materials .... .99 Labor 1.61				
Remove........................ Labor............ .98 Equipment .... .68				
4" concrete sidewalk	sf	$1.66	$3.22	$4.88
Replace Materials ....1.33 Labor 1.89				
Remove........................ Labor............ .98 Equipment .... .68				
6" concrete sidewalk	sf	$1.66	$4.40	$6.06
Replace Materials ....1.99 Labor 2.41				
Remove........................ Labor............ .98 Equipment .... .68				
Minimum charge for concrete sidewalk work	ea	–	$236.00	$236.00
Replace Materials .....120.00 Labor 116.00				
Add for troweled-in concrete dye in flatwork	sf	–	$1.88	$1.88
Replace Materials ....1.52 Labor .... .36				
Add for concrete dye in flatwork per 1" deep layer, blacks and grays	sf	–	$.08	$.08
Replace Materials .... .08				
Add for concrete dye in flatwork per 1" deep layer, blues	sf	–	$.33	$.33
Replace Materials .... .33				
Add for concrete dye in flatwork per 1" deep layer, browns & terra cotta reds	sf	–	$.32	$.32
Replace Materials .... .32				
Add for concrete dye in flatwork per 1" deep layer, bright reds	sf	–	$.33	$.33
Replace Materials .... .33				
Add for concrete dye in flatwork per 1" deep layer, greens	sf	–	$.67	$.67
Replace Materials .... .67				
Add for concrete stamping of slab or sidewalk	sf	–	$2.10	$2.10
Replace .... Labor 2.10				
Add for paver-pattern concrete stamping of slab or sidewalk	sf	–	$1.79	$1.79
Replace .... Labor 1.79				

RELATED ITEMS

Cleaning.....................57
Painting 333

◀ **FLATWORK VAPOR BARRIER**

◀ **SIDEWALK**
Sidewalk to 3' wide.

◁ minimum

◀ **CONCRETE DYE**
For concrete quantities under 350 sf add $32 per truck for wash-out. This charge does not apply to troweled-in dyes.

◀ **STAMPING**

Item Description	Unit	Remove	Replace	Total
STAMPING ▶ continued — **Add for paver stamped slab or sidewalk with grouted joints** *Replace* Materials .... .35 Labor 2.70	sf	–	$3.05	$3.05
EXPOSED ▶ AGGREGATE — **Add for exposed aggregate finish on slab or sidewalk** *Replace* Materials .... .17 Labor .... .75 ▶ Where required, add for disposal of slurry.	sf	–	$.92	$.92
CURB & GUTTER ▶ — **Concrete curb & gutter** *Replace* Materials ....5.45 Labor ....10.60 Equipment .... .93 *Remove* .... Labor ....4.19 Equipment 1.38	lf	$5.57	$16.98	$22.55
Minimum charge for concrete curb & gutter work *Replace* Materials ......41.00 Labor ....142.00 Equipment 87.00	ea	–	$270.00	$270.00
CONCRETE STEP ▶ Includes rebar reinforcement: 2 horizontal pieces on each step with vertical tie-ins. — **Concrete step per cy** *Replace* Materials ....296.00 Labor ....298.00 *Remove* .... Labor ....90.20 Equipment 59.30	cy	$149.80	$594.00	$743.80
Concrete step per lf of step *Replace* Materials ....3.28 Labor ....8.97 *Remove* .... Labor ....1.36 Equipment .... .74	lf	$2.10	$12.25	$14.35
Concrete step landing per sf of landing *Replace* Materials ....8.28 Labor ....2.63 *Remove* .... Labor ....1.33 Equipment .... .90	sf	$2.23	$10.91	$13.14
minimum ▷ — **Minimum charge for a concrete step** *Replace* Materials ......78.00 Labor 232.00	ea	–	$310.00	$310.00
PARGETING ▶ Break ties, prep, and plaster above grade exterior foundation wall. — **Foundation wall pargeting (break ties if necessary)** *Replace* Materials .... .36 Labor .... .98	sf	–	$1.34	$1.34
Minimum charge for foundation wall pargeting *Replace* Materials ......26.00 Labor 44.70	ea	–	$70.70	$70.70
CONCRETE ▶ SAWING Includes blade wear. — **Saw concrete wall with standard rebar package per lf of cut, 1" deep** *Replace* .... Labor ....4.36 Equipment 1.79	lf	–	$6.15	$6.15
Saw concrete wall with CEC rebar package per lf of cut, 1" deep *Replace* .... Labor ....4.91 Equipment 2.60	lf	–	$7.51	$7.51
Saw concrete floor (no rebar) per lf of cut, 1" deep *Replace* .... Labor ....1.97 Equipment .... .69	lf	–	$2.66	$2.66
Saw concrete floor with rebar package *Replace* .... Labor ....2.12 Equipment .... .81	lf	–	$2.93	$2.93
Saw concrete floor with wire mesh reinforcement *Replace* .... Labor ....2.04 Equipment .... .95	lf	–	$2.99	$2.99
Saw expansion joint in "green" concrete pad *Replace* .... Labor ....7.43 Equipment 2.76	lf	–	$10.19	$10.19
minimum ▷ — **Minimum charge for concrete wall sawing** *Replace* .... Labor ....118.00 Equipment 115.00	ea	–	$233.00	$233.00
Minimum charge for concrete slab sawing *Replace* .... Labor ....88.40 Equipment 100.00	ea	–	$188.40	$188.40

CEC = California Earthquake Code.

Item Description			Unit	Remove	Replace	Total	
Core drill 2″ concrete wall per inch of depth			li	–	$3.36	$3.36	◄ **CONCRETE CORE DRILLING** *Includes drill bit wear.*
Replace	Labor 2.59	Equipment .... .77					
Core drill 4″ concrete wall per inch of depth			li	–	$3.76	$3.76	
Replace	Labor 2.87	Equipment .... .89					
Core drill 2″ concrete floor per inch of depth			li	–	$3.24	$3.24	
Replace	Labor 2.52	Equipment .... .72					
Core drill 4″ concrete floor per inch of depth			li	–	$3.46	$3.46	
Replace	Labor 2.63	Equipment .... .83					
Add for pumping footing concrete with pump truck			lf	–	$1.21	$1.21	◄ **PUMP TRUCK** *When pumping concrete 50 feet or less and no more than three stories high.*
Replace		Equipment............1.21					
Add for pumping foundation wall concrete with pump truck			sf	–	$.30	$.30	
Replace		Equipment .... .30					
Add for pumping pier concrete with pump truck			lf	–	$1.73	$1.73	
Replace		Equipment............1.73					
Add for pumping grade-beam concrete with pump truck			lf	–	$.92	$.92	
Replace		Equipment .... .92					
Add for pumping slab or sidewalk concrete with pump truck			sf	–	$.28	$.28	
Replace		Equipment .... .28					
Minimum charge for pump truck			ea	–	$410.00	$410.00	◁ minimum
Replace		Equipment........410.00					
#3 rebar (3/8″)			lf	–	$.72	$.72	◄ **REBAR** *Tied and bent into place.*
Replace Materials .... .19	Labor .... .53						
#4 rebar (1/2″)			lf	–	$.77	$.77	
Replace Materials .... .24	Labor .... .53						
#5 rebar (5/8″)			lf	–	$.90	$.90	
Replace Materials .... .37	Labor .... .53						
#6 rebar (3/4″)			lf	–	$1.10	$1.10	
Replace Materials .... .57	Labor .... .53						
#7 rebar (7/8″)			lf	–	$1.33	$1.33	
Replace Materials .... .77	Labor .... .56						
#8 rebar (1″)			lf	–	$1.57	$1.57	
Replace Materials 1.01	Labor .... .56						
Foundation coating			sf	–	$.57	$.57	◄ **FOUNDATION COATING**
Replace Materials .... .05	Labor .... .52						
Excavate exterior of foundation			sf	–	$8.05	$8.05	◄ **BUTTRESS FOUNDATION** *Excavation, forming, pouring, and finishing of concrete buttress over existing foundation. Does not include shoring.*
Replace	Labor 6.51	Equipment............1.54					
Hand excavate interior of foundation in crawl space			sf	–	$14.30	$14.30	
Replace	Labor............14.30						
Hand excavate interior of footing in basement			sf	–	$6.41	$6.41	
Replace	Labor 6.41						

RELATED ITEMS

Cleaning 57
Excavation 177
Painting 333

Item Description	Unit	Remove	Replace	Total
BUTTRESS FOUNDATION continued				
Backfill foundation when work is complete	sf	–	$1.63	$1.63
Replace .... Labor ....1.51 Equipment .... .12				
Buttress exterior of existing foundation wall	sf	–	$6.70	$6.70
Replace Materials........4.20 Labor 2.50				
Buttress interior of existing foundation with crawl space	sf	–	$7.73	$7.73
Replace Materials........4.20 Labor 3.53				
Buttress interior of existing foundation with basement	sf	–	$12.26	$12.26
Replace Materials........4.20 Labor 8.06				
Minimum charge to buttress existing foundation with concrete	ea	–	$728.00	$728.00
Replace Materials.....195.00 Labor 533.00				
COMPACTION GROUTING				
Does not include excavation. (See excavation under concrete buttress above.) The process can form a "pier" for the foundation and compacts the destabilized soil. An engineer is required to supervise and dictate specifications.				
2" core drill through footings for compaction grouting	ea	–	$26.94	$26.94
Replace .... Labor ....17.70 Equipment..........9.24				
▶ When footings and foundation walls are exposed, 2" holes are core drilled through footings around all corners and approximately 10' on center.				
Insert 2" compaction grouting pipes into ground beneath footings	lf	–	$6.68	$6.68
Replace .... Labor 6.68				
▶ 2" pipes are inserted into the ground through holes in the footing (usually much deeper than is shown in the illustration to the left).				
Pump pressurized concrete grout through pipes	lf	–	$49.99	$49.99
Replace Materials........4.49 Labor ....11.70 Equipment..........33.80				
▶ Pressurized grout is pumped into the ground as the pipe is slowly withdrawn.				
ASPHALT GRADED BASE				
4" graded base for asphalt	sf	–	$.20	$.20
Replace Materials .... .04 Labor .... .04 Equipment .... .12				
6" graded base for asphalt	sf	–	$.24	$.24
Replace Materials ....06 Labor ....04 Equipment..............14				
Minimum grading charge	sf	–	$419.40	$419.40
Replace Materials ......62.00 Labor ....77.40 Equipment........280.00				
ASPHALT DRIVEWAY				
2" asphalt driveway	sf	$.23	$1.53	$1.76
Replace Materials .... .58 Labor .... .46 Equipment .... .49				
Remove................... Labor .... .23				
3" asphalt driveway	sf	$.26	$1.96	$2.22
Replace Materials .... .87 Labor .... .54 Equipment .... .55				
Remove................... Labor .... .26				
4" asphalt driveway	sf	$.29	$2.40	$2.69
Replace Materials ...... 1.17 Labor .... .62 Equipment .... .61				
Remove................... Labor .... .29				
ASPHALT OVERLAY				
1" asphalt overlay	sf	$.26	$1.39	$1.65
Replace Materials .... .30 Labor .... .58 Equipment .... .51				
Remove................... Labor............ .26				
2" asphalt overlay	sf	$.26	$1.80	$2.06
Replace Materials .... .58 Labor .... .66 Equipment .... .56				
Remove................... Labor............ .26				

Item Description		Unit	Remove	Replace	Total	
3" asphalt overlay		sf	$.26	$2.23	$2.49	
Replace Materials .... .87 Labor .... .74 Equipment .... .62						
Remove...................... Labor .... .26						
Fill pothole in asphalt driveway		ea	–	$22.50	$22.50	◄ **FILL ASPHALT POTHOLE**
Replace Materials .... 4.80 Labor 17.70						
Seal crack in asphalt driveway		lf	–	$.88	$.88	◄ **SEAL ASPHALT CRACK**
Replace Materials .... .28 Labor .... .60						
Minimum charge for asphalt paving work		ea	–	$1,414.00	$1,414.00	◄ **MINIMUM ASPAHLT**
Replace Materials .... 150.00 Labor .... 464.00 Equipment 800.00						
Seal asphalt		sf	–	$.14	$.14	◄ **SEAL ASPAHLT**
Replace Materials .... .06 Labor .... .08						
Seal and sand asphalt		sf	–	$.20	$.20	
Replace Materials .... .08 Labor .... .12						

✍ NOTES: _____

_____ end

TIME & MATERIAL CHARTS *(selected items)*

Concrete Materials

DESCRIPTION	MATERIAL PRICE	GROSS COVERAGE	WASTE	NET COVERAGE	UNIT PRICE
Ready mix concrete delivered					
5 bag mix 2,500 psi, per cy	$96.40 cy	1	6%	.94	$103.00 cy
5.5 bag mix 3,000 psi, per cy	$96.90 cy	1	6%	.94	$103.00 cy
6 bag mix, 3,500 psi, per cy	$101.00 cy	1	6%	.94	$107.00 cy
6.5 bag mix, 4,000 psi, per cy	$101.00 cy	1	6%	.94	$107.00 cy
7 bag mix, 4,500 psi, per cy	$104.00 cy	1	6%	.94	$111.00 cy
7.5 bag mix, 5,000 psi, per cy	$106.00 cy	1	6%	.94	$113.00 cy
add for synthetic fiber reinforcing	$11.90 cy	1	0%	1	$11.90 cy
add for high early strength	$12.70 cy	1	0%	1	$12.70 cy
minimum ready mix charge	$124.00 each	1	0%	1	$124.00 ea
Concrete form materials					
form ties	$48.50 box	400	5%	380	$.13 sf
footing forms (2 x lumber, use 6 times, use key 3 times)	$.40 lf	1	0%	1	$.40 lf
Concrete footings					
with rebar per cy	$117.00 cy	1	6%	.94	$124.00 cy
with CEC rebar per cy	$142.00 cy	1	6%	.94	$151.00 cy
16" wide by 10" deep	$101.00 lf	24.3	6%	22.84	$4.42 lf
rebar package for 16" by 10"	$.40 pound	.7	6%	.69	$.58 lf
CEC rebar package for 16" by 10"	$.40 pound	.2	6%	.19	$2.11 lf
20" wide by 10" deep	$101.00 lf	19.44	6%	18.27	$5.53 lf
rebar package for 20" by 10"	$.40 pound	.74	2%	.73	$.55 lf
CEC rebar package for 20" by 10"	$.40 pound	.19	4%	.18	$2.22 lf
24" wide by 12" deep	$101.00 lf	13.5	6%	12.69	$7.96 lf
rebar package for 24" by 12"	$.40 pound	.5	2%	.49	$.82 lf
CEC rebar package for 24" by 10"	$.40 pound	.16	4%	.15	$2.67 lf
32" wide by 14" deep	$101.00 lf	8.68	6%	8.16	$12.40 lf
rebar package for 32" by 14"	$.40 pound	.5	2%	.49	$.82 lf
CEC rebar package for 32" by 14"	$.40 pound	.16	4%	.15	$2.67 lf

. . . More ➢

CEC = California Earthquake Code.

Concrete Materials *continued*

DESCRIPTION	MATERIAL PRICE		GROSS COVERAGE	WASTE	NET COVERAGE	UNIT PRICE	
Foundation wall							
including rebar package per cy	$111.00	cy	1	6%	.94	$118.00	cy
including CEC rebar package per cy	$131.00	cy	1	6%	.94	$139.00	cy
5" wide wall	$101.00	cy	65.06	6%	61.16	$1.65	ea
rebar package for 5" wide	$.40	pound	1.71	2%	1.68	$.24	sf
CEC rebar package for 5" wide	$.40	pound	.55	4%	.53	$.75	sf
6" wide wall	$101.00	cy	54	6%	50.76	$1.99	ea
rebar package for 6" wide wall	$.40	pound	1.71	2%	1.68	$.24	sf
CEC rebar package for 6" wide wall	$.40	pound	.55	4%	.53	$.75	sf
concrete for 8" wide wall	$101.00	cy	40.5	6%	38.07	$2.65	ea
rebar package for 8" wide wall	$.40	sf	1.71	2%	1.68	$.24	sf
CEC rebar package for 8" wide wall	$.40	sf	.55	4%	.53	$.75	sf
concrete for 10" wide wall	$101.00	cy	32.4	6%	30.46	$3.32	ea
rebar package for 10" wide wall	$.40	sf	1.71	2%	1.68	$.24	sf
CEC rebar package for 10" wide wall	$.40	sf	.55	4%	.53	$.75	sf
insulating foam stay-in-place foundation wall forms	$1.47	sf	1	0%	1	$1.47	sf
Pier							
concrete	$101.00	cy	8.6	6%	8.08	$12.50	lf
fiber tube with bracing	$96.40	10' tube	3.33	2%	3.26	$29.60	ea
prefabricated rebar cage	$.40	pound	.01	0%	.01	$40.00	lf
Grade beam							
concrete for 12" by 18"	$101.00	cy	18	6%	16.92	$5.97	lf
concrete for 12" by 24"	$101.00	cy	13.5	6%	12.69	$7.96	lf
concrete for 14" by 18"	$101.00	cy	15.43	6%	14.50	$6.97	lf
concrete for 14" by 24"	$101.00	cy	11.57	6%	10.88	$9.28	lf
concrete for 16" by 18"	$101.00	cy	13.5	6%	12.69	$7.96	lf
concrete for 16" by 24"	$101.00	cy	10.13	6%	9.52	$10.60	lf
concrete for 18" by 18"	$101.00	cy	12	6%	11.28	$8.95	lf
concrete for 18" by 24"	$101.00	cy	9	6%	8.46	$11.90	lf
rebar cage	$.40	pound	.01	0%	.01	$40.00	lf
Lightweight concrete flatwork							
per cy	$126.00	cy	1	6%	.94	$134.00	cy
2" slab	$126.00	cy	162	6%	152.28	$.83	sf
4" slab	$126.00	cy	81	6%	76.14	$1.65	sf
6" slab	$126.00	cy	54	6%	50.76	$2.48	sf
Concrete flatwork							
per cy	$101.00	cy	1	6%	.94	$107.40	cy
4" slab	$101.00	cy	81	6%	76.14	$1.33	sf
6" slab	$101.00	cy	54	6%	50.76	$1.99	sf
8" slab	$101.00	cy	40.5	6%	38.07	$2.65	sf
rebar #4, 24" on center	$.40	pound	.75	2%	.74	$.54	sf
rebar #4, 12" on center	$.40	pound	.37	2%	.36	$1.11	sf
wire mesh (6" x 6" #10)	$125.00	roll	.750	2%	735	$.17	sf
aggregate for 2" slab base	$7.40	cy	162	0%	162	$.05	sf
aggregate for 4" slab base	$7.40	cy	81	0%	81	$.09	sf
sand for 2" slab base	$7.40	cy	162	0%	162	$.05	sf
sand for 4" slab base	$7.40	cy	81	0%	81	$.09	sf
Sidewalk							
3" sidewalk	$101.00	cy	108	6%	101.52	$.99	sf
4" sidewalk	$101.00	cy	81	6%	76.14	$1.33	sf
6" sidewalk	$101.00	cy	54	6%	50.76	$1.99	sf
Rebar							
#3 (3/8" .376 pound per lf)	$3.62	20' bar	20	4%	19.2	$.19	lf
#4 (1/2" .668 pounds per lf)	$4.62	20' bar	20	4%	19.2	$.24	lf
#5 (5/8" 1.043 pounds per lf)	$7.18	20' bar	20	4%	19.2	$.37	lf
#6 (3/4" 1.502 pounds per lf)	$10.90	20' bar	20	4%	19.2	$.57	lf
#7 (7/8" 2.044 pounds per lf)	$14.80	20' bar	20	4%	19.2	$.77	lf
#8 (1" 2.670 pounds per lf)	$19.40	20' bar	20	4%	19.2	$1.01	lf

CEC = California Earthquake Code.

Concrete Rental Equipment

DESCRIPTION	PRICE	COVERAGE	UNIT PRICE
Forms			
plywood wall forms (per sf of form)	$.19 per day	.25 per sf	$.76 sf
steel curb & gutter forms	$.93 per day	1 lf	$.93 lf
Tractor-mounted auger			
hourly charge	$220.00 per hour	90 lf	$2.44 lf
delivery and take-home charge	$465.00 each	1 each	$465.00 ea
Concrete pump truck			
foundation wall	$135.00 hour	450 sf of wall	$.30 sf
footings	$135.00 hour	112 lf of footing	$1.21 lf
flatwork	$135.00 hour	475 sf of flat	$.28 sf
piers	$135.00 hour	78 lf or pier	$1.73 lf
grade beam	$135.00 hour	146 lf of beam	$.92 lf
pressure grout	$135.00 hour	4 lf 2" pipe	$33.80 sf
Dump truck			
5 cy, average aggregate base haul	$67.00 day	540 sf	$.12 sf
Jackhammer with compressor			
foundation wall demo	$200.00 day	110 sf	$1.82 sf
footing demo	$200.00 day	66 lf	$3.03 lf
flatwork demo	$200.00 day	295 sf	$.68 sf
grade beam demo	$200.00 day	46 lf	$4.35 lf
jacket grade beam	$200.00 day	42 lf	$4.76 lf
jacket pier	$200.00 day	5.6 each	$35.70 ea
curb & gutter	$200.00 day	145 lf	$1.38 lf
Portable concrete saw			
wall sawing	$140.00 day	78 1" x 1'	$1.79 lf
floor sawing	$110.00 day	160 1" x 1'	$.69 lf
Concrete core drill			
per day	$96.00 day	125 1" x 1'	$.77 lf
Crane			
concrete pier removal	$639.00 day	98 day	$6.52 lf
Pressure pot			
for pressurized epoxy injection	$187.00 day	120 day	$1.56 lf
Backhoe			
per day	$497.00 day	322 day	$1.54 cy

Concrete Labor

LABORER	BASE WAGE	PAID LEAVE	TRUE WAGE	FICA	FUTA	WORKER'S COMP.	UNEMPLOY. INSUR.	HEALTH INSUR.	RETIRE (401k)	LIABILITY INSUR.	COST PER HOUR
Concrete form installer	$23.80	1.86	$25.66	1.96	.21	6.21	2.23	2.92	.77	3.85	**$43.80**
Concrete finisher	$23.60	1.84	$25.44	1.95	.20	6.16	2.21	2.92	.76	3.82	**$43.50**
Concrete finisher's helper	$19.20	1.50	$20.70	1.58	.17	5.01	1.80	2.92	.62	3.11	**$35.90**
Equipment operator	$30.80	2.40	$33.20	2.54	.27	6.04	2.89	2.92	1.00	4.98	**$53.80**
Plasterer	$23.60	1.84	$25.44	1.95	.20	7.38	2.21	2.92	.76	3.82	**$44.70**
Concrete saw operator	$22.00	1.72	$23.72	1.81	.19	4.31	2.06	2.92	.71	3.56	**$39.30**
Compaction grouter	$34.30	2.68	$36.98	2.83	.30	8.96	3.22	2.92	1.11	5.55	**$61.90**
Laborer	$16.60	1.29	$17.89	1.37	.14	4.33	1.56	2.92	.54	2.68	**$31.40**
Demolition laborer	$14.40	1.12	$15.52	1.19	.12	5.01	1.35	2.92	.47	2.33	**$28.90**

Paid Leave is calculated based on two weeks paid vacation, one week sick leave, and seven paid holidays. Employer's matching portion of **FICA** is 7.65 percent. **FUTA** (Federal Unemployment) is .8 percent. **Worker's Compensation** was calculated using a national average of 24.17 percent for the concrete trade; 18.16 percent for the equipment operator, 18.16 percent for the concrete saw operator; 28.93 percent for the plastering trade; 24.17 percent for the compaction grouting specialist; and 32.20 percent for the demolition laborer. **Unemployment insurance** was calculated using a national average of 8.7 percent. **Health insurance** was calculated based on a projected national average for 2005 of $580 per employee (and family when applicable) per month. Employer pays 80 percent for a per month cost of $464 per employee. **Retirement** is based on a 401(k) retirement program with employer matching of 50 percent. Employee contributions to the 401(k) plan are an average of 6 percent of the true wage. **Liability insurance** is based on a national average of 14.0 percent.

Concrete Labor Productivity

WORK DESCRIPTION	LABORER	COST PER HOUR	PRODUCTIVITY	UNIT PRICE
Demolition				
remove footings including rebar	demolition laborer	$28.90	1.64	$47.40 cy
remove footings including CEC rebar	demolition laborer	$28.90	1.96	$56.60 cy
remove footings with rebar	demolition laborer	$28.90	.121	$3.50 lf
remove footings with CEC rebar	demolition laborer	$28.90	.147	$4.25 lf
remove foundation including rebar	demolition laborer	$28.90	2.44	$70.50 cy
remove foundation including CEC rebar	demolition laborer	$28.90	2.94	$85.00 cy
remove 5" or 6" foundation with rebar	demolition laborer	$28.90	.073	$2.11 sf
remove 5" or 6" foundation with CEC rebar	demolition laborer	$28.90	.088	$2.54 sf
remove 8" or 10" foundation with rebar	demolition laborer	$28.90	.076	$2.20 sf
remove 8" or 10" foundation with CEC rebar	demolition laborer	$28.90	.092	$2.66 sf
remove footing & foundation with rebar	demolition laborer	$28.90	1.96	$56.60 cy
remove footing & foundation with CEC rebar	demolition laborer	$28.90	2.33	$67.30 cy
remove footing & 3' foundation	demolition laborer	$28.90	.346	$10.00 lf
remove footing & 3' foundation with CEC rebar	demolition laborer	$28.90	.418	$12.10 lf
remove footing & 4' foundation	demolition laborer	$28.90	.422	$12.20 lf
remove footing & 4' foundation with CEC rebar	demolition laborer	$28.90	.510	$14.70 lf
remove pier per cy	demolition laborer	$28.90	.699	$20.20 cy
remove pier	demolition laborer	$28.90	.082	$2.37 lf
remove grade beam per cy	demolition laborer	$28.90	2.33	$67.30 cy
remove grade beam	demolition laborer	$28.90	.174	$5.03 lf
remove lightweight slab	demolition laborer	$28.90	.026	$.75 sf
remove lightweight slab with rebar	demolition laborer	$28.90	.029	$.84 sf
remove lightweight slab with wire mesh	demolition laborer	$28.90	.031	$.90 sf
remove slab	demolition laborer	$28.90	.027	$.78 sf
remove slab with rebar	demolition laborer	$28.90	.030	$.87 sf
remove slab with wire mesh	demolition laborer	$28.90	.033	$.95 sf
remove sidewalk	demolition laborer	$28.90	.034	$.98 sf
remove curb & gutter	demolition laborer	$28.90	.145	$4.19 lf
remove step	demolition laborer	$28.90	.047	$1.36 lf
remove step landing	demolition laborer	$28.90	.046	$1.33 sf
Forming and rebar setting crew				
form and set rebar	concrete form installer	$43.80		
form and set rebar	laborer	$31.40		
form and set rebar	**forming crew**	**$37.60**		
Pouring and finishing crew				
pour & finish concrete	concrete finisher	$43.50		
pour & finish concrete	concrete finisher's helper	$35.90		
pour and finish concrete	**finishing crew**	**$39.70**		
Concrete footings				
form, set rebar, pour, & finish per cy	forming & finishing crews	$38.70	2.44	$94.40 cy
form, set CEC rebar, pour, & finish per cy	forming & finishing crews	$38.70	2.94	$114.00 cy
set forms for concrete footings	forming crew	$37.60	.041	$1.54 lf
strip forms from concrete footings & clean	forming crew	$37.60	.009	$.34 lf
set rebar in forms for concrete footings	forming crew	$37.60	.036	$1.35 lf
set CEC rebar in forms for concrete footings	forming crew	$37.60	.067	$2.52 lf
pour and finish 16" by 10" footings	finishing crew	$39.70	.065	$2.58 lf
pour and finish 20" by 10" footings	finishing crew	$39.70	.074	$2.94 lf
pour and finish 24" by 12" footings	finishing crew	$39.70	.081	$3.22 lf
pour and finish 32" by 14" footings	finishing crew	$39.70	.091	$3.61 lf
Concrete foundation wall				
form, set rebar, pour, & finish per cy	forming & finishing crews	$38.70	2.70	$104.00 cy
form, set CEC rebar, pour, & finish per cy	forming & finishing crews	$38.70	3.13	$121.00 cy
set forms	forming crew	$37.60	.029	$1.09 sf
strip forms & clean	forming crew	$37.60	.006	$.23 sf
set rebar package	forming crew	$37.60	.037	$1.39 sf
set CEC rebar package	forming crew	$37.60	.067	$2.52 sf
pour and finish 5" wide wall	finishing crew	$39.70	.024	$.95 sf
pour and finish 6" wide wall	finishing crew	$39.70	.029	$1.15 sf
pour and finish 8" wide wall	finishing crew	$39.70	.039	$1.55 sf
pour and finish 10" wide wall	finishing crew	$39.70	.049	$1.95 sf

. . . More ➤

CEC = California Earthquake Code.

Concrete Labor Productivity *continued*

WORK DESCRIPTION	LABORER	COST	PRODUCTIVITY	UNIT PRICE
Tractor-mounted auger (hole drilling for pier)				
delivery and take home charges (mobilization) .....equipment operator		$53.80	6.25	**$336.00** *ea*
drill pier hole .....equipment operator		$53.80	.083	**$4.47** *sf*
Concrete pier				
form, set rebar cage, pour and finish per cy .....forming & finishing crews		$38.70	14.9	**$577.00** *cy*
set and brace fiber tube cap .....forming crew		$37.60	.125	**$4.70** *lf*
pour concrete pier .....finishing crew		$39.70	1.54	**$61.10** *lf*
set and brace fiber tube for above-grade pier .....forming crew		$37.60	.183	**$6.88** *lf*
strip fiber tube .....forming crew		$37.60	.056	**$2.11** *lf*
pour above-grade concrete pier .....finishing crew		$39.70	.185	**$7.34** *sf*
set rebar cage for concrete pier .....forming crew		$37.60	.091	**$3.42** *lf*
Jacket pier				
jackhammer for jacket, drill for new rebar .....demolition laborer		$28.90	2.32	**$67.00** *ea*
set forms .....forming crew		$37.60	1.09	**$41.00** *ea*
set rebar, secure with epoxy .....forming crew		$37.60	.833	**$31.30** *ea*
pour concrete jacket .....finishing crew		$39.70	1.30	**$51.60** *ea*
Grade beam				
form, set rebar cage, pour, and finish per cy .....forming & finishing crews		$38.70	4.00	**$155.00** *cy*
set forms .....forming crew		$37.60	.127	**$4.78** *lf*
set rebar cage .....forming crew		$37.60	.067	**$2.52** *lf*
pour and finish 12" by 18" .....finishing crew		$39.70	.073	**$2.90** *lf*
pour and finish 12" by 24" .....finishing crew		$39.70	.088	**$3.49** *lf*
pour and finish 14" by 18" .....finishing crew		$39.70	.118	**$4.68** *lf*
pour and finish 14" by 24" .....finishing crew		$39.70	.235	**$9.33** *lf*
pour and finish 16" by 18" .....finishing crew		$39.70	.353	**$14.00** *lf*
pour and finish 16" by 24" .....finishing crew		$39.70	.470	**$18.70** *lf*
pour and finish 18" by 18" .....finishing crew		$39.70	.118	**$4.68** *lf*
pour and finish 18" by 24" .....finishing crew		$39.70	.235	**$9.33** *lf*
Jacket grade beam				
jackhammer for jacket .....demolition laborer		$28.90	.088	**$2.54** *lf*
set forms .....forming crew		$37.60	.150	**$5.64** *lf*
set rebar, secure with epoxy .....forming crew		$37.60	.083	**$3.12** *lf*
pour concrete .....finishing crew		$39.70	.240	**$9.53** *lf*
Lightweight concrete flatwork				
form, pour, and finish per cy .....forming & finishing crews		$38.70	2.04	**$78.90** *cy*
pour and finish 2" slab .....finishing crew		$39.70	.012	**$.48** *sf*
pour and finish 4" slab .....finishing crew		$39.70	.013	**$.52** *sf*
pour and finish 6" slab .....finishing crew		$39.70	.015	**$.60** *sf*
Concrete flatwork				
form, pour, and finish per cy .....forming & finishing crews		$38.70	2.04	**$78.90** *cy*
set forms for concrete slab .....forming crew		$37.60	.011	**$.41** *sf*
set rebar 24" on center .....forming crew		$37.60	.036	**$1.35** *sf*
set rebar 12" on center .....forming crew		$37.60	.080	**$3.01** *sf*
set wire mesh .....forming crew		$37.60	.015	**$.56** *sf*
pour and finish 4" slab .....finishing crew		$39.70	.024	**$.95** *sf*
pour and finish 6" slab .....finishing crew		$39.70	.036	**$1.43** *sf*
pour and finish 8" slab .....finishing crew		$39.70	.036	**$1.43** *sf*
haul aggregate for slab base to job site .....equipment operator		$53.80	.002	**$.11** *sf*
spread 2" aggregate slab base .....laborer		$31.40	.013	**$.41** *sf*
spread 4" aggregate slab base .....laborer		$31.40	.015	**$.47** *sf*
haul sand for slab base to job site .....equipment operator		$53.80	.001	**$.05** *sf*
spread 2" sand slab base .....laborer		$31.40	.012	**$.38** *sf*
spread 4" sand slab base .....laborer		$31.40	.014	**$.44** *sf*
Sidewalk				
form, pour, and finish per cy .....forming & finishing crews		$38.70	4.17	**$161.00** *cy*
set forms .....forming crew		$37.60	.023	**$.86** *sf*
pour and finish 3" sidewalk .....finishing crew		$39.70	.019	**$.75** *sf*
pour and finish 4" sidewalk .....finishing crew		$39.70	.026	**$1.03** *sf*
pour and finish 6" sidewalk .....finishing crew		$39.70	.039	**$1.55** *sf*

. . . More ➤

CEC = California Earthquake Code.

Concrete Labor Productivity *continued*

WORK DESCRIPTION	LABORER	COST	PRODUCTIVITY	UNIT PRICE
Concrete dye				
trowel into wet concrete	finishing crew	$39.70	.009	$.36 sf
Stamp concrete				
slab or sidewalk	finishing crew	$39.70	.053	$2.10 sf
with paver pattern	finishing crew	$39.70	.045	$1.79 sf
grout stamped paver pattern joints	finishing crew	$39.70	.023	$.91 sf
Exposed aggregate				
Finish with exposed aggregate finish	finishing crew	$39.70	.019	$.75 sf
Curb & gutter				
set forms	forming crew	$37.60	.123	$4.62 lf
pour and finish	finishing crew	$39.70	.150	$5.96 lf
Concrete step				
form, set rebar, pour, and finish per cy	forming & finishing crews	$38.70	7.69	$298.00 cy
set forms and rebar per lf of step	forming crew	$37.60	.133	$5.00 lf
pour and finish per lf of step	finishing crew	$39.70	.100	$3.97 lf
set forms and rebar for landing per cubic foot	forming crew	$37.60	.011	$.41 cf
pour and finish landing per cubic foot	finishing crew	$39.70	.056	$2.22 cf
Saw concrete				
wall with rebar per lf, 1" deep	saw operator	$39.30	.111	$4.36 lf
wall with CEC rebar per lf, 1" deep	saw operator	$39.30	.125	$4.91 lf
floor per lf, 1" deep	saw operator	$39.30	.050	$1.97 lf
floor with rebar per lf, 1" deep	saw operator	$39.30	.054	$2.12 lf
floor with wire mesh per lf, 1" deep	saw operator	$39.30	.052	$2.04 lf
expansion joint in "green" slab	saw operator	$39.30	.189	$7.43 lf
Core drill concrete				
2" wall per inch of depth	saw operator	$39.30	.066	$2.59 li
4" wall per inch of depth	saw operator	$39.30	.073	$2.87 li
2" floor per inch of depth	saw operator	$39.30	.064	$2.52 li
4" floor per inch of depth	saw operator	$39.30	.067	$2.63 li
Set rebar				
#3 (3/8")	forming crew	$37.60	.014	$.53 lf
#4 (1/2")	forming crew	$37.60	.014	$.53 lf
#5 (5/8")	forming crew	$37.60	.014	$.53 lf
#6 (3/4")	forming crew	$37.60	.014	$.53 lf
#7 (7/8")	forming crew	$37.60	.015	$.56 lf
#8 (1")	forming crew	$37.60	.015	$.56 lf
Buttress foundation				
machine excavate to 12" to 24" of ext. foundation	equipment operator	$53.80	.027	$1.45 sf
hand excavate exterior of foundation	laborer	$31.40	.161	$5.06 sf
backfill buttressed foundation	laborer	$31.40	.048	$1.51 sf
set forms for exterior buttress	forming crew	$37.60	.021	$.79 sf
set rebar for exterior buttress	forming crew	$37.60	.017	$.64 sf
pour and finish exterior buttress	finishing crew	$39.70	.027	$1.07 sf
hand excavate interior crawl space for buttress	laborer	$31.40	.457	$14.30 sf
set forms for interior buttress in crawl space	forming crew	$37.60	.032	$1.20 sf
set rebar for interior buttress in crawl space	forming crew	$37.60	.023	$.86 sf
pour and finish interior buttress in crawl space	finishing crew	$39.70	.037	$1.47 sf
hand excavate interior foundation in basement	laborer	$31.40	.204	$6.41 sf
set forms for interior buttress in basement	forming crew	$37.60	.025	$.94 sf
set rebar for interior buttress in basement	forming crew	$37.60	.019	$.71 sf
pour and finish interior buttress in basement	finishing crew	$39.70	.032	$1.27 sf
Compaction grouting crew				
core drill, insert pipes, pump grout	compaction grouting specialist	$61.90		
core drill, insert pipes, pump grout	laborer	$31.40		
core drill, insert pipes, pump grout	**compaction grouting crew**	$46.70		
Foundation & footing stabilization with pressurized grout				
2" core drill through footings	compaction grouting crew	$46.70	.379	$17.70 ea
insert 2" pipes into ground beneath footings	compaction grouting crew	$46.70	.143	$6.68 lf
pump pressurized grout through pipes	compaction grouting crew	$46.70	.250	$11.70 lf

CEC = California Earthquake Code.

9 .... *Demolition & Hauling*

Item Description	Unit			Total	
Minimum demolition charge *Demo* .... Labor ....86.70 Equipment 100.00	ea	–	–	$186.70	◄ **MINIMUM**
Dump charge per cy *Demo* Fee 45.70	cy	–	–	$45.70	◄ **DUMP FEE** *Typical metro area landfill fees. Will be up to 60% higher in major metro areas and 30% to 60% lower in rural areas.*
Dump charge per ton *Demo* Fee 85.80	tn	–	–	$85.80	
3 cy dumpster rental per week *Demo* .... Equipment 110.00	ea	–	–	$110.00	◄ **DUMPSTER** *Includes up to two dumps per week.*
5 cy dumpster rental per week *Demo* .... Equipment 190.00	ea	–	–	$190.00	
10 cy dumpster rental per week *Demo* .... Equipment 240.00	ea	–	–	$240.00	
30 cy dumpster rental per week *Demo* .... Equipment 350.00	ea	–	–	$350.00	
Minimum dumpster charge *Demo* .... Equipment 150.00	ea	–	–	$150.00	
Plywood refuse chute *Demo* Materials ....13.10 Labor 47.10	lf	–	–	$60.20	◄ **REFUSE CHUTE**
Minimum charge for plywood refuse chute *Demo* Materials ....69.00 Labor 106.00	ea	–	–	$175.00	
18" prefabricated circular steel refuse chute *Demo* Materials ....14.70 Labor 34.10	lf	–	–	$48.80	
36" prefabricated circular steel refuse chute *Demo* Materials ....26.90 Labor 46.20	lf	–	–	$73.10	
Minimum charge for circular steel refuse chute *Demo* Materials ....78.00 Labor 95.40	ea	–	–	$173.40	
Debris hauling (by trailer or dump truck) per cy *Demo* .... Equipment 21.60	cy	–	–	$21.60	◄ **DEBRIS HAULING**
Debris hauling (by trailer or dump truck) per ton *Demo* .... Equipment 58.80	tn	–	–	$58.80	
Debris hauling per pick-up truck load *Demo* .... Equipment 22.20	ea	–	–	$22.20	
Strip typical room to bare walls and sub-floor *Demo* .... Labor 2.14	sf	–	–	$2.14	◄ **STRIP ROOM** *Remove all wall and floor coverings, doors, trim, and underlayment. Stud walls and plywood subfloor remain. Per sf of floor.*
Strip bathroom to bare walls and sub-floor *Demo* .... Labor 4.34	sf	–	–	$4.34	

Item Description	Unit			Total
STRIP ROOM ▶ *continued*	**Strip kitchen to bare walls and sub-floor**	sf	–	–	$3.32
	Demo .... Labor 3.32				
For rooms with contents add 4%.	**Strip utility room to bare walls and sub-floor**	sf	–	–	$2.49
	Demo .... Labor 2.49				
	Strip laundry room to bare walls and sub-floor	sf	–	–	$2.75
	Demo .... Labor 2.75				

TIME & MATERIAL CHARTS (selected items)

Demolition & Hauling Materials

DESCRIPTION	MATERIAL PRICE	GROSS COVERAGE	WASTE	NET COVERAGE	UNIT PRICE
Refuse chute					
plywood					$13.10 lf
18" prefabricated circular steel					$14.70 lf
36" prefabricated circular steel					$26.90 lf

Demolition & Hauling Rental Equipment

DESCRIPTION	PRICE	COVERAGE	UNIT PRICE
Dumpster rental per week			
3 cy	$100.00 week		$100.00 ea
5 cy	$190.00 week		$190.00 ea
10 cy	$240.00 week		$240.00 ea
30 cy	$350.00 week		$350.00 ea
Truck rental with driver			
3 cy dump truck	$475.00 day	22 cy	$21.60 cy
3 cy dump truck	$475.00 day	8.08 ton	$58.80 ton
pick-up truck	$200.00 day	9 load	$22.20 ea

Demolition & Hauling Labor

LABORER	BASE WAGE	PAID LEAVE	TRUE WAGE	FICA	FUTA	WORKER'S COMP.	UNEMPLOY. INSUR.	HEALTH INSUR.	RETIRE (401K)	LIABILITY INSUR.	COST PER HOUR
Demolition laborer	$14.40	1.12	$15.52	1.19	.12	5.01	1.35	2.92	.47	2.33	$28.90

Paid Leave is calculated based on two weeks paid vacation, one week sick leave, and seven paid holidays. Employer's matching portion of **FICA** is 7.65 percent. **FUTA** (Federal Unemployment) is .8 percent. **Worker's Compensation** for Demolition was calculated using a national average of 32.2 percent. **Unemployment insurance** was calculated using a national average of 8.7 percent. **Health insurance** was calculated based on a projected national average for 2005 of $580 per employee (and family when applicable) per month. Employer pays 80 percent for a per month cost of $464 per employee. **Retirement** is based on a 401(k) retirement program with employer matching of 50 percent. Employee contributions to the 401(k) plan are an average of 6 percent of the true wage. **Liability insurance** is based on a national average of 14.0 percent.

Demolition & Hauling Labor Productivity

WORK DESCRIPTION	LABORER	COST PER HOUR	PRODUCTIVITY	UNIT PRICE
Build / install refuse chute				
plywood	demolition laborer	$28.90	1.63	$47.10 lf
18" prefabricated circular steel	demolition laborer	$28.90	1.18	$34.10 lf
36" prefabricated circular steel	demolition laborer	$28.90	1.60	$46.20 lf
Strip room to bare walls and sub-floor				
typical	demolition laborer	$28.90	.074	$2.14 sf
bathroom	demolition laborer	$28.90	.150	$4.34 sf
kitchen	demolition laborer	$28.90	.115	$3.32 sf
utility	demolition laborer	$28.90	.086	$2.49 sf
laundry	demolition laborer	$28.90	.095	$2.75 sf

10 .... *Doors*

Item Description	Unit	Remove	Replace	Total	
Minimum charge for door work *Replace* Materials ......35.00 Labor.........109.00	ea	–	$144.00	$144.00	◄ **MINIMUM**
Hardboard smooth or wood-textured folding door (per section) *Replace* Materials ......29.20 Labor ....17.10 *Remove*..................... Labor 3.29	ea	$3.29	$46.30	$49.59	◄ **FOLDING DOOR** *Folding doors usually used in closets.* **Priced per section**. *For jamb & casing see page 102.*
Hardboard wood-textured & embossed folding door (per section) *Replace* Materials ......33.40 Labor ....17.10 *Remove*..................... Labor ....3.29 ► Referred to by the brand name "Colonist" in many areas of the country.	ea	$3.29	$50.50	$53.79	
Mahogany (lauan) or birch veneer folding door (per section) *Replace* Materials ......31.30 Labor ....17.10 *Remove*..................... Labor 3.29	ea	$3.29	$48.40	$51.69	
Ash or oak veneer folding door (per section) *Replace* Materials ......34.10 Labor ....17.10 *Remove*..................... Labor 3.29	ea	$3.29	$51.20	$54.49	
Walnut or cherry veneer folding door (per section) *Replace* Materials ......38.90 Labor ....17.10 *Remove*..................... Labor 3.29	ea	$3.29	$56.00	$59.29	
Paint-grade pine panel folding door (per section) *Replace* Materials ......50.70 Labor ....17.10 *Remove*..................... Labor 3.29	ea	$3.29	$67.80	$71.09	
Stain-grade pine panel folding door (per section) *Replace* Materials ......62.60 Labor ....17.10 *Remove*..................... Labor 3.29	ea	$3.29	$79.70	$82.99	
Paint-grade pine full-louvered folding door (per section) *Replace* Materials ......59.80 Labor ....17.10 *Remove*..................... Labor 3.29	ea	$3.29	$76.90	$80.19	
Stain-grade pine full-louvered folding door (per section) *Replace* Materials ......69.50 Labor ....17.10 *Remove*..................... Labor 3.29	ea	$3.29	$86.60	$89.89	
Paint-grade pine half-louvered folding door (per section) *Replace* Materials ......57.00 Labor ....17.10 *Remove*..................... Labor 3.29	ea	$3.29	$74.10	$77.39	
Stain-grade pine half-louvered folding door (per section) *Replace* Materials ......66.00 Labor ....17.10 *Remove*..................... Labor 3.29	ea	$3.29	$83.10	$86.39	
Red oak folding panel door (per section) *Replace* Materials ......76.50 Labor ....17.10 *Remove*..................... Labor 3.29	ea	$3.29	$93.60	$96.89	
Folding mirrored door (per section) *Replace* Materials ......87.60 Labor ....17.10 *Remove*..................... Labor 3.29	ea	$3.29	$104.70	$107.99	

USING DOOR ITEMS

When replacing a door, select the door type, then the jamb type, and add the two together.

Door prices are for the door slab only and include routing and drilling for standard hardware and hinges. Door tear-out is for the door slab only. Use this tear-out price when removing the slab and leaving the jamb and casing intact.

Jamb & casing prices include the cost to pre-hang the door in the jamb and the cost of hinges (but not the door lockset). Tear-out includes removal of the entire door. Use this tear-out price when removing the door, jamb and casing.

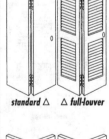

standard △   △ full-louver

half-louver △   △ panel

Item Description			Unit	Remove	Replace	Total
FOLDING DOOR ▶ *continued*	**Remove folding doors for work, then reinstall (per section)**		ea	–	$6.44	$6.44
	Replace	Labor 6.44				
BYPASSING ▶ **DOOR** *Usually used in closets.* **Priced per door sec-** **tion.** *Includes track and* *hardware. For jamb &* *casing see below.*	**Hardboard smooth or wood-textured bypassing door (per section)**		ea	$4.02	$90.50	$94.52
	Replace Materials 57.70	Labor 32.80				
	Remove......................	Labor 4.02				
	Hardboard wood-textured & embossed bypassing door (per section)		ea	$4.02	$97.40	$101.42
	Replace Materials 64.60	Labor 32.80				
	Remove......................	Labor 4.02				
	▶ Referred to by the brand name "Colonist" in many areas of the country.					
	Mahogany (lauan) or birch veneer bypassing door (per section)		ea	$4.02	$95.40	$99.42
	Replace Materials 62.60	Labor 32.80				
	Remove......................	Labor 4.02				
	Ash or oak veneer bypassing door (per section)		ea	$4.02	$98.10	$102.12
	Replace Materials 65.30	Labor 32.80				
	Remove......................	Labor 4.02				
	Walnut or cherry veneer bypassing door (per section)		ea	$4.02	$114.10	$118.12
	Replace Materials 81.30	Labor 32.80				
	Remove......................	Labor 4.02				
	Paint-grade pine panel bypassing door (per section)		ea	$4.02	$133.80	$137.82
	Replace Materials 101.00	Labor 32.80				
	Remove...................:	Labor 4.02				
	Stain-grade pine panel bypassing door (per section)		ea	$4.02	$152.80	$156.82
	Replace Materials 120.00	Labor 32.80				
	Remove......................	Labor 4.02				
	Red oak bypassing panel door (per section)		ea	$4.02	$186.80	$190.82
	Replace Materials 154.00	Labor 32.80				
	Remove......................	Labor 4.02				
	Paint-grade pine full-louvered bypassing door (per section)		ea	$4.02	$149.80	$153.82
	Replace Materials 117.00	Labor 32.80				
	Remove......................	Labor 4.02				
	Stain-grade pine full-louvered bypassing door (per section)		ea	$4.02	$169.80	$173.82
	Replace Materials 137.00	Labor 32.80				
	Remove......................	Labor 4.02				
	Paint-grade pine half-louvered bypassing door (per section)		ea	$4.02	$143.80	$147.82
	Replace Materials 111.00	Labor 32.80				
	Remove......................	Labor 4.02				
	Stain-grade pine half-louvered bypassing door (per section)		ea	$4.02	$162.80	$166.82
	Replace Materials 130.00	Labor 32.80				
	Remove......................	Labor 4.02				
	Mirrored bypassing door (per section)		ea	$4.02	$202.80	$206.82
	Replace Materials 170.00	Labor 32.80				
	Remove......................	Labor 4.02				
	Remove bypassing sliding doors for work, then reinstall (per section)		ea	–	$9.57	$9.57
	Replace	Labor 9.57				
JAMB & CASING ▶ **FOR CLOSET DOOR** *Per lf around opening.*	**Paint-grade jamb & casing for folding or bypassing door opening**		lf	$.75	$5.77	$6.52
	Replace Materials 1.03	Labor 4.74				
	Remove......................	Labor .... .75				

Item Description	Unit	Remove	Replace	Total
Stain-grade pine jamb & casing for folding or bypassing door opening	lf	$.75	$5.88	$6.63
Replace Materials ...... 1.14 Labor 4.74				
Remove .... Labor .... .75				
Birch jamb & casing for folding or bypassing door opening	lf	$.75	$5.85	$6.60
Replace Materials ...... 1.11 Labor 4.74				
Remove .... Labor .... .75				
Mahogany jamb & casing for folding or bypassing door opening	lf	$.75	$6.32	$7.07
Replace Materials ....1.58 Labor 4.74				
Remove .... Labor .... .75				
▶ Deduct **$.18** for mahogany veneer jamb & casing.				
Ash or oak jamb & casing for folding or bypassing door opening	lf	$.75	$6.46	$7.21
Replace Materials ....1.72 Labor 4.74				
Remove .... Labor .... .75				
▶ Deduct **$.15** for ash or oak veneer jamb & casing.				
Walnut or cherry jamb & casing for folding or bypassing door opening	lf	$.75	$7.03	$7.78
Replace Materials ....2.29 Labor 4.74				
Remove .... Labor .... .75				
▶ Deduct **$.13** for walnut or cherry veneer jamb & casing.				
Hardboard smooth or wood-textured interior door	ea	$6.27	$87.25	$93.52
Replace Materials ......77.900 Labor 9.35				
Remove .... Labor 6.27				
Hardboard wood-textured and embossed interior door	ea	$6.27	$117.35	$123.62
Replace Materials ....108.00 Labor 9.35				
Remove .... Labor 6.27				
▶ Called "colonist" style in many areas of the country.				
Mahogany or birch veneer interior door	ea	$6.27	$95.55	$101.82
Replace Materials ......86.20 Labor 9.35				
Remove .... Labor 6.27				
Ash or oak veneer interior door	ea	$6.27	$103.15	$109.42
Replace Materials ......93.80 Labor 9.35				
Remove .... Labor 6.27				
Walnut or cherry veneer interior door	ea	$6.27	$131.35	$137.62
Replace Materials ..... 122.00 Labor 9.35				
Remove .... Labor 6.27				
Mirrored interior door	ea	$6.27	$211.35	$217.62
Replace Materials ....202.00 Labor 9.35				
Remove .... Labor 6.27				
Plastic laminate faced interior door	ea	$6.27	$322.35	$328.62
Replace Materials .....313.00 Labor 9.35				
Remove .... Labor 6.27				
Add for solid-core, fire-rated interior door	ea	–	$111.00	$111.00
Replace Materials 111.00				
▶ 1 hour fire rating.				
Paint-grade wood French door	ea	$6.27	$211.35	$217.62
Replace Materials ....202.00 Labor 9.35				
Remove .... Labor 6.27				

RELATED ITEMS

Cleaning........................57
Door Hardware 127
Finish Carpentry..........201
Painting 334

◀ **INTERIOR DOOR**
Hollow-core interior doors. Pre-drilled and routed for hardware and hinges. For jamb & casing see page 104.

◁ add for fire-rated

◀ **FRENCH DOOR**
For interior French doors Pre-drilled and routed for hardware and hinges. For jamb & casing see page 104.

Item Description	Unit	Remove	Replace	Total
FRENCH DOOR ▶ *continued* **Stain-grade fir French door**	ea	$6.27	$252.35	$258.62
Replace Materials ....243.00 Labor 9.35				
Remove .... Labor 6.27				
Metal French door	ea	$6.27	$218.35	$224.62
Replace Materials....209.00 Labor 9.35				
Remove .... Labor 6.27				
Full-lite door with simulated French door grid	ea	$6.27	$190.35	$196.62
Replace Materials.....181.00 Labor 9.35				
Remove .... Labor 6.27				
add for double-glazed ▷ **Add for double-glazed insulated glass in French door**	ea	–	$78.50	$78.50
Replace Materials 78.50				
add for fire-rated ▷ **Add for fire-rated glass in French door**	ea	–	$90.40	$90.40
Replace Materials......90.40				
▶ 1 hour fire rating.				
FULL-LOUVERED ▶ **DOOR** **Paint-grade full-louvered door**	ea	$6.27	$179.35	$185.62
Replace Materials.....170.00 Labor 9.35				
Remove .... Labor 6.27				
Stain-grade pine full-louvered door	ea	$6.27	$218.35	$224.62
Replace Materials....209.00 Labor 9.35				
Remove .... Labor 6.27				
HALF-LOUVERED ▶ **DOOR** **Paint-grade pine half-louvered door**	ea	$6.27	$162.35	$168.62
Replace Materials.....153.00 Labor 9.35				
Remove .... Labor 6.27				
Stain-grade pine half-louvered door	ea	$6.27	$209.35	$215.62
Replace Materials....200.00 Labor 9.35				
Remove .... Labor 6.27				
REMOVE ▶ **INTERIOR DOOR & REINSTALL** **Remove door slab for work, then reinstall**	ea	–	$6.57	$6.57
Replace .... Labor 6.57				
Remove door, jamb & casing for work, then reinstall	ea	–	$70.90	$70.90
Replace .... Labor...........70.90				
Remove double door slabs for work, then reinstall	ea	–	$12.70	$12.70
Replace .... Labor...........12.70				
Remove double doors, jamb & casing for work, then reinstall	ea	–	$116.00	$116.00
Replace .... Labor..........116.00				
JAMB & CASING ▶ **FOR INTERIOR DOOR** *Per door.* **Paint-grade jamb & casing for interior door**	ea	$11.20	$80.60	$91.80
Replace Materials ......18.40 Labor...........62.20				
Remove...................... Labor 11.20				
Paint-grade jamb & casing for double interior door	ea	$11.20	$96.50	$107.70
Replace Materials ......34.30 Labor...........62.20				
Remove...................... Labor 11.20				
Stain-grade pine jamb & casing for interior door	ea	$11.20	$83.20	$94.40
Replace Materials ......21.00 Labor...........62.20				
Remove...................... Labor 11.20				

Item Description	Unit	Remove	Replace	Total	
Stain-grade pine jamb & casing for double interior door	ea	$11.20	$100.60	$111.80	
Replace Materials......38.40 Labor...........62.20					
Remove....................... Labor...........11.20					
Birch jamb & casing for interior door	ea	$11.20	$84.90	$96.10	
Replace Materials......22.70 Labor...........62.20					
Remove....................... Labor...........11.20					
Birch jamb & casing for double interior door	ea	$11.20	$103.70	$114.90	
Replace Materials ......41.50 Labor...........62.20					
Remove....................... Labor...........11.20					
Mahogany jamb & casing for interior door	ea	$11.20	$89.30	$100.50	
Replace Materials......27.10 Labor...........62.20					
Remove....................... Labor...........11.20					
▶ Deduct **$1.70** for mahogany veneer jamb & casing.					
Mahogany jamb & casing for double interior door	ea	$11.20	$114.50	$125.70	
Replace Materials......52.30 Labor...........62.20					
Remove....................... Labor...........11.20					
▶ Deduct **$.76** for mahogany veneer jamb & casing.					
Ash or oak jamb & casing for interior door	ea	$11.20	$94.90	$106.10	
Replace Materials......32.70 Labor...........62.20					
Remove....................... Labor...........11.20					
▶ Deduct **$3.10** for ash or oak veneer jamb & casing.					
Ash or oak jamb & casing for double interior door	ea	$11.20	$120.60	$131.80	
Replace Materials......58.40 Labor...........62.20					
Remove....................... Labor...........11.20					
▶ Deduct **$2.60** for ash or oak veneer jamb & casing.					
Walnut or cherry jamb & casing for interior door	ea	$11.20	$109.50	$120.70	
Replace Materials ......47.30 Labor...........62.20					
Remove....................... Labor...........11.20					
▶ Deduct **$2.40** for walnut or cherry veneer jamb & casing.					
Walnut or cherry jamb & casing for double interior door	ea	$11.20	$149.80	$161.00	
Replace Materials......87.60 Labor...........62.20					
Remove....................... Labor...........11.20					
▶ Deduct **$4.30** for walnut or cherry veneer jamb & casing.					
Steel jamb & casing for interior door	ea	$11.20	$187.20	$198.40	◁ steel jamb & casing
Replace Materials.....125.00 Labor...........62.20					
Remove....................... Labor...........11.20					
Steel jamb & casing for double interior door	ea	$14.00	$305.20	$319.20	
Replace Materials ....243.00 Labor...........62.20					
Remove....................... Labor...........14.00					
Add for jamb & casing installed for pocket door	ea	–	$29.60	$29.60	◁ add for pocket door
Replace Materials.......15.60 Labor...........14.00					
▶ Add to price above when jamb is installed for a pocket door.					
Add for jamb & casing installed for double pocket door	ea	–	$64.30	$64.30	
Replace Materials......26.40 Labor...........37.90					
▶ Add to price above when jamb is installed for a double pocket door.					
Rough framing package for pocket door in 2" x 4" wall	ea	–	$91.00	$91.00	◀ **ROUGH FRAMING FOR POCKET DOOR**
Replace Materials......25.70 Labor...........65.30					

RELATED ITEMS

Cleaning....................57
Door Hardware 127
Finish Carpentry..........201
Painting 334

continued on next page

	Item Description	Unit	Remove	Replace	Total
ROUGH FRAMING ▶ FOR POCKET DOOR *continued*	**Rough framing package for double pocket doors in 2" x 4" wall** *Replace* Materials ......41.20 Labor 125.00	ea	–	$166.20	$166.20
Includes track, hardware, and side framing kit. Antique systems include framing for walls on each side of the pocket door.	**Rough framing package for pocket door in 2" x 6" wall** *Replace* Materials ......27.80 Labor 66.10	ea	–	$93.90	$93.90
	Rough framing package for double pocket doors in 2" x 6" wall *Replace* Materials ......49.60 Labor 128.00	ea	–	$177.60	$177.60
	Rough framing package for pocket door in 2" x 8" wall *Replace* Materials ......29.90 Labor 67.00	ea	–	$96.90	$96.90
	Rough framing package for double pocket doors in 2" x 8" wall *Replace* Materials ......52.80 Labor 132.00	ea	–	$184.80	$184.80
	Rough framing package for antique pocket door *Replace* Materials ......90.40 Labor 107.00	ea	–	$197.40	$197.40
	Rough framing package for antique double pocket doors *Replace* Materials ......161.00 Labor 223.00	ea	–	$384.00	$384.00
POCKET DOOR ▶ TRACK	**Overhead pocket door track for antique pocket door system** *Replace* Materials ......52.80 Labor ....56.60 *Remove* .... Labor 21.70	ea	$21.70	$109.40	$131.10
	Overhead pocket door track for antique double pocket door system *Replace* Materials ......72.30 Labor ....102.00 *Remove* .... Labor 37.00	ea	$37.00	$174.30	$211.30
	Clean and realign overhead pocket door track *Replace* .... Labor 85.30	ea	–	$85.30	$85.30
	Floor track for antique pocket door system *Replace* Materials ......58.40 Labor ....52.60 *Remove* .... Labor 21.70	ea	$21.70	$111.00	$132.70
	Floor track for antique double pocket door system *Replace* Materials ......78.50 Labor ....95.70 *Remove* .... Labor 37.00	ea	$37.00	$174.20	$211.20
	Clean and realign pocket door floor track *Replace* .... Labor 115.00	ea	–	$115.00	$115.00
REMOVE ▶ POCKET DOOR & REINSTALL	**Remove pocket door and trim for work, then reinstall** *Replace* .... Labor 50.00	ea	–	$50.00	$50.00
	Remove pocket door, jamb & casing for work, then reinstall *Replace* .... Labor 141.00	ea	–	$141.00	$141.00
	Remove double pocket doors & trim for work, then reinstall *Replace* .... Labor 68.70	ea	–	$68.70	$68.70
	Remove double pocket doors, jamb & casing for work, then reinstall *Replace* .... Labor 147.00	ea	–	$147.00	$147.00
PANEL DOOR ▶ *continued on next page*	**Paint-grade panel door** *Replace* Materials ....535.00 Labor ....7.74 *Remove* .... Labor ....6.27 ▶ Add **67%** for panel door custom milled to match.	ea	$6.27	$542.74	$549.01

Item Description	Unit	Remove	Replace	Total
Reconditioned painted antique panel door *Replace* Materials ....431.00 Labor ....7.74 *Remove* .... Labor 6.27	ea	$6.27	$438.74	$445.01
Reconditioned grained antique panel door *Replace* Materials ....626.00 Labor ....7.74 *Remove* .... Labor ....6.27 ▶ "Graining" is a method of painting wood to make it look like the grain of another wood. This process was used extensively in the 19th century, most often to paint pine to appear like quartersawn oak.	ea	$6.27	$633.74	$640.01
Stain-grade fir panel door *Replace* Materials ....709.00 Labor ....7.74 *Remove* .... Labor ....6.27 ▶ Add **35%** for panel door custom milled to match.	ea	$6.27	$716.74	$723.01
Reconditioned stained fir antique panel door *Replace* Materials ....649.00 Labor ....7.74 *Remove* .... Labor 6.27	ea	$6.27	$656.74	$663.01
Redwood panel door *Replace* Materials.....765.00 Labor ....7.74 *Remove* .... Labor ....6.27 ▶ Add **26%** for panel door custom milled to match.	ea	$6.27	$772.74	$779.01
Reconditioned redwood antique panel door *Replace* Materials ....737.00 Labor ....7.74 *Remove* .... Labor 6.27	ea	$6.27	$744.74	$751.01
Cypress panel door *Replace* Materials ....726.00 Labor ....7.74 *Remove* .... Labor ....6.27 ▶ Add **17%** for panel door custom milled to match.	ea	$6.27	$733.74	$740.01
Reconditioned cypress antique panel door *Replace* Materials.....674.00 Labor ....7.74 *Remove* .... Labor 6.27	ea	$6.27	$681.74	$688.01
Oak panel door *Replace* Materials....646.00 Labor ....7.74 *Remove* .... Labor ....6.27 ▶ Add **35%** for panel door custom milled to match.	ea	$6.27	$653.74	$660.01
Reconditioned painted oak antique panel door *Replace* Materials....480.00 Labor ....7.74 *Remove* .... Labor 6.27	ea	$6.27	$487.74	$494.01
Reconditioned stained oak antique panel door *Replace* Materials....556.00 Labor ....7.74 *Remove* .... Labor 6.27	ea	$6.27	$563.74	$570.01
Mahogany panel door *Replace* Materials....744.00 Labor ....7.74 *Remove* .... Labor ....6.27 ▶ Add **29%** for panel door custom milled to match.	ea	$6.27	$751.74	$758.01
Reconditioned mahogany antique panel door *Replace* Materials....688.00 Labor ....7.74 *Remove* .... Labor 6.27	ea	$6.27	$695.74	$702.01

◀ **PANEL DOOR**
continued

6 to 9 panels. Each wood species includes line items for a new door, a reconditioned door, and a door that is custom milled to match a specific pattern. For more see below.

For interior jamb & casing see page 104. For exterior jamb and casing see page 116.

RECONDITIONED DOOR

Reconditioned panel doors have been removed from a historical structure and reconditioned by an architectural salvage company.

These doors will have some scratches, dents, patching and may have been stripped of paint.

CUSTOM-MILLED DOOR

Custom-milled doors include the additional costs for panel doors that are milled to match an existing door pattern.

For these doors it is necessary to cut custom shaper knives for the panels and custom molder (or shaper) knives for the stiles and rails. Add **60%** if milling two or less doors.

RELATED ITEMS

Cleaning......................57
Door Hardware 127
Finish Carpentry..........201
Painting 334

Item Description	Unit	Remove	Replace	Total
PANEL DOOR ▶ *continued* **Walnut panel door**	ea	$6.27	$1,137.74	$1,144.01
Replace Materials ...1130.00 Labor 7.74				
Remove .... Labor 6.27				
▶ Add **17%** for panel door custom milled to match.				
Reconditioned walnut antique panel door	ea	$6.27	$1,001.74	$1,008.01
Replace Materials ....994.00 Labor 7.74				
Remove .... Labor 6.27				
ADDITIONAL ▶ **PANEL DOOR COSTS** **Add for panel door with tempered glass lite**	ea	–	$264.00	$264.00
Replace Materials 264.00				
Add for panel door with beveled or edged glass lite	ea	–	$495.00	$495.00
Replace Materials 495.00				
Add for panel door with leaded or colored glass lite	ea	–	$573.00	$573.00
Replace Materials 573.00				
Add for panel door with round or elliptical top	ea	–	$844.00	$844.00
Replace Materials ....646.00 Labor 198.00				
REMOVE & ▶ **REINSTALL PANEL DOOR** **Remove panel door slab only for work, then reinstall**	ea	–	$6.61	$6.61
Replace .... Labor 6.61				
Remove panel door, jamb, & casing for work, then reinstall	ea	–	$70.90	$70.90
Replace .... Labor 70.90				
PANEL DOOR ▶ **REPAIR** **Replace antique panel door panel (not including custom knife charges)**	ea	–	$227.00	$227.00
Replace Materials ....108.00 Labor 119.00				
Replace antique panel door stile (not including custom knife charges)	ea	–	$187.00	$187.00
Replace Materials ......79.00 Labor 108.00				
Minimum charge to repair antique panel door (no custom milling)	ea	–	$233.00	$233.00
Replace Materials .....125.00 Labor 108.00				
Minimum charge to repair antique panel door (custom milling)	ea	–	$584.00	$584.00
Replace Materials ....431.00 Labor 153.00				
Custom work shaper or molder knife charge	ea	–	$341.00	$341.00
Replace Materials 341.00				
Custom work shaper or molder setup charge	ea	–	$160.00	$160.00
Replace Materials 160.00				
Minimum custom work shaper or molder charge	ea	–	$696.00	$696.00
Replace Materials 696.00				
Repair cracks & dry rot in antique door with epoxy, tighten stiles	ea	–	$351.00	$351.00
Replace Materials .....156.00 Labor 195.00				
Repair cracks & dry rot in antique door jamb with epoxy	ea	–	$238.40	$238.40
Replace Materials ......90.40 Labor 148.00				
Repair cracks & dry rot in antique door casing with epoxy	ea	–	$217.50	$217.50
Replace Materials ......69.50 Labor 148.00				
Remove antique door casing, re-plumb door, & reinstall casing	ea	–	$128.00	$128.00
Replace .... Labor 128.00				

BATTEN DOORS
(on facing page)

Batten doors are built from vertical boards (usually tongue and groove) held in place by horizontal battens and diagonal braces.

STANDARD GRADE Boards held in place by horizontal battens that are braced diagonally. (Sometimes called ledged-and-braced doors.)

HIGH GRADE Boards held in place by a stile frame and a single horizontal batten. Frame is joined with mortise and tenon joints. Also includes diagonal braces. (Sometimes called framed ledged-and-braced doors.)

Item Description	Unit	Remove	Replace	Total
Add 38% for antique panel door transom				
▶ Includes hinges, jamb, casing and brass opening hardware. For newer style transoms see page 118.				
Paint-grade batten door, standard grade	ea	$6.27	$410.74	$417.01
Replace Materials....403.00 Labor 7.74				
Remove .... Labor 6.27				
Paint-grade batten door, high grade	ea	$6.27	$591.74	$598.01
Replace Materials....584.00 Labor 7.74				
Remove .... Labor 6.27				
Stain-grade batten door, standard grade	ea	$6.27	$744.74	$751.01
Replace Materials ....737.00 Labor 7.74				
Remove .... Labor 6.27				
Stain-grade batten door, high grade	ea	$6.27	$1,037.74	$1,044.01
Replace Materials ..1030.00 Labor 7.74				
Remove .... Labor 6.27				
Metal storm/screen door, economy grade	ea	$6.56	$188.60	$195.16
Replace Materials.....136.00 Labor............52.60				
Remove .... Labor 6.56				
Metal storm/screen door, standard grade	ea	$6.56	$252.60	$259.16
Replace Materials....200.00 Labor............52.60				
Remove .... Labor 6.56				
Metal storm/screen door, high grade	ea	$6.56	$343.60	$350.16
Replace Materials ....291.00 Labor............52.60				
Remove .... Labor 6.56				
Metal storm/screen door, deluxe grade	ea	$6.56	$420.60	$427.16
Replace Materials....368.00 Labor............52.60				
Remove .... Labor 6.56				
Wood storm/screen door, economy grade	ea	$6.56	$206.60	$213.16
Replace Materials ....154.00 Labor............52.60				
Remove .... Labor 6.56				
Wood storm/screen door, standard grade	ea	$6.56	$302.60	$309.16
Replace Materials....250.00 Labor............52.60				
Remove .... Labor 6.56				
Wood storm/screen door, high grade	ea	$6.56	$350.60	$357.16
Replace Materials....298.00 Labor............52.60				
Remove .... Labor 6.56				
Wood storm/screen door, deluxe grade	ea	$6.56	$420.60	$427.16
Replace Materials....368.00 Labor............52.60				
Remove .... Labor 6.56				
Victorian style wood storm/screen door, standard grade	ea	$6.56	$455.60	$462.16
Replace Materials....403.00 Labor............52.60				
Remove .... Labor 6.56				
Victorian style wood storm/screen door, high grade	ea	$6.56	$532.60	$539.16
Replace Materials....480.00 Labor............52.60				
Remove .... Labor 6.56				
Victorian style wood storm/screen door, deluxe grade	ea	$6.56	$726.60	$733.16
Replace Materials....674.00 Labor............52.60				
Remove .... Labor 6.56				

◀ **BATTEN DOOR**
For interior jamb & casing see page 104. For exterior jamb and casing see page 116. See "Batten Doors" on facing page.

△ standard   △ high

◀ **STORM DOOR**

METAL . . .

△ economy   △ standard

△ high   △ deluxe

VICTORIAN WOOD . . .

△ standard   △ standard

△ high   △ deluxe

	Item Description		Unit	Remove	Replace	Total
STORM DOOR ▶ *continued*	**Remove storm/screen door for work, then reinstall**		ea	–	$74.00	$74.00
	Replace	Labor 74.00				
EXTERIOR ▶ FRENCH DOOR *For exterior jamb & casing see page 116.*	**Exterior paint-grade wood French door**		ea	$8.18	$412.22	$420.40
	Replace Materials....403.00	Labor 9.22				
	Remove	Labor 8.18				
	Exterior stain-grade fir French door		ea	$8.18	$468.22	$476.40
	Replace Materials.....459.00	Labor 9.22				
	Remove	Labor 8.18				
	Exterior metal French door		ea	$8.18	$457.22	$465.40
	Replace Materials....448.00	Labor 9.22				
	Remove	Labor 8.18				
	Exterior full-lite insulated door with simulated French door grid		ea	$8.18	$393.22	$401.40
	Replace Materials....384.00	Labor 9.22				
	Remove	Labor 8.18				
EXTERIOR ▶ VENEER DOOR *For exterior jamb & casing see page 116.*	**Mahogany (lauan) or birch veneer exterior door**		ea	$8.18	$201.22	$209.40
	Replace Materials.....192.00	Labor 9.22				
	Remove	Labor 8.18				
	Ash or red oak veneer exterior door		ea	$8.18	$218.22	$226.40
	Replace Materials....209.00	Labor 9.22				
	Remove	Labor 8.18				
	Walnut or cherry veneer exterior door		ea	$8.18	$238.22	$246.40
	Replace Materials....229.00	Labor 9.22				
	Remove	Labor 8.18				
	Insulated steel exterior door		ea	$8.18	$200.22	$208.40
	Replace Materials.....191.00	Labor 9.22				
	Remove	Labor 8.18				
ADDITIONAL ▶ EXTERIOR DOOR COSTS	**Add for full-lite in exterior door**		ea	–	$257.00	$257.00
	Replace Materials 257.00					
	Add for leaded or colored glass full-lite in exterior door		ea	–	$573.00	$573.00
	Replace Materials 573.00					
	Add for half-lite in exterior door		ea	–	$111.00	$111.00
	Replace Materials 111.00					
	Add for leaded or colored glass half-lite in exterior wood door		ea	–	$320.00	$320.00
	Replace Materials 320.00					
	Add for 1' by 1' lite in exterior door		ea	–	$34.10	$34.10
	Replace Materials 34.10					
DUTCH DOOR ▶ *See jambs and casing for Dutch doors on pages 116 and 117.*	**Bottom Dutch door section, flush**		ea	$11.30	$203.10	$214.40
	Replace Materials 189.00	Labor..........14.10				
	Remove	Labor..........11.30				
	Bottom Dutch door section, raised panel		ea	$11.30	$298.10	$309.40
	Replace Materials 284.00	Labor..........14.10				
	Remove	Labor..........11.30				
	Bottom Dutch door section, cross buck		ea	$11.30	$381.10	$392.40
	Replace Materials 367.00	Labor..........14.10				
	Remove	Labor..........11.30				

BOTTOM ...

△ flush   raised panel △

Item Description	Unit	Remove	Replace	Total	
Add for shelf on bottom Dutch door section *Replace* Materials.......61.20	ea	–	$61.20	$61.20	BOTTOM . . . △ crossbuck △ shelf
Top Dutch door section with full lite *Replace* Materials....250.00 Labor..........14.10 *Remove* .... Labor 11.30	ea	$11.30	$264.10	$275.40	
Top Dutch door section with four lites *Replace* Materials....300.00 Labor..........14.10 *Remove* .... Labor 11.30	ea	$11.30	$314.10	$325.40	TOP . . .
Top Dutch door section with six lites *Replace* Materials....320.00 Labor..........14.10 *Remove* .... Labor 11.30	ea	$11.30	$334.10	$345.40	△ full lite △ four lite
Top Dutch door section with nine lites *Replace* Materials....346.00 Labor..........14.10 *Remove* .... Labor 11.30	ea	$11.30	$360.10	$371.40	△ six lite △ nine lite
Remove exterior Dutch door, jamb, & casing for work, then reinstall *Replace* .... Labor..........119.00	ea	–	$119.00	$119.00	
Remove exterior Dutch door slabs for work, then reinstall *Replace* .... Labor..........17.10	ea	–	$17.10	$17.10	
Steel entry door, standard grade *Replace* Materials....229.00 Labor ....9.22 *Remove* .... Labor 8.18	ea	$8.18	$238.22	$246.40	◄ **STEEL ENTRY DOOR** For exterior jamb & casing see page 116. Standard grade is flush face and high grade is embossed.
Steel entry door, high grade *Replace* Materials ....307.00 Labor ....9.22 *Remove* .... Labor 8.18	ea	$8.18	$316.22	$324.40	
Steel entry door side-lite, standard grade *Replace* Materials.....118.00 Labor..........49.60 *Remove* .... Labor 14.70	ea	$14.70	$167.60	$182.30	◄ **STEEL ENTRY DOOR SIDE-LITE** Includes jamb & casing.
Steel entry door side-lite, high grade *Replace* Materials.....153.00 Labor..........49.60 *Remove* .... Labor 14.70	ea	$14.70	$202.60	$217.30	
Paint-grade wood entry door, standard grade *Replace* Materials.....247.00 Labor ....9.22 *Remove* .... Labor 8.18	ea	$8.18	$256.22	$264.40	◄ **PAINT-GRADE WOOD ENTRY DOOR** For exterior jamb & casing see page 116. Also see quality indicators on page 112.
Paint-grade wood entry door, high grade *Replace* Materials ....353.00 Labor ....9.22 *Remove* .... Labor 8.18	ea	$8.18	$362.22	$370.40	
Paint-grade wood entry door, deluxe grade *Replace* Materials ....477.00 Labor ....9.22 *Remove* .... Labor 8.18	ea	$8.18	$486.22	$494.40	**ENTRY DOORS** All entry doors are solid wood with occasional veneered wood components in the lower grades.
Paint-grade wood entry door, custom grade *Replace* Materials....688.00 Labor ....9.22 *Remove* .... Labor 8.18	ea	$8.18	$697.22	$705.40	Entry door prices do not include jamb & casing. See page 116 for exterior jambs.
Paint-grade wood entry door, custom deluxe grade *Replace* Materials....799.00 Labor ....9.22 *Remove* .... Labor 8.18	ea	$8.18	$808.22	$816.40	See quality indicators on page 112.

Item Description	Unit	Remove	Replace	Total

PAINT-GRADE ▶
WOOD ENTRY
DOOR SIDE-LITE
*Includes jamb & casing.
Also see quality grades
below.*

Item Description	Unit	Remove	Replace	Total
Paint-grade wood entry door side-lite, standard grade	ea	$14.70	$217.60	$232.30
Replace Materials.....168.00 Labor..........49.60 *Remove* .... Labor..........14.70				
Paint-grade wood entry door side-lite, high grade	ea	$14.70	$280.60	$295.30
Replace Materials ....231.00 Labor..........49.60 *Remove* .... Labor..........14.70				
Paint-grade wood entry door side-lite, deluxe grade	ea	$14.70	$384.60	$399.30
Replace Materials ....335.00 Labor..........49.60 *Remove* .... Labor..........14.70				
Paint-grade wood entry door side-lite, custom grade	ea	$14.70	$512.60	$527.30
Replace Materials ....463.00 Labor..........49.60 *Remove* .... Labor..........14.70				
Paint-grade wood entry door side-lite, custom deluxe grade	ea	$14.70	$608.60	$623.30
Replace Materials ....559.00 Labor..........49.60 *Remove* .... Labor..........14.70				

FIR ENTRY DOOR ▶
*For exterior jamb &
casing see page 116. Also
see quality grades below.*

Item Description	Unit	Remove	Replace	Total
Stain-grade fir entry door, standard grade	ea	$8.18	$558.22	$566.40
Replace Materials ....549.00 Labor ....9.22 *Remove* .... Labor 8.18				
Stain-grade fir entry door, high grade	ea	$8.18	$676.22	$684.40
Replace Materials ....667.00 Labor ....9.22 *Remove* .... Labor 8.18				
Stain-grade fir entry door, deluxe grade	ea	$8.18	$864.22	$872.40
Replace Materials ....855.00 Labor ....9.22 *Remove* .... Labor 8.18				
Stain-grade fir entry door, custom grade	ea	$8.18	$1,269.22	$1,277.40
Replace Materials...1260.00 Labor ....9.22 *Remove* .... Labor 8.18				
Stain-grade fir entry door, custom deluxe grade	ea	$8.18	$1,679.22	$1,687.40
Replace Materials...1670.00 Labor ....9.22 *Remove* .... Labor 8.18				

ENTRY DOOR GRADES

STANDARD GRADE Multiple panel doors (nine and more) with some embossed components. May have lites in place of panels.

HIGH GRADE Same as Standard grade with some embossed and carved components. Also may have carved on-lays.

FIR ENTRY ▶
DOOR SIDE-LITE
*Includes jamb & casing.
Also see quality grades
above and below.*

Item Description	Unit	Remove	Replace	Total
Stain-grade fir entry door side-lite, standard grade	ea	$14.70	$405.60	$420.30
Replace Materials ....356.00 Labor..........49.60 *Remove* .... Labor..........14.70				
Stain-grade fir entry door side-lite, high grade	ea	$14.70	$508.60	$523.30
Replace Materials....459.00 Labor..........49.60 *Remove* .... Labor..........14.70				
Stain-grade fir entry door side-lite, deluxe grade	ea	$14.70	$619.60	$634.30
Replace Materials ....570.00 Labor..........49.60 *Remove* .... Labor..........14.70				
Stain-grade fir entry door side-lite, custom grade	ea	$14.70	$921.60	$936.30
Replace Materials ....872.00 Labor..........49.60 *Remove* .... Labor..........14.70				
Stain-grade fir entry door side-lite, custom deluxe grade	ea	$14.70	$1,219.60	$1,234.30
Replace Materials....1170.00 Labor..........49.60 *Remove* .... Labor..........14.70				

ENTRY DOOR GRADES

DELUXE GRADE Door components have moderate carvings. May have exotic wood components.

CUSTOM GRADE Door components have extensive carvings. May have exotic wood components, leaded glass or beveled glass.

CUSTOM DELUXE GRADE Same as Custom grade with oval or elliptical-top windows.

Item Description	Unit	Remove	Replace	Total
Mahogany entry door, standard grade	ea	$8.18	$483.90	$492.08
Replace Materials....466.00 Labor..........17.90				
Remove .... Labor...........8.18				
Mahogany entry door, high grade	ea	$8.18	$726.90	$735.08
Replace Materials....709.00 Labor..........17.90				
Remove .... Labor...........8.18				
Mahogany entry door, deluxe grade	ea	$8.18	$1,117.90	$1,126.08
Replace Materials...1100.00 Labor..........17.90				
Remove .... Labor...........8.18				
Mahogany entry door, custom grade	ea	$8.18	$1,477.90	$1,486.08
Replace Materials...1460.00 Labor..........17.90				
Remove .... Labor...........8.18				
Mahogany entry door, custom deluxe grade	ea	$8.18	$1,867.90	$1,876.08
Replace Materials ..1850.00 Labor..........17.90				
Remove .... Labor...........8.18				
Mahogany entry door side-lite, standard grade	ea	$14.70	$370.60	$385.30
Replace Materials ....321.00 Labor..........49.60				
Remove .... Labor..........14.70				
Mahogany entry door side-lite, high grade	ea	$14.70	$533.60	$548.30
Replace Materials....484.00 Labor..........49.60				
Remove .... Labor..........14.70				
Mahogany entry door side-lite, deluxe grade	ea	$14.70	$816.60	$831.30
Replace Materials.....767.00 Labor..........49.60				
Remove .... Labor..........14.70				
Mahogany entry door side-lite, custom grade	ea	$14.70	$1,069.60	$1,084.30
Replace Materials ..1020.00 Labor..........49.60				
Remove .... Labor..........14.70				
Mahogany entry door side-lite, custom deluxe grade	ea	$14.70	$1,369.60	$1,384.30
Replace Materials...1320.00 Labor..........49.60				
Remove .... Labor..........14.70				
Ash or oak entry door, standard grade	ea	$8.18	$462.90	$471.08
Replace Materials ....445.00 Labor..........17.90				
Remove .... Labor..........8.18				
Ash or oak entry door, high grade	ea	$8.18	$705.90	$714.08
Replace Materials....688.00 Labor..........17.90				
Remove .... Labor...........8.18				
Ash or oak entry door, deluxe grade	ea	$8.18	$935.90	$944.08
Replace Materials.....918.00 Labor..........17.90				
Remove .... Labor...........8.18				
Ash or oak entry door, custom grade	ea	$8.18	$1,557.90	$1,566.08
Replace Materials ..1540.00 Labor..........17.90				
Remove .... Labor...........8.18				
Ash or red entry door, custom deluxe grade	ea	$8.18	$1,967.90	$1,976.08
Replace Materials...1950.00 Labor..........17.90				
Remove .... Labor...........8.18				

◄ **MAHOGANY ENTRY DOOR**
For exterior jamb & casing see page 116. Also see quality indicators on facing page.

WOOD EMBOSSING

Wood is often embossed to appear like it has been carved. Embossing stamps a pattern onto the wood.

Embossing is far less expensive than carving and can only be used for relatively shallow patterns.

◄ **MAHOGANY DOOR SIDE-LITE**
Includes jamb & casing. Also see quality indicators on facing page.

WOOD ONLAYS

Wood onlays are mass-produced carved wood components that are nailed and glued on doors to give a hand-carved look.

◄ **ASH OR OAK ENTRY DOOR**
See exterior jamb & casing on page 116. Also see quality indicators on facing page.

RELATED ITEMS

Cleaning.......................57
Door Hardware 127
Finish Carpentry...........201
Painting.....................334

	Item Description	Unit	Remove	Replace	Total
ASH OR OAK ▶ **ENTRY DOOR SIDE-LITE** Includes jamb & casing. Also see quality indicators on page 112.	**Ash or oak entry door side-lite, standard grade** *Replace* Materials....300.00 Labor.........49.60 *Remove* .... Labor..........14.70	ea	$14.70	$349.60	$364.30
	Ash or oak entry door side-lite, high grade *Replace* Materials....487.00 Labor.........49.60 *Remove* .... Labor..........14.70	ea	$14.70	$536.60	$551.30
	Ash or oak entry door side-lite, deluxe grade *Replace* Materials....601.00 Labor.........49.60 *Remove* .... Labor..........14.70	ea	$14.70	$650.60	$665.30
	Ash or oak entry door side-lite, custom grade *Replace* Materials....1100.00 Labor.........49.60 *Remove* .... Labor..........14.70	ea	$14.70	$1,149.60	$1,164.30
	Ash or oak entry door side-lite, custom deluxe grade *Replace* Materials ..1380.00 Labor.........49.60 *Remove* .... Labor..........14.70	ea	$14.70	$1,429.60	$1,444.30
REDWOOD ▶ **ENTRY DOOR** For exterior jamb & casing see page 116. Also see quality indicators on page 112.	**Redwood entry door, standard grade** *Replace* Materials ...570.00 Labor...........17.90 *Remove* .... Labor 8.18	ea	$8.18	$587.90	$596.08
	Redwood entry door, high grade *Replace* Materials ...931.00 Labor...........17.90 *Remove* .... Labor 8.18	ea	$8.18	$948.90	$957.08
	Redwood entry door, deluxe grade *Replace* Materials...1180.00 Labor...........17.90 *Remove* .... Labor 8.18	ea	$8.18	$1,197.90	$1,206.08
	Redwood entry door, custom grade *Replace* Materials ..1600.00 Labor...........17.90 *Remove* .... Labor 8.18	ea	$8.18	$1,617.90	$1,626.08
	Redwood entry door, custom deluxe grade *Replace* Materials ..1840.00 Labor...........17.90 *Remove* .... Labor 8.18	ea	$8.18	$1,857.90	$1,866.08
REDWOOD ▶ **ENTRY DOOR SIDE-LITE** Includes jamb & casing. Also see quality indicators on page 112.	**Redwood entry door side-lite, standard grade** *Replace* Materials ....375.00 Labor..........49.60 *Remove* .... Labor..........14.70	ea	$14.70	$424.60	$439.30
	Redwood entry door side-lite, high grade *Replace* Materials....646.00 Labor..........49.60 *Remove* .... Labor..........14.70	ea	$14.70	$695.60	$710.30
	Redwood entry door side-lite, deluxe grade *Replace* Materials....836.00 Labor..........49.60 *Remove* .... Labor..........14.70	ea	$14.70	$885.60	$900.30
	Redwood entry door side-lite, custom grade *Replace* Materials ...1130.00 Labor..........49.60 *Remove* .... Labor..........14.70	ea	$14.70	$1,179.60	$1,194.30
	Redwood entry door side-lite, custom deluxe grade *Replace* Materials...1310.00 Labor..........49.60 *Remove* .... Labor..........14.70	ea	$14.70	$1,359.60	$1,374.30

Item Description	Unit	Remove	Replace	Total	
Cypress entry door, standard grade *Replace* Materials ....520.00 Labor ....17.90 *Remove* .... Labor 8.18	ea	$8.18	$537.90	$546.08	◄ **CYPRESS ENTRY DOOR** *For exterior jamb & casing see page 116. Also see quality indicators on page 112.*
Cypress entry door, high grade *Replace* Materials.....695.00 Labor ....17.90 *Remove* .... Labor 8.18	ea	$8.18	$712.90	$721.08	
Cypress entry door, deluxe grade *Replace* Materials....880.00 Labor ....17.90 *Remove* .... Labor 8.18	ea	$8.18	$897.90	$906.08	
Cypress entry door, custom grade *Replace* Materials...1270.00 Labor ....17.90 *Remove* .... Labor 8.18	ea	$8.18	$1,287.90	$1,296.08	
Cypress entry door, custom deluxe grade *Replace* Materials...1650.00 Labor ....17.90 *Remove* .... Labor 8.18	ea	$8.18	$1,667.90	$1,676.08	
Cypress entry door side-lite, standard grade *Replace* Materials ....355.00 Labor ....49.60 *Remove* .... Labor 14.70	ea	$14.70	$404.60	$419.30	◄ **CYPRESS DOOR SIDE-LITE** *Includes jamb & casing. Also see quality indicators on page 112.*
Cypress entry door side-lite, high grade *Replace* Materials.....475.00 Labor ....49.60 *Remove* .... Labor 14.70	ea	$14.70	$524.60	$539.30	
Cypress entry door side-lite, deluxe grade *Replace* Materials......613.00 Labor ....49.60 *Remove* .... Labor 14.70	ea	$14.70	$662.60	$677.30	
Cypress entry door side-lite, custom grade *Replace* Materials ....897.00 Labor ....49.60 *Remove* .... Labor 14.70	ea	$14.70	$946.60	$961.30	
Cypress entry door side-lite, custom deluxe grade *Replace* Materials....1170.00 Labor ....49.60 *Remove* .... Labor 14.70	ea	$14.70	$1,219.60	$1,234.30	
Walnut or cherry entry door, standard grade *Replace* Materials ....730.00 Labor ....17.90 *Remove* .... Labor 8.18	ea	$8.18	$747.90	$756.08	◄ **WALNUT OR CHERRY ENTRY DOOR** *For exterior jamb & casing see page 116. Also see quality indicators on page 112.*
Walnut or cherry entry door, high grade *Replace* Materials...1100.00 Labor ....17.90 *Remove* .... Labor 8.18	ea	$8.18	$1,117.90	$1,126.08	
Walnut or cherry entry door, deluxe grade *Replace* Materials...1370.00 Labor ....17.90 *Remove* .... Labor 8.18	ea	$8.18	$1,387.90	$1,396.08	
Walnut or cherry entry door, custom grade *Replace* Materials...2050.00 Labor ....17.90 *Remove* .... Labor 8.18	ea	$8.18	$2,067.90	$2,076.08	
Walnut or cherry entry door, custom deluxe grade *Replace* Materials ..2660.00 Labor ....17.90 *Remove* .... Labor 8.18	ea	$8.18	$2,677.90	$2,686.08	

RELATED ITEMS

Cleaning....................57
Door Hardware 127
Finish Carpentry..........201
Painting 334

Item Description	Unit	Remove	Replace	Total
Walnut or cherry entry door side-lite, standard grade	ea	$14.70	$523.60	$538.30
Replace Materials.....474.00 Labor..........49.60				
Remove .... Labor..........14.70				
Walnut or cherry entry door side-lite, high grade	ea	$14.70	$798.60	$813.30
Replace Materials.....749.00 Labor..........49.60				
Remove .... Labor..........14.70				
Walnut or cherry entry door side-lite, deluxe grade	ea	$14.70	$1,005.60	$1,020.30
Replace Materials....956.00 Labor..........49.60				
Remove .... Labor..........14.70				
Walnut or cherry entry door side-lite, custom grade	ea	$14.70	$1,509.60	$1,524.30
Replace Materials...1460.00 Labor..........49.60				
Remove .... Labor..........14.70				
Walnut or cherry entry door side-lite, custom deluxe grade	ea	$14.70	$1,959.60	$1,974.30
Replace Materials ...1910.00 Labor..........49.60				
Remove .... Labor..........14.70				
Remove exterior door, jamb, & casing for work, then reinstall	ea	–	$95.70	$95.70
Replace .... Labor..........95.70				
Remove exterior door slab for work, then reinstall	ea	–	$12.70	$12.70
Replace .... Labor..........12.70				
Remove exterior double door, jamb, & casing for work, then reinstall	ea	–	$136.00	$136.00
Replace .... Labor..........136.00				
Remove exterior double door slab for work, then reinstall	ea	–	$15.90	$15.90
Replace .... Labor..........15.90				
Paint-grade jamb & casing for exterior door	ea	$14.30	$123.40	$137.70
Replace Materials ......47.30 Labor..........76.10				
Remove .... Labor..........14.30				
Paint-grade jamb & casing for double exterior door	ea	$14.30	$219.80	$234.10
Replace Materials......84.80 Labor..........135.00				
Remove .... Labor..........14.30				
Stain-grade pine jamb & casing for exterior door	ea	$14.30	$131.70	$146.00
Replace Materials.....55.60 Labor..........76.10				
Remove .... Labor..........14.30				
Stain-grade pine jamb & casing for double exterior door	ea	$14.30	$236.00	$250.30
Replace Materials.....101.00 Labor..........135.00				
Remove .... Labor..........14.30				
Birch jamb & casing for exterior door	ea	$14.30	$128.90	$143.20
Replace Materials......52.80 Labor..........76.10				
Remove .... Labor..........14.30				
Birch jamb & casing for double exterior door	ea	$14.30	$228.80	$243.10
Replace Materials......93.80 Labor..........135.00				
Remove .... Labor..........14.30				
Mahogany jamb & casing for exterior door	ea	$14.30	$138.70	$153.00
Replace Materials......62.60 Labor..........76.10				
Remove .... Labor..........14.30				
▶ Deduct **$5.80** for mahogany veneer jamb and casing.				

WALNUT OR CHERRY ENTRY DOOR SIDE-LITE
Includes jamb & casing. Also see quality indicators on page 112.

REMOVE EXTERIOR DOOR & REINSTALL

EXTERIOR DOOR JAMB & CASING

Item Description	Unit	Remove	Replace	Total
Mahogany jamb & casing for double exterior door	ea	$14.30	$248.00	$262.30
Replace Materials .....113.00 Labor 135.00				
Remove .... Labor 14.30				
▶ Deduct **$8.70** for mahogany veneer jamb and casing.				
Ash or oak jamb & casing for exterior door	ea	$14.30	$142.10	$156.40
Replace Materials ......66.00 Labor 76.10				
Remove .... Labor 14.30				
▶ Deduct **$5.30** for ash or oak veneer jamb and casing.				
Ash or oak jamb & casing for double exterior door	ea	$14.30	$253.00	$267.30
Replace Materials .....118.00 Labor 135.00				
Remove .... Labor 14.30				
▶ Deduct **$7.00** for ash or oak veneer jamb and casing.				
Redwood jamb & casing for exterior door	ea	$14.30	$135.20	$149.50
Replace Materials ......59.10 Labor 76.10				
Remove .... Labor 14.30				
Redwood jamb & casing for double exterior door	ea	$14.30	$241.00	$255.30
Replace Materials ....106.00 Labor 135.00				
Remove .... Labor 14.30				
Cypress jamb & casing for exterior door	ea	$14.30	$131.00	$145.30
Replace Materials ......54.90 Labor 76.10				
Remove .... Labor 14.30				
Cypress jamb & casing for double exterior door	ea	$14.30	$236.00	$250.30
Replace Materials .....101.00 Labor 135.00				
Remove .... Labor 14.30				
Walnut or cherry jamb & casing for exterior door	ea	$14.30	$154.00	$168.30
Replace Materials ......77.90 Labor 76.10				
Remove .... Labor 14.30				
▶ Deduct **$5.80** for walnut or cherry veneer jamb and casing.				
Walnut or cherry jamb & casing for double exterior door	ea	$14.30	$268.00	$282.30
Replace Materials .....133.00 Labor 135.00				
Remove .... Labor 14.30				
▶ Deduct **$7.00** for walnut or cherry veneer jamb and casing.				
Steel jamb & casing for exterior door	ea	$14.30	$152.60	$166.90
Replace Materials ......76.50 Labor 76.10				
Remove .... Labor 14.30				
Steel jamb & casing for double exterior door	ea	$14.30	$246.00	$260.30
Replace Materials .....111.00 Labor 135.00				
Remove .... Labor 14.30				
Add for hanging exterior Dutch door	ea	–	$76.10	$76.10
Replace .... Labor 76.10				
Add for jamb & casing for a round- or elliptical-top door	ea	–	$160.00	$160.00
Replace Materials 160.00				
Fanlite for single entry door, standard grade	ea	$21.60	$277.50	$299.10
Replace Materials .....197.00 Labor 80.50				
Remove .... Labor 21.60				

RELATED ITEMS

Cleaning 55
Door Hardware 125
Finish Carpentry 201
Painting 336

◀ **ADDITIONAL EXTERIOR JAMB & CASING COSTS**

◀ **ENTRY DOOR FANLITE**
For more info about fanlites see the following page.

Item Description	Unit	Remove	Replace	Total

FANLITE ▶
continued

FANLITE QUALITY

Fanlites are semi-circular or half-elliptical windows that appear above doors. True fanlites have mullions that fan out from the bottom center of the lite. Lower grades will have a simulated fan grid.

All fanlites include jamb and casing. Grades match entry door grades found on page 112.

Item Description	Unit	Remove	Replace	Total
Fanlite for single entry door, high grade	ea	$21.60	$414.50	$436.10
Replace Materials....334.00 Labor..........80.50				
Remove Labor..........21.60				
Fanlite for single entry door, deluxe grade	ea	$21.60	$543.50	$565.10
Replace Materials....463.00 Labor..........80.50				
Remove Labor..........21.60				
Fanlite for single entry door, custom grade	ea	$21.60	$721.50	$743.10
Replace Materials ...641.00 Labor..........80.50				
Remove Labor..........21.60				
Fanlite for single entry door, custom deluxe grade	ea	$21.60	$922.50	$944.10
Replace Materials....842.00 Labor..........80.50				
Remove Labor..........21.60				
Remove entry door fanlite & casing for work, then reinstall	ea	–	$136.00	$136.00
Replace Labor.........136.00				

ADDITIONAL ▶ FANLITE SIZES
Includes jamb & casing.

Add 34% for fanlite for single door with side-lite

Add 85% for fanlite for single door with two side-lites

Add 99% for fanlite for double doors

Add 147% for fanlite for double doors with two side-lites

ENTRY DOOR ▶ FIXED TRANSOM
Includes jamb & casing.

FIXED TRANSOMS

Fixed transoms are rectangular windows that appear above doors. Transoms may have circular, semi-circular, or elliptical components, but the unit fits in a rectangular jamb.

All transoms include jamb and casing. Grades match exterior door grades found on page 112.

Item Description	Unit	Remove	Replace	Total
Fixed transom for entry door, standard grade	ea	$26.70	$175.50	$202.20
Replace Materials.....132.00 Labor 43.50				
Remove Labor..........26.70				
Fixed transom for entry door, high grade	ea	$26.70	$265.50	$292.20
Replace Materials....222.00 Labor..........43.50				
Remove Labor..........26.70				
Fixed transom for entry door, deluxe grade	ea	$26.70	$414.50	$441.20
Replace Materials ....371.00 Labor 43.50				
Remove Labor..........26.70				
Fixed transom for entry door, custom grade	ea	$26.70	$582.50	$609.20
Replace Materials....539.00 Labor 43.50				
Remove Labor..........26.70				
Fixed transom for entry door, custom deluxe grade	ea	$26.70	$810.50	$837.20
Replace Materials.....767.00 Labor 43.50				
Remove Labor..........26.70				
Remove fixed transom & casing for work, then reinstall	ea	–	$119.00	$119.00
Replace Labor.........119.00				

ADDITIONAL ▶ TRANSOM SIZES
Includes jamb & casing.

Add 42% for fixed transom for single door with side-lite

Add 65% for fixed transom for single door with two side-lites

Add 89% for fixed transom for double doors

Add 106% for fixed transom for double doors with two side-lites

CAFE DOORS ▶
Includes hardware.

Item Description	Unit	Remove	Replace	Total
Cafe doors (bar doors) louvered paint-grade	ea	$7.34	$126.90	$134.24
Replace Materials ......97.30 Labor 29.60				
Remove Labor 7.34				

Item Description	Unit	Remove	Replace	Total
Cafe doors (bar doors) louvered stain-grade	ea	$7.34	$151.60	$158.94
Replace Materials ....122.00 Labor 29.60				
Remove .... Labor 7.34				
Cafe doors (bar doors) Victorian spindle & raised-panel paint-grade	ea	$7.34	$154.60	$161.94
Replace Materials.....125.00 Labor 29.60				
Remove .... Labor 7.34				
Cafe doors (bar doors) Victorian spindle & raised-panel stain-grade	ea	$7.34	$185.60	$192.94
Replace Materials.....156.00 Labor 29.60				
Remove .... Labor 7.34				
Remove cafe doors for work, then reinstall	ea	–	$44.40	$44.40
Replace .... Labor 44.40				
6′ wide by 6′8″ tall bronze finish sliding patio door single-glazed	ea	$54.00	$664.00	$718.00
Replace Materials ....473.00 Labor 191.00				
Remove .... Labor 54.00				
6′ wide by 6′8″ tall mill finish sliding patio door double-glazed	ea	$54.00	$830.00	$884.00
Replace Materials ....639.00 Labor 191.00				
Remove .... Labor 54.00				
8′ wide by 6′8″ tall bronze finish sliding patio door single-glazed	ea	$54.00	$764.00	$818.00
Replace Materials ....573.00 Labor 191.00				
Remove .... Labor 54.00				
8′ wide by 6′8″ tall mill finish sliding patio door double-glazed	ea	$54.00	$942.00	$996.00
Replace Materials.....751.00 Labor 191.00				
Remove .... Labor 54.00				
12′ wide by 6′8″ tall bronze finish sliding patio door single-glazed	ea	$81.20	$1,106.00	$1,187.20
Replace Materials ....856.00 Labor 250.00				
Remove .... Labor 81.20				
▶ 3 lites				
12′ by 6′8″ mill finish sliding patio door double-glazed	ea	$81.20	$1,450.00	$1,531.20
Replace Materials ..1200.00 Labor 250.00				
Remove .... Labor 81.20				
▶ 3 lites.				
6′ by 6′8″ wood sliding patio door single-glazed	ea	$54.00	$1,201.00	$1,255.00
Replace Materials...1010.00 Labor 191.00				
Remove .... Labor 54.00				
6′ by 6′8″ wood sliding patio door double-glazed	ea	$54.00	$1,321.00	$1,375.00
Replace Materials...1130.00 Labor 191.00				
Remove .... Labor 54.00				
8′ by 6′8″ wood sliding patio door single-glazed	ea	$54.00	$1,411.00	$1,465.00
Replace Materials...1220.00 Labor 191.00				
Remove .... Labor 54.00				
8′ by 6′8″ wood sliding patio door double-glazed	ea	$54.00	$1,551.00	$1,605.00
Replace Materials...1360.00 Labor 191.00				
Remove .... Labor 54.00				
12′ by 6′8″ wood sliding patio door single-glazed (3 lites)	ea	$81.20	$2,090.00	$2,171.20
Replace Materials...1840.00 Labor 250.00				
Remove .... Labor 81.20				

◀ **SLIDING PATIO DOOR**

△ two lite patio door

△ three lite patio door

RELATED ITEMS
Cleaning.....................57
Door Hardware 127
Finish Carpentry..........201
Painting 334

	Item Description	Unit	Remove	Replace	Total
SLIDING PATIO ▶ DOOR *continued*	12' by 6'8" wood sliding patio door double-glazed (3 lites) *Replace* Materials ..2020.00 Labor ....250.00 *Remove* .... Labor...........81.20	ea	$81.20	$2,270.00	$2,351.20
	6' by 6'8" wood sliding patio door single-glazed clad exterior *Replace* Materials ..1030.00 Labor ....191.00 *Remove* .... Labor...........54.00	ea	$54.00	$1,221.00	$1,275.00
	6' by 6'8" wood sliding patio door double-glazed clad exterior *Replace* Materials ..1250.00 Labor ....191.00 *Remove* .... Labor...........54.00	ea	$54.00	$1,441.00	$1,495.00
	8' by 6'8" wood sliding patio door single-glazed clad exterior *Replace* Materials ..1200.00 Labor ....250.00 *Remove* .... Labor...........54.00	ea	$54.00	$1,450.00	$1,504.00
	8' by 6'8" wood sliding patio door double-glazed clad exterior *Replace* Materials ..1470.00 Labor ....250.00 *Remove* .... Labor...........54.00	ea	$54.00	$1,720.00	$1,774.00
	12' by 6'8" wood sliding patio door single-glazed clad exterior *Replace* Materials ..1870.00 Labor ....250.00 *Remove* .... Labor...........81.20 ▶ 3 lites.	ea	$81.20	$2,120.00	$2,201.20
	12' by 6'8" wood sliding patio door double-glazed clad exterior *Replace* Materials ...2450.00 Labor ....250.00 *Remove* .... Labor...........81.20	ea	$81.20	$2,700.00	$2,781.20
ADDITIONAL ▶ SLIDING PATIO DOOR COSTS	Add for sliding patio door tinted glass (per lite) *Replace* Materials 232.00	ea	–	$232.00	$232.00
	Remove sliding patio door, jamb, & casing for work, then reinstall *Replace* .... Labor 241.00	ea	–	$241.00	$241.00
	Remove sliding patio door lites for work, then reinstall *Replace* .... Labor...........71.80	ea	–	$71.80	$71.80
	Minimum charge for sliding glass patio door work *Replace* Materials ......28.00 Labor 141.00	ea	–	$169.00	$169.00
	Recondition sliding glass patio door, replace hardware *Replace* Materials ......63.00 Labor...........101.00	ea	–	$164.00	$164.00
SLIDING PATIO ▶ DOOR SCREEN	36" sliding patio door screen *Replace* Materials ......62.60 Labor ....5.44 *Remove* .... Labor............3.61	ea	$3.61	$68.04	$71.65
	48" sliding patio door screen *Replace* Materials ......77.90 Labor ....5.44 *Remove* .... Labor............3.61	ea	$3.61	$83.34	$86.95
PET DOOR ▶ *Includes lock, aluminum frame, and PVC door.*	Pet door for small dogs, cats *Replace* Materials ......55.60 Labor ....36.70 *Remove* .... Labor............8.40	ea	$8.40	$92.30	$100.70
	Pet door for average size dogs *Replace* Materials ......97.30 Labor ....36.70 *Remove* .... Labor............8.40	ea	$8.40	$134.00	$142.40

Item Description	Unit	Remove	Replace	Total
Pet door for large dogs	ea	$8.40	$189.70	$198.10
Replace Materials.....153.00 Labor..........36.70				
Remove .... Labor 8.40				
Remove pet door for work, then reinstall	ea	–	$63.10	$63.10
Replace Materials........7.00 Labor 56.10				
8' garage door with hardware, economy grade	ea	$105.00	$668.00	$773.00
Replace Materials ....396.00 Labor.........272.00				
Remove .... Labor..........105.00				
8' garage door with hardware, standard grade	ea	$105.00	$731.00	$836.00
Replace Materials.....459.00 Labor.........272.00				
Remove .... Labor..........105.00				
8' garage door with hardware, high grade	ea	$105.00	$905.00	$1,010.00
Replace Materials....633.00 Labor.........272.00				
Remove .... Labor..........105.00				
8' garage door with hardware, deluxe grade	ea	$105.00	$981.00	$1,086.00
Replace Materials....709.00 Labor.........272.00				
Remove .... Labor..........105.00				
9' garage door with hardware, economy grade	ea	$105.00	$703.00	$808.00
Replace Materials ....431.00 Labor.........272.00				
Remove .... Labor..........105.00				
9' garage door with hardware, standard grade	ea	$105.00	$859.00	$964.00
Replace Materials ....587.00 Labor.........272.00				
Remove .... Labor..........105.00				
9' garage door with hardware, high grade	ea	$105.00	$960.00	$1,065.00
Replace Materials....688.00 Labor.........272.00				
Remove .... Labor..........105.00				
9' garage door with hardware, deluxe grade	ea	$105.00	$1,051.00	$1,156.00
Replace Materials....779.00 Labor.........272.00				
Remove .... Labor..........105.00				
10' garage door with hardware, economy grade	ea	$105.00	$766.00	$871.00
Replace Materials.....494.00 Labor.........272.00				
Remove .... Labor..........105.00				
10' garage door with hardware, standard grade	ea	$105.00	$884.00	$989.00
Replace Materials.....612.00 Labor.........272.00				
Remove .... Labor..........105.00				
10' garage door with hardware, high grade	ea	$105.00	$1,030.00	$1,135.00
Replace Materials ....758.00 Labor.........272.00				
Remove .... Labor..........105.00				
10' garage door with hardware, deluxe grade	ea	$105.00	$1,134.00	$1,239.00
Replace Materials....862.00 Labor.........272.00				
Remove .... Labor..........105.00				
12' garage door with hardware, economy grade	ea	$105.00	$828.00	$933.00
Replace Materials....556.00 Labor.........272.00				
Remove .... Labor..........105.00				
12' garage door with hardware, standard grade	ea	$105.00	$960.00	$1,065.00
Replace Materials....688.00 Labor.........272.00				
Remove .... Labor..........105.00				

◀ **GARAGE DOOR**

GARAGE DOOR GRADES

ECONOMY GRADE
Overhead doors that are plastic-faced polystyrene or flush steel or uninsulated fiberglass. Single-piece doors with flush surface or tongue-and-groove boards in herringbone or chevron patterns.

STANDARD GRADE
Overhead doors that are textured or embossed steel, aluminum or fiberglass, usually insulated. Single-piece doors same as economy grade with lites, and paneled patterns.

HIGH GRADE
Overhead doors are same as standard grade with lites. Single-piece stain-grade wood doors with lites and carvings.

DELUXE GRADE
Overhead doors are stain-grade wood doors, specialty patterns, designed carvings or embossing, fan-tops, and so forth.

△ *economy*

△ *standard*

△ *high*

Item Description		Unit	Remove	Replace	Total
Garage door ▶ *continued*	**12' garage door with hardware, high grade**	ea	$105.00	$1,141.00	$1,246.00
	Replace Materials ....869.00 Labor.........272.00				
	Remove .... Labor.........105.00				
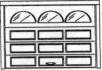	**12' garage door with hardware, deluxe grade**	ea	$105.00	$1,312.00	$1,417.00
	Replace Materials ..1040.00 Labor.........272.00				
	Remove .... Labor.........105.00				
△ deluxe	**14' garage door with hardware, economy grade**	ea	$105.00	$867.00	$972.00
	Replace Materials ....595.00 Labor.........272.00				
	Remove .... Labor.........105.00				
	**14' garage door with hardware, standard grade**	ea	$105.00	$981.00	$1,086.00
	Replace Materials ....709.00 Labor.........272.00				
	Remove .... Labor.........105.00				
△ deluxe (fanlite)	**14' garage door with hardware, high grade**	ea	$105.00	$1,141.00	$1,246.00
	Replace Materials ....869.00 Labor.........272.00				
	Remove .... Labor.........105.00				
	14' garage door with hardware, deluxe grade	ea	$105.00	$1,332.00	$1,437.00
	Replace Materials ..1060.00 Labor.........272.00				
	Remove .... Labor.........105.00				
	16' garage door with hardware, economy grade	ea	$105.00	$918.00	$1,023.00
	Replace Materials ....646.00 Labor.........272.00				
	Remove .... Labor.........105.00				
	16' garage door with hardware, standard grade	ea	$105.00	$1,092.00	$1,197.00
	Replace Materials ....820.00 Labor.........272.00				
	Remove .... Labor.........105.00				
	16' garage door with hardware, high grade	ea	$105.00	$1,245.00	$1,350.00
	Replace Materials ....973.00 Labor.........272.00				
	Remove .... Labor.........105.00				
	16' garage door with hardware, deluxe grade	ea	$105.00	$1,402.00	$1,507.00
	Replace Materials ...1130.00 Labor.........272.00				
	Remove .... Labor.........105.00				
	18' garage door with hardware, economy grade	ea	$105.00	$981.00	$1,086.00
	Replace Materials ....709.00 Labor.........272.00				
	Remove .... Labor.........105.00				
	18' garage door with hardware, standard grade	ea	$105.00	$1,141.00	$1,246.00
	Replace Materials ....869.00 Labor.........272.00				
	Remove .... Labor.........105.00				
	18' garage door with hardware, high grade	ea	$105.00	$1,282.00	$1,387.00
	Replace Materials ...1010.00 Labor.........272.00				
	Remove .... Labor.........105.00				
	18' garage door with hardware, deluxe grade	ea	$105.00	$1,472.00	$1,577.00
	Replace Materials ..1200.00 Labor.........272.00				
	Remove .... Labor.........105.00				
Garage door ▶ opener	**Garage door opener, standard grade**	ea	$22.10	$427.00	$449.10
	Replace Materials ....320.00 Labor.........107.00				
	Remove .... Labor..........22.10				

Item Description	Unit	Remove	Replace	Total
Garage door opener, high grade	ea	$22.10	$455.00	$477.10
Replace Materials....348.00 Labor.........107.00				
Remove .... Labor 22.10				
Garage door opener, deluxe grade	ea	$22.10	$489.00	$511.10
Replace Materials....382.00 Labor.........107.00				
Remove .... Labor 22.10				
Remote radio transmitter for overhead door opener	ea	–	$40.00	$40.00
Replace Materials......40.00				
Remove garage door opener for work, then reinstall	ea	–	$152.00	$152.00
Replace .... Labor 152.00				
Replace garage door spring	ea	–	$145.00	$145.00
Replace Materials......58.00 Labor...........87.00				
Remove single-car garage door for work, then reinstall	ea	–	$335.00	$335.00
Replace .... Labor.........335.00				
Remove two-car garage door for work, then reinstall	ea	–	$402.00	$402.00
Replace .... Labor 402.00				
Minimum charge for garage door work	ea	–	$144.00	$144.00
Replace Materials......35.00 Labor........109.00				
Add 14% for 7' tall doors				
Add 22% for 8' tall doors				

RELATED ITEMS

Cleaning.....................57
Door Hardware 127
Finish Carpentry..........201
Painting 334

◁ garage door spring

◁ remove and reinstall

◀ **ADD FOR TALL DOOR**
All door types.

🖎 NOTES: _____

_____

_____

_____

_____

_____

_____

_____

_____

_____

_____

_____

_____

_____

_____

_____

_____

_____

_____

_____ end

TIME & MATERIAL CHARTS *(selected items)*

Doors Materials

*See **Doors** material prices with the line items and other information in the **QuickFinder** column.*

Doors Labor

LABORER	BASE WAGE	PAID LEAVE	TRUE WAGE	FICA	FUTA	WORKER'S COMP.	UNEMPLOY. INSUR.	HEALTH INSUR.	RETIRE (401K)	LIABILITY INSUR.	COST PER HOUR
Finish carpenter	$24.30	1.90	$26.20	2.00	.21	5.15	2.28	2.92	.79	3.93	$43.50
Demolition laborer	$14.40	1.12	$15.52	1.19	.12	5.01	1.35	2.92	.47	2.33	$28.90

Paid Leave is calculated based on two weeks paid vacation, one week sick leave, and seven paid holidays. Employer's matching portion of **FICA** is 7.65 percent. **FUTA** (Federal Unemployment) is .8 percent. **Worker's compensation** for the doors trade was calculated using a national average of 19.63 percent. **Unemployment insurance** was calculated using a national average of 8.7 percent. **Health insurance** was calculated based on a projected national average for 2005 of $580 per employee (and family when applicable) per month. Employer pays 80 percent for a per month cost of $464 per employee. **Retirement** is based on a 401(k) retirement program with employer matching of 50 percent. Employee contributions to the 401(k) plan are an average of 6 percent of the true wage. **Liability insurance** is based on a national average of 14.0 percent.

Doors Labor Productivity

WORK DESCRIPTION	LABORER	COST PER HOUR	PRODUCTIVITY	UNIT PRICE
Demolition				
folding door	demolition laborer	$28.90	.114	$3.29 ea
bypassing door	demolition laborer	$28.90	.139	$4.02 ea
bypassing or folding door jamb & casing	demolition laborer	$28.90	.026	$.75 lf
pre-hung interior door, jamb, & casing	demolition laborer	$28.90	.388	$11.20 ea
pre-hung interior door slab only	demolition laborer	$28.90	.217	$6.27 ea
double pre-hung interior door, jamb, & casing	demolition laborer	$28.90	.585	$16.90 ea
double pre-hung interior door slabs only	demolition laborer	$28.90	.321	$9.30 ea
garage door, overhead tracks, jamb, & casing	demolition laborer	$28.90	3.65	$105.00 ea
garage door, hardware, jamb, & casing	demolition laborer	$28.90	2.90	$84.00 ea
garage door only	demolition laborer	$28.90	1.82	$52.60 ea
garage door opener	demolition laborer	$28.90	.765	$22.10 ea
pocket door, jamb, & casing	demolition laborer	$28.90	1.02	$29.50 ea
pocket door slab only	demolition laborer	$28.90	.491	$14.20 ea
double pocket door, jamb, & casing	demolition laborer	$28.90	1.86	$53.80 ea
double pocket door slab only	demolition laborer	$28.90	.913	$26.40 ea
pocket door hardware	demolition laborer	$28.90	.496	$14.30 ea
double pocket door hardware	demolition laborer	$28.90	.733	$21.20 ea
panel door, jamb, & casing	demolition laborer	$28.90	.477	$13.80 ea
panel door slab only	demolition laborer	$28.90	.217	$6.27 ea
transom	demolition laborer	$28.90	.451	$13.00 ea
entry door fanlite & casing	demolition laborer	$28.90	.749	$21.60 ea
double entry door fanlite & casing	demolition laborer	$28.90	1.71	$49.40 ea
storm door	demolition laborer	$28.90	.227	$6.56 ea
entry door, jamb, casing, & threshold	demolition laborer	$28.90	.496	$14.30 ea
entry door slab only	demolition laborer	$28.90	.283	$8.18 ea
double entry door, jamb, casing, & threshold	demolition laborer	$28.90	.842	$24.30 ea
double entry door slabs only	demolition laborer	$28.90	.492	$14.20 ea
entry door side-lite	demolition laborer	$28.90	.508	$14.70 ea
Dutch door slabs, jamb, & casing	demolition laborer	$28.90	.883	$25.50 ea
Dutch door slabs only	demolition laborer	$28.90	.321	$9.30 ea
cafe door	demolition laborer	$28.90	.254	$7.34 ea
sliding glass patio door (per lite)	demolition laborer	$28.90	.427	$12.30 ea
pet door	demolition laborer	$28.90	.290	$8.40 ea

. . . More ➤

Doors Labor Productivity *continued*

WORK DESCRIPTION	LABORER	COST PER HOUR	PRODUCTIVITY	UNIT PRICE
Minimum labor charge for door work				
minimum charge	finish carpenter	$43.50	2.50	$109.00 ea
Install interior doors				
folding door per section	finish carpenter	$43.50	.394	$17.10 ea
bypassing door per section	finish carpenter	$43.50	.755	$32.80 ea
bypassing or folding door jamb & casing	finish carpenter	$43.50	.109	$4.74 lf
pre-hung interior door & casing	finish carpenter	$43.50	1.43	$62.20 ea
pre-hung interior door slab only	finish carpenter	$43.50	.215	$9.35 ea
double pre-hung interior door & casing	finish carpenter	$43.50	2.45	$107.00 ea
double pre-hung interior door slabs only	finish carpenter	$43.50	.412	$17.90 ea
Install garage door				
with overhead tracks, jamb, & casing	finish carpenter	$43.50	6.25	$272.00 ea
with hardware, jamb, & casing	finish carpenter	$43.50	5.21	$227.00 ea
door only	finish carpenter	$43.50	3.15	$137.00 ea
opener	finish carpenter	$43.50	2.45	$107.00 ea
Install pocket door				
door slabs	finish carpenter	$43.50	.850	$37.00 ea
door, jamb, trim, & casing	finish carpenter	$43.50	1.35	$58.70 ea
double doors	finish carpenter	$43.50	2.34	$102.00 ea
double door, jamb, trim, & casing	finish carpenter	$43.50	3.12	$136.00 ea
Install pocket door rough framing package including track and hardware				
single door in 2" x 4" wall	finish carpenter	$43.50	1.50	$65.30 ea
double doors in 2" x 4" wall	finish carpenter	$43.50	2.88	$125.00 ea
single door in 2" x 6" wall	finish carpenter	$43.50	1.52	$66.10 ea
double doors in 2" x 6" wall	finish carpenter	$43.50	2.95	$128.00 ea
single door in 2" x 8" wall	finish carpenter	$43.50	1.54	$67.00 ea
double doors in 2" x 8" wall	finish carpenter	$43.50	3.03	$132.00 ea
rough framing for antique door	finish carpenter	$43.50	2.45	$107.00 ea
rough framing for antique double doors	finish carpenter	$43.50	5.12	$223.00 ea
Install pocket door track				
overhead track for antique door	finish carpenter	$43.50	1.30	$56.60 ea
overhead track for antique double door	finish carpenter	$43.50	2.34	$102.00 ea
clean and realign overhead antique door track	finish carpenter	$43.50	1.96	$85.30 ea
floor track for antique door	finish carpenter	$43.50	1.21	$52.60 ea
floor track for antique double door	finish carpenter	$43.50	2.20	$95.70 ea
clean and realign floor antique doors	finish carpenter	$43.50	2.64	$115.00 ea
Install panel door				
hang door & install casing	finish carpenter	$43.50	1.23	$53.50 ea
slab only	finish carpenter	$43.50	.178	$7.74 ea
Install entry door, fanlite, transom				
fanlite & casing	finish carpenter	$43.50	1.85	$80.50 ea
transom & casing	finish carpenter	$43.50	1.00	$43.50 ea
hang entry door & install casing	finish carpenter	$43.50	1.75	$76.10 ea
slab only	finish carpenter	$43.50	.212	$9.22 ea
hang double-entry door & casing	finish carpenter	$43.50	3.11	$135.00 ea
double door slabs only	finish carpenter	$43.50	.330	$14.40 ea
side-lite	finish carpenter	$43.50	1.14	$49.60 ea
Install Dutch door				
hang door & install casing	finish carpenter	$43.50	1.70	$74.00 ea
slabs only	finish carpenter	$43.50	.325	$14.10 ea
Install door lite				
cut hole in door and install	finish carpenter	$43.50	1.12	$48.70 ea
Install cafe door				
per set	finish carpenter	$43.50	.681	$29.60 ea
Install sliding glass patio doors				
with two lites	finish carpenter	$43.50	4.39	$191.00 ea
Install pet door				
per door	finish carpenter	$43.50	.844	$36.70 ea

... More ➤

Doors Labor Productivity *continued*

WORK DESCRIPTION	LABORER	COST PER HOUR	PRODUCTIVITY	UNIT PRICE
Assemble & install storm door				
per door	finish carpenter	$43.50	1.70	$74.00 ea
Remove for work, then reinstall				
folding doors per section	finish carpenter	$43.50	.148	$6.44 ea
bypass sliding doors per section	finish carpenter	$43.50	.220	$9.57 ea
door slab	finish carpenter	$43.50	.151	$6.57 ea
door slab, jamb & casing	finish carpenter	$43.50	1.63	$70.90 ea
double door slabs	finish carpenter	$43.50	.293	$12.70 ea
double door slabs, jamb & casing	finish carpenter	$43.50	2.67	$116.00 ea
pocket door & casing	finish carpenter	$43.50	1.15	$50.00 ea
pocket door, jamb & casing	finish carpenter	$43.50	3.23	$141.00 ea
double pocket doors & casing	finish carpenter	$43.50	1.58	$68.70 ea
double pocket doors, jamb & casing	finish carpenter	$43.50	3.39	$147.00 ea
panel door slab	finish carpenter	$43.50	.152	$6.61 ea
panel door, jamb, & casing	finish carpenter	$43.50	1.63	$70.90 ea
antique door casing & re-plumb door	finish carpenter	$43.50	2.95	$128.00 ea
transom	finish carpenter	$43.50	1.12	$48.70 ea
storm door	finish carpenter	$43.50	1.70	$74.00 ea
Dutch door, jamb, & casing	finish carpenter	$43.50	2.74	$119.00 ea
Dutch door slabs	finish carpenter	$43.50	.394	$17.10 ea
exterior door, jamb, & casing	finish carpenter	$43.50	2.20	$95.70 ea
exterior door slab	finish carpenter	$43.50	.292	$12.70 ea
exterior double door, jamb, & casing	finish carpenter	$43.50	3.12	$136.00 ea
exterior double door slabs	finish carpenter	$43.50	.366	$15.90 ea
entry door fanlite & casing	finish carpenter	$43.50	3.12	$136.00 ea
entry door fixed transom & casing	finish carpenter	$43.50	2.74	$119.00 ea
cafe door	finish carpenter	$43.50	1.02	$44.40 ea
sliding patio door, jamb, & casing	finish carpenter	$43.50	5.55	$241.00 ea
sliding patio door lites	finish carpenter	$43.50	1.65	$71.80 ea
pet door	finish carpenter	$43.50	1.29	$56.10 ea
garage door opener	finish carpenter	$43.50	3.50	$152.00 ea
single-car garage door	finish carpenter	$43.50	7.70	$335.00 ea
two-car garage door	finish carpenter	$43.50	9.25	$402.00 ea
Door repair				
minimum labor to repair antique panel door (no custom milling)	finish carpenter	$43.50	2.49	$108.00 ea
minimum labor charge to repair antique panel door when custom milling is required	finish carpenter	$43.50	3.51	$153.00 ea
replace antique panel door panel (not including custom knife charges)	finish carpenter	$43.50	2.74	$119.00 ea
replace antique panel door stile (not including custom knife charges)	finish carpenter	$43.50	2.49	$108.00 ea
repair cracks & dry rot in antique door with epoxy, tighten stiles	finish carpenter	$43.50	4.49	$195.00 ea
repair cracks & dry rot in antique door jamb with epoxy	finish carpenter	$43.50	3.40	$148.00 ea
repair cracks & dry rot in antique door casing with epoxy	finish carpenter	$43.50	3.40	$148.00 ea
Additional door labor charges				
add for installation of full-lite in exterior door	finish carpenter	$43.50	1.39	$60.50 ea
add for installation of half-lite in exterior door	finish carpenter	$43.50	1.07	$46.50 ea
add for installation of 1' by 1' lite in exterior door	finish carpenter	$43.50	.594	$25.80 ea
recondition sliding glass door, replace hardware	finish carpenter	$43.50	2.33	$101.00 ea
minimum labor for garage door work	finish carpenter	$43.50	2.50	$109.00 ea
minimum labor for sliding glass door work	finish carpenter	$43.50	3.25	$141.00 ea

11 .... *Door Hardware*

Item Description	Unit	Remove	Replace	Total	
Deadbolt, standard grade	ea	$7.98	$53.50	$61.48	◄ DEADBOLT
Replace Material........24.00 Labor 29.50					
Remove .... Labor 7.98					
Deadbolt, high grade	ea	$7.98	$66.50	$74.48	
Replace Material........37.00 Labor 29.50					
Remove .... Labor 7.98					
Deadbolt, deluxe grade	ea	$7.98	$74.50	$82.48	
Replace Material........45.00 Labor 29.50					
Remove .... Labor 7.98					
Remove deadbolt for work, then reinstall	ea	–	$47.90	$47.90	
Replace .... Labor...........47.90					
Exterior door keyed lockset, standard grade	ea	$9.07	$44.10	$53.17	◄ EXTERIOR LOCKSET
Replace Material........24.00 Labor 20.10					
Remove .... Labor 9.07					
Exterior door keyed lockset, high grade	ea	$9.07	$60.10	$69.17	
Replace Material.......40.00 Labor 20.10					
Remove .... Labor 9.07					
Exterior door keyed lockset, deluxe grade	ea	$9.07	$72.10	$81.17	
Replace Material........52.00 Labor 20.10					
Remove .... Labor 9.07					
Remove exterior lockset for work, then reinstall	ea	–	$44.80	$44.80	
Replace .... Labor 44.80					
Entry door keyed lockset, standard grade	ea	$20.10	$152.10	$172.20	◄ ENTRY LOCKSET
Replace Material ....89.00 Labor 63.10					
Remove .... Labor 20.10					
Entry door keyed lockset, high grade	ea	$20.10	$295.10	$315.20	
Replace Material .....232.00 Labor 63.10					
Remove .... Labor 20.10					
Entry door keyed lockset, deluxe grade	ea	$20.10	$455.10	$475.20	
Replace Material .....392.00 Labor 63.10					
Remove .... Labor 20.10					
Entry door keyed lockset, custom grade	ea	$20.10	$608.10	$628.20	
Replace Material .....545.00 Labor 63.10					
Remove .... Labor 20.10					
Remove entry door lockset for work, then reinstall	ea	–	$119.00	$119.00	
Replace .... Labor...........119.00					
Antique style door thumb latch, standard grade	ea	$14.90	$315.30	$330.20	◄ THUMB LATCH
Replace Material.......240.00 Labor...........75.30					
Remove .... Labor...........14.90					

HARDWARE QUALITY

Some rules of thumb:

Standard: Light gauge metal, chrome or brass plated with little or no pattern.

High: Brass, chrome over brass, or nickel over brass with minimal detail, or plated with ornate detail.

Deluxe: Brass, chrome over brass, or nickel over brass with moderate detail.

Custom: Brass, chrome over brass, or nickel over brass with ornate detail.

RELATED ITEMS

Bathroom Hardware......41
Doors.........................101

	Item Description	Unit	Remove	Replace	Total
THUMB LATCH ▶ continued	**Antique style door thumb latch, high grade**	ea	$14.90	$367.30	$382.20
	Replace Material .....292.00 Labor...........75.30				
	Remove .... Labor...........14.90				
INTERIOR ▶ **DOOR LOCKSET** See quality indicators on previous page.	**Interior door lockset, standard grade**	ea	$8.12	$36.60	$44.72
	Replace Material........19.00 Labor...........17.60				
	Remove .... Labor 8.12				
	Interior door lockset, high grade	ea	$8.12	$64.60	$72.72
	Replace Material........47.00 Labor...........17.60				
	Remove .... Labor 8.12				
	Interior door lockset, deluxe grade	ea	$8.12	$91.60	$99.72
	Replace Material........74.00 Labor...........17.60				
	Remove .... Labor 8.12				
	Remove interior door lockset for work, then reinstall	ea	–	$30.90	$30.90
	Replace .... Labor...........30.90				
DOOR CLOSER ▶ See quality indicators on previous page.	**Spring hinge door closer**	ea	$2.61	$29.20	$31.81
	Replace Material........18.00 Labor 11.20				
	Remove .... Labor 2.61				
	Door closer, standard grade	ea	$8.41	$64.70	$73.11
	Replace Material ....46.00 Labor...........18.70				
	Remove .... Labor 8.41				
	Door closer, high grade	ea	$8.41	$99.70	$108.11
	Replace Material........81.00 Labor...........18.70				
	Remove .... Labor 8.41				
	Remove door closer for work, then reinstall	ea	–	$32.30	$32.30
	Replace .... Labor...........32.30				
SECURITY CHAIN ▶ See quality indicators on previous page.	**Security chain**	ea	$7.46	$24.40	$31.86
	Replace Material........13.00 Labor 11.40				
	Remove .... Labor 7.46				
	Remove security chain for work, then reinstall	ea	–	$19.40	$19.40
	Replace .... Labor...........19.40				
DOOR HINGES ▶ See quality indicators on previous page. Deluxe grade hinges include embossed antique patterns.	**Door hinges, standard grade**	ea	$14.00	$31.10	$45.10
	Replace Material........12.00 Labor 19.10				
	Remove .... Labor...........14.00				
	Door hinges, high grade	ea	$14.00	$45.10	$59.10
	Replace Material ....26.00 Labor...........19.10				
	Remove .... Labor...........14.00				
	Door hinges, deluxe grade	ea	$14.00	$60.10	$74.10
	Replace Material........41.00 Labor...........19.10				
	Remove .... Labor...........14.00				
	Batten door hinges	ea	$14.00	$82.50	$96.50
	Replace Material........61.00 Labor...........21.50				
	Remove .... Labor...........14.00				
	Remove door hinges for work, then reinstall	ea	–	$34.20	$34.20
	Replace .... Labor...........34.20				

deluxe grade △

deluxe grade △

Item Description	Unit	Remove	Replace	Total	
Door knocker, standard grade *Replace* Material........19.00 Labor............15.30 *Remove* .... Labor............7.23	ea	$7.23	$34.30	$41.53	◄ **DOOR KNOCKER** See quality indicators on page 127.
Door knocker, high grade *Replace* Material........42.00 Labor............15.30 *Remove* .... Labor............7.23	ea	$7.23	$57.30	$64.53	
Door knocker, deluxe grade *Replace* Material.......82.00 Labor............15.30 *Remove* .... Labor............7.23	ea	$7.23	$97.30	$104.53	
Remove door knocker for work, then reinstall *Replace* .... Labor............27.70	ea	–	$27.70	$27.70	
Storm door hinges *Replace* Material........20.00 Labor............14.90 *Remove* .... Labor............13.20	ea	$13.20	$34.90	$48.10	◄ **STORM DOOR HINGES**
Remove storm door hinges for work, then reinstall *Replace* .... Labor............26.40	ea	–	$26.40	$26.40	
Storm door lockset, standard grade *Replace* Material ....26.00 Labor............16.80 *Remove* .... Labor............9.45	ea	$9.45	$42.80	$52.25	◄ **STORM DOOR LOCKSET**
Storm door lockset, high grade *Replace* Material ....39.00 Labor............16.80 *Remove* .... Labor............9.45	ea	$9.45	$55.80	$65.25	
Remove storm door lockset for work, then reinstall *Replace* .... Labor............29.80	ea	–	$29.80	$29.80	
Hinge door stop *Replace* Material.........5.00 Labor.............5.57 *Remove* .... Labor.............2.43	ea	$2.43	$10.57	$13.00	◄ **DOOR STOP** See quality indicators on page 127.
Flexible spring baseboard door stop *Replace* Material.........6.00 Labor.............6.00 *Remove* .... Labor.............2.43	ea	$2.43	$12.00	$14.43	*flexible spring* △
Rigid baseboard door stop *Replace* Material.........7.00 Labor.............6.00 *Remove* .... Labor.............2.43	ea	$2.43	$13.00	$15.43	*rigid* △
Remove door stop for work, then reinstall *Replace* .... Labor............11.00	ea	–	$11.00	$11.00	
Door push plate, standard grade *Replace* Material ....22.00 Labor............18.10 *Remove* .... Labor.............4.62	ea	$4.62	$40.10	$44.72	◄ **PUSH PLATE** See quality indicators on page 127.
Door push plate, high grade *Replace* Material.......40.00 Labor............18.10 *Remove* .... Labor.............4.62	ea	$4.62	$58.10	$62.72	
Remove door push plate for work, then reinstall *Replace* .... Labor............32.30	ea	–	$32.30	$32.30	△ *high grade* △

RELATED ITEMS

Bathroom Hardware......41
Doors.........................101

	Item Description	Unit	Remove	Replace	Total
KICK PLATE ► *See quality indicators on page 127.*	**Door kick plate, standard grade** *Replace* Material.......37.00 Labor...........19.40 *Remove* .... Labor............6.16	ea	$6.16	$56.40	$62.56
	Door kick plate, high grade *Replace* Material ....54.00 Labor...........19.40 *Remove* .... Labor............6.16	ea	$6.16	$73.40	$79.56
	Remove door kick plate for work, then reinstall *Replace* .... Labor...........35.20	ea	–	$35.20	$35.20
LETTER PLATE ► *See quality indicators on page 127.*	**Letter plate, standard grade** *Replace* Material ....30.00 Labor...........21.80 *Remove* .... Labor............6.24	ea	$6.24	$51.80	$58.04
	Letter plate, high grade *Replace* Material........59.00 Labor...........21.80 *Remove* .... Labor............6.24	ea	$6.24	$80.80	$87.04
	Remove letter plate for work, then reinstall *Replace* .... Labor...........39.20	ea	–	$39.20	$39.20
PEEP HOLE ►	**Door peep hole** *Replace* Material ....20.00 Labor...........21.10 *Remove* .... Labor............5.92	ea	$5.92	$41.10	$47.02
	Remove door peep hole for work, then reinstall *Replace* .... Labor...........38.20	ea	–	$38.20	$38.20
DOOR SWEEP ►	**Door sweep** *Replace* Material ....30.00 Labor...........18.70 *Remove* .... Labor............6.91	ea	$6.91	$48.70	$55.61
	Remove door sweep for work, then reinstall *Replace* .... Labor...........33.20	ea	–	$33.20	$33.20
THRESHOLD ► *Standard grade is aluminum or flat wood.*	**Door threshold, standard grade** *Replace* Material........17.00 Labor...........20.70 *Remove* .... Labor............7.57	ea	$7.57	$37.70	$45.27
	Door threshold, high grade *Replace* Material........31.0000 Labor...........20.70 *Remove* .... Labor............7.57	ea	$7.57	$51.70	$59.27
	Remove door threshold for work, then reinstall *Replace* .... Labor...........37.50	ea	–	$37.50	$37.50
WEATHERSTRIP ►	**Door weatherstripping** *Replace* Material ....20.00 Labor...........18.10 *Remove* .... Labor............5.64	ea	$5.64	$38.10	$43.74
GARAGE DOOR ► **HARDWARE**	**Garage door hardware, standard grade** *Replace* Material........81.00 Labor...........100.00 *Remove* .... Labor...........22.00	ea	$22.00	$181.00	$203.00
	Garage door hardware, high grade *Replace* Material ....110.00 Labor...........100.00 *Remove* .... Labor...........22.00	ea	$22.00	$210.00	$232.00
	Remove garage door hardware for work, then reinstall *Replace* .... Labor...........176.00	ea	–	$176.00	$176.00

TIME & MATERIAL CHARTS (selected items)

Door Hardware Materials

See **Door Hardware** material prices with the line items and other information in the **QuickFinder** column.

Door Hardware Labor

LABORER	BASE WAGE	PAID LEAVE	TRUE WAGE	FICA	FUTA	WORKER'S COMP.	UNEMPLOY. INSUR.	HEALTH INSUR.	RETIRE (401K)	LIABILITY INSUR.	COST PER HOUR
Finish carpenter	$24.30	1.90	$26.20	2.00	.21	5.15	2.28	2.92	.79	3.93	$43.50
Demolition laborer	$14.40	1.12	$15.52	1.19	.12	5.01	1.35	2.92	.47	2.33	$28.90

Paid Leave is calculated based on two weeks paid vacation, one week sick leave, and seven paid holidays. Employer's matching portion of **FICA** is 7.65 percent. **FUTA** (Federal Unemployment) is .8 percent. **Worker's compensation** for the door hardware trade was calculated using a national average of 19.63 percent. **Unemployment insurance** was calculated using a national average of 8.7 percent. **Health insurance** was calculated based on a projected national average for 2005 of $580 per employee (and family when applicable) per month. Employer pays 80 percent for a per month cost of $464 per employee. **Retirement** is based on a 401(k) retirement program with employer matching of 50 percent. Employee contributions to the 401(k) plan are an average of 6 percent of the true wage. **Liability insurance** is based on a national average of 14.0 percent.

Door Hardware Labor Productivity

WORK DESCRIPTION	LABORER	COST PER HOUR	PRODUCTIVITY	UNIT PRICE
Demolition				
deadbolt	demolition laborer	$28.90	.276	$7.98 ea
exterior door keyed lockset	demolition laborer	$28.90	.314	$9.07 ea
entry door keyed lockset	demolition laborer	$28.90	.696	$20.10 ea
antique-style door thumb latch	demolition laborer	$28.90	.516	$14.90 ea
interior door lockset	demolition laborer	$28.90	.281	$8.12 ea
door closer	demolition laborer	$28.90	.291	$8.41 ea
security chain	demolition laborer	$28.90	.258	$7.46 ea
hinges	demolition laborer	$28.90	.485	$14.00 ea
door knocker	demolition laborer	$28.90	.250	$7.23 ea
storm door hinges	demolition laborer	$28.90	.457	$13.20 ea
storm door lockset	demolition laborer	$28.90	.327	$9.45 ea
door stop	demolition laborer	$28.90	.084	$2.43 ea
door push plate	demolition laborer	$28.90	.160	$4.62 ea
door kick plate	demolition laborer	$28.90	.213	$6.16 ea
door letter plate	demolition laborer	$28.90	.216	$6.24 ea
door peep hole	demolition laborer	$28.90	.205	$5.92 ea
door sweep	demolition laborer	$28.90	.239	$6.91 ea
door threshold	demolition laborer	$28.90	.262	$7.57 ea
door weatherstripping	demolition laborer	$28.90	.195	$5.64 ea
garage door hardware	demolition laborer	$28.90	.762	$22.00 ea
Install deadbolt				
install	finish carpenter	$43.50	.678	$29.50 ea
remove for work, then reinstall	finish carpenter	$43.50	1.10	$47.90 ea
Install exterior door keyed lockset				
install	finish carpenter	$43.50	.461	$20.10 ea
remove for work, then reinstall	finish carpenter	$43.50	1.03	$44.80 ea
Install entry door keyed lockset				
install	finish carpenter	$43.50	1.45	$63.10 ea
remove for work, then reinstall	finish carpenter	$43.50	2.73	$119.00 ea
Install antique style door thumb latch				
install	finish carpenter	$43.50	1.73	$75.30 ea

. . . More ➤

Door Hardware Labor Productivity *continued*

WORK DESCRIPTION	LABORER	COST PER HOUR	PRODUCTIVITY	UNIT PRICE
Install interior door lockset				
install	finish carpenter	$43.50	.405	$17.60 ea
remove for work, then reinstall	finish carpenter	$43.50	.710	$30.90 ea
Install door closer				
spring hinge	finish carpenter	$43.50	.257	$11.20 ea
typical	finish carpenter	$43.50	.431	$18.70 ea
remove for work, then reinstall	finish carpenter	$43.50	.742	$32.30 ea
Install security chain				
install	finish carpenter	$43.50	.262	$11.40 ea
remove for work, then reinstall	finish carpenter	$43.50	.445	$19.40 ea
Install door hinges				
typical	finish carpenter	$43.50	.438	$19.10 ea
for batten door	finish carpenter	$43.50	.495	$21.50 ea
remove for work, then reinstall	finish carpenter	$43.50	.786	$34.20 ea
Install door knocker				
install	finish carpenter	$43.50	.351	$15.30 ea
remove for work, then reinstall	finish carpenter	$43.50	.636	$27.70 ea
Install storm door hinges				
install	finish carpenter	$43.50	.342	$14.90 ea
remove for work, then reinstall	finish carpenter	$43.50	.607	$26.40 ea
Install storm door lockset				
install	finish carpenter	$43.50	.387	$16.80 ea
remove for work, then reinstall	finish carpenter	$43.50	.685	$29.80 ea
Install door stop				
hinge	finish carpenter	$43.50	.128	$5.57 ea
baseboard	finish carpenter	$43.50	.138	$6.00 ea
remove for work, then reinstall	finish carpenter	$43.50	.252	$11.00 ea
Install door push plate				
install	finish carpenter	$43.50	.417	$18.10 ea
remove for work, then reinstall	finish carpenter	$43.50	.742	$32.30 ea
Install door kick plate				
install	finish carpenter	$43.50	.445	$19.40 ea
remove for work, then reinstall	finish carpenter	$43.50	.809	$35.20 ea
Install letter plate				
install	finish carpenter	$43.50	.500	$21.80 ea
remove for work, then reinstall	finish carpenter	$43.50	.902	$39.20 ea
Install door peep hole				
install	finish carpenter	$43.50	.484	$21.10 ea
remove for work, then reinstall	finish carpenter	$43.50	.879	$38.20 ea
Install door sweep				
install	finish carpenter	$43.50	.431	$18.70 ea
remove for work, then reinstall	finish carpenter	$43.50	.763	$33.20 ea
Install door threshold				
install	finish carpenter	$43.50	.477	$20.70 ea
remove for work, then reinstall	finish carpenter	$43.50	.862	$37.50 ea
Install door weatherstripping				
install	finish carpenter	$43.50	.417	$18.10 ea
Install garage door hardware				
install	finish carpenter	$43.50	2.30	$100.00 ea
remove for work, then reinstall	finish carpenter	$43.50	4.05	$176.00 ea

✑ NOTES: _____

_____

_____

_____ end

12 .... *Drywall*

Item Description	Unit	Remove	Replace	Total
Remove drywall & prep walls for new installation *Remove*.................... Labor............ .23	sf	$.23	–	$.23
Scrape (remove) acoustic ceiling texture *Remove*.................... Labor............ .32	sf	$.32	–	$.32
Scrape (remove) painted acoustic ceiling texture *Remove*.................... Labor............ .55	sf	$.55	–	$.55
Remove furring strips attached to wood, 16″ on center *Remove*.................... Labor............ .29	sf	$.29	–	$.29
Remove furring strips attached to concrete or masonry, 16″ on center *Remove*.................... Labor............ .32	sf	$.32	–	$.32
Remove furring strips attached to wood, 24″ on center *Remove*.................... Labor............ .26	sf	$.26	–	$.26
Remove furring strips attached to concrete or masonry, 24″ on center *Remove*.................... Labor............ .29	sf	$.29	–	$.29
3/8″ drywall installed with machine texture *Replace* Materials .... .50 Labor ....1.25 *Remove*.................... Labor............ .23	sf	$.23	$1.75	$1.98
3/8″ drywall installed with knock-down machine texture *Replace* Materials .... .50 Labor ....1.30 *Remove*.................... Labor............ .23	sf	$.23	$1.80	$2.03
3/8″ drywall installed with light texture *Replace* Materials .... .50 Labor ....1.34 *Remove*.................... Labor............ .23	sf	$.23	$1.84	$2.07
3/8″ drywall installed with medium texture *Replace* Materials .... .55 Labor ....1.39 *Remove*.................... Labor............ .23	sf	$.23	$1.94	$2.17
3/8″ drywall installed heavy texture *Replace* Materials .... .60 Labor ....1.43 *Remove*.................... Labor............ .23	sf	$.23	$2.03	$2.26
3/8″ drywall installed with smooth-wall finish *Replace* Materials .... .53 Labor ....1.65 *Remove*.................... Labor............ .23	sf	$.23	$2.18	$2.41
3/8″ drywall installed (all coats, no texture) *Replace* Materials .... .40 Labor............ 1.12 *Remove*.................... Labor............ .23	sf	$.23	$1.52	$1.75
3/8″ drywall, hung & fire taped only *Replace* Materials .... .38 Labor............ .82 *Remove*.................... Labor............ .23	sf	$.23	$1.20	$1.43

◄ **DEMOLITION**
Tear-out and debris removal to a truck or dumpster on site. Does not include hauling, dumpster, or dump fees. No salvage value is assumed.

◄ **3/8″ DRYWALL**

DRYWALL INSTALLATION

Drywall is hung and taped according to industry standards. Drywall is attached with nails when hung, then permanently affixed with screws. Perfatape and three coats of mud are applied plus texture.

One lf of corner bead is calculated for every 24 sf of installed drywall.

Productivity is based on repair installations.

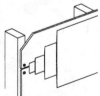

RELATED ITEMS

Cleaning 58
Painting 333
Paneling 347
Plaster 353
Wallpaper 495

	Item Description	Unit	Remove	Replace	Total
3/8" DRYWALL ▶ *continued*	**3/8" drywall, hung only (no tape, coating or texture)** *Replace* Materials .... .36 Labor .... .44 *Remove*...................... Labor .... .23	sf	$.23	$.80	$1.03
	Add for installation of 3/8" drywall over existing plaster wall *Replace* .... Labor .... .13	sf	–	$.13	$.13
	Add for 3/8" foil-backed drywall *Replace* Materials .... .11	sf	–	$.11	$.11
1/2" DRYWALL ▶	**1/2" drywall installed with machine texture** *Replace* Materials .... .48 Labor .... 1.25 *Remove*...................... Labor .... .23	sf	$.23	$1.73	$1.96
	1/2" drywall installed with knock-down machine texture *Replace* Materials .... .48 Labor .... 1.30 *Remove*...................... Labor .... .23	sf	$.23	$1.78	$2.01
	1/2" drywall installed with light texture *Replace* Materials .... .48 Labor .... 1.34 *Remove*...................... Labor .... .23	sf	$.23	$1.82	$2.05
	1/2" drywall installed with medium texture *Replace* Materials .... .53 Labor .... 1.39 *Remove*...................... Labor .... .23	sf	$.23	$1.92	$2.15
	1/2" drywall installed heavy texture *Replace* Materials .... .58 Labor .... 1.43 *Remove*...................... Labor .... .23	sf	$.23	$2.01	$2.24
	1/2" drywall installed with smooth-wall finish *Replace* Materials .... .51 Labor .... 1.65 *Remove*...................... Labor .... .23	sf	$.23	$2.16	$2.39
	1/2" drywall installed (all coats, no texture) *Replace* Materials .... .38 Labor .... 1.12 *Remove*...................... Labor .... .23	sf	$.23	$1.50	$1.73
	1/2" drywall, hung & fire taped only *Replace* Materials .... .36 Labor .... .82 *Remove*...................... Labor .... .23	sf	$.23	$1.18	$1.41
	1/2" drywall, hung only (no tape, coating or texture) *Replace* Materials .... .34 Labor .... .44 *Remove*...................... Labor .... .23	sf	$.23	$.78	$1.01
	Add for installation of 1/2" drywall over existing plaster wall *Replace* .... Labor .... .13	sf	–	$.13	$.13
	Add for 1/2" moisture-resistant drywall *Replace* Materials .... .12	sf	–	$.12	$.12
	Add for 1/2" type X fire-rated drywall *Replace* Materials .... .10	sf	–	$.10	$.10
	Add for 1/2" foil-backed drywall *Replace* Materials .... .16	sf	–	$.16	$.16
	Add for 1/2" type X fire-rated, foil-backed drywall *Replace* Materials .... .24	sf	–	$.24	$.24

Item Description	Unit	Remove	Replace	Total	
5/8" drywall installed with machine texture	sf	$.23	$1.81	$2.04	◄ 5/8" DRYWALL
Replace Materials .... .56 Labor 1.25					
Remove..................... Labor .... .23					
5/8" drywall installed with knock-down machine texture	sf	$.23	$1.86	$2.09	
Replace Materials .... .56 Labor 1.30					
Remove..................... Labor .... .23					
5/8" drywall installed with light texture	sf	$.23	$1.90	$2.13	
Replace Materials .... .56 Labor 1.34					
Remove..................... Labor .... .23					
5/8" drywall installed with medium texture	sf	$.23	$2.00	$2.23	
Replace Materials .... .61 Labor 1.39					
Remove..................... Labor .... .23					
5/8" drywall installed heavy texture	sf	$.23	$2.09	$2.32	
Replace Materials .... .66 Labor 1.43					
Remove..................... Labor .... .23					
5/8" drywall installed with smooth-wall finish	sf	$.23	$2.24	$2.47	
Replace Materials .... .59 Labor 1.65					
Remove..................... Labor .... .23					
5/8" drywall installed (all coats, no texture)	sf	$.23	$1.58	$1.81	
Replace Materials .... .46 Labor 1.12					
Remove..................... Labor .... .23					
5/8" drywall, hung & fire taped only	sf	$.23	$1.26	$1.49	
Replace Materials .... .44 Labor .... .82					
Remove..................... Labor .... .23					
5/8" drywall, hung only (no tape, coating or texture)	sf	$.23	$.86	$1.09	
Replace Materials .... .42 Labor .... .44					
Remove..................... Labor .... .23					
Add for installation of 5/8" drywall over existing plaster wall	sf	–	$.13	$.13	
Replace .... Labor .... .13					
Add for 5/8" moisture-resistant drywall	sf	–	$.11	$.11	
Replace Materials .... .11					
Add for 5/8" foil-backed drywall	sf	–	$.19	$.19	
Replace Materials .... .19					
Acoustic ceiling (cottage cheese) texture, light coverage	sf	$.32	$.50	$.82	◄ ACOUSTIC CEILING
Replace Materials .... .15 Labor .... .35					
Remove..................... Labor .... .32					
Acoustic ceiling (cottage cheese) texture, medium coverage	sf	$.32	$.68	$1.00	
Replace Materials .... .20 Labor .... .48					
Remove..................... Labor .... .32					
Acoustic ceiling (cottage cheese) texture, heavy coverage	sf	$.32	$.92	$1.24	
Replace Materials .... .22 Labor .... .70					
Remove..................... Labor .... .32					
Glitter application to acoustic-ceiling texture	sf	–	$.10	$.10	
Replace Materials .... .01 Labor .... .09					

RELATED ITEMS

Cleaning 58
Painting 333
Paneling 347
Plaster 353
Wallpaper 495

	Item Description	Unit	Remove	Replace	Total
MINIMUM ▶ ACOUSTIC CHARGE	**Minimum charge for acoustic-ceiling texture** *Replace* Materials ....100.00 Labor..........69.00	ea	–	$169.00	$169.00
DRYWALL PATCH ▶	**Drywall patch (match existing texture or finish)** *Replace* Materials ......25.00 Labor..........62.10	ea	–	$87.10	$87.10
MINIMUM ▶ DRYWALL CHARGE	**Minimum charge for drywall repair** *Replace* Materials ......35.00 Labor 253.00	ea	–	$288.00	$288.00
TEXTURE ▶	**Texture drywall with light hand texture** *Replace* Materials .... .100 Labor............ .22	sf	–	$.32	$.32
	Texture drywall with medium hand texture *Replace* Materials .... .150 Labor............ .26	sf	–	$.41	$.41
	Texture drywall with heavy hand texture *Replace* Materials .... .200 Labor............ .26	sf	–	$.46	$.46
	Texture drywall with thin-coat smooth-wall *Replace* Materials .... .130 Labor............ .52	sf	–	$.65	$.65
	Texture drywall, machine applied *Replace* Materials .... .100 Labor............ .17	sf	–	$.27	$.27
	Texture drywall, machine applied and knocked down with trowel *Replace* Materials .... .100 Labor............ .22	sf	–	$.32	$.32
METAL FURRING ▶ *See Rough Carpentry, page 430 for wood furring strips.*	**Metal hat-shaped furring channel, 16" on center on wood** *Replace* Materials .... .180 Labor............ .42 *Remove*........................ Labor............ .29	sf	$.29	$.60	$.89
	Metal hat-shaped furring channel, 24" on center on wood *Replace* Materials .... .140 Labor............ .30 *Remove*........................ Labor............ .26	sf	$.26	$.44	$.70
	Metal sound-resistant furring channel, 16" on center on wood *Replace* Materials .... .200 Labor............ .42 *Remove*........................ Labor............ .29	sf	$.29	$.62	$.91
△ hat-shaped channel	**Metal sound-resistant furring channel, 24" on center on wood** *Replace* Materials .... .150 Labor............ .30 *Remove*........................ Labor............ .26	sf	$.26	$.45	$.71
	Metal hat-shaped furring channel, 16" on center on concrete or masonry *Replace* Materials .... .180 Labor............ .45 *Remove*........................ Labor............ .32	sf	$.32	$.63	$.95
	Metal hat-shaped furring channel, 24" on center on concrete or masonry *Replace* Materials .... .140 Labor............ .30 *Remove*........................ Labor............ .29	sf	$.29	$.44	$.73
△ sound-resistant channel	**Metal sound-resistant furring channel, 16" on center on concrete or masonry** *Replace* Materials .... .200 Labor............ .45 *Remove*........................ Labor............ .32	sf	$.32	$.65	$.97
△ Z channel	**Metal sound-resistant furring channel, 24" on center on concrete or masonry** *Replace* Materials .... .150 Labor............ .30 *Remove*........................ Labor............ .29	sf	$.29	$.45	$.74

Item Description	Unit	Remove	Replace	Total
Metal Z channel, 16" on center on concrete or masonry	sf	$.32	$.59	$.91
Replace Materials .... .140 Labor .... .45				
Remove .... Labor .... .32				
Metal Z channel, 24" on center on concrete or masonry	sf	$.29	$.39	$.68
Replace Materials .... .090 Labor .... .30				
Remove .... Labor .... .29				

RELATED ITEMS

Cleaning 58
Painting 333
Paneling 347
Plaster 353
Rough Carpentry
  furring strips 430
Wallpaper 495

NOTES: _____

_____

_____ end

TIME & MATERIAL CHARTS *(selected items)*

Drywall Materials

DESCRIPTION	MATERIAL PRICE	GROSS COVERAGE	WASTE	NET COVERAGE	UNIT PRICE
3/8" drywall board					
standard	$314.00 per 1,000	1,000	8%	920	$.34 sf
foil-backed	$417.00 per 1,000	1,000	8%	920	$.45 sf
1/2" drywall board					
standard	$300.00 per 1,000	1,000	7%	930	$.32 sf
moisture-resistant	$413.00 per 1,000	1,000	7%	930	$.44 sf
foil-backed	$430.00 per 1,000	1,000	7%	930	$.46 sf
fire-rated type X	$370.00 per 1,000	1,000	7%	930	$.40 sf
fire-rated type X foil-backed	$522.00 per 1,000	1,000	7%	930	$.56 sf
5/8" drywall board					
type X	$368.00 per 1,000	1,000	7%	930	$.40 sf
moisture-resistant	$473.00 per 1,000	1,000	7%	930	$.51 sf
Fasteners					
drywall nails, used to secure when hanging	$52.00 per box	32,000	4%	30,720	$.01 sf
drywall screws, used to attach after hung	$102.00 per box	8,534	3%	8,278	$.01 sf
Drywall taping materials					
perfatape (per 500' roll)	$6.60 per roll	1,111	6%	1,044	$.01 sf
corner bead	$1.00 per stick	204	4%	196	$.01 sf
joint compound	$14.50 per 50 lb box	965	16%	811	$.02 sf
Drywall texture compound					
machine-sprayed	$15.70 per 50 lb box	190	13%	165	$.10 sf
light hand texture	$15.70 per 50 lb box	175	13%	152	$.10 sf
medium hand texture	$15.70 per 50 lb box	120	13%	104	$.15 sf
heavy hand texture	$15.70 per 50 lb box	93	14%	80	$.20 sf
heavy trowel texture	$15.70 per 50 lb box	77	15%	65	$.24 sf
smooth wall	$15.70 per 50 lb box	142	14%	122	$.13 sf
Acoustic ceiling (cottage cheese) texture compound					
light texture	$27.50 per 50 lb bag	220	17%	183	$.15 sf
medium texture	$27.50 per 50 lb box	170	17%	141	$.20 sf
heavy texture	$27.50 per 50 lb box	153	17%	127	$.22 sf
Acoustic ceiling glitter (per pound)					
light to heavy application	$3.40 per pound	2,350	22%	1,833	$.01 sf
Metal furring strips					
hat-shaped channel installed 24" on center	$2.70 per 12' stick	21	3%	20	$.14 sf
sound-resistant channel installed 24" on center	$3.00 per 12' stick	21	3%	20	$.15 sf
Z channel installed 24" on center	$1.40 per 8' stick	15	3%	15	$.09 sf

Drywall Rental Equipment

DESCRIPTION	PRICE	COVERAGE	UNIT PRICE
Ames taping tools	$10.00 per day	416 per day	$.02 sf
texture equipment (gun with hopper & compressor)	$70.00 per day	1,536 per day	$.05 sf
glitter blower for acoustic ceilings	$5.00 per day	5,000 per day	$.001 sf
drywall lifter (for one-person hanging)	$15.00 per day	102 per day	$.15 sf
minimum charge	$40.00 minimum	1 minimum	$40.00 each

Drywall Labor

LABORER	BASE WAGE	PAID LEAVE	TRUE WAGE	FICA	FUTA	WORKER'S COMP.	UNEMPLOY. INSUR.	HEALTH INSUR.	RETIRE (401k)	LIABILITY INSUR.	COST PER HOUR
Drywall hanger	$23.30	1.82	$25.12	1.92	.20	6.51	2.19	2.92	.75	3.77	$43.40
Drywall hanger's helper	$16.90	1.32	$18.22	1.39	.15	4.72	1.59	2.92	.55	2.73	$32.30
Drywall taper	$23.50	1.83	$25.33	1.94	.20	6.57	2.20	2.92	.76	3.80	$43.70
Demolition laborer	$14.40	1.12	$15.52	1.19	.12	5.01	1.35	2.92	.47	2.33	$28.90

Paid Leave is calculated based on two weeks paid vacation, one week sick leave, and seven paid holidays. Employer's matching portion of **FICA** is 7.65 percent. **FUTA** (Federal Unemployment) is .8 percent. **Worker's compensation** for the drywall trade was calculated using a national average of 25.87 percent. **Unemployment insurance** was calculated using a national average of 8.7 percent. **Health insurance** was calculated based on a projected national average for 2005 of $580 per employee (and family when applicable) per month. Employer pays 80 percent for a per month cost of $464 per employee. **Retirement** is based on a 401(k) retirement program with employer matching of 50 percent. Employee contributions to the 401(k) plan are an average of 6 percent of the true wage. **Liability insurance** is based on a national average of 14.0 percent.

Drywall Labor Productivity

WORK DESCRIPTION	LABORER	COST PER HOUR	PRODUCTIVITY	UNIT PRICE
Demolition				
remove drywall and prep walls	demolition laborer	$28.90	.008	$.23 sf
scrape and prep acoustical ceiling	demolition laborer	$28.90	.011	$.32 sf
scrape and prep painted acoustical ceiling	demolition laborer	$28.90	.019	$.55 sf
remove furring strips on wood, 16" oc	demolition laborer	$28.90	.010	$.29 sf
remove furring strips on conc. or masonry, 16" oc	demolition laborer	$28.90	.011	$.32 sf
remove furring strips on wood, 24" oc	demolition laborer	$28.90	.009	$.26 sf
remove furring strips on conc. or masonry, 24" oc	demolition laborer	$28.90	.010	$.29 sf
Hang drywall				
hang drywall	drywall hanger	$43.40		
hang drywall	drywall hanger's helper	$32.30		
hang drywall	drywall hanging crew	$37.90		
Tape and coat drywall				
to finish (no texture)	drywall taper	$43.70	.017	$.74 sf
tape coat only	drywall taper	$43.70	.010	$.44 sf
tape coat and one additional coat only	drywall taper	$43.70	.012	$.52 sf
to finish, apply machine-sprayed texture	drywall taper	$43.70	.020	$.87 sf
to finish, apply machine-sprayed, knock-down texture	drywall taper	$43.70	.021	$.92 sf
to finish, apply light hand texture	drywall taper	$43.70	.022	$.96 sf
to finish, apply heavy hand texture	drywall taper	$43.70	.024	$1.05 sf
to finish, apply smooth-wall texture	drywall taper	$43.70	.029	$1.27 sf
Apply texture				
with compressor and spray gun	drywall taper	$43.70	.004	$.17 sf
with spray gun, then knock down with trowel	drywall taper	$43.70	.005	$.22 sf
light hand texture	drywall taper	$43.70	.005	$.22 sf
heavy hand texture	drywall taper	$43.70	.006	$.26 sf
thin coat smooth-wall finish	drywall taper	$43.70	.012	$.52 sf
Apply acoustical ceiling texture				
light	drywall taper	$43.70	.008	$.35 sf
heavy	drywall taper	$43.70	.016	$.70 sf
apply glitter to freshly sprayed ceiling	drywall taper	$43.70	.002	$.09 sf

13 .... *Electrical*

Item Description	Unit	Remove	Replace	Total	
Minimum charge for electrical work *Replace* Materials......20.00 Labor.........52.80	ea	–	$72.80	$72.80	◄ **MINIMUM**
Complete house wiring, outlets, switches & light fixtures, economy grade *Replace* Materials........1.67 Labor...........2.09	sf	–	$3.76	$3.76	◄ **COMPLETE HOUSE** *Complete house wiring, boxes, switches, outlets and fixtures to code for a house that is not electrically heated. (Electrical hookups for furnace, AC unit, and/or heat pump included.) Does not include breaker panel, main disconnect or service drop. Grades refer to quality of light fixtures (see pages 154-155).*
Complete house wiring, outlets, switches & light fixtures, standard grade *Replace* Materials........1.91 Labor...........3.55	sf	–	$5.46	$5.46	
Complete house wiring, outlets, switches & light fixtures, high grade *Replace* Materials........2.19 Labor...........4.10	sf	–	$6.29	$6.29	
Complete house wiring, outlets, switches & light fixtures, deluxe grade *Replace* Materials........2.32 Labor...........4.29	sf	–	$6.61	$6.61	
Complete house wiring, outlets, switches & light fixtures, low-voltage system *Replace* Materials........2.12 Labor...........3.94	sf	–	$6.06	$6.06	
Add for complete house electrical with wiring in conduit *Replace* Materials........2.15 Labor ....2.17 ► EMT conduit with 4.4 terminations, 7 bends, and 4 clamps per 100 lf.	sf	–	$4.32	$4.32	
Complete house rough electrical (no light fixtures), standard *Replace* Materials...... 1.04 Labor...........2.76	sf	–	$3.80	$3.80	◄ **COMPLETE HOUSE WIRING** *Same as above but does not include fixtures.*
Complete house rough electrical (no light fixtures), in conduit *Replace* Materials........2.31 Labor...........6.07 ► EMT conduit with 4.4 terminations, 7 bends, and 4 clamps per 100 lf.	sf	–	$8.38	$8.38	
Complete house rough electrical (no light fixtures), low-voltage system *Replace* Materials...... 1.14 Labor...........2.96	sf	–	$4.10	$4.10	
Complete house light fixtures, economy grade *Replace* Materials...... 1.08 Labor............ .59	sf	–	$1.67	$1.67	◄ **COMPLETE HOUSE FIXTURES** *See pages 154-155 for info about fixture grades.*
Complete house light fixtures, standard grade *Replace* Materials........1.40 Labor............ .63	sf	–	$2.03	$2.03	
Complete house light fixtures, high grade *Replace* Materials........1.96 Labor............ .63	sf	–	$2.59	$2.59	
Complete house light fixtures, deluxe grade *Replace* Materials........2.57 Labor............ .67	sf	–	$3.24	$3.24	
Complete house light fixtures for low-voltage system *Replace* Materials........1.86 Labor............ .51	sf	–	$2.37	$2.37	
120 volt outlet with wiring run & box *Replace* Materials.......15.00 Labor..........38.50 ► General-purpose use, average of 6 outlets per single-pole breaker (breaker not included). Includes up to 15 lf of #12/2 wire.	ea	–	$53.50	$53.50	◄ **WIRE, OUTLETS & SWITCHES** *Unless otherwise indicated, includes outlet or switch, box, and up to 26 lf of wire.*

> **VOLTAGE**
>
> Voltage listed as "120 volt" applies to 110, 115, 120, and 125 volt applications.
>
> Voltage listed as "240 volt" applies to 220, 240, or 250 volt applications.

Item Description	Unit	Remove	Replace	Total
WIRE, OUTLETS ▶ & SWITCHES *continued*				
120 volt GFCI outlet with wiring run & box	ea	–	**$88.50**	**$88.50**
Replace Materials......50.00 Labor..........38.50				
▶ Average of 3 outlets per single-pole breaker. Includes up to 26 lf of #12/2 wire.				
120 volt exterior waterproof outlet with wiring run & box	ea	–	**$58.50**	**$58.50**
Replace Materials......20.00 Labor..........38.50				
▶ General-purpose use, average of 3 outlets per single-pole breaker (breaker not included). Includes up to 26 lf of #12/2 wire.				
120 volt switch with wiring run & box	ea	–	**$58.50**	**$58.50**
Replace Materials......20.00 Labor..........38.50				
▶ Includes up to 15 lf of #12/2 wire.				
120 volt 3-way switch with wiring run & box	ea	–	**$111.80**	**$111.80**
Replace Materials......35.00 Labor..........76.80				
▶ Includes up to 20 lf of #12/2 wire.				
120 volt exterior waterproof switch with wiring run & box	ea	–	**$58.50**	**$58.50**
Replace Materials......20.00 Labor..........38.50				
▶ Includes up to 26 lf of #12/2 wire.				
240 volt ▷ **240 volt outlet with wiring run & box (30 amp)**	ea	–	**$122.80**	**$122.80**
Replace Materials......70.00 Labor..........52.80				
▶ Includes up to 30 lf of #10/3 wire and a 30 amp double-pole breaker. Common uses: small clothes dryers, through-wall AC / heat units, and baseboard heaters.				
240 volt outlet with wiring run & box (40 amp)	ea	–	**$132.80**	**$132.80**
Replace Materials......80.00 Labor..........52.80				
▶ Includes up to 30 lf of #8/3 wire and a 40 amp double-pole breaker. Common uses: clothes dryers, kitchen ranges.				
240 volt outlet with wiring run & box (50 amp)	ea	–	**$142.80**	**$142.80**
Replace Materials......90.00 Labor..........52.80				
▶ Includes up to 30 lf of #6/3 wire and a 50 amp double-pole breaker. Common use: air conditioning hookup.				
240 volt switch with wiring run & box	ea	–	**$127.80**	**$127.80**
Replace Materials......75.00 Labor..........52.80				
▶ Includes up to 15 lf of #10/2 wire.				
low-voltage ▷ **Low-voltage switch wiring run & box**	ea	–	**$58.50**	**$58.50**
Replace Materials......20.00 Labor..........38.50				
▶ Includes up to 18 lf of #18/2 wire.				
OUTLETS & ▶ SWITCHES *Includes outlet or switch and cover only (no wire or box).* **120 volt outlet with cover**	ea	$4.34	$18.90	$23.24
Replace Materials......10.00 Labor...........8.90				
Remove .... Labor...........4.34				
120 volt GFCI outlet with cover	ea	$4.34	$39.90	$44.24
Replace Materials......31.00 Labor...........8.90				
Remove .... Labor...........4.34				
120 volt exterior waterproof outlet with cover	ea	$4.34	$24.40	$28.74
Replace Materials......15.50 Labor...........8.90				
Remove .... Labor...........4.34				
120 volt switch with cover	ea	$4.34	$15.40	$19.74
Replace Materials........6.50 Labor...........8.90				
Remove .... Labor...........4.34				

Item Description	Unit	Remove	Replace	Total	
120 volt lighted switch with cover	ea	$4.34	$17.90	$22.24	
Replace Materials........9.00 Labor 8.90					
Remove .... Labor 4.34					
120 volt push-button switch with cover	ea	$4.34	$28.40	$32.74	
Replace Materials........19.50 Labor 8.90					
Remove .... Labor 4.34					
► Antique reproduction style, also use this price when replacing an antique rotary snap switch (used between 1900 and 1925).					
120 volt rotary dimmer switch with cover	ea	$4.34	$33.90	$38.24	
Replace Materials......25.00 Labor 8.90					
Remove .... Labor 4.34					
120 volt touch dimmer switch with cover	ea	$4.34	$39.90	$44.24	
Replace Materials ......31.00 Labor 8.90					
Remove .... Labor 4.34					
120 volt exterior waterproof switch with cover	ea	$4.34	$24.90	$29.24	
Replace Materials ......16.00 Labor 8.90					
Remove .... Labor 4.34					
240 volt outlet with cover	ea	$5.78	$26.00	$31.78	◁ 240 volt
Replace Materials ......14.50 Labor 11.50					
Remove .... Labor 5.78					
► 15, 30, or 50 amp style.					
240 volt switch with cover	ea	$5.78	$27.50	$33.28	
Replace Materials ......16.00 Labor 11.50					
Remove .... Labor 5.78					
Low-voltage computer network outlet	ea	$4.34	$43.70	$48.04	◁ low-voltage
Replace Materials......30.50 Labor 13.20					
Remove .... Labor 4.34					
Low-voltage sound system speaker outlet	ea	–	$19.10	$19.10	
Replace Materials........9.00 Labor............10.10					
► Use only when speaker wiring terminates at an outlet for connection to an external speaker. See page 145 for wiring speakers that are mounted in the wall.					
Low-voltage TV outlet	ea	$4.34	$18.60	$22.94	
Replace Materials........8.50 Labor............10.10					
Remove .... Labor 4.34					
Low-voltage phone outlet	ea	$4.34	$16.10	$20.44	
Replace Materials........6.00 Labor............10.10					
Remove .... Labor 4.34					
Low-voltage switch with cover	ea	$4.34	$19.90	$24.24	
Replace Materials........11.00 Labor 8.90					
Remove .... Labor 4.34					
Add for high grade outlet or switch cover	ea	–	$1.00	$1.00	◁ additional outlet covers
Replace Materials........1.00					
► Decorative plastic, over-size plastic, and coated plastic covers.					
Add for deluxe grade outlet or switch cover	ea	–	$3.00	$3.00	
Replace Materials........3.00					
► Brass, chrome, hardwood, or porcelain covers.					

△ *push-button switch*

RELATED ITEMS

Appliances 19
Cleaning 59

	Item Description	Unit	Remove	Replace	Total
OUTLET / SWITCH ▶ COVERS	**Outlet or switch cover, standard grade**	ea	$1.01	$1.79	$2.80
	Replace Materials........1.00 Labor..............79				
	Remove .... Labor............1.01				
	▶ Standard plastic cover style as is provided with typical switch.				
	Outlet or switch cover, high grade	ea	$1.01	$4.79	$5.80
	Replace Materials........4.00 Labor..............79				
	Remove .... Labor............1.01				
	▶ Decorative plastic, wide plastic, and coated plastic covers.				
	Outlet or switch cover, deluxe grade	ea	$1.01	$7.83	$8.84
	Replace Materials........7.00 Labor..............83				
	Remove .... Labor............1.01				
	▶ Brass, chrome, hardwood, or porcelain covers.				
WIRING RUN ▶	**120 volt wiring for typical 120 volt appliance**	ea	–	$80.20	$80.20
	Replace Materials......40.00 Labor..........40.20				
	▶ One direct-wired run per appliance. Includes up to 26 lf of #12/2 wire and box. Does not include breaker or outlet.				
	120 volt wiring for through-wall air conditioner and/or heater	ea	–	$82.80	$82.80
	Replace Materials......33.50 Labor..........49.30				
	▶ One direct-wired run per unit. Includes up to 26 lf of #12/2 wire and box. Does not include breaker or outlet.				
	120 volt wiring for bathroom fan	ea	–	$48.20	$48.20
	Replace Materials.......17.50 Labor..........30.70				
	▶ General-purpose circuit. Includes up to 20 lf of #12/2 wire. Does not include fan or vent hose.				
	120 volt wiring with GFCI for bathroom ceiling heater	ea	–	$79.80	$79.80
	Replace Materials......47.50 Labor..........32.30				
	▶ Includes up to 24 lf of #12/2 wire.				
	120 volt wiring for clothes washer	ea	–	$61.70	$61.70
	Replace Materials......31.00 Labor..........30.70				
	▶ Laundry room outlet includes up to 20 lf of #12/2 wire. 1 to 2 outlets per circuit. Does not include breaker.				
	120 volt wiring for dishwasher	ea	–	$50.20	$50.20
	Replace Materials.......19.50 Labor..........30.70				
	▶ 1 direct-wired run. Includes up to 26 lf of #13/2 wire. Does not include breaker.				
	120 volt wiring for door bell or chime	ea	–	$60.70	$60.70
	Replace Materials......30.00 Labor..........30.70				
	▶ General-purpose circuit. Includes up to 15 lf of #12/2 wire, up to 30 lf of #18 low-voltage wiring, and box. Does not include breaker, transformer, or chime.				
	120 volt wiring for electric baseboard heater	ea	–	$53.30	$53.30
	Replace Materials......21.00 Labor..........32.30				
	▶ 1 direct-wired run per 9 lf of baseboard heater or per location. Includes up to 30 lf of #12/2 wire. Does not include breaker. For 240 volt wiring see page 144.				
	120 volt wiring for electrical-resistance radiant heating system	ea	–	$64.80	$64.80
	Replace Materials......29.50 Labor..........35.30				
	▶ Direct-wired run. Includes up to 30 lf of #12/2 wire and single-pole breaker. Does not include electrical resistance wiring. For 240 volt wiring see page 144.				
	120 volt wiring for furnace	ea	–	$42.70	$42.70
	Replace Materials......12.00 Labor..........30.70				
	▶ 1 direct-wired run. Includes up to 30 lf of #12/2 wire. Does not include breaker.				

Item Description	Unit	Remove	Replace	Total
120 volt wiring for garage door opener	ea	–	$49.30	$49.30
Replace Materials.......17.00 Labor 32.30				
▶ Garage circuit. Includes up to 30 lf of #12/2 wire. Does not include breaker.				
120 volt wiring for garbage disposal	ea	–	$65.90	$65.90
Replace Materials......26.50 Labor 39.40				
▶ 1 direct-wired run. Includes up to 30 lf of #12/2 wire, outlet with box, and switch with box. Does not include breaker.				
120 volt wiring for gas oven or range	ea	–	$48.20	$48.20
Replace Materials.......17.50 Labor 30.70				
▶ Light appliance circuit. 2 to 3 outlets per circuit. Includes up to 20 lf of #12/2 wire. Does not include breaker.				
120 volt wiring for humidifier	ea	–	$47.70	$47.70
Replace Materials.......17.00 Labor 30.70				
▶ With no more than 1 to 3 fixtures or outlets per run. Includes up to 30 lf of #12/2 wire. Does not include breaker.				
120 volt wiring for in-sink hot water dispenser	ea	–	$47.70	$47.70
Replace Materials.......17.00 Labor 30.70				
▶ Direct-wired run. Includes up to 30 lf of #12/2 wire. Does not include breaker.				
120 volt wiring for intercom master station	ea	–	$63.30	$63.30
Replace Materials......28.00 Labor..........35.30				
▶ Up to 20 lf of #12/2 wire. Does not include breaker.				
120 volt wiring for kitchen fan	ea	–	$49.70	$49.70
Replace Materials.......19.00 Labor 30.70				
▶ Includes up to 20 lf of #12/2 wire. Does not include fan or breaker.				
120 volt wiring for light fixture	ea	–	$58.70	$58.70
Replace Materials......28.00 Labor 30.70				
▶ General-purpose circuit, average of 6 outlets or lights per single-pole breaker. Includes up to 15 lf of #12/2 wire and box Does not include breaker or fixture.				
120 volt wiring for range hood fan and light	ea	–	$48.70	$48.70
Replace Materials ......18.00 Labor 30.70				
▶ General-purpose circuit. Includes up to 20 lf of #12/2 wire. Does not include breaker.				
120 volt wiring for security system	ea	–	$61.70	$61.70
Replace Materials ......31.00 Labor 30.70				
▶ General-purpose circuit. Includes up to 15 lf of #12/2 wire and box. Does not include breaker or security system.				
120 volt wiring for smoke or carbon monoxide detector	ea	–	$55.70	$55.70
Replace Materials ......25.00 Labor 30.70				
▶ General-purpose circuit. Includes up to 15 lf of #12/2 wire and box. Does not include breaker or detector. (Also use for direct-wired radon and carbon monoxide detectors.)				
120 volt wiring for sump / water pump	ea	–	$231.50	$231.50
Replace Materials.......19.50 Labor 212.00				
▶ Direct-wired run. Includes up to 50 lf of #12/2 wire, up to 13 lf liquid-tight flexible conduit, remote switch with box, and single-pole breaker.				
120 volt wiring for trash compactor	ea	–	$63.50	$63.50
Replace Materials ......25.00 Labor 38.50				
▶ On garbage disposal run. Includes up to 15 lf of #12/2 wire. Does not include breaker.				

Item Description	Unit	Remove	Replace	Total
WIRING RUN ▶ *continued* **120 volt wiring for built-in vacuum system** *Replace* Materials.......17.00 Labor..........32.30 ▶ Up to 30 lf of #12/2 wire. Does not include breaker.	ea	–	$49.30	$49.30
120 volt wiring run for typical outlet *Replace* Materials......35.00 Labor..........31.60 ▶ General-purpose circuit, average of 6 outlets or lights per single-pole breaker. Includes up to 15 lf of #12/2 wire, box, and outlet. Does not include breaker.	ea	–	$66.60	$66.60
120 volt wiring for water heater *Replace* Materials.......19.50 Labor..........83.10 ▶ Direct-wired run. Includes up to 30 lf of #12/2 wire and single-pole breaker.	ea	–	$102.60	$102.60
120 volt wiring for whole-house fan *Replace* Materials......22.50 Labor..........32.30 ▶ Up to 36 lf of #12/2 wire and remote switch with box. Does not include fan or breaker. For bathroom fan wiring see page 142. For kitchen fan wiring see page 143.	ea	–	$54.80	$54.80
240 volt ▷ **240 volt wiring for air conditioner** *Replace* Materials.....155.00 Labor..........118.00 ▶ Includes up to 36 lf of #6/3 wire, up to 32 lf of #3/2 wire, box, 60 amp discon- nect switch, 40 amp 2 pole breaker, up to 6 lf of liquid-tight flexible conduit.	ea	–	$273.00	$273.00
240 volt wiring, box, & outlet for clothes dryer (30 amp) *Replace* Materials......70.00 Labor..........52.80 ▶ Includes up to 30 lf of #8/3 wire and a 30 amp double-pole breaker.	ea	–	$122.80	$122.80
240 volt wiring, box, & outlet for clothes dryer (40 amp) *Replace* Materials......78.50 Labor..........52.80 ▶ Includes up to 30 lf of #8/3 wire and a 40 amp double-pole breaker.	ea	–	$131.30	$131.30
240 volt wiring for electric cook top *Replace* Materials......84.00 Labor..........52.80 ▶ Includes up to 38 lf of #8/3 wire and a 40 amp double-pole breaker.	ea	–	$136.80	$136.80
240 volt wiring for electric baseboard heater *Replace* Materials......25.00 Labor..........52.80 ▶ 1 direct-wired run per 9 lf of baseboard heater or per location. Includes up to 30 lf of #10/2 wire. Does not include breaker. For 120 volt wiring see page 142.	ea	–	$77.80	$77.80
240 volt wiring for electrical-resistance radiant heating system *Replace* Materials...390.00 Labor..........48.10 ▶ Direct-wired run. Includes up to 30 lf of #8/2 wire and double-pole breaker. Does not include electrical resistance wiring. For 120 volt wiring see page 142.	ea	–	$438.10	$438.10
240 volt wiring, box & outlet for electric oven or range (40 amp) *Replace* Materials......70.00 Labor..........52.80 ▶ Includes up to 30 lf of #8/3 wire and a 40 amp double-pole breaker.	ea	–	$122.80	$122.80
240 volt wiring, box & outlet for electric oven or range (50 amp) *Replace* Materials......89.50 Labor..........52.80 ▶ Includes up to 30 lf of #6/3 wire and a 50 amp double-pole breaker.	ea	–	$142.30	$142.30
240 volt wiring for heat pump *Replace* Materials....345.00 Labor........303.00 ▶ Includes up to 42 lf of #6/3 wire, up to 36 lf of #3/2 wire, box, 60 amp disconnect switch, 100 amp 2 pole breaker, 40 amp 2 pole breaker, up to 6 lf of liquid-tight flexible conduit.	ea	–	$648.00	$648.00

Item Description	Unit	Remove	Replace	Total	
240 volt wiring for water heater	ea	–	$128.30	$128.30	
Replace Materials ......75.50 Labor..........52.80					
▶ Direct-wired run. Includes up to 30 lf of #10/2 wire and double-pole breaker.					
Low-voltage computer network wiring (per outlet)	ea	–	$42.10	$42.10	◁ **low-voltage**
Replace Materials ......28.00 Labor..........14.10					
▶ Up to 28 lf computer network cable.					
Low-voltage wiring for door bell or chime (per button)	ea	–	$25.80	$25.80	
Replace Materials ....3.60 Labor 22.20					
▶ Up to 32 lf #18/2 wire.					
Low-voltage wiring for door or gate latch release	ea	–	$42.70	$42.70	
Replace Materials ......14.50 Labor 28.20					
▶ Up to 40 lf of #18/2 low-voltage wire. Does not include transformer or breaker.					
Low-voltage wiring for intercom (per station)	ea	–	$38.40	$38.40	
Replace Materials ......14.00 Labor..........24.40					
▶ Up to 32 lf #18/2 wire.					
Low-voltage wiring for light fixture	ea	–	$61.70	$61.70	
Replace Materials ......31.00 Labor 30.70					
▶ Average of 6 lights per circuit. Includes up to 24 lf of #18/2 wire and box. Also includes allowance for transformer. Does not include breaker or fixture.					
Low-voltage phone wiring (per outlet)	ea	–	$19.60	$19.60	
Replace Materials ....5.50 Labor 14.10					
▶ Up to 30 lf of 4 or 8 wire bell wire.					
Low-voltage sound system speaker wiring (per speaker)	ea	–	$22.10	$22.10	
Replace Materials ....8.00 Labor 14.10					
▶ Up to 30 lf of #20/2 wire.					
Low-voltage wiring for thermostat	ea	–	$33.70	$33.70	
Replace Materials ......12.50 Labor..........21.20					
▶ Up to 28 lf of #18/2 low-voltage wire.					
Low-voltage TV wiring (per outlet)	ea	–	$21.10	$21.10	
Replace Materials ....7.00 Labor 14.10					
▶ Up to 30 lf shielded coaxial television cable.					
Electric metallic tubing (EMT) conduit, average installation	sf	–	$3.83	$3.83	◀ **CONDUIT** *Based on typical home or light commercial installation. Per sf of floor.*
Replace Materials .... .80 Labor 3.03					
▶ Typical house and light commercial installation per sf of floor, various diameters: 94% 1/2"; 3% 3/4"; 2% misc. flexible and larger IMC and RMC conduit.					
Flexible metal conduit, average installation	sf	–	$3.52	$3.52	
Replace Materials ....1.90 Labor 1.62					
▶ Typical house and light commercial installation per sf of floor, various diameters: 72% 1/2"; 13% 3/4"; 15% misc. EMT, IMC and RMC conduit.					
PVC conduit, average installation	sf	–	$2.27	$2.27	
Replace Materials .... .50 Labor 1.77					
▶ Typical house and light commercial installation per sf of floor, various diameters: 94% 1/2"; 3% 3/4"; 2% misc. larger sizes.					
Intermediate conduit (IMC), average installation	sf	–	$6.15	$6.15	
Replace Materials ....1.70 Labor 4.45					
▶ Commercial and light industrial installation per sf of floor, various diameters: 44% 1/2"; 35% 3/4" or 1"; 22% misc. larger sizes.					

RELATED ITEMS
Cleaning.....................57

Item Description	Unit	Remove	Replace	Total
CONDUIT ▶ continued				
Rigid metal conduit (RMC), average installation	sf	–	$8.24	$8.24
Replace Materials........5.60 Labor............2.64				
▶ Commercial, industrial and exposed installation per sf of floor, various diameters: 44% 1/2"; 35% 3/4" or 1"; 22% misc. larger sizes.				
WIRE ▶ *Average installation and conditions for single family housing and light commercial construction. Per lf of installed wire.*				
#10 2 wire with ground non-metallic sheathed cable (Romex)	lf	–	$2.65	$2.65
Replace Materials........ .64 Labor............2.01				
▶ Typical house or light commercial installation per lf of run.				
#12 2 wire with ground non-metallic sheathed cable (Romex)	lf	–	$2.25	$2.25
Replace Materials........ .40 Labor............1.85				
▶ Typical house or light commercial installation per lf of run.				
#14 2 wire with ground non-metallic sheathed cable (Romex)	lf	–	$1.78	$1.78
Replace Materials........ .20 Labor............1.58				
▶ Typical house installation per lf of run.				
BREAKER PANEL ▶				
100 amp exterior breaker panel	ea	$176.00	$587.00	$763.00
Replace Materials....365.00 Labor........222.00				
Remove .... Labor........176.00				
▶ 20 breaker capacity, 5 breakers installed.				
100 amp interior breaker panel	ea	$176.00	$535.00	$711.00
Replace Materials....340.00 Labor........195.00				
Remove .... Labor........176.00				
▶ 20 breaker capacity, 5 breakers installed.				
150 amp exterior breaker panel	ea	$176.00	$813.00	$989.00
Replace Materials....465.00 Labor........348.00				
Remove .... Labor........176.00				
▶ 20 breaker capacity, 10 breakers installed.				
150 amp interior breaker panel	ea	$176.00	$765.00	$941.00
Replace Materials....440.00 Labor........325.00				
Remove .... Labor........176.00				
▶ 20 breaker capacity, 10 breakers installed.				
200 amp exterior breaker panel	ea	$176.00	$1,084.00	$1,260.00
Replace Materials....595.00 Labor........489.00				
Remove .... Labor........176.00				
▶ 40 breaker capacity, 15 breakers installed.				
200 amp interior breaker panel	ea	$176.00	$1,003.00	$1,179.00
Replace Materials....560.00 Labor........443.00				
Remove .... Labor........176.00				
▶ 40 breaker capacity, 15 breakers installed.				
300 amp exterior breaker panel	ea	$176.00	$1,258.00	$1,434.00
Replace Materials.....610.00 Labor........648.00				
Remove .... Labor........176.00				
▶ 42 breaker capacity, 30 breakers installed.				
300 amp interior breaker panel	ea	$176.00	$1,177.00	$1,353.00
Replace Materials....570.00 Labor........607.00				
Remove .... Labor........176.00				
▶ 42 breaker capacity, 30 breakers installed.				
sub-panel ▷ **40 amp interior breaker sub-panel**	ea	$176.00	$290.00	$466.00
Replace Materials.....155.00 Labor........135.00				
Remove .... Labor........176.00				
▶ 10 breaker capacity, 2 breakers installed.				

Item Description	Unit	Remove	Replace	Total	
50 amp interior breaker sub-panel	ea	$176.00	$348.00	$524.00	
Replace Materials....205.00 Labor.......143.00					
Remove .... Labor.........176.00					
► 10 breaker capacity, 3 breakers installed.					
70 amp interior breaker sub-panel	ea	$176.00	$397.00	$573.00	
Replace Materials ....240.00 Labor.........157.00					
Remove .... Labor.........176.00					
► 10 breaker capacity, 4 breakers installed.					
Remove breaker panel for work, then reinstall	ea	–	$375.00	$375.00	◁ remove & reinstall
Replace .... Labor.........375.00					
100 amp cable service	ea	$303.00	$1,174.00	$1,477.00	◄ **ELECTRIC SERVICE**
Replace Materials....635.00 Labor 539.00					
Remove .... Labor 303.00					
► Overhead installation. Up to 21 lf service entrance cable type SE, insulator, weather head, meter base, main disconnect breaker, up to 6 lf copper ground wire, grounding rod, clamps, fasteners, and waterproof connectors. (Does not include breaker panel.) Add **13%** for underground supply—includes excavation, trench shaping, sand bed, backfill, up to 38 lf USE cable, and underground materials.					
150 amp cable service	ea	$303.00	$1,493.00	$1,796.00	
Replace Materials ....845.00 Labor 648.00					
Remove .... Labor 303.00					
► Overhead installation. Up to 21 lf service entrance cable type SE, insulator, weather head, meter base, main disconnect breaker, up to 6 lf copper ground wire, grounding rod, clamps, fasteners, and waterproof connectors. (Does not include breaker panel.) Add **13%** for underground supply—includes excavation, trench shaping, sand bed, backfill, up to 38 lf USE cable, and underground materials.					
150 amp conduit service	ea	$378.00	$1,593.00	$1,971.00	
Replace Materials ....895.00 Labor 698.00					
Remove .... Labor 378.00					
► Overhead installation. Up to 21 lf service entrance cable type SE, insulator, weather head for conduit, EMT conduit with liquid-tight couplings, conduit straps, conduit entrance ell, meter base, main disconnect breaker, up to 6 lf copper ground wire, grounding rod, clamps, fasteners, and waterproof connectors. (Does not include breaker panel.) *Do not use this item if conduit extends through roof.* See rigid steel mast installations. Add **13%** for underground supply—includes excavation, trench shaping, sand bed, backfill, up to 38 lf USE cable, and underground materials.					

cable service △

Item Description	Unit	Remove	Replace	Total
150 amp rigid steel mast service	ea	$445.00	$1,643.00	$2,088.00
Replace Materials.....945.00 Labor 698.00				
Remove .... Labor.........445.00				
► Overhead installation. Rigid steel conduit extends through roof. Up to 21 lf service entrance cable type SE, insulator (clamps to mast), weather head for conduit, 2" galvanized rigid steel conduit with liquid-tight connections, roof flashing, conduit supports, conduit offset fittings, conduit entrance ell, meter base, main disconnect breaker, up to 6 lf copper ground wire, grounding rod, clamps, fasteners, and waterproof connectors. Add **$125** if guy wire is needed to support mast. (Does not include breaker panel.)				
200 amp cable service	ea	$303.00	$1,938.00	$2,241.00
Replace Materials...1100.00 Labor 838.00				
Remove .... Labor 303.00				
► Overhead installation. Up to 21 lf service entrance cable type SE, insulator, weatherhead, meter base, main disconnect breaker, up to 6 lf copper ground wire, grounding rod, clamps, fasteners, and waterproof connectors. (Does not include breaker panel.) Add **13%** for underground supply—includes excavation, trench shaping, sand bed, backfill, up to 38 lf USE cable, and underground materials.				

△ conduit service

RELATED ITEMS

Cleaning...................57

	Item Description	Unit	Remove	Replace	Total
ELECTRIC SERVICE ▶ *continued*	**200 amp conduit service**	ea	$378.00	$2,051.00	$2,429.00

Replace Materials ...1150.00   Labor.........901.00
Remove ....   Labor.........378.00

▶ Overhead installation. Up to 21 lf service entrance cable type SE, insulator, weatherhead for conduit, EMT conduit with liquid-tight couplings, conduit straps, conduit entrance ell, meter base, main disconnect breaker, up to 6 lf copper ground wire, grounding rod, clamps, fasteners, and waterproof connectors. (Does not include breaker panel.) *Do not use this item if conduit extends through roof.* See rigid steel mast installations. Add **13%** for underground supply—includes excavation, trench shaping, sand bed, backfill, up to 38 lf USE cable, and underground materials.

	Item Description	Unit	Remove	Replace	Total
	200 amp rigid steel mast service	ea	$445.00	$2,101.00	$2,546.00

Replace Materials ..1200.00   Labor.........901.00
Remove ....   Labor.........445.00

▶ Overhead installation. Rigid steel conduit extends through roof. Up to 24 lf service entrance cable type SE, insulator (clamps to mast), weatherhead for conduit, 2" galvanized rigid steel conduit with liquid-tight connections, roof flashing, conduit supports, conduit offset fittings, conduit entrance ell, meter base, main disconnect breaker, up to 6 lf copper ground wire, grounding rod, clamps, fasteners, and waterproof connectors. Add **$125** if guy wire is needed to support mast. (Does not include breaker panel.)

△ *rigid steel mast service*

	Item Description	Unit	Remove	Replace	Total
CIRCUIT BREAKER ▶	**Single pole (120 volt) circuit breaker**	ea	$5.78	$43.80	$49.58

Replace Materials.......15.00   Labor 28.80
Remove......................   Labor 5.78

△ *single pole*

	Item Description	Unit	Remove	Replace	Total
	Double pole (240 volt) circuit breaker	ea	$5.78	$67.40	$73.18

Replace Materials.......38.00   Labor 29.40
Remove......................   Labor 5.78

	Item Description	Unit	Remove	Replace	Total
	Ground fault circuit interrupter breaker	ea	$5.78	$94.20	$99.98

Replace Materials.......63.00   Labor...........31.20
Remove......................   Labor 5.78

△ *double pole*

	Item Description	Unit	Remove	Replace	Total
main disconnect ▷	**Main disconnect circuit breaker**	ea	$5.78	$517.00	$522.78

Replace Materials....360.00   Labor 157.00
Remove......................   Labor 5.78

	Item Description	Unit	Remove	Replace	Total
remove & reinstall ▷	**Remove circuit breaker for work, then reinstall**	ea	—	$48.90	$48.90

Replace ....   Labor 48.90

	Item Description	Unit	Remove	Replace	Total
DOOR BELL ▶ *See page 140 for wiring.*	**Door bell or chime economy grade**	ea	$6.04	$105.90	$111.94

Replace Materials ......57.00   Labor...........48.90
Remove ....   Labor............6.04

▶ Single tone, entry door only.

	Item Description	Unit	Remove	Replace	Total
	Door bell or chime standard grade	ea	$6.04	$150.90	$156.94

Replace Materials ....102.00   Labor...........48.90
Remove ....   Labor............6.04

▶ Separate tones for entry and secondary doors.

	Item Description	Unit	Remove	Replace	Total
	Door bell or chime high grade	ea	$6.04	$188.90	$194.94

Replace Materials ....140.00   Labor...........48.90
Remove ....   Labor............6.04

▶ Select from multiple tones.

	Item Description	Unit	Remove	Replace	Total
	Door bell or chime deluxe grade	ea	$6.04	$313.90	$319.94

Replace Materials ....265.00   Labor...........48.90
Remove ....   Labor............6.04

▶ Programmable, multiple tones.

Item Description	Unit	Remove	Replace	Total	
Door bell or chime button	ea	$2.89	$11.79	$14.68	◁ door bell button
Replace Materials........6.40 Labor 5.39					
Remove........................ Labor 2.89					
► Button only, no wire.					
Remove door chime for work, then reinstall	ea	–	$74.70	$74.70	◁ remove & reinstall
Replace .... Labor 74.70					
Bathroom exhaust fan, economy grade	ea	$14.60	$62.00	$76.60	◀ BATH FAN
Replace Materials ......35.00 Labor............27.00					
Remove .... Labor............14.60					
► 50 cfm. Includes up to 10 lf of 4" flexible vent duct, and wall outlet.					
Bathroom exhaust fan, standard grade	ea	$14.60	$86.00	$100.60	
Replace Materials ......59.00 Labor............27.00					
Remove .... Labor............14.60					
► 65 cfm, low noise. Includes up to 10 lf of 4" flexible vent duct, and wall outlet.					
Bathroom exhaust fan, high grade	ea	$14.60	$112.00	$126.60	
Replace Materials ......85.00 Labor............27.00					
Remove .... Labor............14.60					
► 110 cfm, low noise. Includes up to 10 lf of 4" flexible vent duct, and wall outlet.					
Bathroom exhaust fan, deluxe grade	ea	$14.60	$157.00	$171.60	
Replace Materials ....130.00 Labor............27.00					
Remove .... Labor............14.60					
► 110 cfm, low noise, variable speeds. Includes up to 10 lf of 4" flexible vent duct, and wall outlet.					
Remove bathroom exhaust fan for work, then reinstall	ea	–	$44.30	$44.30	◁ remove & reinstall
Replace .... Labor 44.30					
Bathroom exhaust fan with heat lamp, standard grade	ea	$21.00	$109.80	$130.80	◀ BATH FAN WITH HEAT LAMP
Replace Materials ......75.00 Labor 34.80					
Remove .... Labor...........21.00					
► 75 cfm, single heat lamp in center, single switch. Includes up to 10 lf of 4" flexible vent duct, and wall outlet.					
Bathroom exhaust fan with heat lamp, high grade	ea	$21.00	$144.80	$165.80	
Replace Materials .....110.00 Labor 34.80					
Remove .... Labor...........21.00					
► 110 cfm, double heat lamp in center, separate timer switch for heat lamp. Includes up to 10 lf of 4" flexible vent duct, and wall outlet.					
Bathroom exhaust fan with heater, standard grade	ea	$21.00	$167.50	$188.50	◀ BATH FAN WITH HEATER
Replace Materials ....130.00 Labor...........37.50					
Remove .... Labor...........21.00					
► 110 cfm, 200 watt heater, separate timer switch for heater. Includes up to 10 lf of 4" flexible vent duct, and wall outlet.					
Bathroom exhaust fan with heater, high grade	ea	$21.00	$222.50	$243.50	
Replace Materials .....185.00 Labor...........37.50					
Remove .... Labor...........21.00					
► 110 cfm, 450 watt heater, separate timer switch for heater. Includes up to 10 lf of 4" flexible vent duct, and wall outlet.					
Remove bathroom exhaust fan with heater for work, then reinstall	ea	–	$56.60	$56.60	◁ remove & reinstall
Replace .... Labor 56.60					

	Item Description	Unit	Remove	Replace	Total
KITCHEN FAN ▶ *See page 26 for kitchen exhaust fans in range hoods.*	**Kitchen exhaust fan, economy grade** *Replace* Materials ......70.00 Labor ....44.30 *Remove* .... Labor ....15.60 ▶ 110 cfm, no outside vent, charcoal filtration system.	ea	$15.60	$114.30	$129.90
	Kitchen exhaust fan, standard grade *Replace* Materials ....130.00 Labor ....44.30 *Remove* .... Labor ....15.60 ▶ 200 cfm. Includes up to 10 lf of 4" flexible vent duct, and wall outlet.	ea	$15.60	$174.30	$189.90
	Kitchen exhaust fan, high grade *Replace* Materials ....235.00 Labor ....44.30 *Remove* .... Labor ....15.60 ▶ 300 cfm. Includes up to 10 lf of 4" flexible vent duct, and wall outlet.	ea	$15.60	$279.30	$294.90
remove & reinstall ▷	**Remove kitchen exhaust fan for work, then reinstall** *Replace* .... Labor 63.40	ea	–	$63.40	$63.40
WHOLE-HOUSE ▶ **FAN**	**Whole-house exhaust fan, standard grade** *Replace* Materials ....605.00 Labor ....122.00 *Remove* .... Labor ....43.90 ▶ 4,500 cfm. Two-speed with automatic shutters.	ea	$43.90	$727.00	$770.90
	Whole-house exhaust fan, high grade *Replace* Materials ....700.00 Labor ....122.00 *Remove* .... Labor ....43.90 ▶ 6,500 cfm. Variable speed with automatic shutters.	ea	$43.90	$822.00	$865.90
remove & reinstall ▷	**Remove whole-house exhaust fan for work, then reinstall** *Replace* .... Labor 162.00	ea	–	$162.00	$162.00
INTERCOM ▶ **MASTER STATION**	**Intercom system master station, economy grade** *Replace* Materials ....270.00 Labor ....97.40 *Remove* .... Labor ....21.60 ▶ Push to talk, release to listen.	ea	$21.60	$367.40	$389.00
	Intercom system master station, standard grade *Replace* Materials ....550.00 Labor ....97.40 *Remove* .... Labor ....21.60 ▶ AM/FM radio, room monitor, hands-free answer, privacy.	ea	$21.60	$647.40	$669.00
	Intercom system master station, high grade *Replace* Materials .....715.00 Labor ....97.40 *Remove* .... Labor ....21.60 ▶ AM/FM radio and cassette player, room monitor, hands-free answer, privacy.	ea	$21.60	$812.40	$834.00
	Intercom system master station, deluxe grade *Replace* Materials ...1100.00 Labor ....97.40 *Remove* .... Labor ....21.60 ▶ AM/FM radio with cassette player, built-in telephone, telephone answering machine, room monitor, hands-free answer, privacy, gate or door latch release.	ea	$21.60	$1,197.40	$1,219.00
	Intercom system master station, custom grade *Replace* Materials ...1700.00 Labor ....97.40 *Remove* .... Labor ....21.60 ▶ AM/FM radio with cassette player, built-in telephone, telephone answering machine, room monitor, hands-free answer, privacy, gate or door latch release, door video monitor.	ea	$21.60	$1,797.40	$1,819.00
remove & reinstall ▷	**Remove intercom master station for work, then reinstall** *Replace* .... Labor 128.00	ea	–	$128.00	$128.00

Item Description	Unit	Remove	Replace	Total	
Intercom system remote station, economy grade	ea	$8.67	$92.00	$100.67	◄ INTERCOM REMOTE STATION
Replace Materials ......65.00 Labor...........27.00					
Remove .... Labor 8.67					
► Push to talk, release to listen.					
Intercom system remote station, standard grade	ea	$8.67	$167.00	$175.67	
Replace Materials ....140.00 Labor...........27.00					
Remove .... Labor 8.67					
► Hands-free answer, privacy.					
Intercom system remote station, high grade	ea	$8.67	$292.00	$300.67	
Replace Materials ....265.00 Labor...........27.00					
Remove .... Labor 8.67					
► Built-in telephone, hands-free answer, and privacy.					
Remove intercom remote station for work, then reinstall	ea	–	$40.60	$40.60	◄ remove & reinstall
Replace .... Labor 40.60					
Sound system speaker with grille, economy grade	ea	$6.79	$29.61	$36.40	◄ SOUND SYSTEM
Replace Materials ......20.00 Labor 9.61					
Remove .... Labor 6.79					
► 3" to 5" diameter speaker with plastic grille.					
Sound system speaker with grille, standard grade	ea	$6.79	$34.61	$41.40	
Replace Materials ......25.00 Labor 9.61					
Remove .... Labor 6.79					
► 5" to 8" diameter elliptical speaker with wood-grain plastic grille.					
Sound system speaker with grille, high grade	ea	$6.79	$49.61	$56.40	
Replace Materials ......40.00 Labor 9.61					
Remove .... Labor 6.79					
► 5" to 8" diameter elliptical speaker with 1" to 2" "tweeter" speaker, wood-grain plastic grille.					
Sound system speaker with grille, deluxe grade	ea	$6.79	$69.61	$76.40	
Replace Materials ......60.00 Labor 9.61					
Remove .... Labor 6.79					
► Two 5" to 8" diameter speakers with two or three 1" to 2" "tweeter" speakers, wood-grain plastic grille.					
Check electrical circuits with megameter in small home	ea	–	$177.00	$177.00	◄ CHECK CIRCUITS
Replace .... Labor 177.00					
Check electrical circuits with megameter in average size home	ea	–	$256.00	$256.00	
Replace .... Labor 256.00					
Check electrical circuits with megameter in large home	ea	–	$353.00	$353.00	
Replace .... Labor 353.00					
Smoke detector (battery operated)	ea	$5.78	$49.00	$54.78	◄ SMOKE DETECTOR
Replace Materials ......35.00 Labor 14.00					
Remove .... Labor 5.78					
Smoke detector (direct wired)	ea	$5.78	$60.70	$66.48	
Replace Materials ......45.00 Labor 15.70					
Remove .... Labor 5.78					
Remove smoke detector for work, then reinstall	ea	–	$21.80	$21.80	◄ remove & reinstall
Replace .... Labor...........21.80					

	Item Description	Unit	Remove	Replace	Total
CARBON ► **MONOXIDE** **DETECTOR**	**Carbon monoxide detector (battery operated)** *Replace* Materials......40.00　　Labor.............14.00 *Remove* ....　　Labor 5.78	ea	$5.78	$54.00	$59.78
	Carbon monoxide detector (direct wired) *Replace* Materials......50.00　　Labor.............15.70 *Remove* ....　　Labor 5.78	ea	$5.78	$65.70	$71.48
remove & reinstall ▷	**Remove carbon monoxide detector for work, then reinstall** *Replace* ....　　Labor...........21.80	ea	–	$21.80	$21.80
RADON DETECTOR ►	**Radon detector (battery operated)** *Replace* Materials ......45.00　　Labor............14.00 *Remove* ....　　Labor 5.78	ea	$5.78	$59.00	$64.78
	Radon detector (direct wired) *Replace* Materials......55.00　　Labor............15.70 *Remove* ....　　Labor 5.78	ea	$5.78	$70.70	$76.48
remove & reinstall ▷	**Remove radon detector for work, then reinstall** *Replace* ....　　Labor...........21.80	ea	–	$21.80	$21.80
THERMOSTAT ► *Electrical line thermostat. See HVAC on page 278 for additional thermostats.*	**Thermostat for electric-resistance heating system** *Replace* Materials........8.50　　Labor.............7.21 *Remove* ....　　Labor 5.78	ea	$5.78	$15.71	$21.49
	Thermostat for electric heating system *Replace* Materials......17.50　　Labor............12.80 *Remove* ....　　Labor 5.78	ea	$5.78	$30.30	$36.08
ANTENNA ► *Includes up to 50 lf coaxial cable. Add $200 for ground wire and grounding rod driven 8' deep into ground. (Required by many local codes.)*	**Television antenna, economy grade** *Replace* Materials.....110.00　　Labor...........48.90 *Remove* ....　　Labor...........24.10 ► 55" boom.	ea	$24.10	$158.90	$183.00
	Television antenna, standard grade *Replace* Materials.....185.00　　Labor..........48.90 *Remove* ....　　Labor...........24.10 ► 100" boom.	ea	$24.10	$233.90	$258.00
	Television antenna, high grade *Replace* Materials....280.00　　Labor..........48.90 *Remove* ....　　Labor...........24.10 ► 150" boom.	ea	$24.10	$328.90	$353.00
	Television antenna, deluxe grade *Replace* Materials....400.00　　Labor..........48.90 *Remove* ....　　Labor...........24.10 ► 200" boom.	ea	$24.10	$448.90	$473.00
remove & reinstall ▷	**Remove television antenna for work, then reinstall** *Replace* ....　　Labor...........71.60	ea	–	$71.60	$71.60
WALL HEATER ►	**Electric space heater recessed in wall, economy grade** *Replace* Materials.....215.00　　Labor...........97.40 *Remove* ....　　Labor...........14.60 ► 120 or 240 volt, 1,500 watt.	ea	$14.60	$312.40	$327.00

Item Description	Unit	Remove	Replace	Total	
Electric space heater recessed in wall, standard grade (240 volt)	ea	$14.60	$342.40	$357.00	
Replace Materials.....245.00 Labor...........97.40					
Remove .... Labor...........14.60					
► 2,250 watt.					
Electric space heater recessed in wall, high grade (240 volt)	ea	$14.60	$392.40	$407.00	
Replace Materials....295.00 Labor...........97.40					
Remove .... Labor...........14.60					
► 4,000 watt.					
Remove electric space heater for work, then reinstall	ea	–	$162.00	$162.00	◁ remove & reinstall
Replace .... Labor.........162.00					
Electric-resistance heating cable, ceiling installation	sf	–	$4.22	$4.22	◀ **ELECTRIC-RESISTANCE HEATING CABLE**
Replace Materials........2.80 Labor 1.42					*For 120 volt wiring run*
► Copper inner resistance wire embedded in gypsum.					*see page 142. For 240 volt wiring run see page 144.*
Electric-resistance heating cable, floor installation	sf	–	$7.46	$7.46	
Replace Materials........5.10 Labor 2.36					
► Wire contains copper inner resistance core and is sheathed with aluminum and a cross-linked polyethylene outer layer. Per sf of exposed floor space. Do not measure floor space underneath tubs, cabinets, or appliances.					
Electric-resistance heating floor sensor	ea	–	$109.90	$109.90	
Replace Materials......85.00 Labor...........24.90					
► For use with floor-installed electric-resistance heating that is not the only heat source. Floor sensors determine when floor is below desired temperature.					
Electric baseboard heater, economy grade	lf	$4.77	$38.20	$42.97	◀ **BASEBOARD HEATER**
Replace Materials......18.00 Labor 20.20					*For 120 volt wiring run*
Remove .... Labor 4.77					*see page 142. For 240 volt wiring run see page 144.*
► 3 lf minimum. 165 watts per lf. Thermostat on heater.					
Electric baseboard heater, standard grade	lf	$4.77	$38.70	$43.47	
Replace Materials......18.50 Labor 20.20					
Remove .... Labor 4.77					
► 3 lf minimum. 188 watts per lf. Includes up to 18 lf #18/2 thermostat wire, box and line thermostat.					
Remove electric baseboard heater for work, then reinstall	lf	–	$28.20	$28.20	◁ remove & reinstall
Replace .... Labor 28.20					
Underground wiring for exterior post light fixture (to 30 lf)	ea	–	$258.10	$258.10	◀ **POST FIXTURE WIRING**
Replace Materials.....210.00 Labor 48.10					
► Up to 36 lf #12/2 UF wire, sand bed in trench for wire, and up to 10 lf galvanized conduit. Does not include excavation, see page 178.					
Underground wiring for exterior post light fixture (to 50 feet)	ea	–	$381.20	$381.20	
Replace Materials....330.00 Labor...........51.20					
► Up to 56 lf #12/2 UF wire, sand bed in trench for wire, and up to 10 lf galvanized conduit. Does not include excavation, see page 178.					
Interior incandescent light fixture, economy grade	ea	$8.67	$37.60	$46.27	◀ **LIGHT FIXTURE ALLOWANCE**
Replace Materials.......15.00 Labor 22.60					*Contractor's allowance*
Remove .... Labor 8.67					*per light fixture in complete home.*
Interior incandescent light fixture, standard grade	ea	$8.67	$62.60	$71.27	
Replace Materials......40.00 Labor 22.60					
Remove .... Labor 8.67					

Item Description	Unit	Remove	Replace	Total
LIGHT FIXTURE ▶ *continued* **Interior incandescent light fixture, high grade**	ea	$8.67	$92.60	$101.27
Replace Materials ......70.00 Labor 22.60				
Remove .... Labor 8.67				
Interior incandescent light fixture, deluxe grade	ea	$8.67	$147.60	$156.27
Replace Materials.....125.00 Labor 22.60				
Remove .... Labor 8.67				
remove & reinstall ▷ Remove interior light fixture for work, then reinstall	ea	–	$40.20	$40.20
Replace .... Labor 40.20				
LIGHT BAR ▶ Bathroom light bar with 2 lights, standard grade	ea	$9.10	$74.10	$83.20
Replace Materials ......50.00 Labor 24.10				
Remove .... Labor 9.10				
Bathroom light bar with 2 lights, high grade	ea	$9.10	$84.10	$93.20
Replace Materials ......60.00 Labor 24.10				
Remove .... Labor 9.10				
Bathroom bar light with 3 to 4 lights, standard grade	ea	$9.10	$89.10	$98.20
Replace Materials ......65.00 Labor 24.10				
Remove .... Labor 9.10				
Bathroom bar light with 3 to 4 lights, high grade	ea	$9.10	$99.10	$108.20
Replace Materials ......75.00 Labor 24.10				
Remove .... Labor 9.10				
Bathroom bar light with 5 to 6 lights, standard grade	ea	$9.10	$114.10	$123.20
Replace Materials ......90.00 Labor 24.10				
Remove .... Labor 9.10				
Bathroom bar light with 5 to 6 lights, high grade	ea	$9.10	$134.10	$143.20
Replace Materials .....110.00 Labor 24.10				
Remove .... Labor 9.10				
Bathroom bar light with 7 to 8 lights, standard grade	ea	$9.10	$154.10	$163.20
Replace Materials ....130.00 Labor 24.10				
Remove .... Labor 9.10				
Bathroom bar light with 7 to 8 lights, high grade	ea	$9.10	$184.10	$193.20
Replace Materials.....160.00 Labor 24.10				
Remove .... Labor 9.10				
Remove bathroom bar light for work, then reinstall	ea	–	$42.60	$42.60
Replace .... Labor 42.60				
CHANDELIER ▶ Chandelier, economy grade	ea	$16.10	$200.70	$216.80
Replace Materials.....135.00 Labor 65.70				
Remove .... Labor 16.10				
Chandelier, standard grade	ea	$16.10	$270.70	$286.80
Replace Materials ....205.00 Labor 65.70				
Remove .... Labor 16.10				
Chandelier, high grade	ea	$16.10	$360.70	$376.80
Replace Materials ....295.00 Labor 65.70				
Remove .... Labor 16.10				
Chandelier, deluxe grade	ea	$16.10	$485.70	$501.80
Replace Materials ....420.00 Labor 65.70				
Remove .... Labor 16.10				

LIGHT BAR ▶
Standard grade light bars have decorative light bulbs. High grade light bars have decorative globe covers.

LIGHT FIXTURE QUALITY

Economy Very light-gauge plated metal components, simple, thin glass shades. Chandeliers may contain 4 to 8 arms with turned wood center.

Standard Light-gauge plated metal components, simple glass shades. Chandeliers may contain 4 to 8 arms.

High Heavy-gauge plated metal components, glass shades with some intricate pattern or design, may have antique finish. Chandeliers may contain 4 to 8 arms.

Deluxe Heavy-gauge metal components, solid brass components, intricate glass shades, may have antique finish. Chandeliers may contain 6 to 12 arms.

CHANDELIER ▶
To 28" in diameter. Suitable for installations on 8' and taller ceilings.

FIXTURE QUALITY *continued*

Custom Heavy-gauge metal components, solid brass components, intricate glass shades, specialty antique finishes, polished brass, antiqued brass, polished nickel (or chrome) over brass. Chandeliers may contain 6 to 14 arms.

Item Description	Unit	Remove	Replace	Total
Chandelier, custom grade	ea	$16.10	$605.70	$621.80
Replace Materials....540.00 Labor...........65.70				
Remove .... Labor...........16.10				
Chandelier, custom deluxe grade	ea	$16.10	$750.70	$766.80
Replace Materials....685.00 Labor...........65.70				
Remove .... Labor...........16.10				
Entrance chandelier, economy grade	ea	$16.10	$427.00	$443.10
Replace Materials....295.00 Labor..........132.00				
Remove .... Labor...........16.10				
Entrance chandelier, standard grade	ea	$16.10	$552.00	$568.10
Replace Materials....420.00 Labor..........132.00				
Remove .... Labor...........16.10				
Entrance chandelier, high grade	ea	$16.10	$687.00	$703.10
Replace Materials....555.00 Labor..........132.00				
Remove .... Labor...........16.10				
Entrance chandelier, deluxe grade	ea	$16.10	$832.00	$848.10
Replace Materials....700.00 Labor..........132.00				
Remove .... Labor...........16.10				
Entrance chandelier, custom grade	ea	$16.10	$1,037.00	$1,053.10
Replace Materials....905.00 Labor..........132.00				
Remove .... Labor...........16.10				
Entrance chandelier, custom deluxe grade	ea	$16.10	$1,232.00	$1,248.10
Replace Materials....1100.00 Labor..........132.00				
Remove .... Labor...........16.10				
Grand entrance chandelier, economy grade	ea	$16.10	$746.00	$762.10
Replace Materials....565.00 Labor..........181.00				
Remove .... Labor...........16.10				
Grand entrance chandelier, standard grade	ea	$16.10	$1,111.00	$1,127.10
Replace Materials....930.00 Labor..........181.00				
Remove .... Labor...........16.10				
Grand entrance chandelier, high grade	ea	$16.10	$1,431.00	$1,447.10
Replace Materials...1250.00 Labor..........181.00				
Remove .... Labor...........16.10				
Grand entrance chandelier, deluxe grade	ea	$16.10	$1,781.00	$1,797.10
Replace Materials...1600.00 Labor..........181.00				
Remove .... Labor...........16.10				
Grand entrance chandelier, custom grade	ea	$16.10	$2,181.00	$2,197.10
Replace Materials...2000.00 Labor..........181.00				
Remove .... Labor...........16.10				
Grand entrance chandelier, custom deluxe grade	ea	$16.10	$3,431.00	$3,447.10
Replace Materials...3250.00 Labor..........181.00				
Remove .... Labor...........16.10				
Early American reproduction chandelier, economy grade	ea	$16.10	$355.70	$371.80
Replace Materials....290.00 Labor...........65.70				
Remove .... Labor...........16.10				

▶ Usually contains one or more of the following: hand-soldered brass, tin, or pewter, center wood turning, antique finishes, simulated candles (may be wax coated). 3 to 6 arms, curved metal & scalloped candle escutcheons. 12" to 20" diameter.

RELATED ITEMS
Cleaning........................57

◄ **ENTRANCE CHANDELIER**
To 40" in diameter. Suitable for installations on 12' and taller ceilings.

FIXTURE QUALITY *continued*
Custom deluxe
Designed by prominent designer. Heavy-gauge metal components, solid brass components, intricate glass shades, specialty antique finishes, polished brass, antiqued brass, polished nickel (or chrome) over brass. Chandeliers usually contain 6 to 20 arms, often in two tiers.

◄ **GRAND ENTRANCE CHANDELIER**
To 60" in diameter. Suitable for installations on 18' and taller ceilings.

DESIGNER FIXTURES
The price of a light fixture can vary a great deal, often without any visible explanation.
For example, a light fixture that is designed by a prominent designer may be far more expensive than a light fixture with similar materials and design.

◄ **EARLY AMERICAN CHANDELIER**
Early American candle chandeliers converted to electrical.

continued on next page

Item Description	Unit	Remove	Replace	Total

EARLY AMERICAN ▶ CHANDELIER *continued*

These fixtures are antique reproductions and are hand tooled from tin, distressed tin, pewter, brass, or copper. Joints are hand soldered. The electric "candles" may be coated with bees wax. Although many modern fixtures use a candle style, they should not be confused with early American reproduction fixtures. Look for hand tooling inconsistencies and hand-soldered joints.

EARLY ELECTRIC ▶ CHANDELIER

Reproductions of chandeliers that were made when electricity was first introduced. Use these prices for true design reproductions. See quality indicators on pages 154-155.

*courtesy of **Rejuvenation Lamp & Fixture Co.***

EARLY GAS ▶ CHANDELIER

Electrified reproductions of chandeliers that were originally designed to burn coal gas. Can usually be identified by a fake gas valve on the arm.

continued on next page

Item Description	Unit	Remove	Replace	Total
Early American reproduction chandelier, standard grade	ea	$16.10	$465.70	$481.80
Replace Materials....400.00 Labor..........65.70				
Remove .... Labor..........16.10				
▶ Same quality as economy grade with 4 to 8 arms. 21" to 30" diameter.				
Early American reproduction chandelier, high grade	ea	$16.10	$620.70	$636.80
Replace Materials ....555.00 Labor..........65.70				
Remove .... Labor..........16.10				
▶ Same quality as economy grade with 10 to 18 arms. 21" to 30" diameter.				
Early American reproduction chandelier, deluxe grade	ea	$16.10	$855.70	$871.80
Replace Materials ....790.00 Labor..........65.70				
Remove .... Labor..........16.10				
▶ Simulated candle-style light fixture. Same quality as economy grade with 10 to 18 arms. 21" to 30" diameter, two tiers.				
Early American reproduction chandelier, custom grade	ea	$16.10	$1,015.70	$1,031.80
Replace Materials ....950.00 Labor..........65.70				
Remove .... Labor..........16.10				
▶ Simulated candle-style light fixture. Same quality as economy grade with intricate metalwork. 10 to 18 arms. 21" to 30" diameter, two tiers.				
Early American reproduction chandelier, custom deluxe grade	ea	$16.10	$1,315.70	$1,331.80
Replace Materials ..1250.00 Labor..........65.70				
Remove .... Labor..........16.10				
▶ Simulated candle-style light fixture. Same quality as economy grade with intricate metalwork. 10 to 18 arms. 31" to 44" diameter, two tiers.				
Early electric reproduction chandelier, economy grade	ea	$16.10	$410.70	$426.80
Replace Materials ....345.00 Labor..........65.70				
Remove .... Labor..........16.10				
Early electric reproduction chandelier, standard grade	ea	$16.10	$500.70	$516.80
Replace Materials ....435.00 Labor..........65.70				
Remove .... Labor..........16.10				
Early electric reproduction chandelier, high grade	ea	$16.10	$655.70	$671.80
Replace Materials ....590.00 Labor..........65.70				
Remove .... Labor..........16.10				
Early electric reproduction chandelier, deluxe grade	ea	$16.10	$900.70	$916.80
Replace Materials ....835.00 Labor..........65.70				
Remove .... Labor..........16.10				
Early electric reproduction chandelier, custom grade	ea	$16.10	$1,055.70	$1,071.80
Replace Materials ....990.00 Labor..........65.70				
Remove .... Labor..........16.10				
Early electric reproduction chandelier, custom deluxe grade	ea	$16.10	$1,415.70	$1,431.80
Replace Materials...1350.00 Labor..........65.70				
Remove .... Labor..........16.10				
Early gas reproduction chandelier, economy grade	ea	$16.10	$420.70	$436.80
Replace Materials ....355.00 Labor..........65.70				
Remove .... Labor..........16.10				
Early gas reproduction chandelier, standard grade	ea	$16.10	$500.70	$516.80
Replace Materials ....435.00 Labor..........65.70				
Remove .... Labor..........16.10				

Item Description	Unit	Remove	Replace	Total
Early gas reproduction chandelier, high grade	ea	$16.10	$675.70	$691.80
Replace Materials.....610.00 Labor...........65.70				
Remove .... Labor...........16.10				
Early gas reproduction chandelier, deluxe grade	ea	$16.10	$890.70	$906.80
Replace Materials.....825.00 Labor...........65.70				
Remove .... Labor...........16.10				
Early gas reproduction chandelier, custom grade	ea	$16.10	$1,040.70	$1,056.80
Replace Materials ....975.00 Labor...........65.70				
Remove .... Labor...........16.10				
Early gas reproduction chandelier, custom deluxe grade	ea	$16.10	$1,415.70	$1,431.80
Replace Materials...1350.00 Labor...........65.70				
Remove .... Labor...........16.10				
Early electric / gas combination reproduction chandelier, economy grade	ea	$16.10	$440.70	$456.80
Replace Materials ....375.00 Labor...........65.70				
Remove .... Labor...........16.10				
Early electric / gas combination reproduction chandelier, standard grade	ea	$16.10	$515.70	$531.80
Replace Materials....450.00 Labor...........65.70				
Remove .... Labor...........16.10				
Early electric / gas combination reproduction chandelier, high grade	ea	$16.10	$680.70	$696.80
Replace Materials.....615.00 Labor...........65.70				
Remove .... Labor...........16.10				
Early electric / gas combination reproduction chandelier, deluxe grade	ea	$16.10	$905.70	$921.80
Replace Materials....840.00 Labor...........65.70				
Remove .... Labor...........16.10				
Early electric / gas combination reproduction chandelier, custom grade	ea	$16.10	$1,060.70	$1,076.80
Replace Materials ....995.00 Labor...........65.70				
Remove .... Labor...........16.10				
Early electric / gas combination reproduction chandelier, custom deluxe grade	ea	$16.10	$1,365.70	$1,381.80
Replace Materials ..1300.00 Labor...........65.70				
Remove .... Labor...........16.10				
Imitation crystal chandelier, economy grade	ea	$16.10	$285.70	$301.80
Replace Materials....220.00 Labor...........65.70				
Remove .... Labor...........16.10				
▶ Cut glass imitation crystal. 4 to 8 arms.				
Imitation crystal chandelier, standard grade	ea	$16.10	$360.70	$376.80
Replace Materials ....295.00 Labor...........65.70				
Remove .... Labor...........16.10				
▶ Cut glass imitation crystal. 6 to 14 arms.				
Crystal chandelier, standard grade	ea	$16.10	$780.70	$796.80
Replace Materials.....715.00 Labor...........65.70				
Remove .... Labor...........16.10				
▶ Lower quality crystal components, lightly festooned.				
Crystal chandelier, high grade	ea	$16.10	$975.70	$991.80
Replace Materials.....910.00 Labor...........65.70				
Remove .... Labor...........16.10				
▶ High quality crystal components, moderately festooned. Crystal fixture width is 65% to 80% of the fixture's height.				

◀ **EARLY GAS CHANDELIER** *continued*

Because a flame burns upward, gas reproduction fixture shades always face upward. Also use these prices for electric reproductions of lantern style chandeliers. Modern designs of a gas or lantern style usually fall in the economy and standard grades. See quality indicators on pages 154-155.

◀ **EARLY ELECTRIC / GAS CHANDELIER**

When electricity was first introduced, builders were unsure whether it or gas was the wave of the future. Many builders played it safe by installing fixtures that used both. The original gas components can be identified by the fake valve on the arm. Gas components always face up. Electrical components often have a pull switch and usually, but not always, face down. See quality indicators on pages 154-155.

◀ **IMITATION CRYSTAL CHANDELIER**
Cut glass components.

◀ **CRYSTAL CHANDELIER**
High-quality crystal components. Deduct **15%** for lower quality crystal. To 25" diameter. Suitable for installation on 8' or taller ceilings.

RELATED ITEMS
Cleaning.....................57

	Item Description	Unit	Remove	Replace	Total
CRYSTAL ▶ CHANDELIER *continued*	**Crystal chandelier, deluxe grade**	ea	$16.10	$1,165.70	$1,181.80
	Replace Materials ..1100.00 Labor............65.70				
	Remove .... Labor............16.10				
	▶ High quality crystal components, heavily festooned. Crystal fixture width is 65% to 80% of the fixture's height.				
	Crystal chandelier, custom grade	ea	$16.10	$1,315.70	$1,331.80
	Replace Materials ..1250.00 Labor............65.70				
	Remove .... Labor............16.10				
	▶ High quality crystal components. Crystal fixture width is 50% to 60% of the fixture's height.				
	Crystal chandelier, custom deluxe grade	ea	$16.10	$1,415.70	$1,431.80
	Replace Materials ..1350.00 Labor............65.70				
	Remove .... Labor............16.10				
	▶ High quality crystal components, heavily festooned. Crystal fixture width is 50% to 60% of the fixture's height.				
ENTRANCE ▶ CRYSTAL CHANDELIER *High-quality crystal components. Deduct* **15%** *for lower quality crystal. To 32" diameter. Suitable for installation on 14' or taller ceilings.*	**Entrance crystal chandelier, standard grade**	ea	$16.10	$1,182.00	$1,198.10
	Replace Materials ..1050.00 Labor..........132.00				
	Remove .... Labor............16.10				
	▶ Lower quality crystal components, lightly festooned.				
	Entrance crystal chandelier, high grade	ea	$16.10	$1,382.00	$1,398.10
	Replace Materials ..1250.00 Labor..........132.00				
	Remove .... Labor............16.10				
	▶ High quality crystal components, moderately festooned. Crystal fixture width is 65% to 80% of the fixture's height.				
	Entrance crystal chandelier, deluxe grade	ea	$16.10	$1,532.00	$1,548.10
	Replace Materials ..1400.00 Labor..........132.00				
	Remove .... Labor............16.10				
	▶ High quality crystal components, heavily festooned. Crystal fixture width is 65% to 80% of the fixture's height.				
	Entrance crystal chandelier, custom grade	ea	$16.10	$2,032.00	$2,048.10
	Replace Materials ..1900.00 Labor..........132.00				
	Remove .... Labor............16.10				
	▶ High quality crystal components. Crystal fixture width is 50% to 60% of the fixture's height.				
	Entrance crystal chandelier, custom deluxe grade	ea	$16.10	$2,782.00	$2,798.10
	Replace Materials ..2650.00 Labor..........132.00				
	Remove .... Labor............16.10				
	▶ High quality crystal components, heavily festooned. Crystal fixture width is 50% to 60% of the fixture's height.				
GRAND ▶ ENTRANCE CRYSTAL CHANDELIER *High-quality crystal components. Deduct* **15%** *for lower quality crystal. To 52" diameter. Suitable for installation on 20' or taller ceilings.*	**Grand entrance crystal chandelier, standard grade**	ea	$16.10	$1,731.00	$1,747.10
	Replace Materials ...1550.00 Labor..........181.00				
	Remove .... Labor............16.10				
	▶ Lower quality crystal components, lightly festooned.				
	Grand entrance crystal chandelier, high grade	ea	$16.10	$3,631.00	$3,647.10
	Replace Materials ..3450.00 Labor..........181.00				
	Remove .... Labor............16.10				
	▶ High quality crystal components, moderately festooned. Crystal fixture width is 65% to 80% of the fixture's height.				
	Grand entrance crystal chandelier, deluxe grade	ea	$16.10	$4,781.00	$4,797.10
	Replace Materials ..4600.00 Labor..........181.00				
	Remove .... Labor............16.10				
	▶ High quality crystal components, heavily festooned. Crystal fixture width is 65% to 80% of the fixture's height.				

Item Description	Unit	Remove	Replace	Total
Grand entrance crystal chandelier, custom grade	ea	$16.10	$6,481.00	$6,497.10
Replace Materials..6300.00 Labor 181.00				
Remove .... Labor 16.10				
▶ High quality crystal components. Crystal fixture width is 50% to 60% of the fixture's height.				
Grand entrance crystal chandelier, custom deluxe grade	ea	$16.10	$7,531.00	$7,547.10
Replace Materials..7350.00 Labor 181.00				
Remove .... Labor 16.10				
▶ High quality crystal components, heavily festooned. Crystal fixture width is 50% to 60% of the fixture's height.				
Crystal tier chandelier, standard grade	ea	$16.10	$900.70	$916.80
Replace Materials....835.00 Labor 65.70				
Remove .... Labor 16.10				
▶ 4 to 5 tiers, 6" to 10" diameter. Minimum 8' to 10' ceilings.				
Crystal tier chandelier, high grade	ea	$16.10	$1,091.00	$1,107.10
Replace Materials.....910.00 Labor 181.00				
Remove .... Labor 16.10				
▶ 4 to 5 tiers, 11" to 14" diameter. Minimum 8' to 10' ceilings.				
Crystal tier chandelier, deluxe grade	ea	$16.10	$1,281.00	$1,297.10
Replace Materials...1100.00 Labor 181.00				
Remove .... Labor 16.10				
▶ 4 to 5 tiers, 15" to 20" diameter. Minimum 12' to 14' ceilings.				
Crystal tier chandelier, custom grade	ea	$16.10	$1,431.00	$1,447.10
Replace Materials ..1250.00 Labor 181.00				
Remove .... Labor 16.10				
▶ 4 to 5 tiers, 21" to 25" diameter. Minimum 15' to 18' ceilings.				
Crystal tier chandelier, custom deluxe grade	ea	$16.10	$1,881.00	$1,897.10
Replace Materials...1700.00 Labor 181.00				
Remove .... Labor 16.10				
▶ 4 to 5 tiers, 26" to 34" diameter. Minimum 15' to 18' ceilings.				
Crystal wall fixture, standard grade	ea	$8.67	$271.90	$280.57
Replace Materials....250.00 Labor 21.90				
Remove .... Labor 8.67				
▶ Lower quality crystal components, lightly festooned.				
Crystal wall fixture, high grade	ea	$8.67	$411.90	$420.57
Replace Materials....390.00 Labor 21.90				
Remove .... Labor 8.67				
▶ High quality crystal components, moderately festooned. Crystal fixture width is 65% to 80% of the fixture's height.				
Crystal wall fixture, deluxe grade	ea	$8.67	$596.90	$605.57
Replace Materials ....575.00 Labor 21.90				
Remove .... Labor 8.67				
▶ High quality crystal components, heavily festooned. Crystal fixture width is 65% to 80% of the fixture's height.				
Crystal wall fixture, custom grade	ea	$8.67	$861.90	$870.57
Replace Materials....840.00 Labor 21.90				
Remove .... Labor 8.67				
▶ High quality crystal components. Crystal fixture width is 50% to 60% of the fixture's height.				
Remove crystal wall fixture for work, then reinstall	ea	–	$40.20	$40.20
Replace .... Labor 40.20				

RELATED ITEMS
Cleaning.....................57

◀ **CRYSTAL TIER CHANDELIER**
*High-quality crystal components. Deduct **15%** for lower quality crystal. Crystal tier chandeliers resemble an upside down wedding cake. They are usually 1.5 to 2 times taller than they are wide, so normally are installed on taller ceilings.*

◀ **CRYSTAL WALL FIXTURE**
*High-quality crystal components. Deduct **15%** for lower quality crystal.*

◁ remove & reinstall

Item Description	Unit	Remove	Replace	Total
CRYSTAL ▶ **Repair crystal chandelier, minor repairs**	ea	–	$137.50	$137.50
CHANDELIER *Replace* Materials ......65.00 Labor...........72.50				
REPAIR ▶ Replace 2 to 4 components.				
Repair crystal chandelier, significant repairs	ea	–	$270.00	$270.00
Replace Materials.....125.00 Labor 145.00				
▶ Replace 5 to 10 components.				
Repair crystal chandelier, major repairs	ea	–	$504.00	$504.00
Replace Materials.....215.00 Labor..........289.00				
▶ Replace 11 to 16 components.				
Repair crystal chandelier, rebuild	ea	–	$1,017.00	$1,017.00
Replace Materials.....415.00 Labor 602.00				
▶ Dismantle all or most of fixture, replace 25% to 35% of components.				
Remove chandelier for work, then reinstall	ea	–	$111.00	$111.00
Replace .... Labor..........111.00				
Remove vaulted ceiling chandelier for work, then reinstall	ea	–	$241.00	$241.00
Replace .... Labor 241.00				
▶ For ceiling heights to 14'.				
Remove high vaulted-ceiling chandelier for work, then reinstall	ea	–	$329.00	$329.00
Replace .... Labor 329.00				
▶ For ceiling heights to 22'.				
TALL CEILING ▶ **Add for hanging chandelier on vaulted ceiling 12' to 14' tall**	ea	–	$36.20	$36.20
INSTALLATION *Replace* .... Labor 36.20				
Add for hanging chandelier on vaulted ceiling 14' to 16' tall	ea	–	$65.70	$65.70
Replace .... Labor...........65.70				
Add for hanging chandelier on vaulted ceiling 17' to 22' tall	ea	–	$100.60	$100.60
Replace .... Labor.........100.60				
SINGLE PENDANT ▶ **Single pendant light fixture, economy grade**	ea	$8.67	$87.60	$96.27
FIXTURE *Replace* Materials ......65.00 Labor 22.60				
Remove .... Labor 8.67				
Single pendant light fixture, standard grade	ea	$8.67	$102.60	$111.27
Replace Materials......80.00 Labor 22.60				
Remove .... Labor 8.67				
Single pendant light fixture, high grade	ea	$8.67	$122.60	$131.27
Replace Materials ....100.00 Labor 22.60				
Remove .... Labor 8.67				
Single pendant light fixture, deluxe grade	ea	$8.67	$142.60	$151.27
Replace Materials.....120.00 Labor 22.60				
Remove .... Labor 8.67				
Single pendant light fixture, custom grade	ea	$8.67	$157.60	$166.27
Replace Materials.....135.00 Labor 22.60				
Remove .... Labor 8.67				
Single pendant light fixture, custom deluxe grade	ea	$8.67	$177.60	$186.27
Replace Materials.....155.00 Labor 22.60				
Remove .... Labor 8.67				

Pendant fixtures hang from a chain or rod and connect directly to an electrical box in the ceiling. (For hanging fixtures that connect to a switched outlet, see page 168.) See quality indicators on pages 154-155.

Item Description	Unit	Remove	Replace	Total
Double pendant light fixture, economy grade	ea	$8.67	$132.60	$141.27
Replace Materials.....110.00 Labor 22.60				
Remove .... Labor 8.67				
Double pendant light fixture, standard grade	ea	$8.67	$157.60	$166.27
Replace Materials.....135.00 Labor 22.60				
Remove .... Labor 8.67				
Double pendant light fixture, high grade	ea	$8.67	$182.60	$191.27
Replace Materials.....160.00 Labor 22.60				
Remove .... Labor 8.67				
Double pendant light fixture, deluxe grade	ea	$8.67	$202.60	$211.27
Replace Materials ....180.00 Labor 22.60				
Remove .... Labor 8.67				
Double pendant light fixture, custom grade	ea	$8.67	$227.60	$236.27
Replace Materials ....205.00 Labor 22.60				
Remove .... Labor 8.67				
Double pendant light fixture, custom deluxe grade	ea	$8.67	$262.60	$271.27
Replace Materials ....240.00 Labor 22.60				
Remove .... Labor 8.67				
"Shower" style light fixture, economy grade	ea	$16.10	$220.70	$236.80
Replace Materials.....155.00 Labor...........65.70				
Remove .... Labor 16.10				
"Shower" style light fixture, standard grade	ea	$16.10	$265.70	$281.80
Replace Materials....200.00 Labor...........65.70				
Remove .... Labor 16.10				
"Shower" style light fixture, high grade	ea	$16.10	$330.70	$346.80
Replace Materials ....265.00 Labor...........65.70				
Remove .... Labor 16.10				
"Shower" style light fixture, deluxe grade	ea	$16.10	$375.70	$391.80
Replace Materials.....310.00 Labor...........65.70				
Remove .... Labor 16.10				
"Shower" style light fixture, custom grade	ea	$16.10	$470.70	$486.80
Replace Materials....405.00 Labor...........65.70				
Remove .... Labor 16.10				
"Shower" style light fixture, custom deluxe grade	ea	$16.10	$500.70	$516.80
Replace Materials....435.00 Labor...........65.70				
Remove .... Labor 16.10				
Small bowl-shade or globe light fixture, economy grade	ea	$8.67	$57.60	$66.27
Replace Materials ......35.00 Labor 22.60				
Remove .... Labor 8.67				
Small bowl-shade or globe light fixture, standard grade	ea	$8.67	$67.60	$76.27
Replace Materials ......45.00 Labor 22.60				
Remove .... Labor 8.67				
Small bowl-shade or globe light fixture, high grade	ea	$8.67	$82.60	$91.27
Replace Materials ......60.00 Labor 22.60				
Remove .... Labor 8.67				

◄ **DOUBLE PENDANT FIXTURE**
Pendant fixtures hang from a chain or rod and connect directly to an electrical box in the ceiling. (For hanging fixtures that connect to a switched outlet, see page 168.) See quality indicators on pages 154-155.

◄ **"SHOWER" FIXTURE**
"Shower" style fixtures have a large base. Two to four (sometimes more) small lights with shades hang from the base on chains or rods. See quality indicators on pages 154-155.

◄ **SMALL BOWL-SHADE FIXTURE**
Fixture with a globe or bowl shade. Small sizes are typically found in halls. See quality indicators on pages 154-155.

RELATED ITEMS
Cleaning.....................57

	Item Description	Unit	Remove	Replace	Total
SMALL BOWL- ▶ **SHADE FIXTURE** *continued*	**Small bowl-shade or globe light fixture, deluxe grade** *Replace* Materials......80.00 Labor ....22.60 *Remove* .... Labor 8.67	ea	$8.67	$102.60	$111.27
	Small bowl-shade or globe light fixture, custom grade *Replace* Materials......90.00 Labor ....22.60 *Remove* .... Labor 8.67	ea	$8.67	$112.60	$121.27
	Small bowl-shade or globe light fixture, custom deluxe grade *Replace* Materials.....110.00 Labor ....22.60 *Remove* .... Labor 8.67	ea	$8.67	$132.60	$141.27
BOWL-SHADE ▶ **FIXTURE** *Fixture with a globe or bowl shade. See quality indicators on pages 154-155.*	**Bowl-shade or globe light fixture, economy grade** *Replace* Materials......50.00 Labor ....22.60 *Remove* .... Labor 8.67	ea	$8.67	$72.60	$81.27
	Bowl-shade or globe light fixture, standard grade *Replace* Materials......85.00 Labor ....22.60 *Remove* .... Labor 8.67	ea	$8.67	$107.60	$116.27
	Bowl-shade or globe light fixture, high grade *Replace* Materials.....110.00 Labor ....22.60 *Remove* .... Labor 8.67	ea	$8.67	$132.60	$141.27
	Bowl-shade or globe light fixture, deluxe grade *Replace* Materials ....140.00 Labor ....22.60 *Remove* .... Labor 8.67	ea	$8.67	$162.60	$171.27
	Bowl-shade or globe light fixture, custom grade *Replace* Materials.....170.00 Labor ....22.60 *Remove* .... Labor 8.67	ea	$8.67	$192.60	$201.27
	Bowl-shade or globe light fixture, custom deluxe grade *Replace* Materials.....195.00 Labor ....22.60 *Remove* .... Labor 8.67	ea	$8.67	$217.60	$226.27
SUSPENDED ▶ **BOWL-SHADE FIXTURE** *Bowl-shade suspended on three rods or chains. See quality indicators on pages 154-155.*	**Suspended bowl-shade light fixture, economy grade** *Replace* Materials.....185.00 Labor..........65.70 *Remove* .... Labor..........16.10	ea	$16.10	$250.70	$266.80
	Suspended bowl-shade light fixture, standard grade *Replace* Materials....220.00 Labor..........65.70 *Remove* .... Labor..........16.10	ea	$16.10	$285.70	$301.80
	Suspended bowl-shade light fixture, high grade *Replace* Materials.....310.00 Labor..........65.70 *Remove* .... Labor..........16.10	ea	$16.10	$375.70	$391.80
	Suspended bowl-shade light fixture, deluxe grade *Replace* Materials....390.00 Labor..........65.70 *Remove* .... Labor..........16.10	ea	$16.10	$455.70	$471.80
courtesy of Rejuvenation Lamp & Fixture Co.	**Suspended bowl-shade light fixture, custom grade** *Replace* Materials....430.00 Labor..........65.70 *Remove* .... Labor..........16.10	ea	$16.10	$495.70	$511.80
	Suspended bowl-shade light fixture, custom deluxe grade *Replace* Materials....545.00 Labor..........65.70 *Remove* .... Labor..........16.10	ea	$16.10	$610.70	$626.80

Item Description	Unit	Remove	Replace	Total
Billiard-table style light fixture, economy grade	ea	$16.10	$265.20	$281.30
Replace Materials....205.00 Labor..........60.20				
Remove .... Labor..........16.10				
▶ Single light on rod, with colored glass shade.				
Billiard-table style light fixture, standard grade	ea	$16.10	$510.20	$526.30
Replace Materials....450.00 Labor..........60.20				
Remove .... Labor..........16.10				
▶ Single light on decorative rod, with ribbed glass shade.				
Billiard-table style light fixture, high grade	ea	$16.10	$745.20	$761.30
Replace Materials....685.00 Labor..........60.20				
Remove .... Labor..........16.10				
▶ Double lights on decorative rods, with ribbed glass shades.				
Billiard-table style light fixture, deluxe grade	ea	$16.10	$1,035.20	$1,051.30
Replace Materials....975.00 Labor..........60.20				
Remove .... Labor..........16.10				
▶ Triple lights on decorative rods, with ribbed glass shades.				
Billiard-table style light fixture, custom grade	ea	$16.10	$1,310.20	$1,326.30
Replace Materials..1250.00 Labor..........60.20				
Remove .... Labor..........16.10				
▶ Triple lights on decorative rods with brass scroll work above, ribbed glass shades with brass trim.				
Billiard-table style light fixture, custom deluxe grade	ea	$16.10	$2,010.20	$2,026.30
Replace Materials...1950.00 Labor..........60.20				
Remove .... Labor..........16.10				
▶ Triple lights on decorative rods with elaborate brass scroll work above, ribbed glass shades with brass trim. May have copper shades.				
Remove billiard-table style light fixture for work, then reinstall	ea	–	$103.00	$103.00
Replace .... Labor.........103.00				
Wall-mount light fixture, economy grade	ea	$8.67	$36.90	$45.57
Replace Materials.......15.00 Labor.....21.90				
Remove .... Labor 8.67				
Wall-mount light fixture, standard grade	ea	$8.67	$61.90	$70.57
Replace Materials......40.00 Labor.....21.90				
Remove .... Labor 8.67				
Wall-mount light fixture, high grade	ea	$8.67	$116.90	$125.57
Replace Materials......95.00 Labor.....21.90				
Remove .... Labor 8.67				
Wall-mount light fixture, deluxe grade	ea	$8.67	$186.90	$195.57
Replace Materials.....165.00 Labor.....21.90				
Remove .... Labor 8.67				
Wall-mount light fixture, custom grade	ea	$8.67	$211.90	$220.57
Replace Materials.....190.00 Labor..........21.90				
Remove .... Labor 8.67				
Wall-mount light fixture, custom deluxe grade	ea	$8.67	$296.90	$305.57
Replace Materials ....275.00 Labor.....21.90				
Remove .... Labor 8.67				
Remove wall-mount light fixture for work, then reinstall	ea	–	$40.20	$40.20
Replace .... Labor..........40.20				

◀ **BILLIARD-TABLE STYLE FIXTURE**
See quality indicators on pages 154-155.

◀ **WALL-MOUNT FIXTURE**
See quality indicators on pages 154-155.

RELATED ITEMS
Cleaning.......................57

◁ remove & reinstall

Item Description	Unit	Remove	Replace	Total
FLUORESCENT ► FIXTURE				
1' one-tube surface-mounted fluorescent strip light	ea	$14.50	$56.40	$70.90
Replace Materials......15.00 Labor...........41.40				
Remove .... Labor...........14.50				
1-1/2' one-tube surface-mounted fluorescent strip light	ea	$14.50	$61.40	$75.90
Replace Materials......20.00 Labor...........41.40				
Remove .... Labor...........14.50				
2' one-tube surface-mounted fluorescent strip light	ea	$14.50	$66.40	$80.90
Replace Materials......25.00 Labor...........41.40				
Remove .... Labor...........14.50				
4' one-tube surface-mounted fluorescent strip light	ea	$14.50	$71.40	$85.90
Replace Materials......30.00 Labor...........41.40				
Remove .... Labor...........14.50				
6' one-tube surface-mounted fluorescent strip light	ea	$14.50	$86.40	$100.90
Replace Materials......45.00 Labor...........41.40				
Remove .... Labor...........14.50				
8' one-tube surface-mounted fluorescent strip light	ea	$14.50	$101.40	$115.90
Replace Materials......60.00 Labor...........41.40				
Remove .... Labor...........14.50				
2' one-tube surface-mounted fluorescent strip light with diffuser	ea	$14.50	$71.40	$85.90
Replace Materials......30.00 Labor...........41.40				
Remove .... Labor...........14.50				
4' one-tube surface-mounted fluorescent strip light with diffuser	ea	$14.50	$76.40	$90.90
Replace Materials......35.00 Labor...........41.40				
Remove .... Labor...........14.50				
6' one-tube surface-mounted fluorescent strip light with diffuser	ea	$14.50	$86.40	$100.90
Replace Materials......45.00 Labor...........41.40				
Remove .... Labor...........14.50				
8' one-tube surface-mounted fluorescent strip light with diffuser	ea	$14.50	$111.40	$125.90
Replace Materials......70.00 Labor...........41.40				
Remove .... Labor...........14.50				
two-tube ▷ **2' two-tube surface-mounted fluorescent strip light**	ea	$14.50	$76.40	$90.90
Replace Materials......35.00 Labor...........41.40				
Remove .... Labor...........14.50				
2' two-tube surface-mounted fluorescent strip light with diffuser	ea	$14.50	$96.40	$110.90
Replace Materials......55.00 Labor...........41.40				
Remove .... Labor...........14.50				
2' two-tube surface-mounted fluorescent strip light with vinyl trim & diffuser	ea	$14.50	$101.40	$115.90
Replace Materials......60.00 Labor...........41.40				
Remove .... Labor...........14.50				
2' two-tube surface-mounted fluorescent strip light with solid wood trim & diffuser	ea	$14.50	$111.40	$125.90
Replace Materials......70.00 Labor...........41.40				
Remove .... Labor...........14.50				
4' two-tube surface-mounted fluorescent strip light	ea	$14.50	$91.40	$105.90
Replace Materials......50.00 Labor...........41.40				
Remove .... Labor...........14.50				

Item Description	Unit	Remove	Replace	Total
4' two-tube surface-mounted fluorescent strip light with diffuser	ea	$14.50	$101.40	$115.90
Replace Materials......60.00 Labor..........41.40				
Remove .... Labor..........14.50				
4' two-tube surface-mounted fluorescent strip light with vinyl trim & diffuser	ea	$14.50	$111.40	$125.90
Replace Materials......70.00 Labor..........41.40				
Remove .... Labor..........14.50				
4' two-tube surface-mounted fluorescent strip light with solid wood trim & diffuser	ea	$14.50	$131.40	$145.90
Replace Materials......90.00 Labor..........41.40				
Remove .... Labor..........14.50				
6' two-tube surface-mounted fluorescent strip light	ea	$14.50	$96.40	$110.90
Replace Materials......55.00 Labor..........41.40				
Remove .... Labor..........14.50				
6' two-tube surface-mounted fluorescent strip light with diffuser	ea	$14.50	$111.40	$125.90
Replace Materials......70.00 Labor..........41.40				
Remove .... Labor..........14.50				
6' two-tube surface-mounted fluorescent strip light with vinyl trim & diffuser	ea	$14.50	$136.40	$150.90
Replace Materials......95.00 Labor..........41.40				
Remove .... Labor..........14.50				
6' two-tube surface-mounted fluorescent strip light with solid wood trim & diffuser	ea	$14.50	$146.40	$160.90
Replace Materials....105.00 Labor..........41.40				
Remove .... Labor..........14.50				
8' two-tube surface-mounted fluorescent strip light	ea	$14.50	$116.40	$130.90
Replace Materials......75.00 Labor..........41.40				
Remove .... Labor..........14.50				
8' two-tube surface-mounted fluorescent strip light with diffuser	ea	$14.50	$131.40	$145.90
Replace Materials......90.00 Labor..........41.40				
Remove .... Labor..........14.50				
8' two-tube surface-mounted fluorescent strip light with vinyl trim & diffuser	ea	$14.50	$151.40	$165.90
Replace Materials.....110.00 Labor..........41.40				
Remove .... Labor..........14.50				
8' two-tube surface-mounted fluorescent strip light with solid wood trim & diffuser	ea	$14.50	$171.40	$185.90
Replace Materials....130.00 Labor..........41.40				
Remove .... Labor..........14.50				
4' four-tube surface-mounted fluorescent strip light	ea	$14.50	$116.40	$130.90
Replace Materials......75.00 Labor..........41.40				
Remove .... Labor..........14.50				
4' four-tube surface-mounted fluorescent strip light with diffuser	ea	$14.50	$161.40	$175.90
Replace Materials.....120.00 Labor..........41.40				
Remove .... Labor..........14.50				
4' four-tube surface-mounted fluorescent strip light with vinyl trim & diffuser	ea	$14.50	$176.40	$190.90
Replace Materials.....135.00 Labor..........41.40				
Remove .... Labor..........14.50				
4' four-tube surface-mounted fluorescent strip light with solid wood trim & diffuser	ea	$14.50	$211.40	$225.90
Replace Materials.....170.00 Labor..........41.40				
Remove .... Labor..........14.50				

◁ four-tube

RELATED ITEMS
Cleaning....................57

Item Description	Unit	Remove	Replace	Total
FLUORESCENT ▶ FIXTURE *continued* for suspended ceilings ▷ *add $16 for boxed-in fixture for fire-rated ceiling.*				
2' by 2' drop-in two-tube fluorescent fixture for suspended ceiling	ea	$14.50	$163.40	$177.90
Replace Materials......80.00 Labor 83.40				
Remove .... Labor............14.50				
2' by 4' drop-in two-tube fluorescent fixture for suspended ceiling	ea	$14.50	$178.40	$192.90
Replace Materials......95.00 Labor 83.40				
Remove .... Labor............14.50				
2' by 4' drop-in four-tube fluorescent fixture for suspended ceiling	ea	$14.50	$203.40	$217.90
Replace Materials.....120.00 Labor 83.40				
Remove .... Labor............14.50				
remove & reinstall ▷ **Remove fluorescent light fixture for work, then reinstall**	ea	–	$72.50	$72.50
Replace .... Labor............72.50				
replace ballast ▷ **Remove and replace fluorescent light fixture ballast**	ea	–	$115.70	$115.70
Replace Materials......60.00 Labor............55.70				
FLUORESCENT ▶ CIRCLINE FIXTURE **Fluorescent circline fixture, economy grade**	ea	$10.70	$73.10	$83.80
Replace Materials......35.00 Labor..........38.10				
Remove .... Labor..........10.70				
▶ Single, exposed tube.				
Fluorescent circline fixture, standard grade	ea	$10.70	$93.10	$103.80
Replace Materials......55.00 Labor 38.10				
Remove .... Labor..........10.70				
▶ Double, exposed tubes.				
Fluorescent circline fixture, high grade	ea	$10.70	$123.10	$133.80
Replace Materials......85.00 Labor 38.10				
Remove .... Labor..........10.70				
▶ Double tubes with polystyrene diffuser.				
Fluorescent circline fixture, deluxe grade	ea	$10.70	$208.10	$218.80
Replace Materials.....170.00 Labor 38.10				
Remove .... Labor..........10.70				
▶ Double tubes with polystyrene diffuser and wood or metal trim.				
remove & reinstall ▷ **Remove fluorescent circline light fixture for work, then reinstall**	ea	–	$65.70	$65.70
Replace .... Labor............65.70				
replace ballast ▷ **Remove and replace fluorescent circline light fixture ballast**	ea	–	$115.70	$115.70
Replace Materials......60.00 Labor............55.70				
CEILING FAN ▶ *Fan only, no light.* **Ceiling fan, economy grade**	ea	$14.50	$161.50	$176.00
Replace Materials......65.00 Labor............96.50				
Remove .... Labor............14.50				
▶ 4 blade fan up to 42" diameter. Blades may have painted design. 3 speed pull-chain, reversible.				
Ceiling fan, standard grade	ea	$14.50	$196.50	$211.00
Replace Materials ....100.00 Labor............96.50				
Remove .... Labor............14.50				
▶ 4 to 5 blade fan up to 52" diameter. Plywood blades may have painted design or stained with cane inserts. 3 speed pull-chain, reversible.				
Ceiling fan, high grade	ea	$14.50	$261.50	$276.00
Replace Materials......165.00 Labor............96.50				
Remove .... Labor............14.50				
▶ 4 to 5 blade fan up to 52" diameter. Hardwood stained blades may have cane inserts. Variable speed wall controls, reversible.				

Item Description	Unit	Remove	Replace	Total	
Ceiling fan, deluxe grade	ea	$14.50	$356.50	$371.00	
Replace Materials ....260.00 Labor...........96.50					
Remove .... Labor...........14.50					
► 4 to 5 blade fan up to 52" diameter. Hardwood stained blades may have cane inserts. Brass motor housing contains intricate design. Variable speed wall controls, reversible.					
Remove ceiling fan for work, then reinstall	ea	–	$108.00	$108.00	◁ remove and reinstall
Replace .... Labor..........108.00					
Ceiling fan with light, economy grade	ea	$14.50	$315.00	$329.50	◄ **CEILING FAN WITH LIGHT**
Replace Materials.....170.00 Labor 145.00					
Remove .... Labor...........14.50					
► 4 blade fan up to 42" diameter. Blades may have painted design. 3 speed pull-chain, reversible. 2 to 3 lights with simple glass or metal shades, plated metal escutcheon.					
Ceiling fan with light, standard grade	ea	$14.50	$375.00	$389.50	
Replace Materials....230.00 Labor 145.00					
Remove .... Labor...........14.50					
► 4 to 5 blade fan up to 52" diameter. Plywood blades may have painted design or stained with cane inserts. 3 speed pull-chain, reversible. 3 lights with detailed glass shades, plated metal escutcheon.					
Ceiling fan with light, high grade	ea	$14.50	$425.00	$439.50	
Replace Materials....280.00 Labor 145.00					
Remove .... Labor...........14.50					
► 4 to 5 blade fan up to 52" diameter. Hardwood stained blades may have cane inserts. Variable speed wall controls, reversible. 3 to 4 lights with intricately detailed glass shades, plated metal escutcheon.					
Ceiling fan with light, deluxe grade	ea	$14.50	$545.00	$559.50	
Replace Materials....400.00 Labor 145.00					
Remove .... Labor...........14.50					
► 4 to 5 blade fan up to 52" diameter. Hardwood blades may have cane inserts. Brass motor housing with intricate design. Variable speed wall control, reversible. 3 to 4 lights with intricate, detailed glass shades, solid brass escutcheon.					
Ceiling fan with light, custom grade	ea	$14.50	$620.00	$634.50	
Replace Materials.....475.00 Labor 145.00					
Remove .... Labor...........14.50					
► 4 to 5 blade fan up to 52" diameter. Hardwood stained blades may have cane inserts. Brass motor housing contains intricate design. Variable speed wall controls, reversible. 3 to 4 lights with intricately detailed glass shades, solid brass escutcheon, detailed, curved arms.					
Remove ceiling fan with light for work, then reinstall	ea	–	$111.00	$111.00	◁ remove and reinstall
Replace .... Labor..........111.00					
Light for ceiling fan, economy grade	ea	$8.67	$50.70	$59.37	◄ **LIGHT FOR CEILING FAN**
Replace Materials.......30.00 Labor 20.70					
Remove .... Labor 8.67					
► 2 to 3 lights with simple glass or metal shades, plated metal escutcheon.					
Light for ceiling fan, standard grade	ea	$8.67	$85.70	$94.37	
Replace Materials......65.00 Labor 20.70					
Remove .... Labor 8.67					
► 3 lights with detailed glass shades, plated metal escutcheon.					
Light for ceiling fan, high grade	ea	$8.67	$115.70	$124.37	
Replace Materials.......95.00 Labor 20.70					
Remove .... Labor 8.67					
► 3 to 4 lights with intricately detailed glass shades, plated metal escutcheon.					

RELATED ITEMS

Cleaning.......................57

	Item Description	Unit	Remove	Replace	Total
LIGHT FOR ► CEILING FAN *continued*	**Light for ceiling fan, deluxe grade** *Replace* Materials.....170.00 Labor ....20.70 *Remove* .... Labor ....8.67 ► 3 to 4 lights with intricately detailed glass shades, solid brass escutcheon.	ea	$8.67	$190.70	$199.37
	Light for ceiling fan, custom grade *Replace* Materials....260.00 Labor ....20.70 *Remove* .... Labor ....8.67 ► 3 to 4 lights with intricately detailed glass shades, solid brass escutcheon, detailed, curved arms.	ea	$8.67	$280.70	$289.37
remove & reinstall ▷	**Remove light from ceiling fan for work, then reinstall** *Replace* .... Labor 36.20	ea	–	$36.20	$36.20
HANGING ► FIXTURE *Hanging light fixtures usually hang from ceiling hooks and plug into a switched outlet. For hanging fixtures that connect into a ceiling box, see pendant fixtures on pages 160-161. See quality indicators on pages 154-155.*	**Hanging light fixture, economy grade** *Replace* Materials......40.00 Labor ....12.00 *Remove* .... Labor 2.89	ea	$2.89	$52.00	$54.89
	Hanging light fixture, standard grade *Replace* Materials......50.00 Labor ....12.00 *Remove* .... Labor 2.89	ea	$2.89	$62.00	$64.89
	Hanging light fixture, high grade *Replace* Materials......60.00 Labor ....12.00 *Remove* .... Labor 2.89	ea	$2.89	$72.00	$74.89
	Hanging light fixture, deluxe grade *Replace* Materials......90.00 Labor ....12.00 *Remove* .... Labor 2.89	ea	$2.89	$102.00	$104.89
DOUBLE ► HANGING FIXTURE *Hanging light fixtures usually hang from ceiling hooks and plug into a switched outlet. For hanging fixtures that connect into a ceiling box, see pendant fixtures on pages 160-161. See quality indicators on pages 154-155.*	**Double hanging light fixture, economy grade** *Replace* Materials......55.00 Labor ....12.00 *Remove* .... Labor 2.89	ea	$2.89	$67.00	$69.89
	Double hanging light fixture, standard grade *Replace* Materials......80.00 Labor ....12.00 *Remove* .... Labor 2.89	ea	$2.89	$92.00	$94.89
	Double hanging light fixture, high grade *Replace* Materials.....110.00 Labor ....12.00 *Remove* .... Labor 2.89	ea	$2.89	$122.00	$124.89
	Double hanging light fixture, deluxe grade *Replace* Materials ....150.00 Labor ....12.00 *Remove* .... Labor 2.89	ea	$2.89	$162.00	$164.89
MINIMUM ► FIXTURE CHARGE	**Minimum charge for light fixture work** *Replace* Materials......20.00 Labor...........72.50	ea	–	$92.50	$92.50
PORCELAIN ► FIXTURE	**Porcelain light fixture** *Replace* Materials........4.50 Labor ....9.06 *Remove* .... Labor 2.89	ea	$2.89	$13.56	$16.45
	Porcelain light fixture with pull chain *Replace* Materials........5.50 Labor ....9.06 *Remove* .... Labor 2.89	ea	$2.89	$14.56	$17.45
	Remove porcelain light fixture for work, then reinstall *Replace* .... Labor...........14.50	ea	–	$14.50	$14.50

Item Description	Unit	Remove	Replace	Total	
Recessed spot light fixture, economy grade	ea	$11.60	$82.90	$94.50	◄ **RECESSED SPOT FIXTURE**
Replace Materials......50.00 Labor 32.90					See quality indicators on
Remove .... Labor 11.60					pages 154-155.
► 5" recessed spot.					
Recessed spot light fixture, standard grade	ea	$11.60	$97.90	$109.50	
Replace Materials......65.00 Labor 32.90					
Remove .... Labor 11.60					
► 7" recessed spot.					
Recessed spot light fixture, high grade	ea	$11.60	$117.90	$129.50	
Replace Materials......85.00 Labor 32.90					
Remove .... Labor 11.60					
► 7" recessed spot, reflector in can.					
Recessed spot light fixture, deluxe grade	ea	$11.60	$147.90	$159.50	
Replace Materials .....115.00 Labor 32.90					
Remove .... Labor 11.60					
► 8" recessed spot.					
Recessed spot light fixture, custom grade	ea	$11.60	$187.90	$199.50	
Replace Materials.....155.00 Labor 32.90					
Remove .... Labor 11.60					
► 8" recessed spot, eyeball socket.					
Remove recessed spot light fixture for work, then reinstall	ea	–	$30.20	$30.20	◄ remove and reinstall
Replace .... Labor 30.20					
Remove recessed spot light fixture & can for work, then reinstall	ea	–	$55.70	$55.70	
Replace .... Labor..........55.70					
Electric strip for strip lights (no fixtures) per lf	lf	$3.18	$21.30	$24.48	◄ **ELECTRIC STRIP**
Replace Materials.......11.00 Labor 10.30					Surface-mounted electric
Remove .... Labor 3.18					strip channel. Does
					not include strip-
Remove electric strip for strip lights for work, then reinstall	lf	–	$18.10	$18.10	mounted spot
Replace .... Labor..........18.10					lights. 3 lf
					minimum.
Strip light, economy grade	ea	$4.34	$39.50	$43.84	◄ **STRIP SPOT LIGHT**
Replace Materials......25.00 Labor 14.50					Spot light for surface
Remove .... Labor 4.34					mounted electric strip
► Light gauge metal or plastic.					channel.
Strip light, standard grade	ea	$4.34	$49.50	$53.84	
Replace Materials .....35.00 Labor 14.50					
Remove .... Labor 4.34					
► Light gauge metal or plastic with brass or chrome trim.					
Strip light, high grade	ea	$4.34	$79.50	$83.84	
Replace Materials......65.00 Labor 14.50					
Remove .... Labor 4.34					
► Heavy gauge materials with brass or chrome trim.					
Remove strip light for work, then reinstall	ea	–	$25.40	$25.40	◄ remove and reinstall
Replace .... Labor 25.40					
Exterior flood light fixture, standard grade	ea	$8.67	$68.30	$76.97	◄ **EXTERIOR SPOT LIGHT**
Replace Materials......45.00 Labor 23.30					
Remove .... Labor 8.67					

RELATED ITEMS

Cleaning........................57

Item Description	Unit	Remove	Replace	Total
EXTERIOR ▶ **SPOT LIGHT** *continued* **Exterior flood light fixture, high grade**	ea	$8.67	$83.30	$91.97
Replace Materials......60.00 Labor 23.30				
Remove .... Labor 8.67				
Exterior double flood light fixture, standard grade	ea	$8.67	$78.30	$86.97
Replace Materials ......55.00 Labor 23.30				
Remove .... Labor 8.67				
Exterior double flood light fixture, high grade	ea	$8.67	$98.30	$106.97
Replace Materials ....75.00 Labor 23.30				
Remove .... Labor 8.67				
Exterior triple flood light fixture, standard grade	ea	$8.67	$88.30	$96.97
Replace Materials ......65.00 Labor 23.30				
Remove .... Labor 8.67				
Exterior triple flood light fixture, high grade	ea	$8.67	$108.30	$116.97
Replace Materials ......85.00 Labor 23.30				
Remove .... Labor 8.67				
Remove exterior flood light fixture for work, then reinstall	ea	–	$42.60	$42.60
Replace .... Labor 42.60				
EXTERIOR WALL- ▷ **MOUNT FIXTURE** *See quality indicators on pages 154-155.* **Exterior wall-mount light fixture, economy grade**	ea	$7.23	$57.60	$64.83
Replace Materials ......35.00 Labor 22.60				
Remove .... Labor 7.23				
Exterior wall-mount light fixture, standard grade	ea	$7.23	$77.60	$84.83
Replace Materials ......55.00 Labor 22.60				
Remove .... Labor 7.23				
Exterior wall-mount light fixture, high grade	ea	$7.23	$157.60	$164.83
Replace Materials ......135.00 Labor 22.60				
Remove .... Labor 7.23				
Exterior wall-mount light fixture, deluxe grade	ea	$7.23	$282.60	$289.83
Replace Materials ....260.00 Labor 22.60				
Remove .... Labor 7.23				
remove & reinstall ▷ **Remove exterior wall-mount light fixture for work, then reinstall**	ea	–	$42.60	$42.60
Replace .... Labor 42.60				
EXTERIOR ▶ **RECESSED FIXTURE** **Exterior recessed light fixture, economy grade**	ea	$14.50	$92.90	$107.40
Replace Materials ......60.00 Labor 32.90				
Remove .... Labor 14.50				
▶ 5" recessed spot.				
Exterior recessed light fixture, standard grade	ea	$14.50	$112.90	$127.40
Replace Materials ......80.00 Labor 32.90				
Remove .... Labor 14.50				
▶ 7" recessed spot.				
Exterior recessed light fixture, high grade	ea	$14.50	$177.90	$192.40
Replace Materials .....145.00 Labor 32.90				
Remove .... Labor 14.50				
▶ 7" recessed spot, reflector in can.				
Exterior recessed light fixture, deluxe grade	ea	$14.50	$237.90	$252.40
Replace Materials ....205.00 Labor 32.90				
Remove .... Labor 14.50				
▶ 8" recessed spot.				

courtesy of Rejuvenation Lamp & Fixture Co.

Item Description	Unit	Remove	Replace	Total	
Remove exterior recessed light fixture for work, then reinstall	ea	–	$65.70	$65.70	◁ remove and reinstall
Replace .... Labor...........65.70					
Exterior light fixture, economy grade	ea	$9.10	$48.30	$57.40	◀ **EXTERIOR**
Replace Materials......25.00 Labor 23.30					**LIGHT FIXTURE**
Remove .... Labor 9.10					**ALLOWANCE**
Exterior light fixture, standard grade	ea	$9.10	$73.30	$82.40	*Contractor's allowance*
Replace Materials......50.00 Labor 23.30					*per light fixture in*
Remove .... Labor 9.10					*complete home.*
Exterior light fixture, high grade	ea	$9.10	$113.30	$122.40	
Replace Materials......90.00 Labor 23.30					
Remove .... Labor 9.10					
Exterior light fixture, deluxe grade	ea	$9.10	$198.30	$207.40	
Replace Materials.....175.00 Labor 23.30					
Remove .... Labor 9.10					
Remove exterior light fixture for work, then reinstall	ea	–	$42.60	$42.60	◁ remove and reinstall
Replace .... Labor...........42.60					
Exterior post with light fixture, economy grade	ea	$34.70	$383.00	$417.70	◀ **EXTERIOR POST**
Replace Materials.....170.00 Labor 213.00					**WITH FIXTURE**
Remove .... Labor 34.70					
▶ Redwood post with beveled corners or light turnings or straight metal post, up to 7' tall. Includes post hole, concrete base and hole backfill. Does not include wiring. Plastic or light metal fixture, usually one light with polystyrene lens.					
Exterior post with light fixture, standard grade	ea	$34.70	$458.00	$492.70	
Replace Materials.....245.00 Labor 213.00					
Remove .... Labor 34.70					
▶ Turned redwood post to 7' tall. Includes hole, concrete, and hole backfill. Does not include wiring. Black metal fixture, usually one light with polystyrene lens.					
Exterior post with light fixture, high grade	ea	$34.70	$528.00	$562.70	
Replace Materials.....315.00 Labor 213.00					
Remove .... Labor 34.70					
▶ Turned redwood post, to 7' tall. Includes hole, concrete, and hole backfill. Does not include wiring. Metal fixture, one to two lights clear plastic or glass lens.					
Exterior post with light fixture, deluxe grade	ea	$34.70	$673.00	$707.70	
Replace Materials....460.00 Labor 213.00					
Remove .... Labor 34.70					
▶ Aluminum post, to 7' tall. Includes hole, concrete, J bolts, and hole backfill. Does not include wiring. Metal fixture, one to two lights clear plastic or glass lens.					
Exterior post with light fixture, custom grade	ea	$34.70	$1,033.00	$1,067.70	**RELATED ITEMS**
Replace Materials....820.00 Labor 213.00					Cleaning.....................57
Remove .... Labor 34.70					
▶ Cast-iron post, to 7' tall. Includes post hole, concrete base, J bolts, and hole backfill. Does not include wiring. Cast iron, brass, copper, or pewter fixture, often simulated gas light one to four lights clear plastic or glass lens.					
Remove exterior post with light fixture for work, then reinstall	ea	–	$402.00	$402.00	◁ remove and reinstall
Replace .... Labor........402.00					
Exterior post light fixture (no post), economy grade	ea	$14.50	$105.30	$119.80	◀ **EXTERIOR POST**
Replace Materials......60.00 Labor 45.30					**LIGHT FIXTURE**
Remove .... Labor 14.50					*Fixture only, no post.*
▶ Plastic or light metal fixture. One interior light with polystyrene lens.					

	Item Description	Unit	Remove	Replace	Total
EXTERIOR POST ▶ LIGHT FIXTURE *continued*	**Exterior post light fixture (no post), standard grade**	ea	$14.50	$135.30	$149.80
	Replace Materials......90.00 Labor..........45.30				
	Remove .... Labor..........14.50				
	▶ Metal fixture. Two interior lights with clear polystyrene lens.				
	Exterior post light fixture (no post), high grade	ea	$14.50	$175.30	$189.80
	Replace Materials ....130.00 Labor..........45.30				
	Remove .... Labor..........14.50				
	▶ Metal fixture. 2 to 4 interior lights with clear polystyrene lens.				
	Exterior post light fixture (no post), deluxe grade	ea	$14.50	$250.30	$264.80
	Replace Materials ....205.00 Labor..........45.30				
	Remove .... Labor..........14.50				
	▶ Copper, pewter, or antique finish. 2 to 4 interior light with clear glass lens.				
	Exterior post light fixture (no post), custom grade	ea	$14.50	$340.30	$354.80
	Replace Materials ....295.00 Labor..........45.30				
	Remove .... Labor..........14.50				
	▶ Ornate copper, pewter, brass, or antique finish. 2 to 4 interior lights with clear glass lens.				
remove & reinstall ▷	**Remove exterior post light fixture for work (no post), then reinstall**	ea	–	$76.10	$76.10
	Replace .... Labor..........76.10				
POST FOR ▶ EXTERIOR FIXTURE	**Redwood post for exterior post light fixture, standard grade**	ea	$34.70	$414.00	$448.70
	Replace Materials.....245.00 Labor 169.00				
	Remove .... Labor 34.70				
	▶ To 7' tall. Beveled edges or light turnings. Diameter to 4".				
	Redwood post for exterior post light fixture, high grade	ea	$34.70	$514.00	$548.70
	Replace Materials ....345.00 Labor 169.00				
	Remove .... Labor 34.70				
	▶ Turned post. to 7' tall. Diameter to 4".				
	Metal post for exterior post light fixture, standard grade	ea	$34.70	$316.00	$350.70
	Replace Materials.....155.00 Labor 161.00				
	Remove .... Labor 34.70				
	▶ Straight or tapered aluminum or steel post. Diameter to 4".				
	Metal post for exterior post light fixture, high grade	ea	$34.70	$406.00	$440.70
	Replace Materials.....245.00 Labor 161.00				
	Remove .... Labor 34.70				
	▶ Straight or tapered aluminum or steel post. with flutes and/or simple turned base and cap. Diameter to 4".				
	Metal post for exterior post light fixture, deluxe grade	ea	$34.70	$506.00	$540.70
	Replace Materials ....345.00 Labor 161.00				
	Remove .... Labor 34.70				
	▶ Aluminum post with elaborate turnings, diameter to 6".				
	Metal post for exterior post light fixture, custom grade	ea	$34.70	$596.00	$630.70
	Replace Materials ....435.00 Labor 161.00				
	Remove .... Labor 34.70				
	▶ Aluminum post with elaborate turnings with some cast design (e.g. ivy, inlays, etc.) Diameter to 8".				
	Metal post for exterior post light fixture, custom deluxe grade	ea	$34.70	$841.00	$875.70
	Replace Materials....680.00 Labor 161.00				
	Remove .... Labor 34.70				
	▶ Cast iron with turnings and designs. Diameter to 12".				

Item Description	Unit	Remove	Replace	Total	
Add for exterior light motion sensor or infrared detector	ea	–	$65.00	$65.00	◄ **EXTERIOR LIGHT SENSOR / DETECTOR**
Replace Materials 65.00					
► Add to the cost of an exterior light fixture or lamp post when fixture is equipped with a motion sensor, infrared detector, or both.					
Replace light fixture socket and wiring	ea	–	$25.50	$25.50	◄ **FIXTURE REWIRE**
Replace Materials ....6.50 Labor 19.00					
Replace chandelier socket and wiring, per arm	ea	–	$28.10	$28.10	
Replace Materials ....8.00 Labor 20.10					
Bowl shade or globe for light fixture, economy grade	ea	–	$14.45	$14.45	◄ **REPLACEMENT BOWL SHADE**
Replace Materials ......12.00 Labor 2.45					
► Glass bowl shade or globe only. Light glass with little or no pattern.					
Bowl shade or globe for light fixture, standard grade	ea	–	$21.95	$21.95	
Replace Materials ....19.50 Labor 2.45					
► Glass bowl shade or globe only. Light glass with horizontal turnings.					
Bowl shade or globe for light fixture, high grade	ea	–	$35.95	$35.95	
Replace Materials ......33.50 Labor 2.45					
► Glass bowl shade or globe only. Thick glass with vertical ridges, etched glass, angles in glass, scalloped edges.					
Bowl shade or globe for light fixture, deluxe grade	ea	–	$51.45	$51.45	
Replace Materials ......49.00 Labor 2.45					
► Glass bowl shade or globe only. Thick glass with angles, ornate horizontal turnings, vertical ridges, patterns in glass.					
Bowl shade or globe for light fixture, custom grade	ea	–	$61.95	$61.95	
Replace Materials ......59.50 Labor 2.45					
► Glass bowl shade or globe only. Very thick glass with angles, ornate horizontal turnings, vertical ridges, patterns in glass, specialty gradated colors, flower patterns (Entire shade looks like a flower, not just floral patterns on shade. Flower patterns may be made of thin glass.)					

RELATED ITEMS

Cleaning.........................57

TIME & MATERIAL CHARTS *(selected items)*

Electrical Materials

*See **Electrical** material prices with the line items and other information in the **QuickFinder** column.*

Electrical Labor

LABORER	BASE WAGE	PAID LEAVE	TRUE WAGE	FICA	FUTA	WORKER'S COMP.	UNEMPLOY. INSUR.	HEALTH INSUR.	RETIRE (401K)	LIABILITY INSUR.	COST PER HOUR
Electrician	$26.90	2.10	$29.00	2.22	.23	3.16	2.52	2.92	.87	4.35	**$45.30**
Electrician's helper	$19.40	1.51	$20.91	1.60	.17	2.28	1.82	2.92	.63	3.14	**$33.50**
Demolition laborer	$14.40	1.12	$15.52	1.19	.12	5.01	1.35	2.92	.47	2.33	**$28.90**

Paid Leave is calculated based on two weeks paid vacation, one week sick leave, and seven paid holidays. Employer's matching portion of **FICA** is 7.65 percent. **FUTA** (Federal Unemployment) is .8 percent. **Worker's compensation** for the electrical trade was calculated using a national average of 10.86 percent. **Unemployment insurance** was calculated using a national average of 8.7 percent. **Health insurance** was calculated based on a projected national average for 2005 of $580 per employee (and family when applicable) per month. Employer pays 80 percent for a per month cost of $464 per employee. **Retirement** is based on a 401 (k) retirement program with employer matching of 50 percent. Employee contributions to the 401 (k) plan are an average of 6 percent of the true wage. **Liability insurance** is based on a national average of 14.0 percent.

Electrical Labor Productivity

WORK DESCRIPTION	LABORER	COST PER HOUR	PRODUCTIVITY	UNIT PRICE
Demolition				
remove 240 volt switch or outlet	demolition laborer	$28.90	.200	**$5.78** ea
remove 120 volt switch or outlet	demolition laborer	$28.90	.150	**$4.34** ea
remove bathroom fan	demolition laborer	$28.90	.506	**$14.60** ea
remove bathroom fan / light with heater	demolition laborer	$28.90	.726	**$21.00** ea
remove breaker panel	electrician	$45.30	3.88	**$176.00** ea
remove cable service drop	electrician	$45.30	6.68	**$303.00** ea
remove conduit service drop	electrician	$45.30	8.35	**$378.00** ea
remove rigid steel mast service drop	electrician	$45.30	9.82	**$445.00** ea
remove circuit breaker	demolition laborer	$28.90	.200	**$5.78** ea
remove door bell or chime	demolition laborer	$28.90	.100	**$2.89** ea
remove kitchen exhaust fan	demolition laborer	$28.90	.539	**$15.60** ea
remove whole-house exhaust fan	demolition laborer	$28.90	1.52	**$43.90** ea
remove intercom system master station	demolition laborer	$28.90	.749	**$21.60** ea
remove intercom system remote station	demolition laborer	$28.90	.300	**$8.67** ea
remove low-voltage outlet	demolition laborer	$28.90	.150	**$4.34** ea
remove detector	demolition laborer	$28.90	.200	**$5.78** ea
remove thermostat	demolition laborer	$28.90	.200	**$5.78** ea
remove television antenna	demolition laborer	$28.90	.835	**$24.10** ea
remove recessed electric space heater	demolition laborer	$28.90	.506	**$14.60** ea
remove electric baseboard heater	demolition laborer	$28.90	.165	**$4.77** lf
remove light fixture	demolition laborer	$28.90	.300	**$8.67** ea
remove bathroom light bar	demolition laborer	$28.90	.315	**$9.10** ea
remove chandelier	demolition laborer	$28.90	.557	**$16.10** ea
remove fluorescent light fixture	demolition laborer	$28.90	.500	**$14.50** ea
remove fluorescent circline light fixture	demolition laborer	$28.90	.371	**$10.70** ea
remove ceiling fan	demolition laborer	$28.90	.500	**$14.50** ea
remove hanging light fixture	demolition laborer	$28.90	.100	**$2.89** ea
remove porcelain light fixture	demolition laborer	$28.90	.100	**$2.89** ea
remove recessed spot light fixture	demolition laborer	$28.90	.400	**$11.60** ea
remove electric strip for electric strip lights	demolition laborer	$28.90	.110	**$3.18** lf
remove electric strip light	demolition laborer	$28.90	.150	**$4.34** ea
remove exterior flood light	demolition laborer	$28.90	.300	**$8.67** ea
remove exterior post with light fixture	demolition laborer	$28.90	1.20	**$34.70** ea
remove exterior post light fixture	demolition laborer	$28.90	.500	**$14.50** ea
Electrical crew				
install wiring, boxes, and fixtures	electrician	$45.30		
install wiring, boxes, and fixtures	electrician's helper	$33.50		
install wiring, boxes, and fixtures	electrical crew	$39.40		
Install complete house electrical wiring, outlets, switches & light fixtures				
economy grade	electrical crew	$39.40	.053	**$2.09** ea
deluxe grade	electrical crew	$39.40	.109	**$4.29** ea
low-voltage system	electrical crew	$39.40	.100	**$3.94** ea
add for wiring installation in conduit	electrical crew	$39.40	.055	**$2.17** ea
Install complete house rough electrical (no light fixtures)				
standard	electrical crew	$39.40	.070	**$2.76** ea
in conduit	electrical crew	$39.40	.154	**$6.07** ea
low-voltage system	electrical crew	$39.40	.075	**$2.96** ea
Install complete house light fixtures				
economy grade	electrical crew	$39.40	.015	**$.59** ea
deluxe grade	electrical crew	$39.40	.017	**$.67** ea
for low-voltage system	electrical crew	$39.40	.013	**$.51** ea
Install 240 volt				
outlet or switch with wiring run & box	electrical crew	$39.40	1.34	**$52.80** ea
Install 120 volt				
switch or outlet with wiring run & box	electrical crew	$39.40	.977	**$38.50** ea
3-way switch with wiring run & box	electrical crew	$39.40	1.95	**$76.80** ea
Install electric wiring run				
for typical 120 volt outlet	electrical crew	$39.40	.802	**$31.60** ea
for 120 volt appliance	electrical crew	$39.40	1.02	**$40.20** ea

. . . More ➤

Electrical Labor Productivity *continued*

WORK DESCRIPTION	LABORER	COST PER HOUR	PRODUCTIVITY	UNIT PRICE
Install conduit				
electric metallic tubing (EMT), average installation	electrical crew	$39.40	.077	$3.03 lf
flexible metal, average installation	electrical crew	$39.40	.041	$1.62 lf
PVC, average installation	electrical crew	$39.40	.045	$1.77 lf
intermediate (IMC), average installation	electrical crew	$39.40	.113	$4.45 lf
rigid metal (RMC), average installation	electrical crew	$39.40	.067	$2.64 lf
Install wiring				
#10 2 wire with ground Romex	electrical crew	$39.40	.051	$2.01 lf
#12 2 wire with ground Romex	electrical crew	$39.40	.047	$1.85 lf
#14 2 wire with ground Romex	electrical crew	$39.40	.040	$1.58 lf
Install breaker panel				
100 amp exterior breaker panel (5 breakers)	electrician	$45.30	4.89	$222.00 ea
100 amp interior breaker panel (5 breakers)	electrician	$45.30	4.30	$195.00 ea
150 amp exterior breaker panel (10 breakers)	electrician	$45.30	7.68	$348.00 ea
150 amp interior breaker panel (10 breakers)	electrician	$45.30	7.17	$325.00 ea
200 amp exterior breaker panel (15 breakers)	electrician	$45.30	10.8	$489.00 ea
200 amp interior breaker panel (15 breakers)	electrician	$45.30	9.77	$443.00 ea
300 amp exterior breaker panel (30 breakers)	electrician	$45.30	14.3	$648.00 ea
300 amp interior breaker panel (30 breakers)	electrician	$45.30	13.4	$607.00 ea
40 amp interior breaker sub-panel (5 breakers)	electrician	$45.30	2.99	$135.00 ea
50 amp interior breaker sub-panel	electrician	$45.30	3.16	$143.00 ea
70 amp interior breaker sub-panel	electrician	$45.30	3.47	$157.00 ea
Install electrical service				
100 amp cable service	electrician	$45.30	11.9	$539.00 ea
150 amp cable service	electrician	$45.30	14.3	$648.00 ea
150 amp conduit service	electrician	$45.30	15.4	$698.00 ea
150 amp rigid steel mast service	electrician	$45.30	15.4	$698.00 ea
200 amp cable service	electrician	$45.30	18.5	$838.00 ea
200 amp conduit service	electrician	$45.30	19.9	$901.00 ea
200 amp rigid steel mast service	electrician	$45.30	19.9	$901.00 ea
Install breaker				
single-pole (120 volt) circuit breaker	electrician	$45.30	.636	$28.80 ea
double-pole (240 volt) circuit breaker	electrician	$45.30	.648	$29.40 ea
ground fault circuit interrupter breaker	electrician	$45.30	.689	$31.20 ea
main disconnect circuit breaker	electrician	$45.30	3.47	$157.00 ea
Door bell or chime				
door bell or chime button	electrician	$45.30	.119	$5.39 ea
door bell or chime	electrician	$45.30	1.08	$48.90 ea
low-voltage wiring (per button)	electrician	$45.30	.489	$22.20 ea
Install exhaust fan				
bathroom exhaust fan	electrician	$45.30	.597	$27.00 ea
bathroom exhaust fan with heat lamp	electrician	$45.30	.768	$34.80 ea
bathroom exhaust fan with heater	electrician	$45.30	.827	$37.50 ea
kitchen exhaust fan	electrician	$45.30	.977	$44.30 ea
whole-house exhaust fan	electrician	$45.30	2.69	$122.00 ea
Install intercom				
intercom system master station	electrician	$45.30	2.15	$97.40 ea
intercom system remote station	electrician	$45.30	.597	$27.00 ea
120 volt wiring for intercom master station	electrician	$45.30	.779	$35.30 ea
intercom wiring (per station)	electrician	$45.30	.538	$24.40 ea
Install low-voltage outlet				
Install outlet	electrical crew	$39.40	.256	$10.10 ea
wiring (per outlet)	electrical crew	$39.40	.358	$14.10 ea
Install sound system				
speaker with grille	electrical crew	$39.40	.244	$9.61 ea
Install detector				
battery operated	electrician	$45.30	.308	$14.00 ea
direct-wired	electrician	$45.30	.347	$15.70 ea

. . . More ➤

Electrical Labor Productivity *continued*

WORK DESCRIPTION	LABORER	COST PER HOUR	PRODUCTIVITY	UNIT PRICE
Check electrical circuits				
megameter test small home	electrician	$45.30	3.91	$177.00 ea
megameter test average size home	electrician	$45.30	5.66	$256.00 ea
megameter test large home	electrician	$45.30	7.79	$353.00 ea
Install thermostat				
for electric resistance heating system	electrical crew	$39.40	.183	$7.21 ea
electric heating system	electrical crew	$39.40	.326	$12.80 ea
wiring (per thermostat)	electrical crew	$39.40	.538	$21.20 ea
Install TV antenna				
television antenna	electrician	$45.30	1.08	$48.90 ea
Install recessed electric space heater				
electric space heater recessed in wall	electrician	$45.30	2.15	$97.40 ea
Install electric-resistance heating				
cable, ceiling installation	electrical crew	$39.40	.036	$1.42 ea
cable, floor installation	electrical crew	$39.40	.060	$2.36 ea
electric-resistance heating floor sensor	electrical crew	$39.40	.632	$24.90 ea
Install electric baseboard heater				
electric baseboard heater	electrical crew	$39.40	.512	$20.20 ea
remove for work, then reinstall	electrical crew	$39.40	.717	$28.20 ea
Install underground wiring for exterior post light fixture				
up to 30 feet	electrical crew	$39.40	1.22	$48.10 ea
up to 50 feet	electrical crew	$39.40	1.30	$51.20 ea
Install interior light fixture				
interior incandescent light fixture	electrician	$45.30	.499	$22.60 ea
Install bathroom bar light				
bathroom bar light	electrician	$45.30	.533	$24.10 ea
Install chandelier				
chandelier	electrician	$45.30	1.45	$65.70 ea
entrance chandelier	electrician	$45.30	2.91	$132.00 ea
grand entrance chandelier	electrician	$45.30	3.99	$181.00 ea
Install wall-mount fixture				
wall-mount light fixture	electrician	$45.30	.484	$21.90 ea
Install fluorescent light fixture				
surface-mounted fluorescent light fixture	electrician	$45.30	.913	$41.40 ea
drop-in fluorescent fixture in suspended ceiling	electrician	$45.30	1.84	$83.40 ea
fluorescent circline fixture	electrician	$45.30	.841	$38.10 ea
Install ceiling fan				
assemble and install ceiling fan	electrician	$45.30	2.13	$96.50 ea
remove ceiling fan for work, then reinstall	electrician	$45.30	2.38	$108.00 ea
assemble and install ceiling fan with light	electrician	$45.30	3.20	$145.00 ea
light for ceiling fan	electrician	$45.30	.457	$20.70 ea
Install hanging light fixture				
hanging light fixture	electrician	$45.30	.266	$12.00 ea
Install recessed spot fixture				
recessed spot light fixture	electrician	$45.30	.726	$32.90 ea
Install exterior flood light				
exterior flood light fixture	electrician	$45.30	.515	$23.30 ea
Install exterior post light fixture				
exterior post with light fixture	electrician	$45.30	4.70	$213.00 ea
exterior post light fixture (no post)	electrician	$45.30	.999	$45.30 ea
wood post for exterior post light fixture	electrician	$45.30	3.72	$169.00 ea
metal post for exterior post light fixture	electrician	$45.30	3.55	$161.00 ea

14 .... *Excavation*

Item Description	Unit			Total	
Excavation equipment delivery and take-home charge (mobilization)	ea	–	–	$215.00	◄ **MOBILIZATION**
Excavate .... Labor 215.00					
Excavate for slab-on-grade structure per sf of floor	sf	–	–	$.16	◄ **SLAB-ON-GRADE**
Excavate .... Labor .... .08 Equipment .... .08					*Under-slab excavation up to 1-1/2' deep. Footing*
Excavate for slab-on-grade structure in medium rocky or clay soil	sf	–	–	$.24	*excavation up to 3' deep. Does not include*
Excavate .... Labor .... .14 Equipment .... .10					*mobilization. See above.*
Excavate for slab-on-grade structure in rocky or hardpan soil	sf	–	–	$.28	
Excavate .... Labor .... .17 Equipment .... .11					
Backfill for slab-on-grade structure per sf of floor	sf	–	–	$.13	
Excavate .... Labor .... .08 Equipment .... .05					
Excavate for structure with crawl space per sf of floor	sf	–	–	$.31	◄ **CRAWL SPACE**
Excavate .... Labor .... .17 Equipment .... .14					*Crawl space excavation up to 3' deep. Footing*
Excavate for structure with crawl space in medium rocky or clay soil	sf	–	–	$.38	*excavation up to 4' deep. Does not include*
Excavate .... Labor .... .22 Equipment .... .16					*mobilization. See above.*
Excavate for structure with crawl space in rocky or hardpan soil	sf	–	–	$.40	
Excavate .... Labor .... .22 Equipment .... .18					
Backfill for structure with crawl space per sf of floor	sf	–	–	$.16	
Excavate .... Labor .... .08 Equipment .... .08					
Excavate for structure with basement per sf of floor	sf	–	–	$.82	◄ **BASEMENT**
Excavate .... Labor .... .48 Equipment .... .34					*Basement excavation up to 7' deep. Footing exca-*
Excavate for structure with basement in medium rocky or clay soil	sf	–	–	$.94	*vation up to 8' deep. Does not include*
Excavate .... Labor .... .54 Equipment .... .40					*mobilization. See above.*
Excavate for structure with basement in rocky or hardpan soil	sf	–	–	$1.09	
Excavate .... Labor .... .62 Equipment .... .47					
Backfill for structure with basement per sf of floor	sf	–	–	$.40	
Excavate .... Labor .... .25 Equipment .... .15					
Excavate 3' to 4' deep footings	lf	–	–	$.82	◄ **3' TO 4' DEEP FOOTINGS**
Excavate .... Labor .... .48 Equipment .... .34					*Excavation slopes to 3' width at bottom of*
Excavate 3' to 4' deep footings in medium rocky or clay soil	lf	–	–	$.93	*footing trench. Does not include mobilization. See*
Excavate .... Labor .... .54 Equipment .... .39					*above.*
Excavate 3' to 4' deep footings in rocky or hardpan soil	lf	–	–	$1.08	
Excavate .... Labor .... .62 Equipment .... .46					
Excavate 5' to 6' deep footings	lf	–	–	$1.00	◄ **5' TO 6' DEEP FOOTINGS**
Excavate .... Labor .... .57 Equipment .... .43					*Excavation slopes to 3' width at bottom of*
Excavate 5' to 6' deep footings in medium rocky or clay soil	lf	–	–	$1.15	*footing trench. Does not include mobilization.*
Excavate .... Labor .... .65 Equipment .... .50					

RELATED ITEMS

Concrete
excavate foundation 91
drill pier hole 86

	Item Description	Unit			Total
5' TO 6' DEEP ▶ **FOOTINGS** *continued*	**Excavate 5' to 6' deep footings in rocky or hardpan soil**	If	–	–	**$1.37**
	Excavate .... Labor............ .79 Equipment .... .58				
7' TO 8' DEEP ▶ **FOOTINGS** *Excavation slopes to 3' width at bottom of footing trench. Does not include mobilization. See page 177.*	**Excavate 7' to 8' deep footings**	If	–	–	**$1.25**
	Excavate .... Labor............ .70 Equipment .... .55				
	Excavate 7' to 8' deep footings in medium rocky or clay soil	If	–	–	**$1.47**
	Excavate .... Labor............ .84 Equipment .... .63				
	Excavate 7' to 8' deep footings in rocky or hardpan soil	If	–	–	**$1.69**
	Excavate .... Labor............ .96 Equipment .... .73				
9' TO 10' DEEP ▶ **FOOTINGS** *Excavation slopes to 3' width at bottom of footing trench. Does not include mobilization. See page 177.*	**Excavate 9' to 10' deep footings**	If	–	–	**$1.52**
	Excavate .... Labor............ .87 Equipment .... .65				
	Excavate 9' to 10' deep footings in medium rocky or clay soil	If	–	–	**$1.76**
	Excavate .... Labor............ 1.01 Equipment .... .75				
	Excavate 9' to 10' deep footings in rocky or hardpan soil	If	–	–	**$1.95**
	Excavate .... Labor............ 1.09 Equipment .... .86				
FOUNDATION ▶ **WALL BACKFILL**	**Backfill foundation wall per sf of wall**	If	–	–	**$.53**
	Excavate .... Labor............ .31 Equipment .... .22				
	▶ Typical backfill on flat lot or mild slope per sf of foundation wall. Does not include mobilization.				
1' TO 2' DEEP ▶ **UTILITY TRENCH** *Square trench, 2' wide. Does not include mobilization. See page 177.*	**Excavate utility trench 1' to 2' deep in sandy loam soil**	If	–	–	**$.27**
	Excavate .... Labor............ .17 Equipment .... .10				
	Excavate utility trench 1' to 2' deep in typical soil	If	–	–	**$.28**
	Excavate .... Labor............ .17 Equipment .... .11				
	Excavate utility trench 1' to 2' deep in medium rocky or clay soil	If	–	–	**$.30**
	Excavate .... Labor............ .17 Equipment .... .13				
	Excavate utility trench 1' to 2' deep in rocky or hardpan soil	If	–	–	**$.37**
	Excavate .... Labor............ .22 Equipment .... .15				
	Backfill 1' to 2' utility trench per lf of trench	If	–	–	**$.20**
	Excavate .... Labor............ .11 Equipment .... .09				
3' TO 4' DEEP ▶ **UTILITY TRENCH** *Square trench, 2' wide. Does not include mobilization. See page 177.*	**Excavate utility trench 3' to 4' deep in sandy loam soil**	If	–	–	**$.38**
	Excavate .... Labor............ .22 Equipment .... .16				
	Excavate utility trench 3' to 4' deep in typical soil	If	–	–	**$.40**
	Excavate .... Labor............ .22 Equipment .... .18				
	Excavate utility trench 3' to 4' deep in medium rocky or clay soil	If	–	–	**$.49**
	Excavate .... Labor............ .28 Equipment .... .21				
	Excavate utility trench 3' to 4' deep in rocky or hardpan soil	If	–	–	**$.52**
	Excavate .... Labor............ .28 Equipment .... .24				
	Backfill 3' to 4' utility trench per lf of trench	If	–	–	**$.34**
	Excavate .... Labor............ .16 Equipment .... .18				
5' TO 6' DEEP ▶ **UTILITY TRENCH** *continued on next page*	**Excavate utility trench 5' to 6' deep in sandy loam soil**	If	–	–	**$.50**
	Excavate .... Labor............ .28 Equipment .... .22				

Item Description	Unit			Total
Excavate utility trench 5' to 6' deep in typical soil	lf	–	–	$.53
Excavate .... Labor .... Equipment .... .28				
Excavate utility trench 5' to 6' deep in medium rocky or clay soil	lf	–	–	$.62
Excavate .... Labor .... .33 Equipment .... .29				
Excavate utility trench 5' to 6' deep in rocky or hardpan soil	lf	–	–	$.72
Excavate .... Labor .... .38 Equipment .... .34				
Backfill 5' to 6' utility trench per lf of trench	lf	–	–	$.54
Excavate .... Labor .... .27 Equipment .... .27				
Excavate water-line trench 2' to 3' deep, sandy loam soil	lf	–	–	$.60
Excavate .... Labor .... .38 Equipment .... .22				
Excavate water-line trench 2' to 3' deep, typical soil	lf	–	–	$.63
Excavate .... Labor .... .38 Equipment .... .25				
Excavate water-line trench 2' to 3' deep, medium rocky or clay soil	lf	–	–	$.72
Excavate .... Labor .... .43 Equipment .... .29				
Excavate water-line trench 2' to 3' deep, rocky or hardpan soil	lf	–	–	$.82
Excavate .... Labor .... .48 Equipment .... .34				
Backfill 2' to 3' water-line trench per lf of trench	lf	–	–	$.36
Excavate .... Labor .... .16 Equipment .... .20				
Excavate water-line trench 4' to 5' deep, sandy loam soil	lf	–	–	$.84
Excavate .... Labor .... .48 Equipment .... .36				
Excavate water-line trench 4' to 5' deep, typical soil	lf	–	–	$.96
Excavate .... Labor .... .54 Equipment .... .42				
Excavate water-line trench 4' to 5' deep, medium rocky or clay soil	lf	–	–	$1.08
Excavate .... Labor .... .59 Equipment .... .49				
Excavate water-line trench 4' to 5' deep, rocky or hardpan soil	lf	–	–	$1.20
Excavate .... Labor .... .64 Equipment .... .56				
Backfill 4' to 5' water-line trench per lf of trench	lf	–	–	$.66
Excavate .... Labor .... .32 Equipment .... .34				
Excavate water-line trench 6' to 7' deep, sandy loam soil	lf	–	–	$1.15
Excavate .... Labor .... .64 Equipment .... .51				
Excavate water-line trench 6' to 7' deep, typical soil	lf	–	–	$1.29
Excavate .... Labor .... .70 Equipment .... .59				
Excavate water-line trench 6' to 7' deep, medium rocky or clay soil	lf	–	–	$1.44
Excavate .... Labor .... .75 Equipment .... .69				
Excavate water-line trench 6' to 7' deep, rocky or hardpan soil	lf	–	–	$1.65
Excavate .... Labor .... .86 Equipment .... .79				
Backfill 6' to 7' water-line trench per lf of trench	lf	–	–	$.91
Excavate .... Labor .... .43 Equipment .... .48				
Excavate water-line trench 8' to 9' deep, sandy loam soil	lf	–	–	$1.52
Excavate .... Labor .... .86 Equipment .... .66				

◄ **5' TO 6' DEEP UTILITY TRENCH**
Trench slopes to 2' width at bottom. Does not include mobilization. See page 177.

◄ **2' TO 3' DEEP WATER-LINE TRENCH**
Trench slopes to 2' width at bottom. Does not include mobilization. See page 177.

◄ **4' TO 5' DEEP WATER-LINE TRENCH**
Trench slopes to 3' width at bottom. Does not include mobilization. See page 177.

◄ **6' TO 7' DEEP WATER-LINE TRENCH**
Trench slopes to 3' width at bottom. Does not include mobilization. See page 177.

RELATED ITEMS
Plumbing
repair underground line 364
break-out concrete 364
Concrete
excavate foundation 91
backfill foundation 92
drill pier hole 86

◄ **8' TO 9' DEEP WATER-LINE TRENCH**

	Item Description	Unit			Total
8' TO 9' DEEP ▶ WATER-LINE TRENCH *Trench slopes to 3' width at bottom. Does not include mobilization. See page 177.*	**Excavate water-line trench 8' to 9' deep, typical soil** *Excavate* .... Labor .... .97 Equipment .... .76	If	–	–	$1.73
	Excavate water-line trench 8' to 9' deep, medium rocky or clay soil *Excavate* .... Labor .... 1.08 Equipment .... .89	If	–	–	$1.97
	Excavate water-line trench 8' to 9' deep, rocky or hardpan soil *Excavate* .... Labor ....1.18 Equipment 1.04	If	–	–	$2.22
	Backfill 8' to 9' water-line trench per If of trench *Excavate* .... Labor .... .54 Equipment .... .62	If	–	–	$1.16
3' TO 4' DEEP ▶ SEWER-LINE TRENCH *Trench slopes to 3-1/2' width at bottom. Does not include mobilization. See page 177.*	**Excavate sewer-line trench 3' to 4' deep, sandy loam soil** *Excavate* .... Labor .... .481 Equipment .... .34	If	–	–	$.82
	Excavate sewer-line trench 3' to 4' deep, typical soil *Excavate* .... Labor .... .54 Equipment .... .39	If	–	–	$.93
	Excavate sewer-line trench 3' to 4' deep, medium rocky or clay soil *Excavate* .... Labor .... .59 Equipment .... .46	If	–	–	$1.05
	Excavate sewer-line trench 3' to 4' deep, rocky or hardpan soil *Excavate* .... Labor .... .64 Equipment .... .53	If	–	–	$1.17
	Backfill 3' to 4' sewer-line trench per If of trench *Excavate* .... Labor .... .27 Equipment .... .32	If	–	–	$.59
5' TO 6' DEEP ▶ SEWER-LINE TRENCH *Trench slopes to 3-1/2' width at bottom. Does not include mobilization. See page 177.*	**Excavate sewer-line trench 5' to 6' deep, sandy loam soil** *Excavate* .... Labor .... .64 Equipment .... .51	If	–	–	$1.15
	Excavate sewer-line trench 5' to 6' deep, typical soil *Excavate* .... Labor .... .70 Equipment .... .59	If	–	–	$1.29
	Excavate sewer-line trench 5' to 6' deep, medium rocky or clay soil *Excavate* .... Labor .... .75 Equipment .... .69	If	–	–	$1.44
	Excavate sewer-line trench 5' to 6' deep, rocky or hardpan soil *Excavate* .... Labor .... .86 Equipment .... .80	If	–	–	$1.66
	Backfill 5' to 6' sewer line trench per If of trench *Excavate* .... Labor .... .43 Equipment .... .48	If	–	–	$.91
7' TO 8' DEEP ▶ SEWER-LINE TRENCH *Trench slopes to 3-1/2' width at bottom. Does not include mobilization. See page 177.*	**Excavate sewer-line trench 7' to 8' deep, sandy loam soil** *Excavate* .... Labor .... .75 Equipment .... .68	If	–	–	$1.43
	Excavate sewer-line trench 7' to 8' deep, typical soil *Excavate* .... Labor .... .86 Equipment .... .79	If	–	–	$1.65
	Excavate sewer-line trench 7' to 8' deep, medium rocky or clay soil *Excavate* .... Labor .... .97 Equipment .... .91	If	–	–	$1.88
	Excavate sewer-line trench 7' to 8' deep, rocky or hardpan soil *Excavate* .... Labor .... 1.07 Equipment 1.04	If	–	–	$2.11
	Backfill 7' to 8' sewer-line trench per If of trench *Excavate* .... Labor .... .32 Equipment .... .64	If	–	–	$.96
REPAIR HOLE ▶ *Access hole for repairs, per If of hole depth.*	**Excavate hole for repairs to water, sewer, or utility lines** *Excavate* .... Labor ....1.88 Equipment............1.41	If	–	–	$3.29

Item Description	Unit			Total	
General foundation, slab, & footing excavation	cy	–	–	**$3.46**	◄ **GENERAL**
Excavate .... Labor ....1.97 Equipment...........1.49					General excavation per cy. No mobilization included.
Minimum charge for excavation work	ea	–	–	**$535.00**	◄ **MINIMUM CHARGE**
Excavate .... Labor ....215.00 Equipment........320.00					

TIME & MATERIAL CHARTS _(selected items)_

Excavation Rental Equipment

DESCRIPTION	PRICE	COVERAGE	UNIT PRICE
Backhoe / loader			
excavate slab-on-grade structure			
typical soil	$480.00 _per day_	5,740 _per day_	**$.08** _sf_
rocky or hardpan soil	$480.00 _per day_	4,250 _per day_	**$.11** _sf_
backfill	$480.00 _per day_	9,420 _per day_	**$.05** _sf_
excavate for structure with crawl space			
typical soil	$480.00 _per day_	3,530 _per day_	**$.14** _sf_
rocky or hardpan soil	$480.00 _per day_	2,610 _per day_	**$.18** _sf_
backfill	$480.00 _per day_	6,123 _per day_	**$.08** _sf_
excavate for structure with basement			
typical soil	$480.00 _per day_	1,400 _per day_	**$.34** _sf_
rocky or hardpan soil	$480.00 _per day_	1,030 _per day_	**$.47** _sf_
excavation	$480.00 _per day_	3,140 _per day_	**$.15** _sf_
excavate for 3' to 4' deep footing			
typical soil	$480.00 _per day_	1,420 _per day_	**$.34** _lf_
rocky or hardpan soil	$480.00 _per day_	1,050 _per day_	**$.46** _lf_
excavate for 5' to 6' deep footing			
typical soil	$480.00 _per day_	1,108 _per day_	**$.43** _lf_
rocky or hardpan soil	$480.00 _per day_	830 _per day_	**$.58** _lf_
excavate for 7' to 8' deep footing			
typical soil	$480.00 _per day_	880 _per day_	**$.55** _lf_
rocky or hardpan soil	$480.00 _per day_	660 _per day_	**$.73** _lf_
excavate for 9' to 10' deep footing			
typical soil	$480.00 _per day_	738 _per day_	**$.65** _lf_
rocky or hardpan soil	$480.00 _per day_	560 _per day_	**$.86** _lf_
backfill foundation wall			
backfill	$480.00 _per day_	2,230 _per day_	**$.22** _lf_
excavate for 1' to 2' deep utility trench			
sandy loam soil	$480.00 _per day_	4,930 _per day_	**$.10** _lf_
rocky or hardpan soil	$480.00 _per day_	3,150 _per day_	**$.15** _lf_
backfill	$480.00 _per day_	5,300 _per day_	**$.09** _lf_
excavate for 3' to 4' deep utility trench			
sandy loam soil	$480.00 _per day_	3,057 _per day_	**$.16** _lf_
rocky or hardpan soil	$480.00 _per day_	1,960 _per day_	**$.24** _lf_
backfill	$480.00 _per day_	2,650 _per day_	**$.18** _lf_
excavate for 5' to 6' deep utility trench			
sandy loam soil	$480.00 _per day_	2,219 _per day_	**$.22** _lf_
rocky or hardpan soil	$480.00 _per day_	1,410 _per day_	**$.34** _lf_
backfill	$480.00 _per day_	1,760 _per day_	**$.27** _lf_
excavate for 2' to 3' deep water-line trench			
sandy loam soil	$480.00 _per day_	2,200 _per day_	**$.22** _lf_
rocky or hardpan soil	$480.00 _per day_	1,400 _per day_	**$.34** _lf_
backfill	$480.00 _per day_	2,350 _per day_	**$.20** _lf_

. . . More ➤

Excavation Rental Equipment *continued*

DESCRIPTION	APPLICATION	PRICE	COVERAGE	UNIT PRICE
Backhoe / loader *continued*				
excavate for 4' to 5' deep water-line trench				
sandy loam soil		$480.00 per day	1,330 per day	**$.36** lf
typical soil		$480.00 per day	1,140 per day	**$.42** lf
medium rocky or clay soil		$480.00 per day	980 per day	**$.49** lf
rocky or hardpan soil		$480.00 per day	850 per day	**$.56** lf
backfill		$480.00 per day	1,410 per day	**$.34** lf
excavate for 6' to 7' deep water-line trench				
sandy loam soil		$480.00 per day	940 per day	**$.51** lf
typical soil		$480.00 per day	810 per day	**$.59** lf
medium rocky or clay soil		$480.00 per day	700 per day	**$.69** lf
rocky or hardpan soil		$480.00 per day	610 per day	**$.79** lf
backfill		$480.00 per day	1,010 per day	**$.48** lf
excavate for 8' to 9' deep water-line trench				
sandy loam soil		$480.00 per day	730 per day	**$.66** lf
typical soil		$480.00 per day	630 per day	**$.76** lf
medium rocky or clay soil		$480.00 per day	540 per day	**$.89** lf
rocky or hardpan soil		$480.00 per day	460 per day	**$1.04** lf
backfill		$480.00 per day	780 per day	**$.62** lf
excavate for 3' to 4' deep sewer-line trench				
sandy loam soil		$480.00 per day	1,420 per day	**$.34** lf
typical soil		$480.00 per day	1,220 per day	**$.39** lf
medium rocky or clay soil		$480.00 per day	1,050 per day	**$.46** lf
rocky or hardpan soil		$480.00 per day	900 per day	**$.53** lf
backfill		$480.00 per day	1,520 per day	**$.32** lf
excavate for 5' to 6' deep sewer-line trench				
sandy loam soil		$480.00 per day	940 per day	**$.51** lf
typical soil		$480.00 per day	810 per day	**$.59** lf
medium rocky or clay soil		$480.00 per day	700 per day	**$.69** lf
backfill		$480.00 per day	1,010 per day	**$.48** lf
excavate for 7' to 8' deep sewer-line trench				
sandy loam soil		$480.00 per day	710 per day	**$.68** lf
typical soil		$480.00 per day	610 per day	**$.79** lf
medium rocky or clay soil		$480.00 per day	530 per day	**$.91** lf
rocky or hardpan soil		$480.00 per day	460 per day	**$1.04** lf
backfill		$480.00 per day	750 per day	**$.64** lf
excavate for repairs				
excavate hole		$480.00 per day	340 per day	**$1.41** lf
general excavation				
general excavation		$480.00 per day	322 per day	**$1.49** cy
minimum charge		$320.00 minimum	1 per day	**$320.00** ea
Trenching				
trenching machine		$360.00 per day	1 per day	**$360.00** day
minimum charge for trenching machine		$220.00 minimum	1 each	**$220.00** ea
Compacting				
"jumping jack" compactor		$110.00 per day	1 per day	**$110.00** day
minimum charge for compactor		$90.00 minimum	1 each	**$90.00** ea

Excavation Labor

LABORER	BASE WAGE	PAID LEAVE	TRUE WAGE	FICA	FUTA	WORKER'S COMP.	UNEMPLOY. INSUR.	HEALTH INSUR.	RETIRE (401k)	LIABILITY INSUR.	COST PER HOUR
Equipment operator	$30.80	2.40	$33.20	2.54	.27	6.04	2.89	2.92	1.00	4.98	**$53.80**
Excavation laborer	$15.50	1.21	$16.71	1.28	.13	5.56	1.45	2.92	.50	2.51	**$31.10**

Paid Leave is calculated based on two weeks paid vacation, one week sick leave, and seven paid holidays. Employer's matching portion of **FICA** is 7.65 percent. **FUTA** (Federal Unemployment) is .8 percent. **Worker's compensation** was calculated using a national average of 18.16 percent for the equipment operator and 33.22 percent for the excavation laborer. **Unemployment insurance** was calculated using a national average of 8.7 percent. **Health insurance** was calculated based on a projected national average for 2005 of $580 per employee (and family when applicable) per month. Employer pays 80 percent for a per month cost of $464 per employee. **Retirement** is based on a 401(k) retirement program with employer matching of 50 percent. Employee contributions to the 401(k) plan are an average of 6 percent of the true wage. **Liability insurance** is based on a national average of 14.0 percent.

Excavation Labor Productivity

WORK DESCRIPTION	LABORER	COST PER HOUR	PRODUCTIVITY	UNIT PRICE
Excavation equipment delivery and return labor charges				
backhoe mobilization	machine operator	$53.80	4.00	$215.00 ea
Excavate slab-on-grade structure (per sf of floor)				
typical soil				
machine	machine operator	$53.80	.001	$.05 sf
hand finish	excavation laborer	$31.10	.001	$.03 sf
rocky or hardpan soil				
machine	machine operator	$53.80	.002	$.11 sf
hand finish	excavation laborer	$31.10	.002	$.06 sf
Backfill slab-on-grade structure (per sf of floor)				
all soil types				
machine	machine operator	$53.80	.001	$.05 sf
hand labor	excavation laborer	$31.10	.001	$.03 sf
Excavate for structure with crawl space (per sf of floor)				
typical soil				
machine	machine operator	$53.80	.002	$.11 sf
hand finish	excavation laborer	$31.10	.002	$.06 sf
rocky or hardpan soil				
machine	machine operator	$53.80	.003	$.16 sf
hand finish	excavation laborer	$31.10	.002	$.06 sf
Backfill structure with crawl space (per sf of floor)				
all soil types				
machine	machine operator	$53.80	.001	$.05 sf
hand labor	excavation laborer	$31.10	.001	$.03 sf
Excavate for structure with basement (per sf of floor)				
typical soil				
machine	machine operator	$53.80	.006	$.32 sf
hand finish	excavation laborer	$31.10	.005	$.16 sf
rocky or hardpan soil				
machine	machine operator	$53.80	.008	$.43 sf
hand finish	excavation laborer	$31.10	.006	$.19 sf
Backfill structure with basement (per sf of floor)				
all soil types				
machine	machine operator	$53.80	.003	$.16 sf
hand labor	excavation laborer	$31.10	.003	$.09 sf
Excavate for 3' to 4' deep footings				
typical soil				
machine	machine operator	$53.80	.006	$.32 lf
hand finish	excavation laborer	$31.10	.005	$.16 lf
rocky or hardpan soil				
machine	machine operator	$53.80	.008	$.43 lf
hand finish	excavation laborer	$31.10	.006	$.19 lf
Excavate for 5' to 6' deep footings				
typical soil				
machine	machine operator	$53.80	.007	$.38 lf
hand finish	excavation laborer	$31.10	.006	$.19 lf
rocky or hardpan soil				
machine	machine operator	$53.80	.010	$.54 lf
hand finish	excavation laborer	$31.10	.008	$.25 lf
Excavate for 7' to 8' deep footing				
typical soil				
machine	machine operator	$53.80	.009	$.48 lf
hand finish	excavation laborer	$31.10	.007	$.22 lf
hardpan or rocky soil				
machine	machine operator	$53.80	.012	$.65 lf
hand finish	excavation laborer	$31.10	.010	$.31 lf
Excavate for 9' to 10' deep footing				
typical soil				
machine	machine operator	$53.80	.011	$.59 lf
hand finish	excavation laborer	$31.10	.009	$.28 lf

. . . More ➢

Excavation Labor Productivity *continued*

WORK DESCRIPTION	LABORER	COST PER HOUR	PRODUCTIVITY	UNIT PRICE
Excavate for 9' to 10' deep footing *continued*				
hardpan or rocky soil				
machine	machine operator	$53.80	.014	**$.75** *lf*
hand finish	excavation laborer	$31.10	.011	**$.34** *lf*
Machine backfill foundation wall (per sf of wall)				
machine	machine operator	$53.80	.004	**$.22** *sf*
hand labor	excavation laborer	$31.10	.003	**$.09** *sf*
Machine excavate for 1' to 2' deep utility trench				
sandy loam soil	machine operator	$53.80	.002	**$.11** *lf*
rocky or hardpan soil	machine operator	$53.80	.003	**$.16** *lf*
backfill	machine operator	$53.80	.002	**$.11** *lf*
Machine excavate for 3' to 4' deep utility trench				
sandy loam soil	machine operator	$53.80	.003	**$.16** *lf*
rocky or hardpan soil	machine operator	$53.80	.004	**$.22** *lf*
backfill	machine operator	$53.80	.003	**$.16** *lf*
Machine excavate for 5' to 6' deep utility trench				
sandy loam soil	machine operator	$53.80	.004	**$.22** *lf*
rocky or hardpan soil	machine operator	$53.80	.006	**$.32** *lf*
backfill	machine operator	$53.80	.005	**$.27** *lf*
Hand finish excavation for utility trench				
all soil types	excavation laborer	$31.10	.002	**$.06** *lf*
Excavate for 2' to 3' deep water-line trench				
sandy loam soil	machine operator	$53.80	.004	**$.22** *lf*
rocky or hardpan soil	machine operator	$53.80	.006	**$.32** *lf*
backfill	machine operator	$53.80	.003	**$.16** *lf*
Excavate for 4' to 5' deep water-line trench				
sandy loam soil	machine operator	$53.80	.006	**$.32** *lf*
rocky or hardpan soil	machine operator	$53.80	.009	**$.48** *lf*
backfill	machine operator	$53.80	.006	**$.32** *lf*
Excavate for 6' to 7' deep water-line trench				
sandy loam soil	machine operator	$53.80	.009	**$.48** *lf*
rocky or hardpan soil	machine operator	$53.80	.013	**$.70** *lf*
backfill	machine operator	$53.80	.008	**$.43** *lf*
Excavate for 8' to 9' deep water-line trench				
sandy loam soil	machine operator	$53.80	.011	**$.59** *lf*
rocky or hardpan soil	machine operator	$53.80	.017	**$.91** *lf*
backfill	machine operator	$53.80	.010	**$.54** *lf*
Hand finish excavation for water-line trench				
all soil types	excavation laborer	$31.10	.005	**$.16** *lf*
Excavate for 3' to 4' deep sewer-line trench				
sandy loam soil	machine operator	$53.80	.006	**$.32** *lf*
rocky or hardpan soil	machine operator	$53.80	.009	**$.48** *lf*
backfill	machine operator	$53.80	.005	**$.27** *lf*
Excavate for 5' to 6' deep sewer-line trench				
sandy loam soil	machine operator	$53.80	.009	**$.48** *lf*
rocky or hardpan soil	machine operator	$53.80	.013	**$.70** *lf*
backfill	machine operator	$53.80	.008	**$.43** *lf*
Excavate for 7' to 8' deep sewer-line trench				
sandy loam soil	machine operator	$53.80	.011	**$.59** *lf*
rocky or hardpan soil	machine operator	$53.80	.017	**$.91** *lf*
backfill	machine operator	$53.80	.006	**$.32** *lf*
Hand finish excavation for sewer-line trench				
all soil types	excavation laborer	$31.10	.005	**$.16** *lf*
Machine excavate hole for repairs to water, sewer, or utility lines				
machine excavate per lf of depth	machine operator	$53.80	.024	**$1.29** *lf*
hand finish per lf of depth	excavation laborer	$31.10	.019	**$.59** *lf*
General foundation, slab, & footing machine excavation				
machine excavate per cy	machine operator	$53.80	.025	**$1.35** *cy*
hand-finish per cy	excavation laborer	$31.10	.020	**$.62** *cy*

15 .... *Fees*

Item Description	Unit			Total	
Minimum building permit fee *Fee*..................95.00	ea	–	–	$95.00	◄ **BUILDING PERMIT** *Permit fees vary widely.* *These fees are rules of* *thumb for most areas of* *the country. Rural areas* *will be less and high-* *density areas will be* *more. Includes plan-* *check fees.*
Building permit fee for job $2,001 to $5,000 *Fee*.................100.00	ea	–	–	$100.00	
Building permit fee for job $5,001 to $10,000 *Fee*.................300.00	ea	–	–	$300.00	
Building permit fee for job $10,001 to $20,000 *Fee*.................500.00	ea	–	–	$500.00	
Building permit fee for job $20,001 to $30,000 *Fee*.................700.00	ea	–	–	$700.00	
Building permit fee for job $30,001 to $40,000 *Fee*.................750.00	ea	–	–	$750.00	
Building permit fee for job $40,001 to $50,000 *Fee*.................900.00	ea	–	–	$900.00	
Building permit fee for job $50,001 to $60,000 *Fee*.................1150.00	ea	–	–	$1,150.00	
Building permit fee for job $60,001 to $70,000 *Fee*.................1250.00	ea	–	–	$1,250.00	
Building permit fee for job $70,001 to $80,000 *Fee*.................1400.00	ea	–	–	$1,400.00	
Building permit fee for job $80,001 to $90,000 *Fee*.................1500.00	ea	–	–	$1,500.00	
Building permit fee for job $90,001 to $100,000 *Fee*.................1600.00	ea	–	–	$1,600.00	
Building permit fee for job $100,001 to $150,000 *Fee*.................2050.00	ea	–	–	$2,050.00	
Building permit fee for job $150,001 to $200,000 *Fee*.................2450.00	ea	–	–	$2,450.00	
Building permit fee for job $200,001 to $250,000 *Fee*.................2900.00	ea	–	–	$2,900.00	
Building permit fee for job $250,001 to $300,000 *Fee*.................3350.00	ea	–	–	$3,350.00	
Building permit fee for job $300,001 to $400,000 *Fee*.................4200.00	ea	–	–	$4,200.00	
Building permit fee for job $400,001 to $500,000 *Fee*.................5050.00	ea	–	–	$5,050.00	

Item Description	Unit			Total
SEWER CONNECT ▶				
Rule-of-thumb charge for connecting sewer lines to city service. **Sewer connection fee**	ea	–	–	$2,250.00
Fee.....................2250.00				
▶ Typical charges for labor and materials installed by government entity. Does not include any development upcharges added to the fee. Includes connect to a city sewer line up to 50 lf from the structure, mobilization, excavation, pipe and fittings, backfill, repair to street, curb and gutter, and temporary signs.				
WATER CONNECT ▶				
Rule-of-thumb charge for connecting water lines to city service. **Water connection fee**	ea	–	–	$2,150.00
Fee.....................2150.00				
▶ Typical charges for labor and materials installed by government entity. Does not include any development upcharges added to the fee. Includes connect to a city water line up to 50 lf from the structure, mobilization, excavation, pipe and fittings, water meter, backfill, repair to street, curb and gutter, and temporary signs.				
ESTIMATING ▶				
Typical rates charged to estimate insurance repair damages. **Estimating fees per hour**	hr	–	–	$47.00
Fee.........................47.00				
Estimating fees per day	dy	–	–	$440.00
Fee.........................440.00				
Estimating fees as percentage of estimate	%	–	–	1.5%
▶ Rule of thumb for estimating insurance repair damages on losses under $200,000. Percentage rate drops to as low as **.75%** on large losses or multiple unit losses. This percentage is used across the country. Do not adjust with Area Modification Factor.				
Minimum estimating fee	ea	–	–	$180.00
Fee.........................180.00				
SOILS ENGINEER ▶ **Soils engineer fee per hour**	hr	–	–	$95.00
Fee.........................95.00				
STRUCTURAL ▶ **ENGINEER** **Structural engineer fee per hour**	hr	–	–	$110.00
Fee.........................110.00				
PLAN ▶ **DRAWING FEES** **Plan drawing fee, simple structure per sf of floor**	sf	–	–	$.15
Fee.............................15				
Plan drawing fee, typical structure per sf of floor	sf	–	–	$.25
Fee.............................25				
Plan drawing fee, complex structure per sf of floor	sf	–	–	$.35
Fee.............................35				
Plan drawing fee, ornate structure per sf of floor	sf	–	–	$.50
Fee.............................50				
Minimum plan drawing fee	ea	–	–	$200.00
Fee.........................200.00				

✍ NOTES: _____

_____

_____

_____

_____

_____ end

16 .... *Fences*

Item Description	Unit	Remove	Replace	Total	
Add 11% for redwood wood fences					◄ **OTHER WOODS**
Add 4% for treated-pine wood fences					
4' high cedar post embedded in concrete	ea	$10.60	$56.50	$67.10	◄ **WOOD FENCE POST**
Replace Materials......22.20 Labor 34.30					All wood fence posts include digging of 2' deep hole and setting in con-
Remove........................ Labor...........10.60					crete. Post height is
6' high cedar post embedded in concrete	ea	$10.60	$59.80	$70.40	above ground. For exam-
Replace Materials......25.50 Labor 34.30					ple, a 4' high post is made from a 6' length
Remove........................ Labor...........10.60					with 2' underground and
8' high cedar post embedded in concrete	ea	$10.60	$63.20	$73.80	4' above ground.
Replace Materials......28.90 Labor 34.30					
Remove........................ Labor...........10.60					
4' high cedar basketweave fence	lf	$4.65	$25.30	$29.95	◄ **BASKETWEAVE FENCE**
Replace Materials.......13.30 Labor 12.00					Posts are set in concrete and spaced up to 8' on
Remove........................ Labor 4.65					center with an average
6' high cedar basketweave fence	lf	$4.77	$30.80	$35.57	spacing of 7.2' apart. Fence boards are 1" x 6"
Replace Materials ......18.10 Labor 12.70					to 1" x 10". Gates are
Remove........................ Labor 4.77					3' wide with a frame
8' high cedar basketweave fence	lf	$4.91	$37.30	$42.21	made from 2" x 4" lumber, cross braced with
Replace Materials......23.70 Labor 13.60					turnbuckle and cable.
Remove........................ Labor 4.91					Includes heavy duty
4' high cedar basketweave fence gate with hardware	ea	$9.36	$178.20	$187.56	hinges, latch, and spring closer.
Replace Materials ......76.20 Labor 102.00					
Remove........................ Labor 9.36					
6' high cedar basketweave fence gate with hardware	ea	$9.71	$201.90	$211.61	
Replace Materials ......93.90 Labor 108.00					
Remove........................ Labor 9.71					
8' high cedar basketweave fence gate with hardware	ea	$10.00	$225.10	$235.10	
Replace Materials .....110.10 Labor 115.00					
Remove........................ Labor 10.00					
4' high cedar board fence	lf	$4.65	$23.40	$28.05	◄ **BOARD FENCE**
Replace Materials.......13.30 Labor 10.10					Fence with boards installed vertically or
Remove........................ Labor 4.65					horizontally. Posts are
6' high cedar board fence	lf	$4.77	$28.90	$33.67	set in concrete and spaced up to 8' on center
Replace Materials ......18.10 Labor 10.80					with an average spacing
Remove........................ Labor 4.77					of 7.2' apart. Fence
8' high cedar board fence	lf	$4.91	$35.30	$40.21	boards are 1" x 4" to 1" x 8". 8' tall fence con-
Replace Materials......23.70 Labor 11.60					tains three supporting
Remove........................ Labor 4.91					rails. All other heights contain two. Gates are
4' high cedar board fence gate with hardware	ea	$9.36	$158.20	$167.56	3' wide with horizontal and diagonal rails, heavy
Replace Materials ......76.20 Labor 82.00					duty hinges, latch, and
Remove........................ Labor 9.36					spring closer.

Item Description	Unit	Remove	Replace	Total

BOARD FENCE ▶ *continued*

6' high cedar board fence gate with hardware | ea | $9.71 | $182.00 | $191.71
Replace Materials......93.90   Labor.........88.10
Remove......................   Labor..........9.71

8' high cedar board fence gate with hardware | ea | $10.00 | $202.30 | $212.30
Replace Materials.....110.10   Labor.........92.20
Remove......................   Labor.........10.00

BOARD FENCE ▶ WITH LATTICE CAP
Board fence with 12" cap. Lattice is trimmed with 2" x 4" lattice rails. Posts are set in concrete and spaced up to 8' on center with an average spacing of 7.2'. Gates are 3' wide with a frame made from 2" x 4" lumber, cross braced with turn buckle and cable. Includes heavy duty hinges, latch, and spring closer.

6' high cedar board fence with lattice cap | lf | $4.77 | $36.50 | $41.27
Replace Materials ......24.00   Labor.........12.50
Remove......................   Labor..........4.77

8' high cedar board fence with lattice cap | lf | $4.91 | $43.20 | $48.11
Replace Materials......29.60   Labor.........13.60
Remove......................   Labor..........4.91

6' high cedar board fence gate with lattice cap | ea | $9.67 | $214.80 | $224.47
Replace Materials ....103.80   Labor.........111.00
Remove......................   Labor..........9.67

8' high cedar board fence gate with lattice cap | ea | $9.95 | $250.00 | $259.95
Replace Materials.....120.00   Labor.........130.00
Remove......................   Labor..........9.95

BOARD-ON- ▶ BOARD FENCE
Fence with overlapping boards installed vertically. Posts are set in concrete and spaced up to 8' on center with an average spacing of 7.2' apart. Fence boards are 1" x 4" to 1" x 8". 8' tall fence contains three supporting rails. All other heights contain two. Gates are 3' wide with horizontal and diagonal rails. Includes heavy duty hinges, latch, and spring closer.

4' high cedar board-on-board fence | lf | $4.65 | $30.80 | $35.45
Replace Materials......19.60   Labor.........11.20
Remove......................   Labor..........4.65

6' high cedar board-on-board fence | lf | $4.77 | $39.40 | $44.17
Replace Materials ......27.60   Labor.........11.80
Remove......................   Labor..........4.77

8' high cedar board-on-board fence | lf | $4.91 | $48.90 | $53.81
Replace Materials ......36.40   Labor.........12.50
Remove......................   Labor..........4.91

4' high cedar board-on-board fence gate with hardware | ea | $9.36 | $192.10 | $201.46
Replace Materials......95.30   Labor.........96.80
Remove......................   Labor..........9.36

6' high cedar board-on-board fence gate with hardware | ea | $9.71 | $224.50 | $234.21
Replace Materials ....122.50   Labor.........102.00
Remove......................   Labor..........9.71

8' high cedar board-on-board fence gate with hardware | ea | $10.00 | $256.00 | $266.00
Replace Materials ....148.00   Labor.........108.00
Remove......................   Labor.........10.00

BOARD-AND- ▶ BATTEN FENCE
Vertically installed 1" x 8" to 1" x 12" boards with 1" x 2" to 1" x 4" battens overlapping joints. Posts are set in concrete and spaced up to 8' on center with an average spacing of 7.2' apart. Gates are 3' wide with horizontal and diagonal rails. Includes heavy duty hinges, latch, and spring closer.

4' high cedar board-and-batten fence | lf | $4.65 | $28.10 | $32.75
Replace Materials ......16.70   Labor.........11.40
Remove......................   Labor..........4.65

6' high cedar board-and-batten fence | lf | $4.77 | $34.80 | $39.57
Replace Materials......23.20   Labor.........11.60
Remove......................   Labor..........4.77

8' high cedar board-and-batten fence | lf | $4.91 | $42.70 | $47.61
Replace Materials......30.50   Labor.........12.20
Remove......................   Labor..........4.91

Item Description	Unit	Remove	Replace	Total
4' high cedar board-and-batten fence gate with hardware	ea	$9.36	$186.00	$195.36
Replace Materials......86.60 Labor 99.40				
Remove...................... Labor 9.36				
6' high cedar board-and-batten fence gate with hardware	ea	$9.71	$214.40	$224.11
Replace Materials ....109.40 Labor..........105.00				
Remove...................... Labor 9.71				
8' high cedar board-and-batten fence gate with hardware	ea	$10.00	$241.70	$251.70
Replace Materials ....130.70 Labor..........111.00				
Remove...................... Labor 10.00				
3' high cedar picket fence	lf	$4.65	$16.17	$20.82
Replace Materials........7.78 Labor 8.39				
Remove...................... Labor 4.65				
5' high cedar picket fence	lf	$4.77	$22.04	$26.81
Replace Materials.......13.04 Labor 9.00				
Remove...................... Labor 4.77				
3' high cedar picket fence gate with hardware	ea	$9.36	$134.70	$144.06
Replace Materials ......59.10 Labor.........75.60				
Remove...................... Labor 9.36				
5' high cedar picket fence gate with hardware	ea	$9.71	$167.50	$177.21
Replace Materials......77.50 Labor 90.00				
Remove...................... Labor 9.71				
Minimum charge for board fence work	ea	–	$98.90	$98.90
Replace Materials ......35.00 Labor 63.90				
Remove & reinstall board fence gate	ea	–	$30.40	$30.40
Replace .... Labor 30.40				
Wood gate hardware with self-closing hinges	ea	$5.68	$64.60	$70.28
Replace Materials......36.10 Labor 28.50				
Remove...................... Labor 5.68				
Heavy gauge wood gate hardware with self-closing hinges	ea	$5.68	$88.40	$94.08
Replace Materials......59.90 Labor 28.50				
Remove...................... Labor 5.68				
Wood gate closing spring	ea	$2.90	$34.60	$37.50
Replace Materials......22.10 Labor...........12.50				
Remove...................... Labor 2.90				
3' high chain-link fence	lf	$3.35	$12.25	$15.60
Replace Materials........7.94 Labor 4.31				
Remove...................... Labor 3.35				
▶ With 1-5/8" line posts and 2" terminal posts.				
4' high chain-link fence	lf	$3.50	$16.01	$19.51
Replace Materials ......10.53 Labor 5.48				
Remove...................... Labor 3.50				
▶ With 1-7/8" line posts and 2" terminal posts.				
5' high chain-link fence	lf	$3.61	$20.02	$23.63
Replace Materials.......13.10 Labor 6.92				
Remove...................... Labor 3.61				
▶ With 1-7/8" line posts and 2" terminal posts.				

RELATED ITEMS

Painting 337

◀ **PICKET FENCE**
Posts are set in concrete and spaced up to 8' on center with an average spacing of 7.2' apart. Pickets are factory pre-cut. Gates are 3' wide with horizontal and diagonal rails. Includes heavy duty hinges, latch, and spring closer.

◀ **MINIMUM CHARGE FOR BOARD FENCE**

◀ **REMOVE & REINSTALL GATE**

◀ **WOOD GATE HARDWARE**

◀ **CHAIN-LINK FENCE**
11 gauge chain-link. Line posts and terminal posts are set 2' deep in concrete and spaced up to 10' on center with an average spacing of 9.2' apart. Includes all post caps, tie wire, tension bands, nuts, bolts, and tension rods.

Item Description	Unit	Remove	Replace	Total
CHAIN-LINK FENCE *continued* ► **6' high chain-link fence** *Replace* Materials.......15.70 Labor ....8.81 *Remove*...................... Labor ....3.79 ► With 1-7/8" line posts and 2" terminal posts.	lf	$3.79	$24.51	$28.30
7' high chain-link fence *Replace* Materials ......18.30 Labor ....11.20 *Remove*...................... Labor ....3.93 ► With 1-7/8" line posts and 2" terminal posts.	lf	$3.93	$29.50	$33.43
8' high chain-link fence *Replace* Materials ......20.90 Labor ....14.20 *Remove*...................... Labor ....4.13 ► With 2" line posts and 3" terminal posts.	lf	$4.13	$35.10	$39.23
10' high chain-link fence *Replace* Materials ......26.00 Labor ....18.00 *Remove*...................... Labor ....4.39 ► With 2" line posts and 3" terminal posts.	lf	$4.39	$44.00	$48.39
CHAIN-LINK FENCE GATE *3' wide with all hardware.* ► **3' high chain-link fence gate with hardware** *Replace* Materials....43.50 Labor............96.80 *Remove*...................... Labor 5.87	ea	$5.87	$140.30	$146.17
4' high chain-link fence gate with hardware *Replace* Materials.....56.20 Labor............96.80 *Remove*...................... Labor 5.87	ea	$5.87	$153.00	$158.87
5' high chain-link fence gate with hardware *Replace* Materials ......67.60 Labor............96.80 *Remove*...................... Labor 5.87	ea	$5.87	$164.40	$170.27
6' high chain-link fence gate with hardware *Replace* Materials ......77.80 Labor ....99.40 *Remove*...................... Labor 5.87	ea	$5.87	$177.20	$183.07
7' high chain-link fence gate with hardware *Replace* Materials ......87.70 Labor ....99.40 *Remove*...................... Labor 5.87	ea	$5.87	$187.10	$192.97
8' high chain-link fence gate with hardware *Replace* Materials ......96.30 Labor ....99.40 *Remove*...................... Labor 5.87	ea	$5.87	$195.70	$201.57
10' high chain-link fence gate with hardware *Replace* Materials .....115.00 Labor ....99.40 *Remove*...................... Labor 5.87	ea	$5.87	$214.40	$220.27
CHAIN-LINK DRIVEWAY GATE *Prices per lf. Includes all hardware. Minimum of 6 lf.* ► **3' high chain-link fence driveway gate with hardware** *Replace* Materials ......12.80 Labor............24.20 *Remove*...................... Labor 1.24	lf	$1.24	$37.00	$38.24
4' high chain-link fence driveway gate with hardware *Replace* Materials ......23.60 Labor............24.20 *Remove*...................... Labor 1.24	lf	$1.24	$47.80	$49.04
5' high chain-link fence driveway gate with hardware *Replace* Materials ......38.00 Labor............24.20 *Remove*...................... Labor 1.24	lf	$1.24	$62.20	$63.44
6' high chain-link fence driveway gate with hardware *Replace* Materials ......44.10 Labor............24.90 *Remove*...................... Labor 1.24	lf	$1.24	$69.00	$70.24

Item Description	Unit	Remove	Replace	Total	
7' high chain-link fence driveway gate with hardware	lf	$1.24	$74.70	$75.94	
Replace Materials ......49.80 Labor...........24.90					
Remove....................... Labor 1.24					
8' high chain-link fence driveway gate with hardware	lf	$1.24	$79.80	$81.04	
Replace Materials......54.90 Labor...........24.90					
Remove....................... Labor 1.24					
Add for additional corner in chain-link fence	ea	–	$126.60	$126.60	◄ **ADDITIONAL CHAIN-LINK COSTS**
Replace Materials ......53.60 Labor...........73.00					
► The chain-link fence prices above allow for an average of 1 corner or terminal posts for every 15 lf of fence. Use this price only when estimating a fence that contains more corner or terminal posts.					
Add for vinyl privacy slats (per sf of fence or gate)	sf	–	$.88	$.88	
Replace Materials .... .64 Labor............. .24					
Add for aluminum privacy slats (per sf of fence or gate)	sf	–	$.92	$.92	
Replace Materials .... .68 Labor............. .24					
Add 3% for chain-link fence with top rail					
Add 28% for 9 gauge galvanized chain-link					
Add 25% for 9 gauge vinyl-coated chain-link and posts					
Add 41% for 6 gauge chain-link					
Remove chain-link fence gate for work, then reinstall	ea	–	$11.00	$11.00	◄ **REMOVE CHAIN-LINK & REINSTALL**
Replace .... Labor 11.00					
Remove chain-link fence (posts remain) for work, then reinstall	sf	–	$.49	$.49	
Replace .... Labor .... .49					
Minimum charge for chain-link fence work	ea	–	$145.10	$145.10	◄ **MINIMUM FOR CHAIN-LINK**
Replace Materials ......60.00 Labor...........85.10					
3' high galvanized line post embedded in concrete	ea	$11.60	$50.30	$61.90	◄ **CHAIN-LINK FENCE POST**
Replace Materials.......15.60 Labor 34.70					*All chain-link fence posts*
Remove....................... Labor 11.60					*include digging of 2' deep*
► 1-7/8" diameter post.					*hole and setting in con-*
4' high galvanized line post embedded in concrete	ea	$11.60	$51.50	$63.10	*crete. Post height is*
Replace Materials ......16.80 Labor 34.70					*above ground. For exam-*
Remove....................... Labor 11.60					*ple, a 4' high post is*
► 1-7/8" diameter post.					*made from a 6' length*
5' high galvanized line post embedded in concrete	ea	$11.60	$52.70	$64.30	*with 2' underground and*
Replace Materials ......18.00 Labor 34.70					*4' above ground.*
Remove....................... Labor 11.60					
► 1-7/8" diameter post.					
6' high galvanized line post embedded in concrete	ea	$11.60	$53.90	$65.50	
Replace Materials.......19.20 Labor 34.70					
Remove....................... Labor 11.60					
► 1-7/8" diameter post.					
7' high galvanized line post embedded in concrete	ea	$11.60	$55.10	$66.70	
Replace Materials.......20.40 Labor 34.70					
Remove....................... Labor 11.60					
► 1-7/8" diameter post.					

	Item Description	Unit	Remove	Replace	Total
CHAIN-LINK ▶ FENCE POST *continued*	**8' high galvanized line post embedded in concrete** *Replace* Materials ......22.00 Labor ....34.70 *Remove*........................ Labor ....11.60 ▶ 2" diameter post.	ea	$11.60	$56.70	$68.30
	10' high galvanized line post embedded in concrete *Replace* Materials ......24.50 Labor ....34.70 *Remove*........................ Labor ....11.60 ▶ 2" diameter post.	ea	$11.60	$59.20	$70.80
gate or corner post ▷	**3' high galvanized gate or corner post embedded in concrete** *Replace* Materials ......14.90 Labor ....34.70 *Remove*........................ Labor ....11.60 ▶ 2" diameter post.	ea	$11.60	$49.60	$61.20
	4' high galvanized gate or corner post embedded in concrete *Replace* Materials.......15.90 Labor ....34.70 *Remove*........................ Labor ....11.60 ▶ 2" diameter post.	ea	$11.60	$50.60	$62.20
	5' high galvanized gate or corner post embedded in concrete *Replace* Materials ......16.90 Labor ....34.70 *Remove*........................ Labor ....11.60 ▶ 2" diameter post.	ea	$11.60	$51.60	$63.20
	6' high galvanized gate or corner post embedded in concrete *Replace* Materials.......19.50 Labor ....34.70 *Remove*........................ Labor ....11.60 ▶ 2-1/2" diameter post.	ea	$11.60	$54.20	$65.80
	7' high galvanized gate or corner post embedded in concrete *Replace* Materials ......20.80 Labor ....34.70 *Remove*........................ Labor ....11.60 ▶ 2-1/2" diameter post.	ea	$11.60	$55.50	$67.10
	8' high galvanized gate or corner post embedded in concrete *Replace* Materials ......34.10 Labor ....34.70 *Remove*........................ Labor ....11.60 ▶ 3" diameter post.	ea	$11.60	$68.80	$80.40
	10' high galvanized gate or corner post embedded in concrete *Replace* Materials ......39.60 Labor ....34.70 *Remove*........................ Labor ....11.60 ▶ 3" diameter post.	ea	$11.60	$74.30	$85.90
ADD FOR ▶ ALUMINIZED	**Add 22% for aluminized steel fence post**				
VINYL PICKET ▶ FENCE *36" and 48" fences have 2 rails, 60" and 72" have three. Pickets are 7/8" x 1-1/2" spaced 3-7/8" apart. Top and bottom rails are 1-1/2" x 3-1/2". Bottom rail includes galvanized steel channel. Posts are 4" x 4" and spaced up to 8' on center with an average spacing of 7.2 feet apart. Includes picket and post caps.*	**36" high vinyl picket fence** *Replace* Materials ......14.70 Labor ....13.30 *Remove*........................ Labor 4.02	lf	$4.02	$28.00	$32.02
	48" high vinyl picket fence *Replace* Materials.......17.90 Labor ....13.50 *Remove*........................ Labor 4.02	lf	$4.02	$31.40	$35.42
	60" high vinyl picket fence *Replace* Materials ......21.20 Labor ....13.70 *Remove*........................ Labor 4.02	lf	$4.02	$34.90	$38.92
	72" high vinyl picket fence *Replace* Materials ......24.50 Labor ....13.80 *Remove*........................ Labor 4.02	lf	$4.02	$38.30	$42.32

continued on next page

Item Description	Unit	Remove	Replace	Total
36" high vinyl picket fence gate	If	$4.39	$67.70	$72.09
Replace Materials......43.30 Labor...........24.40				
Remove...................... Labor 4.39				
48" high vinyl picket fence gate	If	$4.39	$70.50	$74.89
Replace Materials......45.50 Labor 25.00				
Remove...................... Labor 4.39				
60" high vinyl picket fence gate	If	$4.39	$73.40	$77.79
Replace Materials......47.70 Labor 25.70				
Remove...................... Labor 4.39				
72" high vinyl picket fence gate	If	$4.39	$76.20	$80.59
Replace Materials......49.90 Labor..........26.30				
Remove...................... Labor 4.39				
36" high vinyl picket fence, large pickets	If	$4.02	$30.20	$34.22
Replace Materials......16.90 Labor...........13.30				
Remove...................... Labor 4.02				
48" high vinyl picket fence, large pickets	If	$4.02	$34.50	$38.52
Replace Materials......21.00 Labor...........13.50				
Remove...................... Labor 4.02				
60" high vinyl picket fence, large pickets	If	$4.02	$38.30	$42.32
Replace Materials......24.60 Labor...........13.70				
Remove...................... Labor 4.02				
36" high vinyl picket fence gate, large pickets	If	$4.39	$69.30	$73.69
Replace Materials......44.90 Labor..........24.40				
Remove...................... Labor 4.39				
48" high vinyl picket fence gate, large pickets	If	$4.39	$72.70	$77.09
Replace Materials......47.70 Labor 25.00				
Remove...................... Labor 4.39				
60" high vinyl picket fence gate, large pickets	If	$4.39	$76.20	$80.59
Replace Materials......50.50 Labor 25.70				
Remove...................... Labor 4.39				
36" high vinyl picket fence, scalloped pickets	If	$4.02	$29.10	$33.12
Replace Materials......15.80 Labor...........13.30				
Remove...................... Labor 4.02				
48" high vinyl picket fence, scalloped pickets	If	$4.02	$32.80	$36.82
Replace Materials......19.30 Labor...........13.50				
Remove...................... Labor 4.02				
60" high vinyl picket fence, scalloped pickets	If	$4.02	$36.40	$40.42
Replace Materials......22.70 Labor...........13.70				
Remove...................... Labor 4.02				
36" high vinyl picket fence gate, scalloped pickets	If	$4.39	$68.40	$72.79
Replace Materials......44.00 Labor...........24.40				
Remove...................... Labor 4.39				
48" high vinyl picket fence gate, scalloped pickets	If	$4.39	$71.30	$75.69
Replace Materials......46.30 Labor 25.00				
Remove...................... Labor 4.39				

◄ **VINYL PICKET FENCE**
continued

Gates are priced per If with a 3 If minimum and a 5 If maximum and include all hardware. For wider gates, measure the gate If, round up to the next even number, multiply by the fence If price, then add $150.

◄ **VINYL LARGE PICKET FENCE**
Same as picket fence discussed on previous page with large 7/8" x 3-1/2" pickets spaced 3-7/8" apart.

VINYL FENCES

Also called PVC fences, vinyl fences are made from a molecularly bonded blend of hi-polymer resin with UV inhibitors to prevent damage from sunlight.

All posts are filled with concrete to about 1/3 of their height and capped with decorative caps

◄ **VINYL SCALLOPED PICKET FENCE**
Same as picket fence discussed above with decorative scalloped pickets.

	Item Description	Unit	Remove	Replace	Total
VINYL SCALLOPED ▶ PICKET FENCE *continued*	60" high vinyl picket fence gate, scalloped pickets *Replace* Materials......48.80 Labor ....25.70 *Remove*........................ Labor 4.39	If	$4.39	$74.50	$78.89
REMOVE & ▶ REINSTALL VINYL FENCE	Remove vinyl fence for work, then reinstall (panels only) *Replace* .... Labor 20.40	If	–	$20.40	$20.40
	Remove vinyl fence gate for work, then reinstall *Replace* .... Labor 25.70	If	–	$25.70	$25.70
VINYL THREE- ▶ RAIL FENCE *Rails are 1-1/2" x 5-1/2". Posts are 5" x 5" and spaced up to 8' apart with an average spacing of 7.2'. Gates priced per If: 3 If minimum, 5 If maximum.*	52" high vinyl three-rail fence *Replace* Materials........9.80 Labor ....7.98 *Remove*........................ Labor 3.01	If	$3.01	$17.78	$20.79
	52" high vinyl three-rail fence gate *Replace* Materials......37.70 Labor ....11.30 *Remove*........................ Labor ....3.01 ▶ For gates longer than 5 If use If fence price, round to even number and add **$105**.	If	$3.01	$49.00	$52.01
REMOVE & ▶ REINSTALL THREE- RAIL FENCE	Remove three-rail vinyl fence for work, then reinstall (rails only) *Replace* .... Labor 14.10	If	–	$14.10	$14.10
	Remove three-rail vinyl fence gate for work, then reinstall *Replace* .... Labor 20.40	If	–	$20.40	$20.40
VINYL SPACED ▶ SLAT FENCE *Contains two widths of slats. The narrow slat is 7/8" x 1-1/2" and the wide slat is 7/8" x 3-1/2". Slats are spaced 2-1/2" apart. Top and bottom rails are 1-1/2" x 3-1/2". Bottom rail includes galvanized steel channel. Posts are 4" x 4" and spaced up to 8' on center with an average spacing of 7.2 feet apart. Includes post caps. Gates are priced per If with a 3 If minimum and a 5 If maximum and include all hardware. For wider gates, measure the gate If, round up to the next even number, multiply by the fence If price, then add $150.*	48" high vinyl spaced slat fence *Replace* Materials.......15.00 Labor ....13.50 *Remove*........................ Labor 4.02	If	$4.02	$28.50	$32.52
	60" high vinyl spaced slat fence *Replace* Materials ......18.40 Labor ....13.70 *Remove*........................ Labor 4.02	If	$4.02	$32.10	$36.12
	72" high vinyl spaced slat fence *Replace* Materials ......21.60 Labor ....13.80 *Remove*........................ Labor 4.02	If	$4.02	$35.40	$39.42
	48" high vinyl spaced slat fence gate *Replace* Materials ......43.50 Labor ....25.00 *Remove*........................ Labor 4.39	If	$4.39	$68.50	$72.89
	60" high vinyl spaced slat fence gate *Replace* Materials ......45.80 Labor ....25.70 *Remove*........................ Labor 4.39	If	$4.39	$71.50	$75.89
	72" high vinyl spaced slat fence gate *Replace* Materials ......48.00 Labor........26.30 *Remove*........................ Labor 4.39	If	$4.39	$74.30	$78.69
VINYL SOLID ▶ SLAT FENCE *Slat is 7/8" x 5-1/2" with no space between slats. Top and bottom rails are 1-1/2" x 3-1/2". Bottom rail includes galvanized steel channel. Posts are 5" x 5" and spaced up to 8' on center with an average spacing of 7.2 feet.*	48" high vinyl solid slat fence *Replace* Materials.......15.70 Labor ....13.50 *Remove*........................ Labor 4.02	If	$4.02	$29.20	$33.22
	60" high vinyl solid slat fence *Replace* Materials ......31.30 Labor ....13.70 *Remove*........................ Labor 4.02	If	$4.02	$45.00	$49.02
	72" high vinyl solid slat fence *Replace* Materials ......22.70 Labor ....13.80 *Remove*........................ Labor 4.02	If	$4.02	$36.50	$40.52

continued on next page

Item Description	Unit	Remove	Replace	Total
48" high vinyl solid slat fence gate *Replace* Materials......43.90 Labor..........25.00 *Remove*...................... Labor...........4.39	If	$4.39	$68.90	$73.29
60" high vinyl solid slat fence gate *Replace* Materials......46.30 Labor..........25.70 *Remove*...................... Labor...........4.39	If	$4.39	$72.00	$76.39
72" high vinyl solid slat fence gate *Replace* Materials......48.70 Labor..........26.30 *Remove*...................... Labor...........4.39	If	$4.39	$75.00	$79.39
60" high vinyl solid slat fence with lattice top *Replace* Materials......26.10 Labor..........14.10 *Remove*...................... Labor...........4.02	If	$4.02	$40.20	$44.22
72" high vinyl solid slat fence with lattice top *Replace* Materials......29.40 Labor..........14.30 *Remove*...................... Labor...........4.02	If	$4.02	$43.70	$47.72
60" high vinyl solid slat fence with lattice top gate *Replace* Materials......51.00 Labor..........27.40 *Remove*...................... Labor...........4.39	If	$4.39	$78.40	$82.79
72" high vinyl solid slat fence with lattice top gate *Replace* Materials......53.20 Labor..........28.60 *Remove*...................... Labor...........4.39	If	$4.39	$81.80	$86.19
60" ornamental iron fence, straight pickets *Replace* Materials......13.80 Labor..........14.10 *Remove*...................... Labor...........5.61	If	$5.61	$27.90	$33.51
72" ornamental iron fence, straight pickets *Replace* Materials......15.90 Labor..........14.30 *Remove*...................... Labor...........5.61	If	$5.61	$30.20	$35.81
60" ornamental iron fence gate, straight pickets *Replace* Materials......55.00 Labor..........27.40 *Remove*...................... Labor...........5.84	If	$5.84	$82.40	$88.24
72" ornamental iron fence gate, straight pickets *Replace* Materials......58.50 Labor..........28.60 *Remove*...................... Labor...........5.84	If	$5.84	$87.10	$92.94
60" ornamental iron fence, twisted pickets *Replace* Materials......14.80 Labor..........14.10 *Remove*...................... Labor...........5.61	If	$5.61	$28.90	$34.51
72" ornamental iron fence, twisted pickets *Replace* Materials......17.20 Labor..........14.30 *Remove*...................... Labor...........5.61	If	$5.61	$31.50	$37.11
60" ornamental iron fence gate, twisted pickets *Replace* Materials......58.90 Labor..........27.40 *Remove*...................... Labor...........5.84	If	$5.84	$86.30	$92.14
72" ornamental iron fence gate, twisted pickets *Replace* Materials......62.60 Labor..........28.60 *Remove*...................... Labor...........5.84	If	$5.84	$91.20	$97.04

◄ **VINYL SOLID SLAT FENCE**
continued

Includes post caps. Gates are priced per If with a 3 If minimum and a 5 If maximum and include all hardware. For wider gates, measure the gate If, round up to the next even number, multiply by the fence If price, then add $150.

◄ **ORNAMENTAL IRON FENCE**
On all grades except fences with ornamental casting, steel pickets are 5/8" square 3-7/8" apart with 1" x 1" top and bottom rails. Posts are 93-1/2" apart. Pickets with decorative scrolls are straight pickets with the decorative scroll-work riveted or screwed to the pickets. Ornamental iron fences with ornamental casting have pickets that are cast in decorative scroll and plant-like patterns. Gates are priced per If with a 3 If minimum and a 5 If maximum. For wider gates, measure the gate If, round up to the next even number, multiply by the fence If price, then add $200.

RELATED ITEMS
Painting..................337

Item Description	Unit	Remove	Replace	Total
ORNAMENTAL IRON FENCE *continued*				
60" ornamental iron fence with decorative scrolls	lf	$5.61	$35.10	$40.71
Replace Materials ......21.00 Labor 14.10				
Remove .... Labor 5.61				
72" ornamental iron fence with decorative scrolls	lf	$5.61	$38.50	$44.11
Replace Materials ......24.20 Labor 14.30				
Remove .... Labor 5.61				
60" ornamental iron fence gate with decorative scrolls	lf	$5.84	$110.60	$116.44
Replace Materials......83.20 Labor...........27.40				
Remove .... Labor 5.84				
72" ornamental iron fence gate with decorative scrolls	lf	$5.84	$117.00	$122.84
Replace Materials......88.40 Labor 28.60				
Remove .... Labor 5.84				
60" ornamental iron fence with ornamental casting	lf	$5.61	$51.20	$56.81
Replace Materials ......37.10 Labor 14.10				
Remove .... Labor 5.61				
72" ornamental iron fence with ornamental casting	lf	$5.61	$57.30	$62.91
Replace Materials......43.00 Labor 14.30				
Remove .... Labor 5.61				
60" ornamental iron fence gate with ornamental casting	lf	$5.84	$174.40	$180.24
Replace Materials.....147.00 Labor...........27.40				
Remove .... Labor 5.84				
72" ornamental iron fence gate with ornamental casting	lf	$5.84	$185.60	$191.44
Replace Materials.....157.00 Labor 28.60				
Remove .... Labor 5.84				
REMOVE & REINSTALL IRON FENCE				
Remove ornamental iron fence for work, then reinstall (panels only)	lf	–	$21.10	$21.10
Replace .... Labor...........21.10				
Remove ornamental iron fence gate for work, then reinstall	lf	–	$36.90	$36.90
Replace .... Labor 36.90				
ELECTRIC GATE OPENER *For swinging or roll-type gates. Includes two remote transmitters, keypad on post by gate, all hardware and electrical wiring up to 45 lf.*				
1/2 horsepower electric gate opener	ea	$22.10	$2,999.00	$3,021.10
Replace Materials ..2850.00 Labor 149.00				
Remove .... Labor 22.10				
3/4 horsepower electric gate opener	ea	$22.10	$3,799.00	$3,821.10
Replace Materials ..3650.00 Labor 149.00				
Remove .... Labor 22.10				
1 horsepower electric gate opener	ea	$22.10	$4,249.00	$4,271.10
Replace Materials ...4100.00 Labor 149.00				
Remove .... Labor 22.10				
2 horsepower electric gate opener	ea	$22.10	$4,949.00	$4,971.10
Replace Materials ..4800.00 Labor 149.00				
Remove .... Labor 22.10				
5 horsepower electric gate opener	ea	$22.10	$5,699.00	$5,721.10
Replace Materials ..5550.00 Labor 149.00				
Remove .... Labor 22.10				
Remove electric gate opener for work, then reinstall	ea	–	$240.00	$240.00
Replace .... Labor.........240.00				

TIME & MATERIAL CHARTS *(selected items)*

Fences Materials *(Also see material prices with the line items and other information in the **QuickFinder** column.)*

DESCRIPTION	MATERIAL PRICE	GROSS COVERAGE	WASTE	NET COVERAGE	UNIT PRICE
4" x 4" posts					
8' cedar	$13.00 *ea*	1	4%	.96	$13.50 *ea*
10' cedar	$16.20 *ea*	1	4%	.96	$16.90 *ea*
12' cedar	$19.50 *ea*	2	4%	1.92	$10.16 *ea*
1" x 2" x 8' fence boards					
#2 cedar	$4.00 *ea*	8	4%	7.68	$.52 *lf*
B grade redwood	$8.80 *ea*	8	4%	7.68	$1.15 *lf*
treated-pine	$2.50 *ea*	8	4%	7.68	$.33 *lf*
1" x 4" x 8' fence boards					
#2 cedar	$5.00 *ea*	8	4%	7.68	$.65 *lf*
B grade redwood	$11.00 *ea*	8	4%	7.68	$1.43 *lf*
treated-pine	$5.00 *ea*	8	4%	7.68	$.65 *lf*
1" x 6" x 8' fence boards					
#2 cedar	$7.60 *ea*	8	4%	7.68	$.99 *lf*
B grade redwood	$16.60 *ea*	8	4%	7.68	$2.16 *lf*
treated-pine	$4.90 *ea*	8	4%	7.68	$.64 *lf*
1" x 8" x 8' fence boards					
#2 cedar	$15.60 *ea*	8	4%	7.68	$2.03 *lf*
B grade redwood	$34.20 *ea*	8	4%	7.68	$4.45 *lf*
treated-pine	$9.90 *ea*	8	4%	7.68	$1.29 *lf*
1" x 10" x 8' fence boards					
#2 cedar	$19.20 *ea*	8	4%	7.68	$2.50 *lf*
B grade redwood	$42.10 *ea*	8	4%	7.68	$5.48 *lf*
treated-pine	$12.40 *ea*	8	4%	7.68	$1.61 *lf*
2" x 4" x 8' fence boards					
#2 cedar	$6.10 *ea*	8	4%	7.68	$.79 *lf*
B grade redwood	$9.60 *ea*	8	4%	7.68	$1.25 *lf*
treated-pine	$9.10 *ea*	8	4%	7.68	$1.18 *lf*
1" x 3" mill-cut fence picket					
3' cedar	$1.50 *ea*	1	4%	.96	$1.56 *ea*
5' cedar	$3.80 *ea*	1	4%	.96	$3.96 *ea*
Lattice					
cedar lattice	$20.50 *sh*	32	4%	30.72	$.67 *sf*
cedar cap mold	$7.90 *ea*	8	4%	7.68	$1.03 *lf*
Chain-link fence materials					
11 gauge chain-link	$1.91 *sf*	1	3%	.97	$1.97 *sf*

Fences Labor

LABORER	BASE WAGE	PAID LEAVE	TRUE WAGE	FICA	FUTA	WORKER'S COMP.	UNEMPLOY. INSUR.	HEALTH INSUR.	RETIRE (401K)	LIABILITY INSUR.	COST PER HOUR
Carpenter	$24.30	1.90	$26.20	2.00	.21	5.15	2.28	2.92	.79	3.93	$43.50
Carpenter's helper	$17.50	1.37	$18.87	1.44	.15	3.71	1.64	2.92	.57	2.83	$32.10
Electrician	$26.90	2.10	$29.00	2.22	.23	3.16	2.52	2.92	.87	4.35	$45.30
Demolition laborer	$14.40	1.12	$15.52	1.19	.12	5.01	1.35	2.92	.47	2.33	$28.90

Paid Leave is calculated based on two weeks paid vacation, one week sick leave, and seven paid holidays. Employer's matching portion of **FICA** is 7.65 percent. **FUTA** (Federal Unemployment) is .8 percent. **Worker's compensation** for the fences trade was calculated using a national average of 19.63 percent. **Unemployment insurance** was calculated using a national average of 8.7 percent. **Health insurance** was calculated based on a projected national average for 2005 of $580 per employee (and family when applicable) per month. Employer pays 80 percent for a per month cost of $464 per employee. **Retirement** is based on a 401(k) retirement program with employer matching of 50 percent. Employee contributions to the 401(k) plan are an average of 6 percent of the true wage. **Liability insurance** is based on a national average of 14.0 percent.

Fences Labor Productivity

WORK DESCRIPTION	LABORER	COST PER HOUR	PRODUCTIVITY	UNIT PRICE
Demolition				
remove 4' high wood fence	demolition laborer	$28.90	.161	$4.65 lf
remove 6' high wood fence	demolition laborer	$28.90	.165	$4.77 lf
remove 8' high wood fence	demolition laborer	$28.90	.170	$4.91 lf
remove wood fence post	demolition laborer	$28.90	.367	$10.60 ea
remove 3' high chain-link fence	demolition laborer	$28.90	.116	$3.35 lf
remove 4' high chain-link fence	demolition laborer	$28.90	.121	$3.50 lf
remove 5' high chain-link fence	demolition laborer	$28.90	.125	$3.61 lf
remove 6' high chain-link fence	demolition laborer	$28.90	.131	$3.79 lf
remove 7' high chain-link fence	demolition laborer	$28.90	.136	$3.93 lf
remove 8' high chain-link fence	demolition laborer	$28.90	.143	$4.13 lf
remove 10' high chain-link fence	demolition laborer	$28.90	.152	$4.39 lf
remove chain-link fence gate	demolition laborer	$28.90	.203	$5.87 ea
remove chain-link fence driveway gate	demolition laborer	$28.90	.043	$1.24 lf
remove chain-link fence post	demolition laborer	$28.90	.402	$11.60 ea
remove vinyl fence	demolition laborer	$28.90	.139	$4.02 lf
remove vinyl rail fence	demolition laborer	$28.90	.104	$3.01 lf
remove vinyl fence gate	demolition laborer	$28.90	.152	$4.39 lf
remove ornamental iron fence	demolition laborer	$28.90	.194	$5.61 lf
remove ornamental iron fence gate	demolition laborer	$28.90	.202	$5.84 lf
remove electric gate opener	demolition laborer	$28.90	.763	$22.10 ea
Fencing crew				
fencing installation	carpenter	$43.50		
fencing installation	carpenter's helper	$32.10		
fencing installation	**fencing crew**	$37.80		
Build basketweave fence				
4' high	fencing crew	$37.80	.318	$12.00 lf
8' high	fencing crew	$37.80	.359	$13.60 lf
4' high gate	fencing crew	$37.80	2.70	$102.00 ea
8' high gate	fencing crew	$37.80	3.03	$115.00 ea
Build board fence				
4' high	fencing crew	$37.80	.268	$10.10 lf
8' high	fencing crew	$37.80	.307	$11.60 lf
4' high gate	fencing crew	$37.80	2.17	$82.00 lf
8' high gate	fencing crew	$37.80	2.44	$92.20 lf
Build board fence with lattice cap				
6' high	fencing crew	$37.80	.331	$12.50 lf
8' high	fencing crew	$37.80	.359	$13.60 lf
6' high gate	fencing crew	$37.80	2.94	$111.00 lf
8' high gate	fencing crew	$37.80	3.45	$130.00 lf
Build board-on-board fence				
4' high	fencing crew	$37.80	.296	$11.20 lf
8' high	fencing crew	$37.80	.331	$12.50 lf
4' high gate	fencing crew	$37.80	2.56	$96.80 lf
8' high gate	fencing crew	$37.80	2.86	$108.00 lf
Build board-and-batten fence				
4' high	fencing crew	$37.80	.301	$11.40 lf
8' high	fencing crew	$37.80	.324	$12.20 lf
4' high gate	fencing crew	$37.80	2.63	$99.40 lf
8' high gate	fencing crew	$37.80	2.94	$111.00 lf
Build picket fence				
3' high	fencing crew	$37.80	.222	$8.39 lf
5' high	fencing crew	$37.80	.238	$9.00 lf
3' high gate	fencing crew	$37.80	2.00	$75.60 lf
5' high gate	fencing crew	$37.80	2.38	$90.00 lf
Install chain-link fence				
3' high	fencing crew	$37.80	.114	$4.31 lf
5' high	fencing crew	$37.80	.183	$6.92 lf
7' high	fencing crew	$37.80	.295	$11.20 lf
10' high	fencing crew	$37.80	.475	$18.00 lf

17 .... *Finish Carpentry*

Item Description	Unit	Remove	Replace	Total	
Minimum charge for finish carpentry work	ea	–	$72.00	$72.00	◄ **MINIMUM**
Replace Materials......25.00 Labor...........47.00					
Add 70% for walnut					◄ **OTHER WOOD SPECIES**
					For moldings made from these species of wood factor the cost of stain-grade pine by the percentage. All grades are kiln-dried select or better.
Add 563% for teak					
Add 73% for cherry					
Add 31% for hard maple					
Add 24% for cypress					
Add 17% for redwood					
Add 0% for cedar					
1-1/2" finger-joint pine clamshell base	lf	$.75	$2.54	$3.29	◄ **1-1/2" CLAMSHELL BASE** *Includes 7% waste.*
Replace Materials .... .89 Labor 1.65					
Remove...................... Labor............ .75					
1-1/2" stain-grade pine clamshell base	lf	$.75	$2.68	$3.43	
Replace Materials ...... 1.03 Labor 1.65					
Remove...................... Labor............ .75					
1-1/2" poplar clamshell base	lf	$.75	$2.76	$3.51	
Replace Materials ...... 1.11 Labor 1.65					
Remove...................... Labor............ .75					
1-1/2" mahogany clamshell base	lf	$.75	$2.97	$3.72	
Replace Materials.......1.32 Labor 1.65					
Remove...................... Labor............ .75					
1-1/2" red oak clamshell base	lf	$.75	$3.07	$3.82	
Replace Materials.......1.42 Labor 1.65					
Remove...................... Labor......... .75					
2-1/2" finger-joint pine clamshell base	lf	$.75	$2.67	$3.42	◄ **2-1/2" CLAMSHELL BASE** *Includes 7% waste.*
Replace Materials ...... 1.02 Labor 1.65					
Remove...................... Labor......... .75					
2-1/2" stain-grade pine clamshell base	lf	$.75	$2.83	$3.58	
Replace Materials ...... 1.18 Labor 1.65					
Remove...................... Labor......... .75					
2-1/2" poplar clamshell base	lf	$.75	$2.92	$3.67	
Replace Materials ...... 1.27 Labor 1.65					
Remove...................... Labor......... .75					
2-1/2" mahogany clamshell base	lf	$.75	$3.17	$3.92	
Replace Materials.......1.52 Labor 1.65					
Remove...................... Labor......... .75					

WOOD EMBOSSING

Wood moldings are often embossed to appear like they have been carved. Embossing stamps a pattern onto the wood.

Embossing is far less expensive than carving and is most successful on softer woods, such as pine.

RELATED ITEMS

Cleaning 61
Painting 337

	Item Description	Unit	Remove	Replace	Total
2-1/2" ▶ **CLAMSHELL BASE** *continued*	**2-1/2" red oak clamshell base** *Replace* Materials....1.63 Labor ....1.65 *Remove*........................ Labor .... .75	lf	$.75	$3.28	$4.03
3-1/2" ▶ **CLAMSHELL BASE** *Includes 7% waste.*	**3-1/2" finger-joint pine clamshell base** *Replace* Materials........1.44 Labor ....1.65 *Remove*........................ Labor .... .75	lf	$.75	$3.09	$3.84
	3-1/2" stain-grade pine clamshell base *Replace* Materials........1.67 Labor ....1.65 *Remove*........................ Labor .... .75	lf	$.75	$3.32	$4.07
	3-1/2" poplar clamshell base *Replace* Materials........1.80 Labor ....1.65 *Remove*........................ Labor .... .75	lf	$.75	$3.45	$4.20
	3-1/2" mahogany clamshell base *Replace* Materials........2.14 Labor ....1.65 *Remove*........................ Labor .... .75	lf	$.75	$3.79	$4.54
	3-1/2" red oak clamshell base *Replace* Materials........2.31 Labor ....1.65 *Remove*........................ Labor .... .75	lf	$.75	$3.96	$4.71
4-1/2" ▶ **CLAMSHELL BASE**	**Add 22% for 4-1/2" clamshell base** ▶ Add to the cost of 3-1/2" clamshell base.				
1-1/2" ▶ **PATTERN BASE** *Includes 7% waste.*	**1-1/2" finger-joint pine pattern base** *Replace* Materials....... 1.09 Labor ....1.65 *Remove*........................ Labor .... .75	lf	$.75	$2.74	$3.49
	1-1/2" stain-grade pine pattern base *Replace* Materials....... 1.26 Labor ....1.65 *Remove*........................ Labor .... .75	lf	$.75	$2.91	$3.66
	1-1/2" poplar pattern base *Replace* Materials........1.34 Labor ....1.65 *Remove*........................ Labor .... .75	lf	$.75	$2.99	$3.74
	1-1/2" mahogany pattern base *Replace* Materials........1.60 Labor ....1.65 *Remove*........................ Labor .... .75	lf	$.75	$3.25	$4.00
	1-1/2" red oak pattern base *Replace* Materials........1.72 Labor ....1.65 *Remove*........................ Labor .... .75	lf	$.75	$3.37	$4.12
2-1/2" ▶ **PATTERN BASE** *Includes 7% waste.*	**2-1/2" finger-joint pine pattern base** *Replace* Materials........1.75 Labor ....1.65 *Remove*........................ Labor .... .75	lf	$.75	$3.40	$4.15
	2-1/2" stain-grade pine pattern base *Replace* Materials........2.03 Labor ....1.65 *Remove*........................ Labor .... .75	lf	$.75	$3.68	$4.43
	2-1/2" poplar pattern base *Replace* Materials........2.17 Labor ....1.65 *Remove*........................ Labor .... .75	lf	$.75	$3.82	$4.57
	2-1/2" mahogany pattern base *Replace* Materials........2.58 Labor ....1.65 *Remove*........................ Labor .... .75	lf	$.75	$4.23	$4.98

Item Description	Unit	Remove	Replace	Total
2-1/2" red oak pattern base	lf	$.75	$4.42	$5.17
Replace Materials........2.77 Labor 1.65				
Remove.................... Labor .... .75				
3-1/2" finger-joint pine pattern base	lf	$.75	$3.96	$4.71
Replace Materials........2.31 Labor 1.65				
Remove.................... Labor .... .75				
3-1/2" stain-grade pine pattern base	lf	$.75	$4.34	$5.09
Replace Materials........2.69 Labor 1.65				
Remove.................... Labor .... .75				
3-1/2" poplar pattern base	lf	$.75	$4.52	$5.27
Replace Materials........2.87 Labor 1.65				
Remove.................... Labor .... .75				
3-1/2" mahogany pattern base	lf	$.75	$5.06	$5.81
Replace Materials........3.41 Labor 1.65				
Remove.................... Labor .... .75				
3-1/2" red oak pattern base	lf	$.75	$5.32	$6.07
Replace Materials........3.67 Labor 1.65				
Remove.................... Labor .... .75				
Add 10% for 5" pattern base				
▶ Add to the cost of 3-1/2" pattern base.				
Add 31% for 8" pattern base				
▶ Add to the cost of 3-1/2" pattern base.				
Remove base for work, then reinstall	lf	–	$2.46	$2.46
Replace .... Labor 2.46				
3/4" finger-joint pine base shoe	lf	$.75	$2.20	$2.95
Replace Materials .... .55 Labor 1.65				
Remove.................... Labor .... .75				
3/4" stain-grade pine base shoe	lf	$.75	$2.28	$3.03
Replace Materials .... .63 Labor 1.65				
Remove.................... Labor .... .75				
3/4" poplar base shoe	lf	$.75	$2.33	$3.08
Replace Materials .... .68 Labor 1.65				
Remove.................... Labor .... .75				
3/4" mahogany base shoe	lf	$.75	$2.46	$3.21
Replace Materials .... .81 Labor 1.65				
Remove.................... Labor .... .75				
3/4" red oak base shoe	lf	$.75	$2.51	$3.26
Replace Materials .... .86 Labor 1.65				
Remove.................... Labor .... .75				
Remove base shoe for work, then reinstall	lf	–	$2.46	$2.46
Replace .... Labor 2.46				
1-1/2" paint-grade clamshell casing	lf	$.92	$2.69	$3.61
Replace Materials .... .91 Labor 1.78				
Remove.................... Labor .... .92				

◀ **3-1/2"
PATTERN BASE**
Includes 7% waste.

◀ **5" PATTERN BASE**

◀ **8" PATTERN BASE**

◀ **REMOVE BASE
& REINSTALL**

◀ **3/4" BASE SHOE**
Includes 7% waste.

┌─────────────────┐
│ **RELATED ITEMS** │
│ Cleaning.............61 │
│ Doors...............101 │
│ Painting............337 │
└─────────────────┘

◀ **1-1/2" CLAM-
SHELL CASING**
Includes 7% waste.

	Item Description	Unit	Remove	Replace	Total
1-1/2" CLAM- ▶ **SHELL CASING** *continued*	**1-1/2" stain-grade pine clamshell casing** *Replace* Materials ...... 1.05 Labor ....1.78 *Remove*....................... Labor .... .92	lf	$.92	$2.83	$3.75
	1-1/2" poplar clamshell casing *Replace* Materials ...... 1.13 Labor ....1.78 *Remove*....................... Labor .... .92	lf	$.92	$2.91	$3.83
	1-1/2" mahogany clamshell casing *Replace* Materials.......1.35 Labor ....1.78 *Remove*....................... Labor .... .92	lf	$.92	$3.13	$4.05
	1-1/2" red oak clamshell casing *Replace* Materials.......1.44 Labor ....1.78 *Remove*....................... Labor .... .92	lf	$.92	$3.22	$4.14
2-1/2" CLAM- ▶ **SHELL CASING** *Includes 7% waste.*	**2-1/2" finger-joint pine clamshell casing** *Replace* Materials ...... 1.04 Labor ....1.78 *Remove*....................... Labor .... .92	lf	$.92	$2.82	$3.74
	2-1/2" stain-grade pine clamshell casing *Replace* Materials ...... 1.20 Labor ....1.78 *Remove*....................... Labor .... .92	lf	$.92	$2.98	$3.90
	2-1/2" poplar clamshell casing *Replace* Materials.......1.29 Labor ....1.78 *Remove*....................... Labor .... .92	lf	$.92	$3.07	$3.99
	2-1/2" mahogany clamshell casing *Replace* Materials.......1.55 Labor ....1.78 *Remove*....................... Labor .... .92	lf	$.92	$3.33	$4.25
	2-1/2" red oak clamshell casing *Replace* Materials.......1.66 Labor ....1.78 *Remove*....................... Labor .... .92	lf	$.92	$3.44	$4.36
3-1/2" CLAM- ▶ **SHELL CASING** *Includes 7% waste.*	**3-1/2" finger-joint pine clamshell casing** *Replace* Materials.......1.46 Labor ....1.78 *Remove*....................... Labor .... .92	lf	$.92	$3.24	$4.16
	3-1/2" stain-grade pine clamshell casing *Replace* Materials.......1.69 Labor ....1.78 *Remove*....................... Labor .... .92	lf	$.92	$3.47	$4.39
	3-1/2" poplar clamshell casing *Replace* Materials.......1.83 Labor ....1.78 *Remove*....................... Labor .... .92	lf	$.92	$3.61	$4.53
	3-1/2" mahogany clamshell casing *Replace* Materials.......2.18 Labor ....1.78 *Remove*....................... Labor .... .92	lf	$.92	$3.96	$4.88
	3-1/2" red oak clamshell casing *Replace* Materials.......2.36 Labor ....1.78 *Remove*....................... Labor .... .92	lf	$.92	$4.14	$5.06
1-1/2" PATTERN ▶ **CASING** *Includes 7% waste.*	**1-1/2" paint-grade pattern casing** *Replace* Materials ...... 1.11 Labor ....1.78 *Remove*....................... Labor .... .92	lf	$.92	$2.89	$3.81

Item Description	Unit	Remove	Replace	Total
1-1/2" stain-grade pine pattern casing Replace Materials ...... 1.28 Labor ....1.78 Remove........................ Labor .... .92	lf	$.92	$3.06	$3.98
1-1/2" poplar pattern casing Replace Materials........1.37 Labor ....1.78 Remove........................ Labor 92	lf	$.92	$3.15	$4.07
1-1/2" mahogany pattern casing Replace Materials........1.63 Labor ....1.78 Remove........................ Labor 92	lf	$.92	$3.41	$4.33
1-1/2" red oak pattern casing Replace Materials........1.75 Labor ....1.78 Remove........................ Labor 92	lf	$.92	$3.53	$4.45
1-1/2" curved pattern casing for half-round top window or door Replace Materials........7.73 Labor ....6.26 Remove........................ Labor 92	lf	$.92	$13.99	$14.91
1-1/2" curved pattern casing for elliptical-top window or door Replace Materials........8.13 Labor ....6.26 Remove........................ Labor 92	lf	$.92	$14.39	$15.31
1-1/2" curved pattern casing for round window per lf of diameter Replace Materials ......18.10 Labor ....12.80 Remove........................ Labor 92	lf	$.92	$30.90	$31.82
2-1/2" finger-joint pine pattern casing Replace Materials........1.79 Labor ....1.78 Remove........................ Labor 92	lf	$.92	$3.57	$4.49
2-1/2" stain-grade pine pattern casing Replace Materials........2.07 Labor ....1.78 Remove........................ Labor 92	lf	$.92	$3.85	$4.77
2-1/2" poplar pattern casing Replace Materials........2.21 Labor ....1.78 Remove........................ Labor 92	lf	$.92	$3.99	$4.91
2-1/2" mahogany pattern casing Replace Materials........2.63 Labor ....1.78 Remove........................ Labor 92	lf	$.92	$4.41	$5.33
2-1/2" red oak pattern casing Replace Materials........2.82 Labor ....1.78 Remove........................ Labor 92	lf	$.92	$4.60	$5.52
2-1/2" curved pattern casing for half-round top window or door Replace Materials........8.29 Labor ....6.26 Remove........................ Labor 92	lf	$.92	$14.55	$15.47
2-1/2" curved pattern casing for elliptical-top window or door Replace Materials........8.72 Labor ....6.26 Remove........................ Labor 92	lf	$.92	$14.98	$15.90
2-1/2" curved pattern casing for round window per lf of diameter Replace Materials........19.50 Labor ....12.80 Remove........................ Labor 92	lf	$.92	$32.30	$33.22

◄ **1-1/2" PATTERN CASING**
Includes 7% waste.

◄ **1-1/2" CURVED PATTERN CASING**
Includes 7% waste. Laminated back, factory fabricated molding. Half-round and elliptical are priced per lf of casing. Round windows are priced per diameter. If curved casing includes wood key see page 204.

◄ **2-1/2" PATTERN CASING**
Includes 7% waste.

RELATED ITEMS
Cleaning 61
Doors 101
Painting 337

◄ **2-1/2" CURVED PATTERN CASING**
Includes 7% waste. Laminated back, factory fabricated molding. Half-round and elliptical are priced per lf of casing. Round windows are priced per diameter. If casing includes wood key see page 204.

	Item Description	Unit	Remove	Replace	Total
3-1/2" PATTERN ▶ CASING *Includes 7% waste.*	**3-1/2" finger-joint pine pattern casing**	lf	$.92	$4.14	$5.06
	Replace Materials........2.36 Labor 1.78				
	Remove Labor .... .92				
	3-1/2" stain-grade pine pattern casing	lf	$.92	$4.52	$5.44
	Replace Materials........2.74 Labor 1.78				
	Remove Labor .... .92				
	3-1/2" poplar pattern casing	lf	$.92	$4.71	$5.63
	Replace Materials........2.93 Labor 1.78				
	Remove Labor .... .92				
	3-1/2" mahogany pattern casing	lf	$.92	$5.25	$6.17
	Replace Materials........3.47 Labor 1.78				
	Remove Labor .... .92				
	3-1/2" red oak pattern casing	lf	$.92	$5.52	$6.44
	Replace Materials........3.74 Labor 1.78				
	Remove Labor .... .92				
3-1/2" CURVED ▶ PATTERN CASING *Includes 7% waste. Laminated back, factory fabricated molding. Half-round and elliptical are priced per lf of casing. Round windows are priced per diameter. If casing includes wood key see below.*	**3-1/2" curved pattern casing for half-round top window or door**	lf	$.92	$14.70	$15.62
	Replace Materials........8.44 Labor 6.26				
	Remove Labor .... .92				
	3-1/2" curved pattern casing for elliptical-top window or door per lf	lf	$.92	$15.13	$16.05
	Replace Materials........8.87 Labor 6.26				
	Remove Labor .... .92				
	3-1/2" curved pattern casing for round window per lf of diameter	lf	$.92	$32.60	$33.52
	Replace Materials......19.80 Labor 12.80				
	Remove Labor .... .92				
5" PATTERN ▶ CASING	**Add 10% for 5" pattern casing**				
	▶ Add to the cost of 3-1/2" pattern casing.				
REMOVE CASING ▶ & REINSTALL	**Remove casing for work, then reinstall**	lf	—	$3.14	$3.14
	Replace .... Labor 3.14				
WOOD KEY ▶	**Wood key for curved molding**	ea	$1.04	$32.10	$33.14
	Replace Materials ......21.20 Labor..........10.90				
	Remove...................... Labor........... 1.04				
	Wood key with light carvings for curved molding	ea	$1.04	$44.50	$45.54
	Replace Materials......33.60 Labor..........10.90				
	Remove...................... Labor........... 1.04				
△ *with rosette*					
	Wood key with medium carvings for curved molding	ea	$1.04	$52.50	$53.54
	Replace Materials ......41.60 Labor..........10.90				
	Remove...................... Labor........... 1.04				
	Wood key with heavy carvings for curved molding	ea	$1.04	$65.30	$66.34
	Replace Materials......54.40 Labor..........10.90				
△ *with carvings*	*Remove*...................... Labor........... 1.04				
remove & reinstall ▷	**Remove wood key for work, then reinstall**	ea	—	$12.20	$12.20
	Replace .... Labor..........12.20				
BASE BLOCK ▶	**Pine base block**	ea	$1.04	$16.04	$17.08
	Replace Materials......13.30 Labor 2.74				
	Remove...................... Labor........... 1.04				

Item Description	Unit	Remove	Replace	Total
Poplar base block	ea	$1.04	$16.64	$17.68
Replace Materials.......13.90 Labor 2.74				
Remove........................ Labor 1.04				
Mahogany base block	ea	$1.04	$18.04	$19.08
Replace Materials.......15.30 Labor 2.74				
Remove........................ Labor 1.04				
Red oak base block	ea	$1.04	$19.94	$20.98
Replace Materials.......17.20 Labor 2.74				
Remove........................ Labor 1.04				
Pine corner block with rosette	ea	$1.04	$13.24	$14.28
Replace Materials ......10.50 Labor 2.74				
Remove........................ Labor 1.04				
Poplar corner block with rosette	ea	$1.04	$14.84	$15.88
Replace Materials ......12.10 Labor 2.74				
Remove........................ Labor 1.04				
Mahogany corner block with rosette	ea	$1.04	$16.34	$17.38
Replace Materials.......13.60 Labor 2.74				
Remove........................ Labor 1.04				
Red oak corner block with rosette	ea	$1.04	$17.74	$18.78
Replace Materials.......15.00 Labor 2.74				
Remove........................ Labor 1.04				
Add 30% for corner block with carvings				
Pine head block with rosette	ea	$1.04	$16.04	$17.08
Replace Materials.......13.30 Labor 2.74				
Remove........................ Labor 1.04				
Poplar head block with rosette	ea	$1.04	$18.04	$19.08
Replace Materials.......15.30 Labor 2.74				
Remove........................ Labor 1.04				
Mahogany head block with rosette	ea	$1.04	$19.94	$20.98
Replace Materials.......17.20 Labor 2.74				
Remove........................ Labor 1.04				
Red oak head block with rosette	ea	$1.04	$21.64	$22.68
Replace Materials ......18.90 Labor 2.74				
Remove........................ Labor 1.04				
Add 31% for head block with carvings				
Remove base, corner, or head block for work, then reinstall	ea	–	$3.02	$3.02
Replace .... Labor 3.02				
Pine overdoor molding	lf	$.81	$14.28	$15.09
Replace Materials ......12.50 Labor 1.78				
Remove........................ Labor .... .81				
Poplar overdoor molding	lf	$.81	$15.88	$16.69
Replace Materials ......14.10 Labor 1.78				
Remove........................ Labor .... .81				
Mahogany overdoor molding	lf	$.81	$17.58	$18.39
Replace Materials.......15.80 Labor 1.78				
Remove........................ Labor .... .81				

△ *with rosette*

◄ **CORNER BLOCK**

◁ *add for carvings*

◄ **HEAD BLOCK**

◁ *add for carvings*

◄ **REMOVE BLOCK & REINSTALL**

◄ **OVERDOOR MOLD**

RELATED ITEMS

Cleaning	.61
Doors	.101
Painting	.337

OVERDOOR MOLD ▶
continued

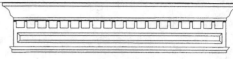

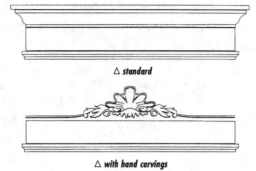

△ *standard*

△ *with vertical milling*

△ *with hand carvings*

△ *with heavy hand carvings*

Item Description	Unit	Remove	Replace	Total
Red oak overdoor molding	lf	$.81	$19.88	$20.69
Replace Materials ......18.10　　　　Labor 1.78				
Remove........................　　　　　Labor .... .81				
other styles ▷ **Add 72% for vertical milling in overdoor molding**				
Add 227% for hand carving in overdoor molding				
Add 411% for heavy hand carving in overdoor molding				
remove & reinstall ▷ **Remove overdoor molding for work, then reinstall**	lf	—	$2.15	$2.15
Replace ....　　　　　Labor 2.15				
Interior architrave, standard grade	lf	$.92	$8.00	$8.92
Replace Materials ....5.30　　　　Labor 2.70				
Remove........................　　　　　Labor .... .92				
▶ Standard casing with rosettes in head and base blocks. Paint-grade pine or poplar or stain-grade pine.				
Interior architrave, high grade	lf	$.92	$9.60	$10.52
Replace Materials ....6.90　　　　Labor 2.70				
Remove........................　　　　　Labor .... .92				
▶ Rosettes or light embossing in base blocks. Overdoor includes horizontal moldings at top and bottom. Stain-grade pine or red oak with simple overdoor.				
Interior architrave, deluxe grade	lf	$.92	$12.30	$13.22
Replace Materials ....9.60　　　　Labor 2.70				
Remove........................　　　　　Labor .... .92				
▶ May have carvings in base blocks. Angled overdoor with horizontal moldings at top and bottom or overdoor with light carvings. Red oak, birch, or similar hardwood or paint grade with more ornate detail.				
Interior architrave, custom grade	lf	$.92	$16.20	$17.12
Replace Materials ....13.50　　　　Labor 2.70				
Remove........................　　　　　Labor .... .92				
▶ May have carvings in base blocks. Angled or curved overdoor with horizontal moldings at top and bottom or overdoor with heavy carvings. Red oak birch or similar hardwood or paint-grade with very ornate carvings.				
Remove interior architrave for work, then reinstall	lf	—	$3.89	$3.89
Replace ....　　　　　Labor 3.89				
Exterior architrave, economy grade	lf	$.92	$8.68	$9.60
Replace Materials ....5.20　　　　Labor 3.48				
Remove........................　　　　　Labor .... .92				
▶ Standard casing with rosettes in head and base blocks. Paint-grade pine or poplar or stain-grade pine. All materials are back-primed.				

INTERIOR ▶
ARCHITRAVE
*Measure lf all around
door: both sides and
over door.*

△ *standard*

△ *high*

EXTERIOR ▶
ARCHITRAVE
*Measure lf all around
door: both sides and
over door.*

Item Description	Unit	Remove	Replace	Total
Exterior architrave, standard grade	lf	$.92	$10.98	$11.90
Replace Materials......7.50 Labor............3.48				
Remove....................... Labor............92				
▶ Wide casing, may be made from two moldings. Rosettes in head and base blocks. Paint-grade pine or poplar or stain-grade pine. All materials are back-primed.				
Exterior architrave, high grade	lf	$.92	$14.18	$15.10
Replace Materials......10.70 Labor............3.48				
Remove....................... Labor............92				
▶ Wide casing, may be made from two moldings. Rosettes or light embossing in base blocks. Overdoor includes horizontal moldings at top and bottom. Stain grade pine or red oak with simple over door. All materials are back-primed.				
Exterior architrave, deluxe grade	lf	$.92	$18.48	$19.40
Replace Materials......15.00 Labor............3.48				
Remove....................... Labor............92				
▶ Wide casing, may be made from two moldings. May have carvings in base blocks. Angled overdoor with horizontal moldings at top and bottom or overdoor with light carvings. Red oak, birch, or similar hardwood or paint grade with more ornate detail. All materials are back-primed.				
Exterior architrave, custom grade	lf	$.92	$22.58	$23.50
Replace Materials......19.10 Labor............3.48				
Remove....................... Labor............92				
▶ Wide casing, may be made from two moldings. May have carvings in base blocks. Angled or curved overdoor with horizontal moldings at top and bottom or overdoor and carvings. Red oak, birch, or similar hardwood or paint-grade with very ornate carvings. All materials are back-primed.				
Exterior architrave, custom deluxe grade	lf	$.92	$30.08	$31.00
Replace Materials......26.60 Labor............3.48				
Remove....................... Labor............92				
▶ Wide casing, may be made from two moldings. May have carvings in base blocks. Curved overdoor with multiple carved moldings. Red oak birch or similar hardwood or paint-grade with very ornate carvings. All materials are back-primed.				
Remove exterior architrave for work, then reinstall	lf	—	$4.80	$4.80
Replace .... Labor............4.80				
Exterior door surround, economy grade	lf	$.98	$42.60	$43.58
Replace Materials......32.40 Labor............10.20				
Remove....................... Labor............98				
▶ See illustration below for representative example.				

◁ remove & reinstall

◀ **EXTERIOR DOOR SURROUND**
Measure lf all around door: both sides and over door. All grades are for wood which is carved with intricate detail in the higher grades. Plastic or other synthetic materials should be considered economy or standard grades. Illustrations show typical complexity, actual door styling varies widely.

△ economy

△ standard

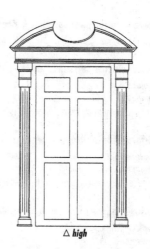
△ high

RELATED ITEMS

Cleaning 61	
Doors 101	
Masonry	
stone architrave 310	
Painting 337	
Plaster	
stucco architrave 359	

**EXTERIOR DOOR ▶
SURROUND**
continued

△ *deluxe*

△ *custom*

△ *custom deluxe*

Item Description	Unit	Remove	Replace	Total
Exterior door surround, standard grade	If	$.98	$65.40	$66.38
Replace Materials......54.20 Labor..........11.20				
Remove........................ Labor............ .98				
▶ See illustration on previous page for representative example.				
Exterior door surround, high grade	If	$.98	$107.40	$108.38
Replace Materials......95.50 Labor..........11.90				
Remove........................ Labor............ .98				
▶ See illustration on previous page for representative example.				
Exterior door surround, deluxe grade	If	$.98	$196.80	$197.78
Replace Materials ....183.00 Labor..........13.80				
Remove........................ Labor............ .98				
▶ See illustration above for representative example.				
Exterior door surround, custom grade	If	$.98	$301.20	$302.18
Replace Materials ....285.00 Labor..........16.20				
Remove........................ Labor............ .98				
▶ See illustration above for representative example.				
Exterior door surround, custom deluxe grade	If	$.98	$495.70	$496.68
Replace Materials ....477.00 Labor..........18.70				
Remove........................ Labor............ .98				
▶ See illustration above for representative example.				
remove & reinstall ▷ **Remove exterior door surround for work, then reinstall**	If	—	$29.30	$29.30
Replace .... Labor 29.30				
EXTERIOR ▶ **Exterior window surround, economy grade**	If	$.98	$35.30	$36.28
WINDOW *Replace* Materials......26.30 Labor 9.00				
SURROUND *Remove*........................ Labor............ .98				
▶ See illustration on facing page for representative example.				
Exterior window surround, standard grade	If	$.98	$53.97	$54.95
Replace Materials......44.10 Labor 9.87				
Remove........................ Labor............ .98				
▶ See illustration on facing page for representative example.				
Exterior window surround, high grade	If	$.98	$88.10	$89.08
Replace Materials......77.70 Labor..........10.40				
Remove........................ Labor............ .98				
▶ See illustration on facing page for representative example.				

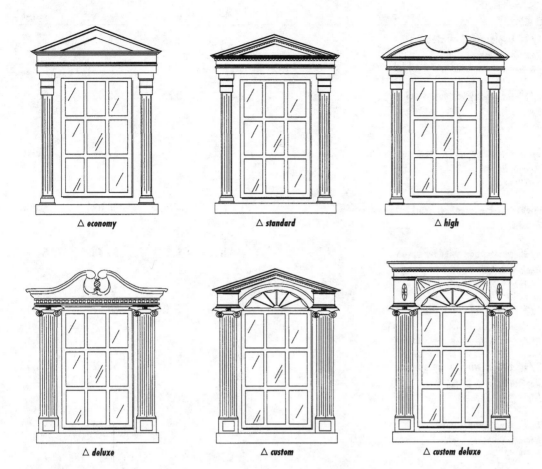

| △ economy | △ standard | △ high |

| △ deluxe | △ custom | △ custom deluxe |

Item Description	Unit	Remove	Replace	Total
Exterior window surround, deluxe grade	lf	$.98	$161.20	$162.18
Replace Materials.....149.00 Labor...........12.20				
Remove........................ Labor............. .98				
▶ See illustration below for representative example.				
Exterior window surround, custom grade	lf	$.98	$246.20	$247.18
Replace Materials....232.00 Labor...........14.20				
Remove........................ Labor............. .98				
▶ See illustration below for representative example.				
Exterior window surround, custom deluxe grade	lf	$.98	$402.00	$402.98
Replace Materials....388.00 Labor...........14.00				
Remove........................ Labor............. .98				
▶ See illustration below for representative example.				
Remove exterior window surround for work, then reinstall	lf	—	$26.10	$26.10
Replace .... Labor...........26.10				
2-1/2" paint-grade window stool	lf	$.75	$4.49	$5.24
Replace Materials........1.97 Labor 2.52				
Remove........................ Labor............. .75				
2-1/2" stain-grade pine window stool	lf	$.75	$4.80	$5.55
Replace Materials........2.28 Labor 2.52				
Remove........................ Labor............. .75				

RELATED ITEMS

Cleaning..............................61
Doors................................101
Masonry
stone architrave 310
Painting............................337
Plaster
stucco architrave 359

◁ remove & reinstall

◀ **WINDOW STOOL**
Includes 4% waste.

Item Description	Unit	Remove	Replace	Total
WINDOW STOOL ▶ *continued* **2-1/2" poplar window stool** *Replace* Materials........2.45 Labor ....2.52 *Remove*....................... Labor .... .75	lf	$.75	$4.97	$5.72
2-1/2" mahogany window stool *Replace* Materials........2.91 Labor ....2.52 *Remove*....................... Labor .... .75	lf	$.75	$5.43	$6.18
2-1/2" red oak window stool *Replace* Materials........3.14 Labor ....2.52 *Remove*....................... Labor .... .75	lf	$.75	$5.66	$6.41
Remove window stool for work, then reinstall *Replace* .... Labor 4.08	lf	–	$4.08	$4.08
WINDOW APRON ▶ *Includes 4% waste.* **3-1/2" paint-grade window apron** *Replace* Materials ...... 1.27 Labor ....2.13 *Remove*....................... Labor .... .81	lf	$.81	$3.40	$4.21
3-1/2" stain-grade pine window apron *Replace* Materials........1.49 Labor ....2.13 *Remove*....................... Labor .... .81	lf	$.81	$3.62	$4.43
3-1/2" poplar window apron *Replace* Materials........1.59 Labor ....2.13 *Remove*....................... Labor .... .81	lf	$.81	$3.72	$4.53
3-1/2" mahogany window apron *Replace* Materials........1.90 Labor ....2.13 *Remove*....................... Labor .... .81	lf	$.81	$4.03	$4.84
3-1/2" red oak window apron *Replace* Materials.......2.03 Labor ....2.13 *Remove*....................... Labor .... .81	lf	$.81	$4.16	$4.97
remove & reinstall ▷ **Remove window apron for work, then reinstall** *Replace* .... Labor 3.02	lf	—	$3.02	$3.02
2-1/2" CHAIR ▶ **RAIL** *Includes 4% waste.* **2-1/2" paint-grade chair rail** *Replace* Materials........1.70 Labor ....1.65 *Remove*....................... Labor .... .75	lf	$.75	$3.35	$4.10
2-1/2" stain-grade pine chair rail *Replace* Materials........1.97 Labor ....1.65 *Remove*....................... Labor .... .75	lf	$.75	$3.62	$4.37
2-1/2" poplar chair rail *Replace* Materials........2.15 Labor ....1.65 *Remove*....................... Labor .... .75	lf	$.75	$3.80	$4.55
2-1/2" mahogany chair rail *Replace* Materials........2.51 Labor ....1.65 *Remove*....................... Labor .... .75	lf	$.75	$4.16	$4.91
2-1/2" red oak chair rail *Replace* Materials........2.71 Labor ....1.65 *Remove*....................... Labor .... .75	lf	$.75	$4.36	$5.11
3-1/2" CHAIR ▶ **RAIL** *Includes 4% waste.* **3-1/2" paint-grade chair rail** *Replace* Materials........2.15 Labor ....1.65 *Remove*....................... Labor .... .75	lf	$.75	$3.80	$4.55

Item Description	Unit	Remove	Replace	Total	
3-1/2" stain-grade pine chair rail *Replace* Materials........2.48 Labor ....1.65 *Remove*..................... Labor .... .75	lf	$.75	$4.13	$4.88	
3-1/2" poplar chair rail *Replace* Materials........2.69 Labor ....1.65 *Remove*..................... Labor .... .75	lf	$.75	$4.34	$5.09	
3-1/2" mahogany chair rail *Replace* Materials........3.17 Labor ....1.65 *Remove*..................... Labor .... .75	lf	$.75	$4.82	$5.57	
3-1/2" red oak chair rail *Replace* Materials........3.45 Labor ....1.65 *Remove*..................... Labor .... .75	lf	$.75	$5.10	$5.85	
Remove chair rail for work, then reinstall *Replace* .... Labor 2.46	lf	–	$2.46	$2.46	◁ remove & reinstall
1-5/8" paint-grade drip cap *Replace* Materials........1.56 Labor ....1.65 *Remove*..................... Labor .... .92	lf	$.92	$3.21	$4.13	◀ **DRIP CAP** *Includes 4% waste.*
1-5/8" redwood drip cap *Replace* Materials........1.82 Labor ....1.65 *Remove*..................... Labor .... .92	lf	$.92	$3.47	$4.39	
1-5/8" cedar drip cap *Replace* Materials........1.70 Labor ....1.65 *Remove*..................... Labor .... .92	lf	$.92	$3.35	$4.27	
2-1/4" paint-grade drip cap *Replace* Materials........1.75 Labor ....1.65 *Remove*..................... Labor .... .92	lf	$.92	$3.40	$4.32	
2-1/4" redwood drip cap *Replace* Materials........2.04 Labor ....1.65 *Remove*..................... Labor .... .92	lf	$.92	$3.69	$4.61	
2-1/4" cedar drip cap *Replace* Materials........1.90 Labor ....1.65 *Remove*..................... Labor .... .92	lf	$.92	$3.55	$4.47	
Remove drip cap for work, then reinstall *Replace* .... Labor 3.14	lf	–	$3.14	$3.14	◁ remove & reinstall
1-3/4" paint-grade astragal *Replace* Materials........3.26 Labor ....1.78 *Remove*..................... Labor .... .92	lf	$.92	$5.04	$5.96	◀ **ASTRAGAL** *Includes 4% waste.*
1-3/4" stain-grade pine astragal *Replace* Materials........3.77 Labor ....1.78 *Remove*..................... Labor .... .92	lf	$.92	$5.55	$6.47	
1-3/4" poplar astragal *Replace* Materials........4.05 Labor ....1.78 *Remove*..................... Labor .... .92	lf	$.92	$5.83	$6.75	
1-3/4" mahogany astragal *Replace* Materials........4.81 Labor ....1.78 *Remove*..................... Labor .... .92	lf	$.92	$6.59	$7.51	

RELATED ITEMS

Cleaning 61
Painting 337

	Item Description		Unit	Remove	Replace	Total
ASTRAGAL ▶ continued	**1-3/4" red oak astragal**		If	$.92	$6.99	$7.91
	Replace Materials.......5.21	Labor 1.78				
	Remove........................	Labor .... .92				
	2-1/4" paint-grade astragal		If	$.92	$5.73	$6.65
	Replace Materials.......3.95	Labor 1.78				
	Remove........................	Labor .... .92				
	2-1/4" stain-grade pine astragal		If	$.92	$6.35	$7.27
	Replace Materials.......4.57	Labor 1.78				
	Remove........................	Labor .... .92				
	2-1/4" poplar astragal		If	$.92	$6.70	$7.62
	Replace Materials.......4.92	Labor 1.78				
	Remove........................	Labor .... .92				
	2-1/4" mahogany astragal		If	$.92	$7.61	$8.53
	Replace Materials.......5.83	Labor 1.78				
	Remove........................	Labor .... .92				
	2-1/4" red oak astragal		If	$.92	$8.09	$9.01
	Replace Materials.......6.31	Labor 1.78				
	Remove........................	Labor .... .92				
remove & reinstall ▷	**Remove astragal for work, then reinstall**		If	–	$3.14	$3.14
	Replace	Labor 3.14				
COVE ▶ Includes 4% waste.	**1/2" paint-grade cove**		If	$.92	$2.38	$3.30
	Replace Materials .... .60	Labor 1.78				
	Remove........................	Labor .... .92				
	1/2" stain-grade pine cove		If	$.92	$2.49	$3.41
	Replace Materials .... .71	Labor 1.78				
	Remove........................	Labor .... .92				
	1/2" poplar cove		If	$.92	$2.56	$3.48
	Replace Materials .... .78	Labor 1.78				
	Remove........................	Labor .... .92				
	1/2" mahogany cove		If	$.92	$2.69	$3.61
	Replace Materials .... .91	Labor 1.78				
	Remove........................	Labor .... .92				
	1/2" red oak cove		If	$.92	$2.74	$3.66
	Replace Materials .... .96	Labor 1.78				
	Remove........................	Labor .... .92				
	3/4" paint-grade cove		If	$.92	$2.47	$3.39
	Replace Materials .... .69	Labor 1.78				
	Remove........................	Labor .... .92				
	3/4" stain-grade pine cove		If	$.92	$2.59	$3.51
	Replace Materials .... .81	Labor 1.78				
	Remove........................	Labor .... .92				
	3/4" poplar cove		If	$.92	$2.68	$3.60
	Replace Materials .... .90	Labor 1.78				
	Remove........................	Labor .... .92				
	3/4" mahogany cove		If	$.92	$2.82	$3.74
	Replace Materials 1.04	Labor 1.78				
	Remove........................	Labor .... .92				

Item Description	Unit	Remove	Replace	Total	
3/4" red oak cove	lf	$.92	$2.87	$3.79	
Replace Materials ...... 1.09 Labor 1.78					
Remove....................... Labor............. .92					
1" paint-grade cove	lf	$.92	$2.63	$3.55	
Replace Materials .... .85 Labor 1.78					
Remove....................... Labor............. .92					
1" stain-grade pine cove	lf	$.92	$2.79	$3.71	
Replace Materials ...... 1.01 Labor 1.78					
Remove....................... Labor............. .92					
1" poplar cove	lf	$.92	$2.89	$3.81	
Replace Materials ...... 1.11 Labor 1.78					
Remove....................... Labor............. .92					
1" mahogany cove	lf	$.92	$3.08	$4.00	
Replace Materials......1.30 Labor 1.78					
Remove....................... Labor............. .92					
1" red oak cove	lf	$.92	$3.14	$4.06	
Replace Materials......1.36 Labor 1.78					
Remove....................... Labor............. .92					
Remove cove for work, then reinstall	lf	–	$2.46	$2.46	◁ remove & reinstall
Replace .... Labor 2.46					
2-1/2" paint-grade ceiling cove	lf	$.92	$3.52	$4.44	◀ **CEILING COVE**
Replace Materials......1.52 Labor 2.00					"Sprung" cove. Includes
Remove....................... Labor............. .92					4% waste.
2-1/2" stain-grade pine ceiling cove	lf	$.92	$3.77	$4.69	
Replace Materials......1.77 Labor 2.00					
Remove....................... Labor............. .92					
2-1/2" poplar ceiling cove	lf	$.92	$3.91	$4.83	
Replace Materials......1.91 Labor 2.00					
Remove....................... Labor............. .92					
2-1/2" mahogany ceiling cove	lf	$.92	$4.29	$5.21	
Replace Materials......2.29 Labor 2.00					
Remove....................... Labor............. .92					
2-1/2" red oak ceiling cove	lf	$.92	$4.49	$5.41	
Replace Materials......2.49 Labor 2.00					
Remove....................... Labor............. .92					
3-1/2" paint-grade ceiling cove	lf	$.92	$3.98	$4.90	
Replace Materials......1.98 Labor 2.00					
Remove....................... Labor............. .92					
3-1/2" stain-grade pine ceiling cove	lf	$.92	$4.30	$5.22	
Replace Materials......2.30 Labor 2.00					
Remove....................... Labor............. .92					
3-1/2" poplar ceiling cove	lf	$.92	$4.48	$5.40	
Replace Materials......2.48 Labor 2.00					
Remove....................... Labor............. .92					
3-1/2" mahogany ceiling cove	lf	$.92	$4.98	$5.90	
Replace Materials......2.98 Labor 2.00					
Remove....................... Labor............. .92					

RELATED ITEMS
Cleaning 61
Painting 337

	Item Description	Unit	Remove	Replace	Total
CEILING COVE ▶ continued	**3-1/2″ red oak ceiling cove** *Replace* Materials........3.24 Labor ....2.00 *Remove*...................... Labor .... .92	lf	$.92	$5.24	$6.16
remove & reinstall ▷	**Remove ceiling cove for work, then reinstall** *Replace* .... Labor 2.46	lf	—	$2.46	$2.46
HALF-ROUND ▶ Includes 4% waste.	**1″ paint-grade half-round** *Replace* Materials .... .70 Labor ....1.78 *Remove*...................... Labor .... .92	lf	$.92	$2.48	$3.40
	1″ stain-grade pine half-round *Replace* Materials .... .83 Labor ....1.78 *Remove*...................... Labor .... .92	lf	$.92	$2.61	$3.53
	1″ poplar half-round *Replace* Materials .... .91 Labor ....1.78 *Remove*...................... Labor .... .92	lf	$.92	$2.69	$3.61
	1″ mahogany half-round *Replace* Materials .... 1.04 Labor ....1.78 *Remove*...................... Labor .... .92	lf	$.92	$2.82	$3.74
	1″ red oak half-round *Replace* Materials .... 1.15 Labor ....1.78 *Remove*...................... Labor .... .92	lf	$.92	$2.93	$3.85
	2″ paint-grade half-round *Replace* Materials .... .99 Labor ....1.78 *Remove*...................... Labor .... .92	lf	$.92	$2.77	$3.69
	2″ stain-grade pine half-round *Replace* Materials ...... 1.18 Labor ....1.78 *Remove*...................... Labor .... .92	lf	$.92	$2.96	$3.88
	2″ poplar half-round *Replace* Materials ...... 1.28 Labor ....1.78 *Remove*...................... Labor .... .92	lf	$.92	$3.06	$3.98
	2″ mahogany half-round *Replace* Materials........1.48 Labor ....1.78 *Remove*...................... Labor .... .92	lf	$.92	$3.26	$4.18
	2″ red oak half-round *Replace* Materials........1.63 Labor ....1.78 *Remove*...................... Labor .... .92	lf	$.92	$3.41	$4.33
	Add 19% for 3″ half-round ▶ Add to the cost of 2″ half-round.				
	Add 40% for 4″ half-round ▶ Add to the cost of 2″ half-round.				
remove & reinstall ▷	**Remove half-round for work, then reinstall** *Replace* .... Labor 3.14	lf	—	$3.14	$3.14
QUARTER-ROUND ▶ Includes 4% waste.	**1/2″ paint-grade quarter-round** *Replace* Materials .... .51 Labor ....1.78 *Remove*...................... Labor .... .92	lf	$.92	$2.29	$3.21

Item Description	Unit	Remove	Replace	Total	
1/2" stain-grade pine quarter-round	If	$.92	$2.44	$3.36	**RELATED ITEMS**
Replace Materials .... .66 Labor 1.78					Cleaning 61
Remove...................... Labor............. .92					Painting 337
1/2" poplar quarter-round	If	$.92	$2.44	$3.36	
Replace Materials .... .66 Labor 1.78					
Remove...................... Labor............. .92					
1/2" mahogany quarter-round	If	$.92	$2.57	$3.49	
Replace Materials .... .79 Labor 1.78					
Remove...................... Labor............. .92					
1/2" red oak quarter-round	If	$.92	$2.66	$3.58	
Replace Materials .... .88 Labor 1.78					
Remove...................... Labor............. .92					
3/4" paint-grade quarter round	If	$.92	$2.38	$3.30	
Replace Materials .... .60 Labor 1.78					
Remove...................... Labor............. .92					
3/4" stain-grade pine quarter-round	If	$.92	$2.51	$3.43	
Replace Materials .... .73 Labor 1.78					
Remove...................... Labor............. .92					
3/4" poplar quarter-round	If	$.92	$2.56	$3.48	
Replace Materials .... .78 Labor 1.78					
Remove...................... Labor............. .92					
3/4" mahogany quarter-round	If	$.92	$2.72	$3.64	
Replace Materials .... .94 Labor 1.78					
Remove...................... Labor............. .92					
3/4" red oak quarter-round	If	$.92	$2.82	$3.74	
Replace Materials ...... 1.04 Labor 1.78					
Remove...................... Labor............. .92					
1" paint-grade quarter-round	If	$.92	$2.85	$3.77	
Replace Materials ...... 1.07 Labor 1.78					
Remove...................... Labor............. .92					
1" stain-grade pine quarter-round	If	$.92	$3.08	$4.00	
Replace Materials ...... 1.30 Labor 1.78					
Remove...................... Labor............. .92					
1" poplar quarter-round	If	$.92	$3.17	$4.09	
Replace Materials ....1.39 Labor 1.78					
Remove...................... Labor............. .92					
1" mahogany quarter-round	If	$.92	$3.45	$4.37	
Replace Materials ....1.67 Labor 1.78					
Remove...................... Labor............. .92					
1" red oak quarter-round	If	$.92	$3.63	$4.55	
Replace Materials ....1.85 Labor 1.78					
Remove...................... Labor............. .92					
Remove quarter-round for work, then reinstall	If	—	$3.14	$3.14	◁ remove & reinstall
Replace .... Labor 3.14					
Paint-grade pine corner bead	If	$1.24	$4.56	$5.80	◀ **CORNER BEAD**
Replace Materials ...... 1.21 Labor 3.35					*Standard corner bead*
Remove...................... Labor............1.24					*includes 4% waste.*

	Item Description	Unit	Remove	Replace	Total
CORNER BEAD ▶ continued	**Stain-grade pine corner bead** *Replace* Materials........1.42 Labor ....3.35 *Remove*..................... Labor 1.24	lf	$1.24	$4.77	$6.01
△ **standard**	**Stain-grade pine corner bead, turned with double finials** *Replace* Materials........15.60 Labor ....3.35 *Remove*..................... Labor 1.24	lf	$1.24	$18.95	$20.19
No waste included for turned corner bead with finials.	**Mahogany corner bead** *Replace* Materials........2.66 Labor ....3.35 *Remove*..................... Labor 1.24	lf	$1.24	$6.01	$7.25
	Mahogany corner bead, turned with double finials *Replace* Materials........19.30 Labor ....3.35 *Remove*..................... Labor 1.24	lf	$1.24	$22.65	$23.89
	Red oak corner bead *Replace* Materials........3.26 Labor ....3.35 *Remove*..................... Labor 1.24	lf	$1.24	$6.61	$7.85
	Red oak corner bead, turned with double finials *Replace* Materials......20.60 Labor ....3.35 *Remove*..................... Labor 1.24	lf	$1.24	$23.95	$25.19
△ **turned with double finials**	**Clear plastic corner bead** *Replace* Materials....... 1.11 Labor ....1.39 *Remove*..................... Labor 1.24	lf	$1.24	$2.50	$3.74
remove & reinstall ▷	**Remove corner bead for work, then reinstall** *Replace* .... Labor 4.27	lf	—	$4.27	$4.27
BED MOLD ▶ *Includes 4% waste.*	**2-1/2" paint-grade pine bed mold** *Replace* Materials........1.70 Labor ....1.65 *Remove*..................... Labor .... .75	lf	$.75	$3.35	$4.10
	2-1/2" stain-grade pine bed mold *Replace* Materials........1.98 Labor ....1.65 *Remove*..................... Labor .... .75	lf	$.75	$3.63	$4.38
	2-1/2" poplar bed mold *Replace* Materials........2.16 Labor ....1.65 *Remove*..................... Labor .... .75	lf	$.75	$3.81	$4.56
	2-1/2" mahogany bed mold *Replace* Materials........2.57 Labor ....1.65 *Remove*..................... Labor .... .75	lf	$.75	$4.22	$4.97
	2-1/2" red oak bed mold *Replace* Materials........2.79 Labor ....1.65 *Remove*..................... Labor .... .75	lf	$.75	$4.44	$5.19
remove & reinstall ▷	**Remove bed mold for work, then reinstall** *Replace* .... Labor 2.46	lf	—	$2.46	$2.46
CROWN ▶ *Includes 4% waste.*	**3-1/2" paint-grade crown** *Replace* Materials........2.18 Labor ....2.00 *Remove*..................... Labor .... .75	lf	$.75	$4.18	$4.93
	3-1/2" stain-grade crown *Replace* Materials........2.54 Labor ....2.00 *Remove*..................... Labor .... .75	lf	$.75	$4.54	$5.29

Item Description		Unit	Remove	Replace	Total
3-1/2" poplar crown		lf	$.75	$4.77	$5.52
Replace Materials........2.77	Labor 2.00				
Remove........................	Labor .... .75				
3-1/2" mahogany crown		lf	$.75	$5.30	$6.05
Replace Materials........3.30	Labor 2.00				
Remove........................	Labor .... .75				
3-1/2" red oak crown		lf	$.75	$5.58	$6.33
Replace Materials........3.58	Labor 2.00				
Remove........................	Labor .... .75				
4-1/2" paint-grade crown		lf	$.75	$5.21	$5.96
Replace Materials........3.21	Labor 2.00				
Remove........................	Labor .... .75				
4-1/2" stain-grade crown		lf	$.75	$5.74	$6.49
Replace Materials........3.74	Labor 2.00				
Remove........................	Labor .... .75				
4-1/2" poplar crown		lf	$.75	$6.08	$6.83
Replace Materials........4.08	Labor 2.00				
Remove........................	Labor .... .75				
4-1/2" mahogany crown		lf	$.75	$7.19	$7.94
Replace Materials........5.19	Labor 2.00				
Remove........................	Labor .... .75				
4-1/2" red oak crown		lf	$.75	$7.64	$8.39
Replace Materials........5.64	Labor 2.00				
Remove........................	Labor .... .75				
Remove crown for work, then reinstall		lf	–	$2.46	$2.46
Replace	Labor 2.46				
Paint-grade hand rail		lf	$.81	$7.02	$7.83
Replace Materials........2.76	Labor 4.26				
Remove........................	Labor .... .81				
Stain-grade pine hand rail		lf	$.81	$8.01	$8.82
Replace Materials........3.75	Labor 4.26				
Remove........................	Labor .... .81				
Mahogany hand rail		lf	$.81	$9.60	$10.41
Replace Materials........5.34	Labor 4.26				
Remove........................	Labor .... .81				
Red oak hand rail		lf	$.81	$9.98	$10.79
Replace Materials........5.72	Labor 4.26				
Remove........................	Labor .... .81				
Remove hand rail for work, then reinstall		lf	–	$5.82	$5.82
Replace	Labor 5.82				
3/4" paint-grade molding with vertical milling		lf	$.92	$4.33	$5.25
Replace Materials........2.55	Labor 1.78				
Remove........................	Labor .... .92				
3/4" stain-grade pine molding with vertical milling		lf	$.92	$4.76	$5.68
Replace Materials........2.98	Labor 1.78				
Remove........................	Labor .... .92				

RELATED ITEMS

Cleaning 61
Painting 337

◁ remove & reinstall

◀ **HAND RAIL**
Includes 4% waste.

◁ remove & reinstall

◀ **SPECIALTY MOLDING**
General moldings for installation as crown, chair rail, panel molds, cabinet trim and so forth.
Includes 4% waste.

Item Description	Unit	Remove	Replace	Total
SPECIALTY ▶ MOLDING continued **3/4" poplar molding with vertical milling** *Replace* Materials........3.21 Labor ....1.78 *Remove*............................ Labor............ .92	lf	$.92	$4.99	$5.91
△ **dentil** *a vertically milled molding.* **3/4" mahogany molding with vertical milling** *Replace* Materials........4.00 Labor ....1.78 *Remove*............................ Labor............ .92	lf	$.92	$5.78	$6.70
3/4" red oak molding with vertical milling *Replace* Materials........4.34 Labor ....1.78 *Remove*............................ Labor............ .92	lf	$.92	$6.12	$7.04
3/4" polyurethane molding with vertical patterns *Replace* Materials........3.83 Labor ....1.78 *Remove*............................ Labor............ .92	lf	$.92	$5.61	$6.53
△ **bead and reel** *a hand-carved molding.* **3/4" stain-grade polyurethane molding with vertical patterns** *Replace* Materials........4.10 Labor ....1.78 *Remove*............................ Labor............ .92	lf	$.92	$5.88	$6.80
other 3/4" styles ▷ **Deduct 41% for 3/4" molding with embossed patterns** ▶ For pine moldings only.				
Add 64% for 3/4" molding with hand carvings				
Add 198% for 3/4" molding with heavy hand carvings				
1-1/2" specialty mold ▷ **1-1/2" paint-grade molding with vertical milling** *Replace* Materials........2.92 Labor ....1.78 *Remove*............................ Labor............ .92	lf	$.92	$4.70	$5.62
△ **bead** *a hand-carved molding.* **1-1/2" stain-grade pine molding with vertical milling** *Replace* Materials........3.40 Labor ....1.78 *Remove*............................ Labor............ .92	lf	$.92	$5.18	$6.10
1-1/2" poplar molding with vertical milling *Replace* Materials........3.67 Labor ....1.78 *Remove*............................ Labor............ .92	lf	$.92	$5.45	$6.37
1-1/2" mahogany molding with vertical milling *Replace* Materials........4.56 Labor ....1.78 *Remove*............................ Labor............ .92	lf	$.92	$6.34	$7.26
△ **rope** *a hand-carved molding.* **1-1/2" red oak molding with vertical milling** *Replace* Materials........4.96 Labor ....1.78 *Remove*............................ Labor............ .92	lf	$.92	$6.74	$7.66
1-1/2" polyurethane molding with vertical patterns *Replace* Materials........6.02 Labor ....1.78 *Remove*............................ Labor............ .92	lf	$.92	$7.80	$8.72
1-1/2" stain-grade polyurethane molding with vertical patterns *Replace* Materials........6.46 Labor ....1.78 *Remove*............................ Labor............ .92	lf	$.92	$8.24	$9.16
other 1-1/2" styles ▷ **Deduct 37% for 1-1/2" molding with embossed patterns** ▶ For pine moldings only.				
Add 66% for 1-1/2" molding with hand carvings				
△ **reed** *a molding with vertical patterns.* **Add 205% for 1-1/2" molding with heavy hand carvings**				

Item Description	Unit	Remove	Replace	Total	
2-1/2″ paint-grade molding with vertical milling *Replace* Materials........3.27 Labor ....1.78 *Remove*....................... Labor .... .92	lf	$.92	$5.05	$5.97	◁ **2-1/2″ specialty mold**
2-1/2″ stain-grade pine molding with vertical milling *Replace* Materials........3.80 Labor ....1.78 *Remove*....................... Labor .... .92	lf	$.92	$5.58	$6.50	△ **acanthus** *a heavy hand-carved molding.*
2-1/2″ poplar molding with vertical milling *Replace* Materials........4.10 Labor ....1.78 *Remove*....................... Labor .... .92	lf	$.92	$5.88	$6.80	
2-1/2″ mahogany molding with vertical milling *Replace* Materials........5.11 Labor ....1.78 *Remove*....................... Labor .... .92	lf	$.92	$6.89	$7.81	△ **leaf and tongue** *a heavy hand-carved molding.*
2-1/2″ red oak molding with vertical milling *Replace* Materials........5.55 Labor ....1.78 *Remove*....................... Labor .... .92	lf	$.92	$7.33	$8.25	
2-1/2″ polyurethane molding with vertical patterns *Replace* Materials........6.74 Labor ....1.78 *Remove*....................... Labor .... .92	lf	$.92	$8.52	$9.44	
2-1/2″ stain-grade polyurethane molding with vertical patterns *Replace* Materials........7.23 Labor ....1.78 *Remove*....................... Labor .... .92	lf	$.92	$9.01	$9.93	△ **laurel and ribbon** *a heavy hand-carved molding.*
Deduct 37% for 2-1/2″ molding with embossed patterns ▶ For pine moldings only.					◁ **other 2-1/2″ styles**
Add 68% for 2-1/2″ molding with hand carvings					
Add 209% for 2-1/2″ molding with heavy hand carvings					
3-1/2″ paint-grade molding with vertical milling *Replace* Materials........3.64 Labor ....1.78 *Remove*....................... Labor .... .92	lf	$.92	$5.42	$6.34	◁ **3-1/2″ specialty mold**
3-1/2″ stain-grade pine molding with vertical milling *Replace* Materials........4.23 Labor ....1.78 *Remove*....................... Labor .... .92	lf	$.92	$6.01	$6.93	△ **shell** *a heavy hand-carved molding.*
3-1/2″ poplar molding with vertical milling *Replace* Materials........4.56 Labor ....1.78 *Remove*....................... Labor .... .92	lf	$.92	$6.34	$7.26	
3-1/2″ mahogany molding with vertical milling *Replace* Materials........5.69 Labor ....1.78 *Remove*....................... Labor .... .92	lf	$.92	$7.47	$8.39	
3-1/2″ red oak molding with vertical milling *Replace* Materials........6.18 Labor ....1.78 *Remove*....................... Labor .... .92	lf	$.92	$7.96	$8.88	△ **oak leaf and ribbon** *a heavy hand-carved molding.*
3-1/2″ polyurethane molding with vertical patterns *Replace* Materials........7.50 Labor ....1.78 *Remove*....................... Labor .... .92	lf	$.92	$9.28	$10.20	
3-1/2″ stain-grade polyurethane molding with vertical patterns *Replace* Materials........8.04 Labor ....1.78 *Remove*....................... Labor .... .92	lf	$.92	$9.82	$10.74	

RELATED ITEMS

Cleaning.....................61
Painting.......................337
"Wood Embossing".......199

	Item Description	Unit	Remove	Replace	Total
SPECIALTY ▶ MOLDING *continued*	**Deduct 38% for 3-1/2" molding with embossed patterns** ▶ For pine moldings only.				
other 3-1/2" styles	**Add 69% for 3-1/2" molding with hand carvings**				
	Add 213% for 3-1/2" molding with heavy hand carvings				
5" specialty mold ▷	**5" paint-grade molding with vertical milling** *Replace* Materials.......5.24 Labor ....2.18 *Remove*...................... Labor.............. .92	If	$.92	$7.42	$8.34
△ **meander** a molding with vertical patterns.	**5" stain-grade pine molding with vertical milling** *Replace* Materials.......6.09 Labor ....2.18 *Remove*...................... Labor.............. .92	If	$.92	$8.27	$9.19
	5" poplar molding with vertical milling *Replace* Materials.......6.57 Labor ....2.18 *Remove*...................... Labor.............. .92	If	$.92	$8.75	$9.67
	5" mahogany molding with vertical milling *Replace* Materials.......8.19 Labor ....2.18 *Remove*...................... Labor.............. .92	If	$.92	$10.37	$11.29
△ **fret** a molding with vertical patterns.	**5" red oak molding with vertical milling** *Replace* Materials.......8.90 Labor ....2.18 *Remove*...................... Labor.............. .92	If	$.92	$11.08	$12.00
	5" polyurethane molding with vertical patterns *Replace* Materials ......10.80 Labor ....2.18 *Remove*...................... Labor.............. .92	If	$.92	$12.98	$13.90
△ **egg and dart** a hand-carved molding.	**5" stain-grade polyurethane molding with vertical patterns** *Replace* Materials......11.60 Labor ....2.18 *Remove*...................... Labor.............. .92	If	$.92	$13.78	$14.70
other 5" styles ▷	**Deduct 39% for 5" molding with embossed patterns** ▶ For pine moldings only.				
	Add 71% for 5" molding with hand carvings				
	Add 219% for 5" molding with heavy hand carvings				
8" specialty mold ▷	**8" paint-grade molding with vertical milling** *Replace* Materials.......8.58 Labor ....2.38 *Remove*...................... Labor.............. .92	If	$.92	$10.96	$11.88
△ **bundled reeds** a hand-carved molding.	**8" stain-grade pine molding with vertical milling** *Replace* Materials.......9.98 Labor ....2.38 *Remove*...................... Labor.............. .92	If	$.92	$12.36	$13.28
	8" poplar molding with vertical milling *Replace* Materials ......10.73 Labor ....2.38 *Remove*...................... Labor.............. .92	If	$.92	$13.11	$14.03
	8" mahogany molding with vertical milling *Replace* Materials.......13.40 Labor ....2.38 *Remove*...................... Labor.............. .92	If	$.92	$15.78	$16.70
△ **ribbon** a heavy hand-carved molding.	**8" red oak molding with vertical milling** *Replace* Materials ......14.60 Labor ....2.38 *Remove*...................... Labor.............. .92	If	$.92	$16.98	$17.90

Item Description	Unit	Remove	Replace	Total	
8" polyurethane molding with vertical patterns *Replace* Materials.......17.70 Labor ....2.38 *Remove*....................... Labor .... .92	lf	$.92	$20.08	$21.00	△ **grape** *a heavy hand-carved molding.*
8" stain-grade polyurethane molding with vertical patterns *Replace* Materials.......19.00 Labor ....2.38 *Remove*....................... Labor .... .92	lf	$.92	$21.38	$22.30	
Deduct 41% for 8" molding with embossed patterns ► For pine moldings only.					◁ *other 8" styles*
Add 75% for 8" molding with hand carvings					
Add 232% for 8" molding with heavy hand carvings					
Remove molding installed on wall for work, then reinstall *Replace* .... Labor 2.46	lf	–	$2.46	$2.46	◁ *remove & reinstall*
Remove window or door casing for work, then reinstall *Replace* .... Labor 3.14	lf	–	$3.14	$3.14	
Molder setup charge *Replace* Materials....200.00	ea	–	$200.00	$200.00	◄ **CUSTOM-MILLED MOLDING** *Custom milled to match existing pattern or a specially designed pattern. All milling is horizontal. Includes 4% waste.*
Molder custom knife charges *Replace* Materials.....415.00	ea	–	$415.00	$415.00	
1" to 2" pine custom-milled molding *Replace* Materials........1.74 Labor ....1.78 *Remove*....................... Labor .... .92	lf	$.92	$3.52	$4.44	
2" to 3" pine custom-milled molding *Replace* Materials........1.95 Labor ....1.78 *Remove*....................... Labor .... .92	lf	$.92	$3.73	$4.65	
3" to 4" pine custom-milled molding *Replace* Materials........2.77 Labor ....2.18 *Remove*....................... Labor .... .92	lf	$.92	$4.95	$5.87	
4" to 5" pine custom-milled molding *Replace* Materials........4.41 Labor ....2.18 *Remove*....................... Labor .... .92	lf	$.92	$6.59	$7.51	
6" to 7" pine custom-milled molding *Replace* Materials........7.24 Labor ....2.38 *Remove*....................... Labor .... .92	lf	$.92	$9.62	$10.54	
7" to 8" pine custom-milled molding *Replace* Materials......10.20 Labor ....2.38 *Remove*....................... Labor .... .92	lf	$.92	$12.58	$13.50	**RELATED ITEMS** Cleaning ....61 Painting ....337 *"Wood Embossing"*......199
Add 7% for poplar custom-milled molding					◁ *other wood species*
Add 21% for mahogany custom-milled molding					
Add 30% for red oak custom-milled molding					
Add for corner radius in panel molding *Replace* Materials........1.95 Labor ....6.48 *Remove*....................... Labor .... .98	ea	$.98	$8.43	$9.41	◄ **PANEL MOLDING CORNER RADIUS** *Includes 4% waste.*

Item Description	Unit	Remove	Replace	Total
PANEL MOLDING ▶ **CORNER RADIUS** Add for corner radius in panel molding with vertical milling	ea	$.98	$11.08	$12.06
Replace Materials........4.60 Labor............6.48 *Remove*........................ Labor............98				
Add for corner radius in panel molding with embossed pattern	ea	$.98	$10.28	$11.26
Replace Materials........3.80 Labor............6.48 *Remove*........................ Labor............98				
Add for corner radius in panel molding with hand carvings	ea	$.98	$13.52	$14.50
Replace Materials........7.04 Labor............6.48 *Remove*........................ Labor............98				
Add for corner radius in panel molding with heavy hand carvings	ea	$.98	$16.43	$17.41
Replace Materials........9.95 Labor............6.48 *Remove*........................ Labor............98				
CLOSET WORK ▶ Closet shelf brackets, shelving, & rod	lf	$1.82	$25.80	$27.62
Replace Materials........11.40 Labor..........14.40 *Remove*........................ Labor............1.82				
Remove closet shelf brackets, shelving, & rod for work, then reinstall	lf	—	$18.90	$18.90
Replace .... Labor............18.90				
closet organizer ▷ Closet organizer system, standard grade	sf	$1.36	$23.70	$25.06
Replace Materials......10.50 Labor............13.20 *Remove*........................ Labor............1.36				
Closet organizer system, high grade	sf	$1.36	$30.80	$32.16
Replace Materials......12.80 Labor............18.00 *Remove*........................ Labor............1.36				
Closet organizer system, deluxe grade	sf	$1.36	$39.00	$40.36
Replace Materials......16.10 Labor..........22.90 *Remove*........................ Labor............1.36				
Remove closet organizer system for work, then reinstall	sf	—	$26.30	$26.30
Replace .... Labor............26.30				
linen closet ▷ Linen closet shelves, standard grade	lf	$.98	$37.71	$38.69
Replace Materials........8.41 Labor..........29.30 *Remove*........................ Labor............98				
Linen closet shelves, high grade	lf	$.98	$38.51	$39.49
Replace Materials........9.21 Labor..........29.30 *Remove*........................ Labor............98				
Linen closet pull-out shelves	lf	$.98	$40.80	$41.78
Replace Materials......10.60 Labor..........30.20 *Remove*........................ Labor............98				
Remove linen closet shelves for work, then reinstall	lf	—	$35.40	$35.40
Replace .... Labor............35.40				
closet rod ▷ Closet rod, pine	lf	$1.01	$6.70	$7.71
Replace Materials........3.22 Labor............3.48 *Remove*........................ Labor............1.01				
Closet rod, hardwood	lf	$1.01	$7.52	$8.53
Replace Materials........4.04 Labor............3.48 *Remove*........................ Labor............1.01				

Item Description	Unit	Remove	Replace	Total	
Remove closet rod for work, then reinstall	lf	–	$4.54	$4.54	
Replace .... Labor 4.54					
Aromatic tongue-&-groove cedar board closet lining	sf	$.81	$2.41	$3.22	◁ cedar closet lining
Replace Materials .... .19 Labor 2.22					
Remove .... Labor 81					
Aromatic 1/4" cedar veneer plywood closet lining	sf	$.64	$4.60	$5.24	
Replace Materials ....2.99 Labor 1.61					
Remove .... Labor 64					
8" deep built-in paint-grade bookcase	sf	$1.47	$19.14	$20.61	◀ **BOOKCASE**
Replace Materials ....7.44 Labor 11.70					Adjustable shelves.
Remove .... Labor 1.47					Shelves approximately
8" deep built-in stain-grade pine bookcase	sf	$1.47	$20.33	$21.80	12" on center. Measure
Replace Materials ....8.63 Labor 11.70					sf of bookcase face.
Remove .... Labor 1.47					
8" deep built-in mahogany bookcase	sf	$1.47	$21.04	$22.51	
Replace Materials ....9.34 Labor 11.70					
Remove .... Labor 1.47					
8" deep built-in oak bookcase	sf	$1.47	$22.70	$24.17	
Replace Materials ....11.00 Labor 11.70					
Remove .... Labor 1.47					
8" deep built-in walnut bookcase	sf	$1.47	$26.80	$28.27	
Replace Materials ....15.10 Labor 11.70					
Remove .... Labor 1.47					
12" deep built-in paint-grade bookcase	sf	$1.47	$22.96	$24.43	◁ 12" deep
Replace Materials ....9.76 Labor 13.20					
Remove .... Labor 1.47					
12" deep built-in stain-grade pine bookcase	sf	$1.47	$24.60	$26.07	
Replace Materials ....11.40 Labor 13.20					
Remove .... Labor 1.47					
12" deep built-in mahogany bookcase	sf	$1.47	$25.50	$26.97	
Replace Materials ......12.30 Labor 13.20					
Remove .... Labor 1.47					
12" deep built-in oak bookcase	sf	$1.47	$27.70	$29.17	
Replace Materials ......14.50 Labor 13.20					
Remove .... Labor 1.47					
12" deep built-in walnut bookcase	sf	$1.47	$33.00	$34.47	
Replace Materials ....19.80 Labor 13.20					
Remove .... Labor 1.47					
18" deep built-in paint-grade bookcase	sf	$1.47	$26.60	$28.07	◁ 18" deep
Replace Materials ......12.80 Labor 13.80					
Remove .... Labor 1.47					
18" deep built-in stain-grade pine bookcase	sf	$1.47	$28.70	$30.17	
Replace Materials ......14.90 Labor 13.80					
Remove .... Labor 1.47					
18" deep built-in mahogany bookcase	sf	$1.47	$29.90	$31.37	
Replace Materials ......16.10 Labor 13.80					
Remove .... Labor 1.47					

RELATED ITEMS

Cleaning 61
Painting 337

Item Description	Unit	Remove	Replace	Total
BOOKCASE ▶ *continued*				
18" deep built-in oak bookcase	sf	$1.47	$32.80	$34.27
Replace Materials......19.00 Labor..........13.80				
Remove.....................Labor..........1.47				
18" deep built-in walnut bookcase	sf	$1.47	$39.70	$41.17
Replace Materials......25.90 Labor..........13.80				
Remove.....................Labor..........1.47				
24" deep built-in paint-grade bookcase	sf	$1.47	$31.30	$32.77
Replace Materials......16.90 Labor..........14.40				
Remove.....................Labor..........1.47				
△ economy mantel **24" deep built-in stain-grade pine bookcase**	sf	$1.47	$34.00	$35.47
Replace Materials......19.60 Labor..........14.40				
Remove.....................Labor..........1.47				
24" deep built-in mahogany bookcase	sf	$1.47	$35.70	$37.17
Replace Materials......21.30 Labor..........14.40				
Remove.....................Labor..........1.47				
24" deep built-in oak bookcase	sf	$1.47	$39.30	$40.77
Replace Materials......24.90 Labor..........14.40				
Remove.....................Labor..........1.47				
△ standard mantel **24" deep built-in walnut bookcase**	sf	$1.47	$48.50	$49.97
Replace Materials......34.10 Labor..........14.40				
Remove.....................Labor..........1.47				
MANTEL BEAM ▶ **Fireplace mantel beam, rough sawn**	lf	$2.31	$33.40	$35.71
Replace Materials......10.00 Labor..........23.40				
Remove.....................Labor..........2.31				
Fireplace mantel beam, glue laminated	lf	$2.31	$52.00	$54.31
Replace Materials......28.60 Labor..........23.40				
Remove.....................Labor..........2.31				
Remove fireplace mantel beam for work, then reinstall	lf	–	$30.20	$30.20
Replace.....................Labor..........30.20				
MANTEL ▶ *Measure the lf of mantel width.* **Fireplace mantel, economy grade**	lf	$2.72	$83.80	$86.52
Replace Materials......55.40 Labor..........28.40				
Remove.....................Labor..........2.72				
▶ Paint-grade wood with simple pattern and moldings. See illustration above.				
Fireplace mantel, standard grade	lf	$2.72	$147.40	$150.12
Replace Materials......119.00 Labor..........28.40				
Remove.....................Labor..........2.72				
▶ Paint-grade wood or stain-grade pine, may have dentil patterns and fluted pilasters. See illustration above.				
△ high **Fireplace mantel, high grade**	lf	$2.72	$284.40	$287.12
Replace Materials......256.00 Labor..........28.40				
Remove.....................Labor..........2.72				
▶ Red oak, birch, stain-grade pine or more ornate paint-grade. May include a combination of some of the following: carved moldings, carved onlays, embossed patterns, fluted pilasters, face projections.				
Fireplace mantel, deluxe grade	lf	$2.72	$603.40	$606.12
Replace Materials......575.00 Labor..........28.40				
Remove.....................Labor..........2.72				
△ deluxe ▶ Cherry, walnut or more ornate red oak, birch, yellow pine, or paint-grade. May include a combination of some of the following: carved moldings, carved onlays, fluted pilasters, face projections, carved corbels, circular patterns and moldings.				

Item Description	Unit	Remove	Replace	Total
Fireplace mantel, custom grade	lf	$2.72	$1,198.40	$1,201.12

Replace Materials....1170.00   Labor 28.40
Remove.......................   Labor 2.72

▶ Cherry, walnut, heart pine or very ornate red oak, birch, or yellow pine. May include a combination of some of the following: carved moldings, carved onlays, fluted pilasters, round columns, capitals (Ionic, Tuscan, contemporary, etc.), face projections, ornately carved corbel (e.g. lion's head), circular openings, paneling above mantel, or mirror.

Fireplace mantel, custom deluxe grade	lf	$2.72	$1,788.40	$1,791.12

Replace Materials...1760.00   Labor 28.40
Remove.......................   Labor 2.72

▶ Cherry, walnut or more ornate red oak, birch, or paint-grade. May include a combination of some of the following: carved moldings, ornate hand-carved patterns, fluted pilasters, round columns, ornate capitals (Scamozzi, Corinthian, etc.), face projections, circular openings, curved pilasters, paneling above mantel, or mirror.

Remove fireplace mantel for work, then reinstall	lf	–	$31.30	$31.30

Replace ....   Labor...........31.30

△ *custom*

△ *custom deluxe*

Coffered ceiling, economy grade	sf	$1.36	$21.60	$22.96

Replace Materials ......10.80   Labor...........10.80
Remove.......................   Labor 1.36

▶ Coffers are finished drywall with corner bead. Inside corners trimmed with 3-1/2" crown mold or similar.

◀ **COFFERED CEILING**
Coffers 42" to 48" on center. Unless otherwise noted, includes wood underframing, and fire-taped drywall. Does not include painting or staining and varnishing. All inside molding joints are coped.

Coffered ceiling, standard grade	sf	$1.36	$27.10	$28.46

Replace Materials.......15.10   Labor...........12.00
Remove.......................   Labor 1.36

▶ Coffers and beams are finished drywall. Inside corners trimmed with vertical pattern moldings. May also include wood onlays (see page 230), plaster enrichments (see page 232), or the raised beams may be cased with hardwood plywood.

Coffered ceiling, high grade	sf	$1.36	$31.00	$32.36

Replace Materials.......17.60   Labor...........13.40
Remove.......................   Labor 1.36

▶ Covered with wood paneling. Inside corners trimmed with vertical-pattern or embossed moldings. Coffers contain panel molding. May also include wood onlays (see page 230).

△ *economy*

△ *standard*

Coffered ceiling, deluxe grade	sf	$1.36	$41.40	$42.76

Replace Materials.......26.30   Labor...........15.10
Remove.......................   Labor 1.36

▶ Covered with hardwood plywood. Inside corners trimmed with hand-carved moldings. May also include wood onlays (see page 230).

△ *high*

Coffered ceiling, custom grade	sf	$1.36	$56.20	$57.56

Replace Materials.......37.50   Labor...........18.70
Remove.......................   Labor 1.36

▶ Covered with wood paneling. Inside corners trimmed with heavy hand-carved moldings. May also include wood onlays at each corner (see page 230), recessed panels on beams or in coffers, and corbels at wall corners.

△ *deluxe*

Coffered ceiling, custom deluxe grade	sf	$1.36	$80.50	$81.86

Replace Materials.......55.80   Labor...........24.70
Remove.......................   Labor 1.36

▶ Covered with wood paneling. Inside corners trimmed with heavy hand-carved moldings. May also include ornate wood onlays at each corner (see page 230), recessed panels on beams or in coffers, and ornately carved corbels at wall corners (e.g. lion's head).

△ *custom*

△ *custom deluxe*

Item Description	Unit	Remove	Replace	Total
NICHE ▶ Niches are high density polyurethane. Opaque bases allow for installation of a light beneath. Add **17%** for niches made from fiber reinforced plaster.				
Niche with casing and shelf bracket	ea	$9.16	$247.00	$256.16
Replace Materials......190.00 Labor...........57.00				
Remove........................ Labor 9.16				
Niche with clamshell top with casing and shelf bracket	ea	$9.16	$390.00	$399.16
Replace Materials....333.00 Labor...........57.00				
Remove........................ Labor 9.16				
Niche with clamshell top, casing, and clamshell shelf bracket	ea	$9.16	$490.00	$499.16
Replace Materials....433.00 Labor...........57.00				
Remove........................ Labor 9.16				
Remove niche for work, then reinstall	ea	–	$80.50	$80.50
Replace .... Labor 80.50				
GINGERBREAD ▶ RUNNING TRIM Paint-grade poplar. Add **30%** for red oak.				
Gingerbread fleur-sawn running trim	lf	$1.10	$36.36	$37.46
Replace Materials......29.40 Labor 6.96				
Remove........................ Labor 1.10				
Gingerbread picket-sawn running trim	lf	$1.10	$45.06	$46.16
Replace Materials......38.10 Labor 6.96				
Remove........................ Labor 1.10				
ball-and-dowel ▷ Gingerbread 2" ball-and-dowel running trim (galley rail)	lf	$1.10	$16.04	$17.14
Replace Materials......9.08 Labor 6.96				
Remove........................ Labor 1.10				
Gingerbread 4" ball-and-dowel running trim	lf	$1.10	$20.56	$21.66
Replace Materials......13.60 Labor 6.96				
Remove........................ Labor 1.10				
Gingerbread 6" ball-and-dowel running trim	lf	$1.10	$22.46	$23.56
Replace Materials......15.50 Labor 6.96				
Remove........................ Labor 1.10				
Gingerbread 8" ball-and-dowel running trim	lf	$1.10	$25.46	$26.56
Replace Materials......18.50 Labor 6.96				
Remove........................ Labor 1.10				
Gingerbread 10" ball-and-dowel running trim	lf	$1.10	$30.26	$31.36
Replace Materials......23.30 Labor 6.96				
Remove........................ Labor 1.10				
Gingerbread 12" ball-and-dowel running trim	lf	$1.10	$34.76	$35.86
Replace Materials......27.80 Labor 6.96				
Remove........................ Labor 1.10				
Gingerbread 14" ball-and-dowel running trim	lf	$1.10	$40.26	$41.36
Replace Materials......33.30 Labor 6.96				
Remove........................ Labor 1.10				
spindle ▷ Gingerbread 2" spindle running trim (galley rail)	lf	$1.10	$15.51	$16.61
Replace Materials.......8.55 Labor 6.96				
Remove........................ Labor 1.10				
Gingerbread 4" spindle running trim	lf	$1.10	$17.66	$18.76
Replace Materials ......10.70 Labor 6.96				
Remove........................ Labor 1.10				
Gingerbread 6" spindle running trim	lf	$1.10	$20.56	$21.66
Replace Materials.......13.60 Labor 6.96				
Remove........................ Labor 1.10				

△ *fleur-sawn*

△ *picket-sawn*

△ *ball-and-dowel*

△ *spindle*

Item Description	Unit	Remove	Replace	Total
Gingerbread 8" spindle running trim	lf	$1.10	$23.36	$24.46
Replace Materials ......16.40　　Labor 6.96				
Remove.........................　　Labor 1.10				
Gingerbread 10" spindle running trim	lf	$1.10	$29.26	$30.36
Replace Materials ......22.30　　Labor 6.96				
Remove.........................　　Labor 1.10				
Gingerbread 12" spindle running trim	lf	$1.10	$34.06	$35.16
Replace Materials ......27.10　　Labor 6.96				
Remove.........................　　Labor 1.10				
Gingerbread 14" spindle running trim	lf	$1.10	$39.86	$40.96
Replace Materials ......32.90　　Labor 6.96				
Remove.........................　　Labor 1.10				
Remove gingerbread running trim for work, then reinstall	lf	–	$8.47	$8.47
Replace ....　　Labor 8.47				
Gingerbread bracket, standard grade	ea	$4.45	$46.50	$50.95
Replace Materials ......31.40　　Labor 15.10				
Remove.........................　　Labor 4.45				
▶ Longest leg up to 12" with simple sawn pattern.				
Gingerbread bracket, high grade	ea	$4.45	$53.20	$57.65
Replace Materials ......38.10　　Labor 15.10				
Remove.........................　　Labor 4.45				
▶ Longest leg up to 23" with simple sawn pattern.				
Gingerbread bracket, deluxe grade	ea	$4.45	$57.00	$61.45
Replace Materials ......41.90　　Labor 15.10				
Remove.........................　　Labor 4.45				
▶ Longest leg up to 30" with ornately sawn pattern.				
Gingerbread bracket, custom grade	ea	$4.45	$62.60	$67.05
Replace Materials ......47.50　　Labor 15.10				
Remove.........................　　Labor 4.45				
▶ Longest leg up to 30" with very ornately sawn pattern.				
Gingerbread fan bracket, standard grade	ea	$4.45	$52.30	$56.75
Replace Materials ......37.20　　Labor 15.10				
Remove.........................　　Labor 4.45				
▶ Longest leg up to 14" with simple pattern.				
Gingerbread fan bracket, high grade	ea	$4.45	$56.90	$61.35
Replace Materials ......41.80　　Labor 15.10				
Remove.........................　　Labor 4.45				
▶ Longest leg up to 25" with simple pattern.				
Gingerbread fan bracket, deluxe grade	ea	$4.45	$66.80	$71.25
Replace Materials ......51.70　　Labor 15.10				
Remove.........................　　Labor 4.45				
▶ Longest leg up to 32" with ornate pattern.				
Gingerbread fan bracket, custom grade	ea	$4.45	$81.40	$85.85
Replace Materials ......66.30　　Labor 15.10				
Remove.........................　　Labor 4.45				
▶ Longest leg up to 32" with very ornate pattern.				

standard bracket △

◀ **GINGERBREAD BRACKET**
Paint-grade poplar corner brackets. Add **30%** for red oak.

high △

deluxe △

◀ **GINGERBREAD FAN BRACKET**
Brackets combining sawn elements with radiating spindles or dowel-and-ball elements. Made from paint-grade poplar. Add **30%** for red oak.

RELATED ITEMS

Cleaning 61
Painting 339

Item Description	Unit	Remove	Replace	Total
GINGERBREAD ▶ POST BRACKET *Made from paint-grade poplar. Add 30% for red oak.*				
Gingerbread post bracket, standard grade	ea	$4.45	$63.20	$67.65
Replace Materials......48.10 Labor...........15.10				
Remove.................. Labor............4.45				
▶ Simple pattern bracket with drop.				
Gingerbread post bracket, high grade	ea	$4.45	$75.00	$79.45
Replace Materials......59.90 Labor...........15.10				
Remove.................. Labor............4.45				
▶ Ornate pattern bracket with drop.				
Gingerbread post bracket, deluxe grade	ea	$4.45	$85.40	$89.85
Replace Materials.......70.30 Labor...........15.10				
Remove.................. Labor............4.45				
▶ Very ornate pattern bracket with drop.				
remove & reinstall ▷ **Remove gingerbread post bracket for work, then reinstall**	ea	—	$16.30	$16.30
Replace .... Labor...........16.30				
GINGERBREAD ▶ CORBEL *Made from paint-grade poplar. Add 30% for red oak.*				
Gingerbread corbel, standard grade	ea	$4.62	$49.90	$54.52
Replace Materials......34.30 Labor...........15.60				
Remove.................. Labor............4.62				
▶ Longest leg up to 12" with simple sawn pattern.				
Gingerbread corbel, high grade	ea	$4.62	$65.70	$70.32
Replace Materials......50.10 Labor...........15.60				
Remove.................. Labor............4.62				
▶ Longest leg up to 16" with simple sawn pattern.				
Gingerbread corbel, deluxe grade	ea	$4.62	$84.80	$89.42
Replace Materials......69.20 Labor...........15.60				
Remove.................. Labor............4.62				
▶ Longest leg up to 20" with ornately sawn pattern.				
Gingerbread corbel, custom grade	ea	$4.62	$114.60	$119.22
Replace Materials......99.00 Labor...........15.60				
Remove.................. Labor............4.62				
▶ Longest leg up to 20" with very ornately sawn pattern.				
remove & reinstall ▷ **Remove gingerbread corbel for work, then reinstall**	ea	—	$16.40	$16.40
Replace .... Labor...........16.40				
GINGERBREAD ▶ HEADER *Made from paint-grade poplar. Add 30% for red oak.*				
Gingerbread door or window header, standard grade	lf	$1.07	$61.40	$62.47
Replace Materials......51.30 Labor.........10.10				
Remove.................. Labor.......... 1.07				
▶ Up to 14" long with sawn pattern.				
Gingerbread door or window header, high grade	lf	$1.07	$81.50	$82.57
Replace Materials......71.40 Labor...........10.10				
Remove.................. Labor.......... 1.07				
▶ Up to 25" long with sawn pattern.				
Gingerbread door or window header, deluxe grade	lf	$1.07	$105.50	$106.57
Replace Materials......95.40 Labor...........10.10				
Remove.................. Labor.......... 1.07				
▶ Up to 36" long with sawn pattern.				
remove & reinstall ▷ **Remove gingerbread header for work, then reinstall**	lf	—	$12.60	$12.60
Replace .... Labor...........12.60				

Item Description	Unit	Remove	Replace	Total
10" gingerbread post drop	ea	$4.45	$21.61	$26.06
Replace Materials.........7.61 Labor............14.00				
Remove.............................. Labor 4.45				
12" gingerbread post drop	ea	$4.45	$23.52	$27.97
Replace Materials.........9.52 Labor............14.00				
Remove.............................. Labor 4.45				
18" gingerbread post drop	ea	$4.45	$25.40	$29.85
Replace Materials........11.40 Labor............14.00				
Remove.............................. Labor 4.45				
24" gingerbread post drop	ea	$4.45	$27.30	$31.75
Replace Materials........13.30 Labor............14.00				
Remove.............................. Labor 4.45				
Remove gingerbread post drop for work, then reinstall	ea	—	$15.50	$15.50
Replace .... Labor............15.50				
Gingerbread spandrel, standard grade	lf	$1.10	$34.70	$35.80
Replace Materials ......24.40 Labor............10.30				
Remove.............................. Labor 1.10				
▶ Up to 6" deep in center and 14" deep on each side.				
Gingerbread spandrel, high grade	lf	$1.10	$41.20	$42.30
Replace Materials ......30.90 Labor............10.30				
Remove.............................. Labor 1.10				
▶ Up to 9" deep in center and 17" deep on each side.				
Gingerbread spandrel, custom grade	lf	$1.10	$50.50	$51.60
Replace Materials ......40.20 Labor............10.30				
Remove.............................. Labor 1.10				
▶ Up to 13" deep in center and 21" deep on each side.				
Gingerbread spandrel, deluxe grade	lf	$1.10	$65.10	$66.20
Replace Materials ......54.80 Labor............10.30				
Remove.............................. Labor 1.10				
▶ Up to 16" deep in center and 24" deep on each side.				
Gingerbread spandrel, custom deluxe grade	lf	$1.10	$78.90	$80.00
Replace Materials ......68.60 Labor............10.30				
Remove.............................. Labor 1.10				
▶ Up to 22" deep in center and 31" deep on each side.				
Gingerbread arch spandrel, standard grade	lf	$1.10	$56.90	$58.00
Replace Materials ......46.60 Labor............10.30				
Remove.............................. Labor 1.10				
▶ Leg against wall up to 12" long.				
Gingerbread arch spandrel, high grade	lf	$1.10	$68.40	$69.50
Replace Materials ......58.10 Labor............10.30				
Remove.............................. Labor 1.10				
▶ Leg against wall up to 20" long, simple pattern.				
Gingerbread arch spandrel, custom grade	lf	$1.10	$77.30	$78.40
Replace Materials ......67.00 Labor............10.30				
Remove.............................. Labor 1.10				
▶ Leg against wall up to 22" long, ornate pattern, often with post drops.				

◀ **GINGERBREAD POST DROP**
Made from paint-grade poplar. Add 30% for red oak.

◁ remove & reinstall

◀ **GINGERBREAD SPANDREL**
Spandrels are horizontal decorative elements for exterior and interior openings. Typically both corners and the center contain sawn elements. The remaining space is filled with either ball-and-dowel or spindle elements. Made from paint-grade poplar. Add 30% for red oak.

high △

deluxe △

◀ **GINGERBREAD ARCH SPANDREL**
Arched spandrels have arched end sections that typically contain either sawn woodwork or a spindle fan. Made from paint-grade poplar. Add 30% for red oak.

custom △

	Item Description	Unit	Remove	Replace	Total
GINGERBREAD ▶ ARCH SPANDREL *continued*	**Gingerbread arch spandrel, deluxe grade**	lf	$1.10	$85.40	$86.50
	Replace Materials ......75.10 Labor...........10.30				
	Remove........................ Labor 1.10				
	▶ Leg against wall up to 26" long, simple pattern.				
custom deluxe △	**Gingerbread arch spandrel, custom deluxe grade**	lf	$1.10	$98.80	$99.90
	Replace Materials ......88.50 Labor...........10.30				
	Remove........................ Labor 1.10				
	▶ Leg against wall up to 28" long, ornate pattern, often with post drops.				
remove & reinstall ▷	**Remove gingerbread spandrel for work, then reinstall**	lf	–	$12.90	$12.90
	Replace .... Labor...........12.90				
GINGERBREAD ▶ WINDOW CORNICE *Made from paint-grade poplar. Add 30% for red oak.*	**Gingerbread window cornice, standard grade**	lf	$1.18	$33.30	$34.48
	Replace Materials ......22.80 Labor...........10.50				
	Remove........................ Labor 1.18				
	▶ Cornice is 5" deep with a height of 6". Made from finish board with bed mold on top and simple panel mold on bottom.				
standard △	**Gingerbread window cornice, high grade**	lf	$1.18	$39.10	$40.28
	Replace Materials ......28.60 Labor...........10.50				
	Remove........................ Labor 1.18				
	▶ Cornice is 5-1/2" deep with a height of 8-1/2". Side brackets are sawn with drop. Front of cornice is made from 2" to 4" ball and dowel running trim.				
high △	**Gingerbread window cornice, deluxe grade**	lf	$1.18	$46.70	$47.88
	Replace Materials ......36.20 Labor...........10.50				
	Remove........................ Labor 1.18				
	▶ Cornice is 8" deep with a height of 9". Side brackets are sawn with drop and spindles. Front of cornice is made from 6" to 8" spindle running trim with sawn woodwork at center.				
deluxe △	**Gingerbread window cornice, custom grade**	lf	$1.18	$47.90	$49.08
	Replace Materials ......37.40 Labor...........10.50				
	Remove........................ Labor 1.18				
	▶ Cornice is 8" deep with a height of 9". Side brackets are sawn with drop and spindles. Front of cornice is made from 6" to 8" spindle running trim with very ornately sawn woodwork at center.				
custom deluxe △	**Gingerbread window cornice, custom deluxe grade**	lf	$1.18	$54.30	$55.48
	Replace Materials ......43.80 Labor...........10.50				
	Remove........................ Labor 1.18				
	▶ Cornice is 8" deep with a height of 9". Side brackets are sawn with drop and ball and dowels. Front of cornice is made from 6" to 8" ball-and-dowel running trim with very ornately sawn woodwork at center.				
remove & reinstall ▷	**Remove gingerbread window cornice for work, then reinstall**	lf	—	$13.30	$13.30
	Replace .... Labor...........13.30				
GINGERBREAD ▶ GABLE ORNAMENT *Gable ornaments can be ordered for roofs of any slope. They are typically found on roofs with a slope of 6 in 12 or more. Ornaments are placed in the gables at the peak of the roof. Made from paint-grade poplar. Add 30% for red oak.*	**Gingerbread gable ornament, standard grade**	ea	$7.34	$158.30	$165.64
	Replace Materials .....133.00 Labor 25.30				
	Remove........................ Labor 7.34				
	▶ Fixed or adjustable ornament. Simple sawn pattern with longest leg up to 32".				
	Gingerbread gable ornament, high grade	ea	$7.34	$249.30	$256.64
	Replace Materials ....224.00 Labor 25.30				
	Remove........................ Labor 7.34				
	▶ Fixed ornament with legs up to 36". May contain some spindles or ball-and-dowel. Often contains drop in center.				

Item Description	Unit	Remove	Replace	Total
Gingerbread gable ornament, deluxe grade	ea	$7.34	$367.30	$374.64
Replace Materials....342.00 Labor 25.30				
Remove........................ Labor 7.34				
▶ Fixed ornament with legs up to 45". May contain some spindles or ball-and-dowel. Often contains drop in center.				
Gingerbread gable ornament, custom grade	ea	$7.34	$630.30	$637.64
Replace Materials....605.00 Labor 25.30				
Remove........................ Labor 7.34				
▶ Fixed ornament with legs up to 48". Ornate combinations of fanned spindles, ball-and-dowel and drops.				
Gingerbread gable ornament, custom deluxe grade	ea	$7.34	$763.30	$770.64
Replace Materials....738.00 Labor 25.30				
Remove........................ Labor 7.34				
▶ Fixed ornament with legs up to 60". Very ornate combinations of fanned spindles, ball-and-dowel and drops.				
Remove gingerbread gable ornament for work, then reinstall	ea	–	$40.80	$40.80
Replace .... Labor 40.80				
Gingerbread gable finial, standard grade	ea	$6.91	$105.30	$112.21
Replace Materials......80.90 Labor 24.40				
Remove........................ Labor 6.91				
▶ Finial with 28" post.				
Gingerbread gable finial, high grade	ea	$6.91	$133.40	$140.31
Replace Materials....109.00 Labor 24.40				
Remove........................ Labor 6.91				
▶ Finial with 34" post.				
Remove gingerbread gable finial for work, then reinstall	ea	–	$38.90	$38.90
Replace .... Labor 38.90				
4" x 4" porch post, standard grade	lf	$3.67	$15.25	$18.92
Replace Materials........9.38 Labor 5.87				
Remove........................ Labor 3.67				
▶ Turned post. Sometimes called colonist style.				
4" x 4" porch post, high grade	lf	$3.67	$24.67	$28.34
Replace Materials......18.80 Labor 5.87				
Remove........................ Labor 3.67				
▶ Turned post with fluted columns. Or square post with flutes. Square post also trimmed with molding at base, at 1/3 shaft, and at about 12" to 16" from top.				
4" x 4" porch post, deluxe grade	lf	$3.67	$55.67	$59.34
Replace Materials......49.80 Labor 5.87				
Remove........................ Labor 3.67				
▶ Turned post with spiral pattern. Or square post with flutes. Square post also trimmed with panels to 1/3 shaft, capped at base and top of panel with moldings, and with molding trim about 12" to 16" from top.				
6" x 6" porch post, standard grade	lf	$3.67	$19.67	$23.34
Replace Materials......13.80 Labor 5.87				
Remove........................ Labor 3.67				
▶ Turned post. Sometimes called colonist style.				
6" x 6" porch post, high grade	lf	$3.67	$33.87	$37.54
Replace Materials......28.00 Labor 5.87				
Remove........................ Labor 3.67				
▶ Turned post with fluted columns. Or square post with flutes. Square post also trimmed with molding at base, at 1/3 shaft, and at about 12" to 16" from top.				

standard △

custom deluxe △

◁ **remove & reinstall**

◀ **GINGERBREAD GABLE FINIAL**
Finials are placed at the peak of the roof on each end. Made from cedar.

◀ **PORCH POST**
For stain-grade add **16%**. Non-laminated posts made from clear, select Douglas fir or clear all-heart redwood. Standard grade posts may be made from cedar. Square posts are hollow and include a structural post inside.

▽ *standard*

high △

Item Description	Unit	Remove	Replace	Total
PORCH POST ▶ *continued*				
6" x 6" porch post, deluxe grade *Replace* Materials......35.30 Labor...........5.87 *Remove*........................ Labor...........3.67 ▶ Turned post with spiral pattern. Or square post with flutes. Square post also trimmed with panels to 1/3 shaft, capped at base and top of panel with moldings, and with molding trim about 12" to 16" from top.	If	$3.67	$41.17	$44.84
8" x 8" porch post, standard grade *Replace* Materials.......15.80 Labor...........5.87 *Remove*........................ Labor...........3.67 ▶ Turned post. Sometimes called colonist style.	If	$3.67	$21.67	$25.34
8" x 8" porch post, high grade *Replace* Materials......32.00 Labor...........5.87 *Remove*........................ Labor...........3.67 ▶ Turned post with fluted columns. Or square post with flutes. Square post also trimmed with molding at base, at 1/3 shaft, and about at 12" to 16" from top.	If	$3.67	$37.87	$41.54
8" x 8" porch post, deluxe grade *Replace* Materials......40.30 Labor...........5.87 *Remove*........................ Labor...........3.67 ▶ Turned post with spiral pattern. Or square post with flutes. Square post also trimmed with panels to 1/3 shaft, capped at base and top of panel with moldings, and with molding trim about 12" to 16" from top.	If	$3.67	$46.17	$49.84
remove & reinstall ▷ Remove porch post for work, then reinstall *Replace* .... Labor...........8.16	If	—	$8.16	$8.16
CARVED ONLAY ▶ Small carved wood onlay, acanthus *Replace* Materials......36.50 Labor...........22.60 *Remove*........................ Labor...........1.79	ea	$1.79	$59.10	$60.89
Small carved wood onlay, ribbon *Replace* Materials......38.20 Labor...........22.60 *Remove*........................ Labor...........1.79	ea	$1.79	$60.80	$62.59
Small carved wood onlay, grape *Replace* Materials......61.20 Labor...........22.60 *Remove*........................ Labor...........1.79	ea	$1.79	$83.80	$85.59
Small carved wood onlay, shell *Replace* Materials......53.50 Labor...........22.60 *Remove*........................ Labor...........1.79	ea	$1.79	$76.10	$77.89
Small carved wood onlay, floral *Replace* Materials......56.10 Labor...........22.60 *Remove*........................ Labor...........1.79	ea	$1.79	$78.70	$80.49
Medium carved wood onlay, acanthus *Replace* Materials......56.90 Labor...........22.60 *Remove*........................ Labor...........1.79	ea	$1.79	$79.50	$81.29
Medium carved wood onlay, ribbon *Replace* Materials......59.50 Labor...........22.60 *Remove*........................ Labor...........1.79	ea	$1.79	$82.10	$83.89
Medium carved wood onlay, grape *Replace* Materials......95.20 Labor...........22.60 *Remove*........................ Labor...........1.79	ea	$1.79	$117.80	$119.59

▽ *high*

deluxe △

*Onlays are available in a wide variety of styles and prices. Use these listings as indicators of complexity and price range. Made from maple. Add **25%** for red oak.*

acanthus △

ribbon △

grape △

Item Description	Unit	Remove	Replace	Total	
Medium carved wood onlay, shell	ea	$1.79	$105.90	$107.69	
Replace Materials......83.30 Labor 22.60					
Remove..................... Labor 1.79					shell △
Medium carved wood onlay, floral	ea	$1.79	$109.30	$111.09	
Replace Materials......86.70 Labor 22.60					
Remove..................... Labor 1.79					
Large carved wood onlay, acanthus	ea	$1.79	$94.80	$96.59	
Replace Materials......72.20 Labor 22.60					
Remove..................... Labor 1.79					
Large carved wood onlay, ribbon	ea	$1.79	$99.10	$100.89	floral △
Replace Materials ......76.50 Labor 22.60					
Remove..................... Labor 1.79					
Large carved wood onlay, grape	ea	$1.79	$141.60	$143.39	
Replace Materials .....119.00 Labor 22.60					
Remove..................... Labor 1.79					
Large carved wood onlay, shell	ea	$1.79	$129.60	$131.39	
Replace Materials.....107.00 Labor 22.60					
Remove..................... Labor 1.79					
Large carved wood onlay, floral	ea	$1.79	$133.10	$134.89	
Replace Materials .....110.50 Labor 22.60					
Remove..................... Labor 1.79					
Remove onlay for work, then reinstall	ea	–	$28.10	$28.10	◁ **remove & reinstall**
Replace .... Labor 28.10					
1" x 2" S4S select pine	lf	$.75	$2.77	$3.52	◀ **FINISH BOARD**
Replace Materials .... .64 Labor 2.13					*Smooth four sides.*
Remove..................... Labor .... .75					*Includes 4% waste.*
1" x 4" S4S select pine	lf	$.75	$3.40	$4.15	
Replace Materials ...... 1.27 Labor 2.13					
Remove..................... Labor .... .75					
1" x 6" S4S select pine	lf	$.75	$4.05	$4.80	
Replace Materials........1.92 Labor 2.13					
Remove..................... Labor .... .75					
1" x 8" S4S select pine	lf	$.75	$4.68	$5.43	
Replace Materials........2.55 Labor 2.13					
Remove..................... Labor .... .75					
1" x 10" S4S select pine	lf	$.75	$5.32	$6.07	
Replace Materials........3.19 Labor 2.13					
Remove..................... Labor .... .75					
1" x 12" S4S select pine	lf	$.75	$5.95	$6.70	
Replace Materials........3.82 Labor 2.13					
Remove..................... Labor .... .75					
Add 3% for S4S poplar					◁ **other wood species**
Add 13% for S4S mahogany					
Add 17% for S4S red oak					

RELATED ITEMS
Cleaning 61
Painting 337

	Item Description	Unit	Remove	Replace	Total
FINISH BOARD ▶ *continued*	**Add for bull nose on 1 x boards** *Replace* Materials .... .58	lf	—	$.58	$.58
remove & reinstall ▷	**Remove finish board trim for work, then reinstall** *Replace* .... Labor 3.02	lf	—	$3.02	$3.02
FINISH PLYWOOD ▶ *Includes* **4%** *waste.*	**1/4" aromatic cedar veneer plywood** *Replace* Materials........2.99 Labor ....1.22 *Remove*....................... Labor............ .64	sf	$.64	$4.21	$4.85
	1/4" birch veneer plywood *Replace* Materials........2.90 Labor ....1.22 *Remove*....................... Labor............ .64	sf	$.64	$4.12	$4.76
	1/4" cherry veneer plywood *Replace* Materials........3.22 Labor ....1.22 *Remove*....................... Labor............ .64	sf	$.64	$4.44	$5.08
	1/4" chestnut veneer plywood *Replace* Materials........5.11 Labor ....1.22 *Remove*....................... Labor............ .64	sf	$.64	$6.33	$6.97
	1/4" knotty pine veneer plywood *Replace* Materials........2.25 Labor ....1.22 *Remove*....................... Labor............ .64	sf	$.64	$3.47	$4.11
	1/4" lauan mahogany veneer plywood *Replace* Materials ...... 1.14 Labor ....1.22 *Remove*....................... Labor............ .64	sf	$.64	$2.36	$3.00
	1/4" mahogany veneer plywood *Replace* Materials........3.26 Labor ....1.22 *Remove*....................... Labor............ .64	sf	$.64	$4.48	$5.12
	1/4" pecan veneer plywood *Replace* Materials........3.32 Labor ....1.22 *Remove*....................... Labor............ .64	sf	$.64	$4.54	$5.18
	1/4" red oak veneer plywood *Replace* Materials........2.93 Labor ....1.22 *Remove*....................... Labor............ .64	sf	$.64	$4.15	$4.79
	1/4" rosewood veneer plywood *Replace* Materials........4.52 Labor ....1.22 *Remove*....................... Labor............ .64	sf	$.64	$5.74	$6.38
	1/4" teak veneer plywood *Replace* Materials........5.99 Labor ....1.22 *Remove*....................... Labor............ .64	sf	$.64	$7.21	$7.85
	1/4" walnut veneer plywood *Replace* Materials........4.30 Labor ....1.22 *Remove*....................... Labor............ .64	sf	$.64	$5.52	$6.16
remove & reinstall ▷	**Remove 1/4" finish plywood for work, then reinstall** *Replace* .... Labor 1.59	sf	—	$1.59	$1.59

✍ NOTES: _____

_____ end

TIME & MATERIAL CHARTS *(selected items)*

Finish Carpentry Materials

DESCRIPTION	MATERIAL PRICE	GROSS COVERAGE	WASTE	NET COVERAGE	UNIT PRICE
Clamshell base					
1-1/2" stain-grade pine	$.96 *lf*	1	7%	.93	$1.03 *lf*
3-1/2" stain-grade pine	$1.55 *lf*	1	7%	.93	$1.67 *lf*
Pattern base					
1-1/2" stain-grade pine	$1.17 *lf*	1	7%	.93	$1.26 *lf*
2-1/2" stain-grade pine	$1.89 *lf*	1	7%	.93	$2.03 *lf*
3-1/2" stain-grade pine	$2.50 *lf*	1	7%	.93	$2.69 *lf*
Base shoe					
3/4" stain-grade pine	$.59 *lf*	1	7%	.93	$.63 *lf*
Clamshell casing					
1-1/2" stain-grade pine	$1.00 *lf*	1	5%	.95	$1.05 *lf*
2-1/2" stain-grade pine	$1.14 *lf*	1	5%	.95	$1.20 *lf*
3-1/2" stain-grade pine	$1.61 *lf*	1	5%	.95	$1.69 *lf*
Pattern casing					
1-1/2" stain-grade pine	$1.22 *lf*	1	5%	.95	$1.28 *lf*
2-1/2" stain-grade pine	$1.97 *lf*	1	5%	.95	$2.07 *lf*
3-1/2" stain-grade pine	$2.60 *lf*	1	5%	.95	$2.74 *lf*
Window moldings					
2-1/2" stain-grade pine stool	$2.19 *lf*	1	4%	.96	$2.28 *lf*
3-1/2" stain-grade pine apron	$1.43 *lf*	1	4%	.96	$1.49 *lf*
Chair rail					
2-1/2" stain-grade pine	$1.89 *lf*	1	4%	.96	$1.97 *lf*
3-1/2" stain-grade pine	$2.38 *lf*	1	4%	.96	$2.48 *lf*
Drip cap					
1-5/8" redwood	$1.75 *lf*	1	4%	.96	$1.82 *lf*
2-1/4" redwood	$1.96 *lf*	1	4%	.96	$2.04 *lf*
Astragal					
1-3/4" stain-grade pine	$3.62 *lf*	1	4%	.96	$3.77 *lf*
2-1/4" stain-grade pine	$4.39 *lf*	1	4%	.96	$4.57 *lf*
Cove					
1/2" stain-grade pine	$.68 *lf*	1	4%	.96	$.71 *lf*
3/4" stain-grade pine	$.78 *lf*	1	4%	.96	$.81 *lf*
1" stain-grade pine	$.97 *lf*	1	4%	.96	$1.01 *lf*
2-1/2" stain-grade pine	$1.70 *lf*	1	4%	.96	$1.77 *lf*
3-1/2" stain-grade pine	$2.21 *lf*	1	4%	.96	$2.30 *lf*
Half-round					
1" stain-grade pine	$.80 *lf*	1	4%	.96	$.83 *lf*
2" stain-grade pine	$1.13 *lf*	1	4%	.96	$1.18 *lf*
Quarter-round					
1/2" stain-grade pine	$.59 *lf*	1	4%	.96	$.61 *lf*
3/4" stain-grade pine	$.70 *lf*	1	4%	.96	$.73 *lf*
1" stain-grade pine	$1.25 *lf*	1	4%	.96	$1.30 *lf*
Corner bead					
stain-grade pine	$1.36 *lf*	1	4%	.96	$1.42 *lf*
turned stain-grade pine with finials	$15.00 *lf*	1	4%	.96	$15.60 *lf*
clear plastic	$1.07 *lf*	1	4%	.96	$1.11 *lf*
Bed mold					
2-1/2" stain-grade pine	$1.90 *lf*	1	4%	.96	$1.98 *lf*

. . . More ➤

Finish Carpentry Materials *continued*

DESCRIPTION	MATERIAL PRICE	GROSS COVERAGE	WASTE	NET COVERAGE	UNIT PRICE
Crown					
3-1/2" stain-grade pine	$2.44 lf	1	4%	.96	$2.54 lf
4-1/2" stain-grade pine	$3.59 lf	1	4%	.96	$3.74 lf
Hand rail					
stain-grade pine	$3.60 lf	1	4%	.96	$3.75 lf
Specialty moldings, 3/4"					
stain-grade pine with vertical milling	$2.86 lf	1	4%	.96	$2.98 lf
stain-grade pine embossed	$1.70 lf	1	4%	.96	$1.77 lf
stain-grade pine with hand carving	$5.28 lf	1	4%	.96	$5.50 lf
stain-grade pine with heavy hand carving	$10.30 lf	1	4%	.96	$10.70 lf
Specialty moldings, 1-1/2"					
stain-grade pine with vertical milling	$3.26 lf	1	4%	.96	$3.40 lf
stain-grade pine embossed	$1.94 lf	1	4%	.96	$2.02 lf
stain-grade pine with hand carving	$6.03 lf	1	4%	.96	$6.28 lf
stain-grade pine with heavy hand carving	$11.80 lf	1	4%	.96	$12.30 lf
Specialty moldings, 2-1/2"					
stain-grade pine with vertical milling	$3.65 lf	1	4%	.96	$3.80 lf
stain-grade pine embossed	$2.17 lf	1	4%	.96	$2.26 lf
stain-grade pine with hand carving	$6.75 lf	1	4%	.96	$7.03 lf
stain-grade pine with heavy hand carving	$13.20 lf	1	4%	.96	$13.80 lf
Specialty moldings, 3-1/2"					
stain-grade pine with vertical milling	$4.06 lf	1	4%	.96	$4.23 lf
stain-grade pine embossed	$2.41 lf	1	4%	.96	$2.51 lf
stain-grade pine with hand carving	$7.51 lf	1	4%	.96	$7.82 lf
stain-grade pine with heavy hand carving	$14.70 lf	1	4%	.96	$15.30 lf
Specialty moldings, 5"					
stain-grade pine with vertical milling	$5.85 lf	1	4%	.96	$6.09 lf
stain-grade pine embossed	$3.47 lf	1	4%	.96	$3.61 lf
stain-grade pine with hand carving	$10.80 lf	1	4%	.96	$11.30 lf
stain-grade pine with heavy hand carving	$21.20 lf	1	4%	.96	$22.10 lf
Specialty moldings, 8"					
stain-grade pine with vertical milling	$9.58 lf	1	4%	.96	$9.98 lf
stain-grade pine embossed	$5.68 lf	1	4%	.96	$5.92 lf
stain-grade pine with hand carving	$17.70 lf	1	4%	.96	$18.40 lf
stain-grade pine with heavy hand carving	$34.70 lf	1	4%	.96	$36.10 lf
Custom-milled moldings					
molder setup charge	$200.00 ea				$200.00 ea
molder custom knife charges	$415.00 ea				$415.00 ea
2" to 3" pine	$1.87 lf	1	4%	.96	$1.95 lf
2" to 3" poplar	$2.07 lf	1	4%	.96	$2.16 lf
2" to 3" mahogany	$2.47 lf	1	4%	.96	$2.57 lf
2" to 3" red oak	$2.69 lf	1	4%	.96	$2.80 lf
Inside corner radius for panel molding					
typical	$1.87 ea	1	4%	.96	$1.95 ea
with heavy carving	$9.55 ea	1	4%	.96	$9.95 ea
Closet work					
shelf brackets, shelving, & rod	$10.90 lf	1	4%	.96	$11.40 lf
organizer system, standard grade	$10.10 sf	1	4%	.96	$10.50 sf
organizer system, deluxe grade	$15.50 sf	1	4%	.96	$16.10 sf
linen closet shelves, standard grade	$8.07 lf	1	4%	.96	$8.41 lf
linen closet pull-out shelves	$10.20 ea	1	4%	.96	$10.60 ea
closet rod, pine	$3.09 lf	1	4%	.96	$3.22 lf
Built-in bookcase					
8" deep stain-grade pine	$8.28 sf	1	4%	.96	$8.63 sf
12" deep stain-grade pine	$10.90 sf	1	4%	.96	$11.40 sf
18" deep stain-grade pine	$14.30 sf	1	4%	.96	$14.90 sf
24" deep stain-grade pine	$18.80 sf	1	4%	.96	$19.60 sf

. . . More ≻

Finish Carpentry Materials continued

DESCRIPTION	MATERIAL PRICE	GROSS COVERAGE	WASTE	NET COVERAGE	UNIT PRICE
Fireplace mantel beam					
rough sawn	$9.64 lf	1	4%	.96	$10.00 lf
glue laminated	$27.50 lf	1	4%	.96	$28.60 lf
Fireplace mantel					
economy grade	$55.40 lf				$55.40 lf
custom deluxe grade	$1,760.00 lf				$1,760.00 lf
Coffered ceiling					
economy grade	$9.52 sf	1	12%	.88	$10.80 sf
custom deluxe grade	$49.10 sf	1	12%	.88	$55.80 sf
Niche with casing and shelf bracket					
typical	$190.00 ea				$190.00 ea
with clamshell top	$333.00 ea				$333.00 ea
clamshell top and clamshell shelf	$433.00 ea				$433.00 ea
Gingerbread running trim					
fleur-sawn	$28.80 lf	1	2%	.98	$29.40 lf
picket-sawn	$37.30 lf	1	2%	.98	$38.10 lf
2" ball-and-dowel	$8.90 lf	1	2%	.98	$9.08 lf
14" ball-and-dowel	$32.60 lf	1	2%	.98	$33.30 lf
2" spindle	$8.38 lf	1	2%	.98	$8.55 lf
14" spindle	$32.20 lf	1	2%	.98	$32.90 lf
Gingerbread bracket					
standard grade	$31.40 ea				$31.40 ea
custom grade	$47.50 ea				$47.50 ea
Gingerbread fan bracket					
standard grade	$37.20 ea				$37.20 ea
custom grade	$66.30 ea				$66.30 ea
Gingerbread post bracket					
standard grade	$48.10 ea				$48.10 ea
deluxe grade	$70.30 ea				$70.30 ea
Gingerbread corbel					
standard grade	$34.30 ea				$34.30 ea
custom grade	$99.00 ea				$99.00 ea
Gingerbread door or window header					
standard grade	$51.30 ea				$51.30 ea
deluxe grade	$95.40 ea				$95.40 ea
Gingerbread post drop					
10"	$7.61 ea				$7.61 ea
24"	$13.30 ea				$13.30 ea
Gingerbread spandrel					
standard grade	$24.40 lf				$24.40 lf
custom deluxe grade	$68.60 lf				$68.60 lf
Gingerbread arch spandrel					
standard grade	$46.60 lf				$46.60 lf
custom deluxe grade	$88.50 lf				$88.50 lf
Gingerbread window cornice					
standard grade	$22.80 lf				$22.80 lf
custom deluxe grade	$43.80 lf				$43.80 lf
Gingerbread gable ornament					
standard grade	$133.00 lf				$133.00 lf
custom deluxe grade	$738.00 lf				$738.00 lf
Gingerbread gable finial					
standard grade	$80.90 ea				$80.90 ea
high grade	$109.00 ea				$109.00 ea

. . . More ➢

Finish Carpentry Materials *continued*

DESCRIPTION	MATERIAL PRICE	GROSS COVERAGE	WASTE	NET COVERAGE	UNIT PRICE
Porch post					
4" x 4", standard grade	$75.00 8' post	8	0%	8	**$9.38** lf
4" x 4", deluxe grade	$398.00 8' post	8	0%	8	**$49.80** lf
6" x 6", standard grade	$110.00 8' post	8	0%	8	**$13.80** lf
6" x 6", deluxe grade	$282.00 8' post	8	0%	8	**$35.30** lf
8" x 8", standard grade	$126.00 8' post	8	0%	8	**$15.80** lf
8" x 8", deluxe grade	$322.00 8' post	8	0%	8	**$40.30** lf
Carved wood onlay					
medium, acanthus	$56.90 ea				**$56.90** ea
medium, ribbon	$59.50 ea				**$59.50** ea
medium, grape	$95.20 ea				**$95.20** ea
medium, shell	$83.30 ea				**$83.30** ea
medium, floral	$86.70 ea				**$86.70** ea
Finish boards					
1" x 12" S4S select pine	$3.67 lf	1	4%	.96	**$3.82** lf
Hardwood plywood					
1/4" aromatic cedar veneer	$91.80 sheet	32	4%	30.72	**$2.99** sf
1/4" birch veneer	$89.00 sheet	32	4%	30.72	**$2.90** sf
1/4" cherry veneer	$99.00 sheet	32	4%	30.72	**$3.22** sf
1/4" chestnut veneer	$157.00 sheet	32	4%	30.72	**$5.11** sf
1/4" knotty pine veneer	$69.00 sheet	32	4%	30.72	**$2.25** sf
1/4" lauan mahogany veneer	$35.00 sheet	32	4%	30.72	**$1.14** sf
1/4" mahogany veneer	$100.00 sheet	32	4%	30.72	**$3.26** sf
1/4" pecan veneer	$102.00 sheet	32	4%	30.72	**$3.32** sf
1/4" red oak veneer	$90.00 sheet	32	4%	30.72	**$2.93** sf
1/4" rosewood veneer	$139.00 sheet	32	4%	30.72	**$4.52** sf
1/4" teak veneer	$184.00 sheet	32	4%	30.72	**$5.99** sf
1/4" walnut veneer	$132.00 sheet	32	4%	30.72	**$4.30** sf

Finish Carpentry Labor

LABORER	BASE WAGE	PAID LEAVE	TRUE WAGE	FICA	FUTA	WORKER'S COMP.	UNEMPLOY. INSUR.	HEALTH INSUR.	RETIRE (401K)	LIABILITY INSUR.	COST PER HOUR
Carpenter	$24.30	1.90	$26.20	2.00	.21	5.15	2.28	2.92	.79	3.93	**$43.50**
Carpenter's helper	$17.50	1.37	$18.87	1.44	.15	3.71	1.64	2.92	.57	2.83	**$32.10**
Demolition laborer	$14.40	1.12	$15.52	1.19	.12	5.01	1.35	2.92	.47	2.33	**$28.90**

Paid Leave is calculated based on two weeks paid vacation, one week sick leave, and seven paid holidays. Employer's matching portion of **FICA** is 7.65 percent. **FUTA** (Federal Unemployment) is .8 percent. **Worker's compensation** for the finish carpentry trade was calculated using a national average of 19.63 percent. **Unemployment insurance** was calculated using a national average of 8.7 percent. **Health insurance** was calculated based on a projected national average for 2005 of $580 per employee (and family when applicable) per month. Employer pays 80 percent for a per month cost of $464 per employee. **Retirement** is based on a 401(k) retirement program with employer matching of 50 percent. Employee contributions to the 401(k) plan are an average of 6 percent of the true wage. **Liability insurance** is based on a national average of 14.0 percent.

Finish Carpentry Labor Productivity

WORK DESCRIPTION	LABORER	COST PER HOUR	PRODUCTIVITY	UNIT PRICE
Demolition				
remove wall molding (base, chair rail, crown)	demolition laborer	$28.90	.026	$.75 lf
remove door and window molding	demolition laborer	$28.90	.032	$.92 lf
remove base or corner block	demolition laborer	$28.90	.036	$1.04 ea
remove head block	demolition laborer	$28.90	.037	$1.07 ea
remove overdoor molding	demolition laborer	$28.90	.028	$.81 lf
remove window stool	demolition laborer	$28.90	.026	$.75 lf
remove window apron	demolition laborer	$28.90	.028	$.81 lf
remove corner bead	demolition laborer	$28.90	.043	$1.24 lf
remove hand rail	demolition laborer	$28.90	.028	$.81 lf
remove shelf brackets, shelving, and rod	demolition laborer	$28.90	.063	$1.82 lf
remove closet organizer system	demolition laborer	$28.90	.047	$1.36 sf
remove linen closet shelves	demolition laborer	$28.90	.034	$.98 lf
remove closet rod	demolition laborer	$28.90	.035	$1.01 lf
remove tongue-&-groove cedar closet lining	demolition laborer	$28.90	.028	$.81 sf
remove cedar veneer plywood closet lining	demolition laborer	$28.90	.022	$.64 sf
remove built-in bookcase	demolition laborer	$28.90	.051	$1.47 sf
remove fireplace mantel beam	demolition laborer	$28.90	.080	$2.31 lf
remove fireplace mantel	demolition laborer	$28.90	.094	$2.72 lf
remove coffered ceiling	demolition laborer	$28.90	.047	$1.36 sf
remove niche	demolition laborer	$28.90	.317	$9.16 ea
remove gingerbread running trim	demolition laborer	$28.90	.038	$1.10 lf
remove gingerbread bracket	demolition laborer	$28.90	.154	$4.45 ea
remove gingerbread corbel	demolition laborer	$28.90	.160	$4.62 ea
remove gingerbread door or window header	demolition laborer	$28.90	.037	$1.07 lf
remove gingerbread post drop	demolition laborer	$28.90	.154	$4.45 ea
remove gingerbread spandrel	demolition laborer	$28.90	.038	$1.10 lf
remove gingerbread window cornice	demolition laborer	$28.90	.041	$1.18 lf
remove gingerbread gable ornament	demolition laborer	$28.90	.254	$7.34 lf
remove gingerbread gable finial	demolition laborer	$28.90	.239	$6.91 ea
remove porch post	demolition laborer	$28.90	.127	$3.67 lf
remove onlay	demolition laborer	$28.90	.062	$1.79 ea
remove finish trim board	demolition laborer	$28.90	.026	$.75 lf
remove finish plywood	demolition laborer	$28.90	.022	$.64 sf
Finish carpentry crew				
finish carpentry	finish carpenter	$43.50		
finish carpentry	finish carpenter's helper	$32.10		
finish carpentry	finish crew	$37.80		
Install molding				
base, chair rail	finish carpenter	$43.50	.038	$1.65 lf
window or door casing or panel moldings	finish carpenter	$43.50	.041	$1.78 lf
crown	finish carpenter	$43.50	.046	$2.00 lf
Install casing on curved window or door				
half-round top window or door per lf	finish carpenter	$43.50	.144	$6.26 lf
elliptical top window or door per lf	finish carpenter	$43.50	.144	$6.26 lf
round window per lf of diameter	finish carpenter	$43.50	.294	$12.80 lf
Install wood key in curved molding				
install	finish carpenter	$43.50	.251	$10.90 ea
Install base, corner, or head block				
install	finish carpenter	$43.50	.063	$2.74 ea
Install overdoor molding				
install	finish carpenter	$43.50	.041	$1.78 lf
Install door architrave				
interior	finish carpenter	$43.50	.062	$2.70 lf
exterior	finish carpenter	$43.50	.080	$3.48 lf
Install exterior door surround				
economy grade	finish carpenter	$43.50	.234	$10.20 lf
custom deluxe grade	finish carpenter	$43.50	.431	$18.70 lf

. . . More ➤

Finish Carpentry Labor Productivity *continued*

WORK DESCRIPTION	LABORER	COST PER HOUR	PRODUCTIVITY	UNIT PRICE
Install exterior window surround				
economy grade	finish carpenter	$43.50	.207	$9.00 lf
custom deluxe grade	finish carpenter	$43.50	.322	$14.00 lf
Install window trim				
stool	finish carpenter	$43.50	.058	$2.52 lf
apron	finish carpenter	$43.50	.049	$2.13 lf
Install corner bead				
wood	finish carpenter	$43.50	.077	$3.35 lf
plastic	finish carpenter	$43.50	.032	$1.39 lf
Install hand rail				
install	finish carpenter	$43.50	.098	$4.26 lf
Install panel molding inside corner radius				
install	finish carpenter	$43.50	.149	$6.48 ea
Install closet shelf brackets, shelving, & rod				
install	finish carpenter	$43.50	.332	$14.40 lf
Install closet organizer system				
standard grade	finish carpenter	$43.50	.304	$13.20 sf
deluxe grade	finish carpenter	$43.50	.526	$22.90 sf
Install linen closet shelves				
typical	finish carpenter	$43.50	.673	$29.30 lf
with pull-out shelves	finish carpenter	$43.50	.695	$30.20 lf
Install closet rod				
install	finish carpenter	$43.50	.080	$3.48 lf
Install closet lining				
tongue-&-groove cedar board	finish carpenter	$43.50	.051	$2.22 sf
1/4" cedar veneer plywood	finish carpenter	$43.50	.037	$1.61 sf
Install built-in bookcase				
8" deep	finish carpenter	$43.50	.269	$11.70 sf
12" deep	finish carpenter	$43.50	.304	$13.20 sf
18" deep	finish carpenter	$43.50	.317	$13.80 sf
24" deep	finish carpenter	$43.50	.332	$14.40 sf
Install fireplace mantel beam				
install	finish carpenter	$43.50	.539	$23.40 lf
Install fireplace mantel				
install	finish carpenter	$43.50	.653	$28.40 lf
Install coffered ceiling				
economy grade	finish carpenter	$43.50	.248	$10.80 sf
custom deluxe grade	finish carpenter	$43.50	.567	$24.70 sf
Install niche				
with casing and shelf bracket	finish carpenter	$43.50	1.31	$57.00 ea
Install gingerbread				
running trim	finish carpenter	$43.50	.160	$6.96 lf
post bracket	finish carpenter	$43.50	.348	$15.10 ea
corbel	finish carpenter	$43.50	.359	$15.60 ea
door or window header	finish carpenter	$43.50	.232	$10.10 lf
post drop	finish carpenter	$43.50	.322	$14.00 ea
spandrel	finish carpenter	$43.50	.237	$10.30 lf
window cornice	finish carpenter	$43.50	.242	$10.50 lf
gable ornament	finish carpenter	$43.50	.582	$25.30 ea
gable finial	finish carpenter	$43.50	.560	$24.40 ea
Install porch post				
install	finish carpenter	$43.50	.135	$5.87 lf
Install carved wood onlay				
install	finish carpenter	$43.50	.519	$22.60 ea
Install finish board trim				
install	finish carpenter	$43.50	.049	$2.13 lf
Install 1/4" hardwood plywood				
install	finish carpenter	$43.50	.028	$1.22 sf

18 .... *Fireplaces*

Item Description	Unit	Remove	Replace	Total
Fireplace, 30" wide by 16" deep by 29" high, open front	ea	$111.00	$1,197.00	$1,308.00
Replace Materials.....424.00 Labor..........773.00				
Remove Labor..........111.00				
Fireplace, 36" wide by 16" deep by 29" high, open front	ea	$111.00	$1,320.00	$1,431.00
Replace Materials....509.00 Labor 811.00				
Remove Labor..........111.00				
Fireplace, 40" wide by 16" deep by 29" high, open front	ea	$111.00	$1,406.00	$1,517.00
Replace Materials....566.00 Labor 840.00				
Remove Labor..........111.00				
Fireplace, 48" wide by 18" deep by 32" high, open front	ea	$111.00	$1,567.00	$1,678.00
Replace Materials ....679.00 Labor 888.00				
Remove Labor..........111.00				
Fireplace, 32" wide by 16" deep by 26" high, open front & one side	ea	$111.00	$1,200.00	$1,311.00
Replace Materials ....398.00 Labor 802.00				
Remove Labor..........111.00				
Fireplace, 40" wide by 16" deep by 29" high, open front & one side	ea	$111.00	$1,395.00	$1,506.00
Replace Materials ....555.00 Labor 840.00				
Remove Labor..........111.00				
Fireplace, 48" wide by 20" deep by 29" high, open front & one side	ea	$111.00	$1,570.00	$1,681.00
Replace Materials ....663.00 Labor..........907.00				
Remove Labor..........111.00				
Fireplace, 32" wide by 28" deep by 29" high, open two faces	ea	$111.00	$1,277.00	$1,388.00
Replace Materials ....389.00 Labor 888.00				
Remove Labor..........111.00				
Fireplace, 36" wide by 28" deep by 29" high, open two faces	ea	$111.00	$1,345.00	$1,456.00
Replace Materials ....438.00 Labor..........907.00				
Remove Labor..........111.00				
Fireplace, 40" wide by 28" deep by 29" high, open two faces	ea	$111.00	$1,409.00	$1,520.00
Replace Materials ....487.00 Labor 922.00				
Remove Labor..........111.00				
Fireplace, 36" wide by 32" deep by 27" high, open three sides	ea	$111.00	$1,399.00	$1,510.00
Replace Materials ....477.00 Labor 922.00				
Remove Labor..........111.00				
Fireplace, 36" wide by 36" deep by 27" high, open three sides	ea	$111.00	$1,497.00	$1,608.00
Replace Materials ....537.00 Labor..........960.00				
Remove Labor..........111.00				
Fireplace, 44" wide by 40" deep by 27" high, open three sides	ea	$111.00	$1,693.00	$1,804.00
Replace Materials.....714.00 Labor..........979.00				
Remove Labor..........111.00				
Prefab. fireplace, 30" wide by 16" deep by 29" high, open front	ea	$70.50	$698.00	$768.50
Replace Materials....480.00 Labor 218.00				
Remove Labor..........70.50				

◄ **FIREPLACE**
Includes concrete reinforced hearth, ash drop, fire brick, damper, throat, smoke shelf and smoke chamber. Does not include foundation, flue or chimney, face, or finish hearth.

◁ **open front**

◁ **open front and side**

RELATED ITEMS

Cleaning
fireplaces.........................62
masonry..........................63
Finish Carpentry
mantel beam, mantel.....224
Masonry........................287
Painting.........................339
Rough Carpentry
chimney cricket 444

◁ **open both faces "see through"**

◁ **open two faces and side**

◄ **PREFABRICATED FIREPLACE**
◁ **open front**

continued on next page

Item Description	Unit	Remove	Replace	Total
PREFABRICATED ▶ FIREPLACE *continued* **Prefab. convection fireplace, 30″ wide by 16″ deep by 29″ high, open front**	ea	$70.50	$781.00	$851.50
Replace Materials ....553.00 Labor ....228.00 *Remove* .... Labor...........70.50				
Zero clearance box. Does not include flue. Actual sizes and style available vary from manufacturer to manufacturer. Choose the size and style that most closely matches. **Prefab. forced-air fireplace, 30″ wide by 16″ deep by 29″ high, open front**	ea	$70.50	$852.00	$922.50
Replace Materials....600.00 Labor...........252.00 *Remove* .... Labor...........70.50				
Prefab. fireplace, 36″ wide by 16″ deep by 29″ high, open front	ea	$70.50	$799.00	$869.50
Replace Materials ....581.00 Labor ....218.00 *Remove* .... Labor...........70.50				
Prefab. convection fireplace, 36″ wide by 16″ deep by 29″ high, open front	ea	$70.50	$898.00	$968.50
Replace Materials.....670.00 Labor ....228.00 *Remove* .... Labor...........70.50				
Prefab. forced-air fireplace, 36″ wide by 16″ deep by 29″ high, open front	ea	$70.50	$979.00	$1,049.50
Replace Materials ....727.00 Labor...........252.00 *Remove* .... Labor...........70.50				
Prefab. fireplace, 40″ wide by 16″ deep by 29″ high, open front	ea	$70.50	$1,179.00	$1,249.50
Replace Materials.....961.00 Labor ....218.00 *Remove* .... Labor...........70.50				
Prefab. convection fireplace, 40″ wide by 16″ deep by 29″ high, open front	ea	$70.50	$972.00	$1,042.50
Replace Materials ....744.00 Labor ....228.00 *Remove* .... Labor...........70.50				
Prefab. forced-air fireplace, 40″ wide by 16″ deep by 29″ high, open front	ea	$70.50	$1,060.00	$1,130.50
Replace Materials....808.00 Labor...........252.00 *Remove* .... Labor...........70.50				
Prefab. fireplace, 48″ wide by 18″ deep by 32″ high, open front	ea	$70.50	$1,368.00	$1,438.50
Replace Materials ....1150.00 Labor ....218.00 *Remove* .... Labor...........70.50				
Prefab. convection fireplace, 48″ wide by 18″ deep by 32″ high, open front	ea	$70.50	$1,121.00	$1,191.50
Replace Materials ....893.00 Labor ....228.00 *Remove* .... Labor...........70.50				
Prefab. forced-air fireplace, 48″ wide by 18″ deep by 32″ high, open front	ea	$70.50	$1,222.00	$1,292.50
Replace Materials ....970.00 Labor...........252.00 *Remove* .... Labor...........70.50				
open front and side ▷ **Prefab. fireplace, 32″ wide by 16″ deep by 26″ high, open front & side**	ea	$70.50	$1,023.00	$1,093.50
Replace Materials....805.00 Labor ....218.00 *Remove* .... Labor...........70.50				
Prefab. fireplace, 40″ wide by 16″ deep by 29″ high, open front & side	ea	$70.50	$1,193.00	$1,263.50
Replace Materials ....965.00 Labor ....228.00 *Remove* .... Labor...........70.50				
Prefab. fireplace, 48″ wide by 20″ deep by 29″ high, open front & side	ea	$70.50	$1,412.00	$1,482.50
Replace Materials ...1160.00 Labor...........252.00 *Remove* .... Labor...........70.50				
open both faces ▷ *"see through"* **Prefab. fireplace, 32″ wide by 28″ deep by 29″ high, open two faces**	ea	$70.50	$1,201.00	$1,271.50
Replace Materials ....983.00 Labor ....218.00 *Remove* .... Labor...........70.50				

Item Description	Unit	Remove	Replace	Total
Prefab. fireplace, 36" wide by 28" deep by 29" high, open two faces *Replace* Materials...1180.00 Labor ....228.00 *Remove* .... Labor...........70.50	ea	$70.50	$1,408.00	$1,478.50
Prefab. fireplace, 40" wide by 28" deep by 29" high, open two faces *Replace* Materials...1420.00 Labor...252.00 *Remove* .... Labor...........70.50	ea	$70.50	$1,672.00	$1,742.50
Prefab. fireplace, 36" wide by 32" deep by 27" high, open three sides *Replace* Materials ...1160.00 Labor.........218.00 *Remove* .... Labor...........70.50	ea	$70.50	$1,378.00	$1,448.50
Prefab. fireplace, 36" wide by 36" deep by 27" high, open three sides *Replace* Materials...1390.00 Labor ....228.00 *Remove* .... Labor...........70.50	ea	$70.50	$1,618.00	$1,688.50
Prefab. fireplace, 44" wide by 40" deep by 27" high, open three sides *Replace* Materials...1670.00 Labor.........252.00 *Remove* .... Labor...........70.50	ea	$70.50	$1,922.00	$1,992.50
Fireplace form, 30" wide by 16" deep by 29" high, open front *Replace* Materials ....553.00 Labor ....145.00 *Remove* .... Labor 80.30	ea	$80.30	$698.00	$778.30
Fireplace form, 36" wide by 16" deep by 29" high, open front *Replace* Materials ....664.00 Labor ....145.00 *Remove* .... Labor 80.30	ea	$80.30	$809.00	$889.30
Fireplace form, 40" wide by 16" deep by 29" high, open front *Replace* Materials ....738.00 Labor ....145.00 *Remove* .... Labor 80.30	ea	$80.30	$883.00	$963.30
Fireplace form, 48" wide by 18" deep by 32" high, open front *Replace* Materials .....910.00 Labor ....145.00 *Remove* .... Labor 80.30	ea	$80.30	$1,055.00	$1,135.30
Fireplace form, 32" wide by 16" deep by 26" high, open front & side *Replace* Materials ..1025.00 Labor ....145.00 *Remove* .... Labor 80.30	ea	$80.30	$1,170.00	$1,250.30
Fireplace form, 40" wide by 16" deep by 29" high, open front & side *Replace* Materials...1230.00 Labor ....145.00 *Remove* .... Labor 80.30	ea	$80.30	$1,375.00	$1,455.30
Fireplace form, 48" wide by 20" deep by 29" high, open front & side *Replace* Materials ..2240.00 Labor ....145.00 *Remove* .... Labor 80.30	ea	$80.30	$2,385.00	$2,465.30
Fireplace form, 32" wide by 28" deep by 29" high, open two faces *Replace* Materials...1240.00 Labor ....145.00 *Remove* .... Labor 80.30	ea	$80.30	$1,385.00	$1,465.30
Fireplace form, 36" wide by 28" deep by 29" high, open two faces *Replace* Materials ..1400.00 Labor ....145.00 *Remove* .... Labor 80.30	ea	$80.30	$1,545.00	$1,625.30
Fireplace form, 40" wide by 28" deep by 29" high, open two faces *Replace* Materials...1560.00 Labor ....145.00 *Remove* .... Labor 80.30	ea	$80.30	$1,705.00	$1,785.30

◁ **open two faces and side**

◀ **FIREPLACE FORM**
Does not include face, hearth, flue or chimney. Actual sizes and style available vary from manufacturer to manufacturer. Choose the size and style that most closely matches.

◁ **open front**

◁ **open front and side**

RELATED ITEMS

Cleaning
fireplaces..........................62
masonry............................63
Finish Carpentry
mantel beam, mantel.......224

◁ **open both faces "see through"**

RELATED ITEMS

Masonry........................287
Painting.........................339
Rough Carpentry
chimney cricket 444

	Item Description	Unit	Remove	Replace	Total
FIREPLACE ▶ FORM *continued*	**Fireplace form, 36" wide by 32" deep by 27" high, open three sides**	ea	$80.30	$1,675.00	$1,755.30
	Replace Materials...1530.00 Labor 145.00				
	Remove .... Labor 80.30				
open two faces and side ▷	**Fireplace form, 36" wide by 36" deep by 27" high, open three sides**	ea	$80.30	$1,875.00	$1,955.30
	Replace Materials...1730.00 Labor 145.00				
	Remove .... Labor 80.30				
	Fireplace form, 44" wide by 40" deep by 27" high, open three sides	ea	$80.30	$2,065.00	$2,145.30
	Replace Materials...1920.00 Labor 145.00				
	Remove .... Labor 80.30				
FIREPLACE ▶ FURNACE *Also called masonry heaters.*	**Fireplace furnace**	ea	$111.00	$6,740.00	$6,851.00
	Replace Materials..5080.00 Labor 1660.00				
	Remove .... Labor 111.00				
	▶ Complete fireplace furnace including two air ducts with automatic dampers, outside air supply, heat exchanger, supply and outlet ducts connected to furnace ducts.				
FIRE BRICK ▶ *Installation of fire brick with fire clay only, no surrounding masonry.*	**Fire brick (complete fireplace)**	ea	$27.50	$280.00	$307.50
	Replace Materials.....135.00 Labor 145.00				
	Remove .... Labor.........27.50				
	Concrete simulated fire brick (complete fireplace)	ea	$15.30	$190.40	$205.70
	Replace Materials.....101.60 Labor 88.80				
	Remove .... Labor...........15.30				
	▶ Three-piece unit stamped and colored to look like fire brick.				
FIREPLACE ▶ CHIMNEY *All brick types. Add 14% for rubble or ashlar stone. Does not include foundation.*	**16" by 16" fireplace chimney with one 8" x 8" flue**	lf	$10.00	$138.00	$148.00
	Replace Materials ......36.00 Labor.........102.00				
	Remove .... Labor...........10.00				
	16" by 24" fireplace chimney with two 8" x 8" flues	lf	$13.60	$189.40	$203.00
	Replace Materials ......47.40 Labor.........142.00				
	Remove .... Labor...........13.60				
	16" by 20" fireplace chimney with one 8" x 12" flue	lf	$10.00	$145.70	$155.70
	Replace Materials ......42.70 Labor.........103.00				
	Remove .... Labor...........10.00				
	20" by 24" fireplace chimney with two 8" x 12" flues	lf	$13.60	$199.70	$213.30
	Replace Materials ......54.70 Labor 145.00				
	Remove .... Labor...........13.60				
	20" by 20" fireplace chimney with one 12" x 12" flue	lf	$10.00	$149.30	$159.30
	Replace Materials ......45.30 Labor.........104.00				
	Remove .... Labor...........10.00				
	20" by 32" fireplace chimney with two 12" x 12" flues	lf	$13.60	$211.00	$224.60
	Replace Materials ......62.00 Labor 149.00				
	Remove .... Labor...........13.60				
	20" by 24" fireplace chimney with one 12" x 16" flue	lf	$10.00	$153.90	$163.90
	Replace Materials ......47.90 Labor.........106.00				
	Remove .... Labor...........10.00				
	20" by 40" fireplace chimney with two 12" x 16" flues	lf	$13.60	$231.60	$245.20
	Replace Materials ......79.60 Labor 152.00				
	Remove .... Labor...........13.60				
	24" by 24" fireplace chimney with one 16" x 16" flue	lf	$10.00	$158.40	$168.40
	Replace Materials ......50.40 Labor.........108.00				
	Remove .... Labor...........10.00				

Item Description	Unit	Remove	Replace	Total
24" by 40" fireplace chimney with two 16" x 16" flues	lf	$13.60	$244.90	$258.50
Replace Materials......89.90 Labor..........155.00				
Remove .... Labor..........13.60				
Add for bend in fireplace chimney with one flue	ea	–	$176.60	$176.60
Replace Materials......23.60 Labor..........153.00				
Add for bend in fireplace chimney with two flues	ea	–	$212.60	$212.60
Replace Materials......26.60 Labor..........186.00				
Add 14% for stone facing on chimney				
Reline chimney using grout and inflatable tube method	lf	–	$35.30	$35.30
Replace Materials........6.30 Labor..........29.00				
Add per bend in chimney when relining	ea	–	$166.50	$166.50
Replace Materials ......18.50 Labor..........148.00				
Minimum charge to reline chimney	ea	–	$262.00	$262.00
Replace Materials ......37.00 Labor..........225.00				
2" concrete single-flue chimney cap	ea	$8.76	$64.30	$73.06
Replace Materials ......16.30 Labor..........48.00				
Remove .... Labor..........8.76				
2" concrete double-flue chimney cap	ea	$10.50	$97.40	$107.90
Replace Materials......25.90 Labor..........71.50				
Remove .... Labor..........10.50				
Cast stone molded chimney cap, standard grade	ea	$10.50	$217.40	$227.90
Replace Materials.....156.00 Labor..........61.40				
Remove .... Labor..........10.50				
▶ With simple pattern moldings on edge.				
Cast stone molded chimney cap, high grade	ea	$10.50	$247.40	$257.90
Replace Materials ....186.00 Labor..........61.40				
Remove .... Labor..........10.50				
▶ With complex pattern moldings on edge.				
Cast stone molded chimney cap, deluxe grade	ea	$10.50	$307.40	$317.90
Replace Materials ....246.00 Labor..........61.40				
Remove .... Labor..........10.50				
▶ With very complex moldings on edge or with curved elements.				
Galvanized steel chimney cap	ea	$5.12	$137.10	$142.22
Replace Materials.....124.00 Labor..........13.10				
Remove .... Labor..........5.12				
▶ For use on metal or masonry flues, with spark arrestor.				
Remove steel chimney cap for work, then reinstall	ea	–	$21.90	$21.90
Replace .... Labor..........21.90				
Chimney pot, standard grade	ea	$13.60	$257.60	$271.20
Replace Materials ....201.00 Labor..........56.60				
Remove .... Labor..........13.60				
▶ No designs on pot or arched design over flue.				
Chimney pot, high grade	ea	$13.60	$351.60	$365.20
Replace Materials ....295.00 Labor..........56.60				
Remove .... Labor..........13.60				
▶ Simple designs on pot.				

◁ add for chimney bend

◁ add for stone face

◀ **RELINE CHIMNEY**
With a technique designed and licensed by Ahrens Chimney Technique.

◀ **CONCRETE CHIMNEY CAP**

◀ **CAST STONE CHIMNEY CAP**
Manufactured cast stone cap with decorative patterns.

◀ **STEEL CHIMNEY CAP**

◀ **CHIMNEY POT**

△ standard

	Item Description	Unit	Remove	Replace	Total
CHIMNEY POT ▶ *continued*	**Chimney pot, deluxe grade**	ea	$13.60	$424.60	$438.20
	Replace Materials ....368.00 Labor 56.60				
	Remove .... Labor 13.60				
	▶ Ornate designs on pot and ornate pattern around top edge.				
△ **high**	**Chimney pot, custom grade**	ea	$13.60	$510.60	$524.20
	Replace Materials ....454.00 Labor 56.60				
	Remove .... Labor 13.60				
	▶ Ornate designs on pot and ornate pattern around top edge with molded bands around pot.				
custom deluxe ▽	**Chimney pot, custom deluxe grade**	ea	$13.60	$634.60	$648.20
	Replace Materials ....578.00 Labor 56.60				
	Remove .... Labor 13.60				
	▶ Ornate designs on pot and ornate pattern around top edge with molded bands around pot. Octagonal or other specialty shape.				
	Remove chimney pot for work, then reinstall	ea	–	$97.90	$97.90
	Replace .... Labor 97.90				
CHIMNEY SCREEN ▶	**Chimney bird screen for single flue chimney**	ea	–	$67.20	$67.20
	Replace Materials ......48.00 Labor 19.20				
	Chimney bird screen for double flue chimney	ea	–	$79.90	$79.90
	Replace Materials ......59.00 Labor 20.90				
FIREPLACE GRATE ▶	**Fireplace grate, 22" x 16"**	ea	$.87	$54.24	$55.11
	Replace Materials ......49.00 Labor 5.24				
	Remove .... Labor .... .87				
	Fireplace grate, 28" x 16"	ea	$.87	$68.24	$69.11
	Replace Materials ......63.00 Labor 5.24				
	Remove .... Labor .... .87				
	Fireplace grate, 32" x 16"	ea	$.87	$76.24	$77.11
	Replace Materials ......71.00 Labor 5.24				
	Remove .... Labor .... .87				
	Fireplace grate, 38" x 16"	ea	$.87	$86.24	$87.11
	Replace Materials ......81.00 Labor 5.24				
	Remove .... Labor .... .87				
	Fireplace grate, 38" x 20"	ea	$.87	$91.24	$92.11
	Replace Materials ......86.00 Labor 5.24				
	Remove .... Labor .... .87				
	Fireplace grate, 32" x 28"	ea	$.87	$98.24	$99.11
	Replace Materials ......93.00 Labor 5.24				
	Remove .... Labor .... .87				
	Fireplace grate, 36" x 28"	ea	$.87	$105.24	$106.11
	Replace Materials ....100.00 Labor 5.24				
	Remove .... Labor .... .87				
	Fireplace grate, 40" x 28"	ea	$.87	$109.24	$110.11
	Replace Materials ....104.00 Labor 5.24				
	Remove .... Labor .... .87				
	Fireplace grate, 36" x 32"	ea	$.87	$113.24	$114.11
	Replace Materials ....108.00 Labor 5.24				
	Remove .... Labor .... .87				

Item Description	Unit	Remove	Replace	Total	
Fireplace grate, 36" x 36"	ea	$.87	$127.24	$128.11	
Replace Materials ....122.00 Labor 5.24					
Remove .... Labor 87					
Fireplace grate, 44" x 40"	ea	$.87	$170.24	$171.11	
Replace Materials.....165.00 Labor 5.24					
Remove .... Labor 87					
Remove fireplace grate for work, then reinstall	ea	–	$6.47	$6.47	
Replace .... Labor 6.47					
Fireplace screen, standard grade	ea	$5.35	$142.90	$148.25	
Replace Materials ....108.00 Labor 34.90					
Remove .... Labor 5.35					
► Plain black with no trim.					
Fireplace screen, high grade	ea	$5.35	$200.90	$206.25	
Replace Materials.....166.00 Labor 34.90					
Remove .... Labor 5.35					
► Plain black with brass or similar trim at top.					
Fireplace screen, deluxe grade	ea	$5.35	$260.90	$266.25	
Replace Materials ....226.00 Labor 34.90					
Remove .... Labor 5.35					
► Brass screen with brass or similar trim at top.					
Remove fireplace screen for work, then reinstall	ea	–	$52.40	$52.40	
Replace .... Labor...........52.40					
Fireplace door, standard grade	ea	$7.31	$229.00	$236.31	
Replace Materials.....185.00 Labor 44.00					
Remove .... Labor 7.31					
► Plain black.					
Fireplace door, high grade	ea	$7.31	$326.00	$333.31	
Replace Materials ....282.00 Labor 44.00					
Remove .... Labor 7.31					
► Brass face.					
Fireplace door, deluxe grade	ea	$7.31	$409.00	$416.31	
Replace Materials ....365.00 Labor 44.00					
Remove .... Labor 7.31					
► Brass face with designs.					
Fireplace door, custom grade	ea	$7.31	$529.00	$536.31	
Replace Materials ....485.00 Labor 44.00					
Remove .... Labor 7.31					
► Brass face with designs and specialty "clear view" glass.					
Remove fireplace door for work, then reinstall	ea	–	$68.60	$68.60	
Replace .... Labor 68.60					
8" x 8" fireplace clean-out door	ea	$1.99	$50.00	$51.99	
Replace Materials ......20.00 Labor 30.00					
Remove .... Labor 1.99					
12" x 12" fireplace clean-out door	ea	$1.99	$73.00	$74.99	
Replace Materials ......43.00 Labor 30.00					
Remove .... Labor 1.99					

RELATED ITEMS

Cleaning
fireplaces........................62
masonry..........................63
Finish Carpentry
mantel beam, mantel 224
Masonry......................287
Painting......................339
Rough Carpentry
chimney cricket 444

◄ **FIREPLACE SCREEN**

◄ **FIREPLACE DOOR**

◄ **FIREPLACE CLEAN-OUT DOOR**
Cast iron door and jamb.

	Item Description	Unit	Remove	Replace	Total
FIREPLACE ▶ **CLEAN-OUT DOOR** *continued*	**18" x 24" fireplace clean-out door** *Replace* Materials.....128.00 Labor ....30.00 *Remove* .... Labor 1.99	ea	$1.99	$158.00	$159.99
	Salvage fireplace clean-out door, then reinstall *Replace* .... Labor 46.60	ea	–	$46.60	$46.60
DAMPER ▶	**Rotary control damper for 30" wide fireplace** *Replace* Materials......86.00 Labor 53.30	ea	–	$139.30	$139.30
	Rotary control damper for 36" wide fireplace *Replace* Materials......93.00 Labor 53.30	ea	–	$146.30	$146.30
	Rotary control for 40" wide fireplace *Replace* Materials .....114.00 Labor 53.30	ea	–	$167.30	$167.30
	Rotary control damper for 48" wide fireplace *Replace* Materials.....135.00 Labor 53.30	ea	–	$188.30	$188.30
	Poker control damper for 30" wide fireplace *Replace* Materials ......67.00 Labor 43.20	ea	–	$110.20	$110.20
	Poker control damper for 36" wide fireplace *Replace* Materials ......73.00 Labor 43.20	ea	–	$116.20	$116.20
	Poker control damper for 40" wide fireplace *Replace* Materials ......89.00 Labor 43.20	ea	–	$132.20	$132.20
	Poker control damper for 48" wide fireplace *Replace* Materials ....105.00 Labor 43.20	ea	–	$148.20	$148.20
DOUBLE WALL ▶ **CHIMNEY PIPE** *stainless steel*	**8" diameter double wall chimney pipe** *Replace* Materials ......29.00 Labor ....25.40 *Remove* .... Labor............ .61	lf	$.61	$54.40	$55.01
	10" diameter double wall chimney pipe *Replace* Materials ......42.00 Labor ....25.40 *Remove* .... Labor............ .61	lf	$.61	$67.40	$68.01
	12" diameter double wall chimney pipe *Replace* Materials ......55.00 Labor ....25.40 *Remove* .... Labor............ .61	lf	$.61	$80.40	$81.01
	14" diameter double wall chimney pipe *Replace* Materials ......68.00 Labor ....25.40 *Remove* .... Labor............ .61	lf	$.61	$93.40	$94.01
TRIPLE WALL ▶ **CHIMNEY PIPE** *stainless steel*	**8" diameter triple wall chimney pipe** *Replace* Materials ......37.00 Labor ....25.40 *Remove* .... Labor............ .61	lf	$.61	$62.40	$63.01
	10" diameter triple wall chimney pipe *Replace* Materials ......53.00 Labor ....25.40 *Remove* .... Labor............ .61	lf	$.61	$78.40	$79.01
	12" diameter triple wall chimney pipe *Replace* Materials ......70.00 Labor ....25.40 *Remove* .... Labor............ .61	lf	$.61	$95.40	$96.01

Item Description	Unit	Remove	Replace	Total	
14" diameter triple wall chimney pipe	lf	$.61	$112.40	$113.01	
Replace Materials ......87.00 Labor 25.40					
Remove .... Labor............ .61					
Add for chimney pipe through interior ceiling	ea	–	$99.80	$99.80	◀ **ADDITIONAL CHIMNEY PIPE COSTS**
Replace Materials ......51.00 Labor 48.80					
▶ Kit to run chimney pipe through interior drywall or plaster ceiling. Includes bracket that allows for 2" clearance.					
Add for chimney pipe through roof	ea	–	$269.00	$269.00	
Replace Materials ....140.00 Labor 129.00					
▶ Kit to run chimney pipe through roof. Includes bracket, boots, and so forth.					
Remove chimney pipe for work, then reinstall	lf	–	$38.90	$38.90	
Replace .... Labor 38.90					
Gas log lighter	ea	$6.56	$147.90	$154.46	◀ **GAS LOG LIGHTER**
Replace Materials ......96.00 Labor............51.90					
Remove .... Labor 6.56					
▶ Log lighter, valve, key and up to 24 lf copper gas piping.					
Remove gas log lighter for work, then reinstall	ea	–	$86.20	$86.20	
Replace .... Labor 86.20					
Gas fireplace kit	ea	$7.25	$639.00	$646.25	◀ **GAS FIREPLACE**
Replace Materials ....584.00 Labor............55.00					
Remove .... Labor 7.25					
▶ Burners, fake logs, valve, key and up to 24 lf copper gas piping.					
Remove gas fireplace kit for work, then reinstall	ea	–	$93.70	$93.70	
Replace .... Labor 93.70					
Marble fireplace face, economy grade	ea	$48.00	$268.00	$316.00	◀ **MARBLE FIREPLACE FACE**
Replace Materials ......97.00 Labor 171.00					
Remove .... Labor 48.00					
▶ Marble tiles laid around inside of mantel.					
Marble fireplace face, standard grade	ea	$87.60	$661.00	$748.60	
Replace Materials ....295.00 Labor 366.00					
Remove .... Labor 87.60					
▶ From single or large pieces up to 5' tall and 4' wide, polished or natural finish.					
Marble fireplace face, high grade	ea	$87.60	$855.00	$942.60	
Replace Materials ....480.00 Labor 375.00					
Remove .... Labor 87.60					
▶ From single pieces or large pieces up to 5' tall and 4' wide, polished or natural finish with simple designs around opening and at corner (cove or similar). Or same as standard grade up to 8' tall and 6' wide.					
Marble fireplace face, deluxe grade	ea	$87.60	$1,099.00	$1,186.60	
Replace Materials ....715.00 Labor 384.00					
Remove .... Labor 87.60					
▶ From single pieces or large pieces up to 5' tall and 4' wide, polished or natural finish with ornate designs around opening and at corner (crown or similar). Or same as high grade up to 8' tall and 6' wide.					
Brick fireplace face, economy grade	ea	$93.30	$1,045.00	$1,138.30	◀ **BRICK FIREPLACE FACE**
Replace Materials ....272.00 Labor 773.00					
Remove .... Labor 93.30					
▶ Brick face in stacked or running bond, up to 5' tall and 5' wide.					

RELATED ITEMS

Cleaning
fireplaces 62
masonry...........................63
Finish Carpentry
mantel beam, mantel........224
Masonry..........................287
Painting...........................339
Rough Carpentry
chimney cricket 444

Item Description	Unit	Remove	Replace	Total
BRICK ▶ **FIREPLACE FACE** *continued* **Brick fireplace face, standard grade** *Replace* Materials....302.00 Labor.........979.00 *Remove* .... Labor ....93.30 ▶ Brick face in specialty bond (see *Masonry,* page 297), up to 5' tall and 5' wide. May include built-in shelf brackets, or small patterns in face. Or same as economy up to 8' tall and 6' wide.	ea	$93.30	$1,281.00	$1,374.30
Brick fireplace face, high grade *Replace* Materials....366.00 Labor.......1200.00 *Remove* .... Labor ....93.30 ▶ Brick face in specialty bond (see *Masonry,* page 297), up to 5' tall and 5' wide. With arch over opening. May include built-in shelf brackets, or small patterns in face. Or same as standard up to 8' tall and 6' wide. Or same as economy up to 11' tall and 7' wide.	ea	$93.30	$1,566.00	$1,659.30
Brick fireplace face, deluxe grade *Replace* Materials....444.00 Labor.......1550.00 *Remove* .... Labor ....93.30 ▶ Brick face in specialty bond like herringbone or basket weave mixed with other patterns (see *Masonry,* page 297), up to 5' tall and 5' wide. May have arched openings or curving sides. Or same as high up to 8' tall and 6' wide. Or same as standard up to 11' tall and 7' wide. Or same as economy up to 15' tall and 10' wide.	ea	$93.30	$1,994.00	$2,087.30
RUBBLE STONE ▶ **FIREPLACE FACE** **Rubble stone fireplace face, economy grade** *Replace* Materials....463.00 Labor.........840.00 *Remove* .... Labor ....99.70 ▶ Up to 5' tall and 5' wide, with flagstone or equivalent stone.	ea	$99.70	$1,303.00	$1,402.70
Rubble stone fireplace face, standard grade *Replace* Materials......515.00 Labor.......1070.00 *Remove* .... Labor ....99.70 ▶ Up to 5' tall and 5' wide, with sandstone, limestone, or similar stone. Or same as economy up to 8' tall and 6' wide.	ea	$99.70	$1,585.00	$1,684.70
Rubble stone fireplace face, high grade *Replace* Materials......624.00 Labor.......1300.00 *Remove* .... Labor ....99.70 ▶ Up to 5' tall and 5' wide, with specialty high priced stones or stones with high priced finishes. Or same as standard up to 8' tall and 6' wide. Or same as economy up to 10' tall and 7' wide.	ea	$99.70	$1,924.00	$2,023.70
Rubble stone fireplace face, deluxe grade *Replace* Materials....756.00 Labor.......1660.00 *Remove* .... Labor ....99.70 ▶ Up to 5' tall and 5' wide, with specialty high priced stones or stones with high priced finishes. With arch over opening or other specialty compartments or designs. Or same as high up to 8' tall and 6' wide. Or same as standard up to 11' tall and 7' wide. Or same as economy up to 14' tall and 8' wide.	ea	$99.70	$2,416.00	$2,515.70
ASHLAR STONE ▶ **FIREPLACE FACE** **Ashlar stone fireplace face, economy grade** *Replace* Materials....539.00 Labor.........826.00 *Remove* .... Labor ....99.70 ▶ Up to 5' tall and 5' wide, with lowest priced stone for your area.	ea	$99.70	$1,365.00	$1,464.70
Ashlar stone fireplace face, standard grade *Replace* Materials ....599.00 Labor.......1040.00 *Remove* .... Labor ....99.70 ▶ Up to 5' tall and 5' wide, with sandstone, limestone, or similar stone. Or same as economy up to 8' tall and 6' wide	ea	$99.70	$1,639.00	$1,738.70

Item Description	Unit	Remove	Replace	Total
Ashlar stone fireplace face, high grade	ea	$99.70	$1,986.00	$2,085.70
Replace Materials ....726.00 Labor.......1260.00				
Remove .... Labor..........99.70				
▶ Up to 5' tall and 5' wide, with specialty high priced stones or stones with high priced finishes. Or same as standard up to 8' tall and 6' wide. Or same as economy up to 10' tall and 7' wide.				
Ashlar stone fireplace face, deluxe grade	ea	$99.70	$2,480.00	$2,579.70
Replace Materials....880.00 Labor.......1600.00				
Remove .... Labor..........99.70				
▶ Up to 5' tall and 5' wide, with specialty high priced stones or stones with high priced finishes. With arch over opening or other specialty compartments or designs. Or same as high up to 8' tall and 6' wide. Or same as standard up to 11' tall and 7' wide. Or same as economy up to 14' tall and 8' wide.				
Tile fireplace face, economy grade	ea	$52.60	$254.00	$306.60
Replace Materials ......76.00 Labor 178.00				
Remove .... Labor..........52.60				
▶ Standard priced tiles laid around inside of mantel.				
Tile fireplace face, standard grade	ea	$85.00	$536.00	$621.00
Replace Materials.....155.00 Labor..........381.00				
Remove .... Labor..........85.00				
▶ High priced tiles laid around inside of mantel.				
Tile fireplace face, high grade	ea	$85.00	$589.00	$674.00
Replace Materials....202.00 Labor..........387.00				
Remove .... Labor..........85.00				
▶ Specialty antique tiles laid around inside of mantel. Including designer hand-painted designs and raised pattern designs. May include tiles in fireback.				
Tile fireplace face, deluxe grade	ea	$85.00	$828.00	$913.00
Replace Materials....432.00 Labor..........396.00				
Remove .... Labor..........85.00				
▶ Same as high with specialty trim pieces and patterns that match antique Victorian styles.				
Marble fireplace hearth, economy grade	ea	$22.40	$250.00	$272.40
Replace Materials ....146.00 Labor..........104.00				
Remove .... Labor 22.40				
Marble fireplace hearth, standard grade	ea	$41.90	$453.00	$494.90
Replace Materials....232.00 Labor..........221.00				
Remove .... Labor..........41.90				
Marble fireplace hearth, high grade	ea	$41.90	$605.00	$646.90
Replace Materials ....378.00 Labor..........227.00				
Remove .... Labor 41.90				
Marble fireplace hearth, deluxe grade	ea	$41.90	$795.00	$836.90
Replace Materials....563.00 Labor..........232.00				
Remove .... Labor..........41.90				
Brick fireplace hearth, economy grade	ea	$43.90	$519.00	$562.90
Replace Materials.....181.00 Labor 338.00				
Remove .... Labor 43.90				
Brick fireplace hearth, standard grade	ea	$43.90	$626.00	$669.90
Replace Materials....201.00 Labor..........425.00				
Remove .... Labor 43.90				

RELATED ITEMS

Cleaning
fireplaces....................62
masonry......................63
Finish Carpentry
mantel beam, mantel.......224
Masonry......................287
Painting......................339
Rough Carpentry
chimney cricket...........444

◀ **TILE FIREPLACE FACE**

◀ **MARBLE HEARTH**
Economy grade is flat hearth. All other grades are raised hearths. See marble fireplace face items for more information about quality.

◀ **BRICK HEARTH**
Economy grade is flat hearth. All other grades are raised hearths. See brick fireplace face items for more information about quality.

Item Description	Unit	Remove	Replace	Total
BRICK HEARTH ▶ **Brick fireplace hearth, high grade**	ea	$43.90	$697.00	$740.90
continued *Replace* Materials ....244.00 Labor..........453.00				
Remove .... Labor..........43.90				
Brick fireplace hearth, deluxe grade	ea	$43.90	$829.00	$872.90
Replace Materials ....296.00 Labor..........533.00				
Remove .... Labor..........43.90				
RUBBLE STONE ▶ **Rubble stone fireplace hearth, economy grade**	ea	$45.10	$675.00	$720.10
HEARTH *Replace* Materials....309.00 Labor 366.00				
Economy grade is flat *Remove* .... Labor..........45.10				
hearth. All other **Rubble stone fireplace hearth, standard grade**	ea	$45.10	$806.00	$851.10
grades are raised *Replace* Materials....344.00 Labor..........462.00				
hearths. See rubble *Remove* .... Labor..........45.10				
stone fireplace face **Rubble stone fireplace hearth, high grade**	ea	$45.10	$907.00	$952.10
items for more *Replace* Materials ....417.00 Labor..........490.00				
information about *Remove* .... Labor..........45.10				
quality. **Rubble stone fireplace hearth, deluxe grade**	ea	$45.10	$1,081.00	$1,126.10
Replace Materials....505.00 Labor..........576.00				
Remove .... Labor..........45.10				
ASHLAR STONE ▶ **Ashlar stone fireplace hearth, economy grade**	ea	$45.10	$717.00	$762.10
HEARTH *Replace* Materials ....359.00 Labor..........358.00				
Economy grade is flat *Remove* .... Labor..........45.10				
hearth. All other **Ashlar stone fireplace hearth, standard grade**	ea	$45.10	$852.00	$897.10
grades are raised *Replace* Materials....399.00 Labor..........453.00				
hearths. See ashlar *Remove* .... Labor..........45.10				
stone fireplace face **Ashlar stone fireplace hearth, high grade**	ea	$45.10	$964.00	$1,009.10
items for more *Replace* Materials....484.00 Labor 480.00				
information about *Remove* .... Labor..........45.10				
quality. **Ashlar stone fireplace hearth, deluxe grade**	ea	$45.10	$1,153.00	$1,198.10
Replace Materials ....587.00 Labor 566.00				
Remove .... Labor..........45.10				
TILE HEARTH ▶ **Tile fireplace hearth economy grade**	ea	$25.30	$222.00	$247.30
Economy grade is flat *Replace* Materials .....114.00 Labor..........108.00				
hearth. All other grades *Remove* .... Labor 25.30				
are raised hearths. See **Tile fireplace hearth standard grade**	ea	$41.30	$384.00	$425.30
tile fireplace face items *Replace* Materials.....155.00 Labor 229.00				
for more information *Remove* .... Labor 41.30				
about quality. **Tile fireplace hearth high grade**	ea	$41.30	$436.00	$477.30
Replace Materials ....202.00 Labor 234.00				
Remove .... Labor 41.30				
Tile fireplace hearth deluxe grade	ea	$41.30	$672.00	$713.30
Replace Materials ....432.00 Labor..........240.00				
Remove .... Labor 41.30				

✏ NOTES: _____

_____

_____ **end**

TIME & MATERIAL CHARTS (selected items)

Fireplaces Materials (Also see material prices with the line items and other information in the **QuickFinder** column.)

DESCRIPTION	UNIT PRICE
Fireplace	
30" wide by 16" deep by 29" high, open front	$424.00 ea
32" wide by 16" deep by 26" high, open front and one side	$398.00 ea
32" wide by 28" deep by 29" high, open two sides	$389.00 ea
36" wide by 32" deep by 27" high, open two faces and one side	$477.00 ea
Prefabricated fireplace	
30" wide by 16" deep by 29" high, open front	$480.00 ea
32" wide by 16" deep by 26" high, open front and one side	$805.00 ea
32" wide by 28" deep by 29" high, open two faces ("see through")	$983.00 ea
36" wide by 32" deep by 27" high, open two faces and one side	$1,160.00 ea
Fireplace form	
30" wide by 16" deep by 29" high, open front	$553.00 ea
32" wide by 16" deep by 26" high, open front and one side	$1,025.00 ea
32" wide by 28" deep by 29" high, open two faces ("see through")	$1,240.00 ea
36" wide by 32" deep by 27" high, open two faces and one side	$1,530.00 ea
Fireplace chimney	
16" by 16" with one 8" x 8" flue	$36.00 lf
16" by 24" with two 8" x 8" flues	$47.40 lf
20" by 32" with two 12" x 12" flues	$62.00 lf
20" by 40" with two 12" x 16" flues	$79.60 lf
24" by 40" with two 16" x 16" flues	$89.90 lf
Fireplace face	
marble	
economy grade	$97.00 ea
deluxe grade	$715.00 ea
brick	
economy grade	$272.00 ea
deluxe grade	$444.00 ea
rubble stone	
economy grade	$463.00 ea
deluxe grade	$756.00 ea
ashlar stone	
economy grade	$539.00 ea
deluxe grade	$880.00 ea
tile	
economy grade	$76.00 ea
deluxe grade	$432.00 ea
Fireplace hearth	
marble	
economy grade	$146.00 ea
deluxe grade	$563.00 ea
brick	
economy grade	$181.00 ea
deluxe grade	$296.00 ea
rubble stone	
economy grade	$309.00 ea
deluxe grade	$505.00 ea
ashlar stone	
economy grade	$359.00 ea
deluxe grade	$587.00 ea
tile	
economy grade	$114.00 ea
deluxe grade	$432.00 ea

Fireplaces Labor

LABORER	BASE WAGE	PAID LEAVE	TRUE WAGE	FICA	FUTA	WORKER'S COMP.	UNEMPLOY. INSUR.	HEALTH INSUR.	RETIRE (401K)	LIABILITY INSUR.	COST PER HOUR
Mason	$25.10	1.96	$27.06	2.07	.22	8.46	2.35	2.92	.81	4.06	$48.00
Mason's helper	$22.90	1.79	$24.69	1.89	.20	7.72	2.15	2.92	.74	3.70	$44.00
Demolition laborer	$14.40	1.12	$15.52	1.19	.12	5.01	1.35	2.92	.47	2.33	$28.90

Paid Leave is calculated based on two weeks paid vacation, one week sick leave, and seven paid holidays. Employer's matching portion of **FICA** is 7.65 percent. **FUTA** (Federal Unemployment) is .8 percent. **Worker's compensation** for the masonry (fireplaces) trade was calculated using a national average of 31.20 percent. **Unemployment insurance** was calculated using a national average of 8.7 percent. **Health insurance** was calculated based on a projected national average for 2005 of $580 per employee (and family when applicable) per month. Employer pays 80 percent for a per month cost of $464 per employee. **Retirement** is based on a 401(k) retirement program with employer matching of 50 percent. Employee contributions to the 401(k) plan are an average of 6 percent of the true wage. **Liability insurance** is based on a national average of 14.0 percent.

Fireplaces Labor Productivity

WORK DESCRIPTION	LABORER	COST PER HOUR	PRODUCTIVITY	UNIT PRICE
Demolition				
remove fireplace	demolition laborer	$28.90	3.85	$111.00 ea
remove prefabricated fireplace	demolition laborer	$28.90	2.44	$70.50 ea
remove fire brick	demolition laborer	$28.90	.952	$27.50 ea
remove concrete simulated firebrick	demolition laborer	$28.90	.529	$15.30 ea
remove fireplace chimney with single flue	demolition laborer	$28.90	.346	$10.00 lf
remove fireplace chimney with double flue	demolition laborer	$28.90	.472	$13.60 lf
remove 2" concrete single flue chimney cap	demolition laborer	$28.90	.303	$8.76 ea
remove 2" concrete double flue chimney cap	demolition laborer	$28.90	.362	$10.50 ea
remove galvanized steel chimney cap	demolition laborer	$28.90	.177	$5.12 ea
remove chimney pot	demolition laborer	$28.90	.469	$13.60 ea
remove fireplace grate	demolition laborer	$28.90	.030	$.87 ea
remove fireplace screen	demolition laborer	$28.90	.185	$5.35 ea
remove fireplace door	demolition laborer	$28.90	.253	$7.31 ea
remove fireplace clean-out	demolition laborer	$28.90	.069	$1.99 ea
remove chimney pipe	demolition laborer	$28.90	.021	$.61 lf
remove gas log lighter	demolition laborer	$28.90	.227	$6.56 ea
remove gas fireplace kit	demolition laborer	$28.90	.251	$7.25 ea
remove marble fireplace face	demolition laborer	$28.90	3.03	$87.60 ea
remove brick fireplace face	demolition laborer	$28.90	3.23	$93.30 ea
remove stone fireplace face	demolition laborer	$28.90	3.45	$99.70 ea
remove tile fireplace face	demolition laborer	$28.90	2.94	$85.00 ea
remove marble fireplace hearth	demolition laborer	$28.90	1.45	$41.90 ea
remove brick fireplace hearth	demolition laborer	$28.90	1.52	$43.90 ea
remove stone fireplace hearth	demolition laborer	$28.90	1.56	$45.10 ea
remove tile fireplace hearth	demolition laborer	$28.90	1.43	$41.30 ea
Fireplace crew				
build fireplace	mason	$48.00		
build fireplace	mason's helper	$44.00		
build fireplace	mason & helper	$46.00		
Build fireplace				
open front				
30" wide by 16" deep by 29" high	mason	$48.00	16.1	$773.00 ea
36" wide by 16" deep by 29" high	mason	$48.00	16.9	$811.00 ea
40" wide by 16" deep by 29" high	mason	$48.00	17.5	$840.00 ea
48" wide by 18" deep by 32" high	mason	$48.00	18.5	$888.00 ea
open front and one side				
32" wide by 16" deep by 26" high	mason	$48.00	16.7	$802.00 ea
40" wide by 16" deep by 29" high	mason	$48.00	17.5	$840.00 ea
48" wide by 20" deep by 29" high	mason	$48.00	18.9	$907.00 ea

Fireplaces Labor Productivity *continued*

WORK DESCRIPTION	LABORER	COST PER HOUR	PRODUCTIVITY	UNIT PRICE
Build fireplace *continued*				
open two faces (see through)				
32" wide by 28" deep by 29" high	mason	$48.00	18.5	$888.00 *ea*
36" wide by 28" deep by 29" high	mason	$48.00	18.9	$907.00 *ea*
40" wide by 28" deep by 29" high	mason	$48.00	19.2	$922.00 *ea*
open two faces and one side				
36" wide by 32" deep by 27" high	mason	$48.00	19.2	$922.00 *ea*
36" wide by 36" deep by 27" high	mason	$48.00	20.0	$960.00 *ea*
44" wide by 40" deep by 27" high	mason	$48.00	20.4	$979.00 *ea*
Install prefabricated fireplace				
radiant	mason	$48.00	4.55	$218.00 *ea*
convection	mason	$48.00	4.76	$228.00 *ea*
forced-air	mason	$48.00	5.26	$252.00 *ea*
Install fireplace form				
form	mason	$48.00	3.03	$145.00 *ea*
Install fireplace furnace				
typical	mason	$48.00	34.5	$1,660.00 *ea*
Install fire brick				
complete fireplace	mason	$48.00	3.03	$145.00 *ea*
concrete simulated firebrick (complete fireplace)	mason	$48.00	1.85	$88.80 *ea*
Build brick chimney				
16" by 16" with one 8" x 8" flue	mason & helper	$46.00	2.21	$102.00 *lf*
16" by 24" with two 8" x 8" flues	mason & helper	$46.00	3.09	$142.00 *lf*
16" by 20" with one 8" x 12" flue	mason & helper	$46.00	2.24	$103.00 *lf*
20" by 24" with two 8" x 12" flues	mason & helper	$46.00	3.15	$145.00 *lf*
20" by 20" with one 12" x 12" flue	mason & helper	$46.00	2.27	$104.00 *lf*
20" by 32" with two 12" x 12" flues	mason & helper	$46.00	3.24	$149.00 *lf*
20" by 24" with one 12" x 16" flue	mason & helper	$46.00	2.31	$106.00 *lf*
20" by 40" with two 12" x 16" flues	mason & helper	$46.00	3.30	$152.00 *lf*
24" by 24" with one 16" x 16" flue	mason & helper	$46.00	2.35	$108.00 *lf*
24" by 40" with two 16" x 16" flues	mason & helper	$46.00	3.36	$155.00 *lf*
add for bend in one flue	mason & helper	$46.00	3.33	$153.00 *ea*
add for bend in two flues	mason & helper	$46.00	4.05	$186.00 *ea*
Pour 2" thick concrete chimney cap				
single-flue	mason	$48.00	1.00	$48.00 *ea*
double-flue	mason	$48.00	1.49	$71.50 *ea*
Install cast stone chimney cap				
typical	mason	$48.00	1.28	$61.40 *ea*
Install galvanized steel chimney cap				
with spark arrestor	mason's helper	$44.00	.298	$13.10 *ea*
Install chimney pot				
typical	mason	$48.00	1.18	$56.60 *ea*
Install chimney bird screen				
for single flue	mason's helper	$44.00	.437	$19.20 *ea*
for double flue	mason's helper	$44.00	.476	$20.90 *ea*
Install fireplace grate				
typical	mason's helper	$44.00	.119	$5.24 *ea*
Install fireplace screen				
typical	mason's helper	$44.00	.794	$34.90 *ea*
Install fireplace door				
typical	mason's helper	$44.00	1.00	$44.00 *ea*
Install fireplace clean-out				
typical	mason	$48.00	.625	$30.00 *ea*
Install fireplace damper				
rotary control	mason	$48.00	1.11	$53.30 *ea*
poker control	mason	$48.00	.901	$43.20 *ea*

. . . More ⟩

Fireplaces Labor Productivity *continued*

WORK DESCRIPTION	LABORER	COST PER HOUR	PRODUCTIVITY	UNIT PRICE
Install chimney pipe				
typical	mason's helper	$44.00	.578	$25.40 lf
add through interior ceiling	mason's helper	$44.00	1.11	$48.80 ea
add through roof	mason's helper	$44.00	2.94	$129.00 ea
Install gas log lighter				
typical	mason's helper	$44.00	1.18	$51.90 ea
Install gas fireplace kit				
typical	mason's helper	$44.00	1.25	$55.00 ea
Install fireplace face				
marble				
economy grade	mason	$48.00	3.57	$171.00 ea
deluxe grade	mason	$48.00	8.00	$384.00 ea
brick				
economy grade	mason	$48.00	16.1	$773.00 ea
deluxe grade	mason	$48.00	32.3	$1,550.00 ea
rubble stone				
economy grade	mason	$48.00	17.5	$840.00 ea
deluxe grade	mason	$48.00	34.5	$1,660.00 ea
ashlar stone				
economy grade	mason	$48.00	17.2	$826.00 ea
deluxe grade	mason	$48.00	33.3	$1,600.00 ea
tile				
economy grade	mason	$48.00	3.70	$178.00 ea
deluxe grade	mason	$48.00	8.26	$396.00 ea
Install fireplace hearth				
marble				
economy grade	mason	$48.00	2.16	$104.00 ea
deluxe grade	mason	$48.00	4.83	$232.00 ea
brick				
economy grade	mason	$48.00	7.04	$338.00 ea
deluxe grade	mason	$48.00	11.1	$533.00 ea
rubble stone				
economy grade	mason	$48.00	7.63	$366.00 ea
deluxe grade	mason	$48.00	12.0	$576.00 ea
ashlar stone				
economy grade	mason	$48.00	7.46	$358.00 ea
deluxe grade	mason	$48.00	11.8	$566.00 ea
tile				
economy grade	mason	$48.00	2.24	$108.00 ea
deluxe grade	mason	$48.00	5.00	$240.00 ea

✐ NOTES: _____

_____

_____

_____

_____

_____

_____

_____

_____

_____ end

19 .... *Flooring*

Item Description		Unit	Remove	Replace	Total	
Carpet, economy grade		sy	$1.79	$22.60	$24.39	◄ **CARPET**
Replace Materials.......17.40	Labor 5.20					*Includes 12% waste.*
Remove	Labor 1.79					*Carpet is available in virtually every price*
Carpet, standard grade		sy	$1.79	$26.50	$28.29	*imaginable. These prices should be considered*
Replace Materials 21.30	Labor 5.20					*allowances for typical*
Remove	Labor 1.79					*grades found in residential and light*
Carpet, high grade		sy	$1.79	$33.30	$35.09	*commercial structures. Top grades include wool*
Replace Materials 28.10	Labor 5.20					*carpets, pattern carpets,*
Remove	Labor 1.79					*and 52 ounce cut pile carpets.*
Carpet, deluxe grade		sy	$1.79	$39.10	$40.89	
Replace Materials 33.90	Labor 5.20					
Remove	Labor 1.79					
Carpet, custom grade		sy	$1.79	$45.50	$47.29	
Replace Materials 40.30	Labor 5.20					
Remove	Labor 1.79					
Remove carpet for work, then re-lay		sy	–	$7.95	$7.95	◄ **REMOVE CARPET AND RE-LAY**
Replace	Labor 7.95					
Glue-down carpet, economy grade		sy	$4.48	$19.30	$23.78	◄ **GLUE-DOWN CARPET**
Replace Materials.......13.00	Labor 6.30					*Includes 12% waste.*
Remove	Labor 4.48					*These prices should be considered allowances for*
Glue-down carpet, standard grade		sy	$4.48	$21.90	$26.38	*typical grades found in residential and light*
Replace Materials.......15.60	Labor 6.30					*commercial structures.*
Remove	Labor 4.48					
Glue-down carpet, high grade		sy	$4.48	$26.80	$31.28	
Replace Materials 20.50	Labor 6.30					
Remove	Labor 4.48					
Glue-down carpet, deluxe grade		sy	$4.48	$30.70	$35.18	
Replace Materials 24.40	Labor 6.30					
Remove	Labor 4.48					
Indoor-outdoor carpet, economy grade		sy	$4.42	$15.96	$20.38	◄ **INDOOR-OUTDOOR CARPET**
Replace Materials........9.66	Labor 6.30					*Includes 12% waste.*
Remove	Labor 4.42					*These prices should be considered allowances for*
Indoor-outdoor carpet, standard grade		sy	$4.42	$20.10	$24.52	*typical grades found in residential and light com-*
Replace Materials.......13.80	Labor 6.30					*mercial structures.*
Remove	Labor 4.42					*Economy grade is plastic*
Indoor-outdoor carpet, high grade		sy	$4.42	$26.80	$31.22	*grass.*
Replace Materials 20.50	Labor 6.30					
Remove	Labor 4.42					
Indoor-outdoor carpet, deluxe grade		sy	$4.42	$37.00	$41.42	
Replace Materials 30.70	Labor 6.30					
Remove	Labor 4.42					

RELATED ITEMS

Cleaning........................62

Item Description			Unit	Remove	Replace	Total
WOOL CARPET ▶	**Wool carpet, standard grade**		sy	**$1.79**	**$31.04**	**$32.83**
Includes 12% waste. These prices should be considered allowances for typical grades found in residential and light commercial structures. Standard and high grade may be used for simulated wool Berber style carpets.	*Replace* Materials......25.80	Labor 5.24				
	Remove	Labor 1.79				
	Wool carpet, high grade		sy	**$1.79**	**$37.74**	**$39.53**
	Replace Materials......32.50	Labor 5.24				
	Remove	Labor 1.79				
	Wool carpet, deluxe grade		sy	**$1.79**	**$48.04**	**$49.83**
	Replace Materials......42.80	Labor 5.24				
	Remove	Labor 1.79				
	Wool carpet, custom grade		sy	**$1.79**	**$59.14**	**$60.93**
	Replace Materials......53.90	Labor 5.24				
	Remove	Labor 1.79				
ADD FOR STAIRS ▶	**Add per step for carpet installation on stairs**		ea	–	**$8.29**	**$8.29**
	Replace Materials........1.50	Labor 6.79				
CARPET PAD ▶	**Carpet pad, urethane rebound**		sy	**$.87**	**$5.37**	**$6.24**
	Replace Materials........4.77	Labor .... .60				
	Remove	Labor .... .87				
	Carpet pad, urethane		sy	**$.87**	**$3.78**	**$4.65**
	Replace Materials........3.18	Labor .... .60				
	Remove	Labor .... .87				
	Carpet pad, rubber waffle		sy	**$.87**	**$4.35**	**$5.22**
	Replace Materials........3.75	Labor .... .60				
	Remove	Labor .... .87				
	Carpet pad, jute		sy	**$.87**	**$3.90**	**$4.77**
	Replace Materials........3.30	Labor .... .60				
	Remove	Labor .... .87				
CARPET COVE ▶	**Add for carpet cove, economy grade**		lf	**$.64**	**$7.25**	**$7.89**
Carpet wrapped up the wall up to 8" high with metal cap. Grades refer to allowances for quality of carpet.	*Replace* Materials........2.16	Labor 5.09				
	Remove	Labor .... .64				
	Add for carpet cove, standard grade		lf	**$.64**	**$7.82**	**$8.46**
	Replace Materials........2.73	Labor 5.09				
	Remove	Labor .... .64				
	Add for carpet cove, high grade		lf	**$.64**	**$8.61**	**$9.25**
	Replace Materials........3.52	Labor 5.09				
	Remove	Labor .... .64				
	Add for carpet cove, deluxe grade		lf	**$.64**	**$9.41**	**$10.05**
	Replace Materials........4.32	Labor 5.09				
	Remove	Labor .... .64				
	Add for carpet cove, custom grade		lf	**$.64**	**$10.20**	**$10.84**
	Replace Materials........5.11	Labor 5.09				
	Remove	Labor .... .64				
	Remove carpet cove for work, then re-lay		lf	–	**$7.62**	**$7.62**
	Replace	Labor 7.62				
CARPET TILE ▶	**Carpet tile, economy grade**		sy	**$4.48**	**$32.43**	**$36.91**
Includes 12% waste. Commercial grades.	*Replace* Materials......28.40	Labor 4.03				
	Remove	Labor 4.48				

Item Description	Unit	Remove	Replace	Total	
Carpet tile, standard grade	sy	$4.48	$38.33	$42.81	**RELATED ITEMS**
Replace Materials......34.30 Labor 4.03					Cleaning.......................62
Remove .... Labor 4.48					*"Stone Quality"*........306
Carpet tile, high grade	sy	$4.48	$47.33	$51.81	
Replace Materials......43.30 Labor 4.03					
Remove .... Labor 4.48					
Minimum charge for carpeting work	ea	–	$97.70	$97.70	◁ minimum carpeting
Replace Materials......60.00 Labor 37.70					
Stone floor, standard grade	sf	$2.37	$13.55	$15.92	◀ **STONE FLOOR**
Replace Materials........6.35 Labor 7.20					*Grades vary by region.*
Remove .... Labor 2.37					*Standard grade includes*
Stone floor, high grade	sf	$2.37	$15.64	$18.01	*flagstone, Chattahoochee,*
Replace Materials........8.44 Labor 7.20					*and some sandstone.*
Remove .... Labor 2.37					*High grade includes better*
					sandstone and lower to
Stone floor, deluxe grade	sf	$2.37	$17.30	$19.67	*medium grade limestone.*
Replace Materials......10.10 Labor 7.20					*Deluxe grade includes*
Remove .... Labor 2.37					*higher grade limestone,*
					sandstone and granite.
Salvage stone floor, then reinstall	sf	$2.37	$20.15	$22.52	
Replace Materials........1.25 Labor...........18.90					
Remove .... Labor 2.37					
▶ Usually only stone floors in grout bed built over wood framing are salvageable. Includes cost to selectively remove and re-lay.					
Regrout stone floor	sf	–	$1.95	$1.95	
Replace Materials .... .52 Labor 1.43					
▶ Regrouting only, for repointing see *Masonry* page 318.					
Minimum charge for stone floor work	ea	–	$50.90	$50.90	◁ minimum stone floor
Replace .... Labor 50.90					
Marble floor, standard grade	sf	$2.31	$17.63	$19.94	◀ **MARBLE FLOOR**
Replace Materials ......10.50 Labor 7.13					*Allowances for typical*
Remove .... Labor 2.31					*grades of marble used in*
Marble floor, high grade	sf	$2.31	$29.53	$31.84	*residential and light com-*
Replace Materials......22.40 Labor 7.13					*mercial structures. See*
Remove .... Labor 2.31					*Masonry, pages 306-307*
					for more information
Marble floor, deluxe grade	sf	$2.31	$41.73	$44.04	*about marble quality.*
Replace Materials......34.60 Labor 7.13					
Remove .... Labor 2.31					
Regrout marble floor	sf	–	$1.70	$1.70	
Replace Materials .... .42 Labor 1.28					
▶ Regrouting only, for repointing see *Masonry* page 318.					
Minimum charge for marble floor work	ea	–	$125.90	$125.90	◁ minimum marble floor
Replace Materials......75.00 Labor 50.90					
Slate floor, standard grade	sf	$2.31	$15.46	$17.77	◀ **SLATE FLOOR**
Replace Materials........8.33 Labor 7.13					*Allowances for typical*
Remove .... Labor 2.31					*grades of marble used in*
					residential and light com-
					mercial structures.

Item Description		Unit	Remove	Replace	Total
SLATE FLOOR ▶ *continued*	**Slate floor, high grade**	sf	$2.31	$17.33	$19.64
	Replace Materials ......10.20 Labor 7.13				
	Remove .... Labor 2.31				
	Slate floor, deluxe grade	sf	$2.31	$19.43	$21.74
	Replace Materials ......12.30 Labor 7.13				
	Remove .... Labor 2.31				
	Regrout slate floor	sf	–	$1.69	$1.69
	Replace Materials .... .41 Labor 1.28				
	▶ Regrouting only, for repointing see *Masonry* page 318.				
	Salvage slate floor, then reinstall	sf	–	$19.26	$19.26
	Replace Materials .... .76 Labor...........18.50				
	▶ Usually only slate floors built in grout bed over wood framing are salvageable. Includes cost to selectively remove and re-lay.				
minimum slate floor ▷	**Minimum charge for slate floor work**	ea	–	$126.90	$126.90
	Replace Materials ......76.00 Labor 50.90				
TILE FLOOR ▶ *Allowances for typical grades of tile used in residential and light commercial structures.*	**Tile floor, standard grade**	sf	$2.31	$12.10	$14.41
	Replace Materials........5.31 Labor 6.79				
	Remove .... Labor 2.31				
	Tile floor, high grade	sf	$2.31	$13.98	$16.29
	Replace Materials........7.19 Labor 6.79				
	Remove .... Labor 2.31				
	Tile floor, deluxe grade	sf	$2.31	$15.75	$18.06
	Replace Materials........8.96 Labor 6.79				
	Remove .... Labor 2.31				
	Regrout tile floor	sf	–	$1.99	$1.99
	Replace Materials .... .67 Labor 1.32				
	▶ Regrouting only, for repointing see *Masonry* page 318.				
minimum tile floor ▷	**Minimum charge for tile floor work**	ea	–	$110.90	$110.90
	Replace Materials......60.00 Labor 50.90				
QUARRY ▶ **TILE FLOOR** *Allowances for typical grades of tile used in residential and light commercial structures.*	**Quarry tile floor, standard grade**	sf	$2.25	$12.58	$14.83
	Replace Materials........7.19 Labor 5.39				
	Remove .... Labor 2.25				
	Quarry tile floor, high grade	sf	$2.25	$15.79	$18.04
	Replace Materials ......10.40 Labor 5.39				
	Remove .... Labor 2.25				
	Quarry tile floor, deluxe grade	sf	$2.25	$19.49	$21.74
	Replace Materials ......14.10 Labor 5.39				
	Remove .... Labor 2.25				
TILE BASE ▶ *Allowances for typical grades of tile used in residential and light commercial structures.*	**Tile base, standard grade**	lf	$1.76	$9.41	$11.17
	Replace Materials........4.58 Labor 4.83				
	Remove .... Labor 1.76				
	Tile base, high grade	lf	$1.76	$10.98	$12.74
	Replace Materials........6.15 Labor 4.83				
	Remove .... Labor 1.76				

Item Description	Unit	Remove	Replace	Total	
Tile base, deluxe grade	lf	$1.76	$12.43	$14.19	**RELATED ITEMS**
Replace Materials........7.60 Labor 4.83					Cleaning........................62
Remove .... Labor 1.76					"Stone Quality"..........306
Precast terrazzo floor tiles, standard grade	sf	$2.34	$17.67	$20.01	◄ **PRECAST**
Replace Materials........13.30 Labor 4.37					**TERRAZZO TILE**
Remove .... Labor 2.34					*Cast in gray cement. Add*
Precast terrazzo floor tiles, high grade	sf	$2.34	$19.47	$21.81	**2%** *for white cement.*
Replace Materials........15.10 Labor 4.37					*Tiles are 12" x 12".*
Remove .... Labor 2.34					*Standard grade is*
Minimum charge for precast terrazzo floor work	ea	–	$118.10	$118.10	*1" thick, high grade is* *1-1/4" thick*
Replace Materials......60.00 Labor 58.10					◄ minimum terrazzo floor
6" high precast terrazzo base	sf	$1.76	$18.71	$20.47	◄ **PRECAST**
Replace Materials........9.06 Labor 9.65					**TERRAZZO BASE**
Remove .... Labor 1.76					*Cast in gray cement.*
8" high precast terrazzo base	sf	$1.76	$19.34	$21.10	
Replace Materials........9.69 Labor 9.65					
Remove .... Labor 1.76					
Cast-in-place thinset terrazzo floor, standard grade	sf	$2.37	$7.78	$10.15	◄ **CAST-IN-PLACE**
Replace Materials........2.95 Labor 4.83					**TERRAZZO FLOOR**
Remove .... Labor 2.37					*Cast in gray cement with*
Cast-in-place thinset terrazzo floor, high grade	sf	$2.37	$9.15	$11.52	*zinc divider strips. Add* **3%** *for brass divider*
Replace Materials........4.32 Labor 4.83					*strips. Standard grade is*
Remove .... Labor 2.37					*1-1/2" deep, high grade*
Minimum charge for cast-in-place terrazzo floor work	ea	–	$241.00	$241.00	*is up to 3" thick. Add* **2%** *for white cement.*
Replace Materials......90.00 Labor 151.00					
Vinyl floor, economy grade	sy	$5.06	$22.60	$27.66	◄ **VINYL FLOOR**
Replace Materials........15.70 Labor 6.90					*Includes 12% waste.*
Remove .... Labor 5.06					*These prices should be*
Vinyl floor, standard grade	sy	$5.06	$27.70	$32.76	*considered allowances for* *typical grades found in*
Replace Materials.......20.80 Labor 6.90					*residential and light*
Remove .... Labor 5.06					*commercial structures.*
Vinyl floor, high grade	sy	$5.06	$32.80	$37.86	*Lower grades have* *smoother faces and are*
Replace Materials.......25.90 Labor 6.90					*thinner. Higher grades*
Remove .... Labor 5.06					*are embossed, marbleized,*
Vinyl floor, deluxe grade	sy	$5.06	$43.00	$48.06	*and thicker vinyl.*
Replace Materials.......36.10 Labor 6.90					
Remove .... Labor 5.06					
Minimum charge for vinyl floor work	ea	–	$92.70	$92.70	◄ minimum vinyl floor
Replace Materials......55.00 Labor...........37.70					
Vinyl tile floor, economy grade	sf	$.69	$2.23	$2.92	◄ **VINYL TILE FLOOR**
Replace Materials...... 1.14 Labor............ 1.09					*Includes 12% waste.*
Remove .... Labor .... .69					*These prices should be*
Vinyl tile floor, standard grade	sf	$.69	$2.79	$3.48	*considered allowances for* *typical grades found in*
Replace Materials........1.70 Labor............ 1.09					*residential and light com-*
Remove .... Labor .... .69					*mercial structures. See*
					vinyl floor above for gen- *eral grade guidelines.*

	Item Description	Unit	Remove	Replace	Total
VINYL TILE FLOOR ▶ *continued*	**Vinyl tile floor, high grade**	sf	$.69	$3.14	$3.83
	Replace Materials........2.05 Labor........... 1.09				
	Remove .... Labor............. .69				
	Vinyl tile floor, deluxe grade	sf	$.69	$4.27	$4.96
	Replace Materials........3.18 Labor........... 1.09				
	Remove .... Labor............. .69				
minimum vinyl tile floor ▷	**Minimum charge for vinyl tile floor work**	ea	–	$72.70	$72.70
	Replace Materials ......35.00 Labor...........37.70				
RESILIENT ▶ **TILE FLOOR** *Allowances for typical grades of resilient tile used in residential and light commercial structures.*	**Resilient tile floor, economy grade**	sf	$.69	$2.23	$2.92
	Replace Materials........1.14 Labor........... 1.09				
	Remove .... Labor............. .69				
	Resilient tile floor, standard grade	sf	$.69	$2.57	$3.26
	Replace Materials........1.48 Labor........... 1.09				
	Remove .... Labor............. .69				
	Resilient tile floor, high grade	sf	$.69	$2.91	$3.60
	Replace Materials........1.82 Labor........... 1.09				
	Remove .... Labor............. .69				
	Resilient tile floor, deluxe grade	sf	$.69	$3.59	$4.28
	Replace Materials........2.50 Labor........... 1.09				
	Remove .... Labor............. .69				
minimum resilient tile ▷	**Minimum charge for resilient tile floor work**	ea	–	$72.70	$72.70
	Replace Materials ......35.00 Labor...........37.70				
ANTIQUE STYLE ▶ **LINOLEUM** *Antique style linoleum is no longer made in the USA and must be imported from Europe. In recent years linoleum has become much more common in commercial and residential applications. Tiles are normally available in limited styles and colors.*	**Antique style linoleum, plain and marbleized**	sy	$5.06	$43.23	$48.29
	Replace Materials......36.10 Labor 7.13				
	Remove .... Labor 5.06				
	Antique style linoleum, inlaid & molded	sy	$5.06	$54.33	$59.39
	Replace Materials ......47.20 Labor 7.13				
	Remove .... Labor 5.06				
	Antique style linoleum, battleship	sy	$5.06	$40.13	$45.19
	Replace Materials ......33.00 Labor 7.13				
	Remove .... Labor 5.06				
	Antique style linoleum tile	sf	$5.06	$6.10	$11.16
	Replace Materials........4.89 Labor 1.21				
	Remove .... Labor 5.06				
minimum linoleum floor ▷	**Minimum charge for antique style linoleum floor work**	ea	–	$163.10	$163.10
	Replace Materials ....105.00 Labor 58.10				
VINYL COVE ▶ *Vinyl wrapped up wall with metal cap. Grades refer to allowances for quality of vinyl.*	**4" high vinyl cove**	lf	$1.04	$5.59	$6.63
	Replace Materials........2.16 Labor 3.43				
	Remove .... Labor........... 1.04				
	6" high vinyl cove	lf	$1.04	$5.82	$6.86
	Replace Materials........2.39 Labor 3.43				
	Remove .... Labor........... 1.04				
	8" high vinyl cove	lf	$1.04	$6.04	$7.08
	Replace Materials........2.61 Labor 3.43				
	Remove .... Labor........... 1.04				

Item Description	Unit	Remove	Replace	Total	
Minimum charge for vinyl cove work	ea	–	$56.00	$56.00	◁ minimum vinyl cove
Replace Materials......30.00 Labor..........26.00					
Rubber base, economy grade	lf	$.32	$2.34	$2.66	◀ **RUBBER BASE**
Replace Materials........1.59 Labor............75					*Economy grade is black or*
Remove .... Labor............32					*brown 2-1/2" high.*
Rubber base, standard grade	lf	$.32	$2.68	$3.00	*Standard grade is 4" high*
Replace Materials........1.93 Labor............75					*standard colors. High*
Remove .... Labor............32					*grade is 6" high. Deluxe*
Rubber base, high grade	lf	$.32	$3.36	$3.68	*grade is 6" high,*
Replace Materials........2.61 Labor............75					*specialty colors.*
Remove .... Labor............32					
Rubber base, deluxe grade	lf	$.32	$3.93	$4.25	
Replace Materials........3.18 Labor............75					
Remove .... Labor............32					
Minimum charge for rubber base work	ea	–	$31.40	$31.40	◁ minimum rubber base
Replace Materials.......15.00 Labor..........16.40					
Maple strip flooring, first grade	sf	$.58	$11.51	$12.09	◀ **MAPLE STRIP**
Replace Materials........8.19 Labor............3.32					**FLOORING**
Remove .... Labor............58					*Strip flooring is up to*
▶ Face almost free of defects. (Variation in color is not a defect.)					*3/4" thick and up to*
Maple strip flooring, second grade	sf	$.58	$9.70	$10.28	*3-1/4" wide. Grading*
Replace Materials........6.38 Labor............3.32					*information based on*
Remove .... Labor............58					*rules established by the*
▶ Small tight knots, slight dressing imperfections.					*Maple Flooring*
					Manufacturers Association
Maple strip flooring, third grade	sf	$.58	$8.21	$8.79	*(MFMA). All wood is kiln-*
Replace Materials........4.89 Labor............3.32					*dried, tongue-and-groove,*
Remove .... Labor............58					*end-matched and hollow*
▶ Larger knots and imperfections that may cause waste.					*or scratch backed.*
Red oak strip flooring, select & better grade	sf	$.58	$9.70	$10.28	◀ **RED OAK STRIP**
Replace Materials........6.38 Labor............3.32					**FLOORING**
Remove .... Labor............58					*Strip flooring is up to*
▶ At least 50% is clear grade. Clear grade face is practically clear, may have very small areas of bright sap. Select grade face may contain very small areas of burl, one small tight knot every 3 lf, pinworm holes and working imperfections.					*3/4" thick and up to 3-1/4" wide. Grading information based on rules established by the National Oak Flooring*
Red oak strip flooring, #1 common grade	sf	$.58	$8.64	$9.22	*Manufacturers Association*
Replace Materials........5.32 Labor............3.32					*(NOFMA). All wood is*
Remove .... Labor............58					*kiln-dried, tongue-and-*
▶ Same as select with larger and more common imperfections with some flags, heavy streaks, and checks.					*groove, end-matched and hollow or scratch backed.*
Red oak strip flooring, #2 common grade	sf	$.58	$7.15	$7.73	
Replace Materials........3.83 Labor............3.32					
Remove .... Labor............58					
▶ Many natural wood imperfections and milling flaws. Used in rustic or general utility applications.					
Red oak strip flooring, quartersawn, clear grade	sf	$.58	$15.72	$16.30	◀ **QUARTERSAWN**
Replace Materials ......12.40 Labor............3.32					**RED OAK STRIP**
Remove .... Labor............58					**FLOORING**
▶ Face is practically clear, may have very small areas of bright sap.					*See grading information above for red oak strip flooring.*

RELATED ITEMS

Cleaning.......................62
Painting....................340

Item Description	Unit	Remove	Replace	Total
QUARTERSAWN ▶ RED OAK STRIP FLOORING *continued*				
Red oak strip flooring, quartersawn, select grade	sf	$.58	$13.75	$14.33
Replace Materials ......10.43 Labor 3.32				
Remove .... Labor .... .58				
▶ Face may contain very small areas of burl, one small tight knot every 3 lf, pinworm holes and working imperfections.				
PREFINISHED ▶ RED OAK STRIP FLOORING				
Prefinished red oak strip flooring, prime grade	sf	$.58	$10.66	$11.24
Replace Materials ....7.23 Labor 3.43				
Remove .... Labor .... .58				
▶ Almost flawless appearance with very small character marks. Sap and color variations are not flaws.				
Prefinished red oak strip flooring, standard & better grade	sf	$.58	$9.60	$10.18
Replace Materials ....6.17 Labor 3.43				
Remove .... Labor .... .58				
▶ Combination of standard and prime grade. See above for prime grade characteristics. Standard grade may contain filled flaws.				
Prefinished red oak strip flooring, standard grade	sf	$.58	$11.83	$12.41
Replace Materials ....8.40 Labor 3.43				
Remove .... Labor .... .58				
▶ May contain filled flaws.				
Prefinished red oak strip flooring, tavern & better grade	sf	$.58	$14.93	$15.51
Replace Materials ....11.50 Labor 3.43				
Remove .... Labor .... .58				
▶ Combination of standard and tavern grade. See above for standard grade characteristics. Tavern grade contains filled flaws and imperfections which produce rustic appearance.				
Prefinished red oak strip flooring, tavern grade	sf	$.58	$19.03	$19.61
Replace Materials ....15.60 Labor 3.43				
Remove .... Labor .... .58				
▶ Contains filled flaws and imperfections which produce rustic appearance.				
RED OAK PLANK ▶ FLOORING				
Red oak plank flooring, select & better grade	sf	$.55	$14.38	$14.93
Replace Materials ....11.40 Labor 2.98				
Remove .... Labor .... .55				
▶ At least 50% is clear grade. Clear grade face is practically clear, may have very small areas of bright sap. Select grade face may contain very small areas of burl, one small tight knot every 3 lf, pinworm holes and working imperfections.				
Red oak plank flooring, #1 common grade	sf	$.55	$12.45	$13.00
Replace Materials ....9.47 Labor 2.98				
Remove .... Labor .... .55				
▶ Same as select with larger and more common imperfections with some flags, heavy streaks, and checks.				
Red oak plank flooring, #2 common grade	sf	$.55	$9.79	$10.34
Replace Materials ....6.81 Labor 2.98				
Remove .... Labor .... .55				
▶ Same as select with larger and more common imperfections with some flags, heavy streaks, and checks.				
MAPLE PARQUET ▶				
Maple parquet unit block flooring, clear grade	sf	$.52	$9.62	$10.14
Replace Materials ....6.15 Labor 3.47				
Remove .... Labor .... .52				
▶ Made from solid wood pieces glued side by side.				
Maple laminated block flooring, clear grade	sf	$.52	$10.76	$11.28
Replace Materials ....7.29 Labor 3.47				
Remove .... Labor .... .52				
▶ Made from at least three laminated layers (like plywood).				

QUARTERSAWN RED OAK STRIP FLOORING *continued*

PREFINISHED RED OAK STRIP FLOORING

Strip flooring is up to 3/4" thick and up to 3-1/4" wide. Grading information based on rules established by the National Oak Flooring Manufacturers Association (NOFMA). All wood is kiln-dried, tongue-and-groove, end-matched and hollow or scratch backed.

RED OAK PLANK FLOORING

Plank flooring is up to 3/4" thick and over 3-1/4" wide. Floors that contain a mix of plank and strip floor widths are usually considered plank floors. Grading information based on rules established by the National Oak Flooring Manufacturers Association (NOFMA). All wood is kiln-dried, tongue-and-groove, end-matched and hollow or scratch backed.

MAPLE PARQUET

Face pieces are practically clear, may have some small areas of bright sap. For select grade deduct **8%**. For #1 common grade deduct **15%**.

Item Description	Unit	Remove	Replace	Total
Maple parquet slat block flooring, clear grade	sf	$.52	$11.28	$11.80

Replace Materials......7.81   Labor 3.47
Remove ....   Labor........... .52
► Made from many wood slats glued side by side with parquet pattern in block.

| **Prefinished maple parquet unit block flooring, prime grade** | sf | $.52 | $10.52 | $11.04 |

Replace Materials......6.98   Labor 3.54
Remove ....   Labor........... .52
► Made from solid wood pieces glued side by side.

| **Prefinished maple laminated block flooring, prime grade** | sf | $.52 | $11.67 | $12.19 |

Replace Materials......8.13   Labor 3.54
Remove ....   Labor........... .52
► Made from at least three laminated layers (like plywood).

| **Prefinished maple parquet slat block flooring, prime grade** | sf | $.52 | $12.19 | $12.71 |

Replace Materials......8.65   Labor 3.54
Remove ....   Labor........... .52
► Made from many wood slats glued side by side with parquet pattern in block.

| **Red oak parquet unit block flooring, clear grade** | sf | $.52 | $9.51 | $10.03 |

Replace Materials......6.04   Labor 3.47
Remove ....   Labor........... .52
► Made from solid wood pieces glued side by side.

| **Red oak laminated block flooring, clear grade** | sf | $.52 | $10.55 | $11.07 |

Replace Materials......7.08   Labor 3.47
Remove ....   Labor........... .52
► Made from at least three laminated layers (like plywood).

| **Red oak parquet slat block flooring, clear grade** | sf | $.52 | $11.18 | $11.70 |

Replace Materials......7.71   Labor 3.47
Remove ....   Labor........... .52
► Made from many wood slats glued side by side with parquet pattern in block.

| **Prefinished red oak parquet unit block flooring, prime grade** | sf | $.52 | $10.42 | $10.94 |

Replace Materials......6.88   Labor 3.54
Remove ....   Labor........... .52
► Made from solid wood pieces glued side by side.

| **Prefinished red oak laminated block flooring, prime grade** | sf | $.52 | $11.46 | $11.98 |

Replace Materials......7.92   Labor 3.54
Remove ....   Labor........... .52
► Made from at least three laminated layers (like plywood).

| **Prefinished red oak parquet slat block flooring, prime grade** | sf | $.52 | $12.08 | $12.60 |

Replace Materials......8.54   Labor 3.54
Remove ....   Labor........... .52
► Made from many wood slats glued side by side with parquet pattern in block.

Add 8% for pickets around unit block
► Add for mitered wood trim around edges of block, called "pickets."

Deduct 7% for beech flooring

Deduct 7% for birch flooring

Deduct 6% for ash flooring

Add 46% for cherry flooring

RELATED ITEMS

Cleaning....................62
Finish Carpentry..........199
Painting....................340

◄ **PREFINISHED MAPLE PARQUET**
Face pieces are almost flawless with very small character marks. (Sap and color variations are not flaws.) For standard grade deduct **10%.** *For tavern grade deduct* **14%.**

◄ **RED OAK PARQUET**
Face pieces are practically clear, may have some small areas of bright sap. For select grade deduct **8%.** *For #1 common grade deduct* **15%.**

◄ **PREFINISHED RED OAK PARQUET**
Face pieces are almost flawless with very small character marks. (Sap and color variations are not flaws.) For standard grade deduct **10%.** *For tavern grade deduct* **14%.**

◄ **ADDITIONAL WOOD SPECIES**
Deduct or add these percentages to the costs listed for red oak.

Item Description	Unit	Remove	Replace	Total

ADDITIONAL ▶ WOOD SPECIES *continued*

Deduct 5% for hickory flooring

Add 182% for teak flooring

Add for 70% walnut flooring

Deduct 7% for white oak flooring

SOUTHERN PINE ▶ STRIP FLOORING
Strip flooring is up to 3/4" thick and up to 3-1/4" wide. Grading information based on rules established by the Southern Pine Inspection Bureau (SPIB). All wood is kiln-dried, tongue-and-groove, end-matched and hollow or scratch backed.

Southern pine strip flooring, B&B grade — sf — $.58 — $6.09 — $6.67
Replace Materials........2.77   Labor 3.32
Remove ....   Labor............ .58
▶ Best quality, allows very small surface checks, pin knots, small closed pitch pockets, light stain and very light warp. Usually no more than one character flaw per 4 lf.

Southern pine strip flooring, C & better grade — sf — $.58 — $5.87 — $6.45
Replace Materials........2.55   Labor 3.32
Remove ....   Labor............ .58
▶ Combination of B&B and C grades. See B&B grade above. C grade is same as B&B with slightly larger and more frequent imperfections with some shakes, wane, splits, and skips.

Southern pine strip flooring, C grade — sf — $.58 — $5.66 — $6.24
Replace Materials........2.34   Labor 3.32
Remove ....   Labor............ .58
▶ C grade is same as B&B (see item above) with slightly larger and more frequent imperfections with some shakes, wane, splits, and skips.

SOUTHERN PINE ▶ PLANK FLOORING
Plank flooring is up to 3/4" thick and over 3-1/4" wide. Floors that contain a mix of plank and strip floor widths are usually considered plank floors. See southern pine strip flooring above for grading information.

Southern pine plank flooring, B&B grade — sf — $.55 — $6.28 — $6.83
Replace Materials........3.30   Labor 2.98
Remove ....   Labor............ .55
▶ See information under same grade of southern pine strip flooring.

Southern pine plank flooring, C & better grade — sf — $.55 — $6.07 — $6.62
Replace Materials........3.09   Labor 2.98
Remove ....   Labor............ .55
▶ See information under same grade of southern pine strip flooring.

Southern pine plank flooring, C grade — sf — $.55 — $5.75 — $6.30
Replace Materials........2.77   Labor 2.98
Remove ....   Labor............ .55
▶ See information under same grade of southern pine strip flooring.

DOUGLAS FIR ▶ STRIP FLOORING
Douglas fir or western hemlock, or white fir, or Sitka spruce. Strip flooring is up to 3/4" thick and up to 3-1/4" wide. Grading information based on rules established by the West Coast Lumbermen's Inspection Bureau (WCLIB). All wood is kiln-dried, tongue-and-groove, end-matched and hollow or scratch backed.

Douglas fir strip flooring, C & better grade — sf — $.58 — $6.30 — $6.88
Replace Materials........2.98   Labor 3.32
Remove ....   Labor............ .58
▶ Highest quality with some pieces perfectly clear. Other pieces may contain infrequent medium stained sapwood, very small seasoning checks, small light skips, light warp, tight knots, and raised grain.

Douglas fir strip flooring, D grade — sf — $.58 — $6.09 — $6.67
Replace Materials........2.77   Labor 3.32
Remove ....   Labor............ .58
▶ Contains some stained wood, medium splits, seasoning checks, small and infrequent holes, torn or raised grain, large pitch streaks, larger and more frequent knots than are found in C grade, and some pieces with medium warp.

Item Description	Unit	Remove	Replace	Total
Douglas fir strip flooring, E grade	sf	$.58	$5.87	$6.45

Replace Materials........2.55   Labor 3.32
Remove ....   Labor............ .58

▶ A subfloor grade that is normally not used in exposed applications. Includes larger and more frequent defects than are found in D grade, with loose knots and knot holes.

Douglas fir plank flooring, C & better grade	sf	$.55	$6.60	$7.15

Replace Materials........3.62   Labor 2.98
Remove ....   Labor............ .55

▶ See information under same grade of Douglas fir strip flooring.

Douglas fir plank flooring, D grade	sf	$.55	$6.28	$6.83

Replace Materials........3.30   Labor 2.98
Remove ....   Labor............ .55

▶ See information under same grade of Douglas fir strip flooring.

Douglas fir plank flooring, E grade	sf	$.55	$5.96	$6.51

Replace Materials........2.98   Labor 2.98
Remove ....   Labor............ .55

▶ See information under same grade of Douglas fir strip flooring.

Reclaimed antique longleaf pine flooring, crown grade	sf	$.58	$15.92	$16.50

Replace Materials ......12.60   Labor 3.32
Remove ....   Labor............ .58

▶ Best grade. 90% is free of knots with 100% dense grade heartwood face and very infrequent nail holes. Knots are tight and less than 1-1/4" in diameter.

Reclaimed antique longleaf pine flooring, select prime grade	sf	$.58	$13.21	$13.79

Replace Materials........9.89   Labor 3.32
Remove ....   Labor............ .58

▶ 75% is free of knots with at least 97% dense grade heartwood and infrequent nail holes. Knots are tight and less than 1-1/2" in diameter.

Reclaimed antique longleaf pine flooring, prime grade	sf	$.58	$13.00	$13.58

Replace Materials........9.68   Labor 3.32
Remove ....   Labor............ .58

▶ Varying degree of knots and nail holes with at least 85% dense grade heartwood. Knots are tight and less than 2" in diameter.

Reclaimed antique longleaf pine flooring, naily grade	sf	$.58	$11.72	$12.30

Replace Materials........8.40   Labor 3.32
Remove ....   Labor............ .58

▶ Same as select prime grade above with many nail holes.

Reclaimed antique longleaf pine flooring, cabin grade	sf	$.58	$11.83	$12.41

Replace Materials........8.51   Labor 3.32
Remove ....   Labor............ .58

▶ Similar to prime grade with more sapwood, larger knots, and some boards with many nail holes.

Reclaimed antique longleaf pine flooring, distressed grade	sf	$.58	$18.62	$19.20

Replace Materials.......15.30   Labor 3.32
Remove ....   Labor............ .58

▶ Crown grade with as-is finish, including gouges, tight cracks, worm holes, worn spots, and raised grain. Boards are also machined to enhance the time-worn look. Edges and back are remilled.

RELATED ITEMS

Cleaning.................62
Finish Carpentry..........199
Painting 340

◀ **DOUGLAS FIR PLANK FLOORING**
Plank flooring is up to 3/4" thick and over 3-1/4" wide. Floors that contain a mix of plank and strip floor widths are usually considered plank floors. See Douglas fir strip flooring on facing page for grading information.

◀ **RECLAIMED ANTIQUE LONGLEAF PINE**
Strip or plank flooring. Although longleaf pine was once common in Southeastern America, new lumber is no longer available. Longleaf pine must be salvaged from existing structures. (Although Goodwin Heart Pine Company of Micanopy, Florida does salvage logs that sank to the bottom of rivers.) Grading is based on grades marketed by Mountain Lumber Company, Inc. of Ruckersville, Virginia.

Item Description	Unit	Remove	Replace	Total
SAND, EDGE, & ▶ **FILL WOOD FLOOR**				
Sand, edge, and fill new wood floor	sf	–	**$1.27**	**$1.27**
Replace Materials .... .29 Labor............. .98				
Light sand, edge, and fill existing wood floor	sf	–	**$1.38**	**$1.38**
Replace Materials .... .25 Labor........... 1.13				
Medium sand, edge, and fill old wood floor	sf	–	**$1.57**	**$1.57**
Replace Materials .... .33 Labor 1.24				
Heavy sand, edge, and fill old wood floor	sf	–	**$1.94**	**$1.94**
Replace Materials .... .39 Labor............1.55				
WOOD FLOOR ▶ **SLEEPERS** *Glued and nailed with case-hardened nails to concrete floor.*				
1" x 2" sleepers on concrete floor, 24" oc	sf	$.20	$.52	$.72
Replace Materials .... .22 Labor............. .30				
Remove .... Labor............. .20				
1" x 3" sleepers on concrete floor, 24" oc	sf	$.20	$.69	$.89
Replace Materials .... .35 Labor............. .34				
Remove .... Labor............. .20				
2" x 4" sleepers on concrete floor, 24" oc	sf	$.20	$1.26	$1.46
Replace Materials .... .81 Labor............. .45				
Remove .... Labor............. .20				
2" x 6" sleepers on concrete floor, 24" oc	sf	$.20	$1.76	$1.96
Replace Materials ....1.27 Labor............. .49				
Remove .... Labor............. .20				
UNDERLAYMENT ▶ *Includes 5% waste. When removing underlayment that has been heavily glued and stapled, double the removal cost.*				
3/8" particleboard floor underlayment	sy	$2.02	$10.44	$12.46
Replace Materials........4.14 Labor 6.30				
Remove .... Labor 2.02				
1/2" particleboard floor underlayment	sy	$2.02	$10.62	$12.64
Replace Materials........4.29 Labor 6.33				
Remove .... Labor 2.02				
5/8" particleboard floor underlayment	sy	$2.02	$11.09	$13.11
Replace Materials........4.76 Labor 6.33				
Remove .... Labor 2.02				
3/4" particleboard floor underlayment	sy	$2.02	$11.90	$13.92
Replace Materials........5.53 Labor 6.37				
Remove .... Labor 2.02				
1/4" hardboard floor underlayment	sy	$2.02	$12.18	$14.20
Replace Materials........5.62 Labor 6.56				
Remove .... Labor 2.02				
1/2" plywood floor underlayment	sy	$2.02	$13.52	$15.54
Replace Materials........7.19 Labor 6.33				
Remove .... Labor 2.02				
Minimum charge for floor underlayment work	ea	–	**$61.90**	**$61.90**
Replace Materials ......35.00 Labor...........26.90				

✍ NOTES: _____

_____

_____ end

TIME & MATERIAL CHARTS *(selected items)*

Flooring Materials

DESCRIPTION	MATERIAL PRICE	GROSS COVERAGE	WASTE	NET COVERAGE	UNIT PRICE
Carpet					
economy grade	$15.30 sy	1	12%	.88	$17.40 sy
custom grade	$35.50 sy	1	12%	.88	$40.30 sy
Glue-down carpet					
economy grade	$11.40 sy	1	12%	.88	$13.00 sy
deluxe grade	$21.50 sy	1	12%	.88	$24.40 sy
Indoor-outdoor carpet					
economy grade	$8.50 sy	1	12%	.88	$9.66 sy
deluxe grade	$27.00 sy	1	12%	.88	$30.70 sy
Wool carpet					
standard grade	$22.70 sy	1	12%	.88	$25.80 sy
custom grade	$47.40 sy	1	12%	.88	$53.90 sy
Simulated wool berber carpet					
standard grade	$20.90 sy	1	12%	.88	$23.80 sy
custom grade	$33.60 sy	1	12%	.88	$38.20 sy
Carpet pad					
urethane rebound	$4.20 sy	1	12%	.88	$4.77 sy
jute	$2.90 sy	1	12%	.88	$3.30 sy
Carpet tile					
standard grade	$25.00 sy	1	12%	.88	$28.40 sy
custom grade	$38.10 sy	1	12%	.88	$43.30 sy
Stone floor					
standard grade	$6.10 sf	1	4%	.96	$6.35 sf
deluxe grade	$9.70 sf	1	4%	.96	$10.10 sf
Marble floor					
standard grade	$10.10 sf	1	4%	.96	$10.50 sf
deluxe grade	$33.20 sf	1	4%	.96	$34.60 sf
Slate floor					
standard grade	$8.00 sf	1	4%	.96	$8.33 sf
deluxe grade	$11.80 sf	1	4%	.96	$12.30 sf
Tile floor					
standard grade	$5.10 sf	1	4%	.96	$5.31 sf
deluxe grade	$8.60 sf	1	4%	.96	$8.96 sf
Quarry tile floor					
standard grade	$6.90 sf	1	4%	.96	$7.19 sf
deluxe grade	$13.50 sf	1	4%	.96	$14.10 sf
Precast terrazzo floor tiles					
standard grade	$12.80 sf	1	4%	.96	$13.30 sf
high grade	$14.50 sf	1	4%	.96	$15.10 sf
Cast-in-place thinset terrazzo floor					
standard grade	$2.60 sf	1	12%	.88	$2.95 sf
high grade	$3.80 sf	1	12%	.88	$4.32 sf
Vinyl floor					
economy grade	$13.80 sy	1	12%	.88	$15.70 sy
deluxe grade	$31.80 sy	1	12%	.88	$36.10 sy
Vinyl tile floor					
economy grade	$1.00 sf	1	12%	.88	$1.14 sf
deluxe grade	$2.80 sf	1	12%	.88	$3.18 sf

. . . More ➤

Flooring Materials *continued*

DESCRIPTION	MATERIAL PRICE	GROSS COVERAGE	WASTE	NET COVERAGE	UNIT PRICE
Resilient tile floor					
economy grade	$1.00 *sf*	1	12%	.88	**$1.14** *sf*
deluxe grade	$2.20 *sf*	1	12%	.88	**$2.50** *sf*
Antique style linoleum					
battleship	$29.00 *sy*	1	12%	.88	**$33.00** *sy*
Rubber base					
economy grade	$1.40 *lf*	1	12%	.88	**$1.59** *lf*
deluxe grade	$2.80 *lf*	1	12%	.88	**$3.18** *lf*
Strip flooring					
maple, first grade	$7.70 *sf*	1	6%	.94	**$8.19** *sf*
red oak, select & better grade	$6.00 *sf*	1	6%	.94	**$6.38** *sf*
red oak, quartersawn, clear grade	$11.70 *sf*	1	6%	.94	**$12.40** *sf*
prefinished red oak, prime grade	$6.80 *sf*	1	6%	.94	**$7.23** *sf*
Plank flooring					
red oak, select & better grade	$10.70 *sf*	1	6%	.94	**$11.40** *sf*
Parquet or block flooring					
maple, slat block, clear grade	$7.50 *sf*	1	4%	.96	**$7.81** *sf*
prefinished maple, slat block, prime grade	$6.70 *sf*	1	4%	.96	**$6.98** *sf*
red oak, slat block, clear grade	$5.80 *sf*	1	4%	.96	**$6.04** *sf*
prefinished red oak, slat block, prime grade	$6.60 *sf*	1	4%	.96	**$6.88** *sf*
Softwood flooring					
Southern pine strip, B&B grade	$2.60 *sf*	1	6%	.94	**$2.77** *sf*
Southern pine plank, B&B grade	$3.10 *sf*	1	6%	.94	**$3.30** *sf*
Douglas fir strip, C & better grade	$2.80 *sf*	1	6%	.94	**$2.98** *sf*
Douglas fir plank, C & better grade	$3.40 *sf*	1	6%	.94	**$3.62** *sf*
reclaimed antique longleaf pine, crown grade	$11.80 *sf*	1	6%	.94	**$12.60** *sf*
Sleepers on concrete floor, 24" on center					
1" x 2"					**$.22** *sf*
2" x 4"					**$.81** *sf*
Floor underlayment					
3/8" particleboard	$14.00 *sheet*	3.56	5%	3.38	**$4.14** *sy*
1/2" particleboard	$14.50 *sheet*	3.56	5%	3.38	**$4.29** *sy*
5/8" particleboard	$16.10 *sheet*	3.56	5%	3.38	**$4.76** *sy*
3/4" particleboard	$18.70 *sheet*	3.56	5%	3.38	**$5.53** *sy*
1/4" hardboard	$9.50 *sheet*	1.78	5%	1.69	**$5.62** *sy*
1/2" plywood	$24.30 *sheet*	3.56	5%	3.38	**$7.19** *sy*

Flooring Labor

LABORER	BASE WAGE	PAID LEAVE	TRUE WAGE	FICA	FUTA	WORKER'S COMP.	UNEMPLOY. INSUR.	HEALTH INSUR.	RETIRE (401K)	LIABILITY INSUR.	COST PER HOUR
Flooring installer	$24.00	1.87	$25.87	1.98	.21	5.42	2.25	2.92	.78	3.88	**$43.30**
Flooring installer's helper	$17.30	1.35	$18.65	1.43	.15	3.91	1.62	2.92	.56	2.80	**$32.00**
Demolition laborer	$14.40	1.12	$15.52	1.19	.12	5.01	1.35	2.92	.47	2.33	**$28.90**

Paid Leave is calculated based on two weeks paid vacation, one week sick leave, and seven paid holidays. Employer's matching portion of **FICA** is 7.65 percent. **FUTA** (Federal Unemployment) is .8 percent. **Worker's compensation** for the flooring trade was calculated using a national average of 20.93 percent. **Unemployment insurance** was calculated using a national average of 8.7 percent. **Health insurance** was calculated based on a projected national average for 2005 of $580 per employee (and family when applicable) per month. Employer pays 80 percent for a per month cost of $464 per employee. **Retirement** is based on a 401(k) retirement program with employer matching of 50 percent. Employee contributions to the 401(k) plan are an average of 6 percent of the true wage. **Liability insurance** is based on a national average of 14.0 percent.

Flooring Labor Productivity

WORK DESCRIPTION	LABORER	COST PER HOUR	PRODUCTIVITY	UNIT PRICE
Demolition				
remove carpet	demolition laborer	$28.90	.062	$1.79 sy
remove glue-down carpet	demolition laborer	$28.90	.155	$4.48 sy
remove indoor-outdoor carpet	demolition laborer	$28.90	.153	$4.42 sy
remove carpet pad	demolition laborer	$28.90	.030	$.87 sy
remove carpet cove	demolition laborer	$28.90	.022	$.64 lf
remove carpet tile	demolition laborer	$28.90	.155	$4.48 sy
remove stone floor	demolition laborer	$28.90	.082	$2.37 sf
remove marble floor	demolition laborer	$28.90	.080	$2.31 sf
remove slate floor	demolition laborer	$28.90	.080	$2.31 sf
remove tile floor	demolition laborer	$28.90	.080	$2.31 sf
remove quarry tile floor	demolition laborer	$28.90	.078	$2.25 sf
remove tile base	demolition laborer	$28.90	.061	$1.76 lf
remove precast terrazzo floor tiles	demolition laborer	$28.90	.081	$2.34 sf
remove cast-in-place terrazzo floor	demolition laborer	$28.90	.082	$2.37 sf
remove vinyl floor	demolition laborer	$28.90	.175	$5.06 sy
remove vinyl tile floor	demolition laborer	$28.90	.024	$.69 sf
remove resilient tile floor	demolition laborer	$28.90	.024	$.69 sf
remove antique style linoleum floor	demolition laborer	$28.90	.175	$5.06 sy
remove vinyl cove	demolition laborer	$28.90	.036	$1.04 lf
remove rubber base	demolition laborer	$28.90	.011	$.32 lf
remove wood strip flooring	demolition laborer	$28.90	.020	$.58 sf
remove wood plank flooring	demolition laborer	$28.90	.019	$.55 sf
remove wood unit block flooring	demolition laborer	$28.90	.018	$.52 sf
remove floor sleepers	demolition laborer	$28.90	.007	$.20 sf
remove floor underlayment	demolition laborer	$28.90	.070	$2.02 sy
Flooring crew				
install flooring	flooring installer	$43.30		
install flooring	flooring installer's helper	$32.00		
install flooring	**flooring crew**	$37.70		
Install carpet				
typical on tackless	flooring crew	$37.70	.138	$5.20 sy
cove	flooring crew	$37.70	.135	$5.09 lf
remove for work, then re-lay	flooring crew	$37.70	.211	$7.95 sy
glue-down	flooring crew	$37.70	.167	$6.30 sy
wool or simulated wool	flooring crew	$37.70	.139	$5.24 sy
add per step for installation on stairs	flooring crew	$37.70	.180	$6.79 ea
pad	flooring crew	$37.70	.0166	$.60 sy
tile	flooring crew	$37.70	.107	$4.03 sy
Install stone floor				
typical	flooring crew	$37.70	.191	$7.20 sf
salvage, then reinstall	flooring crew	$37.70	.500	$18.90 sf
regrout	flooring crew	$37.70	.038	$1.43 sf
Install marble floor				
typical	flooring crew	$37.70	.189	$7.13 sf
regrout	flooring crew	$37.70	.034	$1.28 sf
Install slate floor				
typical	flooring crew	$37.70	.189	$7.13 sf
regrout	flooring crew	$37.70	.034	$1.28 sf
salvage, then reinstall	flooring crew	$37.70	.490	$18.50 sf
Install tile floor				
typical	flooring crew	$37.70	.180	$6.79 sf
regrout	flooring crew	$37.70	.035	$1.32 sf
base	flooring crew	$37.70	.128	$4.83 lf
Install quarry tile floor				
typical	flooring crew	$37.70	.143	$5.39 sf
Install terrazzo floor				
precast tiles	flooring crew	$37.70	.116	$4.37 sf
precast base	flooring crew	$37.70	.256	$9.65 sf
cast-in-place thinset	flooring crew	$37.70	.128	$4.83 sf

. . . More ➤

Flooring Labor Productivity *continued*

WORK DESCRIPTION	LABORER	COST PER HOUR	PRODUCTIVITY	UNIT PRICE
Install vinyl floor				
sheet goods	flooring crew	$37.70	.183	$6.90 sy
cove	flooring crew	$37.70	.091	$3.43 lf
tile	flooring crew	$37.70	.029	$1.09 sf
resilient tile	flooring crew	$37.70	.029	$1.09 sf
Install antique style linoleum				
typical	flooring crew	$37.70	.189	$7.13 sy
tile	flooring crew	$37.70	.032	$1.21 sf
Install rubber base				
typical	flooring crew	$37.70	.020	$.75 lf
Install wood floor				
hardwood strip	flooring crew	$37.70	.088	$3.32 sf
prefinished hardwood strip	flooring crew	$37.70	.091	$3.43 sf
hardwood plank	flooring crew	$37.70	.079	$2.98 sf
parquet or block	flooring crew	$37.70	.092	$3.47 sf
prefinished hardwood block or parquet	flooring crew	$37.70	.094	$3.54 sf
softwood strip	flooring crew	$37.70	.088	$3.32 sf
softwood plank	flooring crew	$37.70	.079	$2.98 sf
Sand, edge, and fill wood floor				
new	flooring crew	$37.70	.026	$.98 sf
light sand	flooring crew	$37.70	.030	$1.13 sf
medium	flooring crew	$37.70	.033	$1.24 sf
heavy sand	flooring crew	$37.70	.041	$1.55 sf
Install sleepers on concrete floor, 24" on center				
1" x 2"	flooring crew	$37.70	.008	$.30 sf
1" x 3"	flooring crew	$37.70	.009	$.34 sf
2" x 4"	flooring crew	$37.70	.012	$.45 sf
2" x 6"	flooring crew	$37.70	.013	$.49 sf
Install floor underlayment				
3/8" particleboard	flooring crew	$37.70	.167	$6.30 sy
1/2" particleboard	flooring crew	$37.70	.168	$6.33 sy
5/8" particleboard	flooring crew	$37.70	.168	$6.33 sy
3/4" particleboard	flooring crew	$37.70	.169	$6.37 sy
1/4" hardboard	flooring crew	$37.70	.174	$6.56 sy
1/2" plywood	flooring crew	$37.70	.168	$6.33 sy

✍ NOTES: _____

_____

_____

_____

_____

_____

_____

_____

_____

_____

_____

_____

_____

_____

_____

_____ end

20 .... *Hazardous Materials*

Item Description	Unit	Remove	Replace	Total	
Minimum asbestos removal charge	ea	$1,033.00	–	$1,033.00	◄ MINIMUM
Remove Materials ....142.00 Labor ....717.00 Equipment.........174.00					
Asbestos analysis	ea	$748.00	–	$748.00	◄ ASBESTOS ANALYSIS
Remove .... Labor.........748.00					
► Includes up to four hours, up to 12 analyzed samples, and a written report indicating severity of asbestos risk for a typical home or small commercial structure.					
Plastic cover attached to ceiling	sf	$3.37	–	$3.37	◄ SEAL AREA
Remove Materials........1.40 Labor 1.97					*Seal area where asbestos exists. Includes tape along all seams, caulk or foam insulation in any cracks, and negative air vent system.*
Plastic cover attached to walls	sf	$3.29	–	$3.29	
Remove Materials........1.41 Labor 1.88					
Plastic cover and plywood over floor (2 layers)	sf	$6.81	–	$6.81	
Remove Materials........2.24 Labor 4.57					
Temporary containment walls with plastic cover	sf	$10.73	–	$10.73	
Remove Materials........2.71 Labor 8.02					
► 2" x 4" walls covered with 1/2" cdx plywood and plastic.					
Prefabricated decontamination unit	dy	$75.00	–	$75.00	◄ DECONTAMINATION UNIT
Remove .... Equipment 75.00					
► Four day minimum. Includes decontamination equipment, shower, and clean room.					
Encapsulate asbestos-based acoustical ceiling with sealant	sf	$1.09	–	$1.09	◄ ENCAPSULATE ASBESTOS
Remove Materials........ .35 Labor .... .63 Equipment .... .11					
► Penetrating sealant sprayed on ceiling with airless sprayer.					
Scrape asbestos-based acoustical ceiling	sf	$1.78	–	$1.78	◄ REMOVE ASBESTOS
Remove Materials........ .09 Labor ....1.52 Equipment .... .17					*Includes full Tyvek suits for workers changed four times per eight hour shift, respirators, (add **20%** for respirators with air supply) air monitoring, supervision by qualified hygiene professionals, final seal of scraped or demo'ed walls, final seal and disposal of plastic cover materials, disposal in fiber drums and hauling to dump. Does not include dump fees (typically about **$12** per drum).*
► Includes disposal in glove bags and fiber drums.					
Remove asbestos-based insulation over 1/2" to 3/4" pipe	lf	$1.42	–	$1.42	
Remove Materials........ .17 Labor .... 1.16 Equipment .... .09					
► Includes disposal in glove bags and fiber drums.					
Remove asbestos-based insulation over 1" to 3" pipe	lf	$4.09	–	$4.09	
Remove Materials........ .32 Labor ....3.58 Equipment .... .19					
► Includes disposal in glove bags and fiber drums.					
Remove asbestos-based siding	sf	$9.16	–	$9.16	
Remove Materials........ .94 Labor ....8.02 Equipment .... .20					
► Includes disposal in fiber drums.					
Remove asbestos-based plaster	sf	$6.94	–	$6.94	
Remove Materials........ .60 Labor ....6.14 Equipment .... .20					
► Includes disposal in fiber drums.					

✍ NOTES: _____

_____ end

TIME & MATERIAL CHARTS *(selected items)*

Materials for Hazardous Materials Removal

DESCRIPTION	MATERIAL PRICE	UNIT PRICE
polyethylene (plastic)	$.20 sf	$.20 sf
Tyvek whole body suit	$17.00 ea	$17.00 ea
respirator cartridge	$4.70 ea	$4.70 ea
glove bag, 7 mil., 50" x 64"	$9.10 ea	$9.10 ea
glove bag, 10 mil., 44" x 60"	$9.70 ea	$9.70 ea
3 cf disposable polyethylene bags, 6 mil	$1.20 ea	$1.20 ea
3 cf disposable fiber drums	$9.90 ea	$9.90 ea
caution labels	$.23 ea	$.23 ea
encapsulation quality sealant	$85.00 gallon	$85.00 gal
vent fan filters	$8.10 ea	$8.10 ea
respirator	$24.00 ea	$24.00 ea

Hazardous Materials Rental Equipment

DESCRIPTION	PRICE	COVERAGE	UNIT PRICE
negative air vent system, two fans	$55.00 per day	1 per day	$55.00 day
HEPA vacuum cleaner, 16 gallon wet/dry	$65.00 per day	1 per day	$65.00 day
airless sprayer unit	$50.00 per day	1 per day	$50.00 day
light stand	$20.00 per day	1 per day	$20.00 day
prefabricated decontamination unit	$75.00 per day	1 per day	$75.00 day

Hazardous Materials Labor

LABORER	BASE WAGE	PAID LEAVE	TRUE WAGE	FICA	FUTA	WORKER'S COMP.	UNEMPLOY. INSUR.	HEALTH INSUR.	RETIRE (401K)	LIABILITY INSUR.	COST PER HOUR
Haz. mat. laborer	$18.90	1.47	$20.37	1.56	.16	14.33	1.77	2.92	.61	3.06	$44.80

Paid Leave is calculated based on two weeks paid vacation, one week sick leave, and seven paid holidays. Employer's matching portion of **FICA** is 7.65 percent. **FUTA** (Federal Unemployment) is .8 percent. **Worker's compensation** for the hazardous materials trade was calculated using a national average of 70.24 percent. **Unemployment insurance** was calculated using a national average of 8.7 percent. **Health insurance** was calculated based on a projected national average for 2005 of $580 per employee (and family when applicable) per month. Employer pays 80 percent for a per month cost of $464 per employee. **Retirement** is based on a 401(k) retirement program with employer matching of 50 percent. Employee contributions to the 401(k) plan are an average of 6 percent of the true wage. **Liability insurance** is based on a national average of 14.0 percent.

Hazardous Materials Labor Productivity

WORK DESCRIPTION	LABORER	COST PER HOUR	PRODUCTIVITY	UNIT PRICE
Minimum				
for asbestos removal	haz. mat. laborer	$44.80	16.0	$717.00 ea
Asbestos analysis				
typical home	haz. mat. laborer	$44.80	16.7	$748.00 ea
Seal area for work				
attach plastic cover to ceiling	haz. mat. laborer	$44.80	.044	$1.97 sf
attach plastic cover to walls	haz. mat. laborer	$44.80	.042	$1.88 sf
attach plastic cover & plywood to floor	haz. mat. laborer	$44.80	.102	$4.57 sf
build walls and attach plastic cover	haz. mat. laborer	$44.80	.179	$8.02 sf
Remove asbestos-based materials				
scrape acoustical ceiling	haz. mat. laborer	$44.80	.034	$1.52 sf
encapsulate acoustical ceiling with sealant	haz. mat. laborer	$44.80	.014	$.63 sf
insulation over 1/2" to 3/4" pipe	haz. mat. laborer	$44.80	.026	$1.16 lf
insulation over 1" to 3" pipe	haz. mat. laborer	$44.80	.080	$3.58 lf
siding	haz. mat. laborer	$44.80	.179	$8.02 sf
plaster	haz. mat. laborer	$44.80	.137	$6.14 sf

21 .... *HVAC*

Item Description	Unit	Remove	Replace	Total	
Duct work per duct *Replace* Materials.....155.00 Labor.........242.00	ea	–	$397.00	$397.00	◀ **Ducts**
Duct work per sf of floor *Replace* Materials .... .50 Labor 1.55	sf	–	$2.05	$2.05	
Forced-air ducting for home to 1,200 sf *Replace* Materials ....575.00 Labor 1730.00	ea	–	$2,305.00	$2,305.00	◀ **Ducts per home**
Forced-air ducting for home 1,200 to 1,900 sf *Replace* Materials ....865.00 Labor 2120.00	ea	–	$2,985.00	$2,985.00	
Forced-air ducting for home 1,900 to 2,400 sf *Replace* Materials...1450.00 Labor.......2600.00	ea	–	$4,050.00	$4,050.00	
Forced-air ducting for home 2,400 to 2,900 sf *Replace* Materials ..2260.00 Labor.......3390.00	ea	–	$5,650.00	$5,650.00	
Forced-air ducting for home 2,900 to 3,400 sf *Replace* Materials .3590.00 Labor 4840.00	ea	–	$8,430.00	$8,430.00	
Forced-air ducting for home 3,400 to 3,900 sf *Replace* Materials ..5880.00 Labor.......6290.00	ea	–	$12,170.00	$12,170.00	
Forced-air ducting for home 3,900 to 4,500 sf *Replace* Materials ..9790.00 Labor 7900.00	ea	–	$17,690.00	$17,690.00	
Electric forced-air furnace 10,200 btu *Replace* Materials....400.00 Labor.........523.00 *Remove* .... Labor 54.60	ea	$54.60	$923.00	$977.60	◀ **Electric furnace** *Includes connection only. Does not include wiring run, plenums, ducts, or flues.*
Electric forced-air furnace 17,100 btu *Replace* Materials ...425.00 Labor.........552.00 *Remove* .... Labor 54.60	ea	$54.60	$977.00	$1,031.60	
Electric forced-air furnace 27,300 btu *Replace* Materials....500.00 Labor ....610.00 *Remove* .... Labor 54.60	ea	$54.60	$1,110.00	$1,164.60	
Electric forced-air furnace 34,100 btu *Replace* Materials....550.00 Labor ....668.00 *Remove* .... Labor 54.60	ea	$54.60	$1,218.00	$1,272.60	
Remove electric forced-air furnace for work, then reinstall *Replace* .... Labor.........252.00	ea	–	$252.00	$252.00	
Gas forced-air furnace 45,000 btu *Replace* Materials ....425.00 Labor.........547.00 *Remove* .... Labor...........52.60	ea	$52.60	$972.00	$1,024.60	◀ **Gas furnace** *Includes connection only. Does not include wiring run, plenums, ducts, or flues.*
Gas forced-air furnace 60,000 btu *Replace* Materials....475.00 Labor.........595.00 *Remove* .... Labor...........52.60	ea	$52.60	$1,070.00	$1,122.60	

RELATED ITEMS

Cleaning 63
Electrical
  baseboard heater..............153
  baseboard
  heater wiring............142, 144
  furnace wiring.................142
  humidifier wiring............143
  resistance wiring run........142
  resistance cable................153
  thermostat............152, 278
  thermostat wiring.............145
  wall heater......................152

Item Description	Unit	Remove	Replace	Total
GAS FURNACE ▶ *continued* **Gas forced-air furnace 75,000 btu**	ea	$52.60	$1,174.00	$1,226.60
Replace Materials ....525.00 Labor..........649.00				
Remove .... Labor...........52.60				
Gas forced-air furnace 100,000 btu	ea	$52.60	$1,326.00	$1,378.60
Replace Materials....600.00 Labor..........726.00				
Remove .... Labor...........52.60				
Gas forced-air furnace, 125,000 btu	ea	$52.60	$1,474.00	$1,526.60
Replace Materials....680.00 Labor..........794.00				
Remove .... Labor...........52.60				
Gas forced-air furnace, 150,000 btu	ea	$52.60	$1,677.00	$1,729.60
Replace Materials....840.00 Labor..........837.00				
Remove .... Labor...........52.60				
Remove gas forced-air furnace for work, then reinstall	ea	–	$246.00	$246.00
Replace .... Labor..........246.00				
OIL FURNACE ▶ *Includes connection only. Does not include wiring run, plenums, ducts, or flues.* **Oil forced-air furnace 56,000 btu**	ea	$59.00	$1,600.00	$1,659.00
Replace Materials ..1000.00 Labor 600.00				
Remove .... Labor...........59.00				
Oil forced-air furnace 84,000 btu	ea	$59.00	$1,770.00	$1,829.00
Replace Materials ...1150.00 Labor..........620.00				
Remove .... Labor...........59.00				
Oil forced-air furnace 95,000 btu	ea	$59.00	$1,870.00	$1,929.00
Replace Materials...1230.00 Labor 640.00				
Remove .... Labor...........59.00				
Oil forced-air furnace 134,000 btu	ea	$59.00	$2,362.00	$2,421.00
Replace Materials ..1500.00 Labor..........862.00				
Remove .... Labor...........59.00				
Remove oil forced-air furnace for work, then reinstall	ea	–	$264.00	$264.00
Replace .... Labor..........264.00				
SERVICE FURNACE ▶ **Service furnace**	ea	–	$92.50	$92.50
Replace Materials........9.50 Labor 83.00				
▶ Check, replace filters, and clean.				
HEAT PUMP ▶ **Heat pump, 2 ton with supplementary heat coil**	ea	$67.30	$3,444.00	$3,511.30
Replace Materials..2500.00 Labor..........944.00				
Remove .... Labor...........67.30				
Heat pump, 4 ton with supplementary heat coil	ea	$67.30	$5,910.00	$5,977.30
Replace Materials..4500.00 Labor........1410.00				
Remove .... Labor...........67.30				
Heat pump, 5 ton with supplementary heat coil	ea	$67.30	$6,690.00	$6,757.30
Replace Materials..5000.00 Labor 1690.00				
Remove .... Labor...........67.30				
Remove heat pump for work, then reinstall	ea	–	$1,060.00	$1,060.00
Replace .... Labor.......1060.00				
HUMIDIFIER ▶ *Centrifugal atomizing.* **Humidifier, 5 pounds per hour**	ea	$48.80	$1,685.00	$1,733.80
Replace Materials ..1500.00 Labor..........185.00				
Remove .... Labor 48.80				

Item Description	Unit	Remove	Replace	Total	
Humidifier, 10 pounds per hour *Replace* Materials...1750.00 Labor ....215.00 *Remove* .... Labor 48.80	ea	$48.80	$1,965.00	$2,013.80	
Remove humidifier for work, then reinstall *Replace* .... Labor.........144.00	ea	–	$144.00	$144.00	
3" diameter double wall furnace vent pipe (all fuels) *Replace* Materials........3.90 Labor ....13.70 *Remove* .... Labor 1.16	lf	$1.16	$17.60	$18.76	◄ **FURNACE VENT PIPE**
4" diameter double wall furnace vent pipe (all fuels) *Replace* Materials........4.80 Labor ....15.40 *Remove* .... Labor 1.16	lf	$1.16	$20.20	$21.36	
5" diameter double wall furnace vent pipe (all fuels) *Replace* Materials........5.60 Labor ....17.00 *Remove* .... Labor 1.16	lf	$1.16	$22.60	$23.76	
6" diameter double wall furnace vent pipe (all fuels) *Replace* Materials........6.60 Labor...........18.90 *Remove* .... Labor 1.16	lf	$1.16	$25.50	$26.66	
7" diameter double wall furnace vent pipe (all fuels) *Replace* Materials........9.80 Labor ....23.50 *Remove* .... Labor 1.16	lf	$1.16	$33.30	$34.46	
8" diameter double wall furnace vent pipe (all fuels) *Replace* Materials......10.90 Labor ....25.80 *Remove* .... Labor 1.16	lf	$1.16	$36.70	$37.86	
Remove furnace vent pipe for work, then reinstall *Replace* .... Labor.........13.70	lf	–	$13.70	$13.70	
Central air conditioning system, complete, 1 ton *Replace* Materials ....770.00 Labor.........296.20	ea	–	$1,066.20	$1,066.20	◄ **CENTRAL AC** *Includes condensing unit, coil, copper lines, and installation.*
Central air conditioning system, complete, 1-1/2 ton *Replace* Materials ....865.00 Labor.........342.70	ea	–	$1,207.70	$1,207.70	
Central air conditioning system, complete, 2 ton *Replace* Materials ....960.00 Labor 412.40	ea	–	$1,372.40	$1,372.40	
Central air conditioning system, complete, 3 ton *Replace* Materials...1550.00 Labor.........355.00	ea	–	$1,905.00	$1,905.00	
Central air conditioning system, complete, 4 ton *Replace* Materials...1930.00 Labor.........784.00	ea	–	$2,714.00	$2,714.00	
Central air conditioning system, complete, 5 ton *Replace* Materials..2380.00 Labor........1130.00	ea	–	$3,510.00	$3,510.00	
Air conditioning unit service *Replace* Materials ......45.00 Labor 84.70	ea	–	$129.70	$129.70	◄ **AC SERVICE**
Recharge AC system, 5 lbs of refrigerant *Replace* Materials .....110.00 Labor...........72.60	ea	–	$182.60	$182.60	◄ **RECHARGE AC UNIT**
Recharge AC system, 10 lbs of refrigerant *Replace* Materials ....225.00 Labor...........79.90	ea	–	$304.90	$304.90	

RELATED ITEMS

Cleaning 63
Electrical
  baseboard heater..............153
  baseboard
  heater wiring.............142, 144
  furnace wiring........................142
  humidifier wiring................143
  resistance wiring run 142
  resistance cable................153
  thermostat................152, 278
  thermostat wiring..............145
  wall heater........................152

	Item Description	Unit	Remove	Replace	Total
RECHARGE ▶ AC UNIT *continued*	**Recharge AC system, 14 lbs of refrigerant** *Replace* Materials.....315.00 Labor...........87.10	ea	–	$402.10	$402.10
THROUGH-WALL ▶ AC UNIT	**Through-wall AC unit, 5,000 btu** *Replace* Materials....800.00 Labor...........427.00 *Remove* .... Labor 43.10	ea	$43.10	$1,227.00	$1,270.10
	Through-wall AC unit, 8,000 btu *Replace* Materials....825.00 Labor...........441.00 *Remove* .... Labor 43.10	ea	$43.10	$1,266.00	$1,309.10
	Through-wall AC unit, 12,000 btu *Replace* Materials ....975.00 Labor.........513.00 *Remove* .... Labor 43.10	ea	$43.10	$1,488.00	$1,531.10
	Through-wall AC unit, 18,000 btu *Replace* Materials..1000.00 Labor..........571.00 *Remove* .... Labor 43.10	ea	$43.10	$1,571.00	$1,614.10
	Remove through-wall AC unit for work, then reinstall *Replace* .... Labor 241.00	ea	–	$241.00	$241.00
THROUGH-WALL ▶ AC & HEAT UNIT	**Through-wall combination 6,000 btu AC and 4,040 btu heat unit** *Replace* Materials ..1250.00 Labor...........494.00 *Remove* .... Labor...........45.10	ea	$45.10	$1,744.00	$1,789.10
	Through-wall combination 9,500 btu AC and 4,040 btu heat unit *Replace* Materials ..1375.00 Labor ....508.00 *Remove* .... Labor...........45.10	ea	$45.10	$1,883.00	$1,928.10
	Through-wall combination 11,300 btu AC and 9,200 btu heat unit *Replace* Materials ..1500.00 Labor..........590.00 *Remove* .... Labor...........45.10	ea	$45.10	$2,090.00	$2,135.10
	Remove combination AC & heat unit for work, then reinstall *Replace* .... Labor..........259.00	ea	–	$259.00	$259.00
EVAPORATIVE ▶ COOLER *Roof mount. Includes up to 36 lf of copper water supply tubing and electrical hookup.*	**Evaporative cooler, 2,000 cfm** *Replace* Materials ....750.00 Labor ....363.00 *Remove* .... Labor...........47.40	ea	$47.40	$1,113.00	$1,160.40
	Evaporative cooler, 4,300 cfm *Replace* Materials ..1000.00 Labor...........462.00 *Remove* .... Labor...........47.40	ea	$47.40	$1,462.00	$1,509.40
	Evaporative cooler, 4,700 cfm *Replace* Materials....1075.00 Labor ....489.00 *Remove* .... Labor...........47.40	ea	$47.40	$1,564.00	$1,611.40
	Evaporative cooler, 5,600 cfm *Replace* Materials....1175.00 Labor ....528.00 *Remove* .... Labor...........47.40	ea	$47.40	$1,703.00	$1,750.40
grille ▷	**Evaporative cooler grille** *Replace* Materials ......65.00 Labor ....32.90 *Remove* .... Labor 4.83	ea	$4.83	$97.90	$102.73
	Remove evaporative cooler for work, then reinstall *Replace* .... Labor..........456.00	ea	–	$456.00	$456.00

Item Description	Unit	Remove	Replace	Total	
Cold-air return grille	ea	$4.83	$76.10	$80.93	◄ **COLD-AIR GRILLE**
Replace Materials......30.00 Labor..........46.10					
Remove .... Labor..........4.83					
Remove cold-air return grille for work, then reinstall	ea	–	$12.00	$12.00	
Replace Materials.......... Labor..........12.00					
Heat register	ea	$3.90	$50.50	$54.40	◄ **HEAT REGISTER**
Replace Materials......20.00 Labor..........30.50					
Remove .... Labor..........3.90					
Remove heat register for work, then reinstall	ea	–	$7.74	$7.74	
Replace .... Labor..........7.74					
Thermostat, heat only	ea	$6.73	$119.10	$125.83	◄ **THERMOSTAT**
Replace Materials......45.00 Labor..........74.10					See Electrical on page 152
Remove .... Labor..........6.73					for electrical system and
Thermostat, heat and air conditioning	ea	$6.73	$190.00	$196.73	baseboard heater
Replace Materials......75.00 Labor..........115.00					thermostats.
Remove .... Labor..........6.73					
Thermostat, programmable	ea	$6.73	$259.00	$265.73	
Replace Materials......90.00 Labor..........169.00					
Remove .... Labor..........6.73					
Thermostat, programmable, with zone control	ea	$6.73	$313.00	$319.73	
Replace Materials....105.00 Labor..........208.00					
Remove .... Labor..........6.73					
Remove thermostat for work, then reinstall	ea	–	$30.10	$30.10	
Replace .... Labor..........30.10					

✍ NOTES: _____

_____

_____ end

TIME & MATERIAL CHARTS (selected items)

HVAC Materials

DESCRIPTION	UNIT PRICE
Ductwork	
per sf of floor...	$.50 sf
Electric forced-air furnace	
10,200 btu..	$400.00 ea
34,100 btu..	$550.00 ea
Gas forced-air furnace	
45,000 btu..	$425.00 ea
150,000 btu..	$840.00 ea
Oil forced-air furnace	
56,000 btu..	$1000.00 ea
134,000 btu..	$1500.00 ea

HVAC Labor

LABORER	BASE WAGE	PAID LEAVE	TRUE WAGE	FICA	FUTA	WORKER'S COMP.	UNEMPLOY. INSUR.	HEALTH INSUR.	RETIRE (401K)	LIABILITY INSUR.	COST PER HOUR
HVAC installer	$28.20	2.20	$30.40	2.33	.24	4.41	2.65	2.92	.91	4.56	**$48.40**
Demolition laborer	$14.40	1.12	$15.52	1.19	.12	5.01	1.35	.47	2.33	28.90	**$28.90**

Paid Leave is calculated based on two weeks paid vacation, one week sick leave, and seven paid holidays. Employer's matching portion of **FICA** is 7.65 percent. **FUTA** (Federal Unemployment) is .8 percent. **Worker's compensation** for the HVAC trade was calculated using a national average of 14.47 percent. **Unemployment insurance** was calculated using a national average of 8.7 percent. **Health insurance** was calculated based on a projected national average for 2005 of $580 per employee (and family when applicable) per month. Employer pays 80 percent for a per month cost of $464 per employee. **Retirement** is based on a 401(k) retirement program with employer matching of 50 percent. Employee contributions to the 401(k) plan are an average of 6 percent of the true wage. **Liability insurance** is based on a national average of 14.0 percent.

HVAC Labor Productivity

WORK DESCRIPTION	LABORER	COST PER HOUR	PRODUCTIVITY	UNIT PRICE
Demolition				
remove electric forced-air furnace	demolition laborer	$28.90	1.89	**$54.60** ea
remove gas forced-air furnace	demolition laborer	$28.90	1.82	**$52.60** ea
remove oil forced-air furnace	demolition laborer	$28.90	2.04	**$59.00** ea
remove heat pump	demolition laborer	$28.90	2.33	**$67.30** ea
remove humidifier	demolition laborer	$28.90	1.69	**$48.80** ea
remove through-wall AC unit	demolition laborer	$28.90	1.49	**$43.10** ea
remove combination AC and heat unit	demolition laborer	$28.90	1.56	**$45.10** ea
remove evaporative cooler	demolition laborer	$28.90	1.64	**$47.40** ea
remove heat register	demolition laborer	$28.90	.135	**$3.90** ea
remove thermostat	demolition laborer	$28.90	.233	**$6.73** ea
Install electric forced air furnace				
10,200 btu	HVAC installer	$48.40	10.8	**$523.00** ea
34,100 btu	HVAC installer	$48.40	13.8	**$668.00** ea
Install gas forced-air furnace				
45,000 btu	HVAC installer	$48.40	11.3	**$547.00** ea
150,000 btu	HVAC installer	$48.40	17.3	**$837.00** ea
Install oil forced-air furnace				
56,000 btu	HVAC installer	$48.40	12.4	**$600.00** ea
134,000 btu	HVAC installer	$48.40	17.8	**$862.00** ea
Install heat pump with supplementary heat coil				
2 ton	HVAC installer	$48.40	19.5	**$944.00** ea
Install humidifier				
5 pounds	HVAC installer	$48.40	3.83	**$185.00** ea
Double wall furnace flue (all fuels)				
4" diameter	HVAC installer	$48.40	.318	**$15.40** lf
8" diameter	HVAC installer	$48.40	.533	**$25.80** lf
Through-wall AC unit				
5,000 btu	HVAC installer	$48.40	8.83	**$427.00** ea
18,000 btu	HVAC installer	$48.40	11.8	**$571.00** ea
Through-wall combination AC and heat unit				
6,000 btu AC and 4,040 btu heat unit	HVAC installer	$48.40	10.2	**$494.00** ea
11,300 btu AC and 9,200 btu heat unit	HVAC installer	$48.40	12.2	**$590.00** ea
Evaporative cooler				
2,000 cfm	HVAC installer	$48.40	7.49	**$363.00** ea
5,600 cfm	HVAC installer	$48.40	10.9	**$528.00** ea
Thermostat				
heat only	HVAC installer	$48.40	1.53	**$74.10** ea
heat and air conditioning	HVAC installer	$48.40	2.38	**$115.00** ea
programmable	HVAC installer	$48.40	3.49	**$169.00** ea
programmable, with zone control	HVAC installer	$48.40	4.29	**$208.00** ea

22 .... *Insulation*

Item Description	Unit	Remove	Replace	Total	
Minimum charge for insulation work *Replace* Material ....40.00 Labor...........69.00	ea	–	$109.00	$109.00	◄ **MINIMUM**
3″ deep vermiculite attic insulation *Replace* Material........ 1.09 Labor............. .25 *Remove* .... Labor............. .40	sf	$.40	$1.34	$1.74	◄ **VERMICULITE** *Poured by hand from 3 cf bags.*
4″ deep vermiculite attic insulation *Replace* Material.........1.46 Labor............. .29 *Remove* .... Labor............. .49	sf	$.49	$1.75	$2.24	
5″ deep vermiculite attic insulation *Replace* Material.........1.82 Labor............. .29 *Remove* .... Labor............. .58	sf	$.58	$2.11	$2.69	
6″ deep vermiculite attic insulation *Replace* Material.........2.20 Labor............. .32 *Remove* .... Labor............. .72	sf	$.72	$2.52	$3.24	
R11 blown mineral wool attic insulation (3-1/2″ deep) *Replace* Material........... .57 Labor............. .32 *Remove* .... Labor............. .35	sf	$.35	$.89	$1.24	◄ **MINERAL WOOL** *See the next page for additional costs to blow into existing walls.*
R19 blown mineral wool attic insulation (6″ deep) *Replace* Material........... .86 Labor............. .35 *Remove* .... Labor............. .38	sf	$.38	$1.21	$1.59	
R30 blown mineral wool attic insulation (10″ deep) *Replace* Material.........1.40 Labor............. .41 *Remove* .... Labor............. .55	sf	$.55	$1.81	$2.36	
R38 blown mineral wool attic insulation (12″ deep) *Replace* Material.........1.89 Labor............. .51 *Remove* .... Labor............. .64	sf	$.64	$2.40	$3.04	
R12 blown cellulose attic insulation (3-1/2″ deep) *Replace* Material........... .55 Labor............. .32 *Remove* .... Labor............. .40	sf	$.40	$.87	$1.27	◄ **CELLULOSE** *See the next page for additional costs to blow into existing walls.*
R21 blown cellulose attic insulation (6″ deep) *Replace* Material........... .83 Labor............. .38 *Remove* .... Labor............. .43	sf	$.43	$1.21	$1.64	
R33 blown cellulose attic insulation (10″ deep) *Replace* Material ....1.35 Labor............. .41 *Remove* .... Labor............. .66	sf	$.66	$1.76	$2.42	
R42 blown cellulose attic insulation (12″ deep) *Replace* Material.........1.81 Labor............. .51 *Remove* .... Labor............. .75	sf	$.75	$2.32	$3.07	
R11 blown fiberglass attic insulation (5″ deep) *Replace* Material........... .48 Labor............. .32 *Remove* .... Labor............. .35	sf	$.35	$.80	$1.15	◄ **BLOWN FIBERGLASS** *See the next page for additional costs to blow into existing walls.*

RELATED ITEMS

Masonry
Polystyrene block inserts....301
loose block insulation 302
2″ polystyrene cavity wall insulation.....295

Rough Carpentry
factory built panels..........443
insulating sheathing..........441

	Item Description	Unit	Remove	Replace	Total
BLOWN ▶ **FIBERGLASS** *continued*	**R19 blown fiberglass attic insulation (8" deep)** *Replace* Material.......... .73 Labor............ .35 *Remove* .... Labor............ .38	sf	$.38	$1.08	$1.46
	R30 blown fiberglass attic insulation (13" deep) *Replace* Material.........1.19 Labor............ .41 *Remove* .... Labor............ .55	sf	$.55	$1.60	$2.15
	R38 blown fiberglass attic insulation (16" deep) *Replace* Material.........1.59 Labor............ .51 *Remove* .... Labor............ .64	sf	$.64	$2.10	$2.74
ADD TO INSULATE ▶ **EXISTING WALLS** *Add to blown in costs.* *Includes holes drilled 16"* *on center every 4' of* *height, patching, and* *painting if necessary.*	**Add 285% to blow insulation into existing wall with stucco** **Add 233% to blow insulation into existing wall with siding** **Add 318% to blow insulation into existing wall with masonry veneer** **Add 216% to blow insulation into existing wall through drywall**				
FIBERGLASS ▶ **BATT IN CEILING** **OR FLOOR** *Based on installation in* *framing 16" on center.* *Add 5% for 12" oc and* *deduct 7% for 24" oc.*	**R11 batt insulation (3-1/2" deep) attic, ceiling or floor installation** *Replace* Material.......... .41 Labor............ .29 *Remove* .... Labor............ .26	sf	$.26	$.70	$.96
	R19 batt insulation (6" deep) attic, ceiling or floor installation *Replace* Material.......... .61 Labor............ .35 *Remove* .... Labor............ .38	sf	$.38	$.96	$1.34
	R30 batt insulation (9-1/2" deep) attic, ceiling or floor installation *Replace* Material........ 1.00 Labor............ .38 *Remove* .... Labor............ .43	sf	$.43	$1.38	$1.81
	R38 batt insulation (12" deep) attic, ceiling or floor installation *Replace* Material.........1.34 Labor............ .48 *Remove* .... Labor............ .52	sf	$.52	$1.82	$2.34
FIBERGLASS ▶ **BATT IN WALL** *Based on installation in* *framing 16" on center.* *Add 5% for 12" oc and* *deduct 7% for 24" oc.*	**R6 batt insulation (1-3/4" deep) wall installation (between furring strips)** *Replace* Material.......... .24 Labor............ .32 *Remove* .... Labor............ .20	sf	$.20	$.56	$.76
	R11 batt insulation (3-1/2" deep) wall installation *Replace* Material.......... .41 Labor............ .35 *Remove* .... Labor............ .26	sf	$.26	$.76	$1.02
	R19 batt insulation (6" deep) wall installation *Replace* Material.......... .61 Labor............ .41 *Remove* .... Labor............ .38	sf	$.38	$1.02	$1.40
	R19 batt insulation (8" deep) wall installation *Replace* Material.......... .81 Labor............ .48 *Remove* .... Labor............ .43	sf	$.43	$1.29	$1.72
ADD FOR ▶ **BATT FACE**	**Add 8% for Kraft face** **Add 10% for foil face** **Add 14% for plastic vapor barrier**				
RIGID FOAM ▶ *Glued and/or nailed in* *place on walls or roof.*	**1/2" rigid foam insulation board** *Replace* Material.......... .50 Labor............ .45 *Remove* .... Labor............ .20	sf	$.20	$.95	$1.15

Item Description	Unit	Remove	Replace	Total
3/4" rigid foam insulation board	sf	$.20	$1.06	$1.26
Replace Material .... .61 Labor .... .45				
Remove .... Labor .... .20				
1" rigid foam insulation board	sf	$.20	$1.26	$1.46
Replace Material .... .81 Labor .... .45				
Remove .... Labor .... .20				
2" rigid foam insulation board	sf	$.20	$1.52	$1.72
Replace Material .... 1.07 Labor .... .45				
Remove .... Labor .... .20				

RELATED ITEMS

Masonry
Polystyrene block inserts ...301
loose block insulation 302
2" polystyrene
  cavity wall insulation 295

Rough Carpentry
factory built panels 443
insulating sheathing..........441

✎ NOTES: _____

_____ end

TIME & MATERIAL CHARTS (selected items)

Insulation Materials

DESCRIPTION	MATERIAL PRICE	GROSS COVERAGE	WASTE	NET COVERAGE	UNIT PRICE
Vermiculite attic insulation					
3" deep	$1.05 sf	1	4%	.96	$1.09 sf
4" deep	$1.40 sf	1	4%	.96	$1.46 sf
5" deep	$1.75 sf	1	4%	.96	$1.82 sf
6" deep	$2.11 sf	1	4%	.96	$2.20 sf
Blown mineral wool insulation					
R 11 (3-1/2" deep)	$.55 sf	1	4%	.96	$.57 sf
R 19 (6" deep)	$.83 sf	1	4%	.96	$.86 sf
R 30 (10" deep)	$1.34 sf	1	4%	.96	$1.40 sf
R 38 (12" deep)	$1.81 sf	1	4%	.96	$1.89 sf
Blown cellulose insulation					
R 12 blown (3-1/2" deep)	$.53 sf	1	4%	.96	$.55 sf
R 21 blown (6" deep)	$.80 sf	1	4%	.96	$.83 sf
R 33 blown (10" deep)	$1.30 sf	1	4%	.96	$1.35 sf
R 42 blown (12" deep)	$1.74 sf	1	4%	.96	$1.81 sf
Blown fiberglass insulation					
R 11 (5" deep)	$.46 sf	1	4%	.96	$.48 sf
R 19 (8" deep)	$.70 sf	1	4%	.96	$.73 sf
R 30 (13" deep)	$1.14 sf	1	4%	.96	$1.19 sf
R 38 (16" deep)	$1.53 sf	1	4%	.96	$1.59 sf
Fiberglass batt insulation in ceiling or floor					
R 11 (3-1/2" deep)	$.39 sf	1	4%	.96	$.41 sf
R 19 (6" deep)	$.59 sf	1	4%	.96	$.61 sf
R 30 (9-1/2" deep)	$.96 sf	1	4%	.96	$1.00 sf
R 38 (12" deep)	$1.29 sf	1	4%	.96	$1.34 sf
Fiberglass batt insulation in wall					
R 6 (1-3/4" deep) (between furring strips)	$.23 sf	1	4%	.96	$.24 sf
R 11 (3-1/2" deep)	$.39 sf	1	4%	.96	$.41 sf
R 19 (6" deep)	$.59 sf	1	4%	.96	$.61 sf
R 25 (8" deep)	$.78 sf	1	4%	.96	$.81 sf
Rigid foam insulation board					
1/2"	$.48 sf	1	4%	.96	$.50 sf
3/4"	$.59 sf	1	4%	.96	$.61 sf
1"	$.78 sf	1	4%	.96	$.81 sf
2"	$1.03 sf	1	4%	.96	$1.07 sf

Insulation Labor

LABORER	BASE WAGE	PAID LEAVE	TRUE WAGE	FICA	FUTA	WORKER'S COMP.	UNEMPLOY. INSUR.	HEALTH INSUR.	RETIRE (401K)	LIABILITY INSUR.	COST PER HOUR
Insulation installer	$16.60	1.30	$17.90	1.37	.14	4.70	1.56	2.92	.54	2.69	**$31.80**
Demolition laborer	$14.40	1.12	$15.52	1.19	.12	5.01	1.35	2.92	.47	2.33	**$28.90**

Paid Leave is calculated based on two weeks paid vacation, one week sick leave, and seven paid holidays. Employer's matching portion of **FICA** is 7.65 percent. **FUTA** (Federal Unemployment) is .8 percent. **Worker's compensation** for the insulation trade was calculated using a national average of 26.20 percent. **Unemployment insurance** was calculated using a national average of 8.7 percent. **Health insurance** was calculated based on a projected national average for 2005 of $580 per employee (and family when applicable) per month. Employer pays 80 percent for a per month cost of $464 per employee. **Retirement** is based on a 401(k) retirement program with employer matching of 50 percent. Employee contributions to the 401(k) plan are an average of 6 percent of the true wage. **Liability insurance** is based on a national average of 14.0 percent.

Insulation Labor Productivity

WORK DESCRIPTION	LABORER	COST PER HOUR	PRODUCTIVITY	UNIT PRICE
Pour vermiculite attic insulation				
3" deep	insulation installer	$31.80	.008	**$.25** sf
4" deep	insulation installer	$31.80	.009	**$.29** sf
5" deep	insulation installer	$31.80	.009	**$.29** sf
6" deep	insulation installer	$31.80	.010	**$.32** sf
Blow in mineral wool insulation				
R11 (3-1/2" deep)	insulation installer	$31.80	.010	**$.32** sf
R19 (6" deep)	insulation installer	$31.80	.011	**$.35** sf
R30 (10" deep)	insulation installer	$31.80	.013	**$.41** sf
R38 (12" deep)	insulation installer	$31.80	.016	**$.51** sf
Blow in cellulose insulation				
R12 (3-1/2" deep)	insulation installer	$31.80	.32	**$.32** sf
R21 (6" deep)	insulation installer	$31.80	.012	**$.38** sf
R33 (10" deep)	insulation installer	$31.80	.013	**$.41** sf
R42 (12" deep)	insulation installer	$31.80	.016	**$.51** sf
Blow in fiberglass insulation				
R11 (5" deep)	insulation installer	$31.80	.010	**$.32** sf
R19 (8" deep)	insulation installer	$31.80	.011	**$.35** sf
R30 (13" deep)	insulation installer	$31.80	.013	**$.41** sf
R38 (16" deep)	insulation installer	$31.80	.016	**$.51** sf
Install fiberglass batt insulation in ceiling or floor				
R11 (3-1/2" deep)	insulation installer	$31.80	.29	**$.29** sf
R19 (6" deep)	insulation installer	$31.80	.011	**$.35** sf
R30 (9-1/2" deep)	insulation installer	$31.80	.012	**$.38** sf
R38 (12" deep)	insulation installer	$31.80	.015	**$.48** sf
Install fiberglass batt insulation in wall				
R6 (1-3/4" deep) (between furring strips)	insulation installer	$31.80	.010	**$.32** sf
R11 (3-1/2" deep)	insulation installer	$31.80	.011	**$.35** sf
R19 (6" deep)	insulation installer	$31.80	.013	**$.41** sf
R25 (8" deep)	insulation installer	$31.80	.015	**$.48** sf
Install rigid foam insulation board				
all thicknesses	insulation installer	$31.80	.014	**$.45** sf

NOTES: _____

_____

_____

_____

_____ end

23 .... *Masking & Moving*

Item Description	Unit			Total	
Minimum charge for masking or moving work *Mask* Material ....17.00 Labor..........59.70	ea	–	–	$76.70	◄ **MINIMUM**
Mask small room *Mask* Material ....3.22 Labor 30.50	ea	–	–	$33.72	◄ **MASK ROOM**
Mask average size room *Mask* Material ....3.68 Labor 35.20	ea	–	–	$38.88	
Mask large room *Mask* Material ....4.29 Labor..........41.80	ea	–	–	$46.09	
Mask very large room *Mask* Material ....4.53 Labor 50.90	ea	–	–	$55.43	
Mask room per lf of wall *Mask* Material .... .11 Labor............. .88	lf	–	–	$.99	◄ **MASK ROOM PER LF**
Mask small window *Mask* Material ....1.63 Labor 7.23	ea	–	–	$8.86	◄ **MASK WINDOW**
Mask average size window *Mask* Material ....1.71 Labor 8.47	ea	–	–	$10.18	
Mask large window *Mask* Material ....1.82 Labor..........10.20	ea	–	–	$12.02	
Mask very large window *Mask* Material ....1.90 Labor..........12.50	ea	–	–	$14.40	
Mask door or opening per lf of opening *Mask* Material .... .07 Labor............. .83	lf	–	–	$.90	◄ **MASK DOOR OR OPENING PER LF**
Mask small door or opening *Mask* Material ....1.79 Labor 7.15	ea	–	–	$8.94	◄ **MASK DOOR OR OPENING**
Mask average size door or opening *Mask* Material ....1.87 Labor 8.33	ea	–	–	$10.20	
Mask large door or opening *Mask* Material ....1.98 Labor..........10.00	ea	–	–	$11.98	
Mask very large door or opening *Mask* Material ....2.06 Labor..........12.20	ea	–	–	$14.26	
Mask woodwork per lf of woodwork *Mask* Material .... .07 Labor............. .80	lf	–	–	$.87	◄ **MASK WOODWORK**
Mask baseboard heater *Mask* Material ....1.36 Labor..........6.11	ea	–	–	$7.47	◄ **MASK HEATER**
Mask light fixture *Mask* Material .... 1.04 Labor..........5.01	ea	–	–	$6.05	◄ **MASK LIGHT FIXTURE**

Item Description	Unit			Total
MASK OUTLET ▶ **Mask outlet or switch (remove cover)**	ea	–	–	**$3.38**
OR SWITCH *Mask* Material .... .24 Labor 3.14				
MASK BATHROOM ▶ **Mask small bathroom**	ea	–	–	**$35.16**
Mask Material ....3.26 Labor............31.90				
Mask average size bathroom	ea	–	–	**$40.82**
Mask Material ....3.72 Labor............37.10				
Mask large bathroom	ea	–	–	**$48.66**
Mask Material ....4.36 Labor 44.30				
Mask very large bathroom	ea	–	–	**$59.65**
Mask Material ....4.65 Labor............55.00				
MASK KITCHEN ▶ **Mask small kitchen**	ea	–	–	**$36.86**
Mask Material ....3.86 Labor 33.00				
Mask average size kitchen	ea	–	–	**$43.00**
Mask Material ....4.20 Labor 38.80				
Mask large kitchen	ea	–	–	**$51.11**
Mask Material ....4.61 Labor 46.50				
Mask very large kitchen	ea	–	–	**$63.40**
Mask Material ....4.80 Labor 58.60				
MASK TILE, ▶ **Mask tile, marble, or stone per lf of edge**	lf	–	–	**$.94**
MARBLE, OR STONE *Mask* Material .... .09 Labor .... .85				
MOVE & COVER ▶ **Move and cover small room contents**	ea	–	–	**$43.55**
ROOM CONTENTS *Move* Material ....9.15 Labor 34.40				
Move and cover average room contents	ea	–	–	**$52.10**
Move Material ....10.30 Labor...........41.80				
Move and cover heavy or above average room contents	ea	–	–	**$64.40**
Move Material...........11.60 Labor...........52.80				
Move and cover very heavy or above average room contents	ea	–	–	**$88.10**
Move Material...........13.80 Labor...........74.30				

TIME & MATERIAL CHARTS (selected items)

Masking & Moving Labor											
LABORER	BASE WAGE	PAID LEAVE	TRUE WAGE	FICA	FUTA	WORKER'S COMP.	UNEMPLOY. INSUR.	HEALTH INSUR.	RETIRE (401K)	LIABILITY INSUR.	COST PER HOUR
Laborer..................	$14.50	1.13	$15.63	1.20	.13	3.48	1.36	2.92	.47	2.34	$27.50

Paid Leave is calculated based on two weeks paid vacation, one week sick leave, and seven paid holidays. Employer's matching portion of **FICA** is 7.65 percent. **FUTA** (Federal Unemployment) is .8 percent. **Worker's compensation** for the masking & movingtrade was calculated using a national average of 22.24 percent. **Unemployment insurance** was calculated using a national average of 8.7 percent. **Health insurance** was calculated based on a projected national average for 2005 of $580 per employee (and family when applicable) per month. Employer pays 80 percent for a per month cost of $464 per employee. **Retirement** is based on a 401(k) retirement program with employer matching of 50 percent. Employee contributions to the 401(k) plan are an average of 6 percent of the true wage. **Liability insurance** is based on a national average of 14.0 percent.

24 .... *Masonry*

Item Description	Unit	Remove	Replace	Total
Minimum charge for masonry work	ea	–	**$429.00**	**$429.00**	◄ **MINIMUM**

    Replace Materials ....150.00   Labor.........279.00

Deduct 16% for common brick   ◄ **COMMON BRICK**

Item Description	Unit	Remove	Replace	Total
4″ wide standard non-modular brick wall	sf	$2.51	$12.70	$15.21

    Replace Materials........5.58   Labor 7.12
    Remove ....   Labor 2.51
    ► Non-modular bricks. Actual dimensions: 3-3/4″ thick by 2-1/4″ high by 8″ long.

◄ **4″ WIDE BRICK WALL**
With 3/8″ wide mortar joints. Includes 4% waste for brick and 25% waste for mortar.

Item Description	Unit	Remove	Replace	Total
4″ wide oversize non-modular brick wall	sf	$2.51	$11.69	$14.20

    Replace Materials........4.65   Labor 7.04
    Remove ....   Labor 2.51
    ► Non-modular bricks. Actual dimensions: 3-3/4″ thick by 2-3/4″ high by 8″ long.

Item Description	Unit	Remove	Replace	Total
4″ wide three-inch non-modular brick wall	sf	$2.51	$11.67	$14.18

    Replace Materials........4.67   Labor 7.00
    Remove ....   Labor 2.51
    ► Non-modular bricks. Actual dimensions: 3″ thick by 2-3/4″ high by 9-3/4″ long. Three-inch bricks also come in lengths of 9-5/8″ and 8-3/4″ and widths vary from 2-5/8″ to 3″. Normally used as a veneer unit.

BRICK WALLS

All brick walls are made from average to high quality face brick. Standard quality bricks will be up to **15%** less and higher quality bricks will vary by as much as **45%**.

Brick sizes come in two general categories: non-modular and modular. Actual dimensions are listed for non-modular bricks.

Item Description	Unit	Remove	Replace	Total
4″ wide standard brick wall	sf	$2.51	$11.03	$13.54

    Replace Materials........3.95   Labor 7.08
    Remove ....   Labor 2.51
    ► Modular bricks. Nominal dimensions: 4″ thick by 2-2/3″ high by 8″ long.

Item Description	Unit	Remove	Replace	Total
4″ wide engineer brick wall	sf	$2.51	$10.03	$12.54

    Replace Materials........4.12   Labor 5.91
    Remove ....   Labor 2.51
    ► Modular bricks. Nominal dimensions: 4″ thick by 3-1/5″ high by 8″ long.

Modular bricks are designed to fit together with a minimum of cutting which saves labor and reduces waste.

Nominal dimensions for modular bricks include the manufactured dimensions *plus* the thickness of the mortar joint for which the unit was designed (usually 1/2″).

Item Description	Unit	Remove	Replace	Total
4″ wide jumbo closure brick wall	sf	$2.51	$9.17	$11.68

    Replace Materials........4.14   Labor 5.03
    Remove ....   Labor 2.51
    ► Also called economy 8. Modular bricks. Nominal dimensions: 4″ thick by 4″ high by 8″ long.

Item Description	Unit	Remove	Replace	Total
4″ wide double brick wall	sf	$2.51	$7.61	$10.12

    Replace Materials........3.38   Labor 4.23
    Remove ....   Labor 2.51
    ► Modular bricks. Nominal dimensions: 4″ thick by 5-1/3″ high by 8″ long.

Actual brick sizes vary from manufacturer to manufacturer. The sizes in this section are typical.

Item Description	Unit	Remove	Replace	Total
4″ wide Roman brick wall	sf	$2.51	$12.20	$14.71

    Replace Materials........5.50   Labor 6.70
    Remove ....   Labor 2.51
    ► Modular bricks. Nominal dimensions: 4″ thick by 2″ high by 12″ long.

Item Description	Unit	Remove	Replace	Total
4″ wide Norman brick wall	sf	$2.51	$9.96	$12.47

    Replace Materials........4.51   Labor 5.45
    Remove ....   Labor 2.51
    ► Modular bricks. Nominal dimensions: 4″ thick by 2-2/3″ high by 12″ long.

RELATED ITEMS

Cleaning 63
Fireplaces.....................241
Painting 340

Item Description	Unit	Remove	Replace	Total
4″ wide Norwegian brick wall	sf	$2.51	$8.13	$10.64

    Replace Materials........3.48   Labor 4.65
    Remove ....   Labor 2.51
    ► Modular bricks. Nominal dimensions: 4″ thick by 3-1/5″ high by 12″ long.

Item Description	Unit	Remove	Replace	Total
4" WIDE ▶ BRICK WALL *continued*				
4" wide jumbo utility brick wall	sf	**$2.51**	**$8.68**	**$11.19**
Replace Materials........4.41 Labor 4.27				
Remove .... Labor 2.51				
▶ Also called economy 12. Modular bricks. Nominal dimensions: 4" thick by 4" high by 12" long.				
4" wide triple brick wall	sf	**$2.51**	**$7.62**	**$10.13**
Replace Materials........3.60 Labor 4.02				
Remove .... Labor 2.51				
▶ Modular bricks. Nominal dimensions: 4" thick by 5-1/3" high by 12" long.				
6" WIDE ▶ BRICK WALL *With 3/8" wide mortar joints. Includes 4% waste for brick and 25% waste for mortar.*				
6" wide Norwegian brick wall	sf	**$3.01**	**$10.01**	**$13.02**
Replace Materials........4.81 Labor 5.20				
Remove .... Labor 3.01				
▶ Modular bricks. Nominal dimensions: 6" thick by 3-1/5" high by 12" long.				
6" wide Norman brick wall	sf	**$3.01**	**$12.06**	**$15.07**
Replace Materials........5.86 Labor 6.20				
Remove .... Labor 3.01				
▶ Modular bricks. Nominal dimensions: 6" thick by 2-2/3" high by 12" long.				
6" wide jumbo brick wall	sf	**$3.01**	**$10.12**	**$13.13**
Replace Materials........5.39 Labor 4.73				
Remove .... Labor 3.01				
▶ Modular bricks. Nominal dimensions: 6" thick by 4" high by 12" long.				
8" WIDE ▶ BRICK WALL				
8" wide jumbo brick wall	sf	**$3.81**	**$11.58**	**$15.39**
Replace Materials........6.26 Labor 5.32				
Remove .... Labor 3.81				
▶ Modular bricks. Nominal dimensions: 8" thick by 4" high by 12" long. With 3/8" wide mortar joints, Includes 4% waste for brick and 25% waste for mortar.				
8" WIDE ▶ DOUBLE WYTHE BRICK WALL *With 3/8" wide mortar joints. Includes 4% waste for brick and 25% waste for mortar.*				
8" wide double wythe standard non-modular brick wall	sf	**$3.81**	**$24.42**	**$28.23**
Replace Materials........11.52 Labor 12.90				
Remove .... Labor 3.81				
▶ Non-modular bricks. Actual dimensions: 3-3/4" thick by 2-1/4" high by 8" long.				
8" wide double wythe oversize non-modular brick wall	sf	**$3.81**	**$22.36**	**$26.17**
Replace Materials........9.66 Labor 12.70				
Remove .... Labor 3.81				
▶ Non-modular bricks. Actual dimensions: 3-3/4" thick by 2-3/4" high by 8" long.				
8" wide double wythe three-inch non-modular brick wall	sf	**$3.81**	**$22.30**	**$26.11**
Replace Materials........9.70 Labor 12.60				
Remove .... Labor 3.81				
▶ Non-modular bricks. Actual dimensions: 3" thick by 2-3/4" high by 9-3/4" long. Three-inch bricks also come in lengths of 9-5/8" and 8-3/4" and widths vary from 2-5/8" to 3". Normally used as a veneer unit.				
8" wide double wythe standard brick wall	sf	**$3.81**	**$21.06**	**$24.87**
Replace Materials........8.26 Labor 12.80				
Remove .... Labor 3.81				
▶ Modular bricks. Nominal dimensions: 4" thick by 2-2/3" high by 8" long.				
8" wide double wythe engineer brick wall	sf	**$3.81**	**$19.20**	**$23.01**
Replace Materials........8.60 Labor 10.60				
Remove .... Labor 3.81				
▶ Modular bricks. Nominal dimensions: 4" thick by 3-1/5" high by 8" long.				
8" wide double wythe jumbo closure brick wall	sf	**$3.81**	**$17.69**	**$21.50**
Replace Materials........8.64 Labor 9.05				
Remove .... Labor 3.81				
▶ Also called economy 8. Modular bricks. Nominal dimensions: 4" thick by 4" high by 8" long.				

Item Description	Unit	Remove	Replace	Total
8" wide double wythe double brick wall	sf	$3.81	$14.70	$18.51
Replace Materials........7.12 Labor 7.58				
Remove .... Labor 3.81				
▶ Modular bricks. Nominal dimensions: 4" thick by 5-1/3" high by 8" long.				
8" wide double wythe Roman brick wall	sf	$3.81	$23.36	$27.17
Replace Materials........11.36 Labor 12.00				
Remove .... Labor 3.81				
▶ Modular bricks. Nominal dimensions: 4" thick by 2" high by 12" long.				
8" wide double wythe Norman brick wall	sf	$3.81	$19.18	$22.99
Replace Materials........9.38 Labor 9.80				
Remove .... Labor 3.81				
▶ Modular bricks. Nominal dimensions: 4" thick by 2-2/3" high by 12" long.				
8" wide double wythe Norwegian brick wall	sf	$3.81	$15.66	$19.47
Replace Materials........7.32 Labor 8.34				
Remove .... Labor 3.81				
▶ Modular bricks. Nominal dimensions: 4" thick by 3-1/5" high by 12" long.				
8" wide double wythe jumbo utility brick wall	sf	$3.81	$16.89	$20.70
Replace Materials........9.18 Labor 7.71				
Remove .... Labor 3.81				
▶ Also called economy 12. Modular bricks. Nominal dimensions: 4" thick by 4" high by 12" long.				
8" wide double wythe triple brick wall	sf	$3.81	$14.81	$18.62
Replace Materials........7.56 Labor 7.25				
Remove .... Labor 3.81				
▶ Modular bricks. Nominal dimensions: 4" thick by 5-1/3" high by 12" long.				
8" wide wall from 4" standard non-mod. brick and 4" block	sf	$3.81	$17.80	$21.61
Replace Materials........8.04 Labor 9.76				
Remove .... Labor 3.81				
▶ Modular bricks. Actual dimensions: 3-3/4" thick by 2-1/4" high by 8" long. Concrete block: 4" thick by 8" high by 16" long.				
8" wide wall from 4" oversize non-mod. brick and 4" block	sf	$3.81	$16.79	$20.60
Replace Materials........7.11 Labor 9.68				
Remove .... Labor 3.81				
▶ Modular bricks. Actual dimensions: 3-3/4" thick by 2-3/4" high by 8" long. Concrete block: 4" thick by 8" high by 16" long.				
8" wide wall from three-inch non-mod. brick and 4" block	sf	$3.81	$16.77	$20.58
Replace Materials........7.13 Labor 9.64				
Remove .... Labor 3.81				
▶ Modular bricks. Actual dimensions: 3" thick by 2-3/4" high by 9-3/4" long. Three-inch bricks also come in lengths of 9-5/8" and 8-3/4" and widths vary from 2-5/8" to 3". Concrete block: 4" thick by 8" high by 16" long.				
8" wide wall from 4" standard brick and 4" concrete block	sf	$3.81	$16.17	$19.98
Replace Materials........6.41 Labor 9.76				
Remove .... Labor 3.81				
▶ Modular bricks. Nominal dimensions: 4" thick by 2-2/3" high by 8" long. Concrete block: 4" thick by 8" high by 16" long.				
8" wide wall from 4" engineer brick and 4" concrete block	sf	$3.81	$15.21	$19.02
Replace Materials........6.58 Labor 8.63				
Remove .... Labor 3.81				
▶ Modular bricks. Nominal dimensions: 4" thick by 3-1/5" high by 8" long. Concrete block: 4" thick by 8" high by 16" long.				

◀ **8" WIDE BRICK & BLOCK WALL**
With 3/8" wide mortar joints. Includes 4% waste for brick and block and 25% waste for mortar.

RELATED ITEMS

Cleaning 63
Fireplaces...................241
Painting 340

Item Description	Unit	Remove	Replace	Total

8" wide wall from 4" jumbo closure brick and 4" concrete block — sf | $3.81 | $14.48 | $18.29
Replace Materials........6.60   Labor 7.88
Remove ....   Labor 3.81
▶ Modular bricks. Nominal dimensions: 4" thick by 4" high by 8" long. Concrete block: 4" thick by 8" high by 16" long.

8" wide wall from 4" double brick and 4" concrete block — sf | $3.81 | $12.96 | $16.77
Replace Materials........5.84   Labor 7.12
Remove ....   Labor 3.81
▶ Modular bricks. Nominal dimensions: 4" thick by 5-1/3" high by 8" long. Concrete block: 4" thick by 8" high by 16" long.

8" wide wall from 4" Roman brick and 4" concrete block — sf | $3.81 | $17.35 | $21.16
Replace Materials........7.96   Labor 9.39
Remove ....   Labor 3.81
▶ Modular bricks. Nominal dimensions: 4" thick by 2" high by 12" long. Concrete block: 4" thick by 8" high by 16" long.

8" wide wall from 4" Norman and 4" concrete block — sf | $3.81 | $15.22 | $19.03
Replace Materials........6.97   Labor 8.25
Remove ....   Labor 3.81
▶ Modular bricks. Nominal dimensions: 4" thick by 2-2/3" high by 12" long. Concrete block: 4" thick by 8" high by 16" long.

8" wide wall from 4" Norwegian and 4" concrete block — sf | $3.81 | $13.48 | $17.29
Replace Materials........5.94   Labor 7.54
Remove ....   Labor 3.81
▶ Modular bricks. Nominal dimensions: 4" thick by 3-1/5" high by 12" long. Concrete block: 4" thick by 8" high by 16" long.

8" wide wall from 4" jumbo utility and 4" concrete block — sf | $3.81 | $14.08 | $17.89
Replace Materials........6.87   Labor 7.21
Remove ....   Labor 3.81
▶ Modular bricks. Nominal dimensions: 4" thick by 4" high by 12" long. Concrete block: 4" thick by 8" high by 16" long.

8" wide wall from 4" triple and 4" concrete block — sf | $3.81 | $13.02 | $16.83
Replace Materials........6.06   Labor 6.96
Remove ....   Labor 3.81
▶ Modular bricks. Nominal dimensions: 4" thick by 5-1/3" high by 12" long. Concrete block: 4" thick by 8" high by 16" long.

10" wide wall from 4" standard non-mod. brick and 6" block — sf | $4.31 | $18.28 | $22.59
Replace Materials........8.39   Labor 9.89
Remove ....   Labor 4.31
▶ Modular bricks. Actual dimensions: 3-3/4" thick by 2-1/4" high by 8" long. Concrete block: 6" thick by 8" high by 16" long.

10" wide wall from 4" oversize non-mod. brick and 6" block — sf | $4.31 | $17.26 | $21.57
Replace Materials........7.46   Labor 9.80
Remove ....   Labor 4.31
▶ Modular bricks. Actual dimensions: 3-3/4" thick by 2-3/4" high by 8" long. Concrete block: 6" thick by 8" high by 16" long.

10" wide wall from three-inch non-mod. brick and 6" block — sf | $4.31 | $17.24 | $21.55
Replace Materials........7.48   Labor 9.76
Remove ....   Labor 4.31
▶ Modular bricks. Actual dimensions: 3" thick by 2-3/4" high by 9-3/4" long. Three-inch bricks also come in lengths of 9-5/8" and 8-3/4" and widths vary from 2-5/8" to 3". Concrete block: 6" thick by 8" high by 16" long.

10" wide wall from 4" standard brick and 6" concrete block — sf | $4.31 | $16.61 | $20.92
Replace Materials........6.76   Labor 9.85
Remove ....   Labor 4.31
▶ Modular bricks. Nominal dimensions: 4" thick by 2-2/3" high by 8" long. Concrete block: 6" thick by 8" high by 16" long.

Item Description	Unit	Remove	Replace	Total

10" wide wall from 4" engineer brick and 6" concrete block — sf — $4.31 — $15.69 — $20.00
Replace Materials........6.93   Labor 8.76
Remove ....   Labor 4.31
▶ Modular bricks. Nominal dimensions: 4" thick by 3-1/5" high by 8" long. Concrete block: 6" thick by 8" high by 16" long.

10" wide wall from 4" jumbo closure and 6" concrete block — sf — $4.31 — $14.91 — $19.22
Replace Materials........6.95   Labor 7.96
Remove ....   Labor 4.31
▶ Modular bricks. Nominal dimensions: 4" thick by 4" high by 8" long. Concrete block: 6" thick by 8" high by 16" long.

10" wide wall from 4" double brick and 6" concrete block — sf — $4.31 — $13.44 — $17.75
Replace Materials........6.19   Labor 7.25
Remove ....   Labor 4.31
▶ Modular bricks. Nominal dimensions: 4" thick by 5-1/3" high by 8" long. Concrete block: 6" thick by 8" high by 16" long.

10" wide wall from 4" Roman brick and 6" concrete block — sf — $4.31 — $17.78 — $22.09
Replace Materials........8.31   Labor 9.47
Remove ....   Labor 4.31
▶ Modular bricks. Nominal dimensions: 4" thick by 2" high by 12" long. Concrete block: 6" thick by 8" high by 16" long.

10" wide wall from 4" Norman and 6" concrete block — sf — $4.31 — $15.70 — $20.01
Replace Materials........7.32   Labor 8.38
Remove ....   Labor 4.31
▶ Modular bricks. Nominal dimensions: 4" thick by 2-2/3" high by 12" long. Concrete block: 6" thick by 8" high by 16" long.

10" wide wall from 4" Norwegian and 6" concrete block — sf — $4.31 — $13.92 — $18.23
Replace Materials........6.29   Labor 7.63
Remove ....   Labor 4.31
▶ Modular bricks. Nominal dimensions: 4" thick by 3-1/5" high by 12" long. Concrete block: 6" thick by 8" high by 16" long.

10" wide wall from 4" jumbo utility and 6" concrete block — sf — $4.31 — $14.55 — $18.86
Replace Materials........7.22   Labor 7.33
Remove ....   Labor 4.31
▶ Modular bricks. Nominal dimensions: 4" thick by 4" high by 12" long. Concrete block: 6" thick by 8" high by 16" long.

10" wide brick wall from 4" triple and 6" concrete block — sf — $4.31 — $13.53 — $17.84
Replace Materials........6.41   Labor 7.12
Remove ....   Labor 4.31
▶ Modular bricks. Nominal dimensions: 4" thick by 5-1/3" high by 12" long. Concrete block: 6" thick by 8" high by 16" long.

12" wide wall from 4" standard non-mod. brick and 8" concrete block — sf — $5.12 — $19.13 — $24.25
Replace Materials........9.03   Labor 10.10
Remove ....   Labor 5.12
▶ Modular bricks. Actual dimensions: 3-3/4" thick by 2-1/4" high by 8" long. Concrete block: 8" thick by 8" high by 16" long.

12" wide wall from 4" oversize non-mod. brick and 8" concrete block — sf — $5.12 — $18.10 — $23.22
Replace Materials........8.10   Labor 10.00
Remove ....   Labor 5.12
▶ Modular bricks. Actual dimensions: 3-3/4" thick by 2-3/4" high by 8" long. Concrete block: 8" thick by 8" high by 16" long.

12" wide wall from three-inch non-mod. brick and 8" concrete block — sf — $5.12 — $18.05 — $23.17
Replace Materials........8.12   Labor 9.93
Remove ....   Labor 5.12
▶ Modular bricks. Actual dimensions: 3" thick by 2-3/4" high by 9-3/4" long. Three-inch bricks also come in lengths of 9-5/8" and 8-3/4" and widths vary from 2-5/8" to 3". Concrete block: 8" thick by 8" high by 16" long.

RELATED ITEMS

Cleaning 63
Fireplaces...................241
Painting 340

◀ **12" WIDE BRICK & BLOCK WALL**
With 3/8" wide mortar joints. Includes 4% waste for brick and block and 25% waste for mortar.

Item Description	Unit	Remove	Replace	Total
12" WIDE BRICK ▶ & BLOCK WALL *continued*				
12" wide wall from 4" standard brick and 8" concrete block	sf	$5.12	$17.50	$22.62
Replace Materials........7.40 Labor...........10.10				
Remove .... Labor...........5.12				
▶ Modular bricks. Nominal dimensions: 4" thick by 2-2/3" high by 8" long. Concrete block: 8" thick by 8" high by 16" long.				
12" wide wall from 4" engineer brick and 8" concrete block	sf	$5.12	$16.54	$21.66
Replace Materials........7.57 Labor 8.97				
Remove .... Labor 5.12				
▶ Modular bricks. Nominal dimensions: 4" thick by 3-1/5" high by 8" long. Concrete block: 8" thick by 8" high by 16" long.				
12" wide wall from 4" jumbo closure brick and 8" concrete block	sf	$5.12	$15.76	$20.88
Replace Materials........7.59 Labor 8.17				
Remove .... Labor 5.12				
▶ Modular bricks. Nominal dimensions: 4" thick by 4" high by 8" long. Concrete block: 8" thick by 8" high by 16" long.				
12" wide wall from 4" double brick and 8" concrete block	sf	$5.12	$14.29	$19.41
Replace Materials........6.83 Labor 7.46				
Remove .... Labor 5.12				
▶ Modular bricks. Nominal dimensions: 4" thick by 5-1/3" high by 8" long. Concrete block: 8" thick by 8" high by 16" long.				
12" wide wall from 4" Roman brick and 8" concrete block	sf	$5.12	$18.63	$23.75
Replace Materials........8.95 Labor 9.68				
Remove .... Labor 5.12				
▶ Modular bricks. Nominal dimensions: 4" thick by 2" high by 12" long. Concrete block: 8" thick by 8" high by 16" long.				
12" wide wall from 4" Norman brick and 8" concrete block	sf	$5.12	$16.51	$21.63
Replace Materials........7.96 Labor 8.55				
Remove .... Labor 5.12				
▶ Modular bricks. Nominal dimensions: 4" thick by 2-2/3" high by 12" long. Concrete block: 8" thick by 8" high by 16" long.				
12" wide wall from 4" Norwegian brick and 8" concrete block	sf	$5.12	$14.77	$19.89
Replace Materials........6.93 Labor 7.84				
Remove .... Labor 5.12				
▶ Modular bricks. Nominal dimensions: 4" thick by 3-1/5" high by 12" long. Concrete block: 8" thick by 8" high by 16" long.				
12" wide wall from 4" jumbo utility brick and 8" concrete block	sf	$5.12	$15.40	$20.52
Replace Materials........7.86 Labor 7.54				
Remove .... Labor 5.12				
▶ Modular bricks. Nominal dimensions: 4" thick by 4" high by 12" long. Concrete block: 8" thick by 8" high by 16" long.				
12" wide wall from 4" triple brick and 8" concrete block	sf	$5.12	$14.34	$19.46
Replace Materials........7.05 Labor 7.29				
Remove .... Labor 5.12				
▶ Modular bricks. Nominal dimensions: 4" thick by 5-1/3" high by 12" long. Concrete block: 8" thick by 8" high by 16" long.				
12" WIDE ▶ TRIPLE WYTHE BRICK WALL *With 3/8" wide mortar joints. Includes 4% waste for brick and 25% waste for mortar.*				
12" wide triple wythe standard non-modular brick wall	sf	$5.12	$35.20	$40.32
Replace Materials........17.10 Labor...........18.10				
Remove .... Labor 5.12				
▶ Non-modular bricks. Actual dimensions: 3-3/4" thick by 2-1/4" high by 8" long.				
12" wide triple wythe oversize non-modular brick wall	sf	$5.12	$32.20	$37.32
Replace Materials ....14.30 Labor...........17.90				
Remove .... Labor 5.12				
▶ Non-modular bricks. Actual dimensions: 3-3/4" thick by 2-3/4" high by 8" long.				

Item Description	Unit	Remove	Replace	Total
12" wide triple wythe three-inch non-modular brick wall	sf	$5.12	$32.20	$37.32
Replace Materials ......14.40 Labor 17.80				
Remove .... Labor 5.12				
► Non-modular bricks. Actual dimensions: 3" thick by 2-3/4" high by 9-3/4" long. Three-inch bricks also come in lengths of 9-5/8" and 8-3/4" and widths vary from 2-5/8" to 3".				
12" wide triple wythe standard brick wall	sf	$5.12	$30.20	$35.32
Replace Materials ......12.20 Labor 18.00				
Remove .... Labor 5.12				
► Modular bricks. Nominal dimensions: 4" thick by 2-2/3" high by 8" long.				
12" wide triple wythe engineer brick wall	sf	$5.12	$27.70	$32.82
Replace Materials ......12.70 Labor 15.00				
Remove .... Labor 5.12				
► Modular bricks. Nominal dimensions: 4" thick by 3-1/5" high by 8" long.				
12" wide triple wythe jumbo closure brick wall	sf	$5.12	$25.60	$30.72
Replace Materials ......12.80 Labor 12.80				
Remove .... Labor 5.12				
► Also called Economy 8. Modular bricks. Nominal dimensions: 4" thick by 4" high by 8" long.				
12" wide triple wythe double brick wall	sf	$5.12	$21.23	$26.35
Replace Materials ......10.53 Labor 10.70				
Remove .... Labor 5.12				
► Modular bricks. Nominal dimensions: 4" thick by 5-1/3" high by 8" long.				
12" wide triple wythe Roman brick wall	sf	$5.12	$34.00	$39.12
Replace Materials ......16.90 Labor 17.10				
Remove .... Labor 5.12				
► Modular bricks. Nominal dimensions: 4" thick by 2" high by 12" long.				
12" wide triple wythe Norman brick wall	sf	$5.12	$27.70	$32.82
Replace Materials ......13.90 Labor 13.80				
Remove .... Labor 5.12				
► Modular bricks. Nominal dimensions: 4" thick by 2-2/3" high by 12" long.				
12" wide triple wythe Norwegian brick wall	sf	$5.12	$22.63	$27.75
Replace Materials ......10.83 Labor 11.80				
Remove .... Labor 5.12				
► Modular bricks. Nominal dimensions: 4" thick by 3-1/5" high by 12" long.				
12" wide triple wythe jumbo utility brick wall	sf	$5.12	$24.50	$29.62
Replace Materials ......13.60 Labor 10.90				
Remove .... Labor 5.12				
► Also called Economy 12. Modular bricks. Nominal dimensions: 4" thick by 4" high by 12" long.				
12" wide triple wythe triple brick wall	sf	$5.12	$21.39	$26.51
Replace Materials ......11.19 Labor 10.20				
Remove .... Labor 5.12				
► Modular bricks. Nominal dimensions: 4" thick by 5-1/3" high by 12" long.				
10" wide cavity wall from 4" standard non-mod. brick and 4" block	sf	$3.81	$18.36	$22.17
Replace Materials ......8.16 Labor 10.20				
Remove .... Labor 3.81				
► Modular bricks. Actual dimensions: 3-3/4" thick by 2-1/4" high by 8" long. Concrete block: 4" thick by 8" high by 16" long.				
10" wide cavity wall from 4" oversize non-mod. brick and 4" block	sf	$3.81	$17.33	$21.14
Replace Materials ......7.23 Labor 10.10				
Remove .... Labor 3.81				
► Modular bricks. Actual dimensions: 3-3/4" thick by 2-3/4" high by 8" long. Concrete block: 4" thick by 8" high by 16" long.				

RELATED ITEMS

Cleaning 63
Fireplaces 241
Painting 340

◄ **10" WIDE BRICK & BLOCK CAVITY WALL** With 2" dead air space. (see page 295 for foam insulation in air space) and 3/8" wide mortar joints. Includes 4% waste for brick and block and 25% waste for mortar.

Item Description	Unit	Remove	Replace	Total
10″ WIDE BRICK ► & BLOCK CAVITY WALL *continued*				
10″ wide cavity wall from three-inch non-mod. brick and 4″ block	sf	$3.81	$17.35	$21.16
Replace Materials........7.25 Labor...........10.10 *Remove* .... Labor ....3.81 ► Modular bricks. Actual dimensions: 3″ thick by 2-3/4″ high by 9-3/4″ long. Three-inch bricks also come in lengths of 9-5/8″ and 8-3/4″ and widths vary from 2-5/8″ to 3″. Concrete block: 4″ thick by 8″ high by 16″ long.				
10″ wide cavity wall from 4″ standard brick and 4″ concrete block	sf	$3.81	$16.73	$20.54
Replace Materials........6.53 Labor...........10.20 *Remove* .... Labor ....3.81 ► Modular bricks. Nominal dimensions: 4″ thick by 2-2/3″ high by 8″ long. Concrete block: 4″ thick by 8″ high by 16″ long.				
10″ wide cavity wall from 4″ engineer brick and 4″ concrete block	sf	$3.81	$15.75	$19.56
Replace Materials........6.70 Labor ....9.05 *Remove* .... Labor ....3.81 ► Modular bricks. Nominal dimensions: 4″ thick by 3-1/5″ high by 8″ long. Concrete block: 4″ thick by 8″ high by 16″ long.				
10″ wide cavity wall from 4″ jumbo closure brick and 4″ concrete block	sf	$3.81	$14.93	$18.74
Replace Materials........6.72 Labor ....8.21 *Remove* .... Labor ....3.81 ► Modular bricks. Nominal dimensions: 4″ thick by 4″ high by 8″ long. Concrete block: 4″ thick by 8″ high by 16″ long.				
10″ wide cavity wall from 4″ double brick and 4″ concrete block	sf	$3.81	$13.42	$17.23
Replace Materials........5.96 Labor ....7.46 *Remove* .... Labor ....3.81 ► Modular bricks. Nominal dimensions: 4″ thick by 5-1/3″ high by 8″ long. Concrete block: 4″ thick by 8″ high by 16″ long.				
10″ wide cavity wall from 4″ Roman brick and 4″ concrete block	sf	$3.81	$17.88	$21.69
Replace Materials........8.08 Labor ....9.80 *Remove* .... Labor ....3.81 ► Modular bricks. Nominal dimensions: 4″ thick by 2″ high by 12″ long. Concrete block: 4″ thick by 8″ high by 16″ long.				
10″ wide cavity wall from 4″ Norman and 4″ concrete block	sf	$3.81	$15.72	$19.53
Replace Materials........7.09 Labor ....8.63 *Remove* .... Labor ....3.81 ► Modular bricks. Nominal dimensions: 4″ thick by 2-2/3″ high by 12″ long. Concrete block: 4″ thick by 8″ high by 16″ long.				
10″ wide cavity wall from 4″ Norwegian brick and 4″ concrete block	sf	$3.81	$13.94	$17.75
Replace Materials........6.06 Labor ....7.88 *Remove* .... Labor ....3.81 ► Modular bricks. Nominal dimensions: 4″ thick by 3-1/5″ high by 12″ long. Concrete block: 4″ thick by 8″ high by 16″ long.				
10″ wide cavity wall from 4″ jumbo utility brick and 4″ concrete block	sf	$3.81	$14.53	$18.34
Replace Materials........6.99 Labor ....7.54 *Remove* .... Labor ....3.81 ► Modular bricks. Nominal dimensions: 4″ thick by 4″ high by 12″ long. Concrete block: 4″ thick by 8″ high by 16″ long.				
10″ wide cavity wall from 4″ triple brick and 4″ concrete block	sf	$3.81	$13.47	$17.28
Replace Materials........6.18 Labor ....7.29 *Remove* .... Labor ....3.81 ► Modular bricks. Nominal dimensions: 4″ thick by 5-1/3″ high by 12″ long. Concrete block: 4″ thick by 8″ high by 16″ long.				
10″ WIDE BRICK ► CAVITY WALL *continued on next page*	**10″ wide cavity wall from 4″ standard non-modular brick, both sides**	sf	$3.81	$25.04	$28.85
Replace Materials.......11.64 Labor...........13.40 *Remove* .... Labor ....3.81 ► Non-modular bricks. Actual dimensions: 3-3/4″ thick by 2-1/4″ high by 8″ long.				

Item Description	Unit	Remove	Replace	Total
10″ wide cavity wall from 4″ oversize non-modular brick, both sides	sf	$3.81	$23.08	$26.89
Replace Materials........9.78 Labor...........13.30				
Remove .... Labor 3.81				
► Non-modular bricks. Actual dimensions: 3-3/4″ thick by 2-3/4″ high by 8″ long.				
10″ wide cavity wall from three-inch non-modular brick, both sides	sf	$3.81	$23.02	$26.83
Replace Materials........9.82 Labor...........13.20				
Remove .... Labor 3.81				
► Non-modular bricks. Actual dimensions: 3″ thick by 2-3/4″ high by 9-3/4″ long. Three-inch bricks also come in lengths of 9-5/8″ and 8-3/4″ and widths vary from 2-5/8″ to 3″.				
10″ wide cavity wall from 4″ standard brick, both sides	sf	$3.81	$21.78	$25.59
Replace Materials........8.38 Labor...........13.40				
Remove .... Labor 3.81				
► Modular bricks. Nominal dimensions: 4″ thick by 2-2/3″ high by 8″ long.				
10″ wide cavity wall from 4″ engineer brick, both sides	sf	$3.81	$19.82	$23.63
Replace Materials........8.72 Labor...........11.10				
Remove .... Labor 3.81				
► Modular bricks. Nominal dimensions: 4″ thick by 3-1/5″ high by 8″ long.				
10″ wide cavity wall from 4″ jumbo closure brick, both sides	sf	$3.81	$18.23	$22.04
Replace Materials........8.76 Labor...........9.47				
Remove .... Labor 3.81				
► Also called Economy 8. Modular bricks. Nominal dimensions: 4″ thick by 4″ high by 8″ long.				
10″ wide cavity wall from 4″ double brick, both sides	sf	$3.81	$15.16	$18.97
Replace Materials........7.24 Labor 7.92				
Remove .... Labor 3.81				
► Modular bricks. Nominal dimensions: 4″ thick by 5-1/3″ high by 8″ long.				
10″ wide cavity wall from 4″ Roman brick, both sides	sf	$3.81	$24.08	$27.89
Replace Materials........11.48 Labor...........12.60				
Remove .... Labor 3.81				
► Modular bricks. Nominal dimensions: 4″ thick by 2″ high by 12″ long.				
10″ wide cavity wall from 4″ Norman brick, both sides	sf	$3.81	$19.80	$23.61
Replace Materials........9.50 Labor...........10.30				
Remove .... Labor 3.81				
► Modular bricks. Nominal dimensions: 4″ thick by 2-2/3″ high by 12″ long.				
10″ wide cavity wall from 4″ Norwegian both sides	sf	$3.81	$16.20	$20.01
Replace Materials........7.44 Labor 8.76				
Remove .... Labor 3.81				
► Modular bricks. Nominal dimensions: 4″ thick by 3-1/5″ high by 12″ long.				
10″ wide cavity wall from 4″ jumbo utility brick, both sides	sf	$3.81	$17.39	$21.20
Replace Materials........9.30 Labor 8.09				
Remove .... Labor 3.81				
► Also called Economy 12. Modular bricks. Nominal dimensions: 4″ thick by 4″ high by 12″ long.				
10″ wide cavity wall from 4″ triple brick, both sides	sf	$3.81	$15.26	$19.07
Replace Materials........7.68 Labor 7.58				
Remove .... Labor 3.81				
► Modular bricks. Nominal dimensions: 4″ thick by 5-1/3″ high by 12″ long.				
Add for 2″ polystyrene insulation in cavity wall	sf	—	$.90	$.90
Replace Materials........ .84 Labor............ .06				

◄ **10″ WIDE BRICK CAVITY WALL**
continued

With 2″ dead air space. (See below for foam insulation in air space.) and 3/8″ wide mortar joints. Includes 4% waste for brick and 25% waste for mortar.

RELATED ITEMS

Cleaning 63
Fireplaces...................241
Painting 340

◄ **ADD FOR CAVITY WALL INSULATION**

Item Description	Unit	Remove	Replace	Total
BRICK VENEER ▶ With 3/8" wide mortar joints and galvanized wall ties. Includes 4% waste for brick and block and 25% waste for mortar.				
Standard non-modular brick veneer	sf	$2.37	$11.61	$13.98
Replace Materials........5.58　　　Labor 6.03				
Remove ....　　　Labor 2.37				
▶ Non-modular bricks. Actual dimensions: 3-3/4" thick by 2-1/4" high by 8" long.				
Oversize non-modular brick veneer	sf	$2.37	$10.64	$13.01
Replace Materials........4.65　　　Labor 5.99				
Remove ....　　　Labor 2.37				
▶ Non-modular bricks. Actual dimensions: 3-3/4" thick by 2-3/4" high by 8" long.				
Three-inch non-modular brick veneer	sf	$2.37	$10.58	$12.95
Replace Materials........4.67　　　Labor 5.91				
Remove ....　　　Labor 2.37				
▶ Non-modular bricks. Actual dimensions: 3" thick by 2-3/4" high by 9-3/4" long. Three-inch bricks also come in lengths of 9-5/8" and 8-3/4" and widths vary from 2-5/8" to 3". Normally used as a veneer unit.				
Used brick veneer	sf	$2.37	$14.12	$16.49
Replace Materials........8.09　　　Labor 6.03				
Remove ....　　　Labor 2.37				
▶ Modular bricks. Nominal dimensions: 4" thick by 2-2/3" high by 8" long.				
Standard brick veneer	sf	$2.37	$9.98	$12.35
Replace Materials........3.95　　　Labor 6.03				
Remove ....　　　Labor 2.37				
▶ Modular bricks. Nominal dimensions: 4" thick by 2-2/3" high by 8" long.				
Engineer brick veneer	sf	$2.37	$9.11	$11.48
Replace Materials........4.12　　　Labor 4.99				
Remove ....　　　Labor 2.37				
▶ Modular bricks. Nominal dimensions: 4" thick by 3-1/5" high by 8" long.				
Jumbo closure brick veneer	sf	$2.37	$8.41	$10.78
Replace Materials........4.14　　　Labor 4.27				
Remove ....　　　Labor 2.37				
▶ Also called Economy 8. Modular bricks. Nominal dimensions: 4" thick by 4" high by 8" long.				
Double brick veneer	sf	$2.37	$6.94	$9.31
Replace Materials........3.38　　　Labor 3.56				
Remove ....　　　Labor 2.37				
▶ Modular bricks. Nominal dimensions: 4" thick by 5-1/3" high by 8" long.				
Roman brick veneer	sf	$2.37	$11.20	$13.57
Replace Materials........5.50　　　Labor 5.70				
Remove ....　　　Labor 2.37				
▶ Modular bricks. Nominal dimensions: 4" thick by 2" high by 12" long.				
Norman brick veneer	sf	$2.37	$9.12	$11.49
Replace Materials........4.51　　　Labor 4.61				
Remove ....　　　Labor 2.37				
▶ Modular bricks. Nominal dimensions: 4" thick by 2-2/3" high by 12" long.				
Norwegian brick veneer	sf	$2.37	$7.42	$9.79
Replace Materials........3.48　　　Labor 3.94				
Remove ....　　　Labor 2.37				
▶ Modular bricks. Nominal dimensions: 4" thick by 3-1/5" high by 12" long.				
Jumbo utility brick veneer	sf	$2.37	$8.06	$10.43
Replace Materials........4.41　　　Labor 3.65				
Remove ....　　　Labor 2.37				
▶ Also called Economy 12. Modular bricks. Nominal dimensions: 4" thick by 4" high by 12" long.				

common bond △

Flemish bond △

English bond △

English cross bond △

stack bond △

header bond △

soldier course △

Item Description	Unit	Remove	Replace	Total
Triple brick veneer	sf	$2.37	$7.04	$9.41

Replace Materials........3.60   Labor 3.44
Remove ....   Labor 2.37
▶ Modular bricks. Nominal dimensions: 4" thick by 5-1/3" high by 12" long.

Add for raked joints	sf	–	$.25	$.25

Replace ....   Labor .... .25
▶ Add for brick walls with raked joints instead of concave.

◀ **RAKED JOINTS**

Add 16% for common bond
▶ Also called American bond. Every sixth course is a full course of full-length headers.

◀ **ADD FOR OTHER BRICK BONDS**

Add 54% for Flemish bond
▶ Each course is made of alternating stretchers and headers.

Add 65% for English bond
▶ Alternating full courses made from stretchers and headers. The joints between stretchers in all courses align vertically.

sailor course △

Add 65% for English cross bond
▶ Also called Dutch bond. A variation of English bond. The vertical joints between stretcher bricks, in alternate courses, align vertically with the center of the stretcher brick in the course above and below.

basketweave △

Add 8% for stack bond
▶ All vertical and horizontal joints align.

Add 116% for false all header bond
▶ All bricks are laid as headers but bricks are cut in half.

Add 115% for all header bond
▶ All bricks are laid as true headers.

diagonal △

Add 15% for soldier course
▶ All bricks are stood on end with edge showing.

Add 5% for sailor course
▶ All bricks are stood on end with face showing.

Add 122% for basketweave
▶ A wide variety of patterns with alternating sections of horizontal and vertical brick.

herringbone △

Add 125% for herringbone weave
▶ Also called diagonal basketweave. Bricks are laid at an angle (usually 45 degree) in alternate sections angling up and down.

Add 90% for diagonal bond
▶ All bricks laid at an angle, usually 45 degree.

Add 70% for coursed ashlar style brick bond with two sizes of bricks
▶ A pattern that uses two sizes of bricks to simulate coursed ashlar stone patterns. Usually one size of brick equals two of the second size.

coursed ashlar style △

Add 27% for curved brick walls

◀ **ADD FOR CURVED INSTALLATION**

Add for opening in 4" brick wall per lf of opening	lf	–	$15.59	$15.59

Replace Materials........4.69   Labor 10.90
▶ Includes angle iron lintel.

◀ **ADD FOR OPENING IN MASONRY WALL**
Use only if sf of opening has been deducted from sf price. Includes angle iron lintel.

Add for opening in 6" brick wall per lf of opening	lf	–	$19.16	$19.16

Replace Materials........8.16   Labor 11.00
▶ Includes angle iron lintel.

Item Description	Unit	Remove	Replace	Total
ADD FOR OPENING ► IN MASONRY WALL *continued*				
Add for opening in 8" brick wall per lf of opening	lf	–	$19.26	$19.26
Replace Materials........8.16 Labor ....11.10 ► Includes angle iron lintel.				
Add for opening in 10" brick wall per lf of opening	lf	–	$20.68	$20.68
Replace Materials........9.38 Labor ....11.30 ► Includes angle iron lintel.				
Add for opening in 12" brick wall per lf of opening	lf	–	$20.78	$20.78
Replace Materials........9.38 Labor ....11.40 ► Includes angle iron lintel.				
ADD FOR ► BRICK ARCH				
Add for flat brick arch	lf	–	$77.10	$77.10
Replace Materials ......14.70 Labor...........62.40 ► Also called a Jack arch. Do not use for standard brick wall openings that use a lintel.				
Add for elliptical brick arch	lf	–	$94.80	$94.80
Replace Materials.......17.30 Labor ....77.50 ► Per lf of arch.				
Add for semi-circular brick arch	lf	–	$99.40	$99.40
Replace Materials.......17.30 Labor ....82.10 ► Per lf of arch.				
Add to brace existing brick arch from below for repairs	lf	–	$36.60	$36.60
Replace Materials.......13.30 Labor ....23.30 ► 2" x 6" or 2" x 8" framing members sheathed with plywood that follows curved shape of arch.				
Minimum charge for arch work	ea	–	$508.00	$508.00
Replace Materials ......89.00 Labor 419.00				
CONCRETE BLOCK ► WALL				
4" wide concrete block wall	sf	$2.51	$5.86	$8.37
Replace Materials........2.13 Labor ....3.73 *Remove* .... Labor 2.51				
6" wide concrete block wall	sf	$3.01	$6.33	$9.34
Replace Materials........2.48 Labor ....3.85 *Remove* .... Labor 3.01				
8" wide concrete block wall	sf	$3.81	$7.18	$10.99
Replace Materials........3.12 Labor ....4.06 *Remove* .... Labor 3.81				
10" wide concrete block wall	sf	$4.31	$8.14	$12.45
Replace Materials........3.82 Labor ....4.32 *Remove* .... Labor 4.31				
12" wide concrete block wall	sf	$5.12	$10.02	$15.14
Replace Materials........4.91 Labor ....5.11 *Remove* .... Labor 5.12				
4" wide lightweight concrete block wall	sf	$2.51	$5.76	$8.27
Replace Materials........2.28 Labor ....3.48 *Remove* .... Labor 2.51				
6" wide lightweight concrete block wall	sf	$3.01	$6.23	$9.24
Replace Materials........2.63 Labor ....3.60 *Remove* .... Labor 3.01				

CONCRETE BLOCK WALLS

Unless otherwise noted all concrete block walls are 8" x 16" face block with 3/8" wide mortar joints.

Cells are grouted 36" on center and at each corner and include one length of #4 rebar in field cells and 2 lengths in corner cells for an average of 1.4 lengths of rebar per grouted cell.

A horizontal bond beam is also calculated for every 8' of wall height which includes two lengths of #4 rebar.

continued on next page

Item Description	Unit	Remove	Replace	Total	
8" wide lightweight concrete block wall	sf	$3.81	$7.13	$10.94	**CONCRETE BLOCK WALLS**
Replace Materials........3.32 Labor 3.81					*continued from prior page*
Remove .... Labor 3.81					Horizontal wire reinforc-
10" wide lightweight concrete block wall	sf	$4.31	$8.12	$12.43	ing appears in every other course.
Replace Materials........4.06 Labor 4.06					Also includes 4% waste
Remove .... Labor 4.31					for block and 25% waste for mortar.
12" wide lightweight concrete block wall	sf	$5.12	$10.02	$15.14	See page 302 for
Replace Materials........5.24 Labor 4.78					block walls with other
Remove .... Labor 5.12					types of reinforcing.
4" wide slump block wall	sf	$2.51	$7.28	$9.79	◄ **SLUMP BLOCK WALL**
Replace Materials........3.55 Labor 3.73					*4" x 16" face block.*
Remove .... Labor 2.51					
6" wide slump block wall	sf	$3.01	$8.20	$11.21	
Replace Materials........4.35 Labor 3.85					
Remove .... Labor 3.01					
8" wide slump block wall	sf	$3.81	$9.45	$13.26	
Replace Materials........5.39 Labor 4.06					
Remove .... Labor 3.81					
10" wide slump block wall	sf	$4.31	$10.76	$15.07	
Replace Materials........6.44 Labor 4.32					
Remove .... Labor 4.31					
12" wide slump block wall	sf	$5.12	$13.24	$18.36	
Replace Materials........8.13 Labor 5.11					
Remove .... Labor 5.12					
4" wide fluted block wall (fluted one side)	sf	$2.51	$6.78	$9.29	◄ **FLUTED BLOCK WALL (ONE SIDE)**
Replace Materials........3.05 Labor 3.73					
Remove .... Labor 2.51					
6" wide fluted block wall (fluted one side)	sf	$3.01	$7.35	$10.36	
Replace Materials........3.50 Labor 3.85					
Remove .... Labor 3.01					
8" wide fluted block wall (fluted one side)	sf	$3.81	$8.46	$12.27	
Replace Materials........4.40 Labor 4.06					
Remove .... Labor 3.81					
10" wide fluted block wall (fluted one side)	sf	$4.31	$9.74	$14.05	
Replace Materials........5.42 Labor 4.32					
Remove .... Labor 4.31					
12" wide fluted block wall (fluted one side)	sf	$5.12	$12.18	$17.30	
Replace Materials........7.07 Labor 5.11					
Remove .... Labor 5.12					
4" wide fluted block wall (fluted two sides)	sf	$2.51	$7.20	$9.71	◄ **FLUTED BLOCK WALL (TWO SIDES)**
Replace Materials........3.47 Labor 3.73					
Remove .... Labor 2.51					
6" wide fluted block wall (fluted two sides)	sf	$3.01	$7.81	$10.82	
Replace Materials........3.96 Labor 3.85					
Remove .... Labor 3.01					

RELATED ITEMS

Cleaning 63
Fireplaces...................241
Painting 340

Item Description	Unit	Remove	Replace	Total
FLUTED BLOCK ▶ WALL (TWO SIDES) *continued*				
8" wide fluted block wall (fluted two sides)	sf	$3.81	$9.05	$12.86
Replace Materials........4.99 Labor ....4.06 *Remove* .... Labor 3.81				
10" wide fluted block wall (fluted two sides)	sf	$4.31	$10.50	$14.81
Replace Materials........6.18 Labor ....4.32 *Remove* .... Labor 4.31				
12" wide fluted block wall (fluted two sides)	sf	$5.12	$13.19	$18.31
Replace Materials........8.08 Labor ....5.11 *Remove* .... Labor 5.12				
GLAZED BLOCK ▶ WALL (ONE SIDE) See "Concrete Block Walls" on page 298.				
4" wide glazed block wall (glazed one side)	sf	$2.51	$15.63	$18.14
Replace Materials........11.90 Labor ....3.73 *Remove* .... Labor 2.51				
6" wide glazed block wall (glazed one side)	sf	$3.01	$16.35	$19.36
Replace Materials ......12.50 Labor ....3.85 *Remove* .... Labor 3.01				
8" wide glazed block wall (glazed one side)	sf	$3.81	$17.26	$21.07
Replace Materials........13.20 Labor ....4.06 *Remove* .... Labor 3.81				
10" wide glazed block wall (glazed one side)	sf	$4.31	$18.22	$22.53
Replace Materials........13.90 Labor ....4.32 *Remove* .... Labor 4.31				
12" wide glazed block wall (glazed one side)	sf	$5.12	$19.71	$24.83
Replace Materials ......14.60 Labor ....5.11 *Remove* .... Labor 5.12				
GLAZED BLOCK ▶ WALL (TWO SIDES) See "Concrete Block Walls" on page 298.				
4" wide glazed block wall (glazed two sides)	sf	$2.51	$21.13	$23.64
Replace Materials........17.40 Labor ....3.73 *Remove* .... Labor 2.51				
6" wide glazed block wall (glazed two sides)	sf	$3.01	$22.55	$25.56
Replace Materials ......18.70 Labor ....3.85 *Remove* .... Labor 3.01				
8" wide glazed block wall (glazed two sides)	sf	$3.81	$23.76	$27.57
Replace Materials........19.70 Labor ....4.06 *Remove* .... Labor 3.81				
10" wide glazed block wall (glazed two sides)	sf	$4.31	$24.62	$28.93
Replace Materials ......20.30 Labor ....4.32 *Remove* .... Labor 4.31				
12" wide glazed block wall (glazed two sides)	sf	$5.12	$26.21	$31.33
Replace Materials ......21.10 Labor ....5.11 *Remove* .... Labor 5.12				
SPLIT-FACE ▶ BLOCK WALL See "Concrete Block Walls" on page 298.				
4" wide split-face block wall	sf	$2.51	$7.02	$9.53
Replace Materials........3.29 Labor ....3.73 *Remove* .... Labor 2.51				
6" wide split-face block wall	sf	$3.01	$7.76	$10.77
Replace Materials........3.91 Labor ....3.85 *Remove* .... Labor 3.01				

Item Description	Unit	Remove	Replace	Total
8" wide split-face block wall	sf	$3.81	$9.23	$13.04
Replace Materials........5.17 Labor 4.06				
Remove .... Labor 3.81				
10" wide split-face block wall	sf	$4.31	$10.11	$14.42
Replace Materials........5.79 Labor 4.32				
Remove .... Labor 4.31				
12" wide split-face block wall	sf	$5.12	$12.61	$17.73
Replace Materials........7.50 Labor 5.11				
Remove .... Labor 5.12				
4" wide split-rib block wall	sf	$2.51	$6.84	$9.35
Replace Materials........3.11 Labor 3.73				
Remove .... Labor 2.51				
6" wide split-rib block wall	sf	$3.01	$7.24	$10.25
Replace Materials........3.39 Labor 3.85				
Remove .... Labor 3.01				
8" wide split-rib block wall	sf	$3.81	$9.16	$12.97
Replace Materials........5.10 Labor 4.06				
Remove .... Labor 3.81				
10" wide split-rib block wall	sf	$4.31	$10.15	$14.46
Replace Materials........5.83 Labor 4.32				
Remove .... Labor 4.31				
12" wide split-rib block wall	sf	$5.12	$11.72	$16.84
Replace Materials........6.61 Labor 5.11				
Remove .... Labor 5.12				
4" wide screen block, pattern two sides	sf	$2.51	$9.80	$12.31
Replace Materials........6.07 Labor 3.73				
Remove .... Labor 2.51				
4" wide screen block, pattern four sides	sf	$2.51	$14.83	$17.34
Replace Materials.......11.10 Labor 3.73				
Remove .... Labor 2.51				

Add 11% for light ochre colored concrete block
▶ Light tans, browns, yellows, light reddish brown, and so forth.

Add 17% darker ochre colored concrete block
▶ Light red, blues, specialty grays, darker yellows, mid-tone browns.

Add 28% for dark or bright colored concrete block
▶ Black, dark blue, terra-cotta red, bright yellow, bright orange, bright red, purple, and so forth.

Add 15% for interlocking concrete block
▶ Add to the cost of *materials* only.

Item Description	Unit	Remove	Replace	Total
Add for polystyrene inserts, 6" block	sf	–	$.95	$.95
Replace Materials .... .95				
Add for polystyrene inserts, 8" block	sf	–	$1.03	$1.03
Replace Materials 1.03				
Add for polystyrene inserts, 10" block	sf	–	$1.15	$1.15
Replace Materials........1.15				

RELATED ITEMS

Cleaning 63
Fireplaces 241
Painting 340

◀ **SPLIT-RIB BLOCK WALL**
See "Concrete Block Walls" on page 298.

◀ **SCREEN BLOCK**
12" x 12" face. See "Concrete Block Walls" on page 298.

◀ **ADD FOR COLORED BLOCK**

◀ **ADD FOR INTERLOCKING BLOCK**

◀ **POLYSTYRENE BLOCK INSERTS**
Additional cost for block with polystyrene inserts already installed.

Item Description	Unit	Remove	Replace	Total
POLYSTYRENE ▶ Add for polystyrene inserts, 12" block **BLOCK INSERTS** *continued* *Replace* Materials........1.24	sf	–	$1.24	$1.24
LOOSE BLOCK ▶ Add for silicone treated perlite or vermiculite loose fill, 6" block **INSULATION** *Includes 3% waste.* *Replace* Materials .... .37 Labor............ .17	sf	–	$.54	$.54
Add for silicone treated perlite or vermiculite loose fill, 8" block *Replace* Materials .... .54 Labor............ .19	sf	–	$.73	$.73
Add for silicone treated perlite or vermiculite loose fill, 10" block *Replace* Materials .... .68 Labor............ .20	sf	–	$.88	$.88
Add for silicone treated perlite or vermiculite loose fill, 12" block *Replace* Materials .... .98 Labor............ .19	sf	–	$1.17	$1.17
BLOCK PILASTER ▶ Add for pilaster in block wall (per vertical lf of pilaster) *Includes 4% waste.* *Replace* Materials........13.70 Labor............12.30 ▶ 16" x 16" pilaster, single piece. For double piece 16" x 20" pilaster add 15%.	lf	–	$26.00	$26.00
BLOCK WALL ▶ Deduct for block walls used as backing **ADDITIONS** **& DEDUCTIONS** *Replace* .... Labor............–.24 *Add or deduct from the* ▶ For walls finished on one side only.	sf	–	– $.24	– $.24

square foot price of
 block walls. **Deduct for wall with no horizontal wire reinforcement**
 Replace Materials ....–.18   Labor............–.04
     ▶ Deduct when ladder or truss style wire reinforcement is not laid between every
       other course of block.
	sf	–	– $.22	– $.22

Deduct for block walls with no vertical reinforcement *Replace* Materials ....–.63 Labor............–.27 ▶ Deduct when block walls contain no grouted cells.	sf	–	– $.90	– $.90
Deduct for block walls with vertical reinforcement every 48" *Replace* Materials ....–.18 Labor............–.21 ▶ Deduct when block walls contain grouted cells with rebar every 48" instead of 36".	sf	–	– $.39	– $.39
Add for block walls with vertical reinforcement every 24" *Replace* Materials .... .22 Labor............ .22 ▶ Add when block walls contain grouted cells with rebar every 24" instead of 36".	sf	–	$.44	$.44
Deduct for block walls with no horizontal bond beam reinforcement *Replace* Materials ....–.47 Labor............–.16 ▶ Deduct when block walls do not contain a bond beam per every 8' of height.	sf	–	– $.63	– $.63

Add for block walls with horizontal bond beam reinforcement 4'
 Replace Materials .... .33   Labor............ .25
     ▶ Add when block walls contain horizontal bond beams with rebar for every 4' of
       wall height instead of every 8'.
	sf	–	$.58	$.58

high-strength block ▷ **Add 19% for high strength concrete block, 3,000 psi** ▶ Add to the cost of *materials* only.				
Add 21% for high strength concrete block, 5,000 psi ▶ Add to the cost of *materials* only.				
BOND BEAM ▶ 6" wide bond beam *Includes two lengths of* *#4 rebar.* *Replace* Materials........1.41 Labor........... 1.09	lf	–	$2.50	$2.50
8" wide bond beam *Replace* Materials........1.65 Labor 1.20	lf	–	$2.85	$2.85

block pilaster ▽

Item Description	Unit	Remove	Replace	Total
10" wide bond beam *Replace* Materials........1.95 Labor 1.31	lf	–	$3.26	$3.26
12" wide bond beam *Replace* Materials........2.26 Labor 1.42	lf	–	$3.68	$3.68
Parge block foundation wall *Replace* Materials........ .36 Labor............. .85 ▶ Up to 1/2" thick.	sf	–	$1.21	$1.21
Add for grade beam cap on 6" wide concrete block wall *Replace* Materials........8.19 Labor............4.44 *Remove* .... Labor............10.50	lf	$10.50	$12.63	$23.13
Add for grade beam cap on 8" wide concrete block wall *Replace* Materials......10.50 Labor............4.61 *Remove* .... Labor............10.50	lf	$10.50	$15.11	$25.61
Add for grade beam cap on 10" wide concrete block wall *Replace* Materials ......12.90 Labor............4.82 *Remove* .... Labor............10.50	lf	$10.50	$17.72	$28.22
Add for grade beam cap on 12" wide concrete block wall *Replace* Materials......15.20 Labor ....5.03 *Remove* .... Labor............10.50	lf	$10.50	$20.23	$30.73
Deduct 8% for concrete block or brick wall installed as fence ▶ Includes wall cap (2" block or masonry rowlock) and horizontal wire reinforcing. Does not include footing, bond beam, coping, or cell grouting.				
4" thick clay backing tile *Replace* Materials........5.03 Labor ....4.69 *Remove* .... Labor 2.51	sf	$2.51	$9.72	$12.23
6" thick clay backing tile *Replace* Materials........5.04 Labor ....5.32 *Remove* .... Labor 3.01	sf	$3.01	$10.36	$13.37
8" thick clay backing tile *Replace* Materials........5.04 Labor ....6.08 *Remove* .... Labor 3.81	sf	$3.81	$11.12	$14.93
4" thick structural tile glazed one side *Replace* Materials........6.77 Labor ....8.55 *Remove* .... Labor 2.51	sf	$2.51	$15.32	$17.83
4" thick structural tile glazed two sides *Replace* Materials......10.31 Labor ....8.97 *Remove* .... Labor 2.51	sf	$2.51	$19.28	$21.79
6" thick structural tile glazed one side *Replace* Materials........8.97 Labor ....10.20 *Remove* .... Labor 3.01	sf	$3.01	$19.17	$22.18
6" thick structural tile glazed two sides *Replace* Materials......13.60 Labor ....10.62 *Remove* .... Labor 3.01	sf	$3.01	$24.22	$27.23
8" thick structural tile glazed one side *Replace* Materials......11.90 Labor ....11.00 *Remove* .... Labor 3.81	sf	$3.81	$22.90	$26.71

RELATED ITEMS

Cleaning 63
Fences 187
Fireplaces 241
Painting 340
Retaining Walls 391

◀ **PARGETING**
Up to 1/2" thick.

◀ **GRADE BEAM FOR BLOCK WALL**
In some states, concrete block walls are capped with a grade beam. This not only adds strength but also levels the wall top. Because the mason does not take care to maintain a level wall, deduct **25%** from the labor cost for block walls capped with a grade beam. Up to 16" tall with four lengths of #4 rebar. Rebar from grouted cells is also bent into the grade beam.

◀ **MASONRY FENCE**

◀ **CLAY BACKING TILE WALL**
12" x 12" face tile with 3/8" wide mortar joints. Includes 4% waste for tile and 25% waste for mortar.

◀ **STRUCTURAL TILE WALL**
8" x 16" face tile with 3/8" wide mortar joints. Includes 4% waste for tile and 25% waste for mortar.

Item Description	Unit	Remove	Replace	Total
GYPSUM PARTITION TILE *12" x 30" face tile with 3/8" wide mortar joints. Includes 4% waste for tile and 25% waste for mortar. (See illustration below.)*				
4" thick gypsum partition tile	sf	$2.51	$4.28	$6.79
Replace Materials........1.89 Labor 2.39				
Remove .... Labor 2.51				
6" thick gypsum partition tile	sf	$3.81	$6.22	$10.03
Replace Materials........2.74 Labor 3.48				
Remove .... Labor 3.81				
GLASS BLOCK WALL *White mortar with 3/8" wide joints and ladder type wire reinforcing every other course. Includes 4% waste for glass blocks and 25% waste for mortar.*				
4" x 8" thinline smooth-face glass blocks	sf	$2.43	$36.60	$39.03
Replace Materials......22.60 Labor 14.00				
Remove .... Labor 2.43				
6" x 6" thinline smooth-face glass blocks	sf	$2.43	$33.80	$36.23
Replace Materials......20.80 Labor 13.00				
Remove .... Labor 2.43				
6" x 8" thinline smooth-face glass blocks	sf	$2.43	$26.90	$29.33
Replace Materials......15.70 Labor 11.20				
Remove .... Labor 2.43				
4" x 8" smooth-face glass blocks	sf	$2.43	$42.20	$44.63
Replace Materials......28.20 Labor 14.00				
Remove .... Labor 2.43				
6" x 6" smooth-face glass blocks	sf	$2.43	$38.10	$40.53
Replace Materials......25.10 Labor 13.00				
Remove .... Labor 2.43				
6" x 8" smooth-face glass blocks	sf	$2.43	$33.90	$36.33
Replace Materials......22.70 Labor 11.20				
Remove .... Labor 2.43				
8" x 8" smooth-face glass blocks	sf	$2.43	$26.22	$28.65
Replace Materials......17.50 Labor 8.72				
Remove .... Labor 2.43				
12" x 12" smooth-face glass blocks	sf	$2.43	$27.93	$30.36
Replace Materials......20.60 Labor 7.33				
Remove .... Labor 2.43				
other glass block costs ▷ **Add 80% for solar UV reflective glass block**				
Add 4% for patterned face on glass block				
Add 12% for tinted glass block				
Deduct 2% for natural gray mortar in glass block wall				
Deduct 1% for colored mortar in glass block wall				
PAVERS *Pavers on sand base have sand embedded in joints with vibrating compactor. Mortar base pavers have grouted joints. Includes 4% waste for pavers and 25% waste for mortar when used.*				
Natural concrete pavers on sand base	sf	$2.43	$10.37	$12.80
Replace Materials........4.21 Labor 6.16				
Remove .... Labor 2.43				
Natural concrete pavers on mortar base	sf	$3.47	$11.75	$15.22
Replace Materials........4.21 Labor 7.54				
Remove .... Labor 3.47				
Adobe pavers on sand base	sf	$2.43	$7.92	$10.35
Replace Materials........1.76 Labor 6.16				
Remove .... Labor 2.43				

gypsum partition tile △

Item Description	Unit	Remove	Replace	Total	
Adobe pavers on mortar base	sf	$3.47	$9.30	$12.77	
Replace Materials........1.76 · · · · Labor 7.54					
Remove .... · · · · Labor 3.47					
Brick paver, standard grade, on sand base	sf	$2.43	$8.47	$10.90	
Replace Materials........2.31 · · · · Labor 6.16					
Remove .... · · · · Labor 2.43					
Brick paver, standard grade, on mortar base	sf	$3.47	$9.92	$13.39	
Replace Materials........2.38 · · · · Labor 7.54					
Remove .... · · · · Labor 3.47					
Brick paver, high grade, on sand base	sf	$2.43	$9.22	$11.65	
Replace Materials........3.06 · · · · Labor 6.16					
Remove .... · · · · Labor 2.43					
Brick paver, high grade, on mortar base	sf	$3.47	$10.60	$14.07	
Replace Materials........3.06 · · · · Labor 7.54					
Remove .... · · · · Labor 3.47					
Brick paver, deluxe grade, on sand base	sf	$2.43	$9.90	$12.33	
Replace Materials........3.74 · · · · Labor 6.16					
Remove .... · · · · Labor 2.43					
Brick paver, deluxe grade, on mortar base	sf	$3.47	$11.35	$14.82	
Replace Materials........3.81 · · · · Labor 7.54					
Remove .... · · · · Labor 3.47					
Brick pavers made from full-size bricks, laid face up	sf	$2.60	$11.85	$14.45	
Replace Materials........4.10 · · · · Labor 7.75					
Remove .... · · · · Labor 2.60					
Brick pavers made from full-size bricks, laid edge up	sf	$2.60	$14.99	$17.59	
Replace Materials........6.27 · · · · Labor 8.72					
Remove .... · · · · Labor 2.60					
Add for curved edges on pavers	lf	–	$4.67	$4.67	◁ additional paver costs
Replace Materials........1.40 · · · · Labor 3.27					
Add for paver steps installed in mortar over concrete per lf of step	lf	–	$11.97	$11.97	
Replace Materials........ .67 · · · · Labor 11.30					
Add for paver steps installed over sand base per lf of step	lf	–	$12.93	$12.93	
Replace Materials........ .63 · · · · Labor 12.30					
Add for separate pattern at edges of pavers	lf	–	$4.55	$4.55	
Replace Materials........1.37 · · · · Labor 3.18					
Add 17% for non-square pavers with interlocking patterns					
Add 8% for pavers installed in diagonal pattern					
Add 17% for pavers installed in basketweave pattern					
Add 14% for pavers installed in herringbone pattern					
Coral stone rubble wall	cf	$12.70	$61.10	$73.80	◀ **RUBBLE STONE**
Replace Materials......39.40 · · · · Labor............21.70					**WALL**
Remove .... · · · · Labor............12.70					

RELATED ITEMS

Cleaning 63
Fireplaces....................241
Painting 340

basketweave △

continued on next page

Item Description	Unit	Remove	Replace	Total
RUBBLE STONE WALL *continued*				
Field-stone rubble wall, no mortar	cf	$7.49	$49.30	$56.79
Replace Materials......29.10 Labor..........20.20				
Remove .... Labor..........7.49				
Field-stone rubble wall	cf	$12.70	$67.80	$80.50
Replace Materials......46.10 Labor..........21.70				
Remove .... Labor..........12.70				
Lava stone rubble wall	cf	$12.70	$66.00	$78.70
Replace Materials......44.30 Labor..........21.70				
Remove .... Labor..........12.70				
River stone rubble wall	cf	$12.70	$68.90	$81.60
Replace Materials ......47.20 Labor..........21.70				
Remove .... Labor..........12.70				
ASHLAR STONE WALL				
Limestone ashlar wall, natural finish	cf	$12.70	$57.00	$69.70
Replace Materials ......37.20 Labor...........19.80				
Remove .... Labor..........12.70				
Limestone ashlar wall, rough finish	cf	$12.70	$61.30	$74.00
Replace Materials ......41.50 Labor,..........19.80				
Remove .... Labor..........12.70				
Limestone ashlar wall, smooth finish	cf	$12.70	$78.90	$91.60
Replace Materials ......59.10 Labor..........19.80				
Remove .... Labor..........12.70				
Marble ashlar wall, natural finish	cf	$12.70	$105.20	$117.90
Replace Materials ......85.40 Labor...........19.80				
Remove .... Labor..........12.70				
Marble ashlar wall, rough finish	cf	$12.70	$111.90	$124.60
Replace Materials ......92.10 Labor 19.80				
Remove .... Labor..........12.70				
Marble ashlar wall, smooth finish	cf	$12.70	$133.60	$146.30
Replace Materials .....113.80 Labor..........19.80				
Remove .... Labor..........12.70				
Sandstone ashlar wall, natural finish	cf	$12.70	$55.60	$68.30
Replace Materials ......35.80 Labor..........19.80				
Remove .... Labor..........12.70				
Sandstone ashlar wall, rough finish	cf	$12.70	$59.60	$72.30
Replace Materials ......39.80 Labor..........19.80				
Remove .... Labor..........12.70				
Sandstone ashlar wall, smooth finish	cf	$12.70	$76.80	$89.50
Replace Materials......57.00 Labor..........19.80				
Remove .... Labor..........12.70				
Add for flat arch in stone wall	lf	–	$207.30	$207.30
Replace Materials ......87.30 Labor..........120.00				
► Also called a Jack arch. See illustration on facing page. Do not use for standard stone wall openings that use a lintel.				
Add for elliptical arch in stone wall	lf	–	$252.80	$252.80
Replace Materials ....102.80 Labor.........150.00				
► Per lf of arch. See illustration on facing page.				

Stone walls laid in a variety of rubble patterns, per cubic foot of stone. Includes an average of 1/3 cubic foot of mortar per cubic foot of wall. To estimate by the perch, multiply the cf price by 24.75. (A perch is 16-1/2' long, 1' high and 1-1/2' wide or 24-3/4 cubic feet.) See illustration below.

Stone walls laid in ashlar patterns, per cf of stone. Stone is 3-1/2" to 6" wide. Lengths and thickness vary. Includes mortar. To estimate by the perch, multiply the cf price by 24.75. (A perch is 16-1/2' long, 1' high and 1-1/2' wide or 24-3/4 cubic feet.)

rubble lay △

ashlar lay △

STONE QUALITY

Stones are quarried within 150 miles of job site.

Cast stone is made from a composite of crushed limestone and quartz sand.

Granite is a good quality gray stone. Add **28%** for light red (pink), light purple, and light brown. Add **88%** for deep green, red, purple, blue, black, charcoal, and brown.

Limestone is standard stock. Add **15%** for select stock and deduct **10%** for rustic stock.

continued on next page

Item Description	Unit	Remove	Replace	Total
Add for semi-circular arch in stone wall *Replace* Materials ....102.80 Labor ....155.00 ▶ Per lf of arch. See illustration below.	lf	–	$257.80	$257.80
Add 27% for curved stone wall				
Coral stone rubble veneer *Replace* Materials.......13.10 Labor...........10.20 *Remove* .... Labor 3.06	sf	$3.06	$23.30	$26.36
Field stone rubble veneer *Replace* Materials.......10.64 Labor...........10.20 *Remove* .... Labor 3.06	sf	$3.06	$20.84	$23.90
Flagstone rubble veneer *Replace* Materials.......6.74 Labor...........10.20 *Remove* .... Labor 3.06	sf	$3.06	$16.94	$20.00
Lava stone rubble veneer *Replace* Materials ......10.24 Labor...........10.20 *Remove* .... Labor 3.06	sf	$3.06	$20.44	$23.50
River stone rubble veneer *Replace* Materials ......10.87 Labor...........10.20 *Remove* .... Labor 3.06	sf	$3.06	$21.07	$24.13
Sandstone rubble veneer *Replace* Materials.......15.10 Labor...........10.20 *Remove* .... Labor 3.06	sf	$3.06	$25.30	$28.36
Flagstone ashlar veneer *Replace* Materials........7.83 Labor ....9.89 *Remove* .... Labor 3.06	sf	$3.06	$17.72	$20.78
Limestone ashlar veneer, natural finish *Replace* Materials........8.55 Labor ....9.89 *Remove* .... Labor 3.06	sf	$3.06	$18.44	$21.50
Limestone ashlar veneer, rough finish *Replace* Materials........9.51 Labor ....9.89 *Remove* .... Labor 3.06	sf	$3.06	$19.40	$22.46
Limestone ashlar veneer, smooth finish *Replace* Materials.......13.40 Labor ....9.89 *Remove* .... Labor 3.06	sf	$3.06	$23.29	$26.35
Marble ashlar veneer, natural finish *Replace* Materials.......19.30 Labor ....9.89 *Remove* .... Labor 3.06	sf	$3.06	$29.19	$32.25
Marble ashlar veneer, rough finish *Replace* Materials......20.80 Labor ....9.89 *Remove* .... Labor 3.06	sf	$3.06	$30.69	$33.75
Marble ashlar veneer, smooth finish *Replace* Materials.......25.70 Labor ....9.89 *Remove* .... Labor 3.06	sf	$3.06	$35.59	$38.65
Sandstone ashlar veneer, natural finish *Replace* Materials........8.25 Labor ....9.89 *Remove* .... Labor 3.06	sf	$3.06	$18.14	$21.20

flat arch △

◀ **RUBBLE STONE VENEER**

STONE QUALITY

continued

Marble is grade A, average to high priced. Marble varies widely in price with little relationship to color and often even the quality of the stone. The more expensive grades are Italian.

Sandstone is standard grade. Varies from very hard rock to fairly soft. Use for Brownstone work.

Slate is standard grade, all colors.

△ *elliptical arch*

◀ **ASHLAR STONE VENEER**

△ *semi-circular arch*

STONE FINISHES

Stone finishes are generally organized in this book as natural, rough, and smooth. In practice there are many variations of each type of finish.

Stone with **natural** finishes show the cleaving or sawing marks made in the quarry.

Rough finishes are applied after the stone is quarried to achieve a specific rough look.

Smooth finishes are achieved by polishing the stone. All molded work is finished smooth.

Item Description	Unit	Remove	Replace	Total
Sandstone ashlar veneer, rough finish	sf	$3.06	$19.04	$22.10
Replace Materials........9.15　　Labor...........9.89				
Remove ....　　Labor...........3.06				
Sandstone ashlar veneer, smooth finish	sf	$3.06	$22.89	$25.95
Replace Materials.......13.00　　Labor...........9.89				
Remove ....　　Labor...........3.06				
Add for flat arch in stone veneer	lf	–	$92.90	$92.90
Replace Materials.......19.60　　Labor...........73.30				
▶ Also called a Jack arch. See illustration on previous page. Do not use for standard stone veneer openings that use a lintel.				
Add for elliptical arch in stone veneer	lf	–	$113.90	$113.90
Replace Materials......23.00　　Labor...........90.90				
▶ Per lf of arch. See illustration on previous page.				
Add for semi-circular arch in stone veneer	lf	–	$119.40	$119.40
Replace Materials......23.00　　Labor...........96.40				
▶ Per lf of arch. See illustration on previous page.				
Add to support arch from below	lf	–	$36.60	$36.60
Replace Materials.......13.30　　Labor...........23.30				
▶ 2" x 6" or 2" x 8" framing members sheathed with plywood that follows curved shape of arch.				
Add 27% for curved stone veneer				
Add 55% for rusticated stone				
▶ Edges of stone rabbeted up to 1" deep.				
Keystone, concrete	ea	$5.72	$77.40	$83.12
Replace Materials......52.00　　Labor...........25.40				
Remove ....　　Labor...........5.72				
▶ Plain key, recessed key, or winged key. See illustrations on page 322.				
Keystone, cast stone	ea	$5.72	$97.40	$103.12
Replace Materials......72.00　　Labor...........25.40				
Remove ....　　Labor...........5.72				
▶ Plain key, recessed key, or winged key. See illustrations on page 322.				
Keystone, natural finish	ea	$5.72	$139.40	$145.12
Replace Materials.....114.00　　Labor...........25.40				
Remove ....　　Labor...........5.72				
▶ Plain key, with natural or rough finish. See illustrations on page 322.				
Keystone, with straight patterns	ea	$5.72	$172.40	$178.12
Replace Materials.....147.00　　Labor...........25.40				
Remove ....　　Labor...........5.72				
▶ Recessed key, or winged key. See illustrations on page 322.				
Keystone, with complex straight patterns (Gothic)	ea	$5.72	$212.40	$218.12
Replace Materials.....187.00　　Labor...........25.40				
Remove ....　　Labor...........5.72				
▶ Key with Gothic patterns over 1" deep.				
Keystone, with light hand carvings	ea	$5.72	$309.40	$315.12
Replace Materials.....284.00　　Labor...........25.40				
Remove ....　　Labor...........5.72				
▶ Light carvings, usually less than 3/4" deep.				

ASHLAR STONE ▶ VENEER *continued*

add for arch ▷

add for curves ▷

add for rustication ▷

△ *rustication*

KEYSTONE ▶ *For use in stone or brick arches.*

Item Description	Unit	Remove	Replace	Total
Keystone, with medium hand carvings	ea	$5.72	$389.40	$395.12
Replace Materials....364.00 Labor 25.40				
Remove .... Labor 5.72				
▶ Heavier carvings like vermiculation, Acanthus, and so forth.				
Keystone, with heavy hand carvings	ea	$5.72	$535.40	$541.12
Replace Materials....510.00 Labor 25.40				
Remove .... Labor 5.72				
▶ Heavy and deep carvings including a lion's face, a human face, and so forth.				
Remove keystone for work, then reinstall	ea	–	$42.70	$42.70
Replace Materials......... Labor.........42.70				
Cast stone quoin	ea	$5.66	$121.87	$127.53
Replace Materials ......115.00 Labor 6.87				
Remove .... Labor 5.66				
Limestone quoin	ea	$5.66	$137.87	$143.53
Replace Materials....131.00 Labor 6.87				
Remove .... Labor 5.66				
Sandstone quoin	ea	$5.66	$130.87	$136.53
Replace Materials....124.00 Labor 6.87				
Remove .... Labor 5.66				
Remove quoin for work, then reinstall (per stone)	ea	–	$18.20	$18.20
Replace Materials......... Labor.........18.20				
Cultured stone veneer panels, smooth finish	sf	$2.14	$16.93	$19.07
Replace Materials.......5.93 Labor 11.00				
Remove .... Labor 2.14				
Cultured stone veneer panels, rough finish	sf	$2.14	$18.96	$21.10
Replace Materials.......7.96 Labor 11.00				
Remove .... Labor 2.14				
Cultured stone veneer panels, terrazzo style finish	sf	$2.14	$29.00	$31.14
Replace Materials ......18.00 Labor 11.00				
Remove .... Labor 2.14				
Ceramic veneer panels	sf	$2.14	$25.60	$27.74
Replace Materials ......14.60 Labor 11.00				
Remove .... Labor 2.14				
Granite veneer panels, natural finish	sf	$2.14	$39.30	$41.44
Replace Materials ......26.80 Labor 12.50				
Remove .... Labor 2.14				
Granite veneer panels, rough finish	sf	$2.14	$40.90	$43.04
Replace Materials ......28.40 Labor 12.50				
Remove .... Labor 2.14				
Granite veneer panels, smooth finish	sf	$2.14	$45.20	$47.34
Replace Materials ......32.70 Labor 12.50				
Remove .... Labor 2.14				
Limestone veneer panels, natural finish	sf	$2.14	$24.70	$26.84
Replace Materials ......12.20 Labor 12.50				
Remove .... Labor 2.14				
Limestone veneer panels, rough finish	sf	$2.14	$30.90	$33.04
Replace Materials ......18.40 Labor 12.50				
Remove .... Labor 2.14				

◀ **STONE QUOIN**
In brick, stone, or stucco walls. Made from alternate courses of headers and stretchers. Price includes one header and one stretcher (two stones). Quoins are plain, beveled, chamfered, rusticated, or rough tooled.

◀ **CULTURED STONE VENEER PANEL**
3/4" to 1-1/2" thick.

◀ **CERAMIC VENEER PANEL**
Precast panels.

◀ **STONE VENEER PANEL**
Granite, slate, and marble panels are 3/4" to 1-1/2" thick. Limestone and sandstone panels are 2" to 3" thick. See page 307 for more information about quality and finishes.

RELATED ITEMS

Cleaning 63
Fireplaces....................241
Painting 340

Item Description	Unit	Remove	Replace	Total
STONE VENEER ▶ PANELS *continued*				
Limestone veneer panels, smooth finish	sf	$2.14	$36.80	$38.94
Replace Materials ......24.30 Labor 12.50				
Remove .... Labor 2.14				
Marble veneer panels, natural finish	sf	$2.14	$43.20	$45.34
Replace Materials ......30.70 Labor 12.50				
Remove .... Labor 2.14				
Marble veneer panels, rough finish	sf	$2.14	$52.60	$54.74
Replace Materials ......40.10 Labor 12.50				
Remove .... Labor 2.14				
Marble veneer panels, smooth finish	sf	$2.14	$62.70	$64.84
Replace Materials ......50.20 Labor 12.50				
Remove .... Labor 2.14				
Sandstone veneer panels, natural finish	sf	$2.14	$34.50	$36.64
Replace Materials ......22.00 Labor 12.50				
Remove .... Labor 2.14				
Sandstone veneer panels, rough finish	sf	$2.14	$36.50	$38.64
Replace Materials ......24.00 Labor 12.50				
Remove .... Labor 2.14				
Sandstone veneer panels, smooth finish	sf	$2.14	$39.30	$41.44
Replace Materials ......26.80 Labor 12.50				
Remove .... Labor 2.14				
Slate veneer panels, natural finish	sf	$2.14	$35.10	$37.24
Replace Materials ......22.60 Labor 12.50				
Remove .... Labor 2.14				
Slate veneer panels, rough finish	sf	$2.14	$37.10	$39.24
Replace Materials ......24.60 Labor 12.50				
Remove .... Labor 2.14				
Slate veneer panels, smooth finish	sf	$2.14	$40.10	$42.24
Replace Materials ......27.60 Labor 12.50				
Remove .... Labor 2.14				
STONE DOOR ▶ ARCHITRAVE **Cast stone door architrave, standard grade**	lf	$3.79	$64.00	$67.79
Replace Materials ......22.90 Labor 41.10				
Remove .... Labor 3.79				
▶ Simple straight patterns. Cast stone is 6" or less wide.				
Cast stone door architrave, high grade	lf	$3.79	$66.10	$69.89
Replace Materials ......25.00 Labor 41.10				
Remove .... Labor 3.79				
▶ Complex straight patterns (Gothic). Cast stone is 6" or less wide.				
Cast stone door architrave, deluxe grade	lf	$3.79	$74.90	$78.69
Replace Materials ......33.80 Labor 41.10				
Remove .... Labor 3.79				
▶ Cast stone 6" or less wide with complex straight patterns (Gothic) with arched top or flat top with decorative work around corners or center of header. Or simple straight patterns with cast stone up to 10" wide.				
Cast stone door architrave, custom grade	lf	$3.79	$82.50	$86.29
Replace Materials ......41.40 Labor 41.10				
Remove .... Labor 3.79				
▶ Cast stone 6" or less wide with hand carvings on header or up to 10" wide with complex straight patterns (Gothic) with arched top. Or simple straight patterns with cast stone up to 12" wide.				

Item Description	Unit	Remove	Replace	Total
Cast stone door architrave, custom deluxe grade	lf	$3.79	$94.20	$97.99
Replace Materials......53.10　　　Labor..........41.10				
Remove ....　　　Labor 3.79				
► Cast stone 6" or less wide with heavy hand carvings on header (e.g. lion's face, human face) or lighter hand carvings throughout or up to 12" wide with complex straight patterns (Gothic). With arched top.				
Limestone door architrave, standard grade	lf	$3.79	$85.50	$89.29
Replace Materials......44.40　　　Labor..........41.10				
Remove ....　　　Labor 3.79				
► Simple straight patterns. Stone is 6" or less wide.				
Limestone door architrave, high grade	lf	$3.79	$122.40	$126.19
Replace Materials......81.30　　　Labor..........41.10				
Remove ....　　　Labor 3.79				
► Complex straight patterns (Gothic). Stone is 6" or less wide.				
Limestone door architrave, deluxe grade	lf	$3.79	$158.10	$161.89
Replace Materials.....117.00　　　Labor..........41.10				
Remove ....　　　Labor 3.79				
► Stone 6" or less wide with complex straight patterns (Gothic) with arched top or flat top with decorative work around corners or center of header. Or simple straight patterns with stone up to 10" wide.				
Limestone door architrave, custom grade	lf	$3.79	$186.10	$189.89
Replace Materials.....145.00　　　Labor..........41.10				
Remove ....　　　Labor 3.79				
► Stone 6" or less wide with hand carvings on header or up to 10" wide with complex straight patterns (Gothic) with arched top. Or simple straight patterns with stone up to 12" wide.				
Limestone door architrave, custom deluxe grade	lf	$3.79	$218.10	$221.89
Replace Materials.....177.00　　　Labor..........41.10				
Remove ....　　　Labor 3.79				
► Stone 6" or less wide with heavy hand carvings on header (e.g. lion's face, human face) or lighter hand carvings throughout or up to 12" wide with complex straight patterns (Gothic). With arched top.				
Marble door architrave, standard grade	lf	$3.79	$107.50	$111.29
Replace Materials......66.40　　　Labor..........41.10				
Remove ....　　　Labor 3.79				
► Simple straight patterns. Stone is 6" or less wide.				
Marble door architrave, high grade	lf	$3.79	$145.10	$148.89
Replace Materials....104.00　　　Labor..........41.10				
Remove ....　　　Labor 3.79				
► Complex straight patterns (Gothic). Stone is 6" or less wide.				
Marble door architrave, deluxe grade	lf	$3.79	$180.10	$183.89
Replace Materials.....139.00　　　Labor..........41.10				
Remove ....　　　Labor 3.79				
► Stone 6" or less wide with complex straight patterns (Gothic) with arched top or flat top with decorative work around corners or center of header. Or simple straight patterns with stone up to 10" wide.				
Marble door architrave, custom grade	lf	$3.79	$208.10	$211.89
Replace Materials.....167.00　　　Labor..........41.10				
Remove ....　　　Labor 3.79				
► Stone 6" or less wide with hand carvings on header or up to 10" wide with complex straight patterns (Gothic) with arched top. Or simple straight patterns with stone up to 12" wide.				

RELATED ITEMS

Cleaning 63
Fireplaces....................241
Painting 340

Item Description	Unit	Remove	Replace	Total
STONE DOOR ARCHITRAVE *continued* · **Marble door architrave, custom deluxe grade**	lf	$3.79	$240.10	$243.89
Replace Materials.....199.00 Labor..........41.10				
Remove .... Labor 3.79				
▶ Stone 6" or less wide with heavy hand carvings on header (e.g. lion's face, human face) or lighter hand carvings throughout or up to 12" wide with complex straight patterns (Gothic). With arched top.				
Sandstone door architrave, standard grade	lf	$3.79	$80.90	$84.69
Replace Materials......39.80 Labor..........41.10				
Remove .... Labor 3.79				
▶ Simple straight patterns. Stone is 6" or less wide.				
Sandstone door architrave, high grade	lf	$3.79	$117.70	$121.49
Replace Materials ......76.60 Labor..........41.10				
Remove .... Labor 3.79				
▶ Complex straight patterns (Gothic). Stone is 6" or less wide.				
Sandstone door architrave, deluxe grade	lf	$3.79	$152.10	$155.89
Replace Materials .....111.00 Labor..........41.10				
Remove .... Labor 3.79				
▶ Stone 6" or less wide with complex straight patterns (Gothic) with arched top or flat top with decorative work around corners or center of header. Or simple straight patterns with stone up to 10" wide.				
Sandstone door architrave, custom grade	lf	$3.79	$180.10	$183.89
Replace Materials.....139.00 Labor..........41.10				
Remove .... Labor 3.79				
▶ Stone 6" or less wide with hand carvings on header or up to 10" wide with complex straight patterns (Gothic) with arched top. Or simple straight patterns with stone up to 12" wide.				
Sandstone door architrave, custom deluxe grade	lf	$3.79	$213.10	$216.89
Replace Materials.....172.00 Labor..........41.10				
Remove .... Labor 3.79				
▶ Stone 6" or less wide with heavy hand carvings on header (e.g. lion's face, human face) or lighter hand carvings throughout or up to 12" wide with complex straight patterns (Gothic). With arched top.				
STONE WINDOW ARCHITRAVE · **Cast stone window architrave, standard grade**	lf	$3.79	$64.20	$67.99
Replace Materials......22.30 Labor..........41.90				
Remove .... Labor 3.79				
▶ Simple straight patterns. Cast stone is 6" or less wide.				
Cast stone window architrave, high grade	lf	$3.79	$66.20	$69.99
Replace Materials ......24.30 Labor..........41.90				
Remove .... Labor 3.79				
▶ Complex straight patterns (Gothic). Cast stone is 6" or less wide.				
Cast stone window architrave, deluxe grade	lf	$3.79	$74.80	$78.59
Replace Materials......32.90 Labor..........41.90				
Remove .... Labor 3.79				
▶ Cast stone 6" or less wide with complex straight patterns (Gothic) with arched top or flat top with decorative work around corners or center of header. Or simple straight patterns with cast stone up to 10" wide.				
Cast stone window architrave, custom grade	lf	$3.79	$82.10	$85.89
Replace Materials......40.20 Labor..........41.90				
Remove .... Labor 3.79				
▶ Cast stone 6" or less wide with hand carvings on header or up to 10" wide with complex straight patterns (Gothic) with arched top. Or simple straight patterns with cast stone up to 12" wide.				

Item Description	Unit	Remove	Replace	Total
Cast stone window architrave, custom deluxe grade	lf	$3.79	$93.40	$97.19
Replace Materials ......51.50 Labor...........41.90				
Remove .... Labor 3.79				
► Cast stone 6" or less wide with heavy hand carvings on header (e.g. lion's face, human face) or lighter hand carvings throughout or up to 12" wide with complex straight patterns (Gothic). With arched top.				
Limestone window architrave, standard grade	lf	$3.79	$85.10	$88.89
Replace Materials ......43.20 Labor...........41.90				
Remove .... Labor 3.79				
► Simple straight patterns. Stone is 6" or less wide.				
Limestone window architrave, high grade	lf	$3.79	$120.90	$124.69
Replace Materials ......79.00 Labor...........41.90				
Remove .... Labor 3.79				
► Complex straight patterns (Gothic). Stone is 6" or less wide.				
Limestone window architrave, deluxe grade	lf	$3.79	$154.90	$158.69
Replace Materials .....113.00 Labor...........41.90				
Remove .... Labor 3.79				
► Stone 6" or less wide with complex straight patterns (Gothic) with arched top or flat top with decorative work around corners or center of header. Or simple straight patterns with stone up to 10" wide.				
Limestone window architrave, custom grade	lf	$3.79	$181.90	$185.69
Replace Materials ....140.00 Labor...........41.90				
Remove .... Labor 3.79				
► Stone 6" or less wide with hand carvings on header or up to 10" wide with complex straight patterns (Gothic) with arched top. Or simple straight patterns with stone up to 12" wide.				
Limestone window architrave, custom deluxe grade	lf	$3.79	$212.90	$216.69
Replace Materials .....171.00 Labor...........41.90				
Remove .... Labor 3.79				
► Stone 6" or less wide with heavy hand carvings on header (e.g. lion's face, human face) or lighter hand carvings throughout or up to 12" wide with complex straight patterns (Gothic). With arched top.				
Marble window architrave, standard grade	lf	$3.79	$106.50	$110.29
Replace Materials ......64.60 Labor...........41.90				
Remove .... Labor 3.79				
► Simple straight patterns. Stone is 6" or less wide.				
Marble window architrave, high grade	lf	$3.79	$142.90	$146.69
Replace Materials .....101.00 Labor...........41.90				
Remove .... Labor 3.79				
► Complex straight patterns (Gothic). Stone is 6" or less wide.				
Marble window architrave, deluxe grade	lf	$3.79	$176.90	$180.69
Replace Materials .....135.00 Labor...........41.90				
Remove .... Labor 3.79				
► Stone 6" or less wide with complex straight patterns (Gothic) with arched top or flat top with decorative work around corners or center of header. Or simple straight patterns with stone up to 10" wide.				
Marble window architrave, custom grade	lf	$3.79	$203.90	$207.69
Replace Materials .....162.00 Labor...........41.90				
Remove .... Labor 3.79				
► Stone 6" or less wide with hand carvings on header or up to 10" wide with complex straight patterns (Gothic) with arched top. Or simple straight patterns with stone up to 12" wide.				

RELATED ITEMS
Cleaning 63
Fireplaces..................241
Painting 340

	Item Description	Unit	Remove	Replace	Total
STONE WINDOW ► **ARCHITRAVE** *continued*	**Marble window architrave, custom deluxe grade**	lf	$3.79	$234.90	$238.69
	Replace Materials.....193.00　　Labor..........41.90				
	Remove ....　　Labor 3.79				
	► Stone 6″ or less wide with heavy hand carvings on header (e.g. lion's face, human face) or lighter hand carvings throughout or up to 12″ wide with complex straight patterns (Gothic). With arched top.				
	Sandstone window architrave, standard grade	lf	$3.79	$83.00	$86.79
	Replace Materials ......41.10　　Labor..........41.90				
	Remove ....　　Labor 3.79				
	► Simple straight patterns. Stone is 6″ or less wide.				
	Sandstone window architrave, high grade	lf	$3.79	$118.70	$122.49
	Replace Materials ......76.80　　Labor..........41.90				
	Remove ....　　Labor 3.79				
	► Complex straight patterns (Gothic). Stone is 6″ or less wide.				
	Sandstone window architrave, deluxe grade	lf	$3.79	$152.90	$156.69
	Replace Materials .....111.00　　Labor..........41.90				
	Remove ....　　Labor 3.79				
	► Stone 6″ or less wide with complex straight patterns (Gothic) with arched top or flat top with decorative work around corners or center of header. Or simple straight patterns with stone up to 10″ wide.				
	Sandstone window architrave, custom grade	lf	$3.79	$179.90	$183.69
	Replace Materials.....138.00　　Labor..........41.90				
	Remove ....　　Labor 3.79				
	► Stone 6″ or less wide with hand carvings on header or up to 10″ wide with complex straight patterns (Gothic) with arched top. Or simple straight patterns with stone up to 12″ wide.				
	Sandstone window architrave, custom deluxe grade	lf	$3.79	$210.90	$214.69
	Replace Materials.....169.00　　Labor..........41.90				
	Remove ....　　Labor 3.79				
	► Stone 6″ or less wide with heavy hand carvings on header (e.g. lion's face, human face) or lighter hand carvings throughout or up to 12″ wide with complex straight patterns (Gothic). With arched top.				
add for round window ▷	**Add 65% for architrave for round or elliptical window**				
	► Measure perimeter of opening.				
replace section to match ▷	**Replace section of stone architrave cut to match**	ea	–	$721.00	$721.00
	Replace Materials ....581.00　　Labor.........140.00				
	► Includes plaster or clay model with work performed on site or in a shop within 150 miles of the site.				
CUT STONE ► **TRIM OR CORNICE** *Per 4″ of width. Use for friezes, architraves, cornices, string courses, band courses, and so on.*	**Cut stone trim or cornice stones, all horizontal patterns**	lf	$3.01	$29.60	$32.61
	Replace Materials ......14.10　　Labor 15.50				
	Remove ....　　Labor 3.01				
	Cut stone trim or cornice stones, complex horizontal patterns (Gothic)	lf	$3.01	$35.20	$38.21
	Replace Materials.......19.70　　Labor 15.50				
	Remove ....　　Labor 3.01				
	Cut stone trim or cornice stones with vertical patterns	lf	$3.01	$37.30	$40.31
	Replace Materials ......21.80　　Labor 15.50				
	Remove ....　　Labor 3.01				
	Cut stone trim or cornice stones with light hand carvings	lf	$3.01	$46.20	$49.21
	Replace Materials ......30.70　　Labor 15.50				
	Remove ....　　Labor 3.01				

Item Description	Unit	Remove	Replace	Total
Cut stone trim or cornice stones with medium hand carvings *Replace* Materials......38.20 Labor...........15.50 *Remove* .... Labor...........3.01	lf	$3.01	$53.70	$56.71
Cut stone trim or cornice stones with heavy hand carvings *Replace* Materials......49.80 Labor...........15.50 *Remove* .... Labor...........3.01	lf	$3.01	$65.30	$68.31
Limestone trim or cornice stones, all horizontal patterns *Replace* Materials......21.60 Labor...........15.50 *Remove* .... Labor...........3.01	lf	$3.01	$37.10	$40.11
Limestone trim or cornice stones, complex horizontal patterns (Gothic) *Replace* Materials......40.80 Labor...........15.50 *Remove* .... Labor...........3.01	lf	$3.01	$56.30	$59.31
Limestone trim or cornice stones with vertical patterns *Replace* Materials......77.70 Labor...........15.50 *Remove* .... Labor...........3.01	lf	$3.01	$93.20	$96.21
Limestone trim or cornice stones with light hand carvings *Replace* Materials.....113.00 Labor...........15.50 *Remove* .... Labor...........3.01	lf	$3.01	$128.50	$131.51
Limestone trim or cornice stones with medium hand carvings *Replace* Materials.....141.00 Labor...........15.50 *Remove* .... Labor...........3.01	lf	$3.01	$156.50	$159.51
Limestone trim or cornice stones with heavy hand carvings *Replace* Materials.....173.00 Labor...........15.50 *Remove* .... Labor...........3.01	lf	$3.01	$188.50	$191.51
Marble trim or cornice stones, all horizontal patterns *Replace* Materials......41.00 Labor...........15.50 *Remove* .... Labor...........3.01	lf	$3.01	$56.50	$59.51
Marble trim or cornice stones, complex horizontal patterns (Gothic) *Replace* Materials......60.50 Labor...........15.50 *Remove* .... Labor...........3.01	lf	$3.01	$76.00	$79.01
Marble trim or cornice stones with vertical patterns *Replace* Materials......97.90 Labor...........15.50 *Remove* .... Labor...........3.01	lf	$3.01	$113.40	$116.41
Marble trim or cornice stones with light hand carvings *Replace* Materials.....133.00 Labor...........15.50 *Remove* .... Labor...........3.01	lf	$3.01	$148.50	$151.51
Marble trim or cornice stones with medium hand carvings *Replace* Materials.....161.00 Labor...........15.50 *Remove* .... Labor...........3.01	lf	$3.01	$176.50	$179.51
Marble trim or cornice stones with heavy hand carvings *Replace* Materials.....193.00 Labor...........15.50 *Remove* .... Labor...........3.01	lf	$3.01	$208.50	$211.51
Sandstone trim or cornice stones, all horizontal patterns *Replace* Materials......17.00 Labor...........15.50 *Remove* .... Labor...........3.01	lf	$3.01	$32.50	$35.51

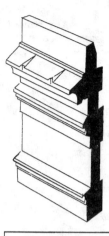

CUT STONE

All horizontal patterns are shallow. Typical depth is 3/4" or less but may be as deep as 1".

Complex horizontal patterns are deep Gothic style reliefs that require two passes through the stone planer.

Vertical patterns are straight vertical cuts like dentil, meander, or fretwork.

Light hand carvings are usually less than 3/4" deep and do not cover the entire face of the stone with detailed work.

Medium hand carvings are heavier carvings like vermiculation, Acanthus, and so forth.

Heavy hand carvings are heavy and deep carvings including a lion's face, a human face, and so forth.

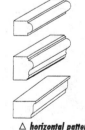

△ *horizontal patterns*

RELATED ITEMS

Cleaning 63
Fireplaces....................241
Painting 340

	Item Description	Unit	Remove	Replace	Total
CUT STONE ▶ **TRIM OR CORNICE** *continued*	**Sandstone trim or cornice stones, complex horizontal patterns (Gothic)** *Replace* Materials ......36.30 Labor ....15.50 *Remove* .... Labor 3.01	lf	$3.01	$51.80	$54.81
	Sandstone trim or cornice stones with vertical patterns *Replace* Materials ......73.10 Labor ....15.50 *Remove* .... Labor 3.01	lf	$3.01	$88.60	$91.61
	Sandstone trim or cornice stones with light hand carvings *Replace* Materials ....108.00 Labor ....15.50 *Remove* .... Labor 3.01	lf	$3.01	$123.50	$126.51
	Sandstone trim or cornice stones with medium hand carvings *Replace* Materials .....136.00 Labor ....15.50 *Remove* .... Labor 3.01	lf	$3.01	$151.50	$154.51
△ *horizontal patterns*	**Sandstone trim or cornice stones with heavy hand carvings** *Replace* Materials .....168.00 Labor ....15.50 *Remove* .... Labor 3.01	lf	$3.01	$183.50	$186.51
replace section to match ▷	**Replace section of stone trim or cornice cut to match** *Replace* Materials .....476.00 Labor ....123.00 ▶ Includes plaster or clay model with work performed on site or in a shop within 150 miles of the site.	ea	–	$599.00	$599.00
CUT STONE SILL ▶ *Up to 10" wide.*	**1-1/2" bluestone window sill or stool** *Replace* Materials ......14.40 Labor ....14.00 *Remove* .... Labor 3.18	lf	$3.18	$28.40	$31.58
4" ▽	**4" cast stone window sill** *Replace* Materials........9.90 Labor ....14.00 *Remove* .... Labor ....3.18 ▶ 4" thick at edge. Up to 6" thick at center or end of sill.	lf	$3.18	$23.90	$27.08
	1-1/2" granite window sill or stool *Replace* Materials........15.60 Labor ....14.00 *Remove* .... Labor 3.18	lf	$3.18	$29.60	$32.78
	4" granite window sill *Replace* Materials ......28.20 Labor ....14.00 *Remove* .... Labor ....3.18 ▶ 4" thick at edge. Up to 6" thick at center or end of sill.	lf	$3.18	$42.20	$45.38
△ *1-1/2"*	**1-1/2" limestone window sill or stool** *Replace* Materials ......14.10 Labor ....14.00 *Remove* .... Labor 3.18	lf	$3.18	$28.10	$31.28
	4" limestone window sill *Replace* Materials ......25.20 Labor ....14.00 *Remove* .... Labor ....3.18 ▶ 4" thick at edge. Up to 6" thick at center or end of sill.	lf	$3.18	$39.20	$42.38
	1-1/2" marble window sill or stool *Replace* Materials ......16.60 Labor ....14.00 *Remove* .... Labor 3.18	lf	$3.18	$30.60	$33.78
	1-1/2" sandstone window sill or stool *Replace* Materials ......10.30 Labor ....14.00 *Remove* .... Labor 3.18	lf	$3.18	$24.30	$27.48

Item Description	Unit	Remove	Replace	Total
4" sandstone window sill	lf	$3.18	$34.20	$37.38
Replace Materials......20.20 Labor............14.00				
Remove .... Labor............3.18				
▶ 4" thick at edge. Up to 6" thick at center or end of sill.				
1-1/2" slate window sill or stool	lf	$3.18	$30.70	$33.88
Replace Materials......16.70 Labor............14.00				
Remove .... Labor............3.18				
10" terra-cotta wall cap	lf	$1.82	$15.32	$17.14
Replace Materials......7.57 Labor............7.75				
Remove .... Labor............1.82				
12" terra-cotta wall cap	lf	$1.82	$20.15	$21.97
Replace Materials......12.40 Labor............7.75				
Remove .... Labor............1.82				
Aluminum wall cap all wall widths	lf	$.55	$21.98	$22.53
Replace Materials......14.40 Labor............7.58				
Remove .... Labor.............55				
10" wide concrete coping	lf	$3.01	$22.60	$25.61
Replace Materials......15.60 Labor............7.00				
Remove .... Labor............3.01				
12" wide concrete coping	lf	$3.01	$23.40	$26.41
Replace Materials......16.40 Labor............7.00				
Remove .... Labor............3.01				
14" wide concrete coping	lf	$3.01	$27.80	$30.81
Replace Materials......20.80 Labor............7.00				
Remove .... Labor............3.01				
8" wide granite coping stone	lf	$3.01	$39.25	$42.26
Replace Materials......31.50 Labor............7.75				
Remove .... Labor............3.01				
10" wide granite coping stone	lf	$3.01	$44.05	$47.06
Replace Materials......36.30 Labor............7.75				
Remove .... Labor............3.01				
12" wide granite coping stone	lf	$3.01	$48.95	$51.96
Replace Materials......41.20 Labor............7.75				
Remove .... Labor............3.01				
8" wide limestone coping stone	lf	$3.01	$26.55	$29.56
Replace Materials......18.80 Labor............7.75				
Remove .... Labor............3.01				
10" wide limestone coping stone	lf	$3.01	$27.05	$30.06
Replace Materials......19.30 Labor............7.75				
Remove .... Labor............3.01				
12" wide limestone coping stone	lf	$3.01	$30.15	$33.16
Replace Materials......22.40 Labor............7.75				
Remove .... Labor............3.01				
8" wide marble coping stone	lf	$3.01	$34.25	$37.26
Replace Materials......26.50 Labor............7.75				
Remove .... Labor............3.01				

◀ **WALL CAP**

◀ **WALL COPING**
From 4" to 6" thick at center with straight or curved taper to edges. Widths over 8" include drip grooves on each side as illustrated below.

RELATED ITEMS

Cleaning 63
Fireplaces....................241
Painting 340

	Item Description	Unit	Remove	Replace	Total
WALL COPING ▶ *continued*	**10" wide marble coping stone** *Replace* Materials......32.90 Labor ....7.75 *Remove* .... Labor 3.01	lf	$3.01	$40.65	$43.66
	12" wide marble coping stone *Replace* Materials ......41.10 Labor ....7.75 *Remove* .... Labor 3.01	lf	$3.01	$48.85	$51.86
REPOINT BRICK ▶ **WALL** *Tuck pointing. To mask and grout deduct 12%.*	**Repoint running bond brick wall** *Replace* Materials .... .36 Labor 4.53	sf	–	$4.89	$4.89
running bond △	**Repoint common bond brick wall** *Replace* Materials .... .36 Labor ....4.65 ▶ Also called American bond. Every sixth course is a full course of full-length headers.	sf	–	$5.01	$5.01
common bond △	**Repoint Flemish bond brick wall** *Replace* Materials .... .36 Labor ....5.07 ▶ Each course is made of alternating stretchers and headers.	sf	–	$5.43	$5.43
Flemish bond △	**Repoint English bond brick wall** *Replace* Materials .... .36 Labor ....5.36 ▶ Alternating full courses made from stretchers and headers. The joints between stretchers in all courses align vertically.	sf	–	$5.72	$5.72
English bond △	**Repoint English cross bond brick wall** *Replace* Materials .... .36 Labor ....5.36 ▶ Also called Dutch bond. A variation of English bond. The vertical joints between stretcher bricks, in alternate courses, align vertically with the center of the stretcher brick in the course above and below.	sf	–	$5.72	$5.72
English cross bond △	**Repoint stack bond brick wall** *Replace* Materials .... .36 Labor ....3.44 ▶ All vertical and horizontal joints align.	sf	–	$3.80	$3.80
stack bond △	**Repoint all header bond brick wall** *Replace* Materials .... .36 Labor ....3.90 ▶ All bricks are laid as headers.	sf	–	$4.26	$4.26
header bond △	**Repoint soldier course brick wall** *Replace* Materials .... .36 Labor ....4.44 ▶ All bricks are stood on end with edge showing.	sf	–	$4.80	$4.80
soldier course △	**Repoint sailor course brick wall** *Replace* Materials .... .36 Labor ....4.15 ▶ All bricks are stood on end with face showing.	sf	–	$4.51	$4.51
sailor course △	**Repoint basketweave brick wall** *Replace* Materials .... .36 Labor ....6.87 ▶ A wide variety of patterns with alternating sections of horizontal and vertical brick.	sf	–	$7.23	$7.23
basketweave △	**Repoint herringbone weave brick wall** *Replace* Materials .... .36 Labor ....7.00 ▶ Also called diagonal basketweave. Bricks are placed at an angle (usually 45 degree) in alternate sections angling up and down.	sf	–	$7.36	$7.36
diagonal △	**Repoint diagonal bond brick wall** *Replace* Materials .... .36 Labor ....6.03 ▶ All bricks laid at an angle, usually 45 degree.	sf	–	$6.39	$6.39

Item Description	Unit	Remove	Replace	Total
Repoint coursed ashlar style bond brick wall with two sizes of bricks	sf	–	$5.39	$5.39
Replace Materials .... .36 Labor 5.03				
► A pattern that uses two sizes of bricks to simulate coursed ashlar stone patterns. Usually one size of brick equals two of the second size.				
Add 12% to repoint brick wall with hard existing mortar				
Add 22% to repoint brick wall with very hard existing mortar				
Add 18% to repoint brick wall with butter joint mortar				
Minimum charge to repoint brick wall	ea	–	$228.00	$228.00
Replace Materials ......18.00 Labor.........210.00				
Repoint rubble lay stone wall	sf	–	$13.27	$13.27
Replace Materials........1.67 Labor...........11.60				
Repoint ashlar lay stone wall	sf	–	$12.21	$12.21
Replace Materials........1.31 Labor...........10.90				
Minimum charge to repoint stone wall	ea	–	$228.00	$228.00
Replace Materials ......18.00 Labor.........210.00				
Remove brick veneer, salvage bricks, and re-lay	sf	–	$38.64	$38.64
Replace Materials........1.94 Labor 36.70				
► Existing bricks are removed and old mortar chipped away. An average of 75% of the bricks are salvaged. To replace the missing bricks, 25% of the salvaged bricks are sawn in half length wise and back filled with mortar to fit. Finish wall includes 50% full bricks and 50% backfilled half bricks. Normally not used for large walls, but on sections of damaged wall where bricks cannot be matched.				
Replace single brick	sf	–	$20.23	$20.23
Replace Materials........2.23 Labor...........18.00				
► A single damaged brick is broken out and replaced.				
Tooth in brick patch up to 4 sf	sf	–	$62.00	$62.00
Replace Materials......40.90 Labor...........21.10				
► A small section of brick (less than 4 sf) is broken out and replaced.				
Tooth in brick patch, 4 to 20 sf	sf	–	$27.30	$27.30
Replace Materials......10.20 Labor...........17.10				
► A small section over 4 sf but less than 20 sf is replaced. Existing bricks remain either above, below, or both. (Does not include demolition.)				
Minimum charge to repair brick wall	ea	–	$547.00	$547.00
Replace Materials ......67.00 Labor 480.00				
Replace single stone	ea	–	$23.20	$23.20
Replace Materials........4.30 Labor...........18.90				
► A single damaged stone is broken out and replaced.				
Tooth in stone patch up to 4 sf	ea	–	$102.80	$102.80
Replace Materials ......79.10 Labor 23.70				
► A small section of stone (less than 4 sf) is broken out and replaced.				
Tooth in stone patch, 4 to 20 sf	ea	–	$44.30	$44.30
Replace Materials.......19.80 Labor...........24.50				
► A section of stone veneer is replaced in an area over 4 sf but less than 20 sf. Existing stones remain either above, below, or both. (Does not include demolition.)				

herringbone △

◁ add for hard mortar

coursed ashlar △

◁ minimum charge

◄ **REPOINT STONE WALL**

rubble lay △

◄ **SALVAGE BRICK**

◄ **BRICK WALL REPAIR**

◁ minimum charge

◄ **STONE WALL REPAIR**

RELATED ITEMS

Cleaning 63
Fireplaces....................241
Painting.................340

Item Description	Unit	Remove	Replace	Total
STONE WALL ▶ **REPAIR** *continued* **Remove segment of rubble stone wall and re-lay** *Replace* Materials........4.76 Labor.........184.00 ▶ Existing stones are removed, old mortar is chipped away and wall is re-laid.	cf	–	**$188.76**	**$188.76**
Remove segment of rubble stone veneer and re-lay *Replace* Materials........1.60 Labor..........88.30 ▶ Existing stones are removed, old mortar is chipped away and veneer is re-laid.	sf	–	**$89.90**	**$89.90**
Remove segment of ashlar stone wall and re-lay *Replace* Materials........3.45 Labor.........177.00 ▶ Existing stones are removed, old mortar is chipped away and wall is re-laid.	cf	–	**$180.45**	**$180.45**
Remove segment of ashlar stone veneer and re-lay *Replace* Materials...... 1.16 Labor..........86.90 ▶ Existing stones are removed, old mortar is chipped away and veneer is re-laid.	sf	–	**$88.06**	**$88.06**
Minimum charge to repair stone wall *Replace* Materials ....130.00 Labor........533.00	ea	–	**$663.00**	**$663.00**
STONE CARVING ▶ *Work performed on site or in a shop within 150 miles of the site. Does not include clay or plaster model.* **Carve stone with light hand carvings** *Replace* .... Labor............1.68 ▶ Light carvings usually less than 3/4" deep and do not cover the entire face of the stone with detailed work.	si	–	**$1.68**	**$1.68**
Carve stone with medium hand carvings \ *Replace* .... Labor............2.46 ▶ Heavier carvings like vermiculation, Acanthus, and so forth.	si	–	**$2.46**	**$2.46**
△ vermiculation **Carve stone with heavy hand carvings** *Replace* .... Labor............3.47 ▶ Heavy and deep carvings including a lion's face, a human face, and so forth.	si	–	**$3.47**	**$3.47**
Add 120% for carving stone to match existing work				
clay or plaster model ▷ **Clay or plaster model for stone carvings** *Replace* Materials........1.58 ▶ Models for light carvings may run 15% less and models for heavy carvings like faces may run 20% to 45% more. It is not unusual for models to cost as much or more as the actual carving.	si	–	**$1.58**	**$1.58**
Minimum charge for clay or plaster model for stone carvings *Replace* Materials 164.00	si	–	**$164.00**	**$164.00**
CARVED STONE ▶ **REPAIR** **Repair carved stone with epoxy** *Replace* Materials .... .25 Labor........... 1.15 ▶ Reattach broken piece of carved stone using epoxy and, when necessary, non-ferrous pins.	si	–	**$1.40**	**$1.40**
Repair carved stone with stucco *Replace* Materials .... .03 Labor........... 1.06 ▶ Reface damaged or weathered stone with stucco and shape stucco to match carving.	si	–	**$1.09**	**$1.09**
minimum charge ▷ **Minimum charge to repair carved stone** *Replace* Materials ......37.00 Labor.........192.00	ea	–	**$229.00**	**$229.00**
STONE REPAIR ▶ **Epoxy repair and pin broken stone** *Replace* Materials........9.68 Labor..........63.80 ▶ Reattach broken piece of stone using epoxy and, when necessary, non-ferrous pins.	ea	–	**$73.48**	**$73.48**

Item Description	Unit	Remove	Replace	Total	
Reconstitute delaminating stone with epoxy and reinforcing pins	si	–	$.90	$.90	
Replace Materials .... .28 Labor .... .62					
► Drill holes and inject epoxy in between layers of delaminating stone. Non-ferrous reinforcing pins are also added for strength.					
Reface damaged stone with grout mixed to match	si	–	$7.18	$7.18	
Replace Materials .... .03 Labor 7.15					
► Grout or plaster colored to match stone is applied over the face of damaged or weathered stone and shaped to match.					
Minimum charge for stone epoxy repair work	ea	–	$170.00	$170.00	◁ minimum charge
Replace Materials ...... 37.00 Labor 133.00					
Hand clean brick wall	sf	–	$1.48	$1.48	◄ CLEAN MASONRY
Replace Materials .... .07 Labor 1.41					
► With bristle brush and muriatic acid (or similar).					
Hand clean stone wall	sf	–	$1.58	$1.58	
Replace Materials .... .07 Labor 1.51					
► With bristle brush and muriatic acid (or similar).					
Pressure spray brick wall	sf	–	$.47	$.47	
Replace Materials .... .10 Labor .... .37					
► With water only or with cleaning chemicals.					
Pressure spray stone wall	sf	–	$.47	$.47	
Replace Materials .... .10 Labor .... .37					
► With water only or with cleaning chemicals.					
Steam clean brick wall	sf	–	$.50	$.50	
Replace .... Labor .... .50					
Steam clean stone wall	sf	–	$.54	$.54	
Replace .... Labor .... .54					
Wet sandblast brick wall	sf	–	$1.86	$1.86	
Replace Materials .... .33 Labor 1.53					
Wet sandblast stone wall	sf	–	$1.95	$1.95	
Replace Materials .... .33 Labor 1.62					
Cut opening in brick wall to 6″ thick	lf	–	$8.23	$8.23	◄ CUT OPENING IN MASONRY WALL
Replace .... Labor 8.23					*Cut masonry wall with*
Cut opening in brick wall 7″ to 12″ thick	lf	–	$9.20	$9.20	*concrete saw. See next*
Replace .... Labor 9.20					*page for prices to insert*
Cut opening in brick veneer wall	lf	–	$7.91	$7.91	*lintels into opening.*
Replace .... Labor 7.91					
Cut opening in stone wall to 6″ thick	lf	–	$9.20	$9.20	
Replace .... Labor 9.20					
Cut opening in stone wall 7″ to 12″ thick	lf	–	$10.40	$10.40	
Replace .... Labor 10.40					
Cut opening in stone veneer wall	lf	–	$8.83	$8.83	
Replace .... Labor 8.83					

RELATED ITEMS

Cleaning 63
Fireplaces 241
Painting 340

Item Description	Unit	Remove	Replace	Total
SHORE MASONRY OPENING ▶ **Shore masonry opening for work per lf of header**	lf	–	$30.30	$30.30
Replace Materials ......12.60 Labor 17.70				
▶ 2" x 6" or 2" x 8" framing members sheathed with plywood.				
Shore arched masonry opening for work	lf	–	$36.50	$36.50
Replace Materials......13.30 Labor 23.20				
▶ 2" x 6" or 2" x 8" framing members sheathed with plywood that follows curved shape of arch.				
CONCRETE LINTEL ▶ **Concrete lintel for opening in 4" thick brick or stone**	lf	–	$13.79	$13.79
Replace Materials ......10.20 Labor 3.59				
Concrete lintel for opening in 6" thick brick or stone	lf	–	$18.20	$18.20
Replace Materials.......13.60 Labor 4.60				
Concrete lintel for opening in 8" thick brick or stone	lf	–	$19.85	$19.85
Replace Materials ......14.70 Labor 5.15				
Concrete lintel for opening in 10" thick brick or stone	lf	–	$31.41	$31.41
Replace Materials ......25.20 Labor 6.21				
Concrete lintel for opening in 12" thick brick or stone	lf	–	$40.45	$40.45
Replace Materials......33.60 Labor 6.85				
Add for key cast into lintel	ea	–	$52.00	$52.00
Replace Materials 52.00				
ANGLE-IRON LINTEL ▶ **Angle iron lintel for opening in 4" thick brick or stone**	lf	–	$6.89	$6.89
Replace Materials........4.08 Labor 2.81				
Angle iron lintel for opening in 6" thick brick or stone	lf	–	$10.97	$10.97
Replace Materials........8.16 Labor 2.81				
Angle iron lintel for opening in 8" thick brick or stone	lf	–	$11.71	$11.71
Replace Materials........8.67 Labor 3.04				
Angle iron lintel for opening in 10" thick brick or stone	lf	–	$12.82	$12.82
Replace Materials........9.74 Labor 3.08				
Angle iron lintel for opening in 12" thick brick or stone	lf	–	$17.23	$17.23
Replace Materials ......14.10 Labor 3.13				

lintel with plain key △

lintel with winged key △

lintel with recessed key △

NOTES: _____

_____

_____

_____

_____

_____

_____

_____

_____

_____ end

TIME & MATERIAL CHARTS (selected items)

Masonry Materials

DESCRIPTION	MATERIAL PRICE	GROSS COVERAGE	WASTE	NET COVERAGE	UNIT PRICE
Rebar					
#3 (3/8" .376 pound per lf)	$3.62 per 20' bar	20	4%	19.2	$.19 lf
#4 (1/2" .668 pounds per lf)	$4.62 per 20' bar	20	4%	19.2	$.24 lf
#5 (5/8" 1.043 pounds per lf)	$7.18 per 20' bar	20	4%	19.2	$.37 lf
#6 (3/4" 1.502 pounds per lf)	$10.90 per 20' bar	20	4%	19.2	$.57 lf
Mortar and grout supplies					
gypsum cement	$17.40 per bag	80	12%	70.4	$.25 lb
masonry cement	$7.40 per bag	70	12%	61.6	$.12 lb
white masonry cement	$22.40 per bag	70	12%	61.6	$.36 lb
hydrated lime	$7.62 per bag	50	12%	44	$.17 lb
double hydrated lime	$10.30 per bag	50	12%	44	$.23 lb
screened and washed sand, delivered	$25.70 per ton	1	0%	1	$25.70 ton
Reinforcing wire strip					
4" ladder style	$.15 lf	1	2%	.98	$.15 lf
12" ladder style	$.21 lf	1	2%	.98	$.21 lf
4" truss style	$.19 lf	1	2%	.98	$.19 lf
12" truss style	$.25 lf	1	2%	.98	$.26 lf
add **30%** for galvanized					
Masonry ties					
galvanized 22 gauge corrugated veneer wall tie	$.19 ea	1	2%	.98	$.19 ea
galvanized 16 gauge corrugated veneer wall tie	$.21 ea	1	2%	.98	$.21 ea
rectangular galvanized wall tie	$.24 ea	1	2%	.98	$.24 ea
galvanized "Z" style cavity wall tie	$.22 ea	1	2%	.98	$.22 ea
Grout					
for 6" wide bond beam	$.83 lf	1	11%	.89	$.93 lf
for 8" wide bond beam	$1.04 lf	1	11%	.89	$1.17 lf
for 10" wide bond beam	$1.31 lf	1	11%	.89	$1.47 lf
for 12" wide bond beam	$1.58 lf	1	11%	.89	$1.78 lf
for cells in 6" wide concrete block	$1.00 lf	1	11%	.89	$1.12 lf
for cells in 8" wide concrete block	$1.46 lf	1	11%	.89	$1.64 lf
for cells in 10" wide concrete block	$1.86 lf	1	11%	.89	$2.09 lf
for cells in 12" wide concrete block	$2.35 lf	1	11%	.89	$2.64 lf
3/8" brick mortar					
for 4" wide standard non-modular or three-inch	$8.40 cf	25	25%	18.75	$.45 sf
for 4" wide oversize non-modular	$8.40 cf	26	25%	19.5	$.43 sf
for 4" wide engineer	$8.40 cf	27	25%	20.25	$.41 sf
for 4" wide jumbo closure	$8.40 cf	31	25%	23.25	$.36 sf
for 4" wide double	$8.40 cf	37	25%	27.75	$.30 sf
for 4" wide Roman	$8.40 cf	21	25%	15.75	$.53 sf
for 4" wide Norman	$8.40 cf	26	25%	19.5	$.43 sf
for 4" wide Norwegian	$8.40 cf	30	25%	22.5	$.37 sf
for 4" wide jumbo utility	$8.40 cf	36	25%	27	$.31 sf
for 4" wide triple	$8.40 cf	44	25%	33	$.25 sf
for 6" wide Norwegian	$8.40 cf	20	25%	15	$.56 sf
for 6" wide Norman	$8.40 cf	16.8	25%	12.6	$.67 sf
for 6" wide jumbo	$8.40 cf	24	25%	18	$.47 sf
for 8" wide jumbo	$8.40 cf	18	25%	13.5	$.62 sf
3/8" concrete block mortar (8" x 16" face)					
for 4" wide	$8.40 cf	40	25%	30	$.28 sf
for 6" wide	$8.40 cf	30	25%	22.5	$.37 sf
for 8" wide	$8.40 cf	25	25%	18.75	$.45 sf
for 10" wide	$8.40 cf	20.5	25%	15.38	$.55 sf
for 12" wide	$8.40 cf	16.6	25%	12.45	$.67 sf

... *More* ➢

Masonry Materials *continued*

DESCRIPTION	MATERIAL PRICE	GROSS COVERAGE	WASTE	NET COVERAGE	UNIT PRICE
3/8" concrete slump block mortar (4" x 16" face)					
for 4" wide	$8.40 cf	.34	25%	25.5	$.33 sf
for 6" wide	$8.40 cf	.24	25%	18	$.47 sf
for 8" wide	$8.40 cf	.21	25%	15.75	$.53 sf
for 10" wide	$8.40 cf	16.5	25%	12.38	$.68 sf
for 12" wide	$8.40 cf	12.6	25%	9.45	$.89 sf
3/8" concrete screen block mortar (12" x 12" face)					
for 4" wide	$8.40 cf	35.6	25%	26.7	$.31 sf
3/8" backing tile mortar (12" x 12" face)					
for 4" thick	$8.40 cf	35.6	25%	26.7	$.31 sf
for 6" thick	$8.40 cf	26.5	25%	19.88	$.42 sf
for 8" thick	$8.40 cf	22.5	25%	16.88	$.50 sf
3/8" structural tile mortar (8" x 16" face)					
for 4" thick	$8.40 cf	40	25%	30	$.28 sf
for 6" thick	$8.40 cf	30	25%	22.5	$.37 sf
for 8" thick	$8.40 cf	25	25%	18.75	$.45 sf
3/8" gypsum partition tile mortar (12" x 30" face)					
for 4" thick	$8.40 cf	78	25%	58.5	$.14 sf
for 6" thick	$8.40 cf	66	25%	49.5	$.17 sf
3/8" white mortar for glass blocks					
for block with 4" x 8" face	$10.60 cf	26	25%	19.5	$.54 sf
for block with 6" x 6" face	$10.60 cf	29	25%	21.75	$.49 sf
for block with 6" x 8" face	$10.60 cf	36	25%	27	$.39 sf
for block with 8" x 8" face	$10.60 cf	44	25%	33	$.32 sf
for block with 12" x 12" face	$10.60 cf	35.6	25%	26.7	$.40 sf
deduct 22% for natural gray mortar in glass block wall					
deduct 8% for colored mortar in glass block wall					
Mortar for stone walls					
mortar for rubble stone wall	$8.40 cf	4.41	32%	3	$2.80 cf
mortar for ashlar stone wall	$8.40 cf	5.5	25%	4.13	$2.03 cf
mortar for rubble stone veneer	$8.40 cf	13.2	32%	8.98	$.94 sf
mortar for ashlar stone veneer	$8.40 cf	16.5	25%	12.38	$.68 sf
Brick					
deduct 16% for common brick					
add $624.00 per thousand for glazed brick					
4" wide standard non-modular	$727.00 per thousand	1,000	4%	960	$.76 ea
4" wide oversize non-modular	$724.00 per thousand	1,000	4%	960	$.75 ea
4" wide three-inch non-modular	$716.00 per thousand	1,000	4%	960	$.75 ea
4" wide standard	$578.00 per thousand	1,000	4%	960	$.60 ea
4" wide used	$1,260.00 per thousand	1,000	4%	960	$1.31 ea
4" wide engineer	$710.00 per thousand	1,000	4%	960	$.74 ea
4" wide jumbo closure	$883.00 per thousand	1,000	4%	960	$.92 ea
4" wide double	$935.00 per thousand	1,000	4%	960	$.97 ea
4" wide Roman	$1,000.00 per thousand	1,000	4%	960	$1.04 ea
4" wide Norman	$978.00 per thousand	1,000	4%	960	$1.02 ea
4" wide Norwegian	$883.00 per thousand	1,000	4%	960	$.92 ea
4" wide jumbo utility	$1,430.00 per thousand	1,000	4%	960	$1.49 ea
4" wide triple	$1,520.00 per thousand	1,000	4%	960	$1.58 ea
6" wide Norwegian	$1,390.00 per thousand	1,000	4%	960	$1.45 ea
6" wide Norman	$1,310.00 per thousand	1,000	4%	960	$1.36 ea
6" wide jumbo	$1,670.00 per thousand	1,000	4%	960	$1.74 ea
8" wide jumbo	$2,220.00 per thousand	1,000	4%	960	$2.31 ea
Concrete block					
4" wide	$997.00 per thousand	1,000	4%	960	$1.04 ea
6" wide	$1,120.00 per thousand	1,000	4%	960	$1.17 ea
8" wide	$1,400.00 per thousand	1,000	4%	960	$1.46 ea
10" wide	$1,750.00 per thousand	1,000	4%	960	$1.82 ea
12" wide	$2,370.00 per thousand	1,000	4%	960	$2.47 ea

. . . More ➤

Masonry Materials *continued*

DESCRIPTION	MATERIAL PRICE	GROSS COVERAGE	WASTE	NET COVERAGE	UNIT PRICE
Lightweight concrete block					
4" wide	$1,130.00 *per thousand*	1,000	4%	960	**$1.18** *ea*
6" wide	$1,260.00 *per thousand*	1,000	4%	960	**$1.31** *ea*
8" wide	$1,580.00 *per thousand*	1,000	4%	960	**$1.65** *ea*
10" wide	$1,960.00 *per thousand*	1,000	4%	960	**$2.04** *ea*
12" wide	$2,670.00 *per thousand*	1,000	4%	960	**$2.78** *ea*
Slump block					
4" wide	$1,060.00 *per thousand*	1,000	4%	960	**$1.10** *ea*
6" wide	$1,290.00 *per thousand*	1,000	4%	960	**$1.34** *ea*
8" wide	$1,590.00 *per thousand*	1,000	4%	960	**$1.66** *ea*
10" wide	$1,880.00 *per thousand*	1,000	4%	960	**$1.96** *ea*
12" wide	$2,400.00 *per thousand*	1,000	4%	960	**$2.50** *ea*
Fluted block (fluted one side)					
4" wide	$1,830.00 *per thousand*	1,000	4%	960	**$1.91** *ea*
6" wide	$2,040.00 *per thousand*	1,000	4%	960	**$2.13** *ea*
8" wide	$2,560.00 *per thousand*	1,000	4%	960	**$2.67** *ea*
10" wide	$3,200.00 *per thousand*	1,000	4%	960	**$3.33** *ea*
12" wide	$4,330.00 *per thousand*	1,000	4%	960	**$4.51** *ea*
Fluted block (fluted two sides)					
4" wide	$2,210.00 *per thousand*	1,000	4%	960	**$2.30** *ea*
6" wide	$2,470.00 *per thousand*	1,000	4%	960	**$2.57** *ea*
8" wide	$3,100.00 *per thousand*	1,000	4%	960	**$3.23** *ea*
10" wide	$3,880.00 *per thousand*	1,000	4%	960	**$4.04** *ea*
12" wide	$5,240.00 *per thousand*	1,000	4%	960	**$5.46** *ea*
Glazed block (glazed one side)					
4" wide	$9,930.00 *per thousand*	1,000	4%	960	**$10.30** *ea*
6" wide	$10,200.00 *per thousand*	1,000	4%	960	**$10.60** *ea*
8" wide	$10,530.00 *per thousand*	1,000	4%	960	**$11.00** *ea*
10" wide	$10,800.00 *per thousand*	1,000	4%	960	**$11.30** *ea*
12" wide	$11,100.00 *per thousand*	1,000	4%	960	**$11.60** *ea*
Glazed block (glazed two sides)					
4" wide	$14,800.00 *per thousand*	1,000	4%	960	**$15.40** *ea*
6" wide	$15,800.00 *per thousand*	1,000	4%	960	**$16.50** *ea*
8" wide	$16,400.00 *per thousand*	1,000	4%	960	**$17.10** *ea*
10" wide	$16,700.00 *per thousand*	1,000	4%	960	**$17.40** *ea*
12" wide	$17,000.00 *per thousand*	1,000	4%	960	**$17.70** *ea*
Split-face block					
4" wide	$2,040.00 *per thousand*	1,000	4%	960	**$2.13** *ea*
6" wide	$2,420.00 *per thousand*	1,000	4%	960	**$2.52** *ea*
8" wide	$3,260.00 *per thousand*	1,000	4%	960	**$3.40** *ea*
10" wide	$3,520.00 *per thousand*	1,000	4%	960	**$3.67** *ea*
12" wide	$4,720.00 *per thousand*	1,000	4%	960	**$4.92** *ea*
Split-rib block					
4" wide	$1,880.00 *per thousand*	1,000	4%	960	**$1.96** *ea*
6" wide	$1,950.00 *per thousand*	1,000	4%	960	**$2.03** *ea*
8" wide	$3,200.00 *per thousand*	1,000	4%	960	**$3.33** *ea*
10" wide	$3,560.00 *per thousand*	1,000	4%	960	**$3.71** *ea*
12" wide	$3,920.00 *per thousand*	1,000	4%	960	**$4.08** *ea*
Screen block					
4" wide, pattern two sides	$5,440.00 *per thousand*	1,000	4%	960	**$5.67** *ea*
4" wide, pattern four sides	$10,300.00 *per thousand*	1,000	4%	960	**$10.70** *ea*
Silicone treated perlite or vermiculite loose fill insulation					
in 6" wide block	$7.62 *4 cf bag*	21	3%	20.37	**$.37** *sf*
in 8" wide block	$7.62 *4 cf bag*	14.5	3%	14.07	**$.54** *sf*
in 10" wide block	$7.62 *4 cf bag*	11.5	3%	11.16	**$.68** *sf*
in 12" wide block	$7.62 *4 cf bag*	8	3%	7.76	**$.98** *sf*

. . . More ➤

Masonry Materials *continued*

DESCRIPTION	MATERIAL PRICE	GROSS COVERAGE	WASTE	NET COVERAGE	UNIT PRICE
Glass block					
4" x 8" thinline smooth-face	$21.20 sf	1	4%	.96	$22.10 sf
6" x 6" thinline smooth-face	$19.50 sf	1	4%	.96	$20.30 sf
4" x 8" smooth-face	$26.60 sf	1	4%	.96	$27.70 sf
6" x 6" smooth-face	$23.60 sf	1	4%	.96	$24.60 sf
8" x 8" smooth-face	$16.50 sf	1	4%	.96	$17.20 sf
add **83%** for solar UV reflective					
add **11%** for patterned face					
add **55%** for tinted					
Rubble stone					
coral-stone rubble	$35.10 cf	1	4%	.96	$36.60 cf
field-stone rubble	$27.90 cf	1	4%	.96	$29.10 cf
flagstone rubble	$16.00 cf	1	4%	.96	$16.70 cf
river stone rubble	$28.60 cf	1	4%	.96	$29.80 cf
lava stone rubble	$26.80 cf	1	4%	.96	$27.90 cf
sandstone rubble	$40.90 cf	1	4%	.96	$42.60 cf
Ashlar stone					
flagstone	$16.70 cf	1	4%	.96	$17.40 cf
limestone, natural finish	$22.70 cf	1	4%	.96	$23.60 cf
limestone, rough finish	$25.40 cf	1	4%	.96	$26.50 cf
limestone, smooth finish	$36.80 cf	1	4%	.96	$38.30 cf
marble, natural finish	$53.80 cf	1	4%	.96	$56.00 cf
marble, rough finish	$58.10 cf	1	4%	.96	$60.50 cf
marble, smooth finish	$72.10 cf	1	4%	.96	$75.10 cf
sandstone, natural finish	$21.80 cf	1	4%	.96	$22.70 cf
sandstone, rough finish	$24.40 cf	1	4%	.96	$25.40 cf
sandstone, smooth finish	$35.40 cf	1	4%	.96	$36.90 cf
Wall coping					
aluminum, all wall widths	$13.80 lf	1	4%	.96	$14.40 lf
10" wide concrete	$14.60 lf	1	2%	.98	$14.90 lf
14" wide concrete	$19.70 lf	1	2%	.98	$20.10 lf
8" wide granite	$30.20 lf	1	2%	.98	$30.80 lf
12" wide granite	$39.70 lf	1	2%	.98	$40.50 lf
8" wide limestone	$17.70 lf	1	2%	.98	$18.10 lf
12" wide limestone	$21.30 lf	1	2%	.98	$21.70 lf
8" wide marble	$26.00 lf	1	2%	.98	$26.50 lf
12" wide marble	$40.30 lf	1	2%	.98	$41.10 lf

Masonry Labor

LABORER	BASE WAGE	PAID LEAVE	TRUE WAGE	FICA	FUTA	WORKER'S COMP.	UNEMPLOY. INSUR.	HEALTH INSUR.	RETIRE (401K)	LIABILITY INSUR.	COST PER HOUR
Mason	$25.10	1.96	$27.06	2.07	.22	8.46	2.35	2.92	.81	4.06	**$48.00**
Mason's helper	$22.90	1.79	$24.69	1.89	.20	7.72	2.15	2.92	.74	3.70	**$44.00**
Hod carrier	$17.10	1.33	$18.43	1.41	.15	5.76	1.60	2.92	.55	2.76	**$33.60**
Plasterer	$23.60	1.84	$25.44	1.95	.20	7.38	2.21	2.92	.76	3.82	**$44.70**
Stone carver	$61.00	4.76	$65.76	5.03	.53	20.56	5.72	2.92	1.97	9.86	**$112.00**
Demolition laborer	$14.40	1.12	$15.52	1.19	.121	5.01	1.35	2.92	.47	2.33	**$28.90**

Paid Leave is calculated based on two weeks paid vacation, one week sick leave, and seven paid holidays. Employer's matching portion of **FICA** is 7.65 percent. **FUTA** (Federal Unemployment) is .8 percent. **Worker's Compensation** was calculated using a national average of 31.20 percent for masonry workers and .28.93 percent for plastering workers. **Unemployment insurance** was calculated using a national average of 8.7 percent. **Health insurance** was calculated based on a projected national average for 2005 of $580 per employee (and family when applicable) per month. Employer pays 80 percent for a per month cost of $464 per employee. **Retirement** is based on a 401(k) retirement program with employer matching of 50 percent. Employee contributions to the 401(k) plan are an average of 6 percent of the true wage. **Liability insurance** is based on a national average of 14.0 percent.

Masonry Labor Productivity

WORK DESCRIPTION	LABORER	COST PER HOUR	PRODUCTIVITY	UNIT PRICE
Demolition				
remove 4" masonry wall	demolition laborer	$28.90	.087	$2.51 sf
remove 12" masonry wall	demolition laborer	$28.90	.177	$5.12 sf
remove brick veneer	demolition laborer	$28.90	.082	$2.37 sf
remove block wall pilaster	demolition laborer	$28.90	.121	$3.50 lf
remove block wall grade beam cap	demolition laborer	$28.90	.363	$10.50 lf
remove terra-cotta wall cap	demolition laborer	$28.90	.063	$1.82 lf
remove coping stone	demolition laborer	$28.90	.104	$3.01 lf
remove glass block wall	demolition laborer	$28.90	.084	$2.43 sf
remove pavers on mortar base	demolition laborer	$28.90	.120	$3.47 sf
remove pavers on sand base	demolition laborer	$28.90	.084	$2.43 sf
remove stone rubble wall with no mortar	demolition laborer	$28.90	.259	$7.49 cf
remove stone rubble wall with mortar	demolition laborer	$28.90	.439	$12.70 cf
remove ashlar wall	demolition laborer	$28.90	.439	$12.70 cf
remove stone veneer	demolition laborer	$28.90	.106	$3.06 sf
remove keystone	demolition laborer	$28.90	.198	$5.72 ea
remove quoin	demolition laborer	$28.90	.196	$5.66 ea
remove veneer panels	demolition laborer	$28.90	.074	$2.14 sf
remove door or window architrave	demolition laborer	$28.90	.131	$3.79 lf
remove trim or cornice stones	demolition laborer	$28.90	.104	$3.01 ea
remove stone window sill	demolition laborer	$28.90	.110	$3.18 lf
remove precast concrete lintel	demolition laborer	$28.90	.120	$3.47 lf
Masonry crew				
install masonry	mason	$48.00		
install masonry	mason's helper	$44.00		
install masonry	hod carrier / laborer	$33.60		
install masonry	**masonry crew**	$41.90		
Mason & helper				
install masonry	mason	$48.00		
install masonry	mason's helper	$44.00		
install masonry	**mason & helper**	$46.00		
Install brick wall				
4" wide standard non-modular	masonry crew	$41.90	.170	$7.12 sf
4" wide oversize non-modular	masonry crew	$41.90	.168	$7.04 sf
4" wide three-inch non-modular	masonry crew	$41.90	.167	$7.00 sf
4" wide standard	masonry crew	$41.90	.169	$7.08 sf
4" wide engineer	masonry crew	$41.90	.141	$5.91 sf
4" wide jumbo closure	masonry crew	$41.90	.120	$5.03 sf
4" wide double	masonry crew	$41.90	.101	$4.23 sf
4" wide Roman	masonry crew	$41.90	.160	$6.70 sf
4" wide Norman	masonry crew	$41.90	.130	$5.45 sf
4" wide Norwegian	masonry crew	$41.90	.111	$4.65 sf
4" wide jumbo utility	masonry crew	$41.90	.102	$4.27 sf
4" wide triple	masonry crew	$41.90	.096	$4.02 sf
6" wide Norwegian	masonry crew	$41.90	.124	$5.20 sf
6" wide Norman	masonry crew	$41.90	.148	$6.20 sf
6" wide jumbo	masonry crew	$41.90	.113	$4.73 sf
8" wide jumbo	masonry crew	$41.90	.127	$5.32 sf
Install 8" wide double wythe brick wall				
with standard non-modular brick	masonry crew	$41.90	.307	$12.90 sf
with oversize non-modular brick	masonry crew	$41.90	.303	$12.70 sf
with three-inch non-modular brick	masonry crew	$41.90	.300	$12.60 sf
with standard brick	masonry crew	$41.90	.305	$12.80 sf
with engineer brick	masonry crew	$41.90	.253	$10.60 sf
with jumbo closure brick	masonry crew	$41.90	.216	$9.05 sf
with double brick	masonry crew	$41.90	.181	$7.58 sf
with Roman brick	masonry crew	$41.90	.287	$12.00 sf
with Norman brick	masonry crew	$41.90	.234	$9.80 sf
with Norwegian brick brick	masonry crew	$41.90	.199	$8.34 sf
with jumbo utility	masonry crew	$41.90	.184	$7.71 sf
with triple brick	masonry crew	$41.90	.173	$7.25 sf

. . . More ➢

Masonry Labor Productivity *continued*

WORK DESCRIPTION	LABORER	COST PER HOUR	PRODUCTIVITY	UNIT PRICE
Install 8" wide wall with 4" wide brick and 4" wide concrete block				
with standard non-modular brick	masonry crew	$41.90	.233	**$9.76** sf
with standard brick	masonry crew	$41.90	.233	**$9.76** sf
with engineer brick	masonry crew	$41.90	.206	**$8.63** sf
with jumbo closure brick	masonry crew	$41.90	.188	**$7.88** sf
with double brick	masonry crew	$41.90	.170	**$7.12** sf
with Roman brick	masonry crew	$41.90	.224	**$9.39** sf
with Norman brick	masonry crew	$41.90	.197	**$8.25** sf
with Norwegian brick	masonry crew	$41.90	.180	**$7.54** sf
with jumbo utility brick	masonry crew	$41.90	.172	**$7.21** sf
with triple brick	masonry crew	$41.90	.166	**$6.96** sf
Install 10" wide wall with 4" wide brick and 6" wide concrete block				
with standard non-modular brick	masonry crew	$41.90	.236	**$9.89** sf
with standard brick	masonry crew	$41.90	.235	**$9.85** sf
with engineer brick	masonry crew	$41.90	.209	**$8.76** sf
with jumbo brick	masonry crew	$41.90	.190	**$7.96** sf
with double brick	masonry crew	$41.90	.173	**$7.25** sf
with Roman brick	masonry crew	$41.90	.226	**$9.47** sf
with Norman brick	masonry crew	$41.90	.200	**$8.38** sf
with Norwegian brick	masonry crew	$41.90	.182	**$7.63** sf
with jumbo utility brick	masonry crew	$41.90	.175	**$7.33** sf
with triple brick	masonry crew	$41.90	.170	**$7.12** sf
Install 12" wide wall with 4" wide brick and 8" wide concrete block				
with standard non-modular brick	masonry crew	$41.90	.240	**$10.10** sf
with standard brick	masonry crew	$41.90	.240	**$10.10** sf
with engineer brick	masonry crew	$41.90	.214	**$8.97** sf
with jumbo closure brick	masonry crew	$41.90	.195	**$8.17** sf
with double brick	masonry crew	$41.90	.178	**$7.46** sf
with Roman brick	masonry crew	$41.90	.231	**$9.68** sf
with Norman brick	masonry crew	$41.90	.204	**$8.55** sf
with Norwegian brick	masonry crew	$41.90	.187	**$7.84** sf
with jumbo utility brick	masonry crew	$41.90	.180	**$7.54** sf
with triple brick	masonry crew	$41.90	.174	**$7.29** sf
Install 12" wide triple wythe wall				
with standard non-modular brick	masonry crew	$41.90	.433	**$18.10** sf
with oversize non-modular brick	masonry crew	$41.90	.427	**$17.90** sf
with three-inch non-modular brick	masonry crew	$41.90	.424	**$17.80** sf
with standard brick	masonry crew	$41.90	.429	**$18.00** sf
with engineer brick	masonry crew	$41.90	.357	**$15.00** sf
with jumbo closure brick	masonry crew	$41.90	.305	**$12.80** sf
with double brick	masonry crew	$41.90	.255	**$10.70** sf
with Roman brick	masonry crew	$41.90	.407	**$17.10** sf
with Norman brick	masonry crew	$41.90	.330	**$13.80** sf
with Norwegian brick	masonry crew	$41.90	.282	**$11.80** sf
with jumbo utility brick	masonry crew	$41.90	.260	**$10.90** sf
with triple brick	masonry crew	$41.90	.244	**$10.20** sf
Install 10" wide cavity wall with 4" brick and 4" concrete block				
with standard non-modular brick	masonry crew	$41.90	.244	**$10.20** sf
with standard brick	masonry crew	$41.90	.243	**$10.20** sf
with engineer brick	masonry crew	$41.90	.216	**$9.05** sf
with jumbo closure brick	masonry crew	$41.90	.196	**$8.21** sf
with double brick	masonry crew	$41.90	.178	**$7.46** sf
with Roman brick	masonry crew	$41.90	.234	**$9.80** sf
with Norman brick	masonry crew	$41.90	.206	**$8.63** sf
with Norwegian brick	masonry crew	$41.90	.188	**$7.88** sf
with jumbo utility brick	masonry crew	$41.90	.180	**$7.54** sf
with triple brick	masonry crew	$41.90	.174	**$7.29** sf
Install 10" wide cavity wall with 4" brick on both sides				
with standard non-modular brick	masonry crew	$41.90	.321	**$13.40** sf
with oversize non-modular brick	masonry crew	$41.90	.317	**$13.30** sf
with three-inch non-modular brick	masonry crew	$41.90	.314	**$13.20** sf
with standard brick	masonry crew	$41.90	.319	**$13.40** sf

... More ➢

Masonry Labor Productivity *continued*

WORK DESCRIPTION	LABORER	COST PER HOUR	PRODUCTIVITY	UNIT PRICE
Install 10" wide cavity wall with 4" brick on both sides *continued*				
with engineer brick	masonry crew	$41.90	.265	**$11.10** *sf*
with jumbo closure brick	masonry crew	$41.90	.226	**$9.47** *sf*
with double brick	masonry crew	$41.90	.189	**$7.92** *sf*
with Roman brick	masonry crew	$41.90	.301	**$12.60** *sf*
with Norman brick	masonry crew	$41.90	.245	**$10.30** *sf*
with Norwegian brick	masonry crew	$41.90	.209	**$8.76** *sf*
with jumbo utility brick	masonry crew	$41.90	.193	**$8.09** *sf*
with triple brick	masonry crew	$41.90	.181	**$7.58** *sf*
Install brick veneer				
with standard brick	masonry crew	$41.90	.144	**$6.03** *sf*
with oversize non-modular brick	masonry crew	$41.90	.143	**$5.99** *sf*
with three-inch non-modular brick	masonry crew	$41.90	.141	**$5.91** *sf*
with standard brick	masonry crew	$41.90	.144	**$6.03** *sf*
with engineer brick	masonry crew	$41.90	.119	**$4.99** *sf*
with jumbo closure brick	masonry crew	$41.90	.102	**$4.27** *sf*
with double brick	masonry crew	$41.90	.085	**$3.56** *sf*
with Roman brick	masonry crew	$41.90	.136	**$5.70** *sf*
with Norman brick	masonry crew	$41.90	.110	**$4.61** *sf*
with Norwegian brick	masonry crew	$41.90	.094	**$3.94** *sf*
with jumbo utility brick	masonry crew	$41.90	.087	**$3.65** *sf*
with triple brick	masonry crew	$41.90	.082	**$3.44** *sf*
Install brick arch				
flat brick arch	masonry crew	$41.90	1.49	**$62.40** *lf*
elliptical brick arch	masonry crew	$41.90	1.85	**$77.50** *lf*
semi-circular brick arch	masonry crew	$41.90	1.96	**$82.10** *lf*
Install block wall with 8" x 16" face				
4" wide	masonry crew	$41.90	.089	**$3.73** *sf*
6" wide	masonry crew	$41.90	.092	**$3.85** *sf*
8" wide	masonry crew	$41.90	.097	**$4.06** *sf*
10" wide	masonry crew	$41.90	.103	**$4.32** *sf*
12" wide	masonry crew	$41.90	.122	**$5.11** *sf*
Install block wall with 4" x 16" face				
4" wide	masonry crew	$41.90	.102	**$4.27** *sf*
6" wide	masonry crew	$41.90	.106	**$4.44** *sf*
8" wide	masonry crew	$41.90	.112	**$4.69** *sf*
10" wide	masonry crew	$41.90	.119	**$4.99** *sf*
12" wide	masonry crew	$41.90	.140	**$5.87** *sf*
Install lightweight block wall with 8" x 16" face				
4" wide	masonry crew	$41.90	.083	**$3.48** *sf*
6" wide	masonry crew	$41.90	.086	**$3.60** *sf*
8" wide	masonry crew	$41.90	.091	**$3.81** *sf*
10" wide	masonry crew	$41.90	.097	**$4.06** *sf*
12" wide	masonry crew	$41.90	.114	**$4.78** *sf*
Form and pour grade-beam cap on block wall				
6" wide	masonry crew	$41.90	.106	**$4.44** *lf*
12" wide	masonry crew	$41.90	.120	**$5.03** *lf*
Install glass block				
4" x 8"	masonry crew	$41.90	.333	**$14.00** *sf*
6" x 8"	masonry crew	$41.90	.267	**$11.20** *sf*
8" x 8"	masonry crew	$41.90	.208	**$8.72** *sf*
12" x 12"	masonry crew	$41.90	.175	**$7.33** *sf*
Install pavers				
on sand base	masonry crew	$41.90	.147	**$6.16** *sf*
on mortar base	masonry crew	$41.90	.180	**$7.54** *sf*
full-size bricks, laid face up	masonry crew	$41.90	.185	**$7.75** *sf*
full-size bricks, laid edge up	masonry crew	$41.90	.208	**$8.72** *sf*
add for paver steps installed in mortar over concrete	masonry crew	$41.90	.270	**$11.30** *lf*
add for paver steps installed over sand base	masonry crew	$41.90	.294	**$12.30** *lf*
add for separate pattern at edges of pavers	masonry crew	$41.90	.076	**$3.18** *lf*

. . . More ➣

Masonry Labor Productivity *continued*

WORK DESCRIPTION	LABORER	COST PER HOUR	PRODUCTIVITY	UNIT PRICE
Lay stone wall				
field stone rubble with no mortar	masonry crew	$41.90	.481	$20.20 cf
rubble wall	masonry crew	$41.90	.518	$21.70 cf
ashlar wall	masonry crew	$41.90	.472	$19.80 cf
add to install flat arch	masonry crew	$41.90	2.86	$120.00 lf
add to install elliptical arch	masonry crew	$41.90	3.57	$150.00 lf
add to install semi-circular arch	masonry crew	$41.90	3.70	$155.00 lf
Lay stone veneer				
rubble	masonry crew	$41.90	.243	$10.20 sf
ashlar	masonry crew	$41.90	.236	$9.89 sf
add to install flat arch	masonry crew	$41.90	1.75	$73.30 lf
add to install elliptical arch	masonry crew	$41.90	2.17	$90.90 lf
add to install semi-circular arch	masonry crew	$41.90	2.30	$96.40 lf
Install veneer panels				
cultured stone	masonry crew	$41.90	.263	$11.00 sf
natural stone	masonry crew	$41.90	.298	$12.50 sf
Install stone architrave				
door	masonry crew	$41.90	.980	$41.10 lf
window	masonry crew	$41.90	1.00	$41.90 lf
Install trim or cornice stones				
all stone types	masonry crew	$41.90	.370	$15.50 lf
Install wall cap or coping				
terra-cotta cap	masonry crew	$41.90	.185	$7.75 lf
aluminum cap	masonry crew	$41.90	.181	$7.58 lf
concrete coping	masonry crew	$41.90	.167	$7.00 lf
stone coping	masonry crew	$41.90	.185	$7.75 lf
Salvage brick veneer				
remove, salvage bricks, and re-lay	masonry crew	$41.90	.877	$36.70 sf
Repoint brick wall				
running bond	masonry crew	$41.90	.108	$4.53 sf
common bond (also called American bond)	masonry crew	$41.90	.111	$4.65 sf
Flemish bond	masonry crew	$41.90	.121	$5.07 sf
English bond	masonry crew	$41.90	.128	$5.36 sf
English cross bond (also called Dutch bond)	masonry crew	$41.90	.128	$5.36 sf
stack bond	masonry crew	$41.90	.082	$3.44 sf
all header bond	masonry crew	$41.90	.093	$3.90 sf
soldier course	masonry crew	$41.90	.106	$4.44 sf
sailor course	masonry crew	$41.90	.099	$4.15 sf
basketweave	masonry crew	$41.90	.164	$6.87 sf
herringbone weave	masonry crew	$41.90	.167	$7.00 sf
diagonal bond	masonry crew	$41.90	.144	$6.03 sf
coursed ashlar style bond	masonry crew	$41.90	.120	$5.03 sf
Repoint stone wall				
rubble	masonry crew	$41.90	.278	$11.60 sf
ashlar	masonry crew	$41.90	.260	$10.90 sf
Stone wall repair				
repair carved stone with epoxy	mason	$48.00	.024	$1.15 si
repair carved stone with stucco or grout	mason	$48.00	.022	$1.06 si
epoxy repair and pin broken stone	mason	$48.00	1.33	$63.80 ea
reconstitute delaminating stone with epoxy	mason	$48.00	.013	$.62 si
reface stone with grout mixed to match	mason	$48.00	.149	$7.15 si
remove segment of rubble wall and re-lay	mason & helper	$46.00	4.00	$184.00 cf
remove segment of rubble veneer and re-lay	mason & helper	$46.00	1.92	$88.30 sf
remove segment of ashlar wall and re-lay	mason & helper	$46.00	3.85	$177.00 cf
remove segment of ashlar veneer and re-lay	mason & helper	$46.00	1.89	$86.90 sf
Carve stone				
with light hand carvings	stone carver	$112.00	.015	$1.68 si
with medium hand carvings	stone carver	$112.00	.022	$2.46 si
with heavy hand carvings	stone carver	$112.00	.031	$3.47 si

25 *Outbuildings*

Item Description	Unit	Remove	Replace	Total	
8′ x 6′ metal storage shed *Replace* Material .....253.00 Labor ....209.00 *Remove*..................... Labor............72.30	ea	$72.30	$462.00	$534.30	◀ **METAL SHED** *Prefabricated metal storage shed with baked enamel finish and gable roof. Includes assembly. Does not include concrete slab or footings. Add 16% for gambrel roof. Add 30% for vinyl covered metal.*
8′ x 10′ metal storage shed *Replace* Material .....340.00 Labor ....225.00 *Remove*..................... Labor............79.20	ea	$79.20	$565.00	$644.20	
9′ x 10′ metal storage shed *Replace* Material .....354.00 Labor ....241.00 *Remove*..................... Labor 82.70	ea	$82.70	$595.00	$677.70	
10′ x 12′ metal storage shed *Replace* Material .....554.00 Labor ....257.00 *Remove*..................... Labor...........87.90	ea	$87.90	$811.00	$898.90	
8′ x 6′ wood storage shed *Replace* Material .....586.00 Labor ....225.00 *Remove*..................... Labor...........94.80	ea	$94.80	$811.00	$905.80	◀ **WOOD SHED** *Pre-built and delivered to site. Painted with trim, truss gambrel roof, panel siding, 1/2″ roof sheathing, 3/4″ tongue and groove floor sheathing with floor skids. Does not include footings or pier blocks. Deduct 12% for gable roof. Deduct 15% for gambrel roof on top of walls that are 5′ tall or less.*
8′ x 10′ wood storage shed *Replace* Material ....1370.00 Labor ....241.00 *Remove*..................... Labor..........111.00	ea	$111.00	$1,611.00	$1,722.00	
9′ x 10′ wood storage shed *Replace* Material ....1570.00 Labor ....257.00 *Remove*..................... Labor 123.00	ea	$123.00	$1,827.00	$1,950.00	
10′ x 12′ wood storage shed *Replace* Material....1850.00 Labor ....273.00 *Remove*..................... Labor 135.00	ea	$135.00	$2,123.00	$2,258.00	
9′ gazebo, standard grade *Replace* Material ....6180.00 Labor ....570.00 *Remove*..................... Labor ....128.00 ▶ With cupola, simple fretwork and rails with cross-grain detailing.	ea	$128.00	$6,750.00	$6,878.00	◀ **GAZEBO** *High quality octagonal gazebos priced by diameter. Made from D grade or better kiln-dried western red cedar surfaced four sides. Wood cedar shingles. Prefabricated parts assembled on site. Add 116% to 15′ diameter price for 21′ diameter triple roof gazebo. Add $175 for bench in 9′ and 12′ diameter gazebos. Add $225 for bench in 15′ diameter gazebo. Add $525 for bow roof (all sizes). Add $325 for steps with balustrades. Deduct 25% for no floor deck. Deduct 17% if made from select #1 grade western red cedar.*
9′ gazebo, high grade *Replace* Material....7520.00 Labor ....653.00 *Remove*..................... Labor ....128.00 ▶ With cupola, fretwork, raised-panel rails.	ea	$128.00	$8,173.00	$8,301.00	
9′ gazebo, deluxe grade *Replace* Material ...8530.00 Labor ....761.00 *Remove*..................... Labor ....128.00 ▶ With cupola, Queen Anne fretwork, and rails.	ea	$128.00	$9,291.00	$9,419.00	
12′ gazebo, standard grade *Replace* Material ...8800.00 Labor ....761.00 *Remove*..................... Labor ....161.00 ▶ With cupola, simple fretwork and rails with cross-grain detailing.	ea	$161.00	$9,561.00	$9,722.00	
12′ gazebo, high grade *Replace* Material....9960.00 Labor ....761.00 *Remove*..................... Labor ....161.00 ▶ With cupola, fretwork, raised-panel rails.	ea	$161.00	$10,721.00	$10,882.00	

	Item Description	Unit	Remove	Replace	Total
GAZEBO ► *continued*	**12′ gazebo, deluxe grade** *Replace* Material ..11600.00 Labor ....761.00 *Remove*........................ Labor ....161.00 ► With cupola, Queen Anne fretwork, and rails.	ea	$161.00	$12,361.00	$12,522.00
 *single roof* △	**15′ gazebo, standard grade** *Replace* Material..12300.00 Labor ....914.00 *Remove*........................ Labor ....206.00 ► Double roof with cupola, simple fretwork and rails with cross-grain detailing.	ea	$206.00	$13,214.00	$13,420.00
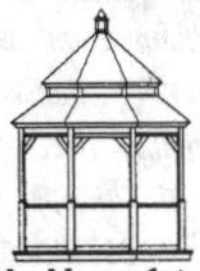 *double roof* △	**15′ gazebo, high grade** *Replace* Material..14600.00 Labor........1140.00 *Remove*........................ Labor ....206.00 ► Double roof with cupola, fretwork, raised-panel rails.	ea	$206.00	$15,740.00	$15,946.00
 *triple roof* △	**15′ gazebo, deluxe grade** *Replace* Material...16100.00 Labor........1140.00 *Remove*........................ Labor ....206.00 ► Double roof with cupola, Queen Anne fretwork, and rails.	ea	$206.00	$17,240.00	$17,446.00
FREE-STANDING ► GREENHOUSE *Residential style, aluminum frame. Automatic electric roof vent.*	**8′ x 9′ free-standing greenhouse** *Replace* Material...4440.00 Labor.........567.00 *Remove*........................ Labor...........87.90	ea	$87.90	$5,007.00	$5,094.90
	8′ x 11′ free-standing greenhouse *Replace* Material...4840.00 Labor.........567.00 *Remove*........................ Labor 99.40	ea	$99.40	$5,407.00	$5,506.40
	8′ x 14′ free-standing greenhouse *Replace* Material...5050.00 Labor.........662.00 *Remove*........................ Labor.........116.00	ea	$116.00	$5,712.00	$5,828.00
	8′ x 17′ free-standing greenhouse *Replace* Material...6040.00 Labor.........662.00 *Remove*........................ Labor.........125.00	ea	$125.00	$6,702.00	$6,827.00
LEAN-TO ► GREENHOUSE *Residential style, aluminum frame. Manually controlled vents.*	**4′ x 8′ lean-to greenhouse** *Replace* Material....1880.00 Labor.........331.00 *Remove*........................ Labor 82.70	ea	$82.70	$2,211.00	$2,293.70
	7′ x 14′ lean-to greenhouse *Replace* Material ...4820.00 Labor.........495.00 *Remove*........................ Labor...........94.80	ea	$94.80	$5,315.00	$5,409.80
	8′ x 16′ lean-to greenhouse *Replace* Material ...5890.00 Labor.........567.00 *Remove*........................ Labor.........101.00	ea	$101.00	$6,457.00	$6,558.00
SCREENED ► SWIMMING POOL ENCLOSURE	**Screened swimming pool enclosure** *Replace* Material ....5.80 Labor............ .68 *Remove*........................ Labor............ .26 ► Aluminum frame, vinyl screen.	sf	$.26	$6.48	$6.74
CHICKHEE HUT ► *Per sf of floor. Typically found in the southern United States.*	**Chickhee hut** *Replace* Material ....23.10 Labor ....39.50 *Remove*........................ Labor 2.89	sf	$2.89	$62.60	$65.49
	Thatched roof for chickhee hut *Replace* Material ....4.60 Labor...........24.20 *Remove*........................ Labor........... 1.10 ► Per sf of roof area.	sf	$1.10	$28.80	$29.90

26 .... *Painting*

Item Description	Unit	prime/stain	1 Coat	2 Coats	3 Coats	
Minimum charge for painting work	ea	—	—	—	$65.00	◄ MINIMUM
Materials Minimum ..34.00						
Labor Minimum 31.00						
Paint acoustic ceiling texture	sf	$.76	$.79	$1.18	$1.59	◄ ACOUSTIC
Materials Prime .... .27 1 Coat........ .30 2 Coats........ .42 3 Coats........ .56						CEILINGS
Labor Prime .... .49 1 Coat........ .49 2 Coats........ .76 3 Coats...... 1.03						
Paint acoustical ceiling tile	sf	$.76	$.79	$1.18	$1.59	
Materials Prime .... .27 1 Coat........ .30 2 Coats........ .42 3 Coats........ .56						
Labor Prime .... .49 1 Coat........ .49 2 Coats........ .76 3 Coats...... 1.03						
Paint aluminum carport or awning	sf	$.46	$.48	$.74	$.97	◄ AWNINGS AND
Materials Prime .... .19 1 Coat........ .21 2 Coats........ .29 3 Coats........ .39						CARPORTS
Labor Prime .... .27 1 Coat........ .27 2 Coats........ .45 3 Coats........ .58						
Paint plaster or drywall	sf	$.40	$.41	$.64	$.83	◄ DRYWALL,
Materials Prime .... .13 1 Coat........ .14 2 Coats........ .19 3 Coats........ .25						PLASTER AND
Labor Prime .... .27 1 Coat........ .27 2 Coats........ .45 3 Coats........ .58						STUCCO
Paint stucco	sf	$.84	$.91	$1.36	$1.78	
Materials Prime .... .22 1 Coat........ .24 2 Coats........ .33 3 Coats........ .44						
Labor Prime .... .62 1 Coat........ .67 2 Coats...... 1.03 3 Coats......1.34						
Paint column	lf	$1.10	$1.14	$1.73	$2.31	◄ COLUMNS
Materials Prime .... .34 1 Coat........ .38 2 Coats........ .53 3 Coats........ .70						Deduct **26%** for
Labor Prime .... .76 1 Coat........ .76 2 Coats......1.20 3 Coats......1.61						pilasters, pilaster capitals,
Stain & varnish column	lf	$1.08	$1.12	$1.69	$2.23	pilaster pedestals, and so
Materials Stain .... .37 1 Coat........ .41 2 Coats........ .57 3 Coats........ .76						on.
Labor Stain .... .71 1 Coat........ .71 2 Coats...... 1.12 3 Coats......1.47						
Paint capital, simple design	ea	$47.70	$50.70	$74.80	$100.80	
Materials Prime ....18.70 1 Coat ....20.80 2 Coats..28.90 3 Coats ...38.40						
Labor Prime ....29.00 1 Coat ....29.90 2 Coats....45.90 3 Coats...62.40						
Paint capital complex design	ea	$61.50	$65.30	$96.50	$129.70	
Materials Prime ....24.10 1 Coat ....26.80 2 Coats....37.20 3 Coats...49.40						
Labor Prime ....37.40 1 Coat ....38.50 2 Coats....59.30 3 Coats....80.30						
Stain & varnish capital, simple design	ea	$50.50	$53.70	$79.10	$106.50	
Materials Stain ....20.60 1 Coat ....22.90 2 Coats....31.80 3 Coats...42.30						
Labor Stain...............29.90 1 Coat ....30.80 2 Coats....47.30 3 Coats...64.20						
Stain & varnish capital complex design	ea	$68.10	$72.30	$106.70	$143.80	
Materials Stain ....26.60 1 Coat ....29.60 2 Coats....41.10 3 Coats...54.60						
Labor Stain ....41.50 1 Coat ....42.70 2 Coats....65.60 3 Coats....89.20						
Paint column pedestal	ea	$39.30	$41.70	$61.50	$82.80	
Materials Prime ....15.40 1 Coat ....17.10 2 Coats....23.70 3 Coats...31.50						
Labor Prime ....23.90 1 Coat ....24.60 2 Coats....37.80 3 Coats...51.30						
Stain & varnish column pedestal	ea	$43.40	$46.10	$68.10	$91.70	
Materials Stain ....17.10 1 Coat ....19.00 2 Coats....26.40 3 Coats...35.10						
Labor Stain...............26.30 1 Coat ....27.10 2 Coats....41.70 3 Coats...56.60						
Paint concrete floor	sf	$.54	$.56	$.82	$1.08	◄ CONCRETE
Materials Prime .... .18 1 Coat........ .20 2 Coats........ .28 3 Coats........ .37						
Labor Prime .... .36 1 Coat........ .36 2 Coats........ .54 3 Coats........ .71						

PAINTING COATS

Prices for one coat, two coats and three coats do *not* include: the primer coat, sealer coat, or stain.

To estimate painting, add the cost of the primer coat to the number of paint coats.

For example, to estimate the cost to prime a wall then paint with two coats, add the prime price to the two coats price.

To estimate the cost to stain an item then cover with two coats of varnish, add the stain cost to the two coats price (unless otherwise noted).

Item Description	Unit	prime/stain	1 Coat	2 Coats	3 Coats
CONCRETE ▶ *continued*					
Paint concrete wall	sf	$.54	$.56	$.86	$1.13
Materials Prime .... .18 1 Coat .... .20 2 Coats .... .28 3 Coats........ .37					
Labor Prime .... .36 1 Coat........ .36 2 Coats .... .58 3 Coats .... .76					
Paint concrete step (per step)	ea	$1.59	$1.69	$2.51	$3.37
Materials Prime .... .56 1 Coat .... .62 2 Coats .... .86 3 Coats 1.14					
Labor Prime .... 1.03 1 Coat ..... 1.07 2 Coats ....1.65 3 Coats 2.23					
DOORS ▶ **Paint folding door**	ea	$28.60	$30.30	$44.90	$60.30
Materials Prime ....10.70 1 Coat......11.90 2 Coats......16.50 3 Coats.....21.90					
Labor Prime...............17.90 1 Coat .....18.40 2 Coats......28.40 3 Coats 38.40					
Stain & varnish folding door	ea	$43.10	$45.60	$67.60	$91.10
Materials Stain ....15.70 1 Coat......17.40 2 Coats......24.20 3 Coats.....32.20					
Labor Stain...............27.40 1 Coat .....28.20 2 Coats......43.40 3 Coats 58.90					
Paint half-louvered folding door	ea	$32.00	$33.90	$50.10	$67.40
Materials Prime ....11.90 1 Coat......13.20 2 Coats......18.30 3 Coats.....24.30					
Labor Prime...............20.10 1 Coat .....20.70 2 Coats......31.80 3 Coats 43.10					
Stain & varnish half-louvered folding door	ea	$48.20	$51.00	$75.50	$101.70
Materials Stain ....17.50 1 Coat......19.40 2 Coats......26.90 3 Coats.....35.70					
Labor Stain...............30.70 1 Coat .....31.60 2 Coats......48.60 3 Coats 66.00					
Paint full-louvered folding door	ea	$35.80	$37.90	$56.10	$75.70
Materials Prime ....13.20 1 Coat......14.70 2 Coats ......20.40 3 Coats.....27.10					
Labor Prime...............22.60 1 Coat .....23.20 2 Coats......35.70 3 Coats 48.60					
Stain & varnish full-louvered folding door	ea	$54.00	$57.20	$84.50	$114.00
Materials Stain ....19.50 1 Coat......21.70 2 Coats .....30.10 3 Coats 40.00					
Labor Stain...............34.50 1 Coat .....35.50 2 Coats......54.40 3 Coats......74.00					
Paint folding panel door	ea	$31.30	$33.20	$49.20	$66.20
Materials Prime ....11.70 1 Coat......13.00 2 Coats......18.10 3 Coats.....24.10					
Labor Prime ....19.60 1 Coat .....20.20 2 Coats......31.10 3 Coats 42.10					
Stain & varnish folding panel door	ea	$47.20	$50.00	$74.20	$99.40
Materials Stain ....17.20 1 Coat......19.10 2 Coats......26.50 3 Coats.....35.20					
Labor Stain...............30.00 1 Coat .....30.90 2 Coats......47.70 3 Coats 64.20					
Paint bypassing door	ea	$50.50	$53.10	$79.70	$107.00
Materials Prime ....13.50 1 Coat......15.00 2 Coats......20.80 3 Coats.....27.60					
Labor Prime ....37.00 1 Coat .....38.10 2 Coats......58.90 3 Coats.....79.40					
Stain & varnish bypassing door	ea	$76.40	$80.40	$120.20	$161.70
Materials Stain ....19.80 1 Coat......22.00 2 Coats......30.60 3 Coats.....40.70					
Labor Stain...............56.60 1 Coat .....58.40 2 Coats......89.60 3 Coats.....121.00					
Paint half-louvered bypassing door	ea	$56.60	$59.50	$89.20	$120.00
Materials Prime ....15.00 1 Coat......16.70 2 Coats .....23.20 3 Coats 30.80					
Labor Prime ....41.60 1 Coat .....42.80 2 Coats .....66.00 3 Coats 89.20					
Stain & varnish half-louvered bypassing door	ea	$85.80	$90.00	$134.90	$181.10
Materials Stain ....22.00 1 Coat......24.40 2 Coats .....33.90 3 Coats.....45.10					
Labor Stain...............63.80 1 Coat .....65.60 2 Coats .....101.00 3 Coats 136.00					
Paint full-louvered bypassing door	ea	$63.50	$66.80	$99.80	$134.20
Materials Prime ....16.70 1 Coat......18.60 2 Coats......25.80 3 Coats 34.30					
Labor Prime ....46.80 1 Coat .....48.20 2 Coats......74.00 3 Coats 99.90					
Stain & varnish full-louvered bypassing door	ea	$95.90	$100.80	$150.80	$203.20
Materials Stain ....24.50 1 Coat......27.20 2 Coats .....37.80 3 Coats 50.20					
Labor Stain...............71.40 1 Coat .....73.60 2 Coats .....113.00 3 Coats 153.00					
Paint bypassing panel door	ea	$55.10	$58.00	$86.50	$116.90
Materials Prime ....15.00 1 Coat......16.70 2 Coats .....23.20 3 Coats 30.80					
Labor Prime...............40.10 1 Coat .....41.30 2 Coats......63.30 3 Coats 86.10					

Doors ▶
Unless otherwise noted,
does not include jamb and
casing. Includes painting
both sides of door.
Folding and bypassing
doors are for both sides of
each section. Add **20%**
for half-round or elliptical
top door.
folding door ▷

bypassing door ▷

Item Description	Unit	prime/stain	1 Coat	2 Coats	3 Coats	
Stain & varnish bypassing panel door	ea	$83.50	$87.70	$131.10	$177.10	
Materials Stain ....22.00 1 Coat .....24.40 2 Coats .....33.90 3 Coats......45.10						
Labor Stain ....61.50 1 Coat.....63.30 2 Coats .....97.20 3 Coats ...132.00						
Paint interior door	ea	$23.31	$24.60	$36.50	$49.40	◁ interior door
Materials Prime..........8.11 1 Coat ....9.00 2 Coats.....12.50 3 Coats ...16.90						
Labor Prime..............15.20 1 Coat.....15.60 2 Coats.....24.00 3 Coats ...32.50						
Stain & varnish interior door	ea	$35.30	$37.50	$55.60	$74.30	
Materials Stain ...12.20 1 Coat.....13.70 2 Coats.....18.90 3 Coats.....24.80						
Labor Stain ....23.10 1 Coat....23.80 2 Coats.....36.70 3 Coats 49.50						
Paint half-louvered door	ea	$26.02	$27.52	$40.80	$55.00	
Materials Prime..........9.02 1 Coat .....10.02 2 Coats.....13.90 3 Coats 18.50						
Labor Prime..............17.00 1 Coat.....17.50 2 Coats.....26.90 3 Coats 36.50						
Stain & varnish half-louvered door	ea	$39.60	$41.90	$62.20	$83.70	
Materials Stain ...13.60 1 Coat.....15.10 2 Coats.....21.00 3 Coats.....27.90						
Labor Stain ....26.00 1 Coat.....26.80 2 Coats.....41.20 3 Coats 55.80						
Paint full-louvered door	ea	$29.13	$30.74	$45.70	$61.50	
Materials Prime.......10.03 1 Coat .....11.14 2 Coats.....15.50 3 Coats 20.60						
Labor Prime..............19.10 1 Coat.....19.60 2 Coats .....30.20 3 Coats 40.90						
Stain & varnish full-louvered door	ea	$44.30	$46.80	$69.70	$93.40	
Materials Stain ...15.10 1 Coat.....16.80 2 Coats.....23.30 3 Coats.....31.00						
Labor Stain ....29.20 1 Coat.....30.00 2 Coats.....46.40 3 Coats 62.40						
Paint door jamb & casing	lf	$.80	$.73	$1.09	$1.47	◁ door jamb and casing
Materials Prime .... .22 1 Coat....... .24 2 Coats....... .33 3 Coats....... .44						
Labor Prime .... .58 1 Coat....... .49 2 Coats....... .76 3 Coats...... 1.03						
Stain & varnish door jamb & casing	lf	$1.17	$1.12	$1.66	$2.22	
Materials Stain.......... .32 1 Coat....... .36 2 Coats....... .50 3 Coats....... .66						
Labor Stain .... .85 1 Coat....... .76 2 Coats.....1.16 3 Coats 1.56						
Paint French door	ea	$50.30	$52.80	$79.20	$106.30	◁ French door
Materials Prime.......13.80 1 Coat.....15.30 2 Coats.....21.20 3 Coats.....28.20						
Labor Prime..............36.50 1 Coat.....37.50 2 Coats.....58.00 3 Coats.....78.10						
Stain & varnish French door	ea	$76.10	$80.10	$119.70	$161.70	
Materials Stain ....20.30 1 Coat.....22.60 2 Coats.....31.40 3 Coats.....41.70						
Labor Stain ....55.80 1 Coat.....57.50 2 Coats.....88.30 3 Coats ...120.00						
Paint full-lite door	ea	$39.60	$41.90	$62.20	$83.70	◁ full-lite door
Materials Prime.......13.40 1 Coat.....14.90 2 Coats.....20.70 3 Coats.....27.50						
Labor Prime..............26.20 1 Coat.....27.00 2 Coats.....41.50 3 Coats.....56.20						
Stain & varnish full-lite door	ea	$59.80	$63.20	$93.70	$126.50	
Materials Stain ....19.70 1 Coat.....21.90 2 Coats.....30.40 3 Coats.....40.40						
Labor Stain ....40.10 1 Coat ....41.30 2 Coats.....63.30 3 Coats 86.10						
Paint panel door	ea	$46.10	$48.60	$72.10	$97.30	◁ panel door
Materials Prime.......14.70 1 Coat.....16.30 2 Coats.....22.60 3 Coats.....30.00						
Labor Prime..............31.40 1 Coat.....32.30 2 Coats.....49.50 3 Coats.....67.30						
Stain & varnish panel door	ea	$69.80	$73.50	$109.10	$147.30	
Materials Stain ....21.60 1 Coat.....24.00 2 Coats.....33.30 3 Coats.....44.30						
Labor Stain ....48.20 1 Coat.....49.50 2 Coats.....75.80 3 Coats ...103.00						
Paint transom	ea	$23.20	$24.44	$36.40	$49.10	◁ transom
Materials Prime..........6.70 1 Coat ....7.44 2 Coats.....10.30 3 Coats ...13.70						
Labor Prime..............16.50 1 Coat.....17.00 2 Coats.....26.10 3 Coats.....35.40						
Stain & varnish transom	ea	$35.03	$36.92	$55.20	$74.20	
Materials Stain ....9.83 1 Coat .....10.92 2 Coats.....15.20 3 Coats 20.20						
Labor Stain ....25.20 1 Coat.....26.00 2 Coats.....40.00 3 Coats 54.00						

RELATED ITEMS
Concrete........................83
Doors.........................101

	Item Description	Unit	prime/stain	1 Coat	2 Coats	3 Coats
storm door ▷	**Paint storm door**	ea	$23.86	$25.13	$37.50	$50.50
	Materials Prime.........6.96 1 Coat......7.73 2 Coats......10.70 3 Coats......14.20					
	Labor Prime.............16.90 1 Coat......17.40 2 Coats......26.80 3 Coats......36.30					
	Stain & varnish storm door	ea	$36.10	$38.00	$56.70	$76.70
	Materials Stain.......10.20 1 Coat......11.30 2 Coats......15.70 3 Coats 20.90					
	Labor Stain...............25.90 1 Coat......26.70 2 Coats......41.00 3 Coats......55.80					
Dutch door ▷	**Paint Dutch door**	ea	$44.20	$46.70	$69.70	$93.60
both sections	*Materials* Prime ......14.50 1 Coat......16.10 2 Coats......22.40 3 Coats 29.80					
both sides	*Labor* Prime.............29.70 1 Coat......30.60 2 Coats......47.30 3 Coats......63.80					
	Stain & varnish Dutch door	ea	$66.80	$70.50	$104.70	$141.40
	Materials Stain.......21.30 1 Coat......23.70 2 Coats......32.90 3 Coats 43.70					
	Labor Stain...............45.50 1 Coat......46.80 2 Coats......71.80 3 Coats......97.70					
entry door ▷	**Paint steel entry door**	ea	$40.80	$43.10	$64.10	$86.30
	Materials Prime ......13.10 1 Coat......14.60 2 Coats ......20.30 3 Coats......27.00					
	Labor Prime.............27.70 1 Coat......28.50 2 Coats......43.80 3 Coats......59.30					
	Paint wood entry door	ea	$47.30	$49.20	$73.20	$99.70
	Materials Prime ......14.20 1 Coat......15.20 2 Coats ......20.60 3 Coats......28.80					
	Labor Prime.............33.10 1 Coat......34.00 2 Coats......52.60 3 Coats......70.90					
	Stain & varnish wood entry door	ea	$70.70	$74.30	$108.70	$147.70
	Materials Stain.......20.30 1 Coat......22.10 2 Coats ......28.40 3 Coats......39.70					
	Labor Stain...............50.40 1 Coat......52.20 2 Coats ......80.30 3 Coats....108.00					
entry door side lite ▷	**Paint entry door side lite**	ea	$41.20	$43.20	$64.50	$87.10
	Materials Prime ......11.20 1 Coat......12.40 2 Coats ......17.20 3 Coats......22.90					
	Labor Prime.............30.00 1 Coat......30.80 2 Coats......47.30 3 Coats......64.20					
	Stain & varnish entry door side lite	ea	$62.30	$65.50	$98.00	$131.70
	Materials Stain.......16.40 1 Coat......18.20 2 Coats ......25.30 3 Coats......33.60					
	Labor Stain...............45.90 1 Coat......47.30 2 Coats......72.70 3 Coats......98.10					
entry door fan lite ▷	**Paint fan lite**	ea	$38.23	$40.20	$60.30	$81.00
	Materials Prime.........9.93 1 Coat......11.00 2 Coats ......15.30 3 Coats 20.30					
	Labor Prime.............28.30 1 Coat......29.20 2 Coats......45.00 3 Coats......60.70					
	Stain & varnish fan lite	ea	$57.90	$60.80	$91.20	$122.70
	Materials Stain.......14.60 1 Coat......16.20 2 Coats ......22.50 3 Coats 29.90					
	Labor Stain...............43.30 1 Coat......44.60 2 Coats ......68.70 3 Coats......92.80					
cafe doors ▷	**Paint cafe doors**	ea	$37.40	$39.40	$58.70	$79.10
	Materials Prime ......11.00 1 Coat......12.20 2 Coats ......16.90 3 Coats 22.50					
	Labor Prime.............26.40 1 Coat......27.20 2 Coats......41.80 3 Coats......56.60					
	Stain & varnish cafe doors	ea	$56.50	$59.50	$88.70	$119.60
	Materials Stain.......16.10 1 Coat......17.90 2 Coats ......24.90 3 Coats......33.10					
	Labor Stain...............40.40 1 Coat ......41.60 2 Coats ......63.80 3 Coats......86.50					
sliding patio door ▷	**Paint wood sliding patio door**	ea	$33.51	$34.93	$52.76	$71.65
	Materials Prime.........4.71 1 Coat......5.23 2 Coats ......7.26 3 Coats......9.65					
	Labor Prime.............28.80 1 Coat......29.70 2 Coats......45.50 3 Coats......62.00					
	Stain & varnish wood sliding patio door	ea	$51.01	$53.18	$80.30	$108.80
	Materials Stain ....6.91 1 Coat......7.68 2 Coats ......10.70 3 Coats......14.20					
	Labor Stain...............44.10 1 Coat......45.50 2 Coats......69.60 3 Coats......94.60					
garage door ▷	**Paint garage door**	sf	$.46	$.48	$.69	$.97
	Materials Prime ....19 1 Coat........21 2 Coats ....29 3 Coats 39					
	Labor Prime ....27 1 Coat........27 2 Coats........40 3 Coats......58					
	Stain & varnish garage door	sf	$.68	$.71	$1.05	$1.42
	Materials Stain ....28 1 Coat........31 2 Coats ....43 3 Coats 57					
	Labor Stain ....40 1 Coat........40 2 Coats........62 3 Coats......85					

Item Description	Unit	prime/stain	1 Coat	2 Coats	3 Coats	
Paint medicine cabinet	ea	$21.22	$22.18	$33.47	$45.30	◄ MEDICINE CABINET
Materials Prime........3.22 1 Coat......3.58 2 Coats ......4.97 3 Coats 6.60						
Labor Prime ....18.00 1 Coat .....18.60 2 Coats......28.50 3 Coats 38.70						
Stain & varnish medicine cabinet	ea	$32.33	$33.66	$50.90	$68.60	
Materials Stain ......4.73 1 Coat......5.26 2 Coats......7.30 3 Coats 9.70						
Labor Stain................27.60 1 Coat .....28.40 2 Coats .....43.60 3 Coats 58.90						
Paint exterior light-fixture post	ea	$7.45	$7.98	$11.65	$15.65	◄ EXTERIOR LIGHT-FIXTURE POST
Materials Prime........3.93 1 Coat......4.37 2 Coats......6.07 3 Coats 8.07						
Labor Prime................3.52 1 Coat......3.61 2 Coats ......5.58 3 Coats 7.58						
Paint 4' high wood fence	lf	$3.15	$3.34	$4.97	$6.67	◄ FENCES
Materials Prime.......... .88 1 Coat....... .98 2 Coats ......1.36 3 Coats 1.81						*Wood fence prices are for one side only.*
Labor Prime................2.27 1 Coat......2.36 2 Coats ......3.61 3 Coats 4.86						*Ornamental iron fence prices are for both sides.*
Seal or stain 4' high wood fence	lf	$4.77	$5.00	$7.48	$10.09	
Materials Seal/stain ..1.29 1 Coat......1.43 2 Coats ......1.99 3 Coats 2.64						
Labor Seal/stain ....3.48 1 Coat......3.57 2 Coats ......5.49 3 Coats 7.45						
Paint 6' high wood fence	lf	$4.72	$4.95	$7.43	$10.00	
Materials Prime........1.29 1 Coat......1.43 2 Coats ......1.99 3 Coats 2.64						
Labor Prime................3.43 1 Coat......3.52 2 Coats ......5.44 3 Coats 7.36						
Seal or stain 6' high wood fence	lf	$7.11	$7.50	$11.22	$15.08	
Materials Seal/stain ..1.89 1 Coat......2.10 2 Coats ......2.92 3 Coats 3.88						
Labor Seal/stain ....5.22 1 Coat......5.40 2 Coats ......8.30 3 Coats 11.20						
Paint 8' high wood fence	lf	$6.24	$6.56	$9.84	$13.24	
Materials Prime........1.69 1 Coat......1.88 2 Coats ......2.61 3 Coats 3.47						
Labor Prime................4.55 1 Coat......4.68 2 Coats ......7.23 3 Coats 9.77						
Seal or stain 8' high wood fence	lf	$9.44	$9.94	$14.83	$19.99	
Materials Seal/stain ..2.48 1 Coat......2.76 2 Coats ......3.83 3 Coats 5.09						
Labor Seal/stain ....6.96 1 Coat......7.18 2 Coats .....11.00 3 Coats 14.90						
Paint 3' high picket fence	lf	$2.50	$2.61	$3.88	$5.25	
Materials Prime.......... .67 1 Coat....... .74 2 Coats ..... 1.03 3 Coats 1.37						
Labor Prime................1.83 1 Coat......1.87 2 Coats ......2.85 3 Coats 3.88						
Paint 5' high picket fence	lf	$4.00	$4.21	$6.28	$8.49	
Materials Prime....... 1.10 1 Coat......1.22 2 Coats ......1.69 3 Coats 2.25						
Labor Prime................2.90 1 Coat......2.99 2 Coats ......4.59 3 Coats 6.24						
Paint 48" high ornamental iron fence	lf	$4.66	$4.89	$7.30	$9.83	◁ ornamental iron
Materials Prime........1.23 1 Coat......1.37 2 Coats ......1.90 3 Coats 2.52						
Labor Prime................3.43 1 Coat......3.52 2 Coats ......5.40 3 Coats 7.31						
Paint 60" high ornamental iron fence	lf	$5.92	$6.19	$9.26	$12.50	
Materials Prime........1.64 1 Coat......1.82 2 Coats ......2.53 3 Coats 3.36						
Labor Prime................4.28 1 Coat......4.37 2 Coats ......6.73 3 Coats 9.14						
Paint 72" high ornamental iron fence	lf	$7.43	$7.82	$11.68	$15.73	
Materials Prime........2.30 1 Coat......2.56 2 Coats ......3.56 3 Coats 4.73						
Labor Prime................5.13 1 Coat......5.26 2 Coats ......8.12 3 Coats 11.00						
Paint wood trim, simple design	lf	$.62	$.63	$.95	$1.28	◄ FINISH CARPENTRY
Materials Prime.......... .13 1 Coat....... .14 2 Coats ..... .19 3 Coats ..... .25						◁ wood trim
Labor Prime .... .49 1 Coat....... .49 2 Coats ..... .76 3 Coats 1.03						
Stain & varnish wood trim, simple design	lf	$.90	$.90	$1.35	$1.81	
Materials Stain .... .19 1 Coat....... .14 2 Coats ..... .19 3 Coats ..... .25						
Labor Stain .... .71 1 Coat....... .76 2 Coats .....1.16 3 Coats 1.56						
Paint wood trim, ornate design	lf	$.74	$.80	$1.19	$1.58	
Materials Prime ..... .16 1 Coat....... .18 2 Coats ..... .25 3 Coats .... .33						
Labor Prime .... .58 1 Coat....... .62 2 Coats .... .94 3 Coats 1.25						

RELATED ITEMS

Bathroom Hardware......41
Doors...........................101
Electrical.....................139
Fences..........................187
Finish Carpentry..........199

Item Description			Unit	prime/stain	1 Coat	2 Coats	3 Coats
FINISH ▶ **CARPENTRY** *continued*	**Stain & varnish wood trim, ornate design**		lf	$1.12	$1.20	$1.79	$2.44
	Materials Stain ....23 1 Coat........26 2 Coats 36	3 Coats .... .48					
	Labor Stain ....89 1 Coat........94 2 Coats 1.43	3 Coats 1.96					
	Paint wood trim, very ornate design		lf	$.95	$.97	$1.45	$1.95
	Materials Prime ....19 1 Coat........21 2 Coats.........29	3 Coats .... .39					
	Labor Prime ....76 1 Coat........ .76 2 Coats 1.16	3 Coats 1.56					
	Stain & varnish wood trim, very ornate design		lf	$1.40	$1.47	$2.21	$2.98
	Materials Stain ....28 1 Coat........31 2 Coats.........43	3 Coats .... .57					
	Labor Stain ....1.12 1 Coat......1.16 2 Coats 1.78	3 Coats 2.41					
interior architrave ▷	**Paint interior architrave, simple design**		lf	$.86	$.88	$1.32	$1.82
	Materials Prime ....19 1 Coat........21 2 Coats.........29	3 Coats .... .39					
	Labor Prime ....67 1 Coat........ .67 2 Coats 1.03	3 Coats 1.43					
	Stain & varnish interior architrave, simple design		lf	$1.31	$1.34	$2.04	$2.71
	Materials Stain ....28 1 Coat........31 2 Coats.........43	3 Coats .... .57					
	Labor Stain ....1.03 1 Coat.... 1.03 2 Coats 1.61	3 Coats 2.14					
	Paint interior architrave, complex design		lf	$1.61	$1.64	$2.52	$3.37
	Materials Prime ....27 1 Coat........30 2 Coats.........42	3 Coats .... .56					
	Labor Prime ....1.34 1 Coat......1.34 2 Coats 2.10	3 Coats 2.81					
	Stain & varnish interior architrave, complex design		lf	$2.41	$2.54	$3.82	$5.14
	Materials Stain ....40 1 Coat........44 2 Coats.........61	3 Coats .... .81					
	Labor Stain ....2.01 1 Coat....2.10 2 Coats 3.21	3 Coats 4.33					
exterior architrave ▷	**Paint exterior architrave, simple design**		lf	$1.84	$1.97	$2.93	$3.97
	Materials Prime ....37 1 Coat........41 2 Coats.........57	3 Coats .... .76					
	Labor Prime ....1.47 1 Coat......1.56 2 Coats 2.36	3 Coats 3.21					
	Paint exterior architrave, complex design		lf	$3.74	$3.91	$5.88	$7.91
	Materials Prime ....75 1 Coat........83 2 Coats 1.15	3 Coats 1.53					
	Labor Prime ....2.99 1 Coat......3.08 2 Coats 4.73	3 Coats 6.38					
exterior door surround ▷	**Paint exterior door surround, simple design**		lf	$6.73	$7.03	$10.58	$14.30
	Materials Prime ....1.51 1 Coat.......1.68 2 Coats 2.33	3 Coats 3.10					
	Labor Prime ....5.22 1 Coat......5.35 2 Coats 8.25	3 Coats 11.20					
	Paint exterior door surround, complex design		lf	$15.99	$16.74	$25.22	$34.04
	Materials Prime ....3.19 1 Coat.......3.54 2 Coats 4.92	3 Coats 6.54					
	Labor Prime ....12.80 1 Coat.....13.20 2 Coats 20.30	3 Coats 27.50					
exterior window ▷ surround	**Paint exterior window surround, simple design**		lf	$6.73	$7.03	$10.58	$14.30
	Materials Prime ....1.51 1 Coat.......1.68 2 Coats 2.33	3 Coats 3.10					
	Labor Prime ....5.22 1 Coat......5.35 2 Coats 8.25	3 Coats 11.20					
	Paint exterior window surround, complex design		lf	$15.99	$16.74	$25.22	$34.04
	Materials Prime ....3.19 1 Coat.......3.54 2 Coats 4.92	3 Coats 6.54					
	Labor Prime ....12.80 1 Coat.....13.20 2 Coats 20.30	3 Coats 27.50					
closets ▷	**Paint closet rod, shelf, and brackets**		lf	$5.89	$6.10	$9.32	$12.68
	Materials Prime ....23 1 Coat........26 2 Coats.........36	3 Coats .... .48					
	Labor Prime ....5.66 1 Coat......5.84 2 Coats 8.96	3 Coats 12.20					
	Paint closet organizer system		sf	$.75	$.78	$1.16	$1.56
	Materials Prime ....26 1 Coat........29 2 Coats.........40	3 Coats .... .53					
	Labor Prime ....49 1 Coat........ .49 2 Coats 76	3 Coats 1.03					
bookcase ▷	**Paint bookcase**		sf	$1.21	$1.33	$1.95	$2.56
	Materials Prime ....59 1 Coat........66 2 Coats.........92	3 Coats 1.22					
	Labor Prime ....62 1 Coat........ .67 2 Coats 1.03	3 Coats 1.34					
	Stain & varnish bookcase		sf	$1.85	$2.00	$2.91	$3.89
	Materials Stain ....87 1 Coat........97 2 Coats 1.35	3 Coats 1.79					
	Labor Stain ....98 1 Coat.... 1.03 2 Coats 1.56	3 Coats 2.10					

Item Description	Unit	prime/stain	1 Coat	2 Coats	3 Coats	
Paint fireplace mantel beam	lf	$1.10	$1.13	$1.71	$2.30	◁ mantel beams and mantels
Materials Prime .... .30 1 Coat........ .33 2 Coats........ .46 3 Coats......... .61						
Labor Prime .... .80 1 Coat........ .80 2 Coats ....1.25 3 Coats 1.69						
Stain & varnish mantel beam	lf	$1.64	$1.74	$2.60	$3.53	
Materials Stain .... .44 1 Coat........ .49 2 Coats........ .68 3 Coats....... .90						
Labor Stain ....1.20 1 Coat....1.25 2 Coats ....1.92 3 Coats......2.63						
Paint fireplace mantel	lf	$1.52	$1.60	$2.39	$3.22	
Materials Prime .... .40 1 Coat........ .44 2 Coats........ .61 3 Coats........ .81						
Labor Prime .... 1.12 1 Coat.......1.16 2 Coats .....1.78 3 Coats 2.41						
Stain & varnish mantel	lf	$2.28	$2.40	$3.64	$4.88	
Materials Stain .... .59 1 Coat........ .66 2 Coats........ .92 3 Coats......1.22						
Labor Stain ....1.69 1 Coat.....1.74 2 Coats .....2.72 3 Coats......3.66						
Paint coffered ceiling, simple design	sf	$1.23	$1.32	$1.92	$2.61	◁ coffered ceiling
Materials Prime .... .47 1 Coat........ .52 2 Coats........ .72 3 Coats........ .96						
Labor Prime .... .76 1 Coat........ .80 2 Coats ....1.20 3 Coats 1.65						
Stain & varnish coffered ceiling, simple design	sf	$1.85	$1.97	$2.94	$3.92	
Materials Stain .... .69 1 Coat........ .77 2 Coats .... 1.07 3 Coats......1.42						
Labor Stain ....1.16 1 Coat.......1.20 2 Coats .....1.87 3 Coats......2.50						
Paint coffered ceiling, complex design	sf	$2.67	$2.80	$4.19	$5.68	
Materials Prime .... .84 1 Coat........ .93 2 Coats ....1.29 3 Coats......1.71						
Labor Prime ....1.83 1 Coat.....1.87 2 Coats .....2.90 3 Coats......3.97						
Stain & varnish coffered ceiling, complex design	sf	$4.04	$4.27	$6.36	$8.54	
Materials Stain ....1.23 1 Coat.......1.37 2 Coats ......1.90 3 Coats......2.52						
Labor Stain ....2.81 1 Coat.......2.90 2 Coats .....4.46 3 Coats......6.02						
Paint niche	ea	$31.67	$33.22	$49.80	$67.00	◁ niche
Materials Prime..........7.67 1 Coat....8.52 2 Coats ....11.80 3 Coats 15.70						
Labor Prime ....24.00 1 Coat ....24.70 2 Coats ....38.00 3 Coats......51.30						
Stain & varnish niche	ea	$48.00	$50.30	$75.50	$101.80	
Materials Stain ....11.30 1 Coat....12.60 2 Coats ....17.50 3 Coats 23.30						
Labor Stain ....36.70 1 Coat....37.70 2 Coats ....58.00 3 Coats......78.50						
Paint gingerbread running trim	lf	$3.20	$3.42	$5.04	$6.76	◁ running trim
Materials Prime..........1.19 1 Coat........1.32 2 Coats ....1.83 3 Coats 2.43						
Labor Prime ....2.01 1 Coat......2.10 2 Coats ....3.21 3 Coats......4.33						
Stain & varnish gingerbread running trim	lf	$4.83	$5.11	$7.60	$10.17	
Materials Stain ....1.75 1 Coat........1.94 2 Coats ....2.69 3 Coats......3.57						
Labor Stain ....3.08 1 Coat.....3.17 2 Coats ....4.91 3 Coats......6.60						
Paint gingerbread bracket	ea	$16.81	$17.41	$26.59	$35.91	◁ bracket
Materials Prime..........1.81 1 Coat......2.01 2 Coats ......2.79 3 Coats 3.71						
Labor Prime ....15.00 1 Coat....15.40 2 Coats ....23.80 3 Coats......32.20						
Stain & varnish gingerbread bracket	ea	$25.66	$26.56	$40.41	$54.56	
Materials Stain ....2.66 1 Coat......2.96 2 Coats ......4.11 3 Coats......5.46						
Labor Stain ....23.00 1 Coat....23.60 2 Coats ....36.30 3 Coats......49.10						
Paint gingerbread corbel	ea	$16.47	$17.17	$26.04	$35.24	◁ corbel
Materials Prime..........1.77 1 Coat.......1.97 2 Coats ......2.74 3 Coats......3.64						
Labor Prime ....14.70 1 Coat....15.20 2 Coats ....23.30 3 Coats......31.60						
Stain & varnish gingerbread corbel	ea	$25.10	$26.09	$39.71	$53.53	
Materials Stain ....2.60 1 Coat......2.89 2 Coats ......4.01 3 Coats......5.33						
Labor Stain ....22.50 1 Coat....23.20 2 Coats ....35.70 3 Coats......48.20						
Paint gingerbread door or window header	lf	$3.00	$3.11	$4.71	$6.35	◁ door or window header
Materials Prime .... .59 1 Coat........ .66 2 Coats........ .92 3 Coats......1.22						
Labor Prime ....2.41 1 Coat.....2.45 2 Coats .....3.79 3 Coats......5.13						

RELATED ITEMS

Finish Carpentry..........199

	Item Description	Unit	prime/stain	1 Coat	2 Coats	3 Coats
FINISH ▶ **CARPENTRY** *continued*	**Stain & varnish gingerbread door or window header**	lf	$4.53	$4.72	$7.15	$9.64
	Materials Stain .... .87 1 Coat .... .97 2 Coats ......1.35 3 Coats 1.79					
	Labor Stain ....3.66 1 Coat ......3.75 2 Coats ......5.80 3 Coats 7.85					
spandrel ▷	**Paint gingerbread spandrel**	lf	$3.97	$4.12	$6.27	$8.46
	Materials Prime .... .62 1 Coat .... .69 2 Coats ...... .96 3 Coats 1.28					
	Labor Prime ....3.35 1 Coat ......3.43 2 Coats ......5.31 3 Coats 7.18					
	Stain & varnish gingerbread spandrel	lf	$6.04	$6.27	$9.52	$12.86
	Materials Stain .... .91 1 Coat ...... 1.01 2 Coats ......1.40 3 Coats 1.86					
	Labor Stain ....5.13 1 Coat ......5.26 2 Coats ......8.12 3 Coats 11.00					
gable ornament ▷ *add 51% to stain & varnish.*	**Paint gingerbread gable ornament**	ea	$46.20	$48.50	$72.50	$97.80
	Materials Prime ......12.90 1 Coat ......14.30 2 Coats ....19.90 3 Coats 26.40					
	Labor Prime ....33.30 1 Coat ......34.20 2 Coats .....52.60 3 Coats 71.40					
gable finial ▷ *add 51% to stain & varnish.*	**Paint gingerbread gable finial**	ea	$13.86	$14.44	$21.84	$29.44
	Materials Prime ....2.56 1 Coat ......2.84 2 Coats ......3.94 3 Coats 5.24					
	Labor Prime ....11.30 1 Coat ......11.60 2 Coats ......17.90 3 Coats 24.20					
porch post ▷	**Paint porch post**	ea	$9.34	$9.97	$14.63	$19.66
	Materials Prime ....4.08 1 Coat ......4.53 2 Coats ......6.29 3 Coats 8.36					
	Labor Prime ....5.26 1 Coat ......5.44 2 Coats ......8.34 3 Coats 11.30					
	Stain & varnish porch post	ea	$14.06	$14.95	$22.04	$29.60
	Materials Stain ....5.99 1 Coat ......6.65 2 Coats ......9.24 3 Coats 12.30					
	Labor Stain ....8.07 1 Coat ......8.30 2 Coats ......12.80 3 Coats 17.30					
FLOORING ▶ *See Flooring for costs to prep wood floors for finish.*	**Seal stone floor**	sf	$.65	$.67	$1.01	$1.36
	Materials Seal .... .16 1 Coat .... .18 2 Coats ...... .25 3 Coats ...... .33					
	Labor Seal .... .49 1 Coat .... .49 2 Coats ...... .76 3 Coats 1.03					
	Paint wood floor	sf	$.75	$.77	$1.17	$1.59
	Materials Prime .... .21 1 Coat .... .23 2 Coats ...... .32 3 Coats ...... .43					
	Labor Prime .... .54 1 Coat .... .54 2 Coats ...... .85 3 Coats 1.16					
	Stain & varnish wood floor	sf	$1.11	$1.19	$1.76	$2.36
	Materials Stain .... .31 1 Coat .... .34 2 Coats ...... .47 3 Coats ...... .62					
	Labor Stain .... .80 1 Coat .... .85 2 Coats ......1.29 3 Coats 1.74					
PANELING ▶	**Paint wall paneling, simple pattern**	sf	$.86	$.90	$1.35	$1.82
	Materials Prime .... .32 1 Coat .... .36 2 Coats ...... .50 3 Coats ...... .66					
	Labor Prime .... .54 1 Coat .... .54 2 Coats ...... .85 3 Coats 1.16					
	Stain & varnish wall paneling, simple pattern	sf	$1.27	$1.37	$2.01	$2.70
	Materials Stain .... .47 1 Coat .... .52 2 Coats ...... .72 3 Coats ...... .96					
	Labor Stain .... .80 1 Coat .... .85 2 Coats ......1.29 3 Coats 1.74					
	Paint wall paneling, ornate pattern	sf	$1.18	$1.23	$1.85	$2.47
	Materials Prime .... .42 1 Coat .... .47 2 Coats ...... .65 3 Coats .... .86					
	Labor Prime .... .76 1 Coat .... .76 2 Coats ......1.20 3 Coats 1.61					
	Stain & varnish wall paneling, ornate pattern	sf	$1.78	$1.89	$2.79	$3.78
	Materials Stain .... .62 1 Coat .... .69 2 Coats ...... .96 3 Coats 1.28					
	Labor Stain ....1.16 1 Coat ......1.20 2 Coats ......1.83 3 Coats 2.50					
	Paint wall paneling, very ornate pattern	sf	$1.76	$1.86	$2.75	$3.73
	Materials Prime .... .51 1 Coat .... .57 2 Coats ...... .79 3 Coats 1.05					
	Labor Prime ....1.25 1 Coat ......1.29 2 Coats ......1.96 3 Coats 2.68					
	Stain & varnish wall paneling, very ornate pattern	sf	$2.67	$2.79	$4.18	$5.68
	Materials Stain .... .75 1 Coat .... .83 2 Coats ......1.15 3 Coats 1.53					
	Labor Stain ....1.92 1 Coat ......1.96 2 Coats ......3.03 3 Coats 4.15					
MASONRY ▶ *Deduct 26% for previously painted block or brick.*	**Paint concrete block**	sf	$.94	$1.03	$1.53	$2.00
	Materials Prime .... .32 1 Coat .... .36 2 Coats ...... .50 3 Coats ...... .66					
	Labor Prime .... .62 1 Coat .... .67 2 Coats ...... 1.03 3 Coats 1.34					

Item Description	Unit	prime/stain	1 Coat	2 Coats	3 Coats
Paint brick	sf	$1.09	$1.13	$1.67	$2.24
Materials Prime ....33 1 Coat........ .37 2 Coats........ .51 3 Coats........ .68					
Labor Prime .... .76 1 Coat........ .76 2 Coats......1.16 3 Coats 1.56					
Paint stone wall	sf	$.70	$.73	$1.10	$1.46
Materials Prime .... .25 1 Coat........ .28 2 Coats........ .39 3 Coats........ .52					
Labor Prime .... .45 1 Coat........ .45 2 Coats........ .71 3 Coats........ .94					
Seal stone wall	sf	$.69	$.77	$1.09	$1.48
Materials Seal .... .33 1 Coat........ .37 2 Coats........ .51 3 Coats........ .68					
Labor Seal .... .36 1 Coat........ .40 2 Coats........ .58 3 Coats........ .80					
Paint metal roofing	sf	$1.12	$1.20	$1.76	$2.39
Materials Prime .... .36 1 Coat........ .40 2 Coats........ .56 3 Coats........ .74					
Labor Prime .... .76 1 Coat........ .80 2 Coats......1.20 3 Coats 1.65					
Treat wood shingles or shakes with shingle oil	sf	$.81	$.88	$1.30	$1.73
Materials Treat .... .23 1 Coat........ .26 2 Coats........ .36 3 Coats........ .48					
Labor Treat................ .58 1 Coat........ .62 2 Coats........ .94 3 Coats 1.25					
Seal wall framing	sf	$.96	$.98	$1.50	$2.02
Materials Seal .... .16 1 Coat........ .18 2 Coats........ .25 3 Coats........ .33					
Labor Seal .... .80 1 Coat........ .80 2 Coats......1.25 3 Coats 1.69					
Seal floor framing	sf	$1.20	$1.27	$1.89	$2.54
Materials Seal .... .22 1 Coat........ .24 2 Coats........ .33 3 Coats........ .44					
Labor Seal .... .98 1 Coat ..... 1.03 2 Coats ......1.56 3 Coats 2.10					
Seal roof framing	sf	$1.52	$1.59	$2.38	$3.19
Materials Seal .... .27 1 Coat........ .30 2 Coats........ .42 3 Coats........ .56					
Labor Seal................1.25 1 Coat......1.29 2 Coats ......1.96 3 Coats 2.63					
Paint exterior siding	sf	$.95	$.98	$1.49	$1.97
Materials Prime .... .24 1 Coat........ .27 2 Coats........ .37 3 Coats........ .50					
Labor Prime .... .71 1 Coat........ .71 2 Coats...... 1.12 3 Coats 1.47					
Stain exterior siding	sf	$1.07	$1.11	$1.64	$2.24
Materials Stain .... .40 1 Coat........ .44 2 Coats........ .61 3 Coats........ .81					
Labor Stain .... .67 1 Coat........ .67 2 Coats...... 1.03 3 Coats 1.43					
Paint window shutter (per shutter, per side)	ea	$22.23	$23.32	$35.02	$47.22
Materials Prime ....5.33 1 Coat.....5.92 2 Coats......8.22 3 Coats....10.92					
Labor Prime ....16.90 1 Coat.....17.40 2 Coats....26.80 3 Coats 36.30					
Stain window shutter (per shutter, per side)	ea	$33.72	$35.29	$53.00	$71.40
Materials Stain ....7.82 1 Coat.....8.69 2 Coats....12.10 3 Coats....16.10					
Labor Stain.................25.90 1 Coat .....26.60 2 Coats....40.90 3 Coats 55.30					
Paint exterior fascia	lf	$.60	$.61	$.93	$1.26
Materials Prime .... .11 1 Coat........ .12 2 Coats........ .17 3 Coats........ .23					
Labor Prime .... .49 1 Coat........ .49 2 Coats........ .76 3 Coats...... 1.03					
Stain exterior wood fascia	lf	$.60	$.62	$.95	$1.26
Materials Stain .... .15 1 Coat........ .17 2 Coats........ .24 3 Coats........ .32					
Labor Stain .... .45 1 Coat........ .45 2 Coats........ .71 3 Coats........ .94					
Paint exterior soffit	sf	$.73	$.81	$1.17	$1.56
Materials Prime .... .24 1 Coat........ .27 2 Coats........ .37 3 Coats........ .49					
Labor Prime .... .49 1 Coat........ .54 2 Coats........ .80 3 Coats...... 1.07					
Stain exterior wood soffit	sf	$.86	$.90	$1.35	$1.82
Materials Stain .... .32 1 Coat........ .36 2 Coats........ .50 3 Coats........ .66					
Labor Stain .... .54 1 Coat........ .54 2 Coats........ .85 3 Coats 1.16					
Paint rain gutter or downspout	lf	$1.01	$1.08	$1.61	$2.17
Materials Prime .... .21 1 Coat........ .23 2 Coats........ .32 3 Coats........ .43					
Labor Prime .... .80 1 Coat........ .85 2 Coats ......1.29 3 Coats 1.74					

RELATED ITEMS

Finish Carpentry 199
Flooring......................257
 sand, edge & fill
 wood floor..............268
Paneling......................347
Masonry......................287
Roofing......................393
Rough Carpentry 409
Siding......................455

◀ **ROOFING**

◀ **ROUGH CARPENTRY**

◁ **seal framing**
 seal smoke-stained framing for odor control

◀ **SIDING**

◁ **shutters**

◁ **fascia**

◁ **soffit**

◁ **gutter or downspout**

Item Description				Unit	prime/stain	1 Coat	2 Coats	3 Coats
STAIRS ▶ **Paint stair balustrade**				lf	$11.38	$11.94	$17.90	$24.20
Materials Prime......2.91	1 Coat......3.24	2 Coats......4.50	3 Coats......6.00					
Labor Prime......8.47	1 Coat......8.70	2 Coats......13.40	3 Coats......18.20					
Stain & varnish stair balustrade				lf	$17.20	$18.03	$27.12	$36.52
Materials Stain......4.30	1 Coat......4.73	2 Coats......6.62	3 Coats......8.82					
Labor Stain......12.90	1 Coat......13.30	2 Coats......20.50	3 Coats......27.70					
Paint stair riser				ea	$7.44	$7.84	$11.65	$15.70
Materials Prime......2.44	1 Coat......2.71	2 Coats......3.76	3 Coats......5.00					
Labor Prime......5.00	1 Coat......5.13	2 Coats......7.89	3 Coats......10.70					
Stain & varnish stair riser				ea	$11.21	$11.83	$17.63	$23.75
Materials Stain......3.58	1 Coat......3.98	2 Coats......5.53	3 Coats......7.35					
Labor Stain......7.63	1 Coat......7.85	2 Coats......12.10	3 Coats......16.40					
Paint stair tread				ea	$8.11	$8.59	$12.74	$17.15
Materials Prime......2.71	1 Coat......3.01	2 Coats......4.18	3 Coats......5.55					
Labor Prime......5.40	1 Coat......5.58	2 Coats......8.56	3 Coats......11.60					
Stain & finish stair tread				ea	$12.23	$12.94	$19.24	$25.96
Materials Stain......3.98	1 Coat......4.42	2 Coats......6.14	3 Coats......8.16					
Labor Stain......8.25	1 Coat......8.52	2 Coats......13.10	3 Coats......17.80					
Paint stair bracket				ea	$6.40	$6.75	$10.03	$13.47
Materials Prime......2.30	1 Coat......2.56	2 Coats......3.56	3 Coats......4.73					
Labor Prime......4.10	1 Coat......4.19	2 Coats......6.47	3 Coats......8.74					
Stain & finish stair bracket				ea	$9.62	$10.18	$15.12	$20.34
Materials Stain......3.38	1 Coat......3.76	2 Coats......5.22	3 Coats......6.94					
Labor Stain......6.24	1 Coat......6.42	2 Coats......9.90	3 Coats......13.40					
WINDOW ▶ **Paint small window (per side)**				ea	$20.94	$22.20	$32.70	$44.00
Materials Prime......7.74	1 Coat......8.60	2 Coats......11.90	3 Coats......15.80					
Labor Prime......13.20	1 Coat......13.60	2 Coats......20.80	3 Coats......28.20					
Paint average size window (per side)				ea	$30.60	$32.40	$47.90	$64.40
Materials Prime......11.80	1 Coat......13.10	2 Coats......18.20	3 Coats......24.20					
Labor Prime......18.80	1 Coat......19.30	2 Coats......29.70	3 Coats......40.20					
Paint large window (per side)				ea	$38.70	$41.10	$60.80	$82.00
Materials Prime......14.90	1 Coat......16.60	2 Coats......23.10	3 Coats......30.70					
Labor Prime......23.80	1 Coat......24.50	2 Coats......37.70	3 Coats......51.30					
Paint very large window (per side)				ea	$51.20	$54.40	$80.40	$107.80
Materials Prime......21.40	1 Coat......23.80	2 Coats......33.10	3 Coats......44.00					
Labor Prime......29.80	1 Coat......30.60	2 Coats......47.30	3 Coats......63.80					
WALLPAPER ▶ **Paint wallpaper**				sf	$.68	$.70	$1.05	$1.42
Materials Prime......19	1 Coat......21	2 Coats......29	3 Coats......39					
Labor Prime......49	1 Coat......49	2 Coats......76	3 Coats......1.03					
STRIP PAINT ▶ **Strip paint or varnish from trim, simple design**				lf	$5.04	$5.39	$7.90	$10.66
Materials Strip......1.43	1 Coat......1.69	2 Coats......2.28	3 Coats......2.99					
Labor Strip......3.61	1 Coat......3.70	2 Coats......5.62	3 Coats......7.67					
Strip paint or varnish from trim, complex design				lf	$8.57	$9.01	$16.09	$27.60
Materials Strip......1.75	1 Coat......1.96	2 Coats......3.09	3 Coats......4.70					
Labor Strip......6.82	1 Coat......7.05	2 Coats......13.00	3 Coats......22.90					
Strip paint or varnish from door (slab only)				ea	$39.00	$42.70	$63.70	$95.30
Materials Strip......15.40	1 Coat......18.40	2 Coats......26.00	3 Coats......38.70					
Labor Strip......23.60	1 Coat......24.30	2 Coats......37.70	3 Coats......56.60					
Strip paint or varnish from door jamb and casing				lf	$6.54	$7.12	$10.39	$13.92
Materials Strip......2.44	1 Coat......2.88	2 Coats......3.88	3 Coats......5.09					
Labor Strip......4.10	1 Coat......4.24	2 Coats......6.51	3 Coats......8.83					

Costs to strip paint that does not contain lead.

RELATED ITEMS

Stairs......................465
Wall Coverings...........495
Windows.................501

TIME & MATERIAL CHARTS *(selected items)*

Painting Materials

DESCRIPTION	APPLIED TO	MATERIAL PRICE		COVERAGE	UNIT PRICE	
Prime or seal						
primer or sealer	plaster or drywall	$22.70	gallon	178	$.13	sf
primer or sealer	interior door	$22.70	gallon	2.8	$8.11	ea
primer or sealer	entry door	$22.70	gallon	1.6	$14.20	ea
primer or sealer	wood trim, simple design	$22.70	gallon	178	$.13	lf
primer or sealer	exterior siding	$22.70	gallon	94	$.24	sf
primer or sealer	stair balustrade	$22.70	gallon	7.8	$2.91	lf
Paint, one coat						
oil or latex paint	plaster or drywall	$28.80	gallon	205	$.14	sf
oil or latex paint	interior door	$28.80	gallon	3.2	$9.00	ea
oil or latex paint	entry door	$28.80	gallon	1.9	$15.20	ea
oil or latex paint	wood trim, simple design	$28.80	gallon	205	$.14	lf
oil or latex paint	exterior siding	$28.80	gallon	108	$.27	sf
oil or latex paint	stair balustrade	$28.80	gallon	8.9	$3.24	lf
Paint, two coats						
oil or latex paint	plaster or drywall	$28.80	gallon	151	$.19	sf
oil or latex paint	interior door	$28.80	gallon	2.3	$12.50	ea
oil or latex paint	entry door	$28.80	gallon	1.4	$20.60	ea
oil or latex paint	wood trim, simple design	$28.80	gallon	151	$.19	lf
oil or latex paint	exterior siding	$28.80	gallon	78	$.37	sf
oil or latex paint	stair balustrade	$28.80	gallon	6.4	$4.50	lf
Paint, three coats						
oil or latex paint	plaster or drywall	$28.80	gallon	113	$.25	sf
oil or latex paint	interior door	$28.80	gallon	1.7	$16.90	ea
oil or latex paint	entry door	$28.80	gallon	1	$28.80	ea
oil or latex paint	wood trim, simple design	$28.80	gallon	113	$.25	lf
oil or latex paint	exterior siding	$28.80	gallon	58	$.50	sf
oil or latex paint	stair balustrade	$28.80	gallon	4.8	$6.00	lf
Stain						
stain	interior door	$30.50	gallon	2.5	$12.20	ea
stain	entry door	$30.50	gallon	1.5	$20.30	ea
stain	wood trim, simple design	$30.50	gallon	159	$.19	lf
stain	exterior siding, one coat	$30.50	gallon	77	$.40	sf
stain	stair balustrade	$30.50	gallon	7.1	$4.30	lf
Varnish, one coat						
varnish, clear	interior door	$39.70	gallon	2.9	$13.70	ea
varnish, clear	entry door	$39.70	gallon	1.8	$22.10	ea
varnish, clear	wood trim, simple design	$39.70	gallon	284	$.14	lf
varnish, clear	stair balustrade	$39.70	gallon	8.4	$4.73	lf
Varnish, two coats						
varnish, clear	interior door	$39.70	gallon	2.1	$18.90	ea
varnish, clear	entry door	$39.70	gallon	1.4	$28.40	ea
varnish, clear	wood trim, simple design	$39.70	gallon	208	$.19	lf
varnish, clear	stair balustrade	$39.70	gallon	6	$6.62	lf
Varnish, three coats						
varnish, clear	interior door	$39.70	gallon	1.6	$24.80	ea
varnish, clear	entry door	$39.70	gallon	1	$39.70	ea
varnish, clear	wood trim, simple design	$39.70	gallon	156	$.25	lf
varnish, clear	stair balustrade	$39.70	gallon	4.5	$8.82	lf

Painting Labor

LABORER	BASE WAGE	PAID LEAVE	TRUE WAGE	FICA	FUTA	WORKER'S COMP.	UNEMPLOY. INSUR.	HEALTH INSUR.	RETIRE (401k)	LIABILITY INSUR.	COST PER HOUR
Painter	$23.90	1.86	$25.76	1.97	.21	6.91	2.24	2.92	.77	3.86	$44.60

Paid Leave is calculated based on two weeks paid vacation, one week sick leave, and seven paid holidays. Employer's matching portion of **FICA** is 7.65 percent. **FUTA** (Federal Unemployment) is .8 percent. **Worker's compensation** for the painting trade was calculated using a national average of 26.77 percent. **Unemployment insurance** was calculated using a national average of 8.7 percent. **Health insurance** was calculated based on a projected national average for 2005 of $580 per employee (and family when applicable) per month. Employer pays 80 percent for a per month cost of $464 per employee. **Retirement** is based on a 401(k) retirement program with employer matching of 50 percent. Employee contributions to the 401(k) plan are an average of 6 percent of the true wage. **Liability insurance** is based on a national average of 14.0 percent.

Painting Labor Productivity

WORK DESCRIPTION	LABORER	COST PER HOUR	PRODUCTIVITY	UNIT PRICE
Prime or seal				
acoustic ceiling texture	painter	$44.60	.011	$.49 sf
plaster or drywall	painter	$44.60	.006	$.27 sf
masonry, block	painter	$44.60	.014	$.62 sf
concrete floor	painter	$44.60	.008	$.36 sf
wood floor	painter	$44.60	.012	$.54 sf
folding door	painter	$44.60	.402	$17.90 ea
bypassing door	painter	$44.60	.830	$37.00 ea
interior door	painter	$44.60	.340	$15.20 ea
door jamb & casing	painter	$44.60	.013	$.58 lf
wood entry door	painter	$44.60	.742	$33.10 ea
wood sliding patio door	painter	$44.60	.646	$28.80 ea
garage door	painter	$44.60	.006	$.27 sf
4' high wood fence (per side)	painter	$44.60	.051	$2.27 lf
48" high ornamental iron fence (both sides)	painter	$44.60	.077	$3.43 lf
wood trim, simple design	painter	$44.60	.011	$.49 lf
wood trim, very ornate design	painter	$44.60	.025	$.76 lf
seal smoke-stained frame walls	painter	$44.60	.018	$.80 sf
seal smoke-stained joists	painter	$44.60	.022	$.98 sf
seal smoke-stained rafters or trusses	painter	$44.60	.028	$1.25 sf
siding	painter	$44.60	.016	$.71 sf
stucco	painter	$44.60	.014	$.62 sf
stair balustrade	painter	$44.60	.190	$8.47 lf
small window	painter	$44.60	.295	$13.20 ea
very large window	painter	$44.60	.668	$29.80 ea
Paint, one coat				
acoustic ceiling texture	painter	$44.60	.011	$.49 sf
plaster or drywall	painter	$44.60	.006	$.27 sf
masonry, block	painter	$44.60	.015	$.67 sf
concrete floor	painter	$44.60	.008	$.36 sf
wood floor	painter	$44.60	.012	$.54 sf
folding door	painter	$44.60	.413	$18.40 ea
bypassing door	painter	$44.60	.854	$38.10 ea
interior door	painter	$44.60	.349	$15.60 ea
door jamb & casing	painter	$44.60	.011	$.49 lf
wood entry door	painter	$44.60	.763	$34.00 ea
wood sliding patio door	painter	$44.60	.665	$29.70 sf
garage door	painter	$44.60	.006	$.27 sf
4' high wood fence (per side)	painter	$44.60	.053	$2.36 lf
48" high ornamental iron fence (both sides)	painter	$44.60	.079	$3.52 lf
wood trim, simple design	painter	$44.60	.011	$.49 lf
wood trim, very ornate design	painter	$44.60	.017	$.76 lf
siding	painter	$44.60	.016	$.71 sf
stucco	painter	$44.60	.015	$.67 sf
stair balustrade	painter	$44.60	.195	$8.70 sf
small window	painter	$44.60	.304	$13.60 ea
very large window	painter	$44.60	.687	$30.60 ea

. . . More ➢

Painting Labor Productivity *continued*

WORK DESCRIPTION	LABORER	COST PER HOUR	PRODUCTIVITY	UNIT PRICE
Paint, two coats				
acoustic ceiling texture	painter	$44.60	.017	$.76 sf
plaster or drywall	painter	$44.60	.010	$.45 sf
masonry, block	painter	$44.60	.023	$1.03 sf
concrete floor	painter	$44.60	.012	$.54 sf
wood floor	painter	$44.60	.019	$.85 sf
folding door	painter	$44.60	.636	$28.40 ea
bypassing door	painter	$44.60	1.32	$58.90 ea
interior door	painter	$44.60	.538	$24.00 ea
door jamb & casing	painter	$44.60	.017	$.76 lf
wood entry door	painter	$44.60	1.18	$52.60 ea
wood sliding patio door	painter	$44.60	1.02	$45.50 sf
garage door	painter	$44.60	.009	$.40 sf
4' high wood fence (per side)	painter	$44.60	.081	$3.61 lf
48" high ornamental iron fence (both sides)	painter	$44.60	.121	$5.40 lf
wood trim, simple design	painter	$44.60	.017	$.76 lf
wood trim, very ornate design	painter	$44.60	.026	$1.16 lf
siding	painter	$44.60	.025	$1.12 sf
stucco	painter	$44.60	.023	$1.03 sf
stair balustrade	painter	$44.60	.300	$13.40 lf
small window	painter	$44.60	.467	$20.80 ea
very large window	painter	$44.60	1.06	$47.30 ea
Paint, three coats				
acoustic ceiling texture	painter	$44.60	.023	$1.03 sf
plaster or drywall	painter	$44.60	.013	$.58 sf
masonry, block	painter	$44.60	.030	$1.34 sf
concrete floor	painter	$44.60	.016	$.71 sf
wood floor	painter	$44.60	.026	$1.16 sf
folding door	painter	$44.60	.861	$38.40 ea
bypassing door	painter	$44.60	1.78	$79.40 ea
interior door	painter	$44.60	.729	$32.50 ea
door jamb & casing	painter	$44.60	.023	$1.03 lf
wood entry door	painter	$44.60	1.59	$70.90 ea
wood sliding patio door	painter	$44.60	1.39	$62.00 sf
garage door	painter	$44.60	.013	$.58 sf
4' high wood fence (per side)	painter	$44.60	.109	$4.86 lf
48" high ornamental iron fence (both sides)	painter	$44.60	.164	$7.31 lf
wood trim, simple design	painter	$44.60	.023	$1.03 lf
wood trim, very ornate design	painter	$44.60	.035	$1.56 lf
siding	painter	$44.60	.033	$1.47 sf
stucco	painter	$44.60	.030	$1.34 sf
stair balustrade	painter	$44.60	.407	$18.20 lf
small window	painter	$44.60	.633	$28.20 ea
very large window	painter	$44.60	1.43	$63.80 ea
Stain				
wood floor	painter	$44.60	.018	$.80 sf
folding door	painter	$44.60	.614	$27.40 ea
bypassing door	painter	$44.60	1.27	$56.60 ea
interior door	painter	$44.60	.519	$23.10 ea
French door	painter	$44.60	1.25	$55.80 ea
panel door	painter	$44.60	1.08	$48.20 ea
door jamb & casing	painter	$44.60	.019	$.85 lf
wood entry door	painter	$44.60	1.13	$50.40 ea
wood sliding patio door	painter	$44.60	.988	$44.10 ea
garage door	painter	$44.60	.009	$.40 sf
4' high wood fence (per side)	painter	$44.60	.078	$3.48 lf
wood trim, simple design	painter	$44.60	.016	$.71 lf
wood trim, very ornate design	painter	$44.60	.025	$1.12 lf
wood paneling, simple pattern	painter	$44.60	.018	$.80 sf
wood paneling, very ornate pattern	painter	$44.60	.043	$1.92 sf
siding	painter	$44.60	.015	$.67 sf
stair balustrade	painter	$44.60	.290	$12.90 lf

. . . More ➤

Painting Labor Productivity *continued*

WORK DESCRIPTION	LABORER	COST PER HOUR	PRODUCTIVITY	UNIT PRICE
Varnish, one coat				
wood floor	painter	$44.60	.019	$.85 sf
folding door	painter	$44.60	.632	$28.20 ea
bypassing door	painter	$44.60	1.31	$58.40 ea
interior door	painter	$44.60	.534	$23.80 ea
French door	painter	$44.60	1.29	$57.50 ea
panel door	painter	$44.60	1.11	$49.50 ea
door jamb & casing	painter	$44.60	.017	$.76 lf
wood entry door	painter	$44.60	1.17	$52.20 ea
wood sliding patio door	painter	$44.60	1.02	$45.50 ea
garage door	painter	$44.60	.009	$.40 sf
4' high wood fence (per side)	painter	$44.60	.080	$3.57 lf
wood trim, simple design	painter	$44.60	.017	$.76 lf
wood trim, very ornate design	painter	$44.60	.026	$1.16 lf
wood paneling, simple pattern	painter	$44.60	.019	$.85 sf
wood paneling, very ornate pattern	painter	$44.60	.044	$1.96 sf
siding	painter	$44.60	.015	$.67 sf
stair balustrade	painter	$44.60	.298	$13.30 lf
Varnish, two coats				
wood floor	painter	$44.60	.029	$1.29 sf
folding door	painter	$44.60	.972	$43.40 ea
bypassing door	painter	$44.60	2.01	$89.60 ea
interior door	painter	$44.60	.822	$36.70 ea
French door	painter	$44.60	1.98	$88.30 ea
panel door	painter	$44.60	1.70	$75.80 ea
door jamb & casing	painter	$44.60	.026	$1.16 lf
wood entry door	painter	$27.10	1.80	$80.30 ea
wood sliding patio door	painter	$44.60	1.56	$69.60 ea
garage door	painter	$44.60	.014	$.62 sf
4' high wood fence (per side)	painter	$44.60	.123	$5.49 lf
wood trim, simple design	painter	$44.60	.026	$1.16 lf
wood trim, very ornate design	painter	$44.60	.040	$1.78 lf
wood paneling, simple pattern	painter	$44.60	.029	$1.29 sf
wood paneling, very ornate pattern	painter	$44.60	.068	$3.03 sf
siding	painter	$44.60	.023	$1.03 sf
stair balustrade	painter	$44.60	.459	$20.50 lf
Varnish, three coats				
wood floor	painter	$44.60	.039	$1.74 sf
folding door	painter	$44.60	1.32	$58.90 ea
bypassing door	painter	$44.60	2.72	$121.00 ea
interior door	painter	$44.60	1.11	$49.50 ea
French door	painter	$44.60	2.68	$120.00 ea
panel door	painter	$44.60	2.31	$103.00 ea
door jamb & casing	painter	$44.60	.035	$1.56 lf
wood entry door	painter	$44.60	2.43	$108.00 ea
wood sliding patio door	painter	$44.60	2.12	$94.60 ea
garage door	painter	$44.60	.019	$.85 sf
4' high wood fence (per side)	painter	$44.60	.167	$7.45 lf
wood trim, simple design	painter	$44.60	.035	$1.56 lf
wood trim, very ornate design	painter	$44.60	.054	$2.41 lf
wood paneling, simple pattern	painter	$44.60	.039	$1.74 sf
wood paneling, very ornate pattern	painter	$44.60	.093	$4.15 sf
siding	painter	$44.60	.032	$1.43 sf
stair balustrade	painter	$44.60	.621	$27.70 lf

NOTES: _____

_____

_____

_____ **end**

27 .... *Paneling*

Item Description	Unit	Remove	Replace	Total	
Minimum charge for paneling work *Replace* Materials......25.00 Labor............31.50	ea	–	$56.50	$56.50	◄ **MINIMUM**
Minimum charge for frame-and-panel wall work *Replace* Materials.......75.00 Labor..........151.00	ea	–	$226.00	$226.00	
Hardboard paneling, economy grade *Replace* Materials........ .80 Labor ....1.25 *Remove* .... Labor............ .20 ► 1/8" thick.	sf	$.20	$2.05	$2.25	◄ **HARDBOARD PANELING** *Prefinished. Installed with adhesive and nails. Includes 5% waste.*
Hardboard paneling, standard grade *Replace* Materials........ .98 Labor ....1.25 *Remove* .... Labor............ .20 ► 1/4" thick, little or no texture.	sf	$.20	$2.23	$2.43	
Hardboard paneling, high grade *Replace* Materials.......1.49 Labor ....1.25 *Remove* .... Labor............ .20 ► 1/4" thick, heavy texture or special finish.	sf	$.20	$2.74	$2.94	
Hardboard wall paneling, with simulated brick face *Replace* Materials...... 1.03 Labor ....1.25 *Remove* .... Labor............ .20 ► 1/4" thick.	sf	$.20	$2.28	$2.48	
Hardboard wall paneling, with simulated stone face *Replace* Materials...... 1.10 Labor ....1.25 *Remove* .... Labor............ .20 ► 1/4" thick.	sf	$.20	$2.35	$2.55	
Pegboard *Replace* Materials........ .77 Labor ....1.13 *Remove* .... Labor............ .20	sf	$.20	$1.90	$2.10	◄ **PEGBOARD** *Tempered. Includes 5% waste.*
1/4" ash plywood paneling *Replace* Materials.......3.39 Labor ....1.36 *Remove* .... Labor............ .23	sf	$.23	$4.75	$4.98	◄ **PLYWOOD PANELING** *Includes 5% waste. Unfinished with top grade veneer.*
1/4" birch plywood paneling *Replace* Materials.......1.69 Labor ....1.36 *Remove* .... Labor............ .23	sf	$.23	$3.05	$3.28	
1/4" cherry plywood paneling *Replace* Materials.......3.85 Labor ....1.36 *Remove* .... Labor............ .23	sf	$.23	$5.21	$5.44	
1/4" hickory plywood paneling *Replace* Materials.......3.62 Labor ....1.36 *Remove* .... Labor............ .23	sf	$.23	$4.98	$5.21	
1/4" knotty pine plywood paneling *Replace* Materials.......2.90 Labor ....1.36 *Remove* .... Labor............ .23	sf	$.23	$4.26	$4.49	

RELATED ITEMS
Cleaning 64
Painting 340
Siding 455

Item Description	Unit	Remove	Replace	Total
PLYWOOD ► PANELING continued. **1/4" mahogany plywood paneling** *Replace* Materials........3.13 Labor ....1.36 *Remove* .... Labor............. .23	sf	$.23	$4.49	$4.72
1/4" white maple plywood paneling *Replace* Materials........2.53 Labor ....1.36 *Remove* .... Labor............. .23	sf	$.23	$3.89	$4.12
1/4" red or white oak plywood paneling *Replace* Materials........1.74 Labor ....1.36 *Remove* .... Labor............. .23	sf	$.23	$3.10	$3.33
1/4" quartersawn red or white oak plywood paneling *Replace* Materials........2.79 Labor ....1.36 *Remove* .... Labor............. .23	sf	$.23	$4.15	$4.38
1/4" walnut plywood paneling *Replace* Materials........4.97 Labor ....1.36 *Remove* .... Labor............. .23	sf	$.23	$6.33	$6.56
1/4" rough-sawn cedar plywood paneling *Replace* Materials........2.36 Labor ....1.36 *Remove* .... Labor............. .23	sf	$.23	$3.72	$3.95

ADD FOR WALL ► MOLDING
Includes 6% waste. Add to plywood paneling prices above for moldings that form repeating squares on wall with radius corners. Add 11% for slope-matched wall molding along stairways.

Add 44% for wall molding, standard grade
► Simple horizontal pattern moldings.

Add 53% for wall molding, high grade
► Vertical or embossed pattern moldings.

Add 70% for wall molding, deluxe grade
► Simple hand-carved moldings.

Add 84% for wall molding, custom grade
► Ornate hand carved moldings.

Item Description	Unit	Remove	Replace	Total
PLYWOOD ► PANELING WITH GROOVES *Prefinished. Includes 5% waste.* **1/4" ash plywood paneling with grooves** *Replace* Materials........3.32 Labor ....1.36 *Remove* .... Labor............. .23	sf	$.23	$4.68	$4.91
1/4" birch plywood paneling with grooves *Replace* Materials........1.65 Labor ....1.36 *Remove* .... Labor............. .23	sf	$.23	$3.01	$3.24
1/4" cherry plywood paneling with grooves *Replace* Materials........3.75 Labor ....1.36 *Remove* .... Labor............. .23	sf	$.23	$5.11	$5.34
1/4" hickory plywood paneling with grooves *Replace* Materials........3.52 Labor ....1.36 *Remove* .... Labor............. .23	sf	$.23	$4.88	$5.11
1/4" knotty pine plywood paneling with grooves *Replace* Materials........2.83 Labor ....1.36 *Remove* .... Labor............. .23	sf	$.23	$4.19	$4.42
1/4" mahogany plywood paneling with grooves *Replace* Materials........3.05 Labor ....1.36 *Remove* .... Labor............. .23	sf	$.23	$4.41	$4.64

Item Description	Unit	Remove	Replace	Total
1/4" white maple plywood paneling with grooves	sf	$.23	$3.83	$4.06
Replace Materials........2.47 Labor 1.36				
Remove .... Labor .... .23				
1/4" red or white oak plywood paneling with grooves	sf	$.23	$3.06	$3.29
Replace Materials........1.70 Labor 1.36				
Remove .... Labor .... .23				
1/4" quartersawn red or white oak plywood paneling with grooves	sf	$.23	$4.08	$4.31
Replace Materials........2.72 Labor 1.36				
Remove .... Labor .... .23				
1/4" walnut plywood paneling with grooves	sf	$.23	$6.20	$6.43
Replace Materials........4.84 Labor 1.36				
Remove .... Labor .... .23				
1/4" rough-sawn cedar plywood paneling with grooves	sf	$.23	$3.66	$3.89
Replace Materials........2.30 Labor 1.36				
Remove .... Labor .... .23				
Pine board-on-board paneling	sf	$.32	$5.58	$5.90
Replace Materials........4.14 Labor 1.44				
Remove .... Labor .... .32				
Pine board-and-batten paneling	sf	$.32	$5.63	$5.95
Replace Materials........4.04 Labor 1.59				
Remove .... Labor .... .32				
Add 10% for chevron installation				
Add 18% for herringbone installation				
Pine tongue-&-groove paneling, simple pattern	sf	$.32	$6.07	$6.39
Replace Materials........4.29 Labor 1.78				
Remove .... Labor .... .32				
► V or bull nose pattern at joints.				
Pine tongue-&-groove paneling, fancy pattern	sf	$.32	$6.36	$6.68
Replace Materials........4.58 Labor 1.78				
Remove .... Labor .... .32				
► V or bull nose pattern at joints with beaded V, nose, or cove in field.				
Pine tongue-&-groove paneling, ornate pattern	sf	$.32	$7.12	$7.44
Replace Materials........5.34 Labor 1.78				
Remove .... Labor .... .32				
► V or bull nose pattern at joints with double beaded V, noses, or coves in field.				
Cedar tongue-&-groove closet lining	sf	$.32	$4.22	$4.54
Replace Materials........2.44 Labor 1.78				
Remove .... Labor .... .32				
Add 14% for paneling installed as wainscoting				
Pine frame-and-panel wall, standard grade	sf	$.55	$48.40	$48.95
Replace Materials......21.00 Labor 27.40				
Remove .... Labor .... .55				
► Simple crown and base if included, panels are 1/4" plywood with no onlays.				
Pine frame-and-panel wall, high grade	sf	$.55	$61.50	$62.05
Replace Materials......28.60 Labor 32.90				
Remove .... Labor .... .55				
► Simple crown and base if included, panels are solid wood, may be raised.				

RELATED ITEMS

Cleaning 64
Painting 340
Siding.......................455

▽ *board-on-board*

board-and-batten △

◄ **BOARD-ON-BOARD OR BOARD-AND-BATTEN PANELING**
Includes 5% waste. Prices for paneling are slightly higher than those for siding because there are more angles indoors.

◁ **add for angled installations**

◄ **TONGUE-&-GROOVE PANELING**
Includes 5% waste.

◁ **add for wainscot installation**

◄ **PINE FRAME-AND-PANEL WALL**
Includes 5% waste. Complete wall systems with furring strips and other backing, moldings between panels, crown and base.

Item Description	Unit	Remove	Replace	Total

PINE FRAME-AND- ▶
PANEL WALL
continued

Pine frame-and-panel wall, deluxe grade	sf	$.55	$73.40	$73.95

Replace Materials......33.70   Labor 39.70
Remove ....   Labor............ .55

▶ Crown and base with vertical patterns if included, panels are solid wood, may be raised, and may have cathedral top. May have bolection molding around panels.

Pine frame-and-panel wall, custom grade	sf	$.55	$97.50	$98.05

Replace Materials......50.20   Labor..........47.30
Remove ....   Labor............ .55

▶ Crown and base with vertical patterns if included, panels are solid wood, may be raised, and may have cathedral top. Panels may be linenfold or wall may contain other components that are hand carved. May also include corbels and pilasters with capitals.

OAK FRAME-AND- ▶
PANEL WALL
See pine frame-and-panel items above and on the previous page for explanation of grades. Includes 5% waste. Complete wall systems with furring strips and other backing, moldings between panels, crown and base.

Oak frame-and-panel wall, standard grade	sf	$.55	$53.00	$53.55

Replace Materials......25.60   Labor............27.40
Remove ....   Labor............ .55

Oak frame-and-panel wall, high grade	sf	$.55	$68.00	$68.55

Replace Materials......35.10   Labor 32.90
Remove ....   Labor............ .55

Oak frame-and-panel wall, deluxe grade	sf	$.55	$81.00	$81.55

Replace Materials ......41.30   Labor 39.70
Remove ....   Labor............ .55

Oak frame-and-panel wall, custom grade	sf	$.55	$108.80	$109.35

Replace Materials.......61.50   Labor............47.30
Remove ....   Labor............ .55

WALNUT FRAME- ▶
AND-PANEL WALL
See pine frame-and-panel items above and on the previous page for explanation of grades. Includes 5% waste. Complete wall systems with furring strips and other backing, moldings between panels, crown and base.

Walnut frame-and-panel wall, standard grade	sf	$.55	$69.50	$70.05

Replace Materials ......42.10   Labor............27.40
Remove ....   Labor............ .55

Walnut frame-and-panel wall, high grade	sf	$.55	$90.70	$91.25

Replace Materials ......57.80   Labor 32.90
Remove ....   Labor............ .55

Walnut frame-and-panel wall, deluxe grade	sf	$.55	$107.60	$108.15

Replace Materials ......67.90   Labor 39.70
Remove ....   Labor............ .55

Walnut frame-and-panel wall, custom grade	sf	$.55	$148.30	$148.85

Replace Materials.....101.00   Labor..........47.30
Remove ....   Labor............ .55

ADD FOR OTHER ▶
WOOD SPECIES
Add to the costs of oak frame-and-panel walls for these wood species.

Add 12% for quartersawn oak frame-and-panel wall

Add 17% for cherry frame-and-panel wall

Add 65% for teak frame-and-panel wall

Add 10% for mahogany frame-and-panel wall

Add 14% for hickory frame-and-panel wall

✐ NOTES: _____

_____

_____ end

TIME & MATERIAL CHARTS (selected items)

Paneling Materials

DESCRIPTION	MATERIAL PRICE	GROSS COVERAGE	WASTE	NET COVERAGE	UNIT PRICE
Hardboard paneling					
economy grade	$24.40 sheet	32	5%	30.4	$.80 sf
high grade	$45.20 sheet	32	5%	30.4	$1.49 sf
1/4" plywood paneling					
rough-sawn cedar	$71.70 sheet	32	5%	30.4	$2.36 sf
ash	$103.00 sheet	32	5%	30.4	$3.39 sf
birch	$51.50 sheet	32	5%	30.4	$1.69 sf
cherry	$117.00 sheet	32	5%	30.4	$3.85 sf
hickory	$110.00 sheet	32	5%	30.4	$3.62 sf
knotty pine	$88.20 sheet	32	5%	30.4	$2.90 sf
mahogany	$95.00 sheet	32	5%	30.4	$3.13 sf
white maple	$77.00 sheet	32	5%	30.4	$2.53 sf
red or white oak	$52.80 sheet	32	5%	30.4	$1.74 sf
quartersawn red or white oak	$84.70 sheet	32	5%	30.4	$2.79 sf
walnut	$151.00 sheet	32	5%	30.4	$4.97 sf
1/4" plywood paneling with grooves					
rough-sawn cedar	$70.00 sheet	32	5%	30.4	$2.30 sf
ash	$101.00 sheet	32	5%	30.4	$3.32 sf
birch	$50.30 sheet	32	5%	30.4	$1.65 sf
cherry	$114.00 sheet	32	5%	30.4	$3.75 sf
hickory	$107.00 sheet	32	5%	30.4	$3.52 sf
knotty pine	$86.10 sheet	32	5%	30.4	$2.83 sf
mahogany	$92.80 sheet	32	5%	30.4	$3.05 sf
white maple	$75.20 sheet	32	5%	30.4	$2.47 sf
red or white oak	$51.60 sheet	32	5%	30.4	$1.70 sf
quartersawn red or white oak	$82.70 sheet	32	5%	30.4	$2.72 sf
walnut	$147.00 sheet	32	5%	30.4	$4.84 sf
Pine board paneling					
board-on-board	$3.97 sf	1	4%	.96	$4.14 sf
board-and-batten	$3.88 sf	1	4%	.96	$4.04 sf
tongue-&-groove, simple pattern	$4.12 sf	1	4%	.96	$4.29 sf
tongue-&-groove, ornate pattern	$5.13 sf	1	4%	.96	$5.34 sf
Frame and panel wall					
pine, standard grade	$19.70 sf	1	6%	.94	$21.00 sf
pine, custom grade	$47.20 sf	1	6%	.94	$50.20 sf
oak, standard grade	$24.10 sf	1	6%	.94	$25.60 sf
oak, custom grade	$57.80 sf	1	6%	.94	$61.50 sf
walnut, standard grade	$39.60 sf	1	6%	.94	$42.10 sf
walnut, custom grade	$95.00 sf	1	6%	.94	$101.00 sf

Paneling Labor

LABORER	BASE WAGE	PAID LEAVE	TRUE WAGE	FICA	FUTA	WORKER'S COMP.	UNEMPLOY. INSUR.	HEALTH INSUR.	RETIRE (401K)	LIABILITY INSUR.	COST PER HOUR
Paneling installer	$24.30	1.90	$26.20	2.00	.21	5.15	2.28	2.92	.79	3.93	$43.50
Paneling installer's helper	$17.50	1.37	$18.87	1.44	.15	3.71	1.64	2.92	.57	2.83	$32.10
Demolition laborer	$14.40	1.12	$15.52	1.19	.12	5.01	1.35	2.92	.47	2.33	$28.90

Paid Leave is calculated based on two weeks paid vacation, one week sick leave, and seven paid holidays. Employer's matching portion of **FICA** is 7.65 percent. **FUTA** (Federal Unemployment) is .8 percent. **Worker's compensation** for the paneling trade was calculated using a national average of 19.63 percent. **Unemployment insurance** was calculated using a national average of 8.7 percent. **Health insurance** was calculated based on a projected national average for 2005 of $580 per employee (and family when applicable) per month. Employer pays 80 percent for a per month cost of $464 per employee. **Retirement** is based on a 401(k) retirement program with employer matching of 50 percent. Employee contributions to the 401(k) plan are an average of 6 percent of the true wage. **Liability insurance** is based on a national average of 14.0 percent.

Paneling Labor Productivity

WORK DESCRIPTION	LABORER	COST PER HOUR	PRODUCTIVITY	UNIT PRICE
Demolition				
remove hardboard paneling	demolition laborer	$28.90	.007	**$.20** sf
remove pegboard	demolition laborer	$28.90	.007	**$.20** sf
remove plywood paneling	demolition laborer	$28.90	.008	**$.23** sf
remove board paneling	demolition laborer	$28.90	.011	**$.32** sf
remove tongue-and-groove paneling	demolition laborer	$28.90	.011	**$.32** sf
remove frame-and-panel wall	demolition laborer	$28.90	.019	**$.55** sf
Paneling installation crew				
install paneling	paneling installer	$43.50		
install paneling	paneling installer's helper	$32.10		
install paneling	paneling crew	$37.80		
Minimum charge				
for paneling work	paneling crew	$37.80	.833	**$31.50** ea
for frame-and-panel wall work	paneling crew	$37.80	4.00	**$151.00** ea
Install paneling				
hardboard	paneling crew	$37.80	.033	**$1.25** sf
pegboard	paneling crew	$37.80	.030	**$1.13** sf
plywood	paneling crew	$37.80	.036	**$1.36** sf
board on board	paneling crew	$37.80	.038	**$1.44** sf
board and batten	paneling crew	$37.80	.042	**$1.59** sf
tongue-&-groove	paneling crew	$37.80	.047	**$1.78** sf
Install frame-and-panel wall				
standard grade	paneling crew	$37.80	.725	**$27.40** sf
high grade	paneling crew	$37.80	.870	**$32.90** sf
deluxe grade	paneling crew	$37.80	1.05	**$39.70** sf
custom grade	paneling crew	$37.80	1.25	**$47.30** sf

NOTES: _____

_____

_____

_____

_____

_____

_____

_____

_____

_____

_____

_____

_____

_____

_____

_____

_____

_____

_____

_____

_____

_____

_____

_____ end

28 _Plaster & Stucco_

Item Description	Unit	Remove	Replace	Total	
Minimum charge to repair plaster wall or ceiling _Replace_ Materials......50.00 Labor 88.40	ea	–	$138.40	$138.40	◄ REPAIR PLASTER
Repair hair-line plaster crack _Replace_ Materials .... .32 Labor 2.70	lf	–	$3.02	$3.02	
Repair plaster crack less than 1″ wide _Replace_ Materials .... .48 Labor 3.36	lf	–	$3.84	$3.84	
Patch small plaster hole less than 2″ square _Replace_ Materials........1.46 Labor 34.90	ea	–	$36.36	$36.36	
Patch plaster hole 2″ to 10″ square _Replace_ Materials........6.59 Labor 44.00	ea	–	$50.59	$50.59	
Patch plaster hole 10″ to 20″ square _Replace_ Materials.......11.40 Labor 54.80	ea	–	$66.20	$66.20	
Patch plaster section _Replace_ Materials........2.42 Labor ....6.47 ► For plaster repair of an area no greater than 20 sf in size.	sf	–	$8.89	$8.89	
Repair plaster wall outside corner damage _Replace_ Materials........3.10 Labor 12.00	lf	–	$15.10	$15.10	
Repair plaster wall inside corner damage _Replace_ Materials........2.55 Labor 8.47	lf	–	$11.02	$11.02	
Repair section of plaster pilaster or column _Replace_ Materials ......21.00 Labor...........37.70	lf	–	$58.70	$58.70	
Repair crack in plaster molding less than 1/4″ wide _Replace_ Materials .... .32 Labor 2.95	lf	–	$3.27	$3.27	◄ REPAIR DECORATIVE PLASTER _Repairs to enrichments, moldings, ceiling rose, ceiling medallion, and so on._
Take flexible mold of plaster molding or decorative plaster _Replace_ Materials ......41.70 Labor...........24.40	ea	–	$66.10	$66.10	
Create running mold for plaster molding _Replace_ Materials......54.90 Labor.........166.00	ea	–	$220.90	$220.90	
Repair section of plaster molding or decorative plaster _Replace_ Materials........6.44 Labor ....53.10 ► Repair section no greater than 3 lf.	ea	–	$59.54	$59.54	
Minimum charge to repair plaster molding or decorative plaster _Replace_ Materials......27.10 Labor.........148.00	ea	–	$175.10	$175.10	
Two coat acoustical plaster on 3/8″ gypsum lath on wall _Replace_ Materials........1.28 Labor ....2.12 _Remove_ .... Labor........... .66	sf	$.66	$3.40	$4.06	◄ ACOUSTICAL PLASTER _Includes lathing and plastering with trowel finish._
Two coat acoustical plaster on 3/8″ gypsum lath on ceiling _Replace_ Materials........1.28 Labor ....2.53 _Remove_ .... Labor........... .66	sf	$.66	$3.81	$4.47	

FLEXIBLE MOLDS

Cracks to decorative plaster that are larger than a hairline are often repaired using flexible molds.

Flexible molds are made by constructing a wood box to fit around the area where the mold will be taken.

A release agent is sprayed on the box and the original plaster to help the mold release when dried.

Cold-cure silicone is usually used to make the mold, although many professionals use hot-melt mold-making compounds.

RELATED ITEMS

Acoustic Ceiling 15
Drywall.....................133
Painting 333
Suspended Ceilings 483

	Item Description	Unit	Remove	Replace	Total
ACOUSTICAL ▶ PLASTER *continued*	**Three coat acoustical plaster on painted metal lath on wall** *Replace* Materials ...... 1.11 Labor ....2.37 *Remove* .... Labor .... .69	sf	$.69	$3.48	$4.17
	Three coat acoustical plaster on painted metal lath on ceiling *Replace* Materials ...... 1.11 Labor ....2.82 *Remove* .... Labor............ .69	sf	$.69	$3.93	$4.62
GYPSUM ▶ PLASTER *Includes lathing and plastering with trowel finish.*	**Two coat gypsum plaster on 3/8" gypsum lath on wall** *Replace* Materials ...... 1.12 Labor ....2.16 *Remove* .... Labor............ .66	sf	$.66	$3.28	$3.94
	Two coat gypsum plaster on 3/8" gypsum lath on ceiling *Replace* Materials ...... 1.12 Labor ....2.57 *Remove* .... Labor............ .66	sf	$.66	$3.69	$4.35
	Three coat gypsum plaster on painted metal lath on wall *Replace* Materials .... .95 Labor ....2.41 *Remove* .... Labor............ .69	sf	$.69	$3.36	$4.05
	Three coat gypsum plaster on painted metal lath on ceiling *Replace* Materials .... .95 Labor ....2.86 *Remove* .... Labor............ .69	sf	$.69	$3.81	$4.50
PERLITE OR ▶ VERMICULITE PLASTER *Includes lathing and plastering with trowel finish.*	**Two coat perlite or vermiculite plaster on 3/8" gypsum lath on wall** *Replace* Materials ...... 1.17 Labor ....2.45 *Remove* .... Labor............ .66	sf	$.66	$3.62	$4.28
	Two coat perlite or vermiculite plaster on 3/8" gypsum lath on ceiling *Replace* Materials ...... 1.17 Labor ....2.95 *Remove* .... Labor............ .66	sf	$.66	$4.12	$4.78
	Three coat perlite or vermiculite plaster on painted metal lath on wall *Replace* Materials........1.91 Labor ....2.86 *Remove* .... Labor............ .69	sf	$.69	$4.77	$5.46
	Three coat perlite or vermiculite plaster on painted metal lath on ceiling *Replace* Materials........1.91 Labor ....3.44 *Remove* .... Labor............ .69	sf	$.69	$5.35	$6.04
KEENE'S CEMENT ▶ PLASTER *Includes lathing and plastering with trowel finish.*	**Two coat Keene's cement plaster on 3/8" gypsum lath on wall** *Replace* Materials........1.39 Labor ....3.11 *Remove* .... Labor............ .66	sf	$.66	$4.50	$5.16
	Two coat Keene's cement plaster on 3/8" gypsum lath on ceiling *Replace* Materials........1.39 Labor ....3.74 *Remove* .... Labor............ .66	sf	$.66	$5.13	$5.79
	Three coat Keene's cement plaster on painted metal lath on wall *Replace* Materials........1.22 Labor ....3.40 *Remove* .... Labor............ .69	sf	$.69	$4.62	$5.31
	Three coat Keene's cement plaster on painted metal lath on ceiling *Replace* Materials........1.22 Labor ....3.86 *Remove* .... Labor............ .69	sf	$.69	$5.08	$5.77
THIN-COAT ▶ PLASTER	**Thin-coat plaster on 3/8" thick gypsum lath** *Replace* Materials .... .41 Labor ....1.83 *Remove* .... Labor............ .61	sf	$.61	$2.24	$2.85
	Thin-coat plaster on 1/2" thick gypsum lath *Replace* Materials .... .29 Labor ....1.83 *Remove* .... Labor............ .61	sf	$.61	$2.12	$2.73

Item Description	Unit	Remove	Replace	Total
Add 28% for curved wall				
Add 60% for plaster installed on old-style wood lath				
Square plaster pilaster, plain	lf	$1.24	$11.47	$12.71
Replace Materials........3.63 Labor 7.84				
Remove .... Labor 1.24				
Square plaster pilaster, rusticated	lf	$1.24	$13.07	$14.31
Replace Materials........3.65 Labor 9.42				
Remove .... Labor 1.24				
Square plaster column, plain	lf	$2.23	$21.56	$23.79
Replace Materials........7.26 Labor 14.30				
Remove .... Labor 2.23				
Square plaster column, rusticated	lf	$2.23	$25.40	$27.63
Replace Materials........7.30 Labor 18.10				
Remove .... Labor 2.23				
Add 30% for round pilaster or column				
Cast-in-place plaster molding to 3″ wide	lf	–	$71.22	$71.22
Replace Materials........6.52 Labor 64.70				
Cast-in-place plaster molding 3″ to 6″ wide	lf	–	$83.10	$83.10
Replace Materials........13.00 Labor 70.10				
Cast-in-place plaster molding 6″ to 14″ wide	lf	–	$102.60	$102.60
Replace Materials......24.20 Labor 78.40				
Add for inside corner in cast-in-place plaster molding	ea	–	$140.59	$140.59
Replace Materials........6.59 Labor 134.00				
Add for outside corner in cast-in-place plaster molding	ea	–	$65.66	$65.66
Replace Materials........1.76 Labor 63.90				
Production plaster molding to 3″ wide	lf	–	$38.00	$38.00
Replace Materials......27.10 Labor 10.90				
Production plaster molding 3″ to 6″ wide	lf	–	$51.50	$51.50
Replace Materials......40.30 Labor 11.20				
Production plaster molding to 6″ to 14″ wide	lf	–	$76.80	$76.80
Replace Materials......64.90 Labor 11.90				
Add for inside corner in production plaster molding	ea	–	$15.24	$15.24
Replace Materials........1.44 Labor 13.80				
Add for outside corner in production plaster molding	ea	–	$15.44	$15.44
Replace Materials........1.64 Labor 13.80				
Plaster enrichment, straight patterns	lf	–	$35.60	$35.60
Replace Materials......24.70 Labor 10.90				
▶ All straight work like scotia, coves, rounds, etc.				
Plaster enrichment, ornate patterns	lf	–	$48.50	$48.50
Replace Materials......37.30 Labor 11.20				
▶ Includes fretwork, meander, fluting, Greek key, bead and reel, and simple egg and dart designs.				

◀ **ADDITIONAL PLASTER COSTS**

◀ **PLASTER PILASTER OR COLUMN**
Additional costs for plaster pilasters and columns.

UNITS OF MEASURE

In some areas, plaster and stucco are estimated by the square yard.

However, computer estimating systems usually calculate plaster and stucco by the square foot. The square foot method is used in this section.

◀ **CAST-IN-PLACE PLASTER MOLD**
For straight-pattern moldings cast in place on walls and/or ceilings using a running mold. Inside corners require a great deal of handwork by a skilled specialist. Outside corners are less complex.

◀ **PRODUCTION PLASTER MOLD**
For moldings available from specialized suppliers in a wide variety of patterns.

◀ **PLASTER ENRICHMENT**
Enrichments are placed on walls or ceilings to further accent friezes, cornices, ceiling medallions and so forth.

	Item Description	Unit	Remove	Replace	Total
PLASTER ▶ **ENRICHMENT** *continued*	**Plaster enrichment, very ornate patterns** *Replace* Materials ......53.80 Labor ....11.90 ▶ Very elaborate designs including figures, harps, Acanthus, swags, festoons, leaf and dart, Anthemion patterns and so forth.	lf	–	$65.70	$65.70
PLASTER FRIEZE ▶ *Usually flat with ornate patterns, plaster friezes can be up to 14" wide.*	**Plaster frieze, straight patterns** *Replace* Materials ......41.10 Labor ....10.90 ▶ All straight work like scotia, coves, rounds, etc.	lf	–	$52.00	$52.00
	Plaster frieze, ornate patterns *Replace* Materials ......62.10 Labor ....11.20 ▶ Includes fretwork, meander, fluting, Greek key, bead and reel, and simple egg and dart style designs.	lf	–	$73.30	$73.30
	Plaster frieze, very ornate patterns *Replace* Materials ......89.60 Labor ....11.90 ▶ Very elaborate designs including figures, harps, Acanthus, swags, festoons, leaf and dart, Anthemion patterns and so forth.	lf	–	$101.50	$101.50
PLASTER ▶ **ARCHITRAVE** *Most complex plaster architraves are production units built by a specialty supplier. See Finish Carpentry, page 206 for more information about architraves.*	**Plaster architrave, plain** *Replace* Materials ....2.90 Labor ....6.39 ▶ Square raised design. Usually raised 1" to 2" and about 4" to 6" wide.	lf	–	$9.29	$9.29
	Plaster architrave, rusticated *Replace* Materials ....3.10 Labor ....7.68 ▶ Same as above with rusticated "stones" shaped into the raised section. Rusticated architrave may also be much wider and show simulated Jack arch "stone" pattern.	lf	–	$10.78	$10.78
	Plaster architrave, straight patterns *Replace* Materials ....3.56 Labor ....19.80 ▶ Molded straight work like scotia, coves, rounds, etc.	lf	–	$23.36	$23.36
	Plaster architrave, ornate patterns *Replace* Materials ....3.66 Labor ....29.00 ▶ Includes fretwork, fluting, Greek key, bead & reel, egg and dart, Acanthus, urns, pediments, etc. All or most of the elaborate work will appear on the header.	lf	–	$32.66	$32.66
PLASTER CEILING ▶ **MEDALLION** *Usually round or oval in shape designed for the center of the ceiling.*	**Plaster ceiling medallion, simple pattern** *Replace* Materials ....144.00 Labor ....37.70 ▶ Round or oval with some simple raised patterns.	ea	–	$181.70	$181.70
	Plaster ceiling medallion, ornate pattern *Replace* Materials ....277.00 Labor ....39.50 ▶ Round or oval with elaborate patterns, like scalloped edges, some simple leaf patterns, ridges, fluting, fretwork, and so forth.	ea	–	$316.50	$316.50
	Plaster ceiling medallion, very ornate pattern *Replace* Materials ....504.00 Labor ....41.50 ▶ Very elaborate designs including figures, harps, Acanthus, swags, festoons, leaf and dart, Anthemion patterns and so forth.	ea	–	$545.50	$545.50
PLASTER ▶ **CEILING ROSE** *Very ornate ceiling medallion common to Victorian homes.*	**Plaster small ceiling rose** *Replace* Materials .....245.00 Labor 37.70	ea	–	$282.70	$282.70
	Plaster average size ceiling rose *Replace* Materials .....376.00 Labor 39.50	ea	–	$415.50	$415.50
	Plaster large ceiling rose *Replace* Materials .....711.00 Labor 41.50	ea	–	$752.50	$752.50

Item Description	Unit	Remove	Replace	Total
Three coat Portland cement stucco, sand float finish	sf	$.78	$4.97	$5.75
Replace Materials .... .99 Labor 3.98				
Remove .... Labor............ .78				
Three coat Portland cement stucco, sand float finish, on masonry	sf	$.78	$3.49	$4.27
Replace Materials .... .38 Labor............3.11				
Remove .... Labor............ .78				
Three coat Portland cement stucco, trowel float finish	sf	$.78	$6.90	$7.68
Replace Materials ...... 1.01 Labor............5.89				
Remove .... Labor............ .78				
Three coat Portland cement stucco, trowel float finish, on masonry	sf	$.78	$5.42	$6.20
Replace Materials .... .40 Labor............5.02				
Remove .... Labor............ .78				
Add 26% for stucco application on soffits				
Add 10% for colors				
Add 19% for white cement				
Add 32% for pebble dash (rough cast) stucco finish				
▶ Colorful aggregate that is "thrown" into the stucco.				
Add 88% for vermiculated stucco finish				
▶ Snake-like pattern found on some historical structures, especially around entries.				
Patch single "stone" section in stucco rustication	ea	–	$36.98	$36.98
Replace Materials ....5.08 Labor............31.90				
Add for stucco quoin	ea	–	$33.81	$33.81
Replace Materials........7.91 Labor 25.90				
Add for stucco key	ea	–	$57.00	$57.00
Replace Materials ......12.20 Labor 44.80				
Add for stucco raised trim	lf	–	$9.27	$9.27
Replace Materials........3.09 Labor 6.18				
▶ For raised trim around doors see architraves on page 357.				
Add for stucco raised curved trim	lf	–	$13.97	$13.97
Replace Materials........3.57 Labor............10.40				
▶ Raised, curved trim over doors, windows, and so forth.				
Add for stucco color change	ea	–	$2.45	$2.45
Replace Materials .... .21 Labor 2.24				
▶ Use when stucco changes colors on a wall. For example, each layer of raised trim may be of a different color.				
Synthetic stucco over 1/2" cement board	sf	$.78	$4.01	$4.79
Replace Materials .... .94 Labor 3.07				
Remove .... Labor............ .78				
Synthetic stucco over 1" insulating foam board	sf	$.78	$3.83	$4.61
Replace Materials .... .76 Labor 3.07				
Remove .... Labor............ .78				
Synthetic stucco over 2" insulating foam board	sf	$.78	$3.88	$4.66
Replace Materials .... .81 Labor............3.07				
Remove .... Labor............ .78				

◄ **STUCCO**
Includes felt or building paper, metal lath, and control joint and corner metal.

◄ **ADDITIONAL STUCCO COSTS**

RELATED ITEMS

Acoustic Ceiling 15
Drywall.......................133
Finish Carpentry..........199
architrave...................206
Masonry.....................287
stone architrave.........310
cut stone trim.............314
Painting 333
Suspended Ceilings 483

◄ **SYNTHETIC STUCCO**
Includes cement board or polystyrene foam insulation board, adhesive primer, color coat stucco, and corner mesh.

	Item Description	Unit	Remove	Replace	Total
ADDITIONAL ▶ SYNTHETIC STUCCO COSTS	**Add for synthetic stucco quoin** *Replace* Materials........4.46　　　Labor 38.80	ea	–	$43.26	$43.26
	Add for synthetic stucco key *Replace* Materials........6.89　　　Labor 66.80	ea	–	$73.69	$73.69
	Add for synthetic stucco raised trim *Replace* Materials........1.74　　　Labor ....9.25 ▶ For raised trim around doors see architraves on facing page.	lf	–	$10.99	$10.99
	Add for synthetic stucco raised curved trim *Replace* Materials........2.02　　　Labor ....15.50 ▶ Raised, curved trim over doors, windows, and so forth.	lf	–	$17.52	$17.52
	Add for synthetic stucco color change *Replace* Materials........ .12　　　Labor ....3.36 ▶ Use when stucco changes colors on a wall. For example, each layer of raised trim may be of a different color.	lf	–	$3.48	$3.48
STUCCO REPAIR ▶ *For repair of standard or synthetic stucco.*	**Minimum charge to repair stucco** *Replace* Materials......56.00　　　Labor 90.10	ea	–	$146.10	$146.10
	Repair hair-line stucco crack *Replace* Materials........ .33　　　Labor 2.74	lf	–	$3.07	$3.07
	Repair stucco crack less than 1" wide *Replace* Materials........ .49　　　Labor 3.44	lf	–	$3.93	$3.93
	Patch small stucco hole less than 2" square *Replace* Materials........1.49　　　Labor 35.50	ea	–	$36.99	$36.99
	Patch stucco hole 2" to 10" square *Replace* Materials........6.74　　　Labor 45.20	ea	–	$51.94	$51.94
	Patch stucco hole 10" to 20" square *Replace* Materials.......11.70　　　Labor 55.20	ea	–	$66.90	$66.90
	Patch stucco section *Replace* Materials........2.47　　　Labor ....6.60 ▶ For stucco repair of an area no greater than 20 sf in size.	sf	–	$9.07	$9.07
	Repair stucco wall outside corner damage per lf of damage *Replace* Materials........3.17　　　Labor 12.30	lf	–	$15.47	$15.47
	Repair stucco wall inside corner damage per lf of damage *Replace* Materials........2.61　　　Labor 8.63	lf	–	$11.24	$11.24
STUCCO PILASTER ▶ OR COLUMN *Additional costs for stucco pilasters and columns. For use with standard or synthetic stucco.*	**Square stucco pilaster, plain** *Replace* Materials........3.77　　　Labor ....7.97 *Remove* ....　　　Labor 1.39	lf	$1.39	$11.74	$13.13
	Square stucco pilaster, rusticated *Replace* Materials........3.79　　　Labor ....9.55 *Remove* ....　　　Labor 1.39	lf	$1.39	$13.34	$14.73
	Square stucco column, plain *Replace* Materials........7.54　　　Labor ....14.50 *Remove* ....　　　Labor 2.40	lf	$2.40	$22.04	$24.44

Item Description	Unit	Remove	Replace	Total
Square stucco column, rusticated	lf	$2.40	$25.88	$28.28
Replace Materials........7.58 Labor...........18.30				
Remove .... Labor...........2.40				
Add 30% for round stucco pilaster or column				
Repair section of stucco pilaster or column	ea	–	$60.40	$60.40
Replace Materials......22.00 Labor..........38.40				
▶ Repair section by hand or by pouring into mold then patching into architrave.				
Minimum charge to repair stucco pilaster or column	ea	–	$79.90	$79.90
Replace Materials......38.00 Labor..........41.90				
Stucco architrave, plain	lf	–	$9.49	$9.49
Replace Materials........3.02 Labor...........6.47				
▶ Square raised design. Usually raised 1" to 2" and about 4" to 6" wide.				
Stucco architrave, rusticated	lf	–	$10.85	$10.85
Replace Materials........3.05 Labor...........7.80				
▶ Same as above with rusticated "stones" shaped into the raised section. Rusticated architrave may also be much wider and show simulated Jack arch "stone" pattern.				
Stucco architrave, straight patterns	lf	–	$23.23	$23.23
Replace Materials........3.23 Labor..........20.00				
▶ Molded straight work like scotia, coves, rounds, etc.				
Stucco architrave, ornate patterns	lf	–	$33.11	$33.11
Replace Materials........3.71 Labor..........29.40				
▶ Includes fretwork, fluting, Greek key, bead & reel, egg and dart, Acanthus, urns, pediments, etc. All or most of the elaborate work will appear on the header.				
Take flexible mold of existing stucco architrave	ea	–	$66.40	$66.40
Replace Materials......41.70 Labor..........24.70				
Create mold for stucco architrave	ea	–	$220.90	$220.90
Replace Materials......54.90 Labor........166.00				
Repair section of stucco architrave	ea	–	$62.74	$62.74
Replace Materials........6.74 Labor..........56.00				
▶ Repair section by hand or by pouring into mold then patching into architrave.				
Minimum charge to repair stucco architrave	ea	–	$181.10	$181.10
Replace Materials......27.10 Labor........154.00				

◀ **STUCCO ARCHITRAVE**
Most complex stucco architraves are production units built by a specialty supplier.

RELATED ITEMS

Acoustic Ceiling 15
Drywall 133
Finish Carpentry 199
    architrave.................206
Masonry.....................287
    stone architrave............310
    cut stone trim.................314
Painting 333
Suspended Ceilings 483

TIME & MATERIAL CHARTS (selected items)

Plaster & Stucco Materials

DESCRIPTION	MATERIAL PRICE	GROSS COVERAGE	WASTE	NET COVERAGE	UNIT PRICE
Plaster and stucco materials					
gauging plaster.......................	$23.20 *100 lb. bag*	1	21%	.79	$29.40 *ea*
gypsum plaster.......................	$18.20 *80 lb. bag*	1	21%	.79	$23.00 *ea*
thin-coat plaster....................	$12.70 *50 lb. bag*	1	21%	.79	$16.10 *ea*
Keene's cement......................	$26.60 *100 lb. bag*	1	21%	.79	$33.70 *ea*
perlite or vermiculite plaster........	$17.80 *100 lb. bag*	1	21%	.79	$22.50 *ea*
3/8" perforated gypsum lath........	$17.70 *sheet*	32	4%	30.72	$.58 *sf*
1/2" perforated gypsum lath........	$18.70 *sheet*	32	4%	30.72	$.61 *sf*
painted metal lath....................	$.29 *sf*	1	4%	.96	$.30 *sf*
painted stucco mesh.................	$.44 *sf*	1	4%	.96	$.46 *ea*

Plaster & Stucco Labor

LABORER	BASE WAGE	PAID LEAVE	TRUE WAGE	FICA	FUTA	WORKER'S COMP.	UNEMPLOY. INSUR.	HEALTH INSUR.	RETIRE (401k)	LIABILITY INSUR.	COST PER HOUR
Plasterer	$23.60	1.84	$25.44	1.95	.20	7.38	2.21	2.92	.76	3.82	$44.70
Plasterer's helper	$20.00	1.56	$21.56	1.65	.17	6.25	1.88	2.92	.65	3.23	$38.30
Demolition laborer	$14.40	1.12	$15.52	1.19	.12	5.01	1.35	2.92	.47	2.33	$28.90

Paid Leave is calculated based on two weeks paid vacation, one week sick leave, and seven paid holidays. Employer's matching portion of **FICA** is 7.65 percent. **FUTA** (Federal Unemployment) is .8 percent. **Worker's compensation** for the plaster and stucco trade was calculated using a national average of 28.93 percent. **Unemployment insurance** was calculated using a national average of 8.7 percent. **Health insurance** was calculated based on a projected national average for 2005 of $580 per employee (and family when applicable) per month. Employer pays 80 percent for a per month cost of $464 per employee. **Retirement** is based on a 401(k) retirement program with employer matching of 50 percent. Employee contributions to the 401(k) plan are an average of 6 percent of the true wage. **Liability insurance** is based on a national average of 14.0 percent.

Plaster & Stucco Labor Productivity

WORK DESCRIPTION	LABORER	COST PER HOUR	PRODUCTIVITY	UNIT PRICE
Demolition				
remove plaster on gypsum lath	demolition laborer	$28.90	.023	$.66 sf
remove plaster on metal lath	demolition laborer	$28.90	.024	$.69 sf
remove thin-coat plaster on gypsum	demolition laborer	$28.90	.021	$.61 sf
remove plaster pilaster	demolition laborer	$28.90	.043	$1.24 lf
remove plaster column	demolition laborer	$28.90	.077	$2.23 lf
remove stucco	demolition laborer	$28.90	.027	$.78 sf
remove synthetic stucco on cement board	demolition laborer	$28.90	.027	$.78 sf
remove stucco pilaster	demolition laborer	$28.90	.048	$1.39 lf
remove stucco column	demolition laborer	$28.90	.083	$2.40 lf
Plaster installation crew				
install plaster	plasterer	$44.70		
install plaster	plasterer's helper	$38.30		
install plaster	**plastering crew**	$41.50		
Install acoustical plaster				
two coat on 3/8" gypsum lath on wall	plastering crew	$41.50	.051	$2.12 sf
two coat on 3/8" gypsum lath on ceiling	plastering crew	$41.50	.061	$2.53 sf
three coat on painted metal lath on wall	plastering crew	$41.50	.057	$2.37 sf
three coat on painted metal lath on ceiling	plastering crew	$41.50	.068	$2.82 sf
Install gypsum plaster				
two coat on 3/8" gypsum lath on wall	plastering crew	$41.50	.052	$2.16 sf
two coat on 3/8" gypsum lath on ceiling	plastering crew	$41.50	.062	$2.57 sf
three coat on painted metal lath on wall	plastering crew	$41.50	.058	$2.41 sf
three coat on painted metal lath on ceiling	plastering crew	$41.50	.069	$2.86 sf
Install perlite or vermiculite plaster				
two coat on 3/8" gypsum lath on wall	plastering crew	$41.50	.059	$2.45 sf
two coat on 3/8" gypsum lath on ceiling	plastering crew	$41.50	.071	$2.95 sf
three coat on painted metal lath on wall	plastering crew	$41.50	.069	$2.86 sf
three coat on painted metal lath on ceiling	plastering crew	$41.50	.083	$3.44 sf
Install Keene's cement plaster				
two coat on 3/8" gypsum lath on wall	plastering crew	$41.50	.075	$3.11 sf
two coat on 3/8" gypsum lath on ceiling	plastering crew	$41.50	.090	$3.74 sf
three coat on painted metal lath on wall	plastering crew	$41.50	.082	$3.40 sf
three coat on painted metal lath on ceiling	plastering crew	$41.50	.093	$3.86 sf
Install thin-coat plaster				
on 3/8" thick gypsum lath	plastering crew	$41.50	.044	$1.83 sf
on 1/2" thick gypsum lath	plastering crew	$41.50	.044	$1.83 sf
Install three-coat Portland cement stucco				
sand float finish	plastering crew	$41.50	.096	$3.98 sf
sand float finish, on masonry	plastering crew	$41.50	.075	$3.11 sf
trowel float finish	plastering crew	$41.50	.142	$5.89 sf
trowel float finish, on masonry	plastering crew	$41.50	.121	$5.02 sf
Install synthetic stucco				
all applications	plastering crew	$41.50	.074	$3.07 sf

29 _____ *Plumbing*

Item Description	Unit	Remove	Replace	Total	
Minimum charge for plumbing work *Replace* Materials......40.00　　　Labor............62.10	ea	–	$102.10	$102.10	◄ **MINIMUM**
1/2″ diameter black steel supply pipe *Replace* Materials........2.31　　　Labor 5.93	lf	–	$8.24	$8.24	◄ **BLACK STEEL PIPE** *Field threaded with fitting or coupling every 8.5 lf and hanger every 10 lf.*
3/4″ diameter black steel supply pipe *Replace* Materials........2.48　　　Labor 6.35	lf	–	$8.83	$8.83	
1″ diameter black steel supply pipe *Replace* Materials........3.30　　　Labor 7.38	lf	–	$10.68	$10.68	
2″ diameter black steel supply pipe *Replace* Materials........6.40　　　Labor............10.80	lf	–	$17.20	$17.20	
Replace section of black steel supply pipe *Replace* Materials......27.30　　　Labor............47.60 ► Includes cut-out in typical drywall wall, replacement section and couplings. Does not include wall repair (see *Drywall* page 136)	ea	–	$74.90	$74.90	
1/2″ diameter brass water supply pipe *Replace* Materials........6.85　　　Labor 8.03	lf	–	$14.88	$14.88	◄ **BRASS WATER SUPPLY PIPE** *Field threaded with fitting or coupling every 8.5 lf and hanger every 10 lf.*
3/4″ diameter brass water supply pipe *Replace* Materials........9.08　　　Labor 8.41	lf	–	$17.49	$17.49	
1″ diameter brass water supply pipe *Replace* Materials ......12.10　　　Labor 8.97	lf	–	$21.07	$21.07	
2″ diameter brass water supply pipe *Replace* Materials......30.00　　　Labor 9.81	lf	–	$39.81	$39.81	
Replace section of brass water supply pipe *Replace* Materials......56.00　　　Labor ....64.90 ► Includes cut-out in typical drywall wall, replacement section and couplings. Does not include wall repair.	ea	–	$120.90	$120.90	◁ replace section
1/2″ diameter type K copper water supply pipe *Replace* Materials........2.37　　　Labor 4.86	lf	–	$7.23	$7.23	◄ **COPPER WATER SUPPLY PIPE TYPE K** *With sweated fitting or coupling every 8.5 lf and hanger every 10 lf.*
3/4″ diameter type K copper water supply pipe *Replace* Materials........2.43　　　Labor 5.09	lf	–	$7.52	$7.52	
1″ diameter type K copper water supply pipe *Replace* Materials........4.55　　　Labor 5.70	lf	–	$10.25	$10.25	
2″ diameter type K copper water supply pipe *Replace* Materials ......10.69　　　Labor 9.43	lf	–	$20.12	$20.12	
1/2″ diameter type L copper water supply pipe *Replace* Materials........2.06　　　Labor 4.86	lf	–	$6.92	$6.92	◄ **COPPER WATER SUPPLY PIPE TYPE L** *With sweated fitting or coupling every 8.5 lf and hanger every 10 lf.*
3/4″ diameter type L copper water supply pipe *Replace* Materials........2.23　　　Labor 5.09	lf	–	$7.32	$7.32	

RELATED ITEMS

Bathroom Hardware......41
Cleaning 64

Item Description	Unit	Remove	Replace	Total
COPPER WATER ▶ SUPPLY PIPE TYPE L *continued*				
1" diameter type L copper water supply pipe *Replace* Materials........3.93 Labor............5.70	lf	–	$9.63	$9.63
2" diameter type L copper water supply pipe *Replace* Materials........9.66 Labor............9.43	lf	–	$19.09	$19.09
COPPER WATER ▶ SUPPLY PIPE TYPE M *With sweated fitting or coupling every 8.5 lf and hanger every 10 lf.*				
1/2" diameter type M copper water supply pipe *Replace* Materials........1.70 Labor............4.86	lf	–	$6.56	$6.56
3/4" diameter type M copper water supply pipe *Replace* Materials........2.23 Labor............5.09	lf	–	$7.32	$7.32
1" diameter type M copper water supply pipe *Replace* Materials........3.08 Labor............5.70	lf	–	$8.78	$8.78
replace section ▷ **Replace section of copper water supply pipe** *Replace* Materials.......20.60 Labor..........38.60 ▶ Includes cut-out in typical drywall wall, replacement section and couplings. Does not include wall repair (see *Drywall* page 136).	ea	–	$59.20	$59.20
GALVANIZED ▶ STEEL WATER SUPPLY PIPE *Field threaded with fitting or coupling every 8.5 lf and hanger every 10 lf.*				
1/2" diameter galvanized steel water supply pipe *Replace* Materials........2.79 Labor............6.02	lf	–	$8.81	$8.81
3/4" diameter galvanized steel water supply pipe *Replace* Materials........3.02 Labor............6.35	lf	–	$9.37	$9.37
1" diameter galvanized steel water supply pipe *Replace* Materials........4.33 Labor............7.24	lf	–	$11.57	$11.57
2" diameter galvanized steel water supply pipe *Replace* Materials........7.96 Labor...........10.80	lf	–	$18.76	$18.76
replace section ▷ **Replace section of galvanized steel water supply pipe** *Replace* Materials......33.50 Labor..........48.60 ▶ Includes cut-out in typical drywall wall, replacement section and couplings. Does not include wall repair (see *Drywall* page 136).	ea	–	$82.10	$82.10
CPVC WATER ▶ SUPPLY PIPE *With fitting or coupling every 8.5 lf and hanger every 3.5 lf.*				
1/2" diameter CPVC schedule 40 water supply pipe *Replace* Materials........3.61 Labor............7.15	lf	–	$10.76	$10.76
3/4" diameter CPVC schedule 40 water supply pipe *Replace* Materials........4.39 Labor............7.57	lf	–	$11.96	$11.96
1" diameter CPVC schedule 40 water supply pipe *Replace* Materials........5.36 Labor............8.83	lf	–	$14.19	$14.19
PVC WATER ▶ SUPPLY PIPE *With fitting or coupling every 8.5 lf and hanger every 3.5 lf.*				
1/2" diameter PVC schedule 40 cold water supply pipe *Replace* Materials........2.09 Labor............7.15	lf	–	$9.24	$9.24
3/4" diameter PVC schedule 40 cold water supply pipe *Replace* Materials........2.15 Labor............7.57	lf	–	$9.72	$9.72
1" diameter PVC schedule 40 cold water supply pipe *Replace* Materials........2.51 Labor............8.83	lf	–	$11.34	$11.34
REPLACE SECTION ▶ OF PVC OR CPVC SUPPLY PIPE				
Replace section of PVC or CPVC water supply pipe *Replace* Materials ......16.40 Labor..........57.40 ▶ Includes cut-out in typical drywall wall, replacement section and couplings. Does not include wall repair (see *Drywall* page 136).	ea	–	$73.80	$73.80

Item Description	Unit	Remove	Replace	Total	
Minimum charge for supply pipe work *Replace* Materials......60.00 Labor..........85.00	ea	–	$145.00	$145.00	◄ **MINIMUM SUPPLY PIPE**
2" cast-iron DWV pipe *Replace* Materials........5.92 Labor...........11.00	lf	–	$16.92	$16.92	◄ **CAST-IRON DWV PIPE** *Lead and oakum joints with fitting every 9.5 lf.*
3" cast-iron DWV pipe *Replace* Materials........8.12 Labor...........11.60	lf	–	$19.72	$19.72	
4" cast-iron DWV pipe *Replace* Materials......10.80 Labor...........12.60	lf	–	$23.40	$23.40	
5" cast-iron DWV pipe *Replace* Materials ......14.10 Labor...........14.20	lf	–	$28.30	$28.30	
6" cast-iron DWV pipe *Replace* Materials........17.30 Labor...........14.80	lf	–	$32.10	$32.10	
Replace section of cast-iron DWV pipe *Replace* Materials ....104.00 Labor...........78.00 ► Includes cut-out in typical drywall wall, replacement section and couplings. Does not include wall repair (see *Drywall* page 136).	ea	–	$182.00	$182.00	◁ replace section
Repack cast-iron DWV pipe joint with oakum and caulk *Replace* Materials ......12.50 Labor............8.45	ea	–	$20.95	$20.95	◁ repack
2" cast-iron no-hub DWV pipe *Replace* Materials........7.01 Labor.............9.81	lf	–	$16.82	$16.82	◄ **CAST-IRON NO-HUB DWV PIPE** *With fitting or coupling every 9.5 lf.*
3" cast-iron no-hub DWV pipe *Replace* Materials........9.42 Labor...........10.40	lf	–	$19.82	$19.82	
4" cast-iron no-hub DWV pipe *Replace* Materials.......11.80 Labor...........11.30	lf	–	$23.10	$23.10	
5" cast-iron no-hub DWV pipe *Replace* Materials ......16.90 Labor...........12.70	lf	–	$29.60	$29.60	
6" cast-iron no-hub DWV pipe *Replace* Materials........19.90 Labor...........13.20	lf	–	$33.10	$33.10	
Replace section of cast-iron no-hub DWV pipe *Replace* Materials ......79.90 Labor...........69.60 ► Includes cut-out in typical drywall wall, replacement section and couplings. Does not include wall repair (see *Drywall* page 136).	ea	–	$149.50	$149.50	◁ replace section
Repair pin-hole leak in cast-iron DWV pipe with epoxy *Replace* Materials........8.79 Labor 25.40	ea	–	$34.19	$34.19	◁ repair pin-hole leak
1-1/4" PVC DWV pipe *Replace* Materials........2.77 Labor 9.25	lf	–	$12.02	$12.02	◄ **PVC DWV PIPE** *With fitting or coupling every 8.5 lf and hanger every 10 lf.*
1-1/2" PVC DWV pipe *Replace* Materials........3.08 Labor...........10.70	lf	–	$13.78	$13.78	
2" PVC DWV pipe *Replace* Materials........3.29 Labor...........11.70	lf	–	$14.99	$14.99	
3" PVC DWV pipe *Replace* Materials........4.83 Labor...........13.10	lf	–	$17.93	$17.93	

RELATED ITEMS

Bathroom Hardware......41
Cleaning 64

	Item Description	Unit	Remove	Replace	Total
PVC DWV PIPE ▶ *continued*	**4" PVC DWV pipe** *Replace* Materials........6.17 Labor...........14.50	lf	–	$20.67	$20.67
	5" PVC DWV pipe *Replace* Materials........8.46 Labor...........16.20	lf	–	$24.66	$24.66
	6" PVC DWV pipe *Replace* Materials.......11.90 Labor...........17.70	lf	–	$29.60	$29.60
replace section ▷	**Replace section of PVC DWV pipe** *Replace* Materials......39.60 Labor..........67.70 ▶ Includes cut-out in typical drywall wall, replacement section and couplings. Does not include wall repair (see *Drywall* page 136).	ea	–	$107.30	$107.30
MINIMUM ▶ **DWV PIPE**	**Minimum charge for DWV line work** *Replace* Materials ......62.00 Labor...........71.90	ea	–	$133.90	$133.90
EXTERIOR LINES ▶ *Includes excavation up to 8' deep, backfill, laying pipe, pipe, and fittings. Does not include mobilization or shoring. Also see Excavation, page 178.*	**4" diameter exterior sewer lines** *Replace* Materials......25.50 Labor..........76.60	lf	–	$102.10	$102.10
	6" diameter exterior sewer lines *Replace* Materials......36.30 Labor..........78.90	lf	–	$115.20	$115.20
	1" diameter exterior water supply line *Replace* Materials.......17.20 Labor..........76.60	lf	–	$93.80	$93.80
	1-1/2" diameter exterior water supply line *Replace* Materials......20.20 Labor..........78.90	lf	–	$99.10	$99.10
minimum ▷	**Minimum charge for exterior line work** *Replace* Materials.....101.00 Labor........467.00	ea	–	$568.00	$568.00
SHUT-OFF AND ▶ **PRESSURE VALVES**	**Interior water supply shut-off valve with pressure valve, 1-1/2" line** *Replace* Materials....399.00 Labor..........51.40	ea	–	$450.40	$450.40
	Interior water supply shut-off valve with pressure valve, 2" line *Replace* Materials....513.00 Labor..........51.40	ea	–	$564.40	$564.40
REPAIR UNDER- ▶ **GROUND LINE** *Includes excavation to specified depth, backfill, laying pipe, pipe, and fittings. Does not include mobilization or shoring. Also see Excavation, page 178.*	**Excavate and repair underground line 4' deep or less** *Replace* Materials......53.70 Labor.........78.00	lf	–	$131.70	$131.70
	Excavate and repair underground line 4' to 8' deep *Replace* Materials......53.70 Labor.......101.00	lf	–	$154.70	$154.70
	Excavate and repair underground line 8' to 12' deep *Replace* Materials......53.70 Labor.........142.00	lf	–	$195.70	$195.70
	Excavate and repair underground line 12' to 16' deep *Replace* Materials......53.70 Labor 203.00	lf	–	$256.70	$256.70
BREAK-OUT ▶ **CONCRETE &** **INSTALL PIPE**	**Install pipe underneath existing concrete slab** *Replace* Materials....17.40 Labor.........104.00 ▶ Saw concrete slab and break-out, hand excavate, lay pipe, hand back fill, and patch concrete. Includes sand bed for pipe as necessary.	lf	–	$121.40	$121.40
minimum ▷	**Minimum charge to install pipe underneath existing concrete slab** *Replace* Materials ....109.00 Labor 584.00	ea	–	$693.00	$693.00

Item Description	Unit	Remove	Replace	Total	
Complete supply lines, waste lines & finish fixtures, economy grade *Replace* Materials........2.22 Labor ....3.78 ▶ With PVC drain, waste, and vent lines, CPVC hot water lines, PVC cold water lines.	sf	–	$6.00	$6.00	◀ **COMPLETE HOUSE ROUGH & FINISH PLUMBING** *Grades refer to quality of plumbing fixtures. For residential structures only. See page 369 for information about plumbing fixture quality.*
Complete supply lines, waste lines, & finish fixtures, standard grade *Replace* Materials........3.56 Labor ....3.97 ▶ With PVC drain, waste, and vent lines, copper water supply lines.	sf	–	$7.53	$7.53	
Complete supply lines, waste lines, & finish fixtures, high grade *Replace* Materials........3.86 Labor ....4.02 ▶ With PVC drain, waste, and vent lines, copper water supply lines.	sf	–	$7.88	$7.88	
Complete supply lines, waste lines, & finish fixtures, deluxe grade *Replace* Materials........4.42 Labor ....4.25 ▶ With cast-iron drain, waste, and vent lines, copper water supply lines.	sf	–	$8.67	$8.67	
Complete supply lines, waste lines, & finish fixtures, custom deluxe grade *Replace* Materials........4.87 Labor ....4.30 ▶ With cast-iron drain, waste, and vent lines, copper water supply lines.	sf	–	$9.17	$9.17	
Complete house rough plumbing (no fixtures), economy grade *Replace* Materials........ .59 Labor ....1.77 ▶ PVC drain, waste, and vent lines, CPVC hot water lines, PVC cold water lines.	sf	–	$2.36	$2.36	◀ **COMPLETE HOUSE ROUGH PLUMBING**
Complete house rough plumbing (no fixtures) standard grade *Replace* Materials........ .86 Labor ....1.96 ▶ PVC drain, waste, and vent lines, copper water supply lines.	sf	–	$2.82	$2.82	
Complete house rough plumbing (no fixtures) high grade *Replace* Materials........1.23 Labor ....2.10 ▶ Cast-iron drain, waste, and vent lines, copper water supply lines.	sf	–	$3.33	$3.33	
Complete house plumbing fixtures, economy grade *Replace* Materials........1.63 Labor 2.01	sf	–	$3.64	$3.64	◀ **COMPLETE HOUSE FINISH PLUMBING (FIXTURES)** *See page 369 for information about plumbing fixture quality.*
Complete house plumbing fixtures, standard grade *Replace* Materials........2.70 Labor 2.05	sf	–	$4.75	$4.75	
Complete house plumbing fixtures, high grade *Replace* Materials........3.00 Labor 2.05	sf	–	$5.05	$5.05	
Complete house plumbing fixtures, deluxe grade *Replace* Materials........3.19 Labor 2.10	sf	–	$5.29	$5.29	
Complete house plumbing fixtures, custom deluxe grade *Replace* Materials........3.64 Labor 2.15	sf	–	$5.79	$5.79	
Rough plumbing, two fixture bathroom, plastic supply, plastic DWV *Replace* Materials ....335.00 Labor 915.00	ea	–	$1,250.00	$1,250.00	◀ **ROUGH PLUMBING TWO FIXTURE BATHROOM** *Typically rough plumbing for one toilet and one sink. Does not include fixtures.*
Rough plumbing, two fixture bathroom, copper supply, plastic DWV *Replace* Materials ....400.00 Labor 953.00	ea	–	$1,353.00	$1,353.00	
Rough plumbing, two fixture bathroom, copper supply, cast-iron DWV *Replace* Materials ....460.00 Labor 995.00	ea	–	$1,455.00	$1,455.00	

RELATED ITEMS
Bathroom Hardware 39
Cleaning....................62

Item Description	Unit	Remove	Replace	Total
ROUGH PLUMBING ▶ THREE FIXTURE BATHROOM *Typically rough plumbing for one toilet, one sink and a shower or bathtub. Does not include fixtures.*				
Rough plumbing, three fixture bathroom, plastic supply, plastic DWV *Replace* Materials....430.00 Labor........1170.00	ea	–	$1,600.00	$1,600.00
Rough plumbing, three fixture bathroom, copper supply, plastic DWV *Replace* Materials.....515.00 Labor.......1230.00	ea	–	$1,745.00	$1,745.00
Rough plumbing, three fixture bathroom, copper supply, cast-iron DWV *Replace* Materials....590.00 Labor........1340.00	ea	–	$1,930.00	$1,930.00
ROUGH PLUMBING ▶ FOUR FIXTURE BATHROOM *Typically rough plumbing for one toilet, one sink one shower and a bathtub. Does not include fixtures.*				
Rough plumbing, four fixture bathroom, plastic supply, plastic DWV *Replace* Materials....535.00 Labor........1560.00	ea	–	$2,095.00	$2,095.00
Rough plumbing, four fixture bathroom, copper supply, plastic DWV *Replace* Materials....640.00 Labor.......1670.00	ea	–	$2,310.00	$2,310.00
Rough plumbing, four fixture bathroom, copper supply, cast-iron DWV *Replace* Materials....735.00 Labor.......1800.00	ea	–	$2,535.00	$2,535.00
ROUGH PLUMBING ▶ FIVE FIXTURE BATHROOM *Typically rough plumbing for one toilet, two sinks one shower and a bathtub. Does not include fixtures.*				
Rough plumbing, five fixture bathroom, plastic supply, plastic DWV *Replace* Materials....640.00 Labor........1950.00	ea	–	$2,590.00	$2,590.00
Rough plumbing, five fixture bathroom, copper supply, plastic DWV *Replace* Materials ....770.00 Labor......2030.00	ea	–	$2,800.00	$2,800.00
Rough plumbing, five fixture bathroom, copper supply, cast-iron DWV *Replace* Materials....880.00 Labor.......2120.00	ea	–	$3,000.00	$3,000.00
ROUGH PLUMBING ▶ LAUNDRY ROOM *Includes supply valves and recessed wall box.*				
Rough plumbing, laundry room, plastic supply, plastic DWV *Replace* Materials......145.00 Labor.........303.00	ea	–	$448.00	$448.00
Rough plumbing, laundry room, copper supply, plastic DWV *Replace* Materials.....170.00 Labor.........318.00	ea	–	$488.00	$488.00
Rough plumbing, laundry room, copper supply, cast-iron DWV *Replace* Materials....200.00 Labor.........336.00	ea	–	$536.00	$536.00
ROUGH PLUMBING ▶ LAUNDRY ROOM WITH SINK *Includes supply valves, recessed wall box, and plumbing for one or two hole laundry sink.*				
Rough plumbing, laundry room with sink, plastic supply, plastic DWV *Replace* Materials....340.00 Labor.........593.00	ea	–	$933.00	$933.00
Rough plumbing, laundry room with sink, copper supply, plastic DWV *Replace* Materials....405.00 Labor.........607.00	ea	–	$1,012.00	$1,012.00
Rough plumbing, laundry room with sink, copper supply, cast-iron DWV *Replace* Materials....465.00 Labor.........621.00	ea	–	$1,086.00	$1,086.00
ROUGH PLUMBING ▶ KITCHEN *Rough plumbing for one, two or three hole kitchen sink. With ice maker includes line from sink to refrigerator ice maker or water dispenser.*				
Rough plumbing, kitchen, plastic supply, plastic DWV *Replace* Materials.....245.00 Labor.........383.00	ea	–	$628.00	$628.00
Rough plumbing, kitchen, copper supply, plastic DWV *Replace* Materials ....270.00 Labor.........399.00	ea	–	$669.00	$669.00
Rough plumbing, kitchen, copper supply, cast-iron DWV *Replace* Materials....300.00 Labor.........410.00	ea	–	$710.00	$710.00
Rough plumbing, kitchen with ice maker, plastic supply, plastic DWV *Replace* Materials....280.00 Labor.........458.00	ea	–	$738.00	$738.00
Rough plumbing, kitchen with ice maker, copper supply, plastic DWV *Replace* Materials....305.00 Labor.........472.00	ea	–	$777.00	$777.00

Item Description	Unit	Remove	Replace	Total
Rough plumbing, kitchen with icemaker, copper supply, cast-iron DWV *Replace* Materials ....335.00 Labor 486.00	ea	–	$821.00	$821.00
Rough plumbing, wet bar sink, plastic supply, plastic DWV *Replace* Materials.....125.00 Labor 346.00	ea	–	$471.00	$471.00
Rough plumbing, wet bar sink, copper supply, plastic DWV *Replace* Materials......145.00 Labor.........359.00	ea	–	$504.00	$504.00
Rough plumbing, wet bar sink, copper supply, cast-iron DWV *Replace* Materials.....175.00 Labor.........371.00	ea	–	$546.00	$546.00
Rough plumbing, bathroom sink, plastic supply, plastic DWV *Replace* Materials.....125.00 Labor 346.00	ea	–	$471.00	$471.00
Rough plumbing, bathroom sink, copper supply, plastic DWV *Replace* Materials ....150.00 Labor.........359.00	ea	–	$509.00	$509.00
Rough plumbing, bathroom sink, copper supply, cast-iron DWV *Replace* Materials ....180.00 Labor.........371.00	ea	–	$551.00	$551.00
Rough plumbing, kitchen sink, plastic supply, plastic DWV *Replace* Materials.....215.00 Labor 383.00	ea	–	$598.00	$598.00
Rough plumbing, kitchen sink, copper supply, plastic DWV *Replace* Materials ....240.00 Labor.........399.00	ea	–	$639.00	$639.00
Rough plumbing, kitchen sink, copper supply, cast-iron DWV *Replace* Materials ....270.00 Labor 410.00	ea	–	$680.00	$680.00
Rough plumbing, laundry sink, plastic supply, plastic DWV *Replace* Materials.....120.00 Labor 303.00	ea	–	$423.00	$423.00
Rough plumbing, laundry sink, copper supply, plastic DWV *Replace* Materials.....145.00 Labor 318.00	ea	–	$463.00	$463.00
Rough plumbing, laundry sink, copper supply, cast-iron DWV *Replace* Materials.....175.00 Labor 336.00	ea	–	$511.00	$511.00
Rough plumbing, bathtub or shower, plastic supply, plastic DWV *Replace* Materials ....180.00 Labor 322.00	ea	–	$502.00	$502.00
Rough plumbing, bathtub or shower, copper supply, plastic DWV *Replace* Materials ....220.00 Labor 339.00	ea	–	$559.00	$559.00
Rough plumbing, bathtub or shower, copper supply, cast-iron DWV *Replace* Materials ....260.00 Labor.........354.00	ea	–	$614.00	$614.00
Rough plumbing, toilet, plastic supply & plastic DWV *Replace* Materials.....155.00 Labor.........273.00	ea	–	$428.00	$428.00
Rough plumbing, toilet, copper supply & plastic DWV *Replace* Materials.....190.00 Labor 290.00	ea	–	$480.00	$480.00
Rough plumbing, toilet, copper supply & cast-iron DWV *Replace* Materials ....225.00 Labor.........301.00	ea	–	$526.00	$526.00
Rough plumbing, bidet, plastic supply & plastic DWV *Replace* Materials.....175.00 Labor.........303.00	ea	–	$478.00	$478.00

◀ **ROUGH PLUMBING WET BAR SINK**
Rough plumbing for one hole bar sink. For feeds only see page 375. For wet bar sink faucets see page 370 and 384. For wet bar sinks see page 374.

◀ **ROUGH PLUMBING BATHROOM SINK**
Rough plumbing for one hole bathroom sink. For feeds only see page 375. For bathroom sink faucets see page 368 and 384. For bathroom sinks see page 371 and 385.

◀ **ROUGH PLUMBING KITCHEN SINK**
Rough plumbing for one, two or three hole kitchen sink. For feeds only see page 375. For kitchen sink faucets see page 369 and 384. For kitchen sinks see page 373.

◀ **ROUGH PLUMBING LAUNDRY SINK**
For one or two hole laundry sink. For feeds only see page 375. For laundry sink faucets see page 369. For laundry sinks see page 374.

◀ **ROUGH PLUMBING BATHTUB OR SHOWER**
For bathtub and shower faucets see page 370 and 384-385. For bathtubs see page 377 and 387. For showers see page 387.

◀ **ROUGH PLUMBING TOILET**
For toilets see page 376 and 386.

RELATED ITEMS
Bathroom Hardware......41
Cleaning 64

◀ **ROUGH PLUMBING BIDET**
For bidets see page 376.

	Item Description	Unit	Remove	Replace	Total
ROUGH PLUMBING ► **BIDET** *continued*	**Rough plumbing, bidet, copper supply & plastic DWV** *Replace* Materials.....215.00 Labor 322.00	ea	–	$537.00	$537.00
	Rough plumbing, bidet, copper supply & cast iron DWV *Replace* Materials ....255.00 Labor 333.00	ea	–	$588.00	$588.00
ROUGH PLUMBING ► **CLOTHES WASHER** *Includes supply valves* *and recessed wall box.* *For clothes washers* *see page 31.*	**Rough plumbing, clothes washer, plastic supply & plastic DWV** *Replace* Materials.....125.00 Labor 339.00	ea	–	$464.00	$464.00
	Rough plumbing, clothes washer, copper supply & plastic DWV *Replace* Materials ...150.00 Labor.........351.00	ea	–	$501.00	$501.00
	Rough plumbing, clothes washer, copper supply & cast iron DWV *Replace* Materials ...180.00 Labor.........362.00	ea	–	$542.00	$542.00
ROUGH PLUMBING ► **DISHWASHER** *Connection from kitchen* *sink (see previous page)* *to dishwasher. For dish-* *washers see* *page 26.*	**Rough plumbing, dishwasher, plastic supply & plastic DWV** *Replace* Materials......22.00 Labor 64.90	ea	–	$86.90	$86.90
	Rough plumbing, dishwasher, copper supply & plastic DWV *Replace* Materials ......27.00 Labor...........69.60	ea	–	$96.60	$96.60
	Rough plumbing, dishwasher, copper supply & cast iron DWV *Replace* Materials ......33.00 Labor...........74.30	ea	–	$107.30	$107.30
ROUGH PLUMBING ► **HOSE BIBB** *Freeze-proof hose bibb.*	**Cold water plastic supply line for exterior hose bibb** *Replace* Materials ......74.00 Labor..........166.00	ea	–	$240.00	$240.00
	Cold water copper supply line for exterior hose bibb *Replace* Materials ....100.00 Labor..........164.00	ea	–	$264.00	$264.00
ROUGH PLUMBING ► **EVAP. COOLER**	**Cold water copper supply line for evaporative cooler** *Replace* Materials ......56.00 Labor 125.00	ea	–	$181.00	$181.00
ROUGH PLUMBING ► **ICE MAKER** *Supply lines only. For* *supply line installation* *including hookup see* *Appliances on page 31.*	**Cold water plastic supply line for refrigerator ice maker** *Replace* Materials ......14.00 Labor...........98.10	ea	–	$112.10	$112.10
	Cold water copper supply line for refrigerator ice maker *Replace* Materials ......35.00 Labor.........103.00	ea	–	$138.00	$138.00
ROUGH PLUMBING ► **FLOOR DRAIN**	**Drain lines for in-floor French drain** *Replace* Materials ....105.00 Labor ....151.00 ► Includes drain, up to 12 lf drain pipe, and two cubic yard gravel drain field. Does not include excavation or backfill.	ea	–	$256.00	$256.00
	Drain lines for in-floor drain connected to sewer *Replace* Materials ....255.00 Labor..........246.00 ► Includes drain, up to 32 lf drain pipe. Does not include excavation or backfill.	ea	–	$501.00	$501.00
BATHROOM SINK ► **FAUCET** *For antique style faucets* *see page 384. For* *bathroom sink rough* *plumbing see page 367.* *For bathroom sinks see* *page 371 and 385.*	**Bathroom sink faucet, economy grade** *Replace* Materials ....95.00 Labor............26.00 *Remove* .... Labor............10.30	ea	$10.30	$121.00	$131.30
	Bathroom sink faucet, standard grade *Replace* Materials.....175.00 Labor............26.00 *Remove* .... Labor............10.30	ea	$10.30	$201.00	$211.30
	Bathroom sink faucet, high grade *Replace* Materials ....335.00 Labor............26.00 *Remove* .... Labor............10.30	ea	$10.30	$361.00	$371.30

Item Description	Unit	Remove	Replace	Total
Bathroom sink faucet, deluxe grade	ea	$10.30	$601.00	$611.30
Replace Materials ....575.00 Labor...........26.00				
Remove .... Labor...........10.30				
Remove bathroom sink faucet for work, then reinstall	ea	–	$38.90	$38.90
Replace .... Labor 38.90				
Bidet faucet, standard grade	ea	$10.30	$317.80	$328.10
Replace Materials....290.00 Labor...........27.80				
Remove .... Labor...........10.30				
Bidet faucet, high grade	ea	$10.30	$487.80	$498.10
Replace Materials....460.00 Labor...........27.80				
Remove .... Labor...........10.30				
Bidet faucet, deluxe grade	ea	$10.30	$782.80	$793.10
Replace Materials ....755.00 Labor...........27.80				
Remove .... Labor...........10.30				
Remove bidet faucet for work, then reinstall	ea	–	$40.60	$40.60
Replace .... Labor 40.60				
Kitchen sink faucet, economy grade	ea	$10.30	$136.20	$146.50
Replace Materials.....110.00 Labor...........26.20				
Remove .... Labor...........10.30				
Kitchen sink faucet, standard grade	ea	$10.30	$221.20	$231.50
Replace Materials.....195.00 Labor...........26.20				
Remove .... Labor...........10.30				
Kitchen sink faucet, high grade	ea	$10.30	$401.20	$411.50
Replace Materials ....375.00 Labor...........26.20				
Remove .... Labor...........10.30				
Kitchen sink faucet, deluxe grade	ea	$10.30	$666.20	$676.50
Replace Materials....640.00 Labor...........26.20				
Remove .... Labor...........10.30				
Remove kitchen sink faucet for work, then reinstall	ea	–	$39.60	$39.60
Replace .... Labor 39.60				
Laundry sink faucet, economy grade	ea	$10.30	$85.50	$95.80
Replace Materials......60.00 Labor 25.50				
Remove .... Labor...........10.30				
Laundry sink faucet, standard grade	ea	$10.30	$130.50	$140.80
Replace Materials ....105.00 Labor 25.50				
Remove .... Labor...........10.30				
Laundry sink faucet, high grade	ea	$10.30	$175.50	$185.80
Replace Materials ....150.00 Labor 25.50				
Remove .... Labor...........10.30				
Laundry sink faucet, deluxe grade	ea	$10.30	$285.50	$295.80
Replace Materials ....260.00 Labor 25.50				
Remove .... Labor...........10.30				
Remove laundry sink faucet for work, then reinstall	ea	–	$38.30	$38.30
Replace .... Labor 38.30				

RELATED ITEMS

Bathroom Hardware......41

Cleaning 64

◁ remove & reinstall

◀ **BIDET FAUCET**
For rough plumbing see page 367. For bidets see page 376.

◁ remove & reinstall

◀ **KITCHEN SINK FAUCET**
For antique style faucets see page 384. For rough plumbing see page 367. For kitchen sinks see page 373.

◁ remove & reinstall

◀ **LAUNDRY SINK FAUCET**
For rough plumbing see page 367. For laundry sinks see page 374.

FAUCET QUALITY

Some faucet quality rules of thumb:

Economy: Light gauge metal, chrome plated. May have some plastic components. Little or no pattern.

Standard: Heavier gauge metal, chrome or brass plated with little or no pattern or with wood handles made of ash or oak.

continued on next page

Item Description	Unit	Remove	Replace	Total
SHOWER FAUCET ▶ *For rough plumbing see page 367. For shower stalls and bathtub surrounds see page 378 and page 491.* **Shower faucet, economy grade** *Replace* Materials ....130.00 Labor............26.90 *Remove* ....Labor............10.30	ea	$10.30	$156.90	$167.20
Shower faucet, standard grade *Replace* Materials ....235.00 Labor............26.90 *Remove* ....Labor............10.30	ea	$10.30	$261.90	$272.20
FAUCET QUALITY *continued* **High:** *Brass, chrome over brass, or nickel over brass with minimal detail or plated hardware with ornate detail, or with European style plastic or porcelain components.* **Shower faucet, high grade** *Replace* Materials....400.00 Labor............26.90 *Remove* ....Labor............10.30	ea	$10.30	$426.90	$437.20
Deluxe: *Brass, chrome over brass, or nickel over brass with ornate detail.* **Shower faucet, deluxe grade** *Replace* Materials ...595.00 Labor............26.90 *Remove* ....Labor............10.30	ea	$10.30	$621.90	$632.20
Remove shower faucet for work, then reinstall *Replace* ....Labor............41.30	ea	–	$41.30	$41.30
BATHTUB FAUCET ▶ *For antique style faucets see page 384. For rough plumbing see page 367. For bathtubs see page 377 and page 386.* **Bathtub faucet, economy grade** *Replace* Materials.....145.00 Labor............26.50 *Remove* ....Labor............10.30	ea	$10.30	$171.50	$181.80
Bathtub faucet, standard grade *Replace* Materials ....265.00 Labor............26.50 *Remove* ....Labor............10.30	ea	$10.30	$291.50	$301.80
Bathtub faucet, high grade *Replace* Materials ....450.00 Labor............26.50 *Remove* ....Labor............10.30	ea	$10.30	$476.50	$486.80
Bathtub faucet, deluxe grade *Replace* Materials ....665.00 Labor............26.50 *Remove* ....Labor............10.30	ea	$10.30	$691.50	$701.80
remove & reinstall ▷ **Remove bathtub faucet for work, then reinstall** *Replace* ....Labor............41.00	ea	–	$41.00	$41.00
BATHUB WITH ▶ SHOWER FAUCET *For antique style faucets see page 384. For rough plumbing see page 367. For bathtubs see page 377 and page 386.* **Bathtub with shower faucet, economy grade** *Replace* Materials.....160.00 Labor ....28.30 *Remove* ....Labor 11.60	ea	$11.60	$188.30	$199.90
Bathtub with shower faucet, standard grade *Replace* Materials....290.00 Labor ....28.30 *Remove* ....Labor 11.60	ea	$11.60	$318.30	$329.90
Bathtub with shower faucet, high grade *Replace* Materials ....490.00 Labor ....28.30 *Remove* ....Labor 11.60	ea	$11.60	$518.30	$529.90
Bathub with shower faucet, deluxe grade *Replace* Materials ....730.00 Labor ....28.30 *Remove* ....Labor 11.60	ea	$11.60	$758.30	$769.90
remove & reinstall ▷ **Remove bathtub with shower faucet for work, then reinstall** *Replace* ....Labor............42.10	ea	–	$42.10	$42.10
WET BAR SINK ▶ FAUCET *For rough plumbing see page 367. For wet bar sink see page 374.* **Wet bar sink faucet, economy grade** *Replace* Materials ......85.00 Labor ....25.30 *Remove* ....Labor...........10.30	ea	$10.30	$110.30	$120.60

Item Description	Unit	Remove	Replace	Total	
Wet bar sink faucet, standard grade	ea	$10.30	$180.30	$190.60	
Replace Materials.....155.00 Labor 25.30					
Remove .... Labor...........10.30					
Wet bar sink faucet, high grade	ea	$10.30	$320.30	$330.60	
Replace Materials ....295.00 Labor 25.30					
Remove .... Labor...........10.30					
Wet bar sink faucet, deluxe grade	ea	$10.30	$535.30	$545.60	
Replace Materials.....510.00 Labor 25.30					
Remove .... Labor...........10.30					
Remove wet bar sink faucet for work, then reinstall	ea	–	$37.40	$37.40	◁ remove & reinstall
Replace .... Labor..........37.40					
Refurbish and repack faucet	ea	–	$41.20	$41.20	◀ **REPACK FAUCET**
Replace Materials......20.00 Labor..........21.20					
Bathroom oval sink, wall-hung porcelain-enamel cast iron	ea	$10.60	$466.00	$476.60	◀ **BATHROOM SINK**
Replace Materials ....425.00 Labor..........41.00					With visible plumbing including water feeds, P trap,
Remove .... Labor...........10.60					escutcheons, and so forth,
Bathroom round sink, wall-hung porcelain-enamel cast iron	ea	$10.60	$461.00	$471.60	to wall or floor. Does not
Replace Materials ....420.00 Labor..........41.00					include faucet. For rough
Remove .... Labor...........10.60					plumbing see page 367.
Bathroom hexagonal sink, wall-hung porcelain-enamel cast iron	ea	$10.60	$496.00	$506.60	For bathroom sink faucets see page 368.
Replace Materials.....455.00 Labor..........41.00					
Remove .... Labor...........10.60					◁ wall-hung
Bathroom oval sink, wall-hung porcelain-enamel steel	ea	$10.60	$396.00	$406.60	
Replace Materials ....355.00 Labor..........41.00					
Remove .... Labor...........10.60					
Bathroom round sink, wall-hung porcelain-enamel steel	ea	$10.60	$391.00	$401.60	
Replace Materials ....350.00 Labor..........41.00					
Remove .... Labor...........10.60					
Bathroom hexagonal sink, wall-hung porcelain-enamel steel	ea	$10.60	$421.00	$431.60	
Replace Materials ....380.00 Labor..........41.00					
Remove .... Labor...........10.60					
Bathroom oval sink, wall-hung vitreous china	ea	$10.60	$386.00	$396.60	
Replace Materials ....345.00 Labor..........41.00					
Remove .... Labor...........10.60					
Bathroom oval sink, wall-hung vitreous china with pattern	ea	$10.60	$491.00	$501.60	
Replace Materials ....450.00 Labor..........41.00					
Remove .... Labor...........10.60					
Bathroom round sink, wall-hung vitreous china	ea	$10.60	$381.00	$391.60	
Replace Materials....340.00 Labor..........41.00					
Remove .... Labor...........10.60					
Bathroom round sink, wall-hung vitreous china with pattern	ea	$10.60	$481.00	$491.60	
Replace Materials....440.00 Labor..........41.00					
Remove .... Labor...........10.60					
Bathroom hexagonal sink, wall-hung vitreous china	ea	$10.60	$391.00	$401.60	
Replace Materials....350.00 Labor..........41.00					
Remove .... Labor...........10.60					

RELATED ITEMS

Bathroom Hardware......41
Cleaning 64

	Item Description		Unit	Remove	Replace	Total
BATHROOM SINK ▶ continued	**Remove wall-hung bathroom sink for work, then reinstall**		ea	–	$50.90	$50.90
	Replace	Labor 50.90				
self-rimming ▷	**Bathroom oval sink, self-rimming vitreous china**		ea	$10.60	$352.50	$363.10
	Replace Materials.....310.00	Labor..........42.50				
	Remove	Labor..........10.60				
	Bathroom oval sink, self-rimming vitreous china with pattern		ea	$10.60	$447.50	$458.10
	Replace Materials....405.00	Labor..........42.50				
	Remove	Labor..........10.60				
	Bathroom round sink, self-rimming vitreous china		ea	$10.60	$347.50	$358.10
	Replace Materials....305.00	Labor..........42.50				
	Remove	Labor..........10.60				
	Bathroom round sink, self-rimming vitreous china with pattern		ea	$10.60	$437.50	$448.10
	Replace Materials 395.00	Labor..........42.50				
	Remove	Labor..........10.60				
	Bathroom hexagonal sink, self-rimming vitreous china		ea	$10.60	$357.50	$368.10
	Replace Materials.....315.00	Labor..........42.50				
	Remove	Labor..........10.60				
	Bathroom oval sink, self-rimming stainless steel		ea	$10.60	$372.50	$383.10
	Replace Materials....330.00	Labor..........42.50				
	Remove	Labor..........10.60				
	Bathroom oval sink, self-rimming scalloped stainless steel		ea	$10.60	$422.50	$433.10
	Replace Materials....380.00	Labor..........42.50				
	Remove	Labor..........10.60				
	Bathroom oval sink, self-rimming polished brass		ea	$10.60	$412.50	$423.10
	Replace Materials 370.00	Labor..........42.50				
	Remove	Labor..........10.60				
	Bathroom oval sink, self-rimming hammered finish brass		ea	$10.60	$462.50	$473.10
	Replace Materials 420.00	Labor..........42.50				
	Remove	Labor 9.04				
	Bathroom oval sink, self-rimming scalloped polished brass		ea	$10.60	$502.50	$513.10
	Replace Materials....460.00	Labor..........42.50				
	Remove	Labor..........10.60				
	Remove self-rimming bathroom sink for work, then reinstall		ea	–	$53.20	$53.20
	Replace	Labor 53.20				
under-counter ▷	**Bathroom oval sink, under-counter vitreous china**		ea	$10.60	$369.50	$380.10
	Replace Materials 325.00	Labor 44.50				
	Remove	Labor..........10.60				
	Bathroom oval sink, under-counter vitreous china with pattern		ea	$10.60	$469.50	$480.10
	Replace Materials 425.00	Labor 44.50				
	Remove	Labor..........10.60				
	Bathroom round sink, under-counter vitreous china		ea	$10.60	$364.50	$375.10
	Replace Materials 320.00	Labor 44.50				
	Remove	Labor..........10.60				
	Bathroom round sink, under-counter vitreous china with pattern		ea	$10.60	$459.50	$470.10
	Replace Materials.....415.00	Labor 44.50				
	Remove	Labor..........10.60				

Item Description	Unit	Remove	Replace	Total
Bathroom hexagonal sink, under-counter vitreous china	ea	$10.60	$374.50	$385.10
Replace Materials ....330.00 Labor 44.50				
Remove .... Labor...........10.60				
Remove under-counter bathroom sink for work, then reinstall	ea	–	$55.10	$55.10
Replace .... Labor...........55.10				
24" by 21" single-bowl porcelain-enamel, cast-iron kitchen sink	ea	$10.70	$378.20	$388.90
Replace Materials ....335.00 Labor 43.20				
Remove .... Labor...........10.70				
30" by 21" single-bowl porcelain-enamel, cast-iron kitchen sink	ea	$10.70	$458.20	$468.90
Replace Materials .....415.00 Labor 43.20				
Remove .... Labor...........10.70				
32" by 21" double-bowl porcelain-enamel, cast-iron kitchen sink	ea	$10.70	$538.20	$548.90
Replace Materials ....495.00 Labor 43.20				
Remove .... Labor...........10.70				
42" by 21" triple-bowl porcelain-enamel, cast-iron kitchen sink	ea	$10.70	$1,143.20	$1,153.90
Replace Materials ...1100.00 Labor 43.20				
Remove .... Labor...........10.70				
24" by 21" single-bowl porcelain-enamel, steel kitchen sink	ea	$10.70	$213.20	$223.90
Replace Materials .....170.00 Labor 43.20				
Remove .... Labor...........10.70				
30" by 21" single-bowl porcelain-enamel, steel kitchen sink	ea	$10.70	$243.20	$253.90
Replace Materials ....200.00 Labor 43.20				
Remove .... Labor...........10.70				
32" by 21" double-bowl porcelain-enamel, steel kitchen sink	ea	$10.70	$248.20	$258.90
Replace Materials ....205.00 Labor 43.20				
Remove .... Labor...........10.70				
42" by 21" triple-bowl porcelain-enamel, steel kitchen sink	ea	$10.70	$968.20	$978.90
Replace Materials ....925.00 Labor 43.20				
Remove .... Labor...........10.70				
19" by 18" single-bowl stainless steel kitchen sink	ea	$10.70	$298.20	$308.90
Replace Materials ....255.00 Labor 43.20				
Remove .... Labor...........10.70				
25" by 22" single-bowl stainless steel kitchen sink	ea	$10.70	$318.20	$328.90
Replace Materials ....275.00 Labor 43.20				
Remove .... Labor...........10.70				
33" by 22" double-bowl stainless steel kitchen sink	ea	$10.70	$413.20	$423.90
Replace Materials ....370.00 Labor 43.20				
Remove .... Labor...........10.70				
43" by 22" double-bowl stainless steel kitchen sink	ea	$10.70	$438.20	$448.90
Replace Materials ....395.00 Labor 43.20				
Remove .... Labor...........10.70				
43" by 22" triple-bowl stainless steel kitchen sink	ea	$10.70	$568.20	$578.90
Replace Materials ....525.00 Labor 43.20				
Remove .... Labor...........10.70				
Remove kitchen sink for work, then reinstall	ea	–	$51.80	$51.80
Replace .... Labor...........51.80				

RELATED ITEMS

Bathroom Hardware......41
Cleaning 64

◄ **KITCHEN SINK**
With visible plumbing including water feeds, P trap, escutcheons, and so forth, to wall or floor. Does not include faucet. For rough plumbing see page 367. For kitchen sink faucets see page 369.

◁ remove & reinstall

Item Description	Unit	Remove	Replace	Total
LAUNDRY SINK ▶ *With visible plumbing including water feeds, P trap, escutcheons, and so forth, to wall or floor. Does not include faucet. For rough plumbing see page 367. For laundry sink faucet see page 369.*				
22" x 17" single-bowl stainless steel laundry sink in countertop	ea	$10.70	$407.10	$417.80
Replace Materials ....365.00 Labor............42.10				
Remove .... Labor............10.70				
19" x 22" single-bowl stainless steel laundry sink in countertop	ea	$10.70	$427.10	$437.80
Replace Materials ....385.00 Labor............42.10				
Remove .... Labor............10.70				
33" x 22" double-bowl stainless steel laundry sink in countertop	ea	$10.70	$457.10	$467.80
Replace Materials .....415.00 Labor............42.10				
Remove .... Labor............10.70				
porcelain-enamel ▷ **24" x 20" single-bowl porcelain-enamel, cast-iron laundry sink on iron frame**	ea	$10.70	$548.90	$559.60
Replace Materials.....510.00 Labor............38.90				
Remove .... Labor............10.70				
24" x 23" single-bowl porcelain-enamel, cast-iron laundry sink on iron frame	ea	$10.70	$588.90	$599.60
Replace Materials.....550.00 Labor............38.90				
Remove .... Labor............10.70				
plastic ▷ **18" x 23" single-bowl plastic laundry sink on plastic legs**	ea	$10.70	$173.90	$184.60
Replace Materials.....135.00 Labor............38.90				
Remove .... Labor............10.70				
20" x 24" single-bowl plastic laundry sink on plastic legs	ea	$10.70	$213.90	$224.60
Replace Materials.....175.00 Labor............38.90				
Remove .... Labor............10.70				
36" x 23" double-bowl plastic laundry sink on plastic legs	ea	$10.70	$248.90	$259.60
Replace Materials.....210.00 Labor............38.90				
Remove .... Labor............10.70				
40" x 24" double-bowl plastic laundry sink on plastic legs	ea	$10.70	$328.90	$339.60
Replace Materials....290.00 Labor............38.90				
Remove .... Labor............10.70				
remove & reinstall ▷ **Remove laundry sink for work, then reinstall**	ea	—	$52.30	$52.30
Replace .... Labor............52.30				
WET BAR SINK ▶ *With visible plumbing including water feeds, P trap, escutcheons, and so forth to wall or floor. Does not include faucet. For rough plumbing see page 367. For wet bar sink faucet see page 370.* **Wet bar sink, self-rimming vitreous china**	ea	$10.30	$587.50	$597.80
Replace Materials ....545.00 Labor............42.50				
Remove .... Labor............10.30				
Wet bar sink, self-rimming vitreous china with pattern	ea	$10.30	$687.50	$697.80
Replace Materials ....645.00 Labor............42.50				
Remove .... Labor............10.30				
self-rimming ▷ **Wet bar sink, self-rimming porcelain-enamel cast iron**	ea	$10.30	$477.50	$487.80
Replace Materials ....435.00 Labor............42.50				
Remove .... Labor............10.30				
Wet bar sink, self-rimming porcelain-enamel steel	ea	$10.30	$287.50	$297.80
Replace Materials.....245.00 Labor............42.50				
Remove .... Labor............10.30				
Wet bar sink, self-rimming stainless steel	ea	$10.30	$232.50	$242.80
Replace Materials.....190.00 Labor............42.50				
Remove .... Labor............10.30				
Wet bar sink, self-rimming scalloped stainless steel	ea	$10.30	$317.50	$327.80
Replace Materials ....275.00 Labor............42.50				
Remove .... Labor............10.30				

Item Description	Unit	Remove	Replace	Total	
Wet bar sink, self-rimming polished brass	ea	$10.30	$422.50	$432.80	**RELATED ITEMS**
Replace Materials....380.00 Labor..........42.50					Bathroom Hardware......41
Remove .... Labor..........10.30					Cleaning 64
Wet bar sink, self-rimming hammered finish brass	ea	$10.30	$477.50	$487.80	
Replace Materials....435.00 Labor..........42.50					
Remove .... Labor..........10.30					
Wet bar sink, self-rimming scalloped polished brass	ea	$10.30	$527.50	$537.80	
Replace Materials....485.00 Labor..........42.50					
Remove .... Labor..........10.30					
Remove self-rimming wet bar sink for work, then reinstall	ea	–	$53.20	$53.20	
Replace .... Labor 53.20					
Wet bar sink, under-counter vitreous china	ea	$10.30	$389.50	$399.80	◁ under-counter
Replace Materials....345.00 Labor..........44.50					
Remove .... Labor..........10.30					
Wet bar sink, under-counter vitreous china with pattern	ea	$10.30	$489.50	$499.80	
Replace Materials....445.00 Labor..........44.50					
Remove .... Labor..........10.30					
Wet bar sink, under-counter porcelain enamel cast iron	ea	$10.30	$469.50	$479.80	
Replace Materials....425.00 Labor..........44.50					
Remove .... Labor..........10.30					
Wet bar sink, under-counter porcelain enamel steel	ea	$10.30	$284.50	$294.80	
Replace Materials....240.00 Labor..........44.50					
Remove .... Labor..........10.30					
Wet bar sink, under-counter stainless steel	ea	$10.30	$229.50	$239.80	
Replace Materials....185.00 Labor..........44.50					
Remove .... Labor..........10.30					
Wet bar sink, under-counter scalloped stainless steel	ea	$10.30	$314.50	$324.80	
Replace Materials....270.00 Labor..........44.50					
Remove .... Labor..........8.84					
Wet bar sink, under-counter polished brass	ea	$10.30	$414.50	$424.80	
Replace Materials....370.00 Labor..........44.50					
Remove .... Labor..........10.30					
Wet bar sink, under-counter hammered finish brass	ea	$10.30	$464.50	$474.80	
Replace Materials....420.00 Labor..........44.50					
Remove .... Labor..........10.30					
Wet bar sink, under-counter scalloped polished brass	ea	$10.30	$514.50	$524.80	
Replace Materials....470.00 Labor..........44.50					
Remove .... Labor..........10.30					
Remove under-counter wet bar sink for work, then reinstall	ea	–	$55.10	$55.10	
Replace .... Labor..........55.10					
Add for brass supply and waste lines	ea	–	$134.00	$134.00	◀ **ADDITIONAL**
					SINK COSTS
Add 33% for almond colored porcelain enamel					
Add 65% for colored porcelain enamel					
Sink plumbing, chrome	ea	–	$142.20	$142.20	◀ **SINK PLUMBING**
Replace Materials....120.00 Labor 22.20					*continued on next page*

Item Description	Unit	Remove	Replace	Total
SINK PLUMBING ▶				
With visible plumbing including water feeds, P trap, escutcheons, and so forth, to wall or floor. Does not include faucet.				
Sink plumbing, brass	ea	–	$217.20	$217.20
Replace Materials.....195.00 Labor..........22.20				
Sink plumbing, chrome-plated brass	ea	–	$267.20	$267.20
Replace Materials.....245.00 Labor..........22.20				
TOILET PLUMBING ▶				
Includes cold water supply, shut-off valve, wax ring, and toilet bolts.				
Toilet plumbing, chrome	ea	–	$96.10	$96.10
Replace Materials......80.00 Labor..........16.10				
Toilet plumbing, brass	ea	–	$146.10	$146.10
Replace Materials ...130.00 Labor..........16.10				
BIDET ▶				
Includes water supply lines with shut-off valves. For rough plumbing see page 367. For bidet faucet see page 369.				
Bidet, standard grade	ea	$10.40	$463.60	$474.00
Replace Materials ...395.00 Labor 68.60				
Remove .... Labor..........10.40				
Bidet, deluxe grade	ea	$10.40	$653.60	$664.00
Replace Materials ...585.00 Labor 68.60				
Remove .... Labor..........10.40				
remove & reinstall ▷				
Remove bidet for work, then reinstall	ea	–	$112.93	$112.93
Replace Materials.........1.93 Labor..........111.00				
TOILET ▶				
Economy grade toilets are typically white with round bowls. Standard grade toilets are typically white with elongated bowls. High and deluxe grades are typically low-tank toilets, in a variety of colors, with elongated bowls. Deluxe grade may also be "jet" toilets which combine low-water consumption with a direct-fed jet, siphon-assisted blow out action. For rough plumbing see page 367. For antique styles see page 386.				
Toilet, economy grade	ea	$10.00	$217.10	$227.10
Replace Materials......155.00 Labor..........62.10				
Remove .... Labor..........10.00				
Toilet, standard grade	ea	$10.00	$247.10	$257.10
Replace Materials......185.00 Labor..........62.10				
Remove .... Labor..........10.00				
Toilet, high grade	ea	$10.00	$332.10	$342.10
Replace Materials ....270.00 Labor..........62.10				
Remove .... Labor..........10.00				
Toilet, deluxe grade	ea	$10.00	$527.10	$537.10
Replace Materials......465.00 Labor..........62.10				
Remove .... Labor..........10.00				
Remove toilet for work, then reinstall	ea	–	$102.93	$102.93
Replace Materials.........1.93 Labor..........101.00				
TOILET SEAT ▶				
Toilet seat, plain round	ea	$4.02	$35.40	$39.42
Replace Materials......25.00 Labor..........10.40				
Remove .... Labor 4.02				
Toilet seat, hardwood	ea	$4.02	$35.40	$39.42
Replace Materials......25.00 Labor..........10.40				
Remove .... Labor 4.02				
Toilet seat, with pattern	ea	$4.02	$50.40	$54.42
Replace Materials......40.00 Labor..........10.40				
Remove .... Labor 4.02				
Toilet seat, elongated	ea	$4.02	$65.40	$69.42
Replace Materials ......55.00 Labor..........10.40				
Remove .... Labor 4.02				
Toilet seat, padded	ea	$4.02	$55.40	$59.42
Replace Materials ......45.00 Labor..........10.40				
Remove .... Labor 4.02				

Item Description	Unit	Remove	Replace	Total
Remove toilet seat for work, then reinstall	ea	–	$15.10	$15.10
Replace .... Labor 15.10				
48" long by 44" deep cast-iron corner bathtub	ea	$46.50	$1,937.00	$1,983.50
Replace Materials ..1800.00 Labor 137.00				
Remove .... Labor 46.50				
48" long by 44" deep acrylic fiberglass corner bathtub	ea	$29.50	$818.60	$848.10
Replace Materials ....735.00 Labor 83.60				
Remove .... Labor 29.50				
60" long by 32" deep acrylic fiberglass bathtub	ea	$29.50	$413.60	$443.10
Replace Materials ....330.00 Labor 83.60				
Remove .... Labor 29.50				
60" long by 32" deep porcelain-enamel, cast-iron bathtub	ea	$46.50	$947.00	$993.50
Replace Materials .....810.00 Labor 137.00				
Remove .... Labor 46.50				
60" long by 32" deep porcelain-enamel, steel bathtub	ea	$46.50	$462.00	$508.50
Replace Materials ....325.00 Labor 137.00				
Remove .... Labor 46.50				
72" long by 36" deep acrylic fiberglass bathtub	ea	$29.50	$778.60	$808.10
Replace Materials ....695.00 Labor 83.60				
Remove .... Labor 29.50				
72" long by 36" deep porcelain-enamel, cast-iron bathtub	ea	$46.50	$1,837.00	$1,883.50
Replace Materials ...1700.00 Labor 137.00				
Remove .... Labor 46.50				
72" long by 36" deep porcelain-enamel, steel bathtub	ea	$46.50	$657.00	$703.50
Replace Materials ....520.00 Labor 137.00				
Remove .... Labor 46.50				
Remove fiberglass bathtub for work, then reinstall	ea	–	$161.00	$161.00
Replace .... Labor 161.00				
Remove cast-iron or steel bathtub for work, then reinstall	ea	–	$246.00	$246.00
Replace .... Labor 246.00				
60" long by 32" deep acrylic fiberglass bathtub with whirlpool jets	ea	$41.90	$1,861.00	$1,902.90
Replace Materials ...1700.00 Labor 161.00				
Remove .... Labor 41.90				
60" long by 32" deep porcelain-enamel, cast-iron bathtub with whirlpool jets	ea	$61.60	$4,287.00	$4,348.60
Replace Materials ...4100.00 Labor 187.00				
Remove .... Labor 61.60				
72" long by 36" deep acrylic fiberglass bathtub with whirlpool jets	ea	$41.90	$3,711.00	$3,752.90
Replace Materials ..3550.00 Labor 161.00				
Remove .... Labor 41.90				
72" long by 36" deep porcelain-enamel, cast-iron bathtub with whirlpool jets	ea	$61.60	$8,687.00	$8,748.60
Replace Materials ..8500.00 Labor 187.00				
Remove .... Labor 61.60				
66" long by 48" deep fiberglass bathtub with whirlpool jets	ea	$41.90	$3,311.00	$3,352.90
Replace Materials ...3150.00 Labor 161.00				
Remove .... Labor 41.90				

◄ **BATHTUB**
Includes standard chrome drain and overflow assembly. Does not include faucet. For rough plumbing see page 367. For bathtub faucets see page 370. For antique style bathtubs see page 386. For antique style faucets see page 384.

◁ *remove & reinstall*

◄ **BATHTUB WITH WHIRLPOOL JETS**
Includes standard chrome drain and overflow assembly and jets and electrical pump hookup. Does not include faucet or electrical rough wiring. For rough plumbing see page 367. For bathtub faucets see page 370. For antique style bathtubs see page 386. For antique style faucets see page 384.

RELATED ITEMS
Bathroom Hardware......41
Cleaning 64

Item Description	Unit	Remove	Replace	Total
BATHTUB WITH ▶ **WHIRLPOOL JETS** *continued*				
72" long by 36" deep fiberglass bathtub with whirlpool jets	ea	$41.90	$3,161.00	$3,202.90
Replace Materials..3000.00 Labor 161.00				
Remove .... Labor 41.90				
60" long by 30" deep fiberglass bathtub with whirlpool jets	ea	$41.90	$2,511.00	$2,552.90
Replace Materials ..2350.00 Labor 161.00				
Remove .... Labor 41.90				
72" long by 42" deep fiberglass bathtub with whirlpool jets	ea	$41.90	$3,911.00	$3,952.90
Replace Materials ..3750.00 Labor 161.00				
Remove .... Labor 41.90				
83" long by 65" deep fiberglass bathtub with whirlpool jets	ea	$41.90	$6,611.00	$6,652.90
Replace Materials ..6450.00 Labor 161.00				
Remove .... Labor 41.90				
▷ *remove & reinstall* **Remove fiberglass bathtub with whirlpool jets for work, then reinstall**	ea	–	$311.00	$311.00
Replace .... Labor 311.00				
Remove cast iron bathtub with whirlpool jets for work, then reinstall	ea	–	$425.00	$425.00
Replace .... Labor 425.00				
BATHTUB & ▶ **SHOWER** **Acrylic fiberglass bathtub & shower combination, standard grade**	ea	$48.80	$606.00	$654.80
Replace Materials.....455.00 Labor 151.00				
Remove .... Labor 48.80				
Acrylic fiberglass bathtub & shower combination, high grade	ea	$48.80	$871.00	$919.80
Replace Materials ....720.00 Labor 151.00				
Remove .... Labor 48.80				
Acrylic fiberglass bathtub & shower combination, deluxe grade	ea	$48.80	$1,061.00	$1,109.80
Replace Materials.....910.00 Labor 151.00				
Remove .... Labor 48.80				
Remove fiberglass bathtub & shower combination for work, then reinstall	ea	–	$260.00	$260.00
Replace .... Labor.........260.00				
SHOWER STALL ▶ **32" wide by 32" deep acrylic fiberglass shower stall**	ea	$35.30	$506.00	$541.30
Replace Materials....380.00 Labor 126.00				
Remove .... Labor...........35.30				
32" wide by 32" deep acrylic fiberglass shower stall with terrazzo base	ea	$35.30	$581.00	$616.30
Replace Materials.....455.00 Labor 126.00				
Remove .... Labor...........35.30				
32" wide by 32" deep metal shower stall	ea	$35.30	$306.00	$341.30
Replace Materials ....180.00 Labor 126.00				
Remove .... Labor...........35.30				
48" wide by 35" deep acrylic fiberglass shower stall	ea	$35.30	$556.00	$591.30
Replace Materials....430.00 Labor 126.00				
Remove .... Labor...........35.30				
60" wide by 35" deep acrylic fiberglass shower stall	ea	$35.30	$601.00	$636.30
Replace Materials.....475.00 Labor 126.00				
Remove .... Labor...........35.30				
▷ *remove & reinstall* **Remove fiberglass shower stall for work, then reinstall**	ea	–	$203.00	$203.00
Replace .... Labor 203.00				
SHOWER PAN ▶ **Shower pan, typical size**	ea	–	$102.60	$102.60
Replace Materials ....55.00 Labor...........47.60				

BATHTUB & SHOWER side note: *Does not include faucet. High and deluxe quality usually indicates thicker fiberglass with glossier finishes and more ornate soap and wash cloth compartments. For rough plumbing see page 367. For bathtub faucets see page 370. For antique style bathtubs see page 386. For antique style faucets see page 384.*

SHOWER STALL side note: *Includes concrete reinforcement under base. Does not include faucet.*

SHOWER PAN side note: *Pan and drain for tile shower.*

Item Description	Unit	Remove	Replace	Total	
Shower pan, large size *Replace* Materials......85.00 Labor...........47.60	ea	–	$132.60	$132.60	
Shower base, fiberglass *Replace* Materials.....120.00 Labor...........49.00	ea	–	$169.00	$169.00	◄ **SHOWER BASE** *Prefabricated*
Shower base, terrazzo style *Replace* Materials....440.00 Labor...........49.00	ea	–	$489.00	$489.00	
Corner entry shower base, fiberglass *Replace* Materials.....145.00 Labor...........49.00	ea	–	$194.00	$194.00	
Corner entry shower base, terrazzo style *Replace* Materials....485.00 Labor...........49.00	ea	–	$534.00	$534.00	
Cultured stone bathtub surround *Replace* Materials....590.00 Labor.........93.40 *Remove* .... Labor...........25.80	ea	$25.80	$683.40	$709.20	◄ **BATHTUB SURROUND** *Three walls surrounding bathtub: two widths and one length. See bathtubs on page 377. For bathtub rough plumbing see page 367. For bathtub faucets see page 370. For antique style bathtubs see page 386. For antique style faucets see page 384.*
Fiberglass bathtub surround, standard grade *Replace* Materials....340.00 Labor.........71.90 *Remove* .... Labor...........25.80	ea	$25.80	$411.90	$437.70	
Fiberglass bathtub surround, high grade *Replace* Materials....535.00 Labor.........71.90 *Remove* .... Labor...........25.80	ea	$25.80	$606.90	$632.70	
Fiberglass bathtub surround, deluxe grade *Replace* Materials....770.00 Labor.........71.90 *Remove* .... Labor...........25.80	ea	$25.80	$841.90	$867.70	
Remove bathtub surround for work, then reinstall *Replace* .... Labor.........123.00	ea	–	$123.00	$123.00	◁ remove & reinstall
Glass shower, with cultured stone slabs on walls, standard grade *Replace* Materials....770.00 Labor.........109.00 *Remove* .... Labor...........35.30	ea	$35.30	$879.00	$914.30	◄ **GLASS SHOWER** *Cultured stone slabs or fiberglass panels on two walls, glass on one wall, and a glass door on one wall. Corner entry showers have two glass walls and a corner entry door.*
Glass shower, with cultured stone slabs on walls, high grade *Replace* Materials....845.00 Labor.........109.00 *Remove* .... Labor...........35.30	ea	$35.30	$954.00	$989.30	
Corner entry glass shower, cultured stone slabs on walls, standard grade *Replace* Materials..1000.00 Labor.........126.00 *Remove* .... Labor...........35.30	ea	$35.30	$1,126.00	$1,161.30	
Corner entry glass shower, cultured slabs on walls, high grade *Replace* Materials...1100.00 Labor.........126.00 *Remove* .... Labor...........35.30	ea	$35.30	$1,226.00	$1,261.30	
Glass shower, fiberglass panels on walls, standard grade *Replace* Materials...700.00 Labor...........97.10 *Remove* .... Labor...........35.30	ea	$35.30	$797.10	$832.40	
Glass shower, fiberglass panels on walls, high grade *Replace* Materials...770.00 Labor...........97.10 *Remove* .... Labor...........35.30	ea	$35.30	$867.10	$902.40	
Corner entry glass shower, fiberglass panels on walls, standard grade *Replace* Materials.....910.00 Labor.........114.00 *Remove* .... Labor...........35.30	ea	$35.30	$1,024.00	$1,059.30	

RELATED ITEMS

Bathroom Hardware.......41
Cleaning 64

	Item Description	Unit	Remove	Replace	Total
GLASS SHOWER ▶ continued	Corner entry glass shower, fiberglass panels on walls, high grade *Replace* Materials ..1000.00 Labor..........114.00 *Remove* .... Labor..........35.30	ea	$35.30	$1,114.00	$1,149.30
remove & reinstall ▷	Remove glass shower for work, then reinstall *Replace* .... Labor..........146.00	ea	–	$146.00	$146.00
SLIDING BATHTUB ▶ **DOOR** *See tubs on page 377.*	Sliding glass bathtub door, mill finish trim *Replace* Materials ....220.00 Labor ....64.00 *Remove* .... Labor 14.90	ea	$14.90	$284.00	$298.90
	Sliding glass bathtub door, mill finish trim with fancy glass *Replace* Materials ....275.00 Labor ....64.00 *Remove* .... Labor 14.90	ea	$14.90	$339.00	$353.90
	Sliding glass bathtub door, gold finish trim *Replace* Materials ....270.00 Labor ....64.00 *Remove* .... Labor 14.90	ea	$14.90	$334.00	$348.90
	Sliding glass bathtub door, gold finish trim with fancy glass *Replace* Materials ....335.00 Labor ....64.00 *Remove* .... Labor 14.90	ea	$14.90	$399.00	$413.90
	Sliding glass bathtub door, brass trim *Replace* Materials.....510.00 Labor ....64.00 *Remove* .... Labor 14.90	ea	$14.90	$574.00	$588.90
	Sliding glass bathtub door, brass trim with etched glass *Replace* Materials ....625.00 Labor ....64.00 *Remove* .... Labor 14.90	ea	$14.90	$689.00	$703.90
remove & reinstall ▷	Remove sliding glass bathtub door for work, then reinstall *Replace* .... Labor..........106.60	ea	–	$106.60	$106.60
FOLDING BATHTUB ▶ **DOOR** *See tubs on page 377.*	Folding plastic bathtub doors *Replace* Materials.....215.00 Labor ....58.40 *Remove* .... Labor 14.50	ea	$14.50	$273.40	$287.90
remove & reinstall ▷	Remove folding plastic bathtub door for work, then reinstall *Replace* .... Labor..........78.90	ea	–	$78.90	$78.90
SHOWER DOOR ▶ *See showers on page 378 and below.*	Shower door, solid glass *Replace* Materials ....260.00 Labor ....56.00 *Remove* .... Labor 14.00	ea	$14.00	$316.00	$330.00
	Shower door, mill finish trim with fancy glass *Replace* Materials ....295.00 Labor ....56.00 *Remove* .... Labor 14.00	ea	$14.00	$351.00	$365.00
	Shower door, gold finish trim *Replace* Materials ....290.00 Labor ....56.00 *Remove* .... Labor 14.00	ea	$14.00	$346.00	$360.00
	Shower door, gold finish trim with fancy glass *Replace* Materials ....330.00 Labor ....56.00 *Remove* .... Labor 14.00	ea	$14.00	$386.00	$400.00
	Shower door, brass finish trim *Replace* Materials.....490.00 Labor ....56.00 *Remove* .... Labor 14.00	ea	$14.00	$546.00	$560.00

Item Description	Unit	Remove	Replace	Total	
Shower doors, brass trim with etched glass *Replace* Materials ...555.00　　Labor ....56.00 *Remove* ....　　Labor 14.00	ea	$14.00	$611.00	$625.00	**RELATED ITEMS** Bathroom Hardware......41 Cleaning 64
Remove shower door for work, then reinstall *Replace* ....　　Labor 76.60	ea	–	$76.60	$76.60	◁ remove & reinstall
10 gallon gas water heater *Replace* Materials.....310.00　　Labor ....156.00 *Remove* ....　　Labor 32.10	ea	$32.10	$466.00	$498.10	◀ **GAS WATER HEATER**
20 gallon gas water heater *Replace* Materials....340.00　　Labor ....156.00 *Remove* ....　　Labor 32.10	ea	$32.10	$496.00	$528.10	
30 gallon gas water heater *Replace* Materials....380.00　　Labor ....156.00 *Remove* ....　　Labor 32.10	ea	$32.10	$536.00	$568.10	
40 gallon gas water heater *Replace* Materials....400.00　　Labor ....156.00 *Remove* ....　　Labor 32.10	ea	$32.10	$556.00	$588.10	
50 gallon gas water heater *Replace* Materials....460.00　　Labor ....156.00 *Remove* ....　　Labor 32.10	ea	$32.10	$616.00	$648.10	
75 gallon gas water heater *Replace* Materials....820.00　　Labor ....156.00 *Remove* ....　　Labor 32.10	ea	$32.10	$976.00	$1,008.10	
Remove gas water heater for work, then reinstall *Replace* ....　　Labor 234.00	ea	–	$234.00	$234.00	◁ remove & reinstall
10 gallon electric water heater *Replace* Materials.....245.00　　Labor ....146.00 *Remove* ....　　Labor 30.60	ea	$30.60	$391.00	$421.60	◀ **ELECTRIC WATER HEATER**
20 gallon electric water heater *Replace* Materials.....310.00　　Labor ....146.00 *Remove* ....　　Labor 30.60	ea	$30.60	$456.00	$486.60	
30 gallon electric water heater *Replace* Materials ...350.00　　Labor ....146.00 *Remove* ....　　Labor 30.60	ea	$30.60	$496.00	$526.60	
40 gallon electric water heater *Replace* Materials....380.00　　Labor ....146.00 *Remove* ....　　Labor 30.60	ea	$30.60	$526.00	$556.60	
50 gallon electric water heater *Replace* Materials ...450.00　　Labor ....146.00 *Remove* ....　　Labor 30.60	ea	$30.60	$596.00	$626.60	
75 gallon electric water heater *Replace* Materials....830.00　　Labor ....146.00 *Remove* ....　　Labor 30.60	ea	$30.60	$976.00	$1,006.60	
Replace element in electric water heater *Replace* Materials ......90.00　　Labor 59.80	ea	–	$149.80	$149.80	◁ replace element
Remove electric water heater for work, then reinstall *Replace* ....　　Labor 222.00	ea	–	$222.00	$222.00	

Item Description	Unit	Remove	Replace	Total
WATER SOFTENER ▶ **Water softener, automatic two tank up to 30 grains per gallon**	ea	$11.80	$711.00	$722.80
Replace Materials ....555.00 Labor..........156.00				
Remove .... Labor...........11.80				
Water softener, automatic two tank up to 100 grains per gallon	ea	$11.80	$1,356.00	$1,367.80
Replace Materials ..1200.00 Labor..........156.00				
Remove .... Labor...........11.80				
remove & reinstall ▷ **Remove water softener for work, then reinstall**	ea	–	$246.00	$246.00
Replace .... Labor.........246.00				
SEPTIC TANK ▶ **1,000 gallon concrete septic tank with 1,000 sf leach field**	ea	–	$6,180.00	$6,180.00
WITH LEACH FIELD *Replace* Materials ..2550.00 Labor 3630.00				
Includes mobilization, **1,000 gallon concrete septic tank with 2,000 sf leach field**	ea	–	$8,930.00	$8,930.00
excavation, backfill, *Replace* Materials ..3700.00 Labor.......5230.00				
gravel, crushed stone, **1,250 gallon concrete septic tank with 1,000 sf leach field**	ea	–	$6,470.00	$6,470.00
pipe, couplings, *Replace* Materials ..2750.00 Labor.......3720.00				
connectors, building **1,250 gallon concrete septic tank with 2,000 sf leach field**	ea	–	$9,170.00	$9,170.00
paper, tank, and *Replace* Materials ..3850.00 Labor.......5320.00				
distribution box. **1,500 gallon concrete septic tank with 1,000 sf leach field**	ea	–	$6,670.00	$6,670.00
Replace Materials ..2900.00 Labor.......3770.00				
1,500 gallon concrete septic tank with 2,000 sf leach field	ea	–	$9,370.00	$9,370.00
Replace Materials ..4000.00 Labor.......5370.00				
1,000 gallon fiberglass septic tank with 1,000 sf leach field	ea	–	$6,070.00	$6,070.00
Replace Materials ...2450.00 Labor.......3620.00				
1,000 gallon fiberglass septic tank with 2,000 sf leach field	ea	–	$8,830.00	$8,830.00
Replace Materials ..3600.00 Labor.......5230.00				
1,250 gallon fiberglass septic tank with 1,000 sf leach field	ea	–	$6,350.00	$6,350.00
Replace Materials ..2650.00 Labor.......3700.00				
1,250 gallon fiberglass septic tank with 2,000 sf leach field	ea	–	$9,070.00	$9,070.00
Replace Materials ..3750.00 Labor.......5320.00				
1,500 gallon fiberglass septic tank with 1,000 sf leach field	ea	–	$6,550.00	$6,550.00
Replace Materials ..2800.00 Labor.......3750.00				
1,500 gallon fiberglass septic tank with 2,000 sf leach field	ea	–	$9,270.00	$9,270.00
Replace Materials ..3900.00 Labor.......5370.00				
1,000 gallon polyethylene septic tank with 1,000 sf leach field	ea	–	$5,870.00	$5,870.00
Replace Materials ..2250.00 Labor.......3620.00				
1,000 gallon polyethylene septic tank with 2,000 sf leach field	ea	–	$8,680.00	$8,680.00
Replace Materials ..3450.00 Labor.......5230.00				
1,250 gallon polyethylene septic tank with 1,000 sf leach field	ea	–	$6,150.00	$6,150.00
Replace Materials ...2450.00 Labor.......3700.00				
1,250 gallon polyethylene septic tank with 2,000 sf leach field	ea	–	$8,920.00	$8,920.00
Replace Materials ..3600.00 Labor.......5320.00				

Item Description	Unit	Remove	Replace	Total
1,500 gallon polyethylene septic tank with 1,000 sf leach field	ea	–	$6,350.00	$6,350.00
Replace Materials ..2600.00 Labor.......3750.00				
1,500 gallon polyethylene septic tank with 2,000 sf leach field	ea	–	$9,070.00	$9,070.00
Replace Materials ..3700.00 Labor.......5370.00				
Submersible 1/2 hp water pump	ea	$50.60	$793.00	$843.60
Replace Materials ....535.00 Labor 258.00				
Remove .... Labor 50.60				
Submersible 3/4 hp water pump	ea	$50.60	$848.00	$898.60
Replace Materials ....590.00 Labor 258.00				
Remove .... Labor 50.60				
Submersible 1 hp water pump	ea	$50.60	$853.00	$903.60
Replace Materials ....595.00 Labor 258.00				
Remove .... Labor 50.60				
Submersible 1-1/2 hp water pump	ea	$50.60	$1,003.00	$1,053.60
Replace Materials.....745.00 Labor 258.00				
Remove .... Labor 50.60				
Submersible 2 hp water pump	ea	$50.60	$1,073.00	$1,123.60
Replace Materials.....815.00 Labor 258.00				
Remove .... Labor 50.60				
Submersible 3 hp water pump	ea	$50.60	$1,323.00	$1,373.60
Replace Materials ..1065.00 Labor 258.00				
Remove .... Labor 50.60				
Submersible 5 hp water pump	ea	$50.60	$1,458.00	$1,508.60
Replace Materials ..1200.00 Labor 258.00				
Remove .... Labor 50.60				
Remove submersible pump for work then reinstall	ea	–	$359.00	$359.00
Replace .... Labor.........359.00				
1/4 hp automatic plastic sump pump	ea	$16.20	$264.90	$281.10
Replace Materials....200.00 Labor 64.90				
Remove .... Labor 16.20				
1/3 hp automatic plastic sump pump	ea	$16.20	$304.90	$321.10
Replace Materials ....240.00 Labor 64.90				
Remove .... Labor 16.20				
1/2 hp automatic plastic sump pump	ea	$16.20	$379.90	$396.10
Replace Materials....315.00 Labor 64.90				
Remove .... Labor 16.20				
1/4 hp automatic cast-iron sump pump	ea	$16.20	$309.90	$326.10
Replace Materials.....245.00 Labor 64.90				
Remove .... Labor 16.20				
1/3 hp automatic cast-iron sump pump	ea	$16.20	$339.90	$356.10
Replace Materials ....275.00 Labor 64.90				
Remove .... Labor 16.20				
1/2 hp automatic cast-iron sump pump	ea	$16.20	$419.90	$436.10
Replace Materials ....355.00 Labor 64.90				
Remove .... Labor 16.20				
Remove sump pump for work, then reinstall	ea	–	$113.00	$113.00
Replace .... Labor..........113.00				

RELATED ITEMS
Bathroom Hardware......41
Cleaning 64

◄ **SUBMERSIBLE WATER PUMP**
Includes wiring and placement for well up to 100' deep.

◁ remove & reinstall

◄ **SUMP PUMP**
Basement style installation, includes up to 45 lf 1-1/2" PVC pipe and wiring hookup. Does not include rough electrical.

◁ remove & reinstall

Item Description	Unit	Remove	Replace	Total
Antique style sink faucet, standard grade	ea	$10.30	$201.00	$211.30
Replace Materials.....175.00 Labor...........26.00				
Remove .... Labor...........10.30				
Antique style sink faucet, high grade	ea	$10.30	$326.00	$336.30
Replace Materials...300.00 Labor...........26.00				
Remove .... Labor...........10.30				
Antique style sink faucet, deluxe grade	ea	$10.30	$431.00	$441.30
Replace Materials...405.00 Labor...........26.00				
Remove .... Labor...........10.30				
Antique style sink faucet, custom grade	ea	$10.30	$616.00	$626.30
Replace Materials...590.00 Labor...........26.00				
Remove .... Labor...........10.30				
Antique style sink faucet, custom deluxe grade	ea	$10.30	$866.00	$876.30
Replace Materials...840.00 Labor...........26.00				
Remove .... Labor...........10.30				
Remove antique style sink faucet for work, then reinstall	ea	–	$38.90	$38.90
Replace .... Labor 38.90				
Claw-foot bathtub faucet, economy grade	ea	$10.40	$266.70	$277.10
Replace Materials...225.00 Labor...........41.70				
Remove .... Labor...........10.40				
Claw-foot bathtub faucet, standard grade	ea	$10.40	$426.70	$437.10
Replace Materials...385.00 Labor...........41.70				
Remove .... Labor...........10.40				
Claw-foot bathtub faucet, high grade	ea	$10.40	$561.70	$572.10
Replace Materials...520.00 Labor...........41.70				
Remove .... Labor...........10.40				
Claw-foot bathtub faucet, deluxe grade	ea	$10.40	$801.70	$812.10
Replace Materials...760.00 Labor...........41.70				
Remove .... Labor...........10.40				
Claw-foot bathtub faucet, custom grade	ea	$10.40	$1,141.70	$1,152.10
Replace Materials...1100.00 Labor...........41.70				
Remove .... Labor...........10.40				
Remove claw-foot bathtub faucet for work, then reinstall	ea	–	$53.20	$53.20
Replace .... Labor...........53.20				
Claw-foot bathtub faucet with hand-held shower, standard grade	ea	$10.50	$396.20	$406.70
Replace Materials....350.00 Labor 46.20				
Remove .... Labor...........10.50				
Claw-foot bathtub faucet with hand-held shower, high grade	ea	$10.50	$646.20	$656.70
Replace Materials....600.00 Labor 46.20				
Remove .... Labor...........10.50				
Claw-foot bathtub faucet with hand-held shower, deluxe grade	ea	$10.50	$856.20	$866.70
Replace Materials....810.00 Labor 46.20				
Remove .... Labor...........10.50				
Claw-foot bathtub faucet with hand-held shower, custom grade	ea	$10.50	$1,246.20	$1,256.70
Replace Materials ..1200.00 Labor 46.20				
Remove .... Labor...........10.50				

ANTIQUE STYLE ▶ SINK FAUCET
See page 369 for information about faucet quality. Antique style faucets are usually brass, chrome over brass, or nickel over brass with ornate detail. Often used in homes that are not historical. For standard faucets see page 368 and 369.

remove & reinstall ▷

ANTIQUE STYLE ▶ BATHTUB FAUCET
See page 369 for information about faucet quality. Antique style are usually brass, chrome over brass, or nickel over brass with ornate detail. Often used in homes that are not historical. For standard faucets see page 370.

remove & reinstall ▷

ANTIQUE STYLE ▶ BATHTUB FAUCET WITH HAND-HELD SHOWER
See page 369 for information about faucet quality. Antique style faucets are usually brass, chrome over brass, or nickel over brass with ornate detail. Often used in homes that are not historical. For standard faucets see page 370.

Item Description		Unit	Remove	Replace	Total	
Remove claw-foot bathtub faucet with hand-held shower for work, then reinstall		ea	–	$55.60	$55.60	◁ remove & reinstall
Replace	Labor............55.60					
Claw-foot bathtub faucet with shower conversion, standard grade		ea	$14.60	$551.00	$565.60	◀ **ANTIQUE STYLE BATHTUB FAUCET WITH SHOWER CONVERSION**
Replace Materials 450.00	Labor..........101.00					
Remove	Labor..........14.60					*With exposed shower supply pipe and circular shower curtain rod. See standard faucets on page 370.*
Claw-foot bathtub faucet with shower conversion, high grade		ea	$14.60	$756.00	$770.60	
Replace Materials 655.00	Labor..........101.00					
Remove	Labor..........14.60					
Claw-foot bathtub faucet with shower conversion, deluxe grade		ea	$14.60	$901.00	$915.60	
Replace Materials....800.00	Labor..........101.00					
Remove	Labor..........14.60					
Claw-foot bathtub faucet with shower conversion, custom grade		ea	$14.60	$1,251.00	$1,265.60	
Replace Materials ...1150.00	Labor..........101.00					
Remove	Labor..........14.60					
Remove claw-foot bathtub faucet with shower conversion, for work, then reinstall		ea	–	$146.00	$146.00	
Replace	Labor..........146.00					
Claw-foot bathtub supply lines, chrome-plated brass		ea	$12.40	$232.30	$244.70	◀ **ANTIQUE STYLE TUB SUPPLY LINES**
Replace Materials 180.00	Labor..........52.30					*Exposed lines used on antique style bathtubs.*
Remove	Labor..........12.40					
Claw-foot bathtub supply lines, brass		ea	$12.40	$207.30	$219.70	
Replace Materials.....155.00	Labor..........52.30					
Remove	Labor..........12.40					
Claw-foot bathtub drain, chrome-plated brass		ea	$11.60	$223.70	$235.30	◀ **ANTIQUE STYLE BATHTUB DRAIN**
Replace Materials.....170.00	Labor 53.70					
Remove	Labor 11.60					
Claw-foot bathtub drain, brass		ea	$11.60	$188.70	$200.30	
Replace Materials.....135.00	Labor 53.70					
Remove	Labor 11.60					
Free-standing water feeds for claw-foot or slipper bathtub, chrome-plated brass		ea	$12.60	$312.00	$324.60	◀ **ANTIQUE STYLE FREE-STANDING SUPPLY LINES**
Replace Materials 255.00	Labor...........57.00					*Exposed lines used on antique style bathtubs that do not rely on the bathtub for support.*
Remove	Labor...........12.60					
Free-standing water feeds for claw-foot or slipper bathtub, brass		ea	$12.60	$362.00	$374.60	
Replace Materials....305.00	Labor...........57.00					
Remove	Labor...........12.60					
Pedestal sink, economy grade		ea	$14.00	$452.00	$466.00	◀ **PEDESTAL SINK**
Replace Materials 395.00	Labor...........57.00					*Antique or contemporary style. See standard sinks on page 371.*
Remove	Labor...........14.00					
Pedestal sink, standard grade		ea	$14.00	$522.00	$536.00	
Replace Materials 465.00	Labor...........57.00					
Remove	Labor...........14.00					
Pedestal sink, high grade		ea	$14.00	$677.00	$691.00	
Replace Materials 620.00	Labor...........57.00					
Remove	Labor...........14.00					
Pedestal sink, deluxe grade		ea	$14.00	$1,132.00	$1,146.00	
Replace Materials...1075.00	Labor...........57.00					
Remove	Labor...........14.00					

RELATED ITEMS
Bathroom Hardware......41
Cleaning 64

Item Description	Unit	Remove	Replace	Total
PEDESTAL SINK ▶ *continued*				
Pedestal sink, custom grade	ea	$14.00	$1,607.00	$1,621.00
Replace Materials...1550.00 Labor..........57.00				
Remove .... Labor..........14.00				
Pedestal sink, custom deluxe grade	ea	$14.00	$2,057.00	$2,071.00
Replace Materials..2000.00 Labor..........57.00				
Remove .... Labor..........14.00				
remove & reinstall ▷ **Remove pedestal sink for work, then reinstall**	ea	–	$99.50	$99.50
Replace .... Labor 99.50				
ANTIQUE STYLE ▶ **PILLBOX TOILET** *Round tank with beaded rim. See standard toilets on page 376.* **Antique style pillbox toilet**	ea	$12.40	$2,054.00	$2,066.40
Replace Materials...1950.00 Labor..........104.00				
Remove .... Labor..........12.40				
Remove antique style pillbox toilet for work, then reinstall	ea	–	$161.00	$161.00
Replace .... Labor 161.00				
ANTIQUE STYLE ▶ **LOW-TANK TOILET** *Identifiable by pipe (usually brass) running from tank to bowl. See standard toilets on page 376.* **Antique style low-tank toilet with porcelain tank**	ea	$12.40	$1,153.70	$1,166.10
Replace Materials ..1050.00 Labor..........103.70				
Remove .... Labor..........12.40				
Antique style low-tank toilet with oak tank	ea	$12.40	$948.70	$961.10
Replace Materials ....845.00 Labor..........103.70				
Remove .... Labor..........12.40				
Remove antique style low-tank toilet for work, then reinstall	ea	–	$162.93	$162.93
Replace Materials........1.93 Labor 161.00				
ANTIQUE STYLE ▶ **HIGH-TANK TOILET** *Tank mounted high on wall. Includes brass pipe and connectors, pull chain, hardwood toilet seat, brass tank support brackets. Wood tanks include plastic liner.* **Antique style high-tank toilet with porcelain tank**	ea	$17.40	$1,423.00	$1,440.40
Replace Materials ..1300.00 Labor..........123.00				
Remove .... Labor..........17.40				
Antique style high-tank toilet with oak tank	ea	$17.40	$1,223.00	$1,240.40
Replace Materials...1100.00 Labor..........123.00				
Remove .... Labor..........17.40				
Remove antique style high-tank toilet for work, then reinstall	ea	–	$174.93	$174.93
Replace Materials........1.68 Labor 173.00				
ANTIQUE BATHTUB ▶ *Claw-foot or ball-foot. Does not include supply lines or faucet. Includes $100 for crating and $290 for shipping. See standard bathtubs on page 377.* **60" antique claw-foot or ball-foot cast-iron bathtub (as is condition)**	ea	$52.60	$986.00	$1,038.60
Replace Materials ....740.00 Labor..........246.00				
Remove .... Labor..........52.60				
66" antique claw-foot or ball-foot cast-iron bathtub (as is condition)	ea	$52.60	$1,080.00	$1,132.60
Replace Materials ....820.00 Labor..........260.00				
Remove .... Labor..........52.60				
REFINISHED ▶ **ANTIQUE BATHTUB** *Claw-foot or ball-foot. Interior and lip refinished exterior surfaces painted. Does not include visible supply lines or faucet. Includes $100 for crating and $290 for shipping. See standard bathtubs on page 377.* **48" refinished antique claw-foot or ball-foot cast-iron bathtub**	ea	$52.60	$2,472.00	$2,524.60
Replace Materials..2250.00 Labor 222.00				
Remove .... Labor..........52.60				
52" refinished antique claw-foot or ball-foot cast-iron bathtub	ea	$52.60	$2,384.00	$2,436.60
Replace Materials...2150.00 Labor 234.00				
Remove .... Labor..........52.60				
60" refinished antique claw-foot or ball-foot cast-iron bathtub	ea	$52.60	$2,196.00	$2,248.60
Replace Materials...1950.00 Labor 246.00				
Remove .... Labor..........52.60				

Item Description	Unit	Remove	Replace	Total
66" refinished antique claw-foot or ball-foot cast-iron bathtub	ea	$52.60	$2,260.00	$2,312.60
Replace Materials..2000.00 Labor.........260.00				
Remove .... Labor.........52.60				
60" antique reproduction claw-foot or ball-foot cast-iron bathtub	ea	$52.60	$1,796.00	$1,848.60
Replace Materials...1550.00 Labor.........246.00				
Remove .... Labor.........52.60				
66" antique reproduction claw-foot or ball-foot cast-iron bathtub	ea	$52.60	$2,210.00	$2,262.60
Replace Materials...1950.00 Labor.........260.00				
Remove .... Labor.........52.60				
60" antique reproduction fiberglass claw-foot or ball-foot bathtub	ea	$41.90	$2,296.00	$2,337.90
Replace Materials...2150.00 Labor.........146.00				
Remove .... Labor.........41.90				
66" antique reproduction fiberglass claw-foot or ball-foot bathtub	ea	$41.90	$3,056.00	$3,097.90
Replace Materials..2900.00 Labor.........156.00				
Remove .... Labor.........41.90				
Remove antique (or antique style) bathtub for work, then reinstall	ea	–	$260.00	$260.00
Replace .... Labor.........260.00				
60" antique cast-iron slipper bathtub	ea	$52.60	$2,996.00	$3,048.60
Replace Materials ..2750.00 Labor.........246.00				
Remove .... Labor.........52.60				
66" antique reproduction fiberglass slipper bathtub	ea	$41.90	$5,310.00	$5,351.90
Replace Materials..5050.00 Labor.........260.00				
Remove .... Labor.........41.90				
Add for solid brass legs	ea	–	$90.00	$90.00
Replace Materials......90.00				
Add for brass-plated legs	ea	–	$50.00	$50.00
Replace Materials......50.00				
Add for oak trim around lip of antique bathtub	ea	–	$1,550.00	$1,550.00
Replace Materials...1550.00				

RELATED ITEMS
Bathroom Hardware......41
Cleaning 64

◀ **REPRODUCTION ANTIQUE BATHTUB**
Claw-foot or ball-foot. New tubs built in the antique style. Does not include supply lines or faucet. Includes $100 for crating and $290 for shipping. ($170 shipping for fiberglass tubs.) See standard tubs on page 377.

slipper bathtub △

◀ **REMOVE ANTIQUE BATHTUB & REINSTALL**

◀ **REPRODUCTION SLIPPER BATHTUB**
Claw-foot or ball-foot. Does not include supply lines or faucet. Includes $100 for crating and $290 for shipping. ($170 shipping for fiberglass tubs.) See standard tubs on page 377.

◀ **ADDITIONAL ANTIQUE BATHTUB COSTS**

TIME & MATERIAL CHARTS *(selected items)*

Plumbing Materials

DESCRIPTION	UNIT PRICE
Black steel pipe	
1/2" pipe	$1.18 lf
3/4" pipe	$1.41 lf
1" pipe	$1.99 lf
2" pipe	$6.34 lf
Brass pipe	
1/2" pipe	$4.09 lf
3/4" pipe	$5.44 lf
1" pipe	$8.89 lf
2" pipe	$13.90 lf
Type K copper pipe	
1/2" pipe	$2.32 lf
3/4" pipe	$3.08 lf
1" pipe	$4.00 lf
2" pipe	$9.69 lf

. . . More ➤

Plumbing Materials *continued*

DESCRIPTION	UNIT PRICE
Type L copper pipe	
1/2" pipe	**$1.37** lf
3/4" pipe	**$2.26** lf
1" pipe	**$3.08** lf
2" pipe	**$7.46** lf
Type M copper pipe	
1/2" pipe	**$1.05** lf
3/4" pipe	**$1.73** lf
1" pipe	**$2.34** lf
Galvanized steel pipe	
1/2" pipe	**$1.44** lf
3/4" pipe	**$1.72** lf
1" pipe	**$2.43** lf
2" pipe	**$7.74** lf
CPVC pipe	
1/2" pipe	**$.84** lf
3/4" pipe	**$1.04** lf
1" pipe	**$1.25** lf
PVC pipe	
1/2" pipe	**$.53** lf
3/4" pipe	**$.57** lf
1" pipe	**$.63** lf
1-1/2" pipe	**$.84** lf
2" pipe	**$1.02** lf
3" pipe	**$1.47** lf
4" pipe	**$1.93** lf
5" pipe	**$2.77** lf
6" pipe	**$3.30** lf
Cast-iron pipe	
2" pipe	**$5.35** lf
3" pipe	**$7.35** lf
4" pipe	**$10.40** lf
5" pipe	**$29.80** lf
6" pipe	**$38.00** lf
No-hub cast-iron pipe	
2" pipe	**$7.41** lf
3" pipe	**$9.49** lf
4" pipe	**$12.30** lf
5" pipe	**$17.90** lf

Plumbing Labor

LABORER	BASE WAGE	PAID LEAVE	TRUE WAGE	FICA	FUTA	WORKER'S COMP.	UNEMPLOY. INSUR.	HEALTH INSUR.	RETIRE (401K)	LIABILITY INSUR.	COST PER HOUR
Plumber	$26.70	2.08	$28.78	2.20	.23	4.85	2.50	2.92	.86	4.32	$46.70
Plumber's helper	$22.50	1.76	$24.26	1.86	.19	4.09	2.11	2.92	.73	3.64	$39.80
Demolition laborer	$14.40	1.12	$15.52	1.19	.12	5.01	1.35	2.92	.47	2.33	$28.90

Paid Leave is calculated based on two weeks paid vacation, one week sick leave, and seven paid holidays. Employer's matching portion of **FICA** is 7.65 percent. **FUTA** (Federal Unemployment) is .8 percent. **Worker's compensation** for the plumbing trade was calculated using a national average of 16.80 percent. **Unemployment insurance** was calculated using a national average of 8.7 percent. **Health insurance** was calculated based on a projected national average for 2005 of $580 per employee (and family when applicable) per month. Employer pays 80 percent for a per month cost of $464 per employee. **Retirement** is based on a 401(k) retirement program with employer matching of 50 percent. Employee contributions to the 401(k) plan are an average of 6 percent of the true wage. **Liability insurance** is based on a national average of 14.0 percent.

Plumbing Labor Productivity

WORK DESCRIPTION	LABORER	COST PER HOUR	PRODUCTIVITY	UNIT PRICE
Demolition				
remove faucet	demolition laborer	$28.90	.357	$10.30 ea
remove bathroom sink	demolition laborer	$28.90	.366	$10.60 ea
remove kitchen or laundry sink	demolition laborer	$28.90	.369	$10.70 ea
remove wet bar sink	demolition laborer	$28.90	.358	$10.30 ea
remove toilet	demolition laborer	$28.90	.346	$10.00 ea
remove fiberglass bathtub	demolition laborer	$28.90	1.02	$29.50 ea
remove cast-iron or steel bathtub	demolition laborer	$28.90	1.61	$46.50 ea
remove fiberglass bathtub with whirlpool jets	demolition laborer	$28.90	1.45	$41.90 ea
remove cast-iron or steel tub with whirlpool jets	demolition laborer	$28.90	2.13	$61.60 ea
remove glass shower	demolition laborer	$28.90	1.22	$35.30 ea
remove bathtub and shower combination	demolition laborer	$28.90	1.69	$48.80 ea
remove shower stall	demolition laborer	$28.90	1.22	$35.30 ea
remove bathtub surround	demolition laborer	$28.90	.893	$25.80 ea
remove sliding glass bathtub door	demolition laborer	$28.90	.515	$14.90 ea
remove shower door	demolition laborer	$28.90	.485	$14.00 ea
remove gas water heater	demolition laborer	$28.90	1.11	$32.10 ea
remove electric water heater	demolition laborer	$28.90	1.06	$30.60 ea
remove water softener	demolition laborer	$28.90	.408	$11.80 ea
remove submersible pump	demolition laborer	$28.90	1.75	$50.60 ea
remove sump pump	demolition laborer	$28.90	.562	$16.20 ea
remove antique style sink faucet	demolition laborer	$28.90	.357	$10.30 ea
remove antique style bathtub faucet	demolition laborer	$28.90	.361	$10.40 ea
remove claw-foot bathtub supply lines	demolition laborer	$28.90	.429	$12.40 ea
remove claw-foot bathtub drain	demolition laborer	$28.90	.403	$11.60 ea
remove free-standing water feeds	demolition laborer	$28.90	.437	$12.60 ea
remove pedestal sink	demolition laborer	$28.90	.483	$14.00 ea
remove antique style pillbox toilet	demolition laborer	$28.90	.429	$12.40 ea
remove antique style low-tank toilet	demolition laborer	$28.90	.429	$12.40 ea
remove antique style high-tank toilet	demolition laborer	$28.90	.602	$17.40 ea
remove cast-iron claw-foot bathtub	demolition laborer	$28.90	1.82	$52.60 ea
remove fiberglass claw-foot bathtub	demolition laborer	$28.90	1.45	$41.90 ea
Install field threaded pipe				
1/2"	plumber	$46.70	.127	$5.93 lf
3/4"	plumber	$46.70	.136	$6.35 lf
1"	plumber	$46.70	.158	$7.38 lf
2"	plumber	$46.70	.231	$10.80 lf
Install copper pipe				
1/2"	plumber	$46.70	.104	$4.86 lf
3/4"	plumber	$46.70	.109	$5.09 lf
1"	plumber	$46.70	.122	$5.70 lf
2"	plumber	$46.70	.202	$9.43 lf
Install plastic pipe				
1/2"	plumber	$46.70	.153	$7.15 lf
3/4"	plumber	$46.70	.162	$7.57 lf
1"	plumber	$46.70	.189	$8.83 lf
2"	plumber	$46.70	.251	$11.70 lf
3"	plumber	$46.70	.281	$13.10 lf
4"	plumber	$46.70	.311	$14.50 lf
5"	plumber	$46.70	.346	$16.20 lf
6"	plumber	$46.70	.380	$17.70 lf
Install cast-iron pipe				
2"	plumber	$46.70	.235	$11.00 lf
3"	plumber	$46.70	.248	$11.60 lf
4"	plumber	$46.70	.270	$12.60 lf
5"	plumber	$46.70	.305	$14.20 lf
6"	plumber	$46.70	.317	$14.80 lf
Install no-hub cast-iron pipe				
2"	plumber	$46.70	.210	$9.81 lf
3"	plumber	$46.70	.222	$10.40 lf
4"	plumber	$46.70	.242	$11.30 lf
6"	plumber	$46.70	.283	$13.20 lf

... More ➤

Plumbing Labor Productivity *continued*

WORK DESCRIPTION	LABORER	COST PER HOUR	PRODUCTIVITY	UNIT PRICE
Install faucet				
bathroom sink	plumber	$46.70	.556	$26.00 ea
kitchen sink	plumber	$46.70	.562	$26.20 ea
laundry sink	plumber	$46.70	.546	$25.50 ea
shower	plumber	$46.70	.575	$26.90 ea
bathtub	plumber	$46.70	.568	$26.50 ea
bathtub with shower	plumber	$46.70	.606	$28.30 ea
Install bathroom sink				
wall-hung	plumber	$46.70	.877	$41.00 ea
self-rimming	plumber	$46.70	.909	$42.50 ea
under-counter	plumber	$46.70	.952	$44.50 ea
Install kitchen sink				
install	plumber	$46.70	.926	$43.20 ea
Install laundry sink				
in countertop	plumber	$46.70	.901	$42.10 ea
on legs or frame	plumber	$46.70	.833	$38.90 ea
Install wet bar sink				
self-rimming	plumber	$46.70	.909	$42.50 ea
under-counter	plumber	$46.70	1.14	$53.20 ea
Install fixtures				
toilet	plumber	$46.70	1.33	$62.10 ea
cast-iron or steel bathtub	plumber	$46.70	2.94	$137.00 ea
fiberglass bathtub	plumber	$46.70	1.79	$83.60 ea
cast-iron or steel bathtub with whirlpool jets	plumber	$46.70	4.00	$187.00 ea
fiberglass bathtub with whirlpool jets	plumber	$46.70	3.45	$161.00 ea
fiberglass bathtub & shower combination	plumber	$46.70	3.23	$151.00 ea
shower stall	plumber	$46.70	2.70	$126.00 ea
Install shower / bathtub door				
sliding bathtub door	plumber	$46.70	1.37	$64.00 ea
shower door	plumber	$46.70	1.20	$56.00 ea
Install water heater				
gas	plumber	$46.70	3.33	$156.00 ea
electric	plumber	$46.70	3.13	$146.00 ea
Install water softener				
install	plumber	$46.70	3.33	$156.00 ea
Install septic system				
with concrete tank				
1,000 gallon with 1,000 sf leach field	plumber	$46.70	77.8	$3,630.00 ea
1,000 gallon with 2,000 sf leach field	plumber	$46.70	112	$5,230.00 ea
with fiberglass tank				
1,000 gallon with 1,000 sf leach field	plumber	$46.70	77.5	$3,620.00 ea
1,000 gallon with 2,000 sf leach field	plumber	$46.70	112	$5,230.00 ea
with polyethylene tank				
1,000 gallon with 1,000 sf leach field	plumber	$46.70	77.5	$3,620.00 ea
1,000 gallon with 2,000 sf leach field	plumber	$46.70	112	$5,230.00 ea
Install water pump				
submersible	plumber	$46.70	5.52	$258.00 ea
automatic sump	plumber	$46.70	1.39	$64.90 ea
Install claw-foot bathtub faucet				
faucet	plumber	$46.70	.893	$41.70 ea
faucet with shower conversion	plumber	$46.70	2.17	$101.00 ea
Install pedestal sink				
install	plumber	$46.70	1.22	$57.00 ea
Install antique style toilet				
pillbox or low tank	plumber	$46.70	2.22	$104.00 ea
high-tank	plumber	$46.70	2.63	$123.00 ea
Install antique style bathtub				
52" cast-iron	plumber	$46.70	5.00	$234.00 ea
60" cast-iron	plumber	$46.70	5.26	$246.00 ea
66" cast-iron	plumber	$46.70	5.56	$260.00 ea
60" reproduction fiberglass	plumber	$46.70	3.13	$146.00 ea
66" reproduction fiberglass	plumber	$46.70	3.33	$156.00 ea

30 .... *Retaining Walls*

Item Description	Unit	Remove	Replace	Total	
Minimum charge for retaining wall work	ea	–	$392.50	$392.50	◄ **MINIMUM**
Replace Materials .....175.00 Labor.........106.00 Equipment 111.50					
Concrete retaining wall	sf	$9.97	$20.33	$30.30	◄ **CONCRETE**
Replace Materials.......7.91 Labor ....9.58 Equipment...........2.84					*See Masonry, page 296 for brick veneer and page*
Remove .... Labor 9.97					*317 for wall caps and*
► Includes 4" perforated pipe drain line at inside base that is set in gravel.					*wall coping.*
Wood pile retaining wall with wood lagging	sf	$5.35	$11.76	$17.11	◄ **PILE WITH**
Replace Materials........6.09 Labor ....4.01 Equipment...........1.66					**LAGGING**
Remove .... Labor 5.35					
Steel pile retaining wall with wood lagging	sf	$5.90	$12.38	$18.28	
Replace Materials........6.33 Labor ....4.39 Equipment...........1.66					
Remove .... Labor 5.90					
Add for anchored tieback	ea	$52.60	$257.80	$257.80	◄ **ANCHORED**
Replace Materials ....122.00 Labor.........103.00 Equipment.........32.80					**TIEBACK**
Remove .... Labor...........52.60					*For all retaining wall types.*
Railroad tie retaining wall with tie tiebacks	sf	$5.78	$18.12	$23.90	◄ **RAILROAD TIE**
Replace Materials........6.22 Labor ....10.30 Equipment...........1.60					
Remove .... Labor 5.78					
Railroad tie retaining wall without tie tiebacks	sf	$5.46	$14.10	$19.56	
Replace Materials........5.62 Labor ....7.05 Equipment...........1.43					
Remove .... Labor 5.46					
Cedar tie retaining wall with tie tiebacks	sf	$5.43	$19.99	$25.42	◄ **CEDAR TIE**
Replace Materials........7.91 Labor ....10.60 Equipment...........1.48					
Remove .... Labor 5.43					
Cedar tie retaining wall without tie tiebacks	sf	$5.14	$16.07	$21.21	
Replace Materials........7.56 Labor ....7.13 Equipment...........1.38					
Remove .... Labor 5.14					
Random stone retaining wall, dry set	sf	$11.10	$37.96	$49.06	◄ **STONE**
Replace Materials.......17.80 Labor ....18.50 Equipment...........1.66					*Includes 4" perforated pipe drain line at inside*
Remove .... Labor 11.10					*base set in gravel.*
Random stone retaining wall, mortar set	sf	$11.10	$36.16	$47.26	
Replace Materials .....18.50 Labor ....16.00 Equipment...........1.66					
Remove .... Labor 11.10					
Cut stone retaining wall, dry set	sf	$11.10	$39.86	$50.96	
Replace Materials......22.50 Labor ....15.70 Equipment...........1.66					
Remove .... Labor 11.10					
Cut stone retaining wall, mortar set	sf	$11.10	$40.46	$51.56	
Replace Materials......23.30 Labor ....15.50 Equipment...........1.66					
Remove .... Labor 11.10					
Interlocking masonry block retaining wall	sf	$9.62	$25.66	$35.28	◄ **INTERLOCKING**
Replace Materials ......10.80 Labor ....13.20 Equipment...........1.66					**BLOCK**
Remove .... Labor 9.62					

> **RETAINING WALLS**
>
> Retaining walls include excavation and backfill. Measure sf of surface area. Includes sand and/or gravel base and 2' to 3' of walls buried beneath exposed surface.

Item Description	Unit	Remove	Replace	Total
INTERLOCKING ▶ BLOCK *continued*				
Add for solid cap on interlocking masonry block retaining wall	If	–	$7.35	$7.35
Replace Materials.......5.32 Labor 2.03				
▶ 4" high by 16" wide by 10" deep. Per If of wall.				
Add for knock-out cap on interlocking masonry block retaining wall	If	–	$8.19	$8.19
Replace Materials.......6.16 Labor 2.03				
▶ Same as above except 3" to 4" back the cap is cut out to about half its thickness to allow soil and vegetation to overlap the top of the wall. Per If of wall.				
ADD FOR FABRIC ▶ REINFORCEMENT *One common brand name is called GeoGrid. Fabric ties retaining walls into hillside.*				
Add for 4-1/2' deep reinforced fabric, one row every 2' of wall height	sf	–	$4.30	$4.30
Replace Materials.......4.00 Labor .... .30				
Add for 4-1/2' deep reinforced fabric, one row every 3' of wall height	sf	–	$2.88	$2.88
Replace Materials.......2.67 Labor .... .21				
Add for 6' deep reinforced fabric, one row every 2' of wall height	sf	–	$5.14	$5.14
Replace Materials.......4.84 Labor .... .30				
Add for 6' deep reinforced fabric, one row every 3' of wall height	sf	–	$3.44	$3.44
Replace Materials.......3.23 Labor .... .21				
SHOTCRETE ▶ **Shotcrete slope stabilization with wire mesh (per inch deep)**	sf	–	$6.49	$6.49
Replace Materials.......1.83 Labor ....4.39 Equipment .... .27				

TIME & MATERIAL CHARTS *(selected items)*

Retaining Walls Materials

See *Retaining Walls* material prices with the line items and other information in the **QuickFinder** column.

Retaining Walls Labor

LABORER	BASE WAGE	PAID LEAVE	TRUE WAGE	FICA	FUTA	WORKER'S COMP.	UNEMPLOY. INSUR.	HEALTH INSUR.	RETIRE (401K)	LIABILITY INSUR.	COST PER HOUR
Retaining wall installer	$23.90	1.86	$25.76	1.97	.21	4.51	2.24	2.92	.77	3.86	**$42.20**
Mason	$25.10	1.96	$27.06	2.07	.22	8.46	2.35	2.92	.81	4.06	**$48.00**
Equipment operator	$30.80	2.40	$33.20	2.54	.27	6.04	2.89	2.92	1.00	4.98	**$53.80**
Demolition laborer	$14.40	1.12	$15.52	1.19	.12	5.01	1.35	2.92	.47	2.33	**$28.90**

Paid Leave is calculated based on two weeks paid vacation, one week sick leave, and seven paid holidays. Employer's matching portion of **FICA** is 7.65 percent. **FUTA** (Federal Unemployment) is .8 percent. **Worker's Compensation** was calculated using a national average of 17.48 percent for the retaining wall installer; 31.20 percent for the mason, and 18.16 percent for the equipment operator. **Unemployment insurance** was calculated using a national average of 8.7 percent. **Health insurance** was calculated based on a projected national average for 2005 of $580 per employee (and family when applicable) per month. Employer pays 80 percent for a per month cost of $464 per employee. **Retirement** is based on a 401(k) retirement program with employer matching of 50 percent. Employee contributions to the 401(k) plan are an average of 6 percent of the true wage. **Liability insurance** is based on a national average of 14.0 percent.

Retaining Walls Labor Productivity

WORK DESCRIPTION	LABORER	COST PER HOUR	PRODUCTIVITY	UNIT PRICE
Install retaining wall				
concrete	retaining wall installer	$42.20	.227	**$9.58** sf
railroad tie with tie tiebacks	retaining wall installer	$42.20	.244	**$10.30** sf
railroad tie, no tie tiebacks	retaining wall installer	$42.20	.167	**7.05** sf
cedar tie with tie tiebacks	retaining wall installer	$42.20	.250	**$10.60** sf
cedar tie, no tie tiebacks	retaining wall installer	$42.20	.169	**$7.13** sf
interlocking masonry block	retaining wall installer	$42.20	.313	**$13.20** sf

31 .... *Roofing*

Item Description	Unit	Remove	Replace	Total	
Minimum charge for roofing work *Replace* Materials......80.00 Labor...........57.80	ea	–	$137.80	$137.80	◄ **MINIMUM**
Add 35% for steep roofs 6-12 to 8-12 slope					◄ **ADD FOR STEEP &** **COMPLEX ROOFS** *Cut-up roofs contain four* *to six intersecting roof* *lines. Very cut-up roofs* *contain seven or more.*
Add 50% for steep roofs greater than 8-12 slope					
Add 30% for cut-up roof					
Add 50% for very cut-up roof					
Aluminum shingles, .02" thick, natural finish *Replace* Materials....263.00 Labor........51.10 *Remove* .... Labor 30.10	sq	$30.10	$314.10	$344.20	◄ **ALUMINUM** **SHINGLES** *See* **Roofing** *box* *on page 394.*
Aluminum shingles, .03" thick, natural finish *Replace* Materials....284.00 Labor........51.10 *Remove* .... Labor 30.10	sq	$30.10	$335.10	$365.20	
Add 20% for colored aluminum shingles (all colors)					◁ add for colored finish
Galvanized steel shingles, 26 gauge, natural finish *Replace* Materials....200.00 Labor ....53.50 *Remove* .... Labor 30.10	sq	$30.10	$253.50	$283.60	◄ **GALVANIZED** **STEEL SHINGLES** *See* **Roofing** *box* *on page 394.*
Galvanized steel shingles, 24 gauge, natural finish *Replace* Materials......211.00 Labor ....53.50 *Remove* .... Labor 30.10	sq	$30.10	$264.50	$294.60	
Galvanized steel shingles, 22 gauge, natural finish *Replace* Materials....232.00 Labor ....53.50 *Remove* .... Labor 30.10	sq	$30.10	$285.50	$315.60	
Add 21% for galvanized steel shingles with baked enamel factory finish					◁ add for colored finish
Add 10% for metal shingles with 1" polystyrene insulation					◁ add for insulation
Minimum charge for metal shingle roof repair *Replace* Materials......50.00 Labor...........96.40	ea	–	$146.40	$146.40	◄ **MINIMUM METAL** **SHINGLES**
20 year asphalt shingles (210 to 230 lb) *Replace* Materials......42.20 Labor........59.80 *Remove* .... Labor 29.50	sq	$29.50	$102.00	$131.50	◄ **ASPHALT** **SHINGLES** *See* **Roofing** *box* *on page 394. Prices are* *for standard three tab* *shingles. Add* **14%** *for 4* *to 6 tab. Add* **16%** *for* *thatch style edge. Add* **15%** *for shingles with* *cut-outs. Add* **10%** *for* *textured shingles.*
25 year asphalt shingles (220 to 240 lb) *Replace* Materials......56.10 Labor........59.80 *Remove* .... Labor 29.50	sq	$29.50	$115.90	$145.40	
30 year asphalt shingles (240 to 260 lb) *Replace* Materials......76.70 Labor...........61.20 *Remove* .... Labor 29.50	sq	$29.50	$137.90	$167.40	
40 year asphalt shingles (260 to 300 lb) *Replace* Materials......92.80 Labor...........61.20 *Remove* .... Labor 29.50	sq	$29.50	$154.00	$183.50	

RELATED ITEMS

Rough Carpentry

chimney cricket 444

Item Description	Unit	Remove	Replace	Total
LAMINATED ▶ ASPHALT SHINGLES *See Roofing box below.*	**Laminated asphalt shingles, standard grade (250 to 300 lb)**	sq	$29.50	$179.70	$209.20
	Replace Materials......80.40 Labor..........99.30				
	Remove .... Labor..........29.50				
	Laminated asphalt shingles, standard grade (300 to 390 lb)	sq	$29.50	$197.90	$227.40
	Replace Materials......98.60 Labor..........99.30				
	Remove .... Labor..........29.50				
	Laminated asphalt shingles, high grade (260 to 300 lb)	sq	$29.50	$213.60	$243.10
	Replace Materials......95.60 Labor..........118.00				
	Remove .... Labor..........29.50				
	Laminated asphalt shingles, high grade (300 to 400 lb)	sq	$29.50	$230.00	$259.50
	Replace Materials .....112.00 Labor..........118.00				
	Remove .... Labor..........29.50				
T-LOCK, DIAMOND ▶ & HEXAGONAL *See Roofing box below.*	**T-lock asphalt shingles (210 to 230 lb)**	sq	$29.50	$101.40	$130.90
	Replace Materials......40.20 Labor..........61.20				
	Remove .... Labor..........29.50				
	Diamond asphalt shingles (210 to 230 lb)	sq	$29.50	$102.40	$131.90
	Replace Materials ......41.20 Labor..........61.20				
	Remove .... Labor..........29.50				
	Hexagonal asphalt shingles (210 to 230 lb)	sq	$29.50	$103.40	$132.90
	Replace Materials......42.20 Labor..........61.20				
	Remove .... Labor..........29.50				
MINIMUM ▶ ASPHALT SHINGLES	**Minimum charge for asphalt shingle roof repair**	ea	–	$126.40	$126.40
	Replace Materials......30.00 Labor..........96.40				
ROLL ROOFING ▶ *Add 82% for double selvage lay.*	**90 lb roll roofing**	sq	$21.20	$60.20	$81.40
	Replace Materials......29.10 Labor..........31.10				
	Remove .... Labor..........21.20				
	110 lb roll roofing	sq	$21.20	$81.40	$102.60
	Replace Materials......50.30 Labor..........31.10				
	Remove .... Labor..........21.20				
	140 lb roll roofing	sq	$21.20	$107.40	$128.60
	Replace Materials ......76.30 Labor..........31.10				
	Remove .... Labor..........21.20				
SLATE ▶ *See Roofing box below.* unfading ▷	**Vermont unfading green slate, clear**	sq	$107.00	$918.00	$1,025.00
	Replace Materials ....725.00 Labor..........193.00				
	Remove .... Labor..........107.00				
	Vermont unfading purple slate, clear	sq	$107.00	$932.00	$1,039.00
	Replace Materials ....739.00 Labor..........193.00				
	Remove .... Labor......107.00				
	Vermont unfading variegated purple slate, clear	sq	$107.00	$1,024.00	$1,131.00
	Replace Materials ....831.00 Labor..........193.00				
	Remove .... Labor......107.00				
	Vermont unfading dark gray or black slate, clear	sq	$107.00	$957.00	$1,064.00
	Replace Materials ....764.00 Labor..........193.00				
	Remove .... Labor......107.00				
	Vermont unfading red slate, clear	sq	$107.00	$2,023.00	$2,130.00
	Replace Materials ..1830.00 Labor.........193.00				
	Remove .... Labor.........107.00				

ROOFING

Roofing costs are based on a typical 2,550 sf house with a 6 in 12 slope roof or less. Roof height is less than 16' so ropes and other safety equipment are not required.

Includes costs for ridges and rakes. Typical roof has an intersecting or L-shaped roof and two dormers. Also includes boots and flashing.

Item Description	Unit	Remove	Replace	Total	
Pennsylvania black weathering slate, clear	sq	$107.00	$902.00	$1,009.00	◁ weathering slate
Replace Materials ....709.00 Labor 193.00					
Remove .... Labor 107.00					
Vermont weathering green slate, clear	sq	$107.00	$879.00	$986.00	
Replace Materials ....686.00 Labor 193.00					
Remove .... Labor 107.00					
Deduct 15% for slate with ribbons of foreign color					◁ deduct for lower grade
Minimum charge for slate roof repair	ea	–	$443.00	$443.00	◁ minimum
Replace Materials ....250.00 Labor 193.00					
Replace single slate	ea	–	$38.60	$38.60	◁ replace single slate
Replace Materials ......20.00 Labor 18.60					
16" blue label cedar shingles (Royals)	sq	$34.70	$414.00	$448.70	◀ WOOD SHINGLES
Replace Materials .....276.00 Labor 138.00					See *Roofing* box on
Remove .... Labor 34.70					facing page.
18" blue label cedar shingles (Perfections)	sq	$34.70	$417.00	$451.70	
Replace Materials ....294.00 Labor 123.00					
Remove .... Labor 34.70					
16" red label cedar shingles (Royals)	sq	$34.70	$405.00	$439.70	
Replace Materials ....267.00 Labor 138.00					
Remove .... Labor 34.70					
18" red label cedar shingles (Perfections)	sq	$34.70	$406.00	$440.70	
Replace Materials ....283.00 Labor 123.00					
Remove .... Labor 34.70					*thatch △*
Minimum charge for wood shingle repair	ea	–	$156.40	$156.40	◁ minimum
Replace Materials ......60.00 Labor 96.40					
Replace single wood shingle	ea	–	$25.00	$25.00	◁ replace single shingle
Replace Materials ......15.00 Labor 10.00					
Deduct 6% for black label shingles					◁ additional costs
Add 20% for 16" wood shingles with 4" exposure					
Deduct 17% for 16" wood shingles with 5-1/2" exposure					
Deduct 20% for 16" wood shingles with 6" exposure					*serrated △*
Add 18% for wood shingles treated with fire retardant					
Add 16% for wood shingles treated with mildew retardant					
Add 16% for wood shingle staggered installation					
Add 26% for wood shingle thatch installation					*Dutch weave △*
Add 24% for wood shingle serrated installation					
Add 38% for wood shingle Dutch weave installation					
Add 45% for wood shingle pyramid installation					*pyramid △*
18" medium handsplit and resawn shakes	sq	$34.70	$342.00	$376.70	◀ WOOD SHAKES
Replace Materials .....181.00 Labor 161.00					See *Roofing* box on fac-
Remove .... Labor 34.70					ing page.

RELATED ITEMS
Rough Carpentry
chimney cricket 444

Item Description			Unit	Remove	Replace	Total
WOOD SHAKES ▶ *continued* handsplit and resawn ▷	**18" heavy handsplit and resawn shakes**		sq	$34.70	$359.00	$393.70
	Replace Materials.....198.00	Labor 161.00				
	Remove	Labor 34.70				
	24" medium handsplit and resawn shakes		sq	$34.70	$379.00	$413.70
	Replace Materials.....241.00	Labor 138.00				
	Remove	Labor 34.70				
	24" heavy handsplit and resawn shakes		sq	$34.70	$405.00	$439.70
	Replace Materials 267.00	Labor 138.00				
	Remove	Labor 34.70				
taper split ▷	**24" tapersplit shakes**		sq	$34.70	$327.00	$361.70
	Replace Materials 189.00	Labor 138.00				
	Remove	Labor 34.70				
straight split ▷	**18" straight split shakes**		sq	$34.70	$323.00	$357.70
	Replace Materials.....162.00	Labor 161.00				
	Remove	Labor 34.70				
	24" straight split shakes		sq	$34.70	$310.00	$344.70
	Replace Materials.....172.00	Labor 138.00				
	Remove	Labor 34.70				
other exposures ▷	**Add 20% for 8" shake exposure**					
	Deduct 20% for 12" shake exposure					
staggered installation ▷	**Add 16% for staggered shake installation**					
minimum charge ▷	**Minimum charge for shake roof repair**		ea	—	$156.40	$156.40
	Replace Materials......60.00	Labor..........96.40				
replace single shake ▷	**Replace single shake**		ea	—	$30.03	$30.03
	Replace Materials......20.00	Labor..........10.03				
FIBER AND CEMENT ▶ **SHINGLES** *Older style shingles may contain asbestos. This is a hazardous material which requires special techniques and equipment to remove.*	**Fiber and cement shingles, weathering shake**		sq	$32.10	$203.60	$235.70
	Replace Materials.....88.60	Labor..........115.00				
	Remove	Labor 32.10				
	Fiber and cement shingles, Spanish tile		sq	$32.10	$231.00	$263.10
	Replace Materials.....110.00	Labor 121.00				
	Remove	Labor 32.10				
minimum ▷	**Minimum charge for fiber and cement shingle roof repair**		sq	—	$115.90	$115.90
	Replace Materials......41.70	Labor..........74.20				
GRANULAR ▶ **COATED METAL TILE** *See* **Roofing** *box on page 394.*	**Granular coated metal tile, simple pattern**		sq	$30.10	$500.00	$530.10
	Replace Materials 294.00	Labor 206.00				
	Remove	Labor 30.10				
	Granular coated metal tile, complex pattern		sq	$30.10	$562.00	$592.10
	Replace Materials 356.00	Labor 206.00				
	Remove	Labor 30.10				
FLAT CLAY TILE ▶ *See* **Roofing** *box on page 394. Old style clay tile shingles.*	**Flat clay tile shingle, terra-cotta red**		sq	$99.70	$259.00	$358.70
	Replace Materials 103.00	Labor..........156.00				
	Remove	Labor 99.70				
	Flat clay tile shingle, glazed red		sq	$99.70	$370.00	$469.70
	Replace Materials.....214.00	Labor.........156.00				
	Remove	Labor 99.70				

Item Description	Unit	Remove	Replace	Total	
Mission tile, terra-cotta red *Replace* Materials....202.00 Labor.........268.00 *Remove* .... Labor 99.70	sq	$99.70	$470.00	$569.70	◄ **MISSION TILE** See **Roofing** box on page 394. Includes 30 lb felt underlayment, doubled
Mission tile, peach *Replace* Materials....232.00 Labor.........268.00 *Remove* .... Labor 99.70	sq	$99.70	$500.00	$599.70	felt on rakes and eaves, bird stop, booster tiles, ridge and rake tiles.
Mission tile, white *Replace* Materials.....269.00 Labor.........268.00 *Remove* .... Labor 99.70	sq	$99.70	$537.00	$636.70	
Mission tile, color blends *Replace* Materials....254.00 Labor.........268.00 *Remove* .... Labor 99.70	sq	$99.70	$522.00	$621.70	
Mission tile, glazed white *Replace* Materials....550.00 Labor.........268.00 *Remove* .... Labor 99.70	sq	$99.70	$818.00	$917.70	
Mission tile, glazed gray *Replace* Materials ...556.00 Labor.........268.00 *Remove* .... Labor 99.70	sq	$99.70	$824.00	$923.70	
Mission tile, glazed burgundy *Replace* Materials ....559.00 Labor.........268.00 *Remove* .... Labor 99.70	sq	$99.70	$827.00	$926.70	
Mission tile, glazed terra-cotta red *Replace* Materials....558.00 Labor.........268.00 *Remove* .... Labor 99.70	sq	$99.70	$826.00	$925.70	
Mission tile, glazed teal *Replace* Materials....700.00 Labor.........268.00 *Remove* .... Labor 99.70	sq	$99.70	$968.00	$1,067.70	
Mission tile, glazed blue *Replace* Materials.....718.00 Labor.........268.00 *Remove* .... Labor 99.70	sq	$99.70	$986.00	$1,085.70	
Add for vertical furring strips under all cap tiles *Replace* Materials.....107.10 Labor 157.00	sq	–	$264.10	$264.10	◁ add for vertical strips
Add for Mission tiles attached with wire *Replace* Materials ......18.10 Labor 107.00	sq	–	$125.10	$125.10	◁ add for other attachment
Add for Mission tiles attached with stainless steel nails *Replace* Materials 25.00	sq	–	$25.00	$25.00	
Add for Mission tiles attached with brass or copper nails *Replace* Materials 33.40	sq	–	$33.40	$33.40	
Add for Mission tiles with wire attached to braided wire runners *Replace* Materials ......32.30 Labor 105.00	sq	–	$137.30	$137.30	
Add for Mission tiles attached with hurricane clips or wind locks *Replace* Materials ......21.90 Labor 146.00	sq	–	$167.90	$167.90	
Add for adhesive between Mission tiles *Replace* Materials.......17.40 Labor 7.40	sq	–	$24.80	$24.80	

RELATED ITEMS
Rough Carpentry
chimney cricket 444

Item Description	Unit	Remove	Replace	Total
SPANISH TILE ▶ See **Roofing** box on page 394. Includes 30 lb felt underlayment, doubled felt on rakes and eaves, bird stop, ridge and rake tiles.				
Spanish tile, terra-cotta red	sq	$99.70	$288.00	$387.70
Replace Materials.....127.00 Labor 161.00				
Remove .... Labor 99.70				
Spanish tile, peach	sq	$99.70	$318.00	$417.70
Replace Materials.....157.00 Labor 161.00				
Remove .... Labor 99.70				
Spanish tile, white	sq	$99.70	$356.00	$455.70
Replace Materials.....195.00 Labor 161.00				
Remove .... Labor 99.70				
Spanish tile, color blends	sq	$99.70	$340.00	$439.70
Replace Materials.....179.00 Labor 161.00				
Remove .... Labor 99.70				
Spanish tile, glazed white	sq	$99.70	$661.00	$760.70
Replace Materials....500.00 Labor 161.00				
Remove .... Labor 99.70				
Spanish tile, glazed gray	sq	$99.70	$663.00	$762.70
Replace Materials....502.00 Labor 161.00				
Remove .... Labor 99.70				
Spanish tile, glazed burgundy	sq	$99.70	$792.00	$891.70
Replace Materials ....631.00 Labor 161.00				
Remove .... Labor 99.70				
Spanish tile, glazed terra-cotta red	sq	$99.70	$666.00	$765.70
Replace Materials....505.00 Labor 161.00				
Remove .... Labor 99.70				
Spanish tile, glazed teal	sq	$99.70	$799.00	$898.70
Replace Materials....638.00 Labor 161.00				
Remove .... Labor 99.70				
Spanish tile, glazed blue	sq	$99.70	$819.00	$918.70
Replace Materials....658.00 Labor 161.00				
Remove .... Labor 99.70				
add for other ▷ attachment **Add for Spanish tiles attached with wire**	sq	–	$99.50	$99.50
Replace Materials.......15.10 Labor 84.40				
Add for Spanish tiles attached with stainless steel nails	sq	–	$21.00	$21.00
Replace Materials 21.00				
Add for Spanish tiles attached with brass or copper nails	sq	–	$28.10	$28.10
Replace Materials 28.10				
Add for Spanish tiles with wire attached to braided wire runners	sq	–	$97.60	$97.60
Replace Materials ....26.70 Labor...........70.90				
Add for Spanish tiles attached with hurricane clips or wind locks	sq	–	$104.40	$104.40
Replace Materials ......16.70 Labor...........87.70				
Add for Spanish tiles attached using mortar set method	sq	–	$176.40	$176.40
Replace Materials ......49.40 Labor 127.00				
Add for adhesive between Spanish tiles	sq	–	$24.00	$24.00
Replace Materials.......17.40 Labor 6.60				

Item Description	Unit	Remove	Replace	Total
Deduct 5% for ASTM grade 2 moderate weathering tiles				
Deduct 11% for ASTM grade 3 negligible weathering tiles				
Deduct 12% for low profile Spanish or Mission tiles				
Furring strips for roofing tiles, vertically laid only	sq	$13.80	$50.40	$64.20
Replace Materials ......21.20 Labor 29.20				
Remove .... Labor 13.80				
Furring strips for roofing tiles, vertically and horizontally laid	sq	$24.30	$77.30	$101.60
Replace Materials ......35.00 Labor 42.30				
Remove .... Labor 24.30				
Corrugated concrete tile, natural gray	sq	$111.00	$259.00	$370.00
Replace Materials ....108.00 Labor 151.00				
Remove .... Labor 111.00				
Corrugated concrete tile, black	sq	$111.00	$273.00	$384.00
Replace Materials ....122.00 Labor 151.00				
Remove .... Labor 111.00				
Corrugated concrete tile, browns and terra-cotta reds	sq	$111.00	$282.00	$393.00
Replace Materials ....131.00 Labor 151.00				
Remove .... Labor 111.00				
Corrugated concrete tile, bright reds	sq	$111.00	$289.00	$400.00
Replace Materials ....138.00 Labor 151.00				
Remove .... Labor 111.00				
Corrugated concrete tile, greens	sq	$111.00	$302.00	$413.00
Replace Materials ....151.00 Labor 151.00				
Remove .... Labor 111.00				
Corrugated concrete tile, blues	sq	$111.00	$310.00	$421.00
Replace Materials ....159.00 Labor 151.00				
Remove .... Labor 111.00				
Flat concrete tile, natural gray	sq	$111.00	$245.00	$356.00
Replace Materials ......99.00 Labor 146.00				
Remove .... Labor 111.00				
Flat concrete tile, black	sq	$111.00	$258.00	$369.00
Replace Materials ....112.00 Labor 146.00				
Remove .... Labor 111.00				
Flat concrete tile, browns and terra-cotta reds	sq	$111.00	$267.00	$378.00
Replace Materials ....121.00 Labor 146.00				
Remove .... Labor 111.00				
Flat concrete tile, bright reds	sq	$111.00	$274.00	$385.00
Replace Materials ....128.00 Labor 146.00				
Remove .... Labor 111.00				
Flat concrete tile, greens	sq	$111.00	$284.00	$395.00
Replace Materials ....138.00 Labor 146.00				
Remove .... Labor 111.00				
Flat concrete tile, blues	sq	$111.00	$290.00	$401.00
Replace Materials ....144.00 Labor 146.00				
Remove .... Labor 111.00				

◄ **OTHER CLAY TILE GRADES**
Deduct from the cost of Spanish or mission tiles.

◄ **FURRING STRIPS**
See **Roofing** box on page 394.

◄ **CONCRETE TILE**
See **Roofing** box on page 394.

◁ flat

RELATED ITEMS
Rough Carpentry
chimney cricket 444

Item Description	Unit	Remove	Replace	Total
CONCRETE TILE ▶ *continued* additional costs ▷ **Add 2% for glazed concrete tiles**				
Add 5% for painted concrete tiles				
ALUMINUM SHEET ▶ **CORRUGATED** *See Roofing box on page 394.* **.016" thick corrugated aluminum roofing, natural finish**	sf	$.29	$2.08	$2.37
Replace Materials .... .92 Labor 1.16				
Remove .... Labor .... .29				
.019" thick corrugated aluminum roofing, natural finish	sf	$.29	$2.17	$2.46
Replace Materials ...... 1.01 Labor 1.16				
Remove .... Labor .... .29				
colored finish ▷ **.016" thick corrugated aluminum roofing, colored finish**	sf	$.29	$2.30	$2.59
Replace Materials .... 1.14 Labor 1.16				
Remove .... Labor .... .29				
.019" thick corrugated aluminum roofing, colored finish	sf	$.29	$2.43	$2.72
Replace Materials .... 1.27 Labor 1.16				
Remove .... Labor .... .29				
ALUMINUM SHEET ▶ **RIBBED** *See Roofing box on page 394.* **.016" thick ribbed aluminum roofing, natural finish**	sf	$.29	$2.22	$2.51
Replace Materials .... .97 Labor 1.25				
Remove .... Labor .... .29				
.019" thick ribbed aluminum roofing, natural finish	sf	$.29	$2.56	$2.85
Replace Materials ....1.31 Labor 1.25				
Remove .... Labor .... .29				
.032" thick ribbed aluminum roofing, natural finish	sf	$.29	$3.14	$3.43
Replace Materials ....1.89 Labor 1.25				
Remove .... Labor .... .29				
.04" thick ribbed aluminum roofing, natural finish	sf	$.29	$3.71	$4.00
Replace Materials ....2.46 Labor 1.25				
Remove .... Labor .... .29				
.05" thick ribbed aluminum roofing, natural finish	sf	$.29	$4.15	$4.44
Replace Materials ....2.90 Labor 1.25				
Remove .... Labor .... .29				
colored finish ▷ **.016" thick ribbed aluminum roofing, colored finish**	sf	$.29	$2.39	$2.68
Replace Materials ....1.14 Labor 1.25				
Remove .... Labor .... .29				
.019" thick ribbed aluminum roofing, colored finish	sf	$.29	$2.53	$2.82
Replace Materials ....1.28 Labor 1.25				
Remove .... Labor .... .29				
.032" thick ribbed aluminum roofing, colored finish	sf	$.29	$3.18	$3.47
Replace Materials ....1.93 Labor 1.25				
Remove .... Labor .... .29				
.04" thick ribbed aluminum roofing, colored finish	sf	$.29	$4.52	$4.81
Replace Materials ....3.27 Labor 1.25				
Remove .... Labor .... .29				
.05" thick ribbed aluminum roofing, colored finish	sf	$.29	$4.99	$5.28
Replace Materials ....3.74 Labor 1.25				
Remove .... Labor .... .29				
FIBERGLASS ▶ **CORRUGATED** *See Roofing page 394.* **8 ounce corrugated fiberglass roofing**	sf	$.26	$3.64	$3.90
Replace Materials ....2.48 Labor 1.16				
Remove .... Labor .... .26				

Item Description	Unit	Remove	Replace	Total	
12 ounce corrugated fiberglass roofing *Replace* Materials........3.30 Labor ....1.16 *Remove* .... Labor........... .26	sf	$.26	$4.46	$4.72	
30 gauge galvanized steel corrugated roofing *Replace* Materials........ .92 Labor ....1.21 *Remove* .... Labor........... .29	sf	$.29	$2.13	$2.42	◄ **GALVANIZED STEEL CORRUGATED** See *Roofing* box on page 394.
28 gauge galvanized steel corrugated roofing *Replace* Materials........ .96 Labor ....1.21 *Remove* .... Labor........... .29	sf	$.29	$2.17	$2.46	
26 gauge galvanized steel corrugated roofing *Replace* Materials...... 1.02 Labor ....1.21 *Remove* .... Labor........... .29	sf	$.29	$2.23	$2.52	
24 gauge galvanized steel corrugated roofing *Replace* Materials........1.14 Labor ....1.21 *Remove* .... Labor........... .29	sf	$.29	$2.35	$2.64	
30 gauge galvanized steel ribbed roofing *Replace* Materials........ .96 Labor ....1.25 *Remove* .... Labor........... .29	sf	$.29	$2.21	$2.50	◄ **GALVANIZED STEEL RIBBED** See *Roofing* box on page 394.
28 gauge galvanized steel ribbed roofing *Replace* Materials...... 1.00 Labor ....1.25 *Remove* .... Labor........... .29	sf	$.29	$2.25	$2.54	
26 gauge galvanized steel ribbed roofing *Replace* Materials...... 1.06 Labor ....1.25 *Remove* .... Labor........... .29	sf	$.29	$2.31	$2.60	
24 gauge galvanized steel ribbed roofing *Replace* Materials........1.20 Labor ....1.25 *Remove* .... Labor........... .29	sf	$.29	$2.45	$2.74	
30 gauge galvanized steel ribbed roofing with colored finish *Replace* Materials........1.31 Labor ....1.25 *Remove* .... Labor........... .29	sf	$.29	$2.56	$2.85	◁ colored finish
28 gauge galvanized steel ribbed roofing with colored finish *Replace* Materials........1.39 Labor ....1.25 *Remove* .... Labor........... .29	sf	$.29	$2.64	$2.93	
26 gauge galvanized steel ribbed roofing with colored finish *Replace* Materials........1.48 Labor ....1.25 *Remove* .... Labor........... .29	sf	$.29	$2.73	$3.02	
24 gauge galvanized steel ribbed roofing with colored finish *Replace* Materials........1.63 Labor ....1.25 *Remove* .... Labor........... .29	sf	$.29	$2.88	$3.17	
16 ounce copper standing seam roofing *Replace* Materials.....616.00 Labor.........321.00 *Remove* .... Labor 29.80	sq	$29.80	$937.00	$966.80	◄ **COPPER** See *Roofing* box on page 394. ◁ standing seam
18 ounce copper standing seam roofing *Replace* Materials....685.00 Labor ....344.00 *Remove* .... Labor 29.80	sq	$29.80	$1,029.00	$1,058.80	
20 ounce copper standing seam roofing *Replace* Materials....783.00 Labor.........371.00 *Remove* .... Labor 29.80	sq	$29.80	$1,154.00	$1,183.80	

RELATED ITEMS
Rough Carpentry
chimney cricket 444

	Item Description	Unit	Remove	Replace	Total
COPPER ▶ continued batten seam ▷	**16 ounce copper batten seam roofing** *Replace* Materials....630.00 Labor.........371.00 *Remove* .... Labor 29.80	sq	$29.80	$1,001.00	$1,030.80
	18 ounce copper batten seam roofing *Replace* Materials....700.00 Labor.........402.00 *Remove* .... Labor 29.80	sq	$29.80	$1,102.00	$1,131.80
	20 ounce copper batten seam roofing *Replace* Materials....803.00 Labor.........438.00 *Remove* .... Labor 29.80	sq	$29.80	$1,241.00	$1,270.80
flat seam ▷	**16 ounce copper flat seam roofing** *Replace* Materials....565.00 Labor.........344.00 *Remove* .... Labor 29.80	sq	$29.80	$909.00	$938.80
	18 ounce copper flat seam roofing *Replace* Materials....631.00 Labor.........371.00 *Remove* .... Labor 29.80	sq	$29.80	$1,002.00	$1,031.80
	20 ounce copper flat seam roofing *Replace* Materials....707.00 Labor.........402.00 *Remove* .... Labor 29.80	sq	$29.80	$1,109.00	$1,138.80
LEAD ▶ See **Roofing** box on page 394.	**3 lb batten seam lead roof** *Replace* Materials....691.00 Labor.........344.00 *Remove* .... Labor 29.80	sq	$29.80	$1,035.00	$1,064.80
	3 lb flat seam lead roof *Replace* Materials....623.00 Labor.........371.00 *Remove* .... Labor 29.80	sq	$29.80	$994.00	$1,023.80
STAINLESS STEEL ▶ See **Roofing** box on page 394. standing seam ▷	**28 gauge stainless steel standing seam roof** *Replace* Materials....451.00 Labor.........344.00 *Remove* .... Labor 29.80	sq	$29.80	$795.00	$824.80
	26 gauge stainless steel standing seam roof *Replace* Materials....504.00 Labor.........321.00 *Remove* .... Labor 29.80	sq	$29.80	$825.00	$854.80
batten seam ▷	**28 gauge stainless steel batten seam roof** *Replace* Materials....464.00 Labor.........371.00 *Remove* .... Labor 29.80	sq	$29.80	$835.00	$864.80
	26 gauge stainless steel batten seam roof *Replace* Materials....518.00 Labor.........344.00 *Remove* .... Labor 29.80	sq	$29.80	$862.00	$891.80
flat seam ▷	**28 gauge stainless steel flat seam roof** *Replace* Materials....430.00 Labor.........344.00 *Remove* .... Labor 29.80	sq	$29.80	$774.00	$803.80
	26 gauge stainless steel flat seam roof *Replace* Materials....481.00 Labor.........321.00 *Remove* .... Labor 29.80	sq	$29.80	$802.00	$831.80
coated finish ▷	**Add 13% for terne coated stainless steel**				
	Add 14% for lead coated stainless steel				
TERNE ▶ See **Roofing** box on page 394.	**40 lb terne standing seam roof** *Replace* Materials...1020.00 Labor.........402.00 *Remove* .... Labor 29.80	sq	$29.80	$1,422.00	$1,451.80

Item Description	Unit	Remove	Replace	Total
40 lb terne batten seam roof	sq	$29.80	$1,411.00	$1,440.80
Replace Materials..1040.00 Labor.........371.00				
Remove .... Labor..........29.80				
40 lb terne flat seam roof	sq	$29.80	$1,410.00	$1,439.80
Replace Materials ....972.00 Labor 438.00				
Remove .... Labor 29.80				
Solder patch into metal roof (less than 1' square)	ea	–	$97.30	$97.30
Replace Materials ......45.00 Labor..........52.30				
Minimum charge for seamed metal roof repair	ea	–	$241.00	$241.00
Replace Materials ......110.00 Labor 131.00				
Built-up 3 ply roofing	sq	$70.50	$226.29	$296.79
Replace Materials ......55.00 Labor ....161.00 Equipment 10.29				
Remove .... Labor..........70.50				
Built-up 4 ply roofing	sq	$87.60	$281.47	$369.07
Replace Materials ......77.00 Labor ....193.00 Equipment...........11.47				
Remove .... Labor..........87.60				
Built-up 5 ply roofing	sq	$111.00	$356.70	$467.70
Replace Materials .....115.00 Labor ....229.00 Equipment 12.70				
Remove .... Labor..........111.00				
Minimum charge for roofing work requiring hot asphalt	ea	–	$401.00	$401.00
Replace Materials.....160.00 Labor 241.00				
Add for built-up roofing gravel surface embedded in flood coat	sq	$24.50	$34.68	$59.18
Replace Materials....13.80 Labor ....19.30 Equipment...........1.58				
Remove .... Labor..........24.50				
Add for flood coat	sq	–	$55.92	$55.92
Replace Materials....17.30 Labor ....34.40 Equipment..........4.22				
Add to paint built-up roof with aluminum UV coating	sq	–	$56.80	$56.80
Replace Materials ......16.60 Labor 40.20				
Add to paint built-up roof with aluminum UV coating with fiber	sq	–	$60.90	$60.90
Replace Materials ......20.70 Labor 40.20				
Add for mineral faced cap sheet	sq	–	$17.30	$17.30
Replace Materials.......17.30				
Remove gravel, flood coat, then replace gravel	sq	–	$173.30	$173.30
Replace Materials ......37.00 Labor ....119.30 Equipment 17.00				
Add per lf of parapet wall on built-up roof	lf	–	$21.45	$21.45
Replace Materials.......9.80 Labor..........10.90 Equipment 75				
45 mil SCPE elastomeric roofing, loose laid and ballasted with stone	sq	$59.00	$218.22	$277.22
Replace Materials.....167.00 Labor ....48.20 Equipment...........3.02				
Remove .... Labor..........59.00				
45 mil SCPE elastomeric roofing, attached at seams with batten strips	sq	$28.30	$222.03	$250.33
Replace Materials.....177.00 Labor ....40.20 Equipment...........4.83				
Remove .... Labor..........28.30				
45 mil SCPE elastomeric roofing, fully attached to deck	sq	$45.10	$244.30	$289.40
Replace Materials.....185.00 Labor ....50.10 Equipment...........9.20				
Remove .... Labor..........45.10				

◀ **TERNE**
Terne is short for Terneplate. Terneplate is sheet iron or steel that is plated with an alloy that is one part tin and three to four parts lead.

◀ **SEAMED METAL ROOF REPAIR**
For repairs to standing seam, batten seam, or flat seam metal roofs.

◀ **BUILT-UP**
Does not include finish coat or wrap up parapet wall (see below).

◁ minimum

◁ surface finish

RELATED ITEMS
Rough Carpentry
chimney cricket 444

◁ replace gravel

◁ add for parapet wall
Includes cant strip and roofing wrap up wall.

◀ **SCPE ELASTOMERIC**
Chlorosulfonated polyethylene-hypalon roofing is abbreviated SCPE. Ballasted roofs contain 1/2 ton of stone per square.

Item Description	Unit	Remove	Replace	Total
EPDM ►				
ELASTOMERIC				
Ethylene propylene diene monomer roofing is abbreviated EPDM. Ballasted roofs contain 1/2 ton of stone per square.				
45 mil EPDM elastomeric roofing, loose laid & ballasted with stone	sq	$59.00	$214.82	$273.82
Replace Materials......93.80 Labor..........118.00 Equipment............3.02				
Remove .... Labor..........59.00				
45 mil EPDM elastomeric roofing, attached to deck at seams	sq	$28.30	$181.83	$210.13
Replace Materials......80.60 Labor..........96.40 Equipment............4.83				
Remove .... Labor 28.30				
45 mil EPDM elastomeric roofing, fully attached to deck	sq	$45.10	$260.20	$305.30
Replace Materials .....113.00 Labor..........138.00 Equipment............9.20				
Remove .... Labor..........45.10				
55 mil ▷ **55 mil EPDM elastomeric roofing, loose laid & ballasted with stone**	sq	$59.00	$232.02	$291.02
Replace Materials ....108.00 Labor..........121.00 Equipment............3.02				
Remove .... Labor..........59.00				
55 mil EPDM elastomeric roofing, attached to deck at seams	sq	$28.30	$198.53	$226.83
Replace Materials .....95.40 Labor..........98.30 Equipment............4.83				
Remove .... Labor..........28.30				
55 mil EPDM elastomeric roofing, fully attached to deck	sq	$45.10	$280.20	$325.30
Replace Materials ....129.00 Labor..........142.00 Equipment............9.20				
Remove .... Labor..........45.10				
60 mil ▷ **60 mil EPDM elastomeric roofing, loose laid & ballasted with stone**	sq	$59.00	$241.02	$300.02
Replace Materials .....115.00 Labor..........123.00 Equipment............3.02				
Remove .... Labor..........59.00				
60 mil EPDM elastomeric roofing, attached to deck at seams	sq	$28.30	$203.33	$231.63
Replace Materials ......98.20 Labor..........100.30 Equipment............4.83				
Remove .... Labor 28.30				
60 mil EPDM elastomeric roofing, fully attached to deck	sq	$45.10	$286.20	$331.30
Replace Materials .....131.00 Labor..........146.00 Equipment............9.20				
Remove .... Labor..........45.10				
PVC ►				
Polyvinyl chloride roofing is abbreviated PVC. Ballasted roofs contain 1/2 ton of stone per square.				
45 mil PVC elastomeric roofing, loose laid & ballasted with stone	sq	$59.00	$144.32	$203.32
Replace Materials .....113.00 Labor..........28.30 Equipment............3.02				
Remove .... Labor..........59.00				
45 mil PVC elastomeric roofing, attached to deck at seams	sq	$28.30	$189.63	$217.93
Replace Materials .....141.00 Labor..........43.80 Equipment............4.83				
45 mil ▷ *Remove* .... Labor 28.30				
45 mil PVC elastomeric roofing, fully attached to deck	sq	$45.10	$226.30	$271.40
Replace Materials.....153.00 Labor..........64.10 Equipment............9.20				
Remove .... Labor..........45.10				
add for reinforced ▷ **Add 22% for 45 mil reinforced PVC elastomeric roofing**				
48 mil ▷ **48 mil PVC elastomeric roofing, loose laid & ballasted with stone**	sq	$59.00	$155.12	$214.12
Replace Materials ....122.00 Labor ....30.10 Equipment............3.02				
Remove .... Labor..........59.00				
48 mil PVC elastomeric roofing, attached to deck at seams	sq	$28.30	$199.03	$227.33
Replace Materials ....146.00 Labor ....48.20 Equipment............4.83				
Remove .... Labor..........28.30				
48 mil PVC elastomeric roofing, fully attached to deck	sq	$45.10	$234.30	$279.40
Replace Materials.....160.00 Labor..........65.10 Equipment............9.20				
Remove .... Labor..........45.10				

Item Description	Unit	Remove	Replace	Total	
60 mil PVC elastomeric roofing, loose laid & ballasted with stone	sq	$59.00	$202.12	$261.12	◁ 60 mil
Replace Materials.....167.00 Labor ....32.10 Equipment...........3.02					
Remove .... Labor..........59.00					
60 mil PVC elastomeric roofing, attached to deck at seams	sq	$28.30	$233.03	$261.33	
Replace Materials.....179.00 Labor..........49.20 Equipment...........4.83					
Remove .... Labor 28.30					
60 mil PVC elastomeric roofing, fully attached to deck	sq	$45.10	$278.20	$323.30	
Replace Materials....202.00 Labor..........67.00 Equipment...........9.20					
Remove .... Labor..........45.10					
120 mil modified bitumen roofing, loose laid & ballasted with stone	sq	$59.00	$140.34	$199.34	◀ **MODIFIED BITUMEN**
Replace Materials......85.10 Labor..........47.70 Equipment...........7.54					*Comes in hot-mop or torch-down styles.*
Remove .... Labor..........59.00					
120 mil modified bitumen roofing, attached to deck at seams	sq	$28.30	$143.54	$171.84	◁ 120 mil
Replace Materials......80.60 Labor..........55.40 Equipment...........7.54					
Remove .... Labor 28.30					
120 mil modified bitumen roofing, fully attached to deck with torch	sq	$45.10	$160.05	$205.15	
Replace Materials......79.20 Labor..........71.80 Equipment...........9.05					
Remove .... Labor..........45.10					
120 mil modified bitumen roofing, fully attached with hot asphalt	sq	$45.10	$171.90	$217.00	
Replace Materials......88.00 Labor..........71.80 Equipment 12.10					
Remove .... Labor..........45.10					
150 mil modified bitumen roofing, loose laid & ballasted with stone	sq	$59.00	$146.64	$205.64	◁ 150 mil
Replace Materials......90.90 Labor ....48.20 Equipment...........7.54					
Remove .... Labor..........59.00					
150 mil modified bitumen roofing, attached to deck at seams	sq	$28.30	$149.54	$177.84	
Replace Materials......85.10 Labor ....56.90 Equipment...........7.54					
Remove .... Labor 28.30					
150 mil modified bitumen roofing, fully attached to deck	sq	$45.10	$165.95	$211.05	
Replace Materials......83.60 Labor..........73.30 Equipment...........9.05					
Remove .... Labor..........45.10					
150 mil modified bitumen roofing, fully attached with hot asphalt	sq	$45.10	$179.70	$224.80	
Replace Materials......92.40 Labor ....75.20 Equipment 12.10					
Remove .... Labor..........45.10					
160 mil modified bitumen roofing, loose laid & ballasted with stone	sq	$59.00	$149.14	$208.14	◁ 160 mil
Replace Materials......92.40 Labor..........49.20 Equipment...........7.54					
Remove .... Labor..........59.00					
160 mil modified bitumen roofing, attached to deck at seams	sq	$28.30	$153.34	$181.64	
Replace Materials......88.00 Labor..........57.80 Equipment...........7.54					
Remove .... Labor 28.30					
160 mil modified bitumen roofing, fully attached to deck	sq	$45.10	$169.75	$214.85	
Replace Materials......86.50 Labor..........74.20 Equipment...........9.05					
Remove .... Labor..........45.10					
160 mil modified bitumen roofing, fully attached with hot asphalt	sq	$45.10	$189.70	$234.80	
Replace Materials.....101.00 Labor..........76.60 Equipment 12.10					
Remove .... Labor..........45.10					
15-pound roofing felt	sq	$4.30	$8.50	$12.80	◀ **ROOFING FELT**
Replace Materials........4.40 Labor 4.10					
Remove .... Labor 4.30					

RELATED ITEMS
Rough Carpentry
chimney cricket 444

	Item Description	Unit	Remove	Replace	Total
ROOFING FELT ▶ *continued*	**30-pound roofing felt**	sq	$4.30	$12.02	$16.32
	Replace Materials......7.92 Labor 4.10				
	Remove .... Labor 4.30				
ICE AND WATER ▶ **SHIELD**	**Ice and water shield**	sf	–	$.91	$.91
	Replace Materials .... .52 Labor .... .39				
DRIP EDGE ▶	**Drip edge**	lf	$.14	$.77	$.91
	Replace Materials .... .48 Labor .... .29				
	Remove .... Labor .... .14				
GRAVEL STOP ▶	**Gravel stop**	lf	$.14	$1.13	$1.27
	Replace Materials .... .84 Labor .... .29				
	Remove .... Labor .... .14				
STEP FLASHING ▶	**Step flashing**	lf	–	$3.29	$3.29
	Replace Materials........1.36 Labor 1.93				
CHIMNEY SAW- ▶ **KERF FLASHING**	**Chimney saw-kerf flashing**	lf	–	$14.32	$14.32
	Replace Materials........6.70 Labor 7.62				
	Minimum charge for chimney saw-kerf flashing	ea	–	$88.40	$88.40
	Replace Materials......40.20 Labor 48.20				
VALLEY METAL ▶	**Valley metal (galvanized or aluminum)**	lf	$.29	$2.62	$2.91
	Replace Materials........1.80 Labor .... .82				
	Remove .... Labor .... .29				
	Copper valley metal	lf	$.29	$8.02	$8.31
	Replace Materials........7.22 Labor .... .80				
	Remove .... Labor .... .29				
PIPE JACK ▶	**Pipe jack**	ea	$9.88	$17.20	$27.08
	Replace Materials........8.76 Labor 8.44				
	Remove .... Labor 9.88				
ROOF VENT ▶	**Roof vent, turbine**	ea	$12.20	$47.90	$60.10
	Replace Materials......33.70 Labor........14.20				
	Remove .... Labor........12.20				
	Roof vent, turtle	ea	$12.20	$28.30	$40.50
	Replace Materials......16.10 Labor........12.20				
	Remove .... Labor........12.20				
	Roof vent, gable	ea	$12.20	$32.90	$45.10
	Replace Materials......20.50 Labor........12.40				
	Remove .... Labor........12.20				
	Remove roof vent for work, then reinstall	ea	–	$23.60	$23.60
	Replace .... Labor 23.60				
FURNACE VENT ▶	**Furnace vent cap**	ea	$12.40	$21.68	$34.08
	Replace Materials........11.80 Labor 9.88				
	Remove .... Labor..........12.40				
	Remove vent cap for work, then reinstall	ea	–	$17.10	$17.10
	Replace .... Labor..........17.10				
REPAIR LEAK ▶ **WITH MASTIC**	**Repair roof leak with mastic**	ea	–	$25.00	$25.00
	Replace Materials........3.20 Labor..........21.80				
	Repair flashing leak with mastic	ea	–	$24.20	$24.20
	Replace Materials........3.20 Labor..........21.00				

TIME & MATERIAL CHARTS *(selected items)*

Roofing Materials

See **Roofing** material prices with the line items and other information in the **QuickFinder** column.

Roofing Labor

LABORER	BASE WAGE	PAID LEAVE	TRUE WAGE	FICA	FUTA	WORKER'S COMP.	UNEMPLOY. INSUR.	HEALTH INSUR.	RETIRE (401K)	LIABILITY INSUR.	COST PER HOUR
Roofer / slater	$23.70	1.85	$25.55	1.95	.20	14.87	2.22	2.92	.77	3.83	$52.30
Roofer's helper	$19.70	1.54	$21.24	1.62	.17	12.36	1.85	2.92	.64	3.19	$44.00
Demolition laborer	$14.40	1.12	$15.52	1.19	.12	5.01	1.35	2.92	.47	2.33	$28.90

Paid Leave is calculated based on two weeks paid vacation, one week sick leave, and seven paid holidays. Employer's matching portion of **FICA** is 7.65 percent. **FUTA** (Federal Unemployment) is .8 percent. **Worker's compensation** for the roofing trade was calculated using a national average of 58.09 percent. **Unemployment insurance** was calculated using a national average of 8.7 percent. **Health insurance** was calculated based on a projected national average for 2005 of $580 per employee (and family when applicable) per month. Employer pays 80 percent for a per month cost of $464 per employee. **Retirement** is based on a 401(k) retirement program with employer matching of 50 percent. Employee contributions to the 401(k) plan are an average of 6 percent of the true wage. **Liability insurance** is based on a national average of 14.0 percent.

Roofing Labor Productivity

WORK DESCRIPTION	LABORER	COST PER HOUR	PRODUCTIVITY	UNIT PRICE
Demolition				
remove metal shingles	demolition laborer	$28.90	1.04	$30.10 sq
remove asphalt shingles	demolition laborer	$28.90	1.02	$29.50 sq
remove roll roofing	demolition laborer	$28.90	.735	$21.20 sq
remove slate shingles	demolition laborer	$28.90	3.70	$107.00 sq
remove wood shingles or shakes	demolition laborer	$28.90	1.20	$34.70 sq
remove fiber and cement shingles	demolition laborer	$28.90	1.11	$32.10 sq
remove mission or Spanish tile shingles	demolition laborer	$28.90	3.45	$99.70 sq
remove vertically laid furring strips	demolition laborer	$28.90	.478	$13.80 sq
remove vertically & horizontally laid furring strips	demolition laborer	$28.90	.840	$24.30 sq
remove concrete shingles	demolition laborer	$28.90	3.85	$111.00 sq
remove preformed metal roofing	demolition laborer	$28.90	.010	$.29 sf
remove preformed fiberglass roofing	demolition laborer	$28.90	.009	$.26 sf
remove seamed metal roofing	demolition laborer	$28.90	1.03	$29.80 sq
remove built-up 3 ply roofing	demolition laborer	$28.90	2.44	$70.50 sq
remove built-up 4 ply roofing	demolition laborer	$28.90	3.03	$87.60 sq
remove built-up 5 ply roofing	demolition laborer	$28.90	3.85	$111.00 sq
add to remove built-up roof with ballast	demolition laborer	$28.90	.847	$24.50 sq
remove single ply roof partially adhered	demolition laborer	$28.90	.980	$28.30 sq
remove single ply roof fully adhered	demolition laborer	$28.90	1.56	$45.10 sq
remove single ply roof with ballast	demolition laborer	$28.90	2.04	$59.00 sq
Roofing crew				
install roofing	roofer	$52.30		
install roofing	roofer's helper	$44.00		
install roofing	roofing crew	$48.20		
Install shingles				
aluminum shingles	roofing crew	$48.20	1.06	$51.10 sq
galvanized steel shingles	roofing crew	$48.20	1.11	$53.50 sq
20 year to 25 year asphalt	roofing crew	$48.20	1.24	$59.80 sq
30 year to 40 year asphalt	roofing crew	$48.20	1.27	$61.20 sq
standard grade laminated asphalt	roofing crew	$48.20	2.06	$99.30 sq
high grade laminated asphalt	roofing crew	$48.20	2.45	$118.00 sq
T-lock asphalt	roofing crew	$48.20	1.27	$61.20 sq
hexagonal asphalt	roofing crew	$48.20	1.27	$61.20 sq
diamond asphalt	roofing crew	$48.20	1.27	$61.20 sq

. . . More ➢

Roofing Labor Productivity *continued*

WORK DESCRIPTION	LABORER	COST PER HOUR	PRODUCTIVITY	UNIT PRICE
Install roll roofing				
all weights	roofing crew	$48.20	.645	$31.10 sq
Install slate				
typical	roofing crew	$48.20	4.00	$193.00 sq
replace single slate shingle	roofing crew	$48.20	.385	$18.60 ea
Install wood shingles				
16"	roofing crew	$48.20	2.86	$138.00 sq
24"	roofing crew	$48.20	2.00	$96.40 sq
replace single wood shingle	roofing crew	$48.20	.208	$10.00 ea
Install wood shakes				
18"	roofing crew	$48.20	3.33	$161.00 sq
24"	roofing crew	$48.20	2.86	$138.00 sq
replace single shake	roofing crew	$48.20	.208	$10.03 ea
Install fiber and cement shingles				
weathering shake style	roofing crew	$48.20	2.38	$115.00 sq
Spanish tile style	roofing crew	$48.20	2.50	$121.00 sq
Install clay tile				
flat	roofing crew	$48.20	3.23	$156.00 sq
Mission tile	roofing crew	$48.20	5.56	$268.00 sq
Spanish tile	roofing crew	$48.20	3.33	$161.00 sq
Install tile furring strips				
vertically laid only	roofing crew	$48.20	.606	$29.20 sq
vertically and horizontally laid	roofing crew	$48.20	.877	$42.30 sq
Install concrete tile				
corrugated	roofing crew	$48.20	3.13	$151.00 sq
flat	roofing crew	$48.20	3.03	$146.00 sq
Install pre-formed roofing				
corrugated aluminum or fiberglass	roofing crew	$48.20	.024	$1.16 sf
corrugated galvanized steel	roofing crew	$48.20	.025	$1.21 sf
ribbed (all types)	roofing crew	$48.20	.026	$1.25 sf
Install standing seam metal roofing				
16 ounce copper	roofing crew	$48.20	6.67	$321.00 sq
20 ounce copper	roofing crew	$48.20	7.69	$371.00 sq
28 gauge stainless steel	roofing crew	$48.20	7.14	$344.00 sq
40 lb terne	roofing crew	$48.20	8.33	$402.00 sq
Install batten seam metal roofing				
16 ounce copper	roofing crew	$48.20	7.69	$371.00 sq
20 ounce copper	roofing crew	$48.20	9.09	$438.00 sq
28 gauge stainless steel	roofing crew	$48.20	7.69	$371.00 sq
26 gauge stainless steel	roofing crew	$48.20	7.14	$344.00 sq
3 lb lead	roofing crew	$48.20	7.14	$344.00 sq
40 lb terne	roofing crew	$48.20	7.69	$371.00 sq
Install flat seam metal roofing				
16 ounce copper	roofing crew	$48.20	7.14	$344.00 sq
20 ounce copper	roofing crew	$48.20	8.33	$402.00 sq
28 gauge stainless steel	roofing crew	$48.20	7.14	$344.00 sq
26 gauge stainless steel	roofing crew	$48.20	6.67	$321.00 sq
3 lb lead	roofing crew	$48.20	7.69	$371.00 sq
40 lb terne	roofing crew	$48.20	9.09	$438.00 sq
Seamed metal roofing repair				
solder patch (less than 1' square)	roofer	$52.30	1.00	$52.30 ea
Install built-up roof				
3 ply	roofing crew	$48.20	3.33	$161.00 sq
4 ply	roofing crew	$48.20	4.00	$193.00 sq
5 ply	roofing crew	$48.20	4.76	$229.00 sq

✍ NOTES: _____

_____ end

32 .... *Rough Carpentry*

Item Description	Unit	Remove	Replace	Total	
Minimum charge for rough carpentry work *Replace* Materials......50.00 Labor 50.30	ea	–	$100.30	$100.30	◄ **MINIMUM**
2" x 4" interior partition wall 8' tall 16" on center *Replace* Materials........9.32 Labor ....9.11 *Remove* .... Labor 1.30	lf	$1.30	$18.43	$19.73	◄ **PER LF** **INTERIOR** **PARTITION WALL**
2" x 4" interior partition wall 8' tall 24" on center *Replace* Materials........7.79 Labor ....7.75 *Remove*........................ Labor 1.30	lf	$1.30	$15.54	$16.84	*Includes 5% waste.* *Based on an average wall* *with 4 openings and 5* *corners per 56 lf of wall.*
2" x 4" interior partition wall 10' tall 16" on center *Replace* Materials.......11.09 Labor ....9.22 *Remove* .... Labor 1.65	lf	$1.65	$20.31	$21.96	*A net of 2.2 studs is* *added for each corner and* *opening. All walls have* *two top plates and a sin-*
2" x 4" interior partition wall 10' tall 24" on center *Replace* Materials........9.17 Labor ....7.82 *Remove* .... Labor 1.65	lf	$1.65	$16.99	$18.64	*gle bottom plate.*
2" x 6" interior partition wall 8' tall 16" on center *Replace* Materials.......13.40 Labor ....9.22 *Remove*........................ Labor 1.39	lf	$1.39	$22.62	$24.01	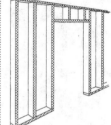
2" x 6" interior partition wall 8' tall 24" on center *Replace* Materials.......11.21 Labor ....7.82 *Remove*........................ Labor 1.39	lf	$1.39	$19.03	$20.42	
2" x 6" interior partition wall 10' tall 16" on center *Replace* Materials.......15.90 Labor ....9.34 *Remove*........................ Labor 1.73	lf	$1.73	$25.24	$26.97	**LUMBER PRICES**
2" x 6" interior partition wall 10' tall 24" on center *Replace* Materials.......13.10 Labor ....7.90 *Remove*........................ Labor 1.73	lf	$1.73	$21.00	$22.73	Some lumber prices, such as oak timbers, vary by as much as 60% depending on the region.
2" x 8" interior partition wall 8' tall 16" on center *Replace* Materials.......17.40 Labor ....9.34 *Remove* .... Labor 1.42	lf	$1.42	$26.74	$28.16	These prices will be 15% to 30% lower in the Northeast, South, and most Great Lake states
2" x 8" interior partition wall 8' tall 24" on center *Replace* Materials ......14.70 Labor ....7.90 *Remove* .... Labor 1.42	lf	$1.42	$22.60	$24.02	and provinces. In many areas of the western mid-west and mountain states
2" x 8" interior partition wall 10' tall 16" on center *Replace* Materials......20.60 Labor ....9.45 *Remove* .... Labor 1.76	lf	$1.76	$30.05	$31.81	and provinces, oak timbers are not available unless specially shipped for a
2" x 8" interior partition wall 10' tall 24" on center *Replace* Materials.......17.10 Labor ....7.98 *Remove* .... Labor 1.76	lf	$1.76	$25.08	$26.84	particular job. For the most accurate results, compare your local prices with the prices found in the material charts for this section
2" x 4" interior bearing wall 8' tall 12" on center *Replace* Materials.......13.50 Labor ....11.60 *Remove*........................ Labor 1.30	lf	$1.30	$25.10	$26.40	starting on page 445 and create a materials factor.
2" x 4" interior bearing wall 8' tall 16" on center *Replace* Materials ......12.01 Labor ....9.87 *Remove*........................ Labor 1.30	lf	$1.30	$21.88	$23.18	◄ **PER LF** **INTERIOR** **BEARING WALL** *continued on next page*

Item Description	Unit	Remove	Replace	Total
2" x 4" interior bearing wall 10' tall 12" on center	lf	$1.65	$27.50	$29.15
Replace Materials.......15.70 Labor...........11.80				
Remove .... Labor...........1.65				
2" x 4" interior bearing wall 10' tall 16" on center	lf	$1.65	$23.82	$25.47
Replace Materials.......13.80 Labor...........10.02				
Remove .... Labor...........1.65				
2" x 6" interior bearing wall 8' tall 12" on center	lf	$1.39	$34.80	$36.19
Replace Materials......23.10 Labor...........11.70				
Remove..................... Labor...........1.39				
2" x 6" interior bearing wall 8' tall 16" on center	lf	$1.39	$30.84	$32.23
Replace Materials......20.90 Labor...........9.94				
Remove..................... Labor...........1.39				
2" x 6" interior bearing wall 10' tall 12" on center	lf	$1.73	$38.00	$39.73
Replace Materials......26.10 Labor...........11.90				
Remove..................... Labor...........1.73				
2" x 6" interior bearing wall 10' tall 16" on center	lf	$1.73	$33.49	$35.22
Replace Materials......23.40 Labor...........10.09				
Remove..................... Labor...........1.73				
2" x 8" interior bearing wall 8' tall 12" on center	lf	$1.42	$42.00	$43.42
Replace Materials......30.20 Labor...........11.80				
Remove .... Labor...........1.42				
2" x 8" interior bearing wall 8' tall 16" on center	lf	$1.42	$37.55	$38.97
Replace Materials......27.50 Labor...........10.05				
Remove .... Labor...........1.42				
2" x 8" interior bearing wall 10' tall 12" on center	lf	$1.76	$46.10	$47.86
Replace Materials......34.10 Labor...........12.00				
Remove .... Labor...........1.76				
2" x 8" interior bearing wall 10' tall 16" on center	lf	$1.76	$40.80	$42.56
Replace Materials......30.60 Labor...........10.20				
Remove .... Labor...........1.76				
2" x 4" exterior wall 8' tall 12" on center	lf	$1.30	$25.61	$26.91
Replace Materials.......13.81 Labor...........11.80				
Remove..................... Labor...........1.30				
2" x 4" exterior wall 8' tall 16" on center	lf	$1.30	$22.37	$23.67
Replace Materials ......12.28 Labor...........10.09				
Remove..................... Labor...........1.30				
2" x 4" exterior wall 8' tall 24" on center	lf	$1.30	$18.91	$20.21
Replace Materials ......10.75 Labor...........8.16				
Remove..................... Labor...........1.30				
2" x 4" exterior wall 10' tall 12" on center	lf	$1.65	$28.00	$29.65
Replace Materials ......16.00 Labor...........12.00				
Remove .... Labor...........1.65				
2" x 4" exterior wall 10' tall 16" on center	lf	$1.65	$24.30	$25.95
Replace Materials ......14.10 Labor...........10.20				
Remove .... Labor...........1.65				
2" x 4" exterior wall 10' tall 24" on center	lf	$1.65	$20.38	$22.03
Replace Materials ......12.14 Labor...........8.24				
Remove .... Labor...........1.65				

PER LF ▶
**INTERIOR
BEARING WALL**
continued

*Includes 5% waste.
Based on an average wall
with 4 openings and 5
corners per 56 lf of wall.
A net of 2.2 studs is
added for each corner and
opening. (Four openings
are, two 3' wide, one 4'
wide, and one 5' wide for
a total of 15 lf.) Headers
in openings are made
from sandwiched 2" x
10" boards with 1/2"
CDX plywood stiffeners
between. All walls have
two top plates and a sin-
gle
bottom plate.*

PER LF ▶
EXTERIOR WALL
*Includes 5% waste.
Based on an average wall
with 4 openings and 5
corners per 56 lf of wall.
A net of 2.2 studs is
added for each corner and
opening. (Four openings
are, two 3' wide, one 4'
wide, and one 5' wide for
a total of 15 lf.) Headers
in openings are made
from sandwiched 2" x
10" boards with 1/2"
CDX plywood stiffeners
between boards. Includes
4 metal let-in braces for
every 56 lf of wall. All
walls have two top plates
and a single bottom
plate. Does not include
exterior sheathing.*

Item Description	Unit	Remove	Replace	Total
2" x 6" exterior wall 8' tall 12" on center *Replace* Materials ....23.40 Labor ....11.90 *Remove* .... Labor 1.30	lf	$1.30	$35.30	$36.60
2" x 6" exterior wall 8' tall 16" on center *Replace* Materials ....21.20 Labor............10.20 *Remove*.................... Labor 1.30	lf	$1.30	$31.40	$32.70
2" x 6" exterior wall 8' tall 24" on center *Replace* Materials.......19.00 Labor ....8.24 *Remove*..................... Labor 1.30	lf	$1.30	$27.24	$28.54
2" x 6" exterior wall 10' tall 12" on center *Replace* Materials ......26.40 Labor............12.10 *Remove*.................... Labor 1.65	lf	$1.65	$38.50	$40.15
2" x 6" exterior wall 10' tall 16" on center *Replace* Materials......23.60 Labor............10.30 *Remove*.................... Labor 1.65	lf	$1.65	$33.90	$35.55
2" x 6" exterior wall 10' tall 24" on center *Replace* Materials......20.90 Labor ....8.35 *Remove*.................... Labor 1.65	lf	$1.65	$29.25	$30.90
2" x 8" exterior wall 8' tall 12" on center *Replace* Materials......30.50 Labor............12.10 *Remove* .... Labor 1.30	lf	$1.30	$42.60	$43.90
2" x 8" exterior wall 8' tall 16" on center *Replace* Materials......27.70 Labor............10.30 *Remove* .... Labor 1.30	lf	$1.30	$38.00	$39.30
2" x 8" exterior wall 8' tall 24" on center *Replace* Materials......25.00 Labor ....8.32 *Remove* .... Labor 1.30	lf	$1.30	$33.32	$34.62
2" x 8" exterior wall 10' tall 12" on center *Replace* Materials......34.30 Labor ....12.20 *Remove* .... Labor 1.65	lf	$1.65	$46.50	$48.15
2" x 8" exterior wall 10' tall 16" on center *Replace* Materials......30.90 Labor............10.40 *Remove* .... Labor 1.65	lf	$1.65	$41.30	$42.95
2" x 8" exterior wall 10' tall 24" on center *Replace* Materials ......27.40 Labor ....8.43 *Remove* .... Labor 1.65	lf	$1.65	$35.83	$37.48
2" x 4" interior partition wall 16" on center *Replace* Materials ...... 1.17 Labor .... 1.13 *Remove*..................... Labor .... .17	sf	$.17	$2.30	$2.47
2" x 4" interior partition wall 24" on center *Replace* Materials .... .97 Labor .... .98 *Remove*..................... Labor .... .17	sf	$.17	$1.95	$2.12
2" x 6" interior partition wall 16" on center *Replace* Materials........1.68 Labor .... 1.13 *Remove* .... Labor .... .17	sf	$.17	$2.81	$2.98
2" x 6" interior partition wall 24" on center *Replace* Materials........1.40 Labor .... .98 *Remove* .... Labor............. .17	sf	$.17	$2.38	$2.55

◁ **2" x 6"**

RELATED ITEMS

Columns 71
Fences 187
Finish Carpentry 199
Outbuildings................331
Painting......................341
Paneling 347
Siding..........................455
Stairs 465

◁ **2" x 8"**

◀ **PER SF INTERIOR PARTITION WALL**
Includes 5% waste. Based on an average wall with 4 openings and 5 corners per 448 sf of wall. A net of 2.2 studs is added for each corner and opening. All walls have two top plates and a single bottom plate.

Item Description	Unit	Remove	Replace	Total
PER SF ▶ **INTERIOR PARTITION WALL** *continued*				
2" x 8" interior partition wall 16" on center	sf	$.17	$5.43	$5.60
Replace Materials........4.26 Labor 1.17				
Remove .... Labor............ .17				
2" x 8" interior partition wall 24" on center	sf	$.17	$4.81	$4.98
Replace Materials........3.83 Labor............ .98				
Remove .... Labor............ .17				
PER SF ▶ **SLOPING INTERIOR PARTITION WALL** *Includes 5% waste. Based on an average wall with one 3' wide opening, two 4'6" wide openings, and 2 corners per 24 lf of wall. A net of 2.4 studs is added per corner or opening. All walls have two top plates and a single bottom plate.*				
2" x 4" sloping interior partition wall 16" on center	sf	$.17	$2.47	$2.64
Replace Materials........ .92 Labor 1.55				
Remove................... Labor............ .17				
2" x 4" sloping interior partition wall 24" on center	sf	$.17	$2.09	$2.26
Replace Materials........ .77 Labor 1.32				
Remove................... Labor............ .17				
2" x 6" sloping interior partition wall 16" on center	sf	$.17	$2.90	$3.07
Replace Materials........1.31 Labor 1.59				
Remove .... Labor............ .17				
2" x 6" sloping interior partition wall 24" on center	sf	$.17	$2.47	$2.64
Replace Materials...... 1.11 Labor 1.36				
Remove .... Labor............ .17				
2" x 8" sloping interior partition wall 16" on center	sf	$.17	$3.29	$3.46
Replace Materials........1.70 Labor 1.59				
Remove .... Labor............ .17				
2" x 8" sloping interior partition wall 24" on center	sf	$.17	$2.80	$2.97
Replace Materials........1.44 Labor 1.36				
Remove .... Labor............ .17				
PER SF ▶ **SLOPING INTERIOR BEARING WALL** *Includes 5% waste. Based on an average wall with one 3' wide opening, two 4'6" wide openings, and 2 corners per 24 lf of wall. A net of 2.4 studs is added per corner or opening. Headers in openings are made from sandwiched 2" x 10" boards with 1/2" CDX plywood stiffeners between boards. All walls have two top plates and a single bottom plate.*				
2" x 4" sloping interior bearing wall 12" on center	sf	$.17	$3.59	$3.76
Replace Materials........1.36 Labor 2.23				
Remove................... Labor............ .17				
2" x 4" sloping interior bearing wall 16" on center	sf	$.17	$3.10	$3.27
Replace Materials...... 1.21 Labor 1.89				
Remove................... Labor............ .17				
2" x 6" sloping interior bearing wall 12" on center	sf	$.17	$4.04	$4.21
Replace Materials........1.81 Labor 2.23				
Remove .... Labor............ .17				
2" x 6" sloping interior bearing wall 16" on center	sf	$.17	$3.50	$3.67
Replace Materials........1.61 Labor 1.89				
Remove .... Labor............ .17				
2" x 8" sloping interior bearing wall 12" on center	sf	$.17	$4.52	$4.69
Replace Materials........2.25 Labor 2.27				
Remove .... Labor............ .17				
2" x 8" sloping interior bearing wall 16" on center	sf	$.17	$3.92	$4.09
Replace Materials........1.99 Labor 1.93				
Remove .... Labor............ .17				
PER SF ▶ **INTERIOR BEARING WALL** *Includes 5% waste. Based on an average wall with 4 openings and 5 corners per 56 lf.*				
2" x 4" interior bearing wall 12" on center	sf	$.17	$3.13	$3.30
Replace Materials........1.69 Labor 1.44				
Remove................... Labor............ .17				
2" x 4" interior bearing wall 16" on center	sf	$.17	$2.75	$2.92
Replace Materials........1.50 Labor 1.25				
Remove .... Labor............ .17				

continued on next page

Item Description	Unit	Remove	Replace	Total	
2″ x 6″ interior bearing wall 12″ on center *Replace* Materials........2.89　　Labor ....1.47 *Remove* ....　　Labor............ .17	sf	$.17	$4.36	$4.53	◄ **PER SF** **INTERIOR** **BEARING WALL** *continued* *A net of 2.2 studs is added for each corner and opening. Openings are two 3′ wide, one 4′ wide, and one 5′ wide for a total of 15 lf. Headers are made from sandwiched 2″ x 10″ boards with 1/2″ CDX plywood stiffeners. All walls have two top plates and a single bottom plate.*
2″ x 6″ interior bearing wall 16″ on center *Replace* Materials........2.61　　Labor ....1.25 *Remove* ....　　Labor............ .17	sf	$.17	$3.86	$4.03	
2″ x 8″ interior bearing wall 12″ on center *Replace* Materials........3.78　　Labor ....1.47 *Remove* ....　　Labor............ .17	sf	$.17	$5.25	$5.42	
2″ x 8″ interior bearing wall 16″ on center *Replace* Materials........3.44　　Labor ....1.25 *Remove* ....　　Labor............ .17	sf	$.17	$4.69	$4.86	
2″ x 4″ exterior wall 12″ on center *Replace* Materials........1.73　　Labor ....1.51 *Remove* ....　　Labor............ .17	sf	$.17	$3.24	$3.41	◄ **PER SF** **EXTERIOR WALL** *Includes 5% waste. Based on an average wall with 4 openings and 5 corners per 56 lf of wall. A net of 2.2 studs is added for each corner and opening. Openings are two 3′ wide, one 4′ wide, and one 5′ wide for a total of 15 lf. Headers in openings are made from sandwiched 2″ x 10″ boards with 1/2″ CDX plywood stiffeners between boards. Includes 4 metal let-in braces for every 56 lf of wall. All walls have two top plates and a single bottom plate. Does not include exterior sheathing.*
2″ x 4″ exterior wall 16″ on center *Replace* Materials........1.54　　Labor ....1.29 *Remove*.....................　　Labor............ .17	sf	$.17	$2.83	$3.00	
2″ x 4″ exterior wall 24″ on center *Replace* Materials........1.34　　Labor .... 1.02 *Remove* ....　　Labor............ .17	sf	$.17	$2.36	$2.53	
2″ x 6″ exterior wall 12″ on center *Replace* Materials........2.93　　Labor ....1.51 *Remove* ....　　Labor............ .17	sf	$.17	$4.44	$4.61	
2″ x 6″ exterior wall 16″ on center *Replace* Materials........2.65　　Labor ....1.29 *Remove* ....　　Labor............ .17	sf	$.17	$3.94	$4.11	
2″ x 6″ exterior wall 24″ on center *Replace* Materials........2.38　　Labor............ 1.02 *Remove* ....　　Labor............ .17	sf	$.17	$3.40	$3.57	
2″ x 8″ exterior wall 12″ on center *Replace* Materials........3.81　　Labor ....1.51 *Remove* ....　　Labor............ .17	sf	$.17	$5.32	$5.49	◁ **2″ x 8″**
2″ x 8″ exterior wall 16″ on center *Replace* Materials........3.46　　Labor ....1.29 *Remove* ....　　Labor............ .17	sf	$.17	$4.75	$4.92	**RELATED ITEMS** **Columns** ....71 **Fences**...................187 **Finish Carpentry** ....199 **Outbuildings**..............331 **Painting**..................341 **Paneling**..................347 **Siding**...................455 **Stairs** 465
2″ x 8″ exterior wall 24″ on center *Replace* Materials........3.13　　Labor........... 1.06 *Remove* ....　　Labor............ .17	sf	$.17	$4.19	$4.36	
2″ x 4″ sloping exterior wall 12″ on center *Replace* Materials........1.56　　Labor ....2.04 *Remove*.....................　　Labor........... .17	sf	$.17	$3.60	$3.77	◄ **PER SF** **SLOPING** **EXTERIOR WALL** *Includes 5% waste. Based on an average wall with one 3′ wide opening, two 4′6″ openings, and 2 corners per 24 lf. A net of 2.? studs is added per co... or opening.* *continued on next*
2″ x 4″ sloping exterior wall 16″ on center *Replace* Materials........1.40　　Labor ....1.74 *Remove*.....................　　Labor........... .17	sf	$.17	$3.14	$3.31	
2″ x 4″ sloping exterior wall 24″ on center *Replace* Materials...... 1.25　　Labor ....1.44 *Remove*.....................　　Labor............ .17	sf	$.17	$2.69	$2.86	

	Item Description	Unit	Remove	Replace	Total
PER SF ► **SLOPING** **EXTERIOR WALL** continued	2" x 6" sloping exterior wall 12" on center *Replace* Materials ....2.06 Labor ....2.04 *Remove* .... Labor .... .17	sf	$.17	$4.10	$4.27
Headers in openings are made from sandwiched 2" x 10" boards with 1/2" CDX plywood stiffeners between boards. Includes 3 metal let-in braces for every 24 lf of wall. All walls have two top plates and a single bottom plate.	2" x 6" sloping exterior wall 16" on center *Replace* Materials ....1.84 Labor ....1.74 *Remove* .... Labor .... .17	sf	$.17	$3.58	$3.75
	2" x 6" sloping exterior wall 24" on center *Replace* Materials ....1.61 Labor ....1.44 *Remove* .... Labor .... .17	sf	$.17	$3.05	$3.22
	2" x 8" sloping exterior wall 12" on center *Replace* Materials ....2.55 Labor ....2.08 *Remove* .... Labor .... .17	sf	$.17	$4.63	$4.80
	2" x 8" sloping exterior wall 16" on center *Replace* Materials ....2.26 Labor ....1.78 *Remove* .... Labor .... .17	sf	$.17	$4.04	$4.21
	2" x 8" sloping exterior wall 24" on center *Replace* Materials ....1.98 Labor ....1.44 *Remove* .... Labor .... .17	sf	$.17	$3.42	$3.59
ADDITIONAL ► **WALL FRAMING** **COSTS**	Add for beam pocket in exterior or bearing wall *Replace* Materials ......46.20 Labor 42.00	ea	–	$88.20	$88.20
	Add to frame round- or elliptical-top door or window per lf of opening *Replace* Materials ....3.74 Labor 22.20	lf	–	$25.94	$25.94
	Add to frame round window per diameter of opening *Replace* Materials ....4.32 Labor 24.10	lf	–	$28.42	$28.42
	Add to frame bay window per lf of wall *Replace* Materials ....4.32 Labor 22.00	lf	–	$26.32	$26.32
	Add to frame bow window per lf of wall *Replace* Materials ....4.32 Labor 24.50	lf	–	$28.82	$28.82
ADDITIONAL ► **COST FOR CEC** **BRACING** *Additional cost to nail, brace, and shear panel to California Earthquake Code standards. Per sf of wall.*	Add for CEC bracing and shear paneling of interior bearing wall *Replace* Materials .... .32 Labor .... .42	sf	–	$.74	$.74
	Add for CEC bracing and shear paneling of sloping interior wall *Replace* Materials .... .35 Labor .... .53	sf	–	$.88	$.88
	Add for CEC bracing and shear paneling of exterior wall *Replace* Materials .... .38 Labor .... .42	sf	–	$.80	$.80
	Add for CEC bracing and shear paneling of sloping exterior wall *Replace* Materials .... .43 Labor .... .57	sf	–	$1.00	$1.00
PER BF ► **WALL FRAMING** *Includes 7% waste.*	Interior wall per bf *Replace* Materials ...... 1.23 Labor ....1.29 *Remove* .... Labor .... .20	bf	$.20	$2.52	$2.72
	Sloping interior wall per bf *Replace* Materials ....1.31 Labor ....1.78 *Remove* .... Labor .... .20	bf	$.20	$3.09	$3.29
	Exterior wall per bf *Replace* Materials ....1.53 Labor ....1.40 *Remove* .... Labor .... .20	bf	$.20	$2.93	$3.13

CEC = California Earthquake Code.

Item Description	Unit	Remove	Replace	Total
Sloping exterior wall per bf	bf	$.20	$3.56	$3.76
Replace Materials........1.63 Labor 1.93				
Remove .... Labor............. .20				
2" x 4" top plate	lf	$.38	$1.45	$1.83
Replace Materials........ .81 Labor............. .64				
Remove .... Labor............. .38				
2" x 6" top plate	lf	$.38	$1.84	$2.22
Replace Materials .... 1.16 Labor............. .68				
Remove .... Labor............. .38				
2" x 8" top plate	lf	$.38	$2.37	$2.75
Replace Materials........1.69 Labor............. .68				
Remove .... Labor............. .38				
2" x 4" treated-wood foundation sill plate	lf	$1.30	$3.86	$5.16
Replace Materials........1.33 Labor 2.53				
Remove .... Labor............1.30				
2" x 6" treated-wood foundation sill plate	lf	$1.30	$4.51	$5.81
Replace Materials........1.98 Labor 2.53				
Remove .... Labor............1.30				
2" x 8" treated-wood foundation sill plate	lf	$1.30	$5.20	$6.50
Replace Materials........2.63 Labor 2.57				
Remove .... Labor............1.30				
2" x 4" con common redwood foundation sill plate	lf	$1.30	$4.01	$5.31
Replace Materials........1.55 Labor 2.46				
Remove .... Labor............1.30				
2" x 6" con common redwood foundation sill plate	lf	$1.30	$4.43	$5.73
Replace Materials........1.97 Labor 2.46				
Remove .... Labor............1.30				
2" x 8" con common redwood foundation sill plate	lf	$1.30	$5.21	$6.51
Replace Materials........2.72 Labor 2.49				
Remove .... Labor............1.30				
4" x 6" header beam	lf	$1.16	$7.44	$8.60
Replace Materials........5.93 Labor 1.51				
Remove .... Labor 1.16				
▶ For 2" x 4". Doubled 2" x 6" with 1/2" CDX plywood stiffener.				
4" x 8" header beam	lf	$1.16	$8.27	$9.43
Replace Materials........6.68 Labor 1.59				
Remove .... Labor 1.16				
▶ For 2" x 4" wall. Doubled 2" x 8" with 1/2" CDX plywood stiffener.				
4" x 10" header beam	lf	$1.16	$10.98	$12.14
Replace Materials........9.35 Labor 1.63				
Remove .... Labor 1.16				
▶ For 2" x 4" wall. Doubled 2" x 10" with 1/2" CDX plywood stiffener.				
4" x 12" header beam	lf	$1.16	$13.00	$14.16
Replace Materials.......11.30 Labor 1.70				
Remove .... Labor 1.16				
▶ For 2" x 4" wall. Doubled 2" x 12" with 1/2" CDX plywood stiffener.				
6" x 6" header beam	lf	$1.16	$13.01	$14.17
Replace Materials ......10.70 Labor 2.31				
Remove .... Labor 1.16				
▶ For 2" x 6" wall. Three 2" x 6" with two 1/2" CDX plywood stiffeners.				

◀ **TOP PLATE**
Includes 5% waste. Cost to remove and replace a damaged top plate on an existing wall.

◀ **FOUNDATION SILL PLATE**
Includes foam sealer strip, hole drilling for anchor bolts, and fastening.

CALIFORNIA EARTHQUAKE CODE

Items that include "CEC" in the description are priced according to California earthquake code requirements.

Although these *Universal Building Code* standards are also required in other areas, they are most commonly associated with efforts initiated in California to improve the construction and engineering of structures in quake zones.

◀ **WALL HEADER**
Includes 5% waste.
◁ for 2" x 4" wall

RELATED ITEMS

Columns 71
Fences 187
Finish Carpentry 199
Outbuildings 331
Painting 341
Paneling 347
Siding 455
Stairs 465

◁ for 2" x 6" wall

	Item Description	Unit	Remove	Replace	Total
WALL HEADER ▶ *continued*	**6" x 8" header beam**	lf	$1.16	$14.37	$15.53
	Replace Materials.......11.91 Labor 2.46				
	Remove .... Labor 1.16				
	▶ For 2" x 6" wall. Three 2" x 8" with two 1/2" CDX plywood stiffeners.				
	6" x 10" header beam	lf	$1.16	$19.01	$20.17
	Replace Materials ......16.40 Labor 2.61				
	Remove .... Labor 1.16				
	▶ For 2" x 6" wall. Three 2" x 10" with two 1/2" CDX plywood stiffeners.				
	6" x 12" header beam	lf	$1.16	$22.80	$23.96
	Replace Materials ......20.00 Labor 2.80				
	Remove .... Labor 1.16				
	▶ For 2" x 6" wall. Three 2" x 12" with two 1/2" CDX plywood stiffeners.				
for 2" x 8" wall ▷	**8" x 6" header beam**	lf	$1.16	$18.26	$19.42
	Replace Materials.......15.50 Labor 2.76				
	Remove .... Labor 1.16				
	▶ For 2" x 8" wall. Four 2" x 6" with three 1/2" CDX plywood stiffeners.				
	8" x 8" header beam	lf	$1.16	$20.05	$21.21
	Replace Materials.......17.10 Labor 2.95				
	Remove .... Labor 1.16				
	▶ For 2" x 8" wall. Four 2" x 8" with three 1/2" CDX plywood stiffeners.				
	8" x 10" header beam	lf	$1.16	$21.91	$23.07
	Replace Materials ......18.70 Labor 3.21				
	Remove .... Labor 1.16				
	▶ For 2" x 8" wall. Four 2" x 10" with three 1/2" CDX plywood stiffeners.				
	8" x 12" header beam	lf	$1.16	$32.12	$33.28
	Replace Materials ......28.60 Labor 3.52				
	Remove .... Labor 1.16				
	▶ For 2" x 8" wall. Four 2" x 12" with three 1/2" CDX plywood stiffeners.				
POSTS ▶ Includes 4% waste. 4" x 4" ▷	**4" x 4" pine post**	lf	$1.71	$4.83	$6.54
	Replace Materials.......3.24 Labor 1.59				
	Remove .... Labor 1.71				
	4" x 4" con common redwood post	lf	$1.71	$5.48	$7.19
	Replace Materials........3.89 Labor 1.59				
	Remove .... Labor 1.71				
	4" x 4" treated pine post	lf	$1.71	$5.81	$7.52
	Replace Materials........4.22 Labor 1.59				
	Remove .... Labor 1.71				
4" x 6" ▷	**4" x 6" pine post**	lf	$1.71	$5.38	$7.09
	Replace Materials.......3.75 Labor 1.63				
	Remove .... Labor 1.71				
	4" x 6" con common redwood post	lf	$1.71	$5.80	$7.51
	Replace Materials........4.17 Labor 1.63				
	Remove .... Labor 1.71				
	4" x 6" treated pine post	lf	$1.71	$6.50	$8.21
	Replace Materials........4.87 Labor 1.63				
	Remove .... Labor 1.71				
x 8" ▷	**4" x 8" pine post**	lf	$1.71	$7.63	$9.34
	Replace Materials........6.00 Labor 1.63				
	Remove .... Labor 1.71				

Item Description	Unit	Remove	Replace	Total
4" x 8" con common redwood post	lf	$1.71	$7.62	$9.33
Replace Materials........5.99 Labor 1.63				
Remove .... Labor 1.71				
4" x 8" treated pine post	lf	$1.71	$9.43	$11.14
Replace Materials........7.80 Labor 1.63				
Remove .... Labor 1.71				
6" x 6" pine post	lf	$1.71	$9.54	$11.25
Replace Materials........7.88 Labor 1.66				
Remove .... Labor 1.71				
6" x 6" con common redwood post	lf	$1.71	$8.39	$10.10
Replace Materials........6.73 Labor 1.66				
Remove .... Labor 1.71				
6" x 6" treated pine post	lf	$1.71	$11.86	$13.57
Replace Materials ......10.20 Labor 1.66				
Remove .... Labor 1.71				
6" x 8" pine post	lf	$1.71	$12.20	$13.91
Replace Materials ......10.50 Labor 1.70				
Remove .... Labor 1.71				
6" x 8" con common redwood post	lf	$1.71	$10.68	$12.39
Replace Materials........8.98 Labor 1.70				
Remove .... Labor 1.71				
6" x 8" treated pine post	lf	$1.71	$15.40	$17.11
Replace Materials ......13.70 Labor 1.70				
Remove .... Labor 1.71				
6" x 10" pine post	lf	$1.71	$14.98	$16.69
Replace Materials ......13.20 Labor 1.78				
Remove .... Labor 1.71				
6" x 10" con common redwood post	lf	$1.71	$12.98	$14.69
Replace Materials ......11.20 Labor 1.78				
Remove .... Labor 1.71				
6" x 10" treated pine post	lf	$1.71	$18.88	$20.59
Replace Materials ......17.10 Labor 1.78				
Remove .... Labor 1.71				
8" x 8" pine post	lf	$1.71	$15.91	$17.62
Replace Materials ......14.10 Labor 1.81				
Remove .... Labor 1.71				
8" x 8" con common redwood post	lf	$1.71	$13.81	$15.52
Replace Materials ......12.00 Labor 1.81				
Remove .... Labor 1.71				
8" x 8" treated pine post	lf	$1.71	$20.01	$21.72
Replace Materials ......18.20 Labor 1.81				
Remove .... Labor 1.71				
Pre-cast concrete pier	ea	$7.80	$29.57	$37.37
Replace Materials........19.70 Labor 9.87				
Remove .... Labor 7.80				
51" to 90" adjustable steel jackpost to 13,000 pound load	ea	$9.05	$69.30	$78.35
Replace Materials ......55.80 Labor 13.50				
Remove .... Labor 9.05				

RELATED ITEMS

Columns 71
Fences...........................187
Finish Carpentry 199
Painting.......................341
Paneling 347
Stairs 465

◁ 6" x 6"

◁ 6" x 8"

◁ 6" x 10"

◁ 8" x 8"

◀ **PRECAST PIER**

◀ **JACKPOST**

Item Description			Unit	Remove	Replace	Total
JACKPOST ▶ continued	20" to 36" adjustable steel jackpost to 16,000 pound load		ea	$9.05	$45.79	$54.84
	Replace Materials......36.60	Labor 9.19				
	Remove	Labor 9.05				
	48" to 100" adjustable steel jackpost to 16,000 pound load		ea	$9.05	$77.60	$86.65
	Replace Materials......63.00	Labor 14.60				
	Remove	Labor 9.05				
	37" to 60" adjustable steel jackpost to 17,500 pound load		ea	$9.05	$56.30	$65.35
	Replace Materials......46.00	Labor...........10.30				
	Remove	Labor...........9.05				
	56" to 96" adjustable steel jackpost to 25,000 pound load		ea	$9.05	$85.20	$94.25
	Replace Materials......71.90	Labor 13.30				
	Remove	Labor...........9.05				
LALLY COLUMN ▶	3-1/2" diameter concrete-filled lally column, 6' to 8'		ea	$10.30	$108.00	$118.30
	Replace Materials......88.10	Labor 19.90				
	Remove	Labor...........10.30				
	3-1/2" diameter concrete-filled lally column, 8' to 10'		ea	$10.30	$119.40	$129.70
	Replace Materials......98.40	Labor...........21.00				
	Remove	Labor...........10.30				
	3-1/2" diameter concrete-filled lally column, 10' to 12'		ea	$10.30	$144.70	$155.00
	Replace Materials 122.50	Labor 22.20				
	Remove	Labor...........10.30				
GLUE-LAMINATED ▶ **BEAM PER BF** *Includes 3% waste.*	Glue-laminated beam per bf		bf	$.72	$8.10	$8.82
	Replace Materials......5.48 Labor 2.27	Equipment .... .35				
	Remove	Labor .... .72				
GLUE-LAMINATED ▶ **BEAM PER LF** *Includes 3% waste.* **3-1/8" wide** ▷	3-1/8" x 7-1/2" glue-laminated beam		lf	$6.42	$16.82	$23.24
	Replace Materials ......10.70 Labor 5.48	Equipment .... .64				
	Remove	Labor 6.42				
	3-1/8" x 9" glue-laminated beam		lf	$6.42	$19.06	$25.48
	Replace Materials ......12.90 Labor 5.52	Equipment .... .64				
	Remove	Labor 6.42				
	3-1/8" x 10-1/2" glue-laminated beam		lf	$6.42	$22.04	$28.46
	Replace Materials ......14.90 Labor 6.50	Equipment .... .64				
	Remove	Labor 6.42				
	3-1/8" x 12" glue-laminated beam		lf	$6.42	$24.88	$31.30
	Replace Materials......17.10 Labor 7.14	Equipment .... .64				
	Remove	Labor 6.42				
	3-1/8" x 13-1/2" glue-laminated beam		lf	$6.42	$27.92	$34.34
	Replace Materials......19.30 Labor 7.98	Equipment .... .64				
	Remove	Labor 6.42				
	3-1/8" x 15" glue-laminated beam		lf	$6.42	$30.05	$36.47
	Replace Materials ......21.40 Labor 8.01	Equipment .... .64				
	Remove	Labor 6.42				
	3-1/8" x 16-1/2" glue-laminated beam		lf	$6.42	$32.33	$38.75
	Replace Materials ......23.60 Labor 8.09	Equipment .... .64				
	Remove	Labor 6.42				
	3-1/8" x 18" glue-laminated beam		lf	$6.42	$34.50	$40.92
	Replace Materials......25.70 Labor 8.16	Equipment .... .64				
	Remove	Labor 6.42				

Item Description	Unit	Remove	Replace	Total	
3-1/2" x 9" glue-laminated beam	If	$6.42	$20.56	$26.98	◁ 3-1/2" wide
Replace Materials ......14.40 Labor ....5.52 Equipment .... .64					
Remove .... Labor 6.42					
3-1/2" x 12" glue-laminated beam	If	$6.42	$26.42	$32.84	
Replace Materials.......19.20 Labor ....6.58 Equipment .... .64					
Remove .... Labor 6.42					
3-1/2" x 15" glue-laminated beam	If	$6.42	$31.97	$38.39	
Replace Materials ......24.00 Labor ....7.33 Equipment .... .64					
Remove .... Labor 6.42					
3-1/2" x 19-1/2" glue-laminated beam	If	$6.42	$40.19	$46.61	
Replace Materials ......31.20 Labor ....8.35 Equipment .... .64					
Remove .... Labor 6.42					
3-1/2" x 21" glue-laminated beam	If	$6.42	$42.67	$49.09	
Replace Materials ......33.60 Labor ....8.43 Equipment .... .64					
Remove .... Labor 6.42					
5-1/8" x 7-1/2" glue-laminated beam	If	$6.42	$24.68	$31.10	◁ 5-1/8" wide
Replace Materials.......17.50 Labor ....6.54 Equipment .... .64					
Remove .... Labor 6.42					
5-1/8" x 9" glue-laminated beam	If	$6.42	$28.36	$34.78	
Replace Materials ......21.10 Labor ....6.62 Equipment .... .64					
Remove .... Labor 6.42					
5-1/8" x 10-1/2" glue-laminated beam	If	$6.42	$32.57	$38.99	
Replace Materials ......24.60 Labor ....7.33 Equipment .... .64					
Remove .... Labor 6.42					
5-1/8" x 12" glue-laminated beam	If	$6.42	$37.58	$44.00	
Replace Materials ......28.70 Labor ....8.24 Equipment .... .64					
Remove .... Labor 6.42					
5-1/8" x 13-1/2" glue-laminated beam	If	$6.42	$40.59	$47.01	
Replace Materials ......31.60 Labor ....8.35 Equipment .... .64					
Remove .... Labor 6.42					
5-1/8" x 15" glue-laminated beam	If	$6.42	$44.31	$50.73	
Replace Materials ......35.20 Labor ....8.47 Equipment .... .64					
Remove .... Labor 6.42					
5-1/8" x 16-1/2" glue-laminated beam	If	$6.42	$47.92	$54.34	
Replace Materials......38.70 Labor ....8.58 Equipment .... .64					
Remove .... Labor 6.42					
5-1/8" x 18" glue-laminated beam	If	$6.42	$51.57	$57.99	
Replace Materials ......42.20 Labor ....8.73 Equipment .... .64					
Remove .... Labor 6.42					
5-1/8" x 19-1/2" glue-laminated beam	If	$6.42	$55.19	$61.61	
Replace Materials ......45.70 Labor ....8.85 Equipment .... .64					
Remove .... Labor 6.42					
5-1/8" x 21" glue-laminated beam	If	$6.42	$58.84	$65.26	
Replace Materials ......49.20 Labor ....9.00 Equipment .... .64					
Remove .... Labor 6.42					
5-1/8" x 22-1/2" glue-laminated beam	If	$6.42	$62.49	$68.91	
Replace Materials ......52.70 Labor ....9.15 Equipment .... .64					
Remove .... Labor 6.42					

RELATED ITEMS

Columns 71
Fences........................187
Finish Carpentry 199
Outbuildings...............331
Painting.....................341
Paneling.....................347
Siding.......................455
Stairs........................465

	Item Description			Unit	Remove	Replace	Total
GLUE-LAMINATED ▶ **BEAM** *continued*	**5-1/8" x 24" glue-laminated beam**			If	$6.42	$66.10	$72.52
	Replace Materials 56.20	Labor 9.26	Equipment .... .64				
	Remove	Labor 6.42					
6-3/4" wide ▷	**6-3/4" x 18" glue-laminated beam**			If	$6.42	$65.46	$71.88
	Replace Materials 55.60	Labor 9.22	Equipment .... .64				
	Remove	Labor 6.42					
	6-3/4" x 19-1/2" glue-laminated beam			If	$6.42	$70.29	$76.71
	Replace Materials 60.20	Labor 9.45	Equipment .... .64				
	Remove	Labor 6.42					
	6-3/4" x 24" glue-laminated beam			If	$6.42	$84.73	$91.15
	Replace Materials 74.00	Labor 10.09	Equipment .... .64				
	Remove	Labor 6.42					
MICRO- ▶ **LAMINATED BEAM** *Includes 4% waste.*	**1-3/4" x 7-1/4" micro-laminated beam**			If	$3.06	$8.12	$11.18
	Replace Materials 6.31	Labor 1.81					
	Remove	Labor 3.06					
	1-3/4" x 9-1/2" micro-laminated beam			If	$3.06	$10.16	$13.22
	Replace Materials 8.27	Labor 1.89					
	Remove	Labor 3.06					
	1-3/4" x 11-7/8" micro-laminated beam			If	$3.06	$12.30	$15.36
	Replace Materials 10.30	Labor 2.00					
	Remove	Labor 3.06					
	1-3/4" x 14" micro-laminated beam			If	$3.06	$14.32	$17.38
	Replace Materials 12.20	Labor 2.12					
	Remove	Labor 3.06					
	1-3/4" x 16" micro-laminated beam			If	$3.06	$16.23	$19.29
	Replace Materials 14.00	Labor 2.23					
	Remove	Labor 3.06					
	1-3/4" x 18" micro-laminated beam			If	$3.06	$18.08	$21.14
	Replace Materials 15.70	Labor 2.38					
	Remove	Labor 3.06					
PINE BEAM ▶ *Includes 4% waste. Deduct 12% for #1 and better grade pine. Rough sawn. Installed as posts, beams, joists, and purlins. Pine species vary by region. Western coastal areas: Douglas fir, hemlock fir; Mountain states and provinces: spruce, pine, Douglas fir, South: southern yellow pine; Midwest: spruce, pine, Douglas fir, southern yellow pine; Southwest: southern yellow pine; Northeast: spruce, pine, Douglas fir, and hemlock fir.*	**4" x 6" pine beam, select structural grade**			If	$6.42	$8.15	$14.57
	Replace Materials 4.56	Labor 2.95	Equipment .... .64				
	Remove	Labor 6.42					
	4" x 8" pine beam, select structural grade			If	$6.42	$10.20	$16.62
	Replace Materials 6.08	Labor 3.48	Equipment .... .64				
	Remove	Labor 6.42					
	4" x 10" pine beam, select structural grade			If	$6.42	$12.55	$18.97
	Replace Materials 7.60	Labor 4.31	Equipment .... .64				
	Remove	Labor 6.42					
	4" x 12" pine beam, select structural grade			If	$6.42	$15.40	$21.82
	Replace Materials 9.13	Labor 5.63	Equipment .... .64				
	Remove	Labor 6.42					
	4" x 14" pine beam, select structural grade			If	$6.42	$17.97	$24.39
	Replace Materials 10.60	Labor 6.73	Equipment .... .64				
	Remove	Labor 6.42					
	4" x 16" pine beam, select structural grade			If	$6.42	$19.64	$26.06
	Replace Materials 12.20	Labor 6.80	Equipment .... .64				
	Remove	Labor 6.42					

Item Description	Unit	Remove	Replace	Total	
6″ x 6″ pine beam, select structural grade *Replace* Materials........6.84 Labor ....3.86 Equipment .... .64 *Remove* .... Labor 6.42	lf	$6.42	$11.34	$17.76	◁ 6″ wide
6″ x 8″ pine beam, select structural grade *Replace* Materials........9.13 Labor ....4.35 Equipment .... .64 *Remove* .... Labor 6.42	lf	$6.42	$14.12	$20.54	
6″ x 10″ pine beam, select structural grade *Replace* Materials.......11.50 Labor ....4.99 Equipment .... .64 *Remove* .... Labor 6.42	lf	$6.42	$17.13	$23.55	
6″ x 12″ pine beam, select structural grade *Replace* Materials.......13.60 Labor ....5.82 Equipment .... .64 *Remove* .... Labor 6.42	lf	$6.42	$20.06	$26.48	
6″ x 14″ pine beam, select structural grade *Replace* Materials.......15.90 Labor ....6.39 Equipment .... .64 *Remove* .... Labor 6.42	lf	$6.42	$22.93	$29.35	
6″ x 16″ pine beam, select structural grade *Replace* Materials.......18.20 Labor ....7.14 Equipment .... .64 *Remove* .... Labor 6.42	lf	$6.42	$25.98	$32.40	
8″ x 8″ pine beam, select structural grade *Replace* Materials.......12.20 Labor ....5.25 Equipment .... .64 *Remove* .... Labor 6.42	lf	$6.42	$18.09	$24.51	◁ 8″ wide
8″ x 10″ pine beam, select structural grade *Replace* Materials.......15.20 Labor ....5.90 Equipment .... .64 *Remove* .... Labor 6.42	lf	$6.42	$21.74	$28.16	
8″ x 12″ pine beam, select structural grade *Replace* Materials.......18.20 Labor ....6.88 Equipment .... .64 *Remove* .... Labor 6.42	lf	$6.42	$25.72	$32.14	
8″ x 14″ pine beam, select structural grade *Replace* Materials.......21.30 Labor ....7.30 Equipment .... .64 *Remove* .... Labor 6.42	lf	$6.42	$29.24	$35.66	
8″ x 16″ pine beam, select structural grade *Replace* Materials.......24.40 Labor ....7.52 Equipment .... .64 *Remove* .... Labor 6.42	lf	$6.42	$32.56	$38.98	
10″ x 10″ pine beam, select structural grade *Replace* Materials.......19.00 Labor ....6.65 Equipment .... .64 *Remove* .... Labor 6.42	lf	$6.42	$26.29	$32.71	◁ 10″ wide
10″ x 12″ pine beam, select structural grade *Replace* Materials.......22.80 Labor ....7.41 Equipment .... .64 *Remove* .... Labor 6.42	lf	$6.42	$30.85	$37.27	
10″ x 14″ pine beam, select structural grade *Replace* Materials.......26.70 Labor ....7.67 Equipment .... .64 *Remove* .... Labor 6.42	lf	$6.42	$35.01	$41.43	
10″ x 16″ pine beam, select structural grade *Replace* Materials.......30.40 Labor ....7.94 Equipment .... .64 *Remove* .... Labor 6.42	lf	$6.42	$38.98	$45.40	
12″ x 12″ pine beam, select structural grade *Replace* Materials.......27.40 Labor ....7.71 Equipment .... .64 *Remove* .... Labor 6.42	lf	$6.42	$35.75	$42.17	◁ 12″ wide

RELATED ITEMS

Columns	71
Fences	187
Finish Carpentry	199
Outbuildings	331
Painting	341
Paneling	347
Siding	455
Stairs	465

Item Description	Unit	Remove	Replace	Total
PINE BEAM ▶ *continued* **12" x 14" pine beam, select structural grade** *Replace* Materials ......32.00　　Labor ....8.05　　Equipment ....64 *Remove* ....　　Labor 6.42	lf	$6.42	$40.69	$47.11
12" x 16" pine beam, select structural grade *Replace* Materials ......36.50　　Labor ....8.39　　Equipment ....64 *Remove* ....　　Labor 6.42	lf	$6.42	$45.53	$51.95
OAK BEAM ▶ *Includes 4% waste. Installed as posts, beams, joists, and purlins.* **4" x 6" oak beam, select structural grade** *Replace* Materials ....9.27　　Labor ....2.95　　Equipment ....64 *Remove* ....　　Labor 6.42	lf	$6.42	$12.86	$19.28
4" x 8" oak beam, select structural grade *Replace* Materials ......12.40　　Labor ....3.48　　Equipment ....64 *Remove* ....　　Labor 6.42	lf	$6.42	$16.52	$22.94
4" x 10" oak beam, select structural grade *Replace* Materials ......15.40　　Labor ....4.31　　Equipment ....64 *Remove* ....　　Labor 6.42	lf	$6.42	$20.35	$26.77
4" x 12" oak beam, select structural grade *Replace* Materials ......18.50　　Labor ....5.63　　Equipment ....64 *Remove* ....　　Labor 6.42	lf	$6.42	$24.77	$31.19
4" x 14" oak beam, select structural grade *Replace* Materials ......21.70　　Labor ....6.73　　Equipment ....64 *Remove* ....　　Labor 6.42	lf	$6.42	$29.07	$35.49
4" x 16" oak beam, select structural grade *Replace* Materials ......24.70　　Labor ....6.80　　Equipment ....64 *Remove* ....　　Labor 6.42	lf	$6.42	$32.14	$38.56
6" wide ▷ **6" x 6" oak beam, select structural grade** *Replace* Materials ......14.00　　Labor ....3.86　　Equipment ....64 *Remove* ....　　Labor 6.42	lf	$6.42	$18.50	$24.92
6" x 8" oak beam, select structural grade *Replace* Materials ......19.40　　Labor ....4.35　　Equipment ....64 *Remove* ....　　Labor 6.42	lf	$6.42	$24.39	$30.81
6" x 10" oak beam, select structural grade *Replace* Materials ......23.20　　Labor ....4.99　　Equipment ....64 *Remove* ....　　Labor 6.42	lf	$6.42	$28.83	$35.25
6" x 12" oak beam, select structural grade *Replace* Materials ......27.80　　Labor ....5.82　　Equipment ....64 *Remove* ....　　Labor 6.42	lf	$6.42	$34.26	$40.68
6" x 14" oak beam, select structural grade *Replace* Materials ......32.50　　Labor ....6.39　　Equipment ....64 *Remove* ....　　Labor 6.42	lf	$6.42	$39.53	$45.95
6" x 16" oak beam, select structural grade *Replace* Materials ......37.10　　Labor ....7.14　　Equipment ....64 *Remove* ....　　Labor 6.42	lf	$6.42	$44.88	$51.30
8" wide ▷ **8" x 8" oak beam, select structural grade** *Replace* Materials ......24.70　　Labor ....5.25　　Equipment ....64 *Remove* ....　　Labor 6.42	lf	$6.42	$30.59	$37.01
8" x 10" oak beam, select structural grade *Replace* Materials ......30.90　　Labor ....5.90　　Equipment ....64 *Remove* ....　　Labor 6.42	lf	$6.42	$37.44	$43.86

Item Description	Unit	Remove	Replace	Total	
8" x 12" oak beam, select structural grade	lf	$6.42	$44.62	$51.04	
Replace Materials......37.10 Labor ....6.88 Equipment 64					
Remove .... Labor 6.42					
8" x 14" oak beam, select structural grade	lf	$6.42	$51.14	$57.56	
Replace Materials......43.20 Labor ....7.30 Equipment 64					
Remove .... Labor 6.42					
8" x 16" oak beam, select structural grade	lf	$6.42	$57.66	$64.08	
Replace Materials......49.50 Labor ....7.52 Equipment 64					
Remove .... Labor 6.42					
10" x 10" oak beam, select structural grade	lf	$6.42	$45.89	$52.31	◁ 10" wide
Replace Materials......38.60 Labor ....6.65 Equipment 64					
Remove .... Labor 6.42					
10" x 12" oak beam, select structural grade	lf	$6.42	$54.45	$60.87	
Replace Materials......46.40 Labor ....7.41 Equipment 64					
Remove .... Labor 6.42					
10" x 14" oak beam, select structural grade	lf	$6.42	$62.41	$68.83	
Replace Materials......54.10 Labor ....7.67 Equipment 64					
Remove .... Labor 6.42					
10" x 16" oak beam, select structural grade	lf	$6.42	$70.38	$76.80	
Replace Materials......61.80 Labor ....7.94 Equipment 64					
Remove .... Labor 6.42					
12" x 12" oak beam, select structural grade	lf	$6.42	$63.95	$70.37	◁ 12" wide
Replace Materials......55.60 Labor ....7.71 Equipment 64					
Remove .... Labor 6.42					
12" x 14" oak beam, select structural grade	lf	$6.42	$73.59	$80.01	
Replace Materials......64.90 Labor ....8.05 Equipment 64					
Remove .... Labor 6.42					
12" x 16" oak beam, select structural grade	lf	$6.42	$83.23	$89.65	
Replace Materials ......74.20 Labor ....8.39 Equipment 64					
Remove .... Labor 6.42					
Add for hand-hewn pine beam per square inch of surface	si	—	$.03	$.03	◀ **ADDITIONAL BEAM COSTS**
Replace Materials .... .03					
Add for curved pine framing member in post & beam framing	lf	—	$42.80	$42.80	
Replace .... Labor..........42.80					
Add for hand-hewn oak beam per square inch of surface	si	—	$.04	$.04	
Replace Materials .... .04					
Add for curved oak framing member in post & beam framing	lf	—	$56.50	$56.50	
Replace .... Labor 56.50					
Pine post & beam single-story bent with simple truss	sf	$2.05	$29.08	$31.13	◀ **PINE POST & BEAM BENT WITH TRUSS**
Replace Materials........3.89 Labor..........24.80 Equipment 39					
Remove .... Labor 2.05					
Pine post & beam single-story bent with king post truss	sf	$2.05	$31.52	$33.57	
Replace Materials........4.33 Labor..........26.80 Equipment 39					
Remove .... Labor 2.05					
Pine post & beam single-story bent with king post & struts truss	sf	$2.05	$34.35	$36.40	
Replace Materials........4.86 Labor ....29.10 Equipment 39					
Remove .... Labor 2.05					

RELATED ITEMS

Columns 71
Fences.....................187
Finish Carpentry 199
Outbuildings...............331
Painting 341
Paneling 347
Siding 455
Stairs 465

◀ **ADDITIONAL BEAM COSTS**

◀ **PINE POST & BEAM BENT WITH TRUSS**

With pine posts and beams, per sf of bent. Post & beam framing styles are nearly unlimited. The following styles are representative.

PINE POST & ▶
BEAM BENT WITH
TRUSS
continued

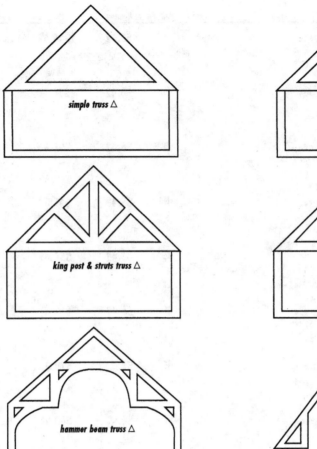

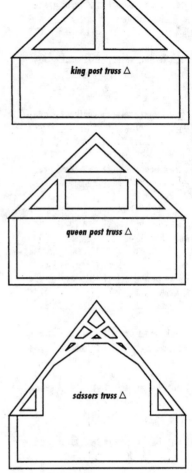

simple truss △

king post truss △

king post & struts truss △

queen post truss △

hammer beam truss △

scissors truss △

Item Description	Unit	Remove	Replace	Total
Pine post & beam single-story bent with queen post truss	sf	$2.05	$33.60	$35.65
Replace Materials........4.51 Labor ....28.70 Equipment .... .39				
Remove .... Labor 2.05				
Pine post & beam single-story bent with hammer beam truss	sf	$2.05	$54.69	$56.74
Replace Materials........4.80 Labor...........49.50 Equipment .... .39				
Remove .... Labor 2.05				
Pine post & beam single-story bent with scissors truss	sf	$2.05	$52.04	$54.09
Replace Materials........5.05 Labor ....46.60 Equipment .... .39				
Remove .... Labor 2.05				
Pine post & beam two-story bent with simple truss	sf	$2.05	$30.87	$32.92
Replace Materials........3.58 Labor...........26.90 Equipment .... .39				
Remove .... Labor 2.05				
Pine post & beam two-story bent with king post truss	sf	$2.05	$33.44	$35.49
Replace Materials........3.85 Labor ....29.20 Equipment .... .39				
Remove .... Labor 2.05				
Pine post & beam two-story bent with king post & struts truss	sf	$2.05	$36.57	$38.62
Replace Materials........4.18 Labor ....32.00 Equipment .... .39				
Remove .... Labor 2.05				
Pine post & beam two-story bent with queen post truss	sf	$2.05	$35.97	$38.02
Replace Materials........3.98 Labor...........31.60 Equipment .... .39				
Remove .... Labor 2.05				

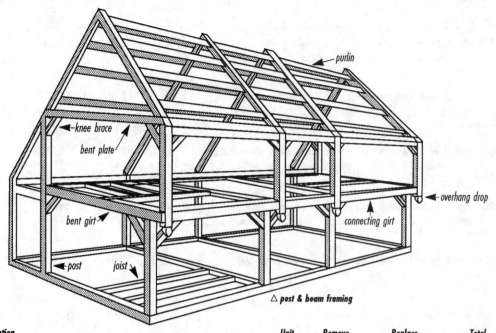

knee brace

bent plate

purlin

overhang drop

bent girt

connecting girt

post

joist

△ **post & beam framing**

Item Description	Unit	Remove	Replace	Total	
Pine post & beam two-story bent with hammer beam truss	sf	$2.05	$63.43	$65.48	
Replace Materials........4.14 Labor ....58.90 Equipment 39					
Remove .... Labor 2.05					
Pine post & beam two-story bent with scissors truss	sf	$2.05	$53.68	$55.73	
Replace Materials........4.29 Labor...........49.00 Equipment 39					
Remove .... Labor 2.05					
Add for overhang drop in pine two-story bent	ea	–	$1,158.39	$1,158.39	◁ add for overhang
Replace Materials.....216.00 Labor.........942.00 Equipment 39					
Pine connecting members between single-story bents and trusses	sf	$6.18	$59.12	$65.30	◀ **PINE CONNECTING MEMBERS BETWEEN BENTS**
Replace Materials........6.82 Labor...........52.30					
Remove .... Labor 6.18					
Pine connecting members between two-story bents and trusses	sf	$8.27	$97.29	$105.56	
Replace Materials ......10.19 Labor...........87.10					
Remove .... Labor 8.27					
Oak post & beam single-story bent with simple truss	sf	$2.05	$33.03	$35.08	◀ **OAK POST & BEAM BENT WITH TRUSS**
Replace Materials........7.84 Labor...........24.80 Equipment 39					
Remove .... Labor 2.05					
Oak post & beam single-story bent with king post truss	sf	$2.05	$35.94	$37.99	
Replace Materials........8.75 Labor...........26.80 Equipment 39					
Remove .... Labor 2.05					
Oak post & beam single-story bent with king post & struts truss	sf	$2.05	$39.30	$41.35	
Replace Materials........9.81 Labor ....29.10 Equipment 39					
Remove .... Labor 1.75					
Oak post & beam single-story bent with queen post truss	sf	$2.05	$38.21	$40.26	
Replace Materials........9.12 Labor ....28.70 Equipment 39					
Remove .... Labor 2.05					
Oak post & beam single-story bent with hammer beam truss	sf	$2.05	$59.55	$61.60	
Replace Materials........9.66 Labor ....49.50 Equipment 39					
Remove .... Labor 2.05					
Oak post & beam single-story bent with scissors truss	sf	$2.05	$57.19	$59.24	
Replace Materials ......10.20 Labor...........46.60 Equipment 39					
Remove .... Labor 2.05					

PINE CONNECTING MEMBERS BETWEEN BENTS
Pine. Includes floor joists, roof purlins, diagonal braces, and beams. Per sf of area beneath roof. Measure only one floor.

OAK POST & BEAM BENT WITH TRUSS
With oak posts and beams, per sf of bent. Post & beam framing styles are nearly unlimited. The following styles are representative.

RELATED ITEMS

Columns 71
Fences 187
Finish Carpentry 199
Outbuildings 331
Painting 341
Paneling 347
Siding 455
Stairs 465

Item Description	Unit	Remove	Replace	Total
Oak post & beam two-story bent with simple truss	sf	$2.05	$34.52	$36.57
Replace Materials.......7.23 Labor...........26.90 Equipment .... .39				
Remove .... Labor 2.05				
Oak post & beam two-story bent with king post truss	sf	$2.05	$37.38	$39.43
Replace Materials.......7.79 Labor ....29.20 Equipment .... .39				
Remove .... Labor 2.05				
Oak post & beam two-story bent with king post & struts truss	sf	$2.05	$40.82	$42.87
Replace Materials.......8.43 Labor ....32.00 Equipment .... .39				
Remove .... Labor 2.05				
Oak post & beam two-story bent with queen post truss	sf	$2.05	$40.02	$42.07
Replace Materials.......8.03 Labor ....31.60 Equipment .... .39				
Remove .... Labor 2.05				
Oak post & beam two-story bent with hammer beam truss	sf	$2.05	$67.65	$69.70
Replace Materials.......8.36 Labor ....58.90 Equipment .... .39				
Remove .... Labor 2.05				
Oak post & beam two-story bent with scissors truss	sf	$2.05	$58.06	$60.11
Replace Materials.......8.67 Labor ....49.00 Equipment .... .39				
Remove .... Labor 2.05				
Add for overhang drop in oak two-story bent	ea	–	$1,336.39	$1,336.39
Replace Materials ....394.00 Labor..........942.00 Equipment .... .39				
Oak connecting members between single-story bents and trusses	sf	$6.18	$66.10	$72.28
Replace Materials.......13.80 Labor..........52.30				
Remove .... Labor 6.18				
Oak connecting members between two-story bents and trusses	sf	$8.27	$107.60	$115.87
Replace Materials......20.50 Labor...........87.10				
Remove .... Labor 8.27				
Minimum charge for post & beam framing work	ea	–	$1,933.00	$1,933.00
Replace Materials ....441.00 Labor.........942.00 Equipment........550.00				
Sill corner half-lap joint	ea	–	$60.70	$60.70
Replace .... Labor 60.70				
▶ Joint connects two timbers that form the sill and intersect at a 90 degree angle.				
Sill corner half-lap joint with through tenon	ea	–	$153.00	$153.00
Replace .... Labor 153.00				
▶ Joint connects three timbers. Two level timbers form the sill and intersect at a 90 degree angle. A mortise is also cut at the corner. The third member is the plumb corner post with a tenon on the bottom.				
Sill corner dovetail joint	ea	–	$110.00	$110.00
Replace .... Labor 110.00				
▶ Joint connects two timbers that form the sill and intersect at a 90 degree angle.				
Sill corner dovetail joint with through tenon	ea	–	$213.00	$213.00
Replace .... Labor 213.00				
▶ Joint connects three timbers. Two level timbers form the sill and intersect at a 90 degree angle. A mortise is also cut at the corner. The third member is the plumb corner post with a tenon on the bottom.				
Sill corner tongue & fork joint	ea	–	$98.80	$98.80
Replace .... Labor...........98.80				
▶ Joint connects two timbers that form the sill and intersect at a 90 degree angle.				

Left margin notes:

OAK POST & BEAM BENT WITH TRUSS *continued*

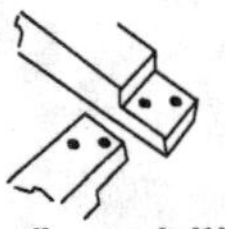

△ *sill corner half-lap*

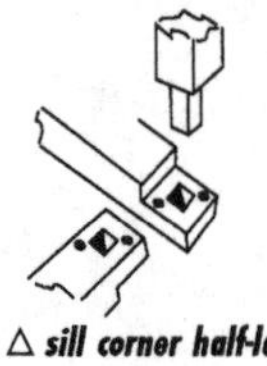

△ *sill corner half-lap with through tenon*

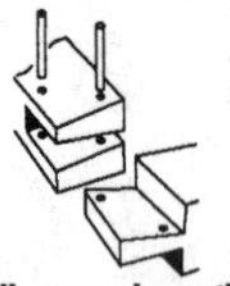

sill corner dovetail △

add for overhang ▷ *see framed overhang illustration on facing page*

OAK CONNECTING MEMBERS BETWEEN BENTS *Includes floor joists, roof purlins, diagonal braces, and beams. Per sf of area beneath roof. Measure only one floor.*

minimum p & b ▷

P & B JOINTS ▶ *Includes cutting, drilling, and joining with pegs.*

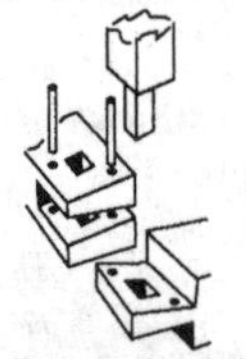

sill corner dovetail △ *with through tenon*

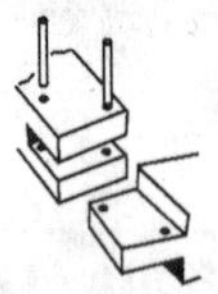

sill corner tongue & fork △

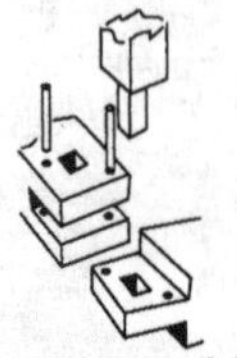

sill corner tongue & fork △ *with through tenon*

Item Description	Unit	Remove	Replace	Total	
Sill corner tongue & fork joint with through tenon	ea	–	$190.00	$190.00	
Replace .... Labor..........190.00					
▶ Joint connects three timbers. Two level timbers form the sill and intersect at a 90 degree angle. A mortise is also cut at the corner. The third member is the plumb corner post with a tenon on the bottom.					*lapped dovetail* △
Lapped dovetail joint	ea	–	$113.00	$113.00	
Replace .... Labor..........113.00					
▶ Joint connects two timbers that intersect at a 90 degree angle. Usually the connection between a purlin and a rafter or a joist and a summer beam.					*housed lapped dovetail* △
Housed lapped dovetail joint	ea	–	$141.00	$141.00	
Replace .... Labor 141.00					
▶ Joint connects two timbers that intersect at a 90 degree angle. Usually the connection between a purlin and a rafter or a joist and a summer beam.					*tusk tenon* △
Tusk tenon joint	ea	–	$153.00	$153.00	
Replace .... Labor 153.00					
▶ Joint connects two timbers that intersect at a 90 degree angle. Usually the connection between a purlin and a rafter or a joist and a summer beam.					
Half-lap joint	ea	–	$59.60	$59.60	
Replace .... Labor...........59.60					
▶ Joint connects two timbers that intersect at a 90 degree angle. Usually the connection between a purlin and a rafter or a joist and a summer beam.					*half-lap* △
Through mortise & tenon with shoulders joint	ea	–	$125.00	$125.00	
Replace .... Labor 125.00					
▶ Joint connects two timbers that intersect at a 90 degree angle. Usually the connection between beam and a post. The level shouldered beam connects into a mortise in the plumb post.					*through mortise & tenon* △
Housed mortise & tenon joint	ea	–	$131.00	$131.00	
Replace .... Labor 131.00					
▶ Joint connects two timbers that intersect at a 90 degree angle. Usually the connection between beam and a post. The level beam connects into a mortise in the plumb post.					*housed mortise & tenon* △
Shouldered mortise & tenon joint	ea	–	$129.00	$129.00	
Replace .... Labor 129.00					
▶ Joint connects two timbers that intersect at a 90 degree angle. Usually the connection between beam and a post. The level beam connects into a mortise in the plumb post.					*shouldered* △ *mortise & tenon*
Wedged dovetail mortise & tenon joint	ea	–	$131.00	$131.00	
Replace .... Labor 131.00					
▶ Joint connects two timbers that intersect at a 90 degree angle. Usually the connection between beam and a post. The level beam connects into a mortise in the plumb post.					*wedged dovetail* △ *mortise & tenon*
Mortise & tenon joint (90 degree intersection)	ea	–	$69.00	$69.00	
Replace .... Labor...........69.00					*mortise & tenon* △
▶ Joint connects two timbers that intersect at a 90 degree angle. A beam or post connects into a mortise in the second beam or post.					
Anchor-beam joint	ea	–	$162.00	$162.00	
Replace .... Labor 162.00					
▶ Joint connects two level beams to opposite sides of a post. The post and beams intersect at 90 degree angles. Each level shouldered beam connects into a mortise in the plumb post.					*anchor beam* △
Framed overhang joint	ea	–	$552.00	$552.00	
Replace .... Labor 552.00					
▶ Includes decorative cutting of the "acorn" on the free-hanging post. Three mortises are cut into the post. One for the cantilevered level beam and two for connecting beams on each side of the post. All three beams are cut with shouldered tenons.					*framed overhang* △

Item Description	Unit	Remove	Replace	Total

P&B JOINTS ▶
continued

Through half-lap joint — ea, Remove —, Replace **$66.20**, Total **$66.20**
Replace .... Labor 66.20
▶ Used when two members cross and neither member terminates at the joint. Both members overlap and continue.

through half-lap △

Mortise & tenon knee brace joint (45 degree intersection) — ea, Remove —, Replace **$86.10**, Total **$86.10**
Replace .... Labor 86.10
▶ Used for diagonal corner braces. Knee brace connects into a post on the bottom and a beam on the top. A mortise is cut into both the post and beam. Tenons are cut at a 45 degree angle in the knee brace. Price is for mortise and tenon on one end only. For a complete knee brace installation use this price twice.

mortise & tenon △
knee brace

Collar tie lapped half dovetail joint — ea, Remove —, Replace **$108.00**, Total **$108.00**
Replace .... Labor 108.00
▶ Used for connecting collar ties to rafters. Collar tie is plumb and intersects with rafters at an angle dictated by the slope of the roof. Price is for joint on one side of the collar tie only. For a complete collar tie use this price twice.

collar tie lapped △
half dovetail

Stopped splayed scarf joint — ea, Remove —, Replace **$178.00**, Total **$178.00**
Replace .... Labor 178.00
▶ Used to splice two level beams together.

stopped splayed scarf △

Stopped splayed scarf joint with through tenon — ea, Remove —, Replace **$276.00**, Total **$276.00**
Replace .... Labor 276.00
▶ Used to splice two level beams together. A mortise is cut through the center of the joint. A tenon is cut at the top of the plumb post that supports the beam.

stopped splayed scarf △
with through tenon

Bladed scarf joint — ea, Remove —, Replace **$135.00**, Total **$135.00**
Replace .... Labor 135.00
▶ Used to splice two level beams together.

bladed scarf △

Bladed scarf joint with through tenon — ea, Remove —, Replace **$240.00**, Total **$240.00**
Replace .... Labor 240.00
▶ Used to splice two level beams together. A mortise is cut through the center of the joint. A tenon is cut at the top of the plumb post that supports the beam.

bladed scarf △
with through tenon

Rafter foot housed bird's mouth joint — ea, Remove —, Replace **$76.70**, Total **$76.70**
Replace .... Labor 76.70
▶ Bird's mouth is cut at foot of rafter. Top plate is cut to receive inside of bird's mouth.

rafter foot housed △
bird's mouth

Rafter foot beveled shoulder bird's mouth joint — ea, Remove —, Replace **$71.80**, Total **$71.80**
Replace .... Labor 71.80
▶ Bird's mouth is cut at foot of rafter. Top plate is bevel-cut to receive inside of bird's mouth.

rafter foot beveled △
shoulder bird's mouth

Rafter foot bird's mouth, purlin, and post joint — ea, Remove —, Replace **$173.00**, Total **$173.00**
Replace .... Labor 173.00
▶ Bird's mouth is cut at foot of rafter. The rafter connects to the timber that is the bottom chord of the truss. A relief for the bird's mouth is cut into the bottom chord. Price also includes the mortise and tenon joint between the bottom chord and the post.

rafter foot bird's △
mouth, purlin, and post

Rafter foot bird's mouth joint — ea, Remove —, Replace **$55.20**, Total **$55.20**
Replace .... Labor 55.20
▶ Bird's mouth is cut at foot of rafter. Rafter connects to beam that forms wall plate. No cut is made in the beam.

Rafter foot bird's mouth with tenon joint — ea, Remove —, Replace **$158.00**, Total **$158.00**
Replace .... Labor 158.00
▶ Direct connection between rafter and a post. (Does not connect with a beam.) Bird's mouth with a tenon is cut at foot of rafter. A mortise is cut in the post. (See illustration on top of facing page.)

rafter foot bird's mouth △

Item Description	Unit	Remove	Replace	Total
Rafter peak tongue & fork joint	ea	–	$98.80	$98.80
Replace .... Labor...........98.80				
▶ The connection between rafters at the peak. One rafter end is cut with a tongue and the other is cut with a fork. The angle of the joint varies with the slope of the roof. (See illustration lower right.)				
2" x 6" joist system for a deck with support beam & posts	sf	$.38	$5.06	$5.44
Replace Materials........2.53 Labor 2.53				
Remove .... Labor .... .38				
2" x 8" joist system for a deck with support beam & posts	sf	$.38	$5.49	$5.87
Replace Materials........2.81 Labor 2.68				
Remove .... Labor .... .38				
2" x 10" joist system for a deck with support beam & posts	sf	$.38	$6.50	$6.88
Replace Materials........3.59 Labor 2.91				
Remove .... Labor .... .38				
2" x 12" joist system for a deck with support beam & posts	sf	$.38	$7.07	$7.45
Replace Materials........3.93 Labor 3.14				
Remove .... Labor .... .38				
2" x 4" redwood decking, con common	sf	$.75	$6.44	$7.19
Replace Materials........4.93 Labor 1.51				
Remove .... Labor .... .75				
2" x 4" redwood decking, con heart	sf	$.75	$7.24	$7.99
Replace Materials........5.73 Labor 1.51				
Remove .... Labor .... .75				
2" x 6" redwood deck, con common	sf	$.75	$5.35	$6.10
Replace Materials........3.95 Labor 1.40				
Remove .... Labor .... .75				
2" x 6" redwood deck, con heart	sf	$.75	$6.00	$6.75
Replace Materials........4.60 Labor 1.40				
Remove .... Labor .... .75				
2" x 8" redwood deck, con common	sf	$.75	$5.48	$6.23
Replace Materials........4.23 Labor 1.25				
Remove .... Labor .... .75				
2" x 8" redwood deck, con heart	sf	$.75	$6.16	$6.91
Replace Materials........4.91 Labor 1.25				
Remove .... Labor .... .75				
2" x 4" treated wood deck	sf	$.75	$5.77	$6.52
Replace Materials........4.26 Labor 1.51				
Remove .... Labor .... .75				
2" x 6" treated wood deck	sf	$.75	$5.54	$6.29
Replace Materials........4.14 Labor 1.40				
Remove .... Labor .... .75				
2" x 8" treated wood deck	sf	$.75	$5.33	$6.08
Replace Materials........4.08 Labor 1.25				
Remove .... Labor .... .75				
Redwood deck railing, con common	lf	$.98	$19.28	$20.26
Replace Materials........8.88 Labor...........10.40				
Remove .... Labor .... .98				
Redwood deck railing, con heart	lf	$.98	$20.69	$21.67
Replace Materials ......10.29 Labor...........10.40				
Remove .... Labor .... .98				

rafter foot bird's △ mouth with tenon

◀ **EXTERIOR DECK JOIST SYSTEM**
Includes 5% waste. Complete joist system. Does not include decking, railing, or stairs. Includes footings, excavation for footings, column stirrups and connectors, posts, and beams on outside edge of deck, connection with joist hangers against house, and joists.

◀ **EXTERIOR DECKING**
Includes 5% waste. Deduct **14%** for 5/4 treated wood decking (decking that is 1-1/4" thick instead of 1-1/2" thick).

rafter peak △ tongue & fork

RELATED ITEMS
Columns 71
Fences.........................187
Finish Carpentry 199
Outbuildings................331
Painting.......................341
Paneling.......................347
Siding..........................455
Stairs 465

◀ **EXTERIOR DECK RAILING**
Includes 5% waste. With 2" x 2" balusters placed approximately 4" on center.

	Item Description	Unit	Remove	Replace	Total
EXTERIOR DECK ▶ RAILING *continued*	**Treated wood deck railing** *Replace* Materials........8.80 Labor...........10.40 *Remove* .... Labor............ .98	lf	$.98	$19.20	$20.18
EXTERIOR ▶ DECK STAIRS *Per step. Includes 5% waste. With three stringers made from 2" x 12" lumber. Each step has up to three 2" x 4" treads. Balusters are approximately 4" on center.*	**2' 6" wide con common redwood deck stairs with railing** *Replace* Materials ......37.20 Labor ....20.40 *Remove* .... Labor 1.76	ea	$1.76	$57.60	$59.36
	2' 6" wide con heart redwood deck stairs with railing *Replace* Materials......40.00 Labor ....20.40 *Remove* .... Labor 1.76	ea	$1.76	$60.40	$62.16
	2' 6" wide treated wood deck stairs with railing *Replace* Materials ......37.00 Labor ....20.40 *Remove* .... Labor 1.76	ea	$1.76	$57.40	$59.16
	3' wide con common redwood deck stairs with railing *Replace* Materials ......39.50 Labor ....22.20 *Remove* .... Labor 1.76	ea	$1.76	$61.70	$63.46
	3' wide con heart redwood deck stairs with railing *Replace* Materials ......42.30 Labor ....22.20 *Remove* .... Labor 1.76	ea	$1.76	$64.50	$66.26
	3' wide treated wood deck stairs with railing *Replace* Materials ......39.40 Labor ....22.20 *Remove* .... Labor 1.76	ea	$1.76	$61.60	$63.36
EXTERIOR ▶ DECK LANDING *Includes 5% waste. 2" x 10" joist system with beams, posts, stirrups, footings, excavation for footings, and all fasteners.*	**Redwood deck stairway landing, con common decking** *Replace* Materials.......13.20 Labor...........2.80 *Remove* .... Labor............. .43	sf	$.43	$16.00	$16.43
	Redwood deck stairway landing, con heart decking *Replace* Materials ......14.60 Labor...........2.80 *Remove* .... Labor............. .43	sf	$.43	$17.40	$17.83
	Treated wood deck stairway landing *Replace* Materials.......13.10 Labor...........2.80 *Remove* .... Labor............. .43	sf	$.43	$15.90	$16.33
FURRING STRIPS ▶ *Includes 5% waste.* **1" x 2" ▷**	**1" x 2" furring strips applied to wood 12" on center** *Replace* Materials .... .23 Labor............. .57 *Remove* .... Labor............. .32	sf	$.32	$.80	$1.12
	1" x 2" furring strips applied to wood 16" on center *Replace* Materials .... .19 Labor............. .49 *Remove* .... Labor............. .32	sf	$.32	$.68	$1.00
	1" x 2" furring strips applied to wood 24" on center *Replace* Materials .... .15 Labor............. .42 *Remove* .... Labor............. .32	sf	$.32	$.57	$.89
	1" x 2" furring strips applied to masonry or concrete 12" on center *Replace* Materials .... .23 Labor............. .76 *Remove* .... Labor............. .35	sf	$.35	$.99	$1.34
	1" x 2" furring strips applied to masonry or concrete 16" on center *Replace* Materials .... .19 Labor............. .60 *Remove* .... Labor............. .35	sf	$.35	$.79	$1.14
	1" x 2" furring strips applied to masonry or concrete 24" on center *Replace* Materials .... .15 Labor............. .53 *Remove* .... Labor............. .35	sf	$.35	$.68	$1.03

Item Description	Unit	Remove	Replace	Total
2" x 2" furring strips applied to wood 12" on center	sf	$.32	$1.10	$1.42
Replace Materials .... .53 Labor............. .57				
Remove .... Labor............. .32				
2" x 2" furring strips applied to wood 16" on center	sf	$.32	$.92	$1.24
Replace Materials .... .43 Labor............. .49				
Remove .... Labor............. .32				
2" x 2" furring strips applied to wood 24" on center	sf	$.32	$.75	$1.07
Replace Materials .... .33 Labor............. .42				
Remove .... Labor............. .32				
2" x 2" furring strips applied to masonry or concrete 12" on center	sf	$.35	$1.29	$1.64
Replace Materials .... .53 Labor............. .76				
Remove .... Labor............. .35				
2" x 2" furring strips applied to masonry or concrete 16" on center	sf	$.35	$1.03	$1.38
Replace Materials .... .43 Labor............. .60				
Remove .... Labor............. .35				
2" x 2" furring strips applied to masonry or concrete 24" on center	sf	$.35	$.86	$1.21
Replace Materials .... .33 Labor............. .53				
Remove .... Labor............. .35				
2" x 4" joist system 12" on center with blocking	sf	$.40	$1.67	$2.07
Replace Materials .... .99 Labor............. .68				
Remove .... Labor............. .40				
2" x 4" joist system 16" on center with blocking	sf	$.40	$1.32	$1.72
Replace Materials .... .79 Labor............. .53				
Remove .... Labor............. .40				
2" x 4" joist system 24" on center with blocking	sf	$.40	$.97	$1.37
Replace Materials .... .55 Labor............. .42				
Remove .... Labor............. .40				
2" x 6" joist system 12" on center with blocking and cross bracing	sf	$.40	$2.41	$2.81
Replace Materials........1.46 Labor............. .95				
Remove .... Labor............. .40				
2" x 6" joist system 16" on center with blocking and cross bracing	sf	$.40	$1.88	$2.28
Replace Materials ...... 1.16 Labor............. .72				
Remove .... Labor............. .40				
2" x 6" joist system 24" on center with blocking and cross bracing	sf	$.40	$1.32	$1.72
Replace Materials .... .83 Labor............. .49				
Remove .... Labor............. .40				
2" x 8" joist system 12" on center with blocking and cross bracing	sf	$.40	$2.88	$3.28
Replace Materials........1.78 Labor............. 1.10				
Remove .... Labor............. .40				
2" x 8" joist system 16" on center with blocking and cross bracing	sf	$.40	$2.32	$2.72
Replace Materials........1.41 Labor............. .91				
Remove .... Labor............. .40				
2" x 8" joist system 24" on center with blocking and cross bracing	sf	$.40	$1.67	$2.07
Replace Materials .... .99 Labor............. .68				
Remove .... Labor............. .40				
2" x 10" joist system 12" on center with blocking and cross bracing	sf	$.40	$4.05	$4.45
Replace Materials.......2.69 Labor............1.36				
Remove .... Labor............. .40				

◁ 2"x 2"

RELATED ITEMS

Columns 71
Fences............................187
Finish Carpentry...........199
Outbuildings..............331
Painting.......................341
Paneling......................347
Siding...........................455
Stairs 465

◀ **JOIST SYSTEM PER SF**
Includes 5% waste. All joist systems include joists, rim joists, blocking, and steel X braces at center span. (Except 2" x 4" joists which include solid blocking at center of span.)

◁ 2"x 6"

◁ 2"x 8"

◁ 2"x 10"

	Item Description	Unit	Remove	Replace	Total
JOIST SYSTEM ► *continued*	**2″ x 10″ joist system 16″ on center with blocking and cross bracing** *Replace* Materials........2.12 — Labor.......... 1.10 *Remove* .... — Labor............ .40	sf	$.40	$3.22	$3.62
	2″ x 10″ joist system 24″ on center with blocking and cross bracing *Replace* Materials........1.46 — Labor............ .83 *Remove* .... — Labor............ .40	sf	$.40	$2.29	$2.69
2″ x 12″ ▷	**2″ x 12″ joist system 12″ on center with blocking and cross bracing** *Replace* Materials........3.08 — Labor ....1.70 *Remove* .... — Labor............ .40	sf	$.40	$4.78	$5.18
	2″ x 12″ joist system 16″ on center with blocking and cross bracing *Replace* Materials........2.42 — Labor ....1.25 *Remove* .... — Labor............ .40	sf	$.40	$3.67	$4.07
	2″ x 12″ joist system 24″ on center with blocking and cross bracing *Replace* Materials........1.66 — Labor........... 1.10 *Remove* .... — Labor............ .40	sf	$.40	$2.76	$3.16
joists per bf ▷	**Joist system per bf** *Replace* Materials........1.44 — Labor............ .79 *Remove* .... — Labor............ .17	bf	$.17	$2.23	$2.40
LAMINATED ► **I JOIST** *Includes 3% waste. The If price includes I joist, rim joists, blocking, and steel X braces at center span.*	**Laminated lumber I joist with 1-3/4″ flange, 9-1/2″ deep** *Replace* Materials........2.85 — Labor ....1.29 *Remove* .... — Labor............ .40	lf	$.40	$4.14	$4.54
	Laminated lumber I joist with 1-3/4″ flange, 11-7/8″ deep *Replace* Materials........3.47 — Labor ....1.36 *Remove* .... — Labor............ .40	lf	$.40	$4.83	$5.23
	Laminated lumber I joist with 1-3/4″ flange, 14″ deep *Replace* Materials........4.25 — Labor ....1.40 *Remove* .... — Labor............ .40	lf	$.40	$5.65	$6.05
2-5/16″ wide ▷	**Laminated lumber I joist with 2-5/16″ flange, 11-7/8″ deep** *Replace* Materials........4.92 — Labor ....1.36 *Remove* .... — Labor............ .40	lf	$.40	$6.28	$6.68
	Laminated lumber I joist with 2-5/16″ flange, 14″ deep *Replace* Materials........6.01 — Labor ....1.44 *Remove* .... — Labor............ .40	lf	$.40	$7.45	$7.85
	Laminated lumber I joist with 2-5/16″ flange, 16″ deep *Replace* Materials........7.11 — Labor ....1.47 *Remove* .... — Labor............ .40	lf	$.40	$8.58	$8.98
FLOOR TRUSS ► *The If price includes cat walks, diagonal braces, fasteners and rim materials.*	**Floor truss** *Replace* Materials........5.00 — Labor ....3.44 *Remove* .... — Labor............ .40	lf	$.40	$8.44	$8.84
	Floor truss designed for heavy loading *Replace* Materials........5.42 — Labor ....3.55 *Remove* .... — Labor............ .40	lf	$.40	$8.97	$9.37
HAND-FRAMED ► **ROOF** *Gable roof. Includes 5% waste. Measure the sf of area beneath roof.* *continued on next page*	**Hand-framed roof 4 in 12 slope with 2″ x 4″ rafters** *Replace* Materials........ .71 — Labor ....1.29 *Remove* .... — Labor............ .46	sf	$.46	$2.00	$2.46
	Hand-framed roof 6 in 12 slope with 2″ x 4″ rafters *Replace* Materials........ .75 — Labor ....1.36 *Remove* .... — Labor............ .49	sf	$.49	$2.11	$2.60

Item Description	Unit	Remove	Replace	Total
Hand-framed roof 8 in 12 slope with 2″ x 4″ rafters *Replace* Materials .... .78 Labor ....1.51 *Remove* .... Labor .... .55	sf	$.55	$2.29	$2.84
Hand-framed roof 10 in 12 slope with 2″ x 4″ rafters *Replace* Materials .... .83 Labor ....1.66 *Remove* .... Labor .... .69	sf	$.69	$2.49	$3.18
Hand-framed roof 12 in 12 slope with 2″ x 4″ rafters *Replace* Materials .... .90 Labor ....1.85 *Remove* .... Labor .... .92	sf	$.92	$2.75	$3.67
Hand-framed roof 14 in 12 slope with 2″ x 4″ rafters *Replace* Materials .... .95 Labor ....2.04 *Remove* .... Labor 1.10	sf	$1.10	$2.99	$4.09
Hand-framed roof 16 in 12 slope with 2″ x 4″ rafters *Replace* Materials ...... 1.01 Labor ....2.27 *Remove* .... Labor 1.45	sf	$1.45	$3.28	$4.73
Hand-framed roof 18 in 12 slope with 2″ x 4″ rafters *Replace* Materials ...... 1.10 Labor ....2.53 *Remove* .... Labor 2.23	sf	$2.23	$3.63	$5.86
Hand-framed roof 4 in 12 slope with 2″ x 6″ rafters *Replace* Materials ...... 1.01 Labor ....1.32 *Remove* .... Labor .... .46	sf	$.46	$2.33	$2.79
Hand-framed roof 6 in 12 slope with 2″ x 6″ rafters *Replace* Materials ...... 1.06 Labor ....1.44 *Remove* .... Labor .... .49	sf	$.49	$2.50	$2.99
Hand-framed roof 8 in 12 slope with 2″ x 6″ rafters *Replace* Materials ...... 1.13 Labor ....1.59 *Remove* .... Labor .... .55	sf	$.55	$2.72	$3.27
Hand-framed roof 10 in 12 slope with 2″ x 6″ rafters *Replace* Materials ...... 1.20 Labor ....1.74 *Remove* .... Labor .... .69	sf	$.69	$2.94	$3.63
Hand-framed roof 12 in 12 slope with 2″ x 6″ rafters *Replace* Materials ...... 1.28 Labor ....1.93 *Remove* .... Labor .... .92	sf	$.92	$3.21	$4.13
Hand-framed roof 14 in 12 slope with 2″ x 6″ rafters *Replace* Materials......1.36 Labor ....2.12 *Remove* .... Labor 1.10	sf	$1.10	$3.48	$4.58
Hand-framed roof 16 in 12 slope with 2″ x 6″ rafters *Replace* Materials......1.46 Labor ....2.34 *Remove* .... Labor 1.45	sf	$1.45	$3.80	$5.25
Hand-framed roof 18 in 12 slope with 2″ x 6″ rafters *Replace* Materials......1.56 Labor ....2.65 *Remove* .... Labor 2.23	sf	$2.23	$4.21	$6.44
Hand-framed roof 4 in 12 slope with 2″ x 8″ rafters *Replace* Materials......1.46 Labor ....1.36 *Remove* .... Labor .... .46	sf	$.46	$2.82	$3.28
Hand-framed roof 6 in 12 slope with 2″ x 8″ rafters *Replace* Materials......1.53 Labor ....1.47 *Remove* .... Labor .... .49	sf	$.49	$3.00	$3.49

◄ **HAND-FRAMED ROOF**
continued

(The sf of bottom floor plus sf under overhangs.) Do not measure the sf of roof. Includes rafters, collar ties, a ridge board that is 2″ wider than the rafter (except for 2″ x 12″ rafters which have a ridge made from a 1-1/2″ x 11-7/8″ micro-laminated beam), rough fascia board, blocking, and wall fasteners. If roof has a hip or a Dutch hip see page 435. There is no additional charge for a Dutch gable. (see illustrations on page 435.)

◁ 2″x 6″

RELATED ITEMS

Columns 71
Fences........................187
Finish Carpentry 199
Outbuildings................331
Painting......................341
Paneling......................347
Siding..........................455
Stairs 465

◁ 2″x 8″

	Item Description	Unit	Remove	Replace	Total
HAND-FRAMED ▶ **ROOF** *continued*	**Hand-framed roof 8 in 12 slope with 2″ x 8″ rafters** *Replace* Materials........1.61 Labor ....1.63 *Remove* .... Labor .... .55	sf	$.55	$3.24	$3.79
	Hand-framed roof 10 in 12 slope with 2″ x 8″ rafters *Replace* Materials........1.71 Labor ....1.78 *Remove* .... Labor .... .69	sf	$.69	$3.49	$4.18
	Hand-framed roof 12 in 12 slope with 2″ x 8″ rafters *Replace* Materials........1.84 Labor ....1.97 *Remove* .... Labor .... .92	sf	$.92	$3.81	$4.73
	Hand-framed roof 14 in 12 slope with 2″ x 8″ rafters *Replace* Materials........1.96 Labor ....2.19 *Remove* .... Labor 1.10	sf	$1.10	$4.15	$5.25
	Hand-framed roof 16 in 12 slope with 2″ x 8″ rafters *Replace* Materials........2.09 Labor ....2.42 *Remove* .... Labor 1.45	sf	$1.45	$4.51	$5.96
	Hand-framed roof 18 in 12 slope with 2″ x 8″ rafters *Replace* Materials........2.24 Labor ....2.72 *Remove* .... Labor 2.23	sf	$2.23	$4.96	$7.19
2″ x 10″ ▷	**Hand-framed roof 4 in 12 slope with 2″ x 10″ rafters** *Replace* Materials........1.89 Labor ....1.40 *Remove* .... Labor .... .46	sf	$.46	$3.29	$3.75
	Hand-framed roof 6 in 12 slope with 2″ x 10″ rafters *Replace* Materials........1.98 Labor ....1.51 *Remove* .... Labor .... .49	sf	$.49	$3.49	$3.98
	Hand-framed roof 8 in 12 slope with 2″ x 10″ rafters *Replace* Materials........2.09 Labor ....1.66 *Remove* .... Labor .... .55	sf	$.55	$3.75	$4.30
	Hand-framed roof 10 in 12 slope with 2″ x 10″ rafters *Replace* Materials........2.24 Labor ....1.85 *Remove* .... Labor .... .69	sf	$.69	$4.09	$4.78
	Hand-framed roof 12 in 12 slope with 2″ x 10″ rafters *Replace* Materials........2.41 Labor ....2.04 *Remove* .... Labor .... .92	sf	$.92	$4.45	$5.37
	Hand-framed roof 14 in 12 slope with 2″ x 10″ rafters *Replace* Materials........2.57 Labor ....2.23 *Remove* .... Labor 1.10	sf	$1.10	$4.80	$5.90
	Hand-framed roof 16 in 12 slope with 2″ x 10″ rafters *Replace* Materials........2.76 Labor ....2.49 *Remove* .... Labor 1.45	sf	$1.45	$5.25	$6.70
	Hand-framed roof 18 in 12 slope with 2″ x 10″ rafters *Replace* Materials........2.95 Labor ....2.84 *Remove* .... Labor 2.23	sf	$2.23	$5.79	$8.02
2″ x 12″ ▷	**Hand-framed roof 4 in 12 slope with 2″ x 12″ rafters** *Replace* Materials........2.57 Labor ....1.44 *Remove* .... Labor .... .46	sf	$.46	$4.01	$4.47
	Hand-framed roof 6 in 12 slope with 2″ x 12″ rafters *Replace* Materials........2.67 Labor ....1.59 *Remove* .... Labor .... .49	sf	$.49	$4.26	$4.75

Item Description	Unit	Remove	Replace	Total
Hand-framed roof 8 in 12 slope with 2" x 12" rafters *Replace* Materials........2.81 Labor ....1.74 *Remove* .... Labor............ .55	sf	$.55	$4.55	$5.10
Hand-framed roof 10 in 12 slope with 2" x 12" rafters *Replace* Materials........2.97 Labor ....1.89 *Remove* .... Labor............ .69	sf	$.69	$4.86	$5.55
Hand-framed roof 12 in 12 slope with 2" x 12" rafters *Replace* Materials........3.15 Labor ....2.12 *Remove* .... Labor............ .92	sf	$.92	$5.27	$6.19
Hand-framed roof 14 in 12 slope with 2" x 12" rafters *Replace* Materials........3.35 Labor ....2.31 *Remove* .... Labor............ 1.10	sf	$1.10	$5.66	$6.76
Hand-framed roof 16 in 12 slope with 2" x 12" rafters *Replace* Materials........3.57 Labor ....2.57 *Remove* .... Labor............1.45	sf	$1.45	$6.14	$7.59
Hand-framed roof 18 in 12 slope with 2" x 12" rafters *Replace* Materials........3.80 Labor ....2.91 *Remove* .... Labor............2.23	sf	$2.23	$6.71	$8.94
Add for each lf of valley in hand-framed roof *Replace* Materials.......15.90 Labor ....29.70 ▶ Includes additional labor, materials, and waste to frame a valley.	lf	–	$45.60	$45.60
For a hand-framed hip roof add for each lf of width *Replace* Materials........2.41 Labor ....8.00 ▶ Includes additional labor, materials, and waste to frame a hip. Per lf of hip. (For a hip on both ends of a roof measure the lf of both sides.)	lf	–	$10.41	$10.41
For a hand-framed Dutch hip roof add for each lf of width *Replace* Materials........2.66 Labor ....8.66 ▶ Includes additional labor, materials, and waste to frame a Dutch hip. Per lf of hip. (For a Dutch hip on both ends of a roof measure the lf of both sides.)	lf	–	$11.32	$11.32
Hand-framed mansard roof with 2" x 4" rafters *Replace* Materials .... .12 Labor............. .19 *Remove* .... Labor............. .06	cf	$.06	$.31	$.37
Hand-framed mansard roof with 2" x 6" rafters *Replace* Materials .... .17 Labor............. .19 *Remove* .... Labor............. .06	cf	$.06	$.36	$.42
Hand-framed mansard roof with 2" x 8" rafters *Replace* Materials .... .24 Labor............. .19 *Remove* .... Labor............. .06	cf	$.06	$.43	$.49
Hand-framed mansard roof with 2" x 10" rafters *Replace* Materials .... .31 Labor............. .19 *Remove* .... Labor............. .06	cf	$.06	$.50	$.56
Hand-framed mansard roof with 2" x 12" rafters *Replace* Materials .... .35 Labor............. .23 *Remove* .... Labor............. .06	cf	$.06	$.58	$.64
Add for each lf of valley in hand-framed mansard roof *Replace* Materials.......19.10 Labor ....40.80 ▶ Includes additional labor, materials, and waste to frame a valley.	lf	–	$59.90	$59.90
Hand-framed gambrel roof with 2" x 4" rafters *Replace* Materials .... .15 Labor............. .15 *Remove* .... Labor............. .06	cf	$.06	$.30	$.36

gable △

hip △

mansard △

gambrel △

Dutch gable △

◀ **ADDITIONAL COSTS FOR HAND-FRAMED ROOFS**

Dutch hip △

◀ **HAND-FRAMED MANSARD ROOF**
Includes 7% waste. Roof area equals roof system width times height times length. Includes rafters, collar ties, ridge boards, hip rafters, rough fascia board, blocking, and wall fasteners.

◁ *mansard roof valley*

◀ **HAND FRAMED GAMBREL ROOF**
continued on next page

Item Description	Unit	Remove	Replace	Total
HAND-FRAMED ▶ **Hand-framed gambrel roof with 2" x 6" rafters**	cf	$.06	$.41	$.47
GAMBREL ROOF *Replace* Materials .... .22 Labor............. .19				
continued *Remove* .... Labor............. .06				
Includes 7% waste. Roof **Hand-framed gambrel roof with 2" x 8" rafters**	cf	$.06	$.50	$.56
area equals roof system *Replace* Materials .... .31 Labor............. .19				
width times height times *Remove* .... Labor............. .06				
length. Includes rafters,				
collar ties, ridge boards, **Hand-framed gambrel roof with 2" x 10" rafters**	cf	$.06	$.59	$.65
valley rafters, rough fas- *Replace* Materials .... .40 Labor............. .19				
cia board, blocking, and *Remove* .... Labor............. .06				
wall fasteners. Does not				
include wall that must be **Hand-framed gambrel roof with 2" x 12" rafters**	cf	$.06	$.69	$.75
built at the intersection of *Replace* Materials .... .46 Labor............. .23				
the top and bottom *Remove* .... Labor............. .06				
sloping roof sections.				
gambrel roof valley ▷ **Add for each lf of valley in hand-framed gambrel roof**	lf	–	$63.00	$63.00
Replace Materials.......19.90 Labor 43.10				
▶ *Includes additional labor, materials, and waste to frame a valley in a gambrel roof.*				
HAND-FRAMED ▶ **Hand-framed gable roof per bf**	bf	$.20	$2.08	$2.28
ROOF PER BF *Replace* Materials ...... 1.21 Labor............. .87				
Includes 5% waste. *Remove* .... Labor............. .20				
Hand-framed hip roof per bf	bf	$.20	$2.21	$2.41
Replace Materials......1.34 Labor............. .87				
Remove .... Labor............. .20				
Hand-framed Dutch hip roof per bf	bf	$.20	$2.27	$2.47
Replace Materials......1.36 Labor............. .91				
Remove .... Labor............. .20				
Hand-framed mansard roof per bf	bf	$.20	$2.46	$2.66
Replace Materials......1.48 Labor............. .98				
Remove .... Labor............. .20				
Hand-framed gambrel roof per bf	bf	$.20	$2.51	$2.71
Replace Materials......1.56 Labor............. .95				
Remove .... Labor............. .20				
MINIMUM FOR ▶ **Minimum charge for roof framing**	ea	–	$97.30	$97.30
ROOF FRAMING *Replace* Materials......50.00 Labor..........47.30				
HAND-FRAMED ▶ **Shed dormer 4 in 12 slope (length x width of dormer)**	sf	$.49	$2.89	$3.38
SHED DORMER *Replace* Materials ...... 1.19 Labor 1.70				
Includes 7% waste. *Remove* .... Labor............. .49				
Complete dormer				
including all side walls **Shed dormer 6 in 12 slope (length x width of dormer)**	sf	$.52	$3.03	$3.55
and roof framing. *Replace* Materials ...... 1.25 Labor 1.78				
Remove .... Labor............. .52				
Shed dormer 8 in 12 slope (length x width of dormer)	sf	$.58	$3.18	$3.76
Replace Materials........1.33 Labor 1.85				
Remove .... Labor............. .58				
Shed dormer 10 in 12 slope (length x width of dormer)	sf	$.72	$3.46	$4.18
Replace Materials........1.42 Labor 2.04				
Remove .... Labor............. .72				
Shed dormer 12 in 12 slope (length x width of dormer)	sf	$.95	$3.78	$4.73
Replace Materials........1.51 Labor 2.27				
Remove .... Labor............. .95				

Item Description	Unit	Remove	Replace	Total
Shed dormer 14 in 12 slope (length x width of dormer) *Replace* Materials........1.60 Labor ....2.34 *Remove* .... Labor 1.16	sf	$1.16	$3.94	$5.10
Shed dormer 16 in 12 slope (length x width of dormer) *Replace* Materials........1.72 Labor ....2.42 *Remove* .... Labor 1.53	sf	$1.53	$4.14	$5.67
Shed dormer 18 in 12 slope (length x width of dormer) *Replace* Materials........1.84 Labor ....2.53 *Remove* .... Labor 2.34	sf	$2.34	$4.37	$6.71
Gable dormer 4 in 12 slope (length of ridge x width of dormer) *Replace* Materials........1.33 Labor ....1.78 *Remove* .... Labor .... .49	sf	$.49	$3.11	$3.60
Gable dormer 6 in 12 slope (length of ridge x width of dormer) *Replace* Materials........1.40 Labor ....1.85 *Remove* .... Labor .... .52	sf	$.52	$3.25	$3.77
Gable dormer 8 in 12 slope (length of ridge x width of dormer) *Replace* Materials........1.49 Labor ....1.93 *Remove* .... Labor .... .58	sf	$.58	$3.42	$4.00
Gable dormer 10 in 12 slope (length of ridge x width of dormer) *Replace* Materials........1.58 Labor ....2.12 *Remove* .... Labor .... .72	sf	$.72	$3.70	$4.42
Gable dormer 12 in 12 slope (length of ridge x width of dormer) *Replace* Materials........1.69 Labor ....2.34 *Remove* .... Labor .... .95	sf	$.95	$4.03	$4.98
Gable dormer 14 in 12 slope (length of ridge x width of dormer) *Replace* Materials........1.80 Labor ....2.46 *Remove* .... Labor 1.16	sf	$1.16	$4.26	$5.42
Gable dormer 16 in 12 slope (length of ridge x width of dormer) *Replace* Materials........1.93 Labor ....2.53 *Remove* .... Labor 1.53	sf	$1.53	$4.46	$5.99
Gable dormer 18 in 12 slope (length of ridge x width of dormer) *Replace* Materials........2.06 Labor ....2.65 *Remove* .... Labor 2.34	sf	$2.34	$4.71	$7.05
Hip dormer 4 in 12 slope (length x width of dormer) *Replace* Materials........1.37 Labor ....1.85 *Remove* .... Labor .... .49	sf	$.49	$3.22	$3.71
Hip dormer 6 in 12 slope (length x width of dormer) *Replace* Materials........1.44 Labor ....1.93 *Remove* .... Labor .... .52	sf	$.52	$3.37	$3.89
Hip dormer 8 in 12 slope (length x width of dormer) *Replace* Materials........1.54 Labor ....2.00 *Remove* .... Labor .... .58	sf	$.58	$3.54	$4.12
Hip dormer 10 in 12 slope (length x width of dormer) *Replace* Materials........1.63 Labor ....2.19 *Remove* .... Labor .... .72	sf	$.72	$3.82	$4.54
Hip dormer 12 in 12 slope (length x width of dormer) *Replace* Materials........1.74 Labor ....2.46 *Remove* .... Labor .... .95	sf	$.95	$4.20	$5.15

◄ **HAND-FRAMED GABLE DORMER**
Includes 7% waste. Complete dormer including all side walls and roof framing.

◄ **HAND-FRAMED HIP DORMER**
Includes 7% waste. Complete dormer including all side walls and roof framing.

RELATED ITEMS

Columns 71
Fences............................187
Finish Carpentry 199
Outbuildings................331
Painting.......................341
Paneling.......................347
Siding...........................455
Stairs 465

Item Description	Unit	Remove	Replace	Total
HAND-FRAMED ▶ HIP DORMER continued				
Hip dormer 14 in 12 slope (length x width of dormer)	sf	$1.16	$4.38	$5.54
Replace Materials........1.85 Labor 2.53				
Remove .... Labor 1.16				
Hip dormer 16 in 12 slope (length x width of dormer)	sf	$1.53	$4.64	$6.17
Replace Materials........1.99 Labor 2.65				
Remove .... Labor 1.53				
Hip dormer 18 in 12 slope (length x width of dormer)	sf	$2.34	$4.88	$7.22
Replace Materials........2.12 Labor 2.76				
Remove .... Labor 2.34				
HAND-FRAMED ▶ DUTCH-HIP DORMER Includes 7% waste. Complete dormer including all side walls and roof framing.				
Dutch-hip dormer 4 in 12 slope (length x width of dormer)	sf	$.49	$3.34	$3.83
Replace Materials........1.41 Labor 1.93				
Remove .... Labor .... .49				
Dutch-hip dormer 6 in 12 slope (length x width of dormer)	sf	$.52	$3.45	$3.97
Replace Materials........1.48 Labor 1.97				
Remove .... Labor .... .52				
Dutch-hip dormer 8 in 12 slope (length x width of dormer)	sf	$.58	$3.62	$4.20
Replace Materials........1.58 Labor 2.04				
Remove .... Labor .... .58				
Dutch-hip dormer 10 in 12 slope (length x width of dormer)	sf	$.72	$3.95	$4.67
Replace Materials........1.68 Labor 2.27				
Remove .... Labor .... .72				
Dutch-hip dormer 12 in 12 slope (length x width of dormer)	sf	$.95	$4.32	$5.27
Replace Materials........1.79 Labor 2.53				
Remove .... Labor .... .95				
Dutch-hip dormer 14 in 12 slope (length x width of dormer)	sf	$1.16	$4.51	$5.67
Replace Materials........1.90 Labor 2.61				
Remove .... Labor 1.16				
Dutch-hip dormer 16 in 12 slope (length x width of dormer)	sf	$1.53	$4.76	$6.29
Replace Materials........2.04 Labor 2.72				
Remove .... Labor 1.53				
Dutch-hip dormer 18 in 12 slope (length x width of dormer)	sf	$2.34	$4.98	$7.32
Replace Materials........2.18 Labor 2.80				
Remove .... Labor 2.34				
HAND-FRAMED ▶ GAMBREL DORMER Includes 7% waste.	**Gambrel dormer (length x width of dormer)**	sf	$.49	$3.68	$4.17
Replace Materials........1.45 Labor 2.23				
Remove .... Labor .... .49				
HAND-FRAMED ▶ ROOF DORMER PER BF	**Shed dormer per bf**	bf	$.29	$3.26	$3.55
Replace Materials........1.97 Labor 1.29				
Remove .... Labor .... .29				
Gable dormer per bf	bf	$.49	$3.38	$3.87
Replace Materials........2.06 Labor 1.32				
Remove .... Labor .... .49				
Hip dormer per bf	bf	$.52	$3.49	$4.01
Replace Materials........2.13 Labor 1.36				
Remove .... Labor .... .52				
Dutch-hip dormer per bf	bf	$.55	$3.63	$4.18
Replace Materials........2.19 Labor 1.44				
Remove .... Labor .... .55				

Item Description	Unit	Remove	Replace	Total
Gambrel dormer per bf	bf	$.66	$3.64	$4.30
Replace Materials.......2.24 Labor 1.40				
Remove .... Labor.............. .66				
Flat roof truss	lf	$1.21	$5.84	$7.05
Replace Materials.......4.80 Labor .... .87 Equipment .... .17				
Remove .... Labor 1.21				
4 in 12 slope truss	lf	$1.21	$6.10	$7.31
Replace Materials.......5.06 Labor .... .87 Equipment .... .17				
Remove .... Labor 1.21				
6 in 12 slope truss	lf	$1.21	$6.50	$7.71
Replace Materials.......5.46 Labor .... .87 Equipment .... .17				
Remove .... Labor 1.21				
8 in 12 slope truss	lf	$1.21	$8.45	$9.66
Replace Materials.......7.37 Labor .... .91 Equipment .... .17				
Remove .... Labor 1.21				
10 in 12 slope truss	lf	$1.21	$9.55	$10.76
Replace Materials.......8.47 Labor .... .91 Equipment .... .17				
Remove .... Labor 1.21				
12 in 12 slope truss	lf	$1.21	$10.94	$12.15
Replace Materials.......9.86 Labor .... .91 Equipment .... .17				
Remove .... Labor 1.21				
14 in 12 slope truss	lf	$1.21	$11.62	$12.83
Replace Materials......10.50 Labor .... .95 Equipment .... .17				
Remove .... Labor 1.21				
16 in 12 slope truss	lf	$1.21	$12.45	$13.66
Replace Materials......11.30 Labor .... .98 Equipment .... .17				
Remove .... Labor 1.21				
17 in 12 slope truss	lf	$1.21	$13.43	$14.64
Replace Materials ......12.20 Labor .... 1.06 Equipment .... .17				
Remove .... Labor 1.21				
Flat roof truss designed for slate or tile roofing	lf	$1.21	$6.14	$7.35
Replace Materials.......5.10 Labor .... .87 Equipment .... .17				
Remove .... Labor 1.21				
4 in 12 slope truss designed for slate or tile roofing	lf	$1.21	$6.50	$7.71
Replace Materials.......5.46 Labor .... .87 Equipment .... .17				
Remove .... Labor 1.21				
6 in 12 slope truss designed for slate or tile roofing	lf	$1.21	$6.84	$8.05
Replace Materials.......5.80 Labor .... .87 Equipment .... .17				
Remove .... Labor 1.21				
8 in 12 slope truss designed for slate or tile roofing	lf	$1.21	$8.83	$10.04
Replace Materials.......7.75 Labor .... .91 Equipment .... .17				
Remove .... Labor 1.21				
10 in 12 slope truss designed for slate or tile roofing	lf	$1.21	$9.94	$11.15
Replace Materials.......8.86 Labor .... .91 Equipment .... .17				
Remove .... Labor 1.21				
12 in 12 slope truss designed for slate or tile roofing	lf	$1.21	$11.28	$12.49
Replace Materials ......10.20 Labor .... .91 Equipment .... .17				
Remove .... Labor 1.21				

◄ **ROOF TRUSS PER LF**
Add **10%** for treated trusses. Per lf of truss bottom chord. The lf price includes cat walks, diagonal braces, fasteners and rough fascia.

◄ **ROOF TRUSS FOR HEAVY LOAD PER LF**
Add **10%** for treated trusses. Per lf of truss bottom chord. The lf price includes cat walks, diagonal braces, fasteners and rough fascia.

RELATED ITEMS

Columns 71
Fences.......................187
Finish Carpentry 199
Outbuildings...............331
Painting.....................341
Paneling....................347
Siding........................455
Stairs 465

	Item Description	Unit	Remove	Replace	Total
ROOF TRUSS FOR ▶ **HEAVY LOAD PER LF** *continued*	**14 in 12 slope truss designed for slate or tile roofing** *Replace* Materials ......10.80 Labor .... .95 Equipment .... .17 *Remove* .... Labor 1.21	lf	$1.21	$11.92	$13.13
	16 in 12 slope truss designed for slate or tile roofing *Replace* Materials.......11.60 Labor .... .98 Equipment .... .17 *Remove* .... Labor 1.21	lf	$1.21	$12.75	$13.96
	17 in 12 slope truss designed for slate or tile roofing *Replace* Materials ......12.50 Labor .... 1.06 Equipment .... .17 *Remove* .... Labor 1.21	lf	$1.21	$13.73	$14.94
ROOF TRUSS ▶ **PER SF** Add **10%** for treated trusses. Per sf of area underneath the roof. For roofs with asphalt, metal, or wood roofing. Includes cat walks, diagonal braces, fasteners and rough fascia.	**Truss roof system 4 in 12 slope** *Replace* Materials........2.93 Labor .... .45 Equipment .... .10 *Remove* .... Labor .... .49	sf	$.49	$3.48	$3.97
	Truss roof system 6 in 12 slope *Replace* Materials........3.17 Labor .... .45 Equipment .... .10 *Remove* .... Labor .... .52	sf	$.52	$3.72	$4.24
	Truss roof system 8 in 12 slope *Replace* Materials........4.27 Labor .... .45 Equipment .... .10 *Remove* .... Labor .... .61	sf	$.61	$4.82	$5.43
	Truss roof system 10 in 12 slope *Replace* Materials........4.91 Labor .... .49 Equipment .... .10 *Remove* .... Labor .... .72	sf	$.72	$5.50	$6.22
	Truss roof system 12 in 12 slope *Replace* Materials........5.72 Labor .... .49 Equipment .... .10 *Remove* .... Labor .... .98	sf	$.98	$6.31	$7.29
	Truss roof system 14 in 12 slope *Replace* Materials........6.09 Labor .... .49 Equipment .... .10 *Remove* .... Labor 1.16	sf	$1.16	$6.68	$7.84
	Truss roof system 16 in 12 slope *Replace* Materials........6.55 Labor .... .49 Equipment .... .10 *Remove* .... Labor 1.53	sf	$1.53	$7.14	$8.67
	Truss roof system 17 in 12 slope *Replace* Materials........7.08 Labor .... .49 Equipment .... .10 *Remove* .... Labor 2.37	sf	$2.37	$7.67	$10.04
ROOF TRUSS ▶ **FOR HEAVY LOAD PER SF** Add **10%** for treated trusses. Per sf of area underneath the roof. For roofs with slate, tile, or other heavy roofing. Includes cat walks, diagonal braces, fasteners and rough fascia.	**Truss roof system 4 in 12 slope designed for slate or tile roofing** *Replace* Materials........3.17 Labor .... .45 Equipment .... .10 *Remove* .... Labor .... .49	sf	$.49	$3.72	$4.21
	Truss roof system 6 in 12 slope designed for slate or tile roofing *Replace* Materials........3.36 Labor .... .45 Equipment .... .10 *Remove* .... Labor .... .52	sf	$.52	$3.91	$4.43
	Truss roof system 8 in 12 slope designed for slate or tile roofing *Replace* Materials........4.50 Labor .... .45 Equipment .... .10 *Remove* .... Labor .... .61	sf	$.61	$5.05	$5.66
	Truss roof system 10 in 12 slope designed for slate or tile roofing *Replace* Materials........5.14 Labor .... .49 Equipment .... .10 *Remove* .... Labor .... .72	sf	$.72	$5.73	$6.45
	Truss roof system 12 in 12 slope designed for slate or tile roofing *Replace* Materials........5.92 Labor .... .49 Equipment .... .10 *Remove* .... Labor .... .98	sf	$.98	$6.51	$7.49

Item Description	Unit	Remove	Replace	Total
Truss roof system 14 in 12 slope designed for slate or tile roofing	sf	$1.16	$6.85	$8.01
Replace Materials.......6.26 Labor............. .49 Equipment .... .10				
Remove .... Labor............ 1.16				
Truss roof system 16 in 12 slope designed for slate or tile roofing	sf	$1.53	$7.32	$8.85
Replace Materials.......6.73 Labor............. .49 Equipment .... .10				
Remove .... Labor............1.53				
Truss roof system 17 in 12 slope designed for slate or tile roofing	sf	$2.37	$7.84	$10.21
Replace Materials.......7.25 Labor............. .49 Equipment .... .10				
Remove .... Labor............2.37				
Add for each lf of valley in truss roof	lf	–	$60.90	$60.90
Replace Materials......30.20 Labor 30.70				
► Includes materials and labor for "California" fill between truss roofs with ridge board and jack rafters. Does not include sheathing.				
Add for each lf of width in a hip truss roof	lf	–	$40.90	$40.90
Replace Materials ......27.30 Labor............13.60				
► Includes additional cost for trusses designed to create a hip. Add per lf of hip.				
Add for each lf of width in a Dutch hip truss roof	lf	–	$45.10	$45.10
Replace Materials......29.70 Labor............15.40				
► Includes additional cost for trusses designed to create a hip. The Dutch hip is stacked and hand framed. Add per lf of Dutch hip.				
Truss mansard roof system	cf	$.17	$.57	$.74
Replace Materials .... .46 Labor............. .11				
Remove .... Labor............. .17				
Truss mansard roof system designed for slate or tile roofing	cf	$.17	$.63	$.80
Replace Materials .... .52 Labor............. .11				
Remove .... Labor............. .17				
Add for each lf of valley in trussed mansard roof	lf	–	$65.90	$65.90
Replace Materials......29.90 Labor 36.00				
► Includes materials and labor to fill between truss roofs with ridge boards and jack rafters. Does not include sheathing.				
Truss gambrel roof system	cf	$.17	$.68	$.85
Replace Materials .... .57 Labor............. .11				
Remove .... Labor............. .17				
Truss gambrel roof system designed for slate or tile roofing	cf	$.17	$.76	$.93
Replace Materials .... .65 Labor............. .11				
Remove .... Labor............. .17				
Add for each lf of valley in trussed gambrel roof	lf	–	$74.00	$74.00
Replace Materials......30.20 Labor 43.80				
► Includes materials and labor to fill between truss roofs with ridge boards and jack rafters. Does not include sheathing.				
Remove truss for work, then reinstall	lf	–	$3.44	$3.44
Replace .... Labor............3.44				
1/2" fiberboard sheathing	sf	$.38	$1.12	$1.50
Replace Materials .... .55 Labor............. .57				
Remove .... Labor............. .38				
3/4" fiberboard sheathing	sf	$.38	$1.32	$1.70
Replace Materials .... .75 Labor............. .57				
Remove .... Labor............. .38				

RELATED ITEMS

Columns.........................71
Fences.........................187
Finish Carpentry..........199
Outbuildings.............331
Painting......................341
Paneling....................347
Siding.........................455
Stairs.........................465

◄ **ADDITIONAL TRUSS ROOF COSTS**

◄ **TRUSS MANSARD ROOF**
*Add **10%** for treated trusses. Roof area equals the roof system width times height times length. Includes cat walks, diagonal braces, fasteners and rough fascia.*

◄ **TRUSS GAMBREL ROOF**
*Add **10%** for treated trusses. Roof area equals the roof system width times height times length. Includes cat walks, diagonal braces, fasteners and rough fascia.*

◄ **REMOVE TRUSS THEN REINSTALL**

◄ **WALL OR ROOF SHEATHING**
Includes 4% waste.

Item Description	Unit	Remove	Replace	Total
WALL OR ROOF ▶ SHEATHING *continued* **1/2″ sound-deadening fiberboard** *Replace* Materials .... .54 Labor .... .57 *Remove* .... Labor .... .38	sf	$.38	$1.11	$1.49
1/2″ foil-faced foam sheathing *Replace* Materials .... .63 Labor .... .57 *Remove* .... Labor .... .38	sf	$.38	$1.20	$1.58
3/4″ foil-faced foam sheathing *Replace* Materials .... .85 Labor .... .57 *Remove* .... Labor .... .38	sf	$.38	$1.42	$1.80
1″ foil-faced foam sheathing *Replace* Materials ...... 1.10 Labor .... .60 *Remove* .... Labor .... .38	sf	$.38	$1.70	$2.08
3/8″ CDX plywood sheathing *Replace* Materials .... .81 Labor .... .60 *Remove* .... Labor .... .38	sf	$.38	$1.41	$1.79
1/2″ CDX plywood sheathing *Replace* Materials .... .76 Labor .... .60 *Remove* .... Labor .... .38	sf	$.38	$1.36	$1.74
1/2″ treated plywood sheathing *Replace* Materials .... .87 Labor .... .60 *Remove* .... Labor .... .38	sf	$.38	$1.47	$1.85
1/2″ waferboard sheathing *Replace* Materials .... .70 Labor .... .60 *Remove* .... Labor .... .38	sf	$.38	$1.30	$1.68
1/2″ oriented strand board (OSB) sheathing *Replace* Materials .... .80 Labor .... .60 *Remove* .... Labor .... .38	sf	$.38	$1.40	$1.78
5/8″ CDX plywood sheathing *Replace* Materials ...... 1.11 Labor .... .60 *Remove* .... Labor .... .38	sf	$.38	$1.71	$2.09
5/8″ treated plywood sheathing *Replace* Materials ...... 1.30 Labor .... .60 *Remove* .... Labor .... .38	sf	$.38	$1.90	$2.28
5/8″ waferboard sheathing *Replace* Materials ...... 1.23 Labor .... .60 *Remove* .... Labor .... .38	sf	$.38	$1.83	$2.21
5/8″ oriented strand board (OSB) sheathing *Replace* Materials ...... 1.23 Labor .... .60 *Remove* .... Labor .... .38	sf	$.38	$1.83	$2.21
3/4″ CDX plywood sheathing *Replace* Materials ...... 1.36 Labor .... .60 *Remove* .... Labor .... .38	sf	$.38	$1.96	$2.34
3/4″ tongue-&-groove plywood sheathing *Replace* Materials ...... 1.37 Labor .... .60 *Remove* .... Labor .... .38	sf	$.38	$1.97	$2.35
3/4″ treated plywood sheathing *Replace* Materials ....1.60 Labor .... .60 *Remove* .... Labor .... .38	sf	$.38	$2.20	$2.58

Item Description	Unit	Remove	Replace	Total
3/4" tongue-&-groove waferboard sheathing	sf	$.38	$2.05	$2.43
Replace Materials........1.45　　　Labor.............60				
Remove ....　　　Labor.............38				
3/4" tongue-&-groove oriented strand board (OSB) sheathing	sf	$.38	$2.06	$2.44
Replace Materials........1.46　　　Labor.............60				
Remove ....　　　Labor.............38				
1" x 6" sheathing	sf	$.40	$3.14	$3.54
Replace Materials........2.50　　　Labor.............64				
Remove ....　　　Labor.............40				
1" x 6" tongue-&-groove sheathing	sf	$.40	$4.56	$4.96
Replace Materials........3.92　　　Labor.............64				
Remove ....　　　Labor.............40				
2" x 6" tongue-&-groove sheathing	sf	$.46	$9.87	$10.33
Replace Materials........9.23　　　Labor.............64				
Remove ....　　　Labor.............46				
2" x 8" tongue-&-groove sheathing	sf	$.43	$6.66	$7.09
Replace Materials........6.02　　　Labor.............64				
Remove ....　　　Labor.............43				
Add for shear-panel sheathing installation	sf	–	$.11	$.11
Replace ....　　　Labor.............11				
► Includes shear paneling installed with nailing patterns and splicing according to code specifications for a shear panel.				
Frame interior soffit (two sides)	lf	$1.30	$7.54	$8.84
Replace Materials........5.31　　　Labor.............2.23				
Remove ....　　　Labor.............1.30				
Frame interior soffit with recess for indirect lighting (two sides)	lf	$1.30	$11.71	$13.01
Replace Materials........7.93　　　Labor.............3.78				
Remove ....　　　Labor.............1.30				
Frame interior soffit (three sides)	lf	$1.30	$10.14	$11.44
Replace Materials........7.12　　　Labor.............3.02				
Remove ....　　　Labor.............1.30				
Frame interior soffit with recess for indirect lighting (three sides)	lf	$1.30	$13.62	$14.92
Replace Materials........8.74　　　Labor.............4.88				
Remove ....　　　Labor.............1.30				
6" thick factory designed & fabricated structural wall panel	sf	$.20	$8.66	$8.86
Replace Materials........6.41　　　Labor.............1.93　　　Equipment.............32				
Remove ....　　　Labor.............20				
8" thick factory designed & fabricated structural wall panel	sf	$.20	$9.50	$9.70
Replace Materials........7.21　　　Labor.............1.97　　　Equipment.............32				
Remove ....　　　Labor.............20				
10" thick factory designed & fabricated structural wall panel	sf	$.20	$10.22	$10.42
Replace Materials........7.86　　　Labor.............2.04　　　Equipment.............32				
Remove ....　　　Labor.............20				
12" thick factory designed & fabricated structural wall panel	sf	$.20	$11.07	$11.27
Replace Materials........8.71　　　Labor.............2.04　　　Equipment.............32				
Remove ....　　　Labor.............20				
6" thick factory designed & fabricated structural floor panel	sf	$.23	$9.13	$9.36
Replace Materials........6.88　　　Labor.............1.93　　　Equipment.............32				
Remove ....　　　Labor.............23				

RELATED ITEMS

Columns 71
Fences............................187
Finish Carpentry 199
Outbuildings................331
Painting........................341
Paneling 347
Siding 455
Stairs 465

◁ shear-panel install

◄ **INTERIOR SOFFIT FRAMING**

◄ **FACTORY BUILT PANELS**
Often called stress-skin panels. Wall panels are installed with dimensional lumber top and bottom plates. Roof and floor panels must be installed between structural members. Does not include the cost for these structural members.

	Item Description	Unit	Remove	Replace	Total
FACTORY BUILT ▶ PANELS *continued*	**8" thick factory designed & fabricated structural floor panel** *Replace* Materials........7.69　　Labor............1.93　　Equipment............32 *Remove* ....　　Labor............ .23	sf	$.23	$9.94	$10.17
	10" thick factory designed & fabricated structural floor panel *Replace* Materials........8.46　　Labor............2.00　　Equipment............32 *Remove* ....　　Labor............ .23	sf	$.23	$10.78	$11.01
	12" thick factory designed & fabricated structural floor panel *Replace* Materials........7.54　　Labor............1.95　　Equipment............31 *Remove* ....　　Labor............ .23	sf	$.23	$9.80	$10.02
	6" thick factory designed & fabricated structural roof panel *Replace* Materials........6.58　　Labor............2.27　　Equipment............31 *Remove* ....　　Labor............ .43	sf	$.43	$9.16	$9.59
	8" thick factory designed & fabricated structural roof panel *Replace* Materials........7.45　　Labor............2.31　　Equipment............31 *Remove* ....　　Labor............ .43	sf	$.43	$10.07	$10.50
	10" thick factory designed & fabricated structural roof panel *Replace* Materials........8.10　　Labor............2.34　　Equipment............31 *Remove* ....　　Labor............ .43	sf	$.43	$10.75	$11.18
	12" thick factory designed & fabricated structural roof panel *Replace* Materials........8.96　　Labor............2.46　　Equipment............31 *Remove* ....　　Labor............ .43	sf	$.43	$11.73	$12.16
CHIMNEY CRICKET ▶ *Includes 5% waste.*	**Wood-frame chimney cricket (length x width)** *Replace* Materials........1.51　　Labor............3.00 *Remove* ....　　Labor............ .52	sf	$.52	$4.51	$5.03
MAIL BOX ▶ *Mail box is standard rural style. Black, white, or gray.*	**Mail box** *Replace* Materials........11.70　　Labor............6.70 *Remove* ....　　Labor............2.20	ea	$2.20	$18.40	$20.60
	Mail-box post *Replace* Materials........28.50　　Labor............23.60 *Remove* ....　　Labor............12.40	ea	$12.40	$52.10	$64.50
	Mail box with post *Replace* Materials........40.20　　Labor............30.30 *Remove* ....　　Labor............15.90	ea	$15.90	$70.50	$86.40
	Remove mail box for work, then reinstall *Replace* Materials........ .32　　Labor............10.40	ea	–	$10.72	$10.72

✍ NOTES: _____

_____

_____

_____

_____

_____

_____

_____

_____ end

TIME & MATERIAL CHARTS (selected items)

Rough Carpentry Materials

DESCRIPTION	MATERIAL PRICE	GROSS COVERAGE	WASTE	NET COVERAGE	UNIT PRICE
Lumber, random lengths per 1,000 bf					
#2 pine or better 2" wide framing lumber	$1,160.00 per mbf.	1,000	7%	930	$1.25 bf
#2 pine or better 1" wide framing lumber	$1,410.00 per mbf.	1,000	7%	930	$1.52 bf
#2 treated pine or better 2" wide framing lumber	$1,450.00 per mbf.	1,000	7%	930	$1.56 bf
redwood con common 2" wide framing lumber	$2,330.00 per mbf.	1,000	7%	930	$2.51 bf
redwood con heart 2" wide framing lumber	$2,700.00 per mbf.	1,000	7%	930	$2.90 bf
heavy oak timber	$4,450.00 per mbf.	1,000	7%	930	$4.78 bf
heavy pine timber	$2,190.00 per mbf.	1,000	7%	930	$2.35 bf
Fasteners and metal braces					
16d gun nails	$74.00 per box	2,500	5%	2375	$.03 ea
12d gun nails	$69.00 per box	2,500	5%	2375	$.05 ea
2" gun staples	$117.00 per box	10,000	5%	9500	$.01 ea
construction adhesive per 29 ounce tube	$8.20 per tube	75	5%	71.25	$.12 lf
metal let-in brace with V-shape for saw kerf	$7.60 per 11.5' stick				$7.60 ea
metal X bracing for between joists	$2.09 per 24" oc				$2.09 ea
Furring strips					
1" x 2" x 8' #2 or better pine	$1.64 ea	8	5%	7.6	$.22 lf
2" x 2" x 8' #2 or better pine	$3.81 ea	8	5%	7.6	$.50 lf
2" x 2" x 8' con heart redwood	$5.63 ea	8	5%	7.6	$.74 lf
2" x 2" x 8' con common redwood	$4.86 ea	8	5%	7.6	$.64 lf
#2 or better pine framing lumber					
2" x 4", random lengths	$6.12 ea	8	5%	7.6	$.81 lf
2" x 6", random lengths	$8.83 ea	8	5%	7.6	$1.16 lf
2" x 8", random lengths	$11.00 ea	8	5%	7.6	$1.45 lf
2" x 10", random lengths	$17.30 ea	8	5%	7.6	$2.28 lf
2" x 12", random lengths	$20.00 ea	8	5%	7.6	$2.63 lf
Redwood framing lumber					
2" x 4" con heart, random lengths	$13.60 ea	8	5%	7.6	$1.79 lf
2" x 6" con heart, random lengths	$15.90 ea	8	5%	7.6	$2.09 lf
2" x 8" con heart, random lengths	$23.90 ea	8	5%	7.6	$3.14 lf
2" x 4" con common, random lengths	$11.70 ea	8	5%	7.6	$1.54 lf
2" x 6" con common, random lengths	$13.70 ea	8	5%	7.6	$1.80 lf
2" x 8" con common, random lengths	$20.60 ea	8	5%	7.6	$2.71 lf
Treated framing lumber					
2" x 4", random lengths	$10.10 ea	8	5%	7.6	$1.33 lf
2" x 6" random lengths	$15.10 ea	8	5%	7.6	$1.99 lf
2" x 8", random lengths	$25.00 ea	8	5%	7.6	$3.29 lf
Posts					
4" x 4"					
#2 or better pine	$24.90 8' post	8	4%	7.68	$3.24 lf
con common redwood	$29.90 8' post	8	4%	7.68	$3.89 lf
treated pine	$32.40 8' post	8	4%	7.68	$4.22 lf
4" x 6"					
#2 or better pine	$28.80 8' post	8	4%	7.68	$3.75 lf
con common redwood	$32.00 8' post	8	4%	7.68	$4.17 lf
treated pine	$37.40 8' post	8	4%	7.68	$4.87 lf
6" x 6"					
#2 or better pine	$60.50 8' post	8	4%	7.68	$7.88 lf
con common redwood	$51.70 8' post	8	4%	7.68	$6.73 lf
treated pine	$78.70 8' post	8	4%	7.68	$10.20 lf
8" x 8"					
#2 or better pine	$108.00 8' post	8	4%	7.68	$14.10 lf
con common redwood	$92.00 8' post	8	4%	7.68	$12.00 lf
treated pine	$140.00 8' post	8	4%	7.68	$18.20 lf

. . . More >

Rough Carpentry Materials *continued*

DESCRIPTION	MATERIAL PRICE	GROSS COVERAGE	WASTE	NET COVERAGE	UNIT PRICE
Adjustable steel jack post					
51" to 90" to 13,000 pound load	$55.80 ea				$55.80 ea
20" to 36" to 16,000 pound load	$36.60 ea				$36.60 ea
37" to 60" to 17,500 pound load	$46.00 ea				$46.00 ea
56" to 96" to 25,000 pound load	$71.90 ea				$71.90 ea
Lally column					
3 1/2" diameter, 6' to 8'	$81.60 ea				$81.60 ea
3 1/2" diameter, 8' to 10'	$91.90 ea				$91.90 ea
3 1/2" diameter, 10' to 12'	$116.00 ea				$116.00 ea
Glue-laminated beam					
per bf	5.32 bf	1	3%	.97	$5.48 bf
Micro-laminated beam					
1-3/4" x 9-1/2"	$7.94 lf	1	4%	.96	$8.27 lf
1-3/4" x 11-7/8"	$9.90 lf	1	4%	.96	$10.30 lf
1-3/4" x 14"	$11.70 lf	1	4%	.96	$12.20 lf
1-3/4" x 18"	$15.10 lf	1	4%	.96	$15.70 lf
Beams, select structural grade, per bf					
pine	$2.19 bf	1	4%	.96	$2.28 bf
oak	$4.45 bf	1	4%	.96	$4.64 bf
Laminated lumber I joist					
1-3/4" flange, 9-1/2" deep	$2.76 lf	1	3%	.97	$2.85 lf
1-3/4" flange, 11-7/8" deep	$3.37 lf	1	3%	.97	$3.47 lf
1-3/4" flange, 14" deep	$4.12 lf	1	3%	.97	$4.25 lf
2-5/16" flange, 11-7/8" deep	$4.77 lf	1	3%	.97	$4.92 lf
Floor truss					
typical loading	$5.00 lf				$5.00 lf
heavy loading	$5.42 lf				$5.42 lf
Roof truss					
flat	$4.80 lf				$4.80 lf
4 in 12 slope	$5.06 lf				$5.06 lf
8 in 12 slope	$7.37 lf				$7.37 lf
12 in 12 slope	$9.86 lf				$9.86 lf
17 in 12 slope	$12.20 lf				$12.20 lf
Roof or wall sheathing					
1/2" fiberboard	$17.00 8' sheet	32	4%	30.72	$.55 sf
3/4" fiberboard	$23.10 8' sheet	32	4%	30.72	$.75 sf
1/2" foil-faced foam	$19.50 8' sheet	32	4%	30.72	$.63 sf
3/4" foil-faced foam	$26.00 8' sheet	32	4%	30.72	$.85 sf
1" foil-faced foam	$33.70 8' sheet	32	4%	30.72	$1.10 sf
1/2" cdx plywood	$23.20 8' sheet	32	4%	30.72	$.76 sf
1/2" waferboard	$21.60 8' sheet	32	4%	30.72	$.70 sf
1/2" oriented strand board (OSB)	$24.50 8' sheet	32	4%	30.72	$.80 sf
5/8" cdx plywood	$34.20 8' sheet	32	4%	30.72	$1.11 sf
5/8" waferboard	$37.70 8' sheet	32	4%	30.72	$1.23 sf
5/8" oriented strand board (OSB)	$37.90 8' sheet	32	4%	30.72	$1.23 sf
3/4" cdx plywood	$41.80 8' sheet	32	4%	30.72	$1.36 sf
3/4" tongue-&-groove plywood	$42.20 8' sheet	32	4%	30.72	$1.37 sf
3/4" tongue-&-groove waferboard	$44.60 8' sheet	32	4%	30.72	$1.45 sf
3/4" tongue-&-groove oriented strand board (OSB)	$44.90 8' sheet	32	4%	30.72	$1.46 sf
1" x 6" tongue-&-groove sheathing	$1.88 lf	50	4%	.48	$3.92 sf
2" x 6" tongue-&-groove sheathing	$4.43 lf	50	4%	.48	$9.23 sf
Factory designed and fabricated building panel					
6" thick wall panel	$6.41 sf				$6.41 sf
8" thick wall panel	$7.21 sf				$7.21 sf
10" thick floor panel	$8.46 sf				$8.46 sf
12" thick floor panel	$9.31 sf				$9.31 sf
6" thick roof panel	$7.91 sf				$7.91 sf
8" thick roof panel	$8.95 sf				$8.95 sf

Rough Carpentry Labor

LABORER	BASE WAGE	PAID LEAVE	TRUE WAGE	FICA	FUTA	WORKER'S COMP.	UNEMPLOY. INSUR.	HEALTH INSUR.	RETIRE (401k)	LIABILITY INSUR.	COST PER HOUR
Carpenter	$24.30	1.90	$26.20	2.00	.21	5.15	2.28	2.92	.79	3.93	**$43.50**
Carpenter's helper	$17.50	1.37	$18.87	1.44	.15	3.71	1.64	2.92	.57	2.83	**$32.10**
Post & beam carpenter	$31.30	2.44	$33.74	2.58	.27	6.63	2.94	2.92	1.01	5.06	**$55.20**
P & B carpenter's helper	$21.60	1.68	$23.28	1.78	.19	4.58	2.03	2.92	.70	3.49	**$39.00**
Equipment operator	$30.80	2.40	$33.20	2.54	.27	6.04	2.89	2.92	1.00	4.98	**$53.80**
Demolition laborer	$14.40	1.12	$15.52	1.19	.12	5.01	1.35	2.92	.47	2.33	**$28.90**

Paid Leave is calculated based on two weeks paid vacation, one week sick leave, and seven paid holidays. Employer's matching portion of **FICA** is 7.65 percent. **FUTA** (Federal Unemployment) is .8 percent. **Worker's Compensation** for the rough carpentry trade was calculated using a national average of 19.63 percent. **Unemployment insurance** was calculated using a national average of 8.7 percent. **Health insurance** was calculated based on a projected national average for 2005 of $580 per employee (and family when applicable) per month. Employer pays 80 percent for a per month cost of $464 per employee. **Retirement** is based on a 401(k) retirement program with employer matching of 50 percent. Employee contributions to the 401(k) plan are an average of 6 percent of the true wage. **Liability insurance** is based on a national average of 14.0 percent.

Rough Carpentry Labor Productivity

WORK DESCRIPTION	LABORER	COST PER HOUR	PRODUCTIVITY	UNIT PRICE
Demolition				
remove 2" x 4" wall 8' tall	demolition laborer	$28.90	.045	**$1.30** lf
remove 2" x 6" wall 8' tall	demolition laborer	$28.90	.048	**$1.39** lf
remove 2" x 8" wall 8' tall	demolition laborer	$28.90	.049	**$1.42** lf
remove wood post	demolition laborer	$28.90	.059	**$1.71** lf
remove glue-laminated beam	demolition laborer	$28.90	.222	**$6.42** lf
remove micro-laminated beam	demolition laborer	$28.90	.106	**$3.06** lf
remove sheathing	demolition laborer	$28.90	.012	**$.35** sf
remove beam	demolition laborer	$28.90	.222	**$6.42** lf
remove deck planking	demolition laborer	$28.90	.026	**$.75** sf
remove deck railing	demolition laborer	$28.90	.034	**$.98** lf
remove deck stairway per step	demolition laborer	$28.90	.061	**$1.76** ea
remove furring strips applied to wood	demolition laborer	$28.90	.011	**$.32** sf
remove joist system	demolition laborer	$28.90	.014	**$.40** sf
remove floor truss system	demolition laborer	$28.90	.014	**$.40** lf
remove hand-framed roof 4 in 12 slope	demolition laborer	$28.90	.016	**$.46** sf
remove hand-framed roof 8 in 12 slope	demolition laborer	$28.90	.019	**$.55** sf
remove hand-framed roof 12 in 12 slope	demolition laborer	$28.90	.032	**$.92** sf
remove hand-framed roof 16 in 12 slope	demolition laborer	$28.90	.050	**$1.45** sf
remove hand-framed roof 18 in 12 slope	demolition laborer	$28.90	.077	**$2.23** sf
remove flat roof truss	demolition laborer	$28.90	.016	**$.46** sf
remove truss roof 4 in 12 slope	demolition laborer	$28.90	.017	**$.49** sf
remove truss roof 8 in 12 slope	demolition laborer	$28.90	.021	**$.61** sf
remove truss roof 12 in 12 slope	demolition laborer	$28.90	.034	**$.98** sf
remove truss roof 16 in 12 slope	demolition laborer	$28.90	.053	**$1.53** sf
remove truss roof 17 in 12 slope	demolition laborer	$28.90	.082	**$2.37** sf
remove hand-framed dormer, 4 in 12 slope	demolition laborer	$28.90	.017	**$.49** sf
remove hand-framed dormer, 10 in 12 slope	demolition laborer	$28.90	.025	**$.72** sf
remove hand-framed dormer, 18 in 12 slope	demolition laborer	$28.90	.081	**$2.34** sf
remove pre-fabricated structural wall panel	demolition laborer	$28.90	.007	**$.20** sf
remove pre-fabricated structural floor panel	demolition laborer	$28.90	.008	**$.23** sf
remove pre-fabricated structural roof panel	demolition laborer	$ 28.90	.015	**$.43** sf
Framing crew				
rough carpentry	carpenter	$43.50		
rough carpentry	carpenter's helper	$32.10		
rough carpentry	**framing crew**	**$37.80**		
Post & beam framing crew				
post & beam framing	post & beam carpenter	$55.20		
post & beam framing	post & beam carpenter's helper	$39.00		
post & beam framing	**post & beam crew**	**$47.10**		

Rough Carpentry Labor Productivity *continued*

WORK DESCRIPTION	LABORER	COST PER HOUR	PRODUCTIVITY	UNIT PRICE
Build interior partition wall				
2" x 4" 8' tall 16" on center	framing crew	$37.80	.241	$9.11 lf
2" x 4" 10' tall 16" on center	framing crew	$37.80	.244	$9.22 lf
2" x 6" 8' tall 16" on center	framing crew	$37.80	.244	$9.22 lf
2" x 6" 10' tall 16" on center	framing crew	$37.80	.247	$9.34 lf
2" x 8" 8' tall 16" on center	framing crew	$37.80	.247	$9.34 lf
2" x 8" 10' tall 16" on center	framing crew	$37.80	.250	$9.45 lf
Build interior bearing wall				
2" x 4" 8' tall 16" on center	framing crew	$37.80	.261	$9.87 lf
2" x 4" 10' tall 16" on center	framing crew	$37.80	.265	$10.02 lf
2" x 6" 8' tall 16" on center	framing crew	$37.80	.263	$9.94 lf
2" x 6" 10' tall 16" on center	framing crew	$37.80	.267	$10.09 lf
2" x 8" 8' tall 16" on center	framing crew	$37.80	.266	$10.05 lf
2" x 8" 10' tall 16" on center	framing crew	$37.80	.270	$10.20 lf
Build exterior wall				
2" x 4" 8' tall 16" on center	framing crew	$37.80	10.09	$10.09 lf
2" x 4" 10' tall 16" on center	framing crew	$37.80	.270	$10.20 lf
2" x 6" 8' tall 16" on center	framing crew	$37.80	.270	$10.20 lf
2" x 6" 10' tall 16" on center	framing crew	$37.80	.273	$10.30 lf
2" x 8" 8' tall 16" on center	framing crew	$37.80	.272	$10.30 lf
2" x 8" 10' tall 16" on center	framing crew	$37.80	.275	$10.40 lf
Build interior partition wall per sf				
2" x 4" 16" on center	framing crew	$37.80	.030	$1.13 sf
2" x 6" 16" on center	framing crew	$37.80	.030	$1.13 sf
2" x 8" 16" on center	framing crew	$37.80	.031	$1.17 sf
Build sloping interior partition wall per sf				
2" x 4" 16" on center	framing crew	$37.80	.041	$1.55 sf
2" x 6" 16" on center	framing crew	$37.80	.042	$1.59 sf
2" x 8" 16" on center	framing crew	$37.80	.042	$1.59 sf
Build sloping interior bearing wall per sf				
2" x 4" 16" on center	framing crew	$37.80	.050	$1.89 sf
2" x 6" 16" on center	framing crew	$37.80	.050	$1.89 sf
2" x 8" 16" on center	framing crew	$37.80	.051	$1.93 sf
Build interior bearing wall per sf				
2" x 4" 16" on center	framing crew	$37.80	.033	$1.25 sf
2" x 6" 16" on center	framing crew	$37.80	.033	$1.25 sf
2" x 8" 16" on center	framing crew	$37.80	.033	$1.25 sf
Build exterior wall per sf				
2" x 4" 16" on center	framing crew	$37.80	.034	$1.29 sf
2" x 6" 16" on center	framing crew	$37.80	.034	$1.29 sf
2" x 8" 16" on center	framing crew	$37.80	.034	$1.29 sf
Build sloping exterior wall per sf				
2" x 4" 16" on center	framing crew	$37.80	.046	$1.74 sf
2" x 6" 16" on center	framing crew	$37.80	.046	$1.74 sf
2" x 8" 16" on center	framing crew	$37.80	.047	$1.78 sf
Build walls per bf				
interior wall	framing crew	$37.80	.034	$1.29 bf
sloping interior wall	framing crew	$37.80	.047	$1.78 bf
exterior wall	framing crew	$37.80	.037	$1.40 bf
sloping exterior wall	framing crew	$37.80	.051	$1.93 bf
Build and install wall header *Made from 2" x dimension lumber and 1/2" cdx plywood*				
4" x 10" header	framing crew	$37.80	.043	$1.63 lf
4" x 12" header	framing crew	$37.80	.045	$1.70 lf
6" x 10" header	framing crew	$37.80	.069	$2.61 lf
6" x 12" header	framing crew	$37.80	.074	$2.80 lf
Install posts				
4" x 4" post	framing crew	$37.80	.042	$1.59 lf
6" x 6" post	framing crew	$37.80	.044	$1.66 lf
8" x 8" post	framing crew	$37.80	.048	$1.81 lf

. . . More ➤

Rough Carpentry Labor Productivity *continued*

WORK DESCRIPTION	LABORER	COST PER HOUR	PRODUCTIVITY	UNIT PRICE
Install adjustable steel jackpost				
20" to 36" adjustable	framing crew	$37.80	.243	**$9.19** *ea*
37" to 60" adjustable	framing crew	$37.80	.272	**$10.30** *ea*
48" to 100" adjustable	framing crew	$37.80	.385	**$14.60** *ea*
56" to 96" adjustable	framing crew	$37.80	.351	**$13.30** *ea*
Install lally column				
3-1/2" diameter, 6' to 8'	framing crew	$37.80	.526	**$19.90** *ea*
3-1/2" diameter, 8' to 10'	framing crew	$37.80	.556	**$21.00** *ea*
3-1/2" diameter, 10' to 12'	framing crew	$37.80	.588	**$22.20** *ea*
Install glue-laminated beam				
per bf	framing crew	$37.80	.060	**$2.27** *bf*
Install micro-laminated beam				
1-3/4" x 7-1/4"	framing crew	$37.80	.048	**$1.81** *lf*
1-3/4" x 9-1/2"	framing crew	$37.80	.050	**$1.89** *lf*
1-3/4" x 11-7/8"	framing crew	$37.80	.053	**$2.00** *lf*
1-3/4" x 14"	framing crew	$37.80	.056	**$2.12** *lf*
1-3/4" x 18"	framing crew	$37.80	.063	**$2.38** *lf*
Install beam				
4" x 10"	framing crew	$37.80	.114	**$4.31** *lf*
4" x 12"	framing crew	$37.80	.149	**$5.63** *lf*
6" x 10"	framing crew	$37.80	.132	**$4.99** *lf*
6" x 12"	framing crew	$37.80	.154	**$5.82** *lf*
8" x 10"	framing crew	$37.80	.156	**$5.90** *lf*
8" x 12"	framing crew	$37.80	.182	**$6.88** *lf*
10" x 10"	framing crew	$37.80	.176	**$6.65** *lf*
10" x 12"	framing crew	$37.80	.196	**$7.41** *lf*
12" x 12"	framing crew	$37.80	.204	**$7.71** *lf*
12" x 16"	framing crew	$37.80	.222	**$8.39** *lf*
Post & beam framing				
Cut and assemble bent with truss				
single-story with simple truss	post & beam crew	$47.10	.526	**$24.80** *sf*
two-story with simple truss	post & beam crew	$47.10	.571	**$26.90** *sf*
single-story with king post truss	post & beam crew	$47.10	.568	**$26.80** *sf*
two-story with king post truss	post & beam crew	$47.10	.621	**$29.20** *sf*
single-story with king post & struts truss	post & beam crew	$47.10	.617	**$29.10** *sf*
two-story with king post & struts truss	post & beam crew	$47.10	.680	**$32.00** *sf*
single-story with queen post truss	post & beam crew	$47.10	.610	**$28.70** *sf*
two-story with queen post truss	post & beam crew	$47.10	.671	**$31.60** *sf*
single-story with hammer beam truss	post & beam crew	$47.10	1.05	**$49.50** *sf*
two-story with hammer beam truss	post & beam crew	$47.10	1.25	**$58.90** *sf*
single-story with scissors truss	post & beam crew	$47.10	.990	**$46.60** *sf*
two-story with scissors truss	post & beam crew	$47.10	1.04	**$49.00** *sf*
add for overhang drop in two-story bent	post & beam crew	$47.10	20.0	**$942.00** *ea*
Cut and assemble connecting members between bents *per sf of area beneath*				
between single-story bents	post & beam crew	$47.10	1.11	**$52.30** *sf*
Cut post & beam framing joint and join timbers				
sill corner half-lap	p & b carpenter	$55.20	1.10	**$60.70** *ea*
sill corner half-lap with through tenon	p & b carpenter	$55.20	2.78	**$153.00** *ea*
sill corner dovetail	p & b carpenter	$55.20	2.00	**$110.00** *ea*
sill corner dovetail with through tenon	p & b carpenter	$55.20	3.85	**$213.00** *ea*
sill corner tongue & fork	p & b carpenter	$55.20	1.79	**$98.80** *ea*
sill corner tongue & fork with through tenon	p & b carpenter	$55.20	3.45	**$190.00** *ea*
lapped dovetail	p & b carpenter	$55.20	2.04	**$113.00** *ea*
housed lapped dovetail	p & b carpenter	$55.20	2.56	**$141.00** *ea*
tusk tenon	p & b carpenter	$55.20	2.78	**$153.00** *ea*
half-lap	p & b carpenter	$55.20	1.08	**$59.60** *ea*
through mortise & tenon with shoulders	p & b carpenter	$55.20	2.27	**$125.00** *ea*
housed mortise & tenon	p & b carpenter	$55.20	2.38	**$131.00** *ea*
shouldered mortise & tenon	p & b carpenter	$55.20	2.33	**$129.00** *ea*
wedged dovetail mortise & tenon	p & b carpenter	$55.20	2.38	**$131.00** *ea*
mortise & tenon (90 degree)	p & b carpenter	$55.20	1.25	**$69.00** *ea*

. . . More ➢

Rough Carpentry Labor Productivity *continued*

WORK DESCRIPTION	LABORER	COST PER HOUR	PRODUCTIVITY	UNIT PRICE
Post & beam framing *continued*				
Cut post & beam framing joint and join timbers *continued*				
anchor-beam	p & b carpenter	$55.20	2.94	**$162.00** *ea*
framed overhang	p & b carpenter	$55.20	10.0	**$552.00** *ea*
through half-lap	p & b carpenter	$55.20	1.20	**$66.20** *ea*
mortise & tenon knee brace (45 degree)	p & b carpenter	$55.20	1.56	**$86.10** *ea*
collar tie lapped half dovetail	p & b carpenter	$55.20	1.96	**$108.00** *ea*
stopped splayed scarf	p & b carpenter	$55.20	3.23	**$178.00** *ea*
stopped splayed scarf with through tenon	p & b carpenter	$55.20	5.00	**$276.00** *ea*
bladed scarf	p & b carpenter	$55.20	2.44	**$135.00** *ea*
bladed scarf with through tenon	p & b carpenter	$55.20	4.35	**$240.00** *ea*
rafter foot housed bird's mouth	p & b carpenter	$55.20	1.39	**$76.70** *ea*
rafter foot beveled shoulder bird's mouth	p & b carpenter	$55.20	1.30	**$71.80** *ea*
rafter foot bird's mouth, purlin, & post joint	p & b carpenter	$55.20	3.13	**$173.00** *ea*
rafter foot bird's mouth joint	p & b carpenter	$55.20	1.00	**$55.20** *ea*
rafter foot bird's mouth with tenon	p & b carpenter	$55.20	2.86	**$158.00** *ea*
rafter peak tongue & fork	p & b carpenter	$55.20	1.79	**$98.80** *ea*
Build joist system for outdoor deck *with support beams, posts and concrete footing*				
2" x 8" joists	framing crew	$37.80	.071	**$2.68** *sf*
2" x 10" joists	framing crew	$37.80	.077	**$2.91** *sf*
2" x 12" joists	framing crew	$37.80	.083	**$3.14** *sf*
Install outdoor deck planking per sf				
2" x 4"	framing crew	$37.80	.040	**$1.51** *sf*
2" x 6"	framing crew	$37.80	.037	**$1.40** *sf*
2" x 8"	framing crew	$37.80	.033	**$1.25** *sf*
Install deck railing and stairs				
deck railing	framing crew	$37.80	.274	**$10.40** *lf*
3' wide deck stairs with balustrades	framing crew	$37.80	.588	**$22.20** *ea*
deck stairway landing per sf	framing crew	$37.80	.074	**$2.80** *sf*
Install furring strips				
on wood 16" on center	framing crew	$37.80	.013	**$.49** *sf*
on wood 24" on center	framing crew	$37.80	.011	**$.42** *sf*
on masonry or concrete 16" on center	framing crew	$37.80	.016	**$.60** *sf*
on masonry or concrete 24" on center	framing crew	$37.80	.014	**$.53** *sf*
Build joist systems with blocking and cross bracing				
per bf	framing crew	$37.80	.021	**$.79** *bf*
Install laminated lumber I truss				
1-3/4" flange, 11-7/8" deep	framing crew	$37.80	.036	**$1.36** *lf*
1-3/4" flange, 14" deep	framing crew	$37.80	.037	**$1.40** *lf*
2-5/16" flange, 11-7/8" deep	framing crew	$37.80	.036	**$1.36** *lf*
2-5/16" flange, 14" deep	framing crew	$37.80	.038	**$1.44** *lf*
2-5/16" flange, 16" deep	framing crew	$37.80	.039	**$1.47** *lf*
Install floor truss				
typical	framing crew	$37.80	.091	**$3.44** *lf*
Hand-frame roof, 24" on center				
with 2" x 4" rafters				
4 in 12 slope	framing crew	$37.80	.034	**$1.29** *sf*
8 in 12 slope	framing crew	$37.80	.040	**$1.51** *sf*
12 in 12 slope	framing crew	$37.80	.049	**$1.85** *sf*
16 in 12 slope	framing crew	$37.80	.060	**$2.27** *sf*
with 2" x 6" rafters				
4 in 12 slope	framing crew	$37.80	.035	**$1.32** *sf*
8 in 12 slope	framing crew	$37.80	.042	**$1.59** *sf*
12 in 12 slope	framing crew	$37.80	.051	**$1.93** *sf*
16 in 12 slope	framing crew	$37.80	.062	**$2.34** *sf*
with 2" x 8" rafters				
4 in 12 slope	framing crew	$37.80	.036	**$1.36** *sf*
8 in 12 slope	framing crew	$37.80	.043	**$1.63** *sf*
12 in 12 slope	framing crew	$37.80	.052	**$1.97** *sf*
16 in 12 slope	framing crew	$37.80	.064	**$2.42** *sf*

. . . More ➤

Rough Carpentry Labor Productivity *continued*

WORK DESCRIPTION	LABORER	COST PER HOUR	PRODUCTIVITY	UNIT PRICE
Hand-frame roof, 24" on center *continued*				
with 2" x 10" rafters				
4 in 12 slope	framing crew	$37.80	.037	$1.40 sf
8 in 12 slope	framing crew	$37.80	.044	$1.66 sf
12 in 12 slope	framing crew	$37.80	.054	$2.04 sf
16 in 12 slope	framing crew	$37.80	.066	$2.49 sf
with 2" x 12" rafters				
4 in 12 slope	framing crew	$37.80	.038	$1.44 sf
8 in 12 slope	framing crew	$37.80	.046	$1.74 sf
12 in 12 slope	framing crew	$37.80	.056	$2.12 sf
16 in 12 slope	framing crew	$37.80	.068	$2.57 sf
additional hand-framed roof labor costs				
add for each lf of valley	framing crew	$37.80	.787	$29.70 lf
add for each lf of hip width	framing crew	$37.80	.211	$8.00 lf
add for each lf of Dutch hip width	framing crew	$37.80	.229	$8.66 lf
Hand-frame mansard roof, 24" on center *per cf of roof*				
2" x 4" rafters	framing crew	$37.80	.005	$.19 cf
2" x 8" rafters	framing crew	$37.80	.005	$.19 cf
2" x 12" rafters	framing crew	$37.80	.006	$.23 cf
add for each lf of valley	framing crew	$37.80	1.08	$40.80 lf
Hand-frame gambrel roof, 24" on center *per cf of roof*				
2" x 4" rafters	framing crew	$37.80	.004	$.15 cf
2" x 8" rafters	framing crew	$37.80	.005	$.19 cf
2" x 12" rafters	framing crew	$37.80	.006	$.23 cf
add for each lf of valley	framing crew	$37.80	1.14	$43.10 lf
Hand-frame roof per bf				
gable roof	framing crew	$37.80	.023	$.87 bf
hip roof	framing crew	$37.80	.023	$.87 bf
Dutch hip roof	framing crew	$37.80	.024	$.91 bf
mansard roof	framing crew	$37.80	.026	$.98 bf
gambrel roof	framing crew	$37.80	.025	$.95 bf
Hand-frame dormer, 24" on center				
shed dormer				
4 in 12 slope	framing crew	$37.80	.045	$1.70 sf
8 in 12 slope	framing crew	$37.80	.049	$1.85 sf
12 in 12 slope	framing crew	$37.80	.060	$2.27 sf
16 in 12 slope	framing crew	$37.80	.064	$2.42 sf
gable dormer				
4 in 12 slope	framing crew	$37.80	.047	$1.78 sf
8 in 12 slope	framing crew	$37.80	.051	$1.93 sf
12 in 12 slope	framing crew	$37.80	.062	$2.34 sf
16 in 12 slope	framing crew	$37.80	.067	$2.53 sf
hip dormer				
4 in 12 slope	framing crew	$37.80	1.85	$1.85 sf
8 in 12 slope	framing crew	$37.80	.053	$2.00 sf
12 in 12 slope	framing crew	$37.80	.065	$2.46 sf
16 in 12 slope	framing crew	$37.80	.070	$2.65 sf
Dutch hip dormer				
4 in 12 slope	framing crew	$37.80	.051	$1.93 sf
8 in 12 slope	framing crew	$37.80	.054	$2.04 sf
12 in 12 slope	framing crew	$37.80	.067	$2.53 sf
16 in 12 slope	framing crew	$37.80	.072	$2.72 sf
gambrel dormer				
per length of ridge x width of dormer	framing crew	$37.80	.059	$2.23 sf
Hand-frame dormer, per bf				
shed dormer	framing crew	$37.80	.034	$1.29 bf
gable dormer	framing crew	$37.80	.035	$1.32 bf
hip dormer	framing crew	$37.80	.036	$1.36 bf
Dutch-hip dormer	framing crew	$37.80	.038	$1.44 bf
gambrel dormer	framing crew	$37.80	.037	$1.40 bf

. . . More ➤

Rough Carpentry Labor Productivity *continued*

WORK DESCRIPTION	LABORER	COST PER HOUR	PRODUCTIVITY	UNIT PRICE
Install roof truss				
flat roof	framing crew	$37.80	.023	**$.87** lf
4 in 12 slope	framing crew	$37.80	.023	**$.87** lf
8 in 12 slope	framing crew	$37.80	.024	**$.91** lf
12 in 12 slope	framing crew	$37.80	.024	**$.91** lf
16 in 12 slope	framing crew	$37.80	.026	**$.98** lf
Install truss system, 24" on center, per sf				
4 in 12 slope	framing crew	$37.80	.012	**$.45** sf
8 in 12 slope	framing crew	$37.80	.012	**$.45** sf
12 in 12 slope	framing crew	$37.80	.013	**$.49** sf
16 in 12 slope	framing crew	$37.80	.013	**$.49** sf
Additional truss roof costs				
add labor for each lf of valley	framing crew	$37.80	.813	**$30.70** lf
add labor for each lf of width in a hip	framing crew	$37.80	.360	**$13.60** lf
add labor for each lf of width in a Dutch hip	framing crew	$37.80	.408	**$15.40** lf
Install mansard truss system, 24" on center, per cf				
per width x height x length	framing crew	$37.80	.003	**$.11** cf
add labor for each lf of valley	framing crew	$37.80	.952	**$36.00** lf
Install gambrel truss system, 24" on center, per cf				
per width x height x length	framing crew	$37.80	.003	**$.11** cf
add labor for each lf of valley	framing crew	$37.80	1.16	**$43.80** lf
Install wall or floor sheathing				
builder board	framing crew	$37.80	.015	**$.57** lf
plywood, waferboard, or OSB	framing crew	$37.80	.016	**$.60** sf
1" x 6" sheathing	framing crew	$37.80	.017	**$.64** sf
1" x 6" tongue-&-groove	framing crew	$37.80	.017	**$.64** sf
2" x 6" tongue-&-groove	framing crew	$37.80	.017	**$.64** sf
2" x 8" tongue-&-groove	framing crew	$37.80	.017	**$.64** sf
add labor for shear-panel installation	framing crew	$37.80	.003	**$.11** sf
Build interior soffit				
two sides	framing crew	$37.80	.059	**$2.23** lf
two sides with recess for indirect lighting	framing crew	$37.80	.100	**$3.78** lf
three sides	framing crew	$37.80	.080	**$3.02** lf
three sides with recess for indirect lighting	framing crew	$37.80	.129	**$4.88** lf
Install factory designed and fabricated structural panel				
6" thick wall panel	framing crew	$37.80	.051	**$1.93** sf
8" thick wall panel	framing crew	$37.80	.052	**$1.97** sf
10" thick wall panel	framing crew	$37.80	.054	**$2.04** sf
12" thick wall panel	framing crew	$37.80	.054	**$2.04** sf
6" thick floor panel	framing crew	$37.80	.051	**$1.93** sf
8" thick floor panel	framing crew	$37.80	.051	**$1.93** sf
10" thick floor panel	framing crew	$37.80	.053	**$2.00** sf
12" thick floor panel	framing crew	$37.80	.054	**$2.04** sf
6" thick roof panel	framing crew	$37.80	.061	**$2.31** sf
8" thick roof panel	framing crew	$37.80	.062	**$2.34** sf
10" thick roof panel	framing crew	$37.80	.063	**$2.38** sf
12" thick roof panel	framing crew	$37.80	.066	**$2.49** sf
Wood-frame chimney cricket				
length of ridge x width	framing crew	$37.80	.083	**$3.14** sf

NOTES: _____

_____

_____

_____

_____

_____ end

33 .... *Security Systems*

Item Description	Unit	Remove	Replace	Total	
Minimum charge for security system work	ea	–	$65.70	$65.70	◄ MINIMUM
Replace Materials......25.00 Labor..........40.70					
Add 37% for security system installed in finished structure					◄ IN EXISTING BUILDING
Security system control panel, standard grade	ea	$7.23	$550.00	$557.23	◄ CONTROL PANEL
Replace Materials....350.00 Labor........200.00					*Includes up to 50 lf of wiring.*
Remove .... Labor 7.23					
► Controls audio alarms and lights.					
Security system control panel, high grade	ea	$7.23	$696.00	$703.23	
Replace Materials....430.00 Labor.........266.00					
Remove .... Labor 7.23					
► Controls audio alarms and lights. Digital read-out reports location of security breach and automatically calls security center.					
Security system key pad	ea	$5.78	$220.70	$226.48	◄ KEY PAD
Replace Materials.....170.00 Labor 50.70					*Includes up to 50 lf of wiring.*
Remove .... Labor 5.78					
► Shows armed / unarmed status with lights, usually red and green.					
Security system key pad with LED read-out	ea	$5.78	$280.70	$286.48	
Replace Materials....230.00 Labor 50.70					
Remove .... Labor 5.78					
► Shows armed / unarmed status with LED read-out that also reports location of security breach.					
Security system outside key control	ea	$4.13	$150.50	$154.63	◄ KEY CONTROL
Replace Materials ....105.00 Labor...........45.50					*Includes up to 50 lf of wiring.*
Remove .... Labor 4.13					
► Shows armed / unarmed status with lights, usually red and green.					
Security system mechanical contact per opening	ea	$4.13	$96.50	$100.63	◄ CONTACT
Replace Materials......58.50 Labor 38.00					*Includes up to 50 lf of wiring.*
Remove .... Labor 4.13					
Security system magnetic contact per opening	ea	$4.83	$124.70	$129.53	
Replace Materials......70.00 Labor 54.70					
Remove .... Labor 4.83					
Security system sound detector	ea	$4.83	$222.20	$227.03	◄ SOUND DETECTOR
Replace Materials.....160.00 Labor...........62.20					*Includes up to 50 lf of wiring.*
Remove .... Labor 4.83					
Security system motion detector	ea	$4.83	$359.50	$364.33	◄ MOTION DETECTOR
Replace Materials....300.00 Labor...........59.50					*Includes up to 50 lf of wiring.*
Remove .... Labor 4.83					
Security system pressure mat detector	lf	$5.35	$110.60	$115.95	◄ PRESSURE MAT
Replace Materials......50.00 Labor 60.60					*Includes up to 50 lf of wiring.*
Remove .... Labor 5.35					

Item Description		Unit	Remove	Replace	Total
SMOKE DETECTOR ▶ Includes up to 50 lf of wiring.	Security system smoke detector	ea	$4.83	$249.50	$254.33
	Replace Materials.....190.00 Labor..........59.50				
	Remove .... Labor 4.83				
	▶ For smoke detectors that are not connected to an alarm system see *Electrical* on page 149. For wiring see page 140.				
HORN OR SIREN ▶ Includes up to 50 lf of wiring.	Security system horn or siren	ea	$4.13	$111.10	$115.23
	Replace Materials......60.00 Labor..........51.10				
	Remove .... Labor 4.13				
	▶ Exterior or interior.				
PANIC BUTTON ▶ Includes up to 50 lf of wiring.	Security system panic button	ea	$3.61	$75.70	$79.31
	Replace Materials......50.00 Labor 25.70				
	Remove .... Labor 3.61				

TIME & MATERIAL CHARTS *(selected items)*

Security Systems Materials

*See Security Systems material prices with the line items and other information in the **QuickFinder** column.*

Security Systems Labor

LABORER	BASE WAGE	PAID LEAVE	TRUE WAGE	FICA	FUTA	WORKER'S COMP.	UNEMPLOY. INSUR.	HEALTH INSUR.	RETIRE (401K)	LIABILITY INSUR.	COST PER HOUR
Security system installer	$23.30	1.82	$25.12	1.92	.20	3.00	2.19	2.92	.75	3.77	$39.90
Demolition laborer	$14.40	1.12	$15.52	1.19	.12	5.01	1.35	2.92	.47	2.33	$28.90

Paid Leave is calculated based on two weeks paid vacation, one week sick leave, and seven paid holidays. Employer's matching portion of **FICA** is 7.65 percent. **FUTA** (Federal Unemployment) is .8 percent. **Worker's compensation** for the security systems trade was calculated using a national average of 11.92 percent. **Unemployment insurance** was calculated using a national average of 8.7 percent. **Health insurance** was calculated based on a projected national average for 2005 of $580 per employee (and family when applicable) per month. Employer pays 80 percent for a per month cost of $464 per employee. **Retirement** is based on a 401(k) retirement program with employer matching of 50 percent. Employee contributions to the 401(k) plan are an average of 6 percent of the true wage. **Liability insurance** is based on a national average of 14.0 percent.

Security Systems Labor Productivity

WORK DESCRIPTION	LABORER	COST PER HOUR	PRODUCTIVITY	UNIT PRICE
Demolition				
remove control panel	demolition laborer	$28.90	.250	$7.23 ea
remove exterior key pad	demolition laborer	$28.90	.200	$5.78 ea
remove contact	demolition laborer	$28.90	.143	$4.13 ea
remove detector (all types)	demolition laborer	$28.90	.167	$4.83 ea
remove pressure mat detector	demolition laborer	$28.90	.185	$5.35 ea
remove horn or siren	demolition laborer	$28.90	.143	$4.13 ea
remove panic button	demolition laborer	$28.90	.125	$3.61 ea
Install security system				
control panel, standard grade	security system installer	$39.90	5.00	$200.00 ea
control panel, high grade	security system installer	$39.90	6.67	$266.00 ea
key pad	security system installer	$39.90	1.27	$50.70 ea
outside key control	security system installer	$39.90	1.14	$45.50 ea
mechanical contact per opening	security system installer	$39.90	.952	$38.00 ea
magnetic contact per opening	security system installer	$39.90	1.37	$54.70 ea
sound detector	security system installer	$39.90	1.56	$62.20 ea
motion detector	security system installer	$39.90	1.49	$59.50 ea
pressure mat detector	security system installer	$39.90	1.52	$60.60 lf
smoke detector	security system installer	$39.90	1.49	$59.50 ea
horn or siren	security system installer	$39.90	1.28	$51.10 ea
panic button	security system installer	$39.90	.645	$25.70 ea

34 *Siding*

Item Description	Unit	Remove	Replace	Total	
Minimum charge for siding work *Replace* Materials ......49.00 Labor...........37.50	ea	–	$86.50	$86.50	◄ **MINIMUM**
Fiberglass corrugated siding, 6 ounce *Replace* Materials........2.03 Labor........... 1.05 *Remove* .... Labor........... .20	sf	$.20	$3.08	$3.28	◄ **FIBERGLASS CORRUGATED SIDING** *Greenhouse style. Includes purlins with corrugated pattern and 4% waste. Weights are per sf.*
Fiberglass corrugated siding, 8 ounce *Replace* Materials........2.20 Labor........... 1.05 *Remove* .... Labor........... .20	sf	$.20	$3.25	$3.45	
Fiberglass corrugated siding, 12 ounce *Replace* Materials........3.03 Labor........... 1.05 *Remove* .... Labor........... .20	sf	$.20	$4.08	$4.28	
Aluminum siding, standard grade *Replace* Materials........1.52 Labor ....1.28 *Remove* .... Labor............. .23 ► .019" to .021" thick. Lightly embossed wood patterns.	sf	$.23	$2.80	$3.03	◄ **ALUMINUM SIDING** *Includes 4% waste.*
Aluminum siding, high grade *Replace* Materials........1.78 Labor ....1.28 *Remove* .... Labor............. .23 ► .024" thick. Embossed patterns with fancy detail work around openings, porches, or in gables.	sf	$.23	$3.06	$3.29	
Aluminum siding, deluxe grade *Replace* Materials........2.11 Labor ....1.28 *Remove* .... Labor............. .23 ► .024" thick. Board-and-batten, board-on-board, or similar embossed patterns.	sf	$.23	$3.39	$3.62	
Aluminum siding, custom grade *Replace* Materials........3.06 Labor ....1.28 *Remove* .... Labor............. .23 ► .024" thick. Shake shingle, or similar embossed patterns.	sf	$.23	$4.34	$4.57	
Add for insulated aluminum siding *Replace* Materials .... .42 ► Add for R-3 to R-4 insulation integrated into siding.	sf	–	$.42	$.42	◁ add for insulation
Cement fiber shingle siding, standard grade *Replace* Materials........1.33 Labor ....1.69 *Remove* .... Labor............. .38 ► 1/8" to 1/4" thick, lightly embossed shingles with square edges.	sf	$.38	$3.02	$3.40	◄ **CEMENT FIBER SHINGLE SIDING** *Includes 4% waste. Also called asbestos cement. Some older styles contain dangerous asbestos which must be removed using hazardous material removal techniques.*
Cement fiber shingle siding, high grade *Replace* Materials........1.67 Labor ....1.69 *Remove* .... Labor............. .38 ► 1/8" to 1/4" thick, heavily embossed shingles with patterned edges.	sf	$.38	$3.36	$3.74	
Replace single cement fiber shingle *Replace* Materials........2.78 Labor...........17.90	sf	–	$20.68	$20.68	◁ single shingle
Minimum charge to repair cement fiber siding *Replace* Materials......40.00 Labor..........37.50	ea	–	$77.50	$77.50	◁ minimum

RELATED ITEMS
Finish Carpentry...........199
Paneling....................347
Rough Carpentry 409

	Item Description	Unit	Remove	Replace	Total
SHAKE OR ▶ WOOD SHINGLE SIDING *Includes 4% waste.*	**Shake or wood shingle siding, standard grade** *Replace* Materials ...... 1.14 Labor ....1.69 *Remove* .... Labor .... .40 ▶ #2 red label wood shingles, straight overlap installation.	sf	$.40	$2.83	$3.23
	Shake or wood shingle siding, high grade *Replace* Materials........1.29 Labor ....1.69 *Remove* .... Labor .... .40 ▶ #1 shakes or #1 blue label wood shingles, straight overlap installation; or #2 red label wood shingles staggered installation.	sf	$.40	$2.98	$3.38
	Shake or wood shingle siding, deluxe grade *Replace* Materials........1.54 Labor ....1.69 *Remove* .... Labor .... .40 ▶ #1 shakes or #1 blue wood shingles, staggered installation; or #2 red label wood shingles double coursed installation.	sf	$.40	$3.23	$3.63
	Shake or wood shingle siding, custom grade (fancy cut) *Replace* Materials........2.07 Labor ....1.69 *Remove* .... Labor .... .40 ▶ #1 shakes or #1 blue fancy cut wood shingle.	sf	$.40	$3.76	$4.16
single shake or shingle ▷	**Replace single shake or wood shingle** *Replace* Materials........3.32 Labor 15.30	ea	–	$18.62	$18.62
minimum ▷	**Minimum charge to repair shake or wood shingle siding** *Replace* Materials......46.00 Labor 37.50	ea	–	$83.50	$83.50
VINYL SIDING ▶ *Includes 4% waste.*	**Vinyl siding, standard grade** *Replace* Materials........1.85 Labor ....1.28 *Remove* .... Labor .... .20 ▶ Lightly embossed wood patterns.	sf	$.20	$3.13	$3.33
	Vinyl siding, high grade *Replace* Materials........2.11 Labor ....1.28 *Remove* .... Labor .... .20 ▶ Heavy embossed patterns such as board-and-batten, board-on-board or similar patterns, with fancy detail work around openings, porches, or in gables.	sf	$.20	$3.39	$3.59
	Vinyl siding, deluxe grade *Replace* Materials........3.19 Labor ....1.28 *Remove* .... Labor .... .20 ▶ Shake shingle, gable fans, or similar embossed patterns.	sf	$.20	$4.47	$4.67
add for insulation ▷	**Add for insulated vinyl siding** *Replace* Materials .... .51 ▶ Add for R-3 to R-4 insulation integrated into siding.	sf	–	$.51	$.51
HARDBOARD ▶ SIDING *Includes 4% waste.*	**7/16" thick hardboard siding, standard grade** *Replace* Materials .... .73 Labor .... .90 *Remove* .... Labor .... .26	sf	$.26	$1.63	$1.89
	7/16" thick hardboard siding, painted-board finish *Replace* Materials .... .82 Labor .... .90 *Remove* .... Labor .... .26	sf	$.26	$1.72	$1.98
	7/16" thick hardboard siding, stained-board finish *Replace* Materials ...... 1.15 Labor .... .90 *Remove* .... Labor .... .26	sf	$.26	$2.05	$2.31

Item Description	Unit	Remove	Replace	Total	
7/16" thick hardboard siding, simulated stucco finish	sf	$.26	$1.80	$2.06	
Replace Materials .... .90 Labor .... .90					
Remove .... Labor .... .26					
Hardboard lap siding	sf	$.29	$1.83	$2.12	◁ lap
Replace Materials .... .85 Labor .... .98					
Remove .... Labor .... .29					
5/8" thick plywood siding, texture 1-11, cedar face	sf	$.29	$2.44	$2.73	◀ **PLYWOOD T1-11**
Replace Materials ....1.50 Labor .... .94					**SIDING**
Remove .... Labor .... .29					*Includes 5% waste.*
5/8" thick plywood siding, texture 1-11, rough-sawn cedar face	sf	$.29	$2.78	$3.07	
Replace Materials ....1.84 Labor .... .94					
Remove .... Labor .... .29					
5/8" thick plywood siding, texture 1-11, fir face	sf	$.29	$2.27	$2.56	
Replace Materials ....1.33 Labor .... .94					
Remove .... Labor .... .29					
5/8" thick plywood siding, texture 1-11, rough-sawn fir face	sf	$.29	$2.46	$2.75	
Replace Materials ....1.52 Labor .... .94					
Remove .... Labor .... .29					
5/8" thick plywood siding, texture 1-11, Southern yellow pine face	sf	$.29	$2.03	$2.32	
Replace Materials ...... 1.09 Labor .... .94					
Remove .... Labor .... .29					
5/8" thick plywood siding, texture 1-11, redwood face	sf	$.29	$3.45	$3.74	
Replace Materials ....2.51 Labor .... .94					
Remove .... Labor .... .29					
Add for factory stained plywood siding	sf	–	$.20	$.20	◁ add for factory stain
Replace Materials .... .20					
1/2" plywood with 1" x 4" stained cedar boards	sf	$.51	$5.96	$6.47	◀ **BOARD OVER**
Replace Materials ....3.82 Labor 2.14					**PLYWOOD SIDING**
Remove .... Labor .... .51					*Includes 4% waste.*
5/8" plywood with 1" x 4" stained cedar boards	sf	$.51	$6.06	$6.57	
Replace Materials ....3.92 Labor 2.14					
Remove .... Labor .... .51					
Pine board-and-batten siding, select grade	sf	$.32	$5.09	$5.41	◀ **BOARD-AND-**
Replace Materials ....3.70 Labor 1.39					**BATTEN SIDING**
Remove .... Labor .... .32					*Includes 4% waste.*
Cedar board-and-batten siding, A grade	sf	$.32	$5.25	$5.57	*Deduct* **9%** *for next*
Replace Materials ....3.86 Labor 1.39					*lower grade, deduct*
Remove .... Labor .... .32					**14%** *for third grade.*
Pine board-on-board siding, select grade	sf	$.32	$5.05	$5.37	◀ **BOARD-ON-BOARD**
Replace Materials ....3.77 Labor 1.28					**SIDING**
Remove .... Labor .... .32					*Includes 4% waste.*
Cedar board-on-board siding, A grade	sf	$.32	$5.22	$5.54	*Deduct* **9%** *for next*
Replace Materials ....3.94 Labor 1.28					*lower grade, deduct*
Remove .... Labor .... .32					**14%** *for third grade.*
Pine channel rustic siding, select grade	sf	$.32	$5.25	$5.57	◀ **CHANNEL RUSTIC**
Replace Materials ....3.79 Labor 1.46					**SIDING**
Remove .... Labor .... .32					*Includes 4% waste.*

RELATED ITEMS

Finish Carpentry 199	
Paneling 347	
Rough Carpentry 409	

Item Description	Unit	Remove	Replace	Total
CHANNEL RUSTIC ▶ SIDING continued				
Deduct **9%** for next lower grade, deduct **14%** for third grade.				
Cedar channel rustic siding, A grade	sf	$.32	$6.22	$6.54
Replace Materials.......4.76 Labor 1.46				
Remove .... Labor .... .32				
Redwood channel rustic siding, clear all heart grade	sf	$.32	$12.56	$12.88
Replace Materials.......11.10 Labor 1.46				
Remove .... Labor .... .32				
SHIPLAP SIDING ▶ Includes 4% waste. Deduct **9%** for next lower grade, deduct **14%** for third grade.				
Pine shiplap siding, select grade	sf	$.32	$5.29	$5.61
Replace Materials.......3.83 Labor 1.46				
Remove .... Labor .... .32				
Cedar shiplap siding, A grade	sf	$.32	$6.27	$6.59
Replace Materials.......4.81 Labor 1.46				
Remove .... Labor .... .32				
Redwood shiplap siding, clear all heart grade	sf	$.32	$12.76	$13.08
Replace Materials.......11.30 Labor 1.46				
Remove .... Labor .... .32				
TONGUE-&- ▶ GROOVE SIDING ▶ Includes 4% waste. Deduct **9%** for next lower grade, deduct **14%** for third grade.				
Pine tongue-&-groove siding, simple pattern, select grade	sf	$.32	$5.38	$5.70
Replace Materials ....3.92 Labor 1.46				
Remove .... Labor .... .32				
Pine tongue-&-groove siding, fancy pattern, select grade	sf	$.32	$5.65	$5.97
Replace Materials........4.19 Labor 1.46				
Remove .... Labor .... .32				
▽ *simple pattern*				
Cedar tongue-&-groove siding, simple pattern, A grade	sf	$.32	$6.38	$6.70
Replace Materials........4.92 Labor 1.46				
Remove .... Labor .... .32				
Cedar tongue-&-groove siding, fancy pattern, A grade	sf	$.32	$6.71	$7.03
Replace Materials........5.25 Labor 1.46				
Remove .... Labor .... .32				
fancy pattern △				
Redwood tongue-&-groove siding, simple pattern, clear all heart grade	sf	$.32	$13.06	$13.38
Replace Materials........11.60 Labor 1.46				
Remove .... Labor .... .32				
Redwood tongue-&-groove siding, fancy pattern, clear all heart grade	sf	$.32	$13.86	$14.18
Replace Materials ....12.40 Labor 1.46				
Remove .... Labor .... .32				
CLAPBOARD ▶ SIDING True clapboard. Based on grades marketed by Donnell's Clapboard Mill of Sedgwick, Maine.				
Radially sawn clapboard siding, eastern pine, #1 premium clear	sf	$.32	$7.58	$7.90
Replace Materials........5.52 Labor 2.06				
Remove .... Labor .... .32				
Radially sawn clapboard siding, eastern pine, #1 New England Cape	sf	$.32	$6.88	$7.20
Replace Materials........4.82 Labor 2.06				
Remove .... Labor .... .32				
BEVELED SIDING ▶ Siding that looks like clapboard but is not radially sawn. (The grain in radially sawn board runs at a consistent 90 degree angle to the board face. In resawn boards grain orientation is inconsistent.)				
Pine resawn beveled siding, select grade	sf	$.32	$3.58	$3.90
Replace Materials........2.04 Labor 1.54				
Remove .... Labor .... .32				
Cedar resawn beveled siding, select grade	sf	$.32	$4.10	$4.42
Replace Materials........2.56 Labor 1.54				
Remove .... Labor .... .32				

Item Description	Unit	Remove	Replace	Total	
Redwood resawn beveled siding, clear all heart grade	sf	$.32	$7.57	$7.89	
Replace Materials........6.03 Labor 1.54					
Remove .... Labor............ .32					
Pine bungalow siding, select grade	sf	$.32	$4.21	$4.53	◀ **BUNGALOW**
Replace Materials........2.75 Labor 1.46					**SIDING**
Remove .... Labor............ .32					*Tapered siding that*
Cedar bungalow siding, select grade	sf	$.32	$4.91	$5.23	*is thicker and wider*
Replace Materials........3.45 Labor 1.46					*than beveled siding.*
Remove .... Labor............ .32					*Includes 4% waste.*
Redwood bungalow siding, clear all heart grade	sf	$.32	$9.56	$9.88	*Deduct **9%** for*
Replace Materials........8.10 Labor 1.46					*next lower grade,*
Remove .... Labor............ .32					*deduct **14%** for*
					third grade.
Pine Dolly Varden siding, select grade	sf	$.32	$4.43	$4.75	◀ **DOLLY VARDEN**
Replace Materials........2.97 Labor 1.46					**SIDING**
Remove .... Labor............ .32					*Includes 4% waste.*
Cedar Dolly Varden siding, select grade	sf	$.32	$5.19	$5.51	*Deduct **9%** for next*
Replace Materials........3.73 Labor 1.46					*lower grade, deduct*
Remove .... Labor............ .32					***14%** for third grade.*
Redwood Dolly Varden siding, clear all heart grade	sf	$.32	$10.23	$10.55	
Replace Materials........8.77 Labor 1.46					
Remove .... Labor............ .32					
Pine log cabin siding, select grade	sf	$.32	$4.24	$4.56	◀ **LOG CABIN**
Replace Materials........2.78 Labor 1.46					**SIDING**
Remove .... Labor............ .32					*Includes 4% waste.*
Cedar log cabin siding, select grade	sf	$.32	$4.95	$5.27	*Deduct **9%** for next*
Replace Materials........3.49 Labor 1.46					*lower grade, deduct*
Remove .... Labor............ .32					***14%** for third grade.*
Add for one coat factory stain	sf	–	$.42	$.42	◀ **ADD FOR FACTORY**
Replace Materials .... .42					**STAINED SIDING**
Add for two coat factory stain	sf	–	$.62	$.62	
Replace Materials .... .62					
Replace section of wood siding	ea	–	$53.00	$53.00	◀ **SIDING REPAIR**
Replace Materials......22.00 Labor...........31.00					
Minimum charge to repair wood siding	ea	–	$98.50	$98.50	◁ minimum
Replace Materials.......61.00 Labor...........37.50					
Aluminum fascia to 6" wide	lf	$.17	$2.96	$3.13	◀ **FASCIA**
Replace Materials........1.68 Labor 1.28					*Includes 4% waste.*
Remove .... Labor............ .17					
Aluminum fascia 6" to 12" wide	lf	$.17	$3.54	$3.71	
Replace Materials........2.26 Labor 1.28					
Remove .... Labor............ .17					
Vinyl fascia to 6" wide	lf	$.17	$3.66	$3.83	
Replace Materials........2.38 Labor 1.28					
Remove .... Labor............ .17					

RELATED ITEMS

Finish Carpentry 199
Paneling 347
Rough Carpentry 409

Item Description	Unit	Remove	Replace	Total
FASCIA ▶ *continued* **Vinyl fascia 6" to 12" wide**	lf	$.17	$4.58	$4.75
Replace Materials.......3.30 Labor 1.28				
Remove .... Labor............ .17				
Cedar fascia to 6" wide	lf	$.20	$3.53	$3.73
Replace Materials.......2.14 Labor 1.39				
Remove .... Labor............ .20				
Cedar fascia 6" to 12" wide	lf	$.20	$4.23	$4.43
Replace Materials.......2.84 Labor 1.39				
Remove .... Labor............ .20				
Redwood fascia to 6" wide	lf	$.20	$6.09	$6.29
Replace Materials.......4.70 Labor 1.39				
Remove .... Labor............ .20				
Redwood fascia 6" to 12" wide	lf	$.20	$7.64	$7.84
Replace Materials.......6.25 Labor 1.39				
Remove .... Labor............ .20				
minimum ▷ **Minimum charge for soffit & fascia work**	ea	–	$100.50	$100.50
Replace Materials......63.00 Labor............37.50				
SOFFIT ▶ *Includes 4% waste.* **Aluminum soffit**	sf	$.26	$4.67	$4.93
Replace Materials.........2.83 Labor 1.84				
Remove .... Labor............ .26				
Vinyl soffit	sf	$.26	$5.91	$6.17
Replace Materials.........4.07 Labor 1.84				
Remove .... Labor............ .26				
Cedar plywood soffit	sf	$.29	$3.99	$4.28
Replace Materials.........2.04 Labor 1.95				
Remove .... Labor............ .29				
Cedar rough-sawn plywood soffit	sf	$.29	$4.02	$4.31
Replace Materials.........2.07 Labor 1.95				
Remove .... Labor............ .29				
Fir plywood soffit	sf	$.29	$3.87	$4.16
Replace Materials.........1.92 Labor 1.95				
Remove .... Labor............ .29				
Fir rough-sawn plywood soffit	sf	$.29	$3.92	$4.21
Replace Materials.........1.97 Labor 1.95				
Remove .... Labor............ .29				
Redwood plywood soffit	sf	$.29	$7.06	$7.35
Replace Materials.........5.11 Labor 1.95				
Remove .... Labor............ .29				
Redwood rough-sawn plywood soffit	sf	$.29	$7.14	$7.43
Replace Materials.........5.19 Labor 1.95				
Remove .... Labor............ .29				
tongue-&-groove soffit ▷ **Cedar tongue-&-groove soffit, simple pattern**	sf	$.35	$6.15	$6.50
Replace Materials.........3.86 Labor 2.29				
Remove .... Labor............ .35				
Cedar tongue-&-groove soffit, fancy pattern	sf	$.35	$6.94	$7.29
Replace Materials.........4.65 Labor 2.29				
Remove .... Labor............ .35				

Item Description	Unit	Remove	Replace	Total
Fir tongue-&-groove soffit, simple pattern	sf	$.35	$5.89	$6.24
Replace Materials........3.60 Labor 2.29				
Remove .... Labor .... .35				
Fir tongue-&-groove soffit, fancy pattern	sf	$.35	$6.08	$6.43
Replace Materials........3.79 Labor 2.29				
Remove .... Labor .... .35				
Redwood tongue-&-groove soffit, simple pattern	sf	$.35	$9.50	$9.85
Replace Materials........7.21 Labor 2.29				
Remove .... Labor .... .35				
Redwood tongue-&-groove soffit, fancy pattern	sf	$.35	$10.12	$10.47
Replace Materials........7.83 Labor 2.29				
Remove .... Labor .... .35				
Aluminum rain gutter	lf	$.32	$5.55	$5.87
Replace Materials........4.01 Labor 1.54				
Remove .... Labor .... .32				
Copper built-in box rain gutter	lf	$.75	$101.80	$102.55
Replace Materials........38.40 Labor 63.40				
Remove .... Labor .... .75				
► Includes additional framing material and labor costs for a typical rain gutter integrated into the roof system and flashed with copper. Removal costs include only copper flashing.				
Copper rain gutter	lf	$.32	$22.64	$22.96
Replace Materials ......21.10 Labor 1.54				
Remove .... Labor .... .32				
Galvanized steel rain gutter	lf	$.32	$12.04	$12.36
Replace Materials ......10.50 Labor 1.54				
Remove .... Labor .... .32				
Plastic rain gutter	lf	$.32	$4.79	$5.11
Replace Materials........3.25 Labor 1.54				
Remove .... Labor .... .32				
Redwood rain gutter	lf	$.32	$46.44	$46.76
Replace Materials ......44.90 Labor 1.54				
Remove .... Labor .... .32				
Tin built-in box rain gutter	lf	$.75	$90.30	$91.05
Replace Materials ......26.90 Labor 63.40				
Remove .... Labor .... .75				
► Includes additional framing material and labor costs for a typical rain gutter integrated into the roof system and flashed with 40 pound terne tin. Removal costs include only copper flashing.				
Tin rain gutter	lf	$.32	$20.34	$20.66
Replace Materials ......18.80 Labor 1.54				
Remove .... Labor .... .32				
Aluminum rain gutter downspout	lf	$.26	$6.33	$6.59
Replace Materials ......4.90 Labor 1.43				
Remove .... Labor .... .26				
Copper built-in box rain gutter downspout	lf	$.26	$45.20	$45.46
Replace Materials ......24.10 Labor 21.10				
Remove .... Labor .... .26				
► Includes additional framing material and labor costs for an enclosed, concealed downspout. Also includes PVC pipe and excavation to drain field.				

RELATED ITEMS

Finish Carpentry 199
Paneling 347
Rough Carpentry 409

◄ **RAIN GUTTER**
Includes 3% waste.

built-in box △

◄ **RAIN GUTTER DOWNSPOUT**
Includes 3% waste.

	Item Description	Unit	Remove	Replace	Total
RAIN GUTTER ▶ DOWNSPOUT *continued*	**Copper rain gutter downspout**	lf	$.26	$27.33	$27.59
	Replace Materials ......25.90 Labor 1.43				
	Remove .... Labor .... .26				
	Galvanized steel rain gutter downspout	lf	$.26	$14.23	$14.49
	Replace Materials ......12.80 Labor 1.43				
	Remove .... Labor .... .26				
	Plastic rain gutter downspout	lf	$.26	$5.40	$5.66
	Replace Materials ....3.97 Labor 1.43				
	Remove .... Labor .... .26				
	Tin built-in box rain gutter downspout	lf	$.26	$19.63	$19.89
	Replace Materials ......18.20 Labor 1.43				
	Remove .... Labor .... .26				
	▶ Includes additional framing material and labor costs for an enclosed, concealed downspout. Also includes PVC pipe and excavation to drain field.				
	Tin rain gutter downspout	lf	$.26	$44.00	$44.26
	Replace Materials ......22.90 Labor 21.10				
	Remove .... Labor .... .26				
DOWNSPOUT ▶ CONDUCTOR	**Copper downspout conductor, standard grade**	ea	–	$68.60	$68.60
	Replace Materials ......52.40 Labor 16.20				
	▶ Simple or clear decorative work.				
	Copper downspout conductor, high grade	ea	–	$115.90	$115.90
	Replace Materials ......99.70 Labor 16.20				
	▶ Decorative embossed design.				
high grade △	**Galvanized steel downspout conductor, standard grade**	ea	–	$58.10	$58.10
	Replace Materials ......41.90 Labor 16.20				
	▶ Simple or clear decorative work.				
	Galvanized steel downspout conductor, high grade	ea	–	$96.00	$96.00
	Replace Materials ......79.80 Labor 16.20				
high grade △	▶ Decorative embossed design.				
POLYPROPYLENE ▶ SHUTTER *Per 16" wide pair. For 12" wide deduct **42%**; for 18" wide add **8%**; for 20" wide add **14%**; for 24" wide add **26%**.*	**24" tall polypropylene fixed shutter**	ea	$4.51	$50.20	$54.71
	Replace Materials ......38.10 Labor 12.10				
	Remove .... Labor 4.51				
	48" tall polypropylene fixed shutter	ea	$4.51	$71.30	$75.81
	Replace Materials ......59.20 Labor 12.10				
	Remove .... Labor 4.51				
	60" tall polypropylene fixed shutter	ea	$4.51	$80.70	$85.21
	Replace Materials ......68.60 Labor 12.10				
	Remove .... Labor 4.51				
	66" tall polypropylene fixed shutter	ea	$4.51	$91.60	$96.11
	Replace Materials ......79.50 Labor 12.10				
	Remove .... Labor 4.51				
WOOD SHUTTER ▶ *Per 16" wide pair. For 12" wide deduct **6%**; for 18" wide add **10%**; for 20" wide add **52%**; for 24" wide add **78%**.*	**36" tall wood fixed shutter**	ea	$4.51	$136.10	$140.61
	Replace Materials .....124.00 Labor 12.10				
	Remove .... Labor 4.51				
	48" tall wood fixed shutter	ea	$4.51	$152.10	$156.61
	Replace Materials ....140.00 Labor 12.10				
	Remove .... Labor 4.51				

Item Description	Unit	Remove	Replace	Total
60" tall wood fixed shutter	ea	$4.51	$170.10	$174.61
Replace Materials.....158.00 Labor..........12.10				
Remove .... Labor 4.51				
72" tall wood fixed shutter	ea	$4.51	$185.10	$189.61
Replace Materials.....173.00 Labor..........12.10				
Remove .... Labor 4.51				
36" tall wood moveable shutter	ea	$4.57	$209.50	$214.07
Replace Materials.....197.00 Labor..........12.50				
Remove .... Labor 4.57				
48" tall wood moveable shutter	ea	$4.57	$240.50	$245.07
Replace Materials....228.00 Labor..........12.50				
Remove .... Labor 4.57				
60" tall wood moveable shutter	ea	$4.57	$278.50	$283.07
Replace Materials....266.00 Labor..........12.50				
Remove .... Labor 4.57				
72" tall wood moveable shutter	ea	$4.57	$340.50	$345.07
Replace Materials....328.00 Labor..........12.50				
Remove .... Labor 4.57				
Remove shutter for work, then reinstall	ea	–	$16.90	$16.90
Replace .... Labor..........16.90				

RELATED ITEMS

Finish Carpentry 199
Paneling 347
Rough Carpentry 409

◄ **WOOD MOVEABLE SHUTTER**
Per 16" wide pair including hardware. For 12" wide deduct 15%; for 18" wide add 7%; for 20" wide add 14%; for 24" wide add 27%. For fixed half circle top add $130 per pair. For moveable louvers with half-circle top add $240 per pair. For raised panel shutter with half-circle top add $150 per pair. For Gothic peaked top (Gothic arch) add $250 per pair.

✍ NOTES: _____

_____

_____

_____ end

TIME & MATERIAL CHARTS *(selected items)*

Siding Materials

*See **Siding** material prices with the line items and waste information in the **QuickFinder** column.*

Siding Labor

LABORER	BASE WAGE	PAID LEAVE	TRUE WAGE	FICA	FUTA	WORKER'S COMP.	UNEMPLOY. INSUR.	HEALTH INSUR.	RETIRE (401K)	LIABILITY INSUR.	COST PER HOUR
Siding installer	$24.10	1.88	$25.98	1.99	.21	5.02	2.26	2.92	.78	3.90	**$43.10**
Siding installer's helper	$17.40	1.36	$18.76	1.44	.15	3.63	1.63	2.92	.56	2.81	**$31.90**
Demolition laborer	$14.40	1.12	$15.52	1.19	.12	5.01	1.35	2.92	.47	2.33	**$28.90**

Paid Leave is calculated based on two weeks paid vacation, one week sick leave, and seven paid holidays. Employer's matching portion of **FICA** is 7.65 percent. **FUTA** (Federal Unemployment) is .8 percent. **Worker's compensation** for the siding trade was calculated using a national average of 19.29 percent. **Unemployment insurance** was calculated using a national average of 8.7 percent. **Health insurance** was calculated based on a projected national average for 2005 of $580 per employee (and family when applicable) per month. Employer pays 80 percent for a per month cost of $464 per employee. **Retirement** is based on a 401(k) retirement program with employer matching of 50 percent. Employee contributions to the 401(k) plan are an average of 6 percent of the true wage. **Liability insurance** is based on a national average of 14.0 percent.

Siding Labor Productivity

WORK DESCRIPTION	LABORER	COST PER HOUR	PRODUCTIVITY	UNIT PRICE
Demolition				
remove fiberglass corrugated siding	demolition laborer	$28.90	.007	**$.20** sf
remove aluminum siding	demolition laborer	$28.90	.008	**$.23** sf
remove cement fiber shingle siding	demolition laborer	$28.90	.013	**$.38** sf
remove shake or wood shingle siding	demolition laborer	$28.90	.014	**$.40** sf
remove vinyl siding	demolition laborer	$28.90	.007	**$.20** sf
remove hardboard siding	demolition laborer	$28.90	.009	**$.26** sf
remove hardboard beveled siding	demolition laborer	$28.90	.010	**$.29** sf
remove plywood siding	demolition laborer	$28.90	.010	**$.29** sf
remove wood siding	demolition laborer	$28.90	.011	**$.32** sf
remove aluminum or vinyl fascia	demolition laborer	$28.90	.006	**$.17** lf
remove wood fascia	demolition laborer	$28.90	.007	**$.20** lf
remove aluminum or vinyl soffit	demolition laborer	$28.90	.009	**$.26** sf
remove plywood soffit	demolition laborer	$28.90	.010	**$.29** sf
remove tongue-&-groove soffit	demolition laborer	$28.90	.012	**$.35** lf
remove rain gutter	demolition laborer	$28.90	.011	**$.32** lf
remove built-in box rain gutter	demolition laborer	$28.90	.026	**$.75** lf
remove downspout	demolition laborer	$28.90	.009	**$.26** lf
remove fixed shutter	demolition laborer	$28.90	.156	**$4.51** ea
remove moveable shutter	demolition laborer	$28.90	.158	**$4.57** ea
Siding installation crew				
install siding	siding installer	$43.10		
install siding	siding installer's helper	$31.90		
install siding	**siding crew**	$37.50		
Install siding				
fiberglass corrugated	siding crew	$37.50	.028	**$1.05** sf
aluminum	siding crew	$37.50	.034	**$1.28** sf
cement fiber shingle	siding crew	$37.50	.045	**$1.69** sf
shake or wood shingle	siding crew	$37.50	.045	**$1.69** sf
vinyl	siding crew	$37.50	.034	**$1.28** sf
7/16" thick hardboard	siding crew	$37.50	.024	**$.90** sf
hardboard lap	siding crew	$37.50	.026	**$.98** sf
5/8" thick plywood	siding crew	$37.50	.025	**$.94** sf
plywood with 1" x 4" boards	siding crew	$37.50	.057	**$2.14** sf
board-and-batten	siding crew	$37.50	.037	**$1.39** sf
board-on-board	siding crew	$37.50	.034	**$1.28** sf
drop siding	siding crew	$37.50	.039	**$1.46** sf
clapboard	siding crew	$37.50	.055	**$2.06** sf
bevel	siding crew	$37.50	.041	**$1.54** sf
Install fascia				
aluminum or vinyl	siding crew	$37.50	.034	**$1.28** lf
wood fascia	siding crew	$37.50	.037	**$1.39** lf
Install soffit				
aluminum or vinyl	siding crew	$37.50	.049	**$1.84** sf
plywood	siding crew	$37.50	.052	**$1.95** sf
tongue-&-groove	siding crew	$37.50	.061	**$2.29** sf
Install rain gutter				
typical	siding crew	$37.50	.041	**$1.54** lf
built-in box	siding crew	$37.50	1.69	**$63.40** lf
Install rain gutter downspout				
typical	siding crew	$37.50	.038	**$1.43** lf
built-in box	siding crew	$37.50	.562	**$21.10** lf
Install downspout conductor				
typical	siding crew	$37.50	.431	**$16.20** ea
Install shutter				
fixed	siding crew	$37.50	.323	**$12.10** ea
moveable	siding crew	$37.50	.333	**$12.50** ea

NOTES: _____

_____ end

35 *Stairs*

Item Description	Unit	Remove	Replace	Total
3' wide utility stairs	st	$2.92	$35.00	$37.92
Replace Materials.......19.30 Labor...........15.70				
Remove......................... Labor 2.92				
▶ Includes three 2" x 12" stringers and 2" dimensional lumber treads.				
3' wide enclosed stairs for covered treads & risers	st	$3.53	$54.80	$58.33
Replace Materials......34.20 Labor 20.60				
Remove......................... Labor 3.53				
▶ Treads and risers are plywood or particleboard with pine risers. Treads and risers will be completely covered by carpeting or other flooring.				
3' wide enclosed stairs with false oak tread & riser	st	$3.53	$95.90	$99.43
Replace Materials ......71.40 Labor...........24.50				
Remove......................... Labor 3.53				
▶ Particleboard treads with pine risers covered with two wall end false red oak tread and riser assemblies. (Carpet runs between false treads.)				
3' wide enclosed stairs with oak treads & paint-grade risers	st	$3.53	$92.80	$96.33
Replace Materials ......72.20 Labor 20.60				
Remove......................... Labor 3.53				
▶ Treads are red oak and risers are paint-grade pine.				
3' wide enclosed stairs with oak treads & oak risers	st	$3.53	$97.80	$101.33
Replace Materials ......77.20 Labor 20.60				
Remove......................... Labor 3.53				
▶ Treads and risers are red oak.				
3' wide stairs, one side open, for covered treads & risers	st	$3.53	$55.30	$58.83
Replace Materials ......34.20 Labor...........21.10				
Remove......................... Labor 3.53				
▶ Particleboard treads and pine risers. Treads and risers will be completely covered by carpeting or other flooring.				
3' wide stairs, one side open, with false oak tread & riser	st	$3.53	$112.40	$115.93
Replace Materials ......87.40 Labor 25.00				
Remove......................... Labor 3.53				
▶ Particleboard treads with pine risers covered with one open end and one wall end false red oak tread and riser assemblies. (Carpet runs between false treads.)				
3' wide stairs, one side open, with oak treads & paint-grade risers	st	$3.53	$93.30	$96.83
Replace Materials ......72.20 Labor...........21.10				
Remove......................... Labor 3.53				
▶ Treads are red oak with easing on open side and 1/2" red oak cove trim beneath tread. Risers are paint-grade pine.				
3' wide stairs, one side open, with oak treads & oak risers	st	$3.53	$98.30	$101.83
Replace Materials ......77.20 Labor...........21.10				
Remove......................... Labor 3.53				
▶ Treads are red oak with easing on open side and 1/2" red oak cove trim beneath tread. Risers are red oak.				
3' wide stairs, two sides open, for covered treads & risers	st	$3.53	$56.70	$60.23
Replace Materials ......34.20 Labor 22.50				
Remove......................... Labor 3.53				
▶ Particleboard tread and pine risers. Treads and risers will be completely covered by carpeting or other flooring.				

◀ **UTILITY STAIRS**
Per step. Does not include railing.

◀ **STRAIGHT STAIRS**
Per step. Each stair system includes four 2" x 12" stringers reinforced with plywood or waferboard. Does not include balustrade.

◁ enclosed

◁ one side open

RELATED ITEMS

Columns 71
Finish Carpentry 199
  porch posts 231
Rough Carpentry 409
  exterior deck stairs 430

◁ two sides open

Item Description	Unit	Remove	Replace	Total
STRAIGHT STAIRS ▶ *continued* **3' wide stairs, two sides open, with false oak tread & riser**	st	$3.53	$129.80	$133.33
Replace Materials ....103.40 Labor..........26.40				
Remove...................... Labor 3.53				
▶ Particleboard treads with pine risers covered with two open end false red oak tread and riser assemblies. (Carpet runs between false treads.)				
3' wide stairs, two sides open, with oak treads & paint-grade risers	st	$3.53	$94.70	$98.23
Replace Materials ......72.20 Labor 22.50				
Remove...................... Labor 3.53				
▶ Treads are red oak with easing on both sides and 1/2" red oak cove trim beneath tread. Risers are paint-grade pine.				
3' wide stairs, two sides open, with oak treads & oak risers	st	$3.53	$99.70	$103.23
Replace Materials ......77.20 Labor 22.50				
Remove...................... Labor 3.53				
▶ Treads are red oak with easing on both sides and 1/2" red oak cove trim beneath tread. Risers are red oak.				
1/4 TURN STAIRS ▶ *Per step. Ten step minimum. L-shaped stair system with 3' by 3' landing. Includes bearing walls beneath landing as indicated, 2" x 8" joists, headers, and 3/4" tongue-&-groove sheathing. Each stair system includes four 2" x 12" stringers reinforced with plywood or waferboard. Does not include balustrade.* **enclosed ▷** **3' wide enclosed 1/4 turn stairs for covered treads & risers**	st	$3.90	$80.10	$84.00
Replace Materials ......44.20 Labor..........35.90				
Remove...................... Labor 3.90				
▶ 6 lf of landing bearing wall. Particleboard treads and pine risers or plywood treads and risers. Treads, risers, and landing will be covered by the flooring.				
3' wide enclosed 1/4 turn stairs with false oak tread & riser	st	$3.90	$136.40	$140.30
Replace Materials ......85.90 Labor 50.50				
Remove...................... Labor 3.90				
▶ 6 lf of landing bearing wall. Particleboard treads with pine risers covered with two wall end false red oak tread and riser assemblies. (Carpet runs between false treads.) Landing covered with oak flooring with stair edged trimmed with landing nose.				
3' wide enclosed 1/4 turn stairs with oak treads & paint-grade risers	st	$3.90	$135.50	$139.40
Replace Materials ......91.10 Labor 44.40				
Remove...................... Labor 3.90				
▶ 6 lf of landing bearing wall. Treads are red oak and risers are paint-grade pine. Landing covered with oak flooring with stair edge trimmed with landing nose.				
3' wide enclosed 1/4 turn stairs with oak treads & oak risers	st	$3.90	$140.50	$144.40
Replace Materials ......96.10 Labor 44.40				
Remove...................... Labor 3.90				
▶ 6 lf of landing bearing wall. Treads and risers are red oak. Landing covered with oak flooring with stair edge trimmed with landing nose.				
one side open ▷ **3' wide 1/4 turn stairs, one side open, for covered treads & risers**	st	$3.90	$81.40	$85.30
Replace Materials ......44.20 Labor..........37.20				
Remove...................... Labor 3.90				
▶ 6 lf of landing bearing wall. Particleboard treads and pine risers. Treads, risers, and landing will be completely covered by carpeting or other flooring.				
3' wide 1/4 turn stairs, one side open, with false oak tread & riser	st	$3.90	$154.10	$158.00
Replace Materials .....101.90 Labor..........52.20				
Remove...................... Labor 3.90				
▶ 6 lf of landing bearing wall. Particleboard treads with pine risers covered with one open end and one wall end false red oak tread and riser assemblies. (Carpet runs between false treads.) Landing covered with oak flooring with stair edge trimmed with landing nose.				
3' wide 1/4 turn stairs, one side open, with oak treads & paint-grade risers	st	$3.90	$136.30	$140.20
Replace Materials ......91.10 Labor..........45.20				
Remove...................... Labor 3.90				
▶ 6 lf of landing bearing wall. Treads are red oak with easing on open side and 1/2" red oak cove trim beneath tread. Risers are paint-grade pine. Landing covered with oak flooring with stair edge trimmed with landing nose.				

Item Description	Unit	Remove	Replace	Total
3' wide 1/4 turn stairs, one side open, with oak treads & oak risers	st	$3.90	$141.30	$145.20

Replace Materials ......96.10   Labor...........45.20
Remove.....................   Labor 3.90

▶ 6 lf of landing bearing wall. Treads are red oak with easing on open side and 1/2" red oak cove trim beneath tread. Risers are red oak. Landing covered with oak flooring with stair edge trimmed with landing nose.

| **3' wide 1/4 turn stairs, two sides open, for covered treads & risers** | st | $3.90 | $82.70 | $86.60 |

Replace Materials ......44.20   Labor 38.50
Remove.....................   Labor 3.90

▶ 12 lf of landing bearing wall. Particleboard treads and pine risers or plywood treads and risers. Treads, risers, and landing will be completely covered by flooring.

| **3' wide 1/4 turn stairs, two sides open, with false oak tread & riser** | st | $3.90 | $171.40 | $175.30 |

Replace Materials .....117.90   Labor 53.50
Remove.....................   Labor 3.90

▶ 12 lf of landing bearing wall. Particleboard treads with pine risers covered with two open end false red oak tread and riser assemblies. (Space is left for carpet to run between treads.) Landing covered with oak flooring with stair edge trimmed with landing nose.

| **3' wide 1/4 turn stairs, two sides open, with oak treads & paint-grade risers** | st | $3.90 | $136.80 | $140.70 |

Replace Materials ......91.10   Labor...........45.70
Remove.....................   Labor 3.90

▶ 12 lf of landing bearing wall. Treads are red oak with easing on both sides and 1/2" red oak cove trim beneath tread. Risers are paint-grade pine. Landing covered with oak flooring with stair edge trimmed with landing nose.

| **3' wide 1/4 turn stairs, two sides open, with oak treads & oak risers** | st | $3.90 | $141.80 | $145.70 |

Replace Materials ......96.10   Labor...........45.70
Remove.....................   Labor 3.90

▶ 12 lf of landing bearing wall. Treads are red oak with easing on both sides and 1/2" red oak cove trim beneath tread. Risers are red oak. Landing covered with oak flooring with stair edge trimmed with landing nose.

| **3' wide enclosed 1/2 turn stairs for covered treads and risers** | st | $4.34 | $93.70 | $98.04 |

Replace Materials ......54.20   Labor 39.50
Remove.....................   Labor 4.34

▶ 9 lf of landing bearing wall. Particleboard treads and pine risers or plywood treads and risers. Treads, risers, and landing will be completely covered by flooring.

| **3' wide enclosed 1/2 turn stairs with false oak tread and riser** | st | $4.34 | $155.20 | $159.54 |

Replace Materials ....100.40   Labor 54.80
Remove.....................   Labor 4.34

▶ 9 lf of landing bearing wall. Particleboard treads with pine risers covered with two wall end false red oak tread and riser assemblies. (Carpet runs between false treads.) Landing covered with oak flooring with stair edged trimmed with landing nose.

| **3' wide enclosed 1/2 turn stairs with oak treads & paint-grade risers** | st | $4.34 | $154.30 | $158.64 |

Replace Materials ....105.60   Labor 48.70
Remove.....................   Labor 4.34

▶ 9 lf of landing bearing wall. Treads are red oak and risers are paint-grade pine. Landing covered with oak flooring with stair edge trimmed with landing nose.

| **3' wide enclosed 1/2 turn stairs with oak treads & oak risers** | st | $4.34 | $159.30 | $163.64 |

Replace Materials .....110.60   Labor 48.70
Remove.....................   Labor 4.34

▶ 9 lf of landing bearing wall. Treads and risers are red oak. Landing covered with oak flooring with stair edge trimmed with landing nose.

RELATED ITEMS

Columns 71
Finish Carpentry...........199
  porch posts....................231
Rough Carpentry 409
  exterior deck stairs 430

◁ **two sides open**

◀ **1/2 TURN STAIRS**
Per step. Ten step minimum. U shaped stair system with 6' by 3' landing. Includes bearing walls beneath landing as indicated, 2" x 8" joists, headers, and 3/4" tongue-&-groove sheathing. Each stair system includes four 2" x 12" stringers reinforced with plywood or waferboard.

◁ **enclosed**

Item Description	Unit	Remove	Replace	Total
1/2 TURN STAIRS ▶ *continued* **one side open** ▷ **3' wide 1/2 turn stairs, one side open, for covered treads & risers** *Replace* Materials......54.20 Labor..........41.00 *Remove*...................... Labor ....4.34 ▶ 9 lf of landing bearing wall. Particleboard treads and pine risers. Treads and risers will be completely covered by carpeting or other flooring.	st	$4.34	$95.20	$99.54
3' wide 1/2 turn stairs, one side open, with false oak tread & riser *Replace* Materials.....132.00 Labor..........57.00 *Remove*...................... Labor ....4.34 ▶ 9 lf of landing bearing wall. Particleboard treads with pine risers covered with one open end and one wall end false red oak tread and riser assemblies. (Space is left for carpet to run between treads.) Landing covered with oak flooring with stair edge trimmed with landing nose.	st	$4.34	$189.00	$193.34
3' wide 1/2 turn stairs, one side open, with oak treads & paint-grade risers *Replace* Materials ....105.60 Labor ....50.00 *Remove*...................... Labor ....4.34 ▶ 9 lf of landing bearing wall. Treads are red oak with easing on open side and 1/2" red oak cove trim beneath tread. Risers are paint-grade pine. Landing covered with oak flooring with stair edge trimmed with landing nose.	st	$4.34	$155.60	$159.94
3' wide 1/2 turn stairs, one side open, with oak treads & oak risers *Replace* Materials.....110.60 Labor ....50.00 *Remove*...................... Labor ....4.34 ▶ 9 lf of landing bearing wall. Treads are red oak with easing on open side and 1/2" red oak cove trim beneath tread. Risers are red oak. Landing covered with oak flooring with stair edge trimmed with landing nose.	st	$4.34	$160.60	$164.94
two sides open ▷ **3' wide 1/2 turn stairs, two sides open, for covered treads & risers** *Replace* Materials......54.20 Labor..........42.20 *Remove*...................... Labor ....4.34 ▶ 18 lf of landing bearing wall. Particleboard treads and pine risers or plywood treads and risers. Treads, risers, and landing will be completely covered by flooring.	st	$4.34	$96.40	$100.74
3' wide 1/2 turn stairs, two sides open, with false oak tread & riser *Replace* Materials.....132.00 Labor ....58.30 *Remove*...................... Labor ....4.34 ▶ 18 lf of landing bearing wall. Particleboard treads with pine risers covered with two open end false red oak tread and riser assemblies. (Space is left for carpet to run between treads.) Landing covered with oak flooring with stair edge trimmed with landing nose.	st	$4.34	$190.30	$194.64
3' wide 1/2 turn stairs, two sides open, with oak treads & paint-grade risers *Replace* Materials ....105.60 Labor ....50.50 *Remove*...................... Labor ....4.34 ▶ 18 lf of landing bearing wall. Treads are red oak with easing on both sides and 1/2" red oak cove trim beneath tread. Risers are paint-grade pine. Landing covered with oak flooring with stair edge trimmed with landing nose.	st	$4.34	$156.10	$160.44
3' wide 1/2 turn stairs, two sides open, with oak treads & oak risers *Replace* Materials.....110.60 Labor ....50.50 *Remove*...................... Labor ....4.34 ▶ 18 lf of landing bearing wall. Treads and risers are red oak with easing on both sides and 1/2" red oak cove trim beneath tread. Landing covered with oak flooring with stair edge trimmed with landing nose.	st	$4.34	$161.10	$165.44
CIRCULAR STAIRS ▶ *Circular stairs usually form half of a circle or less. Based on 9' radius.* **3' wide enclosed circular stairs for covered treads and risers** *Replace* Materials....220.00 Labor ....505.00 *Remove*...................... Labor ....4.57 ▶ Treads and risers are plywood or particleboard treads with pine risers. Treads and risers will be completely covered by carpeting or other flooring.	st	$4.57	$725.00	$729.57

continued on next page

Item Description	Unit	Remove	Replace	Total
3' wide enclosed circular stairs with false oak tread and riser	st	$4.57	$770.00	$774.57
Replace Materials ....257.00 Labor 513.00				
Remove...................... Labor 4.57				
▶ Particleboard treads with pine risers covered with two wall end false red oak tread and riser assemblies. (Carpet runs between false treads.)				
3' wide enclosed circular stairs with oak treads and paint-grade risers	st	$4.57	$763.00	$767.57
Replace Materials ....258.00 Labor 505.00				
Remove...................... Labor 4.57				
▶ Treads are red oak and risers are paint-grade pine.				
3' wide enclosed circular stairs with oak treads and oak risers	st	$4.57	$768.00	$772.57
Replace Materials ....263.00 Labor 505.00				
Remove...................... Labor 4.57				
▶ Treads and risers are red oak.				
3' wide circular stairs, one side open, for covered treads and risers	st	$4.57	$733.00	$737.57
Replace Materials ....220.00 Labor 513.00				
Remove...................... Labor 4.57				
▶ Particleboard treads and pine risers. Treads and risers will be completely covered by carpeting or other flooring.				
3' wide circular stairs, one side open, with false oak tread and riser	st	$4.57	$794.00	$798.57
Replace Materials ....273.00 Labor 521.00				
Remove...................... Labor 4.57				
▶ Particleboard treads with pine risers covered with one open end and one wall end false red oak tread and riser assemblies. (Carpet runs between treads.)				
3' wide circular stairs, one side open, with oak treads and paint-grade risers	st	$4.57	$771.00	$775.57
Replace Materials ....258.00 Labor 513.00				
Remove...................... Labor 4.57				
▶ Treads are red oak with easing on open side and 1/2" red oak cove trim beneath tread. Risers are paint-grade pine.				
3' wide circular stairs, one side open, with oak treads and oak risers	st	$4.57	$776.00	$780.57
Replace Materials ....263.00 Labor 513.00				
Remove...................... Labor 4.57				
▶ Treads are red oak with easing on open side and 1/2" red oak cove trim beneath tread. Risers are paint-grade pine.				
3' wide circular stairs, two sides open, for covered treads and risers	st	$4.57	$738.00	$742.57
Replace Materials ....220.00 Labor 518.00				
Remove...................... Labor 4.57				
▶ Particleboard tread and pine risers. Treads and risers will be completely covered by carpeting or other flooring.				
3' wide circular stairs, two sides open, with false oak tread and riser	st	$4.57	$815.00	$819.57
Replace Materials ....289.00 Labor 526.00				
Remove...................... Labor 4.57				
▶ Particleboard treads with pine risers covered with two open end false red oak tread and riser assemblies. (Carpet runs between false treads.)				
3' wide circular stairs, two sides open, with oak treads and paint-grade risers	st	$4.57	$776.00	$780.57
Replace Materials ....258.00 Labor 518.00				
Remove...................... Labor 4.57				
▶ Treads are red oak with easing on both sides and 1/2" red oak cove trim beneath tread. Risers are paint-grade pine.				
3' wide circular stairs, two sides open, with oak treads and oak risers	st	$4.57	$781.00	$785.57
Replace Materials ....263.00 Labor 518.00				
Remove...................... Labor 4.57				
▶ Treads are red oak with easing on both sides and 1/2" red oak cove trim beneath tread. Risers are red oak.				

◀ **CIRCULAR STAIRS**
Labor prices are for hand-framed open or closed stringer stairs. Overall these prices also apply to purchase and installation of prefabricated circular stairs. Does not include balustrade.

◁ one side open

◁ two sides open

RELATED ITEMS

Columns 71
Finish Carpentry..........199
porch posts...................231
Rough Carpentry 409
exterior deck stairs........430

Item Description	Unit	Remove	Replace	Total

ADD FOR 4' ▶
WIDE STAIRS

Add 12% for 4' wide stairs
▶ For 4' wide straight, 1/4 turn, or 1/2 turn stairs containing the same number of stringers as 3' wide stairs (4) with wider treads and risers. 1/4 turn stair landing is 4' x 4' and 1/2 turn stair landing is 8' x 4'. Add **16%** for 4' wide circular stairs.

ADD FOR STAIR ▶
WINDERS

Add for winder with particleboard tread, paint-grade riser
	ea	—	$67.80	$67.80

Replace Materials......50.40   Labor..........17.40
▶ For use with 1/4 turn and 1/2 turn stairs. Winders are pie-shaped stair treads, usually placed on top of the landing. Each winder is a box made from 2" x 8" boards ripped to the height of the riser. Additional ripped 2" x 8" boards are placed 12" on center inside the box for reinforcement. (Add **3%** for risers over 7-3/8" made from ripped 2" x 10" boards.) Winders are stacked on top of each other.

Add for winder with oak tread, paint-grade riser
	ea	—	$105.80	$105.80

Replace Materials......88.40   Labor..........17.40
▶ For details see above.

Add for winder with oak tread, oak riser
	ea	—	$110.80	$110.80

Replace Materials......93.40   Labor..........17.40
▶ For details see above.

ADD FOR ▶
MITERED STEPS

Add for mitered corners on bottom three treads
	ea	—	$239.00	$239.00

Replace Materials.....138.00   Labor.........101.00
▶ For stairs where the bottom three steps turn at a 45 degree angle (or less) making three steps from the side and front. The three steps on the side are made from stacked boxes made from 2" x 8" boards ripped to the riser height, sheathed with 3/4" plywood then capped with the tread and riser material. Cost per side. (For example, for stairs with mitered corners on both sides, use this price twice.)

ADD FOR ▶
BULL NOSE ON
STARTING STEP

Add for starting step with bull nose one side, standard grade
	ea	—	$274.40	$274.40

Replace Materials....253.00   Labor..........21.40
▶ Red oak up to 4' wide.

Add for starting step with bull nose one side, high grade
	ea	—	$327.40	$327.40

Replace Materials....306.00   Labor..........21.40
▶ Red oak up to 5' wide.

Add for starting step with bull nose two sides, standard grade
	ea	—	$369.40	$369.40

Replace Materials....348.00   Labor..........21.40
▶ Red oak up to 4' wide.

Add for starting step with bull nose two sides, high grade
	ea	—	$442.40	$442.40

Replace Materials ....421.00   Labor..........21.40
▶ Red oak up to 5' wide.

SPIRAL STAIRS ▶
Per step.
Prefabricated spiral
stairs assembled and
installed by carpenter
on site. Includes
balustrade.

Prefabricated spiral stairs, economy grade
	st	$3.55	$241.20	$244.75

Replace Materials....204.00   Labor..........37.20
Remove..........................   Labor............3.55
▶ 48" to 54" diameter. Balusters are made from straight wood, steel, or aluminum with matching hand rail. One baluster per tread. Treads are made from aluminum, steel, or waferboard (for carpet). Add **$60** per lf for landing or balcony railing to match.

Prefabricated spiral stairs, standard grade
	st	$3.55	$397.20	$400.75

Replace Materials....360.00   Labor..........37.20
Remove..........................   Labor............3.55
▶ 48" to 54" diameter. Balusters are made from turned wood, twisted steel, or aluminum with steel or laminated wood hand rail. One baluster per tread. Treads are made from aluminum, steel, or waferboard (for carpet). Add **$80** per lf for landing or balcony railing to match.

Item Description	Unit	Remove	Replace	Total
Prefabricated spiral stairs, high grade	st	$3.55	$433.20	$436.75

Replace Materials ....396.00   Labor...........37.20
Remove........................   Labor 3.55

▶ 55" to 66" diameter. Balusters made from ornate wood or octagonal wood, twisted steel with decorative wrought iron work, or aluminum with matching hand rail. Two balusters per tread. Treads are made from aluminum, steel, or waferboard (for carpet). Add **$90** per lf for landing or balcony railing to match.

Item Description	Unit	Remove	Replace	Total
Prefabricated spiral stairs, custom grade	st	$3.55	$469.20	$472.75

Replace Materials ....432.00   Labor...........37.20
Remove........................   Labor 3.55

▶ 55" to 66" diameter. Balusters made from spiral wood or octagonal wood, steel or cast iron with decorative wrought iron work including brass elements with matching hand rail. Two balusters per tread. Treads are made from aluminum, steel, decorative cast iron, or waferboard (for carpet). Add **$100** per lf for landing or balcony railing to match.

Item Description	Unit	Remove	Replace	Total
Prefabricated spiral stairs, deluxe grade	st	$3.55	$559.20	$562.75

Replace Materials ....522.00   Labor...........37.20
Remove........................   Labor 3.55

▶ 67" to 72" diameter. Balusters made from ornate wood or octagonal wood, twisted steel with decorative wrought iron work with matching hand rail. Two balusters per tread. Treads are made from aluminum, steel, decorative cast iron or waferboard (for carpet). Add **$110** per lf for landing or balcony railing to match.

Item Description	Unit	Remove	Replace	Total
Prefabricated spiral stairs, custom deluxe grade	st	$3.55	$608.20	$611.75

Replace Materials ....571.00   Labor...........37.20
Remove........................   Labor 3.55

▶ 67" to 72" diameter. Balusters made from spiral wood or octagonal wood, steel or cast iron with decorative wrought iron work including brass elements with matching hand rail. Two balusters per tread. Treads are made from aluminum, steel, decorative cast iron, or waferboard (for carpet). Add **$130** per lf for landing or balcony railing to match.

Item Description	Unit	Remove	Replace	Total
Disappearing attic stairs, standard grade	ea	$7.80	$471.00	$478.80

Replace Materials ....367.00   Labor.........104.00
Remove........................   Labor 7.80

▶ Pine components with stain-grade panel door.

Item Description	Unit	Remove	Replace	Total
Disappearing attic stairs, high grade	ea	$7.80	$719.00	$726.80

Replace Materials .....615.00   Labor.........104.00
Remove........................   Labor 7.80

▶ Pine components with stain-grade panel door, spring loaded, heavier quality side rails and treads.

Item Description	Unit	Remove	Replace	Total
Disappearing attic stairs, deluxe grade	ea	$7.80	$1,144.00	$1,151.80

Replace Materials ..1040.00   Labor.........104.00
Remove........................   Labor 7.80

▶ Pine components with stain-grade panel door, spring loaded, heavy duty side rails and treads.

Item Description	Unit	Remove	Replace	Total
Remove disappearing attic stairs for work, then reinstall	ea	—	$145.00	$145.00

Replace ....   Labor 145.00

Item Description	Unit	Remove	Replace	Total
Pine stair balustrade with 1-1/2" balusters	lf	$1.53	$85.90	$87.43

Replace Materials ......28.50   Labor...........57.40
Remove........................   Labor 1.53

Item Description	Unit	Remove	Replace	Total
Pine stair balustrade with 1-1/2" fluted balusters	lf	$1.53	$91.70	$93.23

Replace Materials ......34.30   Labor...........57.40
Remove........................   Labor 1.53

RELATED ITEMS

Columns 71
Finish Carpentry...........199
porch posts...................231
Rough Carpentry 409
exterior deck stairs 430

◀ **DISAPPEARING ATTIC STAIRS**
Fold-up attic access stairs with side rails.

◁ *remove & reinstall*

◀ **PINE STAIR BALUSTRADE**
Add **9%** for red oak rail and newel in pine balustrade. Add **85%** for installation on curved stair. Deduct **10%** for balustrade installed on porch or other level application.

Item Description	Unit	Remove	Replace	Total
PINE STAIR ▶ **Pine stair balustrade with 1-1/2" spiral balusters**	lf	$1.53	$110.60	$112.13
BALUSTRADE *Replace* Materials......53.20 Labor..........57.40				
continued *Remove*...................... Labor............1.53				
with 2-1/2" balusters ▷ **Pine stair balustrade with 2-1/2" balusters**	lf	$1.53	$90.10	$91.63
Replace Materials......32.20 Labor..........57.90				
Remove...................... Labor............1.53				
Pine stair balustrade with 2-1/2" fluted balusters	lf	$1.53	$96.60	$98.13
Replace Materials......38.70 Labor..........57.90				
Remove...................... Labor............1.53				
Pine stair balustrade with 2-1/2" spiral balusters	lf	$1.53	$118.00	$119.53
Replace Materials......60.10 Labor..........57.90				
Remove...................... Labor............1.53				
with 3-1/2" balusters ▷ **Pine stair balustrade with 3-1/2" balusters**	lf	$1.53	$98.00	$99.53
Replace Materials......39.30 Labor..........58.70				
Remove...................... Labor............1.53				
Pine stair balustrade with 3-1/2" fluted balusters	lf	$1.53	$105.90	$107.43
Replace Materials......47.20 Labor..........58.70				
Remove...................... Labor............1.53				
Pine stair balustrade with 3-1/2" spiral balusters	lf	$1.53	$131.80	$133.33
Replace Materials......73.10 Labor..........58.70				
Remove...................... Labor............1.53				
with 5-1/2" balusters ▷ **Pine stair balustrade with 5-1/2" balusters**	lf	$1.53	$123.80	$125.33
Replace Materials......62.50 Labor..........61.30				
Remove...................... Labor............1.53				
Pine stair balustrade with 5-1/2" fluted balusters	lf	$1.53	$135.20	$136.73
Replace Materials......73.90 Labor..........61.30				
Remove...................... Labor............1.53				
Pine stair balustrade with 5-1/2" spiral balusters	lf	$1.53	$171.90	$173.43
Replace Materials......110.60 Labor..........61.30				
Remove...................... Labor............1.53				
POPLAR STAIR ▶ **Poplar stair balustrade with 1-1/2" balusters**	lf	$1.53	$104.90	$106.43
BALUSTRADE *Replace* Materials......47.50 Labor..........57.40				
Includes newel post. *Remove*...................... Labor............1.53				
*Add **9%** for red oak* **Poplar stair balustrade with 1-1/2" fluted balusters**	lf	$1.53	$114.80	$116.33
rail and newel in poplar *Replace* Materials......57.40 Labor..........57.40				
*balustrade. Add **85%*** *Remove*...................... Labor............1.53				
for installation on **Poplar stair balustrade with 1-1/2" spiral balusters**	lf	$1.53	$148.40	$149.93
curved stair. Deduct *Replace* Materials......91.00 Labor..........57.40				
***10%** for balustrade* *Remove*...................... Labor............1.53				
installed on porch or				
other level application.				
with 2-1/2" balusters ▷ **Poplar stair balustrade with 2-1/2" balusters**	lf	$1.53	$111.50	$113.03
Replace Materials......53.60 Labor..........57.90				
Remove...................... Labor............1.53				
Poplar stair balustrade with 2-1/2" fluted balusters	lf	$1.53	$122.70	$124.23
Replace Materials......64.80 Labor..........57.90				
Remove...................... Labor............1.53				
Poplar stair balustrade with 2-1/2" spiral balusters	lf	$1.53	$160.40	$161.93
Replace Materials....102.50 Labor..........57.90				
Remove...................... Labor............1.53				

Item Description	Unit	Remove	Replace	Total	
Poplar stair balustrade with 3-1/2″ balusters *Replace* Materials ......65.30　　Labor ....58.70 *Remove*......................　　Labor 1.53	lf	$1.53	$124.00	$125.53	◁ with 3-1/2″ balusters
Poplar stair balustrade with 3-1/2″ fluted balusters *Replace* Materials ......79.00　　Labor ....58.70 *Remove*......................　　Labor 1.53	lf	$1.53	$137.70	$139.23	
Poplar stair balustrade with 3-1/2″ spiral balusters *Replace* Materials .....125.00　　Labor ....58.70 *Remove*......................　　Labor 1.53	lf	$1.53	$183.70	$185.23	
Poplar stair balustrade with 5-1/2″ balusters *Replace* Materials ....102.30　　Labor ....61.30 *Remove*......................　　Labor 1.53	lf	$1.53	$163.60	$165.13	◁ with 5-1/2″ balusters
Poplar stair balustrade with 5-1/2″ fluted balusters *Replace* Materials ....122.00　　Labor ....61.30 *Remove*......................　　Labor 1.53	lf	$1.53	$183.30	$184.83	
Poplar stair balustrade with 5-1/2″ spiral balusters *Replace* Materials ....187.00　　Labor ....61.30 *Remove*......................　　Labor 1.53	lf	$1.53	$248.30	$249.83	
Redwood stair balustrade with 1-1/2″ balusters *Replace* Materials ......52.60　　Labor..........57.40 *Remove*......................　　Labor 1.53	lf	$1.53	$110.00	$111.53	◀ **REDWOOD STAIR BALUSTRADE** *Includes newel post. Add* **85%** *for installation on curved stair. Deduct* **10%** *for balustrade installed on porch or other level application.*
Redwood stair balustrade with 1-1/2″ fluted balusters *Replace* Materials ......63.50　　Labor..........57.40 *Remove*......................　　Labor 1.53	lf	$1.53	$120.90	$122.43	
Redwood stair balustrade with 1-1/2″ spiral balusters *Replace* Materials ....100.80　　Labor..........57.40 *Remove*......................　　Labor 1.53	lf	$1.53	$158.20	$159.73	
Redwood stair balustrade with 2-1/2″ balusters *Replace* Materials ......59.40　　Labor..........57.90 *Remove*......................　　Labor 1.53	lf	$1.53	$117.30	$118.83	◁ with 2-1/2″ balusters
Redwood stair balustrade with 2-1/2″ fluted balusters *Replace* Materials ......72.00　　Labor..........57.90 *Remove*......................　　Labor 1.53	lf	$1.53	$129.90	$131.43	
Redwood stair balustrade with 2-1/2″ spiral balusters *Replace* Materials .....113.60　　Labor..........57.90 *Remove*......................　　Labor 1.53	lf	$1.53	$171.50	$173.03	
Redwood stair balustrade with 3-1/2″ balusters *Replace* Materials ......72.40　　Labor ....58.70 *Remove*......................　　Labor 1.53	lf	$1.53	$131.10	$132.63	◁ with 3-1/2″ balusters
Redwood stair balustrade with 3-1/2″ fluted balusters *Replace* Materials ......87.60　　Labor ....58.70 *Remove*......................　　Labor 1.53	lf	$1.53	$146.30	$147.83	
Redwood stair balustrade with 3-1/2″ spiral balusters *Replace* Materials ....138.00　　Labor ....58.70 *Remove*......................　　Labor 1.53	lf	$1.53	$196.70	$198.23	
Redwood stair balustrade with 5-1/2″ balusters *Replace* Materials .....113.50　　Labor ....61.30 *Remove*......................　　Labor 1.53	lf	$1.53	$174.80	$176.33	◁ with 5-1/2″ balusters

RELATED ITEMS
Columns 71
Finish Carpentry..........199
　porch posts...................231
Rough Carpentry 409
　exterior deck stairs 430

	Item Description	Unit	Remove	Replace	Total
REDWOOD STAIR ▶ **BALUSTRADE** *continued*	**Redwood stair balustrade with 5-1/2" fluted balusters** *Replace* Materials.....136.00 Labor...........61.30 *Remove*........................ Labor 1.53	lf	$1.53	$197.30	$198.83
	Redwood stair balustrade with 5-1/2" spiral balusters *Replace* Materials ....207.00 Labor...........61.30 *Remove*........................ Labor 1.53	lf	$1.53	$268.30	$269.83
RED OAK STAIR ▶ **BALUSTRADE** *Includes newel post. Add 85% for installation on curved stair. Deduct 10% for balustrade installed on porch or other level application.*	**Red oak stair balustrade with 1-1/2" balusters** *Replace* Materials ......67.00 Labor...........57.40 *Remove*........................ Labor 1.53	lf	$1.53	$124.40	$125.93
	Red oak stair balustrade with 1-1/2" fluted balusters *Replace* Materials......80.60 Labor...........57.40 *Remove*........................ Labor 1.53	lf	$1.53	$138.00	$139.53
	Red oak stair balustrade with 1-1/2" spiral balusters *Replace* Materials.....126.00 Labor...........57.40 *Remove*........................ Labor 1.53	lf	$1.53	$183.40	$184.93
	Red oak stair balustrade with 1-1/2" hand-carved balusters *Replace* Materials ....255.00 Labor...........57.40 *Remove*........................ Labor 1.53	lf	$1.53	$312.40	$313.93
	Red oak stair balustrade with 1-1/2" heavy hand-carved balusters *Replace* Materials ....274.00 Labor...........57.40 *Remove*........................ Labor 1.53	lf	$1.53	$331.40	$332.93
with 2-1/2" balusters ▷	**Red oak stair balustrade with 2-1/2" balusters** *Replace* Materials ......75.00 Labor...........57.90 *Remove*........................ Labor 1.53	lf	$1.53	$132.90	$134.43
	Red oak stair balustrade with 2-1/2" fluted balusters *Replace* Materials......90.40 Labor...........57.90 *Remove*........................ Labor 1.53	lf	$1.53	$148.30	$149.83
	Red oak stair balustrade with 2-1/2" spiral balusters *Replace* Materials.....141.00 Labor...........57.90 *Remove*........................ Labor 1.53	lf	$1.53	$198.90	$200.43
	Red oak stair balustrade with 2-1/2" hand-carved balusters *Replace* Materials ....259.00 Labor...........57.90 *Remove*........................ Labor 1.53	lf	$1.53	$316.90	$318.43
	Red oak stair balustrade with 2-1/2" heavy hand-carved balusters *Replace* Materials ....279.00 Labor...........57.90 *Remove*........................ Labor 1.53	lf	$1.53	$336.90	$338.43
with 3-1/2" balusters ▷	**Red oak stair balustrade with 3-1/2" balusters** *Replace* Materials ......91.30 Labor ....58.70 *Remove*........................ Labor 1.53	lf	$1.53	$150.00	$151.53
	Red oak stair balustrade with 3-1/2" fluted balusters *Replace* Materials ....109.90 Labor ....58.70 *Remove*........................ Labor 1.53	lf	$1.53	$168.60	$170.13
	Red oak stair balustrade with 3-1/2" spiral balusters *Replace* Materials.....172.00 Labor ....58.70 *Remove*........................ Labor 1.53	lf	$1.53	$230.70	$232.23
	Red oak stair balustrade with 3-1/2" hand-carved balusters *Replace* Materials.....317.00 Labor ....58.70 *Remove*........................ Labor 1.53	lf	$1.53	$375.70	$377.23

Item Description	Unit	Remove	Replace	Total	
Red oak stair balustrade with 3-1/2" heavy hand-carved balusters *Replace* Materials....344.00 Labor ....58.70 *Remove*...................... Labor 1.53	lf	$1.53	$402.70	$404.23	
Red oak stair balustrade with 5-1/2" balusters *Replace* Materials.....145.00 Labor ....61.30 *Remove*...................... Labor 1.53	lf	$1.53	$206.30	$207.83	◁ with 5-1/2" balusters
Red oak stair balustrade with 5-1/2" fluted balusters *Replace* Materials.....172.00 Labor ....61.30 *Remove*...................... Labor 1.53	lf	$1.53	$233.30	$234.83	
Red oak stair balustrade with 5-1/2" spiral balusters *Replace* Materials ....258.00 Labor ....61.30 *Remove*...................... Labor 1.53	lf	$1.53	$319.30	$320.83	
Red oak stair balustrade with 5-1/2" hand-carved balusters *Replace* Materials.....310.00 Labor ....61.30 *Remove*...................... Labor 1.53	lf	$1.53	$371.30	$372.83	
Red oak stair balustrade with 5-1/2" heavy hand-carved balusters *Replace* Materials ....342.00 Labor ....61.30 *Remove*...................... Labor 1.53	lf	$1.53	$403.30	$404.83	
Pine stair balustrade with sawn balusters *Replace* Materials ......47.80 Labor ....57.40 *Remove*...................... Labor 1.53	lf	$1.53	$105.20	$106.73	◀ **SAWN STAIR BALUSTRADE** *Includes newel post Deduct **10%** for balustrade installed on porch or other level application.*
Pine stair balustrade with sawn baluster panels *Replace* Materials ......80.70 Labor ....57.40 *Remove*...................... Labor 1.53	lf	$1.53	$138.10	$139.63	
Poplar stair balustrade with sawn balusters *Replace* Materials ......65.10 Labor ....57.40 *Remove*...................... Labor 1.53	lf	$1.53	$122.50	$124.03	
Poplar stair balustrade with sawn baluster panels *Replace* Materials ......98.90 Labor ....57.40 *Remove*...................... Labor 1.53	lf	$1.53	$156.30	$157.83	△ *sawn balusters*
Add for red oak rail & newel in paint-grade sawn stair balustrade *Replace* Materials.......13.70	lf	—	$13.70	$13.70	
Redwood stair balustrade with sawn balusters *Replace* Materials.....107.30 Labor ....57.40 *Remove*...................... Labor 1.53	lf	$1.53	$164.70	$166.23	
Redwood stair balustrade with sawn baluster panels *Replace* Materials.....171.00 Labor ....57.40 *Remove*...................... Labor 1.53	lf	$1.53	$228.40	$229.93	△ *sawn baluster panels*
Red oak stair balustrade with sawn balusters *Replace* Materials ......88.70 Labor ....57.40 *Remove*...................... Labor 1.53	lf	$1.53	$146.10	$147.63	
Red oak stair balustrade with sawn baluster panels *Replace* Materials.....133.00 Labor ....57.40 *Remove*...................... Labor 1.53	lf	$1.53	$190.40	$191.93	
Remove stair balustrade for work, then reinstall *Replace* .... Labor 104.00	lf	—	$104.00	$104.00	◀ **REMOVE & REINSTALL BALUSTRADE**

RELATED ITEMS

Columns 71
Finish Carpentry 199
 porch posts 231
Rough Carpentry 409
 exterior deck stairs 430

	Item Description	Unit	Remove	Replace	Total
ADDITIONAL ▶ BALUSTRADE COSTS	**Add for volute end** *Replace* Materials ....271.00 Labor ....132.00 ▶ Oak, poplar, or pine. Includes additional balusters and labor to install volute end with circled balusters and newel. Usually not used on stairs with balusters larger than 2-1/2".	ea	—	$403.00	$403.00
	Add for goose neck *Replace* Materials ....309.00 Labor ....106.00 ▶ Oak, poplar, or pine.	ea	—	$415.00	$415.00
	Add for 1/4 turn in stair rail *Replace* Materials ......95.60 Labor ....98.70 ▶ Oak, poplar, or pine. 90 degree turn slopes up on one side and down on the other.	ea	—	$194.30	$194.30
	Add for 1/2 turn in stair rail *Replace* Materials .....219.00 Labor ....106.00 ▶	ea	—	$325.00	$325.00
STAIR BRACKET ▶ *Brackets installed beneath open end of tread.*	**Stair bracket, standard grade** *Replace* Materials ......10.70 Labor ....3.96 *Remove* .... Labor ....1.56 ▶ Paint-grade. No inside pattern.	ea	$1.56	$14.66	$16.22
	Stair bracket, high grade *Replace* Materials ......12.50 Labor ....3.96 *Remove* .... Labor ....1.56 ▶ Poplar or red oak. Simple inside pattern.	ea	$1.56	$16.46	$18.02
	Stair bracket, deluxe grade *Replace* Materials ......14.90 Labor ....3.96 *Remove* .... Labor ....1.56 ▶ Poplar or red oak. Ornate inside pattern.	ea	$1.56	$18.86	$20.42
	Stair bracket, custom grade *Replace* Materials ......16.70 Labor ....3.96 *Remove* .... Labor ....1.56 ▶ Poplar or red oak. Very ornate inside pattern.	ea	$1.56	$20.66	$22.22
	Remove stair bracket for work, then reinstall *Replace* .... Labor 6.48	ea	—	$6.48	$6.48
STAIR TREAD ▶ TRIM *Up to 3/4" cove, quarter-round, cove, or similar installed beneath the open end of the tread.*	**Pine molding trim beneath tread** *Replace* Materials .... .62 Labor ....4.70 *Remove* .... Labor .... .55	ea	$.55	$5.32	$5.87
	Red oak molding trim beneath tread *Replace* Materials .... .98 Labor ....4.70 *Remove* .... Labor .... .55	ea	$.55	$5.68	$6.23
PINE NEWEL ▶ *for 1-1/2" balusters ▷ newel is 3-1/2" to 4" wide*	**Pine newel post for 1-1/2" balusters** *Replace* Materials ......48.80 Labor ....41.80 *Remove* .... Labor 5.43	ea	$5.43	$90.60	$96.03
	Pine fluted newel post for 1-1/2" balusters *Replace* Materials ......64.80 Labor ....41.80 *Remove* .... Labor 5.43	ea	$5.43	$106.60	$112.03
	Pine spiral newel post for 1-1/2" balusters *Replace* Materials ......66.60 Labor ....41.80 *Remove* .... Labor 5.43	ea	$5.43	$108.40	$113.83

Item Description	Unit	Remove	Replace	Total	
Pine newel post for 2-1/2″ balusters	ea	$5.43	$100.30	$105.73	◁ for 2-1/2″ balusters newel is 4″ to 4-1/2″ wide.
Replace Materials......58.50 Labor...........41.80					
Remove........................ Labor 5.43					
Pine fluted newel post for 2-1/2″ balusters	ea	$5.43	$119.40	$124.83	
Replace Materials......77.60 Labor...........41.80					
Remove........................ Labor 5.43					
Pine spiral newel post for 2-1/2″ balusters	ea	$5.43	$121.40	$126.83	
Replace Materials......79.60 Labor...........41.80					
Remove........................ Labor 5.43					
Pine newel post for 3-1/2″ balusters	ea	$5.43	$112.00	$117.43	◁ for 3-1/2″ balusters newel is 4-1/2″ to 5″ wide.
Replace Materials......70.20 Labor...........41.80					
Remove........................ Labor 5.43					
Pine fluted newel post for 3-1/2″ balusters	ea	$5.43	$135.00	$140.43	
Replace Materials......93.20 Labor...........41.80					
Remove........................ Labor 5.43					
Pine spiral newel post for 3-1/2″ balusters	ea	$5.43	$137.40	$142.83	
Replace Materials......95.60 Labor...........41.80					
Remove........................ Labor 5.43					
Pine newel post for 5-1/2″ balusters	ea	$5.43	$153.40	$158.83	◁ for 5-1/2″ balusters newel is 6″ to 7″ wide.
Replace Materials......111.60 Labor...........41.80					
Remove........................ Labor 5.43					
Pine fluted newel post for 5-1/2″ balusters	ea	$5.43	$189.80	$195.23	
Replace Materials ....148.00 Labor...........41.80					
Remove........................ Labor 5.43					
Pine spiral newel post for 5-1/2″ balusters	ea	$5.43	$193.80	$199.23	
Replace Materials.....152.00 Labor...........41.80					
Remove........................ Labor 5.43					
Poplar newel post for 1-1/2″ balusters	ea	$5.43	$123.10	$128.53	◀ **POPLAR NEWEL** ◁ for 1-1/2″ balusters newel is 3-1/2″ to 4″ wide.
Replace Materials......81.30 Labor...........41.80					
Remove........................ Labor 5.43					
Poplar fluted newel post for 1-1/2″ balusters	ea	$5.43	$149.80	$155.23	
Replace Materials ....108.00 Labor...........41.80					
Remove........................ Labor 5.43					
Poplar spiral newel post for 1-1/2″ balusters	ea	$5.43	$152.80	$158.23	
Replace Materials .....111.00 Labor...........41.80					
Remove........................ Labor 5.43					
Poplar newel post for 2-1/2″ balusters	ea	$5.43	$139.20	$144.63	◁ for 2-1/2″ balusters newel is 4″ to 4-1/2″ wide.
Replace Materials......97.40 Labor...........41.80					
Remove........................ Labor 5.43					
Poplar fluted newel post for 2-1/2″ balusters	ea	$5.43	$170.80	$176.23	
Replace Materials ....129.00 Labor...........41.80					
Remove........................ Labor 5.43					
Poplar spiral newel post for 2-1/2″ balusters	ea	$5.43	$174.80	$180.23	
Replace Materials.....133.00 Labor...........41.80					
Remove........................ Labor 5.43					
Poplar newel post for 3-1/2″ balusters	ea	$5.43	$158.80	$164.23	◁ for 3-1/2″ balusters newel is 4-1/2″ to 5″ wide.
Replace Materials .....117.00 Labor...........41.80					
Remove........................ Labor 5.43					

RELATED ITEMS

Columns	71
Finish Carpentry	199
porch posts	231
Rough Carpentry	409
exterior deck stairs	430

Item Description	Unit	Remove	Replace	Total
POPLAR NEWEL ▶ *continued*				
Poplar fluted newel post for 3-1/2" balusters	ea	$5.43	$196.80	$202.23
Replace Materials.....155.00 Labor...........41.80				
Remove..................... Labor 5.43				
Poplar spiral newel post for 3-1/2" balusters	ea	$5.43	$200.80	$206.23
Replace Materials.....159.00 Labor...........41.80				
Remove..................... Labor 5.43				
for 5-1/2" balusters ▷ *newel is 6" to 8" wide* **Poplar newel post for 5-1/2" balusters**	ea	$5.43	$227.80	$233.23
Replace Materials ....186.00 Labor...........41.80				
Remove..................... Labor 5.43				
Poplar fluted newel post for 5-1/2" balusters	ea	$5.43	$288.80	$294.23
Replace Materials.....247.00 Labor...........41.80				
Remove..................... Labor 5.43				
Poplar spiral newel post for 5-1/2" balusters	ea	$5.43	$294.80	$300.23
Replace Materials.....253.00 Labor...........41.80				
Remove..................... Labor 5.43				
REDWOOD NEWEL ▶ **for 1-1/2" balusters ▷** *newel is 3-1/2" to 4" wide* **Redwood newel post for 1-1/2" balusters**	ea	$5.43	$132.90	$138.33
Replace Materials ......91.10 Labor...........41.80				
Remove..................... Labor 5.43				
Redwood fluted newel post for 1-1/2" balusters	ea	$5.43	$162.80	$168.23
Replace Materials.....121.00 Labor...........41.80				
Remove..................... Labor 5.43				
Redwood spiral newel post for 1-1/2" balusters	ea	$5.43	$165.80	$171.23
Replace Materials.....124.00 Labor...........41.80				
Remove..................... Labor 5.43				
for 2-1/2" balusters ▷ *newel is 4" to 4-1/2" wide* **Redwood newel post for 2-1/2" balusters**	ea	$5.43	$150.80	$156.23
Replace Materials ....109.00 Labor...........41.80				
Remove..................... Labor 5.43				
Redwood fluted newel post for 2-1/2" balusters	ea	$5.43	$186.80	$192.23
Replace Materials.....145.00 Labor...........41.80				
Remove..................... Labor 5.43				
Redwood spiral newel post for 2-1/2" balusters	ea	$5.43	$190.80	$196.23
Replace Materials.....149.00 Labor...........41.80				
Remove..................... Labor 5.43				
for 3-1/2" balusters ▷ *newel is 4-1/2" to 5" wide.* **Redwood newel post for 3-1/2" balusters**	ea	$5.43	$172.80	$178.23
Replace Materials.....131.00 Labor...........41.80				
Remove..................... Labor 5.43				
Redwood fluted newel post for 3-1/2" balusters	ea	$5.43	$215.80	$221.23
Replace Materials.....174.00 Labor...........41.80				
Remove..................... Labor 5.43				
Redwood spiral newel post for 3-1/2" balusters	ea	$5.43	$220.80	$226.23
Replace Materials.....179.00 Labor...........41.80				
Remove..................... Labor 5.43				
for 5-1/2" balusters ▷ *newel is 6" to 8" wide* **Redwood newel post for 5-1/2" balusters**	ea	$5.43	$249.80	$255.23
Replace Materials....208.00 Labor...........41.80				
Remove..................... Labor 5.43				
Redwood fluted newel post for 5-1/2" balusters	ea	$5.43	$318.80	$324.23
Replace Materials ....277.00 Labor...........41.80				
Remove..................... Labor 5.43				

Item Description	Unit	Remove	Replace	Total
Redwood spiral newel post for 5-1/2" balusters	ea	$5.43	$325.80	$331.23
Replace Materials....284.00 Labor..........41.80				
Remove....................... Labor 5.43				
Red oak newel post for 1-1/2" balusters	ea	$5.43	$161.80	$167.23
Replace Materials.....120.00 Labor..........41.80				
Remove....................... Labor 5.43				
Red oak fluted newel post for 1-1/2" balusters	ea	$5.43	$200.80	$206.23
Replace Materials....159.00 Labor..........41.80				
Remove....................... Labor 5.43				
Red oak spiral newel post for 1-1/2" balusters	ea	$5.43	$204.80	$210.23
Replace Materials.....163.00 Labor..........41.80				
Remove....................... Labor 5.43				
Red oak hand-carved newel post for 1-1/2" balusters	ea	$5.43	$260.80	$266.23
Replace Materials.....219.00 Labor..........41.80				
Remove....................... Labor 5.43				
Red oak heavy hand-carved newel post for 1-1/2" balusters	ea	$5.43	$277.80	$283.23
Replace Materials....236.00 Labor..........41.80				
Remove....................... Labor 5.43				
Red oak newel post for 2-1/2" balusters	ea	$5.43	$177.80	$183.23
Replace Materials.....136.00 Labor..........41.80				
Remove....................... Labor 5.43				
Red oak fluted newel post for 2-1/2" balusters	ea	$5.43	$221.80	$227.23
Replace Materials ....180.00 Labor..........41.80				
Remove....................... Labor 5.43				
Red oak spiral newel post for 2-1/2" balusters	ea	$5.43	$226.80	$232.23
Replace Materials.....185.00 Labor..........41.80				
Remove....................... Labor 5.43				
Red oak hand-carved newel post for 2-1/2" balusters	ea	$5.43	$289.80	$295.23
Replace Materials ....248.00 Labor..........41.80				
Remove....................... Labor 5.43				
Red oak heavy hand-carved newel post for 2-1/2" balusters	ea	$5.43	$309.80	$315.23
Replace Materials ....268.00 Labor..........41.80				
Remove....................... Labor 5.43				
Red oak newel post for 3-1/2" balusters	ea	$5.43	$204.80	$210.23
Replace Materials.....163.00 Labor..........41.80				
Remove....................... Labor 5.43				
Red oak fluted newel post for 3-1/2" balusters	ea	$5.43	$257.80	$263.23
Replace Materials.....216.00 Labor..........41.80				
Remove....................... Labor 5.43				
Red oak spiral newel post for 3-1/2" balusters	ea	$5.43	$263.80	$269.23
Replace Materials....222.00 Labor..........41.80				
Remove....................... Labor 5.43				
Red oak hand-carved newel post for 3-1/2" balusters	ea	$5.43	$312.80	$318.23
Replace Materials ....271.00 Labor..........41.80				
Remove....................... Labor 5.43				
Red oak heavy hand-carved newel post for 3-1/2" balusters	ea	$5.43	$330.80	$336.23
Replace Materials ....289.00 Labor..........41.80				
Remove....................... Labor 5.43				

◀ **RED OAK NEWEL**
◁ **for 1-1/2" balusters**
newel is 3-1/2"
to 4" wide.

◁ **for 2-1/2" balusters**
newel is 4" to
4-1/2" wide.

◁ **for 3-1/2" balusters**
newel is 4-1/2"
to 5" wide.

RELATED ITEMS

Columns 71
Finish Carpentry..........199
porch posts...................231
Rough Carpentry 409
exterior deck stairs 430

Item Description		Unit	Remove	Replace	Total
RED OAK NEWEL ▶ *continued* **for 5-1/2″ balusters** ▷ *newel is 6″ to 8″ wide*	**Red oak newel post for 5-1/2″ balusters** *Replace* Materials ....259.00 Labor ....41.80 *Remove*...................... Labor 5.43	ea	$5.43	$300.80	$306.23
	Red oak fluted newel post for 5-1/2″ balusters *Replace* Materials ....343.00 Labor ....41.80 *Remove*...................... Labor 5.43	ea	$5.43	$384.80	$390.23
	Red oak spiral newel post for 5-1/2″ balusters *Replace* Materials ....353.00 Labor ....41.80 *Remove*...................... Labor 5.43	ea	$5.43	$394.80	$400.23
	Red oak hand-carved newel post for 5-1/2″ balusters *Replace* Materials ....482.00 Labor ....41.80 *Remove*...................... Labor 5.43	ea	$5.43	$523.80	$529.23
	Red oak heavy hand-carved newel post for 5-1/2″ balusters *Replace* Materials.....518.00 Labor ....41.80 *Remove*...................... Labor 5.43	ea	$5.43	$559.80	$565.23
	Remove newel post for work, then reinstall *Replace* .... Labor 61.30	ea	—	$61.30	$61.30
ADD FOR OTHER ▶ **WOOD SPECIES** *Add to the cost of poplar stair components.*	**Add 24% for mahogany** **Add 43% for cherry** **Add 11% for maple** **Add 2% for birch**				

TIME & MATERIAL CHARTS (selected items)

Stairs Materials

See **Stairs** material prices with the line items and waste information in the **QuickFinder** column.

Stairs Labor

LABORER	BASE WAGE	PAID LEAVE	TRUE WAGE	FICA	FUTA	WORKER'S COMP.	UNEMPLOY. INSUR.	HEALTH INSUR.	RETIRE (401k)	LIABILITY INSUR.	COST PER HOUR
Carpenter	$24.30	1.90	$26.20	2.00	.21	5.15	2.28	2.92	.79	3.93	**$43.50**
Demolition laborer	$14.40	1.12	$15.52	1.19	.12	5.01	1.35	2.92	.47	2.33	**$28.90**

Paid Leave is calculated based on two weeks paid vacation, one week sick leave, and seven paid holidays. Employer's matching portion of **FICA** is 7.65 percent. **FUTA** (Federal Unemployment) is .8 percent. **Worker's compensation** for the stairs trade was calculated using a national average of 19.63 percent. **Unemployment insurance** was calculated using a national average of 8.7 percent. **Health insurance** was calculated based on a projected national average for 2005 of $580 per employee (and family when applicable) per month. Employer pays 80 percent for a per month cost of $464 per employee. **Retirement** is based on a 401(k) retirement program with employer matching of 50 percent. Employee contributions to the 401(k) plan are an average of 6 percent of the true wage. **Liability insurance** is based on a national average of 14.0 percent.

Stairs Labor Productivity

WORK DESCRIPTION	LABORER	COST PER HOUR	PRODUCTIVITY	UNIT PRICE
Demolition				
remove utility stairs	demolition laborer	$28.90	.101	$2.92 *st*
remove stairs	demolition laborer	$28.90	.122	$3.53 *st*
remove 1/4 turn stairs	demolition laborer	$28.90	.135	$3.90 *st*
remove 1/2 turn stairs	demolition laborer	$28.90	.150	$4.34 *st*
remove circular stairs	demolition laborer	$28.90	.158	$4.57 *st*
remove spiral stairs	demolition laborer	$28.90	.123	$3.55 *st*
remove disappearing attic stairs	demolition laborer	$28.90	.270	$7.80 *ea*
remove stair balustrade	demolition laborer	$28.90	.053	$1.53 *lf*
remove stair bracket	demolition laborer	$28.90	.054	$1.56 *ea*
remove newel post	demolition laborer	$28.90	.188	$5.43 *ea*
Build 3' wide stairs with three stringers				
utility stairs	finish carpenter	$43.50	.361	$15.70 *st*
Build 3' wide straight stairs with four stringers				
3' wide enclosed	finish carpenter	$43.50	.474	$20.60 *st*
3' wide, one side open	finish carpenter	$43.50	.485	$21.10 *st*
3' wide , two sides open	finish carpenter	$43.50	.518	$22.50 *st*
Build 3' wide 1/4 turn stairs with four stringers, 3' x 3' landing				
3' wide enclosed	finish carpenter	$43.50	.826	$35.90 *st*
3' wide enclosed & oak plank on landing	finish carpenter	$43.50	1.02	$44.40 *st*
3' wide, one side open	finish carpenter	$43.50	.855	$37.20 *st*
3' wide, one side open & oak plank on landing	finish carpenter	$43.50	1.04	$45.20 *st*
3' wide, two sides open	finish carpenter	$43.50	.885	$38.50 *st*
3' wide, two sides open & oak plank on landing	finish carpenter	$43.50	1.05	$45.70 *st*
Build 3' wide 1/2 turn stairs with four stringers, 6' x 3' landing				
3' wide enclosed	finish carpenter	$43.50	.909	$39.50 *st*
3' wide enclosed with oak plank on landing	finish carpenter	$43.50	1.12	$48.70 *st*
3' wide, one side open	finish carpenter	$43.50	.943	$41.00 *st*
3' wide, one side open & oak plank on landing	finish carpenter	$43.50	1.15	$50.00 *st*
3' wide, two sides open	finish carpenter	$43.50	.971	$42.20 *st*
3' wide, two sides open & oak plank on landing	finish carpenter	$43.50	1.16	$50.50 *st*
Additional stair costs				
add to build platform winders	finish carpenter	$43.50	.400	$17.40 *st*
add to build mitered corner on bottom step	finish carpenter	$43.50	2.33	$101.00 *ea*
add to install bull-nose starting step	finish carpenter	$43.50	.493	$21.40 *ea*
Install false treads and risers				
closed end	finish carpenter	$43.50	.070	$3.05 *ea*
open end	finish carpenter	$43.50	.090	$3.92 *ea*
Build 3' wide circular stairs				
enclosed	finish carpenter	$43.50	11.6	$505.00 *st*
one side open	finish carpenter	$43.50	11.8	$513.00 *st*
two sides open	finish carpenter	$43.50	11.9	$518.00 *st*
Install prefabricated spiral stairs				
all grades	finish carpenter	$43.50	.855	$37.20 *st*
Install disappearing attic stairs				
all grades	finish carpenter	$43.50	2.38	$104.00 *ea*
remove for work, then reinstall	finish carpenter	$43.50	3.33	$145.00 *ea*
Install wood stair balustrade				
with 1-1/2" balusters	finish carpenter	$43.50	1.32	$57.40 *lf*
with 2-1/2" balusters	finish carpenter	$43.50	1.33	$57.90 *lf*
with 3-1/2" balusters	finish carpenter	$43.50	1.35	$58.70 *lf*
with 5-1/2" balusters	finish carpenter	$43.50	1.41	$61.30 *lf*
remove for work, then reinstall	finish carpenter	$43.50	2.38	$104.00 *lf*
Install newel post				
install	finish carpenter	$43.50	.962	$41.80 *ea*
remove for work, then reinstall	finish carpenter	$43.50	1.41	$61.30 *ea*

✐ NOTES: _____

_____

_____

_____

_____

_____

_____

_____

_____

_____

_____

_____

_____

_____

_____

_____

_____

_____

_____

_____

_____

_____

_____

_____

_____

_____

_____

_____

_____

_____

_____

_____

_____

_____ end

36 .... *Suspended Ceilings*

Item Description	Unit	Remove	Replace	Total	
12" x 12" concealed grid suspended ceiling tile, smooth face	sf	$.17	$1.88	$2.05	◄ **12" x 12"** TILE
Replace Materials........1.21 Labor............ .67					*Prices are for tile and*
Remove .... Labor............ .17					*installation only. For*
					concealed grid systems,
12" x 12" concealed grid suspended ceiling tile, fissured face	sf	$.17	$2.09	$2.26	*see below.*
Replace Materials........1.42 Labor............ .67					
Remove .... Labor............ .17					
12" x 12" concealed grid suspended ceiling tile, textured face	sf	$.17	$2.30	$2.47	
Replace Materials........1.63 Labor............ .67					
Remove .... Labor............ .17					
12" x 12" concealed grid suspended ceiling tile, patterned face	sf	$.17	$2.43	$2.60	
Replace Materials........1.76 Labor............ .67					
Remove .... Labor............ .17					
Grid for 12" x 12" concealed grid system	sf	$.17	$2.02	$2.19	◄ **12" x 12"** GRID
Replace Materials........1.31 Labor............ .71					
Remove .... Labor............ .17					
► Includes main runners, cross tees, wires, and eyelet screws. Does not include tiles.					
Access panel in 12" x 12" concealed grid system	ea	$2.80	$85.60	$88.40	
Replace Materials......60.00 Labor..........25.60					
Remove .... Labor............2.80					
Re-level sagging 12" x 12" concealed suspended grid	sf	–	$.69	$.69	◁ re-level
Replace Materials.......... Labor............ .69					
2' x 4' suspended ceiling tile, smooth face	sf	$.14	$.85	$.99	◄ **2' x 4'** TILES
Replace Materials........ .52 Labor............ .33					
Remove .... Labor............ .14					
2' x 4' suspended ceiling tile, fissured face	sf	$.14	$1.02	$1.16	
Replace Materials........ .69 Labor............ .33					
Remove .... Labor............ .14					
2' x 4' suspended ceiling tile, textured face	sf	$.14	$1.24	$1.38	
Replace Materials........ .91 Labor............ .33					
Remove .... Labor............ .14					
2' x 4' suspended ceiling tile, patterned face	sf	$.14	$1.50	$1.64	
Replace Materials........1.17 Labor............ .33					
Remove .... Labor............ .14					
Add for fire-rated 2' x 4' suspended ceiling tile installed with clips	sf	–	$.68	$.68	◁ add for fire-rated tile
Replace Materials........ .38 Labor............ .30					
2' x 4' polystyrene cracked-ice or mist-white luminous panel	sf	$.14	$1.58	$1.72	◄ **2' x 4'**
Replace Materials........1.28 Labor............ .30					**LUMINOUS PANEL**
Remove .... Labor............ .14					
2' x 4' acrylic cracked-ice or mist-white luminous panel	sf	$.14	$2.76	$2.90	
Replace Materials........2.46 Labor............ .30					
Remove .... Labor............ .14					

RELATED ITEMS
Acoustic Ceilings............15
Drywall.......................133
Electrical
    drop-in fixtures..............166

	Item Description	Unit	Remove	Replace	Total
2' x 4' **LUMINOUS PANEL** *continued*	**2' x 4' polystyrene egg crate luminous panel** *Replace* Materials........1.25 Labor............. .30 *Remove* .... Labor............. .14	sf	$.14	$1.55	$1.69
	2' x 4' acrylic egg crate luminous panel *Replace* Materials........4.57 Labor............. .30 *Remove* .... Labor............. .14	sf	$.14	$4.87	$5.01
	2' x 4' acrylic egg crate luminous panel with stainless-steel finish *Replace* Materials........4.99 Labor............. .30 *Remove* .... Labor............. .14	sf	$.14	$5.29	$5.43
	2' x 4' acrylic egg crate luminous panel with brass finish *Replace* Materials........5.04 Labor............. .30 *Remove* .... Labor............. .14	sf	$.14	$5.34	$5.48
	2' x 4' square crate polystyrene luminous panel *Replace* Materials........1.21 Labor............. .30 *Remove* .... Labor............. .14	sf	$.14	$1.51	$1.65
	2' x 4' square crate acrylic luminous panel *Replace* Materials........4.30 Labor............. .30 *Remove* .... Labor............. .14	sf	$.14	$4.60	$4.74
	2' x 4' square crate acrylic luminous panel with stainless-steel finish *Replace* Materials........4.86 Labor............. .30 *Remove* .... Labor............. .14	sf	$.14	$5.16	$5.30
	2' x 4' square crate acrylic luminous panel with brass finish *Replace* Materials........4.92 Labor............. .30 *Remove* .... Labor............. .14	sf	$.14	$5.22	$5.36
2' x 4' GRID *Includes main runners 4'* *on center. Cross tees,* *wire, and eyelet screws.* *Does not include tiles or* *luminous panels.*	**2' x 4' suspended grid** *Replace* Materials .... .49 Labor............. .46 *Remove* .... Labor............. .12	sf	$.12	$.95	$1.07
	2' x 4' colored suspended grid *Replace* Materials .... .55 Labor............. .46 *Remove* .... Labor............. .12	sf	$.12	$1.01	$1.13
	2' x 4' brass finish suspended grid *Replace* Materials .... .76 Labor............. .46 *Remove* .... Labor............. .12	sf	$.12	$1.22	$1.34
	2' x 4' stainless steel finish suspended grid *Replace* Materials .... .93 Labor............. .46 *Remove* .... Labor............. .12	sf	$.12	$1.39	$1.51
add for fire-rated grid ▷	**Add for fire-rated 2' x 4' suspended grid** *Replace* Materials .... .32	sf	–	$.32	$.32
2' x 4' **NARROW GRID** *Includes main runners 4'* *on center. Cross tees,* *wire, and eyelet screws.* *Does not include tiles or* *luminous panels.*	**2' x 4' narrow suspended grid** *Replace* Materials .... .52 Labor............. .46 *Remove* .... Labor............. .12	sf	$.12	$.98	$1.10
	2' x 4' colored narrow suspended grid *Replace* Materials .... .52 Labor............. .46 *Remove* .... Labor............. .12	sf	$.12	$.98	$1.10
	2' x 4' brass finish narrow suspended grid *Replace* Materials .... .91 Labor............. .46 *Remove* .... Labor............. .12	sf	$.12	$1.37	$1.49

Item Description	Unit	Remove	Replace	Total	
2' x 4' stainless steel finish narrow suspended grid	sf	$.12	$1.39	$1.51	
Replace Materials .... .93 Labor............ .46					
Remove .... Labor............ .12					
Add for fire-rated 2' x 4' narrow suspended grid	sf	–	$.82	$.82	◁ add for fire-rated grid
Replace Materials .... .36 Labor............ .46					
Re-level sagging 2' x 4' suspended grid	sf	–	$.49	$.49	◀ RE-LEVEL 2' X 4' GRID
Replace Labor............ .49					
Remove 2' x 4' tiles for work, then reinstall	sf	–	$.38	$.38	◀ REMOVE 2' X 4' TILES & REINSTALL
Replace .... Labor............ .38					
Remove 2' x 4' tiles & blanket or insulation for work, then reinstall	sf	–	$.46	$.46	
Replace .... Labor............ .46					
2' x 2' suspended ceiling tile, smooth face	sf	$.12	$.96	$1.08	◀ 2' X 2' TILES
Replace Materials .... .63 Labor............ .33					
Remove .... Labor............ .12					
2' x 2' suspended ceiling tile, fissured face	sf	$.12	$1.47	$1.59	
Replace Materials ...... 1.14 Labor............ .33					
Remove .... Labor............ .12					
2' x 2' suspended ceiling tile, textured face	sf	$.12	$1.42	$1.54	
Replace Materials ...... 1.09 Labor............ .33					
Remove .... Labor............ .12					
2' x 2' suspended ceiling tile, patterned face	sf	$.12	$1.74	$1.86	
Replace Materials ....1.41 Labor............ .33					
Remove .... Labor............ .12					
Add for fire-rated 2' x 2' suspended ceiling tile installed with clips	sf	–	$.78	$.78	◁ add for fire-rated tile
Replace Materials .... .45 Labor............ .33					
2' x 2' recessed edge suspended ceiling tile, smooth face	sf	$.12	$1.05	$1.17	◀ RECESSED 2' X 2' TILES
Replace Materials .... .72 Labor............ .33					
Remove .... Labor............ .12					
2' x 2' recessed edge suspended ceiling tile, fissured face	sf	$.12	$1.28	$1.40	
Replace Materials .... .95 Labor............ .33					
Remove .... Labor............ .12					
2' x 2' recessed edge suspended ceiling tile, textured face	sf	$.12	$1.59	$1.71	
Replace Materials ....1.26 Labor............ .33					
Remove .... Labor............ .12					
2' x 2' recessed edge suspended ceiling tile, patterned face	sf	$.12	$1.95	$2.07	
Replace Materials ....1.62 Labor............ .33					
Remove .... Labor............ .12					
Add for fire-rated 2' x 2' recessed edge tile installed with clips	sf	–	$.36	$.36	◁ add for fire-rated tile
Replace Materials .... .03 Labor............ .33					
2' x 2' polystyrene cracked-ice or mist-white luminous panel	sf	$.12	$1.72	$1.84	◀ 2' X 2' LUMINOUS PANEL
Replace Materials ....1.54 Labor............ .18					
Remove .... Labor............ .12					
2' x 2' acrylic cracked-ice or mist-white luminous panel	sf	$.12	$3.12	$3.24	
Replace Materials ....2.94 Labor............ .18					
Remove .... Labor............ .12					

RELATED ITEMS

Acoustic Ceilings............15
Drywall........................133
Electrical
   drop in fixtures..............166

Item Description	Unit	Remove	Replace	Total
2' x 2' polystyrene egg crate luminous panel	sf	$.12	$1.69	$1.81
Replace Materials........1.51 Labor.............. .18				
Remove .... Labor.............. .12				
2' x 2' acrylic egg crate luminous panel	sf	$.12	$5.67	$5.79
Replace Materials........5.49 Labor.............. .18				
Remove .... Labor.............. .12				
2' x 2' acrylic egg crate luminous panel with stainless steel finish	sf	$.12	$6.17	$6.29
Replace Materials........5.99 Labor.............. .18				
Remove .... Labor.............. .12				
2' x 2' acrylic egg crate luminous panel with brass finish	sf	$.12	$6.22	$6.34
Replace Materials........6.04 Labor.............. .18				
Remove .... Labor.............. .12				
2' x 2' square crate polystyrene luminous panel	sf	$.12	$1.64	$1.76
Replace Materials........1.46 Labor.............. .18				
Remove .... Labor.............. .12				
2' x 2' square crate acrylic luminous panel	sf	$.12	$5.34	$5.46
Replace Materials........5.16 Labor.............. .18				
Remove .... Labor.............. .12				
2' x 2' square crate acrylic luminous panel with stainless-steel finish	sf	$.12	$6.01	$6.13
Replace Materials........5.83 Labor.............. .18				
Remove .... Labor.............. .12				
2' x 2' square crate acrylic luminous panel with brass finish	sf	$.12	$6.09	$6.21
Replace Materials........5.91 Labor.............. .18				
Remove .... Labor.............. .12				
2' x 2' suspended grid	sf	$.12	$1.24	$1.36
Replace Materials........ .78 Labor.............. .46				
Remove .... Labor.............. .12				
2' x 2' colored suspended grid	sf	$.12	$1.34	$1.46
Replace Materials........ .88 Labor.............. .46				
Remove .... Labor.............. .12				
2' x 2' brass finish suspended grid	sf	$.12	$1.58	$1.70
Replace Materials........1.12 Labor.............. .46				
Remove .... Labor.............. .12				
2' x 2' stainless steel finish suspended grid	sf	$.12	$1.64	$1.76
Replace Materials........1.18 Labor.............. .46				
Remove .... Labor.............. .12				
Add for fire-rated 2' x 2' suspended grid	sf	–	$.65	$.65
Replace Materials........ .65				
2' x 2' narrow suspended grid	sf	$.12	$1.27	$1.39
Replace Materials........ .81 Labor.............. .46				
Remove .... Labor.............. .12				
2' x 2' colored narrow suspended grid	sf	$.12	$1.30	$1.42
Replace Materials........ .84 Labor.............. .46				
Remove .... Labor.............. .12				
2' x 2' brass finish narrow suspended grid	sf	$.12	$1.58	$1.70
Replace Materials........1.12 Labor.............. .46				
Remove .... Labor.............. .12				

2' x 2'
LUMINOUS PANEL
continued

2' x 2' GRID ►
*Includes main runners 4'
on center. Cross tees,
wire, and eyelet screws.
Does not include tiles or
luminous panels.*

add for fire-rated grid ▷

2' x 2' ►
NARROW GRID
*Includes main runners 4'
on center. Cross tees,
wire, and eyelet screws.
Does not include tiles or
luminous panels.*

Item Description	Unit	Remove	Replace	Total	
2' x 2' stainless steel finish suspended grid *Replace* Materials........1.45 Labor............ .46 *Remove* .... Labor............ .12	sf	$.12	$1.91	$2.03	
Add for fire-rated 2' x 2' narrow suspended grid *Replace* Materials........ .65	sf	–	$.65	$.65	◁ add for fire-rated grid
Re-level sagging 2' x 2' suspended grid *Replace* Materials.......... Labor............ .57	sf	–	$.57	$.57	◀ **RE-LEVEL 2' x 2' GRID**
Remove 2' x 2' tiles for work, then reinstall *Replace* Materials.......... Labor............ .40	sf	–	$.40	$.40	◀ **REMOVE 2' x 2' TILES & REINSTALL**
Remove 2' x 2' tiles & blanket for work, then reinstall *Replace* Materials.......... Labor............ .49	sf	–	$.49	$.49	
Minimum charge for suspended ceiling work *Replace* Materials......55.00 Labor............62.30	ea	–	$117.30	$117.30	◀ **MINIMUM CHARGE**
Suspended ceiling cold-air return panel *Replace* Materials......50.00 Labor............21.50 *Remove* .... Labor............3.90	ea	3.90	$71.50	$75.40	◀ **DROP-IN HVAC PANELS**
Suspended ceiling air diffuser panel *Replace* Materials......50.00 Labor............21.50 *Remove* .... Labor............3.90	ea	3.90	$71.50	$75.40	
2" sound absorbing blanket above suspended grid system *Replace* Materials........ .44 labor............ .32 *Remove* .... Labor............ .23	sf	$.23	$.76	$.99	◀ **SOUND BLANKET** *Sound absorbing blanket installed above grid.*
3" sound absorbing blanket above suspended grid system *Replace* Materials........ .68 labor............ .32 *Remove* .... Labor............ .26	sf	$.26	$1.00	$1.26	

RELATED ITEMS
Acoustic Ceilings............15
Drywall.....................133
Electrical
   drop in fixtures.............166

✍ NOTES: _____

_____ end

TIME & MATERIAL CHARTS *(selected items)*

Suspended Ceilings Materials

DESCRIPTION	PRICE	GROSS COVERAGE	WASTE	NET COVERAGE	UNIT PRICE
Suspended ceiling with concealed grid					
wall angle............	$6.10 *per 12' stick*	83	4%	79.68	**$.08** *sf*
main tee..............	$7.80 *per 12' stick*	15.00	4%	14.40	**$.54** *sf*
cross tee (12" x 12" installation)...........	$.75 *per 1' stick*	1.14	4%	1.09	**$.69** *sf*
Suspended ceiling grid baked enamel finish					
wall angle............	$4.80 *per 12' stick*	43.20	4%	41.47	**$.12** *sf*
main tee..............	$7.80 *per 12' stick*	27.48	4%	26.38	**$.30** *sf*
cross tee in 2' x 4' installation............	$2.60 *per 4' stick*	41.60	4%	39.94	**$.07** *sf*
cross tee in 2' x 2' installation............	$1.60 *per 2' stick*	4.58	4%	4.40	**$.36** *sf*

. . . More ➤

Suspended Ceilings Materials *continued*

DESCRIPTION	MATERIAL PRICE	GROSS COVERAGE	WASTE	NET COVERAGE	UNIT PRICE
12" x 12" suspended tile for concealed grid system					
smooth face	**$1.15** *per tile*	1	5%	.95	**$1.21** *sf*
patterned face	**$1.67** *per tile*	1	5%	.95	**$1.76** *sf*
add for fire rating	**$.41** *per tile*	1	5%	.95	**$.43** *sf*
2' x 4' suspended tile					
smooth face	**$3.97** *per tile*	8	5%	7.6	**$.52** *sf*
patterned face	**$8.91** *per tile*	8	5%	7.6	**$1.17** *sf*
add for 2' x 4' tile with fire rating	**$2.59** *per tile*	8	5%	7.6	**$.34** *sf*
2' x 4' luminous panel					
polystyrene cracked-ice or mist-white	**$9.80** *per panel*	8	4%	7.68	**$1.28** *sf*
acrylic mist-white	**$18.90** *per panel*	8	4%	7.68	**$2.46** *sf*
polystyrene egg crate	**$9.60** *per panel*	8	4%	7.68	**$1.25** *sf*
acrylic egg crate	**$35.10** *per panel*	8	4%	7.68	**$4.57** *sf*
acrylic egg crate with stainless-steel finish	**$38.30** *per panel*	8	4%	7.68	**$4.99** *sf*
acrylic egg crate with brass finish	**$38.70** *per panel*	8	4%	7.68	**$5.04** *sf*

Suspended Ceiling Labor

LABORER	BASE WAGE	PAID LEAVE	TRUE WAGE	FICA	FUTA	WORKER'S COMP.	UNEMPLOY. INSUR.	HEALTH INSUR.	RETIRE (401K)	LIABILITY INSUR.	COST PER HOUR
Installer	$23.60	1.84	$25.44	1.95	.20	3.18	2.21	2.92	.76	3.82	**$40.50**
Installer's helper	$17.10	1.33	$18.43	1.41	.15	2.31	1.60	2.92	.55	2.76	**$30.10**
Demolition laborer	$14.40	1.12	$15.52	1.19	.12	5.01	1.35	2.92	.47	2.33	**$28.90**

Paid Leave is calculated based on two weeks paid vacation, one week sick leave, and seven paid holidays. Employer's matching portion of **FICA** is 7.65 percent. **FUTA** (Federal Unemployment) is .8 percent. **Worker's compensation** for the suspended ceilings trade was calculated using a national average of 12.48 percent. **Unemployment insurance** was calculated using a national average of 8.7 percent. **Health insurance** was calculated based on a projected national average for 2005 of $580 per employee (and family when applicable) per month. Employer pays 80 percent for a per month cost of $464 per employee. **Retirement** is based on a 401(k) retirement program with employer matching of 50 percent. Employee contributions to the 401(k) plan are an average of 6 percent of the true wage. **Liability insurance** is based on a national average of 14.0 percent.

Suspended Ceiling Labor Productivity

WORK DESCRIPTION	LABORER	COST PER HOUR	PRODUCTIVITY	UNIT PRICE
Demolition				
remove 2' x 4' ceiling tiles	demolition laborer	$28.90	.005	**$.14** *sf*
remove 2' x 4' suspended grid only	demolition laborer	$28.90	.004	**$.12** *sf*
remove 2' x 4' suspended tiles & grid	demolition laborer	$28.90	.009	**$.26** *sf*
remove 2' x 2' suspended tiles only	demolition laborer	$28.90	.004	**$.12** *sf*
remove 2' x 2' grid only	demolition laborer	$28.90	.004	**$.12** *sf*
remove 2' x 2' tiles & grid	demolition laborer	$28.90	.010	**$.29** *sf*
remove 12" x 12" ceiling tiles only	demolition laborer	$28.90	.006	**$.17** *sf*
remove 12" x 12" grid only	demolition laborer	$28.90	.006	**$.17** *sf*
remove 12" x 12" tiles & grid	demolition laborer	$28.90	.011	**$.32** *sf*
Suspended ceiling installation crew				
install suspended ceiling	installer	$40.50		
install suspended ceiling	installer's helper	$30.10		
install suspended ceiling	**installation crew**	$35.30		
Install 2' x 4' suspended ceiling				
grid only	installation crew	$35.30	.013	**$.46** *sf*
grid and tiles	installation crew	$35.30	.025	**$.88** *sf*
ceiling tiles only	installer's helper	$30.10	.011	**$.33** *sf*
luminous panels	installer's helper	$30.10	.010	**$.30** *sf*
Install 12" x 12" concealed suspended ceiling				
grid only	installation crew	$35.30	.020	**$.71** *sf*
grid and tiles	installation crew	$35.30	.038	**$1.34** *sf*
tiles only	installation crew	$35.30	.019	**$.67** *sf*

37 .... *Swimming Pools*

Item Description	Unit	Remove	Replace	Total	
Minimum charge for swimming pool work *Replace* Materials ......41.70 Labor 53.00	ea	–	$94.70	$94.70	◄ **MINIMUM**
Gunite swimming pool with plaster *Replace* Materials......30.90 Labor ....10.80 *Remove* .... Labor 7.08	sf	$7.08	$41.70	$48.78	◄ **SWIMMING POOLS** *Per square feet of walls and bottom of pool. Includes all equipment (average to high quality) and 6" x 6" tile border. Does not includes coping or deck.*
Concrete swimming pool with vinyl liner *Replace* Materials ......21.40 Labor ....8.81 *Remove* .... Labor 6.13	sf	$6.13	$30.21	$36.34	
Galvanized steel swimming pool with vinyl liner *Replace* Materials ......18.40 Labor ....7.17 *Remove* .... Labor 4.10	sf	$4.10	$25.57	$29.67	
Aluminum swimming pool with vinyl liner *Replace* Materials ......18.60 Labor ....7.49 *Remove* .... Labor 4.10	sf	$4.10	$26.09	$30.19	
Fiberglass swimming pool *Replace* Materials ......28.70 Labor ....9.24 *Remove* .... Labor 3.50	sf	$3.50	$37.94	$41.44	
Brick coping *Replace* Materials ......16.70 Labor ....12.10 *Remove* .... Labor 1.45	lf	$1.45	$28.80	$30.25	◄ **COPING**
Precast concrete coping *Replace* Materials ......14.90 Labor ....10.50 *Remove* .... Labor 1.45	lf	$1.45	$25.40	$26.85	
Flagstone coping *Replace* Materials ......18.10 Labor ....13.50 *Remove* .... Labor 1.45	lf	$1.45	$31.60	$33.05	
Remove coping for work, then reinstall *Replace* Materials .... .86 Labor 16.50	lf	–	$17.36	$17.36	
Swimming pool deck, concrete with epoxy aggregate surface *Replace* Materials........2.67 Labor ....2.39 *Remove* .... Labor 1.42	sf	$1.42	$5.06	$6.48	◄ **DECK**
Swimming pool deck, stamped and dyed conrete *Replace* Materials........2.43 Labor ....2.12 *Remove* .... Labor 1.42	sf	$1.42	$4.55	$5.97	
Bond beam repair *Replace* Materials ......10.00 Labor 56.80	lf	–	$66.80	$66.80	◄ **BOND BEAM REPAIR**
Regrout tile swimming pool *Replace* Materials .... .17 Labor 1.27	sf	–	$1.44	$1.44	◄ **REGROUT TILE**
Leak detection *Replace* Materials........3.14 Labor 218.00	ea	–	$221.14	$221.14	◄ **LEAK DETECTION**

Item Description	Unit	Remove	Replace	Total
REPAIR LEAK ▶ Repair pool leak in vinyl lining, underwater	ea	–	$205.10	$205.10
Replace Materials....13.10 Labor 192.00				
Repair pool leak with hydraulic cement, underwater	ea	–	$259.40	$259.40
Replace Materials ......21.40 Labor 238.00				
Remove rusted rebar & stain, patch with plaster, underwater	ea	–	$410.10	$410.10
Replace Materials......38.10 Labor..........372.00				
Repair plaster popoff, underwater	ea	–	$240.70	$240.70
Replace Materials ......16.70 Labor..........224.00				
REPLASTER ▶ Replaster swimming pool	sf	–	$3.66	$3.66
Replace Materials........1.64 Labor 2.02				
PAINT ▶ Paint pool with rubber base paint	sf	–	$2.23	$2.23
Replace Materials .... .80 Labor 1.43				
Paint pool with epoxy paint	sf	–	$2.74	$2.74
Replace Materials .... .88 Labor 1.86				
VINYL LINER ▶ Replace vinyl liner	sf	$.27	$3.85	$4.12
Replace Materials........2.68 Labor 1.17				
Remove .... Labor .... .27				
TILE BORDER ▶ Tile border, 6" x 6"	lf	$1.79	$20.44	$22.23
Replace Materials........8.14 Labor 12.30				
Remove .... Labor 1.79				
Tile border, 12" x 12"	lf	$1.79	$27.40	$29.19
Replace Materials ....10.60 Labor 16.80				
Remove .... Labor 1.79				
Remove tiles for work, then reinstall	lf	–	$34.38	$34.38
Replace Materials .... .88 Labor 33.50				
ACID WASH ▶ Acid wash swimming pool plaster	sf	–	$.35	$.35
Replace Materials .... .14 Labor .... .21				
Minimum charge to acid wash swimming pool	ea	–	$232.70	$232.70
Replace Materials.......20.70 Labor 212.00				
DRAIN ▶ Drain pool	ea	–	$223.00	$223.00
Replace .... Labor 223.00				
Drain and clean pool	ea	–	$516.90	$516.90
Replace Materials.......17.90 Labor..........499.00				
SHOCK TREATMENT ▶ Swimming pool chemical shock treatment	ea	–	$102.10	$102.10
Replace Materials ......35.70 Labor 66.40				
OPEN POOL ▶ Open swimming pool for the summer (cold climates)	ea	–	$226.60	$226.60
Replace Materials......53.60 Labor 173.00				
CLOSE POOL ▶ Close swimming pool for the winter (cold climates)	ea	–	$337.40	$337.40
Replace Materials......71.40 Labor.........266.00				
CAULK ▶ Caulk expansion joint	lf	–	$3.92	$3.92
Replace Materials........2.38 Labor 1.54				

38 .... *Temporary*

Item Description	Unit			Total	
Cover opening with single sheet of plywood Materials ....20.70 Labor..........31.10	ea	–	–	$51.80	◄ **EMERGENCY BOARD UP** *Prices are for work done between 7:00 a.m. and 6:00 p.m. Monday through Friday. Add 25% for emergency work between 6:00 p.m. and 10:00 p.m. Monday through Friday. Add 65% for emergency work between 10:00 p.m. and 7:00 a.m. Monday through Friday, on weekends, or on holidays.*
Cover opening with two sheets of plywood Materials....................41.40 Labor..........39.50	ea	–	–	$80.90	
Install temporary framing and cover opening Materials ....93 Labor.............96	sf	–	–	$1.89	
Cover roof or wall with tarp Materials......................60 Labor.............39	sf	–	–	$.99	
Cover roof or wall with plastic Materials......................30 Labor.............39	sf	–	–	$.69	
Minimum charge for emergency board up Materials ....120.00 Labor..........87.00	ea	–	–	$207.00	◄ minimum
Temporary electrical hookup Materials..................108.00 Labor 60.50	ea	–	–	$168.50	◄ **TEMPORARY POWER**
Temporary electrical, per week Materials 93.00	wk	–	–	$93.00	
Temporary heating, per week Materials...................184.00	wk	–	–	$184.00	◄ **TEMPORARY HEATING**
Scaffolding .... Equipment 20	sf	–	–	$.20	◄ **SCAFFOLDING** *Per week. Per sf of wall that scaffolding covers. 60" wide scaffolding attached with scissor braces.*
Add for hook-end cat walk .... Equipment 1.05	ea	–	–	$1.05	
Add for tented scaffolding .... Labor............22 Equipment 25	sf	–	–	$.47	◄ tented scaffolding
Scaffolding delivery, setup, and take down .... Labor............22	sf	–	–	$.22	◄ setup and take down
Minimum charge for scaffolding .... Labor..........43.50 Equipment..........50.00	ea	–	–	$93.50	◄ minimum
Temporary 5' tall chain-link fence .... Labor ....5.13 Equipment............2.70	lf	–	–	$7.83	◄ **TEMPORARY CHAIN-LINK FENCE** *Per job. Up to 12 months.*
Temporary 6' tall chain-link fence .... Labor ....5.35 Equipment............2.80	lf	–	–	$8.15	
Minimum charge for chain-link fence .... Labor..........87.00 Equipment........140.00	ea	–	–	$227.00	◄ minimum
Security guard .... Labor..........15.10	hr	–	–	$15.10	◄ **SECURITY GUARD** *Per hour.*

	Item Description		Unit			Total
SECURITY GUARD ▶ *continued*	Security guard with dog		hr	–	–	**$20.80**
	Labor 20.80					
minimum ▷	Minimum charge for security guard		ea	–	–	**$302.00**
	Labor 302.00					
OFFICE TRAILER ▶ *Per week.*	8′ x 32′ office trailer	Equipment..........53.00	ea	–	–	**$53.00**
STORAGE TRAILER ▶ *Per week.*	Storage trailer	Equipment..........31.00	ea	–	–	**$31.00**
PORTABLE TOILET ▶ *Chemical. Per week.*	Portable toilet	Equipment..........26.00	ea	–	–	**$26.00**
BARRICADES ▶ *Per week.*	Folding reflective barricades	Equipment..........4.40	ea	–	–	**$4.40**
	Folding reflective barricade with flashing light	Equipment..........5.40	ea	–	–	**$5.40**
TRAFFIC CONE ▶ *Per week.*	28″ traffic cone	Equipment 50	ea	–	–	**$.50**
SAFETY FENCE ▶	4′ tall orange plastic safety fence	Materials ....46 Labor 17	lf	–	–	**$.63**
	5′ tall orange plastic safety fence	Materials ....69 Labor 17	lf	–	–	**$.86**
SAFETY TAPE ▶	Plastic "do not cross" barricade tape	Materials ....03 Labor 09	lf	–	–	**$.12**

TIME & MATERIAL CHARTS *(selected items)*

Temporary Items Labor

LABORER	BASE WAGE	PAID LEAVE	TRUE WAGE	FICA	FUTA	WORKER'S COMP.	UNEMPLOY. INSUR.	HEALTH INSUR.	RETIRE (401K)	LIABILITY INSUR.	COST PER HOUR
Carpenter	$24.30	1.90	$26.20	2.00	.21	5.15	2.28	2.92	.79	3.93	**$43.50**

Paid Leave is calculated based on two weeks paid vacation, one week sick leave, and seven paid holidays. Employer's matching portion of **FICA** is 7.65 percent. **FUTA** (Federal Unemployment) is .8 percent. **Worker's compensation** for carpentry work in the temporary trade was calculated using a national average of 19.63 percent. **Unemployment insurance** was calculated using a national average of 8.7 percent. **Health insurance** was calculated based on a projected national average for 2005 of $580 per employee (and family when applicable) per month. Employer pays 80 percent for a per month cost of $464 per employee. **Retirement** is based on a 401(k) retirement program with employer matching of 50 percent. Employee contributions to the 401(k) plan are an average of 6 percent of the true wage. **Liability insurance** is based on a national average of 14.0 percent.

Temporary Items Labor Productivity

WORK DESCRIPTION	LABORER	COST PER HOUR	PRODUCTIVITY	UNIT PRICE
Temporary board up / fencing				
cover opening with single sheet of plywood	carpenter	$43.50	.714	**$31.10** *ea*
over opening with two sheets of plywood	carpenter	$43.50	.909	**$39.50** *ea*
install temporary framing and cover opening	carpenter	$43.50	.022	**$.96** *sf*
cover roof or wall with tarp	carpenter	$43.50	.009	**$.39** *sf*
cover roof or wall with plastic	carpenter	$43.50	.009	**$.39** *sf*
install temporary 5′ tall chain link fence	carpenter	$43.50	.118	**$5.13** *lf*

39

Tile
with cultured marble

Item Description	Unit	Remove	Replace	Total	
Minimum charge for tile work	ea	–	$140.40	$140.40	◄ **MINIMUM**
Replace Materials......50.00 Labor 90.40					
6' tall tile bathtub surround, adhesive set on moisture-resistant drywall	ea	$82.70	$494.00	$576.70	◄ **TILE TUB**
Replace Materials....280.00 Labor 214.00					**SURROUND**
Remove .... Labor 82.70					*Both sides and one*
6' tall tile bathtub surround, adhesive set on tile backer board	ea	$82.70	$529.00	$611.70	*length of tub including trim tile and one tile*
Replace Materials....315.00 Labor 214.00					*soap dish.*
Remove .... Labor 82.70					◁ **6'**
6' tall tile bathtub surround, mortar set	ea	$103.00	$648.00	$751.00	
Replace Materials ...335.00 Labor 313.00					
Remove .... Labor..........103.00					
7' tall tile bathtub surround, adhesive set on moisture-resistant drywall	ea	$85.00	$584.00	$669.00	◁ **7'**
Replace Materials....330.00 Labor 254.00					
Remove .... Labor...........85.00					
7' tall tile bathtub surround, adhesive set on tile backer board	ea	$85.00	$619.00	$704.00	
Replace Materials....365.00 Labor 254.00					
Remove .... Labor...........85.00					
7' tall tile bathtub surround, mortar set	ea	$107.00	$729.00	$836.00	
Replace Materials ...390.00 Labor 339.00					
Remove .... Labor..........107.00					
8' tall tile bathtub surround, adhesive set on moisture-resistant drywall	ea	$87.60	$666.00	$753.60	◁ **8'**
Replace Materials ....375.00 Labor..........291.00					
Remove .... Labor...........87.60					
8' tall tile bathtub surround, adhesive set on tile backer board	ea	$87.60	$711.00	$798.60	
Replace Materials ...420.00 Labor..........291.00					
Remove .... Labor...........87.60					
8' tall tile bathtub surround, mortar set	ea	$111.00	$815.00	$926.00	
Replace Materials ....445.00 Labor..........370.00					
Remove .... Labor...........111.00					
36" x 36" tile shower, adhesive set on tile backer board	ea	$96.20	$778.00	$874.20	◄ **TILE SHOWER**
Replace Materials ...465.00 Labor 313.00					*Includes walls, floor, all trim,*
Remove .... Labor...........96.20					*and one tile soap dish. Does*
36" x 36" tile shower, mortar set	ea	$107.00	$860.00	$967.00	*not include shower pan, fixtures, door or any plumbing.*
Replace Materials ...490.00 Labor...........370.00					
Remove .... Labor...........107.00					
Add for tile ceiling on 36" x 36" tile shower	ea	–	$110.40	$110.40	
Replace Materials ......75.00 Labor...........35.40					
36" x 48" tile shower, adhesive set on tile backer board	ea	$99.70	$890.00	$989.70	
Replace Materials ...520.00 Labor...........370.00					
Remove .... Labor 99.70					

RELATED ITEMS

Cabinets
tile countertop..................52
Cleaning..........................67
Plumbing
rough plumbing...........365
tub & shower combo.......378
shower stall, pan 378
tub surround..................379
glass shower.................379

Item Description		Unit	Remove	Replace	Total
TILE SHOWER ▶ *continued*	**36" x 48" tile shower, mortar set** *Replace* Materials ....545.00 Labor.........407.00 *Remove* .... Labor 99.70	ea	$99.70	$952.00	$1,051.70
	Add for tile ceiling on 36" x 48" tile shower *Replace* Materials ......85.00 Labor 46.40	ea	–	$131.40	$131.40
TILE ACCESSORY ▶ *Add to above prices for each additional accessory.*	**Add for tile soap holder or other accessory** *Replace* Materials ......32.00 Labor 17.00	ea	–	$49.00	$49.00
CULTURED MARBLE ▶ **TUB SURROUND** *Three-pieces, one length and two widths of tub.*	**Cultured marble tub surround** *Replace* Materials ....345.00 Labor ....157.00 *Remove* .... Labor 37.00	ea	$37.00	$502.00	$539.00
TILE WINDOW SILL ▶	**Tile window sill 4" thick wall** *Replace* Materials ....5.69 Labor ....2.56 *Remove* .... Labor 1.71	lf	$1.71	$8.25	$9.96
	Tile window sill 6" thick wall *Replace* Materials ....6.10 Labor ....2.56 *Remove* .... Labor 1.71	lf	$1.71	$8.66	$10.37
	Tile window sill 8" thick wall *Replace* Materials ....6.64 Labor ....2.65 *Remove* .... Labor 1.71	lf	$1.71	$9.29	$11.00
CULTURED MARBLE ▶ **WINDOW SILL**	**Cultured marble window sill 4" thick wall** *Replace* Materials ....5.89 Labor ....2.16 *Remove* .... Labor .... .52	lf	$.52	$8.05	$8.57
	Cultured marble window sill 6" thick wall *Replace* Materials ....7.51 Labor ....2.16 *Remove* .... Labor .... .52	lf	$.52	$9.67	$10.19
	Cultured marble window sill 8" thick wall *Replace* Materials ......10.10 Labor ....2.20 *Remove* .... Labor .... .52	lf	$.52	$12.30	$12.82
REGROUT TILE ▶	**Regrout tile** *Replace* Materials .... .27 Labor 1.63	sf	–	$1.90	$1.90
REPLACE TILE ▶ *With an original tile furnished by owner.*	**Replace single tile** *Replace* .... Labor.........37.70	ea	–	$37.70	$37.70

TIME & MATERIAL CHARTS *(selected items)*

Tile Labor

LABORER	BASE WAGE	PAID LEAVE	TRUE WAGE	FICA	FUTA	WORKER'S COMP.	UNEMPLOY. INSUR.	HEALTH INSUR.	RETIRE (401k)	LIABILITY INSUR.	COST PER HOUR
Tile layer	$22.80	1.78	$24.58	1.88	.20	4.50	2.14	2.92	.74	3.69	$40.70
Demolition laborer	$14.40	1.12	$15.52	1.19	.12	5.01	1.35	2.92	.47	2.33	$28.90

Paid Leave is calculated based on two weeks paid vacation, one week sick leave, and seven paid holidays. Employer's matching portion of **FICA** is 7.65 percent. **FUTA** (Federal Unemployment) is .8 percent. **Worker's compensation** for the tile trade was calculated using a national average of 18.26 percent. **Unemployment insurance** was calculated using a national average of 8.7 percent. **Health insurance** was calculated based on a projected national average for 2005 of $580 per employee (and family when applicable) per month. Employer pays 80 percent for a per month cost of $464 per employee. **Retirement** is based on a 401(k) retirement program with employer matching of 50 percent. Employee contributions to the 401(k) plan are an average of 6 percent of the true wage. **Liability insurance** is based on a national average of 14.0 percent.

40 .... *Wall Coverings*

Item Description	Unit	Remove	Replace	Total	
Remove wallpaper, strippable	sf	$.48	–	$.48	◄ **STRIP WALLPAPER** Add **25%** for two layers, **36%** for three layers and **42%** for four layers.
Remove .... Labor............ .48					
Remove wallpaper, non-strippable	sf	$.77	–	$.77	
Remove .... Labor............ .77					
Minimum charge for wall covering work	sf	–	$70.70	$70.70	◄ **MINIMUM**
Replace Material ....34.00 Labor 36.70					
Wallpaper underliner	sf	$.48	$1.02	$1.50	◄ **UNDERLINER** Blank stock used to cover flaws in walls or over paneling.
Replace Material .... .54 Labor............ .48					
Remove .... Labor............ .48					
Grass cloth wallpaper, standard grade	sf	$.48	$2.96	$3.44	◄ **GRASS CLOTH** Includes wall sizing and 21% waste. Add **$.35** per sf to patch small holes, gouges, and cracks.
Replace Material ....1.71 Labor 1.25					
Remove .... Labor............ .48					
Grass cloth wallpaper, high grade	sf	$.48	$3.99	$4.47	
Replace Material ....2.74 Labor 1.25					
Remove .... Labor............ .48					
Wallpaper, standard grade	sf	$.48	$1.85	$2.33	◄ **PAPER** From flat to high gloss papers. Includes wall sizing and 21% waste. Add **$.35** per sf to patch small holes, gouges, and cracks.
Replace Material .... .90 Labor............ .95					
Remove .... Labor............ .48					
Wallpaper, high grade	sf	$.48	$2.20	$2.68	
Replace Material ....1.25 Labor............ .95					
Remove .... Labor............ .48					
Vinyl-coated wallpaper, standard grade	sf	$.48	$2.18	$2.66	◄ **VINYL-COATED** Vinyl with paper back. Includes wall sizing and 21% waste. Add **$.35** per sf to patch small holes, gouges, and cracks.
Replace Material ....1.15 Labor............ 1.03					
Remove .... Labor............ .48					
Vinyl-coated wallpaper, high grade	sf	$.48	$2.56	$3.04	
Replace Material ....1.53 Labor............ 1.03					
Remove .... Labor............ .48					
Vinyl wallpaper, standard grade	sf	$.48	$2.25	$2.73	◄ **VINYL** Seams overlapped, then cut. Includes wall sizing and 21% waste. Add **$.35** per sf to patch small holes, gouges, and cracks.
Replace Material ....1.22 Labor............ 1.03					
Remove .... Labor............ .48					
Vinyl wallpaper, high grade	sf	$.48	$2.64	$3.12	
Replace Material ....1.61 Labor............ 1.03					
Remove .... Labor............ .48					
Foil wallpaper, standard grade	sf	$.48	$2.47	$2.95	◄ **FOIL** Includes wall sizing and 21% waste. Add **$.35** per sf to patch small holes, gouges, and cracks.
Replace Material ....1.48 Labor............ .99					
Remove .... Labor............ .48					
Foil wallpaper, high grade	sf	$.48	$2.86	$3.34	
Replace Material ....1.87 Labor............ .99					
Remove .... Labor............ .48					
Wallpaper border, standard grade	lf	$.37	$2.49	$2.86	◄ **BORDER** All styles. Includes 21% waste.
Replace Material ....1.65 Labor............ .84					
Remove .... Labor............ .37					

Item Description	Unit	Remove	Replace	Total
BORDER ▶ *continued* Use remove price when removing border only.	**Wallpaper border, high grade**	If	$.37	$3.11	$3.48
	Replace Material ....2.27 Labor............. .84				
	Remove .... Labor............. .37				
ANAGLYPTA ▶ Brand name for a highly embossed wall or ceiling covering made from material similar to linoleum. Must be painted. Higher grades contain cotton fibers for extra strength and durability. Includes 21% waste.	**Anaglypta embossed wall or ceiling covering, standard grade**	sf	$.66	$2.96	$3.62
	Replace Material ....1.31 Labor............1.65				
	Remove .... Labor............. .66				
	Anaglypta embossed wall or ceiling covering, high grade	sf	$.66	$3.53	$4.19
	Replace Material ....1.88 Labor............1.65				
	Remove .... Labor............. .66				
	Anaglypta embossed wall or ceiling covering, deluxe grade	sf	$.66	$3.73	$4.39
	Replace Material ....2.08 Labor............1.65				
	Remove .... Labor............. .66				
LINCRUSTA ▶ Brand name for a highly embossed wall or ceiling covering made from material similar to linoleum. Lincrusta is typically much heavier than Anaglypta. Must be painted. Includes 21% waste.	**Lincrusta embossed wall or ceiling covering, standard grade**	sf	$.95	$5.86	$6.81
	Replace Material ....3.80 Labor............2.06				
	Remove .... Labor............. .95				
	Lincrusta embossed wall or ceiling covering, high grade	sf	$.95	$7.17	$8.12
	Replace Material ....5.11 Labor............2.06				
	Remove .... Labor............. .95				
	Lincrusta embossed wall or ceiling covering, deluxe grade	sf	$.95	$8.37	$9.32
	Replace Material ....6.31 Labor............2.06				
	Remove .... Labor............. .95				
ANAGLYPTA ▶ FRIEZE See Anaglypta above. Friezes are 12" to 21" wide. Includes 13% waste.	**Anaglypta embossed frieze, standard grade**	If	$.55	$5.62	$6.17
	Replace Material ....4.04 Labor............1.58				
	Remove .... Labor............. .55				
	Anaglypta embossed frieze, high grade	If	$.55	$6.14	$6.69
	Replace Material ....4.56 Labor............1.58				
	Remove .... Labor............. .55				
LINCRUSTA ▶ FRIEZE See Lincrusta above. Friezes are approximately 21" wide. Includes 13% waste.	**Lincrusta embossed frieze, standard grade**	If	$.77	$6.67	$7.44
	Replace Material ....4.72 Labor............1.95				
	Remove .... Labor............. .77				
	Lincrusta embossed frieze, high grade	If	$.77	$7.80	$8.57
	Replace Material ....5.85 Labor............1.95				
	Remove .... Labor............. .77				
ANAGLYPTA ▶ PELMET See Anaglypta above. Pelmets are narrower and often less ornate than friezes. Pelmets are from 4" to 7" wide. Includes 13% waste.	**Anaglypta embossed pelmet, standard grade**	If	$.55	$4.00	$4.55
	Replace Material ....2.53 Labor............1.47				
	Remove .... Labor............. .55				
	Anaglypta embossed pelmet, high grade	If	$.55	$5.06	$5.61
	Replace Material ....3.59 Labor............1.47				
	Remove .... Labor............. .55				
ANAGLYPTA DADO ▶ See Anaglypta above. Dados are heavy, highly embossed wall panels installed as a wainscot. Includes 13% waste.	**Anaglypta embossed dado, standard grade**	If	$3.71	$23.47	$27.18
	Replace Material........19.40 Labor............4.07				
	Remove .... Labor............3.71				
	▶ Typical panels are about 22" wide and 36" tall. Five panels per box.				
	Anaglypta embossed dado, high grade	If	$3.71	$28.07	$31.78
	Replace Material........24.00 Labor............4.07				
	Remove .... Labor............3.71				
	▶ Typical panels are about 24" wide and 40" tall. Five panels per box.				

TIME & MATERIAL CHARTS (selected items)

Wall Coverings Materials

Wallpaper materials were calculated based on double European size rolls with approximately 28 sf per single roll and 56 sf in a double roll. (Most manufacturers no longer make American size rolls which contained approximately 36 sf per single roll and 72 sf in a double roll.) Prices include sizing and glue application, even on pre-pasted rolls.

DESCRIPTION	PRICE		GROSS COVERAGE	WASTE	NET COVERAGE	UNIT PRICE
Minimum						
for wall covering work	$34.00	ea	1	0%	1	$34.00 ea
Wallpaper underliner						
blank stock	$24.10	double roll	56	21%	44.24	$.54 sf
Grass cloth wallpaper						
standard grade	$75.60	double roll	56	21%	44.24	$1.71 sf
high grade	$121.00	double roll	56	21%	44.24	$2.74 sf
Paper wallpaper						
standard grade	$40.00	double roll	56	21%	44.24	$.90 sf
high grade	$55.10	double roll	56	21%	44.24	$1.25 sf
Vinyl-coated wallpaper						
standard grade	$51.00	double roll	56	21%	44.24	$1.15 sf
high grade	$67.60	double roll	56	21%	44.24	$1.53 sf
Vinyl wallpaper						
standard grade	$54.00	double roll	56	21%	44.24	$1.22 sf
high grade	$71.10	double roll	56	21%	44.24	$1.61 sf
Foil wallpaper						
standard grade	$65.60	double roll	56	21%	44.24	$1.48 sf
high grade	$82.70	double roll	56	21%	44.24	$1.87 sf
Wallpaper border						
standard grade	$39.00	bolt	30	21%	23.70	$1.65 lf
high grade	$53.80	bolt	30	21%	23.70	$2.27 lf
Anaglypta embossed wall or ceiling covering						
standard grade	$57.90	double roll	56	21%	44.24	$1.31 sf
high grade	$83.10	double roll	56	21%	44.24	$1.88 sf
deluxe grade	$92.10	double roll	56	21%	44.24	$2.08 sf
Lincrusta embossed wall or ceiling covering						
standard grade	$168.00	double roll	56	21%	44.24	$3.80 sf
high grade	$226.00	double roll	56	21%	44.24	$5.11 sf
deluxe grade	$279.00	double roll	56	21%	44.24	$6.31 sf
Anaglypta embossed frieze						
standard grade	$116.00	bolt	33	13%	28.71	$4.04 lf
high grade	$131.00	bolt	33	13%	28.71	$4.56 lf
Lincrusta embossed frieze						
standard grade	$137.00	bolt	33	12%	29.04	$4.72 lf
high grade	$170.00	bolt	33	12%	29.04	$5.85 lf
Anaglypta embossed pelmet						
standard grade	$72.60	bolt	33	13%	28.71	$2.53 lf
high grade	$103.00	bolt	33	13%	28.71	$3.59 lf
Anaglypta embossed dado *(five panels per box)*						
standard grade	$279.00	box	16	10%	14.40	$19.40 lf
high grade	$346.00	box	16	10%	14.40	$24.00 lf

Wall Coverings Labor

LABORER	BASE WAGE	PAID LEAVE	TRUE WAGE	FICA	FUTA	WORKER'S COMP.	UNEMPLOY. INSUR.	HEALTH INSUR.	RETIRE (401K)	LIABILITY INSUR.	COST PER HOUR
Wallpaper hanger	$19.90	1.55	$21.45	1.64	.17	4.78	1.87	2.92	.64	3.22	$36.70

Paid Leave is calculated based on two weeks paid vacation, one week sick leave, and seven paid holidays. Employer's matching portion of **FICA** is 7.65 percent. **FUTA** (Federal Unemployment) is .8 percent. **Worker's compensation** for the wall coverings trade was calculated using a national average of 22.24 percent. **Unemployment insurance** was calculated using a national average of 8.7 percent. **Health insurance** was calculated based on a projected national average for 2005 of $580 per employee (and family when applicable) per month. Employer pays 80 percent for a per month cost of $464 per employee. **Retirement** is based on a 401(k) retirement program with employer matching of 50 percent. Employee contributions to the 401(k) plan are an average of 6 percent of the true wage. **Liability insurance** is based on a national average of 14.0 percent.

Wall Coverings Labor Productivity

WORK DESCRIPTION	LABORER	COST PER HOUR	PRODUCTIVITY	UNIT PRICE
Remove wallpaper				
strippable	wallpaper hanger	$36.70	.013	$.48 sf
non-strippable	wallpaper hanger	$36.70	.021	$.77 sf
Minimum				
for wall covering work	wallpaper hanger	$36.70	1.00	$36.70 ea
Install wallpaper				
underliner	wallpaper hanger	$36.70	.013	$.48 sf
grass cloth wallpaper	wallpaper hanger	$36.70	.034	$1.25 sf
paper wallpaper	wallpaper hanger	$36.70	.026	$.95 sf
vinyl-coated	wallpaper hanger	$36.70	.028	$1.03 sf
vinyl	wallpaper hanger	$36.70	.028	$1.03 sf
foil	wallpaper hanger	$36.70	.027	$.99 sf
Install border				
all styles	wallpaper hanger	$36.70	.023	$.84 lf
Install Anaglypta embossed wall or ceiling covering				
wall or ceiling	wallpaper hanger	$36.70	.045	$1.65 sf
Install Lincrusta embossed wall or ceiling covering				
wall or ceiling	wallpaper hanger	$36.70	.056	$2.06 sf
Install embossed frieze				
Anaglypta	wallpaper hanger	$36.70	.043	$1.58 lf
Lincrusta	wallpaper hanger	$36.70	.053	$1.95 lf
Install Anaglypta embossed pelmet				
all grades	wallpaper hanger	$36.70	.040	$1.47 lf
Install Anaglypta embossed dado				
all grades	wallpaper hanger	$36.70	.111	$4.07 lf

NOTES: _____

_____

_____

_____

_____

_____

_____

_____

_____

_____ end

41 .... *Water Extraction*

Item Description	Unit			Total	
Minimum charge for water extraction work *Replace* .... Labor..........55.70 Equipment.......100.00	ea	–	–	$155.70	◄ **Minimum**
Equipment delivery, setup, and take-home charge *Replace* .... Equipment..........30.00 ► Per loss charge to deliver water extraction equipment, set the equipment up, and take the equipment home once the water is extracted and drying is complete.	ea	–	–	$30.00	◄ **Setup and take-home charges**
Extract water from lightly soaked carpet *Replace* .... Labor............ .19 Equipment............ .07 ► Carpet and pad are wet but water does not rise around feet as carpet is stepped on.	sf	–	–	$.26	◄ **Extract water**
Extract water from typically wet carpet *Replace* .... Labor............ .26 Equipment............ .07 ► Water in carpet and pad rises around feet as carpet is stepped on.	sf	–	–	$.33	
Extract water from heavily soaked carpet *Replace* .... Labor............ .37 Equipment............ .08 ► Water is visible over the surface of the carpet mat.	sf	–	–	$.45	
Extract water from very heavily soaked carpet *Replace* .... Labor............ .52 Equipment............ .11 ► Standing water over the surface of the carpet.	sf	–	–	$.63	
Treat carpet with germicide *Replace* Material.......... .03 Labor............ .11	sf	–	–	$.14	◄ **Germicide and mildewcide treatment** *Treatments to kill germs and mildew in wet carpet.*
Treat carpet with mildewcide *Replace* Material.......... .03 Labor............ .11	sf	–	–	$.14	
Detach carpet, lift, and block for drying *Replace* .... Labor............ .15	sf	–	–	$.15	◄ **Detach, lift & block carpet for drying**
Remove wet carpet *Remove*.................... Labor 2.97	sy	–	–	$2.97	◄ **Remove wet carpet and pad** *See Flooring chapter, pages 257-258 for prices to tear-out dry carpet and pad.*
Remove wet carpet pad *Remove*.................... Labor............ .19	sf	–	–	$.19	
Dehumidifier unit, 10 gallon daily capacity *Replace*.................... Labor..........15.20 Equipment..........30.00	day	–	–	$45.20	◄ **Dehumidifiers** *Does not include delivery, setup and take-home (see above). Does include daily monitoring and adjustment.*
Dehumidifier unit, 19 gallon daily capacity *Replace*.................... Labor..........15.20 Equipment..........50.00	day	–	–	$65.20	
Dehumidifier unit, 24 gallon daily capacity *Replace*.................... Labor..........15.20 Equipment..........70.00	day	–	–	$85.20	
Drying fan *Replace*.................... Labor..........3.86 Equipment..........25.00	day	–	–	$28.86	◄ **Drying fan** *Does not include delivery, setup and take-home (see above). Does include daily monitoring and adjustment.*

EMERGENCY SERVUCE

All prices are for work done between 7:00 a.m. and 6:00 p.m. Monday through Friday.

Add **25%** for emergency work between 6:00 p.m. and 10:00 p.m. Monday through Friday.

Add **65%** for emergency work between 10:00 p.m. and 7:00 a.m. Monday through Friday, on weekends, or on holidays.

Item Description			Unit			Total
HANG & DRY ▶ **CARPET IN PLANT** *Square foot price to haul carpet to plant, hang, and dry. Includes transport to and from plant. Does not include carpet removal (see page 257-258) or reinstallation (see page 257).*	**Hang and dry carpet in plant** *Replace*............... Labor............ .19 Equipment .... .09		sf	–	–	$.28
	Hang and dry oriental rug in plant *Replace*............... Labor............ .30 Equipment .... .14		sf	–	–	$.44
	Minimum charge to hang and dry carpet in plant *Replace*............... Labor..........75.30 Equipment.........50.00		sf	–	–	$125.30
PAD AND BLOCK ▶ **FURNITURE**	**Pad and block furniture, small room** *Replace*............... Labor..........14.80		ea	–	–	$14.80
	Pad and block furniture, average room *Replace*............... Labor 20.70		ea	–	–	$20.70
	Pad and block furniture, large room *Replace*............... Labor..........26.70		ea	–	–	$26.70
	Pad and block furniture, very large room *Replace*............... Labor..........37.00		ea	–	–	$37.00

TIME & MATERIAL CHARTS *(selected items)*

Water Extraction Materials

*See **Water Extraction** material prices with the line items and other information in the **QuickFinder** column.*

Water Extraction Rental Equipment

DESCRIPTION	UNIT PRICE
Dehumidifier	
10 gallon capacity..	**$30.00** *per day*
19 gallon capacity..	**$50.00** *per day*
24 gallon capacity..	**$70.00** *per day*
Drying fan	
typical..	**$25.00** *per day*

Water Extraction Labor

LABORER	BASE WAGE	PAID LEAVE	TRUE WAGE	FICA	FUTA	WORKER'S COMP.	UNEMPLOY. INSUR.	HEALTH INSUR.	RETIRE (401K)	LIABILITY INSUR.	COST PER HOUR
Water extractor.........	$20.80	1.62	$22.42	1.72	.18	3.85	1.95	2.92	.67	3.36	$37.10

Paid Leave is calculated based on two weeks paid vacation, one week sick leave, and seven paid holidays. Employer's matching portion of **FICA** is 7.65 percent. **FUTA** (Federal Unemployment) is .8 percent. **Worker's compensation** for the water extraction trade was calculated using a national average of 17.13 percent. **Unemployment insurance** was calculated using a national average of 8.7 percent. **Health insurance** was calculated based on a projected national average for 2005 of $580 per employee (and family when applicable) per month. Employer pays 80 percent for a per month cost of $464 per employee. **Retirement** is based on a 401(k) retirement program with employer matching of 50 percent. Employee contributions to the 401(k) plan are an average of 6 percent of the true wage. **Liability insurance** is based on a national average of 14.0 percent.

Water Extraction Labor Productivity

WORK DESCRIPTION	LABORER	COST PER HOUR	PRODUCTIVITY	UNIT PRICE
Extract water				
from lightly soaked carpet.........	water extractor.........	$37.10	.005	$.19 sf
from very heavily soaked carpet.........	water extractor.........	$37.10	.014	$.52 sf
Pad and block furniture				
small room.........	water extractor.........	$37.10	.400	$14.80 ea
very large room.........	water extractor.........	$37.10	.998	$37.00 ea

42 .... *Windows*

Item Description	Unit	small	average	large	very large	
Remove window **Materials** Small ....1.40 Average ....1.40 Large ....1.40 Very Large ....1.40 **Labor** Small ....11.40 Average........11.70 Large........12.10 Very Large........12.40	ea	$12.80	$13.10	$13.50	$13.80	◄ **DEMOLITION**
Remove window for work then reinstall **Materials** Small ....1.40 Average ....1.40 Large ....1.40 Very Large ....1.40 **Labor** Small ....53.50 Average........74.80 Large........109.00 Very Large........161.00	ea	$54.90	$76.20	$110.40	$162.40	◄ **REMOVE &** **REINSTALL**

Item Description	Unit	all types	
Deduct for single-glazed window (all types) **Materials** All types....-4.60	sf	– $4.60	◄ **OTHER OPTIONS** *All windows in this chapter are double-glazed (insulated) units with clear glass. Use for all window types except skylights and roof windows. For information on Low-E and argon see page 503.*
Add for gray or bronze tinted glass (all window types) **Materials** All types......3.00	sf	$3.00	
Add 8% for Low-E between panes (all window types)			
Add 5% for argon fill between panes (all window types)			
Add 11% for thermal break (aluminum windows only)			

RELATED ITEMS

Doors
   sliding patio 119

Item Description	Unit	tempered	laminated	obscure	polished wire	
Add for alternative glazing (all window types) **Materials** Tempered .....8.00 Laminated........5.30 Obscure...... 1.03 Polished wire....24.60	sf	$8.00	$5.30	$1.03	$24.60	◁ other glass types

Item Description	Unit	24" x 12"	36" x 18"	48" x 24"	72" x 36"	
Half-round aluminum window top **Materials** 24" x 12"..302.00 36" x 18"....375.00 48" x 24"....445.00 72" x 36"....659.00 **Labor** 24" x 12"..........43.10 36" x 18".....43.10 48" x 24".....60.50 72" x 36"......87.00	ea	$345.10	$418.10	$505.50	$746.00	◄ **ALUMINUM** ◁ half-round

Item Description	Unit	36" x 15"	48" x 16"	60" x 19"	90" x 20"	
Half-elliptical aluminum window top **Materials** 36" x 15"..575.00 48" x 16"....637.00 60" x 19"....698.00 90" x 20"..1020.00 **Labor** 36" x 15"..........43.10 48" x 16".....43.10 60" x 19".....60.50 90" x 20"......87.00	ea	$618.10	$680.10	$758.50	$1,107.00	◁ half-elliptical

Item Description	Unit	20" x 20"	30" x 30"	40" x 40"	48" x 48"	
Round aluminum window **Materials** 20" x 20".608.00 30" x 30" ...743.00 40" x 40"....857.00 48" x 48"....943.00 **Labor** 20" x 20"..........43.10 30" x 30".....43.10 40" x 40".....60.50 48" x 48"......87.00	ea	$651.10	$786.10	$917.50	$1,030.00	◁ round

Item Description	Unit	15" x 24"	24" x 36"	25" x 40"	30" x 48"	
Elliptical aluminum window **Materials** 15" X 24...1150.00 24" x 36"..1260.00 25" x 40"..1350.00 30" x 48"..1450.00 **Labor** 15" X 24"..........43.10 24" x 36".....43.10 25" x 40".....60.50 30" x 48"......87.00	ea	$1,193.10	$1,303.10	$1,410.50	$1,537.00	◁ elliptical

Item Description	Unit	24" x 24"	36" x 36"			
Quarter round aluminum window **Materials** 24" x 24" ..494.00 36" x 36" ...709.00 **Labor** 24" x 24"..........43.10 36" x 36".....43.10	ea	$537.10	$752.10	—	—	◁ quarter-round

ALUMINUM ▶
continued
casement ▷

Item Description	Unit	36" tall	48" tall	60" tall
18" wide aluminum casement window	ea	$402.10	$431.10	$489.10
Materials 36" tall ...359.00 48" tall ...388.00 60" tall ...446.00				
Labor 36" tall ....43.10 48" tall ....43.10 60" tall ...43.10				
24" wide aluminum casement window	ea	$430.10	$462.10	$534.50
Materials 36" tall ...387.00 48" tall ...419.00 60" tall ...474.00				
Labor 36" tall ....43.10 48" tall ....43.10 60" tall ...60.50				
30" wide aluminum casement window	ea	—	$513.50	$567.50
Materials...................... 48" tall ...453.00 60" tall ...507.00				
Labor.............................. 48" tall ...60.50 60" tall ...60.50				
36" wide aluminum casement window	ea	—	$598.50	$678.50
Materials...................... 48" tall ...538.00 60" tall ...618.00				
Labor.............................. 48" tall ...60.50 60" tall ...60.50				

awning ▷

Item Description	Unit	20" tall	24" tall	30" tall
24" wide aluminum awning window	ea	$375.10	$416.10	$451.10
Materials 20" tall ...332.00 24" tall ...373.00 30" tall ...408.00				
Labor 20" tall ....43.10 24" tall ....43.10 30" tall ...43.10				
30" wide aluminum awning window	ea	$427.10	$464.10	$503.10
Materials 20" tall ...384.00 24" tall ...421.00 30" tall ...460.00				
Labor 20" tall ....43.10 24" tall ....43.10 30" tall ...43.10				
36" wide aluminum awning window	ea	—	$499.10	$555.10
Materials...................... 24" tall ...456.00 30" tall ...512.00				
Labor.............................. 24" tall ...43.10 30" tall ...43.10				
40" wide aluminum awning window	ea	—	$548.10	$613.10
Materials...................... 24" tall ...505.00 30" tall ...570.00				
Labor.............................. 24" tall ...43.10 30" tall ...43.10				

double-hung ▷

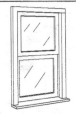

Item Description	Unit	36" tall	48" tall	60" tall	72" tall
24" wide aluminum double-hung window	ea	$237.10	$261.10	$288.10	$317.10
Materials 36" tall ...194.00 48" tall ...218.00 60" tall ...245.00 72" tall ...274.00					
Labor 36" tall ....43.10 48" tall ...43.10 60" tall ...43.10 72" tall ...43.10					
36" wide aluminum double-hung window	ea	$283.10	$310.10	$329.10	$374.50
Materials 36" tall ...240.00 48" tall ...267.00 60" tall ...286.00 72" tall ...314.00					
Labor 36" tall ....43.10 48" tall ...43.10 60" tall ...43.10 72" tall ...60.50					
42" wide aluminum double-hung window	ea	$306.10	$331.10	$374.50	$401.50
Materials 36" tall ...263.00 48" tall ...288.00 60" tall ...314.00 72" tall ...341.00					
Labor 36" tall ....43.10 48" tall ...43.10 60" tall ...60.50 72" tall ...60.50					
24" wide aluminum single-hung window	ea	$204.10	$228.10	$255.10	$284.10
Materials 36" tall ...161.00 48" tall ...185.00 60" tall ...212.00 72" tall ...241.00					
Labor 36" tall ....43.10 48" tall ...43.10 60" tall ...43.10 72" tall ...43.10					
36" wide aluminum single-hung window	ea	$250.10	$277.10	$296.10	$341.50
Materials 36" tall ...207.00 48" tall ...234.00 60" tall ...253.00 72" tall ...281.00					
Labor 36" tall ....43.10 48" tall ...43.10 60" tall ...43.10 72" tall ...60.50					
42" wide aluminum single-hung window	ea	$273.10	$298.10	$341.50	$368.50
Materials 36" tall ...230.00 48" tall ...255.00 60" tall ...281.00 72" tall ...308.00					
Labor 36" tall ....43.10 48" tall ...43.10 60" tall ...60.50 72" tall ...60.50					

Item Description	Unit	24″ tall	36″ tall	48″ tall	60″ tall	
36″ wide aluminum sliding window	ea	$113.10	$121.10	$151.10	$187.10	◁ sliding
Materials 24″ tall .....70.00 36″ tall .....78.00 48″ tall....108.00 60″ tall 144.00						
Labor 24″ tall ....43.10 36″ tall .....43.10 48″ tall .....43.10 60″ tall 43.10						
48″ wide aluminum sliding window	ea	$121.50	$130.10	$164.10	$221.50	
Materials 24″ tall .....78.40 36″ tall .....87.00 48″ tall .....121.00 60″ tall 161.00						
Labor 24″ tall ....43.10 36″ tall .....43.10 48″ tall .....43.10 60″ tall 60.50						
60″ wide aluminum sliding window	ea	$128.80	$138.10	$192.50	$235.50	
Materials 24″ tall .....85.70 36″ tall .....95.00 48″ tall ....132.00 60″ tall 175.00						
Labor 24″ tall ....43.10 36″ tall .....43.10 48″ tall .....60.50 60″ tall 60.50						
72″ wide aluminum sliding window	ea	$144.10	$172.50	$216.50	$294.00	
Materials 24″ tall ....101.00 36″ tall ....112.00 48″ tall .....156.00 60″ tall 207.00						
Labor 24″ tall ....43.10 36″ tall .....60.50 48″ tall .....60.50 60″ tall....87.00						

THERMAL BREAK

Aluminum is an excellent conductor, which means heat and cold easily flow through it, reducing efficiency.

To cure this, a plastic or rubber spacer is introduced into the jamb to break the flow of hot or cold.

Add **11%** for each aluminum window with a thermal break.

Item Description	Unit	36″ tall	48″ tall	60″ tall	72″ tall	
24″ wide aluminum fixed (picture) window	ea	$142.10	$186.10	$214.10	$228.10	◁ fixed (picture)
Materials 36″ tall .....99.00 48″ tall....143.00 60″ tall ....171.00 72″ tall 185.00						
Labor 36″ tall ....43.10 48″ tall .....43.10 60″ tall .....43.10 72″ tall 43.10						
30″ wide aluminum fixed (picture) window	ea	$163.10	$193.10	$208.10	$255.10	
Materials 36″ tall ...120.00 48″ tall....150.00 60″ tall ....165.00 72″ tall 212.00						
Labor 36″ tall ....43.10 48″ tall .....43.10 60″ tall .....43.10 72″ tall 43.10						
36″ wide aluminum fixed (picture) window	ea	$172.10	$215.10	$218.10	$307.50	
Materials 36″ tall ...129.00 48″ tall....172.00 60″ tall ....175.00 72″ tall 247.00						
Labor 36″ tall ....43.10 48″ tall .....43.10 60″ tall .....43.10 72″ tall 60.50						
42″ wide aluminum fixed (picture) window	ea	$186.10	$248.10	$308.50	$345.50	
Materials 36″ tall ...143.00 48″ tall....205.00 60″ tall ....248.00 72″ tall....285.00						
Labor 36″ tall ....43.10 48″ tall .....43.10 60″ tall .....60.50 72″ tall 60.50						
48″ wide aluminum fixed (picture) window	ea	$215.10	$255.10	$331.50	$370.50	
Materials 36″ tall ...172.00 48″ tall....212.00 60″ tall ....271.00 72″ tall 310.00						
Labor 36″ tall ....43.10 48″ tall .....43.10 60″ tall .....60.50 72″ tall 60.50						
60″ wide aluminum fixed (picture) window	ea	$218.10	$280.50	$315.50	$426.00	
Materials 36″ tall ...175.00 48″ tall....220.00 60″ tall ....255.00 72″ tall....339.00						
Labor 36″ tall ....43.10 48″ tall .....60.50 60″ tall .....60.50 72″ tall....87.00						
72″ wide aluminum fixed (picture) window	ea	$334.00	$398.00	$467.00	$533.00	
Materials 36″ tall....247.00 48″ tall ....311.00 60″ tall....339.00 72″ tall 405.00						
Labor 36″ tall ....87.00 48″ tall .....87.00 60″ tall ....128.00 72″ tall 128.00						

LOW-E AND ARGON

Higher quality windows may have Low-E or argon gas or both.

Low-E A coating that increases heat retention in winter and reduces ultraviolet rays that fade carpet and upholstery. Also called high-performance glass and other brand names.

Argon gas An odorless gas that improves the window's energy efficiency when injected between panes of glass.

Argon is usually not available for windows with true divided lights.

See page 501 to add Low-E or argon to windows and page 508 to add to skylights and roof windows.

Item Description	Unit	24″ x 12″	36″ x 18″	48″ x 24″	72″ x 36″	◀ VINYL
Half-round vinyl window top	ea	$253.10	$301.10	$370.50	$546.00	◁ half-round
Materials 24″ x 12″...210.00 36″ x 18″...258.00 48″ x 24″....310.00 72″ x 36″.....459.00						
Labor 24″ x 12″.......43.10 36″ x 18″.....43.10 48″ x 24″ .....60.50 72″ x 36″......87.00						

Item Description	Unit	36″ x 15″	48″ x 16″	60″ x 19″	90″ x 20″	
Half-elliptical vinyl window top	ea	$442.10	$481.10	$548.50	$794.00	◁ half-elliptical
Materials 36″ x 15″ .399.00 48″ x 16″...438.00 60″ x 19″ ..488.00 90″ x 20″ ...707.00						
Labor 36″ x 15 ....43.10 48″ x 16″.....43.10 60″ x 19″ .....60.50 90″ x 20″ 87.00						

Item Description	Unit	20″ x 20″	30″ x 30″	40″ x 40″	48″ x 48″	
Round vinyl window	ea	$467.10	$554.10	$657.50	$742.00	◁ round
Materials 20″ x 20″ ..424.00 30″ x 30″ ....511.00 40″ x 40″ ....597.00 48″ x 48″ 655.00						
Labor 20″ x 20″ ....43.10 30″ x 30″ .....43.10 40″ x 40″ .....60.50 48″ x 48″ 87.00						

Item Description	Unit	15" x 24"	24" x 36"	25" x 40"	30" x 48"
Elliptical vinyl window	ea	$843.10	$911.10	$998.50	$1,097.00
Materials 15" x 24"..800.00 24" x 36"...868.00 25" x 40"....938.00 30" x 48"..1010.00					
Labor 15" x 24"...........43.10 24" x 36".....43.10 25" x 40".....60.50 30" x 48".......87.00					

VINYL ▶
continued
elliptical ▷

Item Description	Unit	24" x 24"	36" x 36"		
Quarter-round vinyl window	ea	$386.10	$532.10		
Materials 24" x 24"..343.00 36" x 36"...489.00					
Labor 24" x 24"...........43.10 36" x 36".....43.10					

quarter-round ▷

Item Description	Unit	36" tall	48" tall	60" tall	
18" wide vinyl casement window	ea	$292.10	$313.10	$354.10	
Materials 36" tall....249.00 48" tall...270.00 60" tall.....311.00					
Labor 36" tall............43.10 48" tall....43.10 60" tall 43.10					
24" wide vinyl casement window	ea	$312.10	$334.10	$390.50	
Materials 36" tall....269.00 48" tall...291.00 60" tall ...330.00					
Labor 36" tall............43.10 48" tall....43.10 60" tall 60.50					
30" wide vinyl casement window	ea	–	$376.50	$412.50	
Materials.................... 48" tall....316.00 60" tall ...352.00					
Labor........................... 48" tall....60.50 60" tall 60.50					
36" wide vinyl casement window (double)	ea	–	$435.50	$490.50	
Materials.................... 48" tall....375.00 60" tall ...430.00					
Labor........................... 48" tall....60.50 60" tall 60.50					

casement ▷

Item Description	Unit	20" tall	24" tall	30" tall	
24" wide vinyl awning window	ea	$274.10	$302.10	$327.10	
Materials 20" tall ...231.00 24" tall ...259.00 30" tall ...284.00					
Labor 20" tall............43.10 24" tall....43.10 30" tall 43.10					
30" wide vinyl awning window	ea	$310.10	$336.10	$363.10	
Materials 20" tall ...267.00 24" tall ...293.00 30" tall ...320.00					
Labor 20" tall............43.10 24" tall....43.10 30" tall 43.10					
36" wide vinyl awning window	ea	–	$361.10	$400.10	
Materials.................... 24" tall....318.00 30" tall ...357.00					
Labor........................... 24" tall....43.10 30" tall 43.10					
40" wide vinyl awning window	ea	–	$395.10	$440.10	
Materials.................... 24" tall ...352.00 30" tall ...397.00					
Labor........................... 24" tall....43.10 30" tall 43.10					

awning ▷

Item Description	Unit	36" tall	48" tall	60" tall	72" tall
24" wide vinyl single-hung window	ea	$156.10	$171.10	$191.10	$212.10
Materials 36" tall ....113.00 48" tall ...128.00 60" tall....148.00 72" tall 169.00					
Labor 36" tall............43.10 48" tall....43.10 60" tall .....43.10 72" tall 43.10					
36" wide vinyl single-hung window	ea	$188.10	$206.10	$220.10	$255.50
Materials 36" tall....145.00 48" tall ...163.00 60" tall ....177.00 72" tall 195.00					
Labor 36" tall............43.10 48" tall....43.10 60" tall .....43.10 72" tall 60.50					
42" wide vinyl single-hung window	ea	$203.10	$221.10	$255.50	$275.50
Materials 36" tall....160.00 48" tall ...178.00 60" tall ....195.00 72" tall 215.00					
Labor 36" tall............43.10 48" tall....43.10 60" tall .....60.50 72" tall 60.50					

single-hung ▷

VINYL

All vinyl windows are double-glazed with clear glass.

All costs are for standard windows. Manu-facturers' window sizes vary. For standard units round measurements to the nearest size. Add approximately **80%** for custom sizes.

Some manufacturers provide a less rigid, lower grade of windows for **15%** less.

GRILLES AND GRID

For aluminum grid between panes or removable grilles outside of window add:

Half-round	**$21**
Half-elliptical	**$33**
Round	**$21**
Elliptical	**$28**
Quarter-round	**$21**
Casement	**$27**
Awning	**$27**
Single-hung	**$21**
Sliding	**$23**
Fixed (picture)	**$25**

Item Description	Unit	24" tall	36" tall	48" tall	60" tall	
48" wide vinyl sliding window	ea	$161.10	$188.10	$207.10	$238.10	◁ sliding
Materials 24" tall ....118.00 36" tall....145.00 48" tall....164.00 60" tall....195.00						
Labor 24" tall ....43.10 36" tall....43.10 48" tall....43.10 60" tall....43.10						
60" wide vinyl sliding window	ea	–	$206.10	$232.10	$293.50	
Materials .... 36" tall....163.00 48" tall....189.00 60" tall....233.00						
Labor .... 36" tall....43.10 48" tall....43.10 60" tall....60.50						
72" wide vinyl sliding window	ea	–	–	$276.50	$312.50	
Materials .... 48" tall....216.00 60" tall....252.00						
Labor .... 48" tall....60.50 60" tall....60.50						

Item Description	Unit	36" tall	48" tall	60" tall	72" tall	
24" wide vinyl fixed (picture) window	ea	$112.80	$142.10	$161.10	$171.10	◁ fixed (picture)
Materials 36" tall....69.70 48" tall....99.00 60" tall....118.00 72" tall....128.00						
Labor 36" tall..........43.10 48" tall....43.10 60" tall....43.10 72" tall....43.10						
30" wide vinyl fixed (picture) window	ea	$126.70	$147.10	$159.10	$191.10	
Materials 36" tall....83.60 48" tall....104.00 60" tall....116.00 72" tall....148.00						
Labor 36" tall..........43.10 48" tall....43.10 60" tall....43.10 72" tall....43.10						
36" wide vinyl fixed (picture) window	ea	$132.30	$163.10	$164.10	$231.50	
Materials 36" tall....89.20 48" tall....120.00 60" tall....121.00 72" tall....171.00						
Labor 36" tall..........43.10 48" tall....43.10 60" tall....43.10 72" tall....60.50						
42" wide vinyl fixed (picture) window	ea	$157.10	$206.10	$259.50	$288.50	
Materials 36" tall....114.00 48" tall....163.00 60" tall....199.00 72" tall....228.00						
Labor 36" tall..........43.10 48" tall....43.10 60" tall....60.50 72" tall....60.50						
48" wide vinyl fixed (picture) window	ea	$163.10	$191.10	$249.50	$276.50	
Materials 36" tall....120.00 48" tall....148.00 60" tall....189.00 72" tall....216.00						
Labor 36" tall..........43.10 48" tall....43.10 60" tall....60.50 72" tall....60.50						
60" wide vinyl fixed (picture) window	ea	$164.10	$213.50	$238.50	$322.00	
Materials 36" tall....121.00 48" tall....153.00 60" tall....178.00 72" tall....235.00						
Labor 36" tall..........43.10 48" tall....60.50 60" tall....60.50 72" tall....87.00						
72" wide vinyl fixed (picture) window	ea	$258.00	$303.00	$363.00	$409.00	
Materials 36" tall....171.00 48" tall....216.00 60" tall....235.00 72" tall....281.00						
Labor 36" tall..........87.00 48" tall....87.00 60" tall....128.00 72" tall....128.00						

RELATED ITEMS
Doors
 sliding patio 119

Item Description	Unit	24" x 12"	36" x 18"	48" x 24"	60" x 30"	
Half-round wood window top	ea	$690.10	$877.10	$883.50	$1,217.00	◀ WOOD
Materials 24" x 12" ..647.00 36" x 18"....834.00 48" x 24"....823.00 60" x 30"...1130.00						◁ half-round
Labor 24" x 12"..........43.10 36" x 18".....43.10 48" x 24" .....60.50 60" x 30"......87.00						

Item Description	Unit	36" x 15"	48" x 16"	60" x 17"	72" x 19"	
Half-elliptical wood window top	ea	$1,053.10	$1,163.10	$1,260.50	$1,517.00	◁ half-elliptical
Materials 36" x 15".1010.00 48" x 16"..1120.00 60" x 17"..1200.00 72" x 19"..1430.00						
Labor 36" x 15"..........43.10 48" x 16".....43.10 60" x 17" .....60.50 72" x 19"......87.00						

Add 114% for true divided light, spoke pattern (half-round or half-elliptical)

Add $20 for 3 spoke hub grille (half-round window)

Item Description	Unit	30" x 30"	48" x 48"	
Round wood window	ea	$1,463.10	$1,673.10	◁ round
Materials 30" x 30" 1420.00 48" x 48"...1630.00				
Labor 30" x 30" ....43.10 48" x 48".....43.10				

Item Description		Unit	25" x 30"	30" x 36"
WOOD ▶ *continued* elliptical ▷	**Elliptical (oval) wood window** *Materials* 25" x 30" 1640.00 30" x 36" .1840.00 *Labor* 25" x 30" ....43.10 30" x 36" 43.10	ea	$1,683.10	$1,883.10
	Add $18 for 4-lite grille in round or elliptical window			
	Add $23 for 9-lite grille in round or elliptical window			
	Add $28 for sunburst grille in round or elliptical window			

Item Description		Unit	24" x 24"	36" x 36"
quarter-round ▷	**Quarter-round wood window** *Materials* 24" x 24" ..795.00 36" x 36" ...937.00 *Labor* 24" x 24" ....43.10 36" x 36" 43.10	ea	$838.10	$980.10

Item Description		Unit	all sizes
	Add for single spoke grille in quarter-round window *Materials* All sizes 24.00	ea	$24.00
	Add for double spoke grille in quarter-round window *Materials* All sizes.....29.00	ea	$29.00
	Add for single radial bar grille in quarter-round window *Materials* All sizes.....33.00	ea	$33.00
	Add for double radial bar grille in quarter-round window *Materials* All sizes.....37.00	ea	$37.00

Item Description		Unit	36" tall	48" tall	60" tall	72" tall
casement ▷	**18" wide wood casement window** *Materials* 36" tall....214.00 48" tall...286.00 60" tall ...343.00 72" tall....401.00 *Labor* 36" tall..........43.10 48" tall.....43.10 60" tall.....43.10 72" tall.....43.10	ea	$257.10	$329.10	$386.10	$444.10
	24" wide wood casement window *Materials* 36" tall ...271.00 48" tall...308.00 60" tall....354.00 72" tall....420.00 *Labor* 36" tall............43.10 48" tall.....43.10 60" tall.....60.50 72" tall.....43.10	ea	$314.10	$351.10	$414.50	$463.10
	30" wide wood casement window *Materials* 36" tall........ 48" tall ...347.00 60" tall....408.00 72" tall ...443.00 *Labor* 36" tall .... 48" tall....60.50 60" tall.....60.50 72" tall.....43.10	ea	–	$407.50	$468.50	$486.10
	36" wide wood casement window *Materials* 36" tall........ 48" tall ...391.00 60" tall....461.00 72" tall ...503.00 *Labor* 36" tall............... 48" tall.....60.50 60" tall.....60.50 72" tall 60.50	ea	–	$451.50	$521.50	$563.50
	Add 87% for authentic divided lites in casement window					
	Add $13 for removable wood grille in casement window					
	Add $12 for aluminum grille between panes in casement window					

Item Description		Unit	20" tall	24" tall	30" tall
awning ▷	**24" wide wood awning window** *Materials* 20" tall....229.00 24" tall.....247.00 30" tall....264.00 *Labor* 20" tall..........43.10 24" tall.....43.10 30" tall.....43.10	ea	$272.10	$290.10	$307.10
	30" wide wood awning window *Materials* 20" tall....240.00 24" tall.....257.00 30" tall....274.00 *Labor* 20" tall..........43.10 24" tall.....43.10 30" tall.....60.50	ea	$283.10	$300.10	$334.50

WOOD

All wood windows are double-glazed with clear glass. Interiors are natural wood and exteriors are primed wood or aluminum clad or vinyl clad.

Hardware on wood windows is bright brass, brushed brass, antique brass, or white.

All costs are for standard windows. Manufacturers' window sizes vary. For standard units, round to the nearest size. Add approximately **80%** for custom sizes.

Item Description	Unit	20" tall	24" tall	30" tall	
36" wide wood awning window	ea	$299.10	$334.50	$350.50	
Materials 20" tall...256.00 24" tall....274.00 30" tall ...290.00					
Labor 20" tall...........43.10 24" tall.....60.50 30" tall 60.50					
48" wide wood awning window	ea	$349.10	$374.50	$410.50	
Materials 20" tall...306.00 24" tall....314.00 30" tall....350.00					
Labor 20" tall...........43.10 24" tall.....60.50 30" tall 60.50					

Add 80% for authentic divided lites in awning window

Add $14 for removable wood grille in awning window

Add $13 for aluminum grille between panes in awning window

Item Description				Unit	36" tall	48" tall	60" tall	72" tall	
24" wide wood double-hung window				ea	$274.10	$311.10	$346.10	$384.10	◁ double-hung
Materials 36" tall ...231.00 48" tall...268.00 60" tall ...303.00 72" tall...341.00									
Labor 36" tall...........43.10 48" tall.....43.10 60" tall .....43.10 72" tall.....43.10									
36" wide wood double-hung window				ea	$324.10	$366.10	$410.10	$476.50	
Materials 36" tall ...281.00 48" tall...323.00 60" tall...367.00 72" tall 416.00									
Labor 36" tall...........43.10 48" tall.....43.10 60" tall .....43.10 72" tall.....60.50									
48" wide wood double-hung window				ea	$401.10	$401.10	$474.50	$538.50	
Materials 36" tall ...358.00 48" tall...358.00 60" tall ....414.00 72" tall....478.00									
Labor 36" tall...........43.10 48" tall.....43.10 60" tall .....60.50 72" tall.....60.50									

Add 105% for authentic divided lites in double-hung window

Add $14 for removable wood grille in double-hung window

Add $13 for aluminum grille between panes in double-hung window

Item Description				Unit	36" tall	48" tall	60" tall	72" tall	
24" wide wood single-hung window				ea	$214.10	$251.10	$286.10	$324.10	◁ single-hung
Materials 36" tall....171.00 48" tall...208.00 60" tall....243.00 72" tall....281.00									
Labor 36" tall...........43.10 48" tall.....43.10 60" tall .....43.10 72" tall.....43.10									
36" wide wood single-hung window				ea	$264.10	$306.10	$350.10	$416.50	
Materials 36" tall....221.00 48" tall...263.00 60" tall...307.00 72" tall...356.00									
Labor 36" tall...........43.10 48" tall.....43.10 60" tall .....43.10 72" tall.....60.50									
40" wide wood single-hung window				ea	$341.10	$341.10	$414.50	$478.50	
Materials 36" tall....298.00 48" tall...298.00 60" tall...354.00 72" tall...418.00									
Labor 36" tall...........43.10 48" tall.....43.10 60" tall .....60.50 72" tall.....60.50									

Add 105% for authentic divided lites in single-hung window

Add $14 for removable wood grille in single-hung window

Add $13 for aluminum grille between panes in single-hung window

Add 97% for segmented top in single-hung window

RELATED ITEMS

Doors
  sliding patio 119

Item Description				Unit	24" tall	36" tall	48" tall	60" tall	
48" wide wood sliding window				ea	$380.10	$406.10	$470.10	$531.10	◁ sliding
Materials 24" tall....337.00 36" tall ...363.00 48" tall ...427.00 60" tall ...488.00									
Labor 24" tall ....43.10 36" tall....43.10 48" tall....43.10 60" tall 43.10									
60" wide wood sliding window				ea	—	$476.10	$533.10	$621.50	
Materials................... 36" tall ...433.00 48" tall....490.00 60" tall ...561.00									
Labor.......................... 36" tall ...43.10 48" tall....43.10 60" tall 60.50									

Item Description					Unit			48" tall	60" tall
WOOD ▶ *continued* **sliding ▷** *continued*	**72" wide wood sliding window**				ea			**$613.50**	**$683.50**
	Materials........ .... 48" tall....553.00 60" tall....623.00								
	Labor........... .... 48" tall....60.50 60" tall 60.50								
	Add 90% for authentic divided lites in sliding window								
	Add $14 for removable wood grille in sliding window								
	Add $13 for aluminum grille between panes in sliding window								

Item Description				Unit	36" tall	48" tall	60" tall	72" tall
fixed (picture) ▷	**24" wide wood fixed (picture) window**			ea	**$238.10**	**$275.10**	**$310.10**	**$348.10**
Materials 36" tall....195.00 48" tall ...232.00 60" tall....267.00 72" tall ...305.00								
Labor 36" tall...........43.10 48" tall.....43.10 60" tall....43.10 72" tall 43.10								
36" wide wood fixed (picture) window				ea	**$288.10**	**$330.10**	**$374.10**	**$440.50**
Materials 36" tall....245.00 48" tall ...287.00 60" tall....331.00 72" tall ...380.00								
Labor 36" tall...........43.10 48" tall.....43.10 60" tall....43.10 72" tall 60.50								
48" wide wood fixed (picture) window				ea	**$365.10**	**$365.10**	**$438.50**	**$502.50**
Materials 36" tall ...322.00 48" tall ...322.00 60" tall....378.00 72" tall....442.00								
Labor 36" tall...........43.10 48" tall.....43.10 60" tall....60.50 72" tall....60.50								
60" wide wood fixed (picture) window				ea	–	**$443.50**	**$500.50**	**$598.00**
Materials................ 48" tall...383.00 60" tall....440.00 72" tall ...511.00								
Labor................ 48" tall....60.50 60" tall ....60.50 72" tall....87.00								
72" wide wood fixed (picture) window				ea	–	–	**$590.00**	**$660.00**
Materials................ .... 60" tall ...503.00 72" tall ...573.00								
Labor................ .... 60" tall.....87.00 72" tall.....87.00								
Add 80% for authentic divided lites in fixed window								
Add $15 for removable wood grille in fixed window								
Add $14 for aluminum grille between panes in fixed window								
Add 97% for segmented top in fixed window								

Item Description	Unit	all types
SKYLIGHT ▶ **additional costs ▷** *See "Low-E and Argon" on page 501. Skylight prices include flashing for roof with low-profile roofing such as asphalt shingles. For tile shingles, or ribbed metal roofing add for high-profile roof. Low-slope roof includes a curb and flat roof includes a special sloped curb.*		
Add for laminated glass over tempered glass in skylight or roof window	ea	**$35.00**
Materials All types 35.00		
Add for Low-E in skylight or roof window	ea	**$9.00**
Materials All types 9.00		
Add for argon gas filled skylight or roof window	ea	**$8.00**
Materials All types 8.00		
Add or bronze or gray tint (all sizes)	ea	**$14.00**
Materials All types.....14.00		
Add for skylight or roof window installed on high-profile roof	ea	**$22.00**
Materials All types....22.00		
Add for skylight or roof window installed on low-slope roof (less than 4-12)	ea	**$289.00**
Materials All types..289.00		
Add for skylight or roof window installed on flat roof (less than 2-12)	ea	**$299.00**
Materials All types..299.00		

Item Description	Unit	24" x 24"	24" x 48"	30" x 30"	48" x 48"	
Single dome skylight	ea	$177.00	$238.00	$212.80	$427.00	◁ dome
Materials 24" x 24"....63.00 24" x 48"....124.00 30" x 30"......98.80 48" x 48"....313.00						
Labor 24" x 24"..........114.00 24" x 48"....114.00 30" x 30".....114.00 48" x 48"....114.00						
Double dome skylight	ea	$197.00	$286.00	$274.00	$483.00	
Materials 24" x 24"....83.00 24" x 48"....172.00 30" x 30"....160.00 48" x 48"....369.00						
Labor 24" x 24"..........114.00 24" x 48"....114.00 30" x 30".....114.00 48" x 48"....114.00						
Triple dome skylight	ea	$221.00	$362.00	$310.00	$587.00	
Materials 24" x 24"....107.00 24" x 48"....248.00 30" x 30"....196.00 48" x 48"....473.00						
Labor 24" x 24"..........114.00 24" x 48"....114.00 30" x 30".....114.00 48" x 48"....114.00						
Single dome ventilating skylight	ea	$252.00	$378.00	$327.00	$772.00	◁ ventilating
Materials 24" x 24"....131.00 24" x 48"....257.00 30" x 30"....206.00 48" x 48"....651.00						
Labor 24" x 24"..........121.00 24" x 48"....121.00 30" x 30".....121.00 48" x 48"....121.00						
Double dome ventilating skylight	ea	$295.00	$480.00	$455.00	$886.00	
Materials 24" x 24"....174.00 24" x 48"....359.00 30" x 30"....334.00 48" x 48"....765.00						
Labor 24" x 24"..........121.00 24" x 48"....121.00 30" x 30".....121.00 48" x 48"....121.00						
Triple dome ventilating skylight	ea	$344.00	$636.00	$530.00	$1,106.00	
Materials 24" x 24"....223.00 24" x 48"....515.00 30" x 30"....409.00 48" x 48"....985.00						
Labor 24" x 24"..........121.00 24" x 48"....121.00 30" x 30".....121.00 48" x 48"....121.00						

Item Description	Unit	28" long	38" long	48" long	55" long	
22" wide fixed skylight	ea	$344.00	$381.00	$412.00	$438.00	◁ fixed
Materials 28" long..227.00 38" long ...264.00 48" long....295.00 55" long...321.00						
Labor 28" long..........117.00 38" long .....117.00 48" long.....117.00 55" long.....117.00						
30" wide fixed skylight	ea	–	$423.00	–	$490.00	
Materials .... 38" long...306.00 55" long....373.00						
Labor .... 38" long ....117.00 55" long.....117.00						
44" wide fixed skylight	ea	$449.00	–	$540.00	–	
Materials 28" long...332.00 48" long....423.00						
Labor 28" long..........117.00 48" long.....117.00						
22" wide fixed skylight with ventilation flap	ea	$373.00	$412.00	$444.00	$463.00	◁ fixed with vent flap
Materials 28" long..256.00 38" long ...295.00 48" long....327.00 55" long ...346.00						
Labor 28" long..........117.00 38" long ....117.00 48" long.....117.00 55" long.....117.00						
30" wide fixed skylight with ventilation flap	ea	–	$461.00	–	$520.00	
Materials .... 38" long...344.00 55" long ...403.00						
Labor .... 38" long ....117.00 55" long.....117.00						
44" wide fixed skylight with ventilation flap	ea	$504.00	–	$580.00	–	
Materials 28" long...387.00 48" long ...463.00						
Labor 28" long..........117.00 48" long.....117.00						
22" wide ventilating skylight	ea	$554.00	$591.00	$634.00	$655.00	◁ ventilating
Materials 28" long..426.00 38" long ...463.00 48" long....506.00 55" long....527.00						
Labor 28" long..........128.00 38" long ....128.00 48" long.....128.00 55" long 128.00						
30" wide ventilating skylight	ea	–	$643.00	–	$723.00	
Materials .... 38" long ....515.00 55" long 595.00						
Labor .... 38" long ....128.00 55" long 128.00						
44" wide ventilating skylight	ea	$671.00	–	$789.00	–	
Materials 28" long .543.00 48" long 661.00						
Labor 28" long ....128.00 48" long 128.00						

RELATED ITEMS

Doors
sliding patio 119

509

Item Description	Unit	28" long	38" long	48" long	55" long
SKYLIGHTS ▶ *continued* roof window ▷ **22" wide roof window**	ea	$711.00	–	$771.00	–
Materials 28" long .583.00 48" long ...643.00 *Labor* 28" long ....128.00 48" long 128.00					
30" wide roof window	ea	–	$775.00	–	$867.00
Materials .... 38" long ...647.00 55" long....739.00 *Labor* .... 38" long ....128.00 55" long 128.00					
44" wide roof window	ea	–	–	–	$935.00
Materials .... 55" long....807.00 *Labor* .... 55" long 128.00					

Item Description	Unit	28" long	38" long	48" long	55" long
accessories ▷ **Add for cord-operated roller shades**	ea	$97.20	$97.20	$97.20	$97.20
Materials 28" long ....61.00 38" long......61.00 48" long ......61.00 55" long ......61.00 *Labor* 28" long...........36.20 38" long......36.20 48" long .....36.20 55" long 36.20					
Add for motorized rod cord control for roller shades	ea	$191.00	$191.00	$191.00	$191.00
Materials 28" long ....191.00 38" long ....191.00 48" long ....191.00 55" long 191.00					
Add for manually controlled Venetian blinds	ea	$86.00	$102.00	$107.00	$136.00
Materials 28" long ....86.00 38" long ...102.00 48" long ....107.00 55" long....136.00					
Add for electrically controlled skylight system	ea	$228.00	$228.00	$228.00	$228.00
Materials 28" long ....141.00 38" long....141.00 48" long....141.00 55" long ...141.00 *Labor* 28" long.......87.00 38" long .....87.00 48" long......87.00 55" long......87.00					
Add for electrically controlled window or skylight opener	ea	$201.50	$201.50	$201.50	$201.50
Materials 28" long ....141.00 38" long....141.00 48" long....141.00 55" long ...141.00 *Labor* 28" long..........60.50 38" long .....60.50 48" long ......60.50 55" long 60.50					
Add for infrared remote control system for opener	ea	$358.30	$358.30	$358.30	$358.30
Materials 28" long ..310.00 38" long....310.00 48" long ....310.00 55" long ...310.00 *Labor* 28" long..........48.30 38" long .....48.30 48" long .....48.30 55" long 48.30					

Item Description	Unit	24" tall	36" tall	48" tall	60" tall
STORM WINDOW ▶ aluminum ▷ **24" wide aluminum storm window**	ea	$109.60	$139.90	$163.50	$178.50
Materials 24" tall .....66.10 36" tall ......96.40 48" tall ....120.00 60" tall ....135.00 *Labor* 24" tall ....43.50 36" tall....43.50 48" tall ....43.50 60" tall 43.50					
36" wide aluminum storm window	ea	$139.90	$170.50	$190.50	$216.00
Materials 24" tall....96.40 36" tall....127.00 48" tall ....147.00 60" tall ....169.00 *Labor* 24" tall ....43.50 36" tall....43.50 48" tall ....43.50 60" tall 47.00					
48" wide aluminum storm window	ea	$163.50	$190.50	$223.00	$252.00
Materials 24" tall....120.00 36" tall....147.00 48" tall ....176.00 60" tall ....205.00 *Labor* 24" tall ....43.50 36" tall....43.50 48" tall ......47.00 60" tall 47.00					
60" wide aluminum storm window	ea	$178.50	$216.00	$252.00	$287.00
Materials 24" tall ....135.00 36" tall....169.00 48" tall....205.00 60" tall ....240.00 *Labor* 24" tall ....43.50 36" tall....47.00 48" tall .....47.00 60" tall......47.00					
72" wide aluminum storm window	ea	$190.50	$237.00	$280.00	$328.10
Materials 24" tall ....147.00 36" tall....190.00 48" tall ....233.00 60" tall....275.00 *Labor* 24" tall ....43.50 36" tall....47.00 48" tall.....47.00 60" tall 53.10					
wood ▷ **24" wide wood storm window**	ea	$124.90	$159.20	$177.50	$194.50
Materials 24" tall.....81.40 36" tall ....115.70 48" tall ....134.00 60" tall ....151.00 *Labor* 24" tall ....43.50 36" tall.....43.50 48" tall ....43.50 60" tall 43.50					

Item Description	Unit	24" tall	36" tall	48" tall	60" tall	
36" wide wood storm window	ea	$159.20	$184.50	$209.50	$237.00	
Materials 24" tall.....115.70 36" tall....141.00 48" tall....166.00 60" tall....190.00						
Labor 24" tall ....43.50 36" tall....43.50 48" tall .....43.50 60" tall.....47.00						
48" wide wood storm window	ea	$177.50	$209.50	$244.00	$277.00	
Materials 24" tall....134.00 36" tall....166.00 48" tall ....197.00 60" tall ...230.00						
Labor 24" tall ....43.50 36" tall....43.50 48" tall......47.00 60" tall.....47.00						
60" wide wood storm window	ea	$194.50	$237.00	$277.00	$315.00	
Materials 24" tall....151.00 36" tall....190.00 48" tall ...230.00 60" tall....268.00						
Labor 24" tall ....43.50 36" tall ...47.00 48" tall......47.00 60" tall.....47.00						
72" wide wood storm window	ea	$209.50	$261.00	$308.00	$361.10	
Materials 24" tall....166.00 36" tall....214.00 48" tall ...261.00 60" tall ...308.00						
Labor 24" tall ....43.50 36" tall ...47.00 48" tall......47.00 60" tall 53.10						
24" wide window screen	ea	$16.54	$19.04	$20.64	$24.44	◄ SCREEN
Materials 24" tall.....11.10 36" tall....13.60 48" tall.....15.20 60" tall.....19.00						
Labor 24" tall ....5.44 36" tall.....5.44 48" tall.......5.44 60" tall......5.44						
36" wide window screen	ea	$18.64	$19.74	$24.84	$26.44	
Materials 24" tall.....13.20 36" tall....14.30 48" tall.....19.40 60" tall....21.00						
Labor 24" tall ....5.44 36" tall.....5.44 48" tall.......5.44 60" tall......5.44						

Item Description	Unit	1/8" thick	3/16" thick	1/4" thick	3/8" thick	
Reglaze window with clear glass	sf	$6.84	$8.24	$7.24	$17.14	◄ REGLAZE
Materials 1/8"..........4.10 3/16" ....5.50 1/4" ......4.50 3/8" 14.40						
Labor 1/8"................2.74 3/16" ....2.74 1/4" ......2.74 3/8" 2.74						
Reglaze window with tempered glass	sf	$9.54	$10.74	$11.24	–	
Materials 1/8"..........6.80 3/16" ....8.00 1/4" 8.50						
Labor 1/8"................2.74 3/16" ....2.74 1/4" 2.74						
Reglaze window with laminated glass	sf	–	–	$12.84	$16.84	
Materials .... 1/4" .....10.10 3/8" 14.10						
Labor .... 1/4" ....2.74 3/8" 2.74						
Reglaze window with polished wire glass	sf	–	–	$29.54	–	
Materials .... 1/4" 26.80						
Labor .... 1/4" 2.74						
Minimum charge for reglazing work	ea	$77.50	–	–	–	◁ minimum
Materials..................34.00						
Labor.......................43.50						

Item Description	Unit	all sizes				
Rehang sash weight in antique double-hung window	ea	$116.70				◄ REPAIR
Materials All sizes 18.00						
Labor All sizes 98.70						
Refurbish antique double-hung window	ea	$167.00				
Materials All sizes 31.00						
Labor All sizes...........136.00						
Recondition antique wood window sash	ea	$106.50				
Materials All sizes 16.00						
Labor All sizes 90.50						

RELATED ITEMS

Doors
sliding patio 119

✍ NOTES: _____

_____ end

TIME & MATERIAL CHARTS *(selected items)*

Windows Materials

*See **Windows** material prices with the line items and other information in the **QuickFinder** column.*

Windows Labor

LABORER	BASE WAGE	PAID LEAVE	TRUE WAGE	FICA	FUTA	WORKER'S COMP.	UNEMPLOY. INSUR.	HEALTH INSUR.	RETIRE (401k)	LIABILITY INSUR.	COST PER HOUR
Installer	$24.30	1.90	$26.20	2.00	.21	5.15	2.28	2.92	.79	3.93	**$43.50**
Demolition laborer	$14.40	1.12	$15.52	1.19	.12	5.01	1.35	2.92	.47	2.33	**$28.90**

Paid Leave is calculated based on two weeks paid vacation, one week sick leave, and seven paid holidays. Employer's matching portion of **FICA** is 7.65 percent. **FUTA** (Federal Unemployment) is .8 percent. **Worker's compensation** for the windows trade was calculated using a national average of 19.63 percent. **Unemployment insurance** was calculated using a national average of 8.7 percent. **Health insurance** was calculated based on a projected national average for 2005 of $580 per employee (and family when applicable) per month. Employer pays 80 percent for a per month cost of $464 per employee. **Retirement** is based on a 401(k) retirement program with employer matching of 50 percent. Employee contributions to the 401(k) plan are an average of 6 percent of the true wage. **Liability insurance** is based on a national average of 14.0 percent.

Windows Labor Productivity

WORK DESCRIPTION	LABORER	COST PER HOUR	PRODUCTIVITY	UNIT PRICE
Remove window				
small (4 to 10 sf)	carpenter	$43.50	.263	$11.40 ea
average size (11 to 16 sf)	carpenter	$43.50	.270	$11.70 ea
large (17 to 29 sf)	carpenter	$43.50	.278	$12.10 ea
very large (30 sf and larger)	carpenter	$43.50	.286	$12.40 ea
Remove window for work & reinstall				
small (4 to 10 sf)	carpenter	$43.50	1.23	$53.50 ea
average size (11 to 16 sf)	carpenter	$43.50	1.72	$74.80 ea
large (17 to 28 sf)	carpenter	$43.50	2.50	$109.00 ea
very large (30 sf and larger)	carpenter	$43.50	3.70	$161.00 ea
Install window				
small (4 to 10 sf)	carpenter	$43.50	.990	$43.10 ea
average size (11 to 16 sf)	carpenter	$43.50	1.39	$60.50 ea
large (17 to 28 sf)	carpenter	$43.50	2.00	$87.00 ea
very large (30 sf and larger)	carpenter	$43.50	2.94	$128.00 ea
Install skylight or roof window				
dome ventilating	carpenter	$43.50	2.78	$121.00 ea
fixed	carpenter	$43.50	2.70	$117.00 ea
ventilating	carpenter	$43.50	2.94	$128.00 ea
cord-operated roller shades	carpenter	$43.50	.833	$36.20 ea
electrically controlled system	carpenter	$43.50	2.00	$87.00 ea
electrically controlled opener	carpenter	$43.50	1.39	$60.50 ea
infrared remote control system for opener	carpenter	$43.50	1.11	$48.30 ea
Install storm window				
small (4 to 14 sf)	carpenter	$43.50	1.00	$43.50 ea
average size (15 to 25 sf)	carpenter	$43.50	1.08	$47.00 ea
large storm (26 sf and larger)	carpenter	$43.50	1.22	$53.10 ea
Reglaze window				
remove and replace glass	carpenter	$43.50	.063	$2.74 sf
Repair antique double-hung window				
rehang sash weight	carpenter	$43.50	2.27	$98.70 ea
refurbish	carpenter	$43.50	3.13	$136.00 ea
recondition	carpenter	$43.50	2.08	$90.50 ea

SELECTED PRICES FROM THE *NATIONAL MANUFACTURED HOUSING ESTIMATOR*

This chapter contains some of the most common items found in manufactured housing. *It is not a complete price list.* A comprehensive costbook of manufactured housing costs is in the planning stages at *Craftsman Book Company*.

Item Description	Unit	Remove	Replace	Total	
APPLIANCES					
Clothes line					
30-line, exterior	ea	$7.64	$175.80	$183.44	◄ **CLOTHES LINE**
Replace Mat..........141.00 Lab. 34.80					*Steel posts, umbrella-style*
Remove .... Lab. 7.64					*supports with vinyl-coated*
					rayon lines.
7-line, exterior	ea	$7.24	$117.70	$124.94	
Replace Mat..........84.30 Lab. 33.40					
Remove .... Lab. 7.24					
remove for work, then reinstall	ea	–	$10.05	$10.05	
Replace .... Lab. 10.05					
Sidewall exhaust ventilator					
for 2" to 3" thick walls	ea	$10.80	$121.70	$132.50	◄ **VENTILATOR**
Replace Mat. ....57.70 Lab. 64.00					*Louvered inside grille,*
Remove .... Lab. 10.80					*insulated outside door,*
					approximately 9" x 9".
for 2-3/4" to 4" thick walls	ea	$10.80	$124.00	$134.80	
Replace Mat..........60.00 Lab. 64.00					
Remove .... Lab. 10.80					
remove for work, then reinstall	ea	–	$101.80	$101.80	
Replace Mat.............2.30 Lab. 99.50					
CABINETS					
Mobile-home type cabinets, average grade					
lower units	lf	$3.35	$61.00	$64.35	◄ **CABINETS**
Replace Mat..........54.30 Lab. 6.70					*Mobile-home style*
Remove .... Lab. 3.35					
upper units	lf	$3.35	$42.53	$45.88	
Replace Mat. ....37.00 Lab. 5.53					
Remove .... Lab. 3.35					
lower island units	lf	$3.35	$84.58	$87.93	
Replace Mat. ....76.20 Lab. 8.38					
Remove .... Lab. 3.35					

Item Description	Unit	Remove	Replace	Total
CABINETS ▶ *continued* **upper island units** *Replace* Mat. ....65.80 Lab. ....6.03 *Remove* .... Lab. 3.35	lf	$3.35	$71.83	$75.18
remove for work, then reinstall *Replace* .... Lab. 7.71	lf	–	$7.71	$7.71

DOORS

ACCESS DOOR ▶ access door

Item Description	Unit	Remove	Replace	Total
for water heater or furnace *Replace* Mat. ....51.00 Lab............26.80 *Remove* .... Lab............16.00	ea	$16.00	$77.80	$93.80
remove for work, then reinstall *Replace* .... Lab...........33.50	ea	–	$33.50	$33.50

ENTRY DOOR ▶ mobile-home type entry door, fiberglass

Item Description	Unit	Remove	Replace	Total
flush *Replace* Mat. ....110.00 Lab............25.20 *Remove* .... Lab............16.80	ea	$16.80	$135.20	$152.00
flush with fixed lite *Replace* Mat..........126.00 Lab............25.20 *Remove* .... Lab............16.80	ea	$16.80	$151.20	$168.00
flush with sliding window *Replace* Mat...........139.00 Lab............25.20 *Remove* .... Lab............16.80	ea	$16.80	$164.20	$181.00
remove for work, then reinstall *Replace* .... Lab............35.20	ea	–	$35.20	$35.20

COMBINATION DOOR ▶ mobile-home type combination entry door (with storm door)

Item Description	Unit	Remove	Replace	Total
flush *Replace* Mat. ....143.00 Lab............28.60 *Remove* .... Lab............20.10	ea	$20.10	$171.60	$191.70
flush with fixed lite *Replace* Mat. ....164.00 Lab............28.60 *Remove* .... Lab............20.10	ea	$20.10	$192.60	$212.70
flush with sliding window *Replace* Mat...........181.00 Lab............28.60 *Remove* .... Lab............20.10	ea	$20.10	$209.60	$229.70
remove for work, then reinstall *Replace* .... Lab............35.80	ea	–	$35.80	$35.80

DOOR HARDWARE

LOCKSET ▶ mobile-home type lockset

Item Description	Unit	Remove	Replace	Total
interior passage *Replace* Mat. ....14.00 Lab. ....13.00 *Remove* .... Lab. 6.95	ea	$6.95	$27.00	$33.95
interior privacy *Replace* Mat. ....16.20 Lab. ....13.00 *Remove* .... Lab. 6.95	ea	$6.95	$29.20	$36.15
remove for work, then reinstall *Replace* .... Lab............15.10	ea	–	$15.10	$15.10

Item Description	Unit	Remove	Replace	Total	
mobile-home type entrance lockset					◄ ENTRANCE LOCKSET
standard quality	ea	$8.57	$50.50	$59.07	
Replace Mat. ....31.90 Lab. 18.60					
Remove .... Lab. 8.57					
remove for work, then reinstall	ea	–	$24.70	$24.70	
Replace .... Lab. 24.70					
mobile-home type deadbolt					◄ DEADBOLT
standard quality	ea	$5.97	$42.10	$48.07	
Replace Mat. ....20.80 Lab. 21.30					
Remove .... Lab. 5.97					
remove for work, then reinstall	ea	–	$25.20	$25.20	
Replace .... Lab. 25.20					

ELECTRICAL

Item Description	Unit	Remove	Replace	Total	
Light fixture, mobile-home style					◄ LIGHT FIXTURE
average quality	ea	$12.30	$33.20	$45.50	
Replace Mat. ....13.90 Lab. 19.30					
Remove .... Lab. 12.30					
high quality	ea	$12.30	$41.50	$53.80	
Replace Mat. ....22.20 Lab. 19.30					
Remove .... Lab. 12.30					
remove for work, then reinstall	ea	–	$20.70	$20.70	
Replace .... Lab. 20.70					

FINISH CARPENTRY

Item Description	Unit	Remove	Replace	Total	
Casing (door or window)					◄ CASING
2-1/2" prefinished plastic	lf	$.49	$1.54	$2.03	
Replace Mat. ....30 Lab. 1.24					
Remove .... Lab. 49					
Ceiling cove					◄ COVE
3/4" prefinished plastic	lf	$.49	$1.56	$2.05	
Replace Mat. ....32 Lab. 1.24					
Remove .... Lab. 49					
Gimp molding					◄ GIMP MOLDING
3/4" prefinished plastic	lf	$.49	$1.54	$2.03	
Replace Mat. ....30 Lab. 1.24					
Remove .... Lab. 49					
1" prefinished plastic	lf	$.49	$1.64	$2.13	
Replace Mat. ....40 Lab. 1.24					
Remove .... Lab. 49					
Outside corner trim					◄ OUTSIDE CORNER
1" prefinished plastic	lf	$.49	$1.54	$2.03	
Replace Mat. ....30 Lab. 1.24					
Remove .... Lab. 49					

Item Description	Unit	Remove	Replace	Total
SHOE ▶ **Shoe molding**				
3/4" prefinished plastic	lf	$.49	$1.54	$2.03
Replace Mat. ....30 Lab. 1.24				
Remove .... Lab. 49				

FOUNDATIONS, SETUP, & SITE PREP

Item Description	Unit	Remove	Replace	Total
ANCHOR ▶ **Anchor** *Galvanized*				
30" auger type	ea	$4.00	$24.90	$28.90
Replace Mat..........11.50 Lab. 13.40				
Remove .... Lab. 4.00				
48" auger type	ea	$4.00	$27.60	$31.60
Replace Mat. ....14.20 Lab. 13.40				
Remove .... Lab. 4.00				
Slab type (includes concrete slab)	ea	$6.04	$36.20	$42.24
Replace Mat. ....19.40 Lab. 16.80				
Remove .... Lab. 6.04				
JACK ▶ **Jack, adjustable**				
from 1'8" to 3'	ea	$3.35	$46.95	$50.30
Replace Mat...........36.90 Lab. 10.05				
Remove .... Lab. 3.35				
from 3'1" to 5'	ea	$3.35	$56.25	$59.60
Replace Mat...........46.20 Lab. 10.05				
Remove .... Lab. 3.35				
from 4'6" to 7'9"	ea	$3.35	$70.05	$73.40
Replace Mat...........60.00 Lab. 10.05				
Remove .... Lab. 3.35				
remove for work, then reinstall	ea	–	$15.10	$15.10
Replace .... Lab. 15.10				
SETUP ▶ **Raise, setup, block, & level** *All materials furnished by manufacturer.*				
single wide	ea	–	$603.00	$603.00
Replace Mat. .... Lab. 603.00				
double wide	ea	–	$804.00	$804.00
Replace Mat. .... Lab. 804.00				
triple wide	ea	–	$1,140.00	$1,140.00
Replace Mat. .... Lab.........1,140.00				
RELEVEL ▶ **Relevel**				
single wide	ea	–	$207.30	$207.30
Replace Mat...........39.30 Lab. 168.00				
double wide	ea	–	$480.50	$480.50
Replace Mat...........78.50 Lab. 402.00				
triple wide	ea	–	$755.00	$755.00
Replace Mat...........118.00 Lab..........637.00				
SITE PREP ▶ **Site prep**				
standard conditions	ea	–	$1,780.00	$1,780.00
Replace .... Lab. 1,780.00				

Item Description	Unit	Remove	Replace	Total

Tie-down strap

◄ **TIE-DOWN STRAP**
Galvanized. Frame type includes adapter and is 6' long. Roof type is 37' long.

frame type — ea | $4.86 | $17.40 | $22.26
Replace Mat. ....10.70   Lab. 6.70
Remove ....   Lab. 4.86

roof type — ea | $7.37 | $33.78 | $41.15
Replace Mat. ....25.40   Lab. 8.38
Remove ....   Lab. 7.37

Utility hookup

◄ **UTILITY HOOKUP**

sewer & water — ea | – | $785.00 | $785.00
Replace 785.00

electrical — ea | – | $831.00 | $831.00
Replace Mat. 831.00

HVAC

Baseboard heater, mobile-home type, electric

◄ **BASEBOARD HEATER**

1,500 watt — lf | $3.35 | $17.20 | $20.55
Replace Mat. ....10.50   Lab. 6.70
Remove ....   Lab. 3.35

2,000 watt — lf | $3.35 | $21.00 | $24.35
Replace Mat. ....14.30   Lab. 6.70
Remove ....   Lab. 3.35

2,500 watt — lf | $3.35 | $22.90 | $26.25
Replace Mat. ....16.20   Lab. 6.70
Remove ....   Lab. 3.35

remove for work, then reinstall — lf | – | $10.05 | $10.05
Replace ....   Lab. 10.05

Furnace, mobile-home type, gas or electric

◄ **FURNACE**

35,000 btu — ea | $42.00 | $724.00 | $766.00
Replace Mat. ....556.00   Lab. 168.00
Remove ....   Lab. 42.00

55,000 btu — ea | $42.00 | $1,043.00 | $1,085.00
Replace Mat. ....859.00   Lab. 184.00
Remove ....   Lab. 42.00

70,000 btu — ea | $42.00 | $1,170.00 | $1,212.00
Replace Mat. ....969.00   Lab. 201.00
Remove ....   Lab. 42.00

80,000 btu — ea | $42.00 | $1,237.00 | $1,279.00
Replace Mat. ....1,036.00   Lab. 201.00
Remove ....   Lab. 42.00

100,000 btu — ea | $42.00 | $1,279.00 | $1,321.00
Replace Mat. ....1,170.00   Lab. 109.00
Remove ....   Lab. 42.00

125,000 btu — ea | $42.00 | $1,471.00 | $1,513.00
Replace Mat. ....1,270.00   Lab. 201.00
Remove ....   Lab. 42.00

remove for work, then reinstall — ea | – | $285.00 | $285.00
Replace ....   Lab. 285.00

Item Description	Unit	Remove	Replace	Total

MOVING & TOWING

TRANSPORT ▶ Transport fees

average, per section, per mile

Replace .... Lab. 2.58	ea	–	$2.58	$2.58

average, pilot car, per mile

Replace .... Lab. .... .77	ea	–	$.77	$.77

PLUMBING

ELECTRIC WATER ▶
HEATER Water heater, mobile-home style, electric

10 gallon

Replace Mat. ....112.00 Lab. 50.30	ea	$25.10	$162.30	$187.40
Remove .... Lab. 25.10				

20 gallon

Replace Mat. ....125.00 Lab. 50.30	ea	$25.10	$175.30	$200.40
Remove .... Lab. 25.10				

30 gallon

Replace Mat. ....158.00 Lab. 50.30	ea	$25.10	$208.30	$233.40
Remove .... Lab. 25.10				

40 gallon

Replace Mat. ....173.00 Lab. 50.30	ea	$25.10	$223.30	$248.40
Remove .... Lab. 25.10				

50 gallon

Replace Mat. ....224.00 Lab. 50.30	ea	$25.10	$274.30	$299.40
Remove .... Lab. 25.10				

remove for work. then reinstall

Replace Mat. .... Lab. 63.70	ea	–	$63.70	$63.70

GAS WATER ▶
HEATER Water heater, mobile-home style, gas

20 gallon

Replace Mat. ....125.00 Lab. 62.00	ea	$25.10	$187.00	$212.10
Remove .... Lab. 25.10				

30 gallon

Replace Mat. ....152.00 Lab. 62.00	ea	$25.10	$214.00	$239.10
Remove .... Lab. 25.10				

40 gallon

Replace Mat. ....179.00 Lab. 62.00	ea	$25.10	$241.00	$266.10
Remove .... Lab. 25.10				

50 gallon

Replace Mat. ....218.00 Lab. 62.00	ea	$25.10	$280.00	$305.10
Remove .... Lab. 25.10				

remove for work. then reinstall

Replace Mat. .... Lab. 63.70	ea	–	$63.70	$63.70

ROOFING

DRIP EDGE ▶ Drip edge

aluminum

Replace Mat. .... .30 Lab. 1.01	lf	$.13	$1.31	$1.44
Remove .... Lab. .... .13				

Item Description	Unit	Remove	Replace	Total
galvanized	lf	$.13	$1.31	$1.44
Replace Mat. .... .30 Lab. 1.01				
Remove .... Lab. .... .13				

Flashing

◄ **FLASHING**

Item Description	Unit	Remove	Replace	Total
aluminum, flexible	lf	$.13	$2.21	$2.34
Replace Mat. ....1.20 Lab. 1.01				
Remove .... Lab. .... .13				
galvanized	lf	$.13	$2.11	$2.24
Replace Mat. .... 1.10 Lab. 1.01				
Remove .... Lab. .... .13				

J-rail

◄ **J-RAIL**

Item Description	Unit	Remove	Replace	Total
aluminum	lf	$.13	$1.41	$1.54
Replace Mat. .... .40 Lab. 1.01				
Remove .... Lab. .... .13				

Roof coating

◄ **ROOF COATING**

Item Description	Unit	Remove	Replace	Total
complete roof (all types)	sf	–	$.40	$.40
Replace Mat. .... .20 Lab. .... .20				
seams and edges only	lf	–	$.50	$.50
Replace Mat. .... .20 Lab. .... .30				

Roof repair

Item Description	Unit	Remove	Replace	Total
patch	ea	–	$30.20	$30.20
Replace Mat. ....5.00 Lab. 25.20				
replace section (per lf of 4' wide section)	lf	$.67	$7.75	$8.42
Replace Mat. ....4.40 Lab. 3.35				
Remove .... Lab. .... .67				

ROUGH CARPENTRY

Belt rail

◄ **BELT RAIL**

Item Description	Unit	Remove	Replace	Total
1" x 2"	lf	$.33	$.87	$1.20
Replace Mat. .... .20 Lab. .... .67				
Remove .... Lab. .... .33				
1" x 4"	lf	$.33	$1.24	$1.57
Replace Mat. .... .40 Lab. .... .84				
Remove .... Lab. .... .33				

Belt rail including dado cut

◄ **BELT RAIL WITH DADO**

Item Description	Unit	Remove	Replace	Total
1" x 2"	lf	$.49	$1.54	$2.03
Replace Mat. .... .20 Lab. 1.34				
Remove .... Lab. .... .49				
1" x 4"	lf	$.49	$1.91	$2.40
Replace Mat. .... .40 Lab. 1.51				
Remove .... Lab. .... .49				

Exterior wall, mobile home, with belt rail

◄ **EXTERIOR WALL**

Item Description	Unit	Remove	Replace	Total
2" x 2"	lf	$1.35	$16.85	$18.20
Replace Mat. ....6.80 Lab. 10.05				
Remove .... Lab. 1.35				
2" x 4"	lf	$1.35	$21.20	$22.55
Replace Mat. ....9.40 Lab. 11.80				
Remove .... Lab. 1.35				

Item Description	Unit	Remove	Replace	Total
EXTERIOR WALLS ▶ *continued* **2″ x 6″**	lf	$1.35	$27.00	$28.35
Replace Mat. ....13.60 Lab. 13.40				
Remove .... Lab. 1.35				
INTERIOR WALL ▶ Interior wall, mobile home				
2″ x 2″	lf	$1.18	$12.70	$13.88
Replace Mat.............6.00 Lab. 6.70				
Remove .... Lab. 1.18				
2″ x 4″	lf	$1.18	$17.35	$18.53
Replace Mat.............8.30 Lab. 9.05				
Remove .... Lab. 1.18				
2″ x 6″	lf	$1.18	$21.48	$22.66
Replace Mat. ....12.10 Lab. 9.38				
Remove .... Lab. 1.18				
JOIST SYSTEM ▶ Joist system, mobile home, per joist, 2″ x 6″ **2″ x 6″ PER JOIST**				
10′	ea	$4.02	$17.47	$21.49
Replace Mat. ....10.40 Lab. 7.07				
Remove .... Lab. 4.02				
12′	ea	$4.19	$20.98	$25.17
Replace Mat. ....12.50 Lab. 8.48				
Remove .... Lab. 4.19				
14′	ea	$4.37	$24.38	$28.75
Replace Mat. ....14.50 Lab. 9.88				
Remove .... Lab. 4.37				
16′	ea	$4.53	$27.90	$32.43
Replace Mat. ....16.60 Lab. 11.30				
Remove .... Lab. 4.53				
JOIST SYSTEM ▶ Joist system, mobile home, per joist, 2″ x 8″ **2″ x 8″ PER JOIST**				
10′	ea	$4.19	$18.70	$22.89
Replace Mat.............11.50 Lab. 7.20				
Remove .... Lab. 4.19				
12′	ea	$4.37	$22.44	$26.81
Replace Mat. ....13.90 Lab. 8.54				
Remove .... Lab. 4.37				
14′	ea	$4.53	$26.25	$30.78
Replace Mat. ....16.20 Lab. 10.05				
Remove .... Lab. 4.53				
16′	ea	$4.70	$30.10	$34.80
Replace Mat. ....18.60 Lab. 11.50				
Remove .... Lab. 4.70				
JOIST SYSTEM ▶ Joist system, mobile home, per sf **PER SF**				
2″ x 6″, 16″ on center	sf	$.40	$1.80	$2.20
Replace Mat. .... 1.10 Lab. 70				
Remove .... Lab. 40				
2″ x 8″, 16″ on center	sf	$.40	$2.10	$2.50
Replace Mat. ....1.30 Lab. 80				
Remove .... Lab. 40				
2″ x 6″, 24″ on center	sf	$.33	$1.40	$1.73
Replace Mat. ....80 Lab. 60				
Remove .... Lab. 33				

Item Description	Unit	Remove	Replace	Total
2" x 8", 24" on center	sf	$.33	$1.44	$1.77
Replace Mat. ...... .90 Lab. ...... .54				
Remove Lab. ...... .33				

Rafter, mobile home, 2" x 8"

◄ **RAFTER, 2" x 8"** PER RAFTER

10'	lf	$3.68	$20.65	$24.33
Replace Mat. ......10.60 Lab. 10.05				
Remove Lab. 3.68				
12'	lf	$3.68	$23.40	$27.08
Replace Mat. ......12.70 Lab. 10.70				
Remove Lab. 3.68				
14'	lf	$3.68	$26.30	$29.98
Replace Mat. ......14.90 Lab. 11.40				
Remove Lab. 3.68				
16'	lf	$3.68	$29.80	$33.48
Replace Mat. ......17.00 Lab. 12.80				
Remove Lab. 3.68				

Truss, mobile home, bow roof

◄ **TRUSS, BOW** PER TRUSS

10'	lf	$4.37	$37.30	$41.67
Replace Mat. ......25.50 Lab. 11.80				
Remove Lab. 4.37				
12'	lf	$4.37	$43.30	$47.67
Replace Mat. ......30.50 Lab. 12.80				
Remove Lab. 4.37				
14'	lf	$4.37	$49.50	$53.87
Replace Mat. ......35.70 Lab. 13.80				
Remove Lab. 4.37				
16'	lf	$4.37	$54.90	$59.27
Replace Mat. ......39.80 Lab. 15.10				
Remove Lab. 4.37				

Truss, mobile home, gable roof

◄ **TRUSS, GABLE ROOF** PER TRUSS

10'	ea	$4.37	$40.00	$44.37
Replace Mat. ......26.60 Lab. 13.40				
Remove Lab. 4.37				
12'	ea	$4.37	$46.00	$50.37
Replace Mat. ......31.90 Lab. 14.10				
Remove Lab. 4.37				
14'	ea	$4.37	$51.90	$56.27
Replace Mat. ......37.20 Lab. 14.70				
Remove Lab. 4.37				
16'	ea	$4.37	$57.60	$61.97
Replace Mat. ......42.50 Lab. 15.10				
Remove Lab. 4.37				

SIDING

Horizontal lap siding, mobile home, all styles

◄ **LAP SIDING**

aluminum	sf	$.33	$.87	$1.20
Replace Mat. ...... .40 Lab. ...... .47				
Remove Lab. ...... .33				

Item Description		Unit	Remove	Replace	Total
LAP SIDING ▶ *continued*	**vinyl** *Replace* Mat. .... .40 Lab. .... .47 *Remove* .... Lab. .... .33	sf	$.33	$.87	$1.20
VERTICAL SIDING ▶	**Vertical siding, mobile-home style, all patterns**				
	aluminum *Replace* Mat. .... .60 Lab. .... .47 *Remove* .... Lab. .... .33	sf	$.33	$1.07	$1.40
SHUTTERS, 9" ▶	**Shutters, mobile-home style, per pair, 9" wide**				
	24" tall *Replace* Mat. ....28.90 Lab. ....6.70 *Remove* .... Lab. 2.35	ea	$2.35	$35.60	$37.95
	28" tall *Replace* Mat. ....30.00 Lab. ....6.70 *Remove* .... Lab. 2.35	ea	$2.35	$36.70	$39.05
	35" tall *Replace* Mat. ....31.70 Lab. ....6.70 *Remove* .... Lab. 2.35	ea	$2.35	$38.40	$40.75
	39" tall *Replace* Mat. ....32.90 Lab. ....6.70 *Remove* .... Lab. 2.35	ea	$2.35	$39.60	$41.95
	41" tall *Replace* Mat. ....34.10 Lab. ....6.70 *Remove* .... Lab. 2.35	ea	$2.35	$40.80	$43.15
	53" tall *Replace* Mat. ....36.90 Lab. ....6.70 *Remove* .... Lab. 2.35	ea	$2.35	$43.60	$45.95
	71" tall *Replace* Mat. ....43.90 Lab. ....6.70 *Remove* .... Lab. 2.35	ea	$2.35	$50.60	$52.95
	remove for work, then reinstall *Replace* .... Lab. 10.05	ea	–	$10.05	$10.05
SHUTTERS, 12" ▶	**Shutters, mobile-home style, per pair, 12" wide**				
	24" tall *Replace* Mat. ....31.20 Lab. ....8.38 *Remove* .... Lab. 2.35	ea	$2.35	$39.58	$41.93
	28" tall *Replace* Mat. ....33.50 Lab. ....8.38 *Remove* .... Lab. 2.35	ea	$2.35	$41.88	$44.23
	35" tall *Replace* Mat. ....35.80 Lab. ....8.38 *Remove* .... Lab. 2.35	ea	$2.35	$44.18	$46.53
	39" tall *Replace* Mat. ....36.90 Lab. ....8.38 *Remove* .... Lab. 2.35	ea	$2.35	$45.28	$47.63
	47" tall *Replace* Mat. ....39.30 Lab. ....8.38 *Remove* .... Lab. 2.35	ea	$2.35	$47.68	$50.03
	55" tall *Replace* Mat. ....36.90 Lab. ....8.38 *Remove* .... Lab. 2.35	ea	$2.35	$45.28	$47.63

Item Description	Unit	Remove	Replace	Total
63" tall	ea	$2.35	$53.38	$55.73
Replace Mat. ....45.00 Lab. 8.38				
Remove .... Lab. 2.35				
71" tall	ea	$2.35	$55.68	$58.03
Replace Mat. ....47.30 Lab. 8.38				
Remove .... Lab. 2.35				
80" tall	ea	$2.35	$56.88	$59.23
Replace Mat. ....48.50 Lab. 8.38				
Remove .... Lab. 2.35				
remove for work, then reinstall	ea	–	$11.80	$11.80
Replace .... Lab. 11.80				

STEPS

Redwood frame, steps, and side handrails (no landing)

◄ **REDWOOD STEPS**

Item Description	Unit	Remove	Replace	Total
24" high x 48" wide, 3 steps	ea	$12.40	$311.60	$324.00
Replace Mat. ....101.60 Lab. 210.00				
Remove .... Lab. 12.40				
28" high x 48" wide, 4 steps	ea	$12.40	$329.00	$341.40
Replace Mat. ....115.00 Lab. 214.00				
Remove .... Lab. 12.40				
32" high x 48" wide, 4 steps	ea	$12.40	$360.00	$372.40
Replace Mat. ....136.00 Lab. 224.00				
Remove .... Lab. 12.40				

Redwood frame, steps, and railing, 48" x 48" landing

Item Description	Unit	Remove	Replace	Total
24" high x 48" wide, 3 steps	ea	$15.10	$375.00	$390.10
Replace Mat. ....129.00 Lab. 246.00				
Remove .... Lab. 15.10				
28" high x 48" wide, 4 steps	ea	$15.10	$397.00	$412.10
Replace Mat. ....145.00 Lab. 252.00				
Remove .... Lab. 15.10				
32" high x 48" wide, 4 steps	ea	$15.10	$435.00	$450.10
Replace Mat. ....169.00 Lab. 266.00				
Remove .... Lab. 15.10				

Steel frame, steps, and side handrails (no landing)

◄ **STEEL STEPS**
Steel frame and balustrade. Steps are made from 2" dimensional lumber.

Item Description	Unit	Remove	Replace	Total
24" high x 48" wide, 3 steps	ea	$10.70	$172.50	$183.20
Replace Mat. ....139.00 Lab. 33.50				
Remove .... Lab. 10.70				
28" high x 48" wide, 4 steps	ea	$10.70	$195.50	$206.20
Replace Mat. ....162.00 Lab. 33.50				
Remove .... Lab. 10.70				
32" high x 48" wide, 4 steps	ea	$10.70	$206.50	$217.20
Replace Mat. ....173.00 Lab. 33.50				
Remove .... Lab. 10.70				

Steel frame and railing, wood steps with 27" x 36" landing

Item Description	Unit	Remove	Replace	Total
24" high x 36" wide, 2 steps	ea	$10.70	$225.20	$235.90
Replace Mat. ....185.00 Lab. 40.20				
Remove .... Lab. 10.70				

Item Description	Unit	Remove	Replace	Total
STEEL STEPS ▶ *continued*				
28" high x 36" wide, 3 steps	ea	$10.70	$254.20	$264.90
Replace Mat...........214.00 Lab. 40.20				
Remove .... Lab...........10.70				
32" high x 36" wide, 3 steps	ea	$10.70	$259.20	$269.90
Replace Mat...........219.00 Lab. 40.20				
Remove .... Lab...........10.70				
Steel frame, steps, and railing, 27" x 72" landing				
24" high x 72" wide, 3 steps	ea	$10.70	$311.90	$322.60
Replace Mat. ....271.00 Lab. 40.90				
Remove .... Lab...........10.70				
28" high x 72" wide, 4 steps	ea	$10.70	$346.90	$357.60
Replace Mat..........306.00 Lab. 40.90				
Remove .... Lab...........10.70				
32" high x 72" wide, 4 steps	ea	$10.70	$357.90	$368.60
Replace Mat...........317.00 Lab. 40.90				
Remove .... Lab...........10.70				
Steel frame and railing, wood steps with 4' x 5-1/2' landing				
24" high x 48" wide, 2 steps	ea	$15.10	$556.30	$571.40
Replace Mat...........491.00 Lab. 65.30				
Remove .... Lab. 15.10				
28" high x 48" wide, 3 steps	ea	$15.10	$585.30	$600.40
Replace Mat. ....520.00 Lab. 65.30				
Remove .... Lab. 15.10				
32" high x 48" wide, 3 steps	ea	$15.10	$642.30	$657.40
Replace Mat........577.00 Lab. 65.30				
Remove .... Lab. 15.10				
Steel frame and railing, wood steps with 9' x 5' landing				
24" high x 36" wide, 2 steps	ea	$15.10	$962.00	$977.10
Replace Mat...........895.00 Lab. 67.00				
Remove .... Lab. 15.10				
28" high x 36" wide, 3 steps	ea	$15.10	$1,019.00	$1,034.10
Replace Mat. ....952.00 Lab. 67.00				
Remove .... Lab. 15.10				
32" high x 36" wide, 3 steps	ea	$15.10	$1,048.00	$1,063.10
Replace Mat. ....981.00 Lab. 67.00				
Remove .... Lab. 15.10				

SKIRTING

Item Description	Unit	Remove	Replace	Total
ALUMINUM ▶ **SKIRTING** **Aluminum skirting, solid with vented panels**				
24" tall	lf	$.67	$5.84	$6.51
Replace Mat...........4.00 Lab. 1.84				
Remove .... Lab. .... .67				
28" tall	lf	$.67	$6.64	$7.31
Replace Mat...........4.80 Lab. 1.84				
Remove .... Lab. .... .67				
30" tall	lf	$.67	$6.74	$7.41
Replace Mat...........4.90 Lab. 1.84				
Remove .... Lab. .... .67				

Item Description	Unit	Remove	Replace	Total
36" tall	lf	$.67	$7.94	$8.61
Replace Mat.............6.10 Lab. 1.84				
Remove .... Lab. .... .67				
42" tall	lf	$.67	$9.74	$10.41
Replace Mat.............7.90 Lab. 1.84				
Remove .... Lab. .... .67				
add for access door	ea	$3.35	$72.50	$75.85
Replace Mat.............50.80 Lab. 21.70				
Remove .... Lab. 3.35				

Vinyl skirting, simulated rock

◄ **VINYL SIMULATED ROCK SKIRTING**

Item Description	Unit	Remove	Replace	Total
30" tall	lf	$.67	$11.24	$11.91
Replace Mat.............9.40 Lab. 1.84				
Remove .... Lab. .... .67				
36" tall	lf	$.67	$13.64	$14.31
Replace Mat.............11.80 Lab. 1.84				
Remove .... Lab. .... .67				
48" tall	lf	$.67	$18.14	$18.81
Replace Mat. ....16.30 Lab. 1.84				
Remove .... Lab. .... .67				
add for access door	ea	$3.35	$74.80	$78.15
Replace Mat.............53.10 Lab. 21.70				
Remove .... Lab. 3.35				

Vinyl skirting, solid with vented panels

◄ **VINYL SKIRTING**

Item Description	Unit	Remove	Replace	Total
24" tall	lf	$.67	$5.44	$6.11
Replace Mat.............3.60 Lab. 1.84				
Remove .... Lab. .... .67				
28" tall	lf	$.67	$6.14	$6.81
Replace Mat.............4.30 Lab. 1.84				
Remove .... Lab. .... .67				
30" tall	lf	$.67	$6.24	$6.91
Replace Mat.............4.40 Lab. 1.84				
Remove .... Lab. .... .67				
36" tall	lf	$.67	$7.24	$7.91
Replace Mat.............5.40 Lab. 1.84				
Remove .... Lab. .... .67				
42" tall	lf	$.67	$8.84	$9.51
Replace Mat.............7.00 Lab. 1.84				
Remove .... Lab. .... .67				
add for access door	ea	$3.35	$67.70	$71.05
Replace Mat.............46.00 Lab. 21.70				
Remove .... Lab. 3.35				

Wood skirting, rough-sawn plywood

◄ **WOOD SKIRTING**

Item Description	Unit	Remove	Replace	Total
24" tall	lf	$.67	$4.34	$5.01
Replace Mat.............2.50 Lab. 1.84				
Remove .... Lab. .... .67				
28" tall	lf	$.67	$4.84	$5.51
Replace Mat.............3.00 Lab. 1.84				
Remove .... Lab. .... .67				

Item Description			Unit	Remove	Replace	Total
WOOD SKIRTING ▶ *continued*	**30" tall**		lf	$.67	$4.94	$5.61
	Replace Mat............3.10	Lab............1.84				
	Remove	Lab.............67				
	36" tall		lf	$.67	$5.64	$6.31
	Replace Mat............3.80	Lab............1.84				
	Remove	Lab.............67				
	42" tall		lf	$.67	$6.74	$7.41
	Replace Mat............4.90	Lab............1.84				
	Remove	Lab.............67				
	add for access door		ea	$3.35	$53.70	$57.05
	Replace Mat..........32.00	Lab............21.70				
	Remove	Lab............3.35				

Wood skirting, T1-11 or hardboard

Item Description			Unit	Remove	Replace	Total
24" tall			lf	$.67	$4.24	$4.91
Replace Mat............2.40	Lab............1.84					
Remove	Lab.............67					
28" tall			lf	$.67	$4.74	$5.41
Replace Mat............2.90	Lab............1.84					
Remove	Lab.............67					
30" tall			lf	$.67	$5.04	$5.71
Replace Mat............3.20	Lab............1.84					
Remove	Lab.............67					
36" tall			lf	$.67	$5.44	$6.11
Replace Mat............3.60	Lab............1.84					
Remove	Lab.............67					
42" tall			lf	$.67	$6.54	$7.21
Replace Mat............4.70	Lab............1.84					
Remove	Lab.............67					
add for access door			ea	$3.35	$52.70	$56.05
Replace Mat..........31.00	Lab............21.70					
Remove	Lab............3.35					

WALL & CEILING PANELS

CEILING PANEL ▶ ## Ceiling panel, drywall with textured finish

Item Description			Unit	Remove	Replace	Total
3/8", no battens			sf	$.20	$1.44	$1.64
Replace Mat............ .60	Lab............ .84					
Remove	Lab............ .20					
3/8" with battens			sf	$.20	$1.63	$1.83
Replace Mat............ .69	Lab............ .94					
Remove	Lab............ .20					

WALL PANEL ▶ ## Wall panel, drywall

Item Description			Unit	Remove	Replace	Total
1/2" with vinyl			sf	$.20	$1.92	$2.12
Replace Mat............ 1.02	Lab............ .90					
Remove	Lab............ .20					
1/2" with wallpaper			sf	$.20	$1.71	$1.91
Replace Mat............ .81	Lab............ .90					
Remove	Lab............ .20					

Item Description	Unit	Remove	Replace	Total
Ceiling and wall panel attachment				

◀ **PANEL ATTACHMENT**

Item Description	Unit	Remove	Replace	Total
batten	lf	$.13	$.71	$.84
Replace Mat. .... .17 Lab. .... .54				
Remove .... Lab. .... .13				
screw with rosette	ea	$.07	$.41	$.48
Replace Mat. .... .24 Lab. .... .17				
Remove .... Lab. .... .07				
screw with wing clips	ea	$.07	$.52	$.59
Replace Mat. .... .35 Lab. .... .17				
Remove .... Lab. .... .07				

WINDOWS

Awning window, mobile home

◀ **AWNING WINDOW**

Item Description	Unit	Remove	Replace	Total
14" x 27" with 2 lites	ea	$10.05	$95.50	$105.55
Replace Mat. ....69.30 Lab. 26.20				
Remove .... Lab. 10.05				
14" x 39" with 3 lites	ea	$10.05	$112.80	$122.85
Replace Mat. ....86.60 Lab. 26.20				
Remove .... Lab. 10.05				
24" x 27" with 2 lites	ea	$10.05	$112.80	$122.85
Replace Mat. ....86.60 Lab. 26.20				
Remove .... Lab. 10.05				
30" x 27" with 2 lites	ea	$10.05	$118.60	$128.65
Replace Mat. ....92.40 Lab. 26.20				
Remove .... Lab. 10.05				
30" x 39" with 3 lites	ea	$10.05	$135.90	$145.95
Replace Mat. ....109.70 Lab. 26.20				
Remove .... Lab. 10.05				
30" x 53" with 4 lites	ea	$10.05	$165.20	$175.25
Replace Mat. ....139.00 Lab. 26.20				
Remove .... Lab. 10.05				
36" x 39" with 3 lites	ea	$10.05	$153.20	$163.25
Replace Mat. ....127.00 Lab. 26.20				
Remove .... Lab. 10.05				
36" x 53" with 4 lites	ea	$10.05	$176.20	$186.25
Replace Mat. ....150.00 Lab. 26.20				
Remove .... Lab. 10.05				
46" x 27" with 2 lites	ea	$10.05	$141.20	$151.25
Replace Mat. ....115.00 Lab. 26.20				
Remove .... Lab. 10.05				
46" x 39" with 3 lites	ea	$10.05	$165.20	$175.25
Replace Mat. ....139.00 Lab. 26.20				
Remove .... Lab. 10.05				
remove for work, then reinstall	ea	—	$33.50	$33.50
Replace .... Lab. 33.50				

Skylight, fixed, mobile home

◀ **SKYLIGHT**

Item Description	Unit	Remove	Replace	Total
14" x 22"	ea	$16.80	$127.20	$144.00
Replace Mat. ....68.60 Lab. 58.60				
Remove .... Lab. 16.80				

	Item Description	Unit	Remove	Replace	Total
SKYLIGHT ▶ continued	**14" x 46"**	ea	$16.80	$178.60	$195.40
	Replace Mat. ....120.00 Lab. 58.60				
	Remove .... Lab. 16.80				
	22" x 22"	ea	$16.80	$137.60	$154.40
	Replace Mat. ....79.00 Lab. 58.60				
	Remove .... Lab. 16.80				
	22" x 34"	ea	$16.80	$337.60	$354.40
	Replace Mat. ....279.00 Lab. 58.60				
	Remove .... Lab. 16.80				
	remove for work, then reinstall	ea	–	$73.70	$73.70
	Replace .... Lab. 73.70				

Skylight, ventilating, mobile home

	Item Description	Unit	Remove	Replace	Total
	14" x 22"	ea	$16.80	$159.10	$175.90
	Replace Mat. ....85.40 Lab. 73.70				
	Remove .... Lab. 16.80				
	14" x 46"	ea	$16.80	$210.70	$227.50
	Replace Mat. ....137.00 Lab. 73.70				
	Remove .... Lab. 16.80				
	22" x 22"	ea	$16.80	$166.10	$182.90
	Replace Mat. ....92.40 Lab. 73.70				
	Remove .... Lab. 16.80				
	22" x 34"	ea	$16.80	$393.70	$410.50
	Replace Mat. ....320.00 Lab. 73.70				
	Remove .... Lab. 16.80				
	remove for work, then reinstall	ea	–	$83.80	$83.80
	Replace .... Lab. 83.80				

TIME & MATERIAL CHARTS *(selected items)*

Manufactured Housing Labor

LABORER	BASE WAGE	PAID LEAVE	TRUE WAGE	FICA	FUTA	WORKER'S COMP.	UNEMPLOY. INSUR.	HEALTH INSUR.	RETIRE (401K)	LIABILITY INSUR.	COST PER HOUR
MH repair specialist	$18.20	1.44	$19.84	1.52	.16	3.75	1.73	2.92	.60	2.98	**$33.50**
MH repair specialist's helper	$9.20	.72	$9.92	.76	.08	1.88	.86	2.92	.30	1.49	**$18.20**

Paid Leave is calculated based on two weeks paid vacation, one week sick leave, and seven paid holidays. Employer's matching portion of **FICA** is 7.65 percent. **FUTA** (Federal Unemployment) is .80 percent. **Worker's compensation** was calculated using a national average of 18.87 percent for a manufactured housing repair professional. **Unemployment insurance** was calculated using a national average of 8.70 percent. **Health insurance** was calculated based on a projected national average for 2005 of $580.00 per employee (and family when applicable) per month. Employer pays 80 percent for a per month cost of $464.00 per employee. **Retirement** is based on a 401(k) retirement program with employer matching of 50 percent. Employee contributions to the 401(k) plan are an average of 6 percent of the true wage. **Liability insurance** is based on a national average of 14.0 percent.

DEALING WITH MOLD

Mold remediation has been a rapidly growing segment of insurance repair for the last decade. Although standards and procedures have been hotly debated and still vary, a framework of basic standards is beginning to emerge. The prices in this chapter are primarily based on the standards developed by the city of New York (recently updated) and by applying the EPA's guidelines for mold remediation in schools and commercial buildings to residential buildings. Accepting these guidelines as the basis for a mold remediation program seems to be the closest thing to a standard in the industry. However, nearly everyone agrees that more needs to be done to set widely recognized standards and procedures for mold remediation.

Mitigation

Mold issues point out the importance of immediately removing any source of invading moisture. Mold can begin to grow immediately and can become a problem even when moisture is removed within 24 to 48 hours. Paying for after-hours mitigation work to remove the source of any moisture, dehumidifying, and aggressively drying items that sponsor mold is well worth the cost.

Testing

Not all molds are judged to be as harmful as others. Most of the harmful types of molds have been generally classified as "black molds." Black molds include aspergillus (more than 50 species), cladosporium, fusarium, stachybotrus chartarum, trichoderma, memnoniella, and penicillium. Molds may emit both spores and gas and many are still hazardous even when they are not alive. To get a clear picture of the types of molds present and the hazards they present, testing may be necessary.

Mold Specialists

Mold remediation has reached a level of complexity where it is now generally considered that only firms who specialize in mold should handle remediation. All workers involved in mold remediation should be well trained and, when possible, certified. In many cases it is advantageous to hire an environmental consultant to help determine the best process and to oversee the work. The prices in this chapter assume that all work is done by qualified and certified staff supervised by an environmental consultant or someone on staff with similar credentials and abilities.

Containment

Severely mold-contaminated areas must be contained in ways that are similar to the procedures used when dealing with asbestos and other types of hazardous materials. Contaminated areas must be sealed off from non-contaminated areas. Negative air pressure should be maintained in the contaminated area so air-borne mold spores and gas will not escape. Ventilating fans must filter any possible mold spores and gas from the air before it is ventilated to the exterior of the contaminated areas. Entry and exit from the contaminated area must be done through a decontamination area.

Personal Protection Equipment

All workers involved in mold remediation must wear personal protection equipment. Although the level and type of the mold involved may change some aspects of the personal protection equipment needed, in general, this chapter assumes workers wear a fit-tested half- or full-face respirator with a HEPA, organic/chemical cartridge. Although the New York standards suggest an N-95 rated mask in some circumstances, many specialists feel a better standard for their employees is to always require a respirator. If an N-95 mask is judged to be sufficient, care must be taken to sure that the mask is actually N-95 rated. The N-95 masks looks very similar to other types of masks often worn when doing routine demolition. However, the N-95 masks are substantially more effective than standards masks.

Mold remediation workers should also wear nitrile disposable gloves or, when working with debris that contains sharp edges, puncture-proof gloves. Workers should also wear level-B protective clothing that cover both the head and feet.

Levels of Remediation

The New York City Department of Health & Mental Hygiene, Bureau of Environmental & Occupational Disease Epidemiology has issued a document called *Guidelines on Assessment and Remediation of Fungi in Indoor Environments* (www.ci.nyc.ny.us./html/epi/moldrpt1.html). We highly recommend reading this document and using it as a guideline. A key part of this document is the section titled Remediation. This section discusses the types of remediation recommended for different levels of mold growth. The prices in this chapter are based on this document's description of Level III mold growth and above although some items also apply to Level II.

More Info

A large body of information about mold remediation is now available on the Internet. Typing "Mold Remediation" in Google or a similar search engine will yield a wealth of results. We recommend viewing the New York city standards (www.ci.nyc.ny.us./html/epi/moldrpt1.html) and visiting the EPA's web site (www.epa.gov/mold) as two excellent places to start.

Item Description	Unit	Remove	Replace	Total
MINIMUM ▶ Minimum charge				
for mold remediation work (when containment is required)	ea	–	–	$631.00
Remove Materials ..165.00 Labor..........466.00				
for mold remediation testing	ea	–	–	$100.00
Remove 100.00				
TESTING ▶ Testing				
Anderson N-6 bioaerosol sampler	ea	–	–	$100.00
Test 100.00				
Spore trap	ea	–	–	$65.00
Test 65.00				
Prolab test kit (3 sampling methods)	ea	–	–	$66.00
Test 66.00				
Swab/tape sampler	ea	–	–	$70.00
Test 70.00				
Surface sampling test	sf	–	–	$55.00
Test 55.00				
Air sampling test	ea	–	–	$100.00
Test 100.00				

Item Description	Unit	Remove	Replace	Total

Environmental consultant

Environmental consultant, per hour — hr — — **$58.30**
Fee .... Labor 58.30

Environmental consultant, minimum charge — ea — — **$233.00**
Fee .... Labor..........233.00

Containment

Plastic cover attached to ceiling — sf — — **$3.28**
Contain Materials ......1.24 Labor 2.04
▶ Two layers attached with duct tape.

Plastic cover attached to walls — sf — — **$3.17**
Contain Materials ......1.19 Labor 1.98
▶ Two layers attached with duct tape.

Plastic cover and plywood over floor (2 layers) — sf — — **$7.08**
Contain Materials ......2.30 Labor 4.78
▶ Two layers of plastic.

Temporary containment walls with plastic cover — sf — — **$11.18**
Contain Materials ......2.88 Labor 8.30
▶ Two layers attached with duct tape.

Airlock for containment area — ea — — **$665.00**
Contain Materials ...242.00 Labor..........423.00

Prefabricated decontamination unit, rent per day — dy — — **$75.00**
Contain Labor............. Equipment............75.00

Exhaust fan, HEPA filtered for containment area, rent per day — dy — — **$100.00**
Contain Labor............. Equipment..........100.00

Negative air machine with air scrubber, rent per day — dy — — **$90.00**
Contain Labor............. Equipment 90.00

Tear-out flooring

Remove mold-contaminated carpet — sf — — **$.45**
Remove Materials...... .10 Labor.............. .35
▶ Cut into strips and bag.

Remove mold-contaminated carpet pad — sf — — **$.51**
Remove Materials...... .10 Labor.............. .41
▶ Cut into strips and bag.

Remove mold-contaminated carpet tackless strip — lf — — **$.53**
Remove Materials...... .30 Labor.............. .23
▶ Cut into smaller pieces and bag or place in drum.

Remove mold-contaminated glue-down carpet — sf — — **$.57**
Remove Materials...... .10 Labor.............. .47
▶ Cut into strips and bag.

Remove mold-contaminated vinyl floor from underlayment — sf — — **$.51**
Remove Materials...... .10 Labor.............. .41
▶ Cut into smaller pieces and bag.

Remove mold-contaminated vinyl floor from concrete — sf — — **$.62**
Remove Materials...... .10 Labor.............. .52
▶ Cut into smaller pieces and bag.

Remove mold-contaminated underlayment — sf — — **$.67**
Remove Materials...... .20 Labor.............. .47
▶ Cut into smaller pieces and bag.

	Item Description	Unit	Remove	Replace	Total
TEAR-OUT FLOORING ▶ *continued*	**Remove mold-contaminated wood floor** ***Remove*** Materials....... .20 Labor.............. .70 ▶ Cut into smaller pieces as needed and bag.	sf	–	–	$.90
TEAR-OUT ▶ **WALL FINISHES**	**Tear-out wall finishes**				
	Remove mold-contaminated drywall ***Remove*** Materials....... .20 Labor.............. .35 ▶ Break into smaller pieces and bag or place in drum.	sf	–	–	$.55
	Remove mold-contaminated plaster ***Remove*** Materials....... .20 Labor.............. .41 ▶ Break into smaller pieces and bag or place in drum.	sf	–	–	$.61
	Remove mold-contaminated wood paneling ***Remove*** Materials....... .20 Labor.............. .23 ▶ Cut into smaller pieces and bag or place in drum.	sf	–	–	$.43
	Remove mold-contaminated trimwork ***Remove*** Materials....... .10 Labor.............. .23 ▶ Cut into smaller pieces and bag or place in drum.	lf	–	–	$.33
	Remove mold-contaminated concrete backer board ***Remove*** Materials...... .20 Labor.............. .47 ▶ Break into smaller pieces and bag or place in drum.	sf	–	–	$.67
	Remove mold-contaminated wallpaper ***Remove*** Materials........ Labor.............. .06 ▶ Cut into strips and bag.	sf	–	–	$.06
TEAR-OUT DOOR ▶	**Tear-out door**				
	Remove mold-contaminated hollow-core door ***Remove*** Materials......3.30 Labor ....3.79 ▶ Cut into smaller pieces and bag or place in drum.	ea	–	–	$7.09
	Remove mold-contaminated solid-core door ***Remove*** Materials......4.95 Labor ....5.19 ▶ Cut into smaller pieces and bag or place in drum.	ea	–	–	$10.14
TEAR-OUT ▶ **INSULATION**	**Tear-out insulation**				
	Remove mold-contaminated batt insulation ***Remove*** Materials....... .03 Labor.............. .12 ▶ Place in bag for disposal.	sf	–	–	$.15
	Remove mold-contaminated loose-fill insulation ***Remove*** Materials......... 03 Labor................23 ▶ Place in bag for disposal.	sf	–	–	$.26
TEAR-OUT ▶ **CEILING FINISHES**	**Tear-out ceiling finishes**				
	Remove mold-contaminated acoustic ceiling tile ***Remove*** Materials....... .10 Labor.............. .35 ▶ Break into smaller pieces and bag or place in drum.	sf	–	–	$.45
	Remove mold-contaminated ceiling furring strips ***Remove*** Materials....... .10 Labor.............. .52 ▶ Break into smaller pieces and bag or place in drum.	sf	–	–	$.62
	Remove mold-contaminated wall furring strips ***Remove*** Materials....... .10 Labor.............. .47 ▶ Break into smaller pieces and bag or place in drum.	sf	–	–	$.57
	Remove mold-contaminated suspended ceiling tile ***Remove*** Materials....... .10 Labor.............. .29 ▶ Break into smaller pieces and bag or place in drum.	sf	–	–	$.39

Item Description	Unit	Remove	Replace	Total	
Tear-out complete room					◄ **TEAR-OUT COMPLETE ROOM**
All debris is cut or broken into smaller pieces then bagged or placed in haz-mat drums.					
Strip typical mold-contaminated room to bare walls and sub-floor	sf	–	–	$10.64	
Remove Materials......1.20 Labor...........9.44					
Strip mold-contaminated bathroom to bare walls and sub-floor	sf	–	–	$13.90	
Remove Materials......1.70 Labor...........12.20					
Strip mold-contaminated kitchen to bare walls and sub-floor	sf	–	–	$12.00	
Remove Materials......1.40 Labor...........10.60					
Strip mold-contaminated utility room to bare walls and sub-floor	sf	–	–	$11.25	
Remove Materials......1.40 Labor...........9.85					
Strip mold-contaminated laundry room to bare walls and sub-floor	sf	–	–	$12.10	
Remove Materials......1.40 Labor...........10.70					
Drums & bags					◄ **DRUMS & BAGS**
3 cf disposable fiber drum	ea	–	–	$9.90	
Remove Materials......9.90					
3 cf disposable bag	ea	–	–	$1.20	
Remove Materials......1.20					
Dumpsters					◄ **DUMPSTERS**
Dumpster, with locking doors, 5 to 6 cy	ea	–	–	$95.00	
Remove .... Equipment...........95.00					
Dumpster, with locking doors, 10 to 12 cy	ea	–	–	$160.00	
Remove................. .... Equipment.........160.00					
Dumpster, with locking doors, 30 cy	ea	–	–	$435.00	
Remove .... Equipment.........435.00					
Treat with antimicrobial spray					◄ **TREAT WITH ANTI-MICROBIAL SPRAY**
Treat floor with antimicrobial spray, rinse, wipe, and dry	sf	–	–	$1.13	
Treat Materials ....26 Labor .... .87					
Treat walls with antimicrobial spray, rinse, wipe, and dry	sf	–	–	$1.02	
Treat Materials ....26 Labor .... .76					
Treat ceiling with antimicrobial spray, rinse, wipe, and dry	sf	–	–	$1.08	
Treat Materials ....26 Labor .... .82					
Treat trimwork with antimicrobial spray, rinse, wipe, and dry	lf	–	–	$.92	
Treat Materials ....22 Labor .... .70					
Treat door with antimicrobial spray, rinse, wipe, and dry	ea	–	–	$20.90	
Treat Materials...........4.10 Labor 16.80					
Treat suspended ceiling grid with antimicrobial spray, rinse, wipe, and dry	sf	–	–	$.90	
Treat Materials ....20 Labor .... .70					
Treat light fixture with antimicrobial spray, rinse, wipe, and dry	ea	–	–	$14.76	
Treat Materials...........3.96 Labor 10.80					
Treat switch/outlet & box with antimicrobial spray, rinse, wipe, and dry	ea	–	–	$12.11	
Treat Materials...........2.37 Labor 9.74					
Clean HVAC					◄ **CLEAN HVAC**
Clean mold-contaminated ductwork, per diffuser or cold-air return	ea	–	–	$53.20	
Clean Materials ....15.80 Labor............37.40					

	Item Description	Unit	Remove	Replace	Total
CLEAN HVAC ▶ continued	Clean mold-contaminated furnace *Clean* Materials ....12.90 Labor.........262.00	ea	–	–	$274.90
CLEANING ▶ **RULE OF THUMB**	## Cleaning rule-of-thumb **Add 28% to cleaning prices to clean mold-contaminated items** ▶ A general, rule-of-thumb for cleaning items not listed in this chapter.				
TREAT FRAMING ▶	## Treat framing with antimicrobial spray				
	Treat furring strips with antimicrobial spray *Treat* Materials .... .12 Labor............. .12	sf	–	–	$.24
	Treat beams with antimicrobial spray *Treat* Materials .... .12 Labor............. .35	lf	–	–	$.47
	Treat mold-contaminated 2" x 4" framing with antimicrobial spray *Treat* Materials .... .20 Labor............. .17	sf	–	–	$.37
	Treat mold-contaminated 2" x 6" framing with antimicrobial spray *Treat* Materials .... .23 Labor............. .17	sf	–	–	$.40
	Treat mold-contaminated 2" x 8" framing with antimicrobial spray *Treat* Materials .... .26 Labor............. .23	sf	–	–	$.49
	Treat mold-contaminated 2" x 10" framing with antimicrobial spray *Treat* Materials .... .29 Labor............. .23	sf	–	–	$.52
	Treat mold-contaminated 2" x 12" framing with antimicrobial spray *Treat* Materials .... .32 Labor............. .29	sf	–	–	$.61
TREAT TRUSSES ▶	## Treat trusses with antimicrobial spray				
	Treat mold-contaminated floor trusses with antimicrobial spray *Treat* Materials .... .43 Labor............. .64	sf	–	–	$1.07
	Treat mold-contaminated 4/12 trusses with antimicrobial spray *Treat* Materials .... .53 Labor.............2.80	sf	–	–	$3.33
	Treat mold-contaminated 6/12 trusses with antimicrobial spray *Treat* Materials .... .65 Labor............3.85	sf	–	–	$4.50
	Treat mold-contaminated 8/12 trusses with antimicrobial spray *Treat* Materials .... .79 Labor............4.90	sf	–	–	$5.69
	Treat mold-contaminated 10/12 trusses with antimicrobial spray *Treat* Materials..........1.08 Labor............5.83	sf	–	–	$6.91
	Treat mold-contaminated 12/12 trusses with antimicrobial spray *Treat* Materials..........1.27 Labor............6.88	sf	–	–	$8.15
	Treat mold-contaminated 17/12 trusses with antimicrobial spray *Treat* Materials..........1.40 Labor............8.28	sf	–	–	$9.68
	Treat mold-contaminated sheathing with antimicrobial spray *Treat* Materials .... .21 Labor............. .12	sf	–	–	$.33
ENCAPSULATE ▶	## Encapsulate with sealer *Cleaning mold-contaminated items and treating with an anitmicrobial spray probably won't remove all mold spores or gas from the air. Since there is always some level of mold in the air, the goal is to reduce the mold to normal levels. In some cases it may be desirable to encapsulate cleaned areas to further reduce the likelihood of continuing problems from previously affected areas.*				
	Encapsulate cleaned floor with sealer *Paint* Materials........... .29 Labor............. .41	sf	–	–	$.70
	Encapsulate cleaned wall with sealer *Paint* Materials........... .29 Labor............. .41	sf	–	–	$.70

Item Description	Unit	Remove	Replace	Total
Encapsulate cleaned ceiling with sealer *Paint* Materials .... .29 Labor .... .41	sf	–	–	$.70

Encapsulate framing

◄ ENCAPSULATE FRAMING

Item Description	Unit	Remove	Replace	Total
Encapsulate treated furring strips with sealer *Paint* Materials .... .36 Labor .... .47	sf	–	–	$.83
Encapsulate treated beams with sealer *Paint* Materials .... .43 Labor .... .47	sf	–	–	$.90
Encapsulate treated 2" x 4" framing with sealer *Paint* Materials .... .52 Labor .... .35	sf	–	–	$.87
Encapsulate treated 2" x 6" framing with sealer *Paint* Materials .... .58 Labor .... .41	sf	–	–	$.99
Encapsulate treated 2" x 8" framing with sealer *Paint* Materials .... .63 Labor .... .47	sf	–	–	$1.10
Encapsulate treated 2" x 10" framing with sealer *Paint* Materials .... .69 Labor .... .52	sf	–	–	$1.21
Encapsulate treated 2" x 12" framing with sealer *Paint* Materials .... .75 Labor .... .58	sf	–	–	$1.33
Encapsulate treated floor trusses with sealer *Paint* Materials .... .83 Labor .... .93	sf	–	–	$1.76
Encapsulate treated 4/12 trusses with sealer *Paint* Materials ....1.30 Labor 1.11	sf	–	–	$2.41
Encapsulate treated 6/12 trusses with sealer *Paint* Materials ....1.44 Labor 2.16	sf	–	–	$3.60
Encapsulate treated 8/12 trusses with sealer *Paint* Materials ....1.58 Labor 3.21	sf	–	–	$4.79
Encapsulate treated 10/12 trusses with sealer *Paint* Materials ....1.73 Labor 4.31	sf	–	–	$6.04
Encapsulate treated 12/12 trusses with sealer *Paint* Materials ....1.87 Labor 5.42	sf	–	–	$7.29
Encapsulate treated 17/12 trusses with sealer *Paint* Materials ....2.10 Labor 6.53	sf	–	–	$8.63
Encapsulate treated sheathing with sealer *Paint* Materials .... .35 Labor .... .47	sf	–	–	$.82

Encapsulation rule-of-thumb

◄ ENCAPSULATION RULE-OF-THUMB

Add 34% to painting cost to encapsulate
► A general, rule-of-thumb for encapsulating items not listed in this chapter.

Fog treatment

◄ FOG TREATMENT

Item Description	Unit	Remove	Replace	Total
Treat area with anti-bacterial and anti-fungal fog *Fog* Materials .... .01 Labor .... .06	cf	–	–	$.07

Dehumidifier

◄ DEHUMIDIFIER

Reducing the relative humidity in the room can be an important part of stopping the growth and spread of mold. Most experts want relative humidity at 60 percent or below and many shoot for around 40 percent.

Item Description	Unit	Remove	Replace	Total
Dehumidifier unit, 5 gallon daily capacity, rental per day *Rent* Labor .... Equipment...........25.00	dy	–	–	$25.00

	Item Description	Unit	Remove	Replace	Total
DEHUMIDIFIER ► *continued*	**Dehumidifier unit, 10 gallon daily capacity, rental per day** *Rent* Labor .... Equipment 30.00	dy	–	–	$30.00
	Dehumidifier unit, 19 gallon daily capacity, rental per day *Rent* Labor .... Equipment 50.00	dy	–	–	$50.00
	Dehumidifier unit, 24 gallon daily capacity, rental per day *Rent* Labor .... Equipment 70.00	dy	–	–	$70.00
	Dehumidifier unit, 28 gallon daily capacity, rental per day *Rent* Labor .... Equipment 75.00	dy	–	–	$75.00
DRYING FANS ►	**Drying fans**				
	Drying fan, rental per day *Rent* Labor .... Equipment 25.00	dy	–	–	$25.00
	Drying fan, large, rental per day *Rent* Labor .... Equipment 30.00	dy	–	–	$30.00
	Drying fan, wall cavity, rental per day *Rent* Labor .... Equipment 35.00	dy	–	–	$35.00

✎ NOTES: _____

_____

_____

_____

_____

_____

_____

_____

_____ end

TIME & MATERIAL CHARTS *(selected items)*

Mold Remediation Labor

LABORER	BASE WAGE	PAID LEAVE	TRUE WAGE	FICA	FUTA	WORKER'S COMP.	UNEMPLOY. INSUR.	HEALTH INSUR.	RETIRE (401k)	LIABILITY INSUR.	COST PER HOUR
Mildew remediation specialist	$38.00	2.96	$40.96	3.13	.33	14.08	3.56	2.92	1.23	6.14	$72.40
Mildew remediation assistant	$22.60	1.76	$24.36	1.86	.19	8.37	2.12	2.92	.73	3.65	$44.20

Paid Leave is calculated based on two weeks paid vacation, one week sick leave, and seven paid holidays. Employer's matching portion of **FICA** is 7.65 percent. **FUTA** (Federal Unemployment) is .8 percent. **Worker's compensation** for the mold remediation trade was calculated using a national average of 34.37 percent. **Unemployment insurance** was calculated using a national average of 8.7 percent. **Health insurance** was calculated based on a projected national average for 2005 of $580 per employee (and family when applicable) per month. Employer pays 80 percent for a per month cost of $464 per employee. **Retirement** is based on a 401(k) retirement program with employer matching of 50 percent. Employee contributions to the 401(k) plan are an average of 6 percent of the true wage. **Liability insurance** is based on a national average of 15.0 percent.

QUICKCALCULATORS

QUANTITY **537–551**
   Bearing Wall (board feet) 538–539
   Concrete Wall & Footing (cubic yards) ...540–541
   Gable Roof Rafters (board feet) 542–543

   Gable Roof Trusses (lineal feet) 544–545
   Gable Roofing (squares) 546–547
   Joist System (board feet) 548–549
   Non-bearing Wall (board feet) 550–551

SURFACE AREA **552–557**
   Prismatic Room 552–553
   Rectangular Room 554–555
   Round Room 556–557

QuickCalculators are designed to help you quickly calculate quantities and the surface areas of some basic room shapes. Pages 537–551 contain *QuickCalculators* that are designed to calculate quantities, and pages 552–557 contain *QuickCalculators* that are designed to calculate the surface area of rooms.

Instruction for each *QuickCalculator* sheet are contained on the left facing page.

The person who purchased this book or the person for whom this book was purchased may photo-copy or otherwise reproduce *QuickCalculator* pages so long as:

❶ the sheets are reproduced for that person's use only.

❷ the sheets are not reproduced for resale or as part of a package that is produced for resale.

❸ the sheets are not used in any promotional or advertising materials.

USING THE BEARING WALL
QuickCalculator

A Calculates the lineal feet of studs in a wall *before* adding for openings and corners.

The length of the wall (Answer 1) is converted into inches by multiplying it by 12.

The number of studs is calculated by dividing the wall length in inches by the stud centers (Answer 8), then adding 1 for the first stud.

The calculation should now be rounded *up*, then multiplied by the wall height (Answer 4).

B Calculates the lineal feet of studs typically added for openings and corners. The number of openings (Answer 6) is multiplied by 2.4 (the *average* additional studs typically needed for an opening). The number of corners (Answer 7) is multiplied by 2.6 (the *average* additional studs typically needed at corners). The studs for openings and corners are added together, then should be rounded *up*. The total additional studs is then multiplied by the wall height (Answer 1).

C Calculates the total lineal feet of lumber in the wall. The length of the wall (Answer 1) is multiplied by the number of plates (Answer 3). The lineal feet of plates is added to the lineal feet of studs (Sum A) and additional studs (Sum B).

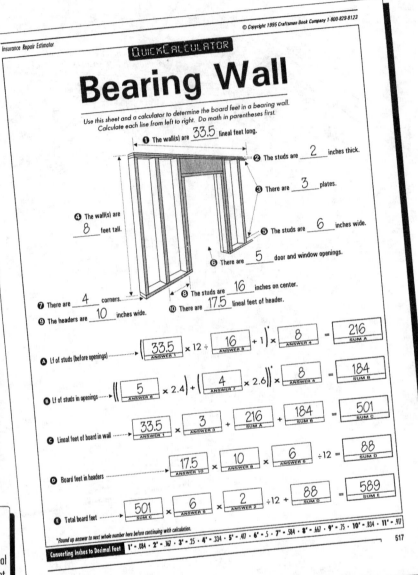

© Copyright 1995 Craftsman Book Company 1-800-829-8123

Insurance Repair Estimator

QuickCalculator

Bearing Wall

Use this sheet and a calculator to determine the board feet in a bearing wall.
Calculate each line from left to right. Do math in parentheses first.

1 The wall(s) are ___33.5___ lineal feet long.

2 The studs are ___2___ inches thick.

3 There are ___3___ plates.

4 The wall(s) are ___8___ feet tall.

5 The studs are ___6___ inches wide.

6 There are ___5___ door and window openings.

7 There are ___4___ corners.

8 The studs are ___16___ inches on center.

9 The headers are ___10___ inches wide.

10 There are ___17.5___ lineal feet of header.

A Lf of studs (before openings) — ([33.5 ANSWER 1] × 12 ÷ [16 ANSWER 8] + 1)* × [8 ANSWER 4] = [216 SUM A]

B Lf of studs in openings — (([5 ANSWER 6] × 2.4) + ([4 ANSWER 7] × 2.6))* × [8 ANSWER 4] = [184 SUM B]

C Lineal feet of board in wall — [33.5 ANSWER 1] × [3 ANSWER 3] + [216 SUM A] + [184 SUM B] = [501 SUM C]

D Board feet in headers — [17.5 ANSWER 10] × [10 ANSWER 9] × [6 ANSWER 5] ÷ 12 = [88 SUM D]

E Total board feet — [501 SUM C] × [6 ANSWER 5] × [2 ANSWER 2] ÷ 12 + [88 SUM D] = [589 SUM E]

*Round up answer to next whole number before continuing with calculation.

Converting Inches to Decimal Feet 1" = .084 · 2" = .167 · 3" = .25 · 4" = .334 · 5" = .417 · 6" = .5 · 7" = .584 · 8" = .667 · 9" = .75 · 10" = .834 · 11" = .917

517

D Calculates the board feet in the headers. The lineal feet of headers (Answer 10) is multiplied by the header width then multiplied by the wall thickness (Answer 5). This total is divided by 12 to convert to board feet.

E Calculates the total board feet in the wall. The lineal feet of board in the wall (Sum C) is multiplied by the wall width (Answer 5) then by the stud thickness (Answer 2). The total is divided by twelve to convert to board feet then added to the board feet in the headers (Sum D).

QUICK FACTS

☞ See page 558 for more information about the geometric formulas used in this *QuickCalculator*. See page 414-415 for wall framing priced per board foot.

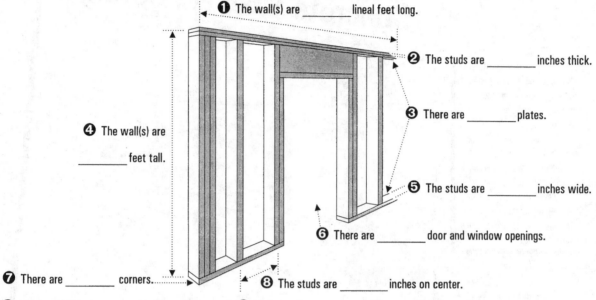

QUICKCALCULATOR

Bearing Wall

Use this sheet and a calculator to determine the board feet in a bearing wall.
Calculate each line from left to right. Do math in parentheses first.

❶ The wall(s) are _____ lineal feet long.

❷ The studs are _____ inches thick.

❸ There are _____ plates.

❹ The wall(s) are _____ feet tall.

❺ The studs are _____ inches wide.

❻ There are _____ door and window openings.

❼ There are _____ corners.

❽ The studs are _____ inches on center.

❾ The headers are _____ inches wide.

❿ There are _____ lineal feet of header.

Ⓐ Lf of studs (before openings) ┄┄┄┄▶ $\left(\boxed{\text{ANSWER 1}} \times 12 \div \boxed{\text{ANSWER 8}} + 1 \right)^{*} \times \boxed{\text{ANSWER 4}} = \boxed{\text{SUM A}}$

Ⓑ Lf of studs in openings ┄┄┄┄▶ $\left(\left(\boxed{\text{ANSWER 6}} \times 2.4 \right) + \left(\boxed{\text{ANSWER 7}} \times 2.6 \right)\right)^{*} \times \boxed{\text{ANSWER 4}} = \boxed{\text{SUM B}}$

Ⓒ Lineal feet of board in wall ┄┄┄▶ $\boxed{\text{ANSWER 1}} \times \boxed{\text{ANSWER 3}} + \boxed{\text{SUM A}} + \boxed{\text{SUM B}} = \boxed{\text{SUM C}}$

Ⓓ Board feet in headers ┄┄┄┄┄┄▶ $\boxed{\text{ANSWER 10}} \times \boxed{\text{ANSWER 9}} \times \boxed{\text{ANSWER 5}} \div 12 = \boxed{\text{SUM D}}$

Ⓔ Total board feet ┄┄┄┄┄▶ $\boxed{\text{SUM C}} \times \boxed{\text{ANSWER 5}} \times \boxed{\text{ANSWER 2}} \div 12 + \boxed{\text{SUM D}} = \boxed{\text{SUM E}}$

*Round up answer to next whole number here before continuing with calculation.

Converting Inches to Decimal Feet   **1"** = .084 • **2"** = .167 • **3"** = .25 • **4"** = .334 • **5"** = .417 • **6"** = .5 • **7"** = .584 • **8"** = .667 • **9"** = .75 • **10"** = .834 • **11"** = .917

USING THE CONCRETE WALL & FOOTING QuickCalculator

A Calculates the cubic yards of footing by multiplying Answer 2 by 12 to convert the length of the footing to inches. The length in inches is then multiplied by the thickness (Answer 4) and by the width (Answer 5) to determine the cubic inches in the footing. The cubic inches are converted to cubic feet by dividing by 1,728. The cubic feet are then converted to cubic yards by dividing by 27.

B Calculates the cubic yards of foundation wall by multiplying Answer 2 by 12 to convert the length of the wall to inches. The length in inches is then multiplied by the thickness (Answer 1) and by the height (Answer 3) to determine the cubic inches in the wall. The cubic inches are converted to cubic feet by dividing by 1,728. The cubic feet are then converted to cubic yards by dividing by 27.

C Calculates the total cubic yards of concrete in the wall & footing by adding the cubic yards of footing (Sum A) to the cubic yards of foundation wall (Sum B).

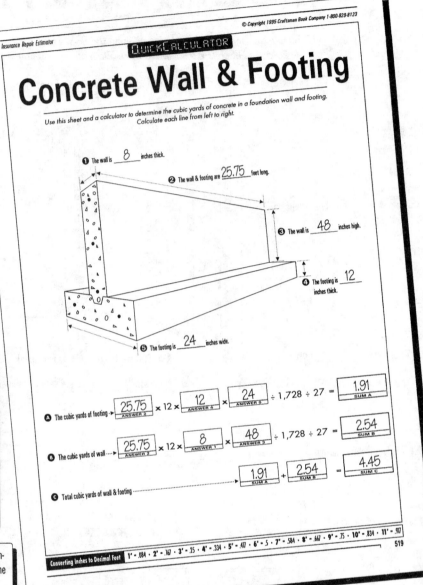

Insurance Repair Estimator

© Copyright 1995 Craftsman Book Company 1-800-829-8123

QUICKCALCULATOR

Concrete Wall & Footing

Use this sheet and a calculator to determine the cubic yards of concrete in a foundation wall and footing. Calculate each line from left to right.

1 The wall is **8** inches thick.

2 The wall & footing are **25.75** feet long.

3 The wall is **48** inches high.

4 The footing is **12** inches thick.

5 The footing is **24** inches wide.

A The cubic yards of footing ➜ | **25.75** ANSWER 2 | × 12 × | **12** ANSWER 4 | × | **24** ANSWER 5 | ÷ 1,728 ÷ 27 = | **1.91** SUM A |

B The cubic yards of wall ➜ | **25.75** ANSWER 2 | × 12 × | **8** ANSWER 1 | × | **48** ANSWER 3 | ÷ 1,728 ÷ 27 = | **2.54** SUM B |

C Total cubic yards of wall & footing ➜ | **1.91** SUM A | + | **2.54** SUM B | = | **4.45** SUM C |

Converting Inches to Decimal Feet **1"** = .084 · **2"** = .167 · **3"** = .25 · **4"** = .334 · **5"** = .417 · **6"** = .5 · **7"** = .584 · **8"** = .667 · **9"** = .75 · **10"** = .834 · **11"** = .917

519

QUICK FACTS

☞ The sample *QuickCalculator* sheet shown above contains quantities that have been rounded. We suggest rounding to two decimal places. We also suggest rounding the final total (Sum C) *up* to the next 1/4 yards since this how concrete must usually be ordered. (In the example above the Sum C total of 4.45 should be rounded up to 4.5 cubic yards.) See pages 83–85 for concrete walls and footings per cubic yard.

☞ See page 558 for more information about the geometric formulas used in this *QuickCalculator*.

Concrete Wall & Footing

Use this sheet and a calculator to determine the cubic yards of concrete in a foundation wall and footing.
Calculate each line from left to right.

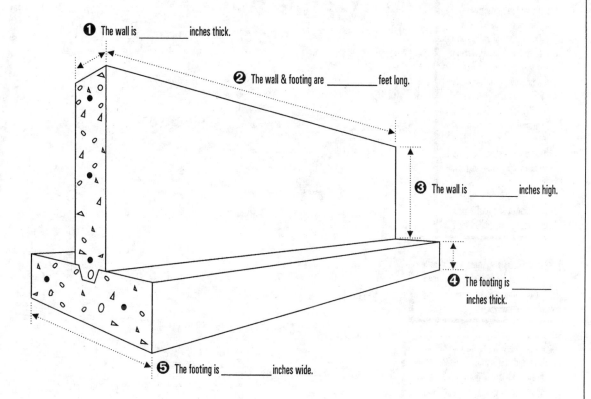

❶ The wall is _____ inches thick.

❷ The wall & footing are _____ feet long.

❸ The wall is _____ inches high.

❹ The footing is _____ inches thick.

❺ The footing is _____ inches wide.

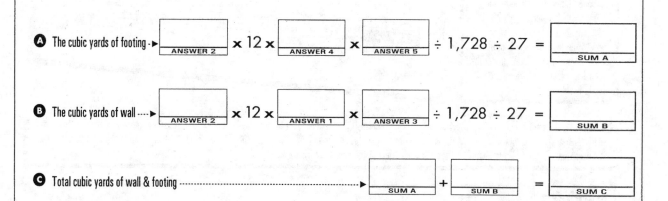

A The cubic yards of footing → [ANSWER 2] **× 12 ×** [ANSWER 4] **×** [ANSWER 5] **÷ 1,728 ÷ 27 =** [SUM A]

B The cubic yards of wall ----→ [ANSWER 2] **× 12 ×** [ANSWER 1] **×** [ANSWER 3] **÷ 1,728 ÷ 27 =** [SUM B]

C Total cubic yards of wall & footing ----------------→ [SUM A] **+** [SUM B] **=** [SUM C]

Converting Inches to Decimal Feet | **1"** = .084 • **2"** = .167 • **3"** = .25 • **4"** = .334 • **5"** = .417 • **6"** = .5 • **7"** = .584 • **8"** = .667 • **9"** = .75 • **10"** = .834 • **11"** = .917

USING THE GABLE ROOF RAFTERS QuickCalculator

A Calculates the total number of rafters in the roof. The length of the roof (Answer 1) is converted into inches by multiplying it by 12.

The number of rafters in the roof is calculated by taking the length in inches and dividing by the rafter centers (Answer 4) then adding 1 for the first rafter.

Because you can never have a fraction of a rafter, the final answer should always be rounded *up* to the next *even* number.

This calculates the total for one side of the roof only so the total is multiplied by 2.

B Calculates the lineal feet of rafters in the roof by multiplying the number of rafters (Sum A) by the rafter length (Answer 2).

C Calculates the board feet in the ridge and sub-fascia. The roof length (Answer 1) is multiplied by 3 (2 sub-fascia boards and 1 ridge) to get the total lineal feet of sub-fascia and ridge. This total is multiplied by the rafter thickness (Answer 5), then by the rafter width (Answer 3) plus 2″ (e.g. a roof with 2″ x 8″ rafters will have 10″ wide ridge and sub-fascia boards).

This total is divided by 12 to get the total board feet in the ridge and sub-fascia boards.

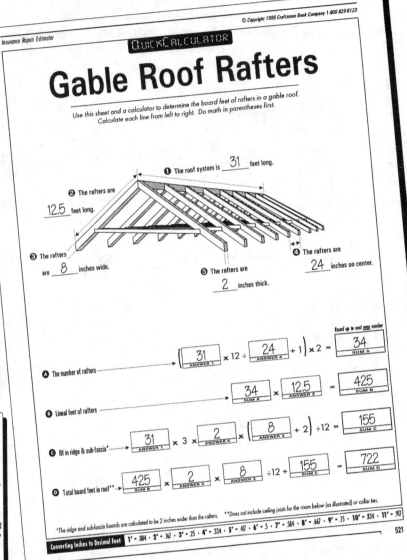

© Copyright 1995 Craftsman Book Company 1-800-829-8123

Insurance Repair Estimator

QuickCalculator

Gable Roof Rafters

Use this sheet and a calculator to determine the board feet of rafters in a gable roof. Calculate each line from left to right. Do math in parentheses first.

① The roof system is __31__ feet long.

② The rafters are __12.5__ feet long.

③ The rafters are __8__ inches wide.

④ The rafters are __24__ inches on center.

⑤ The rafters are __2__ inches thick.

A The number of rafters ············ ($\boxed{31}_{\text{ANSWER 1}}$ × 12 ÷ $\boxed{24}_{\text{ANSWER 4}}$ + 1) × 2 = $\boxed{34}_{\text{SUM A}}$ Round up to next *even* number

B Lineal feet of rafters ············ $\boxed{34}_{\text{SUM A}}$ × $\boxed{12.5}_{\text{ANSWER 2}}$ = $\boxed{425}_{\text{SUM B}}$

C Bf in ridge & sub-fascia* ············ $\boxed{31}_{\text{ANSWER 1}}$ × 3 × $\boxed{2}_{\text{ANSWER 5}}$ × ($\boxed{8}_{\text{ANSWER 3}}$ + 2) ÷ 12 = $\boxed{155}_{\text{SUM C}}$

D Total board feet in roof** ············ $\boxed{425}_{\text{SUM B}}$ × $\boxed{2}_{\text{ANSWER 5}}$ × $\boxed{8}_{\text{ANSWER 3}}$ ÷ 12 + $\boxed{155}_{\text{SUM C}}$ = $\boxed{722}_{\text{SUM D}}$

*The ridge and sub-fascia boards are calculated to be 2 inches wider than the rafters.   **Does not include ceiling joists for the room below (as illustrated) or collar ties.

| Converting Inches to Decimal Feet | 1″ = .084 · 2″ = .167 · 3″ = .25 · 4″ = .334 · 5″ = .417 · 6″ = .5 · 7″ = .584 · 8″ = .667 · 9″ = .75 · 10″ = .834 · 11″ = .917 |

521

D Calculates the total board feet in the roof system. The total lineal feet of rafters (Sum B) is multiplied by the rafter thickness (Answer 5) then by the rafter width (Answer 3). This total is divided by 12 to get the total board feet in the rafters. The total board feet of rafters is then added to the total board feet in the ridge and sub-fascia boards (Sum C) for the total board feet in the entire roof system.

QUICK FACTS

☞ The sample *QuickCalculator* sheet shown above contains quantities that have been rounded. The total number of rafters should always be rounded up to the next even number. We also suggest rounding lineal feet and board feet to the nearest whole number.

☞ See page 558 for more information about the geometric formulas used in this *QuickCalculator*. See page 436 for rafter systems priced per board foot.

Gable Roof Rafters

Use this sheet and a calculator to determine the board feet of rafters in a gable roof.
Calculate each line from left to right. Do math in parentheses first.

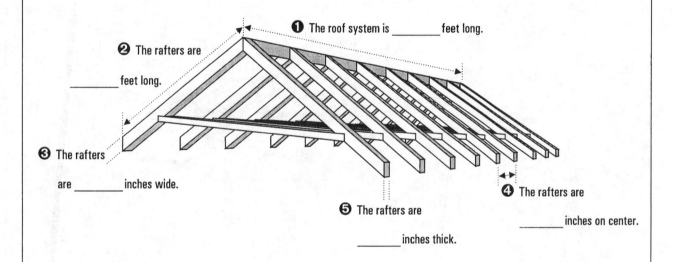

❶ The roof system is _____ feet long.

❷ The rafters are _____ feet long.

❸ The rafters are _____ inches wide.

❹ The rafters are _____ inches on center.

❺ The rafters are _____ inches thick.

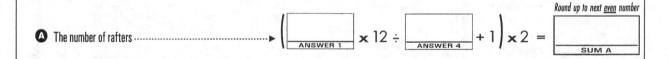

Ⓐ The number of rafters ⟶ $\left(\boxed{\text{ANSWER 1}} \times 12 \div \boxed{\text{ANSWER 4}} + 1\right) \times 2 =$ *Round up to next even number* $\boxed{\text{SUM A}}$

Ⓑ Lineal feet of rafters ⟶ $\boxed{\text{SUM A}} \times \boxed{\text{ANSWER 2}} = \boxed{\text{SUM B}}$

Ⓒ Bf in ridge & sub-fascia* ⟶ $\boxed{\text{ANSWER 1}} \times 3 \times \boxed{\text{ANSWER 5}} \times \left(\boxed{\text{ANSWER 3}} + 2\right) \div 12 = \boxed{\text{SUM C}}$

Ⓓ Total board feet in roof** ⟶ $\boxed{\text{SUM B}} \times \boxed{\text{ANSWER 5}} \times \boxed{\text{ANSWER 3}} \div 12 + \boxed{\text{SUM C}} = \boxed{\text{SUM D}}$

*The ridge and sub-fascia boards are calculated to be 2 inches wider than the rafters.   **Does not include ceiling joists for the room below (as illustrated) or collar ties.*

Converting Inches to Decimal Feet   **1"** = .084 • **2"** = .167 • **3"** = .25 • **4"** = .334 • **5"** = .417 • **6"** = .5 • **7"** = .584 • **8"** = .667 • **9"** = .75 • **10"** = .834 • **11"** = .917

USING THE GABLE ROOF TRUSSES
QuickCalculator

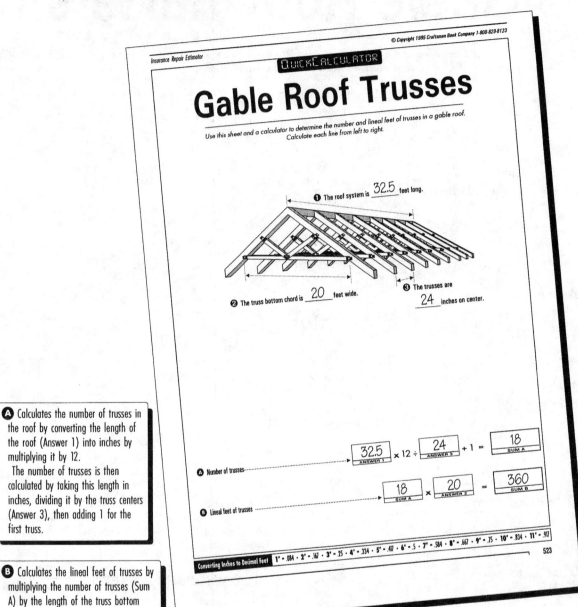

A Calculates the number of trusses in the roof by converting the length of the roof (Answer 1) into inches by multiplying it by 12.

The number of trusses is then calculated by taking this length in inches, dividing it by the truss centers (Answer 3), then adding 1 for the first truss.

B Calculates the lineal feet of trusses by multiplying the number of trusses (Sum A) by the length of the truss bottom chord (Answer 2).

QUICK FACTS

☞ The sample *QuickCalculator* sheet shown above contains quantities that have been rounded. The total number of trusses should always be rounded up to the next whole number. We also suggest rounding lineal feet lineal feet to the nearest whole number.

☞ See page 558 for more information about the geometric formulas used in this *QuickCalculator*. See page 439 for truss systems priced per lineal foot.

Gable Roof Trusses

Use this sheet and a calculator to determine the number and lineal feet of trusses in a gable roof.
Calculate each line from left to right.

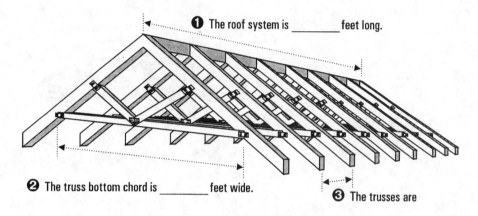

❶ The roof system is _____ feet long.

❷ The truss bottom chord is _____ feet wide.

❸ The trusses are _____ inches on center.

Ⓐ Number of trusses ··················► | ANSWER 1 | x 12 ÷ | ANSWER 3 | + 1 = *Round up to next whole number* | SUM A |

Ⓑ Lineal feet of trusses ··················► | SUM A | x | ANSWER 2 | = | SUM B |

Converting Inches to Decimal Feet   **1″** = .084 • **2″** = .167 • **3″** = .25 • **4″** = .334 • **5″** = .417 • **6″** = .5 • **7″** = .584 • **8″** = .667 • **9″** = .75 • **10″** = .834 • **11″** = .917

USING THE GABLE ROOFING
QuickCalculator

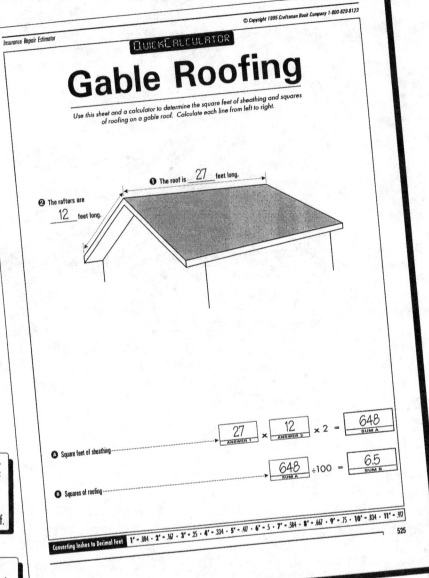

© Copyright 1995 Craftsman Book Company 1-800-829-8123

Insurance Repair Estimator

QuickCalculator

Gable Roofing

Use this sheet and a calculator to determine the square feet of sheathing and squares of roofing on a gable roof. Calculate each line from left to right.

❶ The roof is _27_ feet long.

❷ The rafters are _12_ feet long.

Ⓐ Square feet of sheathing .... $\boxed{27}$ (ANSWER 1) × $\boxed{12}$ (ANSWER 2) × 2 = $\boxed{648}$ (SUM A)

Ⓑ Squares of roofing .... $\boxed{648}$ (SUM A) ÷ 100 = $\boxed{6.5}$ (SUM B)

Converting Inches to Decimal Feet   1" = .084 · 2" = .167 · 3" = .25 · 4" = .334 · 5" = .417 · 6" = .5 · 7" = .584 · 8" = .667 · 9" = .75 · 10" = .834 · 11" = .917

525

Ⓐ Calculates the square feet of sheathing on the roof by multiplying the roof length (Answer 1) by the rafter length (Answer 2), then multiplying this total by 2 to calculate both sides of the roof.

Ⓑ Calculates the squares of roofing by dividing the square feet of roof (Sum A) by 100.

QUICK FACTS

☞ The sample *QuickCalculator* sheet shown above contains quantities that have been rounded. We suggest rounding sheathing to the nearest square foot and rounding squares *up* to the next 1/5 square for shakes, the next 1/4 square for wood shingles and clay tile, and the next 1/3 square for asphalt shingles.

☞ See page 558 for more information about the geometric formulas used in this *QuickCalculator*. Also see *Roofing* beginning on page 393.

Gable Roofing

Use this sheet and a calculator to determine the square feet of sheathing and squares of roofing on a gable roof. Calculate each line from left to right.

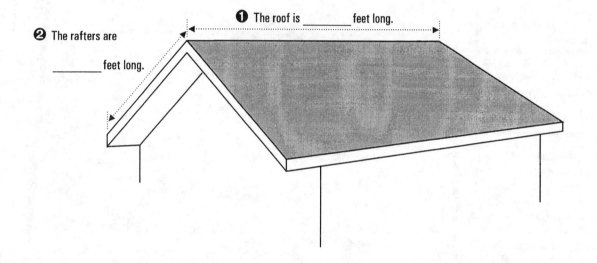

❶ The roof is _____ feet long.

❷ The rafters are

_____ feet long.

🅐 Square feet of sheathing --------------------------------→ | ANSWER 1 | ✕ | ANSWER 2 | ✕ 2 = | SUM A |

🅑 Squares of roofing --------------------------------→ | SUM A | ÷100 = | SUM B |

Converting Inches to Decimal Feet   **1"** = .084 • **2"** = .167 • **3"** = .25 • **4"** = .334 • **5"** = .417 • **6"** = .5 • **7"** = .584 • **8"** = .667 • **9"** = .75 • **10"** = .834 • **11"** = .917

547

USING THE JOIST SYSTEM
QuickCalculator

A Calculates the total number of joists. The length of the joist system (Answer 1) is converted into inches by multiplying it by 12.
The number of joists is calculated by taking the joist system length in inches and dividing it by the joist centers (Answer 4) then adding 1 for the first joist.

B Calculates the lineal feet of joists by multiplying the number of joists (Sum A) by the joist length (Answer 2).

C Calculates the lineal feet in rim joists and in solid blocking. The length of the rim joist (Answer 1) is multiplied by 2 for rim joists on both sides of the joist system. The total lineal feet of rim joists are then added to the lineal feet of solid blocking (Answer 6).

D Calculates total lineal feet of lumber in the joist system by adding the lineal feet of joists (Sum B) to the lineal feet of rim joists and solid blocking (Sum C).

E Calculates the board feet in the joist system by multiplying the total lineal feet of joists (Sum D) by the joist thickness (Answer 5), then by the joist width (Answer 3). This total is then divided by 12.

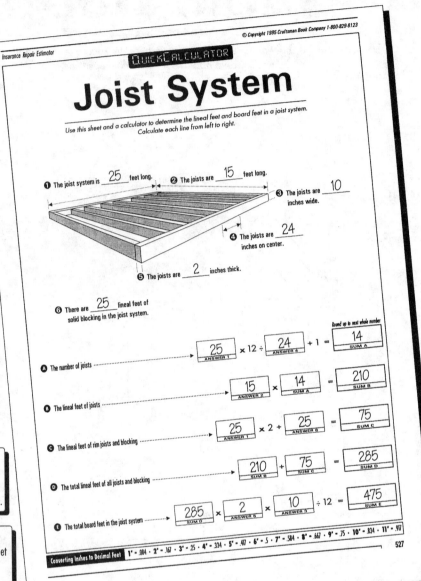

Insurance Repair Estimator

QuickCalculator

Joist System

Use this sheet and a calculator to determine the lineal feet and board feet in a joist system. Calculate each line from left to right.

❶ The joist system is __25__ feet long. ❷ The joists are __15__ feet long.

❸ The joists are __10__ inches wide.

❹ The joists are __24__ inches on center.

❺ The joists are __2__ inches thick.

❻ There are __25__ lineal feet of solid blocking in the joist system.

A The number of joists ········· | 25 ANSWER 1 | × 12 ÷ | 24 ANSWER 4 | + 1 = | 14 SUM A | *Round up to next whole number*

B The lineal feet of joists ········· | 15 ANSWER 2 | × | 14 SUM A | = | 210 SUM B |

C The lineal feet of rim joists and blocking ········· | 25 ANSWER 1 | × 2 + | 25 ANSWER 6 | = | 75 SUM C |

D The total lineal feet of all joists and blocking ········· | 210 SUM B | + | 75 SUM C | = | 285 SUM D |

E The total board feet in the joist system ········· | 285 SUM D | × | 2 ANSWER 5 | × | 10 ANSWER 3 | ÷ 12 = | 475 SUM E |

Converting Inches to Decimal Feet | 1" = .084 • 2" = .167 • 3" = .25 • 4" = .334 • 5" = .417 • 6" = .5 • 7" = .584 • 8" = .667 • 9" = .75 • 10" = .834 • 11" = .917

527

QUICK FACTS

☞ The sample *QuickCalculator* sheet shown above contains quantities that have been rounded. The total number of joists should always be rounded *up* to the next whole number. We also suggest rounding lineal feet and board feet to the nearest whole number.

☞ See page 558 for more information about the geometric formulas used in this *QuickCalculator*. See page 432 for joist systems priced per board foot.

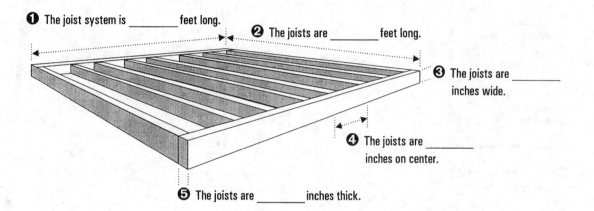

QuickCalculator

Joist System

Use this sheet and a calculator to determine the lineal feet and board feet in a joist system.
Calculate each line from left to right.

❶ The joist system is _____ feet long.

❷ The joists are _____ feet long.

❸ The joists are _____ inches wide.

❹ The joists are _____ inches on center.

❺ The joists are _____ inches thick.

❻ There are _____ lineal feet of solid blocking in the joist system.

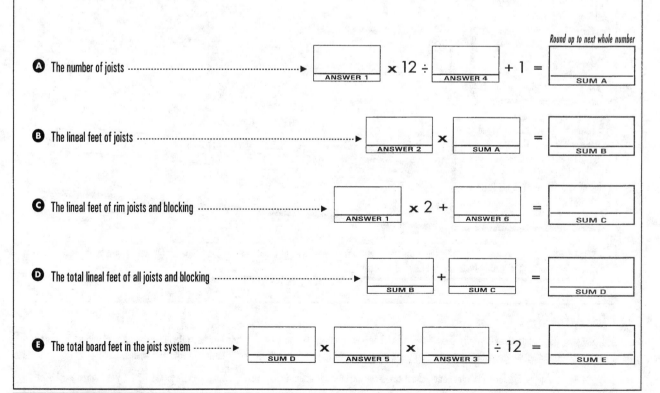

Ⓐ The number of joists ·······► [ANSWER 1] × 12 ÷ [ANSWER 4] + 1 = [SUM A] *Round up to next whole number*

Ⓑ The lineal feet of joists ·······► [ANSWER 2] × [SUM A] = [SUM B]

Ⓒ The lineal feet of rim joists and blocking ·······► [ANSWER 1] × 2 + [ANSWER 6] = [SUM C]

Ⓓ The total lineal feet of all joists and blocking ·······► [SUM B] + [SUM C] = [SUM D]

Ⓔ The total board feet in the joist system ·······► [SUM D] × [ANSWER 5] × [ANSWER 3] ÷ 12 = [SUM E]

Converting Inches to Decimal Feet **1″** = .084 · **2″** = .167 · **3″** = .25 · **4″** = .334 · **5″** = .417 · **6″** = .5 · **7″** = .584 · **8″** = .667 · **9″** = .75 · **10″** = .834 · **11″** = .917

USING THE NON-BEARING WALL
QuickCalculator

Ⓐ Calculates the lineal feet of studs in a wall *before* adding for openings and corners.
The length of the wall (Answer 1) is converted into inches by multiplying it by 12.
The number of studs is calculated by dividing the wall length in inches by the stud centers (Answer 8), then adding 1 for the first stud.
The calculation should now be rounded *up*, then multiplied by the wall height (Answer 4).

Ⓑ Calculates the lineal feet of studs typically added for openings and corners. The number of openings (Answer 6) is multiplied by 2.4 (the *average* additional studs typically needed for an opening). The number of corners (Answer 7) is multiplied by 2.6 (the *average* additional studs typically needed at corners). The studs for openings and corners are added together, then should be rounded *up*. The total additional studs is then multiplied by the wall height (Answer 4).

Ⓒ Calculates the total lineal feet of lumber in the wall. The length of the wall (Answer 1) is multiplied by the number of plates (Answer 3). The lineal feet of plates is added to the lineal feet of studs (Sum A) and additional studs (Sum B).

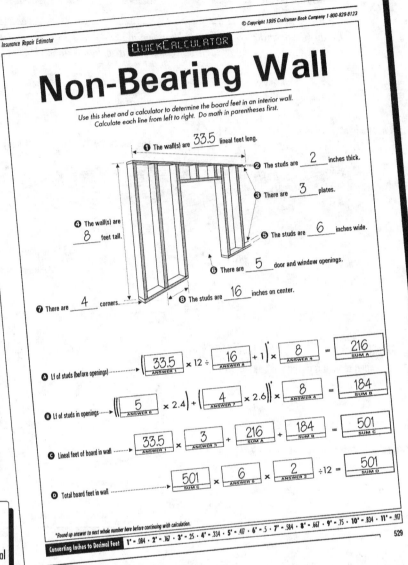

Ⓓ Calculates the total board feet in the wall. The lineal feet of board in the wall (Sum C) is multiplied by the wall width (Answer 5) then by the stud thickness (Answer 2). The total is divided by 12 to convert to board feet.

QUICK FACTS

☞ The sample *QuickCalculator* sheet shown above contains quantities that have been rounded. When calculating Sum A and Sum B we suggest rounding the calculation *up* to the next whole number at the asterisk. Board feet and lineal feet should be rounded.

☞ See page 558 for more information about the geometric formulas used in this *QuickCalculator*. See page 414-415 for walls priced per board foot.

QUICKCALCULATOR

Non-Bearing Wall

Use this sheet and a calculator to determine the board feet in an interior wall.
Calculate each line from left to right. Do math in parentheses first.

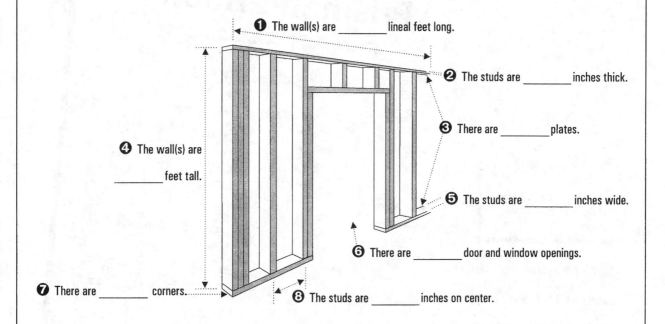

❶ The wall(s) are _____ lineal feet long.

❷ The studs are _____ inches thick.

❸ There are _____ plates.

❹ The wall(s) are _____ feet tall.

❺ The studs are _____ inches wide.

❻ There are _____ door and window openings.

❼ There are _____ corners.

❽ The studs are _____ inches on center.

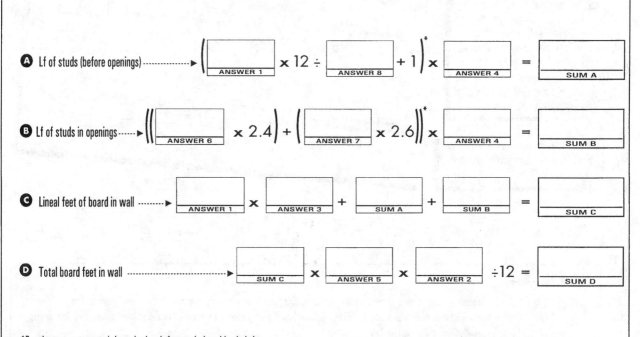

ⓐ Lf of studs (before openings) ⟶ ([ANSWER 1] x 12 ÷ [ANSWER 8] + 1)* x [ANSWER 4] = [SUM A]

ⓑ Lf of studs in openings ⟶ (([ANSWER 6] x 2.4) + ([ANSWER 7] x 2.6))* x [ANSWER 4] = [SUM B]

ⓒ Lineal feet of board in wall ⟶ [ANSWER 1] x [ANSWER 3] + [SUM A] + [SUM B] = [SUM C]

ⓓ Total board feet in wall ⟶ [SUM C] x [ANSWER 5] x [ANSWER 2] ÷12 = [SUM D]

Round up answer to next whole number here before continuing with calculation.

Converting Inches to Decimal Feet   **1"** = .084 • **2"** = .167 • **3"** = .25 • **4"** = .334 • **5"** = .417 • **6"** = .5 • **7"** = .584 • **8"** = .667 • **9"** = .75 • **10"** = .834 • **11"** = .917

USING THE PRISMATIC ROOM
QuickCalculator

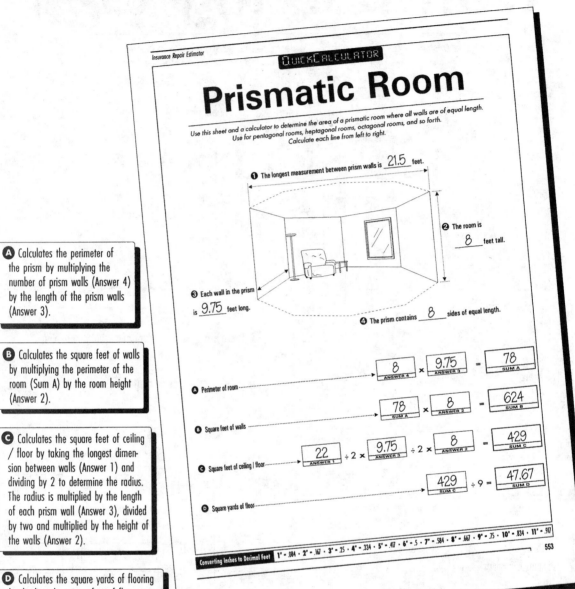

A Calculates the perimeter of the prism by multiplying the number of prism walls (Answer 4) by the length of the prism walls (Answer 3).

B Calculates the square feet of walls by multiplying the perimeter of the room (Sum A) by the room height (Answer 2).

C Calculates the square feet of ceiling / floor by taking the longest dimension between walls (Answer 1) and dividing by 2 to determine the radius. The radius is multiplied by the length of each prism wall (Answer 3), divided by two and multiplied by the height of the walls (Answer 2).

D Calculates the square yards of flooring by dividing the square feet of floor (Sum C) by 9.

Insurance Repair Estimator

QuickCalculator
Prismatic Room

Use this sheet and a calculator to determine the area of a prismatic room where all walls are of equal length.
Use for pentagonal rooms, heptagonal rooms, octagonal rooms, and so forth.
Calculate each line from left to right.

❶ The longest measurement between prism walls is **21.5** feet.

❷ The room is **8** feet tall.

❸ Each wall in the prism is **9.75** feet long.

❹ The prism contains ____ sides of equal length.

A Perimeter of room ...... $\boxed{8}_{\text{ANSWER 4}} \times \boxed{9.75}_{\text{ANSWER 3}} = \boxed{78}_{\text{SUM A}}$

B Square feet of walls ...... $\boxed{78}_{\text{SUM A}} \times \boxed{8}_{\text{ANSWER 2}} = \boxed{624}_{\text{SUM B}}$

C Square feet of ceiling / floor ...... $\boxed{22}_{\text{ANSWER 1}} \div 2 \times \boxed{9.75}_{\text{ANSWER 3}} \div 2 \times \boxed{8}_{\text{ANSWER 2}} = \boxed{429}_{\text{SUM C}}$

D Square yards of floor ...... $\boxed{429}_{\text{SUM C}} \div 9 = \boxed{47.67}_{\text{SUM D}}$

Converting Inches to Decimal Feet **1"** = .084 · **2"** = .167 · **3"** = .25 · **4"** = .334 · **5"** = .417 · **6"** = .5 · **7"** = .584 · **8"** = .667 · **9"** = .75 · **10"** = .834 · **11"** = .917

553

QUICK FACTS

☞ The sample *QuickCalculator* sheet shown above contains quantities that have been rounded. We suggest rounding lineal feet to two decimal places then to the nearest inch when converting to inches. Square feet should probably be rounded to the nearest square foot and square yards should be rounded up to the nearest 1/3 or 1/4 yard.

☞ See page 558 for more information about the geometric formulas used in this *QuickCalculator*.

Prismatic Room

Use this sheet and a calculator to determine the area of a prismatic room where all walls are of equal length.
Use for pentagonal rooms, heptagonal rooms, octagonal rooms, and so forth.
Calculate each line from left to right.

❶ The longest measurement between prism walls is _____ feet.

❷ The room is

_____ feet tall.

❸ Each wall in the prism

is _____ feet long.

❹ The prism contains _____ sides of equal length.

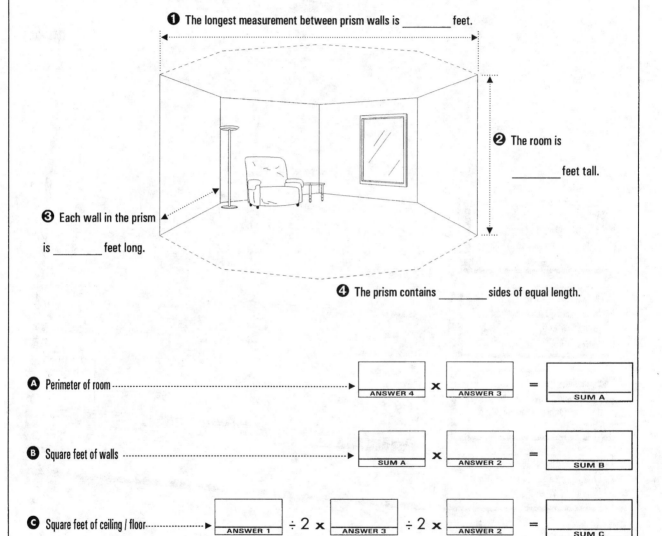

Ⓐ Perimeter of room ···▶ | ANSWER 4 | x | ANSWER 3 | = | SUM A |

Ⓑ Square feet of walls ···▶ | SUM A | x | ANSWER 2 | = | SUM B |

Ⓒ Square feet of ceiling / floor ·················▶ | ANSWER 1 | ÷ 2 x | ANSWER 3 | ÷ 2 x | ANSWER 2 | = | SUM C |

Ⓓ Square yards of floor ···▶ | SUM C | ÷ 9 = | SUM D |

Converting Inches to Decimal Feet   **1"** = .084 · **2"** = .167 · **3"** = .25 · **4"** = .334 · **5"** = .417 · **6"** = .5 · **7"** = .584 · **8"** = .667 · **9"** = .75 · **10"** = .834 · **11"** = .917

USING THE RECTANGULAR ROOM
QuickCalculator

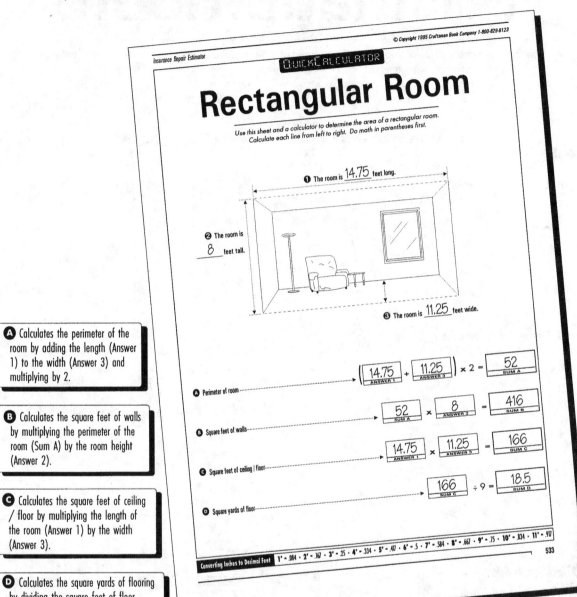

A Calculates the perimeter of the room by adding the length (Answer 1) to the width (Answer 3) and multiplying by 2.

B Calculates the square feet of walls by multiplying the perimeter of the room (Sum A) by the room height (Answer 2).

C Calculates the square feet of ceiling / floor by multiplying the length of the room (Answer 1) by the width (Answer 3).

D Calculates the square yards of flooring by dividing the square feet of floor (Sum C) by 9.

QUICK FACTS

☞ The sample *QuickCalculator* sheet shown above contains quantities that have been rounded. We suggest rounding lineal feet to two decimal places then to the nearest inch when converting to inches. Square feet should probably be rounded to the nearest square foot and square yards should be rounded to the nearest 1/3 or 1/4 yard.

☞ See page 558 for more information about the geometric formulas used in this *QuickCalculator*.

Rectangular Room

Use this sheet and a calculator to determine the area of a rectangular room.
Calculate each line from left to right. Do math in parentheses first.

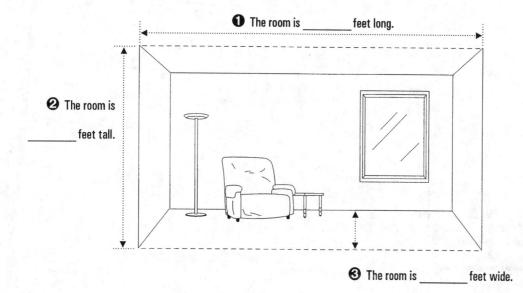

❶ The room is _____ feet long.

❷ The room is _____ feet tall.

❸ The room is _____ feet wide.

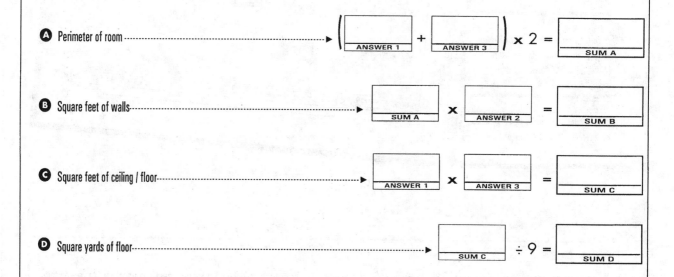

Ⓐ Perimeter of room ·········· ► ([ANSWER 1] + [ANSWER 3]) × 2 = [SUM A]

Ⓑ Square feet of walls ·········· ► [SUM A] × [ANSWER 2] = [SUM B]

Ⓒ Square feet of ceiling / floor ·········· ► [ANSWER 1] × [ANSWER 3] = [SUM C]

Ⓓ Square yards of floor ·········· ► [SUM C] ÷ 9 = [SUM D]

Converting Inches to Decimal Feet   **1"** = .084 • **2"** = .167 • **3"** = .25 • **4"** = .334 • **5"** = .417 • **6"** = .5 • **7"** = .584 • **8"** = .667 • **9"** = .75 • **10"** = .834 • **11"** = .917

USING THE ROUND ROOM
QuickCalculator

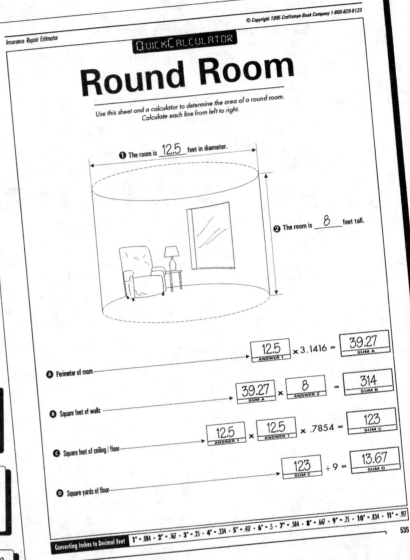

A Calculates the perimeter of the circle by multiplying the diameter (Answer 1) by Pi (3.1416).

B Calculates the square feet of walls by multiplying the perimeter of the room (Sum A) by the room height (Answer 2).

C Calculates the square feet of ceiling / floor by squaring the diameter (Answer 1 times Answer 1) and multiplying by .7854.

D Calculates the square yards of flooring by dividing the square feet of floor (Sum C) by 9.

QUICK FACTS

☞ The sample *QuickCalculator* sheet shown above contains quantities that have been rounded. We suggest rounding lineal feet to two decimal places then to the nearest inch when converting to inches. Square feet should probably be rounded to the nearest square foot and square yards should be rounded to the nearest 1/3 or 1/4 yard.

☞ See page 558 for more information about the geometric formulas used in this *QuickCalculator*.

QUICKCALCULATOR

Round Room

Use this sheet and a calculator to determine the area of a round room.
Calculate each line from left to right.

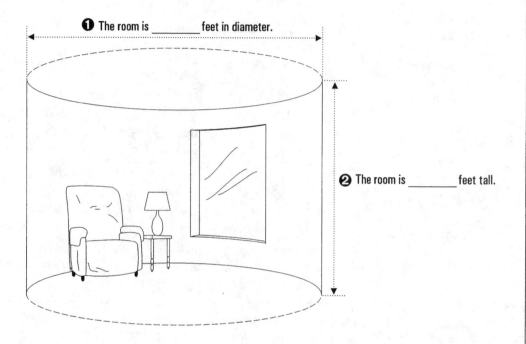

❶ The room is _____ feet in diameter.

❷ The room is _____ feet tall.

🅐 Perimeter of room ┄┄┄┄┄┄┄┄┄┄┄┄┄┄┄┄┄┄┄┄┄┄┄┄┄┄► [ANSWER 1] x 3.1416 = [SUM A]

🅑 Square feet of walls ┄┄┄┄┄┄┄┄┄┄┄┄┄┄┄┄┄► [SUM A] x [ANSWER 2] = [SUM B]

🅒 Square feet of ceiling / floor ┄┄┄┄┄┄┄┄┄► [ANSWER 1] x [ANSWER 1] x .7854 = [SUM C]

🅓 Square yards of floor ┄┄┄┄┄┄┄┄┄┄┄┄┄┄► [SUM C] ÷ 9 = [SUM D]

Converting Inches to Decimal Feet **1"** = .084 • **2"** = .167 • **3"** = .25 • **4"** = .334 • **5"** = .417 • **6"** = .5 • **7"** = .584 • **8"** = .667 • **9"** = .75 • **10"** = .834 • **11"** = .917

QuickCalculator mathematics

CIRCLE

Area

❶ = Pi x radius^2

❷ = .7854 x diameter^2

❸ = .0796 x perimeter^2

Perimeter

❶ = Pi x diameter

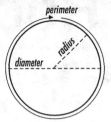

PARALLELOGRAM

Area

❶ = base x height

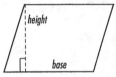

PRISM

Area

❶ = sum of sides ÷ 2 x radius

RECTANGLE

Area

❶ = length x width

TRAPEZOID

Area

❶ = base + top ÷ 2 x height

TRIANGLE

Area

❶ = base x height ÷ 2

PYTHAGOREAN THEOREM

Rafter length

❶ rafter length^2 = rise^2 + run^2

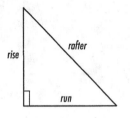

CONVERSION FACTORS

DIVIDE	BY	TO CONVERT TO
square inches	.144	square feet
square inches	.144	board feet
cubic inches	1,728	cubic feet
cubic inches	46,656	cubic yards
square feet	9	square yards
square feet	100	squares
cubic feet	27	cubic yards
feet	16.5	rods
rods	40	furlongs
feet	5,280	miles
meters	1,609	miles
yards	1,760	miles

MULTIPLY	BY	TO CONVERT TO
inches	2.54	centimeters
square inches	6.4516	square centimeters
square inches	.0069	square feet
square feet	9.29	square centimeters
square feet	.0929	square meters
square yards	.8361	square meters
square meters	1.1959	square yards
centimeters	.3937	inches
feet	.3048	meters
meters	3.281	feet
yards	91.44	centimeters
yards	.9144	meters
cubic feet	.0283	cubic meters
cubic meters	35.3145	cubic feet
cubic meters	1.3079	cubic yards
cubic yards	.7646	cubic meters
cubic inches	16.3872	cubic centimeters
cubic centimeters	.0610	cubic inches
cubic meters	1,000	cubic liters

index

A

Abbreviations 7
About this book.................4-6
Access doors,
  mobile home 514
Acknowledgements..................7
Acoustic ceiling 15-18
  1/2" 15
  5/8" 15
  3/4" 16
  aluminum-coated tiles 16
  angled installation..............16
  cleaning 55
  fire-rated tiles 16
  furring strips 16
  minimum charge 16
  paint 335
  repair loose tile.................16
  T&M charts 17-18
Acid wash, swimming pool 490
Acoustical plaster 353-354
Air-born mold.......................529

Air conditioning
  central 277
  recharge...........................277
  through-wall unit..............277
  wiring 142
  with heat...........................277
Alarm system, wiring............142
Allowance,
  light fixture 153-154
Aluminum-coated
  acoustic ceiling tiles 16

Aluminum sheet
  corrugated roofing...........400
  ribbed roofing..................400
Aluminum shingles 393
Aluminum siding.................455
Aluminum,
  swimming pool 489

Aluminum window
  awning 502
  casement 502
  double-hung 502
  elliptical 501
  fixed (picture) 503
  half-elliptical 501
  half-round 501
  quarter round 501
  round 501

sliding................................503
storm window..................510

Anaglypta
  dado................................496
  frieze...............................496
  pelmet..............................496
  wall covering 496
Anchor, mobile home 516
Angle-iron lintel 322
Antenna, TV 152
Antique bathtub...........386-387

Antique style
  bathtub drain....................385
  bathtub faucet 384
  free-standing
    supply lines 385
  sink faucet 384
  toilet 386
  tub faucet 384-385
Appliances 19-34
  cleaning 55-56
  clothes dryer 32
  dishwasher 26-28
  electric 21-25
    cook top...................21-23
    range 23-25
    wall oven.......................25
  garbage disposal..............28
  gas 19-21
    cook top........................19
    range 19-20
    wall oven...................20-21
  microwave oven 28-29
  minimum charge 19
  mobile home 513
  range hood 26
  refinish.............................31
  refrigerator /
    freezer 29-31
  T&M charts 33-34
  trash compactor 31
  washing machine 31-32
  wiring 142
Apron molding,
  window.............................210
Arch
  brick 298
  stone wall 306-307
Arch spandrel,
  gingerbread...............229-230
Architrave
  exterior 206-207
  interior 206

paint 338
plaster 356
stone 310-314
stucco 359
Area modification
  factors 8-9
Art of estimating.....................4
Asbestos removal 273
Ashlar stone
  fireplace face 250-251
  fireplace hearth...............252
  veneer........................307-308
  wall 306
Asphalt 92-93
  driveway 92
  fill pothole........................93
  graded base......................92
  overlay 92-93
  seal 93
Asphalt shingles...........393-394
ASTM clay tile
  roofing grades 399
Astragal molding...........211-212
Attic stair,
  disappearing 471
Awning
  canvas 37
  carport 35
  door 35-36
  downspout 36
  fascia 35
  painting 333
  post 35
  roll-up 37
  roof panel 36
  scroll 35
  T&M charts 38-40
  vinyl 38
  window 36-37
Awning window
  aluminum 502
  vinyl 504
  wood 506-507

B

Backfill,
  foundation wall 178
Backing tile wall 303
Ball-and-dowel
  running trim......................226

Ballast, light fixture 166
Balustrade
  1/4 turn 476
  1/2 turn 476
  goose neck 476
  paint 342
  pine 471-472
  poplar 472-473
  red oak 474-475
  redwood 473-474
  remove &
    reinstall 475
  sawn 475
  volute end 476
Barricade...........................492
Base block....................204-205
Base cabinets
  see: Lower cabinets
Base, column.........................79
Base, for flatwork 88
Base, shower 379
Baseboard
  clamshell.....................199-201
  mask 285
  pattern........................200-201
  remove &
    reinstall 201
  rubber 263
  shoe 201
  tile 260-261
Baseboard heater 153
  mobile home 517
  wiring 142
Basement
  excavation 177
Basketweave fence............187
Bath fan.........................149
  with heat lamp 149
  with heater 149
  wiring 142
Bathroom
  mask 286
  rough plumbing.........365-366
  vanity cabinet 52
Bathroom hardware...39-44
  1/2 bath 41
  bathroom mirror..........45-46
  cleaning 56
  cup & toothbrush
    holder 42
  door clothes
    hanger 42
  glass shelf 41-42

medicine cabinet.........44-45
minimum charge 41
robe hook 42
shower rod 43
soap dispenser.................43
soap holder 42-43
T&M charts 46
tissue holder,
  recessed 43
toilet paper
  dispenser 43-44
towel bar 43
towel ring 44
wash cloth bar 44
Bathroom sink........371-373
  faucet.........................368-369
  rough plumbing 367
Bathtub...............................377
  antique 386
  refinished antique 387
  reproduction
    antique 387
  rough plumbing 367
  slipper 387
  with whirlpool
    jets 377-378
Bathtub & shower
  combination.....................378
Bathtub door
  folding 380
  sliding..............................380
Bathtub drain,
  antique style 385
Bathtub faucet
  antique style.............384-385
  faucet...............................370
  faucet with shower 370
Bathtub surround........379, 494
Batt insulation,
  fiberglass 282
Batten door 109
Batten Doors 108
Batten seam
  copper roofing 402
  lead roofing 402
  terne roofing 403
Beam
  curved 423
  glue-laminated 418-420
  hand-hewn 423
  micro-laminated...............420
  oak 422-423
  pine 420-422

Bearing wall
beam pocket 414
interior, per lf 409-410
interior, per sf 412-413
per bf 414-415
QuickCalculator 538-539
sloping interior,
per sf 412
Bed mold 216
Bent, connecting
members 425
Bent with truss
oak 425-426
pine 423-425
Beveled glass lite
in panel door 108
Beveled siding 458-459
Bibb, rough
plumbing 368
Bidet **376**
faucet 369
rough plumbing 367-368
Billiard-table
style light fixture 163
Bitumen roofing,
modified 405
Black steel pipe 361
Block and brick
cavity wall 293-294
wall 289-292
Block, concrete
colored 301
curved installation 297
inserts,
polystyrene 301-302
insulation, loose 302
interlocking 301
paint 340
pilaster 302
Block wall **298-299**
bond beam 302-303
cut hole in 321
fluted 299-300
glass 304
glazed 300
grade beam 303
pargeting 303
reinforcement 302
retaining,
interlocking 391-392
screen 301
slump 299
split-face 300-301
split-rib 301
Blown fiberglass
insulation 281-282

Board fence **187-188**
with lattice cap 188
Board, finish 233-234
Board over
plywood siding 457
Board up,
emergency 491
Board-and-batten
fence 188-189
paneling 349
siding 457
Board-on-board
fence 188
paneling 349
siding 457
Bond beam,
block wall 302-303
Bond beam repair,
swimming pool 489
Bonds, brick 297
Bookcase **223-224**
paint 338
Border, wallpaper 495-496
Bowl shade
light fixture 161-162
replacement 173
Bracket
fan, gingerbread 227
gingerbread 227
paint 339
post, gingerbread 228
stair 476
Brass pipe 361
Breaker, circuit 148
Breaker panel 146-147
Brick
arch 298
bonds 297
cavity wall 294-295
common 287
curved installation 297
fire 244
fireplace face 249-250
fireplace hearth 251-252
paint 341
raked joints 297
salvage 319
veneer 296-297
Brick and block
cavity wall 293-294
wall 289-292
Brick wall
cut hole 321
double wythe 288-289
repair 319

repoint 318-319
single wythe 287-288
triple wythe 292-293
Brick Walls 287
Building permit fees 185
Built-up roofing 403
Bull nose
starting step 470
Bungalow siding 459
Butcher-block
countertop 52
Buttress foundation 91-92
Bypassing door **102**
paint 334

C

Cabinet Construction 47
Cabinet Grades 47-48
Cabinets **47-54**
bathroom vanity 52
cleaning 56
countertop 51-52
door 50
double oven 49-50
drawer front 50
full-height 48-50
island 48
kitchen 47-48
medicine cabinet 44-45
paint 337
minimum charge 47
mobile home 513
oven 49-50
refinish 50
repair 50
utility 48-49
Cabinets, Foil Face 49
Cafe doors **118-119**
paint 336
*California
Earthquake Code* 83, 415
California earthquake
code (CEC) bracing 414
Calrod burners
see: Appliances, electric
Canvas awning 37
Cap, wall 317
Capital **74-78**
contemporary 74
Corinthian 74-75
Doric or Tuscan 75
empire 75-76
Erechtheum 76

painting 333
repair 78-79
Roman Ionic 77
Scamozzi 77-78
Temple-of-the-Winds 78
Carbon monoxide
detector 152
Carpet **257**
cove 258
germicide and
mildewcide
treatment 499
glue-down 257
hang and dry
in plant 500
indoor-outdoor 257
pad 258
remove wet carpet
and pad 499
stair installation 258
tile 258-259
wool 258
Carport 35
Carved onlay 232-233
Carving, stone 320
Casement window
aluminum 502
vinyl 504
wood 506
Casing
clamshell 201-202
curved pattern 203-204
mask 285
mobile home 515
paint 337
pattern 202-203
remove &
reinstall 204
strip paint from 342
Cast-in-place
plaster mold 355
Cast-iron
DWV pipe 363
pipe, repack 363
Cavity wall **293-295**
insulation 295
Cedar tie
retaining wall 391
Ceiling, coffered **225**
paint 339
Ceiling cove,
mobile home 515
Ceiling fan **166-167**
with light fixture 167
Ceiling
furring strips 430-431

Ceiling medallion,
plaster 356
Ceiling panels,
mobile home 526-527
Ceiling rose,
plaster 356
Cellulose insulation 281
Central air 277
Cement fiber
shingle siding 455
Cement plaster,
Keene's 354
Ceramic veneer
panel 309
Chain, security 128
Chain-link fence **189-191**
post 191-192
temporary 493
Chair rail 210-211
Chandelier **154-155**
crystal 157-158
crystal, entrance 158
crystal, grand
entrance 158-159
crystal, imitation 157
crystal, repair 160
crystal tier 159
early American 155-156
early electric 156
early electric /
gas 157
early gas 156-157
entrance 155
grand entrance 155
tall ceiling
installation 160
Channel rustic
siding 457-458
Chickhee hut 332
Chimney **244-245**
cap 245
cricket 444
flashing 406
pipe 248-249
pot 245-246
reline 245
screen 246
Chute, refuse 99
Circuit breaker 147
Circuits, electrical,
check 151
Circular stair 468-469
Clamshell
base 199-200
casing 201-202
Clapboard siding 458

Clay backing
  tile wall 303
Clean-out door,
  fireplace 247-248
Cleaning 55-70
  acoustic tile 55
  appliances 55-56
  bathroom
    hardware 56
  cabinets 56
    countertops 56
  columns 57
  concrete 57
  doors 57-58
  drywall 58-59
  electrical 59
  fences 60
  finish carpentry 61-62
  fireplaces 62
  flooring 62-63
  HVAC 63
  light fixtures 59
  masonry 63-64, 321
  minimum
    charge 55
  mirror 68
  paneling 64
  plaster 58-59, 64
  plumbing 64-66
  siding 66-67
  stairs 67
  suspended ceiling 67
  tile 67
  T&M charts 68-70
  wallpaper 67
  windows 67-68
Closer, door 128
Closet
  door jamb
    & casing 102-103
  lining, cedar 223
  organizer 222
  paint 338
  rod 222-223
  work 222-223
Clothes dryer 32
  wiring 144
Clothes lines,
  mobile home 513
Clothes washer 31
  rough plumbing 368
  wiring 142
Coffered ceiling 225
  paint 339
Cold air grille 278
Columns 71-82
  12" 71-73

base 79
capitals 74-78
cleaning 57
fluted 72
lally 418
mahogany 80
minimum charge 71
painting 333
pedestal 79-80
pilaster 71-72
pilaster pedestal 80
redwood,
  stain-grade 80
repair 73-74
square 72-73
stucco 358-359
tapered 72
T&M charts 81-82
Combination doors,
  mobile home 514
Common brick 287
Compaction
  grouting 92
Compactor, trash,
  wiring 144
Complete house
  electrical 139
  light fixtures 139
  plumbing 365
  wiring 139
Computer network
  outlet 141
  wiring 145
Concrete 83-98
  cleaning 57
  compaction
    grouting 92
  core drilling 90-91
  curb & gutter 90
  dye 89
  epoxy repair 83
  exposed aggregate 90
  flatwork 88-89
  footing 83-84
  footing &
    foundation,
    single pour 85
  foundation 84-85
  foundation,
    buttress 91-92
  foundation
    coating 91
  grade beam 86-88
  lintel 322
  minimum charge 83
  painting 333-334
  pargeting 90

pier 86
pump truck 91
rebar 91
retaining wall 391
sawing 90
stamping 89-90
step 90
swimming pool 489
T&M charts 92-98
wall & footing
  QuickCalculator 540-541
Concrete block
  wall 298-299
*Concrete Block
  Walls* 298-299
Concrete tile
  roofing 399-400
Conduit 144-145
Connection fees
  sewer 186
  water 186
Contact, security system 453
Containment, mold 529, 531
Contemporary
  capital 74
Control panel,
  security system 453
Cook top
  electric 21-23
  gas 19
  wiring 144
Cooler, evaporative 278
  rough plumbing 368
Coping, wall 317-318
Coping,
  swimming pool 489
Copper pipe 361-362
Copper roofing 401-402
  batten seam 402
  flat seam 402
  standing seam 401
Corbel, gingerbread 228
  paint 339
Core drilling, concrete 91
Corian
  see: Countertops, solid-surface
Corinthian capital 74-75
Corner bead 215-216
Corner block 205
Cornice, cut stone 314-316
Cornice, gingerbread 230
Corrugated roofing
  aluminum sheet 400
  fiberglass 400-401
  galvanized steel 401

Corrugated siding,
  fiberglass 455
Countertop 51-52
  butcher-block 52
  cleaning 56
  cultured 51
  granite 51-52
  plastic laminate 51
  solid-surface 51
  solid-wood 52
  stainless-steel 52
  tile 52
Cove
  carpet 258
  vinyl 262-263
Cove molding 212-213
  ceiling 213-214
CPVC pipe 362
Crawl space excavation 177
Crews 14
Crown molding 216-217
Crystal
  chandelier 157-160
    repair 160
  wall fixture 159
Cultured granite 51
Cultured marble
  bathtub surround 494
  countertop 51
  window sill 494
Cultured onyx 51
Cultured stone
  veneer panel 309
Curb & gutter 90
Curved framing
  member 423
Curved masonry
  installation 297
Curved pattern
  casing 203-204
Custom-Milled Door 107
Custom-milled molding 221
Cut stone
  sill 316-317
  trim or cornice 314-316
Cut Stone 315
Cypress
  entry door 115
  door side lite 115

Dado, Anaglypta 496
Damper 248

Deadbolt 127
  mobile home 515
Debris hauling 99
  removal,
    strip room 99-100
Deck
  decking 429
  joist system 429
  landing 430
  railing 429-430
  stairs 430
Decontamination unit 273
Dehumidifers 499
Demolition & hauling ...99
*also see the
replace column
on most pages*
  debris hauling 99
  dump fee 99
  dumpster 99
  minimum charge 99
  refuse chute 99
  remove wet carpet
    and pad 499
  strip room 99-100
  T&M charts 100
  windows 501
Designer Fixtures 155
Detector
  carbon monoxide 152
  motion,
    security system 453
  radon 152
  smoke 151, 454
  sound,
    security system 453
Determining Costs 4
Diamond shingles 394
Disappearing
  attic stair 471
Dishwasher 26-28
  convertible 27
  electronic 27
  push-button 26-27
  rough plumbing 368
  spacesaver under-sink 28
  wiring 143
Dolly Varden siding 457
Dome skylight 509
Door
  add for tall 123
  architrave, stone 310-312
  awning 35-36
  bathtub folding 380
  batten 109
  bypassing 102
  cabinet 50

D

cafe...............................118-119
casing
    elliptical-top 203
    for closet door..........98-99
    for exterior door 112-113
    for interior door 100-101
    mobile home 515
    round..........................205
    round-top 205
cleaning 57-58
closer..............................126
Dutch door.................110-111
    add to hang................117
entry door
    ash or oak 113
    ash or oak
        side lite 114
    cypress 115
    cypress side lite 115
    fanlite 117-118
    fir 112
    fir side lite.................112
    fixed transom.............118
    mahogany 113
    mahogany side lite 113
    paint-grade wood 111
    paint-grade wood
        side lite 112
    redwood 114
    redwood side lite 114
    steel 111
    steel side lite 111
    walnut or cherry 115
    walnut or cherry
        side lite 116
exterior door
    remove & reinstall 116
    veneer 110
fireplace door 247
    clean-out 247-248
folding door 101-102
French door 103-104
French door,
    exterior 110
full-louvered door 104
garage door 121-122
    opener 122-123
    spring 123
half louvered door 104
interior door 103
    remove & install 104
jamb & casing
    add for round
    or elliptical-top
        door..........................117
    for closet door....102-103
    for exterior door 116-117
    for interior door....104-105

mobile home 514
minimum charge 101
painting 334-336
panel door................106-108
    remove & reinstall 108
    repair 108
    transom 109
    with glass 108
    with round or
        elliptical top 108
pet door 120-121
pocket door
    framing 105-106
shower door 380-381
sliding bathtub
    door 380
sliding patio doors 119-120
stop................................129
storm door 109-110
surround, exterior 207-208
sweep 130
T&M charts 124-126
Victorian wood
    storm door 109
Door bell **148**
    wiring 145
Door, Custom-Milled 107
Door hardware **127-132**
    closer 128
    clothes hanger 42
    deadbolt 127
    door sweep 130
    garage door
        hardware 130
    hinges 128
    hinges, storm door 129
    kick plate 130
    knocker 129
    latch release,
        wiring 144
    letter plate 130
    lockset 127-129
    mobile home 514
    peep hole 130
    push plate 129
    security chain 128
    stop.............................129
    threshold 130
    thumb latch 127-128
    T&M charts 131-132
    weatherstrip 130
Door painting
    Dutch 336
    entry 336
    fanlite 336
    French 335
    full-lite 335

garage 336
gingerbread
    header 339-340
    jamb & casing 335
    panel 334
    side lite 336
    sliding patio door 336
    storm 336
    strip paint from 342
    surround 338
Doric or Tuscan
    capital 75
Dormer, hand-framed
    Dutch-hip.....................438
    gable 437
    gambrel 438
    hip 437-438
    per bf 438-439
    shed 436-437
Double-hung window
    aluminum 502
    wood............................507
Double pendant
    light fixture..................161
Double wythe
    brick wall 288-289
Douglas fir
    plank flooring 267
    strip flooring..........266-267
Downspout............**461-462**
    awning 36
    conductor 462
    paint 341
Drain, bathtub,
    antique style.................385
Drain, floor,
    rough plumbing 368
**Drain, waste, and
    vent (DWV) pipe**
        see: Plumbing, DWV pipe
Drain,
    swimming pool 490
Drawing fees 186
Drip cap molding.............211
Drip edge 406
Driveway, asphalt 92-93
Drop-in suspended
    ceiling HVAC panels.........487
Drying fan 499
Drywall **133-138**
    3/8" drywall...........133-134
    1/2" drywall...............134
    5/8" drywall...............135
    acoustic
        ceiling texture 135-136
    cleaning 58-59

furring 136-137
    masking 285-286
    minimum charge 136
    painting 333
    patch 136
    texture 136
    T&M charts 137-138
Ducting 275
Dump fee 99
Dumpster 99
Dutch door............**110-111**
    add to hang 117
    paint 336
Dutch hip
    hand-framed dormer 438
    hand-framed roof 435
    truss roof 441
DWV pipe
    cast iron 363
    PVC 363-364
Dye, for concrete 89

E

Early American
    chandelier 155-156
Early electric
    chandelier 156
Early electric /
    gas chandelier..............157
Early gas
    chandelier 156-157
Edged glass lite
    in panel door 108
Elastomeric roofing
    EPDM...........................404
    SCPE 403
Electrical
    see also: Appliances, electric
    antenna, TV 152
    baseboard heater............153
    bath fan.......................148
    breaker panel 146-147
    carbon monoxide
        detector 152
    circuit breaker 148
    circuits, check 151
    cleaning 59
    complete house 139
    computer
        network outlet 141
        wiring 145
    conduit 145-146
    door bell 148-149
    electric service.........147-148

furnace...........................275
gate opener 196
intercom 150-151
    wiring 145
kitchen fan 150
light fixture 153-173
    allowance 153-154
    billiard-table
        style fixture 163
    bowl-shade
        fixture 161-162
    ceiling fan...............166-168
    chandelier 154-160
    crystal wall
        fixture 159
    exterior light
        sensor / detector........173
    exterior post
        light fixture 171-172
            wiring 152
    exterior
        recessed
        fixture 170-171
    exterior spot
        light 169-170
    exterior wall-
        mount fixture 170
    fluorescent
        fixture 164-166
            circline
            fixture 166
    hanging fixture............168
    light bar 154
    light fixture
        rewire 173
    minimum light
        fixture charge............168
    pendant fixture.......160-161
    porcelain fixture.........168
    recessed spot
        fixture 169
    replacement
        bowl shade................172
    "shower" fixture 161
    strip spot light............169
    wall-mount
        fixture 163
mask light fixture 287
minimum charge 139
outlet, phone 141
outlet, TV 141
outlets &
    switches................140-141
radon detector 152
resistance
    heating cable..............153
service 147-148
smoke detector 151
sound system...................151

strip..........................169
thermostat..................152
T&M charts.................173
wall heater............152-153
water heater................381
whole-house fan............150
wire.........................146
wire, outlets,
    & switches.........139-140
wiring run.............142-145

Elliptical window
aluminum....................501
vinyl.......................504
wood........................506

Elliptical-top
door, jamb
    & casing................117
door or window,
    casing..................203
panel door.................108

Emergency
board up....................491
Empire capital...........75-76
Engineering fees............186
Enrichment,
plaster.................355-356
Entrance chandelier........155
Entrance crystal
chandelier.................158

Entry door
ash.........................113
cherry......................115
cypress.....................115
fanlite.................117-118
    paint...................336
fir.........................112
fixed transom...............118
lockset.....................127
mahogany....................113
mobile home.................514
oak.........................113
paint.......................336
paint-grade wood............111
redwood.....................114
steel.......................111
walnut......................115
Entry Door Grades.........112

Entry door side lite
ash.........................114
cherry......................116
cypress.....................115
fir.........................112
mahogany....................113
oak.........................114
paint.......................336
paint-grade wood............112

redwood.....................114
steel.......................111
walnut......................116
Entry Doors...............111
Environmental consultant..529,531
EPDM elastomeric............404
Epoxy repair, concrete......83
Equipment, personal
    protection.........529-530
Equipment charts, about..6, 13
Erechtheum capital..........76
Estimating fees.............186

Evaporative cooler...**278**
rough plumbing..............366

Excavation..........**177-184**
basement....................177
crawl space.................177
footings................177-178
foundation wall backfill....178
general.....................181
minimum charge..............181
mobilization................177
repair hole.................180
sewer-line trench...........180
slab-on-grade...............177
T&M charts.............181-184
utility trench.........178-179
water-line trench......179-180
Exhaust ventilator,
mobile home.................513
Exposed aggregate...........90
Exterior architrave.....206-207

Exterior deck
decking.....................429
joist system................429
landing.....................430
railing................429-430
stairs......................430

Exterior door
French......................110
jamb & casing..........116-117
lockset.....................127
remove & reinstall..........116
surround...............207-208
veneer......................110
Exterior fixture, for post..172
Exterior light
sensor / detector...........173
Exterior post
light fixture..........171-172
Exterior recessed
light fixture..........170-171
Exterior spot light.....169-170

Exterior wall
beam pocket.................414

mobile home............519-520
per bf.................414-415
per lf.................410-411
per sf......................413
per sf, sloping........413-414
Exterior wall-mount fixture...170
Exterior water
supply lines................364
Exterior window
surround...............208-209

F

Fabric reinforcement,
retaining wall..............392
Face, fireplace.........249-251
Factory built
panels.................443-444
Factory stained
siding......................459

Fan
bath........................149
    with heat lamp..........149
    with heater.............149
kitchen.....................150
whole house.................150
wiring......................142
Fan bracket,
gingerbread.................227

**Fanlite,
entry door**...........**117-118**
paint.......................336
Fanlite Quality...........118

Fascia................**459-460**
paint.......................341
awning......................35

Faucet
bathtub...........370, 384-385
bidet.......................369
repack......................371
shower......................370
sink
    antique style...........384
    bathroom...........368-369
    kitchen.................369
    laundry.................369
    wet bar.............370-371
Faucet Quality........369-370

Fees..................**185-186**
building permit.............185
estimating..................186
plan drawing................186
sewer connect...............186
soils engineering...........186
structural engineering......186

water connect...............186
Felt, roofing..........405-406

Fences
basketweave.................187
board..................187-188
board-and-batten.......188-189
board-on-board..............188
board with
    lattice cap.............188
chain-link.............189-191
chain-link post........191-192
chain-link,
    temporary..............491
cleaning....................60
electric gate opener........196
masonry.....................303
minimum charge,
    board fence............189
ornamental iron........195-196
painting....................337
picket......................189
post, wood..................187
safety......................492
T&M charts.............197-198
vinyl picket fence.....192-194
vinyl solid-slat.......194-195
vinyl spaced-slat...........194
vinyl three-rail............194
wood gate
    hardware................189
wood post...................187
Fiber and cement
shingles....................396
Fiberglass
corrugated roofing.....400-401
Fiberglass
corrugated siding...........455
Fiberglass
insulation, batt............282
Fiberglass
insulation, blown......281-282
Fiberglass
swimming pool...............489

FICA
see: Time and material charts
Finial, gable...............231
Finish board...........233-234

Finish carpentry....**199-240**
astragal molding.......211-212
base block.............204-205
base shoe...................201
bed mold....................216
book case..............223-224
carved onlay...........232-233
ceiling cove
    molding............213-214
chair rail molding.....210-211

clamshell base.........199-200
clamshell casing.......201-202
cleaning.................61-62
closet work............222-223
coffered ceiling............225
corner bead
    molding............215-216
corner block................205
cove molding...........212-213
crown molding..........216-217
curved pattern
    casing.............203-204
custom-milled
    molding................221
drip cap molding............211
exterior architrave....206-207
exterior door
    surround...........207-208
exterior window
    surround...........208-209
finish board...........233-234
finish plywood..............234
gingerbread............227-231
half-round molding..........214
hand rail...................217
head block..................206
interior architrave.........206
mantel.................224-225
mantel beam.................224
minimum charge..............199
mobile home.................515
niche.......................226
other wood
    species................199
overdoor mold..........205-206
painting...............337-340
panel molding
    corner radius......221-222
pattern base...........200-201
pattern casing.........202-203
porch post.............231-232
post bracket................228
post drop...................229
quarter-round
    molding............214-215
running trim...........226-227
spandrel....................229
specialty molding......217-221
T&M charts.............235-240
window apron
    molding................210
window cornice..............230
window stool
    molding............209-210
wood key....................204
Finish plywood..............234

Fir entry door.........**112**
side lite...................112

Fire brick 244
Fire retardant shingles 395
Fire-rated acoustic ceiling 16
Fireplaces 241-243
  chimney 244-245
    cap 245
    pipe 248-249
    pot 245-246
    reline 245
    screen 246
  cleaning 62
  clean-out door 245-248
  damper 248
  door 247
  face 249-251
  fire brick 244
  fireplace 241
  flue cap 245
  form 243-244
  furnace 244
  gas fireplace 249
  grate 246-247
  hearth 251-252
  prefabricated 241-243
  screen 247
  T&M charts 253-256
Fixed (picture) window
  aluminum 503
  vinyl 505
  wood 508
Fixed skylight 509
Fixed Transoms 118
Fixture rough plumbing
  bathroom sink 367
  bathtub or shower 367
  bidet 367-368
  clothes washer 368
  dishwasher 368
  evaporative cooler 368
  floor drain 368
  hose bibb 368
  ice maker 368
  kitchen sink 367
  laundry sink 367
  toilet 367
  wet bar sink 367
Flashing, roof 406
Flat clay tile roofing 396
Flat seam
  copper roofing 402
  terne roofing 403
Flatwork 88-89
Fleur-sawn
  running trim 226
Flexible Molds 353

Flood light fixture 169-170
Floor drain 368
Floor framing, seal 341
Floor truss 432
Flooring
  carpet 257-259
    cove 258
    glue-down 257
    indoor-outdoor 257
    pad 258
    stair installation 258
    tile 258-259
    wool 258
  cleaning 62-63
  linoleum 262
  marble 259
  quarry tile 260
  resilient tile 262
  rubber base 263
  slate 259-260
  stone 259
  terrazzo, cast-in-place 261
    precast tile 261
    precast base 261
  tile 260
    base 260-261
  T&M charts 269-272
  underlayment 268
  vinyl 261
    cove 264-265
    tile 261-262
  wood floor
    Douglas fir plank 267
    Douglas fir strip 266-267
    maple parquet 264-265
      prefinished 265
    maple strip 263
    other wood
      species 265-266
    painting 340
    reclaimed antique
      longleaf pine 267
    red oak parquet 265
      prefinished 265
    red oak plank 264
    red oak strip 263
      prefinished 264
      quartersawn 263-264
    sand, edge, &
      fill wood floor 268
    sleepers 268
    southern pine plank 266
    southern pine strip 266
Flue
  cap 245
  chimney pipe 248-249

**Fluorescent
light fixture 164-166**
  cirdline 166
Fluted block wall 299-300
Fluted column or pilaster 72
Foam insulation 282-283
Foil wallpaper 495
Foil-Face Cabinets 49
Folding bathtub door 380
Folding door 101-102
  paint 334
Footing 83-84
  excavation 177-178
Footing & foundation,
  single pour 85
Form, fireplace 243-244
Formica
  see: Plastic laminate
Foundation 84-85
  buttress 91-92
  coating 91
  mobile home 516
  sill plate 415
  wall backfill 178
Frame
  see also: Rough Carpentry
  bay window 414
  bow window 414
  round window 414
  round or elliptical top
    door or window 414
Frame-and-panel wall 349-50
Framing, seal 341
Free-standing supply
  lines, antique style 385
Freezer
  see: Refrigerator / freezer
French door 103-104
  exterior 110
  paint 335
Frieze
  Anaglypta 496
  Lincrusta 496
  plaster 356
Full-height cabinets 48-50
Full-lite door, paint 335
Full-louvered door 104
Furnace
  electric 275
  fireplace 244
  gas 275-276
  mobile home 517
  oil 276
  service 276
  vent pipe 277

  wiring 142
Furring strips
  for acoustic ceiling tiles 16
  for tile roofing 399
  metal 136-137
  wood 430-431

G

Gable dormer, hand-framed 437
**Gable finial,
gingerbread 231**
  paint 340
**Gable ornament,
gingerbread 230-231**
  paint 340
Gable roof,
  hand-framed 432-435
Gable roof rafters
  QuickCalculator 542-543
Gable roof trusses
  QuickCalculator 544-545
Gable roofing
  QuickCalculator 546-547
Galvanized
  steel pipe 362
Galvanized steel roofing
  corrugated 401
  ribbed 401
  shingles 393
Galvanized steel
  swimming pool 489
Gambrel
  hand-framed
    dormer 438
  hand-framed roof 435-436
  truss roof 441
Garage door 121-122
  hardware 130
  opener 122-123
    wiring 143
  paint 336
  spring 123
Garage Door Grades 121
Garbage disposal 28
  wiring 143
Gas
  see also: Appliances, gas
  fireplace 249
  furnace 275-276
  water heater 381
Gate
  hardware 189
  latch release, wiring 144
  opener, electric 196

Gazebo 331-332
General excavation 181
Germicide treatment
  for wet carpet 499
Gingerbread
  arch spandrel 229-230
  bracket 227
    paint 339
  corbel 228
    paint 339
  fan bracket 227
  gable finial 231
    paint 340
  gable ornament 230-231
    paint 340
  header 228
    paint 339-340
  post bracket 228
  post drop 229
  running trim 226-227
    paint 339
  spandrel 229
    paint 340
  window cornice 230
Glass block wall 304
Glass lite
  in panel door 108
Glass shower 379-380
Glazed block wall 300
Glazing 501, 511
  skylight 508
Globe, replacement 173
Glue-down carpet 257
Glue-laminated
  beam 418-420
Goose neck,
  balustrade 476
Grade beam 86-88
  for block wall 303
Grand entrance
  chandelier 155
  crystal chandelier 158-159
Granite countertop 51-52
Granular coated
  metal tile roofing 396
Grass cloth wallpaper 495
Grate, fireplace 246-247
Gravel stop 406
Greenhouse 332
Grid, suspended ceiling
  2' x 2' 486-487
  2' x 4' 484-485
  12" x 12" 483
Grille, cold air 278
Grouting, compaction 92

Guard, security 491-492

Gutter **461**
  built-in box.........................461
  down spout..............461-462
    conductor 462
  paint 341

Gypsum drywall
  see: Drywall

Gypsum partition
  tile wall................................304
Gypsum plaster...................354

H

Half-elliptical window
  aluminum 501
  vinyl 503
  wood 505
Half-louvered door 104

Half-round window
  aluminum 501
  molding 214
  vinyl 503
  wood window 505
Hand carved
  moldings...................218-222
Hand rail................................217

Hand-framed
  Dutch-hip roof 435
  Dutch-hip dormer 438
  dormer, per bf..........438-439
  gable dormer 437
  gable roof...............432-435
  gambrel dormer 438
  gambrel roof...........435-436
  hip dormer...............437-438
  hip roof 435
  mansard roof 435
  roof, per bf.........................436
  shed dormer................436-437
  valley.....................................435
Hand-hewn beam................423
Hanging light fixture 168
Hardboard paneling 347
Hardboard siding 456-457
Hauling, debris......................99

Hazardous materials
  asbestos analysis 273
  decontamination
    unit 273
  encapsulate asbestos.......273
  minimum charge 273
  remove asbestos................273
  seal area...............................273

T&M charts.......................274
Head block 206
Header, gingerbread 228
Header, wall 415-416

Health insurance
  see: Time and material charts
Hearth, fireplace..........251-252
Heat and AC,
  through-wall..................277
Heat pump **276**
  wiring 144
Heat register 278

**Heat, vent and
air conditioning**
  see: HVAC
Heater
  baseboard 153
    wiring..................142, 144
  mask 285
  wall 152-153
    wiring..................................142
Heating, temporary 491
Hexagonal shingles 394
High-low gas range 19
High-tank toilet 386

Hinges
  door 128
  screen door 129

Hip
  hand-framed
    dormer.......................437-438
  hand-framed roof 435
  truss roof 441
Horn or siren,
  security system 454
Hose bibb,
  rough plumbing 368
Hot water dispenser,
  in-sink, wiring...................143
Humidifier.........................**276**
  wiring 143
HVAC **275-280**
  cleaning 63
  cold air grille 278
  drop-in suspended
    ceiling panels 487
  ducts 275
  evaporative cooler...........278
  furnace 275-276
    vent pipe.........................277
  heat pump 276
  heat register........................278
  humidifier............................276
  mask heater.........................285
  mobile home 517

thermostat............................278
through-wall
  AC unit 277
through-wall AC
  and heat unit..................277

I

Ice maker,
  rough plumbing 368
Ice shield 406
Indoor-outdoor carpet..........257
Infrared detector 173

Insulation
  blown fiberglass 281-282
  cavity wall 295
  cellulose 281
  fiberglass batt 282
  in existing walls.............282
  loose block 302
  mineral wool......................281
  minimum charge 281
  polystyrene
    block inserts 301-302
  polystyrene on
    steel shingles 393
  rigid foam..................282-283
  T&M charts.................283-284
  vermiculite 281
Intercom **150-151**
  wiring 145
Interior architrave..............206
Interior bearing wall
  per lf.......................409-410
  per sf.......................412-413
Interior door..................**103**
  jamb & casing..........104-105
  lockset.................................128
  paint 335
  remove & install 104
Interior partition wall
  mobile home......................520
  per bf...........................414-415
  per lf....................................409
  per sf....................................411-412
Interlocking block 301
Interlocking block
  retaining wall 391-392
Island cabinets 48

J

Jack, mobile home.............516
Jack, pipe, roofing 406

Jackpost.......................417-418
Jamb & casing
  add for round
    or elliptical
    -top door 117
  closet door 102-103
  exterior door 116-117
  interior door 104-105
  paint 335
  strip paint
    from 342
Joints,
  post & beam 426-429
Joist system
  deck 429
  laminated I..........................432
  mobile home......................520
  per sf.........................431-432
  QuickCalculator.........548-549

K

Keene's cement
  plaster 354
Key control,
  security system 453
Key pad,
  security system 453
Key, wood 204
Keystone....................308-309
Kick plate.............................130
Kitchen
  mask 286
  rough plumbing........366-367
Kitchen fan **150**
  wiring 143
Kitchen sink **373**
  faucet 369
  rough plumbing 367
Knocker, door 129

L

Labor charts, about **13**
  see: Time and material charts
Labor costs, about..................5
**Labor productivity
charts, about** **13**
  see: Time and material charts
Lally column.........................418
Laminated asphalt
  shingles 394
Laminated I joist 432
Landing, deck........................430

Laundry room,
  rough plumbing 366
Laundry sink **374**
  faucet 369
  rough plumbing 367
Leach field................382-383
Lead-coated stainless-
  steel roofing 402
Lead roofing **402**
  batten seam 402
  flat seam 402
Leaded glass lite
  in panel door 108
Leak detection,
  swimming pool 489
Leak repair,
  swimming pool 490
Letter plate..........................130

Liability insurance
  see: Time and material charts
Light bar...............................154
Light fixture **153-173**
  allowance...................153-154
  billiard-table
    style fixture 163
  bowl-shade fixture....161-162
    replacement
    shade 172
  ceiling fan 166-168
  chandelier 154-160
  cleaning 59
  crystal wall
    fixture 159
  electric strip.......................169
  exterior
    post light fixture....171-172
    painting 337
    recessed fixture....170-171
    sensor / detector 173
    spot light.............169-170
    wall-mount
    fixture 170
  fluorescent fixture......164-166
    circline fixture.............166
  for complete house.........139
  hanging fixture.................168
  light bar 154
  low-voltage,
    wiring for 145
  mask.......................................285
  minimum charge 168
  mobile home 515
  pendant fixture..........160-161
  porcelain fixture 168
  recessed spot
    fixture 169
  rewire light fixture...........173

"shower" fixture 161
strip spot light..............169
wall-mount fixture 163
wiring, light fixture 143
*Light Fixture
Quality* 154-155
Lightweight flatwork 88

Lincrusta
frieze......................496
wall covering...............496
Linen closet
shelves.....................222
Liner, vinyl,
swimming pool 490
Linoleum....................262
Lintel 322

Lockset
entry door 127
exterior door...............127
interior door 128
mobile home 514-515
screen door 129
thumb latch 127-128
Log cabin siding............457
Longleaf pine
flooring 267
Loose block
insulation 302
Low-tank toilet.............386
Lower cabinets...............47
Lumber Prices..............409

**Luminous panel
suspended ceiling**
2' x 2' 485-486
2' x 4' 483-484

M

Mail box 444
Main disconnect..............148

Mansard roof
hand-framed.................435
truss 441

Mantel................**224-225**
paint 339

Mantel beam..............**224**
paint 339

Manufactured housing
see: Mobile homes

Marble
fireplace face..............249
fireplace hearth............251
floor 259
Mark up, about..............6

Masking & moving
masking 136, 285-286
minimum
charge 285
moving 286
T&M charts 286

Masonry
architrave 310-314
block 301
loose insulation 302
polystyrene
inserts 301-302
block wall 298-299
bond beam 302-303
fluted 299-300
glazed 300
grade beam 303
pargeting 303
pilaster 302
reinforcement...............302
screen 301
slump 299
split-face 300-301
split-rib 301
brick and block wall...289-292
brick arch 298
brick bonds 297
brick veneer 296-297
brick wall 287-293
repair 319
cavity wall 293-295
brick 294-295
brick and block 293-294
insulation 295
clay backing tile wall 303
cleaning..........63-64, 321
common brick 287
curved installation.........297
cut hole in wall 321
cut stone 314-317
sill 316-317
trim or cornice......314-316
fence 303
glass block wall 304
gypsum partition tile 304
keystone 308-309
lintel 322
masonry fence 303
masonry wall
opening 297-298
minimum charge 287
painting 340-341
pavers 304-305
raked joints 297
repoint brick wall 318-319
repoint stone wall..........319
salvage brick 319

shore masonry opening ...322
stone carving 320
stone quoin 309
stone repair 320-321
stone veneer 307-308
stone wall 305-307
repair 319-320
structural tile
wall........................303
T&M charts 323-330
veneer panel 309-310
wall cap 317
wall coping 317-318
wall opening 297-298
*Material costs,
about*.......................5
Mathematics,
QuickCalculator...........558
Medallion, plaster 356

Medicine cabinet....**45-46**
paint 337
Megameter, check
electrical circuits 151
Metal, roofing 406
Mildew remediation 529-536
Mildewcide treatment
for wet carpet 499
Metal roofing, paint 341
Metal shed 331
Micro-laminated beam 418
Microwave oven 28-29
Mildew retardant,
shingles....................395

Millwork
see also: Finish carpentry
mask 285
Mineral wool
insulation 281

Mirror **45-46**
cleaning 68
Mission tile roofing........397
Mitered steps 470

Mobile homes........**513-528**
access doors 514
anchor 516
appliances 513
baseboard
heaters 517
cabinets 513
casing 515
ceiling cove 515
ceiling panels.........526-527
clothes lines 513
combination doors 514
deadbolts 515
door casing 515

door hardware 514
doors 514
entry doors 514
exhaust ventilator 513
exterior walls.........519-520
finish carpentry 515
foundations 516
furnaces....................517
HVAC........................517
interior walls..............520
jack 516
joist systems 520
light fixtures 515
locksets...............514-515
molding 515-516
moving 518
plumbing 518
rafters 521
relevel 516
roof repair 519
roofing 518-519
rough carpentry 519
setup 516
shutters 522-523
siding 521-522
site prep 516
skirting 524-526
skylights 527-528
steps 523-524
storm doors 514
time-and-material
charts 528
towing 518
trusses 521
utility hookup 517
wall panels 526-527
water heaters 518
window casing 515
windows, awning 527
Mobilization,
excavation 177
Modified
bitumen roofing.............405
Mold remediation 529-536

Molder set up **221**
custom knife
charges 221

Molding....**205-206, 211-222**
mobile home 515-516
Motion detector,
security system 453
Motion sensor,
light fixture 173

Moving **286**
mobile homes................518
pad and block
furniture 500

Mud sill
see: Foundation sill plate

N

**Narrow grid,
suspended ceiling**
2' x 2' 486-487
2' x 4' 484-485

Newel
pine 476-477
poplar 477-478
red oak 479-480
redwood 478-479

Niche **226**
paint 339
Non-bearing wall,
QuickCalculator 550-551

O

Office trailer 492
Oil furnace.................276
Onlay, carved...........232-233

Opener
electric gate 196
garage door 122-123

Opening
mask 285
masonry, shore 322
masonry wall 297-298

**Ornamental
iron fence** **193-194**
paint 337

Outbuildings.........**331-332**
chickhee hut 332
gazebo 331-333
greenhouse 332
metal shed 331
swimming pool
enclosure 332
wood shed 331

Outlet **140-141**
computer
network 141
covers 142
mask 286
phone 141
TV 141
wiring 144
with wire 139-140

Oven
electric wall 25
gas wall 20-21

microwave 28-29
oven or range,
  wiring 144
Overdoor mold..........205-206
Overhead 6
Overlay,
  asphalt driveway 92-93

P

Pad, carpet 258
Paid leave
  see: Time and material charts
Painting
  acoustic ceilings 333
  awnings and
    carports 333
  columns 333
  concrete 333-334
  doors.........................334-336
  drywall 333
  fences 337
  finish carpentry 337-340
  flooring 340
  foundation
    coating 91
  light-fixture
    post 337
  masking 285-286
  masonry 340-341
  medicine cabinet 337
  minimum charge..............333
  moving............................286
  paneling 340
  plaster 333
  roofing 341
  rough carpentry...............341
  seal asbestos 273
  siding 341
  stairs 342
  strip paint 342
  stucco 333
  swimming pool 489
  T&M charts...............343-346
  wallpaper 342
  window 342
Painting Coats..................333
Pan, shower 376-377
Panel, breaker...............145-146
Panel door............**106-108**
  paint...............................335
  remove & reinstall 108
  repair 108
  transom 109
  with glass 108

Panel molding
  corner radius 221-222
Paneling
  board-and-batten 349
  board-on-board 349
  cleaning 64
  frame-and-
    panel wall 349-350
  hardboard 347
  minimum charge 347
  paint...............................340
  pegboard 347
  plywood 347-348
  plywood
    with grooves............348-349
  T&M charts 351-352
  tongue-&-groove 349
  wall molding for.............348
Panels,
  factory built 443-444
Panic button,
  security system 454
Pargeting
  block wall 303
  concrete 90
Parquet flooring
  maple.........................264-265
  maple,
    prefinished 265
  red oak 265
  red oak,
    prefinished 265
Partition tile wall,
  gypsum 304
Partition wall, interior
  per bf 414-415
  per lf 409
  per sf 411-412
  sloping per sf 412
Patch, drywall 136
Patio doors **119-120**
  paint...............................336
Patch roof,
  with mastic.....................406
Pattern base................200-201
Pattern casing 202-203
Pattern, curved
  casing 203-204
Pavers 304-305
Pedestal, column...........**80**
  painting 333
Pedestal, pilaster 80
Pedestal sink 385-386
Peep hole 130
Pegboard paneling............347
Pelmet, Anaglypta 496

Perlite plaster 354
Permit fees 185
Pet door 120-121
Phone outlet 150
Picket fence
  paint 339
  vinyl 192-194
  wood 189
Picket-sawn
  running trim 226
Picture window
  aluminum 503
  vinyl 505
  wood 508
Pier 86
Pier, precast 417
Pilaster
  see also: Columns
  block................................302
  plaster 355
  stucco 358-359
Pile retaining wall
  with lagging 391
Pillbox toilet,
  antique style 386
Pine
  beam.........................420-422
  connecting
    members
    between bents..............425
  flooring,
    reclaimed
    longleaf 267
  newel.........................476-477
  post & beam
    bent with
    truss.........................423-425
  stair balustrade 471-472
Pipe
  black steel 361
  brass 361
  cast-iron DWV 363
  chimney 248-249
  copper........................361-362
  CPVC 362
  galvanized steel 362
  jack 406
  PVC 363
  PVC DWV 363-364
Plan drawing fees..............186
Plank flooring
  Douglas fir 267
  red oak 264
  southern pine 266
Plaster
  see also: Stucco

acoustical 353-354
architrave 356
cast-in-place mold 355
ceiling medallion............356
ceiling rose 356
cleaning 58-59, 64-66
curved wall
  installation 355
enrichment 355-356
frieze 356
gypsum 354
Keene's cement 354
on wood lath 355
painting 335
perlite or
  vermiculite 354
pilaster or column 355
production mold 355
repair 353
thin-coat 354
T&M charts................359-360
Plastic laminate
  countertop 51
Plumbing
  bathtub.......377-378, 385-387
  bathtub &
    shower combination 378
  bathtub door 380
  bathtub surround 379
  bidet................................376
  break-out concrete
    & install pipe.................364
  complete house 365
    finish 365
    rough 365
    rough and finish.............365
  DWV pipe
    cast-iron 363
    minimum charge............364
    PVC 363-364
  exterior lines 364
  faucet
    bathtub.........370, 384-385
    bidet................................369
    sink 368-371, 384
    repack 371
    shower 370
  mobile home 518
  pedestal sink...................385-386
  rough by fixture 367-368
  rough by room 365-367
  septic tank
    with leach field 382-383
  shower base 379
  shower door 380-381
  shower, glass 379-380
  shower pan.................378-379

shower stall......................378
shut-off and
  pressure valve 364
sink
  bathroom 371-373
  kitchen 373
  laundry 374
  plumbing lines 375-376
  wet bar 374-375
submersible water pump 383
sump pump 383
supply pipe
  black steel 361
  brass 361
  copper........................361-362
  CPVC 362
  galvanized steel 362
  minimum charge.........363
  PVC 363
T&M charts 387-390
toilet.......................376, 386
  plumbing lines 376
  seat 376-377
water heater 381
water softener 382
Plywood
  finish 234
  paneling 347-348
  T1-11 siding 457
  with grooves,
    paneling 348-349
Pocket door 105-106
Polypropylene
  shutter 462
Polystyrene
  block inserts 301-302
Porcelain light
  fixture 168
Porch post.............**231-232**
  paint 340
Portable toilet...................492
Post & beam
  joints 426-429
  oak
    bent with truss 425-426
    connecting
      members
      between bents..........425
  pine
    bent with truss.....423-425
    connecting
      members
      between bents..........425
Post 416-417
Post, awning.......................35
Post, mail box 444
Post bracket, gingerbread 228

Post drop,
gingerbread 229

Post fixture
light fixture 171-172
post 172
wiring 153

Post, porch **231-232**
paint 340

Post, fence 187, 191-192

Pothole, fill
with asphalt 93

Power, temporary 491

Precast pier 417

Prefabricated
fireplace 241-243

Prefinished flooring
maple parquet 265
red oak parquet 265
red oak strip
flooring 264

Pressure mat,
security system 453

Pressure valve,
water supply line 364

Prismatic room
QuickCalculator 552-553

Production
plaster mold 355

Profit 6

Pump, submersible
water 383

Pump, sump 383

Pump truck,
concrete 91

Push plate 129

PVC DWV pipe 363-364

PVC, fences
see: Vinyl fences

PVC pipe 363

PVC roofing 404-405

Q

Quarry tile 260

Quarter round window
aluminum 501
molding for 214-215
vinyl 504
wood 506

Quartersawn red
oak strip
flooring 263-264

QuickCalculators **537-557**
bearing wall 530-531

concrete wall
& footing 532-533
gable roof
rafters 534-535
gable roof
trusses 536-537
gable roofing 538-539
joist system 540-541
mathematics 550
non-bearing wall 542-543
prismatic room 544-545
rectangular room 546-547
round room 548-549

*Quickfinder
headings, using* 10

Quoin, stone 309

R

Radiant heating
system, wiring 144

Radon detector 152

Rafters,
mobile home 521

Railing, deck 429-430

Railroad tie
retaining wall 391

Rain gutter **461**
paint 341

Range **19-20, 23-25**
electric 23-25
gas 19-20
wiring 144

Range hood **26**
wiring 143

Rebar
concrete 91
flatwork 88

Recessed 2' x 2'
suspended
ceiling tile 485

Recessed light
fixture, exterior 170-171

Recessed spot
light fixture 169

Recharge central air 277

Reclaimed antique
longleaf pine
flooring 267

Reconditioned Door 107

Rectangular room
QuickCalculator 554-555

Refinish cabinet 50

Refinished
antique bathtub 387

Refreshment center 31

**Refrigerator
/ freezer** **29-31**
over-under 20-31
refinish 31
refreshment center 31
refreshment center
plumbing 31
side-by-side 29-30

Refuse chute 99

Regional pricing 6

Register, heat 278

Reglaze window 511

Regrout tile
swimming pool 489

Regrout tile 494

Reinforcement,
block wall 302

Relevel,
mobile home 516

**Relevel suspended
ceiling grid**
2' x 2' 487
2' x 4' 485

Reline chimney 245

Remediation, mold 529-536

Removal costs
(see replace column on most pages)

Repack faucet 371

Replacement bowl shade 172

Replaster swimming pool 490

Repoint brick wall 318-319

Repoint stone wall 319

Reproduction
antique bathtub 387

Reproduction
slipper bathtub 387

Resilient tile floor 262

Restaurant
style gas range 20

Retaining walls
anchored tieback 391
cedar tie 391
concrete 391
fabric
reinforcement 392
interlocking block 391-392
minimum charge 391
pile with lagging 391
railroad tie 391
shotcrete 392
stone 391
tieback 391

Retaining Walls 391

Retirement

see: Time and material charts

Rewire, light fixture 173

Ribbed roofing
aluminum sheet 400
galvanized steel 401

Rigid foam
insulation 282-283

Robe hook 42

Rock wool insulation
see: Mineral wool insulation

Roll roofing 394

Roll-up awning 37

Roman Ionic capital 77

Roof
hand-framed 432-436
hand-framed dormer ..436-439
repair,
mobile home 519
sheathing 441-443
vent 406

Roof panel, awning 36

Roof curbs, skylight 508

Roof framing, seal 341

Roof truss
per lf 439-440
per sf 440-441

Roof window 510

Roofing
aluminum sheet
corrugated 400
aluminum sheet
ribbed 400
aluminum shingles 393
asphalt shingles 393
asphalt shingles,
laminated 394
built-up 403
clay tile grades 399
concrete tile 399-400
copper 401-402
EPDM elastomeric 404
felt 405-406
fiber and cement
shingles 396
fiberglass
corrugated 400-401
flat clay tile 396
furring strips 399
galvanized steel 393, 401
corrugated 401
ribbed 401
shingles 393
valley metal 406
granular coated
metal tile 396
ice shield 406

lead 402
metal 406
minimum charge 393
mission tile 397
modified bitumen 405
mobile home 518-519
painting 341
PVC 404-405
repair 406
roll roofing 394
SCPE elastomeric 403
seamed metal
roof repair 403
slate shingles 394-395
Spanish tile 398
stainless steel 402
steep and
complex roofs 393
t-lock, diamond,
& hexagonal
shingles 394
terne 402-403
T&M charts 406-408
vents 406
wood shakes 395-396
wood shingles 395

Roofing 394

Room, mask **285**
move contents 286

Rough carpentry
beam
curved, add for 423
glue-laminated 418-420
hand-hewn,
add for 423
micro-laminated 420
oak 422-423
pine 420-422
chimney cricket 444
exterior deck 429-430
factory
built panels 443-44
furring strips 430-431
hand-framed roof
Dutch hip 435
gable 432-435
gambrel 435-436
hip 435
mansard 435
minimum charge 436
per bf 436
valley, add for 435
hand-framed dormer
Dutch-hip 438
gable 437
gambrel 438
hip 437-438

per bf 438-439
shed 436-437
interior soffit
  framing 443
jackpost 417-418
joist, laminated I 432
joist system,
  per sf 431-432
lally column 418
mobile home 519
painting 341
post 416-417
post & beam
  joints 426-429
  oak
    bent
      with truss 425-426
    connecting
      members
      between bents 425
  pine
    bent
      with truss 423-425
    connecting
      members
      between bents 425
precast pier 417
shear panel 443
sheathing,
  wall or roof 441-443
T&M charts 445-452
truss
  Dutch hip roof 441
  floor 432
  gable, per lf 439-440
  gable, per sf 440-441
  gambrel roof 441
  hip roof 441
  mansard roof 441
  remove &
    reinstall 441
  valley in
    truss roof 441
wall
  beam pocket 414
  California
    earthquake
    code (CEC)
    bracing 414
  exterior
    per lf 410-411
    per sf 413
  exterior,
    sloping per sf 413-414
  foundation
    sill plate 415
  frame
    bay window 414
    bow window 414

round window 414
round or
  elliptical
  top door
  or window 414
header 415-416
interior bearing wall
  per lf 409-410
  per sf 412-413
interior partition wall
  per lf 409
  per sf 411-412
interior sloping
  wall, bearing,
  per sf 412
interior sloping
  wall, partition,
  per sf 412
top plate 415
wall, per bf 414-415
Rough framing,
  pocket door 105-106
Rounding 4
Round room
  QuickCalculator 556-557
Round window
  aluminum 501
  vinyl 503
  wood 505
Round-top door,
  jamb & casing 117
Round-top door
  or window, casing 203
Round-top
  panel door 108
Rubber base 263
Rubble stone
  fireplace face 250
  fireplace hearth 252
  veneer 307
  wall 305-306
Run, wiring 142-145
Running trim ...226-227
  ball-and-dowel 226
  fleur-sawn 226
  paint 339
  picket-sawn 226
  spindle 226

S

Safety fence 492
Safety tape 492
Salvage brick 319
Sand, edge, &
  fill wood floor 268

Saw-kerf flashing 406
Sawing, concrete 90
Sawn stair balustrade 475
Scaffolding 489
Scamozzi capital 77-78
Schedule 40 pipe
  see: Plumbing
SCPE elastomeric
  roofing 403
Screen 511
Screen block wall 301
Screen, chimney 246
Screen door
  see: Storm door
Screen, fireplace 247
Screened pool
  enclosure 332
Scroll, awning post 332
Seal asbestos 273
Seal, asphalt
  driveway 93
Seamed metal
  roof repair 403
Security chain 128
Security guard 491-492
Security systems
  contact 453
  control panel 453
  horn or siren 454
  key control 453
  key pad 453
  minimum charge 453
  motion detector 453
  panic button 454
  pressure mat 453
  smoke detector 454
  sound detector 453
  T&M charts 454
  wiring 143
Septic tank
  with leach field 382-383
Service AC unit 276
Service, electrical 147-148
Service furnace 276
Setup,
  mobile home 516
Sewer
  connection fees 186
Sewer-line
  trench excavation 180
Shake or wood
  shingle siding 456
Shakes, wood 395-396
Shear panel 443
Sheathing 441-443

Sheetrock
  see: Drywall
Shed
  dormer 436-437
  storage, metal 331
  storage, wood 331
Shelf, glass 41-42
Shingle siding
  cement fiber 455
  shake or
    wood shingle 456
Shingles
  aluminum 393
  asphalt 393
  diamond 394
  fiber and cement 396
  galvanized steel 393
  hexagonal 394
  laminated asphalt 394
  slate 394-395
  t-lock 394
  wood 395
Shiplap siding 458
Shock treatment,
  swimming pool 490
Shore masonry
  opening 322
Shotcrete slope
  stabilization 392
Shower
  base 379
  bathtub
    combination 378
  door 380-381
  faucet 370
  glass 379-380
  light fixture 161
  pan 378-379
  rod 43
  rough plumbing 367
  stall 378
  tile 493-494
Shut-off and
  pressure valve,
  water supply line 364
Shutter 462-463
  mobile home 522-523
  paint 341
Side lite, entry door
  ash or oak 114
  cypress 115
  fir 112
  mahogany 113
  paint 336
  paint-grade wood 112
  redwood 114

walnut or cherry 116
Sidewalk 89
Siding 455-464
  aluminum 455
  beveled 458-459
  board-and-batten 457
  board-on-board 457
  board over plywood 457
  bungalow 459
  cement fiber
    shingle 455
  channel rustic 457-458
  clapboard 458
  cleaning 66-67
  Dolly Varden 459
  factory stained
    siding 459
  fascia 459-460
  fiberglass
    corrugated 455
  hardboard 456-457
  log cabin 459
  minimum charge 455
  mobile home 521-522
  painting 341
  plywood T1-11 457
  rain gutter 461-462
  repair 459
  shake or wood
    shingle 456
  shiplap 458
  shutter 462-463
  soffit 460-461
  T&M charts 463-464
  tongue-&-groove 458
  vinyl 456
Sill
  cultured marble 494
  cut stone 316-317
  plate 415
  tile 494
Single wythe
  brick wall 287-288
Single-hung window
  vinyl 504
  wood 507
Sink
  bathroom 371-373
    rough plumbing 367
  kitchen 373
    rough plumbing 367
  laundry 374
    rough plumbing 367
  pedestal 385-386
  plumbing lines 375-376
  wet bar 374-375
    rough plumbing 367

Sink faucet
  antique style 384
  bathroom 368-369
  kitchen 369
  laundry 369
  wet bar 370-371
Site prep,
  mobile home 516
Siren,
  security system 454
Skirting,
  mobile home 524-526
Skylight **508-510**
  accessories 510
  dome 509
  fixed 509
  fixed with vent flap 509
  mobile home 527-528
  other glass
    options (glazing) 508
  roof curbs 508
  roof window 510
  ventilating 509
Slab-on-grade
  excavation 177
Slate floor 259-260
Slate shingles 394-395
Sleepers 268
Sliding
  aluminum window 503
Sliding bathtub door 380
Sliding patio door ..**119-120**
  paint 336
Sliding window
  vinyl 505
  wood 507-508
Slipper bathtub 387
Sloping wall
  exterior, per sf 413-414
  interior bearing,
    per sf 412
  interior partition,
    per sf 412
Slump block wall 299
Smoke detector **151, 454**
  wiring 143
Soap holder 42-43
Soffit **460-461**
  paint 341
Soffit framing,
  interior 443
Softener 382
Soils engineering
  fees 186
Solid-slat fence,
  vinyl 194-195

Solid-surface
  countertop 51
Solid-wood
  countertop 52
Sound blanket,
  suspended ceiling 487
Sound detector,
  security system 453
Sound system 151
Southern pine flooring
  plank 266
  strip 266
Space heater,
  electrical 152-153
Spaced-slat
  fence, vinyl 194
Spacesaver
  electric range 24
  gas range 19
  under-sink
    dishwasher 28
Spandrel
  arch, gingerbread 229-230
  gingerbread 229
  paint 340
Spanish tile
  roofing 398
Specialty molding 217-221
Spindle
  running trim 226
Spiral stair 470-471
Split-face
  block wall 300-301
Split-rib
  block wall 301
Spot light,
  exterior 169-170
Spring,
  garage door 123
Sprung cove
  see: Ceiling cove
Stainless-steel
  countertop 52
**Stainless-steel
roofing** **402**
  batten seam 402
  flat seam 402
  lead-coated,
    add for 402
  standing seam 402
  terne-coated,
    add for 402
Stairs **465-482**
  1/4 turn 466-467
  1/2 turn 467-468
  4' wide 470
  balustrade 471-476

balustrade
  handrail 476
  bracket 476
bull nose
  starting step 470
carpet installation 258
circular 468
cleaning 67
disappearing
  attic stair 471
for exterior deck 430
mitered steps 470
newel 476-480
other woods 480
painting 342
spiral 470-471
straight 465-466
T&M charts 480-482
tread trim 476
utility 465
winders 470
Stall, shower 378
Stamping,
concrete 89-90
Standing seam roofing
  copper 401
  stainless steel 402
  terne 402
Steel, black pipe 361
Steel, entry door **111**
  side lite 111
Steel,
  galvanized pipe 362
Steep and
complex roofs,
  add for roofing 393
Steps
  concrete 90
  mobile home 523-524
  paint 334
Step flashing 406
Stone
  architrave, door 310-312
  architrave, window 312-314
  ashlar
    fireplace face 250-251
    fireplace hearth 252
    veneer 307-308
    wall 306
  carving 320
  floor 259
  paint 341
  quoin 309
  repair 320-321
  repoint 319
  retaining wall 391

rubble
  fireplace face 250
  fireplace hearth 252
  veneer 307
  wall 305-306
  veneer panel 309-310
  cultured 309
Stone Finishes 307
Stone Quality 306-307
Stool molding,
  window 209-210
Stop, gravel 406
Storage shed 331
Storage trailer 492
Storm door **109-110**
  hinges 129
  lockset 129
  mobile home 514
  paint 336
  Victorian wood 109
Storm window
  aluminum 510
  wood 510-511
Straight stair 465-466
Strip flooring
  Douglas fir 266-267
  maple 263
  red oak 263
  red oak,
    quartersawn 263-264
  red oak strip,
    prefinished 264
  southern pine 265
Strip paint 342
Strip spot light
  fixture 169
Strip wallpaper 495
Structural
  engineering fees 186
Structural tile wall 303
Stucco **357**
  architrave 359
  curved wall
    installation 355
  painting 333
  pilaster or
    column 358-359
  repair 358
  synthetic 357-358
Submersible
  water pump 383
Sump pump **383**
  wiring 143
Supply lines,
  antique style
  free-standing 385

**Suspended
ceilings** **483-490**
  2' x 2' 485-487
  2' x 4' 483-485
  12" x 12" 483
  cleaning 67
  drop-in
    HVAC panels 487
  minimum charge 487
  sound blanket 487
  T&M charts 488-490
Swamp cooler
  see: Evaporative cooler
Swimming
  pool enclosure 332
Swimming pools ...**489-491**
  acid wash 490
  aluminum 489
  bond beam
    repair 489
  border, tile 490
  caulk expansion
    joint 490
  close for winter 490
  coping 489
  concrete 489
  deck 489
  drain 490
  fiberglass 489
  galvanized steel 489
  leak detection 489
  leak repair 490
  liner, vinyl 490
  open for summer 490
  paint 489
  regrout 489
  replaster 489
  shock treatment 490
Switch **140-141**
  covers 141-142
  mask 286
  with wire 139-140
Synthetic stucco 357-358

T

T-lock shingles 394
T1-11 plywood siding 457
Tape, safety 492
Tapered column
  or pilaster 72
Tempered glass
  lite in panel door 108
Temple-of-the-
  Winds capital 78